The Legal Environment
of Business

THE LEGAL ENVIRONMENT OF BUSINESS

TWELFTH EDITION

ROGER E. MEINERS
University of Texas at Arlington

AL. H. RINGLEB
Consortium International MBA

FRANCES L. EDWARDS
Clemson University

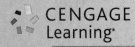

CENGAGE
Learning

Australia • Brazil • Japan • Korea • Mexico • Singapore • Spain • United Kingdom • United States

The Legal Environment of Business, Twelfth Edition
Roger E. Meiners
Al. H. Ringleb
Frances L. Edwards

Senior Vice President, Global Product Management—Higher Ed: Jack W. Calhoun

Vice President, General Manager, Social Science & Qualitative Business: Erin Joyner

Product Director: Michael Worls

Senior Product Manager: Vicky True-Baker

Content Developer: Sarah Blasco

Product Assistant: Tristann Jones

Senior Brand Manager: Kristen Hurd

Marketing Coordinator: Christopher Walz

Art & Cover Direction, Production Management, and Composition: Integra Software Services Pvt. Ltd.

Senior Media Developer: Kristen Meere

Rights Acquisition Director: Audrey Pettengill

Rights Acquisition Specialist, Text and Image: Anne Sheroff

Manufacturing Planner: Kevin Kluck

Spot Illustration: © loops7/ Photos.com, a division of Getty Images

Cover Image(s): AMIEL Jean-Claude/hemis. fr/Getty Images

For product information and technology assistance, contact us at **Cengage Learning Customer & Sales Support, 1-800-354-9706.**

For permission to use material from this text or product, submit all requests online at **www.cengage.com/permissions.** Further permissions questions can be e-mailed to **permissionrequest@cengage.com**

Library of Congress Control Number: 2013952197

ISBN-13: 978-1-285-42822-2

ISBN-10: 1-285-42822-6

Cengage Learning
200 First Stamford Place, 4th Floor
Stamford, CT 06902
USA

Cengage Learning is a leading provider of customized learning solutions with office locations around the globe, including Singapore, the United Kingdom, Australia, Mexico, Brazil, and Japan. Locate your local office at **www.cengage.com/global.**

Cengage Learning products are represented in Canada by Nelson Education, Ltd.

To learn more about Cengage Learning Solutions, visit **www.cengage.com.**

Purchase any of our products at your local college store or at our preferred online store **www.cengagebrain.com.**

Printed in the United States of America
1 2 3 4 5 6 7 17 16 15 14 13

Brief Contents

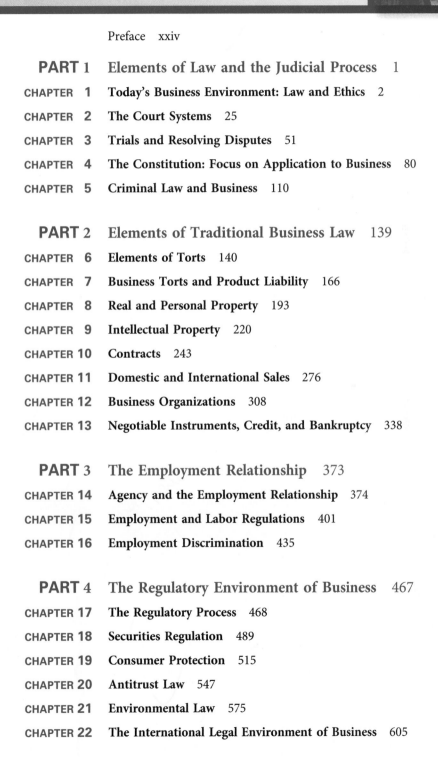

Contents

Table of Cases

The principal cases are in bold type. Cases cited or discussed in the text are roman type. References are to pages. Cases cited in principal cases and within other quoted materials are not included.

Preface

Knowledge of the legal and regulatory environment of business provides practical background for students in many careers. There are legal, social, political, and ethical issues in every profession. Some situations require an understanding of the principles of law to help resolve an issue or to know when legal counsel is needed.

This textbook presents the legal environment from the perspective of the professional who is not a lawyer. Only a few students who take this course will become lawyers, although some students may take additional classes that cover specific legal areas. This course provides the opportunity for people with various interests to learn key points of the law from the standpoint of a working professional.

Over the years, we have received excellent feedback from professors and students who have used the 11 previous editions of this book and have pointed out shortcomings and strong points, and given good advice for improvements. We have taken these comments into account in preparing this edition to make the book even more helpful and practical as we study the complex legal environment that business professionals face.

Essential Organization

In developing a one-semester course in the legal environment of business, you face the problem of determining what to cover in a short time. So many topics; so little time. There is agreement that the key elements of the legal system must be covered. This is done in Part 1 of the book, Elements of Law and the Judicial Process. Parts 2 and 3 from previous editions have been reorganized into three separate parts in this edition to offer a better flow of content. Part 2, Elements of Traditional Business Law, reviews the major areas of the common law that apply to business and statutory law that is oriented to business functions. The new Part 3, The Employment Relationship, addresses a part of the business environment that applies to everyone—employment laws. Part 4, The Regulatory Environment of Business, covers the major regulatory laws that managers of different firms may face and reviews major points of international business law.

Key Features

Edited Cases

A primary way to learn law is to read real cases that the courts had to resolve. Each major case presented in the text has the background facts and legal proceedings summarized by the authors under the label **Case Background**. Then, the court's holding, legal reasoning, and explanation of the law as it applies to the facts at hand are presented from the published opinion in the words of the judge in the **Case Decision**. Because most decisions are long, we present only the key portions of the holding. When there is a long deletion of material from a holding, you see asterisks (***). When the deletion of the logic in a decision is shorter, there are ellipses (…). Finally, **Questions for Analysis** are offered for the reader to consider or for class discussion. (Answers are provided in the *Instructor's Resource Guide*).

Test Yourself

This learning and review tool appears at least twice in each chapter. It provides the student with a quick self-test of material just covered. There are multiple choice, true–false, and fill-in-the-blank questions. They are intended to cover major points in the chapter, not picky details, so if the reader misses questions, the material should be reviewed.

International Perspectives

These boxed features discuss how issues similar to those being reviewed in the text are handled in other countries. As globalization reaches more businesses, managers must know how to deal with different legal systems and cultures. This feature makes clear that legal constraints are different in other nations. Managers must be prepared to resolve problems in different ways in different locales in today's complex legal environment.

Issue Spotter

More than 50 Issue Spotter features are scattered throughout the text. Each briefly presents a business situation that requires application of legal elements just covered. These challenges are a way for students to self-test their retention and ability to reason as they apply newly learned principles to practice. They also remind readers that the material learned in this course is practical and applicable to everyday issues in business. (Discussion points related to these features are provided in the *Instructor's Resource Guide*).

Cyber Law

This feature presents short discussions of applications of the law to developments arising from the information age. E-commerce and e-mail mean legal issues for the courts to resolve as they apply legal principles to never-before-heard-of ways of doing business, transmitting information, and communicating with friends and strangers.

Lighter Side of the Law

These highlights add a light touch to the topic at hand by discussing an actual case or unusual legal situation. While law and business are serious, odd things happen that remind us that trouble can come from unexpected places, that the results of the legal process can be surprising, that scoundrels are among us, and that truth can be stranger than fiction.

Summary

The text of each chapter is summarized in a bulleted format that provides a quick review of the major points of law and rules covered and serves as a self-test of points to be included in examinations.

Terms to Know

After the Summary, there is a list of key terms from the chapter. The reader should know what the terms mean as they are an important part of the vocabulary and substance of the concepts covered in the chapter. Besides being explained in the chapter, each term is also defined in the Glossary at the end of the book.

Discussion Question

Every chapter has a question for general discussion related to major ideas from the chapter. The purpose is to make sure students understand the concepts of the chapter well enough to discuss a topic that was covered and should be expanded upon.

Case Questions

Most problems are solved, but some end up in court where judges decide the resolution based on legal principles. Real case problems are summarized in each case question.

Using the knowledge from the chapter, and maybe some instinct about how a court is likely to resolve a dispute, try to decide which party to a dispute is likely to prevail and why. Some of the questions (marked by a "Check your answer") are answered online at the free companion website at www.cengagebrain.com.

Ethics Question

Each chapter ends with an ethics question that poses a problem related to the legal area covered in the chapter. Remember that ethical issues are different from legal issues, so we go beyond legal reasoning in considering the problem.

Pulling It Together

At the end of the four major sections of the text, several case questions are posed that bring together more than one legal issue covered in more than one chapter. Many situations involve more than one legal issue, so the cases here serve as a refresher to remind students of earlier material and pull in concepts covered there along with legal principles covered in another chapter.

Glossary

At the back of the book is a list of about a thousand key terms covered in the text. The terms are defined here to provide a clear understanding of a legal concept that has a specific application in law.

Appendices

Appendix A is on *Legal Research and the Internet*. Appendix B covers *Case Analysis and Legal Sources*. It explains the structure of court opinions and how they are often briefed by law students and lawyers to give a short summary of a complex matter. The case reporter system and other major legal resources are also reviewed. Appendix C is the full text of the United States Constitution. Appendices that follow give key portions of major statutes, including the Uniform Commercial Code, the National Labor Relations Act, Title VII of the Civil Right Act of 1964, the Americans with Disabilities Act, the Antitrust Statutes, and Securities Statutes.

New to This Edition

Our reviewers agree that this text focuses on practical aspects of the law. We try to keep to a minimum the legal minutia, such as uncommon exceptions or rules peculiar to only a few states. We focus on primary rules and issues that arise most often. We use business situations and examples to highlight legal principles in practice. In selecting cases that appear in the text, the focus is on practical situations in business that students can best relate to and are realistic in a business career. The holdings are straightforward applications of the law to the facts. However, some major cases are included so students can get a sense of how courts announce major rules, and the evolution of law can be discussed.

While the entire text is revised for updates and clarifications, examples of specific changes include:

Chapter 1, clarification of the wide scope of federal criminal law;

Chapter 2, a new case illustrates multiple issues in jurisdiction in a business case;

Chapter 3, how Twitter use can be construed as juror misconduct, the use of online arbitration in Europe, and how global arbitration works in the cotton market;

Chapter 4, new cases illustrate due process and equal protection in business situations;

Chapter 5, a new investment scam case illustrates use of sentencing guidelines;

Chapter 6, gross negligence is clarified, and new cases illustrate assumption of risk and emotional distress in business settings, and another new case discusses the privilege of an employer to share negative information about an employee;

Chapter 7, new cases show how interference with contracts occurs in ordinary business situations;

Chapter 8, new cases help explain how covenants work in property development, and how nuisance law is applied in residential property in a case involving wind turbines;

Chapter 9, enhanced discussion of domain name control and a case involving playing of music without a license on a radio station illustrate copyright issues;

Chapter 10, new cases on contract acceptance and on non-competition agreements;

Chapter 11, the issue of whether the UCC or the common law of contracts applies is reviewed in a new case, another case illustrates how courts settle unclear terms in a contract, and another case involving QVC, a shopping channel, shows how damages are calculated when defective goods are delivered;

Chapter 12, on business organizations, is moved up in sequence and new cases include how a partnership may be formed without formal recognition, as reviewers suggested, and a new review of close corporations and benefit corporations is provided;

Chapter 13, on negotiable instruments, credit, and bankruptcy, is moved back in the sequence, with new discussion of web-based credit scoring as well as new cases showing how mechanic's liens function and on bank liability when an employee abuses check signing privileges;

Chapter 14, the first chapter in the three chapter sequence on agency and employment, has been reorganized as a result of the change in structure and has a new case illustrating the relatively common problem of an employee exercising apparent authority in business dealings not approved by the principal;

Chapter 15 has a simplified discussion of OSHA and a new case showing how it works, and includes new information on social media in the workplace, including limits on employer rights to access employee social media sites;

Chapter 16 contains an updated discussion of employment discrimination law in practice, including a new case that illustrates accommodation for disability in the workplace;

Chapter 17 opens the last section of the text by covering regulatory law procedure, including two new cases that give examples of requirements in practice;

Chapter 18, on securities regulation, has been moved up as suggested by some reviewers and is freshened in its coverage of changes in the requirements in this area;

Chapter 19 updates coverage of consumer protection law and includes a new FTC case that illustrates a "wealth creation" scam;

Chapter 20 shows how the complex antitrust case process may now be aided by computer programs that sort documents;

Chapter 21 includes several new environmental law cases, including a 2013 Supreme Court case regarding application of the Clean Water Act and another case illustrating the international reach of the Endangered Species Act;

Chapter 22 freshens and simplifies the discussion of international business transactions.

Ancillaries

Companion Website

To access additional course materials, including CourseMate, please visit www.cengagebrain.com. At the CengageBrain.com home page, search for this book using the search box at the top of the page. This will take you to the product page where many resources can be found. The book companion website offers answers to selected chapter-ending Case Questions, an interactive quiz with multiple choice questions for each chapter in the text, and case updates.

Instructor's Materials

The electronic *Instructor's Resource Guide* has been revised. As before, it answers all questions in the book. It also provides a detailed outline of each chapter, summarizing the content of the text, including all cases. The instructor can refer quickly to this guide to remember the points that students have covered in the text. The guide also provides numerous additional summarized cases that the instructor can use to illustrate key points of law. Additional material, such as more discussion of certain points and examples of the law in practice, is provided as lecture and discussion enhancements.

The updated electronic *Test Bank* contains true–false questions and more than 6,000 multiple choice questions, totally more than 10,000 available questions. Many questions based on fact have been added to test critical thinking ability. The Test Bank questions vary in levels of difficulty and meet a full range of tagging requirements, so instructors can tailor their testing to meet their specific needs. The Test Bank is available online in Cognero. Cengage Learning Testing Powered by Cognero is a flexible, online system that allows you to:

- *author, edit, and manage test bank content from multiple Cengage Learning solutions*
- *create multiple test versions in an instant*
- *deliver tests from your LMS, your classroom, or wherever you want*

A full set of *PowerPoint* slides keyed to the text with lecture outlines is also available.

CourseMate

CourseMate brings course concepts to life with interactive learning, study, and exam preparation tools—including an e-book—that supports the printed textbook. Revised for this edition, student study materials and a set of auto-gradable, interactive quizzes allow students to instantly gauge their comprehension of the material. Built-in engagement tracking tools allow instructors to follow students' study activities and assess their progress.

CengageNOW™

CengageNOW™ is an online teaching and learning resource that gives you more control in less time and delivers better outcomes—NOW. Brand new to this edition, CengageNOW for *The Legal Environment of Business* allows instructors to customize additional test and study materials for their students. Written by Ray Teske of University of Texas at San Antonio, each of the 22 chapters provides several categories of multiple-choice questions that stress different aspects of the chapter materials: Chapter Review, Business Hypoteticals, Legal Reasoning, and IRAC. Along with pre- and post-test questions, all quiz content is tagged to specific standards. These online resources ensure that students possess the study materials needed to understand and apply the legal principles covered in the book.

Business Law Digital Video Library

Featuring more than 100 video clips that spark class discussion and clarify core legal principles, the Business Law Digital Video Library is organized into six series:

- *Legal Conflicts in Business (includes specific modern business and e-commerce scenarios)*
- *Ask the Instructor (presents straightforward explanations of concepts for student review)*
- *Drama of the Law (features classic business scenarios that spark classroom participation) LawFlix (contains clips from many popular films)*
- *Real World Legal (presents legal scenarios encountered in real businesses)*
- *Business Ethics in Action (presents ethical dilemmas in business scenarios).*

For more information about the Digital Video Library, visit www.cengage.com/blaw/dvl. Access for students is free when bundled with a new textbook or can be purchased separately. Students must register for and purchase access to the Digital Video Library at www.cengagebrain.com.

Acknowledgments

The authors thank the adopters and reviewers from around the country who sent helpful comments and materials for the eleventh edition. Much of the credit for the improvements belongs to them. The reviewers for this edition include:

Cara Anderson (Columbia Basin College)

Robert Barrett (University of La Verne)

Theodore Bolema (Central Michigan University)

S. Whittington Brown (Pulaski Technical College)

James Canarie (University of Southern Maine)

Karen Evans (Lawrence Technological University)

Sean Fields, Esq. (Harrisburg Area Community College)

Samuel B. Garber (DePaul University)

Nathan T. Garrett, Sr. (North Carolina Central University)

Darlene Gerry (Idaho State University)

Margaret Giovannetti (Simpson University)

Roger Goble (College of DuPage)

Glenn Greenfield (Lawrence Technological University)

Joanne Hirase-Stacey (Idaho State University)

Haley Johnson (Northeast Alabama Community College)

Robert K. Johnson (Harrisburg Area Community College)

Jack Karns (East Carolina University)

Joseph F. Lenius (Northeastern Illinois University)

Keith Levinson (LaSalle University)

Cliff Luxion (Waubonsee Community College)

George McNary (Creighton University)

Robert Meisel (Concordia University Texas)

Bret Nelson (LeTourneau University)

Carl Pentis, Esq. (California State University, Fullerton)

Carolyn Plump (LaSalle University)

Darka M. Powers (Northeastern Illinois University)

Nancy Ray (East Carolina University)

Rafique Sheikh (California State University Fullerton)

George Simonof (Pulaski Technical College)

Charles H. Smith (California State University, Fullerton)

Ricky Stacy (Tennessee Technological University)

Andrea Studzinski (College of DuPage)

William H. Volz (Wayne State University)

Rizvana Zameeruddin (University of Wisconsin, Parkside)

The authors also extend thanks to the professionals in business, law, and government who assisted in making this textbook as up-to-date and accurate as possible.

Finally, we thank the editors and staff of Cengage Learning. In particular, we thank the sales representatives who continually give us valuable information on the day-to-day perceptions of the textbook—information provided by the instructors and students who are using it. We thank Carmel Isaac, whose diligence and determination got us through the production process on schedule. Special thanks also go to our content developer, Sarah Blasco, who tolerates us with good humor. The efforts of our previous publisher, Rob Dewey, new product director Mike Worls, and senior product manager, Vicky True-Baker, who manage huge tasks, are much appreciated.

We welcome and encourage comments from the users of this textbook—both students and instructors. By incorporating your comments and suggestions, we can make this text an even better one in the future.

Roger E. Meiners

Al H. Ringleb

Frances L. Edwards

OVERVIEW

Part 1 reviews the major components of the legal system and provides the framework for understanding the material presented in the later two parts of the book. Just as people in business should understand the elements of accounting, economics, finance, management, and marketing, it is important that they also know how the legal environment plays a critical role in the way business and the economy function. Law changes as the structure of business evolves, as social pressures produce changes in the way business operates, as the ethical expectations of business increase, as politics change, and as the economy becomes more interwoven in international operations.

The chapters in Part 1 review the major components of the legal system: the origins of law, constitutional law, the role of law in society and business, the structure and functioning of the court system, the use of alternative forms of dispute resolution, and the key elements of criminal law as it applies to business. These chapters serve as the structural background for the rest of the text, which reviews areas of substantive laws that impact business.

PART 1

Elements of Law and the Judicial Process

Chapter 1
Today's Business Environment: Law and Ethics The evolving legal, social, and ethical pressures that people in business face today in a complex, international political economy are discussed in the context of the origins of our legal system. Our focus is on the purposes, sources, and structure of law and the legal system in the context of the modern economy.

Chapter 2
The Court Systems The structure and power of our federal and state court systems are reviewed, followed by a discussion of how a case gets to a court and what powers the courts have over the parties to a case and its resolution.

Chapter 3
Trials and Resolving Disputes The steps in litigation—from the time a party files a complaint, through the stages of litigation, the forms of relief possible, and the appeals process—are discussed. Many business disputes are not taken to court but to alternate dispute resolution. The key aspects of arbitration and mediation are reviewed.

Chapter 4
The Constitution: Focus on Application to Business The constitutional limits on government actions, especially with respect to business matters, are covered. Congress has nearly unlimited power to regulate and tax, but some protections are provided for civil liberties against an over-reaching state.

Chapter 5
Criminal Law and Business Many statutes, increasingly at the federal level, provide the possibility of criminal penalties for violations that may involve persons in business capacities. The criminal processes are reviewed as are key statutes that specifically target certain actions in business.

CHAPTER 1

Today's Business Environment: Law and Ethics

Getting a good job and building a career after college are major challenges when economic times are difficult. Afraid of being left jobless and needing income, many people take jobs that are less than what they had hoped to find, but these jobs sometimes turn out better than expected, as they provide experience and entry into organizations. On the other hand, some people land prestigious jobs that turn out to present less-than-ideal circumstances.

It is not uncommon for recruiters to puff up the qualities of a position. A job billed as "character-building" may be one of unending stress. One advertised as having a "teamwork environment" may just mean people jammed in cubicles. One person reported that when she was recruited, she was shown a nice office and introduced to her supervisor, whom she liked. When she arrived to start work two weeks later, she was stuck in a tiny back room; the likeable supervisor was gone, replaced by someone less agreeable; and, worst of all, the assignments she was given were not of the quality discussed earlier.

Suppose that happens to you. Can you sue the recruiter who brought you to the employer? Can you sue the company that hired you? Do you have the right to demand a better office? What is your legal status in the situation? These are some of the legal issues in business that we will explore.

In the situation just posed, the new employee probably has little choice but to keep the job as is or leave. The employer is unlikely to have violated any legal obligation. What about the ethical obligation to be honest with current and potential employees? Is overstating the quality of a position unethical, even if it is not a violation of the law? This is another aspect of the modern business environment.

Business is complex. Ethical, legal, social, political, and international issues all impact company operations one way or another. As Exhibit 1.1 indicates, whether your field is human resources, sales, banking, advertising, or software development, you must be familiar with a wide range of subjects to have the skills needed to be aware of possible problems and to recognize potential opportunities that someone with a limited view would likely miss. The topics covered in this book, which focuses on the legal environment of business, help to fit one large piece into the complicated puzzle called the business world.

The study of the legal environment of business begins with an overview of the nature of law and the legal system. Composed of law that comes from different sources, the legal environment is influenced by the needs and demands of the business community, consumers, and government. This chapter helps us understand the functions of law in society, the sources of U.S. law, and the classifications of law. It then considers some major ethical issues that play a role in the modern environment of business.

EXHIBIT 1.1 OVERVIEW OF A BUSINESS'S LEGAL ENVIRONMENT

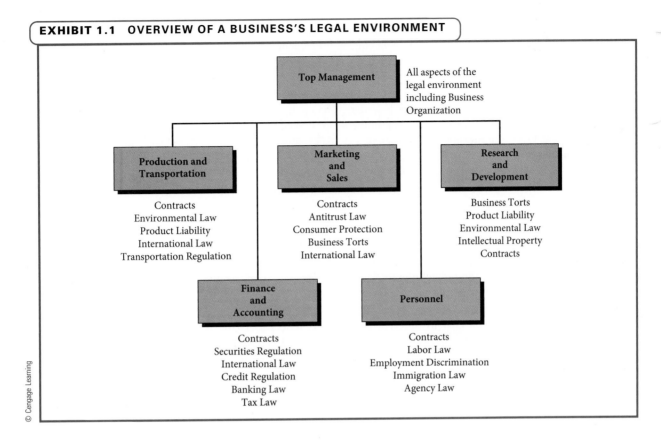

Law and the Key Functions of the Legal System

There is no generally accepted definition of **law**. In the legal environment of business, law refers to the rules, standards and principles that define the behavioral boundaries for business activities. In more general context, law is a more abstract term. According to *Justinian's Institutes*, a summary of Roman law published in 533 in Constantinople, "The commandments of the law are these: live honorably; harm nobody; give everyone his due."

A bit more specific, a century ago Oliver Wendell Holmes, a legal scholar and Supreme Court justice, offered the following definition:

> *Law is a statement of the circumstances, in which the public force is brought to bear ... through the courts.*

In his 1934 book, *Growth of Law*, the famed jurist Benjamin N. Cardozo defined law as follows:

> *A principle or rule of conduct so established as to justify a prediction with reasonable certainty that it will be enforced by the courts if its authority is challenged.*

Also consider these modern definitions from *Black's Law Dictionary*, an authoritative legal dictionary:

1. *Law, in its generic sense, is a body of rules of action or conduct prescribed by [the] controlling authority and having binding legal force.*
2. *That which must be obeyed and followed by [members of a society] subject to sanctions or legal consequences is a law.*

---

*Reprinted from Black's Law Dictionary with permission of Thomson Reuters.

© Cengage Learning

In summary, law may be viewed as a collection of rules or principles intended to limit and direct human behavior. Enforcement of such rules or principles provides some predictability and uniformity to the boundaries of acceptable conduct in a society. Nations have both formal rules that are commonly called laws plus informal rules that come from a society's history, customs, commercial practices, and ethics.

Law and the legal system serve several key roles in society. The most important functions include: (1) influencing the behavior of the members of a society, (2) resolving disputes within society, (3) maintaining important social values, and (4) providing a method for assisting social change. The experience of Haiti and other nations, as discussed in the *International Perspective*, reminds us of how difficult it is to do business in a country with a corrupt government that does not provide a workable legal system.

Improving Social Stability by Influencing Behavior

The legal system helps to define acceptable social behavior. The law limits activities that hurt the public interest. It restricts business practices that are thought to be outside the ethical and social norms of a society. The law can also require or encourage business practices that further social or political goals.

The laws in different jurisdictions reflect social norms. The business of raising and selling marijuana in Amsterdam (Holland) is legal because the government decided that legalizing marijuana would reduce crime in the drug trade and make it less likely that people would use more harmful drugs such as heroin. In the United States, growing and selling marijuana is illegal under federal law and can be punished by long prison terms. Several states have moved to legalize certain marijuana production and use, but

INTERNATIONAL PERSPECTIVE

Emerging Nations and the Law

Haiti was devastated by an earthquake in 2010 that killed hundreds of thousands of people. During coverage of the event, many Americans were shocked to see profound poverty so close to the United States. Haiti's poverty is in contrast to the Dominican Republic that is the other half of the island of Hispaniola. Average income in the Dominican Republic is four times higher than in Haiti. What makes Haiti so poor?

The tragedy of the earthquake caused donors to pledge aid to help rebuild Haiti. It sparked discussion about how to encourage economic development, ensure the aid was used effectively, and prevent corruption. All the aid did little good. Haiti, like many poor countries, suffers under a notoriously corrupt government and a legal system that provides no meaningful law to protect people's lives and property. One businessman with operations in several Caribbean nations said that doing business in Haiti was nearly impossible because the demands for bribes are endless.

This comment is backed up by surveys of Haiti's residents. Transparency International, the Berlin-based organization that studies corruption, ranked Haiti the 168th most corrupt country in the world; only nine countries were worse. Haiti's more prosperous neighbor, the Dominican Republic, ranked 99th. The least corrupt countries—New Zealand and Denmark—are high-income countries. Many studies have found a strong relationship among less corruption, a well-functioning legal system, and the level of economic development.

There are no easy answers for creating a functioning legal system in a country without one and where government authorities make a living by being on the take. Finding the answer to that puzzle is key to helping develop business opportunities that benefit ordinary citizens.

those state laws conflict with federal law. On the other hand, the production and sale of alcoholic beverages to adults is legal in most of the country, although it was illegal nationwide from 1919 to 1933. In Saudi Arabia, people are executed for being involved in the alcohol business, as alcohol violates Sharia law in that country. Other countries also make alcohol a criminal matter, while some countries have few restrictions on its sale, even to minors. This illustrates how different societies use the law to enforce different social norms.

Conflict Resolution

A critical function of the law is dispute resolution. Disagreements are inevitable since societies are made up of people with differing desires and values. Karl N. Llewellyn, a famous legal theorist, stated:

> *What, then, is this law business about? It is about the fact that our society is honeycombed with disputes. Disputes actual and potential, disputes to be settled and disputes to be prevented; both appealing to law, both making up the business of law.... This doing of something about disputes, this doing of it reasonably, is the business of law.*

While most disputes are settled informally, a formal mechanism for the resolution of disputes is the court system. It is used for both private disputes between members of society and public disputes between individuals and the government. Our court system is intended to provide a fair mechanism for resolving these disputes. As we will see in Chapter 3, businesses are increasingly turning to formal private settlement techniques by alternate dispute resolution outside of the courts, often because the courts are expensive and slow.

Social Stability and Change

Every society is shaped in part by its values and customs. It is not surprising, then, that law plays a role in maintaining the social environment. Integrity is reflected in the enforceability of contracts; respect for other people and their property is reflected in tort and property law; and some measures of acceptable behavior are reflected in criminal laws.

Over time, social attitudes change. Not many years ago, gay partners could be subject to criminal prosecution for the fact of a personal, voluntary relationship. Now the discussion has turned to whether such relationships should have the same status as traditional marriages. Some contend that legalizing same-sex marriages would be destructive to the structure of society; others see it as a stabilizing force and a civil right.

The legal system provides a way to bring about changes in "acceptable" behavior. For example, in the past, some states required businesses to discriminate on the basis of race. Attitudes changed, and those laws gradually disappeared, and grossly discriminatory behavior is no longer legally acceptable. Rather than require discrimination, laws now restrict race discrimination in employment decisions. Next, we turn to the sources of law and how law is created.

Sources of Law in the United States

The U.S. and state constitutions created three branches of government—each of which has the ability to make law. Congress—the legislative branch of government—passes statutes. The executive branch—the President and administrative agencies—issues regulations under those statutes. The courts create legal precedents through their decisions.

Constitutions

A **constitution** is the fundamental law of a nation. It establishes and limits the powers of government. Other laws are created through a constitution. The U.S. Constitution (see Appendix C) allocates the powers of government between the states and the federal government. Powers not granted to the federal government are retained by states or are left to the people. Note that a constitution need not be a written document—the United Kingdom's is not—but it is in most nations. It should also be noted that in some countries the constitution is just for show. A document that looks much like the U.S. Constitution may exist, but means little in practice under a dictatorship.

The U.S. Constitution The U.S. Constitution is the oldest written constitution in force in the world. Although it contains some clear rules, such as the President must be at least age 35, it also has many general principles. It sets forth the organizational framework, powers, and limits of the federal government. Specifically, the Constitution creates the legislative, executive, and judicial branches as the primary framework of the U.S. government.

This division of governmental power is referred to as the separation of powers. It arose out of the founders' fear that too much power concentrated in one governmental branch would reproduce the tyranny experienced under King George III. The separation of powers means that each branch of government has functions to perform that can be checked by the other branches. The government structure that has developed is illustrated in Exhibit 1.2.

As the highest legal authority, the U.S. Constitution overrides any state or federal laws that go beyond what the Constitution permits. According to Article VI:

> *This Constitution, and the Laws of the United States which shall be made in Pursuance thereof; and all Treaties made, or which shall be made, under the Authority of the United States, shall be the supreme Law of the Land; and the Judges in every State shall be bound thereby, any Thing in the Constitution or Laws of any State to the Contrary notwithstanding.*

State Constitutions The powers and structures of all state governments are based on written constitutions. Like the federal government, state governments are divided into legislative, judicial, and executive branches. Their constitutions specify how state officials are chosen and removed, how laws are passed, how the court systems run, and, in general terms, how finances and revenues are paid and collected. On matters of state law, each state's constitution is the highest form of law for that state, although the federal Constitution can override the state constitutions. Some state constitutions, unlike the U.S. Constitution, are very long and filled with details, because amending state constitutions is often much easier than changing the U.S. Constitution.

Legislatures and Statutes

Congress and state legislatures are the sources of statutory law. Statutes that are created by legislation make up much of the law that significantly affects business behavior. For example, Congress enacted the Clean Water Act in 1972. It sets standards for water quality for the nation and grants the Environmental Protection Agency the authority to adopt regulations that help make the goals of the statute effective. Similarly at the state level, every state legislature has passed statutes to regulate the insurance industry. The intent of the legislation is fulfilled, in part, through state insurance commissions created for that role.

EXHIBIT 1.2   THE GOVERNMENT OF THE UNITED STATES

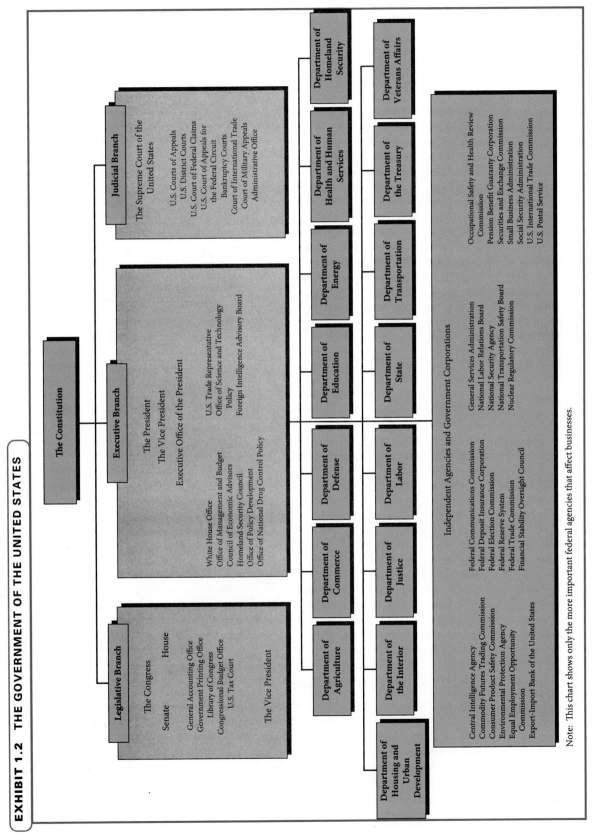

Note: This chart shows only the more important federal agencies that affect businesses.

The Constitution

Legislative Branch

The Congress

Senate   House

General Accounting Office
Government Printing Office
Library of Congress
Congressional Budget Office
U.S. Tax Court

The Vice President

Executive Branch

The President

The Vice President

Executive Office of the President

White House Office
Office of Management and Budget
Council of Economic Advisors
Homeland Security Council
Office of Policy Development
Office of National Drug Control Policy

U.S. Trade Representative
Office of Science and Technology Policy
Foreign Intelligence Advisory Board

Judicial Branch

The Supreme Court of the United States

U.S. Courts of Appeals
U.S. District Courts
U.S. Court of Federal Claims
U.S. Court of Appeals for the Federal Circuit
Bankruptcy Courts
Court of International Trade
Court of Military Appeals
Administrative Office

Department of Agriculture
Department of Commerce
Department of Defense
Department of Education
Department of Energy
Department of Health and Human Services
Department of Homeland Security

Department of Housing and Urban Development
Department of the Interior
Department of Justice
Department of Labor
Department of State
Department of Transportation
Department of the Treasury
Department of Veterans Affairs

Independent Agencies and Government Corporations

Central Intelligence Agency
Commodity Futures Trading Commission
Consumer Product Safety Commission
Environmental Protection Agency
Equal Employment Opportunity Commission
Export-Import Bank of the United States

Federal Communications Commission
Federal Deposit Insurance Corporation
Federal Election Commission
Federal Reserve System
Federal Trade Commission
Financial Stability Oversight Council

General Services Administration
National Labor Relations Board
National Security Agency
National Transportation Safety Board
Nuclear Regulatory Commission

Occupational Safety and Health Review Commission
Pension Benefit Guaranty Corporation
Securities and Exchange Commission
Small Business Administration
Social Security Administration
U.S. International Trade Commission
U.S. Postal Service

© Cengage Learning

Federal courts may review statutes passed by Congress to ensure that they do not violate the U.S. Constitution. State courts may review statutes passed by their legislatures to ensure that they do not violate the constitution of the state or of the United States. If a state legislature enacts a statute that violates the U.S. Constitution, and a state court does not strike down the statute, it may be stricken by a federal court.

United States Congress   Article I, Section 1, of the U.S. Constitution provides that all power to make laws for the federal government is given to Congress, a legislature consisting of the Senate and the House of Representatives. Of the thousands of pieces of legislation proposed in each session of Congress, only about 200 to 300 pass both the House and Senate and go to the President for his signature.

State Legislatures   Every state has lawmaking bodies similar to Congress in their functions and procedures. With the exception of Nebraska, all states have a two-part legislature containing a House of Representatives (sometimes called a House of Delegates or an Assembly) and a Senate. Dividing power between two houses is intended to serve as an added check on government power. The lawmaking process in state legislatures is similar to the procedure followed by the Congress. However, in some states, voters may directly enact legislation through the voting process in referendums or initiatives.

The National Conference of Commissioners on Uniform State Laws works with lawyers, law professors, the business community, and judges. For over a century, it has drafted proposed laws for consideration by state legislatures. Some are ignored, but others have been widely adopted, such as the Uniform Commercial Code (UCC). The UCC, discussed in Chapters 11 and 13, is designed to ease the legal relationship among parties in commercial transactions by making laws uniform among the states. Another important uniform law adopted by most state legislatures is the Uniform Partnership Act, covered in Chapter 12.

Administrative Agencies and Regulations

An administrative agency is created by a delegation of legislative power to the executive branch. Congress or the state legislature enacts a law that directs the agency to issue regulations, bring lawsuits, and otherwise act to fulfill the law's goals. For example, after President Nixon created the Environmental Protection Agency, Congress gave the EPA authority to enact regulations to implement the goals of environmental statutes and to be the primary enforcer of those laws. Similarly, all states have created state environmental agencies to design and enforce state environmental regulation.

Within the boundaries set by the legislature, administrative agencies exercise their powers to enact regulations, supervise compliance with those regulations, and adjudicate violations of regulations. Regulations issued by administrative agencies are among the important sources of law affecting the legal environment of business today. Agency procedures are discussed in Chapter 17.

The Judiciary and Common Law

The **common law**—law made and applied by judges as they resolve disputes among private parties—is a major part of the legal environment of business as it is the foundation of agency (employment), contract, property, and tort law. In addition to applying the common law, the judiciary interprets and enforces laws enacted by legislatures. As we will see, some statutes, such as the antitrust laws, are written in broad terms and require significant court interpretation to be understood. The judiciary also reviews actions taken by the executive branch and administrative agencies to make sure they comply with the Constitution.

The oldest source of law in the United States, the common law, dates to colonial times when English common law governed most internal legal matters. To maintain social order and to encourage commerce, the colonists retained English common law when the United States became an independent nation.

Lighter Side of the Law

Creative Common Law

An 18-year-old high school student in California "earned" over $1 million in a stock scam. When the federal authorities busted his operation, charged him with securities fraud, and made him repay his earnings, he was also booted off his high school baseball team.

He then sued his high school for $50 million. The basis of his suit was that he had planned to be a major league baseball player, but now that he could not play on his high school team he could not perform in front of baseball scouts who would draft him into the pros. He lost.

Source: True Stella Awards.

Case Law Under the common law, a dispute comes to court in the form of a **case**. A case is a dispute between two or more parties that is resolved through the legal process. In common law cases, the judge follows the rules of civil procedure (covered in Chapter 2 and 3) and, to determine the outcome of the matter, follows earlier judicial decisions that resolved similar disputes. For hundreds of years now, the decisions written by judges, often in the courts of appeals, to explain the rulings in important cases and many not-so-newsworthy cases, have been published in books called **case reporters**. The reporters are the official publication of case decisions and are public information. To settle disputes that are similar to past disputes, judges look for guidance by studying decisions from earlier recorded cases. This is referred to as **precedent** that is applied to the facts of the new cases under consideration and helps to guide the decision.

To settle unique or novel disputes, judges create new common law. Even in such cases, their rulings are based on the principles suggested by many previously reported decisions. Since common law is state law, there are some differences across the states in the interpretation of common-law principles, but the judges in one state can look to cases from other states to help resolve disputes if there are not decisions on point from their own state. Sometimes they even look to decisions of courts in other common law countries.

Doctrine of Stare Decisis The deciding of new cases by referencing previous decisions is the foundation of the Anglo-American judicial process used to varying degrees in Australia, the United Kingdom, Canada, New Zealand, India, South Africa, and other former British colonies, including the United States. The use of precedent in deciding current cases is a doctrine called *stare decisis*, meaning "to stand on decided cases." Under this doctrine, judges are expected to stand by established rules of law. According to Judge Richard Posner:

> *Judge-made rules are the outcome of the practice of decision according to precedent (stare decisis). When a case is decided, the decision is thereafter a precedent, i.e., a reason for deciding a similar case the same way. While a single precedent is a fragile thing … an accumulation of precedents dealing with the same question will create a rule of law having virtually the force of an explicit statutory rule.*

Value of Precedent Stare decisis has several benefits. First, consistency in the legal system improves the ability to plan business decisions. Second, as a rule is applied in many disputes involving similar facts, people become increasingly confident that the rule will be followed in the resolution of future disputes and order business and personal affairs given the rules of law. Third, the doctrine creates a legal system that is more just by neutralizing the prejudices of individual judges. If judges use precedent as the basis for decisions, they are less likely to make decisions based on their personal biases.

Changes in Law and Society An advantage of dispute resolution through the common law is its ability to adapt. Although most cases are decided on the basis of precedent, judges are not prohibited from modifying legal principles if conditions justify a new rule. As changes occur in technology or in social values, the common law evolves and provides new rules that better fit the new environment. For example, a court may modify or reverse an existing legal principle. If that decision is appealed to a higher court for review, the higher court may accept the new rule as the one to be followed or retain the existing rule. In the case *Davis v. Baugh Industrial Contractors, Inc.,* that follows, we see a state high court deciding it is time to change a common law rule.

Reporting Court Cases Like all cases presented in this book, the *Davis v. Baugh Industrial Contractors, Inc.* case begins with its legal citation. There were several parties to the case on both sides, but the citation refers only to the lead plaintiff (Davis), who brought the suit, and the first defendant (Baugh) named in the suit. Then we see what court the decision comes from and the reporter citation that tells us where it can be found. The decision was issued by the Washington state Supreme Court in 2007. It is published in volume 159 of the state of Washington official reporter, in its second series, beginning on page 413. It is also published in volume 150 of the *Pacific Reporter* (P), which is in its third series, and the case begins on page 545. The *Pacific Reporter* is a multi-state reporter produced by Westlaw. (See Appendix B for more discussion of case reporting.) We follow the citation with a description of the facts determined at trial (Case Background), which is a summary by the textbook authors. These facts are given by the court at the start of the decision, but are too long to quote in full, so the key points are outlined here. Then we move to the Case Decision, an explanation of the law, and legal reasoning. The judge who authored the decision for the court is named, and the material that follows is quoted from the decision itself. Most decisions are much longer, so we quote only the most important points of law. After the decision, we present Questions for Analysis.

DAVIS V. BAUGH INDUSTRIAL CONTRACTORS, INC.

Supreme Court of Washington 159 Wash.2d 413, 150 P.3d 545 (2007)

Case Background *Glacier Northwest hired Baugh Industrial Contractors to build a processing facility that included a system of underground pipes. Three years later, Glacier suspected a leak in a pipe. It assigned an employee, Alan Davis, to uncover the leak, which he did. While he was down in a hole dug to get to the pipes, a concrete wall collapsed, kill-* *ing him. While the pipes were supposed to last 100 years, it is likely they had been damaged when installed, resulting in a leak. Tami Davis, Alan's daughter, sued Baugh and others, contending their negligent practices were the cause of Alan's death.*

The trial court, called the superior court, held for Baugh and dismissed the suit. Under the traditional common law rule in Washington, the contractor was not liable for such an accident, so the risk of liability was on the property owner, Glacier. This decision was appealed to the Washington state high court that then issued this decision.

Case Decision Chambers, Justice

* * *

Under the completion and acceptance doctrine, once an independent contractor finishes work on a project, and the work has been accepted by the owner, the contractor is no longer liable for injuries to third parties, even if the work was negligently performed. Historically, after completion and acceptance, the risk of liability for the project belonged solely to the property owner. This court has not addressed this doctrine in over 40 years and, in the meantime, 37 states have rejected it. Under the modern … approach, a builder or construction contractor is liable for injury or damage to a third person as a result of negligent work, even after completion and acceptance of that work, when it was reasonably foreseeable that a third person would be injured due to that negligence.

We join the vast majority of our sister states and abandon the ancient Completion and Acceptance Doctrine. We find it does not accord with currently accepted principles of liability …

The Completion and Acceptance Doctrine is also grounded in the assumption that if owners of land inspect and accept the work, the owner should be responsible for any defects in that accepted work. While this assumption may have been well founded in the mists of history, it can no longer be justified. Today, wood and metal have been replaced with laminates, composites, and aggregates. Glue has been replaced with molecularly altered adhesives. Wiring, plumbing, and other mechanical components are increasingly concealed in conduits or buried under the earth. In short, construction has become highly scientific and complex. Landowners increasingly hire contractors for their expertise and a nonexpert landowner is often incapable of recognizing substandard performance…

We conclude that the Doctrine of Completion and Acceptance is outmoded, incorrect, and harmful and join the modern majority of states that have abandoned it in favor of the [modern] approach [holding a builder or contractor liable for injury due to negligent work]. We reverse the superior court order … and remand for further proceedings in keeping with this holding.

Questions for Analysis

1. The court rejected the old common law rule concerning completion and acceptance of a construction job that was in effect prior to this decision and ordered a new trial. What was the key reason for that decision? How does the new rule affect liability?
2. A judge on the court dissented from the decision. Explaining his opposition to the decision of the majority, he said this change in the law should have been done by the legislature in a statute, not the court. Is there a practical problem with that view?

Reported cases are called "primary sources" because they *are* the law. But, when trying to understand an area of law, it is common to rely upon "secondary sources" that explain the law. When secondary sources are respected, they are used by judges when giving decisions in cases. For example, the *Restatement of Torts* is an authoritative source on the law of torts. It is one of the many *Restatements of the Law* that are published on all major areas of common law by the American Law Institute (ALI; see www.ali.org). The ALI describes itself as "the leading independent organization in the United States producing scholarly work to clarify, modernize, and otherwise improve the law." It appoints "reporters" to contribute to *Restatements* according to their area of expertise. The reporters are lawyers, judges, and law professors who contribute to an ongoing review of the law. Every several decades, there may have been enough change in an area of law for reporters to believe that a new *Restatement* should be published. For instance, the *Restatement (Third) of Torts* is now published alongside the older *Restatement (Second) of Torts*. This does not mean that the older *Restatement* is not a good source on the law—indeed it still dominates. However, courts are beginning to refer to the *Restatement (Third) of Torts,* as we will see in later chapters.

INTERNATIONAL PERSPECTIVE

Civil Law Systems

Much of the world has a *civil law* (sometimes called a *civilian system*). Civil law systems are dominant in most countries in Europe and Central and South America, as well as in parts of Asia and Africa. While each civil law system has unique features, there are three major characteristics that differentiate a civil law system from common law:

- Civil law systems are inquisitorial rather than adversarial.
- Civil law is code-based rather than case-based.
- Civil law is influenced more by academic experts than by practicing lawyers.

Civil law has its roots in the Roman Empire. A body of legal experts gradually became prominent in Rome, and their writings on law came to be seen as authoritative. As the Empire grew, Roman law adapted to the needs of commerce across an ever-larger territory and sophisticated concepts of contract and property law developed. The Emperor Justinian (ruled 518–565 C.E.) ordered the compilation of the law (*The Digest of Justinian*) and an introductory text (*The Institutes of Justinian*). These works survived the collapse of the Roman Empire and became the basis for modern European legal systems when copies were rediscovered in libraries in the sixteenth century.

The French Emperor Napoleon initiated the next step in civil law's development. He ordered French legal experts to create a comprehensive code of laws for the French empire. After its adoption in 1804, Napoleon implemented the code in the countries he conquered; it proved so useful that many retained their Napoleonic Codes even after French rule ended. Continental European powers transmitted the civil law to their colonies in the Americas, Asia, and Africa. Other nations, including China and Japan, adopted civil law systems after studying European laws.

There are three key things about the civil law for businesses. First, because the structures of civil law systems are so different from common law ones, doing business in civil law countries requires careful legal review of contracts and other documents. Words that mean one thing in the common law may take on quite different meanings in a civil law system. Second, because civil law systems are inquisitorial, judges have much greater power to direct the course of legal proceedings. Instead of only ruling on matters lawyers bring to them, civil law judges can initiate proceedings on their own. Third, even where the rules are similar, civil law system procedures differ, making it important to have local attorneys who can explain and handle proceedings.

© Cengage Learning

The Executive

In addition to being the one who signs (or vetoes) bills passed by the legislature, the president or governor is another source of law. He or she creates law by issuing **executive orders**, requiring agencies to do certain things within the executive's scope of authority, such as an order to give preference to buying recycled products or to restrict financial transactions by suspected terrorist organizations.

The chief executive can also influence the duties and responsibilities of administrative agencies. One administration, for example, may not pursue environmental, antitrust, or international trade regulation as strongly as another administration. Thus, some industries or companies may face a more hostile legal environment under one administration than under another.

International Sources of Law

A firm doing business in another country is subject to its laws and is still subject to the laws of its home country. International law affecting business also includes treaties, which are international agreements, including trade agreements among countries. There are also rules enacted by multinational regional or global entities, such as the North American Free Trade Agreement (NAFTA) and the World Trade Organization (WTO). The decisions of international tribunals can also affect firms.

Article II, Section 2 of the Constitution requires approval by two-thirds of the Senate before a treaty agreed to by the president becomes binding on the U.S. Treaties of significance to business include the United Nations Convention on Contracts for the International Sale of Goods, which can govern the sale of goods between parties from different countries (discussed in Chapter 11), and the United Nations Convention on the Recognition and Enforcement of Foreign Arbitral Awards, which assists in the enforcement of arbitration clauses in international business contracts. Treaties and laws important in the international legal environment are discussed in Chapter 22 and at various points in other chapters.

Classifications of Law

The organization of law can be thought of in several ways, such as whether it originated from a constitution, a legislative body, or the judiciary. It is common to classify law on the basis of whether it is: (1) public or private, (2) civil or criminal, or (3) procedural or substantive. Laws usually fall into more than one classification. For example, the sale of car insurance is affected by private law (a contract between the company and the buyer) and public law (state regulation of insurance). A violation of law could result in civil law penalties or criminal law penalties for an insurance seller. A violation of a contract could result in a civil suit by the wronged party.

Public and Private Law

Some examples of public and private law are provided in Exhibit 1.3. **Public law** concerns the legal relationship between members of society—businesses and individuals—and the government. Public law includes statutes enacted by Congress and state legislatures and regulations issued by administrative agencies.

Private law sets forth rules governing the legal relationships among members of society. It helps to resolve disputes and to provide a way for the values and customs of society to influence law. Private law is primarily common law and is enforced mostly through the state court systems. Unlike public law, which at times makes major changes in legal rules, private law tends to be quite stable and changes slowly.

EXHIBIT 1.3   MAJOR AREAS OF PUBLIC AND PRIVATE LAW

PUBLIC LAW	PRIVATE LAW
Administrative Law	Agency Law
Antitrust Law	Contract Law
Bankruptcy Law	Corporation Law
Constitutional Law	Partnership Law
Criminal Law	Personal Property Law
Environmental Law	Real Property Law
Labor Law	Tort Law
Securities Regulation	Trusts and Estate Law

© Cengage Learning

Civil and Criminal Law

When a legislative body enacts a statute, it decides whether the law is to be civil, criminal, or both. That is, when Congress or a state legislature passes a statute that contains sanctions for violations, it will state what punishment may be imposed. Many laws—an estimated 3,000 at the federal level—include the possibility of criminal charges in case of violations. Most criminal law statutes may, in case of a claimed violation, have a lesser civil charge brought that could result a fine rather than a criminal charge. Unless a statute is expressly designated as criminal, it is considered to be civil law. Examples of civil and criminal law are provided in Exhibit 1.4.

Criminal law concerns legal wrongs or crimes committed against the state. As determined by federal or state statute, a crime is classified as a **felony** or a **misdemeanor**. A person found guilty of a criminal offense may be fined, imprisoned, or both. To find a person guilty of a crime, the trial court must find that the evidence presented showed beyond a **reasonable doubt** that the person committed the crime. The severity of punishment depends in part on whether the offense is a felony or a misdemeanor. Generally, offenses punishable by imprisonment for more than a year are classified as felonies. Misdemeanors are generally less serious crimes, punishable by a fine and/or imprisonment for less than a year. We discuss criminal law with respect to business in Chapter 5.

Civil law is concerned with the rights and responsibilities that exist among members of society or between individuals and the government in noncriminal matters. A person or business found liable for a *civil wrong* may be required to pay money damages to the injured party, to do or refrain from doing a specific act, or both. In finding the wrongdoer liable, the jury (or the judge in a nonjury trial) must find that the **preponderance of the evidence** favors the injured party, which is a lower standard of proof than is required in criminal cases.

Substantive and Procedural Law

Substantive law includes common law and statutory law that define and establish legal rights and regulate behavior. **Procedural law** determines how substantive law is enforced

EXHIBIT 1.4   EXAMPLES OF CIVIL AND CRIMINAL LAW

CIVIL LAW	CRIMINAL LAW
Contract Law:	**Misdemeanor Offenses:**
Auto Repairs	Simple Assault
Buying Airline Tickets	Disturbing the Peace
Forming a Business	Larceny (Petit)
Sale of Clothing	Public Intoxication
House Insurance	Trespass
Tort Law:	**Felony Offenses:**
Battery	Burglary
Defamation	Homicide
Invasion of Privacy	Larceny (Grand)
Medical Malpractice	Manslaughter
Trespass	Robbery

EXHIBIT 1.5   EXAMPLES OF SUBSTANTIVE AND PROCEDURAL LAW

SUBSTANTIVE LAW	PROCEDURAL LAW
Antitrust Law	Administrative Procedure
Contract Law	Appellate Procedure
Criminal Law	Civil Procedure
Environmental Law	Criminal Procedure
Labor Law	Discovery Rules
Securities Law	Evidence Rules

© Cengage Learning

through the courts by determining how a lawsuit begins, what documents need to be filed, which court can hear the case, how the trial proceeds, and so on.

A criminal trial, for example, follows criminal procedural law that sets deadlines, determines how evidence is introduced, and other steps in the process. The appropriate appellate procedure must be followed when a lower-court decision is appealed to a higher court for review. Similarly, agencies enforcing administrative laws and regulations must follow appropriate procedures. While most of our focus is on substantive law, it is important to keep in mind that all participants in the formal legal system must follow proper procedure. Examples of categories of substantive and procedural law are provided in Exhibit 1.5.

? TEST YOURSELF

1. The U.S. Constitution did not state that there must be a Supreme Court: T—F
2. When a court decides a common law case, it usually relies on _____ from earlier decisions under the doctrine of _____.
3. When the president and Congress both agree to bind the United States to a treaty, it means the treaty:
    a. applies only to federal law, not state law.
    b. affects dealings with foreign nations only.
    c. becomes part of the Constitution.
    d. becomes part of the law of the nation.
4. In the case *Davis* v. *Baugh Industrial Contractors, Inc.*, the Washington state high court held that it would change the common law and abandon an old rule concerning employer liability for worksite injury: T—F
5. Murder or homicide is a(n) _____ offense.

Answers: F; precedent and stare decisis; d; T; felony/criminal.

Business Ethics and Social Responsibility

Public confidence in many major institutions is low. Surveys indicate that the least trusted institutions are law firms, Wall Street, Congress, big companies, labor unions, and the media. Most trusted are most often the military, medical personnel, and small businesses. These findings however must be taken with a grain of salt. Despite not trusting Congress, most people like their members of Congress; reelection rates are high. Despite claiming not to trust big companies or Wall Street, most people buy products and services from big companies and keep their money in Wall Street firms. Nevertheless, when a firm suffers a scandal, the loss of reputation means lost sales and a decline in the value of the company. Trust is critical in business relationships, so building and maintaining a reputation for ethical standards is valuable.

Ethics, Integrity, Morality, and the Law

The concepts of ethics, integrity, morality, and the law are related but are not the same. **Ethics**, in the context of business practitioners, has to do with rules or standards governing the conduct of members of a profession and how standards are put into action within an organization. **Integrity** means living by a moral code and standards of ethics. **Morality** concerns conformity to rules of correct conduct within the context of a society, religion, or other institution.

The law is often distinct from those concepts because ethics, integrity, and morality concern voluntarily adopted standards of conduct. The law contains rules that are not moral or ethical but are imposed upon people. Slavery was legal until the 1860s and, even after it was abolished, there were laws for another century that mandated race discrimination, making it very difficult for African Americans to own property, receive a decent education, or compete in the labor market. During the days of legal segregation, subverting the law may have been unlawful, but few would assert such actions were immoral or unethical. Indeed, people who engaged in acts that intentionally defied the law, such as Martin Luther King, Jr., are regarded as having great integrity.

Business Ethics Peter Drucker, one of the most noted management consultants of all time, said that one should not make a distinction between business ethics and personal ethics. We should put into practice what we believe and not compromise based on moral relativism or business necessity of the time or place.

Consider this situation: The company Lockheed was in a struggle for survival in the 1970s because its commercial aircraft were not selling well. To obtain a large order from All Nippon Airways in Japan, the company had to bribe members of the Japanese government. Paying the bribes and getting the order for new aircraft did not put money in the pockets of the Lockheed executives, but it did save thousands of jobs at Lockheed. When the bribes became known, the top executives at Lockheed were ousted. Forgetting the fact that the bribes were illegal under U.S. law, was the bribe ethical because it saved many jobs?

ISSUE SPOTTER
OK to Grease Palms?

You are hired as a construction supervisor by a firm specializing in multi-story offices. Such construction requires visits by city building inspectors, who must sign off on certain work completed before a permit is issued to begin the next stage. Other supervisors let you know that the inspectors are used to being slipped $100 to $500, depending on the kind of permit being issued. A petty cash fund that is largely for this purpose is used to repay you. What are your options?

Lighter Side **of the Law**

Our Values

Respect: We treat others as we would like to be treated ourselves. We do not tolerate abusive or disrespectful treatment. Ruthlessness, callousness, and arrogance don't belong here.

Integrity: We work with customers and prospects openly, honestly, and sincerely. When we say we will do something, we will do it; when we say we cannot or will not do something, then we won't do it.

Source: Enron 1998 Annual Report.

Drucker said no, a bribe is a bribe. If business is not worth doing on a competitive basis, it should be abandoned. Lockheed should have gotten out of the commercial aircraft business (which it soon did) and looked for something more profitable to pursue, and not rely on paying bribes to stay in a market. A firm that must do that to survive is not one that can survive on its merits. Once business leaders go down the path of justifying various acts, even if not for personal profit, ethics have been lost.

Political Reality Scams do not just occur in other countries. In the United States, for example, many "pay to play" cases have come to light. That is, in some cases firms have had to pay bribes, directly or indirectly, to city, state, or federal government officials to have a chance to receive lucrative contracts. If uncovered, there may be criminal charges involved; but even if you are sure the payments would go undiscovered, you must ask yourself if the business is worth getting in any case.

Campaign contributions by businesses and business leaders are a part of the political economy in which we operate. Many forms of contributions are legal, but the suspicion of influence peddling is always present. If you do not contribute, maybe your firm will get passed by in consideration for contracts that are awarded each year under the direction of political leaders. To get along, you have to go along, so most companies do, but the public regards the practice with great suspicion.

Bribes are illegal and unethical. The hard ethical questions arise when something is not illegal but ethics are in question. In many jurisdictions, discrimination against people on the basis of sexual preference is not illegal. Assuming it is not, is it ethical to allow such discrimination within a business? These are profoundly difficult questions that are more properly addressed in a class on business ethics. Here, we only touch on the interface between law and ethics.

Perceptions of Ethics and Responses

In response to public image and real internal problems, most corporations have written codes of ethics. Making these more than window dressing can be difficult, however. In one study, Professor William Frederick found that corporations with codes of ethics were cited for legal infractions by federal regulatory agencies more frequently than corporations without codes.

Similarly, corporations that made a special effort to improve corporate ethics by placing more people purported to have a socially conscious perspective on their boards of directors witnessed little change in their corporate cultures. That is, building ethical standards into business operations—such that they are more than just slogans—is a complex task. Compliance with legal requirements is one part of that task.

CYBER LAW

Online Ethics and Legal Compliance

The evolution of the Internet has meant changes in the law, as we will see at various points in the text. It also means new ethical challenges—but also some opportunities.

Software allows employers to record every keyboard click an employee makes. Some critics assert that this is an invasion of privacy. Is it wrong for an employee to send personal e-mails from work? Is that really any different from chatting about a basketball game for a few minutes with a co-worker? An employer rarely stops that. However, because employers can be sued for sexual harassment if obscene e-mails are passed around or if pornographic websites are accessed from company computers, managers have good reason to monitor employees' website visits and to keep copies of all e-mail transmissions. They can also watch for breaches in security to be sure that proprietary company information is not being released.

Many companies have employees take online legal and ethics training. It is a cost-effective way to make sure employees are informed about employment discrimination, payoffs, conflicts of interest, and other matters that can spell big trouble for businesses. Employees may also be tested online regarding their knowledge of law and ethics. Many employers find online training more effective than gathering people in auditoriums for instruction, where they may tune out the information presented.

© Cengage Learning

Ethics Codes and Compliance Programs

Ethics codes matter little unless there is a serious effort to ensure compliance within an organization. Ethics and legal requirements may be blended in compliance codes. To be effective, such codes require diligent enforcement by management. According to the Department of Justice (DOJ), the existence of an effective corporate **compliance program** is a key factor in the agency's decision whether to prosecute an organization or to recommend leniency to a court when a legal problem arises. This is discussed more in Chapter 5.

The U.S. Sentencing Guidelines, which list punishment recommendations for various crimes, state that a company found guilty of violating a law may have its fines reduced by as much as 95 percent if it is found to have an effective, strong compliance program in place. A good ethics compliance program can also result in a civil proceeding rather than a criminal prosecution of legal violations. Prevention is less costly than a cure. A survey of 3,000 workers found that more than two-thirds had received ethics training at work. Such training has been rising steadily over time, which is evidence of intent to instill good practices. But remember that compliance programs are internal management tools for helping to avoid legal problems; ethical standards beyond compliance that are required by law, or implemented so as to reduce possible punishment, are management decisions about law, not ethics.

Ethics and Corporate Social Responsibility

Peter Drucker, the "Father of Modern Management," discussed "the ethics of social responsibility." Sometimes this is called **corporate social responsibility**. Drucker asserted that this ethic applied to those in leadership positions. The first responsibility of a business leader is to ensure that the corporate mission is fulfilled. That is why a person is put in a position of leadership—to help make effective use of resources entrusted to a company by investors. To earn a profit is an ethical social responsibility. Part of that

INTERNATIONAL PERSPECTIVE

Does Regulation Improve Business Ethics?

Financial scandals have been a reason for expanded securities regulation. The drug trade has resulted in increased control of money transfers. When problems arise, there is usually a call for more regulation to prevent future problems.

All nations have regulations and bureaucracy. But the wrong kind of regulation, especially when coupled with a corrupt bureaucracy, stifles business and reduces economic opportunities for ordinary people. The World Bank report, *Doing Business*, notes that the more regulation a country has, the more corruption it is likely to have and the lower its standard of living is likely to be.

The World Bank gives some examples. To get government permission to start a business in Indonesia, an entrepreneur must go through nine procedures that take almost two months and cost the equivalent of a quarter of a year of average income. In the United Arab Emirates, to enforce a contract requires 49 procedures that take about a year and a half and cost 20 percent of the value of the claim. In India, to get documents to export goods requires nine steps and takes twice as long as it does in developed countries. Countries that regulate business the most include Bolivia, Congo, Guatemala, Haiti, Mali, Mozambique, Paraguay, the Philippines, and Venezuela. The countries that regulate the least include Australia, Canada, Denmark, Hong Kong, the Netherlands, New Zealand, Norway, Singapore, and the United Kingdom.

To have "good" regulation, there must be ethics in government. In many countries, regulation simply provides a legal excuse to collect bribes. The regulations stay as they are because there are political interests that want to keep the system in place, including established business interests that want to be protected against new competitors.

© Cengage Learning

responsibility is minimizing errors that impose damage. That conforms to the old norm, "first, do no harm."

That is closely related to Google's "Don't Be Evil" rule. The Google Code of Conduct spells this out in detail as it applies to many areas of operation, including serving customers, personnel policy, and privacy issues. The company said it took the Code seriously in

ISSUE SPOTTER
Putting Ethics into Practice

A national chain of stores gives all employees a pamphlet called *Business Conduct Guide.* It states that everyone in the company should be "guided by the highest ethical and legal standards." It then gives brief guidance on a number of legal issues. For example:

> *Antitrust: We must compete vigorously and fairly in the marketplace using our independent judgment to make the best decisions for the Company Credit: We must provide accurate disclosure of credit terms and meet all requirements relating to fair credit reporting and equal credit opportunity.*

Employees are told to report violations either to their supervisor or to the Chief Financial Officer of the company. Is this likely to be part of an effective ethics/compliance program? Can sales clerks relate to these issues? Should such guides focus on relevant issues to different groups of employees?

© Cengage Learning

its struggle with the government of China over censorship of political material. The government stated that Google was breaking Chinese law by refusing to follow censorship rules. After a fight about the matter, Google agreed to follow some government censorship rules. Google has been criticized, but it argues that it is working to reduce censorship. Ethical issues become particularly tricky when in conflict with national laws.

Some companies have staffs dedicated to considering a wide range of impacts from company operations. This can help firms discover issues that may not have been considered when only focusing on, say, the costs of alternative site locations for a facility. Evaluation of social impacts on a community and in a market can reveal issues that affect the long-term costs of operations. There is a wide range of opinions about how much social responsibility, beyond the immediate impact on operations, a company has as part of being a good citizen.

A commitment to a code of ethics, which takes a firm beyond its legal obligations, is generally not binding on a company. Violations that are ignored may cause bad press for a company and bad morale for employees; however, as the *Lamson* v. *Crater Lake Motors* case makes clear, ethics and the law are distinct matters.

LAMSON V. CRATER LAKE MOTORS

Court of Appeals of Oregon 173 P.3d 1242 (2007)

Case Background For 15 years, Kevin Lamson was a sales manager for a car dealership. He liked the company's philosophy that "customers come first." The dealership was respected for not having aggressive sales tactics. Lamson had a reputation "for adhering to a high standard of ethics and integrity."

When sales were lagging, the company hired a sales firm, Real Performance Marketing (RPM), to run a five-day sales promotion. Lamson observed "a number of activities he considered to be unethical or unlawful or both." RPM produced a video that said that "all vehicles" would be cut in price. In fact, only the vehicles pictured in the video were on sale. RPM also tried to "pack the payments" by providing customers with life insurance and service contracts in purchase agreements without the customers' knowledge. When Lamson complained to the general manager (GM), he was told to go home.

After the sale, relations worsened. The GM told Lamson that another sales manager was making an extra $600 profit per sale. Lamson checked the records and found it was $100 per sale. The GM hired RPM to run another sale. He and Lamson argued. Lamson said it sounded as if the GM wanted him out and the GM said, "You're right." He told Lamson

to cooperate with RPM. Lamson sent the company owner a letter complaining of RPM's tactics, saying they violated company rules regarding sales ethics. He did not want to see "the values, ethics, morals, and honorable dealings" of the company lost. He asked him to rethink the "profit at any cost mentality."

The owner said that the company would still be "treating customers with the highest ethical standards" and that RPM promised "no misrepresentations or illegal statements." When Lamson did not cooperate with RPM during the next sale, he was fired. He sued for wrongful discharge, contending that he was fired for complaining about sales tactics that may have been illegal and that violated the company's code of ethics. The jury held for Lamson. The company appealed, contending that Lamson had no cause of action.

Case Decision Edmonds, Presiding Judge

* * *

Nor can we conclude … that plaintiff's internal complaints of unlawful sales practices are of the same public importance as the reports of health and safety violations in our earlier case law. Here, plaintiff did not report or threaten to report RPM's activities to anyone *outside of defendant*, and there is no evidence that defendant intended to "silence" him in a manner that would conceal illegal activities. On these facts, we cannot conclude that plaintiff's internal complaints about defendant's use of a sales firm serves a societal duty. ... Thus, we conclude that plaintiff's internal complaints, standing alone, did not serve an important societal obligation for purposes of a common-law wrongful discharge claim.

* * *

In sum, the evidence, viewed in the light most favorable to plaintiff, does not establish a legally cognizable basis for a claim for wrongful discharge. The employment relationship between plaintiff and defendant was an at-will employment relationship, which meant that plaintiff could be discharged for any reason, unless the discharge was for exercising a job-related right reflecting an important public policy or for fulfilling an important public duty. Here, the evidence is undisputed that plaintiff was not explicitly or impliedly directed to participate in any unlawful activity. ... Even if defendant's actions, viewed together as plaintiff posits, were pretextual because defendant no longer desired to employ plaintiff and expected that he would not attend the March 2004 sale, plaintiff was not discharged for fulfilling what the law would

recognize as an important *public* duty. In other words, defendant took no action concerning plaintiff that amounted to a tort under the applicable law regarding at-will employment relationships. Regardless of whether plaintiff's refusal to work on the ground that his presence would "condone" RPM's sales tactics was laudable, his actions do not fall within the narrowly defined exceptions created by the law of wrongful discharge, and defendant's conduct is not actionable in a court of law.

For all of the reasons stated above, the trial court should have granted defendant's motion for a directed verdict. Reversed.

Questions for Analysis

1. Suppose some of the sale tactics used by RPM violated Oregon law. What could Lamson do about it? Unless he suffered the effects of an illegal practice by making a purchase based on such practice, he had no complaint at law. Who would know more about such practices: those involved in putting them in place or a customer? Do you think any other car dealer would want to hire Lamson if he went public about his complaints?
2. Why do you think the courts are shy to get involved in such incidents? Should the courts be enforcers of a company's ethical practices and codes of ethics?

? TEST YOURSELF

1. Which of the following is generally not held in low esteem by the public?
   a. Congress
   b. Small business
   c. Law firms
   d. Big business
2. A person with a strong set of _____ is more likely to be a person of high _____.
3. Integrity can be defined as living by a moral code and standards of ethics: T—F
4. To reduce the severity of penalty in case of prosecution by the government, many companies have adopted _____.
5. Peter Drucker, like others, argued that it is not unethical for a firm to pay bribes in another country, if that is the norm, and if it protects jobs in the United States: T—F

Answers: b; ethics or morals, integrity; T; codes of compliance; F.

SUMMARY

- The modern environment of business means that managers in firms of all sizes face a variety of ethical, legal, social, political, and international issues that make business increasingly complex.
- Law is a collection of principles and rules that establish, guide, and alter the behavior of members of society. Rules include both the formal rules (law) of society and the informal rules as dictated by customs, traditions, and social ethics.
- Law helps to define acceptable behavior. To ensure order, the legal system provides a formal means through which disputes can be resolved. The law maintains the important values of a society. Finally, the legal system provides a way to encourage changes in social consciousness.
- Sources of law include the U.S. and state constitutions, Congress and the state legislatures, the judiciary branch, the executive branch (the president and governors), state and federal administrative agencies, and multiple sources that form the international legal environment of business.

- Judge-made or common law is the original source of law in this country. This system encourages judges to use prior decisions, or precedents, for guidance in deciding new disputes. The doctrine of *stare decisis*, standing on precedent, gives consistency to case law.
- Law can be classified on the basis of whether it is public or private, civil or criminal, or substantive or procedural.
- The public image of big business and of other major institutions is low. Dishonesty is believed to be common. To overcome problems, many companies use codes of ethics, and firms are enforcing compliance programs to help reduce severity of punishment by regulators in case of law violations.
- Business ethics involve standards and obligations that persons and firms may uphold in business that go beyond the requirements of the law. Some firms have active corporate social responsibility programs that engage the company in activities not required by law.

TERMS TO KNOW

law, 3
constitution, 6
common law, 8
case, 9
case reporters, 9
precedent, 9
stare decisis, 9
executive orders, 12
public law, 13

private law, 13
criminal law, 14
felony, 14
misdemeanor, 14
reasonable doubt, 14
civil law, 14
preponderance of the
   evidence, 14
substantive law, 14

procedural law, 14
ethics, 16
integrity, 16
morality, 16
compliance program, 18
corporate social responsibility, 18

DISCUSSION QUESTION

Should the common-law maxim, "Ignorance of the law is no excuse," apply to an immigrant who speaks little English and was not educated in the United States? How about for a tourist who does not speak English? Everyone knows criminal acts are not allowed, but what about more subtle rules that differ across countries that may not be understood by foreigners?

CASE QUESTIONS

1. Facts from an English judge's decision in 1884: "The crew of an English yacht … were cast away in a storm on the high seas … and were compelled to put into an open boat. … they had no supply of water and no supply of food. … That on the eighteenth day … they … suggested that one should be sacrificed to save the rest. … That next day … they … went to the boy … put a knife into his throat and killed him … the three men fed upon the body … of the boy for four days; [then] the boat was picked up by a passing vessel, and [they] were rescued. … and committed for

trial. … if the men had not fed upon the body of the boy they would probably not have survived to be so picked up and rescued, but would … have died of famine. The boy, being in a much weaker condition, was likely to have died before them. … The real question in this case [is] whether killing under the conditions set forth … be or be not murder." Do you consider the acts to be immoral? [*Regina* v. *Dudley and Stephens*, 14 Queens Bench Division 273 (1884)]

2. We know that smoking is a serious health hazard. Cigarettes are unavoidably dangerous but legal. Should cigarette manufacturers be liable for the serious illnesses and untimely deaths caused by their products, even though they post a warning on the package and consumers voluntarily assume the health risks by smoking? [*Cipollone* v. *Liggett Group, Inc.*, 505 U.S. 504 (1992)]
   ✓ Check your answer

3. Two eight-year-old boys were seriously injured when riding Honda mini-trail bikes. The boys were riding on public streets, ran a stop sign, and were hit by a truck. The bikes had clear warning labels on the front stating that they were only for off-road use. The manual stated the bikes were not to be used on public streets. The parents sued Honda. The Supreme Court of Washington said that there was one basic issue. "Is a manufacturer liable when children are injured while riding one of its mini-trail bikes on a public road in violation of manufacturer and parental warnings?" Is it unethical to make products like mini-trail bikes that will be used by children, when we know accidents like this will happen? [*Baughn* v. *Honda Motor Co.*, 727 P.2d 655 Sup. Ct., Wash. (1986)]

4. Johnson Controls adopted a "fetal protection policy" that women of childbearing age could not work in the battery-making division of the company. Exposure to lead in the battery operation could cause harm to unborn babies. The company was concerned about possible legal liability for injury suffered by babies of mothers who had worked in the battery division. The U.S. Supreme Court held that the company policy was illegal. It was an "excuse for denying women equal employment opportunities." Is the Court forcing the company to be unethical by allowing pregnant women who ignore the warnings to expose their babies to the lead? [*United Auto Workers* v. *Johnson Controls*, 499 U.S. 187 (1991)]
   ✓ Check your answer

5. Noonan worked for Staples, the office supply company. It has a Code of Ethics for employees. One provision states: "We expect you to keep accurate records and reports. … We do not permit … false or misleading entries in the company's books or records for any reason." Noonan was fired for padding expense accounts. The company had the right to fire him, but it also denied him termination benefits that he would otherwise have received. Is it proper for a company to deny such a benefit for an employee for a violation of its Code of Ethics? [*Noonan* v. *Staples*, 556 F.3d 20 (2009)]

6. McGrory worked for Applied Signal in a supervisory position. He was accused of violating the company's policies on sexual harassment. An internal investigation determined he did not violate the policy but that he was evasive and violated the company's personal ethics code. He was fired and sued for wrongful termination, contending that if he did not violate sexual harassment rules, he should not have been subject to termination. Do standards of law and ethics need to be the same for an employer? [*McGrory* v. *Applied Signal Technology*, Cal.Rptr.3d (2013)]

ETHICS QUESTIONS

1. The federal tax code is riddled with special-interest loopholes. Most of these exist because firms and trade associations lobby Congress and provide campaign support to members of Congress to gain special favors to individual firms or industries. Is it ethical for firms to seek special privilege?

2. "Fair trade" goods have become popular, as some people are willing to pay more to know that the goods come from workers paid a decent price for their efforts. However, some retailers who sell fair trade goods mark them up substantially more than non-fair trade goods. One study showed that coffee growers got an average of 44 cents a pound more for fair trade coffee, but the coffee at retail was marked up an additional $3.46 per pound. At one supermarket chain, fair trade bananas that cost an

extra 3.6 cents per pound were marked up four times the price of non-fair trade bananas. Fair trade goods are claimed to be a form of social responsibility. Is that true if it just means higher profit margins?

3. A chemical company located a new plant in a depressed area with high unemployment in West Virginia. It built a state-of-the-art plant that had the latest pollution control technology that met all EPA requirements. It created 2,500 jobs. The company was attacked for polluting a previously pristine area. Had the plant been built in an industrial area, such as the coast near Houston, no one would have been likely to complain. Was the company socially irresponsible for building the plant in such an area?

4. Discussion of ethics issues focuses on company examples. What personal ethics matter? Surveys indicate that many students have cheated in classes one way or another, padded their resumes when seeking jobs, and improperly downloaded copyrighted music. Does ethics "begin at home"?

CHAPTER **2**
The Court Systems

Billy Bones' Longboards of Oregon advertises and sells its products in western states. Its boards and related goods are mostly made in Oregon. If a customer in Arizona buys a Billy Bones' board after seeing it on the Bones' website, and is then injured when skate boarding, can the injured customer bring the lawsuit in the Arizona state court? Must the dispute be decided in an Oregon state court because the business is located in that state? Or would such a dispute be decided in the federal court system? Which substantive law concerning product liability applies? Which court procedure governs the matter? In any dispute, parties must understand and resolve these questions before they can effectively use our court system.

This chapter provides an overview of the American court system and discusses how a party who has suffered a legal wrong can seek relief in the courts. Businesses may face disputes with competitors, suppliers, customers, shareholders, and government agencies. Many problems are resolved directly by the parties with no serious disruption in business relationships or activities. Other problems require resolution in our court system through civil litigation.

A business that has a civil dispute that may go to litigation must first determine, with the help of an attorney, which court has the power and the authority to decide the case. That is, which court has the jurisdiction to take the case for resolution? Today, many businesses operate in multiple states and often in several countries. As a consequence, the choice of the appropriate court may not be clear, or the parties may be in a position to choose between more than one court.

The Court Systems

The federal court system was created in response to the following provision of the United States Constitution:

The judicial Power of the United States shall be vested in one supreme Court and in such inferior Courts [courts subordinate to the Supreme Court] as the Congress may from time to time ordain and establish.

Over many years, the federal court system developed into a three-level system consisting of the U.S. district courts, the U.S. courts of appeals, and the U.S. Supreme Court. In addition, there are specialized courts, such as the bankruptcy courts. Each court has its own role within the federal court system. Since the thirteen original states had courts before the federal system was created, they have the oldest court systems. The state and federal court systems have many similarities, but there are important differences.

Federal Judges

Federal judges are nominated by the president and confirmed by a majority vote in the U.S. Senate. Because the Constitution guarantees federal judges the right to serve "during good behavior," they enjoy a lifetime appointment. Judges below the Supreme Court level retire at age 70, but may remain on "senior status," still hear cases, and be paid. There are about 1,200 federal judges. According to the Constitution, federal judges may be removed from office only if the Congress impeaches them for treason, bribery, or other high crimes and misdemeanors. The impeachment process includes the actual impeachment (indictment) by the House of Representatives, followed by a trial before the Senate. If at least two thirds of the senators vote for removal, the judge is removed from office. This happens rarely; only a handful of federal judges in history have been removed.

While Congress may change the structure of the federal court system, it may not reduce a judge's salary or term of office once an appointment has been made. The writers of the Constitution gave federal judges job security because they wanted to guarantee that judges would be independent and free from the pressure of politics.

State Judges

In contrast to the position enjoyed by federal judges, most state judges serve for a fixed term, whether they are appointed or elected. Terms range from one year for judges in some midwestern states to a fourteen-year term for judges in New York. Massachusetts and New Hampshire appoint judges to serve until they reach age 70; only Rhode Island provides a lifetime term of office.

State judges are chosen by a variety of methods, as Exhibit 2.1 shows. They are elected, appointed, or chosen by a method that mixes the election and appointment processes. In several states with the mixed system, a state bar association committee recommends candidates, and the governor then appoints a judge from its list. The judge selected then serves until the next election, at which time the public is asked to vote for or against him. This system for selecting judges is referred to as the Missouri System.

Some observers claim that appointed judges are of higher average quality than elected judges. Others assert that elected judges work harder than appointed judges. There is statistical evidence that in states with elected judges, the average awards in tort cases are larger and out-of-state companies are treated worse than in states with appointed judges. However, many elected judges are initially appointed to fill vacancies created by retirements. The evidence is that elected and appointed judges are similar in characteristics.

EXHIBIT 2.1 SELECTION METHODS FOR APPEALS COURT AND TRIAL COURT JUDGES

MERIT SELECTION BY NOMINATING COMMIS-SION AND GOVERNOR	GOVERNOR (G) OR LEGISLATURE (L) APPOINTMENT	ELECTIONS BY PARTY	NON-PARTISAN ELECTIONS	COMBINED MERIT SELECTION AND OTHER METHODS
Alaska	California (G)	Alabama	Arkansas	Arizona
Colorado	Maine (G)	Illinois	Georgia	Florida
Connecticut	New Jersey (G)	Louisiana	Idaho	Indiana
Delaware	New Hampshire (G)	Michigan	Kentucky	Kansas
Hawaii	Virginia (L)	Ohio	Minnesota	New York
Iowa		Pennsylvania	Mississippi	Oklahoma
Maryland		Texas	Montana	South Carolina
Massachusetts		West Virginia	Nevada	South Dakota
Missouri			North Carolina	Tennessee
Nebraska			North Dakota	
New Mexico			Oregon	
Rhode Island			Washington	
Utah			Wisconsin	
Vermont				
Wyoming				

Source: American Judicature Society.

Judicial Immunity

Under the **doctrine of judicial immunity**, a judge is absolutely immune from suit for damages for judicial acts. Without this rule, judges could fear being sued by parties unhappy with their judicial decisions. As a result, judges could lose their ability to be independent decision makers. By protecting judges from such suits, judicial immunity aims to keep judges unconcerned about the relative power of parties who appear in court. This immunity extends to parties who perform services that are related to the performance of judicial functions, as we see in the *Davis* case. It also applies to certain quasi-judicial functions, such as officials who perform regulatory duties.

Organization of the Court Systems

Both state and federal court systems have lower courts of **original jurisdiction**, where disputes are first brought and tried, and courts of **appellate jurisdiction**, where the decisions of a lower court may be taken for review. In both systems, the courts of original jurisdiction are trial courts. One judge presides. The courts' principal function is to determine the facts in the dispute and to apply the appropriate law to those facts in making a decision or judgment. As we discuss in the next chapter, the jury is responsible for deciding the facts in a case; if there is no jury in a case, the judge decides the facts.

DAVIS V. WEST
Court of Appeals of Texas, Houston 317 S.W.3d 301 (2009)

Case Background *Houston Reporting Service (HRS) provided court reporting services for attorney Davis. HRS billed Davis for its services, but was not paid. HRS sued Davis for $1,083.98 for a deposition report, plus attorney's fees, interest, and costs. As Davis did not defend herself against the suit, the Justice Court in Harris County entered a default judgment. HRS then began collection efforts. The court appointed Radoff as receiver in the case and issued an order commanding that Radoff take possession of "all ... monies in deposit [by Davis] in financial institutions."*

Radoff sent Davis a letter informing her that he was the receiver and asked her for payment to satisfy the judgment. He sent a letter to Davis' bank demanding that it pay $4,144.91 to Radoff, which the bank did. That satisfied the judgment. HRS was paid and the receivership was closed. Davis then sued Radoff for abuse of process. The trial court granted summary judgment in Radoff's favor on the grounds that he was entitled to derived judicial immunity. Davis appealed.

Case Decision George C. Hanks, Jr., Justice

* * *

A person entitled to derived judicial immunity receives the same absolute immunity from liability for acts performed within the scope of his jurisdiction as a judge. Judicial immunity can attach to certain non-judges because the policy reasons for judicial immunity-protection of individual judges and of the public's interest in an independent judiciary are also implicated when judges delegate their authority, appoint another to perform services for the court, or allow another to otherwise serve as an officer of the court. In those circumstances, the immunity attaching to the judge follows the delegation, appointment, or court employment. The person acting in such a capacity thus also enjoys absolute immunity, which is known as derived judicial immunity.

Texas uses a "functional approach" to determine whether someone is entitled to derived judicial immunity. The "functional approach looks to whether the person seeking immunity is intimately associated with the judicial process" and whether "that person exercises discretionary judgment comparable to that of the judge." The functional approach focuses on the nature of the function performed, not the identity of the actor, and considers whether the court officer's conduct is like that of the delegating or appointing judge.

Radoff contends that, as a court-appointed receiver acting within the scope of his authority, he is entitled to derived judicial immunity. We agree. "Like a court-appointed bankruptcy trustee acting within his authority as trustee, a court-appointed receiver acts as an arm of the court and is immune from liability for actions grounded in his conduct as receiver."

"Once an individual is cloaked with derived judicial immunity because of a particular function being performed for a court, every action taken with regard to that function—whether good or bad, honest or dishonest, well-intentioned or not—is immune from suit. Once applied to the function, the cloak of immunity covers all acts, both good and bad."

* * *

We conclude that the trial court properly granted summary judgment on Radoff's motion for summary judgment as a matter of law on his defense of derived judicial immunity....

Affirmed.

Questions for Analysis

1. Why did Radoff ask for, and get, $4,144.91 when the amount owed was $1,083.98?
2. Do you think Davis could have a cause of action against her bank for giving her money to Radoff without her permission?

EXHIBIT 2.2   THE COURT SYSTEMS

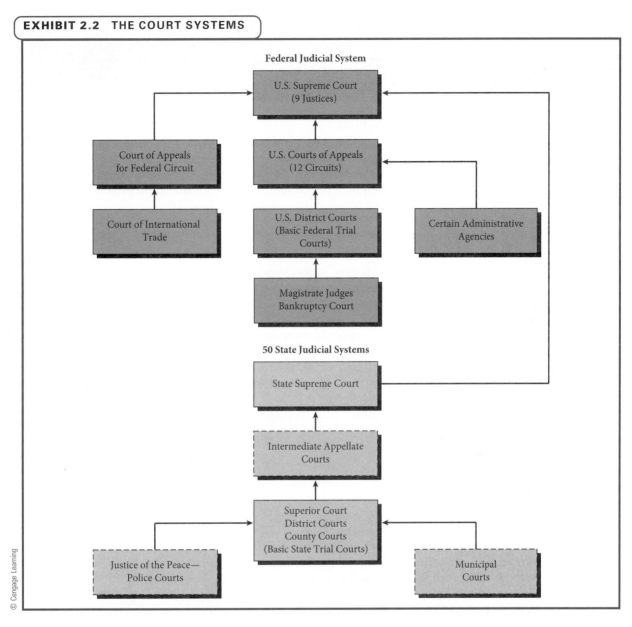

Appellate courts are concerned with correcting errors in the application of the law and making sure proper procedure was followed in the trial court proceeding. Normally three judges review decisions at the intermediate appeals court level. The state supreme courts provide review with participation of all members. The number of judges on the highest appellate court varies across the states from five to nine. The basic structure of the American court system is illustrated in Exhibit 2.2. While we focus more on federal courts here because they serve as a general model, the majority of litigation occurs in state courts.

The Federal Courts

The Constitution intends for the judiciary in the United States to have significant independence from the other branches of government as part of the system of checks and balances. This is unlike most countries, where judges are civil servants who have less independence than judges in the United States enjoy. While some state judges are in political positions, federal judges, once on the bench, are independent. With the exception of bankruptcy judges, federal judges, once appointed and confirmed, are rarely forced from office.

Federal District Courts

As the trial courts of the federal system, U.S. district courts are the courts of original jurisdiction in the federal system. District courts are the only courts in the federal system that use juries. Most cases involving questions of federal law originate in these courts. The geographical boundary of a district court's jurisdiction does not cross state lines. There are a total of 94 federal districts in the court system. Each state has at least one federal district court; the more populated states are divided into two, three, or—as in California, New York, and Texas—four districts. In addition, there are federal district courts in the District of Columbia, Puerto Rico, Guam, and the Virgin Islands. There are 670 federal district judges, so many districts have multiple judges.

In addition to district judges, federal trial courts also use judicial officers called **magistrates**. In each district in which the Judicial Conference of the United States has authorized them to do so, the federal judges may jointly appoint one or more magistrates for eight-year terms. The judges can then send particular matters to the magistrate to be heard, such as discovery disputes, habeas corpus petitions, or civil rights claims filed by prisoners, with the magistrate making a recommendation to the district judge. Cases may even be tried before a magistrate instead of a judge, if both parties agree. This typically happens where courts have a backlog, and the parties want a quicker trial than is available before the district judge. Because magistrates are not appointed under Article III of the Constitution however, they cannot try cases in the place of a district judge without the parties' consent.

Federal Appellate Courts

U.S. courts of appeals may review federal district court decisions. Established in 1891, the U.S. courts of appeals are the intermediate-level appellate courts in the federal system. There are 12 geographically based courts of appeals, one for each of the 11 circuits into which the United States is divided, and one for the District of Columbia that hears many cases involving federal regulations. The division of the states into circuits and the location of the U.S. courts of appeals are presented in Exhibit 2.3.

The U.S. courts of appeals exercise only appellate jurisdiction. If either party to the litigation is not satisfied with a federal district court's decision, it has the right to appeal to the court of appeals for the circuit in which that district court is located. The Fourth Circuit U.S. Court of Appeals headquartered in Richmond, Virginia, for example, hears appeals only from the federal district courts in the states of Maryland, North Carolina, South Carolina, Virginia, and West Virginia.

Although they have many judges, the U.S. courts of appeals assign three-judge panels to review most district courts decisions appealed within their circuits. Occasionally, all the active judges in a circuit hear a case in what is known as an ***en banc* proceeding**. As a practical matter, because it is so difficult to obtain review by the U.S. Supreme Court, the courts of appeals make the final decision in most cases.

Specialized Federal Courts

Although the U.S. Supreme Court, courts of appeals, and district courts are the most visible federal courts, there are also courts with limited or special jurisdiction within

EXHIBIT 2.3 THE FEDERAL JUDICIAL CIRCUITS

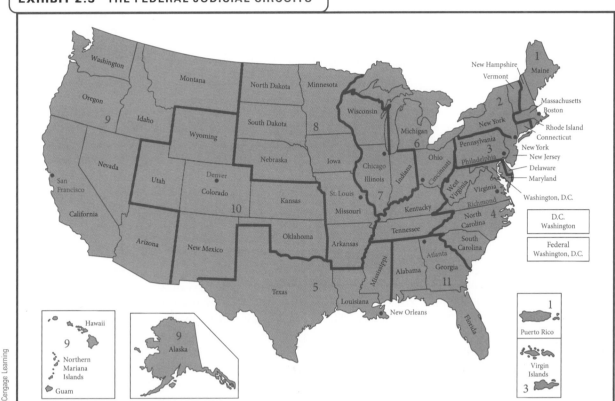

© Cengage Learning

the federal court system. These courts differ from other federal courts in that their jurisdictions are defined in terms of subject matter. U.S. bankruptcy courts exist alongside the district courts. Bankruptcy courts are under the supervision of district courts, but in practice they are accorded great deference. Some districts have multiple bankruptcy judges because there are about 350 such judges, as set by Congress. They handle, of course, cases under federal bankruptcy law. They are appointed by the judges of the courts of appeals and serve 14-year terms.

The U.S. Court of Federal Claims, which is located in Washington, D.C., has 16 judges who serve 15-year terms. They hear cases involving money claims against the federal government. The U.S. Court of International Trade, which sits in New York City, has nine judges. They hear cases involving international customs matters, such as tariff classifications and trade disputes. The U.S. Tax Court consists of 19 judges appointed for 15-year terms. The court primarily hears tax disputes involving the Internal Revenue Service. The court is not a part of the federal judiciary; it is a part of the legislative branch of government.

The Court of Appeals for the Federal Circuit has 12 judges who sit in Washington, D.C. Although its jurisdiction is nationwide, its subject-matter jurisdiction is limited to appeals from the district courts in patent, trademark, and copyright cases; in cases where the United States is a defendant; appeals from the Court of Federal Claims and from the Court of International Trade; and the review of administrative rulings of the U.S. Patent and Trademark Office. Because these matters are technical, Congress established the Federal Circuit so that appeals could be heard by judges who have expertise in these areas.

U.S. Supreme Court

The U.S. Supreme Court is the highest court in the country, as we see in Exhibit 2.2. Created by the U.S. Constitution, the Supreme Court is primarily an appellate review court. Cases reaching the Court are usually heard by nine justices, one of whom is the Chief Justice. The term of the Court begins, by law, on the first Monday in October and continues as long as the business of the Court requires. The Court sits in Washington, D.C.

As an appellate court, the Supreme Court may review appeals from the U.S. district courts, the U.S. courts of appeals, and the highest courts of the states when federal and constitutional issues are at stake. In rare instances, such as in a dispute between two state governments, the U.S. Supreme Court has original and exclusive jurisdiction.

Appellate review is normally obtained by petitioning the court for a writ of certiorari. Appeals to the Supreme Court are heard only at the Court's discretion. The members of the Court determine which cases they wish to review; at least four justices must agree to review a case. If that does not happen, the decision of the lower court becomes final. Although it receives thousands of such petitions each term, the Court accepts few. The Court issues about 70 to 80 opinions per term, down from more than 200 opinions in earlier decades. In contrast, most state high courts issue more opinions, such as the Montana Supreme Court, which issues more than 350 per year. Most petitions granted by the U.S. Supreme Court involve an issue of constitutional importance or a conflict between the decisions of two or more U.S. courts of appeals.

Despite differences in substantive law, foreign courts are often similar in basic structure, but not in procedure, to those in the United States. The *International Perspective* feature looks at the court system in France to contrast it to the system in the United States.

INTERNATIONAL PERSPECTIVE

The French Court System

Like most European countries, France is a civil-law country; its legal system is based on written (code) law rather than on judge-made common law. The structure of the French system appears similar to that of the U.S. federal court system. The French system consists of a supreme court (*cour de cessation*), a court of appeals (*cour d'appel*), and a court of general jurisdiction (*tribunal d'instance*).

The appellate process in France is different from that in the United States, however. In contrast to the powers held by the U.S. Supreme Court, the *cour de cessation* does not have the authority to pronounce judgment. Rather, it has power either to reject an appeal or to invalidate a decision and return the case to the court of appeals for reconsideration.

In the event the appeal is rejected, the proceedings are finished. If, on the other hand, the decision of the *cour d'appel* is invalidated, that court then reconsiders the case before a five-judge panel. However, the judges are not bound by the higher court's determination of the law as they would be in the United States. They may either accept or reject it. They may also consider new facts.

If the case is then appealed a second time to the *cour de cessation*, the case is heard by a panel of 25 judges. If this appeal is rejected, the proceedings end; if the *cour d'appel* decision is invalidated, the case is returned to it for reconsideration. On the second appeal, however, the judges of the *cour d'appel* must follow the higher court's decisions on points of law.

The State Courts

Although the names and organization differ somewhat from state to state, the state court systems are similar in general framework and jurisdictional authorities. Many are three-level systems and many states have local courts of special or limited jurisdiction.

State Courts of Original Jurisdiction

Each state court system has courts of original jurisdiction, or trial courts, where disputes are initially brought and tried. There are often courts of **general jurisdiction** and several courts of **limited** (or **special**) **jurisdiction**. Courts of general jurisdiction have authority to decide almost any kind of dispute and are able to grant virtually every type of relief. In many states, the amount in controversy, however, must generally exceed a specific amount, often $2,000 to $5,000.

The state courts of general jurisdiction, or trial courts, are organized into districts, often on the county level. These district courts have different names in different states, although their jurisdictional limitations are similar. In some states, the courts of general jurisdiction are called superior courts. The same courts in Pennsylvania and Ohio are called the Courts of Common Pleas, but in Florida and Oregon, they are called Circuit Courts. In Kansas, Louisiana, Maine, and other states, the courts of general jurisdiction are called district courts. Oddly, in New York, they are called supreme courts.

Courts of limited or special jurisdiction include municipal courts, justice of the peace courts, and other more specialized courts (such as probate courts, which handle matters related to wills and trusts). The jurisdiction of the municipal courts is similar to that of the district courts, except that municipal courts typically hear claims that involve less money. Litigants not satisfied with the decision of the limited jurisdiction court may appeal to the court of general jurisdiction. On appeal, the parties will get a new trial or, in legal terminology, a **trial *de novo***.

Many states provide small claims courts that have limited jurisdiction. The amount in controversy in most small claims courts may not exceed $5,000 ($7,500 in California). Subject matter includes debts, contract disputes, warranty claims, personal injuries, and security deposits. Small claims courts are particularly good for collecting small debts because procedure is much less formal, and representation by an attorney is not necessary and usually is not permitted. Small claims courts are a faster and less expensive forum than are district courts. Most state courts have websites to guide you through the procedure.

State Courts of Appellate Jurisdiction

Every judicial system allows the review of trial court decisions by a court with **appellate jurisdiction**. In general, a party has the right to appeal a trial court judgment to at least one higher court. When a court system contains two levels of appellate courts, appeal usually is a matter of right at the first level and at the discretion of the court at the second. These courts have different names in different states, such as District Courts of Appeal in Florida and Appellate Division Courts in New York. The most common issues reaching the highest court in a state typically involve the validity of a state law, the state constitution, or a federal law as it is affected by a state law. A party seeking further review from the state supreme court may seek review from the U.S. Supreme Court, but that is rarely granted.

Lighter Side of the Law

In-the-Courtroom Training

Although the failure rate is quite high, it is not uncommon for people to represent themselves in court (called *pro se* litigation). The judges are sympathetic to self-representation in some cases, but not always.

Paul Baldwin appeared in court in Portsmouth, New Hampshire, after being arrested for stealing a can of beer. The judge asked if he wanted to have a lawyer appointed to represent him. Baldwin said, "I don't need a lawyer. I've been in the court more than you have."

After 152 previous arrests, that could be true. The judge was not amused and ordered him held on $10,000 bail.

Source: Portsmouth Herald.

Rules of Civil Procedure

From the moment the **plaintiff**—the party who claims to have suffered an injury that the law can remedy—brings an action, a lawsuit is governed by detailed procedural rules. These force the parties to define the issues in the dispute. The rules also control how the parties to the dispute—the plaintiff and the **defendant** (the party who allegedly injured the plaintiff)—present evidence and arguments in support of their positions.

Although the states are free to develop their own procedural rules, most have adopted the *Federal Rules of Civil Procedure* or rules similar to them. The *Federal Rules*, which have been modified over the years, were developed by an advisory committee appointed by the U.S. Supreme Court and became effective in 1938. The *Federal Rules* govern the procedure of the litigation process, including the pleadings, discovery, trial procedures, and relevant motions. Note that these rules govern only civil litigation; somewhat different procedures are used in criminal and administrative litigation.

The *Federal Rules of Civil Procedure* are contained in the United States Code, Title 28. In addition to establishing trial procedural rules, Title 28 establishes the organization of the federal courts, judicial agencies, and important rules governing jurisdiction and venue. This chapter concentrates on jurisdiction and the organization of the court system. Chapter 3 examines trial procedures and processes.

Jurisdiction

The literal meaning of the term **jurisdiction** is "the power to speak of the law." A court's jurisdiction defines the limits within which it may declare, administer, or apply the law. The limitations imposed upon a court by a constitution, and the statutes that created it, determine what kinds of disputes it may resolve, depending on who the parties to a case are.

When a plaintiff files a lawsuit, the plaintiff must choose the correct court to resolve the dispute. The plaintiff must select a court that has both:

1. Subject-matter jurisdiction, and
2. Personal jurisdiction over (a) the person of the defendant or (b) the property of the defendant.

❓ TEST YOURSELF

1. Most state judges are appointed until age 70, when retirement is usually mandatory: T—F
2. Attorney Davis sued Radoff, the person appointed by the court to be receiver for a debt owed. Radoff convinced Davis' bank to take money out of Davis' account without Davis' permission. The appeals court, in *Davis* v. *West*, held that Radoff:
   a. could be liable for conversion of funds from the account.
   b. was protected against suit by a form of judicial immunity.
   c. could be liable for falsely impersonating a court officer.
   d. could sue Davis for falsely claiming not to have enough money to pay the debt owed.
3. The court that hears suits for money filed against the federal government is called the court of _____. The court that hears cases involving customs and tariffs disputes is called the court of _____.
4. Judicial officials who assist U.S. district court judges in many matters, and may be assigned to hear cases, are called:
   a. clerks.
   b. bailiffs.
   c. receivers.
   d. magistrates.
5. Small claims courts cannot hear disputes involving more than $5,000 in most states: T—F

Answers: F; b; federal claims, international trade; d; T.

If a court should rule in a particular case and it is later determined that jurisdiction was lacking, the judgment of that court will be declared null and void upon appeal. Without jurisdiction a court cannot exercise authority.

Subject-Matter Jurisdiction

Subject-matter jurisdiction is created by a constitution or a statute regarding the types of disputes a court can accept to resolve. It often includes requirements on the amount in controversy and the areas of the law the court may cover. For example, state statutes might restrict disputes in district (trial) courts to civil cases involving more than $2,000, or they might require that all cases involving wills be heard by a probate court. That is, the state legislature places limitations on the subject-matter jurisdiction of various courts.

Subject-Matter Jurisdiction in the Federal Courts Under the U.S. Constitution, the federal courts may hear only those cases within the judicial power of the United States. That is, federal courts have the judicial power to hear cases involving a **federal question**:

> The judicial Power shall extend to all Cases … arising under this Constitution, the Laws of the United States, and Treaties made, or which shall be made, under their Authority.…
>
> This includes cases based on the relationship of the parties involved: [The judicial Power shall extend] to all Cases affecting Ambassadors, other public Ministers … to Controversies between two or more States;—between a State and Citizens of another State;—between Citizens of different States … and between a State, or the Citizens thereof, and foreign States, Citizens or Subjects.

Lighter Side **of the Law**

It's Only Taxpayer Money

If someone applies for Social Security Disability benefits and is not awarded benefits, an appeal may be filed. There are 1,500 judges who handle such appeals; on average they grant disability status about 60 percent of the time.

Judge David Daugherty found for claimants 99 percent of the time. Commenting on other judges who were not so generous, he said they "act like it's their own damn money we're giving away." After the *Wall Street Journal* reported Daugherty's generosity, especially for clients of certain lawyers who received benefits without a hearing, he retired. Later, suit was filed against him and a lawyer who often presented cases to him for defrauding the government of millions of dollars.

Sources: Wall Street Journal; Associated Press.

When federal jurisdiction is based on the parties involved, most litigation is generated by cases (1) in which the United States is a party to the suit or (2) involving citizens of different states. The purpose for allowing federal jurisdiction when a dispute arises between citizens of different states—referred to as **diversity-of-citizenship** or **diversity jurisdiction**—is to provide a neutral forum for handling such disputes.

The writers of the Constitution worried that state courts might be biased in favor of their own citizens and against "strangers" from other states or countries. To obtain diversity jurisdiction, there must be total diversity of citizenship among the parties. That is, all parties on one side of the lawsuit must have state citizenship different from all the parties on the other side of the lawsuit. To establish federal jurisdiction in a diversity case, the parties must also show two things: (1) that they are from different states and (2) that the **amount in controversy** (the sum the plaintiff is suing the defendant for) is more than $75,000. In cases involving questions of federal law, there is no minimum dollar requirement.

Personal Jurisdiction

Once it is established that the court has subject-matter jurisdiction, the plaintiff must meet the **personal jurisdiction** requirements. A court's jurisdictional authority is generally limited to the boundaries of the state in which it is located. Territorial jurisdiction usually does not become an issue unless the defendant is not a resident of the state in which the plaintiff wishes to bring the lawsuit. In such a case, the plaintiff must determine how to bring the defendant—or the defendant's property—before the court.

A court's power over the person ("person" may be a business) of the defendant is referred to as *in personam* **jurisdiction**. The defendant is served with a **summons**, a notice of the lawsuit (see Exhibit 2.4). That is, after selecting the appropriate court, the plaintiff must properly notify the defendant of the action filed by **service of process**. The summons directs the defendant to appear before the court to defend against the plaintiff's allegations. The court will issue a **default judgment** against a defendant who fails to appear.

EXHIBIT 2.4   A TYPICAL SUMMONS

United States District Court
for the
Southern District of California

Elena Gori	Civil Action, File Number 80151
Plaintiff	
v.	Summons
Tom Eyestone	
Defendant	

To the above-named Defendant:
You are hereby summoned and required to serve upon *Carol Chapman*, plaintiff's attorney, whose address is *3620 San Felipe, San Diego, California*, an answer to the complaint which is herewith served upon you, within 20 days after service of this summons upon you, exclusive of the day of service. If you fail to do so, judgment by default will be taken against you for the relief demanded in the complaint.

Gloria Hernandez
Clerk of Court

[Seal of the U.S. District Court]
Dated 2/5/15

© Cengage Learning

Service of process is usually achieved by **personal service**. The plaintiff, the plaintiff's attorney, a private process server, or a public official, such as a sheriff or a U.S. marshal, delivers the summons to the defendant. In civil litigation, a private process server usually serves process. If the defendant cannot be located, courts allow the limited use of substituted service, such as publication of the pending lawsuit in a newspaper. The U.S.

INTERNATIONAL PERSPECTIVE

London's Commercial Court

When international contracts are signed, the parties can specify how future disputes will be resolved, including the choice of a court. If a court is not agreed upon initially, parties can agree at the time of a dispute where to resolve the matter. The Commercial Court in London is a popular forum; many of its cases involve parties from more than one country.

Created in 1895, the court is often chosen because London is a major business city; most firms have assets in the U.K. that the court can control; and the judges are experienced in commercial matters. Over 1,000 cases are filed each year; about a quarter of them actually go to trial.

As the court's website notes, it "deals with complex cases arising out of business disputes, both national and international. There is particular emphasis on international trade, banking, commodity, and arbitration disputes." Smaller and less complex cases are assigned to the London Mercantile Court, and cases involving shipping disputes go to the Admiralty Court.

One judge handles each trial; there is no jury. Trials usually occur within months of when requested and are finished quickly; the losing party pays the winner's attorney fees. Because English courts are respected, their judgments are likely to be enforced in other countries, and the remedies used by the court have been innovative and relevant to commercial matters.

© Cengage Learning

Supreme Court has emphasized that substituted service must be reasonably calculated to alert the defendant of the action. Although television shows sometimes show clever tricks being used to serve process on a defendant attempting to dodge a suit, most business cases involve direct service on a business's registered agent. There is little drama involved.

Jurisdiction over Out-of-State Defendants If both parties to a lawsuit are residents of the same state, the courts of the state clearly have jurisdiction over both persons. Within a state, the proper court should be used. If both parties are residents of Dallas County, Texas, the state district court in Dallas County would be proper. If the defendant is a resident of another state, obtaining jurisdiction can be more difficult. The most obvious method for obtaining *in personam* jurisdiction over nonresident defendants is to serve them with process while they are within the state. The nonresident defendant need only be passing through the state to be legally served with a summons.

While it would seem as if defendants could avoid lawsuits by staying out of state, often the court can still exert jurisdiction. If the defendant committed a wrong, such as causing an automobile accident within the court's territorial boundaries, or has done business within the state, the court can exercise jurisdiction under the authority of the state's **long-arm statute** (see Exhibit 2.5). A long-arm statute is a state law that permits a state's courts to reach beyond the state's boundaries for jurisdiction over nonresident defendants.

Jurisdiction over Out-of-State Business Defendants The long-arm statutes are aimed primarily at nonresident businesses. Do business defendants receive less favorable treatment by courts when it comes to jurisdiction than do individual defendants? Juries tend to be more hostile to business defendants, viewing them as more powerful, wealthy, and unfair, an entity against whom the state's citizens need protection. True or not, courts primarily have jurisdiction over a corporation in the following three situations:

1. The court is in the state in which the corporation was incorporated.
2. The court is in the state where the corporation has its headquarters or its main plant.
3. The court is in a state in which the corporation is doing business.

While the first two points rarely create legal issues, the third basis for jurisdiction—doing business in a state—has been subject to constitutional scrutiny by the U.S. Supreme Court. In reaching out-of-state corporate defendants, states rely upon

---

EXHIBIT 2.5   LONG-ARM STATUTE: GENERAL LAWS OF MASSACHUSETTS

CHAPTER 223A. Jurisdiction of Courts of the Commonwealth over Persons in Other States and Countries

Section 3. A court may exercise personal jurisdiction over a person, who acts directly or by an agent as to a cause of action in law or equity arising from the person's
  (a) transacting any business in this commonwealth;
  (b) contracting to supply services or things in this commonwealth;
  (c) causing tortious injury by an act or omission in this commonwealth;
  (d) causing tortious injury in this commonwealth by an act or omission outside this commonwealth, if he regularly does or solicits business, or engages in any other persistent course of conduct, or derives substantial revenue from goods used or consumed or services rendered in this commonwealth;
  (e) having an interest in, using, or possessing real property in this commonwealth;
  (f) contracting to insure any person, property, or risk located within this commonwealth at the time of contracting.

CYBER LAW

The Long Arm of the Internet

Sales on the Internet allow a business to try for nationwide exposure. When does a website advertiser become subject to jurisdiction in other states if a buyer wishes to sue the online seller?

In general, personal jurisdiction is appropriate when the defendant has engaged in business in a state. Hence, Amazon.com, which does active business in every state by selling directly online, is subject to court jurisdiction in every state.

Jurisdiction is not appropriate when the defendant's contact with the forum state is only informational. Even if the website is interactive, if it is only informative, no jurisdiction is created. Similarly, if a website provides information about sales, allows customers to download order forms, and provides an e-mail address for inquiries, that is not enough to subject the defendant to jurisdiction.

An area that is unclear is how much activity must occur with residents in a state for a web-based business to be subject to jurisdiction. Courts have ruled in different ways in nearly identical cases involving disputes over cars sold on eBay. In one case, an Indiana appeals court held that Indiana courts had personal jurisdiction over an Idaho buyer of a car sold by a seller in Indiana. In another case, a federal appeals court held that courts in California did not have personal jurisdiction over the seller of a car in Wisconsin. The unhappy California buyer would have to go to Wisconsin to sue.

When technology or business conditions change, it may take some years of litigation for consistent rules to evolve.

© Cengage Learning

long-arm statutes. As Exhibit 2.5 shows, the statutes often list "transacting any business" in the state as a basis for jurisdiction. According to the Supreme Court in the landmark case of *International Shoe Company* v. *Washington* (66 S.Ct. 154, 1945), a state's long-arm statutes must identify certain minimum contacts between the corporation and the state where the suit is being filed to qualify as transacting business.

In the *Blimka* case, we see an example of long-arm jurisdiction being established in state court over a company from another state doing business over the Internet.

BLIMKA V. MY WEB WHOLESALERS, LLC
Supreme Court of Idaho 143 Idaho 723, 152 P.3d 594 (2007)

Case Background *My Web Wholesalers, a company in Maine, used the Internet to do business around the country. It made offers on its website but did not distribute e-mails to customers who did not request information.*

Blimka, an Idaho resident, discovered My Web when surfing the net. He called My Web to discuss bulk merchandise offered on the website. DePalma, a My Web manager, agreed to sell Blimka 26,500 pairs of jeans for $20,935. Blimka wired the money to My Web. When a shipment of 16,000 pairs of jeans arrived, Blimka called My Web to complain

that the jeans were not of the quality discussed. My Web's response was not satisfactory.

Blimka sued My Web and DePalma in state court in Idaho for the tort of fraud. Defendants were properly served in Maine, but did not respond to the complaint, so the district court issued a judgment against My Web and DePalma. Defendants filed a motion for relief from the judgment, claiming it was void for lack of personal jurisdiction. The district court held that it had personal jurisdiction. Defendants appealed to the high court of Idaho.

Case Decision Jones, Justice

* * *

This case concerns the exercise of personal jurisdiction by an Idaho court over nonresident defendants, a small Maine-based company and its manager, who utilized the Internet to advertise and conduct business on a national scale.

* * *

The proper exercise of personal jurisdiction over nonresident defendants by an Idaho court involves satisfying two criteria: First, the court must determine that the nonresident defendant's actions fall within the scope of Idaho's long-arm statute. Second, the court must determine that exercising jurisdiction over the nonresident defendant comports with the constitutional standards of the Due Process Clause of the U.S. Constitution....

Blimka alleges that the defendants directed misrepresentations to him in Idaho via electronic means and that he sustained injury when he took delivery of the jeans in Idaho, only then learning that they had been misrepresented....

In this case, the allegedly fraudulent representations were directed at an Idaho resident and the injury occurred in this state. Thus, we hold that Blimka's allegation of fraud was sufficient to invoke the tortious acts language of [the long-arm statute] with respect to both defendants....

Where an Idaho resident alleges that a defendant in Maine intentionally directed false representations to, and caused injury in, Idaho that resident need not travel to Maine to pursue his or her claim against the perpetrator of the fraud. The defendants' actions satisfy minimum contacts with respect to the fraud allegations.

Additionally, because the defendants purposefully directed their allegedly false representations into Idaho, the exercise of personal jurisdiction is presumed not to offend traditional notions of fair play and substantial justice. Idaho has an ever-increasing interest in protecting its residents from fraud committed on them from afar by electronic means....

In sum, neither the Idaho long-arm statute nor the Due Process Clause precluded the district court from exercising personal jurisdiction over the defendants and entering a binding judgment against them in this case. As a result, the district court's decision to deny the defendants' motion for relief from judgment was not an abuse of that court's discretion and will not be disturbed by this Court....

We hold that the acts of the defendants were sufficient to subject them to the jurisdiction of the Idaho courts for the purpose of this litigation. The decision of the district court is affirmed. Blimka is awarded attorney fees and costs on appeal.

Questions for Analysis

1. The Idaho high court held that Idaho courts have jurisdiction over an out-of-state seller who misrepresented goods sold over the Internet. Does this mean most Internet-based sellers are subject to jurisdiction in every state where they have a customer?
2. Why did My Web not move the case from Idaho state court to federal court?

ISSUE SPOTTER
Can Your Firm Be Reached?

You work for a Florida real estate development firm, GoldenShores. Many clients come from the New York area to retire or to have a second home. To help marketing, a colleague suggests sending e-mails to potential clients advertising property and offering a five percent discount to buyers who respond to the e-mail and then buy property. New York requires real estate agents who offer property for sale to be registered in the state of New York. Your colleague says that this requirement does not apply to your company because it is located in Florida and sells property only in Florida. He claims it does not matter if the state of New York likes the advertisements or not; it cannot come after GoldenShores. Is that right?

Jurisdiction over Property

In lawsuits based on a dispute over property, a court in the state where the property is located has jurisdiction to resolve claims against that property—whether the property owner is there or not. The court is said to have **in rem** **jurisdiction** (*rem* means "the thing"). Property in an *in rem* proceeding can include tangible property, such as real estate and personal property, and intangible property, including bank accounts and stocks. Even if a court cannot obtain jurisdiction over the person of the defendant, it still may have authority to establish jurisdiction based on the existence of the defendant's property within the state. Suppose Andy and Carol are in a dispute over who owns a piece of property in Illinois. Andy sues Carol in state court in Illinois to obtain a court decree about property ownership. Carol lives in Alabama and refuses to respond to the suit. While the Illinois court does not have jurisdiction over Carol in Alabama, it has jurisdiction over the property in Illinois, so it may decide who the rightful owner is.

Relations Between the Court Systems

Some disputes can be resolved only in the state courts, some disputes only in the federal courts, and some disputes in either the federal or the state court systems. If a case could go to either federal or state court, one party may choose to file quickly before the other party if it has a preference as to which court is chosen for trial.

Exclusive Jurisdiction

Courts in the federal system have **exclusive jurisdiction** over certain disputes. State courts do not have subject matter jurisdiction over such cases and so may not try them. Congress specifies by statute matters over which the federal courts have exclusive jurisdiction. For example, federal courts have exclusive jurisdiction in cases involving federal crimes, bankruptcy, patents, and copyrights.

State courts have exclusive jurisdiction over disputes such as divorce, adoption, and other matters controlled by state governments. A state government may confer exclusive jurisdiction on its courts as long as it does not infringe on the supremacy of federal law. If a plaintiff seeks relief for such a state matter in a federal court, the case would be dismissed for lack of jurisdiction. The plaintiff would need to refile the case in the appropriate state court.

With exclusive jurisdiction, the court hearing the case—whether a federal court or a state court—applies its procedural rules and follows its substantive law. If the court with jurisdiction is a state court in California, for example, it follows California procedural rules and applies the laws of the state of California. If the court is a federal court, it follows federal rules of procedure and applies federal law.

Concurrent Jurisdiction

As Exhibit 2.6 illustrates, both the federal and the state court systems have jurisdiction in some disputes. When both systems have the power to hear a case, **concurrent jurisdiction** exists. In such cases, where the case is heard usually depends on which court the plaintiff picks. As Exhibit 2.6 also illustrates, both systems may have jurisdiction when either of the following is the case:

1. There is diversity of citizenship and the amount in controversy exceeds $75,000.
2. The dispute involves a federal question and Congress has not conferred exclusive jurisdiction on the federal courts.

EXHIBIT 2.6   JURISDICTION RELATIONSHIPS BETWEEN COURT SYSTEMS

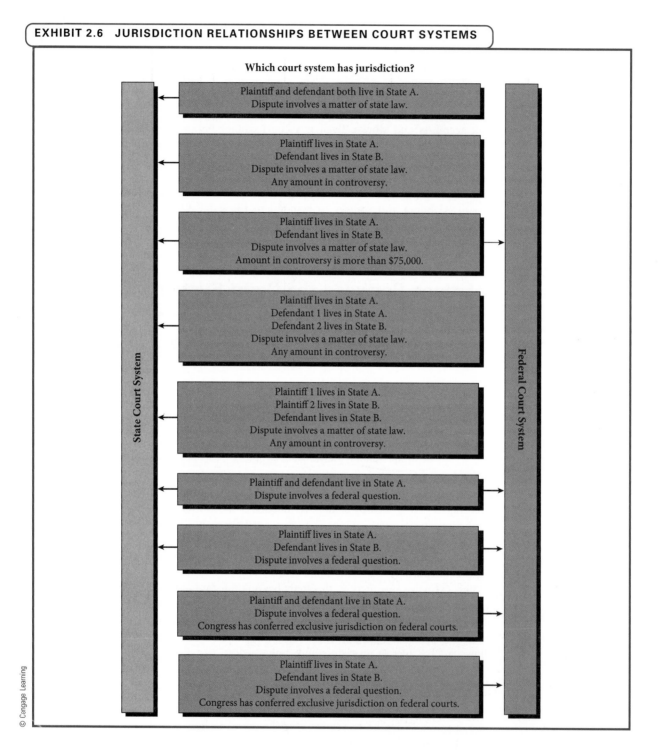

Federal Question Jurisdiction Congress may provide that state courts do not have jurisdiction over a particular matter of federal law. That is, Congress explicitly gives federal courts exclusive jurisdiction over an area of law, or Congress provides exclusive jurisdiction "by unmistakable implication from the legislative history, or by a clear incompatibility between state-court jurisdiction and federal interests." In such cases, only the federal court system has jurisdiction over the case. If a plaintiff seeks relief for such a matter in a state court, the case would be dismissed for lack of jurisdiction.

Concurrent Jurisdiction and Removal When concurrent jurisdiction exists, the plaintiff may bring suit in either the state court or the federal court system. For example, a suit by an employee for race discrimination in employment under 42 U.S.C. § 1983 (discussed in Chapter 16) could be brought in either federal or state court because Congress did not choose to limit such actions to federal courts. If the plaintiff chooses the state court system, the defendant could have the right to have the case removed to a federal court if diversity of citizenship exists and more than $75,000 is at stake. This right of removal is intended to protect out-of-state defendants from state courts that might be biased in favor of their own citizens.

A plaintiff considers several issues when deciding which court system best suits her legal needs. For example, the rules of procedure in federal and state courts may be different, and the plaintiff's attorney may be more familiar with (and more successful using) one set of rules than the other. Also, local politics may be an issue for state judges. The plaintiff can do little to prevent the defendant from removing the case to the federal court if the defendant has the right to do so. However, if the plaintiff filed suit in the defendant's home state court, rather than the plaintiff's home state, then the defendant cannot remove the case to federal court.

Applying the Appropriate Law in Federal Court

When there is diversity of citizenship, and the case is in federal court, the central question becomes which body of substantive law should the court apply to resolve the dispute—federal law or state law?

Suppose that Lil Wayne and Jay-Z were involved in a dispute over rights to revenue from a concert, and Lil Wayne sued Jay-Z in California. If both were from California, the case would be tried in a California state court, and California law would be applied to resolve the dispute. However, if Jay-Z was from Florida and Lil Wayne was from California, and the amount in controversy exceeded $75,000, the dispute could be decided by a federal court because of diversity of citizenship. If the issue in dispute was governed by statutory law, federal and California courts would apply the same law—the statutory law of California—and the outcomes should be the same. But what would happen if the case involved common-law issues? Would a federal court and a state court hearing similar cases reach different decisions? This is what used to happen in the United States until the Supreme Court decided the landmark 1938 case of *Erie Railroad Co.* v. *Tompkins*.

In *Erie Railroad Co.* v. *Tompkins*, the Supreme Court overturned an old Supreme Court case, *Swift* v. *Tyson* (1842) and held that except in matters governed by the federal Constitution or by acts of Congress (statutes), federal courts must apply state law. Thus, federal judges must apply both a state's common law and a state's statutory law when deciding cases in federal court because of diversity of citizenship. The federal court, however, follows federal procedural law.

Applying the Appropriate Law in State Court

When a state court hears a case involving events that took place in more than one state or entirely in another state, a conflict-of-law problem may arise. The court determines whether its own law or the law of another state should be applied. To help courts in such situations, states have enacted statutes that provide conflict-of-law rules. Some general **conflict-of-law** rules that affect businesses are presented in Exhibit 2.7.

ERIE RAILROAD CO. V. TOMPKINS
United States Supreme Court 304 U.S. 64, 58 S.Ct. 817 (1938)

Case Background *Tompkins was injured on "a dark night" by something protruding from a passing freight train owned by Erie Railroad Company as Tompkins stood next to the tracks in Pennsylvania, He claimed the accident occurred because of negligent operation of the train. Tompkins was a citizen of Pennsylvania, and Erie was a company incorporated in New York, but operated the railroad in Pennsylvania. Tompkins (the plaintiff) brought suit in federal district court.*

Erie argued that the court, in deciding the case, should apply the law of Pennsylvania. Under Pennsylvania law, Tompkins was a trespasser, and Erie would not be liable for his injuries. Tompkins argued that because of diversity of citizenship, *federal common law should apply. Under federal common law, Erie could be liable for Tompkins's injuries.*

The trial court agreed with Tompkins, and the jury awarded him $30,000 in damages. The decision was affirmed by the court of appeals. Erie appealed to the U.S. Supreme Court, arguing that in diversity-of-citizenship cases, federal courts must apply the appropriate state law.

Case Decision Brandeis, Justice

* * *

First. *Swift v. Tyson* held that federal courts exercising jurisdiction on the ground of diversity of citizenship need not, in matters of general jurisprudence, apply [the common law] of the state as declared by its highest court; that they are free to exercise an independent judgment as to what the common law of the State is—or should be....

Second. Experience in applying the doctrine of *Swift v. Tyson* had revealed its defects....Diversity of citizenship jurisdiction was conferred [by the Constitution] to prevent discrimination in state courts against those not citizens of the State. *Swift v. Tyson* introduced grave discrimination by non-citizens against citizens. It made rights enjoyed under the [state's common law] vary according to whether enforcement was sought in the state or in the federal court.... Thus, the doctrine rendered impossible equal protection of the law. In attempting to promote uniformity of law throughout the United States, the doctrine had prevented uniformity in the administration of the law of the State.

* * *

Third. Except in matters governed by the Federal Constitution or by Acts of Congress, the law to be applied in any case is the law of the State. And whether the law of the State shall be declared by its Legislature in a statute or by its highest court in a decision is not a matter of federal concern.... Congress has no power to declare substantive rules of common law applicable in a State.... And no clause in the Constitution purports to confer such a power upon the federal courts.

Fourth. The defendant contended that by the common law of Pennsylvania ... the only duty owed to the plaintiff was to refrain from willful or wanton injury.... The Circuit Court of Appeals ... declined to decide the issue of state law. As we hold this was error, the judgment is reversed and the case remanded to it for further proceedings in conformity with our opinion.

Reversed.

Case Note The concept of federal common law in diversity-of-citizenship cases was ended. Hence, Pennsylvania law applied and Tompkins was a trespasser and Erie was not liable for his injuries.

Questions for Analysis

1. Why had the decision in *Swift* v. *Tyson* prevented uniformity in the administration of state law?
2. After *Erie*, which court's procedural law must be applied in a diversity-of-citizenship case?

EXHIBIT 2.7 CONFLICT-OF-LAW RULES FREQUENTLY AFFECTING BUSIN.

SUBSTANTIVE LAW ISSUE	APPLY STATE LAW
Contract Disagreement	State in which contract was formed or in which contract was to be performed or most significantly affected by the contract or designated in the contract
Liability Issues Arising from Injury	State in which injury occurred
Workers' Compensation	State of employment or in which injury occurred

© Cengage Learning

Conflict-of-law, or **choice-of-law**, rules vary according to the nature of the dispute. In contract cases, for example, the traditional rule is that the law of the state in which the contract was made determines the interpretation of the contract. In tort cases, the general rule is that courts apply the law of the place where the tort occurred. However, the rules are not always simple. Courts evaluate the interests of the states involved in a dispute. The state with the most significant interest in the case would be the state whose law would be applied.

States do not all use the same rules, but they tend to be similar. They try to account for the interests of parties in the fair resolution of the dispute, for the interests of the governments in the effective application of laws and the policy rationales upon which they are based, and for the benefits that result from the ability of citizens to predict the legal consequences of their actions.

Venue

A lawsuit must be brought in a court having **venue**, the proper place where a lawsuit is heard. On the basis of fairness, state statutes generally provide that a lawsuit be brought in a court located in the county in which either the plaintiff or the defendant lives. Similarly, the defendant can be sued in a federal court only in a district where either the defendant or the plaintiff lives or where the dispute arose. Sometimes a court is referred to as a **forum**, a public place where judicial proceedings occur.

Lighter Side of the Law

The Law Applies to Me?

You owe a bank a bunch of money for a mortgage on your house in Michigan. To dump the mortgage, you claim to be broke and hide your assets in deals with relatives. In one deal, you "sell" a Florida vacation home to a relative for $10. The relative later "sells" it back for a trivial amount. A similar transaction can be used for the Michigan house, allowing a $600,000 mortgage to be unloaded.

Maybe the scam was noticed because a member of the Michigan Supreme Court, Diane Hathaway, executed it. Her lawyer said her resignation from the court had nothing to do with the land deals that appeared to cheat the bank. Federal prosecutors disagreed and brought criminal fraud charges before she had time to resign.

Sources: Associated Press; Washington Post.

Change of Venue

In some controversial or well-publicized cases, defendants request a change of venue from the court where the plaintiff filed the case. In such cases, defendants worry that because of the publicity surrounding their case, they will be unable to get a fair trial. Another court in a different location is chosen, but it has to be in the same state court system if the matter is in state court. While change of venue can arise in criminal cases, the matter of proper venue—state court versus federal court—can arise in civil litigation. A party can demand to be moved from, say, federal court to state court. Such instances may also involve questions of proper jurisdiction, as we see in the *BancorpSouth Bank* v. *Hazelwood Logistics Center, LLC* case.

BANCORPSOUTH BANK V. HAZELWOOD LOGISTICS CENTER, LLC

United States Court of Appeals, Eighth Circuit, 706 F.3d 888 (2013)

Case Background *HLC was formed to build a commercial real estate development project in Missouri known as the Hazelwood Logistics Center. HLC, a Missouri company, got a loan from BancorpSouth Bank (the Bank), a Mississippi company. Later, four Missouri banks (called participating banks) joined in to lend more money for HLC, but the Bank was the lead lender on the project. The owners of HLC provided a guaranty that they would make good on the loan to HLC in case of problems.*

The property HLC had chosen turned out to have major environmental problems, so development came to a halt, and the loan came due. The Bank sued for payment from HLC's owners in federal district court in Missouri. Hazelwood moved for dismissal of the action, contending the choice of venue was improper and that the federal district court lacked subject matter jurisdiction. The court held it did have jurisdiction and that venue was proper. HLC appealed.

Case Decision William J. Riley, Circuit Judge

* * *

In this diversity case, we apply the substantive law that would be applied by a Missouri state court. The loan agreements and guaranty provide Missouri law governs the interpretation and application of the contracts. Under Missouri law, "a valid choice of law provision in a contract binds the parties," and the parties here ... do not contend any law other than Missouri law applies. The loan agreements each additionally provide the "Loan Agreement and other Loan Documents shall not be construed against [the bank] merely because of

the involvement of [the bank] in the preparation of such documents and agreements."

We first address whether the district court had subject matter jurisdiction over this case. Diversity of citizenship is determined by reference to the parties named in the proceeding before the district court, as well as any indispensable parties who must be joined pursuant to Rule 19 of the Federal Rules of Civil Procedure. ... Hazelwood asserts a lack of complete diversity of citizenship because both Hazelwood and (at least some of) the participating banks are Missouri citizens. The participating banks were not named parties in the action below [in district court], and Hazelwood has not demonstrated the participating banks were necessary parties to the suit under Rule 19. We therefore reject Hazelwood's argument. ...

In this case, the bank has legal title; manages the assets; and controls the litigation. The participating banks are not necessary parties and their citizenship is immaterial. ... The district court properly exercised jurisdiction.

* * *

Hazelwood also maintains the action in federal court violated the loan agreements' and the guaranty's choice of venue provisions. We disagree.

The loan agreements provide:

Any legal action or proceeding with respect to this Loan Agreement or any of the other Loan Documents may be brought in the Courts of the County of St. Louis, State of Missouri, and ...

[HLC] and [the bank] consent, for itself and in respect of its property, to the jurisdiction of those Courts.... *Nothing in this section ... shall ... limit the right of [the bank] to bring any action or proceeding against [HLC] or its property in the Courts of any other jurisdiction.*

The guaranty also contained a choice of venue provision. This provision stated, "at [the bank's] sole and absolute election, all legal and other proceedings of any kind arising out of or related to this Guaranty shall be litigated in courts having sites in the County of St. Louis, Missouri."

Under Missouri law, a forum selection clause is enforceable so long as "the clause [was] obtained through freely negotiated agreements absent fraud and overreaching and its enforcement must not be unreasonable and unjust."

In this case, the forum selection clauses are unambiguous and will be enforced as written. The loan agreements simply provide an action *may be brought* in the courts of St. Louis County, but do not indicate such actions *must* be brought there....

We hold the forum selection clauses are permissive and did not prohibit the bank from bringing suit in the United States District Court for the Eastern District of Missouri. ...

We affirm the district court's entry of summary judgment in favor of the bank.

Questions for Analysis

1. What law will the federal district court use to resolve the matter?
2. Could HLC have avoided being in federal court despite the diversity of citizenship?

Forum Non Conveniens

Related to venue is the doctrine *forum non conveniens* (the forum is not suitable). A party asks the court to transfer a case to another court, even though the original court has jurisdiction, because there is a more convenient court that could hear the case. When considering the motion, a court considers where the actions related to the case took place, where the witnesses and evidence are located, whether the parties will be unfairly burdened by using a particular court, and whether problems of conflicts of law might be avoided by transferring the case.

❓ *TEST YOURSELF*

1. In some cases that would normally be heard in state court, and in which state law applies, the cases will be heard in federal court on the basis of _____.
2. In *Erie Railroad Co.* v. *Tompkins*, the Supreme Court held that federal courts should apply federal common law in suits involving parties from multiple states: T—F
3. The law that states have that help state courts obtain jurisdiction over out-of-state business defendants is called _____.
4. In *Blimka* v. *My Web Wholesalers, LLC*, the Supreme Court of Idaho held that an Idaho resident who bought goods from an out-of-state Internet seller:
   a. could sue the seller in Idaho state court.
   b. had to sue the seller in federal court in Idaho.
   c. would have to travel to the home state of the seller due to insufficient Idaho contacts.
   d. would have to take the case to arbitration as required by the purchase contract.
5. When a court obtains jurisdiction over property, it is called _____ jurisdiction.
6. In the *BancorpSouth Bank* v. *Hazelwood Logistics Center, LLC* case, the appeals court held that because the contract called for Missouri law to govern disputes, the parties must go to Missouri courts for proper resolution of their dispute: T—F

Answers: diversity of citizenship; F; long-arm statute; a; in rem; F.

SUMMARY

- Civil litigation involves the use of law and the legal process to resolve disputes among businesses, individuals, and governments. Litigation through the court systems provides a means of resolving disputes without the need to resort to force.
- Most U.S. judges are attorneys. It is their responsibility to uphold the legal system's reputation for honesty and impartiality. Federal judges are nominated by the president and confirmed by the Senate. They enjoy lifetime employment once appointed. State judges are appointed or elected.
- The court system is made up of the state court systems and the federal court system. Most courts follow the Federal Rules of Civil Procedure to govern the important procedural aspects of the litigation process.
- Jurisdiction means "the power to speak of the law." A court must have jurisdiction to hear and resolve a dispute. A court's jurisdiction is divided into two basic categories: subject-matter jurisdiction and personal jurisdiction.
- Subject-matter jurisdiction is a constitutional or statutory limitation on the types of disputes a court can resolve. Typical subject-matter constraints include minimum requirements on the amount in controversy in the dispute and restrictions on the types of disputes the court has authority to resolve.
- The jurisdiction of a court varies according to its position in a particular court system. Courts of original jurisdiction in the federal and the state court systems are trial courts. They have authority to hear virtually any kind of dispute and provide any kind of relief. Courts with appellate jurisdiction have the power to review cases decided by courts below them. Most state court systems and the federal court system have two levels of appellate courts. The highest appellate court in the federal system is the U.S. Supreme Court.
- The federal court system has limited subject-matter jurisdiction. The federal courts are limited by the U.S. Constitution to hearing cases involving (1) a federal question or (2) diversity-of-citizenship cases where the amount in controversy exceeds $75,000 and parties are from more than one jurisdiction. The state court systems can hear most disputes, including federal question cases where Congress has not limited jurisdiction to the federal court system.
- In addition to meeting the subject-matter jurisdictional requirements of a court, the parties—the plaintiff and the defendant—must meet personal jurisdictional requirements of the court. A state court's personal jurisdiction is generally limited to the boundaries of its state.
- Personal jurisdiction normally is not an issue, unless the defendant is not a resident of the state in which the plaintiff wants to bring the action. Jurisdiction of the court over the defendant is obtained by personal service of process. For out-of-state defendants, however, the court may need to exercise jurisdiction under authority of the state's long-arm statute. Generally, the plaintiff must show that the out-of-state defendant is transacting business or has some other interest in the state.
- When the court is unable to establish its jurisdiction through personal service on the defendant, the court may be able to establish *in rem* jurisdiction over property owned by the defendant that is located within the state.
- The federal courts in diversity-of-citizenship cases must apply the appropriate state common and statutory law.
- In state court cases, when the incident in question took place in another state, the court must look to the forum state's conflict-of-law or choice-of-law rule to determine what substantive law will apply to resolve the dispute.
- Litigation must occur in the proper venue. In the interest of fairness, a case may be moved to another forum in the same court system, usually because of strong publicity that makes a fair trial difficult. A case may also be moved because the forum for a trial is not convenient for most parties relevant to litigation.

TERMS TO KNOW

doctrine of judicial immunity, 27
original jurisdiction, 27
appellate jurisdiction, 27
magistrate, 30

en banc proceeding, 30
general jurisdiction, 33
limited (special) jurisdiction, 33
trial *de novo*, 33

appellate jurisdiction, 33
plaintiff, 34
defendant, 34
jurisdiction, 34

DISCUSSION QUESTION

Judges in many nations are trained for their offices in law school. They are hired into the judicial system and work their way up through that system. In the United States, there is no special training to be a judge; it is an honor bestowed, usually on senior attorneys, or it is an office one runs for in some states. What advantages might the other system have over the U.S. method?

CASE QUESTIONS

1. Ocean World, a foreign corporation, operates Ocean World Adventure Park in the Dominican Republic (DR). It contracted to buy 12 dolphins from Japan for delivery in the DR. The DR denied a permit to import the dolphins. Ocean World sued various defendants including Columbia University of New York. Suit was filed in Florida, contending that Columbia was "doing business" in Florida through its alumni association and online courses for students. Columbia also owns property in Florida. Ocean World contended that Columbia encouraged the DR to refuse to allow the dolphins to be imported, which was interference with a business relationship. Columbia moved for dismissal for lack of jurisdiction in Florida courts. Should Florida courts have jurisdiction over Columbia? [*Trustees of Columbia University* v. *Ocean World*, 12 So.3d 788, Ct. App., Fla. (2009)]

2. Charlotte Chambers and other South Dakota residents chartered a bus in South Dakota from Dakotah Charter, a South Dakota corporation, to attend a Tae Kwon Do tournament in Arkansas. While en route from South Dakota to Arkansas, the bus stopped in Missouri. Chambers fell on the steps in the bus and broke her ankle. She sued, claiming that Dakotah failed to maintain the bus in a safe condition. Dakotah contended that the plaintiff's carelessness caused her injury. Which law should apply to the case—the law of South Dakota, where the contract was made; Missouri, where the injury occurred; or Arkansas, where the contract was ultimately to be per-

formed? [*Charlotte Chambers* v. *Dakotah Charter*, 488 N.W.2d 63, Sup. Ct., S.D. (1992)]
   ✓ Check your answer

3. Edwards received unsolicited faxes from Direct Access in violation of the Federal Telephone Consumer Protection Act, which makes it illegal to send unsolicited faxes. Edwards, a Nevada resident, sued Direct, not a Nevada resident, in state court in Nevada for damages allowed under the law. Direct contended that the suit could not be filed in state court because it concerned federal law, so Nevada courts did not have jurisdiction. Is that correct? [*Edwards* v. *Direct Access*, 124 P.3d 1158, Sup. Ct., Nev. (2005)]

4. Pueblo De Bahia Lora, S.A., is a Costa Rican corporation owned by U.S. citizens. It operates a fishing resort in Costa Rica called "Parrot Bay Village." Oldfield, a Florida resident, saw the Parrot Bay website, which is in English and lists a U.S. mailing address and provides a toll-free number for potential guests to call. Oldfield made a reservation online. When at the resort, he went on a fishing trip on a chartered boat. That arrangement was made by Parrot Bay, but the boat was owned and operated by a Costa Rican. Oldfield suffered an injury that he claims was the result of the negligence of the boat operator. He sued Parrot Bay in federal court, claiming diversity of citizenship. Parrot Bay did not respond; Oldfield was awarded a default judgment for $750,000 as requested. Parrot Bay appealed. What argument is on Parrot Bay's side? [*Oldfield*

v. *Pueblo de Bahia Lora, S.A.*, 558 F.3d 1210, 11th Cir. (2009)]

✓ Check your answer

5. An accident in Florida killed three of the four members of a family from Alabama who were riding in their Kia automobile that had been bought in Alabama. Suit was filed in Alabama state court against Kia by the survivor of the accident. Kia requested that the trial be moved to Florida on the ground of *forum non conveniens* because almost all of the witnesses were in Florida. Was that motion reasonable? [*Ex parte Kia Motors America*, 881 So.2d 396, Sup. Ct., Ala. (2003)]

6. Jones lived in California. She met Williams, a therapist, in New Mexico. For four years, Williams provided Jones weekly psychotherapy and dream counseling by telephone from New Mexico. Several times, Williams went to California to provide treatment for Jones there. Williams' wife, Ritzman, provided Jones weekly Shamanic counseling over the phone. Jones then sued Williams and Ritzman in federal court in California for medical malpractice. Defendants moved to dismiss the complaint for lack of personal jurisdiction. Did Williams or Ritzman have sufficient contacts in California to be subject to jurisdiction? [*Jones* v. *Williams*, 660 F.Supp.2d 1145, N.D. Calif. (2009)]

✓ Check your answer

7. Koh, a California resident, won a judgment in California of $240,000 against Inno-Pacific, a Singapore company, but Inno-Pacific did not pay the judgment. Koh discovered that the company had an interest in land in Washington State, so he filed suit in Washington to seize the property to satisfy his judgment. The trial court in Washington dismissed the suit because it lacked personal jurisdiction over Inno-Pacific. Koh appealed. On what basis could the Washington court have jurisdiction? [*Koh* v. *Inno-Pacific Holdings, Ltd.*, 54 P.3d 1270, Ct. App., Wash. (2002)]

8. A Volkswagen on a highway in Dallas was hit from behind and pushed into a truck parked on the side of a freeway. One person in the VW was injured and one was killed. The survivor sued VW, contending that design defects in the car caused the injury and death. The survivor filed sued in federal court in Marshall, Texas, 155 miles east of Dallas. VW moved to transfer venue to federal court in Dallas, contending that the VW was bought in Dallas, the accident occurred there, witnesses were in Dallas, Dallas police responded to the accident, medical care was given in Dallas, the driver who struck the VW was in Dallas, and no party related to the litigation lived in Marshall. The district court refused to move the case. VW appealed. Do you think the case should be moved and what would the reason be? [*In re: Volkswagen of America*, 545 F.3d 304, 5th Cir. (2008)]

ETHICS QUESTION

Should judges consider the social consequences of their decisions that go beyond legal issues? What if the case involves an individual who has committed a crime and the judge is asked to release the defendant on a mere legal "technicality"?

CHAPTER **3**

Trials and Resolving Disputes

Jaime Sanchez took years to work his way up from day laborer to owning a company that imported doors from Latin America for sale to homebuilders. Sanchez had suffered through turbulent times in the construction market. Sometimes he did not get paid for doors he delivered. When that happened, at times he could not pay his suppliers. Sometimes he sued builders who did not pay him, and sometimes he was sued by creditors. But, as in other areas of litigation, such suits are often settled or dropped before trial. Of all civil cases filed in court, about 90 percent are resolved before a judgment is entered at trial.

Why resolve a suit out of court or not even bring one? Experienced lawyers can make pretty good estimates of the outcomes of most cases that go to trial, so they can recommend resolution that heads off costly litigation. Litigated cases consume more hours of lawyers' time and so are expensive. Litigation also takes a great deal of company personnel time and effort—time that could be spent on the business. Sanchez and others in the construction business realized there was little to be gained by floundering businesses suing each other.

Trials involving businesses can be costly and uncertain. Some involve complex facts that require extensive evidence, including mountains of business records. Trials often require testimony by managers and, in some cases, high-priced experts. There is good evidence that juries tend to be less sympathetic to businesses than to individuals.

Over time, because of the expense, time, and uncertainty of litigation, alternative dispute resolution (ADR), such as arbitration, has become ever more common. Courts and Congress encourage the use of arbitration, mediation, and negotiation to settle disputes, and parties often find these preferable to litigation. In this chapter, we first discuss litigation and then the alternatives.

Basic Trial Procedures

A distinctive element of our judicial system is that it is an **adversary system of justice**. It requires the parties to represent themselves, usually through their lawyers, and to argue their positions before a neutral court. The responsibility for bringing a lawsuit, shaping its issues, and presenting evidence rests upon the parties to the dispute.

Courts play a small role in establishing the facts of a case. Unlike countries that use a system of inquiry run by judges, as described in the previous chapter and in the International Perspective in this chapter about procedure in Germany, judges in the United States do not investigate the parties or the facts of a case. Instead, the courts apply legal rules to the facts that the parties establish under rules of procedure and evidence. This section discusses the major procedural rules governing the civil litigation process.

Pleadings Stage

As we discussed in the last chapter, to begin a lawsuit, the plaintiff files the first **pleading**, known as the complaint. In the **complaint**, the plaintiff must state the basis of the court's subject-matter jurisdiction and jurisdiction over the parties to the dispute. The plaintiff then gives notice to the defendant by **service of process**, including a **summons**, an example of which is in Exhibit 2.4. Along with the summons, the plaintiff serves the defendant with a copy of the complaint.

Pleadings are the formal statements made to the court by the parties to a case that list their claims and defenses. The complaint is a statement that sets forth the plaintiff's claim against the defendant. As illustrated in Exhibit 3.1, the complaint contains statements:

- alleging the essential facts necessary for the court to take jurisdiction.
- of the facts necessary to claim that the plaintiff is entitled to a remedy.
- of the remedy the plaintiff is seeking.

Exhibit 3.1 is quoted from a complaint filed in federal court in New York. Billionaire casino owner Steve Wynn owns a lot of highly valued artwork, including a painting by Pablo Picasso, which he bought for $48.4 million. He claimed to have a contract to sell it for $139 million, one of the highest prices ever received, when he managed to poke a hole in the painting. The painting was repaired, but the deal was called off because the value was decreased as a result of the damage. Wynn claimed the value fell by $54 million and that the loss should be covered by an insurance policy issued by Lloyd's of London; but Lloyd's was not keen to pay. As you see, the complaint lays out the bare facts, legal issues, and remedy sought. (Note: The case was later settled out of court and the painting later sold, after being repaired, for $155 million.)

Responses to the Complaint

Following the service by the plaintiff's complaint, the defendant must file an answer. If the defendant does not respond, the court will presume the claims of the plaintiff are true and grant the plaintiff the relief requested in the complaint. Depending on the circumstances, the defendant may file (1) a motion to dismiss, (2) an answer with or without an affirmative defense, and/or (3) a counterclaim.

Motion to Dismiss A **motion to dismiss** by the defendant asks the court to dismiss the case because it does not have jurisdiction over either the subject matter of the dispute or the defendant's person. The defendant may also file a **motion to dismiss for failure to state a claim** or a **demurrer** (some states do not use the term "demurrer"; they use only the term "motion to dismiss"). This is an assertion that even if the

EXHIBIT 3.1   EXCERPT FROM ACTUAL COMPLAINT

United States District Court Southern District of New York

07 CV 202

Stephen and Elaine Wynn, Plaintiffs

—against—   Complaint

Lloyd's, London and Certain Underwriters at
Lloyd's, London, Defendants

Plaintiffs, by and through its attorneys Buchanan Ingersoll & Rooney PC, by way of its complaint and against the Defendants, alleges as follows:

The Parties

1. Plaintiffs, Stephen and Elaine Wynn ("Wynn" or "Plaintiffs") are individuals who are citizens of the State of Nevada.
2. Defendant, Lloyd's, London ("Lloyds") is an underwriting company with a principal place of business located at 1 Lime Street, London EC3M 7HA, United Kingdom.
3. Certain Underwriters at Lloyd's, London ("Certain Underwriters," and together with Lloyds, the "Defendants"). ...

Jurisdiction and Venue

4. This Court has jurisdiction over this action pursuant to 28 U.S.C. § 1332(a)(1), in that the matter in controversy exceeds the sum of $75,000, exclusive of interest and costs, and is between citizens of the State of Nevada and citizens or subjects of a foreign country.
5. Venue in this District is proper under 28 U.S.C. § 1391(a)(2), since a part of the events giving rise to the claim occurred in this judicial district, and a part of the policy proceeds that are the subject of the action relates to the restoration of the damaged painting situated in this judicial district, and defendants.
6. Venue is further appropriate in this district under 28 U.S.C. paragraph 1391(a)(1), as the Defendants reside and/or conduct business in this district.

Statement of Facts

7. At all relevant times mentioned herein, Plaintiffs are individuals involved in, among other things, the buying, selling and collecting of artwork.
8. At all relevant times mentioned herein, Defendants were and are engaged in the business of underwriting specialized insurance coverage, including but not limited to, providing insurance coverage on artwork.
9. On or about June 8, 2006, Plaintiffs and Defendants entered into an insurance policy...for all risks of physical loss or damage for the coverage of fine arts. ...
18. On or about September 30, 2006, while demonstrating the painting to colleagues and friends, plaintiff and insured, Stephen Wynn, unintentionally placed a tear in a Picasso painting titled "Le Reve" owned by the Plaintiffs. ... The painting is admittedly covered under the Agreement. ... [Lloyd's was notified; the painting went to New York for inspection, repair and appraisal.]
25. By letter dated November 3, 2006, Plaintiffs notified the Defendants that the post-restoration market value will be approximately $85 million dollars. ...
30. Defendants have not submitted the appraisers' reports and continue to wrongfully withhold from Plaintiffs such reports.
31. Plaintiffs are therefore entitled to receive Defendants' appraisal reports, which will reveal the Defendants' appraised depreciated value of the restored painting. ...

Count I Declaratory Judgment

36. The Plaintiffs therefore, respectfully request that this Court issue a declaratory ruling directing Defendants to provide the Plaintiffs with an appraisal report or initial damages assessment so the appraisal process set forth in the Policy can timely take place. ...

Count II Breach of Covenant of Good Faith and Fair Dealing

39. The Defendants breached their implied covenant of good faith and fair dealing by reasons, among other things, intentionally, knowingly, willfully, unreasonably, recklessly, arbitrarily, frivolously and/or maliciously:

   a. Failing to render a sincere and substantial performance of their obligations under the Agreement;
   b. Arbitrarily, recklessly and frivolously refusing to provide either an appraisal report or a post restoration value on the restored painting. ...

EXHIBIT 3.1   EXCERPT FROM ACTUAL COMPLAINT *(Continued)*

42. By virtue of the foregoing, Plaintiffs have suffered loss and damage. Wherefore, Plaintiffs respectfully request that this Court enter an Order:

   a. Directing Defendants to provide a copy of their appraisal reports to the Plaintiffs;

   b. Directing Defendants to provide the Plaintiffs with a post restoration value of the Painting in furtherance of settlement;

   c. Awarding Plaintiffs all consequential losses resulting from the Defendants' breach of the covenant of good faith and fair dealing;

   d. Granting Plaintiff's attorneys' fees and costs; and

   e. Granting Plaintiffs such other and further relief as the Court deems just and proper.

Dated: New York, New York
January 10, 2007

> Barry I. Slotnick, Esq, (BS-1398)
> Attorney for Plaintiffs
> One Chase Manhattan Plaza, 35th Floor
> New York, New York 10005

---

facts asserted are true, the injury claimed by the plaintiff is one for which the law furnishes no remedy.

Answer If the defendant's motion to dismiss is denied, or if the defendant does not make such a motion, the defendant must file an **answer** with the court. In this pleading, the defendant responds to the allegations made by the plaintiff. The defendant will admit, deny, or say that he does not know the truth, with respect to each assertion of the plaintiff.

In answering a complaint, the defendant may also assert additional facts that should result in the action being dismissed. Called an **affirmative defense**, the defendant admits to the facts claimed by the plaintiff but offers additional facts he asserts constitute a defense—a legal excuse—to the plaintiff's complaint. The defendant could admit to being in a car accident involving the plaintiff, but could assert that the claim is now barred by the statute of limitations; that is, the plaintiff waited too long to file suit. Other examples of affirmative defenses include self-defense, assumption of risk, contributory negligence, and other defenses we will study later. The defendant typically bears the burden of proving the facts necessary to establish an affirmative defense.

Counterclaim In addition to responding to the plaintiff's allegations in the answer, the defendant can assert a claim against the plaintiff. The defendant's claim is a **counterclaim** and may be based on the same events that the plaintiff bases the complaint on. The counterclaim is a complaint by the defendant, and the plaintiff must respond to it just as the defendant responded to the original complaint. Combining claims and counterclaims into a single lawsuit makes the process less costly. Some claims by defendants against plaintiffs must be brought in the same lawsuit as counterclaims; other claims may be brought in separate lawsuits, if desired.

Reply Any new matters raised by the defendant's answer are automatically taken as denied by the plaintiff. When the defendant files a counterclaim, the plaintiff answers with a *reply*, which is an answer to the counterclaim. We see these steps outlined in Exhibit 3.2.

EXHIBIT 3.2   STAGES OF A TYPICAL CIVIL LAWSUIT

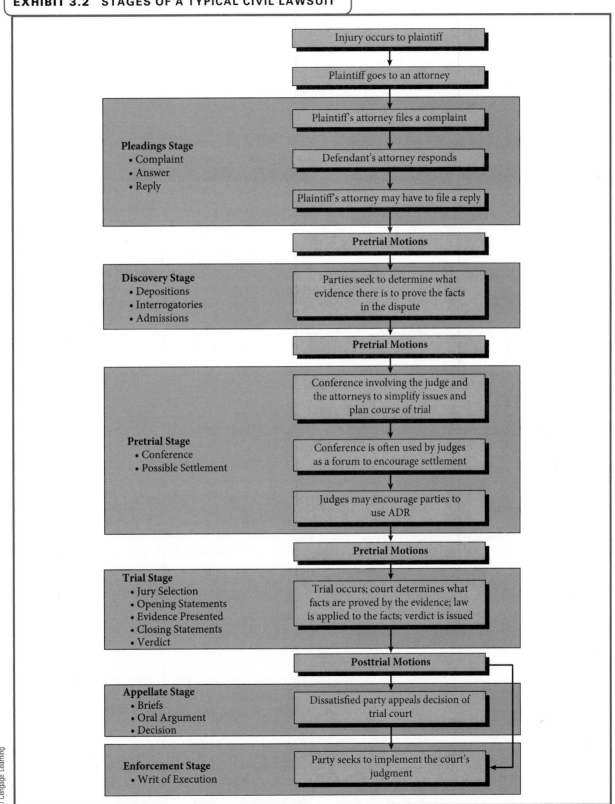

Discovery Stage: Obtaining Information before Trial

After the initial exchange of pleadings, litigation enters the discovery stage. The parties use various legal tools to obtain evidence from each other and outsiders about the dispute. The process of obtaining information is known as **discovery**. The Federal Rules of Civil Procedure and the corresponding state procedural rules set down the guidelines for the discovery process.

Purpose of Discovery   Discovery serves several functions. Years ago, disputes moved from the pleadings directly to the trial stage. As a result parties had little information about the specific evidence the other party was going to use. The evidence presented could catch the opposing party by surprise—a "trial by ambush." The discovery process now prevents surprises by giving the parties access to each others' information.

Discovery also preserves evidence of witnesses who might not be available at the time of the trial, as well as the testimony of witnesses whose memory may fade over time. Finally, by allowing both parties the opportunity to learn what evidence would be available at trial, discovery encourages pretrial settlements. Parties can assess the strengths of both sides' cases and estimate what a reasonable settlement would be. Most cases are settled, but if the case goes to trial, discovery narrows the issues by revealing what the parties actually disagree about, so the trial can focus on the important questions in the case. Notice in the Wynn case in Exhibit 3.1 how there is a laundry list of claims. If the case goes to trial, it will be narrowed down to specifics as the parties learn which claims are best supported by evidence. One important difference between criminal and civil cases is that there is very little discovery in criminal trials, an issue to be discussed more in Chapter 5.

Tools of the Discovery Process   The discovery rules offer several ways to get information from an opposing party: depositions, written interrogatories, orders for production of documents, requests for admissions, and orders for a mental or physical examination. According to the Federal Rules of Civil Procedure, a party seeking information must select a discovery tool that is not "unduly burdensome" to the other party. In practice, parties can force out nearly any information related to the legal issues. The opposing party cannot refuse to comply just because compliance is time consuming or costly.

Depositions and Interrogatories   A principal discovery tool is the **deposition**—the sworn, in-person testimony of a witness recorded by a court reporter. Attorneys from both sides may question the person whose deposition is taken, perhaps an eyewitness to an accident or an expert witness expected to provide testimony at trial. Sometimes depositions are videotaped.

The deposition is a useful way to find information relevant to the dispute, including leads to other witnesses or documents. It may be used at trial to impeach, or challenge, a witness who attempts to change his story at the trial. The deposition of a witness who is unavailable at the time of the trial may be allowed in place of live testimony.

Written **interrogatories** are questions submitted by a party to a case to the other party, or a witness, or another person with relevant information. The party receiving the interrogatories prepares written answers, usually with the aid of an attorney, and signs them under oath. Although the interrogatories lack the face-to-face spontaneity of a deposition, they can require the party to provide information from her records and files—the kind of information not carried in one's head.

Expert Witnesses   Many trials involving businesses use expert witnesses to help establish facts critical to a case, such as the value of lost profits, the costs to a victim of an accident, or the scientific evidence of harm from a product. These witnesses usually

Lighter Side of the Law

Come to the Judge's Party!

U.S. District Judge Sam Sparks became irritated by the motions filed by a defense attorney and the difficulties imposed on the plaintiff, so he issued the following order:

Greetings and Salutations!

You are invited to a kindergarten party on Thursday, September 1, 2011, at 10:00 a.m. in Courtroom 2 of the United States Courthouse, 200 W. Eighth Street, Austin, Texas. The party will feature many exciting and informative lessons, including:

- *How to telephone and communicate with a lawyer*
- *How to enter into reasonable agreements about deposition dates*
- *How to limit depositions to reasonable subject matter*
- *Why it is neither cute nor clever to attempt to quash a subpoena for technical failures or service when notice is reasonable given; and*
- *An advanced seminar on not wasting the time of a busy federal judge and his staff because you are unable to practice law at the level of a first-year law student.*

Invitation to this exclusive event is not RSVP. Please remember to bring a sack lunch! The United States Marshals may have beds available if necessary, so you may wish to bring a toothbrush in case the party runs late.

Source: *Theresa Morris* v. *John Coker*, Case 1:11-mc-00712-SS.

have their depositions taken before trial so that the other side knows the essence of their testimony and can prepare questions for trial.

There have been abuses by experts who want to please their clients and overstate the case by inflating damages or asserting harm to exist based on reasoning that violates general scientific opinion. The Supreme Court instructed courts in the *Daubert* case to exclude evidence that was not reliable and was contrary to scientific standards. The Court has held that when expert testimony is critical to a case but is rejected because it is not scientifically sound, then it is proper to grant summary judgment to the defendant and not allow another trial on the matter. The Court does not want to encourage parties to use hired guns who provide evidence that is not credible, so trial judges are to screen the reliability of experts.

We see an example of faulty expert testimony in the *Barabin* v. *AstenJohnson, Inc.* case. Faulty testimony can mean the plaintiff loses the case because it relied on the claims made by an unqualified expert. In the *Barabin* case, we see that faulty expert testimony procedure required a new trial.

BARABIN V. ASTENJOHNSON, INC.

United States Court of Appeals, Ninth Circuit, 700 F.3d 428 (2012)

Case Background *Henry Barabin was exposed to asbestos from 1964 to 1984. For much of that time he worked at a paper mill that used dryer felts containing asbestos supplied by AstenJohnson. In 2006, Barabin was diagnosed with a rare lung cancer known to be caused by exposure to asbestos. He sued.*

AstenJohnson moved to exclude expert testimony by Barabin's expert Dr. Cohen because of his "dubious credentials and his lack of expertise with regard to dryer felts and paper mills." The district court chose not to hold a Daubert hearing to determine if Cohen was a qualified expert and allowed the jury to *determine if Cohen's testimony was credible. The jury found for Barabin and awarded damages of $10,200,000. AstenJohnson appealed.*

Case Decision Rawlinson, Circuit Judge

* * *

In its role as gatekeeper, the district court determines the relevance and reliability of expert testimony and its subsequent admission or exclusion. Admission or exclusion under *Daubert* rests on the scientific reliability and relevance of the expert testimony. The expert's opinion must be deduced from a "scientific method" to be admissible. "The test under *Daubert* is not the correctness of the expert's conclusions but the soundness of his methodology...."

Daubert provided the following non-exhaustive factors for consideration in assessing the reliability of proffered expert testimony: (1) whether the scientific theory or technique can be (and has been) tested, (2) whether the theory or technique has been subjected to peer review and publication, (3) whether there is a known or potential error rate, and (4) whether the theory or technique is generally accepted in the relevant scientific community. ...

Unfortunately, because no *Daubert* hearing was conducted as requested, the district court failed to assess the scientific methodologies, reasoning, or principles Dr. Cohen applied. None of the *Daubert* factors was considered. Instead, the court allowed the parties to submit the experts' unfiltered testimony to the jury. ...

* * *

Under our precedent, the district court's decision to allow presentation of the expert testimony to the jury without making any gateway determinations regarding relevance and reliability constituted an abuse of discretion requiring a new trial.

The district court committed reversible error when it failed to assess the proffered expert testimony for relevance and reliability. ... A new trial will be provided in this circumstance. Accordingly, the district court abused its discretion when it denied AstenJohnson's ... motions for a new trial.

Judgment vacated and case remanded for a new trial.

Questions for Analysis

1. Why did the trial judge not hold a *Daubert* hearing?
2. Since Barabin's expert may be disqualified, what can he do?

Sanctions for Failing to Respond to a Discovery Request   Judges have broad powers to impose sanctions against a party who fails to comply with discovery requirements. If a party fails to comply with the requirements, of, say, a deposition, the requesting party can make a motion to the judge to require compliance. If the party does not comply with a court order, the court may order a **default judgment** granting victory to the other party or find the noncomplying party in **contempt of court** and order the party to jail or impose a fine. For example, one federal judge fined Walmart $18 million for having "a corporate policy" of frustrating discovery and withholding evidence in cases. Judges may also require the party or attorney who caused the problem to pay the costs of the other party arising from a discovery dispute.

Orders for the Production of Documents   A party may access information in the possession of the other party by an order for the production of documents. The kinds of information that are often sought are e-mails, medical bills, business records, letters, and repair bills. The party seeking the information usually has the right to inspect, examine, and reproduce it. Businesses have an obligation to maintain company records in a coherent manner, so they may be accessed in case of a lawsuit. Failure to do so may result in sanctions by the court and even a judgment for the opposing party. If a trade secret or other confidential information is involved, a company can get a **protective order** that limits access to the material so as to ensure confidentiality.

Requests for Admissions   Either party can serve the other with written requests for an admission of the truth in matters relating to the dispute. Requests are used to settle facts

INTERNATIONAL PERSPECTIVE

British Courtroom Procedure

Although both British and American court proceedings are based on the adversarial model, there are some significant differences. The British bar is divided into *solicitors* and *barristers.* Solicitors handle matters such as advising private clients on business and property matters. Barristers mostly do litigation. A business client involved in a legal dispute would typically hire a solicitor for advice before litigation and then add a barrister to the legal team once a decision to litigate had been made. Although U.S. attorneys typically specialize as well, the degree of specialization is much greater in the British system.

British courts have what commentators describe as "a more civil and cooperative atmosphere" than their American counterparts. British barristers typically remain behind one long table and stay there while questioning witnesses or speaking to the judge, rather than walking about as in American courtrooms. Most objections about evidence are raised outside the presence of the jury and resolved before the witness is called. As a result, barristers rarely, if ever, object to a line of questioning by the other side, relying on the judge to redirect the opposing barrister. As a result, the jury sees a more continuous flow of information and is less distracted by legal maneuverings by the attorneys.

At the end of the evidence phase in a British court, the judge summarizes the evidence for the jury before instructing them on the relevant laws. In U.S. courts, judges do not discuss the evidence with the jury. The order of trial is also different, with the defense opening statement coming at the end of the plaintiff or prosecution's evidence rather than at the start of the trial.

Some comparative law scholars believe that these procedural differences make British trials superior in helping the jurors to understand the evidence. However, others worry that the more active role of the judge makes it more likely that one party will be prejudiced by the judge's nonverbal behavior (frowning, etc.) during the trial. Because judges know quite a bit about a case by the time it reaches trial, some scholars worry that judges' views, based on their information, affects their facial expressions, tone of voice, and so forth. U.S. appeals courts have overturned trial verdicts because of such behavior, making this a real concern.

Some social science experiments have shown recordings of trials conducted under both U.S. and UK rules to audiences. Participants generally see the UK version as more civil and view the judge more positively than the U.S. version, but participants still prefer the U.S. procedure overall.

about which there are no real disputes. That eliminates the need to establish such matters at trial. For example, in a contract dispute over the price of a product, one party may ask the other to admit that deliveries were made according to the terms of the contract. If admitted, these facts need not be proven at trial.

Mental and Physical Examinations   When the physical or mental condition of a party is an issue, the court may be asked to order that party to submit to an examination. Because of concerns for privacy, the party requesting the order must show a greater need for the information than in requests for most forms of discovery. Generally, the party requesting the order specifies the exact type of mental or physical examination desired and the time, the place, and the specialists who are to conduct it.

Discovery: Impacts on Business Discovery can impose significant costs on businesses. Firms can be forced to endure expense and disruption, while managers answer questions and produce documents. For example, in one regulatory dispute between Ford Motor and the Federal Trade Commission, it cost Ford $4 million just to copy required documents. The burdens are heavy when executives have to take time to prepare for and provide a deposition. In disputes involving technical matters or significant detail, a deposition may take two weeks or more, plus days or even weeks of preparation time.

It is not uncommon for the chief executive of a corporation to get a subpoena requesting that he appear for a deposition. In most cases, the information sought is in the hands of subordinates. Courts protect executives if the purpose of a deposition is to harass them, but their participation is not uncommon. The disruption of business caused by having executives away from work for several days to prepare for and give a deposition is one more reason out-of-court settlements are likely.

Summary Judgment At the close of discovery, either party may move for a **summary judgment**. The Federal Rules of Civil Procedure state in Rule 56(c) that summary judgment "shall be rendered … if the pleadings, depositions, answers to interrogatories, and admissions on file, together with affidavits, if any, show that there is no genuine issue as to any material fact and that the moving party is entitled to judgment as a matter of law."

The key is not that there are no differences over what happened but that, despite those differences, when the court looks at the undisputed facts, it can apply the law to the facts and resolve the dispute. If the motion is granted, the case is over or the judgment may apply to only some issues, which are eliminated, and the trial proceeds on the remaining issues.

Pretrial Conference Either party or the court may request a pretrial conference. These commonly held conferences normally involve only the attorneys and the judge. The conferences often simplify the issues and plan the course of the trial, agreeing on witness lists, exhibits, and the schedule. To ensure more efficient trials, judges urge the parties to focus on the key issues. Also at pretrial conferences, judges usually encourage the parties to attempt to reach an out-of-court settlement.

❓ TEST YOURSELF

1. In *Barabin* v. *AstenJohnson, Inc.,* the appeals court held that:
   a. Barabin's attorney failed to file motions properly on time, so Barabin lost his right to sue AstenJohnson.
   b. AstenJohnson would be fined $1 million for failure to respond in a timely manner to documents properly requested by Barabin.
   c. AstenJohnson's requests for many depositions were not justified; they were an attempt to run up costs on Barabin.
   d. Barabin's expert witness was not determined by the trial judge to be qualified to testify, so the jury determination would be thrown out in favor of a new trial.
2. Sworn, in-person testimony of a witness recorded by a court reporter is called a(n) _____.
3. A case begins by the _____ filing a(n) _____ against the _____ who may have claims and files a(n) _____.
4. Parties are not allowed to see "critical documents" that support an argument being made by the opposition in a case: T—F
5. A party may not demand a physical examination of an opposing party in any legal proceeding due to constitutional protection of personal privacy: T—F

Answers: d; deposition; plaintiff, complaint, defendant, counterclaim; F; F.

Trial Stage

After discovery is complete, if there has been no dismissal, summary judgment, or settlement, the dispute is set for **trial**. In many court systems, the trial calendar is long. Delays of two or three years before a noncriminal case comes to trial are not uncommon, even in courts without large backlogs. In courts in border regions or with international airports, the large criminal case load arising from illegal immigration and smuggling cases can mean civil trial delays may be up to five years.

Lighter Side **of the Law**

The Dog Ate My Summons

Trying to avoid jury duty is common. The Harris County (Houston, Texas) District Court clerk compiled the following list of excuses offered by jury duty dodgers:

"I have to feed my bird during the day."

"I take care of three cats during the day."

"I have to pee—a lot."

"I shot holes in my daughter's boyfriend's car."

"My wife killed someone."

"I had something removed from my head this morning."

Source: National Law Journal.

The Jury   The Sixth and Seventh Amendments to the U.S. Constitution, as well as state constitutions, provide for the right to a **jury** in certain cases. In criminal cases, there is a right to a jury trial. In the federal court system, this right is guaranteed if the amount in controversy exceeds $20 and is a common-law claim. Most state court systems have similar guarantees, although the minimum amount in controversy may be higher. There is no right to a jury trial when a private plaintiff requests an equitable remedy, rather than money damages, or in civil cases in which the government seeks non-criminal penalties for violations of federal law.

Decision to Use a Jury   The right to a jury trial does not have to be exercised. If a jury is not requested, the judge hears and determines the facts in the dispute and applies the law to resolve the matter. The judge's temperament, the complexity of the evidence, and the degree to which the emotions of the jury are likely to affect the judgment, influence decisions to request jury trials. Prosecutors often request jury trials in criminal cases even when defendants do not.

Selection of the Jury   Jury selection begins when the clerk of the court sends a notice instructing citizens to appear on a particular day for jury duty. The people called are in a jury pool.

The process used to select jury members is called ***voir dire***. Depending upon the court, either the judge or the attorneys conduct *voir dire*. The purpose is to determine whether a prospective juror is likely to be so biased that he or she could not reach a fair decision based on the evidence presented. The jurors are asked questions to see if they know any of the witnesses, parties, or lawyers, or have heard about the case. If an attorney thinks a juror is biased, she can challenge the juror and, if she persuades the judge that the juror in question may be biased, have the juror removed. Attorneys are also allowed a limited number of challenges that permit them to reject prospective jurors without stating a reason. Juries traditionally involve a panel of 12 persons, but in many states, panels of fewer than 12—frequently 6—are used.

The Trial Although judges have some freedom to change the details of how a trial proceeds, most follow the general order summarized in Exhibit 3.3. Jury and nonjury trials are handled in much the same way, but they have a number of procedural differences. In nonjury trials, the judge may put more limits on the attorneys' opening statements and closing arguments, but is likely to put fewer restrictions on witnesses' testimony. The following discussion details the steps involved in a typical jury trial.

Start of the Trial After the jurors have been sworn in, both attorneys make **opening statements**. The attorneys tell the jury what the crucial facts are and how they will prove that those facts support their position. Opening statements are often limited to 20 minutes. These statements are the lawyers' chances to explain their clients' view of the case to the jury, tell the jury who the witnesses will be, and provide a roadmap of the trial. The plaintiff's attorney normally presents the first statement.

Presentation of Direct Testimony Following the opening statement, the plaintiff's attorney begins to call witnesses and present evidence. The plaintiff has the burden of proving that his claims are correct. Each witness is first questioned by the plaintiff's attorney on **direct examination**. The defendant's attorney then examines that witness on **cross-examination**. Cross-examination may be followed by redirect examination by the plaintiff's attorney and then by re-cross examination by the defendant's attorney. While cross-examination is usually the highlight of courtroom dramas in movies or on television, real-life cross-examinations are rarely dramatic. The judge controls the length and the course of these examinations.

Closing Arguments Before the case goes to the jury, the attorneys each present a **closing argument**. They summarize the evidence for the jury in a manner most favorable to their case. As in the opening statement, the judge limits the amount of time available to the attorneys for their closing arguments.

EXHIBIT 3.3   SUMMARIES OF TYPICAL JURY AND NONJURY TRIALS

JURY TRIAL	NONJURY TRIAL
1. The selection of a jury	1. Plaintiff's opening statement
2. Plaintiff's opening statement	2. Defendant's opening statement
3. Defendant's opening statement	3. Plaintiff's presentation of direct evidence
4. Plaintiff's presentation of direct evidence	4. Defendant's presentation of direct evidence
5. Defendant's presentation of direct evidence	5. Plaintiff's presentation of rebuttal evidence
6. Plaintiff's presentation of rebuttal evidence	6. Defendant's presentation of rebuttal evidence
7. Defendant's presentation of rebuttal evidence	7. Defendant's final argument
8. Opening final argument by the plaintiff	8. Plaintiff's closing argument
9. Defendant's final argument	9. Judge's deliberation and verdict
10. Plaintiff's closing argument	
11. Instruction to the jury	
12. Jury deliberation and verdict	

© Cengage Learning

Instructions to the Jury Before the jury retires to deliberate and reach a verdict, the judge gives the jury **instructions,** or **charges**. In the instructions, the judge tells the jury the applicable law, summarizes the issues of the dispute, and states which of the parties has the burden of persuasion. After the instructions, the jurors are placed in the custody of the bailiff or other court official, who will see that they remain together and that there is no misconduct.

One form of misconduct is contact about the case with people outside of the jury. Increasingly, this has come to include jurors posting information on Facebook or tweeting about a trial. When a juror in Florida used Facebook to "friend" a defendant in a personal-injury case, the juror was sentenced to three days in jail. A murder conviction was thrown out in Arkansas because a juror tweeted information about the trial despite warnings from the judge not to do so. How to limit misconduct arising from social media use is still being determined by the courts.

Reaching a Verdict The jury deliberates to reach an agreement and find for the plaintiff or the defendant. In a civil trial, the parties must prove their contentions to the jury by a **preponderance of the evidence**. If jurors are unable to reach a unanimous decision, the jury is said to be **hung**, and a new trial before a different jury may be necessary. The jury is discharged and a **mistrial** declared.

Because of the cost and delay associated with a new trial, judges are reluctant to allow hung juries. Although many jurisdictions require a unanimous jury decision, some states allow verdicts in civil disputes to be less than unanimous, such as 10 of 12 jurors.

After the jury has reached a verdict, the verdict is read in court by the foreman of the jury or by the judge or the clerk of the court. The judgment is then entered. In some cases, the jury deliberates a second time to determine damages to be awarded if they found for the plaintiff on liability.

Lighter Side of the Law

You Got Me There, Counselor!

The editor of the Massachusetts Bar Association's *Lawyers Journal* has a collection of courtroom bloopers by lawyers when questioning parties at trial. Among them:

"Were you present when your picture was taken?"

"Are you qualified to give a urine sample?"

"Did he kill you?"

"Were you alone or by yourself?"

"How many times have you committed suicide?"

Source: Wall Street Journal.

Motions for a Verdict The parties may ask the judge to issue a favorable verdict that makes jury deliberation unnecessary. Most common is a motion for a **directed verdict** or a motion for **judgment as a matter of law** (also called *judgment on the pleadings*). These are much the same thing; different jurisdictions use different terms or procedures. After the cases have been presented, but before the case goes to the jury, a party may request that the court enter a judgment in its favor because there is not legally sufficient evidence on which a jury could find for the other party. The defense is more likely to prevail on such a motion. That is, the judge holds that the plaintiff failed to provide sufficient grounds, even if what is claimed is true, to be able to win a verdict.

Similarly, after a jury returns a verdict, the losing party may make a motion for judgment as a matter of law or motion for **judgment notwithstanding the verdict**. The judge is asked to hold that there were not legally sufficient grounds to support the jury's verdict and to either overturn the entire verdict or a portion of it. Courts prefer post-verdict motions to pre-verdict motions because, if an appeals court reverses a post-verdict motion, there is no need to redo the entire trial.

Remedies in Civil Litigation

A plaintiff brings a civil suit seeking a remedy from the court. A *remedy* is the way a right is enforced or how a violation of a right is compensated or prevented. The remedies awarded by courts in civil disputes are classified as either **equitable remedies** or **remedies at law**, usually **monetary damages**. Most cases are for monetary damages, but in some cases a remedy in equity is more appropriate. Exhibit 3.4 summarizes the remedies available in civil litigation.

Monetary Damages If a court finds that a party has suffered a legally recognized harm, monetary damages may be awarded. The general categories of monetary damage awards are *compensatory, punitive,* and *nominal.*

Compensatory Damages To award injured parties enough money to restore them to the economic position they were in before the injury, or to cover the losses caused by

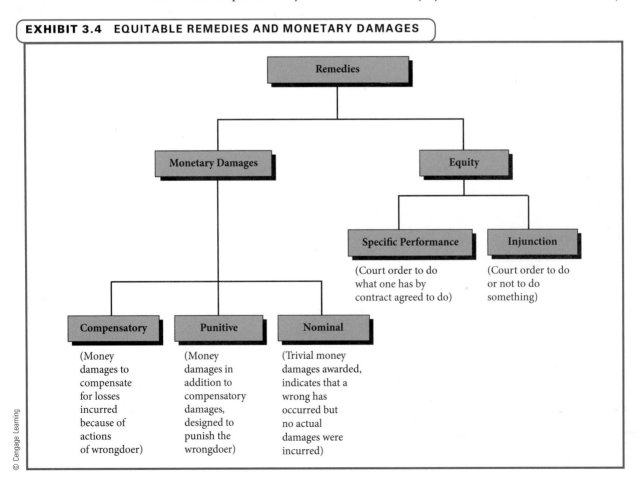

EXHIBIT 3.4   EQUITABLE REMEDIES AND MONETARY DAMAGES

Remedies

Monetary Damages — Equity

Equity:
- Specific Performance (Court order to do what one has by contract agreed to do)
- Injunction (Court order to do or not to do something)

Monetary Damages:
- Compensatory (Money damages to compensate for losses incurred because of actions of wrongdoer)
- Punitive (Money damages in addition to compensatory damages, designed to punish the wrongdoer)
- Nominal (Trivial money damages awarded, indicates that a wrong has occurred but no actual damages were incurred)

© Cengage Learning

the injury, **compensatory damages** are granted. These may be awarded for loss of time and money, pain and suffering, injury to reputation, and mental anguish, depending on the circumstances. When losses are purely monetary, the court looks for evidence of reasonable costs, as discussed in the *Naples* case.

NAPLES V. KEYSTONE BUILDING AND DEVELOPMENT CORP.
Supreme Court of Connecticut 295 Conn. 214, 990 A.2d 326 (2010)

Case Background *Frank and Karen Naples contracted with Keystone to build a new home for them for $620,500. The work was warranted by the contract. Soon after they moved into the home, major problems were noticed. The builder sent crews several times to do repair work, but problems continued. An expert, Dykins, was hired to evaluate the home. He stated that to repair the problems, extensive work would be needed that he detailed. The estimated cost was $113,511. Painting would be an additional $15,819. The Naples sued Keystone for that amount.*

The trial court held for the Naples but awarded them $59,140, stating that the higher damage figure had "not been established with a sufficient degree of certainty." The Naples appealed the damage award.

Case Decision Norcott, J.

* * *

"As a general rule, in awarding damages upon a breach of contract, the prevailing party is entitled to compensation which will place [it] in the same position [it] would have been in had the contract been properly performed.... Such damages are measured as of the date of the breach.... For a breach of a construction contract involving defective or unfinished construction, damages are measured by computing either (i) the reasonable cost of construction and completion in accordance with the contract, if this is possible and does not involve unreasonable economic waste; or (ii) the difference between the value that the product contracted for would have had and the value of the performance that has been received by the plaintiff, if construction and completion in accordance with the contract would involve unreasonable economic waste." The court may consider evidence demonstrating that the repairs undertaken by the plaintiff were necessary to restore the facility to the condition that it would have been in had it been constructed as warranted. "The repairs, however, may not result in improvements to the property, in the sense that they may not be of a different and superior type than they would have been had they been constructed as warranted."...

We conclude that the trial court's damages award was clearly erroneous because of its failure to award the plaintiffs damages adequate to pay for the labor necessary to replace the trim and siding, as well as to repair and repaint damaged portions of the home's interior.... The court did not point to any conflicting evidence or explain why it elected to discredit those discrete portions of the estimate while accepting the others verbatim. The apparent illogic in the award leaves us with a definite and firm conviction that a mistake has been committed;... the trial court plainly credited Dykins' testimony... yet it failed to compensate the plaintiffs for the expense of installing new materials on the house. Moreover, there is no evidence in the record contradicting the reasonableness of [Dykins' estimate]. Thus, we conclude that a new trial limited to the issue of damages is necessary to ensure that the plaintiffs are compensated adequately for the damages caused by the defendants' breach of the contract....

Questions for Analysis

1. Suppose the Naples are awarded all damages requested but have the work done for less than the amount awarded. Should the difference between the award and the actual costs incurred have to be returned?
2. Do you think it would be reasonable for the Naples to receive compensation for the time cost of their troubles?

Punitive Damages   When the wrongdoer's actions are particularly reprehensible, or when the defendant's conduct is willful or malicious, the court may award the injured party **punitive** (or **exemplary**) **damages** in addition to compensatory damages. These may be awarded in some tort cases, as we will see in Chapters 7 and 8. Punitive damages are intended to punish the wrongdoer and discourage others from engaging in similar conduct in the future.

Juries have substantial discretion in determining punitive damages when they are warranted. One federal appeals court, citing Florida law, explained some of the factors:

> *Under Florida law, the purpose of punitive damages is not to further compensate the plaintiff, but to punish the defendant for its wrongful conduct and to deter similar misconduct by it and other actors in the future. The Supreme Court of Florida ... has determined that the wealth of the defendant is a factor for consideration in determining the reasonableness of a punitive award: "an award must be reviewed to ensure that it bears some relationship to the defendant's ability to pay and does not result in economic castigation or bankruptcy of the defendant." While it is not "an accurate rule of law that the greater a defendant's wealth, the greater must be punitive damages," a "jury may properly punish each wrongdoer by exacting from his pocketbook a sum of money which, according to his financial ability, will hurt, but not bankrupt." [Myers v. Central Florida Investments, 592 F.3d 1201, 11th Cir., 2010]*

As we will see in Chapter 4, the Supreme Court has reviewed some of the constitutional issues related to punitive damages.

Nominal Damages   If a plaintiff suffers a legal wrong but has not suffered actual damages to person or property, or if the damages are considered trivial by the court, the court may award **nominal damages**. The plaintiff may recover as little as one dollar. Although winning $1 may seem pointless, an award of nominal damages may be enough for a party to prevail on a motion for attorney fees and costs, which could be significant.

Equitable Remedies
The courts recognize that there are times when monetary damages are neither practical nor effective. Money may not be able to compensate for the loss, or the defendant may not be able to pay damages but could do certain things to help rectify a wrong. Using their broad powers of equity, courts have developed remedies in equity that can be imposed when remedies at law, such as monetary damages, are inadequate.

Specific Performance   In equity, courts can order **specific performance** as a remedy and require the offending party to do what it had promised. This remedy may apply in contract cases, when monetary damages would not be adequate or the subject matter is unique. If the owner of a unique piece of land has a contract to sell the land and then changes her mind, a court may order her to perform as promised and transfer title to the land to the buyer for the promised payment. Specific performance is more likely when the subject matter is land or rare properties, such as art, antiques, or even baseball cards, because such items may be unique and irreplaceable, or because the other party may have incurred substantial expense in expectation of the deal.

Courts rarely order someone to perform personal services. Suppose Beyoncé agreed to appear in a Paramount movie, but then refused. A court would not order Beyoncé to appear because courts do not want to become involved in supervising services, such as making sure that Beyoncé acts well and to Paramount's satisfaction. Courts also do not want to force people into involuntary servitude, doing work they do not want to do. Monetary damages are appropriate in such cases.

Injunction   An **injunction** is a court order directing a person to do or not do something. The court is using its equitable powers when it issues such an order. There are three types of injunctive relief available. A **temporary restraining order** (TRO) is a short-term court order, generally lasting just a few days, and which is primarily used by a court to preserve the status quo until a more formal hearing can be held. A TRO proceeding is often a hearing conducted with just the judge and the parties' lawyers present. Sometimes a court will issue an *ex parte* TRO, where only the party requesting the order is present. Such orders are almost always for a short time and are intended to prevent the destruction of evidence, removal of assets, or otherwise maintain the court's jurisdiction over matters pending a hearing with all parties.

A **preliminary injunction** (or interlocutory injunction) is a longer-term court order, usually in force until the dispute is resolved. It is issued after more formal proceeding at which there may be live witness testimony. Before issuing a preliminary injunction, a court generally weighs four factors: (1) the parties' relative likelihood of success on the merits; (2) the likelihood that the plaintiff will suffer an irreparable injury if the injunction is not granted; (3) the balance of the equities; and (4) the public interest. The most difficult of these for non-lawyers to understand is the notion of "irreparable injury." An irreparable injury is generally one for which a payment of money would be insufficient to compensate the harmed party. The *Pre-Paid Legal Services, Inc.* case provides an example of the standards for issuing a preliminary injunction.

PRE-PAID LEGAL SERVICES, INC. V. CAHILL

United States District Court, Eastern District, Oklahoma F.Supp.2d (2013)

Case Background *Pre-Paid Legal Services, Inc. (PPLSI) sells legal service plans. Members pay a monthly fee and may call a toll-free number to be connected to law firms that have contracted with PPLSI to provide free or discounted legal assistance.*

Cahill was a successful sales representative for PPLSI who rose to a senior position. He had access to the sales records of all representatives so he knew the top performers around the country. Like all sales representatives, he had signed an agreement with PPLSI that prohibited use of such information outside of PPLSI. Cahill met with other top sales associates, including Cabradilla, and told them that he was going to work for another company, Nerium, and he wanted them to come with him. He resigned from PPLSI and posted material about Nerium on a PPLSI private website seen only by top sales associates. Cahill's access to PPLSI materials and websites was terminated.

PPLSI sued Cahill for breach of contract and in tort. As it would be some time before that dispute would go to arbitration, PPLSI requested the court issue a preliminary injunction to prohibit Cahill from exploiting the information he learned at PPLSI. The Magistrate Judge reviewed the request and issued

a report and recommendation that was reviewed by the District Judge.

Case Decision James H. Payne, District Judge

* * *

A preliminary injunction is an extraordinary remedy; it is the exception rather than the rule.... The main purpose of a preliminary injunction is simply to preserve the status quo pending the outcome of the case.... In order for a preliminary injunction to issue, the movant must satisfy a four-part test:

> The requesting party must demonstrate (1) that it has a substantial likelihood of prevailing on the merits; (2) that it will suffer irreparable harm unless the preliminary injunction is issued; (3) that the threatened injury outweighs the harm the preliminary injunction might cause the opposing party; and (4) that the preliminary injunction if issued will not adversely affect the public interest.

* * *

[The Magistrate Judge] finds that should Defendant be permitted to breach the non-solicitation agreement…PPLSI will suffer irreparable harm. While PPLSI has not shown that Defendant has made initial contact with any other PPLSI sales associate since the August 10, 2012 meeting, the fact that Defendant continued to send text messages to Cabradilla after he rejected his offer to go to Nerium combined with the fact that Defendant is engaged in another multi-level marketing company and will need to recruit sales associates to Nerium in the San Diego market shows that PPLSI faces a significant risk that Defendant will solicit current PPLSI associates if he is not enjoined from initiating contact with current PPLSI associates…. Next…the harm to the Defendant in being enjoined from initiating contact with PPLSI is minimal. Defendant will still be able to recruit sales associates to Nerium and build his business. The only restriction Defendant will face is that he will be required to abide by the contractual provisions that he *agreed* to at the start of his association with PPLSI. Finally, the public interest is promoted through the judicial enforcement of valid contracts. Thus, the [Magistrate] finds that PPLSI has successfully satisfied each of the four requirements for the issuance of a preliminary injunction on this issue, and recommends that a preliminary injunction should issue barring Defendant from initiating contact with PPLSI sales associates in an effort to solicit them to join Nerium.

* * *

In summary, the [Magistrate] finds that Plaintiff has shown that it is entitled to a preliminary injunction on the claim of breach of the non-solicitation agreement with respect to Michael Cabradilla. The [Magistrate] therefore recommends the issuance of a preliminary injunction barring the Defendant from initiating contact with current PPLSI sales associates or employees. The preliminary injunction should be valid until the issues can be presented to the arbitrators for consideration….

It is so ordered.

Questions for Analysis

1. Assuming PPLSI is correct, and might win a damage award for Cahill's actions, what difference does the preliminary injunction make?
2. Would an injunction be a limitation on Cahill's right to engage in free speech by talking to other sales associates?

A **permanent injunction** is a final court order, issued after the conclusion of the trial or as part of a settlement agreement. It usually remains in force indefinitely. To get a permanent injunction, a party must persuade the court that money damages are inadequate. For example, a court might enjoin a party from storing dangerous chemicals in a building next to a school.

Appellate Stage

The decision in a case may be appealed if one of the parties believes an **error of law** was made during the trial. These errors include mistakes about the substantive law or procedural and evidentiary matters. The parties cannot appeal the factual determinations made at trial. Bases for appeal include failure by the trial judge to admit or exclude certain evidence, improper instructions being given to the jury, and the granting or denying of motions to dismiss the case. Usually the party appealing must show that the mistake would have affected the outcome. Appellate courts ensure that the trial court judge correctly applied the law.

Arguments before Appeals Courts The parties present their arguments to the appellate court through **written briefs** and **oral arguments**, which focus on the law, not the facts in the case. Usually, three judges hear an appeal. The appellate court has authority to review any ruling of law by the trial judge. It has the power to **affirm**, **reverse**, or **modify** the judgment of the trial court. The decision of the appellate court is the one that receives the majority vote of the judges.

Decisions by Appeals Courts An appellate court's majority decision is referred to as the court's **majority opinion**. This opinion gives the legal rationale for the court's decision. It also provides guidance to judges and attorneys for the resolution of similar disputes. A judge may also write a **concurring opinion**, if he agrees with the outcome but has different reasons or wishes to make an additional argument, or a **dissenting opinion**, if she disagrees with the decision of the majority. While concurring and dissenting opinions may influence future thinking about the dispute, the majority decision decides the case and has the force of law.

When the appeals court's majority agrees with the trial court's decision, the court affirms that decision. When the majority disagrees with the trial court, the appellate court's decision reverses the trial court's decision. The appellate court may also affirm the decision but modify it in some way—for example, by reducing the damages awarded by the trial court. In such situations, the appeals court is likely to **remand** the case— return the case—to the trial court for retrial. The trial court must then retry the case, in part or in whole, taking into account the appellate court's ruling.

Lighter Side **of the Law**

The Legal Magic of Spell Check

California attorney Arthur Dudley prepared a brief for an appeals court case. The term *sua sponte*, which means "on its own motion," appeared five times. When he ran spell check, it replaced *sua sponte* with "sea sponge." He did not notice, but the judges did.

One line in the brief now read: "It is well settled that a trial court must instruct sea sponge on any defense." Other lawyers told him he invented a new defense: the sea sponge duty to instruct.

Source: www.law.com.

Enforcement Stage

After a trial, if no appeal is taken or if no further appeal is available, the **judgment**, or decision, of the court becomes final. The same dispute cannot be considered again in that or any other forum. It is *res judicata*—a thing decided by judgment.

The judgment may be a monetary award to the plaintiff, a declaration of the rights between the parties, or an order prohibiting some activity. When the defendant wins, the judgment generally does not involve an award of money. It states that the defendant is not responsible for the plaintiff's injuries. In some instances, the court may require that the losing party pay the other party's legal expenses, but in the United States, each side is usually responsible for their own costs. This is not true in Britain, where the loser must usually pay the winner's legal costs. Many proposals for legal reform in the United States include advocacy of the "loser pays" or "English rule."

Enforcing Judgments When the plaintiff recovers a damage award and the defendant does not pay, the plaintiff can seek a **writ of execution**. The writ is a court order to an official, such as the sheriff, to seize the property of the defendant to satisfy the judgment. Courts may order **garnishment** of a debtor's property, such as a checking account, which usually involves an order to a third party who owes the debtor money to pay the money to the plaintiff instead. When the debtor is an individual, his wages may be garnished, and his employer will pay part of his wages to the plaintiff.

INTERNATIONAL PERSPECTIVE

German Trial Procedure

The rules governing trial procedures can vary substantially from country to country. In Germany, trials are conducted much differently from trials in the United States. Perhaps most striking to U.S. observers is the fact that judges in Germany play a much more active role in the trial process than do American judges. In Germany, civil procedure is governed by rules called the Zivilprozessordnung (ZPO). Under these rules, the judge holds hearings to gather evidence to help him reach a decision in the case. The trial progresses informally (compared to trials in the United States) through these hearings.

In the United States, the role of the judge is usually limited to applying the law to the facts of the case. In Germany, the judge decides the facts of the case and then applies the law to those facts. The judge, not the lawyers, decides which witnesses to call. The judge, not the lawyers, interrogates the witnesses and records their testimony. Judges may ask questions only about the evidence that the parties to the case present themselves. And what is presented is much more limited than what is typically presented at U.S. trials. This is because German courts protect many more confidential relationships than do U.S. courts.

Although obtaining a writ of execution to enforce a judgment may be easy, it is often difficult to collect a judgment. If a party does not have valuable property to seize, or if the losing party flees the jurisdiction with his property or hides property out of the country, it may be nearly impossible for the plaintiff to collect a judgment. In other cases, the losing party, by stalling or otherwise failing to comply with the writ of execution, makes it difficult and costly for the plaintiff to collect. This is one of the many complexities of the litigation process that cause parties to use alternative forms of dispute resolution.

❓ *TEST YOURSELF*

1. If a court issues an order of indefinite length to a party, instructing them to do something or not to do something, it is called _____.
2. In the *Naples* v. *Keystone Building* case, the court issued a temporary restraining order against Keystone instructing it to stop harassing the Naples: T—F
3. The process used to select members of a jury is called _____; an attorney may have the right to _____ the selection of a person to a jury.
4. In the *Pre-Paid Legal Services, Inc.* v. *Cahill* case, where Cahill was soliciting other sales representatives from the company to go with him to another company, the court held that:
   a. it would violate freedom of speech to prevent Cahill from talking to other PPLSI employees about possible alternative employment.
   b. Cahill was liable for damages to PPLSI for lost sales as a result of his recruiting away top sales representatives.
   c. a preliminary injunction against Cahill's solicitation of other employees would be granted.
   d. a preliminary injunction against Cahill's solicitation of other employees would not be proper, but a temporary restraining order prior to trial would be granted.
5. After a jury return a verdict, the losing party may ask the judge to overturn the verdict by granting a motion for judgment as a matter of law: T—F

Answers: permanent injunction; F; voir dire, challenge; c; T.

© Cengage Learning

Alternate Dispute Resolution

If you have a checking account or a credit card, most likely you have agreed to an arbitration agreement, even though you may not have read the details of the contract when you signed up for the account. Many contracts contain arbitration clauses that obligate the parties to the contract to submit disputes to arbitration, not litigation. **Arbitration** is the most widely recognized form of **alternate dispute resolution** (ADR). ADR consists of various ways to resolve disputes outside of the court system. Its use is widespread domestically and internationally. Besides arbitration, which is structured, parties may also agree to use other, less formal, forms of ADR, such as mediation or negotiation.

Arbitration

Arbitration is a process similar to litigation in which two or more persons agree to allow a neutral person or panel to resolve a dispute. The advantages of using a neutral party, called an **arbitrator** or **arbiter**, are threefold: (1) the arbitrator is mutually agreed upon by the parties and has the trust of both parties; (2) because the arbitrator is usually an expert in the subject matter, less time is needed to educate her about the dispute, which usually results in a faster resolution of the matter; and (3) because arbitrators do not usually issue public decisions or hold public hearings, the parties can keep the evidence and decision private.

In the *Federal Arbitration Act* (FAA), Congress states in the strongest terms that agreements to arbitrate must be upheld. A "written provision in any … contract evidencing a transaction involving commerce to settle by arbitration a controversy thereafter arising out of such contract or transaction … shall be valid, irrevocable, and enforceable, save upon such grounds as exist at law or in equity for the revocation of any contract" (9 U.S.C. § 2). If a party tries to avoid arbitration, the courts are instructed by the FAA to compel and enforce arbitration.

Similarly, most states have adopted the *Uniform Arbitration Act* (UAA), which has provisions similar to those in the FAA. Even states that have not adopted the UAA have laws that are similar. All of these laws strongly uphold the integrity of the arbitration process.

There are frequent challenges in court to arbitration awards, but the courts uphold the vast majority of arbitration decisions. The Supreme Court frequently corrects lower federal courts and state courts that try to restrict arbitration. The Court unanimously reiterated in 2012 that there is "a national policy favoring arbitration" in *Nitro-Life Technologies* v. *Eddie Lee Howard* (133 S.Ct. 500). In that case, the Court overturned an Oklahoma high court decision that restricted certain arbitration clauses in employment. Once arbitration has been agreed to by contract, the party is not likely to be able to evade that in favor of litigation.

The Arbitration Agreement

It is common for parties to provide for arbitration of future disputes by inserting an arbitration clause in a contract, such as this standard arbitration clause:

> *Any controversy or claim arising out of or relating to this contract, or the breach thereof, shall be settled by arbitration administered by the American Arbitration Association under its Commercial Arbitration Rules, and the judgment on the award rendered by the arbitrator(s) may be entered in any court having jurisdiction thereof.*

Similarly, parties to a dispute not already covered by an arbitration clause may agree to submit the dispute to arbitration. Arbitration begins when a party files a submission to refer a dispute to arbitration. If you go to the website of the American Arbitration Association (www.adr.org), you see forms used to submit a dispute to arbitration. The time in which a dispute must be filed is usually much shorter than the time in which a lawsuit must be filed. Some commercial arbitration clauses require that cases be filed within a couple of months of the claim or the right to contest the matter is lost.

Selection of Arbitrators In arbitration, the parties agree on who the arbitrator will be or they agree to a selection method given the arbitration rules specified in the arbitration agreement. One arbitrator arbitrates most matters, but panels of three arbitrators are not unusual.

Arbitrators are often attorneys, but that is not required. Rather, arbitrators are required to be impartial, which means that they must avoid conflicts of interest and should uphold the integrity of the arbitration process as spelled out in codes of ethics. Because arbitration is common in many areas, such as labor disputes, the parties usually insist on arbitrators with experience in the field. Having an expert decision maker involved results in faster proceedings because the parties need not explain industry terms or practices to the arbitrator. As a result, arbitrators often have more expertise in their case area than most judges, who hear certain kinds of cases rarely.

Hearing Procedure Arbitration associations have rules that guide participants and arbitrators. For example, the JAMS alternate dispute resolution service (www.jamsadr.com) requires parties to cooperate in good faith in the "voluntary, prompt, and informal exchange of all nonprivileged documents … relevant to the dispute immediately upon commencement of the Arbitration." If a party does not comply with document requests, the arbitrator may order compliance. There is no power to find a party in contempt, as a judge may do, but an arbitrator can order the uncooperative party to pay fees, compensation, and expenses. In practice, because the arbitrator determines the award in the matter, failure to comply may result in loss of a case.

The hearing is normally a closed-door proceeding conducted like a trial but without a trial's restrictive procedural rules. For example, evidence can be presented in an arbitration hearing in a less rigid manner. Because the arbitrator is an expert in the field, he is less likely to be persuaded by improperly presented evidence.

Hearing procedures may take a variety of forms, including online arbitration. General Electric (GE) has used online arbitration in Europe to resolve commercial disputes for amounts less than $60,000. Each side submits their estimate of what proper payment

---

ISSUE SPOTTER
Are There Limits on the Terms of Arbitration?

As a manager at WeLuvPets, you wish to keep down the cost of possible litigation that arises from unhappy former and current employees. You draw up a contract that all new employees must sign as a condition of employment. It says that any and all employment disputes, including claims made under laws against discrimination in employment, will be subject to binding arbitration. It also stipulates that WeLuvPets will choose the arbitrator and that both parties to the dispute will pay one-half of the costs of arbitration. Is the agreement binding on all who sign it? Are all the conditions you put in the arbitration agreement sensible and ethical?

© Cengage Learning

would be in a contract dispute and an arbitrator looks to see if the parties agree. If they do not, the arbitrator provides the settlement based on documents submitted online. GE notes that arbitration for a small dispute, say $10,000, can cost each side that much to handle by in-person arbitration, so it is not as cost effective as the online process.

The Award After the hearing, the arbitrator reaches a decision, called an **award**, which is usually given within 30 days. The award is usually in writing. However, the arbitrator need not state the legal basis of a decision unless the parties have requested it and are willing to pay for that extra work it takes to write the rationale for an award.

The arbitrator makes an award based on application of law to the evidence presented. Besides deciding if one party owes the other party cash, goods, or something else, the arbitrator decides how the parties will split her fee and the administrative fees. In some arbitration, the arbitrator does not construct an award but chooses between the claims of the two parties. Under the rules regarding salary disputes in Major League Baseball, for example, the arbitrator picks either the salary requested by the player or the salary offered by the baseball team, but cannot split the difference.

Arbitrators have wide latitude in making awards. For example, in a case involving a claim by a stockbroker against his former employer, an arbitration panel of the National Association of Securities Dealers (NASD, now FINRA) ordered the employer to pay $2.7 million in compensatory damages and $25 million in punitive damages. The panel also ordered the company to eliminate defamatory materials from the broker's records. The panel held that the employer engaged in reprehensible conduct in smearing the broker's name after he was fired. While only a small percentage of arbitration cases involve punitive damages, arbitrators can have the authority to order such damages based on the arbitration agreement. Some agreements prohibit the award of punitive damages.

Appealing the Award Just as parties who lose in court may be dissatisfied, parties who lose in arbitration may want to carry the matter further. However, errors of fact or law by an arbitrator are not reviewable by the courts. According to the Federal Arbitration Act, there are only four grounds for overturning an award:

1. The award was obtained by corruption or fraud.
2. There was evidence of partiality or corruption by an arbitrator.
3. An arbitrator was guilty of serious procedural misconduct, such as refusing to hear relevant evidence that prejudiced the rights of a party.
4. An arbitrator exceeded his power, and an award was made on a subject not relevant to the proceeding.

Under the doctrine *of res judicata*, the final judgment on the merits of a case by a court prevents an issue from being relitigated. This doctrine also applies to arbitration awards. While this doctrine has a few limitations in arbitration cases, in general, an arbitration award is final, and the matter cannot be litigated again or appealed. This point is worth repeating: once arbitration is agreed to, it is very rare that a party in the case will be allowed to reject it in favor of litigation.

Negotiation

The least formal form of ADR is **negotiation**. It is almost voluntary and, unlike arbitration, has no mandatory procedure, but there can be legal consequences for lying. Negotiation occurs when parties decide to settle a matter between themselves; the use of lawyers or representatives is not required but is common. For an example of one organization active in the area, see CPR International Institute for Conflict Prevention and Resolution (www.cpradr.org).

Issues in Negotiation Whenever people bargain about something, they are engaged in negotiation. Many contracts are formed after negotiation. A negotiated settlement of a dispute is usually a contract that, like other contracts, is enforced by the courts. When parties enter into negotiation, it is often with the intention of making a deal; that is, they are looking forward to forming a contract.

Stages of Negotiation While the steps of negotiation may be much the same in all situations, negotiation in a dispute involves parties at odds with one another. Because the parties to the dispute are unlikely to be experienced negotiators and may be influenced by their anger about what has happened, negotiation to settle a dispute is often handled by an attorney or other experienced person who is not emotionally involved in the matter.

The first stage of negotiation involves studying the issues. A party should gather facts and relevant information and not rely personal opinions; understand the weak points of his own position as well as the other party's; consider the objectives of negotiation; know the law that would be applied to the situation if litigated; know the alternative routes that can be taken; and decide how to handle the negotiation process, such as whether the parties to the dispute will be present.

Next, the parties must exchange information. At this point, the style of the negotiator plays a role. Some negotiators are combative tough guys, while others are thoughtful problem solvers. In either case, the negotiator must know what information to present, such as an offer to settle.

Most negotiators expect to compromise. Some concessions are planned in advance to help get the parties closer to a realistic settlement. Because the courts encourage negotiation, settlement offers presented in negotiation may not be used as evidence in court. If a negotiation is properly handled, almost nothing said in the negotiation can be used in court later, if the negotiation fails. The fact that a negotiation that fails will not come back to haunt a party in court encourages integrity in the process. If an agreement is reached, it is usually presented in writing and becomes a contract that can be enforced in court. The courts have a policy of enforcing negotiated settlements.

CYBER LAW

International Arbitration and Mediation of Domain Name Disputes

The global use of domain names means that they must be unique to be effective in the server system. The World Intellectual Property Organization (WIPO), as part of its function to establish international rules for trademarks and other forms of intellectual property, has a domain name dispute resolution service that protects the integrity of country code top-level domains (such as .mx for Mexico) and for generic top-level domains (gTLDs), such as .edu for education.

WIPO, headquartered in Switzerland, has a Uniform Dispute Resolution Policy (UDRP) that deals with problems such as cybersquatting. Parties can go to the WIPO Arbitration and Mediation Center for dispute resolution. Experts from many countries are available to handle disputes. Most are law professors or lawyers who specialize in this area of law. If only one panelist is requested to settle a dispute, the fee for one to five domain names included in a complaint is $1,500; the fee is $3,000 if three panelists are requested. Such resolution has the advantage of global acceptance of the results. Over a thousand disputes a year are submitted to the Center.

Mediation

Unlike negotiation, where the parties to a dispute or their representatives meet to try to settle a matter, in **mediation** a third party—the **mediator**—is always used to help the parties try to reach a solution by coming to an acceptable agreement. Unlike arbitration, where the arbitrator imposes an award on the parties, the mediator cannot impose a decision, but can only help resolve a conflict.

The American Arbitration Association suggests the following provision be included in contracts:

> *If a dispute arises out of or relates to this contract or the breach thereof and if the dispute cannot be settled through negotiation, the parties agree first to try in good faith to settle the dispute by mediation administered by the American Arbitration Association under its Commercial Mediation Rules before resorting to arbitration, litigation, or some other dispute-resolution procedure.*

Mediation is commonly used to resolve disputes that start out in the courts. Many federal and state courts require that mediation be attempted before trial or at least offered as an alternative. Surveys indicate that attorneys prefer to go to mediation rather than to arbitration.

Mediation is also often used to help resolve labor disputes. The Federal Mediation and Conciliation Service helps unions and employers bargain to a contract. Mediation is also commonly used to help resolve marital problems and, if not successful, to help set the terms of divorce. In all such instances, mediation is a voluntary process that helps avoid litigation.

In general, there is little formal regulation of mediation, but there are professional organizations that assist in training and in setting standards. Those who offer their services as mediators and fail to act in a professional manner may be subject to liability by a party to the dispute unhappy with the outcome.

INTERNATIONAL PERSPECTIVE

Arbitration and Cotton Contracts

Tens of billions of dollars are involved in more than 100,000 cotton contracts made annually around the world. Farmers contract to sell to cotton brokers who contract to sell to textile mills. When prices go up or down after contracts are made, one side of the contract suffers a loss; the other side makes a gain.

A standard clause in cotton contracts requires disputes to be handled by arbitration through the International Cotton Association (ICA) in Liverpool, England, which has been handling such matters for 170 years. Most years, the ICA handles about 75 cases, but when cotton prices change radically, the number can jump to 250 cases or more, as happened in 2011 and 2012 when cotton prices were exceptionally volatile. Cotton prices rose to a high level, and some farmers refused to deliver to brokers at the older, lower price they had agreed to. When cotton prices fell, some textile mills refused to take delivery at the old, higher price they had agreed to.

When the losing party ignores an arbitration award, the winning party can begin the costly process of litigation to get enforcement of the ICA award. Many textile mills are in countries with courts of dubious integrity. However, courts in China have upheld some awards against mills in China, but the defendants still refused to pay.

The ICA provides an efficient, low-cost mechanism to resolve disputes, but when it is ignored, the integrity of cotton contracting comes into question. To try to discipline firms that refuse to abide by the arbitration system they agreed to, the ICA publishes a list of parties who are in default so cotton market participants will know to avoid them.

Mediation Process When both parties agree to mediation, a mediator may review the issues to prepare to handle the matter. The mediator explains the process involved and makes clear that he is a neutral party. The mediator collects information, outlines the key issues, listens, asks questions, observes the parties, discusses options, and encourages compromise. If successful, the mediator helps draft an agreement between the parties that settles the dispute. The agreement is an enforceable contract that therefore settles the matter.

A standard part of the mediation process is an agreement by the parties to maintain confidentiality. Nothing said in the mediation can be made public or be used in court as evidence if mediation should fail and a suit follows. Regardless of what the parties agree upon, there is a presumption in law that information revealed during negotiation or mediation should not be used in evidence. To encourage honesty in negotiation and mediation, most discussions are privileged, and mediators cannot be required to testify later in court. Some states, including Colorado, have made this a firm rule by statute:

> *Mediation proceedings shall be regarded as settlement negotiations, and no admission, representation, or statement made in mediation not otherwise discoverable or obtainable shall be admissible as evidence or subject to discovery. In addition, a mediator shall not be subject to process requiring the disclosure of any matter discussed during mediation proceedings.* [Colo. Rev. Stat. 13-22-307]

❓ TEST YOURSELF

1. When parties to a dispute agree to meet before a private decision maker who has authority to impose a binding resolution to the dispute, the process is called:
   a. mediation.
   b. arbitration.
   c. *res judicata*.
   d. negotiation.
2. The majority of states now require mediators to be licensed, which is usually accomplished by passing a state examination: T—F
3. At the end of arbitration, the decision is called _____.
4. If an arbitrator makes a mistake of law, not a mistake of fact, there is a right to appeal the decision to the proper court for review of the decision: T—F

Answers: b; F; award; F.

SUMMARY

- The American legal system is an adversary system of justice. The responsibility for bringing and presenting a lawsuit rests upon the litigants. The system reflects the belief that truth is best discovered through the presentation of competing ideas.
- Litigation begins with pleadings. The plaintiff must notify the defendant by service of process that a complaint has been filed with a court. The

defendant must answer the complaint with a motion to dismiss, a defense, or a counterclaim, or the plaintiff wins by default. The plaintiff may respond to the defendant's answer with a reply.

- Before trial, the discovery process allows the parties to gather evidence. Depositions or interrogatories may be taken from both the parties and the witnesses. The discovery process allows parties to know what the trial is to be about so that few surprises arise. Gathering evidence may cause the parties to settle the case as the likely outcome becomes clear.

- At most trials, the defendant has the right to ask for a jury trial. Attorneys discuss with clients the advisability of a jury trial or a trial where the judge hears and determines the entire matter. When a jury is used, it is the finder of fact.

- At trial, after opening statements by both parties, the plaintiff presents witnesses and evidence to prove the facts of her case. Witnesses are questioned by both sides. After the cases have been stated, either party can request that the judge give a directed verdict to end the case. In most cases, the matter goes to the jury after closing arguments and instructions by the judge. The jury determines the facts of the case and applies the law as explained by the judge.

- The remedies awarded by the courts in resolving civil disputes include monetary damages and equitable relief. Monetary damages include compensatory, punitive, and nominal damages. Equitable remedies include specific performance and injunctions.

- A party unhappy with the result may appeal the decision. The court of appeals reviews the case to determine whether any errors were made in the application of the law to the facts as the judge or jury determined them. The court of appeals may affirm, reverse, or modify the trial court's decision.

- Plaintiffs winning judgments are responsible for attempting to collect the judgment, which is difficult if the defendant leaves the state or has few assets. The plaintiff may have to return to the court to obtain orders to force compliance with the judgment. A writ of execution allows the property of the defendant to be seized to satisfy the judgment.

- Arbitration is the most formal ADR process. A decision to enter into arbitration is a binding contract. The parties who agree to arbitration choose an arbitrator, a neutral party who arbitrates the dispute and issues a binding decision, called an award, much like a judge resolves a case.

- Arbitration hearings are run somewhat like a trial, but the rules of evidence are not as strict, and the procedure is more informal. Each side presents its case to the arbitrator and may call witnesses and experts to testify. An arbitrator's award need not be justified in writing. Appeals of awards to the courts are rarely successful because the parties have agreed to be bound by the decision. Unless fraud or other misconduct by the arbitrator can be shown, the courts are very unlikely to intervene.

- Arbitration is often a standard part of employment contracts, insurance and commercial sale contracts, and agreements with stockbrokers.

- Negotiation is the least formal kind of ADR. The parties deal directly with each other or do so through attorneys or other agents who represent them in confidential discussions to resolve a matter. The parties exchange information, make offers, compromise, and move toward a formal settlement.

- Mediation is a more structured form of negotiation; a neutral mediator helps the parties come to a resolution of a dispute. Both parties must agree upon a mediator. A mediator gets the parties to agree on a process, explains the rules, gathers information, outlines key issues, talks to and listens to the parties, suggests options, encourages compromise, and may help draft an enforceable settlement. Mediation is usually confidential.

TERMS TO KNOW

adversary system of justice, 52
pleading, 52
complaint, 52
service of process, 52
summons, 52
motion to dismiss, 52
motion to dismiss for failure to
   state a claim, 52
demurrer, 52
answer, 54

affirmative defense, 54
counterclaim, 54
discovery, 56
deposition, 56
interrogatories, 56
default judgment, 58
contempt of court, 58
protective order, 58
summary judgment, 60
trial, 61

jury, 61
voir dire, 61
opening statement, 62
direct examination, 62
cross-examination, 62
closing argument, 62
instructions (charges), 63
preponderance of the evidence, 63
hung jury, 63
mistrial, 63

DISCUSSION QUESTION

In many aspects of business, a manager can choose to include an arbitration or mediation clause to govern disputes, such as with customers and employees, or can leave that out and use litigation. What are the pros and cons of such alternatives in regular business practice?

CASE QUESTIONS

1. Bonnie Weisgram died from smoke inhalation during a fire in her home. Her son, Chad Weisgram, sued Marley, the maker of a heater, claiming it was defective and caused the fire. At trial, Weisgram offered expert witness testimony to prove that the heater was defective. Marley objected that the testimony was unreliable and therefore inadmissible, but the judge overruled the objections; the jury found for Weisgram. The appeals court held that the testimony of Weisgram's expert was not scientifically sound. The appeals court directed a judgment for Marley, holding that there were no grounds for a new trial. Weisgram appealed; does he have a good reason for a new trial? [*Weisgram* v. *Marley Co.*, 120 S.Ct. 1011 (2000)]
   ✓ Check your answer

2. Curtis and Bruce Wenzel jointly owned land, buildings, and machinery used for agricultural purposes. After Bruce died, Curtis and Bruce's estate could not agree on how to sell or partition the assets. Curtis continued to use the machinery without paying rent to the estate, but paid certain bills related to the care of the assets. The estate disputed the need for several of the bills paid by Curtis. The dispute over the assets went to trial. The court divided the land and ordered Curtis to buy out the estate's share of the machinery for $74,300—after the court had made adjustments for use and expenses. Curtis appealed, contending that as a matter of law, the court could not order him to pay the estate for half the value of the jointly owned machinery. Is it reasonable for the court to use such powers in equity in this manner? [*Bruce J. Wenzel Estate* v. *Wenzel*, 747 N.W.2d 103, Sup. Ct., N.D. (2008)]
   ✓ Check your answer

3. A franchise agreement between the parent company franchisor and the franchisees who operated 7-Eleven stores said that any dispute between the franchisor and franchisees would be settled by arbitration. A franchisee sued the franchisor in state court, claiming that some actions of the franchisor were in violation of state law concerning franchises. The state supreme court ruled that the issues covered by the state law could be tried in state court and did not have to go to arbitration. What did the U.S. Supreme Court hold about the choice between arbitration and litigation? [*Southland Corp.* v. *Keating*, 465 U.S. 1 (1984)]

4. Hammond, a mediator, assisted in negotiations between a union and a company. After mediation, the union declared that an agreement had been reached. The employer denied that an agreement had been reached and refused to sign

the union contract. The union filed an unfair labor practice complaint with the National Labor Relations Board. The company claimed that it had the right to call the mediator as a witness in the unfair labor practice complaint. Could the mediator be called to give testimony in the case? [*National Labor Relations Board* v. *Joseph Macaluso, Inc.*, 618 F.2d 51, 9th Cir. (1980)]

✓ Check your answer

5. People who borrowed money from Buckeye Check Cashing signed an agreement that included a clause requiring any dispute to go to arbitration. Suit was filed by some customers against Buckeye, claiming their service violated the lending laws of Florida, which would make the agreement invalid. The Florida high court held that because the legality of the contract was in question, the matter had to go to court for review, not arbitration. Do you think that ruling was upheld on review by the U.S. Supreme Court? [*Buckeye Check Cashing* v. *Cardegna*, 126 S.Ct. 1204 (2006)]

6. Paranzino claimed she deposited $200,000 in a bank but was given a receipt for only $100,000, but she did not notice the mistake until later. She sued the bank, but attended court-ordered mediation. The mediation required parties to sign a confidentiality agreement. At mediation, the bank offered $25,000 to settle the matter. Paranzino rejected that and called the newspaper to explain the details of the story. This violated the confidentiality agreement. What can be done in such a case? [*Paranzino* v. *Barnett Bank*, 690 So.2d 725, Ct. App., Fla. (1997)]

✓ Check your answer

ETHICS QUESTION

Because litigation is so costly, many firms settle suits that they are quite sure they would win if litigated. It is cheaper to settle for $10,000 or $50,000 rather than consume management time and litigation fees. While it is unethical to bring dubious suits that are largely intended to extract a settlement, is it ethical for firms to settle such cases rather than spend additional resources and defeat such suits?

CHAPTER **4**

The Constitution: Focus on Application to Business

George Washington presided over a convention in Philadelphia in 1787, at which the Constitution of the United States was drafted. The Constitution became effective in 1789, after it was ratified by the legislatures of 9 of the 13 original states. It is composed of the preamble and seven Articles. The preamble reads:

We the People of the United States, in Order to form a more perfect Union, establish Justice, insure domestic Tranquility, provide for the common defence, promote the general Welfare, and secure the Blessings of Liberty to ourselves and our Posterity, do ordain and establish this Constitution for the United States of America.

The Articles of the Constitution are:

   I. Composition and powers of Congress
  II. Selection and powers of the president
 III. Creation and powers of the federal judiciary
 IV. Role of the states in the federal system
  V. Methods of amending the Constitution
 VI. Declaring the Constitution to be supreme law of the land
VII. Method for ratifying the Constitution

The Constitution was amended almost immediately. The concern was that there was not enough protection for individual rights. In 1791, the first 10 amendments—the Bill of Rights—were ratified by the states after having been approved by the First Session of Congress. A proposed amendment must be passed by a two-thirds vote in the House and Senate and then be ratified by three-fourths of the state legislatures. An amendment may also be proposed by two-thirds of the state legislatures by calling for a constitutional convention, the results of which must be ratified by three-fourths of the state legislatures. That has never happened. The Constitution is reprinted in Appendix C.

All citizens and businesses are affected by the Constitution. Court rulings about the rights of people accused of crimes draw the most popular attention. Supreme Court interpretation of the rights of the accused and of other constitutionally protected rights changes over time. The Court has reversed itself on major constitutional issues over the years, reading the same words in an opposite manner. Some would say this means the Court is political, but it may also reflect changes in technology, social values, economic conditions, and political realities.

The Commerce Clause

While all parts of the Constitution have application to businesses and to individuals, certain provisions have a particular impact on businesses. In that respect, perhaps the most important part of the Constitution is Article I, Section 8: "The Congress shall have Power ... To regulate Commerce with foreign Nations, and among the several States. ..." Known as the **commerce clause**, these words have been interpreted to give Congress the power to enact most of the federal regulation of business. When combined with the **necessary and proper clause**, this gives Congress tremendous regulatory power.

The Necessary and Proper Clause

The Constitution lists specific congressional powers (including collecting taxes, regulating commerce, and providing for national defense). At the end of the list, Clause 18 of Article I, Section 8, gives Congress power "to make all Laws which shall be necessary and proper for carrying into Execution the foregoing Powers and all other Powers vested by this Constitution in the Government of the United States, or in any Department or Officer thereof." This is called the necessary and proper clause.

McCulloch *v.* Maryland   Chief Justice John Marshall gave a broad reading to the necessary and proper clause in 1819 in *McCulloch* v. *Maryland* (17 U.S. 316). In that case, the state of Maryland questioned whether Congress had the right to establish a national bank because banking was not a power of Congress specified in the Constitution. The Supreme Court upheld the constitutionality of the bank under the necessary and proper clause. The Court held that the clause expands the power of Congress:

> *1st. The clause is placed among the powers of Congress, not among the limitations on those powers.*
>
> *2nd. Its terms purport to enlarge, not to diminish the powers vested in the government. It purports to be an additional power, not a restriction on those already granted.*

Over the years, the Supreme Court has upheld most federal statutes challenged under that clause as necessary and proper, even if the subject of the legislation could not have been contemplated when the Constitution was written. For example, the Court upheld a federal statute limiting liability from nuclear accidents as necessary and proper to achieve the government's objective of encouraging the development of private nuclear power plants. The authors of the Constitution knew nothing about nuclear power, the Internet, or other things that Congress would deal with eventually. The Supreme Court has used the necessary and proper clause to allow Congress to respond to such developments without requiring amendments to the Constitution.

Federal Supremacy   Another key point made in the *McCulloch* decision is that when the federal government has the power to act under the Constitution, its actions are supreme; that is, they take precedence over the actions of other governments. The state of Maryland had argued that even if the federal government had the right to establish a national bank, the state could tax the national bank just as it did private banks. The Court struck down the Maryland tax as in violation of Article VI, Paragraph 2, the **supremacy clause**: "The Constitution, and the Laws of the United States ... shall be the supreme Law of the Land; and the judges in every State shall be bound thereby...." If Congress did not want Maryland to tax a bank created by Congress, Maryland could not do so because, so long as they are constitutional, federal laws are supreme over state laws.

Defining "Commerce among the Several States"

Although most federal regulation of business began after the Civil War, Congress has had broad regulatory powers since the early days of the Republic. In 1824, Chief Justice Marshall established some of the basic guidelines of the commerce clause in *Gibbons* v. *Ogden* (22 U.S. 1). He held that commerce among the states means **interstate commerce**, that is, business that concerns more than one state. Further, Chief Justice Marshall held:

> *What is this power? It is the power to regulate; that is, to prescribe the rule by which commerce is to be governed. This power, like all others vested in Congress, is complete in itself, may be exercised to its utmost extent, and acknowledges no limitations other than are prescribed in the Constitution.*

Power over Interstate Commerce Is Extensive Congress can regulate almost any form of commerce, even if the impact on interstate commerce is tiny. In the landmark case of *Wickard* v. *Filburn* (317 U.S. 111, 1942), the Supreme Court upheld federal regulations of what farmers could grow. Filburn had a 90-acre family farm in Ohio. According to the U.S. Department of Agriculture, which was authorized by Congress to set the price of wheat and tell every farmer how much wheat they could grow, Filburn produced 239 bushels of wheat more than he was allowed. He was fined $117 and ordered not to plant more than he was told.

Filburn protested that the law was unconstitutional because he should be free to plant crops on his land and, furthermore, he did not sell the wheat. He used it to feed his chickens and cows and to make bread for his family, so there was no effect on interstate commerce. The Court held that although Filburn's effect on the market for wheat was "trivial," it was still subject to federal control. Since "home-consumed wheat would have a substantial influence on price and market conditions," Congress could regulate its price and the quantity allowed grown by every farmer. Since this case, almost all commerce is defined as interstate commerce. For example, in the *Katzenbach* v. *McClung* decision, the Court used the commerce clause to extend nondiscrimination requirements of the 1964 Civil Rights Act to local businesses.

KATZENBACH V. MCCLUNG

United States Supreme Court 379 U.S. 294, 85 S.Ct. 377 (1964)

Case Background *Ollie's Barbecue was a restaurant in Birmingham, Alabama, owned by McClung. It had 220 seats for white customers. Although most employees were black, black customers were allowed to buy food only at a take-out window. The Department of Justice (Attorney General Katzenbach) sued the restaurant for violating Title II of the 1964 Civil Rights Act, which prohibits racial segregation in places of public accommodation. This includes restaurants that offer "to serve interstate travelers [if] a substantial portion of the food which it serves ... has moved in interstate commerce." McClung contended that because his customers were local, not traveling*

interstate, he should be exempt from the law. The government noted that half of the food McClung bought came from out of state, which was enough to make the business interstate.

The district court held for McClung and refused to enforce the Act. The government appealed directly to the Supreme Court.

Case Decision Clark, Justice

* * *

Much is said about a restaurant business being local but "even if appellee's activity is local and though it may not be regarded as commerce, it may still, whatever its nature, be reached by Congress if it exerts a substantial economic effect on interstate commerce." *Wickard* v. *Filburn.*

This Court has held time and again that this power extends to activities of retail establishments, including restaurants, which directly or indirectly burden or obstruct interstate commerce.

* * *

Confronted as we are with the facts laid before Congress, we must conclude that it had a rational basis for finding that racial discrimination in restaurants had a direct and adverse effect on the free flow of interstate commerce. Insofar as the sections of the Civil Rights Act here relevant are concerned, Congress prohibited discrimination only in those establishments having a close tie to interstate commerce, that is, those, like McClung's, serving food that has come from out of the State. We think in so doing that Congress acted well within its power to protect and foster commerce in extending the coverage of Title II only to those restaurants offering to serve interstate travelers or serving food, a substantial portion of which has moved in interstate commerce.

The absence of direct evidence connecting discriminatory restaurant service with the flow of inter-state food, a factor on which the appellees place much reliance, is not, given the evidence as to the effect of such practices on other aspects of commerce, a crucial matter.

The power of Congress in this field is broad and sweeping; where it keeps within its sphere and violates no express constitutional limitation it has been the rule of this Court, going back almost to the founding days of the Republic, not to interfere. The Civil Rights Act of 1964, as here applied, we find to be plainly appropriate in the resolution of what the Congress found to be a national commercial problem of the first magnitude. We find in it no violation of any express limitations of the Constitution and we therefore declare it valid.

The judgment is therefore reversed.

Questions for Analysis

1. Might the Court have found that the Civil Rights Act did not apply to a local restaurant if the restaurant could show that all of its food was produced in the state?
2. Suppose evidence showed that when restaurants were required to integrate, they often closed their doors and refused to do more business. Does this go against the argument that the law improves interstate commerce?

Federal and State Regulatory Relations

There are tens of thousands of pages of federal and state laws and even more pages of regulations issued under these laws. The responsibility for regulating a particular activity may fall to a state governing body or a federal governing body, or state and federal governments may share it. Federal environmental regulation, for example, requires the Environmental Protection Agency to set national pollution control standards. Once those are set, state environmental regulators must then create specific requirements to be met within a state and issue permits for dischargers to the air and water, inspect landfills, and many other tasks. As Exhibit 4.1 illustrates, regulation may be exclusive to one level of government or may overlap.

States often legislate on a matter on which Congress has legislated. When can state law exist along with federal law? Federal regulation takes precedence over state regulation, so state regulations may not contradict or reduce the standards imposed by federal law. States also may not enact laws that burden interstate commerce by imposing restrictions on businesses from other states.

In some areas, such as postal authority, the courts have ruled that the states may not regulate at all. In *U.S.* v. *Locke* (529 U.S 89) the Supreme Court struck down Washington state regulations regarding oil tanker design and operation. State rules are preempted by the comprehensive federal regulatory scheme governing tankers. Congress clearly wished

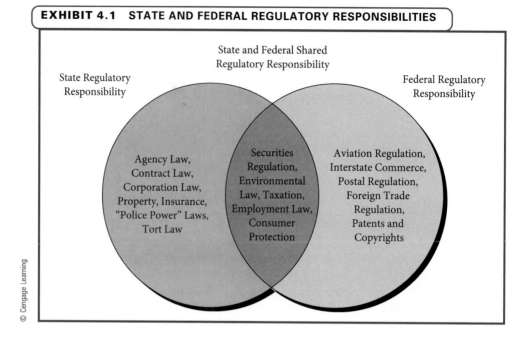

EXHIBIT 4.1   STATE AND FEDERAL REGULATORY RESPONSIBILITIES

State and Federal Shared
Regulatory Responsibility

State Regulatory
Responsibility

Federal Regulatory
Responsibility

Agency Law,
Contract Law,
Corporation Law,
Property, Insurance,
"Police Power" Laws,
Tort Law

Securities
Regulation,
Environmental
Law, Taxation,
Employment Law,
Consumer
Protection

Aviation Regulation,
Interstate Commerce,
Postal Regulation,
Foreign Trade
Regulation,
Patents and
Copyrights

© Cengage Learning

to have uniform rules governing tanker operations in all waters, so the states may not intervene.

In some areas, states may add their own rules to strengthen the impact of a federal rule, so long as the rules do not conflict with the intent of the law and do not impede interstate commerce. For example, states may pass air pollution regulations to apply to their industries that are stricter, but not less strict, than the federal air pollution rules. Similarly, states are allowed to prohibit discrimination based on sexual orientation, which is not covered by federal law.

In other areas that Congress could regulate, such as insurance, Congress has authorized states to regulate the business within state borders.

When State Law Impedes Interstate Commerce   In 1911, the Supreme Court, in *Southern Railway Co.* v. *Arizona* (222 U.S. 20), had to consider Arizona regulations that required trains to be shorter in Arizona than in other states for "safety considerations." The effect of the Arizona requirement was to impede interstate commerce. At the Arizona border, trains had to stop and be broken up into shorter trains with additional engines and train crews. The Supreme Court struck down the Arizona law. Chief Justice Stone said, "The decisive question is whether in the circumstances the total effect of the law as a safety measure in reducing accidents and casualties is so slight or problematical as not to outweigh the national interest in keeping interstate commerce free from interferences which seriously impede it."

Because state legislatures often pass laws creating safety standards or other regulations inconsistent with other states' laws, there are many Supreme Court cases in this area. The Supreme Court consistently takes a hard line against state regulations that restrict interstate commerce or are designed to help local businesses at the expense of out-of-state competitors:

- In *Chemical Waste Management* v. *Hunt* (504 U.S. 334), the Court held it violated the commerce clause for Alabama to impose a higher fee for hazardous waste generated outside the state than it charged for hazardous waste generated within the state, when both were disposed at commercial disposal facilities in Alabama.

- Oklahoma required coal-burning power plants in the state to burn at least 10 percent Oklahoma-mined coal. Wyoming challenged the regulation because it meant less Wyoming coal was sold to Oklahoma power plants. The Court held in *Wyoming* v. *Oklahoma* (502 U.S. 437) that the Oklahoma law was discriminatory and interfered with interstate commerce.

The states have a legitimate interest in protecting public health, safety, and other public policies. When such goals are the reason for a state law, the regulation chosen must be designed to achieve its legitimate interest with minimal impact on interstate business. The *Hughes* decision concerned a minor matter—the sale of bait fish to people in Texas—but was a case used by the Court to lay out the three steps still used today to guide evaluation of state regulations that affect interstate commerce.

HUGHES V. OKLAHOMA

United States Supreme Court 441 U.S. 322, 99 S.Ct. 1727 (1979)

Case Background *To protect minnows that live in state waters, Oklahoma prohibited shipping or selling minnows out of state. Hughes was convicted of transporting minnows from Oklahoma to Texas. He bought the minnows from a dealer licensed in Oklahoma. If the minnows had been sold and used within the state, it would have been legal. It was illegal to take the fish across the state line. The Oklahoma Court of Criminal Appeals upheld the statute and Hughes' conviction as consistent with Oklahoma's interest in protecting its natural resources. Hughes appealed.*

Case Decision Brennan, Justice

* * *

We turn then to the question whether the burden imposed on interstate commerce in wild game by [the Oklahoma law] is permissible under the general rule articulated in our precedents governing other types of commerce. Under the general rule, we must inquire (1) whether the challenged statute regulates even-handedly with only "incidental" effects on interstate commerce, or discriminates against interstate commerce either on its face or in practical effect; (2) whether the statute serves a legitimate local purpose; and, if so, (3) whether alternative means could promote this local purpose as well without discriminating against interstate commerce. The burden to show discrimination rests on the party challenging the validity of the

statute, but "when discrimination against commerce ... is demonstrated, the burden falls on the State to justify it both in terms of the local benefits flowing from the statute and the unavailability of nondiscriminatory alternatives adequate to preserve the local interests at stake." Furthermore, when considering the purpose of a challenged statute, this Court is not bound by "the name, description, or characterization given it by the legislature or the courts of the State," but will determine for itself the practical impact of the law.

[The Oklahoma law] on its face discriminates against interstate commerce. It forbids the transportation of natural minnows out of the State for purposes of sale, and thus "overtly blocks the flow of interstate commerce at the State's borders." Such facial discrimination by itself may be a fatal defect, regardless of the State's purpose, because "the evil of protectionism can reside in legislative means as well as legislative ends." At a minimum such facial discrimination invokes the strictest scrutiny of any purported legitimate local purpose and of the absence of nondiscriminatory alternatives.

Oklahoma argues that [its law] serves a legitimate local purpose in that it is "readily apparent as a conservation measure." The State's interest in maintaining the ecological balance in state waters by avoiding the removal of inordinate numbers of minnows may well qualify as a legitimate local purpose.

* * *

Far from choosing the least discriminatory alternative, Oklahoma has chosen to "conserve" its minnows in the way that most overtly discriminates against interstate commerce. The State places no limits on the numbers of minnows that can be taken by licensed minnow dealers; nor does it limit in any way how these minnows may be disposed of within the State. Yet it forbids the transportation of any commercially significant number of natural minnows out of the State for sale. [Its law] is ... a choice of the most discriminatory means even though nondiscriminatory alternatives would seem likely to fulfill the State's purported legitimate local purpose more effectively....

Reversed.

Questions for Analysis

1. The Court held that the Oklahoma law unfairly discriminated against interstate commerce. How could the state have designed a regulation to achieve the same result, to protecting minnows, without harming interstate commerce?
2. Suppose Oklahoma got other states to agree to a restriction on the interstate shipment of minnows to help other states protect their resources. Would that be a reasonable compromise?

Imitation Not Allowed The states may not copy federal regulations if such imitation inhibits interstate commerce. Consider the following situation. Congress has long required that timber removed from federal lands in Alaska may not be shipped out of state unless processed into boards in Alaska. The state of Alaska imitated the federal rule, requiring that timber cut on state lands be processed in the state before shipment out of state.

The Supreme Court struck down the state law in *South-Central Timber Development* v. *Wunnicke* (467 U.S. 82). "Although the Commerce Clause is by its text an affirmative grant of power to Congress to regulate interstate and foreign commerce, the Clause has long been recognized as a self-executing limitation on the power of the States to enact laws imposing substantial burdens on such commerce." That is, although Congress could impose such a requirement on timber, the state could not do so, unless authorized by Congress. Congress may regulate interstate commerce, but the states have much more limited powers.

 ## Lighter Side of the Law

I Am My Own Sovereign

Justin Wayne Gray was pulled over for speeding in Austin, Texas. Having no license or insurance, he was arrested. Representing himself in court, he stated that he was "a sovereign political power holder" and that the state could not bring charges against him because he was "a sovereign man" and "sovereigns are excluded from all the statutes."

Furthermore, the state violated the war powers clause of the U.S. Constitution and because the state refused to respond to his pleadings, the case should be dismissed. The appeals court disagreed, finding that he was "a person" subject to the traffic laws of Texas.

Source: Gray v. *State,* Ct. App., Tx. (2010).

The Taxing Power

Congress is given the power to "lay and collect Taxes, Duties, Imposts, and Excises" by Article I, Section 8, Clause 1, of the Constitution. Although this text does not cover tax law (it is a complex topic requiring specialized courses), keep in mind that taxation is a potent tool of regulation. In *McCulloch* v. *Maryland*, Chief Justice Marshall noted "the power to tax includes the power to destroy." Taxes can be used for more than raising revenue to pay for government services. They can deter and punish certain behavior. For example, a tax may be tied to a requirement to keep detailed records about goods subject to the tax. This way, goods such as explosives, firearms, drugs, and liquors can be kept under close federal supervision.

Federal Taxation

Since the 16th Amendment gave the federal government the power to impose income taxes, the Supreme Court has rarely questioned the constitutionality of federal taxing schemes. Even if the taxpayer alleges an improper or discriminatory motive behind a tax, the Court has refused to consider such claims. The Court noted in *Sonzinsky* v. *United States* (300 U.S. 506):

> *Inquiry into the hidden motives which may move Congress to exercise a power constitutionally conferred upon it is beyond the competency of courts.... We are not free to speculate as to the motives which moved Congress to impose it, or as to the extent to which it may operate to restrict the activities taxed.*

The Court has upheld taxes on illegal gambling and illegal drugs. This makes it easier for the government to prosecute people involved in illegal activities. If the income from such activities is reported, the government has evidence of illegal dealings. If the income is not reported and money is found, then the tax laws have been violated. As the Court held in *United States* v. *Kahriger* (345 U.S. 22), "the power of Congress to tax is extensive and sometimes falls with crushing effect on businesses."

State Taxation

The Constitution protects interstate commerce from discriminatory state taxes. As the Supreme Court ruled in *Northwestern States Portland Cement Co.* v. *Minnesota* (358 U.S. 450):

> *A State cannot impose taxes upon persons passing through the state or coming into it merely for a temporary purpose. ... Moreover, a State may not lay a tax on the "privilege" of engaging in interstate commerce. ... Nor may a State impose a tax which discriminates against interstate commerce either by providing a direct commercial advantage to local business ... or by subjecting interstate commerce to the burden of "multiple taxation."... States, under the Commerce Clause, are not allowed "one single tax-dollar worth of direct interference with the free flow of commerce."*

Consider the following cases in which the Supreme Court reviewed state taxing schemes to decide whether they interfered with interstate commerce:

- The state of Hawaii imposed a 20 percent tax on all alcoholic beverages except for local products. The Court struck this down (*Baccus Imports* v. *Bias*, 468 U.S. 263), holding that the tax imposed on alcoholic products had to be the same regardless of origin.
- Michigan exempted from state income taxes the retirement benefits paid to state employees. The state taxed all other retirement income, such as retired federal

government employees' benefits. The Supreme Court struck this down in *Davis* v. *Michigan Dept. of Treasury* (489 U.S. 803) as discriminatory. State income taxes must apply equally to all retirement benefits.

- In *Quill Corp.* v. *North Dakota* (504 U.S. 298), state sales taxes imposed on out-of-state firms doing mail-order business with North Dakota residents were stricken as a violation of the commerce clause. Mail-order firms that do not have a physical presence in the state may not be taxed. As firms such as Amazon have become more important in retailing, the practicality of this rule has come under question, and some online retailers are collecting sales taxes rather than fight the states.

- Illinois imposed a 5 percent tax on all long-distance calls to or from the state. If a taxpayer can show that another state has billed the call, the Illinois tax is refunded. This tax was held not to violate the commerce clause in *Goldberg* v. *Sweet* (488 U.S. 252) because it satisfies a four-part test of the constitutionality of state tax schemes. The tax:
  1. applies to an activity having a substantial nexus (connection) with the state.
  2. is fairly apportioned to those inside and outside the state.
  3. does not discriminate against interstate commerce.
  4. is fairly related to services provided by the state.

The kind of tax imposed by states—income, property, or sales—does not matter, nor does the tax rate; the issue is if the tax is imposed in such a way as to discriminate against income and businesses from other states.

Apportioning State Tax Burden   The Supreme Court has held that business income may be taxed by the states as long as they use formulas that divide a company's income fairly into the portion attributable to their state. There are two important limitations on states' ability to tax multistate corporations' profits. First, states can only tax profits if a multistate business does at least a minimal amount of business in that state. The business must have a "nexus" with the state. Second, each state with which a company has a nexus must have rules for dividing the company's income into an in-state and an out-of-state portion, a process known as "apportionment." The state can only tax the in-state portion. The reason for these limits is to prevent a company from being taxed on more than 100% of its income, which could happen if the company's income was not apportioned.

 ISSUE SPOTTER
Unconstitutional Business Activity?

Your company, an auto parts maker in Michigan, belongs to the Michigan Industrial Alliance (MIA), a trade association that lobbies on behalf of its members' interests in the state and federal legislatures. The MIA has succeeded in getting influential members of the Michigan legislature to propose legislation that would exempt auto parts produced in Michigan from sales tax, while auto parts brought to Michigan from other states or foreign countries would be subject to the tax. The legislation was designed to encourage auto manufacturers in Michigan to buy more auto parts made in Michigan.

Should your company support this lobbying activity in the legislature? Is it likely to succeed if the bill becomes law?

States use different formulas to apportion taxes. About half the states have adopted the Uniform Division of Income for Tax Purposes Act (UDITPA), so that companies operating in those states face the same formula across the board. UDITPA uses three factors to divide a company's income: (1) the percentage of a corporation's nationwide property located in the state, (2) the percentage of a corporation's nationwide sales made to residents of the state, and (3) the percentage of a corporation's nationwide payroll paid to residents of the state. Most states give twice the weight to the sales factor as to the other factors. More than a dozen states use only sales to determine the share of the profits they can tax.

Because different companies benefit from different formulas, businesses lobby states to adopt a particular formula that will help them. For example, Raytheon, which had major operations in Massachusetts, would pay less if employment and property did not count, so it pushed Massachusetts to adopt the sales-only formula by threatening to move operations elsewhere. Businesses also make decisions about where to locate their facilities and employees based on the impact on their state tax bills, making this a complex subject.

State Taxes May Not Impede Foreign Trade Although Congress has nearly unlimited taxing power, the states may not interfere with interstate commerce through their taxing schemes. Further, because the Constitution gives Congress the power to regulate international trade as well, the states may not interfere with international commerce through taxation.

The Supreme Court emphasized that point in *Japan Line* v. *County of Los Angeles* (441 U.S. 434). Several California cities and counties imposed a property tax on cargo-shipping containers owned by Japanese companies. The containers were used only in international commerce on Japanese ships. The California taxes were imposed on the containers in the state during loading and unloading. The Supreme Court held the tax to be unconstitutional because the commerce clause reserves to Congress the power over foreign commerce. Foreign commerce may not be subject to discriminatory state taxes. If such taxes could be imposed, the states would be able to regulate foreign trade, which the Constitution forbids.

❓ TEST YOURSELF

1. The first ten amendments to the Constitution are known as The Bill of Rights: T—F
2. The Constitution holds that federal law takes precedence over state law in the _____.
3. In *Hughes* v. *Oklahoma*, the Supreme Court held that Oklahoma could impose:
   a. "all rational" regulations to protect the state's environment.
   b. no environmental regulations without permission of the Environmental Protection Agency.
   c. environmental regulations so long as they did not discriminate against interstate commerce.
   d. environmental regulations that were shown not to take private property without just compensation.
4. According to the taxing powers allowed by the Constitution, states may impose any tax "substantially identical" to any tax imposed by Congress: T—F
5. When a state taxes the income of multi-state businesses, the taxes imposed must be _____ according to how much income was generated in the state.

Answers: T; supremacy clause; c; F; apportioned.

Business and Free Speech

The First Amendment restricts control of freedom of speech: "Congress shall make no law … abridging the freedom of speech. …" Despite this language, this right is not absolute. As Justice Holmes said in *Schenck* v. *United States* (249 U.S. 47), "The most stringent protection of free speech would not protect a man in falsely shouting fire in a theatre and causing a panic." The Constitution prohibits laws "abridging the freedom of speech," but it does not prohibit all laws regulating communication. For example, as the Supreme Court noted in *Ward* v. *Rock Against Racism* (491 U.S. 781), the City of New York could require a city sound technician to be present to regulate the volume at which music was played at an outdoor concert, but the technician could not control the content of the sound.

Do commercial speech (advertisements) and political statements by corporations about public issues deserve the same freedoms? In both cases, the parties are trying to convince some people about something—to buy soap or to support a political program. While the text of the Constitution does not distinguish between the two kinds of speech, traditionally there have been more restrictions on commercial speech than on political speech by businesses. The Supreme Court has been more sympathetic in recent decades to commercial speech than it had been in the past.

Business and Political Speech

The Supreme Court has emphasized the right of businesses to speak out on political issues. In 1978, the Court struck down a Massachusetts law that prohibited corporations from making contributions that could influence certain political issues. In *First National Bank of Boston* v. *Bellotti* (535 U.S. 765), the Court noted that "The freedom of speech … guaranteed by the Constitution embraces at the least the liberty to discuss publicly and truthfully all matters of public concern without previous restraint or fear of subsequent punishment…."

INTERNATIONAL PERSPECTIVE

Freedom of Speech

In the United States, there are few restrictions on what the media may investigate. There is a tradition of media attempts to uncover bad deeds by public officials. Unless a statement is published about a person that the publisher knew was false and harmful, there is little legally that the subject of a critical report can do in response. Suits against the media for defamation and attempts by the government to prevent publication of sensitive material are rarely successful.

In the rest of the world, there are more restraints on speech. In the United Kingdom, it is common for politicians to sue the media successfully for defamation. In many European countries, books asserted to contain hateful material may not be published. In Belgium, journalists must reveal their sources of information.

Hans Tillack, a reporter for a German magazine, *Stern*, was arrested in Brussels, all his files were seized, and he was not allowed access to a lawyer for a while. What was he accused of doing? Publishing articles alleging that members of the European Parliament engage in fraud by collecting pay when they are not working. The rest of the media said little about the matter, but one Danish member of European Parliament said: "The practice of the EU [European Union] is to stop those who reveal fraud, instead of stopping the fraud."

Three years after his arrest, a court held that Tillack's "freedom of expression" had been violated. Two years after that, the Belgians closed the case against Tillack and his research materials were returned to him.

The Court soon followed this decision with the *Consolidated Edison* decision. In the case, the Court explained the three-part test that restrictions must pass to be allowed to regulate **political speech** made by businesses. This is still the key test that is used by courts today.

CONSOLIDATED EDISON COMPANY V. PUBLIC SERVICE COMMISSION OF NEW YORK

United States Supreme Court 447 U.S. 530, 100 S.Ct. 2326 (1980)

Case Background *Consolidated Edison inserted material in favor of nuclear power in monthly bills sent to its electricity customers. The Public Service Commission of New York ruled that Consolidated Edison could not discuss its opinions on controversial issues of public policy it its bills. The New York Court of Appeals upheld the Commission's prohibition. Consolidated Edison appealed to the Supreme Court. The issue is whether the First Amendment of the Constitution is violated by the Commission's order prohibiting the inclusion of inserts discussing public policy issues in customers' electric bills.*

Case Decision Powell, Justice

* * *

The Commission's ban on bill inserts is not, of course, invalid merely because it imposes a limitation upon speech. We must consider whether the State can demonstrate that its regulation is constitutionally permissible.... We must determine whether the prohibition is (1) a reasonable time, place, or manner restriction, (2) a permissible subject-matter regulation, or (3) a narrowly tailored means of serving a compelling state interest....

A restriction that regulates only the time, place or manner of speech may be imposed so long as it is reasonable. But when regulation is based on the content of speech, governmental action must be scrutinized more carefully to ensure that communication has not been prohibited "merely because public officials disapprove the speaker's views."...

The Commission does not pretend that its action is unrelated to the content or subject matter of bill inserts. Indeed, it has undertaken to suppress certain

bill inserts precisely because they address controversial issues of public policy. The Commission allows inserts that present information to consumers on certain subjects, such as energy conservation measures, but it forbids the use of inserts that discuss public controversies. The Commission... justifies its ban on the ground that consumers will benefit from receiving "useful" information, but not from the prohibited information. The Commission's own rationale demonstrates that its action cannot be upheld as a content-neutral time, place, or manner regulation. ...

The First Amendment's hostility to content-based regulation extends not only to restrictions on particular viewpoints, but also to prohibition of public discussion of an entire topic.... To allow a government the choice of permissible subjects for the public debate would be to allow that government control over the search for political truth.

* * *

Where a government restricts the speech of a private person, the state action may be sustained only if the government can show that the regulation is a precisely drawn means of serving a compelling state interest. ...

Where a single speaker communicates to many listeners, the First Amendment does not permit the government to prohibit speech as intrusive unless the "captive" audience cannot avoid objectionable speech.

Passengers on public transportation or residents of a neighborhood disturbed by the raucous broadcasts from a passing sound truck may well be unable to escape an unwanted message. But customers who encounter an objectionable billing insert may "effectively avoid further bombardment of their sensibilities simply by averting their eyes." The customer of Consolidated Edison may escape exposure to objectionable material simply by transferring the bill insert from envelope to wastebasket.

* * *

Reversed.

Questions for Analysis

1. The court held the company could discuss controversial political issues. Should a distinction be drawn between political speech paid for by private persons and that paid for by customers who may not want the speech?
2. Would you distinguish between speech that addresses issues and corporate political speech that endorses particular candidates for office?

A major decision regarding business and political speech, *Citizens United* v. *Federal Election Commission* (130 S.Ct. 876), has been controversial. A sharply divided Court struck down portions of a federal law, the McCain-Feingold Act. The Act prohibited for-profit and nonprofit corporations and unions from broadcasting "electioneering communication." That was defined as any communication that mentioned a candidate for office within 60 days of a general election or 30 days of a primary election. Justice Kennedy, writing for the majority, stated: "If the First Amendment has any force, it prohibits Congress from fining or jailing citizens, or associations of citizens from simply engaging in political speech." Because there is no distinction between media and other corporations, such restrictions would allow Congress to suppress political speech in all media outlets—newspapers, books, blogs, movies, and television.

Business and Commercial Speech

The modern **commercial speech** doctrine first came about as restrictions on advertising were attacked as anticompetitive. Some commercial speech restrictions violated antitrust laws, but most such restrictions also violated the rights of sellers of legal products and services to inform citizens of the availability and merits of their goods. This trend began in the 1970s.

CYBER LAW

Freedom of Speech on the Net

Georgia passed a statute making it a crime for "any person ... knowingly to transmit any data through a computer network ... for the purpose of setting up, maintaining, operating, or exchanging data with an electronic mailbox, home page, or any other electronic information storage bank or point of access to electronic information if such data uses an individual name ... to falsely identify the person." That is, there could be no anonymous communications.

In *American Civil Liberties Union of Georgia* v. *Miller* (977 F.Supp. 1228), the federal court issued an injunction preventing Georgia from enforcing the statute. Statutes that regulate speech must be narrowly tailored to survive First Amendment challenges. The Georgia statute was too sweeping in its coverage to stand.

Similarly, the Supreme Court, in *Reno* v. *American Civil Liberties Union* (117 S.Ct. 2329), struck down the Communications Decency Act. While the supposed intent of the law was to restrict pornography for children on the Web, the court held that the act went too far in restricting First Amendment rights; it was like "burning the house to roast the pig."

In 1975, in *Bigelow* v. *Virginia* (421 U.S. 809), the Supreme Court reversed the conviction of a Virginia newspaper editor who published ads about the availability of low-cost abortions in New York City. A Virginia law prohibited publications from encouraging abortions. The Court held that speech that is related to legal products or services has value in the marketplace of ideas.

The following year, in *Virginia State Board of Pharmacy* v. *Virginia Citizens Consumer Council* (425 U.S. 748), the Court struck down a Virginia law prohibiting the advertising of prices of prescription drugs. "It is clear … that speech does not lose its First Amendment protection because money is spent … as in a paid advertisement…." The Board of Pharmacy argued that the restrictions on advertising were needed to protect the public from their ignorance about drugs. The Court rejected that, holding, "that people will perceive their own best interests if only they are well enough informed, and that the best means to that end is to open the channels of communication rather than to close them."

While commercial speech that is not truthful may be regulated (unlike political speech), the Court finds little justification for extensive controls on truthful commercial speech. In the *Central Hudson Gas and Electric* decision, the Court established a four-part test that must be met to justify restrictions on commercial speech. This is the leading case on this issue.

CENTRAL HUDSON GAS AND ELECTRIC CORPORATION V. PUBLIC SERVICE COMMISSION OF NEW YORK

United States Supreme Court 447 U.S. 557, 100 S.Ct. 2343 (1980)

Case Background *The winter of 1973-1974 was difficult because of the Organization of Petroleum Exporting Countries (OPEC) oil embargo and shortages of natural gas. The Public Service Commission of New York ordered electric utilities in New York to end all advertising that "promotes the use of electricity." The order was based on the commission's finding that New York utilities might not have enough power to meet all customer demands for the winter. The Commission declared all promotional advertising contrary to the national policy of conserving energy. It offered to review any proposed advertising that would encourage energy conservation. The New York high court upheld the constitutionality of the Commission's regulation. The utility appealed to the Supreme Court.*

Case Decision Powell, Justice

* * *

The Commission's order restricts only commercial speech, that is, expression related solely to the economic interests of the speaker and its audience…. The First Amendment, as applied to the States through the Fourteenth Amendment, protects commercial speech from unwarranted government regulation. Commercial expression not only serves the economic interest of the speaker, but also assists consumers … in the fullest possible dissemination of information. In applying the First Amendment to this area, we have rejected the "highly paternalistic" view that government has complete power to suppress or regulate commercial speech. "People will perceive their own best interests if only they are well enough informed and … the best means to that end is to open the channels of communication, rather than to close them…." Even when advertising communicates only an incomplete version of the relevant facts, the First Amendment presumes that some accurate information is better than no information at all….

The Constitution … accords a lesser protection to commercial speech than to other constitutionally guaranteed expression. The protection available for particular commercial expression turns on the nature both of the expression and of the governmental interests served by its regulation.

The First Amendment's concern for commercial speech is based on the informational function of advertising. Consequently, there can be no constitutional objection to the suppression of commercial messages that do not accurately inform the public about lawful activity. The government may ban forms of communication more likely to deceive the public than to inform it, to commercial speech related to illegal activity.

If the communication is neither misleading nor related to unlawful activity, the government's power is more circumscribed.

* * *

In commercial speech cases … a four-part analysis has developed. (1) At the outset, we must determine whether the expression is protected by the First Amendment. For commercial speech to come within that provision, it at least must concern lawful activity and not be misleading. (2) Next, we ask whether the asserted governmental interest is substantial. If both inquiries yield positive answers, (3) we must determine whether the regulation directly advances the governmental interest asserted, and (4) whether it is not more extensive than is necessary to serve the interest.

We now apply this four-step analysis for commercial speech to the Commission's arguments in support of its ban on promotional advertising.

The Commission does not claim that the expression at issue is inaccurate or relates to unlawful activity.…

The commission offers two state interests as justifications for the ban on promotional advertising. The first concerns energy conservation. Any increase in demand for electricity—during peak or off-peak periods—means greater consumption of energy. The Commission argues … that the State's interest in conserving energy is sufficient to support sup-

pression of advertising designed to increase consumption of electricity.… Plainly, therefore, the state interest asserted is substantial.

* * *

We come finally to the critical inquiry in this case: whether the Commission's complete suppression of speech ordinarily protected by the First Amendment is no more extensive than necessary to further the State's interest in energy conservation. The Commission's order reaches all promotional advertising, regardless of the impact of the touted service on overall energy use. But the energy conservation rationale, as important as it is, cannot justify suppressing information about electric devices or services that would cause no net increase in total energy use. In additional, no showing has been made that a more limited restriction on the content of promotional advertising would not serve adequately the State's interests.

* * *

Reversed.

Questions for Analysis

1. Because the Court found that the state had a substantial interest in the subject in question (electricity conservation), why did it find the ad restrictions to be unconstitutional? Which part of the four-part test was not met?
2. Suppose the Commission had said that only advertising designed to promote energy conservation was allowed. Would that have met the Supreme Court test?

The Supreme Court has ruled that First Amendment rights are violated by restrictions on advertising for professional services, such as by lawyers or doctors. In *Shapero* v. *Kentucky Bar Association* (484 U.S. 814), the Court held that the state bar association violated the First Amendment by prohibiting lawyers from soliciting business by sending truthful letters to prospective clients known to face possible legal action. If an attorney engages in misleading or deceptive solicitation practices, the attorney may be punished by the bar for doing so, but the bar may not act as a barrier to truthful commercial speech.

The Court further discussed the regulation of commercial speech in *Board of Trustees of the State University of New York* v. *Fox* (492 U.S. 469). The standard for judging commercial speech regulation is one that is "not necessarily perfect but reasonable" and one "narrowly tailored to achieve the desired objective." The basis of the regulation must be a substantial state interest in controlling an undesirable activity, balanced against the cost imposed by the restrictions. When regulations are challenged, the state bears the burden of justifying restrictions on commercial speech.

Lighter Side **of the Law**

Freedom of Bark but Not Burn in Ohio

Gilchrist was charged with taunting a dog when he barked at a police dog sitting in an unattended police car. He argued that he was not taunting but rather engaging in "unrestrained late-night enthusiasm." Besides, the dog barked first. An Ohio appeals court upheld dismissal of the charges.

Another Ohio appeals court held that burning a rainbow flag at a gay pride parade was not protected speech because the burners did not obtain a burn permit first. Requiring such a permit is "unquestionably within the city's constitutional power."

Sources: State of Ohio v. Gilchrist; City of Columbus v. Meyer.

Freedom to Criticize Freedom of speech can mean that a business is criticized. A report in *Consumer Reports* was critical of the quality of a stereo speaker made by Bose. Bose sued. The Supreme Court upheld the right to be critical of a product in a review of the product in *Bose Corp.* v. *Consumers Union* (466 U.S. 485).

The Supreme Court held that for a public figure, such as a corporation selling products, to recover damages for a defamatory falsehood, the trial court must find clear and convincing evidence that there was actual malice in publishing a knowing or reckless falsehood. Because actual malice was not shown in this case, the suit was dismissed. This principle applies to Internet-based speech. Federal appeals courts have held that websites dedicated to mocking or negative opinions about a business are protected speech.

 TEST YOURSELF

1. With respect to business, the primary issue involving the First Amendment to the Constitution involves _____.
2. The Supreme Court held, in the *Consolidated Edison Co.* case, that there may be no restrictions on political speech by business: T—F
3. What two kinds of commercial speech are not protected by the First Amendment?
4. In the case *Citizens United* v. *Federal Election Commission*, the Supreme Court held that Congress could impose significant restrictions on political speech by business, but not upon persons: T—F

Answers: freedom of speech; F; misleading speech and speech about unlawful activities; F.

INTERNATIONAL PERSPECTIVE

The (Partially) Unwritten Constitution of the United Kingdom

Unlike the U.S. Constitution, the constitution of the United Kingdom is a collection of laws, treaties, statutes, and unwritten principles. These laws are no different from other Parliamentary Acts and can be amended by Parliament at any time.

The constitution of the UK has two central principles: the rule of law and the supremacy of Parliament. The UK view of Parliament as supreme is different from the separation of powers at the center of the U.S. Constitution. Because Parliament is supreme, a government with a majority of the seats in Parliament can do almost anything it wishes, limited by tradition and popular opinion.

Key parts of the constitution of the United Kingdom include:

- The Magna Carta (or Great Charter), signed by King John in 1215 to limit the monarch's power over the nobility. Although much of the Magna Carta is no longer relevant, three provisions of it still apply. Most important is the provision that "No free man shall be seized or imprisoned, or stripped of his rights or possessions, or outlawed or exiled nor will we proceed with force against him except by the lawful judgment of his equals or by the law of the land. To no one will we sell, to no one deny or delay right or justice."
- The Bill of Rights 1689 that prohibits the monarch from interfering with the law.
- The Act of Union 1707 that united England and Wales with Scotland. The Scottish independence movement, led by the Scottish National Party, seeks to undo this.

The constitution of the United Kingdom today is much different than it was 100 years ago. The European Communities Act allows the European Parliament to overrule the Parliament of the United Kingdom. The Human Rights Act of 1998 (HRA) allows UK courts to issue a "declaration of incompatibility" for legislation that violates the HRA. Unlike when a law is declared unconstitutional in the United States, this action does not strike the statute from the books but instead creates an unenforceable obligation on the government to change the law to conform to the HRA. The government made a number of such constitutional reforms, including reducing the number of hereditary peers in the House of Lords.

© Cengage Learning

Other Key Parts of the Bill of Rights

The Bill of Rights is the first ten amendments to the Constitution. Some amendments, while providing important rights for citizens, have little special impact on business. Most of the rest of the amendments, numbered 11 through 27, also have no special impact on business, although we will see that the Fourteenth Amendment has important consequences. No amendment was written specifically to address a business issue. Some just happen to have an impact on the legal environment of business. Managers want to be aware of how specific parts of the Constitution may impact business operations.

Right to Bear Arms

The Second Amendment is brief: "A well regulated Militia, being necessary to the security of a free State, the right of the people to keep and bear Arms, shall not be infringed." Those 27 words are controversial. What restrictions the government may place on gun ownership and possession is not a settled area of law. Some jurisdictions, such as New York City, have very tight controls. Other jurisdictions impose few controls.

Some employers and businesses ban the possession of firearms on company property. The state of Oklahoma passed a statute prohibiting employers from preventing employees from storing firearms in their personal, locked vehicles on company property. The law was upheld by the Tenth Circuit Court of Ap... (555 F.3d 1199). Businesses must comply with city ...

Unreasonable Search and Seizure

The Fourth Amendment reads: "The right of the peo... houses, papers, and effects against unreasonable search... lated, and no Warrants shall issue, but upon probable c... der this amendment are criminal and concern the prope... of suspected criminals and evidence. Searches by governm... ...ce reg- ulations that may result in criminal charges are subject to ... ...ourth Amendment cases, key issues are whether government authorities used proper search and seizure procedures and whether a person has a constitutionally protected reasonable expectation of privacy.

Limits on Searches and Inspections If a government inspector shows up at a business to inspect the premises or to search company records for some purpose related to the law being enforced by the inspector, does the business have to allow admission? Not without a warrant in many instances, the Supreme Court held in *Marshall* v. *Barlow's* (436 U.S. 307). In that case, an inspector for the Occupational Safety and Health Administration (OSHA) arrived at Barlow's plant in Idaho and asked to search the work areas. Barlow asked the inspector if he had a warrant. He did not. Barlow refused him admission to the plant unless he got a warrant. OSHA asked the Court to require businesses to admit inspectors to conduct warrantless searches.

The Court refused, saying that warrantless searches are generally unreasonable and that this rule applies to commercial premises as well as homes. The government argued that if inspectors had to obtain warrants, businesses would have time to hide safety and health defects on worksites. The Court responded:

> We are unconvinced ... that requiring warrants to inspect will impose serious burdens on the inspection system or the courts, will prevent inspections necessary to enforce the statute, or will make them less effective. In the first place the great majority of business-men can be expected in normal course to consent to inspection without warrant; the Secretary [of Labor] has not brought to this Court's attention any widespread pattern of refusal.

As the Court predicted would be the case, most businesses allow warrantless searches; the requirement to obtain a warrant when demanded is not burdensome, nor has it much affected enforcement of regulatory law.

Warrantless Searches Warrantless searches are allowed for closely regulated businesses. For example, in *New York* v. *Burger* (482 U.S. 691), the Supreme Court held the state could impose warrantless searches on auto junkyards. They are closely regulated because they can become chop shops for stolen vehicles and parts. The Court noted that the government had a substantial interest behind the regulatory scheme (to reduce auto thefts), and the warrantless inspections were necessary to make the regulatory scheme work. Those who run junkyards (and other closely regulated businesses) know that a condition of their being licensed to have such an operation is that they must submit to warrantless searches of the grounds as outlined in the state statute.

Gathering Evidence Evidence improperly gathered by law enforcement officials violates Fourth Amendment rights regarding search and seizure and may not be used in court under the **exclusionary rule.** Generally, this means that evidence gathered from a home or business without a warrant was improperly obtained and cannot be used. Businesses have fewer constitutional rights in this respect than persons in their homes. This contrasts with the law in most other countries, where police or regulators might be reprimanded for an improper search, but the evidence would still be admissible in court proceedings.

In *Skinner* v. *Railway Labor Executives' Association* (489 U.S. 602), the Court approved warrantless searches of railroad employees involved in train accidents or safety violations. The searches consist of blood, breath, and urine tests for evidence of alcohol or drugs. These searches do not violate the Fourth Amendment because they are in a "closely regulated" industry, are based on compelling public interest in safety, and may be used only in specific situations. The employees know they are subject to this requirement, so the limited invasion of privacy is acceptable.

Self-Incrimination

The Fifth Amendment protects individuals against **self-incrimination**: "No person shall be … compelled in any criminal case to be a witness against himself." This protection applies to persons, not to corporations. Although corporate executives cannot be made to testify against themselves, business records that might incriminate the corporation—and the executives—must be produced since the Fifth Amendment does not protect such records.

Corporations are not given the same Fifth Amendment protection as are individuals, the Supreme Court noted in *Braswell* v. *United States* (487 U.S. 99). Braswell was president and sole shareholder of a corporation. Claiming Fifth Amendment privilege against self-incrimination, he refused to produce company records ordered under a federal grand jury subpoena. The Court rejected this claim, holding that the corporation was an entity not protected by the Fifth Amendment; hence, Braswell, acting as corporate representative, had to produce corporate records, even though the records might incriminate him as an individual.

Just Compensation

The Fifth Amendment also states, "… nor shall private property be taken for public use, without just compensation." Termed the **just compensation** or **takings clause**, it requires governments to pay for property when a government requires an owner to sell because public officials determined that the property should be used for some public purpose, such as for the construction of a highway, school, or military base.

The power of governments to condemn or take private property for such public uses is ancient, so the use of **eminent domain** is common. Compensation is based on fair market value. While some property owners are not happy about being forced to move, the relatively small amount of litigation over the values paid for property indicates that the compensation provided is usually adequate.

Eminent Domain and Economic Development A controversial use of eminent domain is when government takes private property for the benefit of another private party. A common economic development tactic is for a city to use its power to piece together land desired by a party who promises to build a facility, shopping center, or high-valued homes on property. If a developer must deal with sellers individually, the process can take longer and will be more costly than if the government forces sales at existing market prices. Cities like the new development, as it means higher tax revenues and more residents. To avoid the claim that property is being transferred from one private party to another, a 99-year lease from the government to the developer is often used. The practice is legal in some states and illegal in others. The Supreme Court set off a national discussion of the issue when it handed down the *Kelo* decision.

KELO V. CITY OF NEW LONDON, CONNECTICUT
United States Supreme Court 545 U.S. 469, 125 S.Ct. 2655 (2005)

Case Background *The City of New London wanted to encourage development. It worked on a plan to piece together property along a riverfront to be used for upscale housing, a new shopping center, and a facility for the Pfizer Company. Some homeowners refused to sell, including Suzette Kelo, who prized her waterfront home, and Wilhelmina Deny, who was born in her home in 1918 and lived there her entire life. The City then used its power of eminent domain to buy the property and provide it to the developers. The homeowners protested that this taking violated the "public use" provision of the Fifth Amendment. The Connecticut courts held the taking as proper. Homeowners appealed.*

Case Decision Stevens, Justice

* * *

The trial judge and all the members of the Supreme Court of Connecticut agreed that there was no evidence of an illegitimate purpose in this case. Therefore … the City's development plan was not adopted "to benefit a particular class of identifiable individuals."

On the other hand, this is not a case in which the City is planning to open the condemned land—at least not in its entirety—to use by the general public. Nor will the private lessees of the land in any sense be required to operate like common carriers, making their services available to all comers. But although such a projected use would be sufficient to satisfy the public use requirement, this "Court long ago rejected any literal requirement that condemned property be put into use for the general public."… The disposition of this case, therefore, turns on the question whether the City's development plan serves a "public purpose."

* * *

For more than a century, our public use jurisprudence has wisely eschewed rigid formulas and intrusive scrutiny in favor of affording legislatures broad latitude in determining what public needs justify the use of the takings power.

Those who govern the City were not confronted with the need to remove blight … but their determination that the area was sufficiently distressed to justify a program of economic rejuvenation is entitled to our deference. The City has carefully formulated an economic development plan that it believes will provide appreciable benefits to the community, including—but by no means limited to—new jobs and increased tax revenue.… Because that plan unquestionably serves a public purpose, the takings challenged here satisfy the public use requirement of the Fifth Amendment.…

Petitioners contend that using eminent domain for economic development impermissibly blurs the boundary between public and private takings. Again, our cases foreclose this objection. Quite simply, the government's pursuit of a public purpose will often benefit individual private parties.

* * *

The judgment of the Supreme Court of Connecticut is affirmed.

Questions for Analysis

1. The Court upheld the use of eminent domain to further private economic development. Does this mean any government can force one private landowner to sell so that another private party who wants the land can get it?
2. Why would government favor such actions when local property owners oppose it?

As a result of *Kelo*, many states passed laws or amended their constitutions to restrict the use of eminent domain at the state and local level on behalf of private beneficiaries. Some of these restrictions are weak because they allow eminent domain to benefit private developers if the property is declared to be "blighted"—which generally means low-income housing exists on the property now.

Regulatory Takings Beyond eminent domain, which requires governments to pay fair market value for property taken, governments have regulatory powers that can change property values. A change in zoning rules or land use rules can greatly decrease the value of property.

The Supreme Court decision, *Nollan* v. *California Coastal Commission* (483 U.S. 825), addressed compensation in case of changing land-use rules. The Nollans wanted to tear down their house and build a larger one on their beach property in Ventura, California. The Coastal Commission said that their permit would be granted only if they agreed to allow the public an easement (access) to private land. The Commission wanted the public to have the right to use what had been the Nollans' backyard—above the high-tide line—along the beach.

The Supreme Court held that the takings clause of the Fifth Amendment had been violated. The state could not tie a rebuilding permit to an easement (land use) that it would have to pay for if it simply imposed the easement. "California is free to advance its 'comprehensive program,' if it wishes, [of increased beach access] by using its power of eminent domain for this 'public purpose,' but if it wants an easement across the Nollans' property, it must pay for it."

In general, the **regulatory takings** cases indicate that the destruction of property value must be almost complete for compensation to be due. If a regulation, such as a decision by a government to build a garbage dump next to a house, reduces the value of property by, say, 60 percent, it is very unlikely that compensation is due. That is not an uncommon result of a change in zoning laws or a rule that eliminates the ability of a company to produce a particular product or for certain residential property to be desirable.

Right to Trial

The Sixth Amendment addresses the right of persons to trial by jury in criminal cases. The Seventh Amendment provides for the right to jury trial in common-law cases. Although the law is well established about the constitutional right to jury trial in criminal cases and common-law cases, what about cases in which a business is charged with a violation of a statute that regulates the business? If the charge is criminal, the right to request a jury trial remains. What if the charge is civil, such as the government demanding a fine of $20 million?

If the only question at trial arises under a statute that may impose civil penalties, such as money fines, or issue an injunction, no right to jury trial exists. Because civil penalties are imposed by statute, there is no constitutional right to trial on such matters.

CYBER LAW

No Right of Privacy in Chat Rooms

An FBI agent monitored online chat rooms to uncover distribution of child pornography. He would enter the chat rooms, so his user name was seen, but he would not participate. Based on the agent's observations, Charbonneau was accused of distributing child pornography to contacts made in the chat room. Charbonneau contended that this method of collecting evidence violated his Fourth Amendment right to a reasonable expectation of privacy.

A federal court held that the evidence collected was good. "The expectation of privacy in E-mail transmissions depends in large part on both the type of E-mail sent and recipient of the E-mail." Messages sent to a chat room, unlike personally addressed e-mails, lose their privacy, so the evidence may be used against him. More than one court has held this to be the rule.

Sources: U.S. v. Charbonneau (979 F.Supp. 1177); *U.S. v. Dietz* (452 F.Supp.2d 611).

Excessive Fines

The Eighth Amendment is best known for its restriction on "cruel and unusual punishments," but it also holds that no **excessive fines** may be imposed. As large jury awards have become more common in recent years, defendants have sought to use the Eighth Amendment for protection against huge punitive damage awards. The Supreme Court has applied the Eighth Amendment through the Fourteenth Amendment to limit excessive punitive damages.

The claim of excessive fines also has been raised in suits that allow the government to press for large damages. For example, when illegal drug dealing occurs on private property, the property may be confiscated. Even if the property is worth a thousand times what the drugs were worth, this has generally been held not to be an excessive fine in violation of the Eighth Amendment, so long as the fines are part of a rational and consistent scheme to deter certain behavior.

A restriction imposed on forfeiture arose in the Supreme Court case, *United States* v. *Bajakajian* (118 S.Ct. 2028). The Bajakajians were leaving the country with $357,144 in cash. The money was legally earned; they were taking the money to repay relatives who had given them money to start their business. While it was legal to take the money out of the country, the Bajakajians failed to report that they were leaving with more than $10,000. Government agents seized all the money, contending that it could be kept because it was an "instrumentality" of the crime committed—not reporting the fact of carrying the money. The Court held that the forfeiture was an "excessive fine" in violation of the Eighth Amendment, as it was grossly disproportional to the seriousness of the offense.

Fourteenth Amendment

Recall that in the *Central Hudson Gas and Electric* case the Supreme Court noted: "The First Amendment, as applied to the States through the Fourteenth Amendment, protects commercial speech from unwarranted government regulation." That is, the Fourteenth Amendment incorporates protections from the Bill of Rights and applies them to state governments. Before the Fourteenth Amendment was adopted, unless similar protections were offered in a state constitution, such liberties might not have applied in instances of actions by state and local governments.

The Fourteenth Amendment holds, in part, "No State shall … deprive any person of life, liberty, or property, without due process of law; nor deny to any person within its jurisdiction the equal protection of the laws." This amendment has been a powerful device for extending federal constitutional guarantees to the states and preventing states from passing laws that diminish federal constitutional protections.

The Fourteenth Amendment, which was passed after the Civil War to try to prevent Southern states from passing laws to reinstitute some aspects of slavery, has two key provisions concerning substantive and procedural law: the **due process clause** and the equal protection clause. Substantive due process comes into play whenever the courts review the ability of the government to restrict the freedoms of life, liberty, or property. Equal protection is an issue when the courts are called upon to review a classification of persons that has been established by a government.

Bringing suit under the Fourteenth Amendment is made easier by Section 1983 of Chapter 42 of the United States Code (42 U.S.C. § 1983). As you can see, it provides broad language for suit, and many are brought under it:

Every person who, under color of any statute, ordinance, regulation, custom, or usage, of any State or Territory or the District of Columbia, subjects, or causes to be subjected, any citizen of the United States or other person within the jurisdiction thereof to the deprivation of any rights, privileges, or immunities secured by the Constitution and laws, shall be liable to the party injured in an action at law, suit in equity, or other proper proceeding for redress, except that in any action brought against a judicial officer for an act or omission taken in such officer's judicial capacity, injunctive relief shall not be granted unless a declaratory decree was violated or declaratory relief was unavailable.

This is sweeping language. In applying the statute, the Supreme Court has explained that fundamental liberty interests are deeply rooted in our history. They require a "careful description" of an asserted fundamental liberty interest before it is presumed to be included. Protected liberty interests are carefully defined. There must be a strong basis for this designation to be applied.

Due Process

In general, **due process** claims can be stated in two ways. First, due process is violated when the state infringes on fundamental liberty interests without narrowly tailoring that infringement to serve a compelling state interest. Second, due process is infringed when state action either shocks the conscience or offends judicial notions of fairness and human dignity.

Suppose a state prohibited all persons from making or selling tobacco products in the state. A challenge to the law could be based on due process. The person claiming he or she should be allowed to make, consume, or sell tobacco products would claim that the Fourteenth Amendment was violated because the substance of the law, not the procedures used to enforce the law, restricted the freedom of persons in the state without a constitutional rationale. When governments restrict the rights of citizens, unless a fundamental constitutional liberty is at stake (would that include access to tobacco products?), the law needs to relate rationally to a legitimate government interest, such as public health, to satisfy due process requirements.

Most due process cases involve protection of individual liberties, but the constitutional standard extends to businesses when governments go beyond the discretion they are ordinarily allowed and do not have a rational basis for a law or do not follow proper procedure. A claim of due process violation is common but, as the *Fresenius Medical Care* case indicates, they are often not successful.

FRESENIUS MEDICAL CARE HOLDINGS, INC. V. TUCKER

United States Court of Appeals, Eleventh Circuit, 704 F.3d 935 (2013)

Case Background *Florida's "Patient Self-Referral Act" prohibits Florida physicians from referring their patients for services to businesses in which referring physicians have a financial interest, unless the physician only owns a small share in a large company. Fresenius Medical Care Holdings and other companies provide renal (kidney) dialysis service and laboratory blood work. As various physicians owned parts of companies providing these services, they could not refer their patients to*

those companies. They sued, seeking a declaration that the Florida act is unconstitutional in part because it violates due process. They contended that the law was not effective and, indeed, might actually reduce competition in medical services. The district court held for the state of Florida. The physicians appealed.

Case Decision Dubina, Chief Judge

* * *

When a challenged law does not infringe upon a fundamental right, we review substantive due process challenges under the rational basis standard. Under the rational basis standard, the law requires only that the Florida Act's prohibition on physician self-referrals be rationally related to the Florida Legislature's goal of reducing conflicts of interest, lowering health care costs, and improving the quality of health care services. The Act will be upheld so long as "there is any reasonably conceivable state of facts that could provide a rational basis for [the regulation]." Appellants bear the burden of demonstrating that the law lacks a rational basis. We agree with the district court that the Florida Act passes rational basis-scrutiny because, no matter how ineffective the law might actually be, it was not irrational for the Florida Legislature to conclude that the amendments to the law would accomplish the legislative objectives identified in [the Florida statute]. ...

Appellants' arguments miss the mark of a rational basis inquiry. Their evidence casts doubt on the wisdom of the statute and suggests that perhaps a competitor out-lobbied Appellants before the Florida Legislature, but the evidence does not demonstrate that the Florida Legislature could not have

possibly believed that removing the ESRD (end-state renal disease) exemption would reduce conflicts and improve health care in the renal-dialysis field. Appellants fail to convince the court that the purported reasons given for the enactment of the law " 'could not reasonably be conceived to be true by the governmental decisionmaker.' " Because it is reasonably conceivable that Florida ESRD patients would be better served if their physicians were prohibited from making self-referrals to associated laboratories, we conclude that the Florida Act survives rational basis scrutiny and that the law does not deprive Appellants of their rights to substantive due process. ...

Affirmed.

Questions for Analysis

1. Is there an ethical issue when physicians own firms they refer patients to?
2. Suppose the physicians were right and that lobbyists for competitor firms helped obtain passage of a law that benefited them in a way that causes patients to pay more for service than they might get from a physician-owned service provider. Would that change the outcome?

Equal Protection

The Fourteenth Amendment provides, "No state shall ... deny ... the equal protection of the laws." The **equal protection clause** has come to mean that governments must treat people equally. However, equal protection does not extend to all government activities. Some actions by government that discriminate are held to tougher standards than others.

Going back to our example concerning state limits on tobacco, suppose a state passed a law prohibiting people under age 25 or over age 65 from making, consuming, or selling tobacco products. A challenge to the law could be brought by someone under age 25 or over age 65 claiming that the equal protection clause of the Fourteenth Amendment is violated. That is, persons in those age groups belong to the class of persons affected by the law, which they claim is constitutionally wrong because it creates a class that suffers a loss of freedom.

To uphold such a law that classifies persons differently, the court must find a valid governmental interest, such as public health. Perhaps evidence shows that people under 25 may have higher addiction rates than older people who have access to tobacco. The government may also wish to keep down expenditures on health care for people over age 65, who are in the Medicare program. While it may be rational to have age restrictions on access to tobacco, such restrictions on tobacco based on race or sex would be harder to meet a constitutional challenge.

Lighter Side **of the Law**

Drop That Fry! Hands over Your Head!

Twelve-year-old Ansche Hedgepeth was arrested for eating french fries at a Washington, D.C. subway (Metro) station in violation of the rules. She was searched, put in handcuffs behind her back, and had her shoelaces removed until she was released to her mother several hours later. She sued for violation of equal protection.

She lost. "There is no fundamental right to freedom from physical restraint in cases where probable cause for arrest is present."

Source: Hedgepeth v. Washington Metro Area Transit, 284 F.Supp.2d 145.

Government action that discriminates on the basis of race is held to a standard of strict scrutiny. Hence, government programs that discriminate are not likely to meet a Fourteenth Amendment challenge unless there is a compelling state interest. This meant, of course, that "Jim Crow" laws that discriminated against minorities were stricken as unconstitutional.

State classifications based on sex are also subject to scrutiny. To be allowed to stand, such laws must substantially relate to important government objectives and provide "exceeding persuasive justification," as the Supreme Court held in *United States v. Virginia* (518 U.S. 515). It held the state of Virginia violated the equal protection clause by excluding women from attending the Virginia Military Institute.

Claims of violations of protection are strongest when they involve sex or race discrimination, but these constitutional protections are due all persons and businesses. Claims of equal protection violation, like claims of due process violation, are common. How the issue is raised in a business setting is shown in the *Corey Airport Services* case, where a business claims that it was cheated out of the opportunity to compete for a city contract.

COREY AIRPORT SERVICES, INC. V. CLEAR CHANNEL OUTDOOR, INC.

United States Court of Appeals, Eleventh Circuit, 682 F.3d 1293 (2012)

Case Background *The City of Atlanta requested bids for a five-year advertising contract at the Atlanta airport. The winning bidder would manage hundreds of advertising displays at the airport. Before this bid request, Clear Channel held the advertising concession. Three companies bid for the new concession.*

Clear Channel won; Corey was second. Corey appealed, but the appeal was rejected, so Corey sued in federal court contending that Clear Channel had conspired with the City to deprive Corey of its equal rights. The jury found for Corey and awarded millions in damages. Defendants appealed.

Case Decision Per Curiam

* * *

Underlying Corey's conspiracy claim against Defendants is its assertion that the City violated Corey's equal protection rights by selecting Defendants' bid for the airport advertising contract after conducting a biased bid process. Without an underlying violation of equal protection, no valid conspiracy claim can be shown in this case; and judgment as a matter of law must be granted to Defendants.

Equal protection jurisprudence is typically concerned with governmental classification and treatment that affects some discrete and identifiable group of citizens differently from other groups. Defining an "identifiable group" that has been discriminated against is critical to establishing a claim under the Equal Protection Clause. ...

While the proposed definitions differ in their words, Corey chiefly attempts to identify itself as a member of a group of bidders who were not "politically connected" to the City or to influential persons in City government and who were bidders that lost the bid based on this status.

Corey's proposed group definitions fail to support a claim under the Equal Protection Clause. For a group to qualify properly as identifiable for the purposes of an Equal Protection Clause claim, substantive group characteristics must pop out that allow us to separate entities or people into discrete groupings and clearly identify those persons that suffered the alleged discrimination and those persons that did not. Many substantive characteristics of this kind exist that allow for separation of entities or people into discrete groupings and that could potentially support an Equal Protection Clause claim. Groups based on race, sex, or even longer-term and discrete political affiliation—Republican as opposed to non-Republican or Democrat as opposed to non-Democrat—all potentially allow courts to identify clearly the parties involved, separate the parties into strongly defined groupings, and discern the existence of an identifiable group whose members may have suffered discrimination.

Corey does not offer sufficient substantive group characteristics. Instead, Corey attempts to identify groups based on affiliation or connection to the City, the supposed discriminator: "insiders" and "outsiders." This vague category is inadequate because these idea-based characteristics do not allow us to separate people and entities into discrete groupings—a necessary part of identifying the group that suffered the alleged discrimination. The proposed categories are too loose, too shifting to be useful to courts. ...

Every government-run bid process involves winners and losers: selection of a winner inherently involves a kind of discrimination in itself. If the law allowed groups defined basically as the "bid-losers" to be the basis for an Equal Protection Clause claim, every government bid process—with winners and losers—would theoretically support such an equal protection claim. ...

Plaintiff's conspiracy claims fail against Defendants because the underlying proposed equal protection claim fails, lacking the sufficient identifiable group required. ...

Vacated and remanded.

Questions for Analysis

1. Would Corey have had a chance of making this claim if the firm was minority-owned and the others were not?
2. Regardless of what happened here, many government contracts are given to firms that are politically favored. Does this case indicate there is no equal protection claim in such instances?

SUMMARY

- The commerce clause and the necessary and proper clause give Congress nearly unlimited discretion to regulate and tax business. Unless a statute specifies that certain businesses are exempt, regulations apply to all because even local (intrastate) business has been held to affect interstate business.

- States may impose regulations that do not conflict with federal regulations or may impose regulations in areas in which Congress gives them specific regulatory authority, but states may not impose burdens on interstate commerce. Numerous state regulatory and taxing schemes have been limited because they violate the commerce clause of the Constitution.

- The taxing power of the federal government is nearly unlimited. Taxes may be used for purposes other than just to raise revenues. They may be used to regulate and may be punitive in nature. The Supreme Court rarely questions the taxing schemes of Congress. State taxing schemes may not discriminate against interstate or international commerce.

- Commercial speech is afforded a high level of First Amendment protection. Businesses have the right to participate in political discussion whether or not it concerns an issue that directly affects business.

- Restrictions on commercial speech are subject to constitutional guidelines concerning strong public necessity. Truthful speech about lawful activities may be regulated only if the regulation would advance a substantial governmental interest and the regulation is no more extensive than is necessary.

- Because companies have Fourth Amendment guarantees against unreasonable searches and seizures, law enforcement authorities can be required to obtain warrants for most inspections. The main exception is in the case of closely regulated industries. The business sensibility of requiring an inspector to obtain a warrant for a routine inspection is dubious.

- Companies may not withhold documents or testimony requested by prosecutors on the grounds that the evidence might incriminate the company; only individuals may invoke that Fifth Amendment right. Efforts to evade the requirement to testify by holding corporate evidence out of the country will not necessarily work.

- When government agencies prevent property from being used in a legitimate manner because of long, unjustified procedural delays, or if agencies impose rules that substantially change property values, compensation may be sought under the just compensation clause of the Fifth Amendment.

- The Supreme Court has held that large damage awards—including punitive damages—by juries against businesses do not violate the Eighth Amendment protection against excessive fines, nor do they violate Fourteenth Amendment due process clause protections of fair play and substantial justice.

- The due process clause of the Fourteenth Amendment has been used to extend constitutional protections to matters subject to state regulation. Economic regulations must be shown to be related to a legitimate government interest, such as public safety. The clause is also used to ensure fairness in law enforcement procedures.

- The equal protection clause of the Fourteenth Amendment is used to protect individuals from suffering a loss of freedom from state laws that discriminate against a particular class of persons when there is no compelling governmental interest in the law, such as public health or safety.

TERMS TO KNOW

commerce clause, 81
necessary and proper clause, 81
supremacy clause, 81
interstate commerce, 82
political speech, 91

commercial speech, 92
exclusionary rule, 97
self-incrimination, 98
just compensation (takings clause), 98

eminent domain, 98
regulatory takings, 100
excessive fines, 101
due process clause, 101
equal protection clause, 103

DISCUSSION QUESTION

Congress requires, via the Internal Revenue Service (IRS), that you report any income from illegal activities, such as drug dealing. If you report the income, you reveal your illegal activities. If you do not report the income and the dealing is discovered, you can be charged with income tax evasion. Does this violate the Fifth Amendment? If not, why not?

CASE QUESTIONS

1. Many states prohibit their lottery tickets from being sold out of the state, so Pic-A-State would have its agents buy lottery tickets in various states and hold them there; someone in Pennsylvania would buy a claim on the tickets held in the other states. Congress passed a law prohibiting interstate transmission of lottery ticket information to be used for lottery ticket sales. Pic-A-State, which was being put out of business, challenged the law as unconstitutional. Was it correct? [*Pic-A-State Pa.* v. *Reno*, 76 F.3d 1294 3rd Cir. (1996)]

2. The state of Iowa had a statute limiting to 55 feet the length of trucks on its highways. This made it illegal for commonly used double-trailer trucks 65 feet long to use Iowa highways. The shippers had to either use shorter trucks or go around the state. Iowa justified the regulation on the basis of safety on the highways, and because the bigger trucks caused more damage to its highways. Was this regulation constitutional? [*Kassel* v. *Consolidated Freightways Corp.*, 450 U.S. 662 (1981)]

3. When margarine was invented, it cut into the butter market. The dairy lobby begged Congress for help and got it in the form of a federal tax on margarine of one quarter of a cent per pound on white margarine and ten cents per pound on

yellow margarine. Obviously, because people were used to yellow butter, white margarine was unattractive and less competitive. This discriminatory tax on margarine, especially yellow margarine, was challenged. Would such a tax be improper? [*McCray* v. *United States*, 195 U.S. 27 (1904)]

✓ Check your answer

4. Montana imposed a tax on coal that ran as high as 30 percent of its value. The tax generated as much as 20 percent of all state revenues. Because more than 90 percent of the coal was shipped to other states, the tax was mostly borne by non-Montanans through higher utility prices. Was this tax constitutional? [*Commonwealth Edison* v. *Montana*, 453 U.S. 609 (1981)]

5. Massachusetts imposed a tax on all milk sold in the state. The tax proceeds, collected by the state, were distributed to dairy farmers in Massachusetts. Milk buyers who bought milk from out-of-state dairies contested the tax as unconstitutional for interfering with interstate commerce. Were they correct? [*West Lynn Creamery* v. *Healy*, 114 S.Ct. 2205 (1994)]

✓ Check your answer

6. Mahaney owns Headed West, a shop selling pipes and other smoking accessories. He hired artists to paint murals on the building's exterior. The murals showed musicians such as Jimi Hendrix, Jerry Garcia, and others. The city of Englewood cited Mahaney for three sign code violations: (1) failing to obtain a permit; (2) failing to obtain city manager approval before the murals were painted; and (3) exceeding the maximum sign area allowed. Mahaney brought an action for declaratory and injunctive relief, alleging that the city ordinances violate the First Amendment. The district court granted summary judgment in favor of the city. Mahaney appealed. Do you think he has a case? Why? [*Mahaney* v. *City of Englewood*, 226 P.3d 1214, Ct. App., Colo. (2009)]

7. The city of Cincinnati, for reasons of the safety and appearance of its streets and sidewalks, would not allow new racks on public property that distributed "commercial handbills" (free newspapers and advertising papers). Regular newspapers were allowed to have racks. The publishers of the free circulars sued the city for violating their First Amendment rights. Did they win? [*Cincinnati* v. *Discovery Network*, 113 S.Ct. 1505 (1993)]

✓ Check your answer

8. Under the Hazardous Materials Transportation Act, the Secretary of Transportation regulates the transportation of hazardous materials. The regulatory scheme includes warrantless, unannounced inspections of property and records involved in transporting hazardous materials. A propane gas dealer contested the constitutionality of surprise, warrantless inspections of its transport facilities. The government sued to force such inspections. Was that position upheld? [*U.S.* v. *V-l Oil Co.*, 63 F.3d 909, 9th Cir. (1995)]

9. Albert Wild was served a summons by the Internal Revenue Service to appear and testify about the tax records of Air Conditioning Supply Company, of which Wild was owner and president. He appeared but refused to produce the records, claiming Fifth Amendment protection against self-incrimination. The IRS wanted to force him to produce the records of the company. Could they do so? [*Wild* v. *Brewer*, 329 F.2d 924, 9th Cir. (1964)]

✓ Check your answer

10. A jury in West Virginia held that a coal company was liable for various claims made against it. They awarded the plaintiffs $50 million in punitive damages. Knowing that the decision would be appealed, the coal company donated $3 million to the election campaign of a successful candidate for the West Virginia high court. When the case was heard on appeal, plaintiffs contended that the justice who received the campaign contribution should not participate in the decision. He did participate and held for the coal company, reversing the trial court decision. What basis would the plaintiffs have to complain about participation by the judge? [*Caperton* v. *A.T. Massey Coal Co.*, 129 S.Ct. 2252 (2010)]

✓ Check your answer

ETHICS QUESTION

A firm subject to OSHA inspections requires an OSHA inspector, who shows up unexpectedly one day, to get a warrant before engaging in the search. The firm owner knows that the inspector is a genuine inspector and that there is no question that the warrant to search will be issued. However, requiring the inspector to get the warrant takes half a day of the inspector's time (which is paid for by taxpayers). Is it ethical to slow the process of such inspections?

CHAPTER 5

Criminal Law and Business

Scott Levine owned Snipermail, a Florida company that distributed Internet ads to e-mail addresses. Through his business, Levine had access to certain Acxiom databases. Acxiom provides data management services for marketing and other business purposes to various companies. Levine went beyond his authorized access and collected data including names, telephone numbers, addresses, e-mail addresses, and detailed demographics on many people. He did not use the data to steal from anyone, but sold it to a company to use in an ad campaign.

Levine was charged with several crimes: unauthorized access to data, access device fraud, and obstruction of justice. At trial, a friend of Levine's, a police officer, testified that Levine helped many people and was not violent. He thought Levine should not go to prison "because of addresses and e-mails and phone numbers." The friend argued that he should be given home detention, not prison time. The Secret Service argued that the Internet and cyberspace should be free from cybercrime. The judge noted that, as a result of Levine's actions, Acxiom lost $850,000, and sentenced him to eight years in prison plus three years probation. His access to the Internet was also restricted.

Crime

Scott Levine violated laws passed by Congress that make it a federal criminal offense to hack into secured computer databases. These laws are newer versions of existing criminal statutes prohibiting physically breaking into property belonging to another. Although the common law was once a primary source of criminal law, today criminal law is primarily made up of statutes passed by Congress and state legislatures. Hence, we have a federal criminal code and a criminal code in each state. These laws define the scope of offenses against the public that make an offense a crime.

A **crime** may be a positive or negative act that violates a penal law; that is, it is an offense against a state or the federal government. According to *Black's Law Dictionary*, a crime is "any act done in violation of those duties which an individual owes to the community, and for the breach of which the law has provided that the offender shall make satisfaction to the public." What crimes exist and what punishments may be imposed for committing a crime are determined by statutes passed by federal and state legislatures, within limits set by federal and state constitutions.

As discussed in Chapter 1, we distinguish between **civil law** and **criminal law**. Civil law concerns civil and private rights and remedies. That is, some laws passed by legislatures are declared to be civil in nature. The government enforces those laws at the federal, state, or local level, but there are no criminal penalties. Violations of civil statutes result in fines or orders to do or not do something, but not jail time. In the United States, only the government can bring criminal charges. Private rights are enforced by common-law actions when private parties bring suit, usually regarding torts, contracts, or property law. These are not criminal law actions, although many criminal acts are also torts. However, those are distinct legal issues and proceedings.

Crime Categories

Upon being found by a court to have committed a crime, that is, to be convicted, the range of possible punishments is set out in the statute that declared the matter to be criminal. Some crimes may be punishable by death, but most are punishable by imprisonment and/or by paying a fine. Because of a crime, a person may be removed from public office and may be disqualified from holding office, owning a firearm, or voting in public elections.

Crimes are divided into felonies and misdemeanors. A **felony** is a serious crime. In many states, a crime declared to be a felony may be punished by more than a year in prison. That is the definition used in the *Model Penal Code* adopted by the American Law Institute. That Code has been adopted in part by a majority of the states. **Misdemeanors** are less serious crimes, usually punished by a fine or a year or less in prison. Many states classify misdemeanors by their level of severity: Class A, B, and C. The term "petty offense" may also describe misdemeanors in some jurisdictions.

Some crimes are referred to as victimless criminal acts in which no other party is injured, such as possession of illegal drugs. These may be classified as felonies or misdemeanors.

In the federal criminal code and in many states, felonies are listed in classes (Class A, Class B, etc.) or in degrees (first degree, second degree, etc.) to denote the seriousness of a criminal charge. First degree murder is the most serious. It is a murder that was planned or was committed with extreme cruelty. Second degree murders are not premeditated and generally receive lesser punishments. Manslaughter, which may be voluntary or involuntary, is an unlawful killing committed recklessly or under the influence of extreme mental distress. A killing done in the "heat of passion" may be declared manslaughter and subject to lesser punishment than a murder. Similarly, other crimes may have different degrees or classes of severity.

EXHIBIT 5.1   ESTIMATED CRIMES IN THE UNITED STATES

TOTAL VIOLENT CRIMES	**1,246,248**
Murder and Manslaughter	14,748
Forcible Rape	87,767
Robbery	367,832
Aggravated Assault	778,901
TOTAL PROPERTY CRIMES	**9,082,887**
Burglary	2,159,878
Larceny-theft	6,185,867
Motor vehicle theft	737,142

Source: FBI for 2010.

Types of Felonies

Exhibit 5.1 shows the estimated number of major crime categories, which are generally classified as being against persons or against property. The number of crimes reported varies quite a bit compared to the estimated numbers. Most murders and vehicle thefts are reported, but many rapes are not. Violent crimes are ones where physical force is used: murder, rape, armed robbery, and assault and battery. Such crimes generally carry the most severe penalties. Crimes against property include burglary and theft, which includes the receipt of stolen goods. **White-collar crimes**, discussed more below, include nonviolent crimes committed by corporations or individuals. Embezzlement, bribery, fraud, and violations of federal and state laws regulating business, such as securities laws, generally fall into this category.

Lesser Offenses

Local levels of government may enact ordinances that are the equivalent of municipal (city) or county statutes. The powers that local governments have to write ordinances are determined by state law. The ordinances usually deal with zoning, building regulations, and local safety issues. In most instances, violations may be punished only by fine or by short amounts of jail time, much like a misdemeanor.

Lighter Side of the Law

They Think Big in Chicago

A Chicago zoning inspector was convicted of taking two $600 bribes to issue certificates of occupancy for new houses. The conviction was overturned on appeal as the court noted that under the law in question, the bribe must be a minimum of $5,000 for a violation. Small bribes were not enough.

Chicago Mayor Rahm Emanuel disbanded the city's ethics board. In its 25-year history, it never found a city alderman doing anything wrong, even though 20 of them were convicted of felonies during that time.

Sources: U.S. v. Owens, 697 F.3d 657; Chicago Tribune.

Crimes and Elements of Crime

Legislatures decide what will be criminal offenses. Government agencies charged with enforcing the laws decide who will be charged with committing crimes. Public prosecutors, after receiving reports from the police or other investigators, may decide whether or not to bring charges. Because all law-enforcement agencies have limited resources, not all reports of alleged crimes are investigated or result in charges being brought.

While it is not supposed to happen, this is where politics and personal preference can come into play. Prosecutors cannot charge favored parties with crimes or bring lesser charges against them, but may go hard after parties who are not in favor. While we want unbiased prosecution of crimes, it is not a perfect process. Because many state and local prosecutors are elected or rely on appointment by political leaders, it is difficult to keep politics out of all such decisions.

Standard for Conviction

To be convicted of a crime, the government must prove beyond a reasonable doubt that (1) the accused committed the illegal act, and (2) that there was necessary intent or state of mind to commit the act. When one commits a criminal act, they perform a wrongful deed, an ***actus reus***. That is the existence of the crime—the guilty act. That fact must be established at trial. There must also be ***mens rea***; this is the criminal intent that must be established, the "guilty mind" or showing of wrongful purpose in the criminal act committed. If both are present such that it is shown that the defendant caused the act involved, then guilt can be established.

Criminal acts need not be planned. They may occur as a result of negligence. **Criminal negligence**, as explained by *Black's Law Dictionary*, is "a degree of carelessness amounting to a culpable disregard of rights and safety of others." That is, it is criminal conduct that is not intentional, but occurred because one failed to act with the reasonable care that is expected under the circumstances. For example, if someone gets drunk and drives the wrong way down a highway and kills a person in an accident, there may be guilt for negligent homicide or manslaughter. There was no intent to kill the person who was the victim, but the act showed a disregard for the safety of others and violated the obligation to be prudent. A driver knows, or should know, that reckless driving, drunk or not, can lead to death or injury.

A business can be convicted of a crime. Many statutes do not specify that there can be corporate criminal liability, but it is generally inferred to be possible because the wording of statutes discuss the liability of "the person" or of "whoever" committed a certain act, as the *Angela Todesca Corp.* case discusses. The liability may arise as a result of business responsibility for the actions of an employee, an issue we discuss in Chapter 14, or it may arise from the collective action of people within the organization.

Constitutional Right: Fifth Amendment

When a person is arrested on suspicion of a crime, they must be read their **Miranda rights**. This refers to a Supreme Court opinion in 1966 that held that, under the Constitution, persons accused of a crime, or held in suspicion of a crime, must be informed of their right to remain silent, as provided by the Fifth Amendment, of their right to be represented by counsel, and that statements they make can be used as evidence against them.

COMMONWEALTH V. ANGELO TODESCA CORPORATION

Supreme Judicial Court of Massachusetts 842 N.E.2d 930 (2006)

Case Background *Gauthier drove a truck for the Angelo Todesca Corporation to a highway construction site near a busy intersection. A police officer directing traffic at the intersection was run over and killed by the truck when Gauthier backed up to deliver asphalt. The back-up horn on the truck was not working. Gauthier and his employer, Todesca, knew the horn was not working, a violation of safety procedures.*

Gautier was charged with driving offenses. He paid a fine and had his driving privileges restricted. The Commonwealth of Massachusetts charged Todesca with motor vehicle homicide. The jury convicted the company, and it was fined $2,500. The appeals court reversed the conviction. The Commonwealth appealed.

Case Decision Spina, Justice

* * *

As a threshold matter, the parties agree that corporate criminal liability is governed by the standards outlined in *Commonwealth* v. *Beneficial Fin. Co.,* 275 N.E.2d 33 (1971).... In [that case] we held that before criminal liability may be imposed on a corporate defendant:

> The Commonwealth must prove that the individual for whose conduct it seeks to charge the corporation criminally was placed in a position by the corporation where he had enough power, duty, responsibility and authority to act for and in behalf of the corporation to handle the particular business or operation or project of the corporation in which he was engaged at the time that he committed the criminal act ... and that he was acting for and in behalf of the corporation in the accomplishment of that particular business or operation or project, and that he committed a criminal act while so acting.

We rejected the argument that corporations can be liable criminally for conduct of employees only if such conduct "was performed, authorized, ratified, adopted or tolerated by" corporate officials or managers....

The Appeals Court correctly summarized the elements of corporate criminal liability:

> To prove that a corporation is guilty of a criminal offense, the Commonwealth must prove the following three elements beyond a reasonable doubt: (1) that an individual committed a criminal offense; (2) that at the time of committing the offense, the individual 'was engaged in some particular corporate business or project'; and (3) that the individual had been vested by the corporation with the authority to act for it, and on its behalf, in carrying out that particular corporate business or project when the offense occurred....

We agree with the Commonwealth. Because a corporation is not a living person, it can act only through its agents.... A "corporation" can no more serve alcohol to minors, or bribe government officials, or falsify data on loan applications, than operate a vehicle negligently: only human agents, acting for the corporation, are capable of these actions. Nevertheless, we consistently have held that a corporation may be criminally liable for such acts when performed by corporate employees, acting within the scope of their employment and on behalf of the corporation.... Because no intention to exclude corporations from the definition of "persons" or "whoever" appears in [traffic statutes] we conclude that a corporation may be criminally liable for violation of [the traffic statute]....

Judgment of trial court affirmed.

Questions for Analysis

1. Why would the fine be so small for such an incident?
2. Why would the Todesca Corporation incur the cost of appealing such a small fine? The legal fees are much greater than the fine.

Defenses

If proper procedure is not followed in a criminal case, prosecution will not be successful. If a crime is not prosecuted within the time set by the **statute of limitations**, then the state loses the right to bring suit. That time varies by crime and state. For unsolved murders, it may never end. The statute of limitations may **toll**; that is, the legal clock stops running under certain circumstances, such as if one has fled the country to avoid prosecution.

A criminal defendant may offer a variety of defenses to the charges. He may attempt to raise doubts in the jurors' minds by offering an **alibi** or other evidence that he did not commit the crime. For example, a bank robbery defendant may have witnesses testify he was away from the scene of the crime at the time of the robbery. The defendant does not have to prove his alibi, only make the jury have a reasonable doubt about the prosecution's claim.

The defendant may also raise an **affirmative defense**. That is, the defendant may attempt to show that even if the prosecution's claims are true, there are other facts that prevent the claims from constituting the crime charged. For example, specific defenses may be raised in criminal cases. These include intoxication and insanity, but in practice these defenses rarely succeed. In some violent crimes, the claim of self-defense may be made. The defendant admits to the use of physical force but argues it was justifiable to protect himself against another person.

Conviction may be avoided also if one can show that law enforcement authorities set up a trap to lure someone into a crime there was no intent to commit. While it is legitimate to spring traps on criminals, **entrapment** can be a successful defense. On these matters, the defendant has the burden of proof.

Evidence

While evidence in civil trial must be properly gathered and presented, the standards in criminal trials are more strict. The state gathers the evidence to be used in prosecution in criminal cases. It must be shown that the evidence was gathered, handled, and presented properly. This is often called the chain of custody. If evidence is not handled properly, it is excluded and the prosecution may fail. Hence, defendants pay close attention to procedural aspects of evidence in criminal trials.

To obtain evidence, law enforcement authorities may search property and persons and seize documents and other physical items that they think may be relevant. As discussed in the previous chapter, the Fourth Amendment protects against improper search and seizure. It violates our privacy interests to have our person and property subject to unjust searches. If evidence is gathered improperly, it may be referred to as "the fruit of the poisonous tree" and may not be used at trial under the **exclusionary rule**. Many cases turn on this issue and the Supreme Court addresses some aspect of search and seizure every year.

Before authorities may search property or persons and seize evidence, unless they are in "hot pursuit" of a suspected criminal, a warrant must be obtained first. A judge or magistrate issues a **warrant**. It authorizes an officer to search for and seize property, often called *personal effects*, that may be evidence of a crime. To obtain the warrant, the law enforcement officials must show **probable cause** to the judge. That means that they have reasonable grounds, based on knowledge to date, to believe that a person should be searched or arrested. The *Young* case discusses a search incident.

Prosecution Process

Suppose you have an employee you are sure has been stealing from your store. You call the police to report this matter. Because the person suspected of a crime was not caught

UNITED STATES V. YOUNG

United States Court of Appeals, Eleventh Circuit, 350 F.3d 1302 (2003)

Case Background *Under Internal Revenue Service (IRS) regulations, federal taxes on gasoline and diesel fuel do not apply to sales of fuels for marine use. Marinas that sell tax-free fuel must obtain a "637 certificate" from the IRS. Young obtained a certificate for his business, a marine retailer in Marco Island, Florida. The IRS believed Young never used the fuel for marine purposes, but sold it in cash deals to truck stops and service stations, thereby evading paying fuel taxes.*

The IRS believed that Young shipped his sale proceeds by Federal Express, which agreed to let the IRS X-ray packages shipped by Young. Packages were found to contain large amounts of cash. Based on the X-rays, the IRS obtained a warrant to seize and open Young's packages, which did contain cash. At trial, Young moved to suppress that evidence, because the IRS did not obtain a warrant to X-ray the packages originally. The trial court rejected that motion and Young was convicted. He appealed.

Case Decision Fay, Circuit Judge

* * *

The Federal Express packages were "effects" in the context of the Fourth Amendment, and therefore defendants presumptively possessed a legitimate expectation of privacy in their contents....

However ... every Federal Express airbill utilized by defendants states "We may, at our option, open and inspect your packages prior to or after you give them to us to deliver."

* * *

No reasonable person would expect to retain his or her privacy interest in a package shipment after signing an airbill containing an explicit, written warning that the carrier is authorized to act in direct contravention to that interest. Federal Express told its customers two things: (1) do not ship cash, and (2) we may open and inspect your packages at our option. As a matter of law, this simply eliminates any expectation of privacy. We affirm the district court's finding that Young did not have any legitimate expectation of privacy in the packages x-rayed by the IRS agents....

Young assumed the risk that Federal Express might consent to a search. When Federal Express did consent, Young's Fourth Amendment rights were not offended.

Affirmed.

Questions for Analysis

1. The IRS could X-ray the FedEx packages without a warrant, but if the FedEx notice did not say anything about contents being subject to search, would the IRS have been allowed to X-ray the packages without a warrant?
2. Suppose Young had been carrying a briefcase filled with cash and was driving along the highway in Florida. Could an IRS agent stop him and demand to inspect the briefcase?

red-handed in the act, there is no immediate arrest, as would be the case if the police caught someone breaking into your store at night. If law enforcement authorities, after reviewing your evidence, decide to bring criminal charges against your employee, certain steps are followed, with some variation.

A prosecuting attorney would consider your evidence. More evidence might be requested, and the prosecutor's office might do its own investigation. Assuming the prosecutor agrees to go forward, a determination would be made as to what kind of charges to bring—misdemeanor or felony. In some instances a **grand jury** is used to review potential felony cases. The grand jury determines probable cause. It is uncommon for a grand jury not to issue an **indictment** when so requested by a prosecutor.

Arraignment

When criminal charges are filed, the accused is arrested by the police who have been issued a warrant. In many non-violent matters, a date is set by which the accused must surrender to the court, rather than have the police take the person into custody. The suspect is booked at the police station, photographed, fingerprinted, and searched. The matter is entered in the police record and the accused must be allowed the chance to contact a lawyer. There is a court appearance called an **arraignment**, at which time the district attorney gives the accused a copy of the criminal charges. The appearance may be before a judge or a magistrate, and the defendant may plead guilty, no contest (*nolo contendere*), or innocent.

If the judge allows the matter to proceed, the accused is usually released and ordered to appear once a court date is set. In some cases, the defendant has to post bail to be released prior to trial. Violent criminals who pose a threat to the community, or defendants who may flee before trial, may be held without bail; or bail may be set so high that it is unlikely to be met.

In many misdemeanor cases, there may be a settlement conference to save court time. The attorneys attempt to resolve the matter without trial, but under the supervision of a judge. If there is no agreement, then trial is scheduled.

In felony cases, the judge decides at the arraignment whether there is sufficient evidence to proceed or if the matter should be reduced to a misdemeanor or dismissed. In practice, most cases proceed based on the charges brought by the state. If a trial date for the felony charges is set, there is likely to be an attempt to obtain a **plea bargain** to save the time, cost, and uncertainty of a trial. A plea bargain allows the matter to be settled under supervision of a judge, by having the defendant plead guilty or plead no contest, in exchange for an agreement by the prosecutor to recommend a lesser punishment, to reduce the charges, or to make some concession to the defendant. In business cases where both a company and executives are charged, the plea bargain often is for the company to plead guilty and to drop charges against the executives.

Discovery

One of the major differences between civil court procedure, reviewed in Chapter 3, and in criminal proceedings is how discovery is conducted. Civil procedure discovery rules focus on reducing surprises. The parties are intended to exchange all the relevant information before trial. Civil trial verdicts can even be reversed where one party surprises another with important evidence. In contrast, the parties in a criminal case are expected to do their own investigations, disclosing only a subset of what they find to the other side before trial. Long before the defendant even has a lawyer in a criminal matter, law enforcement authorities may be conducting an investigation that the defendant knows nothing about.

The prosecution must disclose to the defendant any exculpatory evidence, that is, evidence that might show that the defendant is not guilty. But the prosecution lawyers make the decision about which evidence is exculpatory, and the defendant's lawyers may not learn of evidence that the prosecutors choose not to disclose.

In civil cases, both sides must turn over anything requested by the other side that might be relevant, and then the parties can dispute whether the evidence is admissible before the judge. The lack of civil discovery tools can be a serious handicap for criminal defense lawyers. Two law professors who compared the two systems, wrote "Civil litigators who venture into criminal cases tend to be stunned and often outraged by their inability to depose government witnesses or even to file interrogatories or requests for admissions."

EXHIBIT 5.2   GENERAL STEPS IN CRIMINAL PROCEDURE

Event Happens
  Law enforcement authorities notified, respond, investigate; an arrest may occur
Reports Filed
  Prosecutor evaluates matter; may dismiss, order arrest, or issue a warrant
  Charges filed seeking conviction if matter proceeds; more evidence gathered
  Arraignment—Indictment Read
  Settlement, Dismissal, or Trial

© Cengage Learning

However, in criminal cases, the defendant also has no obligation to disclose to the prosecution any evidence it has that shows the defendant is guilty. Further, the Fifth Amendment protects defendants from being questioned under oath by prosecutors in advance of trial, as would occur in a civil case. In some states, defendants have an obligation to reveal if they intend to pursue some specific, special defenses such as insanity as well as alibis that may be offered.

The defense avoids disclosing much of its strategy to the prosecution, much more than would be possible in a civil case. Not until just before a criminal trial do the prosecution and the defendant exchange witness and exhibit lists, together with any written statements by the witnesses, i.e., long after they would have done so in a civil matter. Thus, although the criminal discovery rules appear to favor the prosecution because it usually has the advantage in terms of investigative resources, defense attorneys can use their lack of obligation to disclose information to their advantage and often give the prosecution less than complete information. As one former prosecutor put it, "When it comes to discovery, the prosecutors play chess and the defense plays street hockey."

Trial

If there is a trial, the government attorney presents the prosecution's case. Both sides have opening statements and then present their cases, just as in a civil trial. As previously noted, all evidence must have been properly gathered and handled to protect the rights of the accused. As the store owner, you would likely be called to testify about the matter. In this case, you would be both a victim and a witness, but the charge of, say, embezzlement, is a crime against the state. That is why most criminal cases are called something like *State* v. *Obama* or *People* v. *Obama*. If the employee stole money from your business, you could sue the employee for the common law tort of conversion, but that is a separate legal matter from the criminal case brought by the state.

As discussed in Chapter 1, to be convicted in a criminal case, the defendant must be found guilty "beyond a reasonable doubt." That means the evidence fully satisfies and convinces the court to a moral certainty. The facts presented at trial must, by virtue of their value when subjected to study, prove guilt.

If the jury finds the accused not guilty, that is the end of that criminal matter. Note that those who are acquitted are not found innocent but are declared not guilty. This signifies that the state has failed in its burden of proof, not that the defendant proved she was innocent.

The constitutional rule against **double jeopardy** prevents a defendant from being tried a second time for the same charges. However, prosecutors may not bring all possible charges against a defendant, so if they fail to obtain a conviction at trial, different charges related to the same event may be brought so the defendant is tried again.

If the jury cannot agree on a verdict, then a mistrial may be declared. At that point, it is up to the prosecutor to decide if time and resources will be invested in another trial, if the matter will be dropped, or if lesser charges will be filed. If the defendant is found guilty, depending on the severity of the charges and the criminal history of the defendant, there may be prison time, jail time, probation, fine, and/or restitution to be paid to the victim included in the sentence

❓ TEST YOURSELF

1. In *Commonwealth* v. *Angelo Todesca Corporation,* criminal charges were brought against a highway construction firm because one of its trucks backed over and killed a police officer when the backup warning horn on the truck was out of order. The high court in Massachusetts held that the trucking company could:
   a. be liable for civil damages for the loss of life, but not convicted of a crime.
   b. not be convicted of a crime because only real persons can be convicted.
   c. be convicted of a crime which, by law, meant prison time for the company CEO.
   d. be convicted of a crime just as a real person could be.
2. Federal Express allowed the IRS to search a package sent by a customer. As a result of the search, the evidence helped lead to the customer's conviction. The appeals court held the evidence was improperly gathered as it violated the right to privacy: T—F
3. When a person is arrested on suspicion of a crime they must be read their _____.
4. If a city enacts a law, often called a(n) _____, violations are most likely classified as a(n) _____.
5. If, rather than go to trial, a defendant agrees to plead guilty, that is called a plea of *nolo contendere*: T—F
6. A degree of carelessness amounting to a culpable disregard of rights and safety of others is the definition of _____.

Answers: d; F; Miranda rights; ordinance, misdemeanor; F; criminal negligence.

White-Collar Crime

Google the term "white-collar crime" and you will get millions of hits. The term is reputed to have originated in 1939, when used in a speech to mean a "crime committed by a person of respectability and high social status in the course of his occupation." At that time, businessmen wore "white collar" dress shirts daily. "Blue collar" refers to the color of shirts worn by construction workers, truck drivers, and other "service" personnel. Today white-collar crime generally refers to any criminal activity for financial advantage. A person need not be of "high social status" to commit such crimes.

The acts declared to be crimes have expanded greatly over the years, as more things have been defined as criminal activities and penalties have been stiffened. The FBI estimates that such crimes cause economic losses of at least a third of a trillion dollars a year. While most cases are against individuals, corporations can be subject to prosecution. Many areas are covered by federal and state statutes that can impose criminal liability for violations.

What follows is a list of the major areas of white-collar crime that can result in criminal convictions. Some areas of law will be covered in detail later in the text; others are mentioned only here.

Lighter Side of the Law

Crime May or May Not Pay

Antoinette Galluzzo admitted to stealing more than $50,000 from a youth agency in Englewood, New Jersey. She was put on probation for three years and ordered to pay $10 a month restitution for the 36 months while on probation.

Not far away, Kerry Haggard was convicted of selling counterfeit movie posters. In federal court in New York City, he was sentenced to six and a half years in prison.

Sources: Associated Press; NJ.com; Banner-Herald.

Antitrust   Under the Sherman Act and Clayton Acts, discussed in Chapter 20, prison terms may be imposed on those involved in price fixing by competitors and certain other anti-competitive practices, and such terms can be as long as 10 years. Antitrust prosecutions by the Department of Justice result in about 80 criminal cases being filed annually, fines average more than a half-billion dollars a year in total, and a couple dozen people are sent to prison. There are also several hundred civil antitrust investigations each year, and state attorneys' general offices add to this total.

Bankruptcy Fraud   This crime occurs when a person or corporation hides or lies about assets in bankruptcy proceedings, which will be discussed in Chapter 12. It also applies when creditors are given false information or when improper pressure is applied to bankruptcy petitioners.

Bribery   The offer of or taking of money, goods, services, or other things of value to influence official actions or decisions may be **bribery**.

> *U.S. Code Section 201. Bribery of public officials and witnesses...*
>
> *(b) Whoever—1) directly or indirectly, corruptly gives, offers or promises anything of value to any public official or person who has been selected to be a public official, or offers or promises any public official or any person who has been selected to be a public official to give anything of value to any other person or entity, with intent—(A) to influence any official act... 2) being a public official or person selected to be a public official, directly or indirectly, corruptly demands, seeks, receives, accepts, or agrees to receive or accept anything of value personally or for any other person or entity, in return for: (A) being influenced in the performance of any official act ....*

For example, a member of Congress from California was sentenced to over eight years in prison for taking cash in exchange for legislative favors.

Counterfeiting   The copying of a genuine item without authorization, especially when it is passed off for the genuine item, constitutes counterfeiting. This is discussed further in Chapter 9 with respect to the counterfeiting of trademarked and copyrighted goods. It also applies to illegal copying of currency, most of which happens outside of the country.

Credit Card Fraud   The unauthorized use of a credit card to obtain goods, services, or cash. The Federal Trade Commission gives some common examples:

1. A thief goes through trash to find discarded receipts and then uses your account numbers illegally.
2. A dishonest clerk makes an extra imprint from your credit or charge card and uses it to make personal charges.

3. You respond to a mailing asking you to call a long distance number for a free trip or bargain-priced travel package. You're told you must join a travel club first, and you're asked for your account number, so you can be billed. The catch: Charges you did not make are added to your bill, and you never get your trip.

Some issues regarding credit card fraud are reviewed in Chapter 19.

Computer and Internet Fraud A thief goes through trash to find discarded receipts or carbons and then uses your account numbers illegally. This often includes credit card fraud or other unauthorized access to financial accounts, as well as unauthorized use of computers and computer files and sabotage of computers. See U.S. Code, Title 18, Sections 1029, 1030, 1362, 2511, 2701-03.

Economic Espionage The theft or misappropriation of valuable business information, such as a trade secret (discussed in Chapter 9), is generally called **economic espionage**. Such information theft may be performed by a person or a business. As the U.S. Code indicates, the penalties are harshest when such activities involve foreign businesses.

> *§ 1831. Economic espionage (a) In General—Whoever, intending or knowing that the offense will benefit any foreign government, foreign instrumentality, or foreign agent, knowingly—1) steals, or without authorization appropriates, takes, carries away, or conceals, or by fraud, artifice, or deception obtains a trade secret; 2) without authorization copies, duplicates, sketches, draws, photographs, downloads, uploads, alters, destroys, photocopies, replicates, transmits, delivers, sends, mails, communicates, or conveys a trade secret … shall … be fined not more than $500,000 or imprisoned not more than 15 years, or both.*

Embezzlement When someone is in a position of trust with money or other valued property, and they take it for their use, they have committed **embezzlement**. A number of federal and state laws could apply in such cases.

Lighter Side **of the Law**

That Wasn't Me!

Phyllis Stevens' employer confronted her with evidence that she had embezzled $6 million. She and her husband had a great time spending the money. She did not deny that she ended up with the money. Her defense was that the crime was committed by "hundreds" of personalities created by her dissociative identity disorder. Indeed, one of those persons, "Robin" took off for Las Vegas to spend more money right after being confronted. The judge was not impressed and gave her six years in prison.

Source: Des Moines Register.

Environmental Law Violations Most federal and state environmental statutes provide for the possibility of criminal conviction for environmental harm. The Environmental Protection Agency states:

> *The criminal enforcement program has successfully prosecuted significant violations across all major environmental statutes, including: data fraud cases (e.g., private laboratories submitting false environmental data to state and federal environmental*

agencies); indiscriminate hazardous waste dumping that resulted in serious injuries and death; industry-wide ocean dumping by cruise ships; oil spills that caused significant damage to waterways, wetlands, and beaches; international smuggling of CFC refrigerants that damage the ozone layer and increase skin cancer risk; and illegal handling of hazardous substances such as pesticides and asbestos that exposed children, the poor, and other especially vulnerable groups to potentially serious illness.

While the EPA, reviewed in Chapter 21, collects significant fines, its primary settlement goal is to force additional private sector spending, running in the billions of dollars per year, on new pollution reduction measures. There are hundreds of criminal prosecutions per year, resulting in about 200 years of prison time imposed on various defendants.

Financial Fraud   Federal regulatory agencies oversee banks and other financial institutions. Financial firms and their employees are subject to potential criminal liability for fraud in loans, financial documents, mortgages, and other abuses.

Government Fraud   Various laws govern contracts with public agencies for the provision of supplies and for construction. Besides billing for goods not delivered and double-billing, agencies must watch to be sure they are not delivered inferior goods. Fraud laws also apply to federal payment programs, including farm subsidies, public housing, and educational programs.

Healthcare Fraud   Because one in every six dollars in the United States is spent on healthcare, and most of that is through government agencies or insurance companies, various laws deal with over-billing and other scams by hospitals, doctors, ambulance services, laboratories, pharmacies, and extended-care facilities.

Insider Trading   According to the Securities and Exchange Commission:

The securities laws broadly prohibit fraudulent activities of any kind in connection with the offer, purchase, or sale of securities. These provisions are the basis for many types of disciplinary actions, including actions against fraudulent insider trading. Insider trading is illegal when a person trades a security while in possession of material nonpublic information in violation of a duty to withhold the information or refrain from trading.

As discussed in Chapter 18, it is not only company heads who may be convicted of insider trading, but rather, a range of people with an obligation not to use such information for personal gain may be subject to criminal prosecution.

Insurance Fraud   Insurance companies can engage in fraud by charging higher rates than allowed by state regulators, but most fraud is by policy holders who lie about the condition of their property to get lower rates or who pad their claims.

Mail Fraud   Because a great deal of fraud is committed by distributing materials that help create a fraud, **mail fraud** is a common basis for the government to prosecute those involved in some sort of trickery. According to U.S. Code, Title 18, Section 1341:

Whoever, having devised or intending to devise any scheme or artifice to defraud, or for obtaining money or property by means of false or fraudulent pretenses, representations, or promises, or to sell, dispose of, loan, exchange, alter, give away, distribute, supply, or furnish or procure for unlawful use any counterfeit or spurious coin, obligation, security, or other article, or anything represented to be or intimated or held out to be such counterfeit or spurious article, for the purpose of executing such scheme or artifice or attempting so to do, places in any post office or authorized depository for mail matter, *any matter or thing whatever to be sent or delivered by the Postal Service ... shall be fined under this title or imprisoned not more than 20 years, or both. If the violation affects a financial institution, such person shall be fined not more than $1,000,000 or imprisoned not more than 30 years, or both.*

The mail fraud statute is wide-reaching. For example, in one case, a businessman obtained more than $100 million worth of contracts from the City of Chicago by claiming his companies were minority- or woman-owned, so he had a better chance to win contracts. He did all work properly under the contract, but when it was revealed that he lied about the ownership status of his companies, he was convicted of mail fraud, because he had sent materials containing false information through the mails. That was held to be the "scheme or artifice" that violated the statute. He was sentenced to 10 years in prison.

Money Laundering   Just as the mails are often used in the commission of a crime, so too is money. Hiding the truth about the origins of money is called **money laundering**. If one is engaged in illegal activities, such as drug dealing, there is still an obligation to report the income from transactions to the government for tax purposes. To avoid charges of income tax evasion, and to report a legitimate source for such

INTERNATIONAL PERSPECTIVE

Multinational Employers and Criminal Charges Abroad

When people work in another nation, they are subject to its laws and procedures. We can see how this can affect a multinational employer through the experience of Rio Tinto, a global mining and resource company with headquarters in London and Melbourne. It is a supplier of iron ore to China, the world's largest steel market, and has many Chinese and non-Chinese employees working in China.

Four Rio Tinto employees in Shanghai were arrested and held in jail, accused of taking bribes and stealing commercial secrets. The four were tried, convicted, and received sentences ranging from 7 to 14 years each. Three defendants were Chinese nationals working for Rio Tinto; the fourth was an Australian citizen working in China. All four confessed to the crimes.

The details of the case are not known. Criminal trials in China are held in secret. The Australian Prime Minister said that China "missed an opportunity to demonstrate to the world at large transparency that would be consistent with its emerging global role." He was rebuked by the Chinese Ministry of Foreign Affairs for not respecting Chinese law and for making "irresponsible comments."

Despite an international agreement signed in 1999 that allows an Australian representative to sit in on legal proceedings involving Australian citizens in China, no Australian official was allowed into the courtroom until the day the verdicts were announced at the Shanghai No. 1 Intermediate People's Court. The defendants had lawyers, but they would not talk to the media. Some details of the alleged bribes were provided when the verdicts were read, but no evidence was made public. The damage to the Chinese steel industry was claimed to be 1.02 billion yuan ($150 million) because, the judge said, the actions of the defendants "put the Chinese steel industry in a powerless position."

An investigation by Rio Tinto found no evidence of the bribes, but the company fired the four men when they were convicted and described their behavior as "deplorable." Because the company obtains about a quarter of its annual revenue from sales to China, it had an incentive not to irritate the government.

Firms doing business in China, and in many other nations around the world, must remember that the rule of law can be quite different there. Foreign citizens working in those countries can become enmeshed in criminal proceedings that their home countries can do little about.

ISSUE SPOTTER
Internal Fraud

Businesses tend to focus on problems with those outside of the firm—theft by customers, improper billing by suppliers, and relations with regulatory authorities, Audits of firms indicate internal problems that are often missed because of the trust we tend to place in each other within an organization. "A lot of times a small business will close its doors, and may never know they were defrauded … that employees were stealing," says James Ratley, president of the Association of Certified Fraud Examiners.

A study by that organization found that one-quarter of companies with fewer than 100 employees suffered from check tampering—company checks used for improper purposes, and 21 percent suffer from skimming—when cash is taken before it is recorded on the books. Rigging the payroll and falsifying reimbursement expenses, such as for travel, are also common. What can managers do to help control such problems?

© Cengage Learning

income, drug money may be laundered by creating a paper trail that claims a legitimate business origin for the money. Section 1956 of Title 18 is entitled "Laundering of Monetary Instruments." It states:

> *Whoever, knowing that the property involved in a financial transaction represents the proceeds of some form of unlawful activity, conducts or attempts to conduct such a financial transaction, which in fact involves the proceeds of specified unlawful activity … with the intent to promote the carrying on of specified unlawful activity; or … knowing that the transaction is designed in whole or in part … to conceal or disguise the nature, the location, the source, the ownership, or the control of the proceeds of specified unlawful activity … shall be sentenced to a fine of not more than $500,000 or twice the value of the property involved in the transaction, whichever is greater, or imprisonment for not more than 20 years, or both.*

Hundreds of defendants are convicted of money laundering annually by the Treasury Department. The average prison time is over five years. In similar cases brought under bank secrecy laws, which can be closely related, hundreds of people are convicted annually and given average prison sentences of 42 months.

Racketeer Influenced and Corrupt Organizations (RICO) Act   Congress passed **RICO** in 1970 to provide an extra weapon against organized crime, such as the Mafia. In practice, RICO has been used in a wide range of actions against persons, businesses, political protest groups, and terrorist organizations. Although aimed primarily at the Mafia, it has broad reach because, as a key drafter of the statute said, "We don't want one set of rules for people whose collars are blue or whose names end in vowels, and another set for those whose collars are white and have Ivy League diplomas."

Dozens of other statutes, such as mail fraud and money laundering, may be the basis of a RICO claim of **racketeering**. Racketeering traditionally meant a pattern of illegal activity, such as bribery or extortion, which was part of an enterprise controlled by those engaged in the illegal activity. The more modern meaning comes from the RICO statute, which broadened the term to include such activities as mail fraud and many other illegal activities.

When the government brings a RICO action, it can seek a court order to seize a defendant's assets, prevent the transfer of assets, or require a defendant to post a performance bond. These steps can make it difficult for a defendant to pay for a lawyer and often help persuade the defendant to agree to a plea bargain. The government may also press for imprisonment for criminal RICO violations.

The Act allows civil claims to be brought by a person injured in their business by a RICO violation. A plaintiff who succeeds in a civil RICO claim gets triple actual damages plus costs and attorneys' fees. The large damage award available under RICO has inspired expanded private causes of action under the statute.

RICO's broad application is the result of Congress' inclusion of many crimes as the basis of a RICO claim. Such litigation is complex, but it allows injured parties expanded opportunities for claims, as the Supreme Court explains in the *Bridge* case, where we see mail fraud as the basis of a RICO claim by private litigants. This case is not a criminal prosecution by the state, but rather private enforcement under the civil litigation provision of the statute.

BRIDGE V. PHOENIX BOND & INDEMNITY CO.
United States Supreme Court 553 U.S. 639, 128 S.Ct. 2131 (2008)

Case Background *Cook County, Illinois, holds public auctions to sell tax liens on delinquent taxpayers' property. To keep the system honest, the County requires buyers to submit bids in their own names. One may not use "agents, employees, or related entities" to submit bids for the same property by disguising the real bidder.*

Phoenix Bond and some others, who regularly compete to buy the tax liens, sued Bridge for fraudulently getting tax liens by filing false documents that swore they were in compliance with the open bidding process when they were not. As a result, plaintiffs lost possible tax lien purchases. They claimed defendants violated RICO through a pattern of racketeering activity involving mail fraud by sending false documents related to the tax lien purchases.

The district court dismissed the RICO claims. It held that plaintiffs were not protected by the mail fraud statute because the scam was not directed at them as they were not the "first party" to rely on the false information. If there was a scam, it was directed at the County and the property owners, so they would be the ones to have a cause of action, not the competitor bidders. The RICO claim was being carried too far. The appeals court reversed, *holding that plaintiffs could state a claim as victims of the fraud and could sue under RICO. Defendants appealed.*

Case Decision Justice Thomas

* * *

RICO provides a private right of action for treble damages to any person injured in his business or property by reason of the conduct of a qualifying enterprise's affairs through a pattern of acts indictable as mail fraud. Mail fraud, in turn, occurs whenever a person, "having devised or intending to devise any scheme or artifice to defraud," uses the mail "for the purpose of executing such scheme or artifice or attempting so to do." The gravamen of the offense is the scheme to defraud, and any "mailing that is incident to an essential part of the scheme satisfies the mailing element," even if the mailing itself "contains no false information."

Once the relationship among these statutory provisions is understood, respondents' theory of the case is straightforward. They allege that petitioners devised a scheme to defraud when they agreed to submit false attestations of compliance with the ... Bidder Rule to the county. In furtherance of this scheme, petitioners used the mail on numerous occasions to send the requisite notices to property owners. Each of these mailings was an "act which is indictable" as mail fraud, and together they constituted a "pattern of racketeering activity." By conducting the affairs of their enterprise through this pattern of racketeering activity, petitioners violated [the mail fraud statute]. As a result, respondents lost the opportunity to acquire valuable liens. Accordingly, respondents were injured in their business or property by reason of petitioners' violation of [the mail fraud statute], and RICO's plain terms give them a private right of action for treble damages.

* * *

Whatever the merits of petitioners' arguments as a policy matter, we are not at liberty to rewrite RICO to reflect their—or our—views of good policy. We have repeatedly refused to adopt narrowing constructions of RICO in order to make it conform to a preconceived notion of what Congress intended to proscribe.

We see no reason to change course here. RICO's text provides no basis for imposing a first-party reliance requirement. If the absence of such a requirement leads to the undue proliferation of RICO suits, the "correction must lie with Congress." "It is not for the judiciary to eliminate the private action in situations where Congress has provided it."

For the foregoing reasons, we hold that a plaintiff asserting a RICO claim predicated on mail fraud need not show, either as an element of its claim or as a prerequisite to establishing ... causation, that it relied on the defendant's alleged misrepresentations. Accordingly, the judgment of the Court of Appeals is affirmed.

Questions for Analysis

1. How were Phoenix Bond and other plaintiffs allegedly injured by the bidding scheme of Bridge and others?
2. Why was it to the advantage of plaintiffs to bring a cause of action under RICO?

Securities Fraud   While insider trading gets a lot of press, securities fraud in the form of market rigging, theft from accounts of clients of securities firms, and other violations of securities laws are in fact much more common. Chapter 17 on securities regulation covers various aspects of the requirements imposed on professionals in the securities industry.

Tax Evasion   The Internal Revenue Service devotes significant resources to tracking down persons and businesses that fail to file tax returns, fail to report all of their income, or overstate their expenses. The federal tax code states:

> *Any person who willfully attempts in any manner to evade or defeat any tax imposed by this title or the payment thereof shall, in addition to other penalties provided by law, be guilty of a felony and, upon conviction thereof, shall be fined not more than $100,000 ($500,000 in the case of a corporation), or imprisoned not more than five years, or both, together with the costs of prosecution.*

Most investigations carried on by thousands of IRS agents are settled without litigation, but each year about 2,000 people are imprisoned for tax fraud. Cases include fraud by tax preparers; fraud for pocketing but not reporting income; and fraud in the health care industry. All areas of economic activity are under scrutiny. Each year the IRS also obtains injunctions to shut down tax avoidance scams. IRS jurisdiction can be international. For example, in 2013 a Swiss bank agreed to pay $74 million to settle a criminal complaint for helping Americans hide income outside of the United States.

Telephone and Telemarketing Fraud   According to the Department of Justice:

> *Telemarketing fraud is a term that refers generally to any scheme to defraud in which the persons carrying out the scheme use the telephone as their primary means of communicating with prospective victims and trying to persuade them to send money*

to the scheme. When it solicits people to buy goods and services, to invest money, or to donate funds to charitable causes, a fraudulent telemarketing fraud operation typically uses numerous false and misleading statements, representations, and promises, for three purposes: 1) To make it appear that the good, service, or charitable cause their tele-marketers offer to the public is worth the money that they are asking the consumer to send. 2) To obtain immediate payment before the victim can inspect the item of value they expect to receive. 3) To create an aura of legitimacy about their operations, by trying to resemble legitimate telemarketing operations, legitimate businesses, or legitimate government agencies.

Fraud committed on the Internet is essentially the same and is also subject to criminal prosecution. The Justice Department notes that it is "any type of fraud scheme that uses one or more components of the Internet—such as chat rooms, e-mail, message boards, or Web sites—to present fraudulent solicitations to prospective victims, to conduct fraudulent transactions, or to transmit the proceeds of fraud to financial institutions or to others connected with the scheme."

Wire Fraud   This is much like mail fraud and telephone or Internet fraud. If there is any electronic communication involved in illegal activities, it may be referred to as **wire fraud** and be the basis of federal prosecution for an activity that traditionally would have been subject only to state prosecution. Now either federal or state authorities can prosecute for a wide range of activities. U.S. Code, Title 18, Section 1343 provides:

Whoever, having devised or intending to devise any scheme or artifice to defraud, or for obtaining money or property by means of false or fraudulent pretenses, representations, or promises, transmits or causes to be transmitted by means of wire, radio, or television communication in interstate or foreign commerce, any writings, signs, signals, pictures, or sounds for the purpose of executing such scheme or artifice, shall be fined under this title, or imprisoned not more than 20 years, or both. If the violation affects a financial institution, such person shall be fined not more than $1,000,000, or imprisoned not more than 30 years, or both.

CYBER LAW

Your Laptop Is an Open Book

When Arnold arrived at the Los Angeles International airport from the Philippines, a U.S. Customs officer asked him to turn on his laptop. He did. One icon said "Kodak Pictures." The officer opened the folder, looked around in it, and found child pornography. Arnold was indicted for the felony of transporting child pornography. He protested that the evidence was improperly obtained, but the federal appeals court held that the evidence could be used. "Reasonable suspicion" is not needed for customs officers to search laptops, the court held.

Businesses are learning the consequences of this rule. Two executives from BAE Systems, a large British defense and aerospace company, had their laptops seized at the border—and all the data copied from them. The Justice Department said that action was consistent with its intensified investigations into foreign corrupt payments. The individuals were not under suspicion; the government simply wanted to see the information in their computers. Similar rules apply to smartphones and other electronic devices one carries in international business travel. Careful thought must be given about what information is contained in such electronic records.

© Cengage Learning

The sweeping nature of such statutes is seen in the Supreme Court case, *Pasquantino* v. *United States* (125 S.Ct. 1766), where Americans bought liquor in the United States and smuggled it into Canada for resale to avoid high Canadian taxes. The real violation was of Canadian tax law, but since electronic communications were used to engage in illegal activities that originated in the United States, two people were sent to prison in the United States for five years each.

Business Implications from Money Laundering

We just reviewed a long list of major areas of activity that are often called white-collar crime. Increasingly, businesses are expected to be proactive in helping head off problems, even if they are not the origin of illegal activity. Next we consider only the area of money laundering to give an indication of obligations created in normal business operations.

Law enforcement authorities estimate that $1 to $2 trillion is laundered worldwide each year. As noted before, money laundering is taking the proceeds of criminal activities, such as the revenue from drug smuggling, and transforming the cash into what appears to be the proceeds of legitimate businesses, enabling the criminals to spend money without attracting law enforcement attention. Exhibit 5.3 illustrates the common steps in a complicated process. To help prevent money laundering or other financial crimes, legitimate businesses are required to have internal procedures that help spot problems.

Suppose Tony Soprano earns $1 million in cash from his loan sharking and drug dealing businesses. If he has no legitimate source of income and is observed spending $1 million, federal or state authorities may investigate. If he creates Soprano Coin Laundry, Inc., and gradually deposits cash in his corporate bank account, claiming it to be income from the laundry, then he can pay himself a salary from that business and have legitimate income. Because the coin laundry business involves a great deal of cash, he has an explanation for

EXHIBIT 5.3   TYPICAL MONEY LAUNDERING SCHEME

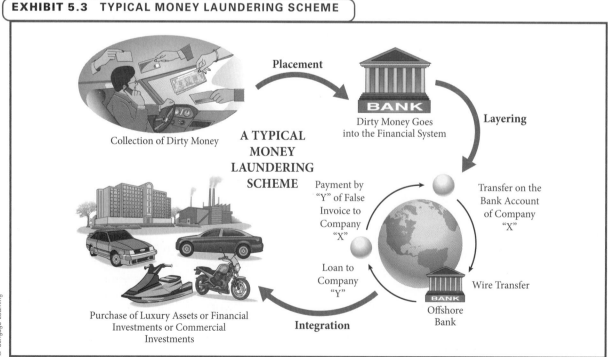

why he is making large cash deposits in the bank. **Anti-money laundering** (AML) measures are regulations aimed at making it difficult for Tony to accomplish this. Soprano's bank and other financial institutions must comply with federal regulations.

Elements of Control within Business Operations Over time, AML measures have expanded in scope. At the heart of all AML are three key goals: (1) identify the beneficial owner of assets; (2) trace the transmission of assets; and (3) report suspicious transactions. All three have impacts on legitimate businesses.

Who Owns What? The beneficial owner of an asset is the person who enjoys the benefits of ownership, regardless of whose name appears on records as the legal owner of the asset. If Tony owns Soprano Coin Laundry, he is the beneficial owner of the money in the company's bank accounts. AML measures seek to ensure that financial records reflect who is the beneficial owner of assets, so law enforcement and tax authorities can know to whom assets really belong. This is to prevent the common money laundering technique of transferring ownership of assets through a string of legal entities to disguise their origins in criminal activity.

AML regulations increasingly force businesses to look past the legal forms of ownership and seek to identify beneficial owners. Regulators want financial institutions to adopt *Know Your Customer* (KYC) or *Customer Due Diligence* (CDD) programs. The Financial Crimes Enforcement Network says that "the cornerstone of a strong Bank Secrecy Act/Anti-Money Laundering (BSA/AML) compliance program is the adoption and implementation of internal controls, which include comprehensive CDD policies, procedures, and processes for all customers, particularly those that present a high risk for money laundering or terrorist financing." Among the examples it lists for financial institutions are:

- Determine if the customer is acting as an agent for another, and, if so, obtain information about the capacity in which the customer is acting.
- Where the customer is a legal entity not publicly traded in the United States, such as a private investment company or trust, get information about the entity to allow the institution to determine if the account poses heightened risk.
- Where the customer is a trustee, obtain information about the trust structure and determine the provider of funds and any parties that have control over the funds or over the trustees.

Track It Down Tracing asset flows requires businesses to ask customers about where the assets used in a transaction come from and document the path the funds took to get to the recipient. Banks need to know the source of funds used to make down payments on real estate or to repay loans; vendors want to know where the money came from to fund large purchases. Regulators apply AML procedures to businesses where there are large cash transactions, including jewelry and auto dealers. To prevent criminals from buying diamonds or cars with cash, and then reselling those assets to launder their funds, governments want businesses to insist that buyers prove their assets came from legitimate sources before accepting payments.

Who Is Up to What? Reporting suspicious transactions is already a requirement for banks and other financial institutions. Banks must file a currency transaction report for any cash transaction over a set amount (currently $10,000) and a suspicious activity report for any transactions that appear odd. For example, if a customer consistently makes cash deposits of $9,900, just under the reporting limit for the currency reports, a suspicious activity report would be required.

These regulations apply to a wide range of firms classified as *Money Services Business.* The Financial Crimes Enforcement Network of the Treasury Department notes that this includes companies that issue or redeem money orders; that transmit money; that offer regular check cashing services; that deal in securities; that exchange foreign currency; that run gambling operations; or that store high-valued items. The Internal Revenue Service lists as examples of suspicious activities:

- The customer pays cash for products/services using bills having an unusual or chemical-like odor.
- A 16-year-old brings bags of cash to a money transmitter to make a transfer from New York City to Miami.
- A customer, a retired CPA, frequently sends and receives money transfers of more than $2,000 to and from many different people.
- A customer conducting an $11,000 cash transaction attempts to bribe a Money Services Business employee not to file the required Currency Transaction Report.

Consequences of Non-Compliance Failing to file a suspicious activity report may lead to civil and criminal penalties or both. Civil penalties can apply for each willful violation of the reporting requirements, meaning that failing to report a series of 10 transactions could lead to 10 penalties. The civil penalty can be up to the greater of the amount involved in a transaction (with a maximum of $100,000), or $25,000. Willful violations can lead to criminal penalties, including a fine of up to $250,000 or five years

INTERNATIONAL PERSPECTIVE

White-Collar Crime in France

French and U.S. law are quite different in their assessment of criminal liability to corporations. Article 121-2 of the French Penal Code provides that corporations are liable for "offenses committed on their account by their organs or representatives." Corporations can be criminally liable in France only when it is established that: (1) an offense was committed, (2) by an organ or representative of the corporation, and (3) the act was committed on the corporation's behalf.

A company's "organs" are defined as those bodies that either the law or the company's organizational documents have designated as being responsible for managing and directing the company or for representing the company in dealings with third parties. "Organs" thus include a company's board of directors and senior management. Representatives include persons who have received a delegation of power from the corporation's organs.

French courts will not base a corporate conviction upon acts of employees who have not been delegated

representative authority by the corporation's board, even when the acts were intended to benefit the corporation. For example, a French court rejected application of criminal responsibility for the French railway company SNCF based on actions committed by engineers and ground-level employees.

The requirement that individuals play a key function within a corporation's decision-making structure before liability significantly restricts corporate criminal liability in France. The emphasis on the role of the board and senior management makes it important both for foreigners joining French firms to understand the greater impact on liability that their actions may have. Similarly, French managers joining U.S. firms should be aware that their actions could lead to criminal prosecution of the entire firm in the United States even if it could not in France. Such differences in law are a major reason that international mergers require careful preparation and legal advice for the new management and employees of the merged firm.

imprisonment. These penalties apply to the Money Services Business firm, not the originator of the cash from illegal operations, so increasingly firms must be sure they are in compliance with a host of regulatory controls.

Sentencing Guidelines and Compliance

When federal prosecutors go after someone, the chances are better than 90 percent that a conviction will result. Prosecutors do not like to bring cases they are not quite sure about winning. When there is a conviction in a federal case, the judge will look to the **Sentencing Guidelines** to determine punishment.

The Guidelines are a controversial aspect of federal criminal law. They were created when Congress mandated that the courts be given clear rules about what sentences are to be imposed by judges for criminal law violations in an effort to make sentences consistent across the country. To do that, the Sentencing Commission has a list of factors to consider for each conviction (see www.ussc.gov for details). Punishment is reduced when a company has a program in place to help ensure that problems do not occur within the organization. If problems do happen, the existence of a program can reduce punishment even if it failed in another particular case. Justice Department guidelines for effective compliance programs require:

1. Compliance standards and procedures that are reasonably capable of reducing the prospect of criminal conduct.
2. High-level persons within the organization to have overall responsibility to oversee compliance with standards and procedures.
3. Effective communication of standards and procedures to all employees and agents, such as by training.
4. Reasonable steps to achieve compliance with standards by monitoring and auditing the program.
5. Consistent enforcement of standards.
6. When offenses do occur, reasonable steps to respond to the problem and to prevent further such offenses.

Some companies have compliance committees to look for evidence of proper activities within the organization that go beyond the traditional accounting and financial reporting concerns of audit committees. Hiring an outsider to be on the committee can bring a fresh perspective. Some companies use whistleblower hotlines to encourage employees to report possible problems anonymously. Such steps can aid in the compliance effort. However, some European countries, such as France, prohibit such hotlines, contending that those who are accused of improper behavior have a right to know who complained. So companies with international operations need to be careful about such hotlines as they are encouraged in some places and forbidden in others.

When sentencing guidelines were first proposed, there were supporters, because some judges were "too easy" on criminals; others thought some judges were "too tough" on criminals, and it was argued that it was unfair for the same crime to result in wide variations in punishment from court to court. The Supreme Court has held that the Guidelines are advisory, but federal judges are expected to follow them closely and must give substantive reasons for departures from the Guidelines. Application of the Guidelines is a common issue in appeals, as the *United States* v. *Allmendinger* case shows.

UNITED STATES V. ALLMENDINGER
United States Court of Appeals, Fourth Circuit, 706 F.3d 330 (2013)

Case Background *Allmendinger, Oncale, and others were the brains behind an insurance investment scam that imposed $100 million in losses on 800 investors. They misrepresented what they were selling and pocketed a lot of cash rather than investing it in the manner promised. When federal investigators began to poke around, Allmendinger began to hide assets. The ringleaders were indicted by a grand jury for mail fraud, money laundering, and securities fraud. The court ordered them to freeze all accounts, but Allmendinger transferred yet more money to secret accounts.*

After they were convicted, the judge imposed sentences based on Sentencing Guideline measures. Given the size of the loss, the fact that Allmendinger did not cooperate with investigators and that he hid money, he was given a 45-year sentence. Oncale was given a 10 year sentence. Allmendinger appealed.

Case Decision Traxler, Chief Judge

* * *

Since the Supreme Court issued its decision in *United States v. Booker,* the Sentencing Guidelines are no longer mandatory but rather are "effectively advisory." When sentencing criminal defendants after *Booker,* district courts must begin by correctly calculating the defendant's sentencing range under the Sentencing Guidelines. The court is next required to give the parties the opportunity to argue for what they believe to be an appropriate sentence, and the court must consider those arguments in light of the factors set forth in 18 U.S.C.A. § 3553(a).

Our review of Allmendinger's sentence can be divided into two steps. First, we must consider whether the district court committed a significant procedural error, such as improperly calculating the appropriate guideline range or inadequately explaining the sentence imposed. If it did, then we must vacate the sentence and remand for resentencing. If it did not, then we consider whether the sentence imposed was substantively reasonable under an abuse-of-discretion standard. ...

As the district court found, Allmendinger built a business permeated by fraud in which the principals, instead of paying the premiums immedi-

ately or putting the money in escrow, placed them in an account that they used as their own piggy bank. ...

The district court heard extensive argument from Allmendinger and the government concerning the extent to which Allmendinger was similarly situated to his co-conspirator Oncale. The district court's lengthy explanation for the sentence imposed left no doubt regarding the court's reasons for selecting the particular sentence that it did. Indeed, the court specifically noted that it was considering unwarranted disparities both among defendants in general and among co-defendants within the case. We therefore conclude that the district court's explanation satisfied the requisite standard. ...

Oncale and Allmendinger were situated differently in that Oncale was confronted by the government early in the investigation and admitted to his culpability and immediately agreed to plead guilty. He liquidated his assets and gave the money to the government, and he cooperated extensively with the government, including by pleading guilty. Allmendinger, on the other hand, refused to accept responsibility for his actions when confronted by the government. He instead sought to squirrel away cash with his father in anticipation of his indictment and continued to live a lavish lifestyle with this money. He also hid money in violation of the restraining order and attempted to flee just days before the trial. And he eventually proceeded to trial, failing to accept responsibility. ...

In sum, finding no error, we affirm Allmendinger's convictions and sentence.

Questions for Analysis

1. Oncale got 10 years while Allmendinger got 45 years. Both were involved in the same scam for years. Should sentences be that much lower for defendants who cooperate?
2. Defendants were guilty of multiple counts of mail fraud and other violations. Why would they be convicted on multiple counts, rather than just one count for their illegal activity? Is that just piling on more punishment for the same event?

? TEST YOURSELF

1. The offer of or taking of money, goods, services, or other things of value to influence official actions or decisions is _____.
2. Federal courts have the ability to impose sentences on convicted felons that do not follow the Sentencing Guidelines exactly: T—F
3. In *Bridge* v. *Phoenix Bond & Indemnity*, some bidders at government auctions cheated on the rules. Other bidders sued them. The Supreme Court held that:
   a. the losing bidders could sue under RICO for mail fraud.
   b. the losing bidders could not sue under RICO, because there was no racketeering, but could sue for mail fraud.
   c. only the government could sue the bid riggers because only the government suffered losses from the cheating.
   d. the bid riggers could be prosecuted for criminal violations, but there could be no civil actions for damages.
4. _____ is a pattern of illegal activity, such as bribery or extortion that is part of an enterprise controlled by those engaged in the illegal activity.
5. Telemarketing fraud is subject to civil penalties, such as fines and injunctions, but Congress did not provide for criminal penalties: T—F
6. Copying of a genuine item without authorization is called _____.

Answers: bribery; T; a; Racketeering; F; counterfeiting.

SUMMARY

- Crimes are actions that violate a law of the federal or state government that has been declared to be enforceable by criminal penalties. Most crimes are matters of state law.

- Felonies are more serious crimes for which prison may be imposed. Misdemeanors are lesser crimes that usually are punishable by a year or less in jail or a fine.

- For a person to be convicted of a crime, the person must have committed a wrongful act, or *actus reus*, and must have had the necessary intent or state of mind, or *mens rea*, to commit the crime.

- Criminal acts need not be intentional; they may be based on criminal negligence, a careless disregard of the rights and safety of others, which is a violation of our duty to act with reasonable care.

- A criminal case must be prosecuted during the statute of limitations. Other defenses include entrapment—when the state has tricked someone to commit a crime that would not otherwise have occurred—and a failure to allow the defendant to exercise constitutional rights, such as be made aware of Miranda rights.

- In criminal cases, evidence must be handled with special care to ensure that it has not been tainted. If not treated properly, it will be excluded from trial.

- Unless a person is caught in the act of committing a crime, there is usually a warrant issued for arrest. Judges or magistrates issue arrest warrants based on presentation of probable cause by law enforcement officials.

- When a person is arrested, there is an arraignment before a judge or magistrate to read the charges. In serious cases, there may be a grand jury used to issue an indictment. Parties may plead guilty, no contest, or not guilty.

- Most cases, especially misdemeanors, are settled by pleas without a trial. Judges must approve plea bargain agreements. If there is a trial and the jury finds the defendant innocent of the charge, there may not be another trial on that charge.

- White collar crimes include a wide range of actions where persons or corporations are accused of violating federal or state statutes that concern the abuse of business processes.

- Areas in which white collar crimes occur include: antitrust, bankruptcy fraud, bribery, counterfeiting, credit card fraud, computer and internet fraud, economic espionage, embezzlement, environmental law, financial fraud, government fraud, health care fraud, insider trading, insurance fraud, mail fraud, money laundering, securities fraud, tax evasion, telephone and telemarketing fraud, and wire fraud.
- Congress has imposed Sentencing Guidelines to tell judges the ranges of sentences to be imposed for various crimes. The Supreme Court has held these to be advisory, and they remain controversial, because they cut into the traditional powers of judges to determine punishment in crime cases.
- Companies that have taken active steps to ensure compliance with various legal duties can lessen punishment in case a problem does arise. Lesser charges may be filed, and the penalty for violations may be lighter, if the company is shown to have a reasonable compliance program in place.

TERMS TO KNOW

crime, 111
civil law, 111
criminal law, 111
felony, 111
misdemeanor, 111
white-collar crime, 112
actus reus, 113
mens rea, 113
criminal negligence, 113
Miranda rights, 113
statute of limitations, 115
toll, 115

alibi, 115
affirmative defense, 115
entrapment, 115
exclusionary rule, 115
warrant, 115
probable cause, 115
grand jury, 116
indictment, 116
arraignment, 117
nolo contendere, 117
plea bargain, 117
double jeopardy, 118

bribery, 120
economic espionage, 121
embezzlement, 121
mail fraud, 122
money laundering, 123
RICO, 124
racketeering, 124
wire fraud, 127
anti-money laundering, 129
Sentencing Guidelines, 131

DISCUSSION QUESTION

Proof in criminal cases must be "beyond a reasonable doubt" for there to be a conviction. Is such a high standard likely to lead to many defendants getting off too easily? What is the purpose of such a standard?

CASE QUESTIONS

1. Brogan lied when IRS agents asked if he had received gifts from a company whose employees were represented by the union in which he was an officer. Brogan was convicted on federal bribery charges and for making a false statement to a federal agency. He appealed, contending that false statements to federal investigators are protected by the Fifth Amendment, which holds that a person cannot be forced to testify against himself. Did Brogan have a right to use the Fifth Amendment in this situation? [*Brogan* v. *U.S.*, 118 S.Ct. 805 (1998)]

2. Hsu was indicted for violating the Economic Espionage Act by conspiring to steal corporate trade secrets for an anti-cancer drug. The defense requested a copy of the trade secret documents. The government contended that the defense did not need access to the documents except under supervision of the judge. The defense maintained a right of full access to the documents so the defense of impossibility could be established— Hsu could not steal trade secrets that did not exist. District court agreed with the defense; government appealed. Must the defendant be allowed full access to trade secrets that are a key part of a case? [*U.S.* v. *Hsu*, 155 F.3d 189, 3rd Cir. (1998)]
   ✓ Check your answer

3. Jolivet was convicted of mail fraud and money laundering in connection with an insurance fraud scheme she carried out with her husband. They provided fraudulent documents to insurance

companies to extract settlements for auto accidents that never occurred. She appealed the conviction, contending that she was not guilty of money laundering because she never hid the funds that were taken improperly. Was Jolivet correct? [*U.S.* v. *Jolivet*, 204 F.3d 902, 8th Cir. (2000)]

✓ Check your answer

4. Hector was prosecuted following police seizure of 80 pounds of drugs from his airplane. The seizure was held to be unlawful, the evidence was suppressed, and the suit against Hector was dismissed. He then sued the government officials involved in his arrest and prosecution to recover $3,500 in bail-bond expenses, $23,000 in attorney's fees, and $2,000 in travel costs. The district court held that he could not recover the costs incurred during the criminal prosecution. Hector appealed. Can he recover those costs? [*Hector* v. *Watt*, 235 F.3d 154, 3rd Cir. (2000)]

5. Wyoming police were told that Barekman was selling large quantities of marijuana from his residence. The police went to Barekman's residence and took a bag of trash out of a trashcan in front of the residence. In the trash they found marijuana residue. Obtaining a warrant, they searched the residence and found all kinds of drugs. Barekman was convicted. He appealed, contesting that the taking of his trash was an improper search and seizure that violated his expectation of privacy under the Fourth Amendment. Do you think he had a right to privacy? [*Barekman* v. *State*, 200 P.3d 802, Sup. Ct., Wyo. (2009)]

✓ Check your answer

6. Highgate LTC operated a nursing home. Following an investigation into patient records, five employees were convicted of crimes relating to their failure to provide required care. Highgate was convicted of criminal liability for willful violation of health laws and for falsifying business records related to the care of the patient. The company was prohibited from operating nursing homes in New York for a year and fined $15,000. The company appealed that it could not be convicted for the actions of its employees. Does that argument hold? [*People* v. *Highgate LTC Management*, 887 NYS.2d 298, App. Div., N.Y. (2009)]

7. Farraj worked at a law firm that represented plaintiffs in a suit against tobacco companies. Plaintiffs' lawyers prepared a trial plan over 400 pages long that included strategy, deposition summaries, and lists of exhibits to be used. Farraj, accessing the plan on secure computers at the law firm, e-mailed 80 pages of the plan to defense attorneys and offered to sell them the entire plan. The FBI was brought in to pose as a defense attorney to arrange the purchase. Farraj was charged with transporting stolen property across state lines. He moved to have the charge dismissed, contending that the content of an e-mail is not "property." He transmitted information, not goods. Do you think that position correct? [*U.S.* v. *Farraj*, 142 F.Supp.2d 484, S.D. NY. (2001)]

8. Tatum ran a pawnshop. Police became suspicious that one of Tatum's employees, Newton, was accepting stolen goods from known burglars. Undercover cops gained Newton's confidence and sold him and Tatum some jewelry. Evidence was presented at trial that Tatum knew or should have known that the jewelry was stolen. He was convicted of violating the RICO Act for conspiring to deal in stolen property. He was sentenced to 7½ years in prison. His criminal intent was based on his and Newton's dealings with the undercover officers during the sting operation. Tatum appealed. What do you think the rule should be regarding Tatum? [*Tatum* v. *State of Florida*, 857 So.2d 331, Ct. App., Fla. (2003)]

9. Corner pleaded guilty to possessing more than five grams of cocaine base, with intent to distribute. He was sentenced to 188 months imprisonment, as called for by the Sentencing Guidelines because he had a previous conviction. He appealed, contending that the trial judge is entitled to disagree with the Guideline and impose a lesser sentence. Is that argument correct? [*U.S.* v. *Corner*, 598 F.3d 411, 7th Cir. (2010)]

✓ Check your answer

ETHICS QUESTION

Recall the discussion in International Perspectives about the conviction of four Rio Tinto employees in China, accused by the government of China of bribing Chinese officials. The company asserted that it had no evidence that such activity took place, but, nevertheless, fired the imprisoned employees.

If Rio Tinto management truly believed no bribery had occurred, was it ethical to fire employees convicted of a crime related to the business? Does your answer depend on whether or not the company officials believed the Chinese government would punish the company if it did not fire them? Why or why not?

PULLING IT TOGETHER

We have covered a number of key concepts in Chapters 1 through 5, so here we consider some cases that bring in legal issues from more than one area for you to identify. Part 1 of the text reviewed the key elements of the legal system—the sources and roles of law, the structure of the legal system, the court system, alternate dispute resolution, the Constitution as it applies to business, and criminal law. Here we consider cases that overlap more than one area, so we can see the interconnection of multiple areas of law.

1. JURISDICTION AND CONSTITUTIONAL LAW

A Japanese company, Asahi, sold parts to a Taiwanese company that then sold finished products in the United States. One of the products, claimed to be defective, injured a consumer who sued the Taiwanese company in state court in California. The company settled the case and then sued Asahi in a California state court. The Taiwanese company contended that the part Asahi had sold it in Taiwan was the cause of the defect in the product. Can the Taiwanese company make Asahi appear in court in California? What constitutional issues would be involved in such a jurisdictional question? [*Asahi Metal Industry Co.* v. *Superior Court of California*, 480 U.S. 1026 (1987)]

2. DUE PROCESS AND CRIMINAL LAW

Dixon bought guns at gun shows while she was under indictment for a felony in violation of federal law that bars those under felony indictment from firearms ownership. She made false statements on the applications to buy the guns. She was indicted and convicted of receiving a firearm while under indictment and for making false statements. She admitted that she bought the guns and lied, but said she did it because her boyfriend threatened to kill her or hurt her daughters if she did not buy the guns for him. She appealed, contending due process had been violated, because the judge did not agree with her claim that her defense—that she acted under duress—should be held to a preponderance of the evidence standard, while the government should have to prove beyond a reasonable doubt that she did not act under duress. Instead, the trial judge said both positions on duress would be held to a preponderance of the evidence standard. Did the trial court violate her Fourteenth Amendment due process rights? [*Dixon* v. *United States*, 126 S.Ct. 2427 (2006)]

OVERVIEW

Common-law rules evolved over centuries as judges and juries responded to changes in business and social norms. In countries with legal systems derived from the present-day United Kingdom, the common law is the traditional basis of private legal relationships that dominate the business legal environment. While the common law evolved differently than the major codes of other nations, the basic elements of how private relationships are governed are not radically different around the world. Over the years, the common law has been modified by and codified in various statutes and regulations.

These chapters in Part 2 review the core topics of business law. This part of the law concerns the rights and obligations of parties to each other in business formation and in various working relationships.

Contracts, especially those formed in domestic and international sales of goods, are a key part of business relationships. To make contracts work, credit is often extended, and various forms of negotiable instruments are often used. We begin by studying tort law: the common-law obligations and rights we have to protect the sanctity of each others' persons and property. We also study the law of property itself: physical property and—of rapidly growing importance—intellectual property.

PART 2

Elements of Traditional Business Law

CHAPTER **6**

Elements of Torts

Litigation is distressing to business operators, but fear of tort suits may be the worst. Other areas of law are more predictable and are generally more controllable. Tort suits tend to arise from unexpected instances that involve momentary carelessness or bad behavior. Text on your smartphone to a customer while making a delivery and you might cause an accident by carelessly running a stop sign. Your mistake makes you responsible for damages that could be catastrophic. Leave a wet spot on the floor of your store and you could be responsible if a customer falls and breaks a hip. Become furious at the stupid mistakes of an employee that caused you to lose valuable business, and you might do something foolish that could result in a rash of suits.

The biggest jury verdict in history was a tort case. In 1984, Pennzoil agreed to buy a large share of Getty Oil. Texaco, knowing of the agreement, offered more money for Getty and got Getty's owners to refuse Pennzoil's offer in favor of Texaco's. Pennzoil then sued Texaco for the common-law tort of inducement of breach of contract. A Houston jury awarded Pennzoil $10.5 billion in damages. Texaco did not have that much cash and could not raise it, making it impossible for the company to stop execution of the judgment pending an appeal. To put the suit behind it, Texaco agreed to pay about one-third the agreed verdict to Pennzoil and to abandon its appeal. While the dollars in that case are huge, we see the same point in many tort cases—juries often place a high value on the enforcement of legal rights.

Like other parts of the common law, the law of torts evolves through case decisions that reflect social values, community standards, and the way we deal with each other in the current environment. Common law tort cases go back centuries. In recent years, tort law has become a major issue for business; tort liability is a significant expense, and some claim that tort judgments bear little relation to reality.

Torts and the Legal System

The word **tort** is derived from the Latin *tortus*, or twisted, and it means "wrong" in French. Although the word faded from common use, it has acquired meaning in the law. A tort is generally defined as a civil wrong, other than a breach of contract, for which the law provides a remedy. Tort is a breach of a duty owed to another that causes harm. That is, liability is imposed for conduct that unreasonably interferes with the legally protected interests of another.

Business and Torts

As we are about to review, torts fall into three groups: negligence, intentional, and strict liability. Regardless of how a tort is classified, businesses become involved in a tort action in one of three ways: (1) a person is harmed by the actions of a business or its employees, (2) a person is harmed by a product manufactured or distributed by the business, or (3) a business is harmed by the wrongful actions of another business or person. The principles of tort law covered in this chapter are applicable to persons in everyday life, but the focus is on business applications. Chapter 7 discusses torts that are unique to business. Chapter 8 discusses torts that are specific to property.

Role of Tort Law

Many accidents result in personal injury and property damage. To have a legal action in tort, the injury suffered by a person or their property must legally be the consequence of the actions of another. In a tort action, the party whose interests have been injured sues the party allegedly responsible.

As discussed in Chapter 1, one act may result in both a criminal case and a tort case. For example, the famous football player O. J. Simpson was tried by the state of California for murder but was found not guilty. In a tort suit that followed, based on the same incident, he was found liable for the tort of assault and battery.

A criminal case is brought by the government against the alleged wrongdoer for violating a rule imposed by the legislature. The victim of the crime, if alive, is a witness in a criminal case. The criminal case does not result in compensation for the injured party, although a convicted criminal may be ordered to pay restitution. The injured party is the plaintiff in the tort suit. An attorney is hired to sue for compensation for injuries wrongfully inflicted by the defendant (the accused criminal in the criminal case). In practice, it is not common for there to be both a criminal case and a tort case based on the same incident because most criminals do not have enough assets to be worth suing in tort.

While most criminal acts, especially violent ones, involve a tort, most torts do not involve criminal acts. The rules vary from state to state, but tort principles are similar across the states. Tort law is private law. It is intended, as the Alaska Supreme Court has said, to place an injured party "as nearly as possible in the position he would have occupied had it not been for the defendant's tort." In a small percentage of tort suits, punitive damages are awarded in addition to compensation for injury. Punitive damages are intended to punish the defendant financially for malicious behavior and to send a message that such behavior will not be tolerated by society.

Negligence-Based Torts

Torts based on **negligence** protect people from harm from others' unintentional but legally careless conduct. As a general rule, we have a duty to conduct ourselves in all situations so as not to create an unreasonable risk of harm, including financial harm, or injury to others. Persons and businesses that do not exercise due care in their conduct may be liable for negligence in tort in a wide range of situations if the following elements can be shown by an injured party:

1. The wrongdoer owed a duty to the injured party. The legal standard created is often called **due care** or **ordinary care**.
2. The duty of care owed to the injured party was breached through some act or omission on the part of the wrongdoer. This breach itself is often called "negligence."
3. There is a causal connection between the wrongdoer's negligent conduct and the resulting harm to the injured party.
4. The injured party suffered actual harm or damage recognized as actionable by law as a result of the negligent conduct.

Negligence is conduct—an act or **omission** (a failure to act)—by a person or business that results in harm to another to whom the person owes a duty of care. If conduct creates an unreasonable risk of harm to others, such conduct may be found to be negligent even though there was no intent to cause harm. In contrast to an intentional tort, in negligence, the harmful results of a party's conduct are not based on an intended invasion of another person's rights or interests. Thus, the person who intentionally runs over another person while driving has committed the intentional tort of battery. A person who unintentionally runs over another while driving carelessly has committed a tort of battery based on negligence.

If negligence is based on a conscious and voluntary disregard for the need to use reasonable care, then there may be a **gross negligence**. This is a stronger claim than ordinary negligence as it involves an assertion that the defendant was engaged in willful and wanton misconduct. A finding of gross negligence is more likely to lead to the imposition of punitive damages in addition to ordinary or compensatory damages, as discussed in Chapter 3.

INTERNATIONAL PERSPECTIVE

No Litigation Jackpots in New Zealand

Events that are classified as torts in the United States also occur in New Zealand, but the consequences are very different. Although New Zealand is a common-law nation with an English legal heritage, it abandoned tort suits for damages in personal injuries. Tort litigation was replaced by the Accident Compensation Corporation (ACC), a body that makes payments to people injured in accidents.

Personal injury tort suits for damages are not allowed. Instead, an injured party is compensated for injuries, including lost wages, from a social insurance fund. Hence, there are no mega-damage awards as occur now and then in the U.S. Those injured, regardless of fault, receive compensation based on cost recovery of losses incurred. There is no waiting

for years for cases to come to trial; ACC payments come quickly by comparison. Coverage applies to mental injury (similar to mental distress) and medical misadventure (similar to medical malpractice). Because there is a "single-payer" health care system in New Zealand, recovery for medical expenses is generally not an issue.

While no one gets a giant damage award in New Zealand, people who have the misfortune to be the victim of an injury caused by a negligent party with no money have their costs covered. In the United States, if you suffer an injury at the hands of a party with little cash, you bear your own costs. The ACC makes payments on a consistent basis, so there is not the wide disparity observed in the United States, and many fewer lawyers are needed.

Duty of Care

In determining whether a person's conduct is negligent, that is, whether it violates the duty of care in any given situation, the law applies a standard of reasonableness. The standard is usually stated as ordinary care or due care as measured against the conduct of a hypothetical person, called the **reasonable person**.

The reasonable person standard represents how persons in the relevant community ought to behave. If the person is a skilled professional, such as a doctor, engineer, or financial consultant, the standard is that of a reasonably skilled, competent, and experienced person in that profession. To decide if a person's conduct was negligent, the question is, what would a reasonable, qualified person have done under the same or similar circumstances? If the conduct was not what is expected of such a person in the eyes of the court, the person has failed the reasonableness test and acted negligently. Tort law does not make us responsible for every injury our actions cause, only those that result from unreasonable behavior.

The reasonableness standard, or the reasonable person standard, is a theoretical concept. It describes a hypothetical person who acts in a reasonable manner under the circumstances. Perfection is not required, but errors in judgment must be reasonable or excusable under the circumstances, or negligence will be found. In a professional relationship, a mistake can result in a suit for negligent misrepresentation. It may be a careless, unintended error, but it does harm. If a loss occurs, liability may be borne by the party who failed to provide the services expected. In the *Squish La Fish* case, we see an example of bad information causing a small firm to suffer a large loss. The question was whether the representative of the company providing information failed to take reasonable care.

SQUISH LA FISH V. THOMCO SPECIALTY PRODUCTS

United States Court of Appeals, Eleventh Circuit, 149 F.3d 1288 (1998)

Case Background *Squish La Fish holds a patent on a plastic device called "Tuna Squeeze" that squeezes oil and water from cans of tuna. A distributor ordered two million units. Squish hired ProPack to affix each Tuna Squeeze to preprinted cardboard "point of purchase" cards for display in stores. Pro-Pack brought in Thomco to advise it as to the kind of adhesive to use to make the Tuna Squeeze stick to the cardboard. The Thomco representative recommended a 3M adhesive called Extra High Tack Adhesive Transfer and said that the adhesive would easily wash off of the Tuna Squeeze in warm water. Pro-Pack and Squish relied on Thomco's advice.*

After 8,600 units had been produced, it was discovered that the adhesive would not wash off of the Tuna Squeeze and the distributor was not happy with the results. The adhesive was replaced with two-sided tape, but the distributor wanted a guarantee that the product would be delivered on time and that there would not be adhesive problems. Squish could not make the promise because there were problems finding a proper adhesive. The distributor canceled the contract.

Squish sued Thomco for negligent misrepresentation. The district court granted summary judgment for Thomco; Squish appealed.

Case Decision Cohill, Senior District Judge

* * *

The Georgia Supreme Court adopted the "negligent misrepresentation exception" from the *Restatement (Second) of Torts* § 522 (1977). Under this now well-established rule,

One who supplies information during the course of his business, profession, employment, or in any transaction in which he has a pecuniary interest has a duty of reasonable care and competence to parties who rely upon the information in circumstances in which the maker was manifestly aware of the use to which the information was to be put and intended that it be so used.

This liability is limited to a foreseeable person or limited class of persons for whom the information was intended, either directly or indirectly.

The elements of this cause of action have recently been formulated as follows: (1) the negligent supply of false information to foreseeable persons, known or unknown; (2) such persons' reasonable reliance upon that false information; and (3) economic injury approximately resulting from such reliance.

* * *

We find that the district court committed an error of law when it failed to acknowledge that Squish La Fish's indirect reliance, through ProPack, on Thomco's alleged representations concerning the … adhesive, were sufficient to bring the company within the negligent misrepresentation rule….

Applying the three-part test for negligent misrepresentation to the facts before the district court, it is clear that Squish La Fish, as the manufacturer of the product being affixed by Thomco's adhesive, was a foreseeable user of Thomco's representations concerning that adhesive. The parties dispute the remaining two prongs of the analysis: whether any false information was conveyed about the adhesive's removability, and whether Squish La Fish indirectly relied upon any such information. The record shows that disputed issues of material fact remain for trial as to both issues.

* * *

Reversed and remanded.

Questions for Analysis

1. The appeals court held that Thomco could be liable for negligent misrepresentation to Squish La Fish. Did Thomco intend to mislead Squish about the adhesive used in the packaging?
2. Would it seem a good defense for Thomco to say that Squish and ProPack should have tested the adhesive before going into production?

Causation

A basic element of a tort based on negligence is **causation** between one party's act and another's injury. For a party to have caused an injury to another and be held negligent, the act must have been the cause of the other's injury.

Res Ipsa Loquitur   In some cases the plaintiff states a case that is so obvious that the doctrine of *res ipsa loquitur*—"the thing speaks for itself"—applies. It does not always mean the plaintiff wins the case, but the showing is strong enough to prevent dismissal of the claim without further examination. Suppose someone had surgery. Three years later, because of ongoing pain, x-rays show that a scalpel was left inside the body at the point of surgery. Assuming there were no other surgeries, the fact that the scalpel is there "speaks for itself"—it must have been carelessly left there during the earlier surgery and is the cause of the injury.

Cause in Fact   **Cause in fact** is established by evidence showing that a defendant's action or inaction is the actual cause of an injury that would not have occurred but for the defendant's behavior. Courts express this in the form of a rule commonly referred to as the "but for" or *sine qua non* rule. That is, the injury would not have occurred but for the conduct of the party accused of committing a tort. Suppose a hotel has a pile of trash, stored improperly, that catches fire and causes a person in the hotel to die from smoke inhalation. Failure to attend to the trash was the failure by the defendant hotel to take steps to protect its guests. A hotel's failure to install a proper fire escape, for example, is not the cause in fact of the death of a person who suffocated in bed from smoke. The person would have died regardless of whether the hotel had a proper fire escape.

Lighter Side **of the Law**

Extending the Concept of Negligence

Police were sure Timothy Pereira was at fault in an accident. He was driving 85 mph in a 35-mph zone when he swerved into on-coming traffic and hit Christine Speliotis's car head-on.

Four months later, Timothy's 17-year-old cousin, Brandon Pereira, who was injured in the accident, sued Speliotis for negligence, claiming that the collision would not have occurred if she had gotten out of the way.

Source: Salem (Mass.) News.

Proximate Cause In most jurisdictions, the injured party must prove that the defendant's act was not only the cause in fact of the injury but also the proximate cause or legal cause of the injury. **Proximate cause** limits liability to consequences that bear a reasonable relationship to the negligent conduct. Consequences that are too remote or too far removed from negligent conduct will not result in liability.

A person's act may set off a chain of events and injuries that were not foreseeable. The principal cause in fact of the Great Chicago Fire of 1871 that destroyed much of the city may have been Mrs. O'Leary's negligent conduct of leaving an oil lamp in the barn that her cow kicked over, but no court would hold her liable for the full consequences of her initial act. The results were too far-fetched. The chain of events must be foreseeable, as New York's highest court explained in the famous *Palsgraf* case.

PALSGRAF V. LONG ISLAND RAILROAD COMPANY

Court of Appeals of New York 48 N.Y. 339, 162 N.E. 99 (1928)

Case Background *Helen Palsgraf was waiting at a train station platform for her train. While she was there, another train stopped and then began to leave. A man who was late for the train ran to catch it and jumped on the moving train while holding a package. A train guard helped pull the man onto the train and another guard helped push him from behind. The man dropped his package. It fell and was run over by the train. The package was full of fireworks, which exploded. The explosion caused some scales on the platform to fall, striking Palsgraf in the head, seriously injuring her.*

Palsgraf sued the railroad for negligence by its employees during the event. The jury found for the plaintiff and the appellate division affirmed the judgment. The railroad appealed to the New York high court.

Case Decision Justice Cardozo

* * *

Negligence is not actionable unless it involves the invasion of a legally protected interest, the violation of a right. "Proof of negligence in the air, so to speak, will not do." "Negligence is the absence of care, according to the circumstances." The plaintiff, as she stood upon the platform of the station, might claim to be protected against intentional invasion of her bodily security. Such invasion is not charged.... If no hazard was apparent to the eye of ordinary vigilance, an act innocent and harmless ... with reference to her, did not take to itself the quality of a tort because it happened to be a wrong.... "In every instance, before negligence can be predicated of a given act, back of the act must be sought and found a duty to the individual complaining, the observance of which would have averted or avoided the injury." The plaintiff sues in her own right for a wrong personal to her, and not as the vicarious beneficiary of a breach of duty to another. ...

The argument for the plaintiff is built upon the shifting meanings of such words as "wrong" and "wrongful," and shares their instability. What the plaintiff must show is "a wrong" to herself; i.e., a violation of her own right, and not merely a wrong to someone else, nor conduct "wrongful" because unsocial, but not "a wrong" to anyone…. Here, by concession, there was nothing in the situation to suggest to the most cautious mind that the parcel wrapped in newspaper would spread wreckage through the station. If the guard had thrown it down knowingly and willfully, he would not have threatened the plaintiff's safety, so far as appearances could warn him. His conduct would not have involved, even then, an unreasonable probability of invasion of her bodily security. Liability can be no greater where the act is inadvertent.

Negligence, like risk, is thus a term of relation. Negligence in the abstract, apart from things related, is surely not a tort, if indeed it is understandable at all. Negligence is not a tort unless it results in the commission of a wrong, and the commission of a wrong imports the violation of a right, in this case, we are told, the right to be protected against interference with one's bodily security. But bodily security is protected, not against all forms of interference or aggression, but only against some. One who seeks redress at law does not make out a cause of action by showing without more that there has been damage to his person. If the harm was not willful, he must show that the act as to him had possibilities of danger so many and apparent as to entitle him to be protected against the doing of it though the harm was unintended.

The law of causation, remote or proximate, is thus foreign to the case before us. The question of liability is always anterior to the question of the measure of the consequences that go with liability. If there is no tort to be redressed, there is no occasion to consider what damage might be recovered if there were a finding of a tort. We may assume, without deciding, that negligence, not at large or in the abstract, but in relation to the plaintiff, would entail liability for any and all consequences, however novel or extraordinary….

The judgment…should be reversed, and the complaint dismissed, with costs in all courts.

Questions for Analysis

1. Why was there no negligence on the part of the railroad?
2. Why is there no proximate cause in this situation?

Over the years, state supreme courts have restated proximate cause in terms similar to the *Palsgraf* case. The Missouri high court has held that the duty owed by the plaintiff to the defendant "is generally measured by whether or not a reasonably prudent person would have anticipated danger and provided against it…." The New Mexico supreme court explained that "A duty to the individual is closely intertwined with the foreseeability of injury to *that individual* resulting from an activity conducted with less than reasonable care…." And the Texas high court stated that "before liability will be imposed, there must be sufficient evidence indicating that the defendant knew of or should have known that harm would eventually befall a victim."

Substantial Factor Proximate cause has been criticized as difficult to understand and apply. The California Supreme Court, in *Mitchell* v. *Gonzales* (819 P.2d 872), joined some other states in replacing the traditional proximate cause rule in negligence actions in favor of the **substantial factor test**.

The substantial factor test states: "A legal cause of injury is a cause which is a substantial factor in bringing about the injury." That is, as the Pennsylvania Supreme Court has explained, the jury is asked to determine whether a defendant's conduct "has such an effect in producing the harm as to lead reasonable men to regard it as a cause, using that word in the popular sense." As Exhibit 6.1 indicates, defendants could be liable even if their negligent behavior was only one factor contributing to an injury, so long as the behavior was found to be a substantial factor in causing the injury.

Intervening Conduct One issue in determining proximate cause is the possibility of **intervening conduct**. Even if negligence occurred, if the causal connection to the resulting harm is broken by an intervening act or event, there is a **superseding cause**. If the

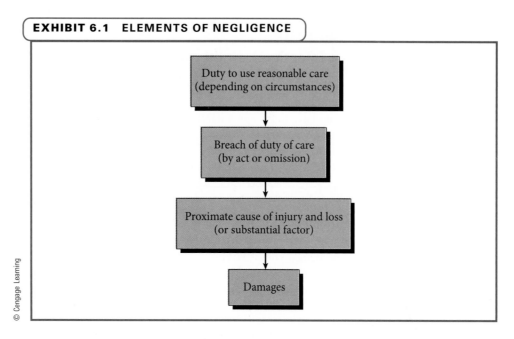

EXHIBIT 6.1   ELEMENTS OF NEGLIGENCE

Duty to use reasonable care
(depending on circumstances)

Breach of duty of care
(by act or omission)

Proximate cause of injury and loss
(or substantial factor)

Damages

© Cengage Learning

causal relationship between the defendant's act and resulting harm is broken by the intervening act, which was unforeseeable under the circumstances, the defendant will likely not be liable.

Suppose Colbert Construction has dug a ditch across a sidewalk to lay some pipe. When the workers quit for the night, they left the ditch uncovered and did not place any warnings around the hole. That night, if Lady Gaga shoves Jay-Z into the ditch and Jay-Z is hurt, Gaga's act is intervening conduct that relieves Colbert of liability. However, suppose Jay-Z had accidentally fallen into the ditch at night and was drowning because the ditch was filled with rainwater. Tiger Woods dives into the ditch to save Jay-Z and Woods drowns. Colbert Construction may well be liable to Jay-Z and Woods. Because of the **danger-invites-rescue doctrine**, the common law holds the negligent party responsible for the losses suffered by those who attempt to save people who are in danger as the result of the torts of others.

Evolving Changes in the Law of Negligence

As noted in Chapter 1, the *Restatement of Torts* is an authoritative secondary source on the law of torts (case law being primary source). While the *Restatement (Second) of Torts* is still the source most cited, we see increasing references to the newer *Restatement (Third) of Torts*. Over time, that will mean new interpretations of some of tort law.

In *Thompson* v. *Kaczinski* (774 N.W.2d 329), the Iowa Supreme Court decided, in a case involving negligence, to adopt some portions of the *Restatement (Third) of Torts*. That means some changes in how negligence is viewed. The Court held that, henceforth, in Iowa, courts need not focus on the ordinary duty of reasonable care because the duty is presumed to almost always exist where there is a risk of physical harm. Instead, the courts should "proceed directly to the elements of liability." The Court also noted that there is less reliance on the notion of proximate cause, as it "has been the source of significant uncertainty and confusion."

There is also a move away from the notion of "substantial factor" that is used in some states. Instead, the *Restatement (Third)* refers to the "scope of liability" related to the risks present in a specific situation. Considering a situation, the court will use a "risk standard" to help judge when liability should be imposed. These changes are subtle and take years to become apparent in the practical consequences in the workings of tort law.

ISSUE SPOTTER
Effective Liability Releases

You help run a resort that in the winter offers snow-tubing. Patrons pay to slide down a snow hill on an inflated tube. Because they can fall off or run into each other and get hurt, you have them sign a liability release that says they will not sue the resort if they get hurt while snow-tubing. Is such a release sufficient? What if they claim the injury was due to the negligence of the resort? Will the liability release protect your company against litigation that could bankrupt the resort?

© Cengage Learning

Defenses to a Negligence Action

Even if an injured party has established the required elements of negligence, the plaintiff may be denied compensation if the defendant establishes a valid defense. As a general rule, any defense to an intentional tort is also available in a negligence action. In addition, other defenses are available to defendants in negligence actions, including assumption of risk and comparative negligence.

Assumption of Risk An injured party who voluntarily assumed the risk of harm arising from the negligent or reckless conduct of another may not be allowed to recover compensation for such harm. Such action by the injured party is called **assumption of risk** and creates a defense for the negligent defendant. The defense requires that the injured party knew or should have known of the risk and that the risk was voluntarily assumed. Thus, spectators at sporting events such as basketball games assume the risk for injuries that result from the usual playing of the game and the reaction of the crowd. Similarly, if you play in a game of pickup basketball, you may get bumped, fall down, and break a leg. That is rarely considered a tort. It is just an accident that happens in such events.

Assumption of risk is an affirmative defense. It may be based on a **liability waiver** or an **exculpatory clause** in a contract by which the plaintiff promised not to sue in case of injury. To take advantage of this defense, the defendant must specifically raise the issue. When established, assumption of risk usually bars the plaintiff from recovery. The *Geczi* v. *Lifetime Fitness* case raises several of these issues.

GECZI V. LIFETIME FITNESS
Court of Appeals of Ohio, 973 N.E.2d 801 (2012)

Case Background *Jodi Geczi was a member of Lifetime Fitness in Columbus, Ohio. One day when she was using a treadmill, it began to jerk violently. When she tried to steady herself, she was pulled sideways and suffered an arm injury. Two Lifetime employees told her they knew the machine was broken, but no sign had been put on it to indicate that it did not work properly. Geczi sued Lifetime for negligence and gross negligence, claiming she suffered lost income, pain, and medical* *expenses as a result of the injury caused by the malfunctioning machine.*

Lifetime defended that as part of the membership agreement, Geczi agreed to an exculpatory clause that barred her claim. She admitted she knew of the clause, which stated that Lifetime was not liable for any negligence on its party that resulted in injury to her while using equipment. Geczi claimed that Lifetime was liable for willful and wanton behavior for failure to warn of the danger posed by the malfunctioning machine. The jury held for Lifetime. Geczi appealed.

Case Decision Dorrian, Justice

* * *

In the case at bar, the parties agree concerning the material facts. The determinative issue is whether reasonable minds can only conclude that the documents Geczi signed constituted a valid release of her claims against Lifetime.

This court has previously considered releases executed in favor of recreational facilities, including fitness centers. We have recognized that the law does not favor releases from liability for future tortious conduct, which will be narrowly construed. ...

But clear and unambiguous contract clauses relieving a party from liability for its own negligence are generally upheld in Ohio.

* * *

[In addition to other discussion of the risk of injury, including injury from use of machines] the new member policy checklist Geczi signed contained the following provision:

> I accept full responsibility for my use, as well as the use by any other person under my membership, of any and all equipment and fixtures as well as for any participation in the activities provided by the Club. *I agree that I will hold the Club*, its shareholders, directors, officers, employer's representative, agents and landlord *harmless from any and all loss, claim, injury, damage, or liability incurred by me* or any other person using the Club under my membership. I further agree that I fully understand all of the Club's policies and agree to abide by them at all times while using the Club....

The only reasonable interpretation of Lifetime's release is that it reflected the parties' intent to release Lifetime from negligence claims of the nature asserted by Geczi....

The release did not distinguish between types of negligence, exempting some types of negligence from liability while preserving liability for other types of negligence. Rather, the clause extended to liability for *any* injury resulting from Lifetime's negligence. The scope of that broad language extends to negligence in maintaining equipment, negligence in leaving defective equipment available to users, and negligence in failing to warn patrons of defective equipment. The trial court did submit to the jury the question whether Lifetime's failure to act or failure to warn rose to the level of willful or wanton conduct, liability for which would not have been affected by the release signed by Geczi. But the jury did not find Lifetime to have acted willfully or wantonly.

Judgment affirmed.

Questions for Analysis

1. The court held that because of the liability waiver, the defendant was released from liability even if the defendant had been grossly negligent. Should gross negligence be treated differently than ordinary negligence?
2. Even if Lifetime had no obligation, would there be an ethical duty to put a sign on the machine saying it was not working?

Comparative Negligence Most states now use the rule of **comparative negligence**. A few states still retain the traditional rule of **contributory negligence**. Under that rule, if a plaintiff who contends that a defendant inflicted a tort injury can be shown to have contributed his or her own negligence to the situation, there may be no recovery.

More common now is comparative negligence, which is a form of modified contributory negligence. It holds that the court, in evaluating the actions, should compare the possible negligence of both parties and allocate the liability. Hence, if a plaintiff contributes 25 percent of the fault in a tort, then the defendant would be liable for 75 percent of the damages found to arise. In some states, if the plaintiff contributes 50 percent of the negligence, there is no recovery for damages. In other states the plaintiff must contribute at least 51 percent of the negligence for no recovery to be allowed. In some states, even if the plaintiff contributed 95 percent of the negligence that caused the event, the plaintiff still recovers for the 5 percent of the damages assigned to the defendant.

> **EXHIBIT 6.2   TERMS OF AN EFFECTIVE LIABILITY WAIVER**
>
> A liability waiver is more likely to be upheld if:
>
> 1. The disclaimer is placed in a prominent place in the document.
> 2. The print size is larger than surrounding print (courts do not like fine print).
> 3. The word, Disclaimer, appears in all capital letters, in bold, or in some color different from other print.
>
> Include such key terms as:
>
> I knowingly and freely assume all risks, known and unknown, even if arising from negligence of the seller.
>
> I hereby release and hold harmless the seller with respect to any and all injury, disability, death, loss, or damage.
>
> I have read this release of liability and assumption of risk agreement, fully understand its terms, understand that I have given up substantial rights by signing it, and sign it voluntarily without any inducement.
>
> [Signature and date]

© Cengage Learning

? TEST YOURSELF

1. The elements of a tort based on negligence include a duty of _____ that was _____ by the defendant.
2. In *Squish La Fish* v. *Thomco Specialty Products*, the appeals court held that Thomco could not be liable because there was no intent to inflict economic harm on Squish La Fish: T—F
3. When the cause of something seems to be the obvious reason for an injury that has been suffered, it is said that the doctrine of _____ may apply.
4. In *Palsgraf* v. *Long Island Railroad*, where Palsgraf was injured when there was an explosion at a train station, the New York high court held that the railroad was:
   a. liable for her injuries due to the Interstate Commerce Act rule for safety.
   b. liable for her injuries due to careless storage of materials that could fall.
   c. not liable because the explosion was not the cause in fact of her injury.
   d. not liable for her injuries because proximate cause was not established.
5. In some states, courts have replaced proximate cause with _____.
6. In the case *Geczi* v. *Lifetime Fitness*, the appeals court held that public policy that favors safety negated effect of the liability waiver signed by McCune: T—F
7. In the *Lifetime Fitness* case, the court held that because Geczi was warned of the dangers and expressly agreed to not sue in case of injury arising from negligence, there was an assumption of risk by Geczi: T—F

Answers: ordinary care, breached; F; res ipsa loquitur; d; substantial factor; F; T.

Intentional Torts against Persons

Some tort liability is based on the intent of a defendant to interfere with the protected interests of a plaintiff. **Intentional torts** are classified on the basis of the interests the law seeks to protect: personal rights and property rights. Here we review intentional torts against persons. In Chapter 8, we look at intentional torts against property. The law imposes a greater degree of responsibility on **tortfeasors**, persons who commit torts, for intentional acts that harm legally protected interests than is imposed for unintentional or negligent acts. As Justice Holmes said, it is the difference between kicking a dog and tripping over a dog. In both cases, the dog gets kicked, but one case is intentional, while the other case is carelessness.

Establishing Intent

Several elements establish the legal requirement of intent. First is the state of mind of the defendant, which means that the person knew what he was doing. Second is that the person knew, or should have known, the possible consequences of his act. The third factor is knowing that certain results are likely to occur.

While these elements are tied together, there may be legal differences between act, intent, and motive. To be liable, a defendant must have acted; that is, there must have been voluntary action. An act is to be distinguished from its consequences. Intent is the fact of doing an act, such as firing a gun. The motive—why the person wanted to fire the gun—is legally distinct. If Britney fires a gun into a crowd of people, that is a wrongful act for which she may be held liable regardless of her motives. Even if she had no bad motive—when she fired the gun she really wished no one would be hurt—that does not relieve her of liability. Under tort law, she acted voluntarily, so she is presumed to have intended the consequences of her act, or should have known what the consequences could be, and so is responsible for them.

Intentional torts are based on willful acts that invade protected interests. Intentional torts occur when a jury finds that, under the circumstances, a reasonable person would have known that harmful consequences were likely to follow from the act. Intent matters much less than the act of invading the interests of another person. Even in cases in which the defendant did not have a bad motive (such as when the defendant was playing a trick), if the tortfeasor intended to commit the act that inflicted injury on another, the willful intent would be present for tort liability. Next we review the major categories of intentional torts.

Assault

Assault is intentional conduct directed at a person that places the person in fear of immediate bodily harm or offensive contact. That is, a person is subject to liability if he or she intends to act to cause a harmful or offensive contact, or an immediate apprehension of such contact, and the other person is thereby put in imminent apprehension or fear. There is a protected interest in freedom from fear of harmful or offensive contact. Actual contact with the body is not necessary.

Pointing a gun or swinging a club at a person can constitute an assault. The requirement of "fear" is satisfied if a reasonable person under the same or similar circumstances would have apprehension of bodily harm or offensive contact. An essential element of

---

EXHIBIT 6.3   MAJOR CATEGORIES OF INTENTIONAL TORTS AGAINST PERSONS

Assault
Battery
False Imprisonment or False Arrest
Emotional or Mental Distress
Invasion of Privacy
Defamation: Libel and Slander

this tort is that the person in danger of harm or injury must know of the danger of suffering a battery and be apprehensive of its threat. If, for example, a person points a gun at another while the other person is sleeping, there is no assault because there was no fear of harm while sleeping.

Battery

Battery is an unlawful touching, which is intentional physical contact without consent. In such cases, a defendant would be subject to liability to another if he acted intending to cause a harmful or offensive contact and such contact actually resulted. There is a protected interest in freedom from unpermitted contact with one's person. Even if the contact does not cause actual physical harm, it is unlawful if it would offend a reasonable person's sense of dignity. This is the case in many batteries that occur in the workplace that involve inappropriate sexual contact. There may be no physical injury, but the contact is not permissible. The following case involves a joke at work not taken well.

FUERSCHBACH V. SOUTHWEST AIRLINES

United States Court of Appeals, Tenth Circuit, 439 F.3d 1197 (2006)

Case Background *Fuerschbach worked as a customer service representative for Southwest Airlines at the Albuquerque airport. The airline prides itself on being a "fun-loving, spirited company." When new employees successfully complete a probationary period, they may be subject to a prank to celebrate the event. Some pranks have been elaborate, and Fuerschbach was aware that one might be pulled on her.*

Her supervisor had been subject to a mock arrest once, and thought it was fun, so she set one up for Fuerschbach. Supervisors got two Albuquerque police to come and pretend to arrest Fuerschbach. The officers approached her at the ticket counter, told her she had outstanding warrants against her, and that she was under arrest. They handcuffed her. She began to cry, so the officers took her to the back, where other employees yelled "congratulations for being off probation." The handcuffs were removed so a little party could begin. But Fuerschbach could not stop crying and was eventually sent home. She saw a psychologist who said she suffered from post-traumatic stress disorder.

Fuerschbach sued everyone connected with the event on numerous grounds, including assault and battery. The district court granted summary judgment for defendants. Fuerschbach appealed.

Case Decision Lucero, Circuit Judge

* * *

Fuerschbach's claim of assault and battery by [the police officers] survives summary judgment.... For there to be an assault, there must have been an act, threat, or menacing conduct which causes another person to reasonably believe that he is in danger of receiving an immediate battery. Battery occurs when an individual acts intending to cause a harmful or offensive contact with the person of the other or a third person, or an imminent apprehension of such a contact, and ... an offensive contact with the person of the other directly or indirectly results. The district court granted the defendants' motion for summary judgment, finding that the officers did not intend to cause an offensive contact, but rather that "the officers were courteous and professional," and that in any event, placing an individual in handcuffs is not an offensive contact.

Any bodily contact is offensive if it offends a reasonable sense of personal dignity. Viewing the evidence in the light most favorable to Fuerschbach, a jury could conclude that the officers' actions offended a reasonable sense of personal dignity. A jury could find that placing a person's hands in position to be handcuffed, handcuffing the individual, and then leading the individual to walk 15 feet offends a reasonable sense of personal dignity.

Moreover, the officers' demeanor is not probative of their intent to cause an offensive contact. Nor is the officers' intent merely to pull a prank on Fuerschbach an excuse. The record reveals that the officers intended to touch Fuerschbach's arms, to place her arms in position to be handcuffed, and to then handcuff her tightly, thus intending to cause an offensive contact. Viewing the evidence in the light most favorable to Fuerschbach, the officers intended to cause an offensive contact with Fuerschbach's person and did cause an offensive contact. Accordingly, we reverse the district court's grant of summary judgment to the officers on Fuerschbach's assault and battery claim.

[Note: Some other claims were allowed to proceed, some were denied. Fuerschbach could only make a workers' compensation claim against Southwest, as there was no intent by anyone at the airline to harm her, and the actions involved occurred at work.]

Questions for Analysis

1. The appeals court held that Fuerschbach could sue the officers for assault and battery. The officers clearly did not mean to harm her; it was a joke. Why could they be liable?
2. Would you suppose Fuerschbach continued to work for Southwest?

Assault and Battery Assault and battery are often the same, although they are separate offenses in some states. The principal distinction is the difference between the requirements of apprehension of an offensive physical contact for an assault and of actual physical contact for a battery. Either of the torts may exist without the other. An individual may strike another who is asleep, for example, thus committing battery but not assault. On the other hand, an individual may shoot at another and miss, thereby creating an assault but no battery. In common discussion, and in some states, the term "assault" is used to cover both assault and battery.

Defenses There are situations in which assault and battery are permitted. A person accused of a tort may have a defense, a legally recognized justification for the actions that relieves the defendant of liability. Defenses include consent, privilege, self-defense, and defense of others and of property. These defenses can be used in any tort but are most common in cases of assault and battery.

Consent occurs when the injured party gave permission to the alleged wrongdoer to interfere with a personal right. Consent may be either expressed or implied by words or conduct. An example of consent in battery includes voluntary participation in a contact sport, such as boxing or football. Of course, you consent only to the normal contacts that occur in a game. When Mike Tyson bit off Evander Holyfield's ear in a heavyweight championship boxing match, Holyfield had not consented to such contact, although he has consented to Tyson punching him.

A **privilege** can give immunity from liability. It can excuse what would have been a tort had the defendant not acted to further an interest of social importance that deserves protection. For example, breaking into a burning store to save someone trapped inside would not be trespass because of the privilege to save someone.

ISSUE SPOTTER
Dealing with Drunks

You have a convenience store. In the evenings, it is not uncommon for people to come in who seem to have had a bit too much to drink. They pick up a six-pack of beer and buy gasoline. Should you refuse to sell them beer and gas? Can you be liable if you do sell them what they want, and they go out and plow into someone while driving? What sort of policy should you have?

© Cengage Learning

Self-defense is a privilege based on the need to allow people who are attacked to take steps to protect themselves. The force allowed is that which a reasonable person may have used under the circumstances. A person may take a life to protect his own life, but the measures used in self-defense should be no more than are needed to provide protection. If an attacker has been stopped and made helpless, a person has no right to continue to inflict a beating on the attacker as punishment. Most states have "stand your ground" doctrines, by common law or statute. A person need not retreat in the face of danger and may meet force with force. As explained by the Washington State Supreme Court, "there is no duty to retreat when a person is assaulted in a place where he or she has a right to be."

Similarly, in defense of other persons or in defense of property, one may use force reasonable under the circumstances. If someone is being threatened with an attack, other persons have a privilege to defend the victim by using force. We have the right to defend our property to keep others from stealing or abusing it, but again, the force used must be reasonable under the circumstances. Because the law places a higher value on human life than on property, it is unlikely that killing or inflicting serious bodily injury on someone invading property will be allowed. It is not reasonable to shoot a person stealing a smartphone from a store.

Lighter Side **of the Law**

Not Good Policy or Advertising

Forest Whitaker, who won the Best Actor Oscar for "Last King of Scotland," was in New York filming a new movie. He went into a deli on Broadway looking for something. Not finding it, he went back out to his car, but was stopped by an employee who accused him of shoplifting. The employee patted Whitaker down but found nothing.

Realizing he made a mistake, the employee offered Whitaker some food. When the media showed up, store employees denied anything happened. Because there were witnesses, that did not hold, and the store manager apologized. The manager said the employee was "just doing his job" but fired him anyway. Whitaker just asked the store to use proper procedure in handling suspected shoplifters.

Sources: New York Post; ABC News.

False Imprisonment

The tort of **false imprisonment**, or false arrest, is the intentional holding, detaining, or confining of a person that violates the protected interest in freedom from restraint of movement. The detention need not be physical; verbal restraints, such as threats, may be the basis of an action for false imprisonment. This often arises in retail businesses when employees or customers are detained by store security personnel. Most states have anti-shoplifting statutes, which provide businesses with an affirmative defense to a charge of false imprisonment for detaining a shoplifter. However, the store must have reasonable cause to believe the person has shoplifted, and the person must be delayed for a reasonable time and in a reasonable manner.

One employer was successfully sued for keeping an employee in an office for an hour, accusing her of stealing, while a security guard stood by. She probably could have walked out, but in such situations, people tend to submit to those in positions of authority. Hence, discussions should be professional, to the point, and not threatening. In the *Forgie-Buccioni* case, we see what happens when the line is crossed.

FORGIE-BUCCIONI V. HANNAFORD BROTHERS
United States Court of Appeals, First Circuit, 13 F.3d 175 (2005)

Case Background *Forgie-Buccioni went into a grocery store. He paid for various items and left the store. He realized he bought the wrong kind of Drixoral, a cold medication, so left the other items in his car and went back into the store. He told a clerk he was going to exchange the Drixoral and left the box he had paid for on a counter. Buccioni found the box of Drixoral he wanted and picked up some other items to buy. He told the clerk, who was different than the one he had seen before, that he had already paid for the Drixoral and he paid for the new items.*

When he left the store, the manager went out to the parking lot and asked him to come back in the store because he did not pay for the Drixoral. The manager, Frender, took Buccioni back to the store's security room to discuss the matter and called the police. The officer was called and arrested Buccioni but the charges were later dropped. He sued for false imprisonment and the jury awarded him $100,000. Hannaford Brothers appealed.

Case Decision Baldock, Senior Circuit Judge

* * *

Under New Hampshire law, "false imprisonment is the unlawful restraint of an individual's personal freedom" (citing *Restatement (Second) of Torts* § 35). The essential elements of false imprisonment are:

(1) defendant acted with the intent to restrain or confine plaintiff within boundaries fixed by the defendant;
(2) defendant's act directly or indirectly resulted in such restraint or confinement of plaintiff; and
(3) plaintiff was conscious of and harmed by the restraint or confinement. Confinement can be imposed by physical barriers or physical force.

The district court did not err when it denied Defendant's motion for judgment as a matter of law on Plaintiff's false imprisonment claim. Drawing all reasonable inferences in Plaintiff's favor and assuming the jury resolved credibility issues consistent with the verdict, a reasonable jury could have concluded:

Defendant's employees intended to confine Plaintiff; Defendant's actions resulted in such confinement; and Plaintiff was aware of the confinement. Plaintiff testified that Frender escorted him back into Defendant's store with his hand on his arm. Although Plaintiff testified he voluntarily returned to the store, he later explained that he did not feel free to leave the store any time thereafter. Once inside the store, Frender "kept pushing" Plaintiff towards the store's security room. Plaintiff explained: "I wasn't free to leave, and I was being very matter of factly taken to the back of this area of the store escorted by not one but two people." Frender sat Plaintiff in the back of the security room and a store employee sat next to Plaintiff "the entire time."… Plaintiff again explained: "I was being detained. I wasn't free to leave." Plaintiff also explained that he waited thirty to forty minutes until Officer Tompkins arrived.… Based upon this and other evidence in the record, a reasonable jury could have easily concluded that Defendant unlawfully restrained or confined Plaintiff.

* * *

Based upon the evidence in the record, the jury's damage award of $100,000 is not so grossly excessive that justice would be denied if we permitted the award to stand.… Affirmed.

Questions for Analysis

1. How should the manager have handled this situation?
2. Does $100,000 for an hour of Buccioni's time seem reasonable?

Infliction of Emotional Distress

The tort of intentional infliction of **emotional** (or **mental**) **distress** involves conduct that is so outrageous that it creates severe mental or emotional distress in another person. The protected interest is peace of mind. This cause of action protects us from conduct that goes way beyond the bounds of decency, but not from annoying behavior, petty insults, or bad language. Many states also provide compensation to third parties based on emotional distress. For example, a Louisiana court provided compensation for emotional distress to a woman who found her comatose husband being chewed on by rats while in a hospital.

Bill collectors, landlords, and insurance adjusters are often involved in emotional-distress suits. Badgering, late-night phone calls, profanity, threats, and name calling lay the groundwork for potential emotional distress suits. Employers have been sued for the distress suffered by employees, as the *Lawler* v. *Montblanc North America* case discusses.

LAWLER V. MONTBLANC NORTH AMERICA, LLC

United States Court of Appeals, Ninth Circuit, 704 F.3d 1235 (2013)

Case Background *Montblanc makes high-end writing implements, jewelry, and other luxury products that it sells wholesale and at boutique retail stores. Cynthia Lawler was manager of a retail store in California for eight years. As the manager, she was expected to work full time. In her eighth year at the store, Lawler developed medical conditions that her doctor said meant she could only work 20 hours a week. She informed Montblanc of this and was told that, as manager, she had to work at least 40 hours a week.*

Soon after, the president of the company, Schmitz, visited and was critical of the way the store was run. Lawler testified that he was unpleasant. She again told the company her doctor said she should not work full time. The company said that was part of her position, so offered her severance pay. She refused and sued for disability discrimination and intentional infliction of emotional distress. The district court held for Montblanc. Lawler appealed.

Case Decision Duffy, Judge

[First, the appeals court affirmed that Lawler had no claim for disability discrimination, as she was unable to perform the duties of her job. It then turned to the emotional distress claim.]

* * *

California recognizes a cause of action for intentional infliction of emotional distress when there is: (1) extreme and outrageous conduct by the defendant with the intention of causing, or reckless disregard of the probability of causing, emotional distress; (2) the plaintiff's suffering severe or extreme emotional distress; and (3) actual and proximate causation of the

emotional distress by the defendant's outrageous conduct. A defendant's conduct is "outrageous" when it is so extreme as to exceed all bounds of that usually tolerated in a civilized community. Liability for intentional infliction of emotional distress does not extend to mere insults, indignities, threats, annoyances, petty oppressions, or other trivialities.

Here, Schmitz's "gruff," "abrupt," and "intimidating" conduct cannot be characterized as exceeding all bounds of that tolerated in a civilized community. His conduct and criticisms relate to the store's business operations and Lawler's performance as a manager. While Schmitz may have inconsiderately and insensitively communicated his dissatisfaction of Lawler's managerial performance, this is not conduct from which California tort law protects employees.

Lawler's alleged emotional distress is not "severe." Severe emotional distress means emotional distress of such substantial quality or enduring quality that no reasonable [person] in civilized society should be expected to endure it. Lawler testified that her emotional injuries manifest as "anxiety, sleeplessness, upset stomach, and sometimes muscle twitches." Clearly, these injuries alone do not rise to the level of "severe."…

For the foregoing reasons, we affirm the district court's order granting summary judgment to Defendants on each of Lawler's claims.

Questions for Analysis

1. Why do you think the standard for emotional distress is so tough to meet?
2. Was the behavior of Lawler's boss ethical in how he treated her?

ISSUE SPOTTER
Dealing with the Elderly and Their Heirs

Your company runs assisted-care facilities. Most of your clients are elderly people in poor health. Most of your clients die within two years of entering a facility. Unfortunately, some of the clients never have visitors. They seem to have no relationships with any family members, but you know that legally they have heirs. If they provide no information about whom to contact in the event of death, their body is cremated. You have heard of instances when a family member suddenly appears after a death and is irate that the family was not contacted. Suits for emotional distress, negligence, and other torts have been filed. How should you handle this matter to cover your legal obligations? What are your ethical obligations?

© Cengage Learning

 TEST YOURSELF

1. In the case *Fuerschbach* v. *Southwest Airlines*, the appeals court held that Fuerschbach may have a claim for assault and battery against police officers who participated in a prank celebrating her work accomplishment: T—F
2. For there to be liability in case of assault, there must be some "clearly defined" offensive contact with the body: T—F
3. When playing soccer you collide with another player and break that player's leg. Most likely, you have the defense of _____.
4. In *Forgie-Buccioni* v. *Hannaford Brothers*, where Buccioni was arrested because the store manager mistakenly thought he did not pay for some merchandise, when in fact he had paid, the appeals court held that:
   a. Buccioni could win a judgment for false imprisonment.
   b. Buccioni could win a judgment for mental distress.
   c. the store was not liable due to state law that permits merchants to detain suspected shoplifters "for a reasonable time."
   d. the store was not liable because the police took charge of the matter.
5. One may not use deadly force to prevent the theft of property unless there is no reasonable alternative so as to stop the thief: T—F

Answers: T; F; consent; a; F.

Invasion of Privacy

The concept behind the tort of **invasion of privacy** is a person's right to solitude and to be free from unwarranted public exposure. The tort may be committed in a number of ways:

1. The use of a person's name or picture without permission (which can make advertisers and marketing companies liable).
2. The intrusion into a person's solitude (illegal wiretapping or searches of a residence; harassment by unwanted and continual telephoning).

3. The placing of a person in a false light (publishing of a story with serious misinformation).
4. The public exposure of facts that are private in nature (such as public disclosure of a person's drug use or debts).

While we often think of invasion-of-privacy cases involving the rich and famous, in fact, most such cases come about from more ordinary situations, as the *James* v. *Bob Ross Buick* case indicates.

JAMES V. BOB ROSS BUICK, INC.

Court of Appeals of Ohio, Second District, 855 N.E.2d 119 (2006)

Case Background *James worked at a Mercedes dealership owned by Bob Ross Buick (BRBI). In 2002, James was named sales representative of the year. None of the sales representatives met sales quotas established for 2003. James was fired in January 2004. Soon after, BRBI sent batches of letters to customers who had dealt with James, encouraging them to shop for Mercedes. The letters were addressed as if they were from James, and a clerk at BRBI signed James's name to the letters.*

James became aware of the letters when a number of former clients told him they had received them. He sued for misappropriation of his name, a form of invasion of privacy. The trial court granted summary judgment in favor of BRBI. James appealed.

Case Decision Wolff, Judge

* * *

The tort of invasion of privacy includes four separate torts: "(1) intrusion upon the plaintiff's seclusion or solitude, or into his private affairs; (2) public disclosure of embarrassing private facts about the plaintiff; (3) publicity which places the plaintiff in a false light in the public eye; and (4) appropriation, for the defendant's advantage, of the plaintiff's name or likeness."

The forgery of the signature of another is a recognized variant of the tort known generally as invasion of privacy. More specifically, forgery amounts to the appropriation of the name or likeness of another. Ohio has adopted the tort of misappropriation of the name or likeness of another....

The [Ohio] Supreme Court has distinguished "the mere incidental use of a person's name and likeness, which is not actionable, from appropriation

of the benefits associated with the person's identity, which is." The court cited with approval the *Restatement of the Law 2d, Torts* (1965), Section 652C, including the portion regarding the incidental use of name or likeness. That portion reads:

The value of the plaintiff's name is not appropriated by mere mention of it, or by reference to it in connection with legitimate mention of his public activities; nor is the value of his likeness appropriated when it is published for purposes other than taking advantage of his reputation, prestige, or other value associated with him, for purposes of publicity. No one has the right to object merely because his name or his appearance is brought before the public, since neither is in any way a private matter and both are open to public observation. It is only when the publicity is given for the purpose of appropriating to the defendant's benefit the commercial or other values associated with the name or the likeness that the right of privacy is invaded.

In our view, BRBI's conduct cannot reasonably be viewed as the incidental use of James's name. [BRBI employees] stated in their affidavits that, pursuant to BRBI policy, batches of these form letters were printed out on a daily basis and given to the salespeople to sign and mail to their assigned customers to maintain a relationship with them. James's name was signed to correspondence that was sent to his former clients at BRBI. In this context, his name clearly had a commercial value, as personal letters are used to induce future sales to customers who have established a client relationship with the dealership.

* * *

The monetary benefit that BRBI received as a result of its wrongful use of James's name is an appropriate (although not exclusive) measure of James's actual damages.... BRBI could have benefited from the use of James's name. Accordingly, upon remand, James may seek nominal, compensatory, and, if appropriate, punitive damages at trial.... [Reversed and remanded.]

Questions for Analysis

1. The appeals court held that James did have a claim for a kind of invasion of privacy based on the misappropriation of his name. What value would there be in a company using the name of a sales representative?
2. What would the damages likely be in such a case? What might make them higher or lower?

Defenses In addition to common-law protection, some states have statutes to recognize a right to privacy. In either case, the right to privacy is largely waived when a person becomes a public figure, such as an entertainer, a politician, or a sports personality. In addition, the publication of information about an individual taken from public files and records does not constitute an invasion of privacy.

Lighter Side **of the Law**

How Dare You List My Phone Calls!

Gabriella Nagy's husband was looking through their phone bill and saw many calls to a strange number. He called the number and the man on the other end admitted they had been having an affair. Mr. Nagy dumped his wife.

She sued the wireless company for invasion of privacy for publishing the list of phone calls, which were bundled with the television and Internet services. She said she had asked the company to send her the phone bill in her name alone; the company said the couple requested the package service. Ms. Nagy demanded $600,000.

Source: Telegraph (UK).

Defamation

The tort of **defamation** is an intentional false communication that injures a person's reputation or good name. If the defamatory communication was spoken, **slander** is the tort. If the communication was in the form of a printing, a writing, a picture, or a radio or television broadcast, the tort is **libel**. The elements that must be shown to exist for both torts to be actionable are:

1. Making a false or defamatory statement about another person.
2. Publishing or communicating the statement to a third person.
3. Causing harm to the person about whom the statement was made.

If a false statement is said directly to a person about that person, there is no defamation because the false information was not communicated to a third party. If the person who had the false statement said to them tells a third party what was said, it is "self-publication" of the defamatory information, and there is no tort.

Some statements are considered **defamation** *per se*. That is, they are presumed by law to be harmful to the person to whom they were directed and therefore require no proof of harm or injury. Statements, for example, that a person has committed a crime or has

CYBER LAW

Tort Liability for Internet Servers

Internet users do things that are illegal or violate the rights of others. Are the Internet service providers liable? In general, no, so long as they were not aware of, or had no reason to be aware of, the improper activity occurring on their system.

In *Zeran* v. *America Online* (129 F.3d 327), a federal appeals court held that America Online (AOL) could not be sued for tort liability for a defamatory message that an AOL user sent. The sender may be liable, but AOL was not. However, if a site contains defamatory material, the host of the site may be required to provide the identity of the party who posted the material. The Delaware high court held, in *Doe* v. *Cahill* (884 A.2d 451), that First Amendment protections extend to anonymous Internet speech, but not if it is defamatory. When defamatory statements are posted, the victim of the statements has the right to obtain the identity of Doe, the otherwise anonymous defendant. Similar rules apply to cyberbullying that occurs on Facebook and other social websites. Once website hosts are aware of significant problems, they will usually end the offending party's right to communicate via the service.

© Cengage Learning

engaged in shady business activities can be defamatory *per se*. Defamation does not only include damage to the reputation of a person; it can involve damage to the good name of a business. Therefore companies must be careful about what they say about competitors and their products.

Workplace Defamation Most defamation suits come about from former employees suing for negative statements made about them by their ex-bosses. As a result, many companies have a policy of providing no information about job performance, good or bad, for current or past employees to outsiders who inquire about performance. When managers talk about the negative aspects of an employee's performance, they must remember that if the information is spread to those who do not have a business reason to know the information, then the company could be exposed to tort liability. An employer does have the right to share negative information for business purposes with people within an organization who should know why someone was fired or involved in some other negative event that has consequences for the company and is useful information for other employees.

ISSUE SPOTTER
Say Good Things about a Good Employee?

Jeff was a good employee at a company you both worked at. He was laid off three years ago when conditions forced the company to release 20 percent of the workforce. Since then, he has worked for another firm, but you know he has been looking for a better job. Jeff has listed you as a reference. A company interested in hiring Jeff has asked for a letter of recommendation. Your firm does not provide such letters because of the possibility of being sued. But you feel that you can write a positive letter about Jeff, which would help a good person who was a loyal employee. Should you write the letter? Can there be a downside to writing a positive letter?

© Cengage Learning

INTERNATIONAL PERSPECTIVE

Libel in Foreign Courts

Many countries do not have constitutional freedom of speech. The news media in the United States can communicate defamatory material about public officials or persons of legitimate public interest as long as the material is provided without actual malice. In the United Kingdom, the news media do not have this extensive privilege. Plaintiffs need show only that the defamatory statement was communicated and that their reputations were damaged. To avoid liability, a defendant must demonstrate that the statements made were true or that they had been made either in court or in Parliament.

As a result of this difference in the law of defamation, a number of U.S. media companies have found themselves in foreign courts, especially in the United Kingdom, defending against defamation suits. Although the broadcasts in question may have originated in the U.S. and may have been republished in the foreign country without the consent of the U.S. company, the U.S. company is not be relieved of liability on that basis alone.

© Cengage Learning

Defenses Truth and privilege are defenses to an action for defamation. If the statement that caused harm to a person's reputation is in fact the truth, some states hold that truth is a complete defense regardless of the purpose or intent in publishing the statement. Truth is an important defense in a defamation suit.

Depending on the circumstances, three privileges—absolute, conditional, and constitutional—may be used as a defense to a defamation action. **Absolute privilege** is an immunity applied in those situations where public policy favors complete freedom of speech. For example, state legislators in legislative sessions, participants in judicial proceedings, and government executives in the discharge of their duties have absolute immunity from liability resulting from their statements.

A **conditional** (or **qualified**) **privilege** eliminates liability when the false statement was published in good faith and with proper motives, such as for a legitimate business purpose. Individuals have a conditional privilege to publish defamatory matter to protect their legitimate interests, such as to defend their reputation against defamation by another. Businesses have a privilege to communicate information believed to be true. Hence, businesses generally have a qualified privilege to share information about employees' performance, as the *Chambers* v. *Travelers Companies* case explains.

CHAMBERS V. TRAVELERS COMPANIES, INC.

United States Court of Appeals, Eighth Circuit, 668 F.3d 559 (2012)

Case Background *Karen Chambers worked for Travelers from 1987 to 2008. In 2007, employees (underwriters) under her supervision began to file complaints about her. The Human Resources Manager, Cady, investigated the complaints along with Chambers' superior, Werner. The results were not good. Chambers was warned about her behavior and given* *specific management issues to address. She was not in agreement.*

Two months later, her superior asked her if it was true that she took her daughter with her on a business trip. She admitted she did but did not volunteer that her grandson came along too. When that came to light, she was fired. She sued for defamation. The district court held for Travelers; she appealed.

Case Decision Loken, Circuit Judge

* * *

Defamation under Minnesota law requires proof that the alleged defamatory statement (1) was communicated to someone other than the plaintiff, (2) was false, and (3) tended to harm the plaintiff's reputation and lower her in the estimation of the community. Whether a communication is actionable because it contained a provably false statement of fact is a question of law. If a plaintiff presents sufficient evidence of these three elements, the defendant may nonetheless be entitled to a qualified privilege that defeats the defamation claim if its statement was made upon a proper occasion, from a proper motive, and based upon reasonable or probable cause. The existence of the privilege is a matter of law for the court.

The district court concluded that the statements made by Travelers agents ... were entitled to a qualified privilege. We agree. An underwriter's telephone complaint to Cady gave Travelers reasonable ground to investigate staff morale in the unit managed by Chambers. Cady surveyed the entire staff and reported the concerns they expressed about Chambers' performance to supervisor Werner, who then summarized the negative comments to Chambers and sought her response. Communications between an employer's agents made in the course of investigating or punishing employee misconduct are made upon a proper occasion and for a proper purpose, as the employer has an important interest in protecting itself and the public against dishonest or otherwise harmful employees.

A qualified privilege is abused and therefore lost if the plaintiff demonstrates that the defendant acted with actual malice. ... Chambers argues that Travelers lost any privilege through abuse because Cady and Werner did not adequately investigate the truth of the underwriters' defamatory comments before presenting those statements to Chambers. ... Travelers investigated the initial complaint regarding Chambers' managerial deficiencies by surveying each member of her staff before asking Chambers to respond. Though the underwriters' survey responses were not uniformly negative, an employer may act on reports of employee misconduct, even if it receives conflicting reports during its investigation. On this summary judgment record, we agree with the district court that Chambers presented no evidence from which actual malice or ill will could reasonably be inferred and therefore Travelers was entitled to the qualified privilege as a matter of law. ...

The judgment of the district court is affirmed.

Questions for Analysis

1. Could Chambers have sued employees under her supervision for giving negative feedback about her?
2. Do you think Chambers had adequate opportunity to respond to the negative aspects of the information provided about her?

As discussed in Chapter 4, the First Amendment to the Constitution guarantees freedom of speech and freedom of press. This **constitutional privilege** protects members of the press who publish "opinion" material about public officials, public figures, or persons of legitimate public interest. This privilege is lost if the statement was made with **actual malice**, that is, the false statement was made with reckless disregard for the truth.

? TEST YOURSELF

1. In the case *James* v. *Bob Ross Buick, Inc.,* where James sued his former employer, the appeals court held that James:
   a. had no case because while he may have been defamed, there were no damages.
   b. could sue for invasion of privacy due to exploitation of his name.
   c. could sue for defamation because prospective customers may have been dissuaded from dealing with him.
   d. could sue for defamation because his ability to obtain future employment had been damaged.
2. For there to be a possible suit for defamation, false information *must* have been provided to a third party: T—F
3. When there is defamation, if it is spoken, it is called _____; if it is in writing, it is called _____.
4. In *Chambers* v. *Travelers Companies, Inc.,* the court held that Chambers had no cause of action for defamation despite employees saying she was a bad boss: T—F
5. In *Lawler* v. *Montblanc North America, LLC,* where Lawler suffered from a medical condition and was fired, the court held that there was no cause of action for emotional distress: T—F
6. If someone falsely tells other people that you were convicted of armed robbery, that may be a tort called _____.

Answers: b; T; slander, libel; T; T; defamation per se.

SUMMARY

- Tort law concerns legal wrongs inflicted by one party on another by interfering with an interest protected by common law. Tort law changes over time as social values, technology, and business practices change. The primary purpose is to compensate the injured party and to put the burden on the tortfeasor.
- Tort liability for negligence arises when the duty of ordinary care—the care expected of a reasonable person under the circumstances—to another person is breached, usually by an act that is the proximate cause, or substantial factor of harm, to the other person.
- For a tort to be established, it must be shown that the act or failure to act on the part of the defendant was the cause in fact of the injury sustained. When the causation appears to be clear, the doctrine of *res ipsa loquitur* applies. After the cause is shown, then proximate cause in the logical

sequence of events leading to the injury must be established. Liability may be avoided if some intervening conduct by another party becomes the superseding cause of the injury that occurred.

- A defendant in a negligence case may pose a defense of assumption of the risk on the part of the plaintiff. The plaintiff knew or should have known the risk, or may have accepted it by signing a liability waiver. There may also be a comparison of the behavior of the plaintiff and defendant under the rule of comparative negligence.
- Intentional torts are based on willful misconduct that invades the rights of another and causes injury. The rights can be the rights of persons to be safe and secure in their person or in their property. Wrongdoers will be expected to pay damages to compensate for injuries.
- Intentional interference with personal rights includes assault, when a person is placed in fear

of bodily harm or offensive contact; battery, or unlawful physical contact without consent; false imprisonment, which is detaining someone within boundaries against his or her will; emotional distress, caused by outrageous conduct; invasion of privacy, which is a violation of a person's right to be free from unwanted exposure; defamation, or false communication that injures a person's reputation, including slander and libel; and malicious prosecution, or the unjustified use of the law to injure another.

- Defenses raised in tort lawsuits include truth in defamation cases; consent, or that the plaintiff had approved of the interference that led to injury; privilege, or that the defendant had a right to take the actions now challenged, including self-defense in case of assault; inflicting injury on another to defend someone else being attacked; and physically defending property. Force used should be no more than reasonable under the circumstances. The law places a higher value on human life than on property.

TERMS TO KNOW

tort, 141
negligence, 141
due care, 142
ordinary care, 142
omission, 142
gross negligence, 142
reasonable person, 143
causation, 144
res ipsa loquitur, 144
cause in fact, 144
sine qua non, 144
proximate cause, 145
substantial factor test, 146
intervening conduct, 146

superseding cause, 146
danger-invites-rescue
    doctrine, 147
assumption of risk, 148
liability waiver, 148
exculpatory clause, 148
comparative negligence, 149
contributory negligence, 149
intentional tort, 150
tortfeasor, 151
assault, 151
battery, 152
consent, 153
privilege, 153

self-defense, 154
false imprisonment, 154
emotional (mental) distress, 155
invasion of privacy, 157
defamation, 159
slander, 159
libel, 159
defamation *per se*, 159
absolute privilege, 161
conditional (qualified)
    privilege, 161
constitutional privilege, 162
actual malice, 162

DISCUSSION QUESTION

Are most accidents and injuries covered by tort law?

CASE QUESTIONS

1. Senna owned Flipper's Fascination, an arcade game on the boardwalk in New Jersey. His rival, defendant Florimont, ran Olympic Fascination, a competitor. Fascination is a game of chance regulated by the New Jersey Chance Control Commission. Winners get tickets that can be redeemed for prizes. Olympic broadcast over a public address system that Flipper's was "dishonest" and "a crook" and said other negative things. Olympic employees told customers that Flipper's did not honor winning tickets. Senna sued Florimont, contending that he defamed his business. The trial court dismissed the suit, holding that actual malice had not been shown. Senna appealed; did he have a

case? [*Senna* v. *Florimont*, 958 A.2d 427, Sup. Ct., N.J. (2008)]

2. Charlotte Newsom worked as a cashier at a store. One day she was told to report to the manager's office, where she was accused by two security staff members of stealing $500. She denied stealing the money. The meeting lasted two hours. The security staff asserted to have evidence of theft, although Newsom constantly denied the claim. Whenever Newsom said she wanted to leave, the staff told her she would be arrested for theft if she left. Finally, Newsom wrote a statement denying the charge. She was fired on the spot and left the store. Did she have a case for false imprisonment? [*Newsom* v. *Thalhimer*

Brothers, 901 S.Wd.2d 365, Ct. App., Tenn. (1994)]

✓ Check your answer

3. When States was operated on at a hospital, an IV was put in her right arm to administer anesthesia. After the surgery, her arm, which had been fine before, was seriously damaged. What doctrine would States likely invoke to support her claim against the doctor and hospital? [*States* v. *Lourdes Hospital*, 792 N.E.2d 151, Ct. App., NY (2003)]

4. A patron at a casino in Nevada got into a fight with another customer. The bouncer went to throw out the patron and got into a fight with him. The bouncer took the patron to a back room to photograph him (they keep photos of troublemakers), which resulted in another fight in which the patron suffered injury to his arm. What torts could the patron bring against the casino? What defenses may work for the casino? [*Cerminara* v. *California Hotel and Casino*, 760 P.2d 108, Sup. Ct., Nev. (1988)]

✓ Check your answer

5. Jerry Katz, a politician, stated that he would not raise taxes if elected. The local newspaper supported Katz, who won the election. At his first board meeting, Katz moved to raise taxes. That prompted an editorial that began, "Jerry Katz is a liar. He has lied to us in the past, and he will lie to us in the future." Katz sued the newspaper. What would that action be, and what would be the likely result? [*Costello* v. *Capital Cities Communications*, 505 N.E.2d 701, App. Ct., Ill. (1987)]

6. After Scarfo quit working for Ginsberg, she claimed that he subjected her to unwelcome sexual conduct and sued him for battery, emotional distress, and invasion of privacy. Does Scarfo potentially have a claim? [*Allstate Insurance* v. *Ginsberg*, 863 So.2d 156, Sup. Ct., Fla. (2003)]

✓ Check your answer

7. Huggins's identity was stolen by an unknown person, who used it to obtain credit cards from various banks in Huggins's name. Huggins suffered the grief of cleaning up the identity theft. He sued the banks and credit card companies for negligence for issuing credit cards without more verification of the identity of the applicant and for failing to adopt other policies to prevent successful identity theft. Do the banks have a duty to protect potential victims of identity theft from imposter fraud? [*Huggins* v. *Citibank*, 585 S.E.2d 275, Sup. Ct., S.C. (2003)]

8. A police officer was served a hamburger at a Burger King at the checkout window. Thinking something was not right, he took off the top bun and saw that an employee had spit on the burger, which was shown to be the case. He sued for emotional distress. Could he have a case? [*Bylsma* v. *Burger King Corp.*, 293 P.3d 1168, Sup. Ct., Wash. (2013)]

✓ Check your answer

9. Barrett was injured when he struck a snowboard rail while he was skiing at a ski resort. He sued the resort for negligence for failure to warn of the presence of the snowboard rail. The resort owner moved to have the suit dismissed, but the trial court and court of appeals refused that motion. The resort owner appealed. Was there likely to be negligence? [*Barrett* v. *Mt Brighton, Inc.*, 712 N.W.2d 154, Sup. Ct., Mich. (2006)]

10. Reynolds worked in the Sioux Falls office of a company that decided to close the office. She was offered a position in another city or a severance package. She did not want to move and suffered a miscarriage. She sued for emotional distress. Do you think she had a case? [*Reynolds* v. *Ethicon Endo-Surgery*, 454 F.3d 868, 8th Cir. (2006)]

ETHICS QUESTION

Some businesses are aggressive at suing the media that reports negative news about them. For example, a cigarette company sued CBS for interviewing a disgruntled former executive; an infomercial producer sued *Forbes* for $420 million for a negative article about infomercials; ABC paid $15 million and made on-the-air apologies to settle a suit by two tobacco companies demanding $10 billion for a report about "spiking" cigarettes with nicotine. It is claimed that such suits are primarily to deter the media from negative reporting. The use of the law seems to be mostly strategic—to discourage the media from being critical of company practices. Is this a defensible business tactic?

CHAPTER **7**

Business Torts and Product Liability

There is no legal category called "business torts." Many torts involve businesses as defendants, as we saw in the last chapter, but some torts, in practice, involve only businesses. This chapter focuses on the areas of tort law that are of special concern to businesses. About 5 percent of all civil suits are tort actions, but the huge amount of money involved in some tort cases draws attention to this area of law. The statistics are a bit soft in this area, but in general:

- Plaintiffs win half of personal injury suits and less than half of product defect suits.
- The median award in product liability suits has been about $400,000.
- Ten percent of personal injury suit awards are for more than $1 million.
- The average jury award for sexual assault on business property is $1.8 million.
- The median jury award for paraplegia is $6.5 million.

Because defendants who expect to lose usually settle out of court, reported awards do not reflect the totality of what happens under tort law. Little information is available about such settlements, so the full magnitude of litigation is not known.

According to the *U.S. Tort Liability Index*, New Jersey, New York, Florida, and Illinois are the states in which a defendant is most likely to lose a tort case; Alaska and North Carolina are among the states least favorable to tort litigation. Businesses take such factors into consideration in location decisions and in deciding what products to offer. For example, Volkswagen cited product liability concerns when it decided not to market a small vehicle that would get 46 miles per gallon.

Tort Law and Business

As seen in Chapter 6, there are several categories of intentional torts. Those torts occur when the tortfeasor is found to have intended to invade a protected interest, and the tortfeasor knew, or should have known, of the consequences of the act that resulted in an injury.

Other torts are based on negligence, which is carelessness in a legal sense. When we fail to act the way we are obligated to behave and, as a result, others suffer an injury, we can be held liable. Persons in business are presumed to have a level of expertise that holds them to a higher level of care than is expected of a nonprofessional in the same situation.

While businesses may be defendants in suits for assault, such actions are not as peculiar to business as are the tort actions covered in this chapter. The actions we look at here involve only business and can be big-dollar cases. As we will see, suits may involve both claims of intentional tort and claims of negligence. Plaintiffs make many claims in one case because when they file suit, they may not be sure which claims will be supported by the facts and be allowed to proceed. As we study later in the chapter, certain cases involve strict liability in tort.

Fraud

When a person suffers an injury (most injuries we study here are financial, not physical) resulting from deliberate deception, there may be a tort of fraud, misrepresentation, fraudulent misrepresentation, or deceit involved. When this issue arises in a business relationship, there is often a breach of contract or some other tort issue present. **Fraud** is a broad concept and may be held to be an intentional tort or to be a tort based on negligence. In the last chapter, we looked at negligent misrepresentation. Here, we consider the more serious charge of fraud as **intentional misrepresentation**. As we noted before, a claim of misrepresentation or fraud is very common in litigation.

Although the Federal Rules of Civil Procedure generally require that the complaint contain only "a short and plain statement of the claim," Rule 9(b) requires that "In alleging fraud or mistake, a party must state with particularity the circumstances constituting fraud or mistake. Malice, intent, knowledge, and other conditions of a person's mind may be alleged generally." Fraud is treated differently because, as the federal court in *Miller* v. *Merrill, Lynch, Pierce, Fenner & Smith* (572 F.Supp. at 1184), noted, "a claim of fraud is so much more amorphous than, for example, a claim of battery, it is often more difficult for a defendant to know exactly what conduct of his the plaintiff believes constitutes fraud. Rule 9(b) therefore requires a greater degree of particularity where claims of fraud are made than where other, less amorphous, allegations are made."

Intentional Misrepresentation or Fraud When misrepresentation is an intentional tort, there must be proof, as the United Kingdom's House of Lords expressed in a famous case in 1889, "that a false representation has been made 1) knowingly, or 2) without belief in its truth, or 3) recklessly, careless whether it be true or false." [*Deny* v. *Peek,* 14 A.C. 337 at 374] While misrepresentation is a common-law rule subject to different interpretations, as the law has evolved, the following key elements generally have been agreed upon to establish fraud or intentional misrepresentation:

1. There was a **misstatement** of an important or **material fact**; that is, false information was presented as fact. The misstatement is usually about a key fact relevant to trying to induce someone to enter into a contract or some sort of business relationship. Unrelated or unimportant misstatements, such as claiming that Abraham Lincoln was president during the Vietnam War, cannot be the basis of fraud since they are

not material. Hyping a product—such as by saying "This is the most fun computer game ever invented," is not sufficient to indicate intent to defraud.

2. There must be **scienter** or intent to defraud; that is, the party wanted to mislead the other party and intentionally deceived him. Scienter means that the court finds that there is something rotten about the deal about which the seller could not be ignorant.

3. The seller must know, or have reason to know, that the statement she is making is false. That is, there was an intent to induce reliance on the false information presented. If you sell your car, which you bought used, and you believe that the mileage is correct, when in fact the person who owned it before you had turned the odometer back, then you do not know you are not telling the truth.

4. The recipient of the false information must justifiably rely on that information in making the decision to go ahead with the deal. The plaintiff had good reason to believe the misrepresentation offered by the defendant. If a seller tells you false information intending to deceive you, but you are not fooled and go ahead with the deal anyway, there is no fraud. Similarly, if you believe information that you should know to be false, such as a claim that the engine in a car is made out of gold, there is no justifiable reliance.

5. There must be **privity** between the parties; that is, the parties must have been in a relationship that created a legal obligation. A third party observing fraud cannot sue.

6. There must be causation: a logical link existed between reliance on the misstatement and the losses that were then suffered by the plaintiff. That is, there must be proximate cause. The fact that there was false information that caused a relationship to be entered into must be related to losses that were suffered for there to be a cause of action for damages.

7. There must be **damages** that were caused by the fraud. That is, even if there is fraud, if there are no damages, there should be no award. Damages are the losses suffered by the plaintiff resulting from reliance on the fraud.

As with other torts, the relationship of the parties can be significant in determining whether legal responsibility is created. If a stranger walking down the street tells you to invest all of your money in Cool Video Company stock, you do not have a cause of action against the stranger when all of your money is lost when the company collapses because there is no justification to believe a stranger about such a decision, nor is there a business relationship—it was just friendly, if stupid advice. But if your stockbroker tells you to invest all of your money in Cool Video Company stock and tells you it is a safe, sure investment, when she knows it is a highly risky venture but she gets high commissions for sales, then your reliance may be justified. She and her employing company may well be responsible for your losses when the Cool Video Company goes broke.

Fraud or intentional misrepresentation comes up in a wide variety of circumstances in business. It is a claim frequently added to a suit for breach of contract because damages for an intentional tort have a chance of including punitive damages, which contract damages alone do not allow. While swindles are easily understood to fall into this category, overly aggressive behavior by a real estate agent trying to ensure a house sale can also fall into this category, such as in *Lightle* v. *Real Estate Commission*.

Interference with Contractual Relations

One of the more common business torts is intentional **interference with contract** or *interference with business relations* or *interference with contractual relations*. As noted at

LIGHTLE V. REAL ESTATE COMMISSION

Supreme Court of Alaska 146 P.3d 980 (2006)

Case Background *Lightle, a real estate agent in Anchorage, listed the Leighs' house for sale. The Williams made an offer to buy the house, and the offer was accepted based on their obtaining a mortgage. Later, another realtor had a client, Seeley, who was interested in the house. Lightle said the house was available as "the first offer was dead." Seeley made an offer that the Leighs accepted. Believing she had a deal on the house, Seeley canceled her existing lease and prepared to move. Unknown to her, Lightle wrote on her offer that it was a back-up contract only if the Williams could not get a mortgage.*

Seeley found out, rescinded her offer, demanded her deposit back, and filed a claim against the Alaska Real Estate Commission's real estate surety fund, a state-administered program to compensate people who lose money in real estate transactions as a result of fraud. The Commission heard the case and held that Lightle committed fraudulent misrepresentation. It awarded Seeley damages and suspended Lightle's real estate license. Lightle appealed, but the decision was upheld by the superior court, which acts as an appeals court for Commission decisions. Lightle appealed again.

Case Decision Bryner, Chief Justice

* * *

Alaska follows the *Restatement (Second) of Torts* on what constitutes an intentional or fraudulent misrepresentation. As described in the *Restatement*, the elements of fraudulent misrepresentation are: (1) a misrepresentation of fact or intention, (2) made fraudulently (that is, with "scienter"), (3) for the purpose or with the expectation of inducing another to act in reliance, (4) with justifiable reliance by the recipient, (5) causing loss....

As used in the *Restatement*, the word "fraudulent" refers "solely to the maker's knowledge of

the untrue character of his representation. This element of the defendant's conduct frequently is called 'scienter.'" Under Section 526 of the *Restatement*, (a) misrepresentation is fraudulent if the maker (a) knows or believes that the matter is not as he represents it to be, (b) does not have the confidence in the accuracy of his representation that he states or implies, or (c) knows that he does not have the basis for his representation that he states or implies. ...

The *Restatement* defines this requirement of a "purpose to induce" action as follows:

> One who makes a fraudulent misrepresentation is subject to liability to the persons or class of persons whom he intends *or has reason to expect to act or to refrain from action in reliance upon the misrepresentation*, for pecuniary loss suffered by them through their justifiable reliance in the type of transaction in which he intends or has reason to expect their conduct to be influenced. ...

Lightle ... said that the prior deal "is dead," that Seeley's offer had been accepted, and that "the house is yours."... Lightle made a partial disclosure that failed to reveal facts that "might have affected the recipient's conduct in the transaction in hand."...

For these reasons, we affirm the superior court's ruling upholding the commission's decision.

Questions for Analysis

1. The court held that Lightle committed fraud by not telling the truth about the contract status of the house. Did he intend to deceive the buyer?
2. Since Lightle was the representative of the sellers, the Leighs, why should he have any obligation to the buyer, Seeley?

the beginning of Chapter 6, it was the basis for the largest tort jury verdict in the United States in the *Pennzoil* case. In such cases, the claim is that another party wrongfully interfered with the injured business's contractual relations. The elements of this tort, which are illustrated in Exhibit 7.1, were explained by a Maryland court, citing Indiana law on point, as follows: "1) the existence of a valid and enforceable contract or business

EXHIBIT 7.1   EXAMPLE: TORT OF INTERFERENCE WITH A CONTRACT

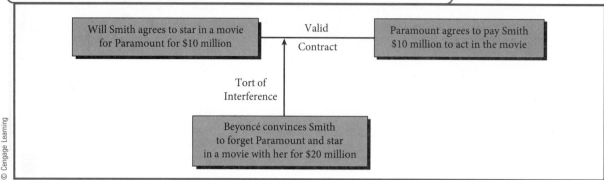

relationship; 2) the defendant's knowledge of the contract or relationship; 3) the defendant's intentional inducement of the breach of contract or interference with the relationship; 4) the absence of justification; and 5) damages resulting from the wrongful interference" (57 A.3d 1041).

When a wrongdoer intentionally causes another party to break a good contract, the motive does not matter. The point is that breaking the contract is done to benefit the tortfeasor. This causes injury to the party who suffers the breach of contract. The party who suffers the breach may sue both the party who breached the contract for breach and the wrongdoer for the tort of interference with contract. The *Slater Numismatics* case discusses the elements of this kind of tort.

SLATER NUMISMATICS, LLC V. DRIVING FORCE, LLC

Colorado Court of Appeals ---P.3d--- (2012)

Case Background *Slater bought and sold rare and modern coins. It worked with ICG to grade and ship coins to Cable Shopping Network which advertised the coins for sale. ICG and Slater shared revenues from that work. Cable was Slater's most important client. Taylor and Williams worked at ICG; they left the company and set up Driving Force, LLC, which operated ANACS in the coin business. ANACS hired away most of ICG's key employees, essentially driving it out of business, and then, knowing the terms of Slater's deal with Cable, offered Cable a better deal and took the account away from Slater.*

Slater then sued for intentional interference with contractual relations. The trial court granted summary judgment for Driving Force. Slater appealed.

Case Decision Terry, Judge

* * *

Colorado Supreme Court precedents rely on the definition of the tort of intentional interference with contractual relations contained in § 766 of the *Restatement (Second) of Torts*, which provides:

One who intentionally and improperly interferes with the performance of a contract (except a contract to marry) between another and a third person *by inducing or otherwise causing the third person not to perform* the contract, is subject to liability to the other for the pecuniary loss resulting to the other from the failure of the third person to perform the contract.

Given the evidence presented to the trial court here, a reasonable jury could conclude that ANACS purposefully depleted the ranks of ICG, significantly impairing its ability to fulfill Cable's coin grading needs. When that circumstance is combined with ANACS's use of Plaintiff's confidential information … to make a play for Cable's business while undercutting ICG's pricing, a reasonable jury could conclude that ANACS caused ICG "not to perform" its contract with Plaintiff, within the meaning of § 766.

* * *

We can think of no principled reason for rejecting a theory of intentional interference with contract that would insulate ANACS's alleged conduct from liability to Plaintiff. While an outside observer could chalk up such collateral damage to Plaintiff by remarking, "That's just the nature of competition," we believe such alleged conduct fits within the very purpose for imposing tort liability on intentional interference with contractual relations. …

We conclude that Plaintiff here has established a triable claim for intentional interference with contractual relations. The evidence submitted to the trial court in opposition to the summary judgment motion was sufficient to create triable issues of fact, such that summary judgment should have been denied as to this claim. …

[Reversed and remanded.]

Questions for Analysis

1. Why is the behavior of the defendant not allowed as fair competition?
2. Cable Shopping was happy to move its business to ANACS. Should it be liable to Slater for damages?

Interference with Prospective Advantage

Similar to the tort of interference with contractual rights is the tort of **interference with prospective advantage**, also called interference with prospective economic advantage or interference with prospective contractual relationship. Businesses devise countless schemes to attract customers, which are a good part of competition. But there can be a tort when a business attempts to improve its place in the market by interfering with another's attempt to gain new business by use of improper acts.

An employee of Kim's Hot Threads, for example, cannot be positioned at the entrance of U2 Runners Sportswear to tell customers to go to Kim's. Such conduct is predatory behavior. If the behavior of the defendant is merely competitive and not predatory in nature—for example, the defendant is so effective in advertising that customers are drawn from the losing business—the courts do not find improper interference.

Many of the cases in this area cover a wide range of actions where one party has made it difficult or impossible for another party to continue in certain or all business dealings. The *Gieseke* case provides an example.

GIESEKE V. IDCA, INC.

Court of Appeals of Minnesota, 826 N.W.2d 816 (2013)

Case Background *Brothers Michael Hogenson (MH) and Arthur Hogenson (AH) owned Standard Water together. Gieseke worked for them. MH and AH got into a dispute and they stopped working together. MH kept Standard and fired Gieseke because he was friendly with AH. Gieseke and AH then started Diversified Water, each owning half. Later, MH bought AH's half interest in Diversified Water and merged that into a*

new company, IDCA, which, MH testified, he wanted to close after settling debts. Without Gieseke's consent, MH changed all business correspondence for Diversified Water to another address and hauled away some of its physical equipment, making it nearly impossible for Gieseke to continue operations.

Gieseke sued MH and IDCA for interference with prospective advantage. The district court awarded

Gieseke $220,000 in damages for that tort. IDCA and MH appealed.

Case Decision Schellhas, Judge

* * *

The [Minnesota Supreme Court] expressly stated, "This state *has recognized* a cause of action for wrongful interference with both present and *prospective* contractual relations." And the court described the elements for "intentional interference with prospective contractual relations" from the *Restatement (Second) on Torts* § 766B (1979). Section 766B broadly defines intentional interference with prospective contractual relations in a way that fully encompasses the subject tort:

> The relations protected against intentional interference by the rule stated in this Section include *any prospective contractual relations,* except those leading to contracts to marry..., if the potential contract would be of pecuniary value to the plaintiff. Included are interferences with the prospect of obtaining employment or employees, the opportunity of selling or buying land or chattels or services, and *any other relations leading to potentially profitable contracts.* Interference with the exercise by a

third party of an option to renew or extend a contract with the plaintiff is also included. *Also included is interference with a continuing business or other customary relationship not amounting to a formal contract....*

The expression, prospective contractual relation, is not used in this Section in a strict, technical sense. *It is not necessary that the prospective relation be expected to be reduced to a formal, binding contract.* It may include prospective quasi-contractual or other restitutionary rights or even the voluntary conferring of commercial benefits in recognition of a moral obligation....

* * *

The jury could reasonably have found that Diversified Water had a reasonable expectation of economic advantage before IDCA interfered with that prospective advantage....

Affirmed.

Questions for Analysis

1. IDCA was part owner of Diversified Water. Did that not give it the right to shut down Diversified?
2. Why do you think MH would go to all the trouble he did with respect to Diversified Water?

ISSUE SPOTTER
Hiring Employees from Competitors

© Cengage Learning

When opening a new office in a new city for your company, a quick way to get qualified employees who know the market is to bid away people now working for competitors. What legal issues in tort could arise in that regard? What precautions should you take if you use this strategy?

Product Liability

Product liability is a general term applied to an area of the law that is primarily tort law but also involves some contract law and statutory law. This concerns the liability that producers and sellers of goods have to those injured by their products. Because some cases involve thousands of people and billions of dollars, product liability gets a lot of media attention and is controversial. Major companies have been bankrupted by product liability decisions. The primary political issue is whether the law has become so strict in assigning liability to producers that the legislature should intervene and set limits on liability. On the one hand, we want companies to have incentives to ensure their products

❓ TEST YOURSELF

1. To establish fraud or intentional misrepresentation, one must show misrepresentation of a(n) _____ fact, and that there was _____ by the plaintiff on the misinformation.
2. In the *Lightle* v. *Real Estate Commission* case, where Seeley's attempt to buy a house through real estate agent Lightle failed, the Alaska high court held that Lightle was not responsible for wrongdoing because the sellers of the house, the Leighs, backed out of the deal: T—F
3. The tort of interference with contractual relations does *not* require which of the following elements:
   a. existence of a contractual relationship between the injured party and another party
   b. that a third party, the alleged wrongdoer, knew of the contractual relationship
   c. the wrongdoer intentionally interfered with the relationship
   d. the injured party sued the other party for breach of contract
   e. all of the other choices are necessary elements to establish the tort
4. In establishing fraud, one must show that the defendant knew there was false information being transmitted; that is called _____.
5. In *Gieseke* v. *ICDA, Inc.*, the Minnesota appeals court held that there was no tort because a defendant cannot be liable for interfering with a company it partly owns: T—F
6. In *Slater Numismatics, LLC* v. *Driving Force, LLC*, where a coin appraisal firm sued a firm established by executives of a company Slater used to work closely with for interference with contractual relations, the appeals court held that Slater had a cause of action for interference: T—F

Answers: material, justifiable reliance; F; d; scienter; F; T.

are safe. On the other hand, we do not want companies to pay for injuries consumers suffer while using products improperly or keep products off the market that are, in net, beneficial.

Holding a company liable for a lawn mower made with improperly exposed blades that injure consumers during normal use is different than holding a company liable for an injury caused by a consumer sticking a hand under a running lawn mower. Producers redesign products in response to liability concerns. "Dead man" switches on lawn mowers, which cut off the engine when the user lets go of the handle, is one such innovation that now prevents some injuries each year. But some consumers found the switches annoying and tie the control to stay in the on-position. Makers have to balance such real-world issues in the design of products. The evolution of the common law of product liability over the past century provides a good example of how the law changes as technology and expectations change.

Consumer Products and Negligence

A century ago, the rule was that a manufacturer was liable for injuries caused by defects in its products only to parties with whom the manufacturer had a contractual relationship. The term **privity of contract** refers to the relationship that exists between contracting parties. It is essential to a contract that privity, a legal relationship, exist between the parties. Since modern consumers rarely buy products directly from manufacturers, there often is no privity between consumer and producer. The requirement of privity arose in a time when people were more likely to buy directly from product makers, before mass production of consumer goods came to dominate. Privity thus effectively isolated most manufacturers from liability for most product-related injuries.

Rule of Caveat Emptor   Injured parties who did not have privity of contract with the manufacturer of the defective products operated under the rule of ***caveat emptor***, which means "let the buyer beware." According to the U.S. Supreme Court, the rule of *caveat emptor* "requires that the buyer examine, judge, and test [the product] for himself." Thus, a consumer without privity took the risk that a product was safe. If a product was not safe and there was an injury, the loss fell on the consumer.

Negligence in Tort   The privity rule often left innocent, injured consumers without any remedy. In response to the harsh result the rule could impose, the courts began to recognize exceptions. Then, in 1916, in the famous *MacPherson* decision, New York's highest court eliminated the privity requirement and held a manufacturer liable in tort for negligence for a product-related injury to a consumer despite the lack of privity. This case is still good law today.

MACPHERSON V. BUICK MOTOR COMPANY

Court of Appeals of New York, 217 N.Y. 382, 111 N.E. 1050 (1916)

Case Background *Buick produced cars and sold them to dealers. MacPherson bought a new Buick from a dealer in New York. The wheels on MacPherson's car were made by another company for Buick. Soon after he bought the car, one of the wheels collapsed, causing an accident that injured MacPherson, who sued Buick.*

His suit against Buick traditionally would have been barred because of lack of privity. That is, Buick sold the car to the dealer. The dealer then sold the car to MacPherson. The dealer had a contract with MacPherson but the dealer was not responsible for the defect and MacPherson had no privity with Buick. Nevertheless, the lower courts ruled for MacPherson, finding Buick liable in tort for injuries caused by the defect. Buick appealed to the highest court in New York.

Case Decision Cardozo, Justice

* * *

One of the wheels was made of defective wood, and its spokes crumbled into fragments. The wheel was not made by the defendant; it was bought from another manufacturer. There is evidence, however, that its defects could have been discovered by reasonable inspection, and that inspection was omitted. There is no claim that Buick knew of the defect and willfully concealed it.... The charge is one, not of fraud, but of negligence. The question to be determined is whether the defendant owed a duty of care and vigilance to anyone but the immediate purchaser.

* * *

If the nature of a thing is such that it is reasonably certain to place life and limb in peril when negligently made, it is then a thing of danger. Its nature gives warning of the consequences to be expected. If to the element of danger there is added knowledge that the thing will be used by persons other than the purchaser, and used without new tests, then, irrespective of contract, the manufacturer of this thing of danger is under a duty to make it carefully. That is as far as we are required to go for the decision of this case. There must be knowledge of a danger, not merely possible, but probable.... We are dealing now with the liability of the manufacturer of the finished product, who puts it on the market to be used without inspection by his customers. If he is negligent, where danger is to be foreseen, a liability will follow.

* * *

We think the defendant was not absolved from a duty of inspection because it bought the wheels from a reputable manufacturer. It was not merely a dealer in automobiles. It was a manufacturer of automobiles. It was responsible for the finished product. It was not at liberty to put the finished product on the market without subjecting the component parts to ordinary and simple tests. Under the charge of the trial judge, nothing more was required of it. The obligation to inspect must vary with the

nature of the thing to be inspected. The more probable the danger, the greater the need of caution.

* * *

The judgment should be affirmed.

Questions for Analysis

1. The court held Buick liable in tort for negligence in manufacturing a product with a danger. Buick argued that it should not be liable because it did not make the wheels. Why not make the injured party sue the producer of the defective part?
2. Buick argued that this was the only wheel out of 60,000 sold (15,000 cars) that had been shown defective. Should 1/60,000 be sufficient to establish negligence?

Manufacturers must produce products using proper care to eliminate foreseeable harm or risk being found negligent in tort if a consumer is injured by a defective product. The rule originating with *MacPherson*, and adopted in every state in the following decades, can be summarized:

> *The manufacturer of a product is liable in the production and sale of a product for negligence, if the product may reasonably be expected to inflict harm on the user if the product is defective.*

A manufacturer is required to exercise **reasonable care** in the production of its product. Liability may be imposed on a manufacturer for negligence in the preparation of the

INTERNATIONAL PERSPECTIVE

Is Japan Really Different?

Some politicians want legislation to restrict tort litigation. Japan is often cited as an example of where there is less litigation and fewer lawyers. This is claimed to make Japan more cost competitive than the United States, where tort cases are claimed to be out of control.

The United States has 25 times more lawyers per person than Japan because the government of Japan allows only between 300 and 500 new attorneys to be licensed each year. However, Japanese universities produce 50 percent more legal specialists per person than do American universities. These Japanese "non-lawyers" do all legal work except represent clients in

court for a fee. Although the non-lawyers are not called lawyers, they are paid to do what Americans call legal work.

A study of fatal traffic accidents in Japan by American and Japanese law professors found that the American and Japanese tort systems are not that different. The systems are organized differently, but the results are much the same. Japanese plaintiffs win a higher percentage of tort liability suits than do American plaintiffs. Payments to Japanese plaintiffs are close to those given to American plaintiffs in similar suits. A close examination makes the actual operation of the two tort systems look more alike than is often claimed.

product—for failing to inspect or test the materials used in the product, for below-normal-quality workmanship, or for failing to discover possible defects. Defects must be revealed even if the manufacturer becomes aware of them after the sale of the product. Reasonable care must also be taken in presenting the product to the public—through advertisements or other promotions—to avoid misrepresentation.

If a causal connection can be established between the failure of the manufacturer to exercise reasonable care in any of these areas and an injury suffered by a consumer, liability based on negligence for damages may be imposed on the manufacturer. Producers are responsible for damages inflicted in such cases and punitive damages may be added.

Lighter Side **of the Law**

You Can't Be Too Careful

Multiple websites provide examples of highly dubious warning labels:

- On the underside of a cereal bowl: Always use this product with adult supervision.
- On a washing machine: DO NOT put any person in this washer.
- On the wheels of a skateboard: Warning: This product moves when used.
- On Scrubbing Bubbles bathroom cleaner: Not a body wash.
- On the Yellow Pages: Please do not use this directory while operating a moving vehicle.
- On a gas can: Never use a lit match or open flame to check fuel level.

© Cengage Learning 2015

Strict Liability under Contract Law

Negligence in tort meant more injured consumers recovered than when privity was required to have a chance for recovery. Nevertheless, the law did not provide relief for all injured consumers in product-related cases. Injured parties sometimes had a hard time showing that manufacturers had not exercised reasonable care in the production of their product, in part because the evidence about the product usually belonged to the manufacturer, making it hard for plaintiffs to know whether there had been negligence or not.

The **strict liability** doctrine resolved this by holding manufacturers liable to consumers injured by defective products regardless of whether the manufacturer had been negligent. Thus, the injured party is not required to attack the reasonableness of the conduct of the manufacturer, but rather focus on product problems.

Strict liability was first applied to product-related injuries through a warranty theory under contract law. Later, the adoption of strict liability in tort by the American Law Institute in the authoritative *Restatement (Second) of Torts* helped spur the adoption of strict liability in tort. We now have a mix of contract law and tort law applied in product liability cases.

Strict liability under contract law is based on the relationship between the injured party and the manufacturer because of the existence of a **warranty**. A warranty is a manufacturer's assurance that a product will meet certain quality and performance standards. Such warranties may be either expressed or implied. An **express warranty** is when the manufacturer contractually provides performance promises to the consumer. An **implied warranty** is when the law inserts quality standards into the relationship regardless of the actual contract terms.

ISSUE SPOTTER
Understanding Product Problems

Your company makes products that are sometimes involved in consumer injuries. What would you suggest doing with respect to managing the information about defects so that the company can better understand its products' problems and address them more quickly? Is there a systematic way to deal with the problem?

Strict Liability Based on Implied Warranty The first applications of the doctrine of strict liability for defective consumer products were in the area of food and drink. For example, in a 1913 case from the state of Washington, *Mazetti* v. *Armour* (135 P. 633), the court held "a manufacturer of food products ... impliedly warrants his goods when dispensed in original packages." Consumer injury caused by defective food or drink is a breach of implied warranty of safety, and the manufacturer is strictly liable for the injury.

The Supreme Court of New Jersey extended implied warranty of safety to other consumer products in a decision in 1960. In *Henningsen* v. *Bloomfield Motors* (161 A.2d 69), the New Jersey court held the manufacturer of an automobile strictly liable to the buyer's wife for her injuries when the brakes failed and an accident occurred.

Strict Liability Based on Express Warranty Strict liability under contract law is also applied in cases in which a manufacturer makes an express warranty about its products to consumers. Manufacturers often advertise quality or performance characteristics of their products. When such claims become part of the bargain between a manufacturer and a consumer, the manufacturer is held to have a duty of performance as to that representation.

Strict liability based on an express warranty does not require that injured consumers have purchased the product directly from the manufacturer. The courts have long allowed the consumer to sue the manufacturer, not the retail dealer. Injured consumers are not required to prove fault because the law requires manufacturers to guarantee the truthfulness of their representations. **Misrepresentation** about a product may be the basis for strict liability in tort.

For example, back in 1932, Ford was found liable for failing to provide a shatterproof windshield on a car. As a result, a driver lost an eye when a rock hit the windshield and the glass shattered. [*Baxter* v. *Ford Motor*, 12 P.2d 409] The contract for sale did not say the car had a shatterproof windshield, but Ford advertised that the car had that safety feature. The court held the advertisement created an express warranty of safety that Ford breached when it failed to provide the safety glass. An express warranty was a part of the contract in the sale of the car because of the advertising promise made to consumers.

Strict Liability in Tort

Strict liability may be imposed today under contract law. This can be the basis for a strong liability suit. However, the plaintiff can be faced with the problem of showing a warranty existed. In response to such difficulties, the courts simplified the legal basis for injured plaintiffs by adopting the rule of strict liability in tort. In the *Greenman* decision, the Supreme Court of California was the first court to adopt a general rule of strict liability in tort in product injury cases.

GREENMAN V. YUBA POWER PRODUCTS

Supreme Court of California 7 Cal.Rptr. 697, 377 P.2d 897 (1963)

Case Background *Greenman's wife bought him a Shopsmith—a power tool that could be used as a saw, drill, and wood lathe. Greenman had studied material about the product and asked his wife to buy it. Two years later, while Greenman was using the machine, a piece of wood flew out of the machine and struck him on the forehead, inflicting serious injuries.*

Greenman sued the manufacturer, Shopsmith, and the retail dealer, Yuba Power, alleging breaches of warranties and negligence. The verdict in Greenman's favor against Shopsmith was appealed.

Case Decision Traynor, Justice

* * *

Plaintiff introduced substantial evidence that his injuries were caused by defective design and construction of the Shopsmith. His expert witnesses testified that inadequate set screws were used to hold parts of the machine together so that normal vibration caused the tailstock of the lathe to move away from the piece of wood being turned, permitting it to fly out of the lathe. They also testified that there were other more positive ways of fastening the parts of the machine together, the use of which would have prevented the accident. ...

A manufacturer is strictly liable in tort when an article he places on the market, knowing that it is to be used without inspection for defects, proves to have a defect that causes injury to a human being. Recognized first in the case of unwholesome food products, such liability has now been extended to a variety of other products that create as great or greater hazards if defective.

* * *

The purpose of such liability is to insure that the costs of injuries resulting from defective products

are borne by the manufacturers that put such products on the market rather than by the injured persons who are powerless to protect themselves. Sales warranties serve this purpose fitfully at best. ... Implicit in the machine's presence on the market, however, was a representation that it would safely do the jobs for which it was built. Under these circumstances, it should not be controlling whether plaintiff selected the machine because of the statements in the brochure, or because of the machine's own appearance of excellence that belied the defect lurking beneath the surface, or because he merely assumed that it would safely do the jobs it was built to do. It should not be controlling whether the details of the sales from manufacturer to retailer and from retailer to Greenman's wife were such that one or more of the implied warranties of the sales act arose. The remedies of injured consumers ought not to be made to depend upon the intricacies of the law of sales. To establish the manufacturer's liability it was sufficient that plaintiff proved that he was injured while using the Shopsmith in a way it was intended to be used as a result of a defect in design and manufacture, of which plaintiff was not aware, that made the Shopsmith unsafe for its intended use.

* * *

The judgment is affirmed.

Questions for Analysis

1. The court adopted the rule of strict liability in tort. What is the advantage of this compared to strict liability imposed on the basis of implied warranty in contract?
2. Would strict liability be imposed on the manufacturer if a friend of Greenman's had used the machine and was hurt while using it?

Section 402A In the *Restatement (Second) of Torts*, the American Law Institute adopted a strict liability in tort rule in product injury cases similar to that imposed in *Greenman*. This helped bring about nationwide acceptance of the strict liability in tort rule. The *Restatement's* strict liability in tort rule is found in Section 402A:

(1) One who sells any product in a defective condition unreasonably dangerous to the user or consumer, or to his property, is subject to liability for physical harm thereby caused to the ultimate user or consumer, or to his property, if
   (a) the seller is engaged in the business of selling such a product, and
   (b) it is expected to and does reach the user or consumer without substantial change in the condition in which it is sold.
(2) The rule stated in Subsection (1) applies, although
   (a) the seller has exercised all possible care in the preparation and sale of his product, and
   (b) the user or consumer has not bought the product from or entered into any contractual relation with the seller.

While this is still the law in most states, as we see next, the standard appears to be evolving.

Lighter Side of the Law

I'm From the FBI; I Know the Law

FBI Special Agent Clymer jumped the curb with his pickup and was found in it, passed out drunk—his blood alcohol was 0.306—after it caught fire, along with an empty bottle of rum. Police pulled him from the vehicle.

Clymer claims he stopped along the road to make a call, had the pickup in Park, then "somehow lost consciousness," and the truck "somehow produced a heavy smoke that filled the passenger cab." He sued Chevy and the Chevy dealer who sold him the truck for selling him a defective vehicle.

Source: Las Vegas Review-Journal.

Restatement (Third) of Torts *on Products Liability* The American Law Institute's (ALI) definition of strict liability in Section 402A of the *Restatement (Second) of Torts* has been the leading rule adopted by states to define liability for product-related injury. Over the years, a review of court decisions applying Section 402A led the ALI to revise the standard in its newer *Restatement (Third) of Torts*. The new language is proving influential with courts. Section 2 of the *Restatement (Third) of Torts* expresses a key part of product liability as follows:

Section 2. Categories of Product Defect A product is defective when, at the time of sale or distribution, it contains a manufacturing defect, is defective in design, or is defective because of inadequate instructions or warnings. A product:

(a) contains a manufacturing defect when the product departs from its intended design even though all possible care was exercised in the preparation and marketing of the product;

(b) is defective in design when the foreseeable risks of harm posed by the product could have been reduced or avoided by the adoption of a reasonable alternative design by the seller or other distributor, or a predecessor in the commercial chain of distribution, and the omission of the alternative design renders the product not reasonably safe;

(c) is defective because of inadequate instructions or warnings when the foreseeable risks of harm posed by the product could have been reduced or avoided by the provision of reasonable instructions or warnings by the seller or other distributor, or a predecessor in the commercial chain of distribution, and the omission of the instructions or warnings renders the product not reasonably safe.

Although Section 2 is a refinement rather than a major change from Section 402A of the *Restatement (Second)*, the newer version focuses on what it calls "risk-utility balancing." That is, some products cannot be made completely safe. For example, gasoline is explosive and its use as a fuel requires it to be so. Carrying a tankful of explosive fuel in a car means there are risks, but those risks are necessary for gasoline to serve its function. If gasoline could not explode, its utility would be lost. So the courts consider the reality of technology, costs, and use in practice.

The *Restatement (Third)* also encourages courts to move away from the distinction between negligence and strict liability. The focus is on functionality, not traditional categories, so all producers are expected, given the risks and utility of their products, to meet the standard expressed in Section 2 of the *Restatement (Third)*. Although the *Restatement* expresses a trend in the law, recognition of its new language by courts takes time. Iowa's Supreme Court, for example, has expressly adopted the newer version of product liability; others are exploring the matter. It will not cause a great change in the impact of the law in practice because the kinds of cases will remain much the same. That is what we turn to now.

Primary Areas of Product Liability Law

We refer to strict liability in tort, as that is still the most common way to discuss liability for defective products, although *Restatement (Third)* just calls this product defect law. In either case, the chain of events needed to establish liability in tort is outlined in Exhibit 7.2. There are four key areas: (1) a defect in the product from manufacturing; (2) the manufacturer failed to warn the consumer of risks of use or of known hazards in certain uses of the product; (3) the product had a design defect in it that could have been avoided; and (4) the product resulted in latent injuries that may not become known for years. We consider each of these areas in turn.

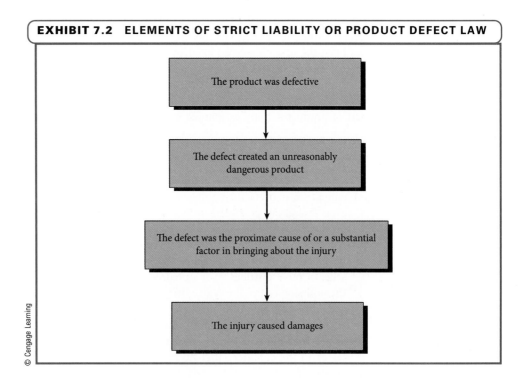

EXHIBIT 7.2   ELEMENTS OF STRICT LIABILITY OR PRODUCT DEFECT LAW

The product was defective

↓

The defect created an unreasonably dangerous product

↓

The defect was the proximate cause of or a substantial factor in bringing about the injury

↓

The injury caused damages

© Cengage Learning

Manufacturing Defect This area is straightforward, so we spend little time on it. It is what the law was clearly intended to address: someone buys a new toaster, plugs it in, and is electrocuted because of a defect in the product from the manufacturing stage. Consumers do not expect such defects and will be compensated for them. The *Restatement* makes clear that liability is imposed when a product comes off the assembly line with a defect that makes it dangerous to any user. It is other areas of greater uncertainty that we study in more detail next.

Failure to Warn A manufacturer's **failure to warn** consumers of dangers in the use of a product, or to instruct consumers about proper procedures in using a product, has long been actionable. This applies where the manufacturer knows of a danger caused by the product's use that cannot be prevented entirely, but about which users could be warned. For example, lawn mowers now routinely have warning labels telling users not to try to unclog blocked grass discharge chutes while the mower is running.

In cases that fall into this category, the defect in the product is in the failure to warn, not necessarily in the product itself. Failure to warn includes a wide variety of circumstances, from failure to give information about specific dangers, to failure to issue added warnings about problems that become known after a product has been in use for some time, to failure to give special emphasis to the biggest dangers posed by a product. In the *Parish* v. *ICON* case, we see an analysis of the failure to warn claim under the standards of *Restatement (Third) of Torts*.

PARISH V. ICON
Supreme Court of Iowa 719 N.W.2d 540 (2006)

Case Background *Parish was jumping on a backyard trampoline, made by Jumpking, that was surrounded by a safety net, called a fun ring, made by ICON. He did a back somersault but landed on his head and was rendered a quadriplegic. He sued ICON and Jumpking for failure to warn of the dangers involved in using the products. The district court granted summary judgment for the manufacturers; Parish appealed.*

Case Decision Larson, Justice

* * *

Under the *Restatement*, a product is defective because of inadequate instructions or warnings when the foreseeable risks of harm posed by the product could have been reduced or avoided by the provision of reasonable instructions or warnings by the seller or other distributor, or a predecessor in the commercial chain of distribution, and the omission of the instructions or warnings renders the product not reasonably safe. Restatement § 2(c).

The trampoline in this case, and its surrounding fun ring, together provide numerous warnings. Three warnings are placed permanently on the pad of the trampoline and advise the user:

Warning

Do not land on head or neck.

Paralysis or death can result, even if you land in the middle of the trampoline mat (bed).

To reduce the chance of landing on your head or neck, do not do somersaults (flips).

Only one person at a time on trampoline.

Multiple jumpers increase the chances of loss of control, collision, and falling off.

This can result in broken head, neck, back, or leg.

This trampoline is not recommended for children under 6 years of age.

These warnings also include nationally recognized warning symbols cautioning against those activities. During manufacture, Jumpking also places one warning on each of the eight legs of the trampoline, and the design is such that the only way to assemble the trampoline is to have these warnings facing out so they are visible to the user. Jumpking further manufactures two printed (nonpictorial) warnings that are sewn onto the trampoline bed itself. It also provides a warning placard for the owner to affix to the trampoline that contains both the pictorial warning and the language regarding safe use of the trampoline, and it provides an owner's manual that contains the warnings as found on the trampoline, as well as additional warnings regarding supervision and education. It is undisputed that these warnings exceed the warnings required by the American Society for Testing and Material (ASTM)....

Warnings are also provided with the fun ring.... The fun ring comes with a separate owner's manual that provides additional warnings.

The *Restatement* recognizes that users must pay some attention for their own safety:

Society does not benefit from products that are excessively safe—for example, automobiles designed with maximum speeds of 20 miles per hour—any more than it benefits from products that are too risky. Society benefits most when the right, or optimal, amount of

product safety is achieved. *From a fairness perspective, requiring individual users and consumers to bear appropriate responsibility for proper product use prevents careless users and consumers from being subsidized by more careful users and consumers, when the former are paid damages out of funds to which the latter are forced to contribute through higher product prices. Restatement § 2 comment (a) (emphasis added)....*

We conclude that a reasonable fact finder could not conclude that the defendant's warnings were inadequate, and we affirm the district court's summary judgment on that claim.

Affirmed.

Questions for Analysis

1. The Iowa high court held that there was no failure to warn of the dangers of a trampoline, so the maker was not liable for injuries suffered. Could it be that the dangers of such a product are such that it should simply be banned because it is too dangerous and simply cannot be made safe?

2. The plaintiff here was an adult. Would it be different if a small child, who would be less likely to pay attention to the warnings, had been injured?

Manufacturers must warn of possible dangers in the use, storage, and handling of their products. For example, although household cleansers are dangerous and not intended for consumption, manufacturers know that adults often leave such products in places where children might get them. Thus, liability may be imposed for not warning people sufficiently of such dangers and for not taking steps to reduce possible tragedies, such as by using containers that are not attractive to children, using hard-to-remove caps, and putting danger labels or symbols on the containers. How far does the failure-to-warn liability in tort extend? The outside limits of the application are illustrated by the following cases:

- A Pennsylvania court found a gun manufacturer that failed to warn users of damage to hearing from long-term exposure to gunfire was liable for injuries.
- The Supreme Court of Alaska upheld a verdict against a diet food producer that failed to provide adequate warnings about using the adult diet food as baby food. Although the food was safe for dieting adults, it was not for infants because of the low-calorie level, and the company should have stated so on its product.
- New York's highest court held the producer of a commercial pizza dough roller machine liable for injuries suffered by a worker who stuck his hands in the machine when he tried to clean it. Although the machine had a safety switch to be used when cleaning the machine, the worker had turned off the switch so he could stick his

hands in the machine. The manufacturer failed to warn by not clearly explaining the dangers of turning off the switch.

- A jury in a federal court ordered Johnson & Johnson to pay $8.85 million to a man who had to have a liver transplant because years of drinking alcohol and taking Tylenol had destroyed his liver. Johnson & Johnson had not warned Tylenol users that liver damage could occur in heavy drinkers who used Tylenol often.

Design Defects Unlike defective product cases, **design defect** cases are not concerned with a product that has been poorly manufactured and causes an injury. Rather, such cases focus on the determination of whether an injury to users could have been prevented by designing the product differently. In that regard, consider the following design defect cases:

- In a Washington state case, a worker received $750,000 for the loss of a leg. While repairing a machine, coworkers had removed a metal plate from the top of the machine. When they finished, the workers covered the machine with cardboard. The plaintiff walked on what he thought was the metal plate and fell into the machine. The court held that a design defect had allowed the machine to be able to run when the metal plate was removed.
- A restaurant employee was seriously burned when he tried to retrieve something that fell out of his shirt pocket and into a commercial French fryer machine. The D.C. Circuit Court of Appeals reversed a summary judgment for the manufacturer and allowed the case to go to a jury, holding that a jury could find that a safer alternative design of the machine was possible, in which case it could impose liability.
- A child pushed the emergency stop button on an escalator, causing a person to fall and be injured. The Seventh Circuit Court of Appeals ruled that it was a design defect both to make the button red, because that color is attractive to children, and to place the button so that it was accessible to children.
- A group of Chicago firefighters won an award against the maker of sirens used on fire trucks because the sirens caused "excessive exposure to noise" and were, therefore, unreasonably dangerous and defective.

Lighter Side **of the Law**

Reason #4 Why West Virginia Is Considered a Litigation Hellhole

"As long as I am allowed to redistribute wealth from out-of-state companies to injured in-state plaintiffs, I shall continue to do so. Not only is my sleep enhanced when I give someone else's money away, but so is my job security, because the in-state plaintiffs, their families, and their friends will re-elect me."

Source: West Virginia Supreme Court Justice Richard Neely, *The Product Liability Mess*, p. 4.

The court in the *Timpte* case discusses the **risk-utility test** that is often applied in design defect cases.

TIMPTE INDUSTRIES, INC. V. GISH
Supreme Court of Texas 86 S.W.3d 306 (2009)

Case Background *Gish, a trucker, arrived at a plant to pick up a load of fertilizer. His truck pulled a trailer made by Timpte. It is a twin-hopper trailer loaded from above by a downspout that pours fertilizer into the hoppers. Because the downspout was not going into position, Gish climbed on top of the trailer. He walked out along a top rail that is about five inches wide so he could grab the downspout and put it in position to pour in the fertilizer. When he was on the rail, a gust of wind blew and he fell to the ground, suffering severe injuries.*

Gish (and his workers' compensation insurance carrier) sued for design defect contending that the trailer should not have had a ladder that allowed a person to climb up to the rail and that the rail on top of the trailer is too narrow to walk on safely. Timpte argued that the danger of being on the rail was open and obvious. The district court granted summary judgment for Timpte; the appeals court reversed. Timpte appealed.

Case Decision Justice Medina

* * *

To remedy these alleged design defects, Dr. Gary Nelson, Gish's expert witness, proposed three design changes:

- Remove the top two rungs of the ladders attached to the trailer to make it impossible for a person to climb atop the trailer;
- Provide an adequate foothold and handhold at the top of the trailer so that a user on top of the trailer can maintain three-point contact [two feet and one hand] with the trailer at all times; and
- If an adequate handhold cannot be provided, then widen the side rail to at least 12 inches to provide an adequate foothold. ...

To recover for a product liability claim alleging a design defect, a plaintiff must prove that (1) the product was defectively designed so as to render it unreasonably dangerous; (2) a safer alternative design existed; and (3) the defect was a producing cause of the injury for which the plaintiff seeks recovery. To determine whether a product was defectively designed

so as to render it unreasonably dangerous, Texas courts have long applied a risk-utility analysis that requires consideration of the following factors:

(1) the utility of the product to the user and to the public as a whole weighed against the gravity and likelihood of injury from its use; (2) the availability of a substitute product which would meet the same need and not be unsafe or unreasonably expensive; (3) the manufacturer's ability to eliminate the unsafe character of the product without seriously impairing its usefulness or significantly increasing its costs; (4) the user's anticipated awareness of the dangers inherent in the product and their avoidability because of general public knowledge of the obvious condition of the product, or of the existence of suitable warnings or instructions; and (5) the expectations of the ordinary consumer.

The risk-utility analysis does not operate in a vacuum, but rather in the context of the product's intended use and its intended users. ...

The focus of a design defect claim ... is whether there was a reasonable alternative design that, at a reasonable cost, would have reduced a foreseeable risk of harm. ...

The risk-utility factors here confirm that the design of the Super Hopper trailer was not defective as a matter of law. Timpte warned users to always maintain three-point contact with the trailer, which is impossible for a user standing on the top rail. Had Gish adhered to this warning, his accident would not have happened. Additionally, widening the side walls of the trailer so as to convert the top rail into a safe walkway, as Gish's expert proposed, would have increased the cost and weight of the trailer while decreasing its utility. ... The width of the top rail of the Super Hopper trailer is therefore not a design defect that renders the trailer unreasonably dangerous.

There is also no evidence that the top two rungs of the ladder are a design defect that renders the trailer unreasonably dangerous. Thompson testified that the top two rungs are necessary to maintain the structure and stability of the ladder when the side rails are under pressure; without them, the ladder could twist or bend. Additionally, even though Timpte warned users to use the side rails of the ladder as a handhold when climbing the ladder, were a user's hands to slip, the additional rungs provided additional handholds and an additional measure of safety....

Because there is no evidence that the design defects alleged by Gish rendered the trailer unreasonably dangerous, we reverse the court of appeals' judgment and render judgment reinstating the trial court's summary judgment.

Questions for Analysis

1. What could Gish have done to protect himself better from the risk, given what he was trying to accomplish?
2. This is a commercial truck trailer. Would the risk-utility analysis be likely to produce the same result if this were a consumer product?

Unknown Hazards   The largest dollar volume and greatest number of product liability cases are based on **unknown hazards** or latent defects—dangers that were not known or not fully appreciated at the time the product was manufactured. Because the hazard associated with the product may not be learned for years, neither the producer nor the consumer may be able to prevent injury.

Tens of billions of dollars have been awarded in tens of thousands of claims (often joined as class actions) involving the health effects of asbestos, injuries caused by IUDs, and damage caused by drug side effects that did not appear for years. The single largest area of litigation for unknown hazard has involved asbestos. Companies in the asbestos industry, of which dozens have filed for bankruptcy-court protection, have devoted more than $100 billion to help resolve litigation that has been proceeding for more than 40 years. Although hundreds of thousands of plaintiffs have agreed to settlements, many more have not reached resolution. How to deal with a huge number of injured parties, all with large claims that sometimes involve generic products, has been a struggle for the courts.

Joint and Several Liability   Most states have held that plaintiffs may sue any or all of the manufacturers of a defective product where the identity of the actual manufacturer is not clear, as is the case with asbestos. The manufacturers are then allowed to fight it out among themselves as to which should pay the damages. This is termed **joint and several liability**. It may be applied where two or more defendants are found liable for damages. The plaintiff may collect the entire judgment from any one of the defendants or from any and all of the defendants in varying amounts until the judgment is paid. If the plaintiff sues one company, it may then seek to recover a share of the damages from the others, but the company sued must pay the plaintiffs' damages.

Suppose there are a dozen defendants in a suit, and all are held liable. If all are insolvent except one, the one defendant with money may have to pay the entire judgment. Plaintiffs obviously have an incentive to make sure a defendant in a suit has "deep pockets" so there can be collection of a judgment. This has resulted in limits on the application of joint and several liability in some areas, such as medical malpractice, in many states.

ISSUE SPOTTER
Cheaper Can Be More Expensive

In the supply chain, your company may find suppliers in China or Vietnam that offer to provide inputs at lower cost than would domestic suppliers. You can write careful contracts specifying the quality of materials that must be used to make sure you meet U.S. safety standards. But things can go wrong that result in tort liability. Can you protect yourself against shoddy inputs?

Defenses in Product Liability Suits

Strict liability and the rule of negligence hold manufacturers to a high standard of product safety. This does not mean absolute liability. Manufacturers are generally not liable if the consumer has engaged in improper activity that increases the risk of injury. Most courts recognize product misuse and assumption of risk as defenses in product-related injury cases. Some other defenses to tort actions were discussed in Chapter 6. The rules vary somewhat from state to state, and regulations may also affect liability.

Product Misuse If it can be shown that the product was misused, combined with another product to make it dangerous, used in some improper and unforeseen manner, or not maintained properly, the injured consumer's behavior may preclude recovery for damages.

In one case, the court barred recovery by plaintiffs who were injured when the blowout of a fairly new tire was shown to be caused by plaintiff over-inflating the tires. The court noted, "To hold otherwise would be to convert a strict liability cause of action into one of absolute liability." In another case, drunkenness by a consumer was held to have led to product misuse that resulted in injury.

Assumption of Risk As we saw in the last chapter, one may consent to assume risk. Playing contact sports and engaging in many other activities that can lead to injury are voluntary choices that include a chance of injury. Certain consumer products are unavoidably dangerous, such that so long as the risks are understood, consumers are presumed to accept the bad with the good. Medicinal drugs are understood to be inherently

INTERNATIONAL PERSPECTIVE

Asbestos Litigation in the United States and United Kingdom

Asbestos, a naturally occurring mineral, was widely used as a fire retardant in construction and consumer products. Unfortunately, it is also a carcinogen that causes lung cancer and other debilitating lung conditions. Some of the dangers of asbestos use were known decades ago but little was done about it.

By the mid-1970s, litigation over asbestos-exposure claims exploded; by the twenty-first century more than 850,000 individual claimants had sued over 8,400 defendants, including manufacturers, distributors, installers, and sellers of asbestos-containing products and owners of properties in which asbestos was present. Asbestos litigation has resulted in the bankruptcy reorganizations of many defendants and changing the interpretation of insurance contracts to hold insurers liable for additional claims.

The scale of American asbestos litigation is difficult to comprehend. Its scope has spread well beyond the makers of asbestos products to virtually all parts of the U.S. economy. The scale of its cost dwarfs that of natural disasters or the most significant regulations; former U.S. Attorney General Griffin Bell contends that asbestos litigation's costs are greater than the estimates of the costs of "all Superfund cleanup sites combined, Hurricane Andrew, or the September 11 terrorist attacks."

Some asbestos firms were not American companies, and here we can see a major difference between U.S. and foreign laws. In one famous case, Cape, a UK-based company, was sued in U.S. courts by plaintiffs alleging injury from asbestos sold by a U.S. sales company affiliated with Cape. The UK company ignored the U.S. suit, and the plaintiffs obtained a default judgment against it. Because the U.S. sales company had no assets and the UK company had no assets in the United States, the plaintiffs took their judgment to the UK courts for enforcement.

UK law did not recognize the theory adopted in the United States however, and so the UK court refused to enforce the judgment. The court held that, to collect against Cape, the U.S. plaintiffs would have to sue Cape under UK law. Then Cape would have defenses not available to it under U.S. law and the "loser pays" rule for attorneys' fees would be a powerful deterrent to suit.

dangerous. Most have known side effects about which physicians and consumers should be informed, but we must accept the fact that given the current state of scientific knowledge, these beneficial products cannot be made safer.

Another class of goods, which are more controversial, are products such as tobacco and alcohol that inflict well-known undesirable side effects. If a person smokes cigarettes for 40 years and contracts lung cancer, should the cigarette producer be liable? If a person drinks large quantities of alcohol for years and develops cirrhosis of the liver, should the liquor industry be liable? In general, the courts have said no; the persons using the cigarettes and alcohol know of the risks involved and should bear the costs. It is not hard to imagine the impact on the liquor and cigarette industries if they were held liable for health problems believed to be associated with the use of their products.

Bulk-Supplier Doctrine and Sophisticated User Defense These defenses usually apply in business settings. The **bulk-supplier doctrine** holds that when a supplier sells a product to an intermediary in bulk, the supplier can discharge its duty to warn the ultimate users if it provides adequate instructions to the distributor next in line, or determines that the intermediary party is adequately trained in the use of the product. The bulk supplier has a duty to take reasonable steps to ensure that its buyer is knowledgeable and equipped to provide warnings to the ultimate users, but it does not have to police the details of what is done as the product continues down the chain of use.

Similarly, the **sophisticated user** (or knowledgeable purchaser) defense, as the Massachusetts high court explains, relieves a manufacturer of liability for failing to warn of a product's characteristics or dangers when "the end user knows or reasonably should know of a product's dangers" (852 N.E.2d 100). This is similar to the more traditional open-and-obvious doctrine—no warning is needed when the danger is obvious.

For example, employees at Tinker Air Force Base in Oklahoma sued several suppliers of chemicals to the Air Force for toxic tort arising out of exposure to chemicals. The appeals court upheld the dismissal of the case. "Because of the wealth of research available, the ability of the Air Force to conduct studies, and its extremely knowledgeable staff, we find that the Air Force easily qualifies as a 'knowledgeable purchaser' that should have known the risks involved with low-level chemical exposure. Employees of the Air Force are also deemed to possess the necessary level of sophistication, so that defendants had no duty to warn the Air Force or its employees of the potential hazards" (156 F.3d 1030).

Statutory Limits on Liability

Various laws are specifically designed to limit potential tort liability:

- Worker compensation statutes usually make that program the exclusive remedy for injured workers, unless an intentional tort was involved.
- Federal regulations that prescribe maximum allowable radiation exposure levels set the standard of care upon which liability is based.
- As government contractors, manufacturers of products made to government specifications may be immune from product liability.
- Products that must follow federal regulations regarding label requirements, including warnings of possible injuries, may not be subject to common-law failure-to-warn actions although such defenses are limited.
- State laws may specify limits on liability, such as Colorado's statutory limits on the liability of ski resorts for injuries suffered by skiers.

Lighter Side **of the Law**

Busted!

Michigan judge Robert Colombo quashed thousands of apparently bogus lawsuits for asbestos-related injuries. The principal examining doctor, Michael Kelly, had diagnosed injuries on 7,323 patients' X-rays over 15 years (at $500 each). His detection rate of abnormalities was 58 times the detection rate by independent radiologists.

The judge found that Kelly was neither a radiologist nor a pulmonologist and had failed the certification test for reading X-rays. The day Judge Colombo commenced the investigation of the X-ray evidence, the plaintiffs' attorneys withdrew all lawsuits except one.

Source: Wall Street Journal.

Ultrahazardous Activity

Long before the development of strict liability for defective products, the common law had developed a rule of strict liability for injuries resulting from **ultrahazardous** (or abnormally dangerous) **activity**. This rule, which is in effect in most states, goes back to the 1868 British case, *Rylands* v. *Fletcher*. The *Restatement of Torts* defines such activity as one that "necessarily involves a risk of serious harm to the person, land, or chattels of another, which cannot be eliminated by the exercise of the utmost care" and "is not a matter of common usage."

This rule has applied to such things as blasting with explosives, allowing chemicals to seep into water supplies, crop dusting, and transporting chemicals in a city. Actually, most of these activities are not all that uncommon, but they are ultrahazardous. The party in charge of such acts is generally responsible for whatever happens that is logically related.

As the Kansas high court explained in a case (287 P.3d 214) involving groundwater contamination from an oil refinery, "The general rule imposing strict liability in tort law for abnormally dangerous activities provides: (a) one who carries on abnormally dangerous activity is subject to liability for harm to the person, land, or chattels of another resulting from the activity, although he or she has exercised the utmost care to prevent the harm; and (b) this strict liability is limited to the kind of harm the possibility of which makes the activity abnormally dangerous."

Does Product Liability Need Reform?

We started the chapter by noting the big dollars that can be involved in tort suits. The numbers can be high, but injuries can produce medical expenses in the millions of dollars. While we hear of juries that award massive sums, many of those startling figures are greatly reduced or thrown out by the trial judge or by the appeals court. Does a costly tort system make American firms less competitive than foreign firms? Not likely, as any company selling products in the United States must meet the same liability standard. The high standard of safety that has evolved becomes the standard for products marketed in much of Europe and Japan because markets are increasingly global. Chinese companies, wanting increased access to world markets, have had to improve quality to meet the high standards demanded in wealthy nations.

What has been called a "tort crisis" has abated in recent years as the Supreme Court has cracked down on massive punitive damage awards and doubtful expert testimony. There has also been reform legislation from Congress to make class-action suits more difficult, and state laws have capped liability for certain damages. Tort payouts, which had been growing rapidly since the 1970s, may have stabilized. In recent years, the growth seems to have stopped.

Tort litigation involving companies continues to be a flashpoint in the law, as injured people seek relief from what they see as heartless companies not caring about ordinary people. On the other side, firms subject to dubious suits feel wronged as they devote resources to fending off deep-pocket tort litigators. In the middle are the courts, attempting to continue to craft a set of fair rules for all.

? TEST YOURSELF

1. Major defenses in product liability suits include _____ and _____.
2. In *Parish* v. *ICON*, where a serious injury was suffered on a trampoline, the Iowa high court held that the maker of the trampoline was:
   a. liable for defective product under the *Restatement (Second) of Torts*.
   b. liable for defective product under the *Restatement (Third) of Torts*.
   c. not liable due to lack of privity with the injured party.
   d. not liable due to adequate warnings of the dangers involved.
3. Strict liability in tort for a defective product requires showing that the producer failed to exercise all possible care in the preparation and marketing of the product: T—F
4. The *Greenman* v. *Yuba Power Products* case is noteworthy because it was the first case where a state supreme court adopted a general rule of strict liability in tort in product injury cases: T—F
5. In *MacPherson* v. *Buick Motor Company*, where MacPherson was injured when a defective wheel on his Buick collapsed, the New York high court held that Buick:
   a. could be held liable for negligence in tort.
   b. could be held liable in tort on the theory of strict liability for defective product.
   c. could not be held liable; the wheel maker was liable.
   d. could not be held liable because of abuse of the wheel by MacPherson.
6. The old rule "let the buyer beware" is _____.
7. The courts have held that for strict liability to apply to a producer, there must have been some knowledge of the problem at the time the product was made and distributed: T—F
8. If a firm sells a large quantity of toxic chemicals to another firm, which uses the chemical in its production process, and an employee of that firm is injured by the chemical, there may be a defense called _____ or the sophisticated user defense.

Answers: misuse, assumption of risk; d; F; T; a; caveat emptor; F; bulk-supplier doctrine.

SUMMARY

- Misrepresentation, or fraud, is a general category of tort that can be intentional or based on negligence. When intentional, it must be shown that there was an intent to provide misleading information to convince someone to do something they would not have otherwise, and that the party had

good reason to rely on the deceit, which was then the cause of a loss suffered.

- The tort of interference with contractual relations occurs when ongoing contractual deals are wrongfully and knowingly interfered with by another party who wants the existing contract to be broken.

- Interference with prospective advantage or prospective economic advantage is an unreasonable interference in another party's business dealings so as to prevent an ongoing relationship from succeeding.
- The rule of negligence in tort dominated product liability the first half of the twentieth century. Still good law, it requires producers to take the care of a reasonable person when making products to prevent foreseeable injury. The reasonable person is held to the skill of an expert in the industry.
- Strict liability for defective products began in contract law based on implied warranty inferred by the courts from a review of the parties' dealings or based on express warranty about the quality of a product.
- Strict liability in tort became widely accepted after the 1963 *Greenman* decision in California. Section 402A of the *Restatement (Second) of Torts* imposes strict liability on the manufacturer when a "product in a defective condition unreasonably dangerous to the user or consumer or to his property" is sold. Besides a flaw in the product at the time of manufacture, strict liability is imposed for failure to warn of hazards in using the product and for defects in the design of the product that make it less safe than it could reasonably be.
- The newer *Restatement (Third) of Torts*, Section 2, regarding product defects, moves away from a distinction between strict liability and negligence. In assigning liability, it encourages the use of a risk-utility analysis for products that are defective at the time of manufacture as a result of poor design or failure to warn of dangers.
- Many strict liability suits have concerned unknown hazards, such as those associated with asbestos, where the danger did not become known until many years later. When claims of thousands of persons exceed the funds of the defendants, the courts strive to find fair ways to allocate money among claimants. When many companies have made the same product, they may be held jointly and severally liable, potentially requiring all producers to pay compensation.
- A defense that may be raised in product liability suits is negligence by the user, which can include product misuse. There also can be assumption of risk by the consumer, especially for products, such as medicinal drugs, that are beneficial but have unavoidable side effects and products, such as tobacco and alcohol, that are legal but have bad effects. Producers do not have to constantly warn sophisticated buyers, such as producers, about all dangers in products.
- Strict liability in tort has long been imposed on those who engage in ultrahazardous activities, such as using explosives, and on those who handle unusually dangerous substances, such as toxic chemicals. If the party involved in the ultrahazardous activity causes an injury to an innocent party, regardless of the degree of care taken to prevent harm, liability is imposed.

TERMS TO KNOW

fraud, 167
intentional misrepresentation, 167
misstatement, 167
material fact, 167
scienter, 168
privity, 168
damages, 168
interference with contract, 168
interference with prospective
   advantage, 171

product liability, 172
privity of contract, 173
caveat emptor, 174
reasonable care, 175
strict liability, 176
warranty, 176
express warranty, 176
implied warranty, 176
misrepresentation, 177
failure to warn, 181

design defect, 183
risk-utility test, 183
unknown hazard, 185
joint and several liability, 186
bulk-supplier doctrine, 187
sophisticated user, 187
ultrahazardous activity, 188

DISCUSSION QUESTION

Refer to Section 402A of the *Restatement (Second) of Torts*: What does "the seller is engaged in the business of selling such a product" mean? Who is excluded by this? What does "it is expected to and does reach the user or consumer without substantial change in the condition in which it is sold" mean? What situations does this cover? What is the difference between the idea that the rule applies although "the seller has exercised all possible care in the preparation and sale of his product" and the rule of negligence? What does "the user or consumer has not bought the product from or entered into any contractual relation with the seller" mean?

CASE QUESTIONS

1. The buyers of residential property mistakenly believed that the 3.5 acres of land included a well, which they later found out was not on the property. The previous owner and the real estate agent had pointed out the well, but had not stated that it was on the property. The buyers did not examine the existing survey of the property, nor did they order a new survey done. Did the buyers have a basis for a suit for fraud? [*Crawford* v. *Williams*, 375 S.E.2d 223, Sup. Ct., Ga. (1989)]

2. Eating bags of microwave popcorn for years is claimed to cause "popcorn" lung from inhalation of the flavoring used on the popcorn. Plaintiffs with the medical problem sued the popcorn makers and the maker of the flavoring. The flavoring maker asserted it was not liable under the bulk-supplier defense. Would that apply? [*Daughetee* v. *Chr. Hansen, Inc.*, 2013 WL 828126, N.D. Iowa (2013)]
   ✓ Check your answer

3. Overstock and SmartBargains (SB) both sold brand-name products through their websites. Overstock sued SB, complaining that pop-up ads for SB appeared when customers accessed Overstock's website. Overstock contended the ads were a tortious interference with prospective economic advantage. Was there a tort? [*Overstock.com* v. *SmartBargains*, 192 P.3d 858, Sup. Ct., Utah (2008)]

4. Florida land developer Lehigh would show prospective buyers Lehigh Acres and have the buyers stay at its motel. Competitor Azar would watch for the buyers, contact them at the motel, tell them that under federal law they had three days to cancel any contract with Lehigh, and then show them less expensive property that he was selling. What tort could apply in this circumstance? [*Azar* v. *Lehigh Corp.*, 364 So.2d 860, Dist. Ct. App., Fla. (1978)]
   ✓ Check your answer

5. Woeste ate raw oysters at a restaurant and died a week later from the bacteria *Vibrio vulnificus*. The bacteria naturally occur in oysters from warm water. *Vibrio* has no effect on most people, but can be fatal to people with a weak immune system—as Woeste had as a result of Hepatitis C and cirrhosis of the liver. The restaurant menu warned of the danger of eating raw oysters, especially for persons with "chronic illness of the liver." Woeste ordered without reading the menu warning. His estate sued the restaurant and the Texas company that harvested the oysters for negligence and strict liability. Would they have a good case? [*Woeste* v. *Washington Plaform Saloon*, 836 N.E.2d 52, Ct. App., Ohio (2005)]

6. Some crimes involve the use of cheap handguns. Sellers of such handguns know that some of these guns will be used in crimes by the purchaser or by a criminal who steals the gun. Could the producers and retailers of such handguns be held liable for the injuries suffered by persons shot during a crime? That is, could such a producer be held strictly liable or negligent for selling a "defective" product in that one of its known end uses is crime? [See *Patterson* v. *Rohm Geselkchaft*, 608 F.Supp. 1206, N.D. Tex. (1985)]
   ✓ Check your answer

7. Wilspec and DunAn both produce parts for air conditioning (AC) units. Wilspec contracted with DunAn, a Chinese corporation, for it to make certain parts for AC units sold in North America. The DunAn parts were to be sold under the Wilspec name and Wilspec would be the exclusive distributor in North America. Wilspec claimed that DunAn then solicited the sale of products to Wilspec's customers in North America and made disparaging remarks to Wilspec's customers about its ability to perform. What tort might there be? [*Wilspec Technologies* v. *DunAn Holding Group*, 204 P.3d 69, Sup. Ct., Okla. (2009)]

8. A 4-year-old child used a Bic lighter to start a house fire that killed a 2-year-old child. The lighter had a warning: "KEEP OUT OF REACH OF CHILDREN." The dead child's parents sued Bic for strict liability based on inadequate

warning and because the lighter was unreasonably dangerous. What was the result? [*Todd* v. *SocieteBic*, 21 F.3d 1402, 7th Cir. (1994)]

✓ Check your answer

9. Two experienced welders were working inside a barge. A gas hose leading to the welding torch developed a leak that the workers apparently could not smell because of "nasal fatigue" from having inhaled so much gas. One worker lit a cigarette, igniting the gas, killing both workers. The workers' heirs sued the gas and gas hose producers in strict liability. Was either company liable? [*Littler* v. *Liquid Air Corp.*, 37 F.3d 1069, 5th Cir. (1994)]

10. Old Island Fumigation pumped poison into two of the three buildings in a condominium complex to kill bugs. Old Island was told that the third building was sealed from the other two, but in fact it was not. Residents of the third building became ill. The opening that let the fumes into the third building was a mistake made by the architect or contractor who built the buildings. Is Old Island liable? On what theory? [*Old Island Fumigation* v. *Barbee*, 604 So.2d 1246 (1992)]

ETHICS QUESTION

Various industries have lobbied for legislative restrictions on tort liability. For instance, the nuclear power industry has long been protected by a statute that limits its upper-dollar liability in the event of a serious accident that is much lower than the potential losses from such an accident. Also, the industry cannot be held liable in tort for radiation releases so long as federal guidelines are not exceeded. Many companies in other industries would like similar protection. Is it ethical to seek statutory limits on liability? Is it ethical for legislators to grant such protection? What limits would be acceptable?

CHAPTER **8**

Real and Personal Property

When Baron Leo von Rozmital traveled with King Edward IV across the English Channel in 1466 to the French port of Calais, he reported that most members of the royal court were seasick. It was so common that it was the duty of the owner of the Manor of Archer's Court, as a condition of ownership of that property, that he "should hold the King's head when he passes to Calais and by the workings of the sea should he be obliged to vomit."

Property owners today need not worry about holding the King's head to be allowed to retain property, but most property owners hold property once claimed by a king or queen of England, France, or Spain. The title to much of the property in the United States can be traced to a grant from a sovereign to a party he or she favored by title to a large tract of land. Over the centuries, the large estates have been divided into many smaller parcels owned by millions of people. For many people and businesses, property is one of their most valued assets.

We begin our study of the law of **property**—the oldest part of the common law—focusing on its application to business. Property refers to rights that are legally protected. That includes things visible and invisible—tangible and intangible—that have value. This chapter focuses on real property: things that are immovable, such as land; and personal property: physical things that are movable, such as furniture and clothing (traditionally called chattel). We consider ownership of property, in the many forms it can take, the legal basis for controls on private property imposed by governments and the liability that may rest with property owners when accidents happen on their property.

Real Property

The review of tort law was concerned mostly with personal interests protected by the law. Property interests differ from personal interests in that property refers to physical things, such as land and objects, in which one can have recognized interests against other persons. That is, a person has the right to deny others the use of the "things" in which there is a legal interest. Tort law is often used to protect interests in property. Contract law is used to make arrangements with others about the use of property. **Real property** refers to land, which includes things under the land, such as oil and minerals, and things solidly attached to the land, such as buildings and trees.

At law, property is a legally protected expectation of being able to use a thing for one's advantage. The owner of property is said to have a "bundle of legal rights." That is, it is not the physical existence of property that matters so much as the right to use property for certain purposes. Someone may have strong rights to use a piece of land for many purposes, or one may have rights to use the land only for certain purposes. Expectations about land can change because legal interests may change. For example, if your land is found to contain a rare plant protected under the Endangered Species Act (discussed in Chapter 21), how you may use the land will be limited by regulations concerning protection for the plant.

English Origins

Some of the terms that describe the law regarding real property appear a bit peculiar because the terms and concepts come from the common law as developed in England from the twelfth to the sixteenth centuries. Because much of the United States was a British colony at one time, English property law was applied and retained after independence. While some terms are old, some of the law has changed over the years. Statutory law has modified the common law, although in many cases, statutes primarily provide procedures for enforcing common-law property rules. Next, we look at some of the traditional elements of property law.

Deeds and Titles

Ownership of land is evidenced by various documents. The deed and the title are among the most important. A **deed** is the primary way to transfer ownership interests (title) in property. Deeds are in writing and transfer or convey title from the current property owner to the new owner. Deeds identify the current owner (grantor), describe the land, identify the new owner, and state that ownership is being transferred, possibly subject to certain conditions. Different deeds are used for different purposes. The most common are:

- A **quitclaim deed** is a conveyance that passes whatever interests the grantor had in the property. This might not provide any assurance of good title to the property; it may only terminate the interest of the previous possessor of the property. The rights conveyed by such a deed vary from state to state. Quitclaim deeds are often used in settlements of property suits, with one party passing his interest to another party.
- A **warranty deed** (also called a general warranty deed) promises that a good, clear title to the property is being conveyed by the grantor. This is the deed most often used in both personal and business property transactions and provides the buyer the most protection. The seller or grantor warrants that the property is free of any **liens** or encumbrances unless they are revealed in the title. Hence, the title is warranted to be good against third parties attempting to claim title to the property.

- A **special warranty deed** is not as protective as a general warranty deed. By it, the grantor warrants that the buyer or grantee has received title, and that the property was not encumbered during the ownership by the grantor, but does not warrant things that may have happened prior to ownership by the grantor.

The **title**, which comes from receipt of a valid deed, is the means by which the owner of property has legal possession of the property. The rights normally possessed by the holder of title to property, the formal right of ownership, usually includes the right to possess the property, the right to control the property, the right to exclude others from use of the property, the right to enjoy the property in legal manners, and the right to dispose of the property—sell it, rent it, or give it to another person.

A clear title means that no other party can claim valid ownership. Titles may be held by one or more persons or by a business. Titles to land are recorded by state officials, usually at the county level. Title recording provides a public record of who owns what and of limitations or claims on titles, such as the claim that mortgage lenders usually hold on real estate. The appropriate state or county office maintains a deed registry along with a grantor index, a grantee index, and a plat index. By tracing back the chain of ownership for land, a prospective buyer can determine exactly what the seller owns.

When property is transferred, it is common to obtain title insurance. A title company searches the public record and issues a title insurance binder or commitment. It binds the title company to insure that the title is as declared in the conveyance from the grantor to the grantee. Usually, the title company is looking to be sure the seller's mortgage is paid off, that there are no taxes owed on the property, that any liens (claims) on the property have been satisfied, that the boundaries of the property are clearly established, and that the deed transferring the property is properly prepared.

Title insurance may not protect against claims against the property that were not known in the public records at the time the title search was done. If a search reveals "defects" in a title, the title is said to be "clouded." This could arise from a boundary dispute with a neighbor, tax liens placed against the property, or liens imposed for work done on the property or for uncertain claims of ownership by heirs to property.

Fee Simple

The law often refers to one's interest or legal rights in real property as an estate. According to the *Restatement (Third) Property*, an **estate** is "an interest in land which (a) is or may become possessory and (b) is ownership measured in terms of duration." That is, one may have possession of land now or may have the right to take possession of land at some point in the future. There are time limits on the length of ownership. Ownership may be for life, which is uncertain in length, but one cannot take property to the grave—one's interests in an estate must pass to other persons.

The most common form of real property ownership is **fee simple** or fee simple absolute. Fee simple means the right to exclusive possession of a particular piece of land for an indefinite time, as well as the right to dispose of the land as the owner pleases. Most real estate in the United States today is held in fee simple, meaning it may be inherited, transferred to others, or sold in part or in whole. In general, it is the strongest form of real property control.

Traditionally, ownership in fee simple was said to extend to the skies, but air travel limited that concept. Ownership is also said to extend "to the center of the earth," meaning fee simple ownership includes the right to minerals and oil under the land. Those assets, like other features of land, can be sold or rented separately from the main piece of property. Subsurface **mineral rights** are often legally separated from ownership of the surface land. In contrast to the United States, in other countries all mineral rights belong to the government, not the landowner.

Lighter Side of the Law

Is It Real Property or Personal Property?

Chen knew that his dog bit his neighbor, Liu, on the hand and caused a serious injury. Knowing he could be liable for medical expenses while Liu was in the hospital, Chen and his wife moved their entire house, hoping they would not be found and forced to pay. Police were able to follow the trail anyway.

Source: China Daily News.

Tenancies Property is often held in the name of a husband and wife, family member, business partnership, trust, or corporation. There are three forms by which people may hold property jointly without creating a business entity to do so: tenancy in common, joint tenancy, and tenancy by the entirety. Because each individual's interest is different depending which form is used, businesses must be careful to understand exactly what a potential business partner owns based on which ownership form is used.

Tenancy refers to possession or use of lands by any kind of right or title, whether in fee simple or for a limited purpose or time periods. When we consider the ownership of property, different forms of tenancy are used.

A **tenancy in common** is a form of ownership in which each tenant (owner) has an undivided interest in the property. Suppose Angelina Jolie and Halle Berry each contributes half the money to buy a piece of property they own equally. They are said to have a tenancy in common, although such tenancy need not be equal shares. If Jolie dies, her interest in the property passes to her estate or to the heirs she has named; it does not go to Berry. If Jolie or Berry no longer wants to own the property with the other, either can force a division of the property by going to court, often to request a judicial sale.

It is common for married couples or partners to own property in the form of a **joint tenancy**. This is a property purchase by two or more persons who have the same interest in the undivided possession of property. The primary difference from the tenancy in common is that in a joint tenancy, there is a right of survivorship, which means that if one owner dies, the deceased owner's interest ends, and the survivor is left in sole possession. Joint tenants can force an end to the joint tenancy by transferring their interest into a tenancy in common. Tenancy by the entirety is available only for married couples and only in about half the states. As with a joint tenancy, there is a right of survivorship, but unlike a joint tenancy, one tenant cannot force an end to it except by divorcing the other tenant.

The law places few restrictions on the forms used to hold property. For example, one may grant a **life estate** in a piece of property that gives a person the right to be a tenant for life. This may be done so that a family member has the right to occupy a piece of property until death, at which point title to the property passes to someone designated by the former owner of the property.

Centuries ago in England, many complex interests were used to achieve certain types of control of property. Today, the most common means of ownership is the fee simple absolute. Those seeking to do more complex property structures generally use trusts.

Trusts A **trust** is a form of property ownership created by the common law that separates the legal and beneficial ownership of property. A settlor (or grantor) places property into a trust through a trust instrument (sometimes called a deed of trust). The **trustee** holds the legal title to the property and can make all decisions with respect to it. The **beneficiary** of the trust holds an equitable title to the property. Hence, the trustee has a duty to manage the property for the benefit of the beneficiary.

For example, Jenny could place $200,000 in stocks and bonds and the title to a piece of property, Blackacre (pieces of property are often referred to in law as "Blackacre," an old tradition), into a trust for the benefit of her daughter, Emma, naming Ethan as trustee. Ethan would have the power to make decisions about how to invest the money, whether to sell or rent Blackacre, and so on, but must do so with a view to protect the assets and maximize the return so that Emma could receive the income. Ethan has no right to sell the trust assets and bet the money on horse races, as he would if Jenny had simply given him the assets. Such trusts are often called "spend-thrift trusts." Similarly, if Ethan sold Blackacre at a discount to his partner, Emma could sue him for breaching his duty as trustee.

Business trusts may be used in place of a partnership or corporation, with the beneficiaries receiving certificates of beneficial ownership that can be traded like stocks and bonds. Walmart, for example, uses the Walmart Real Estate Business Trust to handle a portion of its real estate operations. Delaware created a special statute governing business trusts to codify the common law and provide more certainty for these trusts. The main advantages of using a business trust rather than a partnership or corporation are flexibility and security.

Flexibility exists because the trust agreement can set up whatever structure of rights and obligations the trustees and the beneficial owners involved think is most desirable. For example, the voting power given the various trustees can be whatever the organizer of the trust wishes rather than the equal power partnership law establishes. Using a trust instead of a partnership allows such flexibility.

Security comes from having business trusts serve as bankruptcy-remote vehicles. That is, the trust is not connected legally to any business entity and so would not be affected by the bankruptcy of the business that is the beneficiary of its assets. Suppose a company wanted to borrow money against some real estate. Putting that real estate into a business trust, with the company as beneficiary, gives the creditors of the business trust greater protection from the possibility of bankruptcy by the borrower than would be the case if the company owned the real estate directly. Because the trust is a separate entity, the lender would not have to worry that other creditors of the beneficiary would seize the real estate to satisfy their claims.

Evolving Property Law: Condominiums While property law is old in origin, it adapts to changes in society. Condominiums were not common before the 1960s, but the law concerning fee simple estates has been applied to such living arrangements. Each living space in a building may be owned in fee simple (with numerous conditions attached), yet the land the building sits on, as well as common areas, such as elevators and lobbies, is held in common for the benefit of the condo owners as a group. To help adapt property law to such arrangements, all states have statutes that simplified the legal process of having condos and other modern living arrangements consistent with traditional property law.

Servitudes

Servitudes are limitations or requirements about the use of property. Servitudes attach to the estate or property itself and impose certain use limits on the owner of the property. The most important forms of servitudes are easements and covenants.

Easements An **easement** is a right to enter land owned by another and make certain use of it. An easement is not ownership or right of possession of an estate but a "burden"

INTERNATIONAL PERSPECTIVE

Insecure Property Rights

In the United States, property ownership is clear. Land is owned by a private party or by the government. There are few disputes over title to land, and no one would think of building a house on land unless clear title was assured. But in much of the world, rights to property are muddled and highly political. Hernando de Soto, head of a think tank in Peru, studied land ownership in several nations. He found that most farmers do not own the land they farm and that city dwellers do not own the land under their houses.

In the Philippines, only one-third of agricultural land has clear title and only 43 percent of dwellings have clear title to the land they occupy. In Peru, 81 percent of farmed land is not owned; only half the urban dwellings are on titled land. The poorest nation in the Western Hemisphere is Haiti, where 97 percent of farm land is not owned and 68 percent of urban dwellings are in the "informal" sector. In Egypt, 92 percent of urban dwellings are on "unowned" land, as are 83 percent of all farms.

De Soto attributes the persistence of poverty in such countries to the inability of most people to have the chance to capitalize on the value they have put into their farms and houses. There is no possibility to use property as collateral for a loan to start a business or improve a farm. Sales of property are for low prices because the transfer is informal; there is no deed to be recorded. Without secure property rights, economic progress is enjoyed primarily by a minority of people who live in the formal economy that we recognize as critical to global commerce.

Source: The Mystery of Capital (Basic Books).

on another person's estate; that is, the right to use it for some purpose without payment for each use. The document that creates an easement is much like a deed: it explains the use of certain property that is conveyed from the property owner to the easement holder.

Positive easements allow the easement holder to go onto the estate for certain purposes. A negative easement would be giving up a right that the owner of an estate would normally have, such as agreeing with the Nature Conservancy to preserve and protect certain rare plants that exist on the property. Easements are becoming common in connection with solar and wind energy, to guarantee that neighbors will not block sunlight for solar collectors or wind from turbines. One may also give or sell someone the right to remove valuable things from one's estate, such as oil, minerals, or trees; this right may be referred to as a **profit**.

Unless the easement is for a set time, it will be attached permanently to the property. An easement right is said to "run with the land." As with ownership arrangements, parties are generally free to agree upon any kind of easement they wish. Almost all homes have easements for utilities and for public sidewalks. Once an easement is granted, the property owner may not interfere with it unless the easement holder agrees. That is, if a gas line needs to be dug up for repair, the gas company has the right, doing as little damage as possible, to go on the property to dig up the yard, and later repair the yard, to get to the pipe.

Easements are often sold to a neighbor who needs the use of someone else's property. If Harry buys twenty acres in the woods and the property is behind Nancy's land, which faces the road, to have access to his property, Harry must get an easement from Nancy to build a road across her property. It is obviously a good idea to get needed easements to property settled before buying such property. However, easements can also arise by implication if a landowner sells part of a property without clearly providing a means of access to it.

Adverse Possession   One way that a party may come to own property or an easement is by **adverse possession** or by **easement by prescription**. These are called hostile uses of another person's land; that is, someone who has no right to occupy or use an estate does so without permission. The use may be in the form of an easement, such as driving across another's property regularly, or may be actual possession, such as building a house and living on another's property. In such cases, the user of the property may obtain a legally recognized easement, such as the right to continue driving across the land, or may even obtain title to the land on which the house is built, so long as taxes have been paid.

The general conditions needed for adverse possession are that it must be:

1. Actual: the adverse user in fact uses or possesses the property in question.
2. Open: the use or possession must be visible so that the owner is on notice.
3. Hostile: the use or possession is without permission of the owner.
4. Exclusive: the use or possession is not shared with others who also have no right to use the property.
5. Continuous: the use or possession must go on without major interruption for as much time as required by law to obtain the easement by prescription or title by adverse possession.

All states have rules, called **statutes of limitations**, for the number of years the adverse possession must occur before it becomes a legally protected possession. State law varies on the time required from 5 to 20 years. Issues involving prescriptive easement and adverse possession are seen in the *Moran* case.

MORAN V. SIMS

Court of Appeals of Mississippi 873 So.2d 1067 (2004)

Case Background *Sims owned property surrounded by the Morans' property. His deed was recorded in 1985, but the property had been in his family for over 50 years. He built a home in 1991. The property was accessed by a driveway across the property bought by the Morans in 1996. Sims asked the court to grant him an easement. The trial court held that Sims had a prescriptive easement that allowed use of the driveway on the Morans' property. They appealed.*

Case Decision Southwick, Presiding Judge

* * *

An easement may be acquired by ten years possession. ... Prescription occurs if there is ten years of use that is open, notorious, and visible; hostile; under a claim of ownership; exclusive; peaceful; and continuous and uninterrupted. Permission from the record title owner will make the use permissive and not adverse. ...

The elements for a prescriptive easement will be examined individually.

a. Open, notorious and visible At trial, Sims testified that he had used the driveway running across Moran's property since he purchased the parcel in 1985. ... Among the testimony was from a school bus driver who testified that he had driven the bus down the driveway to pick up children in 1956-1957. ... This was sufficient under this factor.

b. Hostile Moran argues that Sims and his predecessors had implied permission to use the property. That allegedly is proved by the fact that the owners of the land across which the driveway ran never objected to his use. A prescriptive easement cannot originate from a permissive use of land because it would not be hostile. However, the absence of an objection is not the equivalent of consent.

Here, there was no evidence that Sims or his predecessors had permission to use the driveway. Consent may be inferred from evidence, but it will not be presumed in the absence of evidence ... consent must be shown. Here it was not.

c. **Claim of ownership** Sims presented testimony which showed a claim of ownership, including the fact that he purchased gravel for the driveway. There was testimony on that from the person whom Sims hired to deliver and spread the gravel. This element was properly established.

d. **Exclusive** "Exclusive" use does not mean that no one else used the driveway. Exclusivity here means that the use was consistent with an exclusive claim to the right to use. There was evidence that the driveway was used by the Sims family and those whom they implicitly permitted to do so. The Sims' home was the only home located on the driveway.

e. **Peaceful** Sims testified that there was no controversy concerning the driveway prior to Moran's purchase of property. There was no evidence of a dispute with prior owners. By the time that Moran complained, the period of prescription had long since run.

f. **Continuous and uninterrupted for ten years** Sims recorded the deed to his property in 1985. His family had owned the property for at least fifty years before. During this time, the driveway had been in use. That is ten years, and more.

The elements of adverse possession were sufficiently proven....

Affirmed.

Questions for Analysis

1. The appeals court held that Sims did have an easement by prescription across the Moran's property. Sims asked them to give it to him, but they would not. Why not?
2. The Morans did not own the property for the ten years during which Sims used the driveway. Why did Sims not have to wait ten years?

Covenants A **covenant**, or covenant running with the land, is a means by which owners of estates in land can make agreements that bind their successors. One property is benefitted by the covenant and the other property is burdened by it. Most often, covenants are restrictions that attach to the deed when a home is sold. The agreement made in a covenant is said to "run" with the land. That is, the covenant is a binding obligation that goes with property when it is transferred to a new owner, who must abide by the covenant.

Most covenants create value by restricting rights that the burdened property owner values little but the benefitted owner values a lot; otherwise, why would many people agree to them? The most common forms are residential subdivision covenants; for example, only single-family homes are allowed; every home must be at least 2,000 square feet; no prefabricated homes are allowed; no dog kennels are allowed; no businesses may operate from a home; and homes must be painted pastel colors. Such covenants ensure certain attributes to a subdivision that the owners of the homes think desirable. Because each owner values the absence of dog kennels among his neighbors more than he values his own right to have one, the trade makes everyone better off. Most new residential construction in the United States has been in subdivisions with covenants for the past several decades. Covenants in conflict with public policy are not enforceable. For example, years ago some covenants prohibited the sale of homes to members of racial and religious minorities. The courts no longer enforce these today.

Assuming no violation of public policy, covenants are enforced by the courts. Changing them can be difficult because that may require getting everyone affected by the covenants to agree to a change. In practice, covenants are often a critical tool in developing real estate because they set the rules for the character of the development. But later, when rules are violated, enforcement is often neglected because it means a homeowner or group of homeowners must band together and use their resources to enforce the rules. That means suing your neighbors, which is unpleasant and costly. Disputes over easements and covenants generate a lot of litigation because people are not clear as to what rights they have over access to property, or, after time has passed, they think they have rights that they may not in fact possess, as the *Thayer* case illustrates.

THAYER V. HOLLINGER

Supreme Court of Montana 296 P.3d 1183 (2013)

Case Background *Hollinger and Williams bought a lake and 800 acres around the lake in 1965. They subdivided the land around the lake into 75 lots, which were sold as lakeshore lots. The developers of Big Sky Lake also built Perimeter Road around the lake. Homeowner lots are on the lakeside of the road. The homeowners association now owns the road.*

Hollinger and Williams kept land on the outside of the road. The land has trails on it that Hollinger allowed lakeside lot owners to use for hiking and horseback riding. When lot owners began to drive motorized vehicles, including ATVs, snowmobiles, and motorcycles on the trails, Hollinger blocked access. A group of lot owners sued, contending they had an easement to use the trails with motorized vehicles as established by covenants on the property. The district court held they had no right of access; the lot owners appealed.

Case Decision Chief Justice McGrath

* * *

An easement for a right of way is a servitude which may be imposed upon a parcel of land, which is the servient tenement, in favor of another parcel of land, which is the dominant tenement. In this case the Homeowners claim a right of way attached to their lakeshore lots as the dominant tenements, to travel over the four roads or trails through the servient tenement of the Hollingers' land. The Homeowners claim that their right of way arises expressly from several identified documents that establish their easement rights across the Hollingers' land. In such a case, the easement must be described with "reasonable certainty" in documents conveying land, or may be depicted or described in expressly referenced documents such as a recorded plat or certificate of survey. . . .

The Homeowners rely upon several documents to support their claimed easements across the

Hollingers' land. First they argue that "Restrictive Covenants for Big Sky Lake," recorded in 1968, are a source of the claimed easements. In those Covenants the Company granted the persons owning lakeshore lots a 60–foot wide easement and right of way for ingress and egress "over roads as the same have been constructed by the Company." The easement was "applicable to the perimeter road, which shall be the outer boundary of each tract and subdivision," and to the "middle access roads" connecting the perimeter road to the roads leading to each lakeshore lot. . . .

The District Court properly determined that the Restrictive Covenants granted an easement only for ingress and egress to the lakeshore lots, and only within the Perimeter Road system. The Hollingers' land at issue is all outside of the Perimeter Road. The easements were also expressly limited to roads constructed by the Company after 1965. There is no evidence that the Company constructed the Hollinger roads after 1965. In addition, the Restrictive Covenants do not provide any clear description or depiction, expressly or by reference, of any roads on the Hollingers' land. The Restrictive Covenants are therefore not a source of easements in favor of the Homeowners across the Hollingers' land. . . .

The District Court properly applied the facts and the law to conclude that the Homeowners had not established any right to easements over the Hollingers' land. The District Court is affirmed.

Questions for Analysis

1. Why, after so many decades, would the homeowners think they have the right to drive on the Hollingers' land?
2. Because the homeowners had been allowed to hike and ride horses on the trail, would that not give them a constructive easement to use the trails for other uses?

Landlord and Tenants

When we rent property, our interest is called a **leasehold**. The property may be owned in fee simple by the **landlord**, but that is not necessary to create a leasehold with a tenant. A **tenant** is a party with possessory rights for a fixed time period or at will as agreed upon. That is, the lease gives the tenant certain rights to occupy and use the property. The tenant has possession of the estate; the landlord has the right to reclaim the estate after the lease ends. Generally, unless prohibited by the leasehold, the tenant may sublease all or a portion of the property to a subtenant; many leases require the landlord's consent for a sublease.

Leases A **lease** is an agreement that creates a leasehold out of an estate and contains conditions, such as how much rent is to be paid and what restrictions have been placed on the use of the property. All leases are subject to a large body of statutory and common law that sets boundaries on what is legal in a leasehold and on how a dispute about any issue is to be resolved.

Many states have adopted all or part of the Uniform Residential Landlord and Tenant Act, a statute designed to modernize and clarify standard terms of leases. Although state laws may require certain terms, in general, the courts want leases to:

1. Identify the parties.
2. Describe the premises (address or legal description of the property) being leased.
3. State how long the lease is to be in effect.
4. State how much rent is to be paid.

Note that a lease does not have to end at a specific date but can go from month to month. Most leases also specify who is responsible for utility bills, when and where the rent is to be paid, the terms of a damage deposit, and the tenants' responsibility for wear and tear of the property.

Rights of a Tenant A tenant has a legal interest in rented property and has the right of possession during the term of the lease. Other parties may be kept out of the property, including the landlord, with some exceptions. The landlord has a privilege to enter the premises to make needed repairs. Leases often state that the landlord has the right to enter the property to inspect it or to show it to future tenants, but there is no general right for the landlord to pop in any time.

Leased property is assumed at law to have an implied warranty of habitability. Even if not spelled out in a written lease, it is presumed at law that landlords protect

Lighter Side of the Law

The Tenants Who Would Not Go Away

Teeman rented an apartment in New York in 1968. She subleased the apartment to the Levys in 1977, year-by-year, intending to return to the city after she had helped her ailing parents. Teeman told the Levys in1985 that the lease would not be renewed and that she was returning. The Levys refused to vacate and began a series of lawsuits, court motions, and appeals to keep control of the apartment.

The Levys ignored court orders to vacate. Finally, in late 1999, an appeals court upheld the Levys' ejection, calling their many legal tactics "abject nonsense couched as legal argument." The court ordered them to pay Teeman's legal fees and $8,000 in sanctions to the Lawyers' Fund for Client Protection because of their "reprehensible" actions.

Source: Levy v. Carol Management, 698 N.Y.S.2d 226.

tenants from known hazards (a loose stair), that the fixtures work (the toilets flush and the bathtub drains), that the building is structurally sound (no holes in the floor), and that there are not recurring problems (the air conditioner never really gets fixed).

If a landlord fails to make essential repairs in a timely manner, such as keeping the air conditioning working during the summer, or otherwise allows the premises to be uninhabitable, there may be "constructive eviction." In such cases, the landlord has broken the lease, and the tenant has the right to terminate the tenancy, leave, and, in some cases, sue to recover costs incurred by the untimely move.

Duties of a Tenant   A tenant has the right to use leased property, but not to abuse it by making changes that will affect the property beyond the lease term. Abuse can come from negligence, failure to prevent damage from problems such as a leaking pipe. Abuse may take the form of **waste**, which is the intentional destruction or removal of valuable property, such as trees, from the premises. A tenant may not be a nuisance to neighbors and may not engage in illegal activities on the premises.

Most landlord-tenant leases are straightforward. About a third of the states have adopted all or part of the Uniform Residential Landlord and Tenant Act issued by the National Conference of Commissioners on Uniform State Law. Such statutes set many background standards for landlords and tenants that cannot be evaded, making detailed leases not as necessary as they otherwise might be. Lease agreements for business spaces are different.

Commercial Leases

Commercial leases are often drafted by the lessor's legal department based on state law requirements and experience with previous tenants. They tend to be long because they cover many issues, so expertise is needed. The description of leased space is often defined by terms used by the Building Owners and Managers Association (BOMA), the recognized authority in setting such standards.

To get an idea of the detail that must be considered, in BOMA's *Office Buildings: Methods of Measurement and Calculating Rentable Area*, the "Single Load Factor Method" is "a new calculation applied to the occupant area of each floor to determine the rentable area and is the same for all floor levels of a building. This method is referred

---

INTERNATIONAL PERSPECTIVE

Americans Crossing into Mexico for Land

Millions of Americans own second homes, and many look to Mexico as a warm-weather destination for that investment. It is estimated that a million American citizens live in Mexico, and the number is rising quickly. Real estate prices on the Yucatan peninsula doubled in five years as a result of the American influx.

Mexican property law is complex. Foreigners are allowed to own land only in certain locations; elsewhere, they can hold the property in trust, *fideicomiso*, which gives them a right to use the land for 50 years. A number of foreigners have "bought" land in Mexico, presuming the law of title to be much like in the U.S., but found out differently. More than 200 American "homeowners" were evicted from a luxury development on the Baja coast after a court held against the developer in a title dispute.

Just as in the U.S., good local counsel is important. Some Mexican attorneys are fluent in English and can guide clients through the complexities of using a *notario* (public notary) and other steps unfamiliar under American law. Title registries in Mexico are not as reliable as in the U.S., so independent reviews are desirable. Due diligence in real estate is always a good idea; how it is performed varies greatly from country to country. U.S. law does not apply.

to as 'Method B.' This method was not permitted in the 1996 version." A lease using BOMA standards may choose "either the new Method B or the measurement methodology of the 1996 standard, referred to as 'Legacy Method A.'" There are also regional leasing practices, such as a "new standard to allow for enclosure requirements and limited (unenclosed) circulation" in tropical climates. Because of such complexity in commercial leases, it is common for a building manager to provide a tenant a schematic of the floor plan from which space is leased. The leased space is "hatch marked" and incorporated in the lease as an exhibit.

Leases identify the lessor and lessee; the legal description of the property (including square footage); rent; additional payment, such as "net," which is typically the percent of the space leased in relationship to property taxes, utilities, and insurance. In addition to the "nets," common-area maintenance charges may be added for lighting, cleaning, parking lot maintenance, and so forth. When rent includes these additional charges, it is referred to as "gross rents."

Common terms in commercial leases cover:

- security deposits
- use of the property, which is usually specific
- maintenance and repair responsibilities
- how alterations, including structural changes, will be handled
- right to sublease
- early termination provision
- insurance
- responsibility for attorney's fees
- prohibitions on hazardous substances
- right of inspection
- taxes
- utilities
- what signage will be allowed
- liability waivers
- damage provisions
- what happens in case of eminent domain that forces relocation
- subordination to mortgage
- dispute resolution

Commercial landlords often want control over the type of uses, to ensure that an office building or shopping center has the right mix of tenants; tenants often want clauses restricting the landlord's ability to rent to potential competitors.

Many commercial properties are shell buildings. Leases may use terms such as a "grey shell" without interior finish or a "vanilla shell" with four finished walls, heating and cooling, a restroom, and suspended ceiling. Depending on negotiations, the lease or a

ISSUE SPOTTER
Would Tighter Leases Help?

As manager of an apartment complex, you know that a nontrivial number of tenants not only make a mess that is not covered by their damage deposit, but some stop paying rent so they must be evicted. You win the eviction battles, but they incur some legal fees and, because the tenants do not have resources and often leave town, you lose the rent for a couple of months, too. What can you do to reduce your losses? Can you write leases that are more effective at making the tenants pay?

separate agreement grant a "tenant allowance," an amount per square foot for interior finishes. The landlord must approve alterations. Failure to write the lease properly can result in problems, as we see in the *Gold's Gym* case.

NIELSEN V. GOLD'S GYM
Supreme Court of Utah 78 P.3d 600 (2003)

Case Background *Peterson signed a preprinted commercial lease agreement with Nielsen to lease the "premises" in a "strip mall at 1341 E. Center, Spanish Fork, UT," to be used as a "health club and gym" for three years at $0.85 annually per square foot. Nielsen was still constructing the building at the time the lease was signed. A contractor then told Peterson it would cost $168,000 to improve the building shell to be ready for the gym. Peterson went back to Nielsen to discuss who would pay for the interior improvements. When an agreement could not be reached, Peterson walked away and Nielsen leased to another party.*

Nielsen sued for $112,000 in damages for breach of contract for having to rent the space for less than Peterson had agreed. The trial court held the lease to be unenforceable for lack of agreement as to the nature and extent of the property to be leased. Nielsen appealed.

Case Decision Wilkins, Justice

* * *

In this case, the building shell itself was still under construction when the lease was signed. Uncontroverted trial testimony establishes that the contractor had not completed the floor of the building shell because he anticipated that tenant improvements would require modification to the original building plans for plumbing and electrical configurations. Nor were the roof and walls completed. This renders the question of payment even more important because it is not clear from the lease who was required to pay for those tenant-based modifications to the building shell. Furthermore, there was no

evidence at trial concerning industry customs or standards, or any other extrinsic evidence that would aid the court in determining responsibility for payment. Finally, even Nielsen notes that the cost of improvements "would have consumed more than half of the total rents over the three-year term of the lease," constituting a significant portion of the overall costs associated with the lease. While payment for tenant improvements is by no means an essential term in every commercial lease agreement, the facts of this case persuade us that it was an essential part of the bargain to be reached here.

We uphold the trial court's legal determination that the lease agreement was ambiguous due to missing terms, specifically, those terms governing payment of tenant improvements. The trial court's interpretation of the contract after finding ambiguity was not challenged on appeal; thus, we also uphold the trial court's ruling that the contract was unenforceable for lack of mutual assent as to the essential terms governing which party was to pay for tenant improvements. The judgment of dismissal is affirmed.

Questions for Analysis

1. The Utah high court held that no commercial lease was ever formed because key terms to the lease were never set. Given that the building was still under construction, how could they have set all these details?
2. Why did the court not make the lease work or assign the appropriate costs of the construction to the parties?

Public Control of Real Property

Many statutes modify the common law. Some statutes make property law operate more smoothly by providing offices for the registration of titles to private property, for listing loans taken out against property, and for noting claims made against property—often

? TEST YOURSELF

1. The most common form of real property ownership in the United States is fee simple: T—F

2. The right to remove minerals or oil from someone's property is called a(n) _____; the right to drive across that property to get to another piece of property is called a(n) _____.

3. Tenants in common are when two or more people rent property together for a period of at least one year: T—F

4. To gain ownership of land by open occupation of it over time, despite not owning the land, is called:

   a. a covenant.

   b. adverse possession.

   c. life tenancy.

   d. a profit.

5. When we rent property from someone, our interest is called a(n) _____.

6. In *Moran* v. *Sims*, where Sims wanted the right to drive across Moran's property, the court held that Sims:

   a. would have to pay the fair market value for such an easement.

   b. would receive a life tenancy regarding the driveway usage.

   c. had a prescriptive easement to use the driveway.

   d. had no right to demand to use the driveway; he got the property cheap because it was difficult to access.

7. In *Nielsen* v. *Gold's Gym*, regarding a lease for space for a gym, the courts held that there was not an enforceable lease: T—F

8. A corporation or a partnership may find it desirable to hold ownership in property through a(n) _____ so as to increase the security of ownership.

Answers: T; profit, easement; F; b; leasehold; c; T; trust.

---

called liens—that are filed by people who assert they are owed money by the property owner, such as for failure to pay for putting a new roof on a house. A lien is a legal interest that a creditor has in another's property. It usually is kept in place until a debt has been repaid. The process for filing liens and the rights involved in liens are detailed in state law (discussed in Chapter 12). Governments also have strong powers over the use of private property. Most important are the power of eminent domain and the broad police powers that include control of property by zoning rules. That is what we review next.

Eminent Domain

If a government wants to build a road, it can negotiate with property owners to acquire the land needed and use tax dollars to buy the land through voluntary sales. Many landowners are happy to sell some land for roads at it may make their remaining land more valuable. However, some landowners may refuse to sell. The government may then use its power of **eminent domain** to "condemn" property to force its sale or to force the granting of an easement.

Eminent domain is the power to take private property for public use without the consent of the owner. As the Supreme Court noted in 1875 (91 U.S. 367), "The right of eminent domain always was a right at common law. It was not a right in equity, nor was it even the creature of a statute. The . . . right itself was superior to any statute." That is, it comes from the right of the government as sovereign to control property for its purposes.

The Fifth Amendment states that "private property" shall not "be taken for public use, without just compensation." Governments are allowed to force a property owner to give up title to part or all of her land or to force a property owner to give an easement on the land for some public purpose. Governments must pay compensation, which is generally determined by statutes that allow "fair market value" for the property interests taken. When the landowner and the government disagree on how much should be paid, statutes provide for a method for valuation that may involve a trial.

While governments have long condemned property to use for building a school, a road, or for some other public purpose, a major issue has arisen in recent years over the use of eminent domain to benefit a private party as part of economic development plans. When a business wishes to locate in a particular place, it may face the problem that some property owners may refuse to sell or will sell only at very high prices. To encourage business location, governments, especially at the local level, have used their power of eminent domain to allow a private party to get specific property at current market value and not have to bargain with current property owners. As we saw in the *Kelo* case in Chapter 4, the Supreme Court holds this practice to be a legitimate use of eminent domain. Many states adopted restrictions on the use of eminent domain in response to *Kelo*.

Police Powers

Eminent domain is government taking of land, but government also controls private land use by regulation. Except for some environmental regulations, most land regulation is done at the state and local level. This is generally called the **police power** to regulate behavior to protect or to promote the "general welfare." While the general welfare usually means health or safety, in practice it means very general power to control private use of property.

Often the key issue is not whether there is such a power to regulate but whether government must provide compensation when land-use controls reduce property values. No one questions that when the government takes property by eminent domain it must pay for the property. But in general, even when the government greatly reduces the value of property by regulation, compensation might not be due. As discussed in Chapter 4, the Supreme Court has declared that when almost all value of property is destroyed by regulation, it is protected by the Fifth Amendment rule of just compensation. But when regulation causes property to lose only part of its value, even a large part, compensation is rarely required, so long as the government can show a rational reason for the police power that caused the economic damage and that there was no violation of due process with respect to the injured property owner. Owners who object must turn to the political process to try to change the regulation.

Zoning Governments have long mandated controls on land use. More than 200 years ago, regulation stated that dangerous businesses such as gunpowder factories, and smelly businesses such as slaughterhouses, must be located away from residential areas. Since the 1920s, **zoning** has become the primary method of local land control. Zoning rules commonly limit building height and size, require green areas, set population-density limits, decide what kinds of buildings and businesses can be built where, and set many rules about the quality and type of construction that must be used.

So long as zoning regulations do not violate a provision of the Constitution, such as free speech, or violate due process rules, they are likely to be upheld. However, if the zoning authorities do not follow proper procedure and interpret zoning statutes properly, their decisions may be overturned, as we see in the *Saadala* case. After the case, we turn to issues that arise when parties become involved in tort actions involving property.

SAADALA V. EAST BRUNSWICK ZONING BOARD OF ADJUSTMENT

Superior Court of New Jersey, Appellate Division 991 A.2d 866 (2010)

Case Background *7-Eleven has a store with six parking spaces on a half-acre lot in East Brunswick, New Jersey. Part of the 7-Eleven lot is zoned residential, but the store existed before the residential zoning, so it was "grandfathered in" as a preexisting nonconforming use. Next to the 7-Eleven was a vacant gasoline station, which was also protected as a preexisting nonconforming use. 7-Eleven wanted to take over the gas station property and a neighboring vacant lot zoned residential and build a retail gas operation as part of the 7-Eleven. It requested that the preexisting nonconforming use be extended.*

Saadala, a resident in the area, opposed the classification requested by 7-Eleven, but the Zoning Board approved it. The county trial court affirmed that decision. Saadala appealed.

Case Decision Skillman, Presiding Judge

* * *

Since the Zoning Board granted 7-Eleven's application on the theory that its redevelopment plan involves an expansion of a nonconforming use or uses, and the trial court affirmed the Board on this same basis, we first consider the law governing the continuation of nonconforming uses. The statutory authorization for such continuation is provided by *N.J.S.A.* [*New Jersey Statutes Annotated*] 40:55D-68, which states:

> Any nonconforming use or structure existing at the time of the passage of an ordinance may be continued upon the lot or in the structure so occupied and any such structure may be restored or repaired in the event of partial destruction thereof.

In construing *N.J.S.A.* 40:55D-68, our courts have held that "because nonconforming uses are inconsistent with the objectives of uniform zoning...they should be reduced to conformity as quickly as is compatible with justice. The method generally used to limit nonconforming uses is to prevent any increase or change in the nonconformity."...

Under 7-Eleven's redevelopment plan, what was formerly a nonconforming convenience store on one lot and a nonconforming gasoline station on another lot would be replaced by an integrated nonconforming business operating on both lots as well as a third lot not formerly used for any nonconforming business operation. The establishment of this new business operation would involve the construction of three new islands for the dispensing of gasoline, on which three new gasoline pumps and a kiosk would be erected, and the creation of eleven new parking spaces. Therefore, we conclude that 7-Eleven's plan for the establishment of a mini-mart, which would add the retail sale of gasoline to its current operation of a convenience store, would not involve simply an expansion of the convenience store or the former Shell gas station but rather a substantial change in the use of the properties....

Although the Board stated in its resolution approving 7-Eleven's application that "7-Eleven's proposed uses...are particularly suited to and peculiarly situated in an area where numerous commercial uses are located," this statement...lacks evidential support in the record. 7-Eleven has not shown that there is anything about its property that makes it "peculiarly fitted" for a mini-mart. Indeed, as previously discussed, the East Brunswick zoning ordinance expressly permits this type of commercial use in another zoning district.

Therefore, 7-Eleven failed to make the showing of "special reasons" required for approval of a use variance for its redevelopment plan.

Accordingly, the judgment of the Law Division is reversed.

Questions for Analysis

1. Why would Saadala and other people living nearby oppose this improved use of the land?
2. What practical reasons might there be for the Zoning Board to approve the plan?

Torts against Property

Some acts harm people's property or property interests rather than the people themselves. "Property" refers to real property, such as land, personal property (a person's possessions), and intellectual property, such as trade secrets. We discuss intellectual property in the next chapter (see Chapter 9); here we review the torts that interfere with the right to enjoy and control one's property. Tort actions that may be initiated for violations of the property rights of another include trespass to land, nuisance, trespass to personal property, conversion, and misappropriation.

Trespass to Land

The tort of **trespass** to land is an unauthorized intrusion by a person or a thing on land belonging to another. A belief of the trespasser that she is on her own land or does not know who the land belongs to is not a defense—intent to trespass is not relevant. Nor is it necessary for the property owner to demonstrate actual injury to the property for there to be a trespass. For example, shooting a gun across another's property may be a trespass to land despite the fact that no physical damage occurs. Landowners have a right of peaceful enjoyment of their property. If, however, a person enters another's property to protect it from damage or to help someone on the property who is in danger, that is a defense against the tort of trespass to land.

The original idea of possession of land included dominion over a space "from the center of the earth to the heavens." A trespass could be committed on, beneath, or above the surface of the land. That rule is much more relaxed today. An airplane flying over a property owner's airspace does not create an action in trespass so long as it is flying at a reasonable altitude.

In general, unless we invite people onto our property, they are trespassers, and we have no obligation to protect them against accidents, as the *Smith* case discusses. A property owner may not intentionally harm a trespasser or set a trap for one, but there is no duty to warn trespassers of dangerous conditions on property.

SMITH V. KULIG

Supreme Court of North Dakota 696 N.W.2d 521 (2005)

Case Background *Kulig owns a building with businesses on the ground floor and apartments on the second floor. The street door to the apartments is kept locked so only tenants and their guests have access. At the back of the building is a fire escape. The tenants were told not to use the fire escape unless there was an emergency. "No trespassing" signs were posted on the fire escape. Smith was visiting Wolf at his apartment in the building. Apparently, Smith went on to the fire escape, some bolts that attached it to the wall came out, and Smith fell to his death. His estate sued Kulig. The trial court dismissed the suit, holding Smith to be a trespasser. The holding was appealed.*

Case Decision Maring, Justice

* * *

The word "trespasser" is legally defined as a person who enters or remains upon premises in possession of another without a privilege to do so created by the possessor's consent, either express or implied. . . .

Here, the trial court found the fire escape on the back side of Kulig's building contained *no trespass* signs, as did the doors leading to and from the fire escape. . . . The court also found that the ladder to the fire escape had a *no trespassing* sign mounted on it. . . . The court found that Smith was a trespasser on the premises because Smith did not have a right to use the fire escape as an entry or exit to the building and there was no emergency situation which would reasonably require him to have used it for that purpose... the *no trespassing* signs on the property negated any implied consent upon which Smith could claim to have been a lawful occupant of the premises while using the fire escape in contravention of the warnings against such use....

An occupier of premises owes no duty to a trespasser other than to refrain from harming the trespasser in a willful and wanton manner until such time as the trespasser's presence in a place of danger becomes known, at which point the occupier's duty is to exercise ordinary care to avoid injuring him.

Thus, a landowner does not owe a duty to a trespasser other than to refrain from harming the trespasser in a willful and wanton manner. We, therefore, conclude the court did not err in applying the willful and wanton conduct standard of liability under the circumstances of this case....

With respect to trespassers, a landowner is not under any affirmative duty to give a trespasser warning of concealed perils, although, by the exercise of reasonable care, the owner might have discovered the defect or danger which caused the injury. The person in charge only owes a duty to not knowingly or willfully expose a trespasser to hidden danger or peril.... In this case, there is no evidence that Kulig knew or had reason to know the fire escape was in a dangerous condition....

We affirm the judgment dismissing the wrongful death action with prejudice.

Questions for Analysis

1. The North Dakota high court held the landlord had no duty to protect trespassers from dangers on the property. Because Smith was a guest of Wolf, a tenant, why was he a trespasser?
2. The fire escape was in poor condition and may have collapsed if people had used it in case of a fire. Why was that not a failure by the landlord to exercise due care?

Nuisance (Private and Public)

The common law of torts recognizes two kinds of nuisance: private nuisance and public nuisance. A **private nuisance** is an activity that substantially and unreasonably interferes with the use and enjoyment of someone's land. The interference may be physical, such as vibration, the destruction of crops, or the throwing of objects on to the land. The interference may cause discomfort or a health risk from pollution, odors, excessive noise, dust, or noxious fumes. A nuisance may include offensive conditions on neighboring land that injure the occupants' mental peace through the problems those conditions create or threaten to create through their offensive nature. Most people would find, for example, that the use of the house next door for drug deals is upsetting to their mental peace while in their own house.

Common-law nuisance actions have been useful for challenging environmental damage. In fact, nuisance actions have challenged virtually every major industrial activity that causes some form of pollution, as we see in Chapter 21.

A **public nuisance** is an unreasonable interference with a right held in common by the general public. A public nuisance usually involves interference with the public health and welfare. For example, an illegal gambling establishment, bad odors, and the blockage of a highway would be grounds for a public nuisance action. In addition to the common law, states have statutes that define various activities as being public nuisances.

Whether an action creates a private or a public nuisance depends who is affected by it. The pollution of a well by a factory, for example, is a private nuisance if it interferes only with the rights of landowners living next to the plant. The suit is brought by those landowners against the owners of the plant. However, if the pollution hurts the public water supply, it is a public nuisance. In such circumstances, the legal representative of the community, such as the county district attorney, brings the action on behalf of the citizens against the polluters.

Public nuisance actions are often based on enforcement of statutes and city ordinances as the court explains in the *Sowers* case.

SOWERS V. FOREST HILLS SUBDIVISION
Supreme Court of Nevada 294 P.3d 427 (2013)

Case Background *Sowers decided he would build a wind turbine to generate electricity on his residential property. His neighbors were not pleased, as the turbine would generate noise, cause shadow flicker, ruin the view, and reduce property values. Members of the subdivision sued to permanently enjoin construction of the turbine as a nuisance. The district court granted the injunction. Sowers appealed.*

Case Decision Hardesty, Justice

* * *

A nuisance is anything which is injurious to health, or indecent and offensive to the senses, or an obstruction to the free use of property, so as to interfere with the comfortable enjoyment of life or property. There are several kinds of nuisances, two of which are pertinent to this discussion. A nuisance at law, also called a nuisance *per se*, is a nuisance at all times and under any circumstances, regardless of location or surroundings. A nuisance in fact, also called a nuisance *per accidens*, is one which becomes a nuisance by reasons of circumstances and surroundings. ...

We do not believe that wind turbines are severe interferences in all circumstances, and thus wind turbines are not nuisances at law.

However, even when a structure or act is not a nuisance *per se*, a nuisance may arise from a lawful activity conducted in an unreasonable and improper manner. Thus, a wind turbine may be or become a nuisance by reason of the improper or negligent manner in which it is conducted, or by reason of its locality, as where it is done or conducted in a place where it necessarily tends to the damage of another's property. Accordingly, a fair test as to whether a business or a particular use of a property in connection with the operation of the business constitutes a nuisance is the reasonableness or

unreasonableness of the operation or use in relation to the particular locality and under all existing circumstances.

When deciding whether one's use of his or her property is a nuisance to his neighbors, it is necessary to balance the competing interests of the landowners, using a commonsense approach. ... Thus, in resolving this issue on appeal, we must determine whether the proposed wind turbine is so unreasonable and substantial as to amount to a nuisance and warrant an injunction by balancing the gravity of the harm to the plaintiff against the utility of the defendant's conduct, both to himself and to the community. ...

To sustain a claim for private nuisance, an interference with one's use and enjoyment of land must be both substantial and unreasonable. Interference is substantial if normal persons living in the community would regard the alleged nuisance as definitively offensive, seriously annoying or intolerable." Interference is unreasonable when "the gravity of the harm outweighs the social value of the activity alleged to cause the harm. ...

We conclude that this evidence concerning the noise, diminution in property value, shadow flicker, and aesthetics far outweighs any potential utility of the proposed wind turbine within the Forest Hills Subdivision. Accordingly, we conclude that the proposed wind turbine constitutes a nuisance in fact. ...

Accordingly, we affirm the district court's order granting a permanent injunction.

Questions for Analysis

1. Why is this conclusion called a nuisance in fact instead of a nuisance *per se*?
2. If public policy supports the production of renewable energy, should that be allowed to overcome the objections?

Trespass to Personal Property

The intentional and wrongful interference with possession of personal property of another without consent is a **trespass to personal property**. An important element in this tort is that someone has interfered with the right of the owner to exclusive possession and enjoyment of personal property. Liability usually occurs when the trespasser damages the property or deprives the owner of the use of the property for a time. However, if the interference with the personal property of another is warranted, there is a defense to the trespass. Many states assist this ruling by statutes that allow motel operators to hold the personal property of guests who have not paid their bills.

Conversion

The tort of **conversion** is an intentional and unlawful control or appropriation of the personal property of another. In contrast to trespass on personal property, conversion requires that the control or appropriation so seriously interferes with the owner's right of control that it justifies payment for the property. Several factors are considered in determining whether the interference warrants a finding of conversion: the extent of dominion or control, the duration of the interference, the damage to the property, and the inconvenience and expense to the owner.

Generally, one who wrongfully acquires possession of another's personal property—by theft, duress, or fraud—is said to have committed the tort of conversion. In most states, a *bona fide* purchaser (a good-faith purchaser who thought the seller was the rightful owner of the property) is liable for conversion if the property was purchased from a thief, but this rule has exceptions.

Misappropriation

Some forms of intellectual property, including trademarks and trade secrets, are highly valued and are protected by tort law from **misappropriation** or theft by others. We discuss intellectual property in detail in Chapter 9, where we see that some statutes specify the damages that may be incurred when others take such property without permission. As with other forms of property, owners may sue those who invade their property rights for damages and may ask a court to issue an injunction against further unauthorized use of the property. Next, we turn to a common tort action filed against property owners.

ISSUE SPOTTER
Protecting Company Property

At your office, employees often walk out with assorted supplies. Pencils and paper clips are cheap, but the cost of pens, staplers, reams of paper, and more expensive items can quickly add up. Multiply this amount by the number of employees, and losses can be significant. Can a company have a policy informing employees that taking supplies is theft of company property that makes them subject to dismissal? Does the company need to notify the employees that it is theft, or should they know this without it being said? How should these losses be handled? As you think about this, remember that theft by employees costs businesses more in total than theft by non-employees.

Lighter Side **of the Law**

The FBI Negligent? No, Just Doing Law Enforcement

A rare Ferrari was stolen in Pennsylvania and was recovered six years later in Kentucky. Before the car could be returned, an FBI agent—for reasons "not entirely clear"—took the car out of storage, gave a U.S. attorney for a ride, and ultimately wrecked the car. The insurance company that owned the car claimed the government was liable for negligence and conversion for $750,000, which was the market value of the car.

The judge held the matter to be "unfortunate" but the government cannot be sued in such instances because the "purpose in holding the vehicle was ... to control and preserve relevant evidence" related to a criminal matter.

Source: Motors Insurance Corp. v. *U.S.,* 2011 WL 4506103.

Torts against Property Owners

Remember Humpty Dumpty who sat on a wall and had a great fall? Did he have a cause of action against the wall owner? It depends on several factors. Was Humpty invited to sit on the wall or was he a trespasser? If he was committing a trespass by sitting on the wall without permission, then the owner of the wall owed him no duty of care, other than not to take steps that could cause him to suffer an injury. If Humpty had been invited to a party and, during the party, decided to sit on the wall, then the property owner would not be liable to Humpty unless the owner was aware of some danger involved in sitting on the wall and failed to tell Humpty about it. The principles we have discussed come together for businesses in what is generally called **premises liability**.

Premises Liability

There are many cases involving someone slipping and falling on business property. The customer of a business, presumed by law to be invited to be on the premises to shop or just look around, suffers an injury resulting from slipping on a wet spot. The general rule is that the owner of the property has a duty to keep the premises reasonably safe under the circumstances. Customers are not trespassers; they are **invitees** welcome on business property. Invitees have an express or implied invitation to enter another's premises. Property owners have a duty to inspect premises for dangers and correct the problem or warn invitees of the dangers. This rule holds for social guests and business invitees.

Suppose it is raining, and water splashes into the front of the store. The property owner has a duty to limit any slips that could occur by mopping the area, putting down an extra doormat, and perhaps a warning sign, but customers are also expected to use common sense in such conditions. If a danger is obvious, people have a duty to protect themselves from it. What if the danger is not so obvious? If a patron is injured, is the property owner liable? The legal standard is discussed by the Connecticut high court in the *DiPietro* case.

Premises liability may also occur when a business does not provide sufficient security to help prevent crimes from occurring on its property. For instance, in another Supreme Court of Connecticut case, a $1.5 million verdict was upheld in favor of the heirs of a woman who was robbed and murdered in the parking garage of a Bloomingdale's department store. The

DIPIETRO V. FARMINGTON SPORTS ARENA, LLC
Supreme Court of Connecticut 49 A.3d 951 (2012)

Case Background *Michelle DiPietro, age 11, was playing soccer at the Farmington Indoor Sports Arena when her foot "stuck" on the playing surface (an Astroturf-like carpet). She fell and suffered a severe ankle injury. Her mother brought suit on her behalf, contending that the fall resulted from a "dangerous and defective condition with the playing surface." An inspection found the playing surface to be in good condition with no evident problems such as a tear or hole. No other player ever complained of a problem. The trial court granted defendants summary judgment. The matter was appealed.*

Case Decision Rogers, Chief Justice

* * *

The relevant principles of premises liability are well established. A business owner owes its invitees a duty to keep its premises in a reasonably safe condition. In addition, the possessor of land must warn an invitee of dangers that the invitee could not reasonably be expected to discover. Nevertheless, for a plaintiff to recover for the breach of a duty owed to him as a business invitee, it is incumbent upon him to allege and prove that the defendant either had actual notice of the presence of the specific unsafe condition which caused his injury or constructive notice of it. … The notice, whether actual or constructive, must be notice of the very defect which occasioned the injury and not merely of conditions

naturally productive of that defect even though subsequently in fact producing it. … In the absence of allegations and proof of any facts that would give rise to an enhanced duty … a defendant is held to the duty of protecting its business invitees from known, foreseeable dangers.

Accordingly, business owners do not breach their duty to invitees by failing to remedy a danger unless they had actual or constructive notice of that danger. To defeat a motion for summary judgment in a case based on allegedly defective conditions, the plaintiff has the burden of offering evidence from which a jury reasonably could conclude that the defendant had notice of the condition and failed to take reasonable steps to remedy the condition after such notice. …

Because the plaintiff failed to establish a genuine issue of material fact as to the defendants' actual or constructive notice of the dangerousness of the carpet, the defendants were entitled to summary judgment. …

[We] affirm the judgments of the trial court.

Questions for Analysis

1. Suppose the surface was found not to comply with an industry standard or federal regulation. Could that have made a difference?
2. Can a business evade responsibility by saying it never knew of a problem?

ISSUE SPOTTER
Duties to Elderly Customers

The number of persons over age 65 will double in the coming decades. More patrons at businesses will be frail, have poor balance, weak eyesight, and other age-related issues. The Metropolitan Opera in New York was sued when an elderly patron fell and injured another patron in the fall. To avoid claims of negligence when falls and other problems occur, what changes may need to be made in business operations? Is your answer different if the business has a particularly high or particularly low proportion of elderly customers?

© Cengage Learning

Lighter Side of the Law

Pesky Surveillance Cameras

Benedict Harkins filed an insurance claim against Farm Fresh Market in Jamestown, N.Y., for having tripped over a rug and fallen at the front door. After he filed suit, he was told that the store surveillance camera showed him sitting down and adjusting the rug to make it look like he tripped on it. He withdrew his claim but was arrested for attempted petty larceny.

Source: Buffalo News.

store was found negligent for not having a security guard on duty. The store was in a high-crime area and other customers had been robbed in the garage.

Commercial property cannot provide protection against every criminal act that may occur, but property owners cannot ignore crime problems that may be in the area, as the *Erichsen* case discusses.

ERICHSEN V. NO-FRILLS SUPERMARKETS OF OMAHA

Supreme Court of Nebraska 518 N.W.2d 116 (1994)

Case Background *Erichsen went grocery shopping at No-Frills one morning. When she returned to her car, she was assaulted, beaten, robbed, and dragged over one mile hanging from the car of her assailant, suffering serious injuries. She sued No-Frills and the owner of the shopping center for negligently failing to warn her of criminal activity and for failing to protect her from criminal activities that were foreseeable because of 10 criminal events in the previous 16 months. The trial court held that defendants did not violate a duty of care to Erichsen. She appealed.*

Case Decision Lanphier, Justice

* * *

We have adopted the rule regarding landlord liability to business invitees, as set forth in *Restatement (Second) of Torts* § 344 (1965). It provides:

A possessor of land who holds it open to the public for entry for his business purposes is subject to liability to members of the public while they are upon the land for such a pur-

pose, for physical harm caused by the accidental, negligent, or intentionally harmful acts of third persons or animals, and by the failure of the possessor to exercise reasonable care to (a) discover that such acts are being done or are likely to be done, or (b) give a warning adequate to enable the visitors to avoid the harm, or otherwise to protect them against it.

Comment *f.* to § 344 makes it clear that the owner of the property is not an insurer of the land or the visitor's safety while on it. However, liability will be found under certain circumstances:

Since the possessor is not an insurer of the visitor's safety, he is ordinarily under no duty to exercise any care until he knows or has reason to know that the acts of the third person are occurring, or are about to occur. *He may, however, know or have reason to know, from past experience, that there is a likelihood of conduct on the part of third persons in general which is likely to endanger the safety of the visitor, even though he has no reason to expect it on the part of any particular individual. If the place or character of his business, or his past experience, is* such that he should reasonably anticipate careless or criminal conduct on the part of third persons, *either generally* or at some particular time, he may be under a duty to take precautions against it, and to provide a reasonably sufficient number of servants to afford reasonable protection. We have interpreted the *Restatement* and have held that a landlord is under a duty to exercise reasonable care to protect his patrons. Such care many require giving a warning or providing greater protection where there is a *likelihood* that third persons will endanger the safety of the visitors....

This court has denied relief where the appellant based his or her allegations of negligence on a single act of violence. In those cases, we held that one incident did not, under the facts presented in those cases, constitute sufficient notice to make the criminal acts sued upon reasonably foreseeable. However ... a duty to undertake reasonable precautionary measures will be imposed on the landlord when there is a sufficient amount of criminal activity to make further criminal acts reasonably foreseeable....

We find that appellant has alleged sufficient facts in her petition to overcome the demurrer of appellees. The cause is therefore remanded for further proceedings consistent with this opinion.

Questions for Analysis

1. The Nebraska high court held it was for the jury to determine if the store violated its duty to take more precautions to protect patrons against criminal attack. Why should this store do any more than any other store?
2. Can a store afford to have full-time security guards? Is that required in cases such as this one?

❓ *TEST YOURSELF*

1. Governments often control the use of land through _____ and may obtain ownership of land, if the owner does not want to sell, by _____.
2. State and local governments impose land use controls under their police powers: T—F
3. In the case *Saadala* v. *East Brunswick Zoning Board*, concerning zoning for retail gas sales at a 7-Eleven, the appeals court held that the Zoning Board had:
   a. improperly allowed 7-Eleven's request.
   b. used "proper discretion" under state zoning law to decide to grant 7-Eleven's request.
   c. apparently taken bribes in return for the zoning request and were subject to criminal prosecution.
   d. allowed the request as the area was clearly zoned for such commercial sales and Saadala had no grounds to oppose the 7-Eleven request.
4. An activity that substantially and unreasonably interferes with the use and enjoyment of land is a(n) _____.
5. In *Smith* v. *Kulig*, where Smith was killed when a fire escape collapsed, the court found the fire escape to be a nuisance as an "unreasonable danger": T—F
6. An intentional and wrongful interference with possession of personal property of another without consent is _____.
7. In *DiPietro* v. *Farmington Sports Arena*, where the DiPietro child suffered an ankle injury attributed to the playing surface on an indoor soccer field, the court found the failure to properly maintain the surface to create an unreasonable hazard to invitees: T—F
8. In *Sowers* v. *Forest Hills Subdivision*, where neighbors wanted to block construction of a wind turbine that would generate electricity, the court held that the turbine was a nuisance: T—F

Answers: zoning, eminent domain; T; a; nuisance; F; trespass to personal property; F; T.

ISSUE SPOTTER
Protecting Customers' Kids

As a manager of a department store, you know that it is not uncommon for kids to run around in the store with little adult supervision. Some kids have been hurt when they run into display cabinets. The edges of the cabinets are sharp and hard. Kids have cut themselves, requiring trips to the emergency room for stitches. While most customers have not asserted that the store should be liable for the uncontrolled behavior of their kids, some have. Given that this happens at least several times a year, should the store take extra steps to protect itself from possible liability? What sort of steps could be taken?

© Cengage Learning

SUMMARY

- Property law focuses on real property, which is land, houses, and things attached to the land: and personal property, which is movable property, such as furniture, books, and cars. The owners of property have legal interests or rights in property. Property rights are limited by common law and by statutes that restrict the use of property.

- Written deeds are used to transfer ownership interests in real property. Many forms of deeds exist that provide different levels of assurances of the quality of ownership rights being provided. Titles to property, which constitute the formal right of ownership, are passed by deeds.

- The strongest form of ownership of real property is fee simple, which is how most real estate in the United States is held. When more than one party owns real estate, it is often held in a tenancy in common, where the parties have an undivided interest that passes to their heirs on death; or it may be in a joint tenancy, which is also an undivided interest, but the other owner has a right of survivorship.

- Property is often held in a trust for a business so as to protect the property against being lost if the business has financial problems. Trusts are also used by people who wish to keep property under certain controls for the beneficiary of the trust.

- Servitudes are restrictions or requirements imposed on the use of property, most commonly easements and covenants. Such legal rights are held to run with the land, as they usually stay in place when title to property passes. Most easements grant the right to another party to enter property for some purpose, such as to have access to power lines. Covenants are often used in real estate developments to impose requirements on the design of houses and characteristics of the property that must be maintained.

- Real estate may be leased to tenants for any terms the parties agree on so long as it does not conflict with state law. Any details not covered in a lease fall under state landlord-tenant law. The parties have obligations. Tenants may not abuse the property, and landlords must make certain key repairs in a timely manner and must not invade the privacy of the tenants.

- Leases for commercial property tend to be highly specific on many details about the property. Unlike most residential leases, which are often governed by state landlord-tenant statutes, commercial leases are determined by the parties to the bargain and so require care by the parties to the transaction.

- Governments have the power of eminent domain. It allows them to condemn private property and take it for public use, so long as fair market value compensation is paid to the owners. Destruction of substantial property value by regulations such as zoning is generally not compensable. A controversial form of eminent domain in recent years is its use to turn the property over to a private party for profitable use.

- Torts against property include trespass, or the unauthorized intrusion on the land of another, and nuisance, which is a substantial and unreasonable interference with the right of persons to use and enjoy their property. A nuisance may be private, in which case a property owner sues, or public, when many people suffer from the interference, and a public attorney acts on their behalf.

- Other torts include trespass to personal property, which is wrongful interference with the right of persons to use their property in a lawful manner, and conversion, which is the unlawful appropriation (theft) of the personal property of another person.
- Property owners may be sued for premises liability by those they have invited to come on their property, such as store customers. If the property owner has been negligent in maintaining the condition of the property and that negligence violates the duty of ordinary care and results in an injury, liability may be imposed. Liability may also arise from the failure of a property owner to provide reasonable security against criminal attacks.

TERMS TO KNOW

property, 193
real property, 194
deed, 194
quitclaim deed, 194
warranty deed, 194
lien, 194
special warranty deed, 195
title, 195
estate, 195
fee simple, 195
mineral rights, 195
tenancy in common, 196
joint tenancy, 196
life estate, 196

trust, 196
trustee, 196
beneficiary, 197
business trust, 197
servitude, 197
easement, 197
profit, 198
adverse possession, 198
easement by prescription, 198
statute of limitations, 199
covenant, 200
leasehold, 202
landlord, 202
tenant, 202

lease, 202
waste, 203
eminent domain, 206
police power, 207
zoning, 207
trespass, 209
private nuisance, 210
public nuisance, 210
trespass to personal property, 212
conversion, 212
misappropriation, 212
premises liability, 213
invitee, 213

DISCUSSION QUESTION

A century ago, the common law regarding landlords and tenants held the tenant responsible for major repairs to residences, such as roof repairs. Over the years, the common law changed to put such responsibility on the landlords. Why did the law evolve in that direction? What factors may have brought about the change?

CASE QUESTIONS

1. Peterson operated a private golf course. In 1964, he sold property next to the golf course, including a restaurant and parking lot, to AL. The parking lot was used by the golfers on Peterson's golf course and by restaurant patrons. In 1978, AL sold the property containing the parking lot to VBC. Peterson had always maintained the parking lot. In 1992, VBC demanded Peterson pay rent for the use of the parking lot by the golfers. Peterson sued, claiming title to the parking lot by adverse possession. Is Peterson right? [*Peterson* v. *Beck*, 537 N.W.2d 375, Sup. Ct., S.D. (1995)]

2. The Gleasons owned a large piece of property. Part of it was subject to a public drainage easement. Taub went into the drainage area with a bulldozer and removed 16,000 cubic feet of dirt to use as fill on other land. The Gleasons sued him for trespass. He defended that he had a right to go on the public easement and, furthermore that his dirt removal improved the drainage in the easement. Who would you think correct? [*Gleason* v. *Taub*, 180 S.W.3d 711, Ct. App., TX (2005)]

3. A KFC restaurant was on a major street in town until the city redesigned the road, leaving the KFC at the end of a dead-end road, which caused business to fail. The KFC owners sued the city for inverse condemnation—a taking of their property by reducing the value of it. Can they demand compensation for this loss of value? [*Kau Kau Take Home* v. *City of Wichita*, 135 P.3d 1221, Sup. Ct., Kan. (2006)]
   ✓ Check your answer

4. The City of New York sued a web-based business, smartapartments.com, that connected

people who wanted to rent their apartments for less than a month to people who want to rent apartments for less than a month. The City contended this would create a public nuisance. Does the City have a good case? [*City of New York* v. *Smart Apartments, LLC,* 2013 WL 692880 (2013)]

5. Fox rented a house from Chiodini, but he noticed exposed electrical wiring in the basement, so he refused to move in. City inspectors confirmed a code violation, and Chiodini fixed the wiring a month after the lease was to start. By that time, Fox had moved elsewhere. Because Chiodini was willing to begin the lease the day the wiring was fixed, did Fox break the lease by refusing to move in? [*Chiodini* v. *Fox,* 207 S.W.3d 174, Ct. App., Mo. (2006)]
    ✓ Check your answer

6. Smith, a sales rep for Ziva, left $850,000 in jewelry in the trunk of his car when he took it to a car wash to be cleaned. Smith watched the procedure to make sure no one opened the trunk, but while it was being dried, someone jumped in the car, took off, and stole the jewelry. He sued the car wash for allowing the theft of his personal property. While the car wash had possession of his car, was it responsible for the jewelry? [*Ziva Jewelry* v. *Car Wash Hq.,* 897 So.2d 1011, Sup. Ct., Ala. (2004)]

7. While Rouse was looking at new cars at a dealership, he gave his car keys to a sales rep so that his car could be examined for trade-in. When Rouse decided to leave without buying, the keys were hidden from him—supposedly lost—for about a half hour. The sales rep thought this was a joke. Rouse sued and was awarded $5,000 in punitive damages. What was the tort claimed? [*Russell-Vaughn Ford* v. *Rouse,* 206 So.2d 371, Sup. Ct., Ala. (1968)]
    ✓ Check your answer

8. Allen slipped and fell on a grape that was on the floor at a grocery store. No one saw the accident, and no one was sure how the grape ended up on the floor. The manager claimed that the area had been recently checked to make sure it was clean. A jury awarded Allen $10,000 for her injuries. The store appealed. Does the verdict hold? [*Brookshire Food Stores* v. *Allen,* 93 S.W.3d 897, Ct. App., Tx. (2002)]

9. Members of Earth First! demonstrated in a forest against logging. Protestors chained themselves to logging machinery. Logging operations had to be stopped for a day because of the protest and occupation of machinery (which was not damaged). What cause of action does the logging company have against the protesters or does the First Amendment protect them? [*Huffman and Wright Logging Co.* v. *Wade,* 857 P.2d 101, Sup. Ct., Ore. (1993)]
    ✓ Check your answer

10. Strahs, age 84, slipped on an icy spot in the parking lot of a drugstore, fell, and broke her hip. She sued the drugstore and the company that was under contract to keep the parking lot plowed for snow. While it had been plowed, there were icy spots remaining in the parking lot. Did she have a case against either of those parties? [*Strahs* v. *Tovar's Snowplowing,* 812 N.E.2d 441, Ct. App., Ill. (2004)]

ETHICS QUESTION

A real estate development sells houses with a covenant that prohibits the sale to buyers under the age of 55 so as to discourage children from living in the area. The covenant may even prohibit children from being permanent residents of the area; they can come as visitors, but not residents. Is that sort of restriction ethically acceptable?

CHAPTER 9

Intellectual Property

You can find most software at a fraction of the normal retail price because it is pirated. Suppose you get a pirated program and install it on the 14 computers at your company. Do you have proper licensing? No? This can be a poor move if you are charged with illegal use of software that was pirated or illegally copied (see the Software & Information Industry Association, www.siia.net; an unhappy worker could turn you in for a reward). Illegal software is a serious problem for a business, involving fines and the cost of legal defense, as well as possible public exposure and damage to the company's reputation.

Reputation, or how others view you or a company, is one part of intellectual property. **Intellectual property** is created by mental effort, not by physical labor. It is often called **intangible property** because it may be invisible, impossible to hold, and harder to value than the physical property we discussed in the previous chapter (see Chapter 8).

Intellectual property is more valuable than the real property owned by many companies. For example, it is estimated that almost half of the market value of the Coca-Cola Company rests in its brand value. The aggregate value of brand names of American firms is estimated to be around $1.5 trillion, which represents about 40 percent of global brand value.

In this chapter, we will look at the four major forms of intellectual property:

- Trademarks
- Copyrights
- Patents
- Trade secrets

The law has a long tradition of providing protection for intellectual property. The first modern patent statute was created in the Republic of Venice in 1474. The Constitution expresses its importance; Article I, Section 8, authorizes Congress "To promote the Progress of Science and useful Arts, by securing for limited Times to Authors and Inventors the exclusive Right to their respective Writings and Discoveries." Many of the Founders of the Republic were involved in intellectual property. Not only was Thomas Jefferson an inventor, but George Washington was involved in controversies over patents for steamboats, and one of Alexander Hamilton's aides hired an industrial spy to try to steal British technology. Today, the Commissioner of Patents and Trademarks issues more than 200,000 patents annually—half to Americans and half to foreigners. The Trademark Office receives about 400,000 trademark filings annually. The Copyright Office receives more than 600,000 copyrights annually.

Just as the common law protects real property, it also works with various statutes to protect intellectual property by allowing property owners to sue in cases of **infringement.** Wrongful, unauthorized use of intellectual property in violation of the owner's rights is the basis for a tort action. When intellectual property rights are infringed, or misappropriated, damages may be awarded to the property holder, and an injunction against further unauthorized use may be issued. Various statutes enhance this protection. How important is protection of intellectual property? The U.S. government estimates that counterfeit and fraudulent use of intellectual property costs business tens of billions of dollars a year.

Trademarks

A **trademark** is a commercial symbol—a design, logo, phrase, distinctive mark, name, or word—that a manufacturer puts on its goods so they can be readily identified in the marketplace. We often recognize them as brand names, such as Nike, or a symbol, such as the Nike "swoosh." Other producers may not legally imitate genuine trademarks. Because companies spend large sums so consumers will recognize and trust their products, the common law has long recognized the right to protect this property. This common-law protection was made a part of federal law by the **Lanham Act**. Federal trademark law allows trademarks to be registered if they are distinctive and nonfunctional. As long as the owner continues to use and protect the trademark, the trademark's exclusive use can be perpetual.

Traditionally, trademark protection was created by priority of use. The first person to use a symbol in a business or geographic area has the right to stop others from using the same or very similar trade symbols in that business or area. The Lanham Act allows a person to register a symbol with the Patent and Trademark Office in Washington, D.C. The Trademark Revision Act allows nationwide claim to a mark from the moment it is registered, as long as sincere intent exists to use the symbol in commerce.

The advantages of registration of trademarks with the U.S. Patent and Trademark Office, rather than relying only on common-law protection of trademarks, include the following:

1. Nationwide notice of the trademark owner's claim.
2. Legal presumption of the registrant's ownership of the mark in the event of a dispute.
3. Federal court jurisdiction, if desired.
4. Forming the basis for obtaining registration in other nations.
5. Filing the registration with U.S. Customs Service to help prevent importation of foreign goods that infringe on the trademark.

Most colleges have trademarks for their names or employ a distinctive use of letters in their names and for their sports team names and mascots. Collegiate Licensing is a licensing agent for many universities and the manufacturers that make clothing and various items with university logos. This licensing allows colleges to collect royalties from and control the use of their trademarks so that they are not used in ways the colleges do not approve.

Registration

The registration process, which can be done online, includes payment of a fee ($325 per class of goods using a mark); submission of a copy of the mark, called a specimen; a description of the goods that will use the mark; and a declaration that, to the best of the applicant's knowledge, the mark does not conflict with other marks (see the U.S. Patent and Trademark office at www.uspto.gov for a clear guide to the process).

The applicant is responsible for searching existing trademarks to make sure there is no confusion with or infringement on existing marks. A trademark examiner reviews

ISSUE SPOTTER
Establishing Your Name

As even more business is done on the Internet, a company's domain name is critical. While established companies have registered their domain names, what if you have a new company or a small company that has never had one before? How do you go about getting a good, secure name? Should you also secure names that are close to your name?

Lighter Side **of the Law**

Discrimination against Men?

Chippendales strip club in Los Angeles has bare-chested male performers wear wrist cuffs and a bow tie without a shirt as part of their routine. The club submitted a trademark application for "Cuffs & Collar" for "adult entertainment services, namely exotic dancing for women."

The Trademark Office rejected the application, noting that the mark is not inherently distinctive. The club appealed. The federal appeals court upheld the rejection, explaining that the Playboy bunny costume included cuffs and collars for many years. The proposed mark was too similar to the distinctive Playboy brand.

Source: In re Chippendales USA, 622 F.3d 1346.

the request to make sure the mark does not conflict with existing marks, is not descriptive, and does not claim too much coverage. That is, if you wish to trademark a word for a brand of perfume, you cannot register the word "perfume" because that is the generic term for that product. If the word "Charlie" is registered as a trademark for perfume, other people may be allowed to use the word in other contexts, such as "Charlie's Motel," as no one will confuse the perfume with the motel.

Registration is good for ten years, after which it must be renewed. You can make sure people know a mark is protected by stating "Registered in U.S. Patent and Trademark Office" or by using the circle-R (® symbol). You also see the symbol "TM," which puts people on notice, but is not specified in the Lanham Act. However, lack of notice that a mark is a trademark does not mean the owner of the mark is not due legal protection for the mark.

International protection of trademarks is encouraged by the International Bureau of the World Intellectual Property Organization (www.wipo.int). Through the "Madrid System" a trademark holder from most countries can file an existing trademark for international registration. This is much less costly than going through the process of registering individually in each country where trademark protection is desired. The Trademark Office website explains the international application process and fees.

Classifications of Trademarks

Trademarks are classified as arbitrary and fanciful, suggestive, descriptive, or generic (see Exhibit 9.1).

EXHIBIT 9.1   TYPES OF TRADEMARKS

ARBITRARY AND FANCIFUL	SUGGESTIVE	DESCRIPTIVE	GENERIC (NO LONGER TRADEMARKS)
Polaroid	Orange Crush	Raisin Bran	Trampoline
Lexus	Roach Motel	Holiday Inn	Nylon
Virginia Slims	Dairy Queen	Musky (perfume)	Thermos
Ivory (soap)	Passion (Perfume)	Yellow Pages	Shredded Wheat
Clorox	Coppertone	After Tan	Zipper
Camel (cigarettes)	Playboy	Vision Center	Outlet Store

© Cengage Learning

Arbitrary and fanciful trademarks are most favored by the courts because they are inherently distinctive (fanciful), such as the made-up names Exxon or Reebok, or they are names not related to the product (arbitrary), such as Captain Morgan for rum and Apple for computers.

Suggestive marks hint at the product, such as Chicken of the Sea for canned tuna. They are due legal protection, but establishing that can be more difficult than if the mark is arbitrary and fanciful.

Descriptive marks are not as favored by the law and must be shown to have acquired customer recognition to be allowed protection. Examples of successful descriptive marks are Bufferin for aspirin with acid buffering and Holiday Inn for hotels.

Generic marks are words that are common and do not refer to products from a specific producer. Some words that were once trademarks have become generic or unprotected marks, for example, *thermos* for vacuum-insulated bottles, *aspirin* for acetylsalicylic acid, and *escalator* for moving stairways. If trademark owners do not protect their marks, it is presumed they do not care about ownership, and the marks become generic. Many people refer to facial tissues as Kleenex, but Kleenex® is a trademark for a brand of tissue made by Kimberly-Clark, so the company must be sure the word does not become generic by defending the use of the mark. Similarly, Google gets a benefit from many people referring to web searches as "googling," but it takes steps to protect the term from becoming generic and freely used by anyone.

Extent of Coverage

Trademarks, service marks, and other marks cannot claim too much. For example, if you go to the Trademark Office website (www.uspto.gov) and search for the Shox trademark, you will see more than 60 claims. One claim was Nike Shox. The listing shows the address of the company in Beaverton, Oregon, and gives the serial number assigned to Nike Shox (78406612). Nike sold athletic apparel that was called Shox, but it stopped using the term and its registration is now dead, as are about half of the other Shox claims.

Trademarks that are dead or abandoned are listed. For example, the word *Shox* was once claimed for "plastic step supports for ladders" by a Kentucky company, but it no longer claims the mark, so it is listed as dead for that use. Other marks that used the word Shox are active, such as for "polyurethane tires for wheelchairs" for an Indiana company. Most mark claims are narrow so marks can be used across an array of unrelated products.

Trademark protection applies to a wide range of creative property other than the names of products. Trademark law applies to titles of movies, advertising slogans, titles of comic books, and fictional characters, such as Batman. This allows the producers of highly popular movies and cartoon characters to license use of the names, such as Star Wars, which showed up in toys and premiums at fast-food restaurants.

Infringement, Dilution, and Cybersquatting

The extent of trademark protection depends on how well known a mark is and whether a similar mark could be confused with the original mark. The holders of marks must actively protect them, or they will be presumed to have been given up, as happened to marks that became generic.

Infringement occurs when a seller causes confusion about the origins of a product by improper use of a trademark. If a company other than Reebok makes and sells shoes using that famous name, there is infringement; consumers will be confused, thinking the counterfeit shoes to be genuine Reebok, even if the shoes are not designed to look like genuine

CYBER LAW

Who Controls Domain Names?

The International Corporation for Assigned Names and Numbers (ICANN) is in charge of preserving the organizational and operational stability of the Internet (see www.icann.org). The Department of Commerce granted control of the domain-name system (DNS) to this global organization. ICANN coordinates the top-level domain (TLD) system, such as *.com*, and it decides on additional TLDs. For example, it refused to allow the TLD *.xxx*, which was desired by "adult" material website operators. It also coordinates IP addresses and country codes.

ICANN does not issue individual domain names. It accredits firms such as Network Solutions that meet its standards for proper registry of domain names. ICANN does not control spam and other problems; those issues are left to national law and Internet service providers. If a domain name owner does not

keep registration current, which costs about $40 a year, the site goes dormant. At one point, the Dallas Cowboys failed to renew DallasCowboys.com, so visitors saw only a page that noted that the team was delinquent on renewing its domain name.

The World Intellectual Property Organization (see www.wipo.int) handles many disputes over domain names—about 3,000 a year. Other disputes are handled by organizations accredited by ICANN to resolve problems, including the National Arbitration Forum in the United States. The regulation of domain names is global and largely handled by private organizations through arbitration under the Uniform Domain-Name Dispute-Resolution Policy. Individual disputes may end up in court, but such cases represent only a very small fraction of the total number of intellectual property legal issues that need to be resolved.

Reebok-brand shoes. Similarly, if a company sells shoes called *Rebok*, while not identical, that too would cause confusion because the name "Reebok" is famous. Essentially, it is stealing the good name of another. The Lanham Act specifically allows suit for infringement.

Dilution is another violation of trademark rights. The Trademark Dilution Act expanded the rights of famous and distinctive trademarks under the Lanham Act. This right was strengthened by the Trademark Revision Dilution Act of 2006, which holds that:

> *The owner of a famous mark that is distinctive, inherently or through acquired distinctiveness, shall be entitled to an injunction against another person who, at any time after the owner's mark has become famous, commences use of a mark or trade name in commerce that is likely to cause dilution by blurring or dilution by tarnishment of the famous mark, regardless of the presence or absence of actual or likely confusion, of competition, or of actual economic injury.*

That is, if a company sold guitars under the name Nike Guitars, that would be dilution. No one would think the guitars to be Nike athletic wear, but they may presume Nike has gotten into the guitar business, thereby diluting the strength of the Nike mark.

Cybersquatting occurs when a trademark is used improperly in a domain name. That practice is expressly restricted by the Anticybersquatting Consumer Protection Act (ACPA), which prevents a website from capturing value from another's trademark. So, to register the domain name reebokshoes.com without permission from Reebok would be cybersquatting.

To pursue a cybersquatting claim under the ACPA, a plaintiff must show that: (1) the defendant registered, trafficked in, or used a domain name; (2) the domain name is identical or confusingly similar to the protected mark owed by the plaintiff; and (3) the defendant acted "with bad faith intent to profit from that mark." Such claims are usually part of larger litigation involving other trademark violation claims under the Lanham Act.

Defenses in all of these situations include: (1) fair use, such as to mention a mark in comparative advertising; (2) noncommercial uses, such as parody or editorial commentary; and (3) news reporting or educational use, such as using the word "Reebok" here. In the *Audi* case that follows, we see a discussion of all of these points (which is why the case is long) and the standards set by the statutes and courts in applying the law when disputes arise.

AUDI AG V. D'AMATO

United States Court of Appeals, Sixth Circuit, 469 F.3d 534 (2006)

Case Background *D'Amato registered the domain name www.audisport.com. He sold goods with Audi logos. His site used various Audi trademarks. He claimed to have permission from a salesman at an Audi dealership to use the marks. Even if he did, Audi dealerships have no right, by contract, to grant any use of Audi trademarks. Audi's website sells assorted goods with the Audi name and logo on it. Audi sued D'Amato for infringement, dilution, and cybersquatting of its famous trademarks including Audi and the Audi four-ring logo. The district court held for Audi and issued a permanent injunction against D'Amato, his website, and domain name. He appealed.*

Case Decision Martin, Circuit Judge

* * *

A trademark is a designation used "to identify and distinguish" the goods of a person. Under the Lanham Act, we use the same test to decide whether there has been trademark infringement, unfair competition, or false designation of origin: the likelihood of confusion between the two marks. D'Amato argues that the district court's finding of a likelihood of confusion should be reversed, because Audi did not offer evidence demonstrating *actual* confusion. However, although proof that the buying public was actually deceived is necessary in order to recover *statutory damages* under the Lanham Act, only a "likelihood of confusion" must be shown in order to obtain *equitable relief*, which is at issue in this appeal.

We have held that in determining whether there is a likelihood of confusion, the following eight factors should be considered: (1) strength of plaintiff's mark; (2) relatedness of the goods; (3) similarity of the marks; (4) evidence of actual confusion; (5) marketing of channels used; (6) degree of purchaser care; (7) defendant's intent in selecting the mark; and (8) likelihood of expansion in selecting the mark....

In light of these factors, we agree with the district court's conclusion that there was a likelihood of confusion....

D'Amato contends that any proof of consumer confusion is rebutted by a disclaimer on his Web site, which stated, "This page is not associated with Audi GmbH or Audi USA in any way." First, such a disclaimer does not absolve D'Amato of liability for his unlawful use of marks identical to Audi's trademarks. In addition ...:

> An infringing domain name has the potential to misdirect consumers as they search for Web sites associated with the owner of a trademark. A disclaimer disavowing affiliation with the trademark owner read by a consumer after reaching the Web site comes too late. This "initial interest confusion" is recognized as an infringement under the Lanham Act....

D'Amato also defends his actions on the ground that his "Web site merely had hyperlinks to goods (hats and shirts)"... and that such "hyperlinks create no liability for [him]." However, even if D'Amato's intention was in fact noncommercial (which it does not appear to be), the issue is whether his actions had a commercial *effect*. We have stated that "the proper inquiry is not one of intent. ... If consumers are confused by an infringing mark, the offender's motives are largely irrelevant." Even "minimal" advertisements constitute use of the owner's trademark in connection with the advertising of the goods, which the Lanham Act proscribes. ...

Even when we construe the facts in a light most favorable to D'Amato, Audi has shown that there is a clear likelihood of confusion based on D'Amato's use of the Audi Trademarks. ...

Dilution law, unlike traditional trademark infringement law ... is not based on a likelihood of confusion standard, but only exists to protect the quasi-property rights a holder has in maintaining the integrity and distinctiveness of his mark. We use a five-point test to determine whether a plaintiff will succeed in a federal dilution claim. Audi must show that its trademark is (1) famous, (2) distinctive, and that D'Amato's use of the mark (3) was in commerce, (4) began after Audi's mark became famous, and (5) "caused dilution of the distinctive quality" of Audi's mark.

It is clear from the record that Audi's trademarks, on which Audi has spent millions of dollars and which are known worldwide, satisfy the first two factors. Further, because the Web site sold merchandise, e-mail subscriptions, and advertising space, all with Audi's logo, the third factor is satisfied. The fourth factor is met, as there is no dispute that www .audisport.com came after the Audi trademarks. As for the fifth element—whether the junior mark dilutes the senior mark—the Supreme Court has noted that "direct evidence of dilution such as consumer surveys will not be necessary if actual dilution can reliably be proven through circumstantial evidence—the obvious case is one where the junior and senior marks are identical." ...

The Anticybersquatting Consumer Protection Act (ACPA) was enacted to curb the proliferation of cybersquatting—the Internet version of a land grab. With respect to a famous mark, ACPA provides that a person will be civilly liable when he or she has a bad faith intent to profit from the mark, and "registers, traffics in, or uses a domain name that ... is identical or confusingly similar to or dilutive of that mark."

In order to prevail under the ACPA, a plaintiff must show that a defendant's use of a domain name was done in bad faith. ACPA provides a list of nine nonexclusive factors which a court should consider in determining whether a defendant acted in bad faith:

(I)   the trademark or other intellectual property rights of the person, if any, in the domain name;

(II) the extent to which the domain name consists of the legal name of the person or a name that is otherwise commonly used to identify that person;

(III) the person's prior use, if any, of the domain name in connection with the *bona fide* offering of any goods or services;

(IV) the person's *bona fide* noncommercial or fair use of the mark in a site accessible under the domain name;

(V)   the person's intent to divert consumers from the mark owner's online location to a site accessible under the domain name that could harm the goodwill represented by the mark, either for commercial gain or with the intent to tarnish or disparage the mark, by creating a likelihood of confusion as to the source, sponsorship, affiliation, or endorsement of the site;

(VI) the person's offer to transfer, sell, or otherwise assign the domain name to the mark owner or any third party for financial gain without having used, or having an intent to use, the domain name in the *bona fide* offering of any goods or services, or the person's prior conduct indicating a pattern of such conduct;

(VII) the person's provision of material and misleading false contact information when applying for the registration of the domain name, the person's intentional failure to maintain accurate contact information, or the person's prior conduct indicating a pattern of such conduct;

(VIII) the person's registration or acquisition of multiple domain names which the person knows are identical or confusingly similar to marks of others that are distinctive at the time of registration of such domain names, or dilutive of famous marks of others that are famous at the time of registration of such domain names, without regard to the goods or services of the parties; and

(IX) the extent to which the mark incorporated in the person's domain name registration is or is not distinctive and famous. ...

We affirm the judgment of the district court.

Questions for Analysis

1. The court affirmed that D'Amato engaged in infringement, dilution, and cybersquatting with respect to Audi's marks. His website stated that he was not affiliated with Audi, so why did that not protect him? How could Audi be harmed?
2. Why does the law focus on marks that are distinctive and famous?

Counterfeiting

Counterfeiting of trademarks means the copying or imitating of a mark without authority to do so. It usually means passing off goods as if they were original. Hence, marks owned by universities, Major League Baseball, and well-known companies such as Nike and Disney, must be protected by their owners. Levi's has seized millions of pairs of counterfeit pants. Not only are profits lost to counterfeiters, but also, counterfeit goods are usually of lower quality than the originals. So, consumers might think the trademarks do not represent quality, and the reputation of the owner can suffer.

Even if people are told that the counterfeit goods are counterfeit—so that no one is being fooled—the trademark has still been counterfeited. For example, Ferrari makes very expensive cars with distinctive body designs. Ferrari sued companies that made fiberglass imitations of its car bodies that could be placed on car frames. Everyone knew the bodies were not Ferrari, and there was a name other than Ferrari on the bodies, but the distinctive design of Ferrari was held to be a trademark that could be protected against imitators.

INTERNATIONAL PERSPECTIVE

Costs of Counterfeiting

The World Customs Organization estimates that counterfeit goods generate more than $500 billion in sales a year, including $200 billion in the United States. Some of that represents sales lost by owners of intellectual property (IP) rights from goods produced illegally.

The European Union estimates that as a result of the loss of revenues and sales to counterfeiters—most located in China and other countries with weak IP enforcement practices—120,000 jobs in the United States and 100,000 jobs in Europe have been lost. These estimates are probably high however, because they assume anyone who bought a cheap counterfeit would have bought an expensive genuine article if the counterfeit were not available.

Fake sunglasses are one thing; the problem is more serious when it involves counterfeit items with health and safety consequences. Counterfeit drug sales are common around the world. Those taking such drugs receive no benefit or may be harmed by the unknown substance. In San Diego, baby formula that could cause allergy and nutrition problems in infants was sold with counterfeit labels. Aircraft parts are very expensive (a single screw can cost $600) because they must meet strict standards. Counterfeit parts have been found infiltrating military supplies, endangering aircraft and helicopter crews.

Congress toughened criminal penalties through the Stop Counterfeiting in Manufactured Goods Act. European nations have also cracked down; Google was ordered to pay $400,000 to Louis Vuitton for allowing fake Vuitton goods to be advertised on Google. Firms invest in detectives to uncover counterfeit trade routes. They sue vendors and landlords who rent space to those who are clearly selling knockoffs. It is a complicated, sophisticated market with much at stake. Any business that makes use of trademarks needs a strategy for enforcement.

Private Enforcement The Lanham Act allows private parties to obtain search-and-seizure orders to grab counterfeit goods. A private investigator hired by the mark owner provides a U.S. Attorney with evidence of the existence and location of the counterfeit goods. The U.S. Attorney may take action directly, but usually approves the private party going to a judge to obtain a warrant. The party shows up unannounced at the location of the goods with a police officer, searches the premises, and seizes any counterfeit goods. For example, the National Football League seized 160,000 counterfeit NFL-related goods, such as football jerseys, before the 2013 Super Bowl. Such goods may be used as evidence in a civil suit for damages, but often no suit is brought if the person with the goods cooperates in providing information about their origins.

Trade Dress

A commercial symbol also protected by trademark law and the Lanham Act is **trade dress**, which has been given more attention in recent years, although it is often not registered. Trade dress concerns the "look and feel" of products and of service establishments. This includes the size, shape, color, texture, graphics, and even certain sales techniques of products. This has been applied to many products, such as teddy bears, luggage, greeting cards, romance novels, and folding tables.

The Supreme Court supported a trade dress claim in *Two Pesos* v. *Taco Cabana* (112 S.Ct. 2753). One Mexican-style restaurant could not copy its competitor's decor, which included distinctive exterior decorations and interior design. Trade dress that is "inherently distinctive" is protected under the Lanham Act and by common-law principles concerning unfair competition.

The Supreme Court further explained the standards for trade dress in *Wal-Mart Stores* v. *Samara Brothers* (120 S.Ct. 1339). The Court held that Wal-Mart had not infringed on Samara's designs of children's clothing when it produced its own clothing with designs similar to those sold by Samara. The reason Samara had no protection is because trade dress must be distinctive and must have **secondary meaning.** That is, the primary significance of trade dress is to identify the source of the product, rather than the product itself; it is not functional. Samara's design of children's clothing was not inherently distinctive on sight to many people so as to earn protection under the Lanham Act. Trade dress protection would be possible if many consumers did recognize a design as Samara, but its products did not have that level of recognition.

On the other hand, pink is protected trade dress for Owens Corning fiberglass insulation. The roar of a lion is trade dress for MGM movie introductions. Green is trade dress for Deere brand farm equipment. Orange is trade dress for the exterior of Home Depot stores. However, orange cannot be protected trade dress for the taste of a product, whether the product is orange-colored or not. Orange flavor is functional. Orange color is not functional, so it can have secondary meaning.

ISSUE SPOTTER
Knock Off the Knock-Offs?

Your company makes expensive leather products, such as purses, briefcases, and carrying bags. The company has a well-known logo that is on all the products. Knock-off versions of the product are produced in China and sold by street vendors in the United States and in stores in other countries. At times, the imitation products end up in stores in the United States. What steps can you take to protect your trademark? Should you ignore it because customers generally can distinguigh the real thing from the knock-off?

Other Marks

The Lanham Act also recognizes service marks. These marks, denoted by SM, apply to services, such as Jiffy Lube, rather than to goods; but the law is the same as it is for trademarks. **Service marks** apply to services such as advertising, insurance, hotels, restaurants, and entertainment. For example, the International Silk Association uses the motto "Only silk is silk." That is a service mark. Burger King is a trademark. The phrase "Home of the Whopper" is a service mark that is owned by Burger King.

A **certification mark** is any word, symbol, device, or any combination of these that is used, or intended to be used, in commerce to certify regional or other geographic origin ("Made in Montana"). It may also signify the type of material used, mode of manufacture, quality, accuracy, or other characteristics of someone's goods or services, or that the work was performed by members of a union ("Union Made in the USA") or another organization.

A trademark or service mark that is used in commerce by members of a cooperative, an association, or other collective group or organization is a **collective mark**. This includes a mark that indicates membership in a union, an association, or other organization.

Trade Names

A **trade name** is the name of a company or a business. Some products, such as Coca-Cola, have the same trademark as the trade name of their producer. Trade names cannot be registered under the Lanham Act, but they are protected by the common law. Many states allow trade names to be registered, but the rule is that trade name protection belongs to the first to actually use the name in a given functional area of business or in a particular geographic area.

Protection applies to the areas in which the name has meaning; national protection of the name cannot be claimed because there might be confusion. For example, because Coca-Cola operates and is known worldwide, no one may use the trade name in any business, such as by opening a Coca-Cola Motel. Even though Coca-Cola is not in the motel business, its name is protected in all uses. Because the name Coca-Cola has tremendous goodwill value, the company could license its use to motel operators. Usage of the good name of the company is thus prohibited without the company's permission. For example, the owner of the term "Rollerblade" has been careful to protect its name from becoming the generic term for in-line skates.

Goodwill

It is the reputation of a firm that gives value to trademarks and other such forms of intellectual property. This is a prized asset of many firms. The trademarks Coke and Coca-Cola are far more valuable assets than the physical property owned by the Coca-Cola Company. When firms have created such value, and have gained the trust of many customers, it is called **goodwill**.

Goodwill is the benefit or advantage of having an established business and secured customers. When a business is sold, the real property assets, such as buildings and equipment, can be evaluated precisely, as they can be replicated in the market. However, the sale price must also take into account the value of the goodwill that a business has established. Two businesses may have identical physical operations, but perhaps only one has an excellent reputation and strong customer base. That is goodwill, and it is an intangible asset. It is often closely tied to trademark or brand name. When a trademark or other form of intellectual property suffers an injury, damage estimates must include the loss of profits due to damage to the trade name, or goodwill, of the firm.

TEST YOURSELF

1. The copying or imitating of a trademark without authority to do so is called _____.
2. Trademarks are called "trade dress" if they apply to items of clothing: T—F
3. When a trademark holder suspects another party of violating a trademark, enforcement efforts must be initiated by filing a complaint with the Patent and Trademark Office: T—F
4. In the case *Audi AG* v. *D'Amato*, where D'Amato ran a business using the domain name audisport.com, and Audi sued to stop him from using the domain name. The appeals court held that:
   a. there was no likelihood of confusion, so D'Amato could keep the name because he had a legitimate business.
   b. there was no likelihood of confusion, but D'Amato could not keep the name because he did not have a legitimate business; he was only a cybersquatter.
   c. under ICANN rules, first-come, first-serve is the general rule for legitimate businesses, which D'Amato had, so he could retain the name.
   d. there was a likelihood of confusion, so D'Amato had to stop using the name.
5. If a seller causes confusion about the origins of a product by improper use of a trademark there is infringement: T—F
6. A new hotel chain names its hotels Arranllianna. The classification of trademark that name would likely have is _____.
7. The improper use of a trademark in a domain name is called _____.
8. Producers in Indiana decide that all products actually made in Indiana can have the label "Made in Indiana." That kind of mark is a _____ mark.

Answers: infringement; F; F; d; T; arbitrary and fanciful; cybersquatting; certification.

Copyright

Copyrights are rights of literary property as recognized by law. They are intangible assets that are held by the author or owner for a certain time period. More than 600,000 items are copyrighted each year. About half are books and other written works; the other half are musical compositions. Copyrights exist at common law and are supplemented by federal statutes. Copyrights are easy to obtain, and the legal protection is strong.

The Copyright Act of 1976 (amended several times since) created statutory protection for all copyrightable works. It protects an original expression automatically from the time it is fixed in a tangible medium of expression—printed, sung, used in a computer, or whatever form expression takes. The length of copyright protection depends on when the work was produced, as Congress has changed the terms of protection numerous times. Most copyrighted materials in the United States now have the same protection term: the life of the author plus 70 years, as is the case in the European Union. For works for hire, such as material written by employees of a company, the copyright is 95 years from the date of publication.

Lighter Side **of the Law**

You Owe Us the World and More!

LimeWire was a peer-to-peer file-sharing service commonly used to share copyrighted music. If you visit its website, you will see it was shut down by court order for assisting in copyright violations.

Not satisfied with that outcome, the Recording Industry Association of America sued the defunct company for $72 trillion for multiple copying of at least 11,000 songs. That is more than the GDP of the world. Federal Judge Kimba Woods called that demand "absurd." The matter was settled for a much more modest sum.

Source: PCWorld.

The Copyright Act gives a copyright owner five rights over copyrighted works:

1. The right to reproduce the work.
2. The right to publish or distribute the work.
3. The right to display the work in public.
4. The right to perform the work in public.
5. The right to prepare derivative works based on the original work.

The 1990 amendment added what are called **moral rights**, which include the right of the author to have proper attribution of authorship and to prevent unauthorized changes in or destruction of an artist's work.

Copyrighted work must be original. You cannot copyright a 200-year-old song because you did not create it; the song is in the public domain and may be used, performed, or reproduced by anyone. The Supreme Court noted that copyrighted works must be original in *Feist Publications* v. *Rural Telephone Service Co.* (111 S.Ct. 1282), in which one company copied the white-page telephone listings of another company. The Court ruled that there is nothing original in listing telephone user names, addresses, and phone numbers alphabetically; it is "devoid of even the slightest trace of creativity." Public facts not presented in an original manner cannot obtain copyright protection. There must be an original element in the work.

Registration

Copyright registration is simple (see www.copyright.gov). Fill out an online registration form from the Copyright Office (a part of the Library of Congress) in Washington, D.C.; send two copies of the copyrighted work; and pay a $35 fee. The Copyright Office simply records the registration; it does not check to make sure that the material is in fact original or that all the information provided is accurate. Unlike patents, copyrights are not issued by the government; it provides only a registration process effective the day received.

Registration provides important evidence of copyright ownership in the event of an infringement suit, and it is required for federal courts to have jurisdiction in copyright cases. A notice of copyright consists of the circle-C (©) symbol, followed by the year of first publication and the name of the copyright owner. Notice is not required but is encouraged by the Copyright Act because it helps provide proof of ownership in case of a dispute.

Infringement and Fair Use

We have all made copies of copyrighted works without getting permission. Is that illegal infringement? Not if the copying is considered **fair use**. The Copyright Act allows use of original material "for purposes such as criticism, comment, news reporting, teaching …

ISSUE SPOTTER
Fair Sharing of Educational Information?

Your company makes electrical components for jet engines. The engineers who do the designing subscribe to a number of electrical engineering journals. The subscriptions are quite expensive, so they order one subscription of each journal and make copies of articles to give to all the engineers who might be interested. Is this copying fair use, as it is for educational purposes, or could it be copyright infringement that could lead to trouble? How should this practice be handled?

scholarship, or research." If copying is not authorized for fair use, it is infringement. When considering whether a use is fair, the courts apply four factors:

1. The purpose and character of the copying (for commercial use or for nonprofit educational use).
2. The nature of the copyrighted work.
3. The extent of the copying.
4. The effect of the copying on the market for the work.

In the 1984 Supreme Court case, *Sony* v. *Universal City Studios* (104 S.Ct. 774), the fact that video owners can copy copyrighted television programs for personal use was held to be covered by the fair-use exception. Sony, the maker of video recorders, could not be sued for infringement by Sony video users. However, it is not proper for publishers to publish works in ways not anticipated by original contracts with authors. In *New York Times* v. *Tasini* (121 S.Ct. 2381), the Supreme Court held that it was copyright infringement for electronic databases, such as Lexis/Nexis, to publish stories online that were originally published in print. Because the authors had agreed to paper publication only, "reprinting" in electronic media without permission of the authors was infringement.

Claims of copyright infringement are common. Damages for violations of copyright law focus on the economic loss to the copyright holder. Federal law mandates minimum damage awards for some kinds of violations, such as copying and distributing copyrighted songs without permission. Some infringement claims fail for lack of proper procedure, as seen in the *Latin American Music* case. If copyright infringement is tied to criminal activity that occurs by mail or wire fraud, then felonies may be involved, and penalties can include imprisonment.

LATIN AMERICAN MUSIC CO., INC. V. MEDIA POWER GROUP, INC.
United States Court of Appeals, First Circuit, 705 F.3d 34 (2013)

Case Background *Media Power Group (MPG) owns four ratio stations, called "Radio Isla," in Puerto Rico, and has affiliated stations that rebroadcast its programming. It was notified by Latin American Music Company (LAMCO) and Asociación de Compositores y Editores de Música Latinoamericana (ACEMLA) that it was infringing on copyrights by* *playing songs without a license. After MPG refused to pay, LAMCO and ACEMLA sued for damages. The jury found that plaintiffs failed to show that it had copyrights on certain songs that it asserted could be played on the radio station only if a license had been purchased. Plaintiffs appealed.*

Case Decision Howard, Circuit Judge

* * *

To establish copyright infringement, the plaintiff must prove two elements: (1) ownership of a valid copyright, and (2) copying of constituent elements of the work that are original. Provided that a copyright claim is registered with the Copyright Office within five years of first publication of the work, the certificate of registration is *prima facie* evidence of ownership and the validity of the copyright. Upon the plaintiff's production of such a certificate, the burden shifts to the defendant to demonstrate some infirmity in the claimed copyright.

The jury determined that LAMCO did not prove that it owned copyrights in any of the nine songs that the defendants allegedly infringed. ...

The district court granted the defendants' motion for summary judgment as to four songs on the ground that LAMCO failed to produce evidence of registration. Registration of a copy-right is a precondition to filing a copyright infringement claim. ...

For the four songs, LAMCO submitted certificates of recordation containing assignments of rights to either the specific song at issue or all of the relevant composer's works. The district court correctly determined that a certificate of recordation is not evidence of registration because it merely indicates that the document attached was recorded in the Copyright Office on a specific date. Because recordation of an instrument relating to a work does not indicate that the work itself has been registered, a certificate of recordation does not suffice to prove compliance with the registration requirement. ...

We affirm the judgments of the district court.

Questions for Analysis

1. Did the plaintiff's case fail as a result of a technicality of registering with the Copyright Office?
2. How do radio stations pay the copyright holders given the huge number of stations and songs?

Patents

A **patent** is a grant from the government to an inventor for "the right to exclude others from making, using, offering for sale, or selling" the invention for 20 years after the inventor files a patent application. Since the Leahy-Smith America Invents Act became effective in 2013, patents are granted based on a "first-to-file" rule, as has long been the practice in other countries. Previously, the rule was the "first-to-invent" system, which meant the Patent Office granted patents to those who could prove they were the first to come up with the idea, even if they were not the first to apply for the patent.

Unlike other forms of intellectual property that have common-law roots, patents are purely statute-based. According to patent law, a person who "invents or discovers any new and useful process, machine, manufacture, or composition of matter, or any new and useful improvement thereof, may obtain a patent." The Supreme Court has explained that this does not include a human gene that has been isolated because DNA or genetic material is naturally occurring.

A process generally means an industrial or technical process, act, or method. Manufacture refers to articles that are made by manufacturing, and composition of matter relates to chemical compositions and other mixtures of ingredients. For something to be useful means the invention must have a use and be operative; patents are not given for theories. Most patents are **utility patents**, the kind just described, but there are also design patents for original and ornamental designs for manufactured articles and plant patents for new varieties of botanical plants.

The patent statute states that an invention cannot be patented if "(a) the invention was known or used by others in this country, or patented or described in a printed publication in this or a foreign country, before the invention thereof by the applicant for patent," or "(b) the invention was patented or described in a printed publication in this or a foreign country or in public use of no sale in the country more than one year prior to the application for patent in the United States." That means that even if the inventor is the first to describe the invention or to show it in public, if a patent application is not filed within one year of publication, the right to a patent is lost.

Some historians believe that the U.S. system of inexpensive, reliable patents played a major role in turning the country into a major industrial power, compared to Europe, in the nineteenth century. In the United States, ordinary people could obtain patents for innovations without political favor. A major advantage of patents is the strong protection provided. For the life of the patent, its owner has the right to exclude all others from making or using the patented invention. For example, Polaroid won a billion-dollar judgment against Kodak for infringement on its instant camera and film patents. Those patents are irrelevant today, but were hugely valuable at one time.

However, the patent process has drawbacks. The application process is technical, expensive, and time-consuming. The approval process usually takes about two years, and only about half of all patent applications are approved. Because patenting takes so long unless an extra fee is paid for quicker review, industries where technological change is rapid, such as computer software, have a hard time relying on patents. In other industries, where research and development costs are high and products can have long lives, such as pharmaceuticals, there is strong reliance on patents. There may be disputes over how the pharmaceutical patents are applied, but the technology in that industry does not change as fast as it does in software development.

Lighter Side **of the Law**

Why Many Patents Are Overturned when Challenged

The Patent Office awarded patent number 6,368,227: Method of swinging on a swing. Here is the abstract from the PTO website: "A method of swinging on a swing is disclosed, in which a user positioned on a standard swing suspended by two chains from a substantially horizontal tree branch induces side-to-side motion by pulling alternately on one chain and then the other."

This was awarded to Steve Olson, age 7, who reportedly excelled at swinging on a swing.

Source: U.S. Patent and Trademark Office.

Eighteen months after a patent application is filed that contains all the details, it is made public. That means competitors can gain a lot of valuable information even before a patent is issued. As a result, inventors prefer to use trade secrets for some innovations. More than 100 years ago, the Coca-Cola Company decided to keep the formula for Coke a secret. Had it obtained a patent instead, the formula could have been used by anyone after about 1907. Some firms use a combination of trade secrets and patents to protect their innovations.

The Federal Circuit Court of Appeals has primary responsibility for reviewing patent cases. Patents may be stricken when challenged if the court determines that the patent office did not apply the proper standards when issuing a patent. If the court upholds a patent that is challenged, then the patent holder has a good chance of recovering damages from a party accused of infringing on the patent. A few cases, such as the *Bowman* case, go to the Supreme Court. It addresses the issue of the right of a buyer of a patented product to reproduce the product.

BOWMAN V. MONSANTO CO.

Supreme Court of the United States 133 S.Ct. 1761 (2013)

Case Background *Monsanto invented and patented Roundup Ready® soybean seeds. They contain a genetic alteration that allows them to survive application of a weed killer. The seeds are sold with a licensing agreement that permits farmers to plant the seeds or resell the seeds. Buyers may not reproduce the seeds for future plantings. Bowman bought seeds, grew soybeans, then saved the soybean seeds to use for the next planting cycle; that is, he reproduced the patented seeds. Monsanto sued him for patent infringement. He defended on the basis of patent exhaustion. It holds that the buyer of a patented product has the right to use or resell the item. The lower courts held for Monsanto. Bowman appealed.*

Case Decision Justice Kagan

* * *

The doctrine of patent exhaustion limits a patentee's right to control what others can do with an article embodying or containing an invention. Under the doctrine, the initial authorized sale of a patented item terminates all patent rights to that item. ...

Consistent with that rationale, the doctrine restricts a patentee's rights only as to the "particular article" sold; it leaves untouched the patentee's ability to prevent a buyer from making new copies of the patented item. "The purchaser of the [patented] machine... does not acquire any right to construct another machine either for his own use or to be vended to another."...

Unfortunately for Bowman, that principle decides this case against him. Under the patent exhaustion doctrine, Bowman could resell the patented soybeans he purchased from the grain elevator; so too he could consume the beans himself or feed them to his animals. Monsanto, although the patent

holder, would have no business interfering in those uses of Roundup Ready beans. But the exhaustion doctrine does not enable Bowman to make additional patented soybeans without Monsanto's permission (either express or implied). And that is precisely what Bowman did. ... Because Bowman thus reproduced Monsanto's patented invention, the exhaustion doctrine does not protect him.

Were the matter otherwise, Monsanto's patent would provide scant benefit. After inventing the Roundup Ready trait, Monsanto would, to be sure, receive its reward for the first seeds it sells. But in short order, other seed companies could reproduce the product and market it to growers, thus depriving Monsanto of its monopoly. And farmers themselves need only buy the seed once, whether from Monsanto, a competitor, or (as here) a grain elevator. The grower could multiply his initial purchase, and then multiply that new creation, ad infinitum–each time profiting from the patented seed without compensating its inventor. Bowman's late-season plantings offer a prime illustration. After buying beans for a single harvest, Bowman saved enough seed each year to reduce or eliminate the need for additional purchases. Monsanto still held its patent, but received no gain from Bowman's annual production and sale of Roundup Ready soybeans. ...

[Affirmed.]

Questions for Analysis

1. If Monsanto could not prevent reproduction, what incentive would it have to invest in developing such products?
2. Should the court take into account the commercial success of a patented product when considering a challenge to a patent?

Lack of Global Uniformity

Part of the complexity and cost of patents comes from the variation of patent laws around the world. To ensure wide protection, firms must patent in the United States, Europe, and Japan, just to cover those markets. Much of the rest of the world is left uncovered as the cost of registration in every country would be too high and enforcement dubious in small-market countries with court systems of doubtful integrity. The cost of European protection is dropping as 25

INTERNATIONAL PERSPECTIVE

Patent Differences

The World Intellectual Property Organization (WIPO) encourages legal protection of intellectual property (IP) around the world and has encouraged IP laws to become more alike to avoid duplication costs and create consistency in standards. Important differences still remain, however.

In Europe, unlike the United States, patents may not be obtained for surgery or therapy methods, or for new plant or animal varieties, and there are more patent restrictions on software than in the United States.

A co-owner of a United States patent has the right, unless otherwise agreed, to exploit the patent fully, including licensing it. In Japan, all co-owners of a patent must agree as to how it will be exploited. In Europe, the law varies from country to country.

In Japan, unlike in Europe and the United States, employees who create patentable inventions on the job must receive compensation by employers according to the value of the patent. In one case, such compensation was $180 million, so choosing where to do research involves important patent law considerations.

Despite the move to patent laws that are more similar and the Patent Cooperation Treaty, valuable products are still patented in dozens of countries at once, at a cost of hundreds of thousands of dollars.

nations in the European Union agreed to create a single patent system (Italy and Spain refused to participate) beginning in 2014. The cost of filing patents in Europe could fall by as much as 80 percent. Still, global rules vary, often forcing firms to file and litigate in many nations.

Trade Secrets

Coca-Cola has kept a valuable secret—the formula for Coke—for more than 100 years. Businesses have many **trade secrets**, and tort law protects such information. The *Restatement (Second) of Torts* defines such information as follows: "A trade secret may consist of any formula, pattern, device, or compilation of information which is used in one's business, and which gives him an opportunity to obtain an advantage over competitors who do not know or use it." Information such as the Coke formula could have been patented. Some information may not be eligible for patent or copyright protection but is still a valuable secret. Information is a trade secret if:

1. It is not known by the competition.
2. The business would lose its advantage if the competition were to obtain it.
3. The owner has taken reasonable steps to protect the secret from disclosure.

If the owner of a trade secret has taken reasonable steps to protect secret information, and it is stolen by a competitor—either by the abuse of confidence of an employee or by trespass, electronic surveillance, or bribery—the courts can provide relief to the injured business in the form of damages and an injunction against further use of the secret. While some secrets are technical, a common trade secret is a customer list. Sales representatives know a lot about the best customers, how much they buy, and at what price. That knowledge is valuable to a competitor who may hire away such personnel. The FBI estimates that annual losses from trade secret theft are about $13 billion.

Generally, businesses with trade secrets protect themselves by having employees agree in their employment contracts not to divulge those secrets. The classic example of a theft of a trade secret involves an employee who steals a secret and then uses it in direct competition with the former employer or sells it to a competitor for personal gain. In the *Bohnsack* case, we see an example of an inventor who had his trade secret stolen by a potential manufacturer.

© Cengage Learning

BOHNSACK V. VARCO, L.P.

United States Court of Appeals, Fifth Circuit, 668 F.3d 262 (2012)

Case Background *Bohnsack is an engineer. Based on long experience, he invented the "Pit Bull," a machine to make the process of cleaning drilling fluids used in drilling oil wells more efficient. Varco is a company that cleans drilling fluids. Under a secrecy agreement, Varco negotiated the possibility of manufacturing Pit Bull, but the talks fell apart. Varco's lawyer had filed a patent application for Pit Bull, claiming the invention for Varco. Bohnsack sued Varco. The jury awarded $600,000 for misappropriation of trade secrets. Varco appealed.*

Case Decision Stewart, Circuit Judge

* * *

The elements of misappropriation of trade secrets are the following: (1) existence of a trade secret; (2) breach of a confidential relationship or improper discovery of a trade secret; (3) use of the trade secret; and (4) damages. ...

Varco first contends that Bohnsack presented no evidence that Varco used the trade secret. We have relied on the *Restatement* test to determine what constitutes a "use":

Any exploitation of the trade secret that is likely to result in injury to the trade secret owner or enrichment to the defendant is a "use" under this Section. Thus, marketing goods that embody the trade secret, employing the trade secret in manufacturing or production, relying on the trade secret to assist or accelerate research or development, or soliciting customers through the use of information that is a trade secret ... all constitute "use."

Under this broad definition of "use," a reasonable jury had sufficient evidence to conclude that Varco exploited Bohnsack's idea for the Pit Bull in a way that was likely to result in injury to the trade secret owner or enrichment to the defendant. ... It is common sense that when Varco has obtained rights to obtain profits from the Pit Bull, Varco's competitors become significantly less interested in compensating Bohnsack for the use of the Pit Bull. From these facts, a reasonable juror could infer that Varco's act of filing a patent application to the Pit Bull was likely to result in injury to the trade secret owner because it lowered the market value of Bohnsack's invention. Further, by making it less likely that Bohnsack would sell his invention to Varco's competitors, its decision to pursue rights to the Pit Bull was likely to result in ... enrichment to the defendant by protecting Varco from competition to the agitators it produced. We therefore hold that a reasonable jury had sufficient evidence that Varco's actions constituted a "use" in this case. ...

Varco argues that Bohnsack must prove his precise damages to recover for misappropriation. This is incorrect. A jury need only have sufficient evidence to determine the value a reasonably prudent investor would pay for the trade secret. Here, the final terms negotiated between Varco and Bohnsack are sufficient evidence to prove the value of the Pit Bull to a reasonably prudent investor. Those terms demonstrated Varco's willingness to pay at least $600,000, and possibly much more, for the Pit Bull. ...

For the foregoing reasons, we affirm the jury's award of compensatory damages for misappropriation of trade secrets.

Questions for Analysis

1. Do you think punitive damages should be awarded in such instances?
2. Why would Varco steal the invention? Why not pay for it?

Economic Espionage

While trade secrets are based on common law and are generally enforced by tort litigation claiming misappropriation or other violations of a trade secret or secrecy agreement, in some cases the government will intervene. The Economic Espionage Act of 1996 contains a provision concerning theft of commercial trade secrets, that is, **economic espionage**: "Whoever, with intent to convert a trade secret that is related to or included

ISSUE SPOTTER
Protecting Valuable Information

At many companies, employees carry valuable information in their heads. At a sales-based organization, sales representatives know many of the clients and their volume of purchases of various products. If the representatives leave to go to work for a competitor, that information, which can be a trade secret, is carried out the door with them. If you are a manager in such a company, what steps can you take to try to prevent the exploitation of such information when the sales representatives leave?

in a product that is produced for or placed in interstate or foreign commerce to the economic benefit of anyone other than the owner thereof, and intending or knowing that the offense will injure any owner of that trade secret" is subject to prosecution. Punishment for an individual can be as high as ten years in prison, and fines up to $5 million may be levied against firms.

The *Yang* case illustrates the application of this statute. Note that the case also helps us understand what is involved in a criminal conspiracy.

UNITED STATES V. YANG
United States Court of Appeals, Sixth Circuit, 281 F.3d 534 (2002)

Case Background *Lee, a native of Taiwan, worked in research for Avery, an adhesives manufacturer. When Lee was visiting Taiwan, he was approached by Yang and Yang's daughter about providing information to their Taiwanese adhesives company. Lee agreed and was paid $25,000 per year for confidential information from Avery about new products. When the arrangement was uncovered, the FBI confronted Lee, who agreed to participate in a sting operation to help arrest and prosecute Yang. When the Yangs visited the United States, Lee met with them and discussed confidential information. The meeting was filmed. The Yangs were arrested, convicted, and fined $5 million. They appealed, contending the materials used in the sting operation were not actual trade secrets, so they could not have violated the law.*

Case Decision Batchelder, Circuit Judge

* * *

[The Economic Espionage Act] provides:

(a) Whoever, with intent to convert a trade secret that is related to or included in a product that is produced for or placed in interstate or foreign commerce, to the economic benefit of anyone other than

the owner thereof, and intending or knowing that the offense will injure any owner of that trade secret, knowingly [steals, copies, buys such information, or conspires with others to do so, may be fined up to $5 million and imprisoned for up to 10 years]....

Because [under the Model Penal Code] the defendant's guilt turns on the circumstances as he believes them to be, the court held that the government was not required to prove that what the defendant sought to steal was in fact a trade secret, but only that the defendant believed it to be one....

The Yangs' conspiracy to steal the trade secrets in violation of The Economic Espionage Act was completed when, with the intent to steal the trade secrets, they agreed to meet with Lee in the hotel room and they took an overt act towards the completion of the crime, that is, when the Yangs went to the hotel room. The fact that the information they conspired to obtain was not what they believed it to be does not matter, because the objective of the Yangs' agreement was to steal trade secrets, and they took an overt step toward achieving that objective. Conspiracy is nothing more than the parties to the conspiracy coming to a mutual understanding to try to accomplish a common and unlawful plan, where at least one of the conspirators knowingly commits an overt act in pursuit of the conspiracy's objective. It is the mutual understanding or agreement itself that is criminal, and whether the object of the scheme actually is as the parties believe it to be, unlawful is irrelevant. ...

We affirm the judgments of conviction.

Questions for Analysis

1. The appeals court held that the Yangs conspired to buy information they believed to be trade secrets, which is a criminal offense. How could Avery prove the information involved was secret?
2. Do you think the fine, with no prison time, is sufficient to discourage such activity?

? TEST YOURSELF

1. Key conditions for an invention to be patented are that it is _____ and _____.
2. Patents have always been statutory law going back to the writing of the Constitution: T—F
3. The theft of commercial trade secrets may be held to be a felony: T—F
4. There is no infringement of a copyright if the copying is considered to be _____.
5. In the case *Nystrom* v. *Trex Co.*, the appeals court held the patent claimed for the shape of a board cut was:
   a. valid and could be enforced against infringement.
   b. invalid because the method of cutting was not novel.
   c. invalid because the cutting method is "obvious."
   d. invalid because the firm had failed to protect the patent for more than two years.
6. If a trade secret becomes known by a competitor, the secret is held to be lost: T—F
7. For a trade secret to be valid, a firm must have all employees sign an agreement to protect the secret for a minimum of two years after leaving the place of employment: T—F

Answers: original, novel; T; T; fair use; a; T; F.

SUMMARY

- Intellectual property is intangible property, which is legally protected property created mostly by mental effort. The scope of interests in intellectual property is determined by a mix of common law and statutory law that restricts infringement by others.
- Trademarks are designs, logos, distinctive marks, or words that manufacturers put on their goods for identification by consumers. At common law, the first producer to use a mark in a given area establishes priority of use. Under the Lanham Act, marks may be registered with the Patent and Trademark Office. Rights to a mark continue for as long as the mark is used and protected.

- The strongest trademarks are arbitrary and fanciful, including made-up words or real words applied to a product not related to the word as commonly used. Suggestive marks that hint at the kind of product are also provided strong protection. Less protection is available for descriptive marks, where the mark directly implies what the good is. Generic marks are words that were once protected trademarks but were lost as a result of common usage and lack of protection.
- Trade dress is trademark law applied to the look and feel of a product, such as a distinctive color or design. Service marks are the same as trademarks, but apply to services instead of goods. Trade

names are business names and are protected in the market in which the business is recognized.

- Goods that are sold pretending to be genuine trademarked goods are counterfeits and are illegal. It is also a violation of trademark law to infringe on a mark by using it improperly or by using a version of the mark that is so close to the original that it could cause confusion in the market.
- Infringement often draws sales away from the original mark holder. Related to this is the dilution of marks. Rules against dilution protect the integrity and distinctiveness of the mark by prohibiting their use in unrelated markets without permission.
- Copyrights allow exclusive control over original written works, musical compositions, art, and photography. Control extends to reproduction, publication, displays, performances, or derived works. While copyright exists at common law, registration under the Copyright Act provides clear evidence of ownership and is good for 70 years plus the lifetime of the creator.
- While copyright ownership is based on the common law, the Copyright Act specifies a fair use

defense to avoid a charge of infringement. The factors the courts consider in ruling on fair use include: (1) the purpose and character of the copying, (2) the nature of the copyrighted work, (3) the extent of the copying, and (4) the effect of copying on the market for the original work.

- Patents are exclusive statutory grants to protect an invention, design, or process that is genuine, useful, novel, and not obvious. Protection runs for 20 years from the time of patent application, which reveals to the public all details about the innovation.
- Trade secrets are formulas, patterns, devices, or compilations of information used in business that give an economic advantage over competitors who do not have the information. They are protected by tort law from theft. Trade secret owners must take reasonable steps to protect the information from disclosure, including obtaining employee agreements not to reveal the information.
- The Economic Espionage Act makes it a federal criminal offense to steal a trade secret and give it or sell it to another in commerce for economic benefit.

TERMS TO KNOW

intellectual property, 220
intangible property, 220
infringement, 220
trademark, 221
Lanham Act, 221
arbitrary and fanciful, 223
suggestive, 223
descriptive, 223
generic, 223

dilution, 224
cybersquatting, 224
counterfeiting, 227
trade dress, 228
secondary meaning, 228
service mark, 229
certification mark, 229
collective mark, 229
trade name, 229

goodwill, 229
copyright, 230
moral right, 231
fair use, 231
patent, 233
utility patent, 233
trade secrets, 236
economic espionage, 237

DISCUSSION QUESTION

Garden Company sells wheelbarrows under the name Garden Wheelbarrow. Its sales are not doing well around the country. In an effort to achieve greater standing in the

industry, Garden claims the trademark "Wheelbarrow's Wheelbarrows" for its wheelbarrows. If no one else has used that mark before, can Garden claim it?

CASE QUESTIONS

1. Martin worked for AMA, a firm that designs and administers retirement plans for 500 clients. The client list is confidential, but no agreement about that existed. When Martin left AMA after five years, he set up a competing firm and successfully solicited 15 AMA clients based on infor-

mation of who they were from his memory. AMA sued for theft of trade secrets. The trial court awarded AMA damages for fees that it would have earned from the clients. Martin appealed. Is he liable? [*Al Minor & Assoc.* v. *Martin*, 881 N.E.2d 850, Sup. Ct., Ohio (2008)]

2. OBX-Stock created OBX as an abbreviation for the Outer Banks of North Carolina. OBX-Stock used OBX on oval stickers for cars and applied OBX to souvenirs sold in the Outer Banks. The company obtained trademark registration for OBX for a range of goods. In practice, OBX was widely used by many businesses that advertise their Outer Banks location. Bicast began to sell stickers printed with "OB Xtreme." OBX-Stock sued Bicast for trademark infringement. The district court held for Bicast, finding that OBX was either a generic mark or a descriptive mark without secondary meaning and so not valid. OBX-Stock appealed. What would support OBX-Stock's position? [*OBX-Stock* v. *Bicast,* 558 F.3d 334, 4th Cir. (2009)]

3. Beacon Mutual Insurance Company sold insurance in Rhode Island under its name and also under the marks Beacon Insurance and The Beacon. It uses a lighthouse logo. A competitor changed its name to OneBeacon Insurance Group and used a lighthouse logo. Beacon sued OneBeacon for infringement. What claims could it make, and do you think will prevail? [*Beacon Mutual Ins.* v. *OneBeacon Ins.*, 376 F.3d 8, 1st Cir. (2004)]
   ✓ Check your answer

4. Lucky Break Wishbone designed, copyrighted, and produced wishbones. While they looked like a wishbone, they were thinner in the arms, more rounded on the edges, and made of graphite. Sears then produced similar wishbones for sale. Lucky Break sued for copyright infringement. Sears contended that the wishbones did not meet the elements needed to obtain a copyright. The trial court held that the copyright was valid, and the jury awarded Lucky Break $1.7 million in damages. Sears appealed. Do you think an imitation wishbone can be copyrighted? [*Lucky Break Wishbone* v. *Sears,* 373 Fed.Appx. 752, 9th Cir. (2010)]

5. Milano worked for Twentieth Television. She developed the concept for a reality television series called "From Fat to Phat," which had contestants losing weight. A number of people knew of the idea. Twentieth decided not to pursue it. Later, NBC announced a new show, "The Biggest Loser," which has a similar concept. Milano sued NBC and others for infringement of her copyrighted "treatments" for the program and for misappropriation of her ideas. Who should prevail and why? [*Milano* v. *NBC Universal,* 584 F.Supp.2d 1288, C.D. Calif. (2008)]
   ✓ Check your answer

6. An American company imported video game cartridges from China that were pirated from copyrighted originals made by Nintendo. The counterfeit copies also were sold with the Nintendo name on them. What laws have been violated, and what are the damages? [*Nintendo of America* v. *Dragon Pacific,* 40 F.3d 1007, 9th Cir. (1994)]

7. Hormel is the maker of SPAM® luncheon meat, trademarked since 1937. Hormel sued Jim Henson Productions for trademark infringement for using a Muppet character "Spa'am" in its *Muppet Treasure Island* movie. "Spa'am is the high priest of a tribe of wild boars that worships Miss Piggy as its Queen.... Henson hopes to poke a little fun at Hormel's famous luncheon meat by associating its processed, gelatinous block with a humorously wild beast." The district court denied Hormel's request for an injunction against the name Spa'am. Do you think Hormel could win on appeal? Why? [*Hormel Foods* v. *Jim Henson Productions,* 73 F.3d 497, 2nd Cir. (1996)]
   ✓ Check your answer

8. Qualitex makes press pads used in dry cleaning and laundry establishments. It is well known in the industry and always made its products in a special shade of green-gold. A competitor, Jacobson, began to use a similar shade on its own press pads. Qualitex registered its color as a trademark and sued Jacobson for trademark infringement for using the same color in its products. Does Qualitex have a good claim? [*Qualitex* v. *Jacobson Products,* 115 S.Ct. 1300 (1995)]
   ✓ Check your answer

9. United States Gypsum developed a new putty to use on walls and ceilings to cover cracks. A key ingredient in the compound was a silicon product made by another company. The patent application did not list that as an ingredient in the putty. A competitor started to make and sell the same putty, and the two companies ended up in court. Could USG win for patent infringement? [*United States Gypsum* v. *National Gypsum,* 74 F.3d 1209, Fed. Cir. (1996)]

10. Defendant flew his plane over a chemical plant being built by DuPont and took

numerous photos of the construction. Although the plant was guarded on the ground from outsiders, it was not guarded from aerial inspection. The photographs revealed a lot about secret processes.

ETHICS QUESTION

Poor countries assert that patented drugs are too expensive for most of their people to afford. The issue became especially noteworthy over drugs for AIDS sufferers in Africa. Monthly drug expenses are above average total income levels. Countries have been

Defendant said that if DuPont cared, it would have covered the construction site. Does DuPont have a legitimate trade secret action against the photographer? [*E. I. DuPont* v. *Christopher*, 431 F.2d 1012, 5th Cir. (1970)]

changing their drug laws to eliminate patent rights in certain cases. Do drug companies have an ethical duty to sell their products for the lowest possible price? Should countries abolish patent protection for drugs?

CHAPTER 10
Contracts

A customer sends an inquiry by e-mail to your electronics distribution company. The customer asks if there is a quantity discount for large orders for flat-screen, 55-inch Samsung LED HD television sets. The customer service representative responds that yes, there is a ten-percent discount off the list price of $700 per television for orders of 20 or more. The customer says: "Great, I'll take 50 of the 55-inch Samsung televisions at $630 each." The customer says to send a bill, and he will pay before delivery. The person filling the order accidentally types $63 instead of the correct price of $630 per television. The customer happily sends a check for that amount and says to ship the televisions. The rep who receives the check notices the mistake and calls the customer to apologize for the mistake and notes the correct price. The customer demands the televisions at $63, noting that the televisions were offered at that price in writing, and he accepted that price by paying. "We have a contract," he says.

Is there a contract? Did the information and money exchange create a binding contract? Does your company have to absorb the loss? Can you tell the customer there was no contract?

Pricing mistakes are only one issue that can arise in the daily business of making contracts with customers and suppliers. Whether it is buying gas at the pump with a credit card, a meal at a drive-through window, or a dress that needs alterations, the transactions are all contracts.

The law of contracts evolved in commerce over the centuries. There are specific rules that involve the creation of a contract. The freedom of contract, which is a hallmark of the law, means that there are also responsibilities imposed on parties who commit to binding relationships. Here we study the key elements of the creation of contracts and the rights and duties that accompany common-law contracts.

Contract Law

Contract law is primarily state common law. It has developed through decades of judicial opinions that have resolved virtually every kind of contract dispute. When English courts began to consider more contract disputes in the early 1800s, they made express reference to the **law merchant** (*lex mercatoria*), which were commercial rules that merchants devised over centuries of doing business across national boundaries. One important source was the Roman law of contracts, a sophisticated body of law that reflected the extensive commercial relationships of an empire covering much of Europe, North Africa, and the Middle East. That Contract law reflects real business experience and time-tested principles. Today, the *Restatement (Second) of Contracts* is an authoritative document that provides a summary of the common law of contracts.

The common law of contracts that comes from the courts is modified by various statutes. Of particular importance is Article 2 of the Uniform Commercial Code (UCC), a state statute that applies to sales of goods. It is designed to promote uniformity of the laws relating to commercial sales of goods. The next chapter studies the role that law plays.

Definition of a Contract

Sir William Blackstone, a famous English jurist, defined a **contract** as "an agreement, upon sufficient consideration, to do or not to do a particular thing." Modern definitions of contract center on a **promise**. It is the element common to all contracts. Section I of the *Restatement (Second) of Contracts* defines a contract as "a promise or a set of promises for the breach of which the law gives a remedy, or the performance of which the law in some way recognizes as a duty." It defines a promise as "a manifestation of the intention [of a party] to act or refrain from acting in a specified manner."

A contract, then, is the legal relationship consisting of the rights and duties of the agreeing parties that arise from promises exchanged. Contract law governs that relationship. Contracts are particularly important for businesses as they usually concern arrangements that are more complex than the simultaneous exchange of money for goods.

Not all promises are enforceable contracts. A promise may be binding (contractual) or nonbinding (noncontractual). For a promise to be binding and enforceable, it must meet the essential requirements of a contract. If a party fails to perform a nonbinding promise, contract law will not provide a remedy. This makes clear the need to meet the requirements of a contract when parties want their exchange of promises to be legally binding.

Formal writing or oral discussions may create contracts or contracts may be inferred by the actions of the parties. A contract is called an **express contract** if there is a written or oral expression of intent by the parties to enter into a legally binding agreement. A contract is an **implied contract** if it arises from the actions rather than the expressions of the parties. That is, given the way the parties have acted with respect to each other, the court may infer that a contract exists. As we saw in the discussion of torts, the law may also imply particular terms into contracts, such as implied warranties of safety. The essence of a contract is illustrated in Exhibit 10.1, regardless of whether the contract is express or implied.

Elements of a Contract

A contract gives parties greater confidence that bargained-for exchanges are enforceable. This section discusses the basic elements so a bargain forms a valid contract. While many contracts consist of standardized forms, the basic elements of a contract are constant: agreement, consideration, legal capacity to contract, lawful subject matter, and genuine consent to the contract (see Exhibit 10.2). In addition, compliance with the Statute of Frauds may be necessary.

EXHIBIT 10.1 ESSENCE OF A CONTRACT

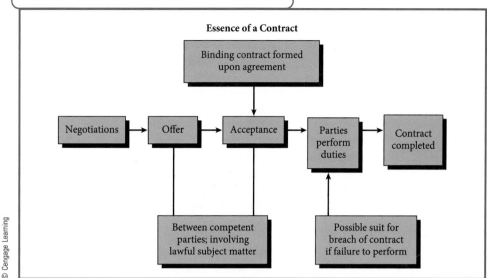

Essence of a Contract

Offer and Acceptance

The essence of a contract is a legally binding agreement, that is, a mutual understanding between the parties as to the substance of the contract. This agreement between the parties is reached through a process of offer and acceptance.

The Offer An **offer** is a promise to do something or to refrain from doing some specific thing. As defined in the *Restatement (Second) of Contracts*, "An offer is the manifestation of willingness to enter into a bargain, so made as to justify another person in understanding that his assent to that bargain is invited and will conclude it." The party making an offer is called the **offeror** or offerer; the **offeree** is the party to whom the offer is made.

You offer to obligate yourself through a contract. Because the offeror is allowing the offeree the opportunity to create a binding promise by making a valid acceptance of the offer, the offeror controls the terms of the offer. To be an effective offer, three requirements must be met:

1. There must be a clear intent by the offeror to become contractually bound.
2. The basic terms and conditions of the offer must be clear and certain.
3. The offer must be properly communicated.

Manifestation of Intent To make an offer, the offeror must have the intent to be bound to the contract, and that intent must be clearly expressed or manifested. Preliminary negotiations

EXHIBIT 10.2 KEY ELEMENTS OF A CONTRACT

A. Offer and Acceptance: An Agreement
B. Consideration
C. Contractual Capacity
D. Legality
E. Genuine Consent

© Cengage Learning

are not offers but are invitations to negotiate or to make an offer. Dickering with a salesperson about the price of a car is negotiation, not an offer.

A person's intent is tested by an objective standard. The court decides from the evidence whether a reasonable person familiar with the business being transacted would be justified in believing an offer had been made. If, under the circumstances, the court decides that intent was lacking, a contract could not be formed. For example, if Shakira says, "I would like to sell my car for $5,000," there is no offer to sell that allows Sean Paul to form a contract by saying, "Sold. I will pay you $5,000."

Many things that are stated as being for sale are not definite offers that can be accepted to create a contract. For example, when a jacket worn by Beyoncé is put on the auction block, unless otherwise stated, it is an invitation for people to submit offers on the jacket. Under common auction rules, such as one with a reserve price, the owner of the jacket can withdraw it if the highest price offered is not sufficient. However, if the auction rules say that the highest bid must be accepted, then putting the jacket up for auction is an offer.

Similarly, most advertisements are regarded as invitations for others to submit offers to buy. If a company website lists a particular model of laser printers for $219.99, it is likely that if you order one, the order will be accepted and a contract formed. But the seller listing the printers for sale can reject offers to buy, as ads are legally generally considered to be requests for offers to buy, rather than offers themselves. No seller wants to give up profitable sales, but if inventory is not adequate, offers by customers to buy will be rejected unless they are willing to wait for the next shipment from China.

Definite Terms and Conditions   Not every tiny detail of an offer must be present for it to be a valid offer. If you order a laptop on the Internet, the contract does not have to say it will be properly packed for shipment; that is presumed. Under common law, however, terms of an offer must be sufficiently detailed so each party's promises are certain. An offer that has unclear major terms or is missing important terms cannot be the basis for a contract. Sometimes the courts supply minor missing terms, so the offer does not fail because it is indefinite. By doing this, the courts prevent a party from backing out of a contract after the fact by claiming that there never was an offer because some trivial point was not clear.

Lighter Side **of the Law**

No Extra Charge for the Smell

Salais bought a four-year-old car from a dealership during the winter. When the weather warmed up, the car began to smell. The warmer it got, the worse the smell. She took the car back to the dealership, and someone told her the smell was from a dead animal. Doubtful about that, she filed a claim with her insurance company.

State Farm hired a biohazard clean-up company. It determined the odor was human. State Farm also learned the car had been stolen three times and that it had been used as a rental vehicle. Salais sued the dealership to undo the deal and return her money plus extra for her trouble.

Source: Detroit News.

EXHIBIT 10.3	LEGAL EFFECT OF OFFER AND ACCEPTANCE COMMUNICATIONS	
COMMUNICATION	**TIME EFFECTIVE**	**LEGAL EFFECT**
By Offeror		
1. Offer	When received by offeree	Offeree has the power to accept
2. Revocation	When received by offeree	Ends offeree's power to accept
By Offeree		
1. Rejection	When received by offeror	Terminates the offer
2. Counteroffer	When received by offeror	Terminates the offer
3. Acceptance	When sent by offeree	Forms a contract

© Cengage Learning

Communication of the Offer   Exhibit 10.3 summarizes the timing of communication of offer and acceptance. An acceptance requires knowledge of the offer by the offeree. The case of a person who finds and returns a lost dog and later learns of a reward is an example of an offer failing for lack of communication. Because communication of the offer occurred after the act of acceptance (returning the dog to its owner), a proper acceptance did not take place. We cannot form a contract by accepting an unknown offer.

Terminating an Offer   **Termination** of an offer can occur by the action of the parties or by the operation of law. The parties can terminate an offer by withdrawing it (by the offeror), rejecting it (by the offeree), or through lapse of time (by the inaction of the offeree).

An **option contract** is different because it is a binding promise to keep an offer open for a specified period of time. For example, one may pay $100 to have an option to buy a house for $200,000 any time in the next ten days. The offer to sell the house may not be withdrawn during that time; there is an exclusive right to exercise the option to buy at $200,000 for ten days. Of course, the option contract itself must have been formed through an offer and acceptance.

Termination by the Parties   Offerors can terminate most offers by withdrawing the offer before it has been accepted by the offeree. The withdrawal of the offer by the offeror is a **revocation**. To be effective, the revocation must be communicated to the offeree before acceptance. An offer can state that it must be accepted within a designated time period. The end of that time period terminates the offer.

After an offer has been made, the offeree can create a contract by accepting the offer or can terminate the offer by rejecting it. One important form of rejection is a **counteroffer**, a proposal by the offeree to change the terms of the original offer. For example, if Johnny Depp offers to buy Brad Pitt's old laptop for $500, and Pitt says that he will sell it for $600, a counteroffer has been made. The original offer by Depp is terminated by the counteroffer. By making a counteroffer, Pitt became the offeror and Depp became the offeree. Depp's original offer no longer exists, although it can be revived.

An offer may also terminate by lapse of time. If an offer does not state a specific time for acceptance, the passage of a reasonable length of time after the offer has been made terminates it. What is reasonable depends upon the circumstances. An offer to buy stock in a company at a set price terminates by lapse of time almost immediately, while an offer to sell a car expires after a longer time. It depends on the normal practices of the businesses involved.

Termination by the Operation of Law   An offer may terminate by operation of law through intervening illegality. That occurs when a court decision or, usually, legislation makes an offer illegal. Suppose Lindsay Lohan has an Internet-based business that offers to take bets on college football games. Congress then enacts a law forbidding gambling by Internet. Lohan's offer to take bets is terminated by an intervening illegality.

An offer also terminates by law if the subject matter is destroyed. Suppose Shakira offers to sell Rihanna her car. Before Rihanna accepts Shakira's offer, the car is wrecked in an accident. The offer terminated when the accident occurred. Note that if Shakira had offered to sell Rihanna a type of car rather than a particular car, the offer would not have been terminated by the accident.

The mental or physical incapacity or death of the offeror or the offeree also terminates an offer by operation of law. An offer is terminated because the person does not have the mental capacity to enter into a contract; or physical limitations, such as a severe injury, may make a party unable to perform a contract that requires certain skills. Similarly, an offeror or offeree who dies cannot execute a contract.

The Acceptance   In contract law, **acceptance** is an offeree's expression of assent or agreement to the terms of an offer. In most contracts, this means the offeree accepts by making a promise in exchange for the original promise. To be effective, an acceptance must be unconditional, unequivocal, and properly communicated. A supposed acceptance that lacks one of these elements generally does not bring about a binding contract.

Most contracts are called **bilateral contracts** when there is an exchange of promises. For example, you say to a friend, "I will sell you my car for $2,000"; he responds, "Fine, I will pay that." In some states, certain contracts are referred to as **unilateral contracts** when there is acceptance by **performance**. For example, your neighbor says to you, "I will pay you $30 to mow my lawn." You say nothing in response, but the next day you mow the lawn—so the offer was accepted by performance. Such contracts are valid whether they are called unilateral or bilateral.

Must Be Unconditional   An offeree must accept an offer as presented by an offeror. Traditionally, it was said that the acceptance must be the **mirror image** of the offer. In other words, the key parts of the offer must be in the acceptance. The common-law rule is that a supposed acceptance that adds conditions to the original offer is a counteroffer. By changing the terms of the offer, there is not unconditional acceptance; the offeree rejects the offer. Failure of the parties to clearly agree is seen in the *Certified Fire Protection* case.

CERTIFIED FIRE PROTECTION, INC. V. PRECISION CONSTRUCTION, INC.

Supreme Court of Nevada 283 P.3d 250 (2012)

Case Background *Precision Construction is a general contractor that bid on a construction job. It solicited bids from subcontractors for, among other things, the design and installation of a sprinkler system for fire suppression. Based on the specifications,* *Certified Fire submitted a bit of $480,000. Precision later notified Certified that it had won the bid and that Precision was beginning construction. On December 5, Certified got a copy of the contract from Precision along with a set of construction plans* and sprinkler requirements. The contract required Certified to have the preliminary design drawings of the sprinkler system within two weeks and to provide an insurance certificate.

Over the next several weeks, Precision told Certified it must have the documents. Certified objected to certain terms of the contract. On January 19, with no signed contract or insurance certificate, Certified billed Precision for $33,575 for its work on the sprinkler plans, although the plans were not yet ready for Certified. On January 26, Precision told Certified that it was holding up the whole project and that it would move ahead without Certified. Certified submitted drawings on February 1, but still objected to terms in the contract. On February 8, Precision was informed of mistakes in the sprinkler system drawings. On February 16, it told Certified that it was ending its relationship because the contract was not signed, there was no insurance certificate, and the drawings were incorrect.

Certified sued for breach of contract, contending it was due payment for the drawings on the sprinkler system. The trial court held for Precision as no contracted existed. Certified appealed.

Case Decision Pickering, Justice

* * *

Basic contract principles require, for an enforceable contract, an offer and acceptance, meeting of the minds, and consideration. A meeting of the minds exists when the parties have agreed upon the contract's essential terms. Which terms are essential "depends on the agreement and its context and also on the subsequent conduct of the parties, including the dispute which arises and the remedy sought." *Restatement (Second) of Contracts* § 131 comment g (1981). Whether a contract exists is a question of fact, requiring this court to defer to the district court's findings unless they are clearly erroneous or not based on substantial evidence.

Certified argues that the progress bill it sent to Precision established the price term and Precision's urging that Certified get started on the designs established the scope of work for the express design-work-only contract it claims. But the record does not establish that Precision agreed to pay a sum certain for the design-related work. Certified's $33,575 progress bill—which represented seven percent of the whole subcontract—went unpaid, and Precision told Certi-

fied it would not make a progress payment until the whole subcontract had been executed. Beyond this, witness testimony established that a party in Precision's position would not execute a contract for only design drawings; such drawings are specifically tailored for the company rendering them and not useful to another installer. Thus, Certified's argument that Precision was parceling out the work—with Certified doing the designs only—makes no sense.

Not only were price and scope of work terms missing from the claimed design-work contract, the parties never agreed to a time for performance. Certified objected to Precision's proposed two-week timeline for producing the design drawings as "not realistic," and the parties never agreed to another time frame. That the time-for-performance term mattered is demonstrated by Precision's repeated prompting of Certified to complete the designs and Certified's refusal to bind itself to Precision's desired two-week turnaround. When essential terms such as these have yet to be agreed upon by the parties, a contract cannot be formed.

And while the district court's judgment on partial findings does not reference a design-only contract, the record substantially supports its conclusion that no enforceable contract existed.

Next, Certified argues that absent an express contract, it should be able to recover under a theory of implied contract. ...

A contract implied-in-fact must be "manifested by conduct," it is a true contract that arises from the tacit agreement of the parties. To find a contract implied-in-fact, the fact-finder must conclude that the parties intended to contract and promises were exchanged, the general obligations for which must be sufficiently clear. ...

Certified maintains that it had an implied contract with Precision for the design-related work. As discussed above, however, substantial evidence supports the district court's finding that there was no contract, express or implied, for the design work standing alone. There are simply too many gaps to fill in the asserted contract. ... Precision never agreed to a contract for only design-related work, the parties never agreed to a price for that work, and they disputed the time of performance. When Precision selected Certified, it did so on the basis that Certified would design *and install* the fire suppression system, not that it would draft the designs and leave installation to someone else. The evidence established that design drawings are installer-specific and so not useful to a replacement subcontractor. Accordingly, the district court properly denied recovery...for an implied-in-fact contract....

Affirmed.

Question for Analysis

1. The appeals court held that no contract ever came into existence, so there could be no breach of contract. But Certified did some work, so why could it not recover for that?

Must Be Unequivocal Acceptance must be unequivocal or definite. Suppose an offeree receives an offer to buy a car for $10,000. If the offeree says "I see" or "What a good idea," either expression fails the unequivocal test. There is no acceptance.

While the words "I accept" are a clear acceptance, any words or conduct expressing the offeree's intent to accept an offer is an effective acceptance. When negotiations take place, much is expressed in words and conduct that is not a rejection or acceptance. In such cases, the courts look (as in the *Certified Fire* case) at the offeree's expressions to determine whether a reasonable person would consider them as an acceptance of the offer.

As a general rule, silence is not acceptance because it is not unequivocal. It could mean yes or no. However, past business dealings of the offeror and the offeree may allow silence by the offeree to be acceptance. For example, if a company has serviced a copier for a customer every month for several years, an express statement every month that copier service is desired is not necessary. Service will continue until one party says it will end.

Must Be Properly Communicated The final requirement of acceptance is that it is properly communicated. Three factors can be important in meeting this requirement: (1) the method of acceptance, (2) the timeliness of acceptance, and (3) in some cases, performance as acceptance. Exhibit 10.4 summarizes the elements of offer and acceptance.

The general rule in communicating an acceptance is that any reasonable method is adequate. Problems arise when the offeror authorizes one way to communicate acceptance, but the offeree uses another. If, for example, the offeror requires a signed contract to make an acceptance, a response by telephone does not create an acceptance.

EXHIBIT 10.4 ALTERNATIVE RESULTS IN THE CONTRACTING PROCESS

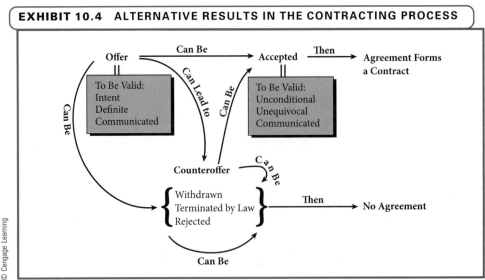

© Cengage Learning

If no method of acceptance is specified, the offeree may use any reasonable means to communicate. The safest approach is to use the method used by the offeror in communicating the offer.

The timeliness of acceptance is important, especially when the value of goods or services being offered changes rapidly. To deal with time problems, the courts created the general rule that if the method of acceptance is reasonable under the circumstances, the acceptance is effective when it is sent.

Consideration

Consideration is something of value or something bargained for in exchange for a promise; that is, both parties to a contract get something and give up something. Consideration is what distinguishes contracts from gifts. If consideration is absent, neither party can enforce the promise or agreement.

The traditional rule is that an exchange is consideration if it creates a legal detriment to the **promisee** (the party to whom a promise is made) or a legal benefit to the **promisor** (the party making a promise). A **legal detriment** is an act, a promise to act, or a promise to refrain from acting, such as giving up a legal right. For example, if you are hit by a careless driver and accept an out-of-court settlement of $20,000, you give up the right to sue in court for damages. A legal benefit to the promisor exists when the promisor acquires some legal right through the promisee's act, promise to act, or promise to refrain from doing some act.

Consideration requires either a legal detriment to the promisee or a legal benefit to the promisor, although both usually occur at the same time. Suppose Def Jam buys a watch from Seiko for $100. Def Jam suffers a legal detriment (gives up the right to keep $100) in exchange for a benefit (the watch). Seiko suffers a legal detriment (gives up the watch) in exchange for a benefit ($100). As the following case illustrates, courts use this detriment-benefit test to determine whether there is consideration for a contract.

Adequacy of Consideration For the most part, courts do not inquire into the adequacy of consideration given in a contract. The bargaining is the responsibility of the parties to the contract. Even if one party bargains poorly, and the values of the items to be exchanged are very unequal, the courts generally do not interfere. Courts support contracts that are bargained for, even if the consideration is not related to market value. The main concern for the courts is to see that there was a trade of mutual promises and obligations as discussed in the *Caley* case.

CALEY V. GULFSTREAM AEROSPACE CORP

United States Court of Appeals, Eleventh Circuit, 28 F.3d 1359 (2005)

Case Background *Gulfstream adopted a dispute resolution policy (DRP). It mailed the policy to all employees. It said the DRP would be the only procedure to resolve disputes between Gulfstream and employees. It would begin in two weeks and would be "a condition of continued employment." For*
employees to continue to work at Gulfstream, they had to accept the DRP as a condition of employment. A group of employees sued, contending that there was no contract, so the DRP could not be enforced. The district court held for Gulfstream. The employees appealed.

Case Decision Hull, Circuit Judge

* * *

1. Offer The plaintiffs argue that the DRP does not constitute an "offer." We disagree. "An offer is the manifestation of willingness to enter into a bargain, so made as to justify another person in understanding that his assent to that bargain is invited and will conclude it." *Restatement (Second) of Contracts,* § 24. The DRP clearly states that it is a contract, establishes the terms of the contract, and explains the means of accepting the contract. Thus, the DRP plainly constituted an offer....

2. Acceptance The plaintiffs also contend that they cannot be deemed to have accepted the terms of the DRP simply by their continued employment, even though the DRP expressly provides that continued employment is the proper means of acceptance. However, we agree with the district court that the employees accepted the DRP through continued employment....

An offer maybe accepted ... either by a promise to do the thing contemplated therein, or by the actual doing of the thing. However, the offer must be accepted in the manner specified by it; and if it calls for a promise, then a promise must be made; or if it calls for an act, it can be accepted only by the doing of the act....

By specifying the manner of acceptance as continued employment and announcing that the DRP was a condition of employment, the DRP and accompanying letter plainly set forth two options for Gulfstream employees: (1) continue in employment, thereby accepting the DRP, or (2) terminate employment. Thus, given these two options, the employees remaining in Gulfstream's employ after notice of the DRP was an unambiguous act of acceptance of the DRP....

3. Consideration The plaintiffs next argue that the arbitration agreement is unenforceable because there is no "bargained for consideration" for their relinquishment of trial rights. They argue that the employees got nothing in return.

This argument is unavailing. Georgia law provides that mutual promises and obligations are sufficient consideration to support a contract. Here, the plaintiffs received reciprocal promises from Gulfstream to arbitrate and be bound by arbitration in covered claims. In addition, the DRP provides that Gulfstream will pay the arbitration and mediation costs. These promises constitute bargained-for consideration....

Affirmed.

Questions for Analysis

1. The appeals court held that continued employment was evidence of acceptance of the offer and employment was consideration. Because the employees were already working, why was there consideration? Was there a change in anything?
2. If the case had come out the opposite, how could an employer change the terms of the working arrangement (contract)?

Enforceable Promises without Consideration Under certain circumstances, the courts do not require consideration for a promise to be enforceable. The doctrine used by the courts is called **promissory estoppel** (or *detrimental reliance*). The rationale for the doctrine is that it will avoid an injustice resulting from the promisee's reasonable reliance on the promisor's promise.

Under the doctrine, the promisor is estopped (prevented) from denying a promise. The *Restatement (Second) of Contracts* explains promissory estoppel this way: "A promise which the promisor should reasonably expect to induce action or forbearance on the part of the promise ... and which does induce such action or forbearance is binding if injustice can be avoided only by enforcement of the promise." We see an application of this doctrine in the *Hinson* case, which also notes that oral promises can be the basis of a contract.

HINSON V. N&W CONSTRUCTION COMPANY
Court of Appeals of Mississippi 890 So.2d 65 (2004)

Case Background *N&W Construction prepared a bid for the Mississippi Job Corps Center (MJCC) to build a kitchen facility at a training center. In preparing the bid, N&W received oral bids from several plumbing contractors. Hinson quoted $92,000 as his bid for the plumbing job. The next-lowest plumbing subcontractor bid was $139,000. N&W used Hinson's bid in preparing its general contracting bid for the whole project.*

N&W was the low bidder and was awarded the MJCC contract. N&W notified Hinson that he was needed to do the plumbing work when construction began. Hinson refused the job. N&W had to hire the next-lowest bidder and pay an additional $47,000 to get the plumbing work done.

N&W sued Hinson on the basis of promissory estoppel. The trial court granted summary judgment to N&W and awarded $47,000 in damages. Hinson appealed.

Case Decision Irving, Justice

* * *

The doctrine of promissory estoppel has been stated as follows:

> An estoppel may arise from the making of a promise, even though without consideration, if it was intended that the promise should be relied upon and in fact it was relied upon, and if a refusal to enforce it would be virtually to sanction the perpetuation of fraud or would result in other injustice.

A review of the undisputed facts of this case and the evidence submitted by the parties to N&W's motion for summary judgment ... clearly indicate that the circuit court correctly granted N&W's motion for summary judgment on the theory of promissory estoppel....

Hinson admits that he provided a verbal quote to N&W in the amount of $92,000 for plumbing work on the building....

Hinson testified that he reviewed the plans and specifications for the building, worked on his quote for approximately a week, and was satisfied with his price of $92,000....

Moreover, Hinson does not dispute that N&W used his quote for the plumbing work in its bid for the building contract.... Hinson later explained ... that he refused to do the plumbing work.... "I just had a lot of other jobs going." ...

Affirmed.

Questions for Analysis

1. The appeals court held there was an enforceable promise. Because Hinson did not sign a contract and never received any payment from N&W, should Hinson be responsible? Why did N&W not get an agreement in writing?

2. Because the next bid was 50 percent higher than Hinson's, is it likely that Hinson's bid was poorly done and that he would have suffered a big loss had he done the work?

This is not a burden imposed lightly by the courts, because they do not want to impose obligations that were not really agreed to. Promissory estoppel also arises in some cases of promises to charities. Suppose an art museum is raising $50 million for an expansion. It collects promises from various donors, but none of the money is collected until there are enough promises to make the project feasible and construction begins. Once that happens, if a big donor backs out, the courts may rule that promissory estoppel applies, and the gift must be made; because the building contract was entered into on reliance of the donation being made.

Lighter Side of the Law

You Can't Trust Anyone These Days

Fugitive murder suspect Jesse Dimmick was on the run when he broke into a home in Kansas and held a couple at knifepoint. While being held, the couple convinced Dimmick that they would hide him from the police if he paid them some money. He agreed and fell asleep while watching a movie. The couple escaped and Dimmick was shot when trying to escape from the police.

Dimmick sued the couple for $235,000 for breach of contract. "As a result of the breech (sic) of contract, I suffered a gunshot to my back, which almost killed me," he noted in his claim. "I asked the Rowleys to hide me because I feared for my life. I offered the Rowleys an unspecified amount of money which they agreed upon, thereby forging a legally binding oral contract."

Source: Topeka Capital-Journal.

Capacity to Contract

One element of a contract is **contractual capacity**, or legal ability, to create a contract. Capacity refers to a party's ability to perform legally valid acts, acquire legal rights, and incur legal liabilities. Generally, minors, intoxicated persons, and the mentally disabled have limited capacity to contract. Until the mid-nineteenth century, most states added married women to that list. They did not have the capacity to contract independent of their husbands. A party claiming incapacity has the burden of proving it.

Most adults have complete capacity to contract. If a person, perhaps as a result of mental disability, does not have capacity to contract, a contract entered into is not enforceable. If a person has partial capacity, the contract is enforceable unless the person with partial capacity exercises the right to disaffirm the contract. Contracts created by those with partial capacity are voidable.

Void and Voidable Contracts A contract that does not exist at law, and so cannot be enforced, is a **void contract**. A contract is void if it concerns illegal subject matter, such as a contract to sell cocaine. The courts do not accept disputes over such matters.

A **voidable contract** is when one party to the contract has the right to avoid a legal obligation. As we discuss below, this can be the case when minors or persons with limited mental ability enter into contracts. If a person is so stoned when he makes a contract that he does not know what he is doing, then because he did not have the capacity to contract, he may later have the right to have the contract declared voidable. A contract is also voidable if there is fraud involved in making the contract.

Minors A *minor* is a person under the legal age of majority. The age of majority is 18 for most contracts and younger for some. The general rule is that a minor may enter into contracts but the contracts are voidable at the option of the minor. A company that contracts with a minor may find itself with relatively few rights if the minor disaffirms the contract. If a minor has received benefits, such as a 16-year-old buying a car on credit and driving it for six months, *restitution* must be paid by the minor for the value of the benefit received, even if the minor is not liable on the contract itself.

After a minor reaches the age of majority, the person may ratify contracts made while a minor. **Ratification** may be expressed through words, in writing, or implied by conduct, such as continued use of a car. There are some contracts that minors may not disaffirm. Enlistment contracts to join the Army and marriage contracts are nonvoidable contracts. Some states have statutes that do not allow minors to disaffirm certain other type of contracts as well, such as contracts for insurance, educational loans, medical care, and bank account agreements.

❓ TEST YOURSELF

1. In the *Caley* v. *Gulfstream Aerospace Corp* case, where the employees were told to sign an arbitration agreement regarding employment disputes or lose their jobs, the court held that there was no contract because there was no real consent: T—F
2. Something of value or something bargained for in exchange for a promise is called _____.
3. In *Certified Fire Protection, Inc.* v. *Precision Construction, Inc.*, where Precision decided it did not want to use Certified for work on a project and refused to pay for work done, the court held that:
   a. the oral agreement was sufficient to create a contract, so it could be enforced.
   b. Certified had a right to specific enforcement of the contract as agreed upon.
   c. there was no contract; it was not properly accepted by Certified.
   d. there was no contract because the written terms deviated, in part, from the oral agreement.
4. An exchange of promises is called a(n) _____ contract. When an offer is accepted by performance, it may be called a(n) _____ contract.
5. In some circumstances, consideration for a promise is not required for the promise to be enforceable. This is called detrimental reliance or _____.
6. When a party to a contract has the right to avoid fulfilling the terms of the contract, the contract is said to be voidable: T—F

Answers: F; consideration; c; bilateral, unilateral; promissory estoppel; T.

Legality

For a contract to be valid, its subject matter must be lawful. A contract is illegal and unenforceable if its subject matter violates a state or federal statute or common law or is contrary to public policy. The terms "illegal bargain" and "illegal agreement", rather than illegal contract, may be more proper because contract by definition refers to a legal and enforceable agreement.

Illegal Agreements Promises that violate the law are illegal agreements that the courts do not recognize, regardless of the intent of the parties. Deals for prohibited drugs, such as cocaine, are illegal agreements, as are other contracts to engage in criminal activities. State law controls some activities, such as gambling. Hence, gambling contracts are often illegal, and the person who won an illegal wager cannot seek help from the courts in collecting his winnings. Some states have limits on interest rates that can be charged on certain loans; charges above the maximum allowed are called **usury** and are illegal. When a court is asked to enforce a contract, and it finds the contract to be in violation of law, it may strike the entire bargain as unenforceable or strike the part of the bargain that concerns illegal subject matter.

Unenforceable Contracts Some contracts were legal and enforceable when they were made, but a change in the law made them **unenforceable contracts**. For example, suppose a company agreed to sell a shipload of wheat to the government of Iran. While the shipment is at sea, the U.S. government declares that no U.S. firms may trade with Iran. The contract at that point becomes unenforceable under U.S. contract law, even if it is

INTERNATIONAL PERSPECTIVE

Problems Enforcing Contracts

An ongoing study by the World Bank looks at the problem of enforcing a contract in countries around the world. Lack of both effective contract law and honest, efficient judicial enforcement in certain countries discourages foreign firms from investing in those countries or doing business there and makes it difficult for residents of a country to do business in an above-board, sophisticated manner.

The Doing Business website explains: "This topic looks at the efficiency of contract enforcement by following the evolution of a sale of goods dispute and tracking the time, cost, and number of procedures involved from the moment the plaintiff files the lawsuit until actual payment." The study examined the following variables in many countries: (1) the number of procedures mandated by law that are required to file a contract case and take it through the court system; (2) the average number of days to complete the legal process from service of process to trial and enforcement; and (3) the cost of a legal action as a percent of the value of the claim that is in dispute.

Country	Number of Procedures	Time (days)	Cost (as % of claim)
Canada	36	570	22.3
China	37	406	11.1
Germany	30	394	14.4
India	46	1,420	39.6
Mexico	38	415	31.0
United Kingdom	28	399	25.9
United States	32	370	14.4

The United States is no paragon of efficiency, but the cost of legal action is relatively low compared to most countries. If contract enforcement takes too much time, is too costly, or is too complex, ordinary people are unlikely to integrate it into the way they do business.

Source: Doing Business, www.doingbusiness.org.

seen as legal in Iran. The seller must end the effort to sell the goods or face prosecution for trying to fulfill a contract about a matter that is now illegal.

Contracts Contrary to Public Policy Some contracts are unenforceable because their subject matter is contrary to public policy. Some contracts may not violate any particular statute yet may injure public welfare. Some contracts that courts have held to be contrary to public policy are exculpatory agreements, unconscionable contracts, and contracts in restraint of trade.

Exculpatory Agreements An **exculpatory agreement** (or exculpatory clause) releases one party from the consequences brought about by wrongful acts or negligence. An example is an employment contract stating that the employee will not hold the employer liable for any harm to her caused by the employer while on the job. With such a clause, the employer is no longer concerned about being sued for intentional torts. Such clauses generally violate public policy and are not enforceable.

Unconscionable Contracts The courts usually do not concern themselves with the fairness of a bargain struck by contracting parties. But in some cases, if a contract is grossly unfair to an innocent party, the courts, in equity, will not enforce it. These are called **unconscionable contracts** and occur when one of the parties, being in a strong position, takes advantage of the other party. The stronger party convinces the other party to enter into a contract contrary to his well-being. Such agreements may violate public policy and may not be enforceable.

A famous case on unconscionability is *Williams* v. *Walker-Thomas Furniture* (350 F.2d 445, 1965). A furniture store sold many items on credit to an unsophisticated, low-income person. Under the contract, none of the goods were paid for until every item had been paid for. When the buyer failed to make payments on the last thing bought, the store wanted to repossess everything, not just the last item purchased. The appeals court held that the contract was unconscionable and that the trial court would not enforce it.

Contracts in Restraint of Trade   Contracts that restrain trade or unreasonably restrict competition are considered contrary to public policy and are not enforced by the courts. Part of the common law on this subject became part of modern antitrust law, discussed later in the text.

Even if a contract does not violate a statute, it still may be an unenforceable restraint of trade. A **covenant not to compete**, for example, may be unenforceable if it does not meet certain guidelines. These usually arise in contracts for the sale of a business and for employment. The seller (or employee) agrees not to compete with the buyer (or employer).

Suppose you buy a restaurant. You do not want the previous owner to move across the street and open up a new restaurant in competition with you, so the sale is likely to have a provision that the former owner will not open a restaurant within five miles for three years. Such restrictions are usually upheld if reasonable. A restriction on national competition would not make sense in a case like this, but local restrictions would.

More controversial, and an area in which state law varies quite a bit, are restrictions on competition by former employees. In states where such restrictions can be legal, many employers have employees sign an agreement not to work for a competitor, or go into competition against the employer, for a certain length of time after leaving. For example, when a senior sales manager left Nike to go to work for Reebok, the court held that a one-year noncompete agreement in the athletic footwear market was enforceable.

In the *Gallagher* case, we see such a contractual restriction upheld. In the decision, we also see that states may differ in their rules. The court explains that under Louisiana law, as in other states, courts may "reform" a noncompete agreement. In some other states, if the noncompete agreement is too broad, it is rejected, not reformed.

ARTHUR J. GALLAGHER & CO. V. BABCOCK
United States Court of Appeals, Fifth Circuit, 703 F.3d 284 (2012)

Case Background *Arthur J. Gallagher & Co. is in the insurance business. A subsidiary, GBSI, handles employee-benefit insurance programs. GBSI purchased a Louisiana insurance broker, Babcock, paying almost $3 million for his business. As part of the deal, Babcock and several of his employees went to work for GBSI and agreed to a restrictive covenant that if they left GBSI, they would not compete with GBSI in Louisiana for two years. A few years later, Babcock and the others quit GBSI and went to work for a competitor, drawing away 13 clients to their new employer.*

Gallagher sued Babcock for violating his agreement that contained a non-solicitation agreement and a non-competition agreement. Gallagher contended that Babcock, and the employees he took with him, solicited GBSI clients in competition with

their former employer. The trial court upheld the agreements, but limited the geographic restriction to nine parishes (counties) in which Babcock could not compete with GBSI, rather than the whole state. The jury awarded Gallagher $1.2 million in damages plus attorneys' fees. Babcock and the other former GBSI employees appealed.

Case Decision Higgenbotham, Circuit Judge

* * *

Defendants argue that their employment agreements do not contain valid and enforceable non-competition provisions, both because of (1) their language and (2) their geographic scope. We are not persuaded. ...

The agreements unambiguously prohibit Defendants from competing against Gallagher or soliciting its clients for two years after the termination of their employment. Defendants agreed not to "solicit" certain of Gallagher's existing and prospective clients. And they agreed they would not "serve," "sell to," "market," "accept," "aid," "consult," "place," "counsel" or "consult" regarding insurance-related services with customers (or prospective customers) of Gallagher on whose accounts they had worked while employed by Gallagher....

Louisiana does, of course, restrict and narrowly construe non-competition agreements. As the Louisiana Supreme Court has explained, this policy "is based upon an underlying state desire to prevent an individual from contractually depriving himself of the ability to support himself and consequently becoming a public burden." But over time, the Legislature has broadened the kinds of non-competition agreements into which employers and employees may enter.

The provisions at issue here are *less* restrictive than allowed under state law. Instead of preventing its former employees from engaging in a similar business, Gallagher prohibits employees from competing for accounts on which they actually worked while at Gallagher, a restriction perhaps uncommon, but not unenforceable....

Under Louisiana law, non-solicitation and non-competition clauses must be limited to geographic areas in which the employer conducts "a like business," and the agreement must make this limitation clear by specifying the "parish or parishes, municipality or municipalities, or parts thereof" in which the employer operates. A court may, however, rely on a contractual severability clause to excise the geographic areas in which an employer does not conduct such business....

The district court agreed with Defendants and eliminated the fifty-five parishes in which Gallagher did not provide life and health insurance services. This was not error. We have already made clear that these provisions were not invalid merely because they attempted to reach every Louisiana parish. Similarly, Defendants may not defeat restrictions on competition in these nine parishes by showing that the restrictions were not enforceable in other parishes....

We affirm the judgment insofar as it directs a verdict against the Defendants.

Questions for Analysis

1. Why would the court limit the application to a few counties, rather than the whole state?
2. Suppose such noncompete agreements were illegal. Would Gallagher pay Babcock the same price for his business?

Reality and Genuineness of Consent

Freedom of contract is based on the right of individuals to enter freely into the bargains of their choice. As part of this, the parties must mutually consent to the proposed terms of a contract for it to be enforceable. The manifestation of the intent of the parties to be bound to terms of an agreement is discerned from their conduct or exchanges.

Under some circumstances, a person may enter into an agreement without knowing key information about the real nature of the transaction. Without knowledge, there is no **reality of consent** (or **genuine consent**) by the parties, and the contract may be void. This may happen for different reasons.

It is possible that a contract is not formed because of a **mistake**. A unilateral mistake occurs when one party to a contract enters into it with false information or accidentally makes an error in a significant matter. If, for example, a contract to buy a house says the price is $20,000, when the buyer knows it should be $200,000, the contract cannot be enforced at the lower price because of the mistake made in typing the contract (as happened in the sale of televisions at the start of the chapter).

In general, if the other party should have known of the error, the contract cannot be enforced to allow one party to profit from a simple error. A bilateral mistake is when both parties are wrong about presumed facts important to the making of a contract.

This does not happen often, but can be the basis for finding that no contract was ever entered into by the parties. In such a situation, either party has the right to rescind (terminate) such a contract.

Fraud and Misrepresentation A person who "agrees" to a contract as a result of **fraud, misrepresentation, duress,** or **undue influence** has the right to disaffirm the contract because there was not genuine consent. Duress occurs when someone is "forced" to sign a contract; that is, the contract is made because of a threat that presented no sensible way out. In the case of undue influence, a person enters into a contract because they are so dominated by another person or have so much trust in that person that they are subject to improper persuasion. This happens sometimes to elderly people who rely on a trusted caretaker.

Fraud or intentional misrepresentation, as discussed in Chapter 7, is an effort by a party to induce another party to enter into a contract based on false information. This may be either negligent misrepresentation or intentional misrepresentation (fraud). If so, there never was a good contract. The injured party may sue in tort and is likely to seek punitive damages.

Misrepresentation can be intentional, in which case it is fraud or much like it—different states use different names for this. But misrepresentation can also be based on negligence, as we saw in the *Squish La Fish* case in Chapter 6. Incorrect information can be made innocently in ignorance. If a false statement is made innocently, it is possible that the contract may be rescinded if the misstatement was material, or key, to the decision to make the contract and the value of the contract. If losses were incurred, there may also be a cause of action to recover the losses suffered as a result of the false information. But there would be less reason for punitive damages because the use of false information was not willful.

Statutory Exceptions Some statutes deal with high-pressure selling techniques by some door-to-door salespeople. These "home solicitation" statutes allow contracts to be cancelled if the buyer entered into the contract under pressure by a salesperson. For example, the Federal Trade Commission's Cooling-Off Rule allows buyers in door-to-door sales with a value more than $25 to void the contract in writing within three business days. An employer subject to the law may want to structure its compensation for sales representatives to count only sales that are not cancelled.

Contracts in Writing and the Statute of Frauds

Contracts do not always have to be in writing to be enforceable. Written contracts are generally a good idea, because they are difficult to deny, and courts prefer written documents over conflicting oral claims. Some contracts must be evidenced by a writing to be enforceable. They are subject to the **Statute of Frauds**, which evolved from a 1677 English statute called "An Act for the Prevention of Frauds and Perjuries." The purpose is to prevent parties from claiming that a contract existed when in fact it did not. To reduce such fraud, the statute requires that for certain contracts to be enforceable, they must be in writing.

In most states, several types of contracts are covered by the Statute of Frauds and must be evidenced in writing to be enforced by a court in the event of a dispute:

1. Contracts for the sale of real property (land).
2. Contracts that cannot be performed within one year.
3. Promises to pay the debt of another, including the debts of an estate.
4. Promises made in consideration of marriage.

CYBER LAW

Digital Signatures and Contracts

The Electronic Signatures in Global and National Commerce Act (E-Sign) became part of federal law in 2000. It is based on the Uniform Electronic Transactions Act, which had been adopted by most states. The purpose of E-Sign is to leave the substance of contract law unchanged, but to be neutral about the use of technology in creating contracts.

E-Sign removes obstacles to the use of electronic media in contract formation. A valid signature includes any "electronic sound, symbol, or process, attached to or logically associated with a contract or other record and executed or adopted by a person with the intent to sign the record." The primary

impact of the law is in internal business record keeping, such as employee timesheets, business-to-business (B2B) transactions that tend to be more complex than consumer transactions, and business-to-government dealings, such as compliance with regulatory procedures over the Internet.

As in the days when written signatures dominated contracts, the authenticity of a "signature" is still critical. Companies such as Symantec provide SSL (secure socket layer) certificates to guarantee Internet security. Signatures also include such things as the PIN number used at an ATM machine. The law does not dictate the specific technology that must be used for a signature to be accepted as genuine because such technology changes rapidly.

Sufficiency of the Writing For a writing to be sufficient under the Statute of Frauds, it must give the material terms of the contract and be signed by at least the defendant. Courts usually also require the writing to have the names of the parties, the consideration offered, the subject matter of the contract, and other material terms. The writing need not look like a contract. Confirmations, invoices, e-mails, sales orders, and even checks may satisfy the writing requirement.

Parol Evidence Rule Negotiations often come before contracts. The parties may exchange e-mails or other communications before signing the actual contract. Parties may omit from the final contract some terms agreed upon in negotiations. Later, the parties may disagree about those terms.

The **parol evidence rule** restricts the use of oral (parol) statements in a lawsuit when the evidence is contrary to the terms of a written contract. Oral evidence cannot contradict, change, or add terms to a written contract. Parol evidence may be introduced when the written contract is incomplete or ambiguous; when it proves fraud, mistake, or misrepresentation; or when the parol evidence explains the written instrument through previous trade usage or course of dealing. We see these issues arise in the *Deschamps* case.

DESCHAMPS V. TREASURE STATE TRAILER COURT, LTD.

Supreme Court of Montana 230 P.3d 800 (2010)

Case Background *In 2003, Rasmussen agreed to sell Deschamps a mobile home trailer park in Great Falls, Montana, with 96 residential spaces, for $1,445,000. The contract explained how Deschamps would pay Rasmussen over time. Right after the sale was completed, Rasmussen died and his estate*

inherited his assets. Deschamps found significant problems with the trailer park water system that required $400,000 in repairs. In 2006, he quit making payments to the estate, claiming that the cost of the water system repairs made payments impossible.

The estate sued for payment; Deschamps sued for breach of contract and fraud, contending that Rasmussen told him the water system was in good condition and that the occupancy rate was higher than it was in fact. The trial court held for the estate, finding that Deschamps' claims were precluded by the parol evidence rule. He appealed.

Case Decision Justice Patricia O. Cotter

* * *

The parol evidence rule, codified [in Montana law], states: "The execution of a contract in writing, whether the law requires it to be written or not, supersedes all the oral negotiations or stipulations concerning its matter which preceded or accompanied the execution of the instrument." The District Court determined this rule precluded Deschamps' claims for (1) negligent misrepresentation of the water system's condition, (2) breach of implied covenant of good faith and fair dealing as to the condition of the water system, and (3) both fraud claims pertaining to the water system. The court ruled that the Agreement ... memorialized the parties' buy/sell transaction and Deschamps could not introduce evidence of oral agreements or statements ostensibly made by Rasmussen that were not included in the Agreement. Therefore, Deschamps was not allowed to claim that Rasmussen told him the water system was in "good" or "fine" condition, when Rasmussen, according to Deschamps, knew that was untrue. Deschamps also was constrained from testifying that Rasmussen claimed the Park had at least 90 percent occupancy with a low turnover rate.

In its legal analysis, the court referenced several relevant clauses in the Buy-Sell Agreement upon which it relied. Without repeating lengthy portions of the Agreement, it is undisputed that the Agreement provided: (1) that Rasmussen had not conducted an inspection and did not warrant the property's condition, (2) Deschamps had the right and obligation to inspect the property prior to purchase, (3) a special disclaimer of reliance on any assurances given by Rasmussen as to the condition

of the property, (4) an inspection contingency waiver provision that indicated the inspection was satisfied or waived, (5) a merger clause specifying that the Agreement was the entire agreement and superseded any oral agreements between the parties, and (6) that the Agreement could only be amended in writing. The District Court ... noted that Deschamps had signed a contract prepared by *his* real estate agent that contained an unequivocal statement that Deschamps had not relied "upon any assurances by ... the Seller as to the condition of the property..." The court concluded that Deschamps, by claiming Rasmussen had misled him as to the condition of the water supply system, was now arguing that he *had* relied, to his detriment, on Rasmussen's assurances. This argument was a direct contradiction to the express content of the contract and therefore was precluded under the parol evidence rule.

It is well established that when the language of a contract is clear and unambiguous, we are "to ascertain and declare what is in terms or in substance contained therein, not to insert what has been omitted or to omit what has been inserted." Here, the contract drafted by Deschamps and presented to Rasmussen for signature clearly and expressly stated that Deschamps did not rely on any oral assurances or representations by Rasmussen. Deschamps cannot now claim otherwise. Therefore, in that his allegations of reliance on alleged fraudulent statements specifically contradict the language of the Agreement, consideration of them is barred under the parol evidence rule.

* * *

Affirmed.

Questions for Analysis

1. What is the key lesson from this case—and many others like it? Do you think the court believed that Rasmussen never made the claims that Deschamps claimed?
2. Would Deschamps' claim of fraud, a tort, avoid the parol evidence rule?

❓ TEST YOURSELF

1. In *Arthur J. Gallagher & Co.* v. *Babcock*, where Babcock signed noncompete and non-solicitation agreements that stated he would not work for a competitor for two years after leaving Gallagher, the appeals court held that the agreements could:
   a. not be enforced because the two-year period was too long.
   b. not be enforced because they were "overly broad."
   c. be enforced only for personnel in "managerial positions."
   d. be enforced as reasonable in a specific region in Louisiana.
2. If one party to a contract accidentally writes in a contract that the price of something is one-tenth of what it was supposed to be, such as a house for $30,000 instead of $300,000, there is said not to be genuine consent to the lower price: T—F
3. If someone points a gun at another person and tells them to sign a contract, there is no real consent because of _____. If someone takes advantage of another person and convinces them to do something they would likely not have done otherwise, there may be found to be _____.
4. In *Deschamps* v. *Treasure State Trailer Court, LTD.*, where Deschamps bought a trailer court and then found out the water system needed costly repairs, the appeals court held that the contract was:
   a. invalid because of fraud.
   b. not enforceable because of unilateral mistake.
   c. not enforceable because of mutual mistake.
   d. enforceable as written.
5. An unconscionable contract may violate "public policy" and not be enforceable: T—F
6. Some contracts must be in writing to be enforceable. Such contracts are subject to _____.

Answers: d; T; duress, undue influence; d; T; the Statute of Frauds.

ISSUE SPOTTER
Liars' Contest?

You go to look at new cars at a dealership that is having a sale. You like one particular vehicle. The salesperson tells you that the sale ends today and the cars are going fast, so you better buy now. You are not sure. The salesperson says that to guarantee that you get the sale price, you must sign a contract today and write a check for $500. But, she knows you are not ready to commit, so she will hold the contract and check for three days while you decide for sure. If you decide not to buy, you get your money back, and the contract is torn up. You have nothing to lose. You sign the contract and write a check. Two days later, you call to say you have decided not to buy; but the dealer says that there is a signed contract, and you'll lose your $500 if you back out. Can you explain to the judge what happened and get your money back?

© Cengage Learning

Performance, Discharge, and Breach of Contracts

Eventually all contracts end. When the obligations have been performed, the contract is terminated or discharged. Just as there are rules governing the creation of contracts, there are rules concerning the performance and discharge of contracts. The various ways a contract can be discharged are summarized in Exhibit 10.5.

Performance

Most contracts come to an end by **performance** of the parties' obligations under the contract. Contracts may be for one sale or for provision of a service. If a contract is to be completed over time, such as for NightStaff to clean the offices in BigBank's office building for two years, once NightStaff has done the cleaning for two years and BigBank has paid, the contract terminates. No further obligation is owed by either party.

Substantial Performance Suppose Microsoft delivers a computer program written specifically for HP. The product is delivered on time, but a couple of bugs in the program are discovered. Has Microsoft performed its obligation so that HP must pay, or is there a lack of performance such that HP may refuse or can sue Microsoft for breach of contract? Generally, **substantial performance** means that the contract basically has been fulfilled, and payments must be made. The parties are expected to act in good faith. Refusing to pay when most of the contract was properly completed would not be acceptable. HP could delay final payment to Microsoft until the bugs were worked out, but there is no justification to rescind the agreement for lack of performance. Of course, if HP incurs costs as a result of the bugs, Microsoft is liable for those damages.

EXHIBIT 10.5   DISCHARGE OF A CONTRACT AND ITS EFFECTS ON THE PARTIES

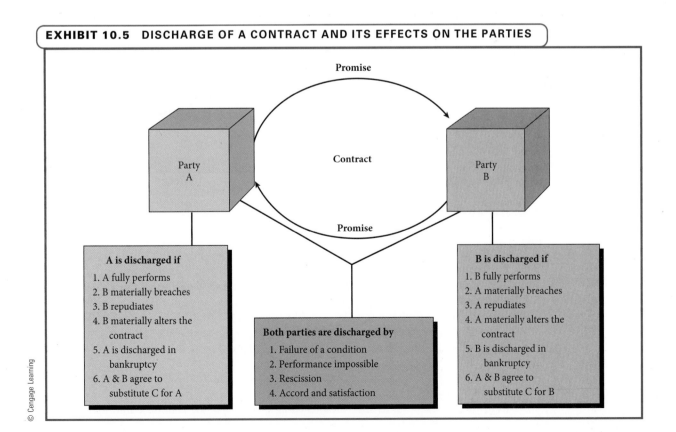

Promise

Party A

Contract

Party B

Promise

A is discharged if
1. A fully performs
2. B materially breaches
3. B repudiates
4. B materially alters the contract
5. A is discharged in bankruptcy
6. A & B agree to substitute C for A

Both parties are discharged by
1. Failure of a condition
2. Performance impossible
3. Rescission
4. Accord and satisfaction

B is discharged if
1. B fully performs
2. A materially breaches
3. A repudiates
4. A materially alters the contract
5. B is discharged in bankruptcy
6. A & B agree to substitute C for B

The difference between a breach where there has been substantial performance and a **material breach** (significant breach) of contract can be a judgment call. If a party wants to make sure things are done to perfection, that fact must be made clear in the contract. Many business contracts specify milestones that trigger payment obligations so there is a way for the parties to measure performance along the way. Construction contracts usually include provisions for the buyer to give the builder a list of all things that must be done for performance to be complete after the buyer has inspected a new building.

Assignment and Delegation

Some contracts may be performed by a third party. A transfer of contract rights to another party is an **assignment**; a transfer of contractual duties to a third party is a **delegation**. Many contracts are for services (duties) that cannot be assigned. Kobe Bryant cannot delegate his duty to play for the Los Angeles Lakers to any other person. If a dentist has agreed to cap your teeth, you cannot assign your right to have your teeth capped to someone else. However, many contracts are capable of being assigned or delegated to third parties.

For example, if HP contracted with Microsoft to develop some software for HP, unless prohibited in the contract, Microsoft may delegate some of the software creation to a company that does contract work for it. When that company delivers the software, Microsoft can integrate it into the final product it delivers to HP. Similarly, if NightStaff has contracted to provide cleaning services for BigBank for two years, it may assign the contract to another cleaning company, unless the contract prohibits that, perhaps for security reasons. NightStaff is liable for problems that arise as a result of poor performance by the other company, however.

Third-Party Beneficiaries A **third-party beneficiary** is a party who is not part of an original contract who acquires rights under the contract. This happens mostly in credit contracts. For example, suppose Sting loans Bono $5,000. In consideration for the loan, Bono promises to pay $5,000 to Diddy, to whom Sting already owes $5,000. If Bono fails to pay Diddy, then Diddy may sue Bono to collect the $5,000, even though Diddy and Bono did not enter into a contract. Diddy is a third-party beneficiary of the contract between Sting and Bono.

Breach

When a party to a contract does not perform as required, there is a **breach of contract**. If one party prevents or hinders the other party to a contract from performing her duties, then a breach occurs. The party injured by the breach may be entitled to a remedy (discussed below). To determine the remedy that may be provided, the court looks at the extent of the breach.

Material Breach If the performance provided by a party is substantially less than the requirements of the contract, there is a **material breach**. Suppose Microsoft fails to deliver the program to HP on time, or it delivers seriously defective software. As a result, HP cannot deliver its computers. HP would have a cause of action against the breaching party, Microsoft, for damages. HP would be discharged from the performance promised under the contract, i.e., HP would not have to accept delivery of the defective program nor accept the corrected version if it arrived too late to be useful.

Anticipatory Breach Before the performance of a contract takes place, an **anticipatory breach**, or **repudiation**, occurs if one party indicates inability or lack of desire to perform the contract. Sometimes the breaching party does not volunteer information that it is going to breach, but the fact that the contract is not performed becomes clear. If Microsoft was scheduled to ship the program to HP by August 1, but HP learns on July 15 that Microsoft forgot to assign anyone to work on the program and has not completed any code, HP does not have to wait until August 1 to look for replacements, because HP already knows that Microsoft cannot deliver on time. HP may be able to sue Microsoft for costs it incurred as a result of Microsoft's failure to deliver on time.

Discharge by Agreement of the Parties

Just as parties have the freedom to contract, they are also free to agree to modify or to terminate—that is, **discharge**—their obligations under the contract. Discharge by agreement between the parties can take various forms. Among the most important are rescission, novation, and accord and satisfaction.

Rescission A **rescission** occurs when both parties agree that the contract should be terminated without performance. A rescission discharges the obligations of both parties under the contract. For example, Avon contracted with Sears to sell cosmetics at Sears' stores. Sears decided to cancel the deal and paid Avon $20 million to agree to terminate the arrangement. The parties agreed to rescind, or cancel, the contract.

Novation In a **novation**, all the parties agree to discharge one party from the contract and create a new contract with another party, who becomes responsible for the discharged party's performance. Suppose JLo was contracted to star in a movie, but decides she does not want to. She asks Beyoncé if she would like the part instead. If the movie studio agrees on that replacement, then the new agreement is a novation, and JLo is released from liability for not doing the movie.

Accord and Satisfaction Another way parties may agree to discharge their duties to one another under a contract is through **accord and satisfaction**. An **accord** is an agreement by the parties to offer and accept performance that differs from the original agreement. **Satisfaction** is the actual performance of the new obligation. The original obligation is discharged when the consideration for the accord is provided.

Suppose Spielberg owes DiCaprio $1,000. If Spielberg offers to direct a movie for DiCaprio in place of paying him the $1,000, and DiCaprio accepts, then there is an accord. If Spielberg then directs a movie for DiCaprio, there is accord and satisfaction. The new consideration discharges the original claim. If Spielberg fails to direct the movie, then DiCaprio could still sue him for the $1,000, because there was no satisfaction of the accord.

Discharge by Impossibility

The doctrine of **impossibility of performance** is used to end the obligations to a contract when an event occurs that makes performance impossible. Impossibility occurs when a party who was to provide services dies or is incapacitated, a law is passed making performance of the contract illegal, or the subject matter of the contract is destroyed (e.g., a house you wanted to buy burns down before the deal is done). Impossibility discharges the obligations of the parties to the contract.

An extension of impossibility is **impracticability** or **frustration**. The *Restatement (Second) of Contracts* holds, at § 262, that impracticability may be applied because of "extreme or unreasonable difficulty, expense, injury or loss..." The term means more than unexpected difficulty and cost. The concept may be applied to wartime shortages, crop failures, or loss of needed supplies as a result of international embargos. Courts

ISSUE SPOTTER
Do You Have to Eat the Loss?

At the start of the chapter, we posed the problem of the sales rep who accidentally billed a customer for the wrong price. All the terms of the contract were in place except for the misquoted price of $63. That issue was resolved, and the televisions were ordered from Korea. A fire at the Samsung factory stops production for several months, and the order cannot be fulfilled. Is there a contract, or can the seller tell the customer their deal is off for at least several months without facing the likelihood of successful litigation by the customer?

© Cengage Learning 2015

generally expect at least partial performance, even if full performance is excused by impracticability.

Remedies

Parties to contracts usually perform their obligations. Still, thousands of disputes must be resolved every year. There is a basic premise that after a breach, innocent parties should be placed in the economic position they would have enjoyed had the contract been performed. If, however, the circumstances are such that the legal remedy of monetary damages is inadequate, the court may grant the injured party an appropriate equitable remedy. The major classes of remedies available are presented in Exhibit 10.6.

Damages

The most common remedy for breach of contract is monetary damages. The party who suffered from a breach seeks a judgment for lost profits and for other expenses particular to the breach. A variety of types of damage awards may be awarded by the courts under different circumstances, including compensatory, expectancy, liquidated, nominal, and special damages.

Economic Loss Rule The **economic loss rule** means that when a breach of contract does not include a tort, such as injury to persons, the damages only relate to economic losses suffered from a breach. As the Wisconsin Supreme Court explained (573 N.W.2d at 846), the "application of the economic loss doctrine to tort actions between commercial parties is generally based on three policies… 1) to maintain the fundamental distinction between tort law and contract law; 2) to protect commercial parties' freedom to allocate economic risk by contract; and 3) to encourage the party best situated to assess the risk of economic loss."

EXHIBIT 10.6   CONTRACT REMEDIES

MONETARY DAMAGES	EQUITABLE REMEDIES
Compensatory Damages	Specific performance
Expectancy Damages	Injunction
Liquidated Damages	Restitution
Nominal Damages	Reformation
Special Damages	

© Cengage Learning

Because the damages should be related only to lost profits and costs incurred as a result of a breach, which require accounting evidence and specific calculations, i.e., not punitive damages or mental distress awards, it is common to try to assert that a tort occurred in a breach of contract case. Look back at the complaint in the *Wynn* v. *Lloyd's* case in Chapter 3's Exhibit 3.1. There is a claim the defendant acted "intentionally" and "maliciously." This is an effort to try to wriggle a tort claim into a breach of contract case in an effort to obtain higher damages.

Calculating Damages Suppose you arrange for Lil Wayne and Justin Bieber to appear together at a concert. That is an odd pairing, but you think it is a great idea. They will each get 20 percent of the gate and a $10,000 guarantee, plus all revenues from t-shirt sales at the concert. The concert arena will hold 10,000 fans; average ticket price will be $80, so revenues will be $800,000 if you sell out, of which $320,000 will go to the performers. The concert hall charges a flat $100,000 to host the show. That would leave you $380,000 for other expenses and profit. You get local radio stations to hype the concert. A week before the concert, both artists cancel because they decide the idea is insane. The arena charges you a $50,000 cancellation fee. You have sold 6,000 tickets that must be refunded. You sue the performers for breach of contract.

You win, but what are the damages? First, you have the market value of your time spent, say 200 hours. What is your usual wage rate? At $40 an hour, it would be an $8,000 cost you incurred by devoting time to event planning. You spent $1,000 having the tickets printed. Each ticket costs $1 to process and mail, so there is another $6,000, plus the $50,000 arena fee, plus the cost of mailing refunds, which would likely be $6,000, or $71,000 in direct costs incurred. Those costs are covered by **compensatory damages** or actual damages. These damages, in contract cases, are to allow the party suffering the breach to recover costs incurred as a result of relying on the promise of the other party.

What about lost profits? If you only sold 6,000 tickets by the time of the concert, there would likely have been no profit, in which case you could not claim **expectancy damages**. These damages cover the profits you reasonably expected to make if the contract had been fulfilled. However, if you could show that most tickets for a concert are usually sold in the last days, and selling out was likely, then you would have suffered lost profits and may collect expectancy damages. What about the fact that you cannot sleep nights worrying about this and feeling that your career as a concert promoter has been ruined? Too bad; there is no recovery for mental distress or some other tort. It was a business deal gone bad. The rule is to stick to measurable costs.

The *DeRosier* case discusses damage calculation, the issue of mitigation of damages, and why a party may not want to have a breaching party correct a problem.

DEROSIER V. UTILITY SYSTEMS OF AMERICA, INC.

Court of Appeals of Minnesota 780 N.W.2d 1 (2010)

Case Background *DeRosier owned land on a hill-side. Before a house could be built, the lot needed to be filled with dirt. DeRosier saw Utility Systems of America (USA) doing road construction nearby. He asked USA if it would be willing to dump excess fill dirt on his lot. Because DeRosier's land was close to*

the construction, USA saved money by doing that instead of hauling the dirt further away. DeRosier obtained a permit from the city that would allow 1,500 cubic yards of fill to be dumped on his property, which was the amount needed for the lot to be made level. DeRosier gave the permit to USA.

Later, DeRosier found that USA dumped 6,500 cubic yards of fill, so 5,000 yards had to be removed because the amount violated the fill permit and was way too much to be useful for construction. USA denied responsibility but offered to move the excess dirt for $9,500.

DeRosier sued. The trial court granted him $22,829 in general damages to pay another company to remove 5,000 yards of fill. It also awarded him $8,000 in consequential or delay damages for the time lost to be able to construct a new house while waiting for the dirt to be moved. USA appealed, contending that DeRosier failed to mitigate the damages by not having USA move the dirt for only $9,500 rather than the $22,829 he paid another contractor.

Case Decision   Minge, Judge

* * *

General damages, as opposed to special damages, naturally and necessarily result from the act complained of. Minnesota courts have stated, "the term 'consequential damages' usually ... refers to those items of damages which, because of particular circumstances, are to be distinguished from 'general' damages." Consequential damages are commonly called special damages. Special damages are the natural, but not the necessary, result of a breach. Although special or consequential damages flow naturally from the breach, they are not recoverable unless they are reasonably foreseeable to the parties at the time of the breach. ...

USA's counsel pointed out that there was no claim for delay damages in the pleadings or discovery. Perhaps most significantly, no evidence of monetary loss caused by delay was introduced at trial. Although the district court observed that DeRosier's attorney specifically mentioned delay in his prelitigation demand, that did not constitute evidence of such damages. ...

Because consequential (or delay) damages were not pleaded and not supported by any evidence in the record, we conclude that the district court erred in awarding DeRosier $8,000 as consequential damages for delay in construction and we reverse that portion of the judgment.

* * *

Based on the record and the deference we afford the fact finder, we conclude the district court had a sufficient basis for calculating and did not abuse its discretion in granting $22,829 in general damages.

The third issue is whether DeRosier had a duty to mitigate damages that was breached by his failure to accept USA's offer to remove excess fill for $9,500. USA claims that, even if the actual-damage award was supported by the evidence, recoverable damages are limited to its $9,500 offer. DeRosier responds that he was not obligated to do business with USA after its breach and that such an arrangement would have jeopardized his ability to sue by acting as a form of settlement. ...

We conclude that when one party to the contract defectively performs and subsequently offers to correct the breach through a new contract, the non-breaching party may generally decline the offer and still recover its full damages. Special circumstances may rebut the reasonableness of the rejection and call for exceptions to this rule. The facts before us support DeRosier's decision: (1) the $9,500 payment demanded was substantial; (2) DeRosier was not unreasonable in believing that acceptance could constitute an accord and satisfaction; (3) other hauling services were readily available; and (4) DeRosier's relationship with USA was strained as USA was blaming DeRosier. ...

Although the district court erred in awarding DeRosier $8,000 in consequential damages, the district court did not abuse its discretion in awarding DeRosier general damages. DeRosier did not unreasonably reject USA's $9,500 offer, and therefore did not improperly fail to mitigate his general damages. We modify the judgment to the amount of the award for general damages: $22,829.

Affirmed in part and reversed in part.

Questions for Analysis

1. Why could DeRosier's paying USA to haul the excess dirt away be considered an accord and satisfaction?
2. Explain why were there no consequential damages.

INTERNATIONAL PERSPECTIVE

Contracting with the Japanese

A typical U.S. view is that a contract defines the rights and responsibilities of the parties and seeks to cover all possible contingencies. The traditional Japanese view is that a contract is secondary in a business transaction. Business is an ongoing relationship with both parties committed to the pursuit of similar objectives. Consequently, relationships, not contracts, are negotiated.

Major concepts are negotiated in Japan, but the details that are more common in a contract in the United States are often not included. As a result, Americans are often somewhat uncomfortable with Japanese contract because of their lack of specificity. Some Japanese accept more details in a contract, knowing it is what Americans expect, but brief and flexible contracts are preferred. Contracts are often viewed as agreements to be refined as circumstances change. Lengthy legal agreements drafted by the other party are likely to be viewed with suspicion in Japanese business. Relationships should take precedence over formal rights and obligations. Problems can be resolved by compromise.

Japanese contract-negotiating teams are often larger than American teams. Japanese groups may excuse themselves during sessions so members can discuss issues among themselves. Strong statements such as, "that would not work," may be seen as rude. Japanese business people work for a consensus within the team and the company. Negotiations may proceed slowly. Japanese business people do not usually operate with the urgency typical of Americans because they wish to develop a lasting relationship.

Liquidated Damages **Liquidated damages** are an amount specified in the contract to be paid in the event of breach. Liquidated damages are not allowed if the court finds that they are so excessive that they actually impose a **penalty**. That is, the damages specified in the contract must be reasonably related to actual losses that could be suffered. For example, if a small office building is supposed to ready for occupancy by May 15, the contract may require the builder to pay liquidated damages of $1,000 per day after May 15 until the building is ready. But the contract could not call for "damages" of $1 million per day; that would be a penalty, which is against public policy.

Nominal Damages When a plaintiff suffers a breach of contract but does not suffer a measurable economic loss, a court may award **nominal damages**. The amount of recovery to the injured party may be as little as a dollar, but attorney fees, which can be huge, and court costs may also be awarded. Such awards can be important because proof of breach may be related to other legal issues.

Punitive Damages **Punitive damages** or **exemplary damages** are usually awarded when the wrongdoer's conduct has been willful or malicious and fraud was involved, bringing in tort issues. They punish the wrongdoer by allowing the plaintiff to receive relief beyond compensatory and expectancy damages. Punitive damages are relatively rare in contract cases as a tort must be proven.

Mitigation of Damages

When a breach of contract does occur, the injured party is required to make reasonable efforts to **mitigate**, or lessen, the losses that may be incurred. When Lil Wayne and Justin Bieber decided not to show for the concert, you had to stop work on it, take the steps necessary to call it off, and refund money to those who bought tickets. You could not keep

© Cengage Learning

Lighter Side **of the Law**

Me, Read the Rules?

Struna bought 52 lottery tickets with the same numbers on each. The top prize was $100,000 for a winning ticket, but the lottery rules hold that the maximum any one person can win in a drawing is $1 million. So when Struna's number won, he got $1 million, not the $5.2 million he expected.

He sued Convenient Food Mart, where he bought the tickets, for fraud, because the clerk did not tell him the terms of the lottery contract, which were printed on the ticket. The jury awarded him $250,000 in compensatory damages and $1.1 million in punitive damages.

The appeals court threw out the judgment.

Source: Struna v. Convenient Food Mart, 828 N.E.2d 647, Ct App., Ohio.

incurring new costs by selling more tickets in the hope that they might change their minds and perform after all. Once there is a clear breach, business as usual must resume.

Equitable Remedies

If money damages are inadequate to compensate for the injury caused by a breach of contract, or if they do not resolve the problem properly, **equitable remedies**, such as specific performance or an injunction, may be available. These remedies are available to injured parties only at the discretion of the court. They generally are not granted if an adequate damage remedy exists, or where enforcement would impose a great burden on the defendant. The remedy of equity requires the party seeking such remedy to have "clean hands" and to have not engaged in any bad behavior.

Specific Performance **Specific performance** is an order by a court requiring a party who created a wrong to perform the obligations promised in a contract. The remedy is granted for breach of a contract when the payment of money damages is inadequate. Contracts for the sale of a particular piece of real property (land) or of a unique good, such as a piece of art, are the types of contracts in which specific performance may be granted by the courts.

Courts do not order people to perform personal service or to do some particular job, because that would be involuntary servitude. Moreover, it would be very hard for a court to monitor the quality of performance in such cases—judges do not want to listen to disputes over whether Lil Wayne's decision to rap seventeenth-century poetry was a breach or not. That is, a court would not force Lil Wayne and Justin Bieber to appear at a concert and perform. Damages would be imposed instead for their failure to appear.

Injunction As with specific performance, the remedy of an injunction is allowed when the payment of damages does not offer a satisfactory substitute for the performance promised. An **injunction** is a court order requiring a party to perform or to refrain from performing certain acts.

Suppose a partnership agreement stated that a partner who quits to go into business for herself or with another firm would not compete against the partnership for three years. If a partner then quits the partnership to start a new competing firm, the payment of damages may be an inadequate remedy for the partnership. The court, through the granting of an injunction, may order the departing partner not to compete with the partnership. Violating the injunction can subject a party to contempt of court penalties, including jail time.

Restitution

The remedy of **restitution** may be used to prevent unjust enrichment. That is, if one party has unjustly enriched himself—received a benefit not paid for—at the expense of another party, the court can order payment to be made or the goods involved to be returned. Closely related to this is the idea of quasi contract.

Quasi Contracts

A **quasi contract** is not a contract. The courts created the concept of quasi contract to give relief to innocent parties or to prevent injustice, even though no true contract exists. In the words of New York's highest court in *Bradkin* v. *Leverton* (309 N.Y.S.2d 192):

> *Quasi contracts are not contracts at all.... The contract is a mere fiction, a form imposed in order to adapt the case to a given remedy.... Briefly stated, a quasi-contractual obligation is one imposed by law where there has been no agreement or expression of assent, by word or act, on the part of either party involved. The law creates it, regardless of the intention of the parties, to assure a just and equitable result.*

The idea of quasi contract is closely related to *quantum meruit* recovery. The doctrine of *quantum meruit* is used by the courts to avoid injustice. Something of value has been provided, but there was no contract or a contract was not completed. We see the application of *quantum meruit* in the *Scheerer* case.

SCHEERER V. FISHER

Court of Appeals of North Carolina 688 S.E.2d 471 (2010)

Case Background *Scheerer, a real estate agent, helped arrange for Fisher to buy some commercial real estate for $20 million. The seller and Fisher, the buyer, each promised to pay Scheerer a 2 percent commission, but the deal fell apart before it was completed. Fisher then formed a new company and had a third party, Antonio, buy the property and sell it to Fisher's new company. Scheerer learned of the deal, from which he got no commission, and sued for breach of contract or* quantum meruit *for reasonable compensation. The trial court held there was no contract or basis for payment to Scheerer. He appealed.*

Case Decision Calabria, Judge

* * *

Plaintiffs argue that the trial court erred in dismissing their claim of *quantum meruit* for failure to state a claim upon which relief can be granted. We agree.

Under Rule 8(a)(2) of the North Carolina Rules of Civil Procedure, plaintiffs are entitled to seek alternative forms of relief.... If plaintiffs' allegations in their claim for *quantum meruit* are accepted as true, no contract exists and *quantum meruit* is not excluded as a remedy *per se*.

Recovery in *quantum meruit* will not be denied where a contract may be implied from the proven facts but the express contract alleged is not proved. The rationale for allowing a plaintiff to plead both breach of express contract and breach of implied contract is that if the plaintiff fails to prove the existence of an express contract, he or she is not foreclosed from recovery in *quantum meruit* if a contract can be implied and the reasonable value of his or her services can be drawn from the evidence.

To recover in *quantum meruit*, plaintiffs must show: (1) services were rendered to defendants; (2) the services were knowingly and voluntarily accepted; and

(3) the services were not given gratuitously. In short, if plaintiffs alleged and proved acceptance of services and the value of those services, they were entitled to go to the jury on *quantum meruit....*

In the instant case, as to their claim for *quantum meruit*, plaintiffs alleged that: (1) defendants had a prior professional relationship with Scheerer and therefore knew Scheerer was a real estate agent; (2) defendants knew plaintiffs were working on behalf of defendants to find property suitable for defendants to purchase; (3) plaintiffs told defendants that such property was for sale; (4) both parties expected plaintiffs to be paid a commission for their work; and (5) defendants were ready, willing, and able buyers and in fact purchased the properties located by plaintiffs.

... The undisputed facts establish conduct demonstrating that defendants took action to deny Scheerer compensation that was earned for the services he rendered. Although the original contract he negotiated failed to close, the law implies a promise to pay some reasonable compensation for services rendered. Plaintiffs' allegations state a valid claim for relief in *quantum meruit....*

Reversed.

Questions for Analysis

1. There was no written contract involving Scheerer and the purchase of the property by Fisher from Antonio, so why should Scheerer receive payment?
2. Does this rule allow many parties to claim they were cheated out of a deal, thereby generating a lot of litigation?

? TEST YOURSELF

1. The transfer of contract rights to another party is called _____. A transfer of contractual duties to a third party is called _____.
2. If both parties to a contract agree that the contract should be terminated without performance, there is said to be a novation: T—F
3. In *DeRosier* v. *Utility Systems of America*, where DeRosier had more dirt dumped on his property than he requested, the appeals court held that he:
   a. could receive compensatory damages for the cost of removal of excess dirt.
   b. had failed to take advantage of the offer to remove the dirt at low cost, so he failed to mitigate the damages.
   c. could receive consequential (or delay) damages for lost time in construction.
   d. could receive punitive damages for defendant's malicious act.
4. If a breach of contract has occurred, the party suffering a loss from the breach has an obligation to mitigate the damages: T—F
5. A quasi contract is a type of contract that is held to exist when one key term is missing, but a court finds that the parties intended to enter into a contract, so one does exist: T—F
6. If a party does everything required under a contract except for some small bit, and a dispute arises, the court is likely to find that there has been _____.

Answers: assignment, delegation; F; a; T; F; substantial performance.

SUMMARY

- Basic to the law of contracts is freedom of contract. However, because of public policy goals, state and federal laws place some restrictions on the kinds of contracts businesses can enter into.
- Contract law is based on a large body of common or judge-made law. The *Restatement of Contracts* is an authoritative document providing a summary of the common law of contract, which is quite consistent across the states.
- A contract is a promise or set of promises that creates an agreement between parties. It creates legal rights and duties enforceable under the law.
- Under the common law, a contract must meet several elements to be enforceable:

  1. There must be an agreement (offer and acceptance).
  2. The parties to a contract must provide consideration.
  3. The parties must have the legal capacity to contract.
  4. The subject matter of the contract must be legal.
  5. The consent of the parties must be genuine.

- An offeror has the right to terminate an offer without warning, before it is accepted, unless there was an option granted, which is a contract in itself, giving the offeree a certain time in which to decide. If an offer is not specifically ended, it is presumed to end in a reasonable time, given usual practices in that area of business.
- Acceptance of an offer must be clear and, to be effective, must not make changes in the terms offered. When an offeree makes changes to an offer, a new offer has been created. If an offeror states that acceptance must follow a specific form, such as signing a piece of paper, then that must be done for acceptance to be effective.
- Consideration is something of value bargained for in an exchange. The courts do not care much about the "fairness" of an exchange, only that there

has been a voluntary exchange of mutual promises to give something of value. A legal detriment exists for both parties to the contract, which distinguishes contracts from gifts.
- A promise that falls short of meeting the terms of a contract may still be held to be enforceable under the doctrine of promissory estoppel. That occurs when a promise is made that the other party can reasonably rely upon in their decision making.
- Parties to a contract must have capacity to contract, meaning they must be of legal age and not suffering from a disability that precludes their understanding the matter. The subject matter of a contract must be legal for the courts to be willing to consider enforcement; deals for subjects that are illegal by statute, or that violate public policy, are not recognized.
- Consent must be genuine; no force or duress may be used. If a supposed contract was based on fraud or fraudulent misrepresentation, there was no real consent. This can fall into tort law, which allows greater damages, including punitive damages.
- Some contracts must be in writing to fulfill requirements of the Statute of Frauds. They include contracts for the sale of land and real property, promises made in consideration of marriage, contracts that cannot be completed within one year, and promises to pay the debt of another.
- Contracts may be discharged, or terminated, in several ways: by performance, through a breach by one or both of the parties to the contract, by the impossibility of performance, by operation of law, or by mutual agreement of the parties.
- In the event of a breach of contract, the injured party may ask the court for relief. Most common are money damages to compensate for expenses incurred and for lost profits. The injured party has a responsibility to minimize losses from the breach. The courts can also provide equitable relief, such as specific performance, in certain cases.

TERMS TO KNOW

law merchant, 244
contract, 244
promise, 244
express contract, 244
implied contract, 244

offer, 245
offeror, 245
offeree, 245
termination, 247
option contract, 247

revocation, 247
counteroffer, 247
acceptance, 248
bilateral contract, 248
unilateral contract, 248

performance, 248
mirror image, 248
consideration, 251
promisee, 251
promisor, 251
legal detriment, 251
promissory estoppel, 252
contractual capacity, 254
void contract, 254
voidable contract, 254
ratification, 254
usury, 255
unenforceable contract, 255
exculpatory agreement, 256
unconscionable contract, 256
covenant not to compete, 257
reality of consent, 258
genuine consent, 258
mistake, 258
fraud, 259

misrepresentation, 259
duress, 259
undue influence, 259
Statute of Frauds, 259
parol evidence rule, 260
performance, 263
substantial performance, 263
material breach, 264
assignment, 264
delegation, 264
third-party beneficiary, 264
breach of contract, 264
material breach, 264
anticipatory breach, 264
repudiation, 264
discharge, 265
rescission, 265
novation, 265
accord and satisfaction, 265
accord, 265

satisfaction, 265
impossibility of performance, 265
impracticality, 265
frustration, 265
economic loss rule, 266
compensatory damages, 267
expectancy damages, 267
liquidated damages, 269
penalty, 269
nominal damages, 269
punitive damages, 269
exemplary damages, 269
mitigate, 269
equitable remedy, 270
specific performance, 270
injunction, 270
restitution, 271
quasi contract, 271
quantum meruit, 271

DISCUSSION QUESTION

Jones walks into a grocery store, puts 75 cents down on the counter, and says, "A Coke please." Under contract law, what has just occurred? If the grocery store owner takes the 75 cents, what type of contract has been agreed upon?

CASE QUESTIONS

1. Polk listed property to sell with a real estate agent. Avon made an offer, and the two parties went back and forth on terms. When Polk rejected an offer from Avon, Avon then accepted an earlier offer from Polk and gave a $25,000 deposit check to cinch the deal. Polk refused to sell. Avon sued, claiming there was a contract or, at a minimum, an option contract formed by the deposit check. Is there a contract? [*Polk* v. *Avon Properties*, 946 So.2d 1120, Dist. Ct. App., Fla. (2006)]
   ✓ Check your answer

2. Barry hired Anglin to produce engineering drawings for work Barry was doing at a brewery. Anglin said it would charge "street" rates for the work, which meant $35 an hour for regular work, $40 an hour for overtime work, and $45 an hour for its time. Barry gave Anglin a "purchase order" for the work, but no rate was specified. Barry paid bills for two months. Barry insisted that the work be done, but constantly complained about the rates and did not pay bills for four months. Anglin sued for $98,618, the amount it was due for work at the "street" rate. Barry claimed there was no contract, because there was no meeting of the minds about the rate to be paid. Who prevails? [*Anglin* v. *Barry*, 912 S.W.2d 633, Ct. App., Mo. (1995)]
   ✓ Check your answer

3. At the end of a two-year lease, a landlord and tenant discussed a new lease. The tenant sent a letter to the landlord stating that it would pay rent of $1,800 per month, and that "all other terms and conditions of the [original] lease, including taxes, insurance, utilities, etc., shall remain the same." The letter also said the tenant was to be advised "by confirmation letter if the terms of the two-year lease extension were acceptable to the lessor." The landlord never responded. The tenant paid rent for a couple months, then moved out. The landlord sued for breach, claiming there was an agreement evidenced by the letter from the tenant; the tenant claimed there was no contract. Who is correct and why? [*Valiant Steel* v. *Roadway Express*, 421 S.E.2d 773, Ct. App., Ga. (1992)]
   ✓ Check your answer

4. Mary Lowe, in the presence of her son, David, and Allen Amdahl, wrote: "January 26, 1987. I, Mary Lowe, in the presence of David Lowe received from Allen Amdahl $1.00 in cash binding the sale of my farm (of 880 acres) for the amount of $210,000 with final payment due Nov. 1, 1989. Terms of Agreement have been mutually agreed to by both parties. Contract drawn up as soon as possible." She signed this statement, and David Lowe witnessed it. Amdahl wrote on the back of the paper a payment schedule but did not sign the paper. When he returned with a formal contract, Lowe refused to sign. Amdahl sued. Was there an enforceable contract? [*Amdahl* v. *Lowe*, 471 N.W.2d 770, Sup. Ct., N.D. (1991)]

5. Rose, a minor, purchased a new car from Sheehan Buick for $5,000. Rose later, while still a minor, elected to disaffirm the purchase and notified Sheehan of her decision. She also requested a full refund of the purchase price. Sheehan refused, and Rose brought an action to invalidate the contract and to seek a refund of the purchase price. What will be the likely result? [*Rose* v. *Sheehan Buick*, 204 So.2d 903, Fla. App. (1967)]
   ✓ Check your answer

6. To help in a fund raising drive for a hospital, Burt gave a pledge for $100,000 that provided, "In consideration of and to induce the subscription of others, I promise to pay to Mount Sinai Hospital of Greater Miami, Inc. the sum of $100,000 in ten installments." Burt made two installment payments of $10,000 each before his death. The hospital filed a claim for the unpaid balance against his estate. Is this a contract for which the estate is now liable? [*Mount Sinai Hospital* v. *Jordan*, 290 So.2d 484, Sup. Ct., Fla. (1974)]

7. BP sells gasoline under various brands. It sold a gas station to Stanley. The sale agreement stated that Stanley would only sell BP-branded gas for 15 years. After four years, he switched to another brand. BP sued for breach. Stanley claimed the restrictive covenant was commercially unreasonable. Would it be upheld? [*BP Products* v. *Stanley*, 669 F.3d 184, 4th Cir. (2012)]

8. Copenhaver contracted to put pay washers and dryers in an apartment complex owned by Berryman. With four years still left on the contract, Berryman kicked Copenhaver out. Within six months, Copenhaver had put all equipment back into service in other locations. He sued for compensatory damages for the cost of moving and for profits he lost over the rest of the four years of the contract. What damages is he owed? [*Copenhaver* v. *Berryman*, 602 S.W.2d 540, Ct. App., Tex. (1980)]

9. A builder constructed a house according to detailed plans provided by the owner. The contract specified that only Reading brand pipe was to be used in the plumbing. After the house was completed, the owner discovered that another brand of pipe had been used. The owner refused final payment and demanded that the pipe be replaced with Reading pipe, which would have involved major reconstruction. Evidence at trial was that the two brands of pipe were of the same general quality. Did the owner have to pay the builder or did the pipe have to be replaced? [*Jacob & Youngs* v. *Kent*, 129 N.E. 889, Ct. App., NY (1921)]

10. GE contracted to provide kitchen appliances for an apartment complex for $93,500. Several months later, GE discovered that a mathematical error had been made in the bid and that the bid should have been for an additional $30,150. GE demanded rescission of the contract. Did it get it? [*General Electric Supply* v. *Republic Construction*, 272 P.2d 201, Sup. Ct., Ore. (1954)]

ETHICS QUESTION

The Metropolitan Museum of Art in New York City is one of the best in the world. Under an 1893 law, it must admit the public free of charge five days and two evenings a week. The Met has a long practice of posting a sign at all times at the entrance that says $25 admission. In small letters, it says "recommended." About half of the visitors pay that amount, many not knowing they do not have to pay. The Met says it needs the revenue. A class action suit was filed on behalf of those who paid (how the enterprising attorneys are supposed to track down visitors is unclear). Is it unethical for the nonprofit museum to imply that a price must be paid when it is really a donation?

CHAPTER **11**
Domestic and International Sales

As a food broker, you fulfill orders from retailers. You deal directly with food processors and specialize in knowing who has what and how to get it delivered promptly by trusted shipping companies. Mostly, you rely on your reputation and the reputation of those you deal with, rather than formal contracts, in your dealing with vendors. You know most of the sellers, buyers, and truckers, and they know you. There is little time for formal contracting. Most of the work is done on the phone and by e-mail. It is not possible to draw up contracts for every deal. If you sent a contract to a client you have dealt with for a long time, the client would probably wonder what was up.

But things can go wrong. A truck makes a delivery in July from Cleveland to Phoenix and arrives Friday night. The buyer thought the load would arrive on Monday, so the load sits over the weekend without refrigeration. A half-million dollars' worth of food is spoiled. Who is responsible for the bill? Did the trucker promise to cover such losses? As the broker, you bought and resold the food, picking up a commission in the middle. Are you stuck or does the buyer suffer the loss? If you have a contract with each party, what does it say? What if you do not have a contract that covers such problems?

These are the kinds of issues addressed in this chapter on the sale of goods under the **Uniform Commercial Code** (UCC). Article 2 of the UCC governs the law of commercial sales. Because buying and selling goods is the primary activity of many commercial enterprises, it is not surprising that the law of sales is an important part of the legal environment of business. This chapter provides an overview of the law of sales in Article 2. It considers the nature of sales contracts under the UCC and the requirements the UCC places upon merchants. The chapter then examines some key aspects of international commercial sales.

Introduction to the UCC

The Uniform Commercial Code governs many contracts for the sale of goods. The UCC does not apply to the sale of services such as website design or maintenance, real estate sales, or professional services such as provided by physicians and accountants. Like the common law of contract, commercial law is primarily state, not federal, law.

History of Commercial Law

Commercial rules governing trade—"codes"—existed almost 4,000 years ago in the *Code of Hammurabi* in ancient Babylon. Later, the Roman Empire had highly developed commercial laws, which still influence modern contract law, especially in western European countries. Over a thousand years later, in medieval Europe, merchants developed rules governing trade issues such as sales, payment, insurance, and shipping. These were known as the *lex mercatoria*, or law merchant, and covered transactions in different countries.

So, a fourteenth-century merchant who sold cloth would be likely to use the same rules if the sale took place in London, England; Marseilles, France; or Prague, Bohemia. Merchants themselves, rather than governments, generally enforced this law through merchant courts at trade fairs. Although merchant courts had few formal enforcement powers, a merchant who disregarded their rulings would be shunned by other merchants, making it very difficult to make a living.

By the eighteenth century, judges in England began to incorporate the customary law merchant into the common law of England to resolve contract disputes. As the economy developed during the nineteenth century, so too did commercial law. As new technologies emerged—railroads, steamships, telegraphs—commercial law evolved to accommodate the changing needs of merchants.

In the early twentieth century, each state in the United States had a different, but related, set of commercial laws. One of the costs of doing business in different states was dealing with somewhat different rules. There was no explicit reason for many of these differences; they simply reflected differences in the evolution of common law rules. Some legal scholars and people in business decided it would be efficient to have a more consistent set of rules for commercial transactions.

The National Conference of Commissioners on Uniform State Laws and the American Law Institute began drafting a proposed commercial law to apply in many states. In the 1950s, the groups presented the Uniform Commercial Code to the states. Every state adopted most of the UCC, although Louisiana has still not adopted Article 2. Over the years, the UCC has been modified to reflect changes in the way businesses operate. Exhibit 11.1 notes the major sections of the UCC.

Application of the UCC

We refer here to the "model" UCC and cite specific sections of it (denoted as §). Some states modified the UCC somewhat when it was made part of their law, and so the UCC is not quite uniform across all states. The benefits to the states of lowering the costs of doing business across state lines were so great however, that most states accepted the UCC's provisions on most topics. The UCC's purpose is "to simplify, clarify and modernize the law governing commercial transactions" (§ 1-102). When does the UCC apply rather than the common law of contracts? It applies when "the item involved is movable and is not money or an investment security" (§ 2-102). Examples of movable goods include clothing and computers. Land and houses are not movable. Article 2 covers the sale of goods, not services, so, for example, if you contract with a lawyer to represent you, that would be under the common law of contracts.

EXHIBIT 11.1   THE ARTICLES OF THE UNIFORM COMMERCIAL CODE

ARTICLE NUMBER AND TITLE	COVERAGE
1. General Provisions	Purpose of the UCC; general guidance and definitions
2. Sale of Goods	Applies to sales and leases of goods
3. Negotiable Instruments	Use of checks, promissory notes, and other financial instruments
4. Bank Deposits and Collections	Rights and duties of banks and their clients
5. Letters of Credit	Guaranteed payment by a bank that extends credit on behalf of a client
6. Bulk Transfers	Sales of a large part of a company's material
7. Warehouse Receipts, Bills of Lading, and Other Documents of Title	Papers proving ownership of goods being shipped
8. Investment Securities	Rights and duties related to stock or other ownership interests
9. Secured Transactions	Sales in which seller holds a financial interest in goods sold

© Cengage Learning

Despite all the lawyers who draft contracts and all the business students who have taken courses such as this one, many contracts fail to state what law governs a contract. Also, there may be more than one contract in place at the same time affecting a business relationship between parties. These issues may not matter unless there is a dispute, at which point it can make a difference if the UCC or the common law governs.

Suppose, as often happens, a contract is for a mix of goods and services, and the contract does not specify common law or UCC. Which law governs a dispute? The rule is to look to whether goods or services dominate the contract. If the contract is for $180,000 total and, in breaking it down, the court sees that $70,000 covers the cost of goods and $100,000 is for services such as installation and maintenance, then the value of the services dominates and the common law governs. Note, however, that in such a deal, the parties could specify in their contract that one law or the other governs the resolution of a dispute. That is, the common law of contracts would be the default rule applied in this case, but if the parties agreed in the contract that the UCC would govern it, then the court would apply the UCC. An illustration of this is provided in the *Paramount Contracting* case.

Goods, Merchants, Sales, and Titles under the UCC

Unlike the common law of contracts, Article 2 of the Uniform Commercial Code provides specific terminology and definitions that are applied to many of the key terms involved in establishing a contract for the sale of goods. It also gives default rules to resolve many disputes that arise under a business relationship not based on a contract. These UCC default rules clearly determine which party may be responsible for certain costs.

Goods The UCC defines **goods** as "all things (including specially manufactured things) which are movable at the time of identification to the contract for sale" [§ 2-105(l)]. In other words, the subject matter of a sales contract is not considered a good under Article 2 unless it is movable and tangible. A good is movable if it can be carried from one

PARAMOUNT CONTRACTING COMPANY V. DPS INDUSTRIES, INC.

Court of Appeals of Georgia, 709 S.E.2d 288 (2011)

Case Background *Paramount Contracting needed hundreds of truckloads of dirt for a construction project. DPS offered to sell dirt and haul the dirt to the construction site. DPS claimed that Paramount accepted the offer; Paramount denied it. It hired another company. DPS sued for breach of contract. The jury found for DPS and awarded damages. Paramount appealed, contending no contract had ever been made.*

Case Decision Blackwell, Judge

* * *

The question of contract formation was a disputed issue at the trial of this case, and the parties disagreed about whether the issue is governed by Article 2 of the Uniform Commercial Code or the common law. We have observed before that it is easier, generally speaking, to form a binding contract under Article 2 than under the common law. Article 2 applies, however, only to contracts for the sale of goods, and it does not apply to contracts for the mere provision of services or labor. When a transaction involves both the sale of a good and the provision of services or labor, whether the transaction is governed by Article 2 depends upon the "predominant purpose" of the transaction. . . .

At the trial of this case, the parties disputed not only the predominant purpose of the contemplated transaction, but also the scope and nature of the transaction. DPS said that the parties contemplated only that DPS would sell and deliver dirt, and DPS urged that Article 2 applies because, according to DPS, the sale of goods—the dirt that DPS offered to furnish to Paramount—was the predominant purpose of the contemplated transaction. Paramount, on the other hand, said that the parties also contemplated that DPS would perform other tasks, such as placing and compacting dirt at the construction site. And even if the par-

ties contemplated nothing more than the sale and delivery of dirt, Paramount argued that the common law applies nonetheless because, Paramount said, the provision of a service—the hauling of the dirt—was the predominant purpose of the transaction. . . . We do not agree. . . .

Paramount, a civil engineering firm and general contractor, was awarded a contract in early 2006 to construct runway improvements at the Atlanta Hartsfield–Jackson International Airport. When Paramount had prepared its bid for this construction project, it had asked DPS to quote a price for supplying the fill dirt that Paramount would need to complete the project. In response to this request, DPS had given Paramount a written quote for the price of furnishing and hauling fill dirt, and Paramount had incorporated this price into its bid. . . .

When Paramount learned in January 2006 that it had submitted the low bid for the construction project, it contacted DPS again about the volume of dirt that it would need and the number of trucks that would be needed to haul the dirt to the Airport. At that point, DPS believed that the parties had reached a definitive agreement for DPS to sell and deliver the dirt that Paramount needed, and on January 25, DPS memorialized its understanding in a letter to Paramount. In this letter, DPS confirmed that it was "holding approximately 45,000 [cubic yards] of borrow dirt ready to be hauled in to your project once we receive the 10–day notice from you." Paramount did not respond in writing to this letter. . . .

Finally, after officers of DPS and Paramount met in person on April 7, 2006, Paramount sent a letter to DPS in which it disputed that the parties had reached a definitive agreement. In this letter, Paramount referred repeatedly to the purchase and sale of dirt, but the letter says nothing about the transportation of the dirt. . . .

Ultimately, Paramount decided to buy the dirt it needed from another vendor.

Viewed in this light, the evidence is consistent with a finding that the sale of dirt was the predominant purpose of the contemplated transaction. . . .

Affirmed.

Questions for Analysis

1. Why did Paramount push for this to be seen as a common law contract?
2. Why do you suppose Paramount failed to make its position clear earlier?

location to another, such as dirt in the *Paramount* case above. Real estate does not come under Article 2 because land cannot be moved. A good is tangible when it has a physical existence; that is, it can be seen and touched. Thus, services and intangible interests—such as stocks, bank accounts, patents, and copyrights, which are intangible forms of personal property—are not goods under Article 2. A contract involving such items would be governed by the common law of contracts or by another part of the UCC in some cases.

Merchants Section 1-203 holds all parties who enter into an Article 2 sales contract to a standard of **good faith**. Good-faith dealing is defined by UCC § 1-201 as "honesty in fact in the conduct or transaction concerned." Article 2 places a higher duty of conduct on merchants, who are treated differently from members of the public, because they have business expertise. A **merchant** is recognized by § 2-104 as a person who:

1. regularly deals in goods of the kind involved in the transaction,
2. by occupation presents himself as having knowledge or skill specialized to the transaction, or
3. employs an agent who holds herself out as having particular knowledge or skill about the goods involved.

Sales Article 2 applies to contracts for the sale of goods. A **sale** occurs when there is a "passing of title from the seller to the buyer for a price" [§ 2-106(1)]. The title represents the legal rights to ownership of a thing, such as a car or a computer. It need not be an actual piece of paper; what is important is that the right of ownership passes. If legal title does not pass, there has not been a sale under the UCC. Article 2 does not apply to the lease of goods, such as the lease of a car, but most states have adopted Article 2A, a newer part of the UCC that deals with certain leases of personal property.

Titles How do we determine who holds title to goods? We look to UCC § 2-401. A party may hold legal **title** to a good if (1) the good exists, and (2) the good has been identified—such as by the serial number on a car—to the contract, meaning that the seller has specified which goods are being sold to the buyer. Then § 2-401 allows title to be passed however the parties see fit. For example, the UCC would allow title to pass in any of the following situations, if that is what the parties bargain for, as determined by contract language, custom, or past practices:

- When the goods arrive for shipment at a port
- When the goods arrive at the buyer's warehouse
- When the goods leave the seller's warehouse
- When the goods are halfway between the seller's factory and the buyer's warehouse

If the parties disagree about whether title has passed, or they failed to specify when title passed, then the courts look to § 2-401, which states that (1) title passes to the buyer when the seller completes all her obligations regarding delivery of the goods; or (2) title passes to the buyer when the seller delivers the title documents, if the goods did not have to be moved.

If a seller sells stolen goods, then good title does not pass to the buyer (§ 2-403). For example, if someone steals a computer from a university and sells the computer to a buyer who does not know it is stolen, and then the university finds the stolen property, it gets it back. A thief has no title and so cannot pass good title.

Forming a Sales Contract

Contracts are governed by the common law of contracts unless the UCC changes or modifies the rule. The UCC tends to reduce the formality of contract law. It recognizes that many deals are not formal, so UCC rules are used to "fill the gap" when a contract is silent on an issue. This section considers the effect of Article 2 on contract principles. As you read this, keep in mind the basic differences between the UCC and the common law of contracts, some of which are outlined in Exhibit 11.2.

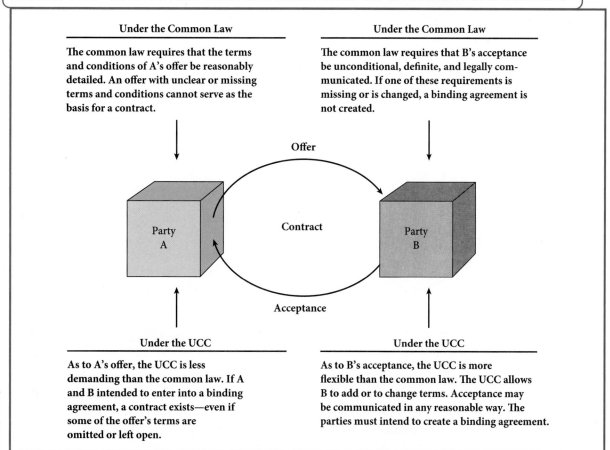

EXHIBIT 11.2   OFFER AND ACCEPTANCE: COMPARING THE UCC AND THE COMMON LAW OF CONTRACTS

Under the Common Law

The common law requires that the terms and conditions of A's offer be reasonably detailed. An offer with unclear or missing terms and conditions cannot serve as the basis for a contract.

Under the Common Law

The common law requires that B's acceptance be unconditional, definite, and legally communicated. If one of these requirements is missing or is changed, a binding agreement is not created.

Offer

Party A

Contract

Party B

Acceptance

Under the UCC

As to A's offer, the UCC is less demanding than the common law. If A and B intended to enter into a binding agreement, a contract exists—even if some of the offer's terms are omitted or left open.

Under the UCC

As to B's acceptance, the UCC is more flexible than the common law. The UCC allows B to add or to change terms. Acceptance may be communicated in any reasonable way. The parties must intend to create a binding agreement.

© Cengage Learning

Intent to Contract

Under the common law, a contract cannot be formed until an offer is clearly accepted. Article 2 relaxes this rule; § 2-204 provides that a **sales contract** "may be made in any manner sufficient to show agreement" between the parties. Suppose a seller delivers various restaurant supplies to a buyer's restaurant based on orders given by phone and e-mail. Prices are often not discussed or known to the buyer, who pays the invoice by mail. Under the UCC, a contract is formed by the conduct of the parties. It does not matter that the moment of contract formation is uncertain. In the *Crest Ridge* case, we see an example of this.

CREST RIDGE CONSTRUCTION V. NEWCOURT
United States Court of Appeals, Fifth Circuit, 78 F.3d 146 (1996)

Case Background *John and Joe Brower worked for a construction company before setting up their own company, Crest Ridge. They were awarded a subcontract on a job to provide wall panels. They wanted to use panels made by Newcourt, which set the price at $760,000. The contract stated it was "subject to credit department approval." Because it was a new company, the Newcourt credit department could not find much information about Crest Ridge, but over the next six months, detailed discussions about specifications of panels continued and shipment was set.*

Newcourt then demanded payment in full before delivery of the panels. Industry practice was payment 45 days after shipment, so the subcontractor could collect payment from the general contractor. When Crest Ridge could not pay up front, Newcourt cancelled the order. Because of the cancellation, Crest Ridge had to find another supplier at a higher price to fill the order. It sued Newcourt. The jury awarded $70,214 in damages. Newcourt appealed.

Case Decision Higginbotham, Circuit Judge

* * *

Newcourt argues that the phrase "subject to credit department approval" illustrated that it never agreed to extend credit to Crest Ridge and thus its demand of payment up front constituted no breach of contract. ...

The jury heard evidence sufficient to allow it to conclude that Newcourt and Crest Ridge formed a contract. The UCC provides that "a contract for the sale of goods may be made in any manner sufficient to show agreement, including conduct by both parties which recognizes the existence of such a contract." Newcourt and Crest

Ridge exchanged a price quotation and a purchase order, documents the construction industry considered to have binding effect. Moreover, the parties' conduct illustrated that they thought they had a deal. ... [For six months] the parties engaged in an extended exchange designed to clarify the details of the project. Newcourt itself provided material samples, three revisions of shop drawings, fastening details, stipulations as to the color of each panel, and final drawings showing where each panel would go. ...

For two reasons, we find unpersuasive Newcourt's ... argument that insufficient evidence supported the jury's finding that Newcourt breached its contract with Crest Ridge. First, the phrase "subject to credit department approval" does not constitute a refusal to grant credit. Indeed, the requirement of credit department approval would be unnecessary unless the parties contemplated some form of credit. Second because Newcourt and Crest Ridge left the terms of payment blank in their exchange of price quotation and purchase order, payment was due either upon delivery, or perhaps according to "general usage." In either case, Newcourt breached the agreement by demanding full payment in advance. ...

Affirmed.

Questions for Analysis

1. The appeals court affirmed that a contract existed, even though a specific term had been ignored. Did Newcourt have reason to worry about the ability of a company like Crest Ridge to pay its bill?
2. Suppose a credit check found that Crest Ridge had serious financial problems. Could Newcourt have ended the deal then?

Lighter Side **of the Law**

Be Honest, Not Necessarily Kind

The UCC requires merchants to operate in "good faith." That means "honesty in fact in the conduct or transaction concerned." In a dispute between two companies, where one refused to continue to do business with the other and there was a claim of a violation of "good faith," the court explained that "There is no duty to be kind, or considerate, or make concessions in bargaining."

Source: Digital Equipment v. Uniq Digital Technologies, 73 F.3d 756.

An Indefinite Offer Under Article 2, if parties intended to enter into an agreement on the basis of the offer, a contract exists. This can be the case even though some of the offer's major terms—such as price, delivery, or payment terms—are omitted or are left open for later determination. UCC § 2-204(3) states that a contract does not fail for indefiniteness "if the parties have intended to make a contract and there is a reasonably certain basis for giving an appropriate remedy." When terms are left open by the parties, Article 2 has rules for determining what they should be.

Merchant's Firm Offer Article 2 modifies the contract rules governing when an offer may be revoked. Under the common law, an offer can be revoked any time before acceptance. The main common-law exception is the option contract, under which the offeree gives consideration for the offeror's promise to keep the offer open for a stated time period. Section 2-205 provides another exception: If a merchant-offeror gives assurances in a signed writing that the offer will remain open for a given period, then the merchant's **firm offer** is irrevocable. No consideration is needed. If the period is not stated in the offer, it stays open for a reasonable time not to exceed three months.

Acceptance

Article 2 modifies the common-law rules for acceptance in several important ways. To bring the rules of acceptance more in line with business practices, the UCC provides greater flexibility in the way acceptance can be communicated. If the offeror does not clearly demand a particular method of acceptance, § 2-206 holds that a contract is formed when the offer is accepted in any reasonable manner under the circumstances. This flexibility allows the legal rules governing acceptance to adapt to new methods of communication such as the Internet.

The UCC provides that an acceptance may be valid even if the offeree includes additional terms or changes existing terms in an offer. Under the common law, an acceptance cannot deviate from the terms of the offer without being considered either a rejection or a counteroffer. Article 2 makes an acceptance valid when the parties intend to form a contract—even though the offeree's acceptance contains different terms from those in the offer.

Conflicting Terms It is not uncommon for an offeror to send an offer on a company form that lists standard terms, such as when payment is due. The offeree may accept the offer but send acceptance on its own standard form that does not contain all the terms that were stated in the original offer. UCC § 2-207(1) states that in such cases, there is a valid acceptance if the parties proceed. However, the contract is generally based on the offeror's original terms. If there are significantly different terms, called "material alterations" to the contract, contained in the acceptance, they become a part of the contract only if the offeror accepts the terms posed by the offeree in acceptance. In some cases, such as when much time has passed, acceptance may be shown by a failure to object to the additional terms in the offeree's form.

When terms in contracts conflict, it is called the "battle of the forms." It is not uncommon for both companies in a transaction to send their own standard forms, possibly by e-mail, to each other. Under the UCC, small differences in the writings do not matter. No one may even care about material differences until a dispute arises, as we see in the *Orkal* case.

ORKAL INDUSTRIES, LLC V. ARRAY CONNECTOR CORPORATION

Supreme Court, Appellate Division New York 948 N.Y.S.2d 318 (2012)

Case Background *Orkal, a New York company, bought airplane-related products from Array, a Florida company, by sending purchase order forms. Array confirmed the orders with "customer order acknowledgment" forms that contained a forum selection clause. It stated that in case of any contract disputes, the buyer would have to bring suit in a Florida court. Orkal did not object to the clause.*

Later, Orkal sued Array (defendant) in court in New York for breach of contract. Array moved for summary judgment to dismiss the complaint based on the forum selection clause—Orkal had to sue in Florida. The trial court (called Supreme Court) agreed. Orkal appealed.

Case Decision Skelos, Associate Justice

* * *

Pursuant to UCC-2-207(2), additional terms of a contract between merchants become part of the parties' contract unless they are specifically objected to within a reasonable time, or unless the additional

terms materially alter the contract. The party opposing the inclusion of the additional terms bears the burden of proving that the additional terms are material changes and, thus, are rendered nonbinding.

Under the circumstances of this case, and given the distance between the New York and Florida forums, the defendant's inclusion of a forum selection clause in its customer order acknowledgment forms constitutes a material alteration to the parties' initial contracts. Therefore … the Supreme Court should have denied … defendant's motion. …

Reversed.

Questions for Analysis

1. The forum selection clause was held to be a material change to the original offer, so it was not binding. How could Array have made the clause binding?
2. How do you know if a term that is changed is material or not?

Contract Modifications

Under the common law, contract modifications must be supported by new consideration to be binding on the parties. The UCC§ 2-209 makes a significant change in the common-law rule by providing that the parties need not provide new consideration to modify an existing contract. A modification to a sales contract, however, must meet the UCC's test of good-faith dealing and usually must be in writing.

CYBER LAW

Shrinkwrap Your Contract

Many goods are now sold with a "shrinkwrap" agreement. If you buy a new laptop, it likely has an agreement written in the materials, or on the box, that states that it is the controlling terms of the agreement. This generally precludes a "battle of the forms" when parties argue over the terms of the agreement.

As federal Judge Easterbrook explains, "Practical considerations support allowing vendors to enclose the full legal terms with their products. Cashiers cannot be expected to read legal documents to customers before ringing up sales. ... And oral recitation would not avoid customers' assertions (whether true or feigned) that the clerk did not read term X to them,

or that they did not remember or understand it" (104 F.3d at 1149). The Supreme Court of Rhode Island agreed: "It is simply unreasonable to expect a seller to apprise a consumer of every term and condition at the moment he or she makes a purchase" (984 A.2d at 1071).

While most courts subscribe to this view and find it consistent with the UCC, a minority of courts have not, and "battle of the forms" cases have arisen. The best defense against such suits is that the terms of the agreement are clear and not grossly biased against the consumer, and attempts are made to ensure that consumers, when viewing the product, see the agreement so they cannot claim lack of knowledge.

© Cengage Learning

Statute of Frauds

Article 2 § 2-201 provides a **statute of frauds** provision. The basic rule is that a contract for the sale of goods for $500 or more is not enforceable unless it is in writing and signed by the party against whom enforcement is sought. Compared to the common law, the UCC relaxes the requirements for the sufficiency of a writing to satisfy the Statute of Frauds. Under Article 2, the writing need not list all material terms in the contract. The key element is that there is some basis for believing that the parties made a contract for the sale of goods.

Failure to Respond to a Writing The UCC recognizes that it is common in business for contract writings to be incomplete. This is especially the case when parties discuss a deal, and one sends a writing to confirm what was discussed, but the other party does not send a written reply. The parties may be too busy, they may deal with each other regularly and do not see the need for a formal reply. Hence, even when there is a failure to respond to a writing signed by the other party, there may be a good contract. The UCC recognizes that businesses behave less formally than the common law requires as a part of the informal nature of much business and the fact that we do not want to get lawyers involved in every step of business.

Section 2-201(2) states: "Between merchants, if within a reasonable time a writing in confirmation of the contract and sufficient against the sender is received and the party receiving it has reason to know its contents, it satisfies the [writing] requirements ... against such party unless written notice of objection to its contents is given within ten days after it is received." This applies only to contracts between merchants; the writing must be complete as to essential terms; and the writing must be sent and received soon after the contract has been formed.

Parol Evidence Because the UCC is more generous than common-law contract law in presuming contracts to exist when terms are not all set, oral testimony is more likely to be needed to clarify disputes over terms of a contract subject to the UCC. Section 2-202 states that written documents may not be contradicted by oral testimony, but that such testimony may be used to explain customary trade dealings or the meaning of certain terms. Parol evidence may not be used "if the court finds the writing to have been intended also as a complete and exclusive statement of the terms of the agreement."

Filling the Gaps

Courts try to make sense out of contracts that have become the basis of a legal dispute. The UCC especially prefers to keep parties working and fills in parts of contracts that are left open or otherwise need to be made clear to make a contract complete. The intent is to deal with the reality of business operations where contracts may not be highly formal or circumstances force changes to occur. The UCC instructs the courts how to resolve uncertain terms.

In § 1-205, the Code states that when parties have had regular dealings, their previous conduct will be looked to as the basis for resolving the current situation. Further, the courts look to **trade usage**—the regular practice and methods of dealings in a given trade—to resolve an unsettled transaction. We see an example of the court filling the gaps in the *Clear Lakes Trout* case.

GRIFFITH V. CLEAR LAKES TROUT

Supreme Court of Idaho 143 Idaho 733, 152 P.3d 604 (2007)

Case Background *Clear Lakes, a fish hatchery, sold Griffith, a trout grower, small trout. Griffith sold them back to Clear Lakes after they had grown to "market size." Trout were priced at a set rate per pound. The deal was for six years. After three years, Clear Lake's customers began to demand larger fish than the 12- to 16-ounce fish delivered by Griffith. Clear Lakes began to take fewer fish and waited longer to get them, leaving Griffith with too many fish. Griffith was deeply in debt and could not easily change his operations to grow larger fish.*

He sued Clear Lakes for breach for "refusing to accept and purchase in a timely manner the trout that Griffith had grown to market size." Clear Lakes claimed no contract existed because there was no meeting of the minds as to what was market size. The district court found for Griffith, holding that the parties knew that market size was 12 to 16 ounces. The holding was appealed by Clear Lake.

Case Decision Schroeder, Chief Justice

* * *

Under the Uniform Commercial Code, "a contract for sale does not fail for indefiniteness if the parties

have intended to make a contract and there is a reasonably certain basis for giving an appropriate remedy." Thus, "in order to have an enforceable contract, the UCC does not require a document itemizing all the specific terms of the agreement. Rather, the UCC requires a determination whether the circumstances of the case, including the parties' conduct, are 'sufficient to show agreement.' "...

The district court found that "the parties undoubtedly intended to make a contract and there is a 'reasonably certain basis for giving an appropriate remedy.' " The district court's statement is consistent with UCC § 2-204(3):

> Even though one or more terms are left open, a contract for sale does not fail for indefiniteness if the parties have intended to make a contract and there is a reasonably certain basis for giving an appropriate remedy. ...

The district court found that at the time of contract formation "Clear Lakes and Griffith had an understanding about what fish were 'market size.' "...

The district court found that the course of performance between the parties over the first three years of the contract, as well as their course of dealing prior to executing the Agreement, confirmed that the parties intended market size to indicate trout approximating one pound live weight. Griffith also presented evidence of similar trade usage pre-dating the contract. ...

The evidence cited by the district court is sufficient to support its finding that both parties understood the term "market size" to refer to a fixed range approximating one pound live weight. ...

Affirmed.

Questions for Analysis

1. The Idaho high court held that by their actions the parties understood the meaning of "market size," so there was an agreement. How could Clear Lakes have avoided this problem?
2. Because market conditions changed, and customers began to want bigger fish, how could Clear Lakes and Griffith have adjusted their relationship in a friendly manner?

Price While price is usually specified, in some contracts price is not clear or is to be set over time as the parties work together. For example, if a supplier is asked to provide a new product, the price may depend on things the parties do not know at the start of the contract, so price terms are left vague. If price is unclear when a contract is found to exist, § 2-305 directs the courts to determine "a reasonable price." Reasonable price may or may not be "fair market value," depending on the past dealings and conduct of the parties.

If the price referred to in the contract relies on benchmarks, such as "the price of wheat on August 15" or "cost plus 10 percent," disputes may arise as to whether the price of wheat included delivery or the cost was determined in good faith. In such cases, the courts attempt to determine what the parties intended when they formed the contract and what is the most reasonable method to determine the price to fulfill the contract, given usual business practices.

Quantity The UCC generally requires that a contract specify the quantity to be bought. However, § 2-306(1) recognizes requirements contracts and output contracts, in which the quantities may not be specified. A **requirements contract** is one in which a seller agrees to provide all of a certain good that a buyer needs. For example, Michelin may agree to provide Ford all of the tires it needs to install on all new models of the Ford Flex it produces next year. Ford is not certain how many that will be, but Michelin says it will produce whatever is required. An **output contract** is when a buyer agrees to take all of the output of a certain seller. If Foot Locker wants to push a hot line of LeBron James shoes made by Nike, it could agree to take all the LeBron James shoes that Nike produces next year. In both cases, the law imposes a duty to act in good faith. The buyer and seller are expected to act in a reasonable manner, given the customs of their industry.

Delivery Terms Most sales contracts specify how goods are to be delivered and who is responsible for the cost of transportation. At some point, responsibility for transportation and control of the goods, such as storage, switches from the seller to the buyer. Sections 2-319 to 2-324 detail the definition of delivery terms, such as "free on board" (F.O.B.), often used in contracts. If delivery is not specified, the UCC fills the gaps so long as a contract exists. Section 2-309 states that the time for delivery is to be within a "reasonable time."

ISSUE SPOTTER
Gouge the Wholesaler

Your chain of six gas stations has a requirements contract with a gasoline wholesaler. The wholesaler promised to deliver to you all the gasoline you need for two years at a price of $2.53 per gallon. After several months, because the price of oil shot up, the wholesaler is losing 30 cents on every gallon delivered to you. You are making so much money on every gallon you sell that you begin to order more tanker loads and resell it to other gas stations. This may be unethical, but does it violate the requirements contract?

What is reasonable depends, of course, on factors such as trade custom, the apparent intentions of the parties, and the availability of transportation services. If the parties do not state what is to determine the time of delivery, § 2-311 provides that "specifications or arrangements relating to shipment are at the seller's option." Section 2-308 presumes that delivery is to be at the seller's place of business. When the seller turns goods over to a shipping company, § 2-504 holds that the seller has a duty to assure that the carrier is competent and that all parties understand who bears the risk of loss at various points before the buyer gets possession of the goods.

Performance and Obligations

Both parties must perform their obligations under that contract or risk being found in breach. The general duties and obligations assumed by each party to a contract for the sale of goods include those specified by the contract, those imposed by the UCC, and, where necessary, those provided by trade custom.

INTERNATIONAL PERSPECTIVE
How to Assure Foreign Buyers of Product Quality

Reputation in business is critical for a company to be accepted into commerce. When a firm is unknown, especially when it moves into foreign markets, it needs to demonstrate that its goods are of a quality worthy of consideration.

One way to demonstrate quality is to obtain certification from a private organization that has global acceptance as a measure of quality assurance. For many buyers, such certification is much better information than a statement by the company itself—or a government agency promoting the company—that its goods are of high quality.

Many companies seek certification from the International Organization for Standardization (ISO),

headquartered in Geneva, Switzerland. The ISO is a network of national standards institutes from around the world that coordinates the system and sets standards. ISO certification is required by many firms before they even consider buying goods from a supplier.

Firms apply for ISO certification, are visited by a certified registrar, and follow a complex procedure to document and organize production procedures. Firms are audited for compliance to ensure that they follow their own stated procedures. The ISO does not tell firms how to implement all aspects of the program; rather, firms must demonstrate that they know and follow quality-assurance procedures.

Seller's Rights and Obligations

The seller's basic obligation under the UCC is to transfer and deliver goods that conform to the contract to the buyer. The seller must be concerned about the appropriate manner and timeliness of delivery, the place of delivery, and the quality of the goods provided.

Tender   The proper tender of goods to, and their acceptance by, the buyer entitles the seller to be paid according to the contract. **Tender** is a valid and sufficient offer of performance under a contract. When a seller offers conforming goods to the buyer under the terms of the contract, there is tender of delivery. Under the contract, the seller may be obliged to tender the goods at the buyer's place of business, or the buyer may have contracted to accept the goods at the point of production.

Under the common law, a seller's delivery was supposed to conform to all terms of the agreement. This is called the **perfect tender rule**—the seller must tender the quality, quantity, and delivery method as specified in the contract or the buyer has the right to reject the goods. The UCC expects parties to meet obligations but provides greater flexibility. UCC § 2-601 states: "if the goods … fail in any respect to conform to the contract, the buyer may: (a) reject the whole; (b) accept the whole; or (c) accept any commercial unit or units and reject the rest." This modifies the common-law rule by allowing the buyer to accept less than the entire shipment.

On the other hand, allowing a buyer to reject a shipment when the problems are slight would allow the buyer to escape payment obligations. This is a problem particularly when the market price of the goods is falling. The buyer could look for some minor problem, cancel the contract, and buy the goods at a lower price from another seller. Article 2's policy of enforcing contracts when performance is reasonable discourages such behavior.

Right to Cure by the Seller   UCC § 2-508 provides some opportunities for a seller to **cure** an improper tender of goods that have been rejected by the buyer. After the buyer has rejected a shipment as not conforming to the contract, the seller may cure the defective tender or delivery if:

- the time for the seller's performance under the contract has not yet passed;
- the seller notifies the buyer in a timely manner of an intent to cure the defect; and
- the seller properly repairs or replaces the defective goods within the time allowed for his performance.

Buyer's Rights and Obligations

In general, a buyer's obligations begin when the seller delivers goods that conform to the contract. The buyer is required by § 2-507 to accept conforming goods and to pay for them according to the contract. If the buyer accepts the goods, the seller awaits payment. If the buyer rejects the goods as nonconforming, the seller may need to remedy the problem or may have to sue for breach of contract.

Buyer's Right of Inspection   Unless the parties have otherwise agreed, under § 2-513 the buyer has a right to inspect goods before accepting them. Inspection allows the buyer to verify that the goods received are of the quality that the seller had agreed to deliver. The buyer must pay for expenses associated with an inspection. However, the expenses can be recovered from the seller as damages if the goods do not conform to the contract.

Buyer's Right of Rejection   According to § 2-601 and § 2-602, a buyer who receives goods that are nonconforming may reject them as a breach of contract and withhold payment. The buyer may also cancel the contract and recover any prepayments made to the seller. The buyer must notify the seller of a rejection in a timely manner to allow the seller to either cure the nonconformity if realistic, or to reclaim the goods.

Buyer's Duty of Acceptance   When the seller has delivered conforming goods, the buyer has a duty to accept. That is, under § 2-606 and § 2-607, the buyer has a duty to become the owner of goods. If the goods are nonconforming but have been accepted under § 2-608, the buyer may later revoke acceptance only if the nonconformity "substantially impairs" the value of the goods. Of course, if the buyer is willing to accept nonconforming goods, they must be paid for, although the price paid may be lower if the parties so agree.

Obligation of Payment   Unless otherwise agreed, § 2-507 requires payment when and where the buyer receives the goods. Even when the contract calls for the seller to deliver the goods to a transportation company for shipment to the buyer, the buyer's payment for the goods is not due until the goods are received. Payment upon receipt gives the buyer a chance to inspect the goods before paying for them.

❓ *TEST YOURSELF*

1. If the parties to a contract under the UCC do not specify all terms, the courts may use the UCC to help _____. To do so, the courts look to _____ for ideas on practice or methods relevant to the contract.
2. The UCC allows a contract to exist even if some terms are missing, but there must be written evidence of intent of both parties to form the initial contract: T—F
3. The UCC requires good-faith dealings on the part of _____.
4. In the *Crest Ridge Construction* v. *Newcourt* case, where Newcourt refused to supply construction goods to Crest Ridge because of a lack of credit history, the appeals court held that Newcourt, as a merchant:
   a. must sell merchantable goods to all buyers who request the goods.
   b. had no obligation to sell to Crest Ridge because no contract was ever entered into.
   c. had an obligation to sell to Crest Ridge because the parties had entered into a contract.
   d. not only failed to act in good faith, but "maliciously misled" Crest Ridge, so could be sued for fraud.
5. Under the UCC, unless specifically required in a particular manner, acceptance of an offer can be communicated in any "reasonable" manner: T—F
6. The main purpose of the International Organization for Standardization (ISO) is to serve as a "clearing house" for potential sellers and buyers of commercial, wholesale products: T—F
7. In the case *Griffith* v. *Clear Lakes Trout,* where Griffith raised trout for Clear Lakes, the court held that Clear Lakes had the right to demand "market size" trout from Griffith, which were larger than the ones he had been providing: T—F
8. If a seller delivers a product with a defect in it, and the time for completion of the contract has not ended, the seller has the right to try to _____ the defect.

Answers: *fill the gap, trade usage; F; merchants; c; T; F; F; cure.*

> **EXHIBIT 11.3 SUMMARY OF WARRANTIES UNDER THE UCC**

Warranty to Title § 2-312	Seller is the rightful owner of the goods, the goods are free of any liens or claims of infringement
Express Warranty § 2-313	Seller's promise as to quality, safety, or performance; may be created by the seller's statements, description, or models
Implied Warranties of Merchantability § 2-314	Imposed on the seller by the UCC; requires that the goods are reasonably fit and safe for the purposes they are being sold for; also applies to packaging and labeling
Fitness for a Particular Purpose § 2-315	If the buyer relies on the seller's skill or judgment in selecting goods for a particular purpose, the goods must be able to perform that purpose

Sales Warranties

A **warranty** is a statement or representation made by a seller that goods meet certain standards of quality, safety, performance, and title. If the goods do not conform to the standards created by the warranty, the seller can be held liable for damages for breach of warranty. Article 2 imposes certain various warranties by law and explains how the parties may create additional warranties or amend the terms of warranties by contract. The warranties are summarized in Exhibit 11.3.

Warranty of Title

Under § 2-312, a seller warrants that good title is being transferred to the buyer and that goods will be delivered free of any claims against them, such as liens, unless those have been revealed to the buyer. As the UCC describes **warranty of title** in its official comments, the purpose of this is to ensure that a buyer gets "a good, clean title" and that the buyer "will not be exposed to a lawsuit in order to protect it." This means that a seller is responsible to the buyer if the seller sells a good that does not have good title, such as a stolen property.

Warranty of title also means that the seller warrants that goods being sold are free of any claim of infringement. If a seller has infringed on a trademark, copyright, or patent owned by a third party, the seller is responsible for expenses incurred by a buyer who is ignorant of the infringement. For example, a department store was sued because the store was selling goods that infringed on trademarks. The department store sued its supplier for violating the trademarks and was awarded damages to cover costs incurred.

Express Warranties

An **express warranty** is created by a seller's promise or guarantee as to the quality, safety, performance, and durability of goods being sold. During negotiations, a seller may induce a buyer to purchase goods by making representations about the goods, which become warranties under certain circumstances. Section 2-313 lists three circumstances where an express warranty may be created:

1. A seller provides a sample or model of the good that the buyer relies upon as evidence of what the goods will be like.
2. A seller describes attributes about the goods to the buyer.
3. A seller makes specific oral or written statements or promises to the buyer about the goods that are a part of the basis of the bargain.

Statements about goods are more likely to be express warranties when the claims are specific, rather than general statements about "how nice" the goods are or other happy talk (puffery). Similarly, an express warranty is created if statements are made about attributes of the goods that are not obvious, such as claims about the quality of steel used in production of a good, or if it is a case in which the buyer has good reason to rely on the expertise of the seller. When statements are made in writing, they are more likely to be held to be express warranties. It does not matter that a seller does not intend to create an express warranty by making claims about a product; if it is reasonable that buyers rely on the seller's claims, then those claims are likely to be construed as express warranties. This is particularly the case for goods sold to consumers.

Implied Warranties

An **implied warranty** is a quality and safety standard imposed by Article 2. This part of the UCC has important implications, for it establishes a standard similar to that imposed by product liability law in tort. Implied warranties exist at law. Unlike express warranties, which are based on representations made by the seller, implied warranties are automatically imposed on sellers unless they specifically disclaim them.

Implied Warranty of Merchantability Section 2-314 states that unless the parties to the contract explicitly agree otherwise, an implied warranty of merchantability accompanies every sale by a merchant. This provision of the UCC applies to sellers who are merchants of the kind of goods in question. That is, it applies to those who routinely deal in such goods or offer their expertise to others about such goods, such as jewelers selling jewelry and furniture companies selling furniture.

Merchantable means that the good "must be of a quality comparable to that generally acceptable in that line or trade." That is, industry standards must be met. Obviously, for such things as jet engines, industry standards are very high, and any seller must offer products to meet current standards. If the product is a common one, such as bushels of hard red winter wheat, the quality must be of the industry standard; one cannot pass off a load of bad bottom-of-the-silo, moldy, rat-dropping-infested wheat. Further, the goods must be able to do the tasks expected of them. If the goods are one-ton trucks, they must be able to carry the loads expected of such trucks. Also, goods must be adequately packaged and labeled and conform with claims made on labels or sales materials.

Implied Warranty of Fitness for a Particular Purpose In some situations, a buyer orders a good with a special use in mind. Section 2-315 is more demanding of a seller who has reason to know the buyer's particular purpose for purchasing certain goods. If the buyer relies on the seller's skill or judgment to select the goods for

 ISSUE SPOTTER
How Much Advice Should Retailers Give?

At self-service home-center stores, where you can buy plumbing, electrical, and other supplies, the employees try to be helpful in giving advice. You explain the problem, and they point you to the supplies you need to fix the problem. Can the retailers be setting themselves up to be sued for breach of implied warranty of fitness for a particular purpose? That is, if you go into the store, tell an employee what is wrong with your sink—or at least what you think is wrong—and the employee advises you to change a fitting, and shows you what to buy, and the result is you flood your kitchen, could you have a suit against the retailer for the damages you suffered? Is it a good idea for store employees to give a lot of advice?

© Cengage Learning

that purpose, and the seller knows that is this case, an implied warranty of **fitness for a particular purpose** is created.

The buyer is required to demonstrate "actual reliance" on the seller's expertise. The buyer must also show that the seller had "reason to know" of the buyer's purpose. Suppose that Oprah needs paint to apply to a new line of products. She tells the paint company representative what she needs. She is concerned about chipping and peeling and asks for a recommendation. The salesperson recommends Pittura paint for the product. If Oprah buys Pittura based on the salesperson's recommendation, and the paint chips and peels the next year because Pittura actually is not suitable for use on such material, there is a breach of implied warranty of fitness for a particular purpose.

Warranty Disclaimers

The warranty requirements imposed on sellers by the UCC can be thought of as a form of strict liability under contract law. Because it is a tough standard, sellers may wish to reduce their liability by issuing **warranty disclaimers**. If a seller has made an express warranty, the courts do not want to see disclaimers that are inconsistent with the promises made in that warranty. Under § 2-316, boilerplate language that attempts to dismiss an express warranty is not effective when the disclaimer is inconsistent with the warranty.

Disclaimers of implied warranties of merchantability and of fitness for a particular purpose are permitted if the disclaimer uses the word "merchantability" and the disclaimer is conspicuous. Under UCC § 1-201, conspicuous means that it is written so that a reasonable person would notice it; for example, it would conspicuous if written in all capital letters or in a different color than the rest of the text. Furthermore, a seller is more likely held to have disclaimed warranties if there is a conspicuous notice that the goods are being sold "as is." As the *Lee* case indicates, disclaimers mean consumers should beware.

LEE V. R & K MARINE

Court of Appeals of North Carolina, 598 S.E.2d 683 (2004)

Case Background *Lee bought a new boat from R & K Marine and signed a standard purchase agreement. On the agreement, all in capital letters, it stated: "EXCEPT TO THE EXTENT REQUIRED BY STATE LAW, SELLER EXPRESSLY DISCLAIMS ALL WARRANTIES, EXPRESS OR IMPLIED, INCLUDING ANY IMPLIED WARRANTY OF MERCHANTABILITY OR FITNESS FOR A PARTICULAR PURPOSE."*

Three years later, Lee took the boat in for repairs when cracks and extensive deterioration were discovered in the hull. An appraiser determined that the problems resulted from defects in manufacturing, and the boat was a complete loss. The manufacturer was bankrupt, so Lee sued the retailer who sold him the boat, claiming breach of warranties *of merchantability and fitness for a particular purpose. Defendant was granted summary judgment. Lee appealed.*

Case Decision Tyson, Judge

* * *

UCC § 2-316(2) provides, "to exclude or modify the implied warranty of merchantability or any part of it, the language must mention merchantability and in case of a writing must be conspicuous, and to exclude or modify any implied warranty of fitness the exclusion must be by a writing and conspicuous." UCC § 1-201(10) defines the term "conspicuous" as:

A term or clause is conspicuous when it is so written that a reasonable person against whom it is to operate ought to have noticed it. A printed heading in capitals (as: NONNEGOTIABLE BILL OF LADING) is conspicuous. Language in the body of a form is "conspicuous" if it is in larger or other contrasting type of color. ...

The disclaimer here met all the requirements and was conspicuous. Defendant effectively disclaimed any and all warranties of merchantability and fitness for a particular purpose. The trial court did not err in granting defendant's motion for summary judgment on plaintiff's breach of warranty claim.

Questions for Analysis

1. The appeals court affirmed that the warranty disclaimer was valid. There was no evidence that the retailer knew that the boat was junk, but suppose that could have been shown. How might that have changed the case?
2. Would there be any reason to sue the boat manufacturer?

Remedies and Damages

When a buyer or seller breaches a contract for the sale of goods, the UCC provides the nonbreaching party with a number of remedies. The remedies are intended to place the nonbreaching party in the same position as if the contract had been performed according to its terms. In applying its remedies, § 1-106 of the UCC directs the courts to interpret the remedies liberally.

Seller's Remedies

A buyer may default on contractual obligations by rejecting a tender of goods that conform to the contract, wrongfully revoking an acceptance, repudiating the contract, failing to make a payment, or failing to complete some other performance required by the contract. In each situation, the UCC provides the seller with remedies. As Exhibit 11.4 indicates, the seller is not restricted to any one remedy. Rather, § 2-703 states that the seller may use several remedies at the same time.

Lighter Side **of the Law**

Does It Come with a Warranty?

The inventor of the Quadro Tracker said that the device could locate drugs, bombs, and just about anything else, whether behind walls, inside cars, on persons, or out in fields. A brochure claimed that it could even detect drugs in a person's bloodstream just by being pointed at a person. An MIT physics professor said that the chances of the Quadro Tracker's working were zero and that there were many hoaxes involving such incredible claims.

Nevertheless, dozens of law enforcement agencies and schools bought the device, also called the Positive Molecular Locator, for prices ranging from $400 to $8,000. Over 1,000 of the plastic boxes were sold, making more than $1 million for the seller, before a federal judge issued an injunction banning the sale or distribution of the product. An FBI agent said, "The only thing this accurately detects is your checkbook."

Source: Atlanta Journal and Constitution.

EXHIBIT 11.4 SUMMARY OF SELLER'S RIGHTS AND REMEDIES

STATUS OF THE GOODS	SELLER'S RIGHTS AND REMEDIES
Buyer breaches before receiving the goods	The seller may: 1. Cancel the contract 2. Identify the goods; minimize losses if necessary by stopping production and salvaging the goods 3. Withhold delivery or, if needed, stop delivery 4. Resell the goods in a reasonable manner 5. Sue the buyer to recover the loss suffered by having to resell the goods and related costs

Buyer breaches after receiving the goods	The seller may:
	1. If buyer does not pay, sue to recover the purchase price and resulting incidental damage
	2. Be entitled to remedies if the buyer wrongfully rejects the goods, depending on whether the seller reclaims the goods:
	   a. If so, the remedies are the same as if the buyer had breached before receiving the goods
	   b. If not, the seller can sue to recover the purchase price and any related costs

© Cengage Learning

The remedies available to the seller depend on whether the buyer breached before or after receiving the goods (see Exhibit 11.4). When the buyer breaches before receiving the goods, the seller may elect to cancel the contract, resell or salvage (recycle) the goods, and withhold or stop delivery. If the buyer breaches after receiving the goods, the remedies available to the seller depend upon whether the seller reclaims the goods. If unable to reclaim the goods, the seller may sue the buyer to recover the purchase price and any resulting incidental damages. If the seller reclaims the goods, the seller may use any of the same remedies available had the buyer's breach occurred before receiving the goods.

Seller's Damages When reclaiming and reselling the goods does not fully compensate the seller for the buyer's breach, damages are the proper remedy. UCC's damage measures are designed to put the seller in as good a position as if the buyer had performed contractual obligations. The seller is also allowed to seek incidental damages. Under § 2-710, such costs may include expenses associated with stopping delivery, transporting and taking care of the goods after the breach, returning or reselling the goods, and taking any other necessary action.

Buyer's Remedies

A seller usually breaches a sales contract in one of the following ways:

1. The seller repudiates the contract before tendering the goods.
2. The seller fails to make a scheduled delivery on time.
3. The seller delivers nonconforming goods.

The buyer's remedies vary somewhat depending on the type of breach by the seller. In any case, the buyer may respond by canceling the contract, arranging to obtain the goods from another supplier, and suing the nonperforming seller for damages. The buyer's rights and remedies are summarized in Exhibit 11.5.

EXHIBIT 11.5 SUMMARY OF BUYER'S RIGHTS AND REMEDIES

STATUS OF THE GOODS	BUYER'S RIGHTS AND REMEDIES
Seller repudiates the contract before delivery	The buyer may: 1. Cancel the contract 2. Obtain goods from another supplier 3. Sue the seller for damages and recover advance payments
Seller fails to deliver	The buyer may: 1. Cancel the contract 2. Obtain goods from another supplier 3. Sue the seller for damages
Seller delivers nonconforming goods; buyer rejects them	The buyer may: 1. Cancel the contract 2. Obtain goods from another supplier if goods are rejected 3. Sue the seller for damages 4. Sell rejected goods to recover advance payments 5. Store or reship goods, if no advance payment was made
Seller delivers nonconforming goods; buyer accepts them	The buyer may: 1. Deduct damages from the price of goods 2. Sue the seller for damages 3. Sue for breach of warranty

© Cengage Learning

Buyer's Damages   Like the seller's damage provisions, the buyer's damage provisions under the UCC are designed to put the buyer in the same financial position as if the seller had performed according to the contract. The terminology for damages is a bit different under the UCC than in the common law, so we consider the main damages specified in the UCC.

Cover   When a seller fails to deliver goods, either by being too late to be useful or because the goods are nonconforming, the buyer is entitled to buy substitute goods and recover the price difference. This is referred to as **cover** in § 2-712 of the UCC. The cover price is what is paid for the substitute goods, or the market price may be used to measure the damages. Of course, if similar goods are available at the same or a lower price, then the breaching seller does not have to provide cover. The UCC does not permit overcompensation for losses by requiring the seller to pay the full cost of substitute goods.

Incidental Damages   When the buyer properly rejects a delivery or does not receive the goods, under § 2-710 **incidental damages** include the reasonable costs of inspecting, receiving, transporting, and taking care of the goods while they remain in her possession. If there was no delivery at all, or if delivery is late, § 2-715 states that the buyer's incidental damages include all reasonable costs or direct expenses associated with the delay in receiving the goods or in tracking down substitute goods.

Consequential Damages   Foreseeable damages that result from the seller's breach are called **consequential damages**. They differ from incidental damages in that these damages may result from the buyer's relations with parties other than the seller; that is, the breach may cause the buyer to lose sales and, most importantly, lose profits.

   In sum, the UCC provides more structure to the measure of damages in commercial settings than may occur in the case of common law contracts, and tort claims are difficult to bring. Parties to commercial contracts are expected to allocate the risks carefully among themselves and not hope that claims of fraud will later allow for generous damage awards. Some of the different kinds of damages and the factors taken into account in their calculation are discussed in the *QVC* case.

QVC, INC. V. MJC AMERICA, LTD.
United States District Court, Eastern District of Pennsylvania
904 F.Supp.2d 466 (2012)

Case Background *The television shopping network QVC offered customers Soleus-brand portable electric heaters. They were made in China for Soleus. QVC sold 19,100 heaters in late 2007 and early 2008. Customers immediately reported safety problems. QVC stopped sales and had the product evaluated by an expert firm. It showed quality problems. QVC ordered a recall and refunded money to customers who wanted to return the product or return the electric cord to the heater.*

QVC's contract with Soleus contained strong warranty terms, holding the seller responsible for all costs related to defective products, including recall costs. Soleus disputed that there was a problem. QVC sued. The district court held that Soleus breached its warranty and held in favor of QVC and determined damages.

Case Decision O'Neill, District Judge

* * *

In Section 4 of the Purchase Orders, Soleus agreed to hold harmless and indemnify QVC from and against any "direct, special, incidental, exemplary, and consequential damages and losses of any kind," specifically including lost profits and reasonable attorneys' fees "based upon or resulting from ... any alleged or actual defect" in the Heaters....

QVC seeks damages for the cost price of the Heaters in addition to lost profits, refunded outbound customer shipping costs, shipping costs for the return of Heater Cords to QVC, refunded customer shipping costs for Heaters returned to QVC, return-to-vendor shipping costs, returns center processing costs and other costs associated with the recall.

A. Cost Price Damages

Each Heater had a cost price to QVC of $41.07—$36.00 to Soleus and $5.07 to third parties for landed costs. QVC's claimed cost price damages for all of the Heaters at issue in this action is $1,046,176. ...

QVC's claimed cost price damages for the Shipped Customer Return Heaters total $175,943.88—or the cost price of $41.07 multiplied by 4,284. ...

QVC's claimed cost price damages for the Unshipped Customer Return Heaters are $74,911.68. ...

QVC had in its inventory 8,752 Heaters that had never been sold to its retail customers (the "Unsold Heaters"). QVC's claimed cost price damages for the Unsold Heaters are $359,444.64. ...

QVC had received 10,613 customer returned cords as a result of the recall (the "Heater Cords"). QVC's claimed cost price damages for the Heater Cords are $435,875.91.

B. Lost Profit

Upon receipt of a Customer Return Heater or a Heater Cord, QVC refunded to its customer the full value that the customer paid to QVC for the Heater. The Today's Special Value® price for the Heaters was $67.86, the lowest per unit price at which QVC offered the Heaters for sale. QVC claims that $26.49 constituted its profit on the sale of each Heater—profit that QVC would have realized had it not refunded the sales price to its customers. QVC's total claimed lost profit damages for the Heaters or Heater Cords that were returned to QVC are $442,939.29.

[Other damages approved by the court were:]

C. Refunded Outbound Customer Shipping Costs ... $134,436.84.

D. Costs for Heater Cord Returns ... $21,226.

E. Refunded Customer Shipping Costs for Heaters Returned to QVC ... $49,108.32.

F. Return-to-Vendor Shipping Costs ... $6,092.60.

G. Returns Center Processing Costs ... $27,589.65.

H. Other Recall Costs [customer notification letters, service calls, testing by expert, recall letters, phone calls to customers, customer contact letters] ... $111,286.78.

[After noting other costs and credits, the court concluded:]

The Clerk of Court shall enter judgment in favor of Plaintiff QVC, Inc. and against Defendant MJC America, Ltd. d/b/a Soleus International, Inc. in the amount of $1,681,806.84.

Questions for Analysis

1. Why does the UCC detail such costs rather than allow general lump-sum judgments that the court may think appropriate?

2. Can Soleus recover against the Chinese manufacturer?

International Sales

Global commerce means businesses must deal with the laws and customs of other countries as well as American law. Litigation everywhere is costly and people are often suspicious about the fairness of legal rules and procedures in other nations. As a result, there are strong reasons to give business partners around the world reasons to believe that everyone plays by the same "rules of the game," and that those who serve as "referees" to disputes are qualified and impartial. Effective legal rules substantially reduce the cost of doing international business. While we discuss other aspects of international law in detail in Chapter 22, here we focus on how the law of the international sale of goods has developed.

General Principles

Parties who make contracts for the sale of goods that cross national borders are generally free to choose the law they want to apply to their contract, given limits set by nations' domestic laws. That is, if a company in Tennessee is buying shirts from Bangladesh, the two parties can specify the law that governs their contract. They can specify that the Uniform Commercial Code of Tennessee governs the contract and that disputes are to be resolved by the arbitration rules of the International Chamber of Commerce.

If the parties do not specify how contract disputes are to be resolved, conflict-of-law rules determine what law governs a dispute and what court system or arbitrator governs the matter. Most people prefer to control their legal destiny, so most contracts for the sale of goods specify what governs the contract and where disputes must be resolved. Alternatively, as we see next, many disputes are now governed by a common set of rules.

The Convention on Contracts for the International Sale of Goods

The Convention on Contracts for the International Sale of Goods (CISG) was adopted by the United Nations to provide a commercial code that parties would think unbiased. It has been ratified by most nations, including the United States. Because the CISG is a treaty adopted by Congress, it prevails over state laws, such as the UCC.

Contracts for the sale of goods that fall under the CISG between a party in, for example, Florida, and a party in another nation that has adopted the CISG are resolved by the CISG. So, if an auto parts company in the United States buys parts from a German

INTERNATIONAL PERSPECTIVE

Contracts in China

China's basic contract law, the Uniform Contract Law (UCL), was adopted in 1999. Although there are similarities between the Chinese UCL and the American UCC, there are important differences, and business people considering contracting with a Chinese business need to pay attention to these:

Offer and Acceptance Like the UCC, the UCL requires an offer and acceptance to create a contract. Thus, as under the UCC, price lists, advertisements, bids, and auction announcements are merely invitations to make offers, not offers themselves.

Terms Required The UCL requires that contracts include the names and addresses of the parties, subject matter, quantity, quality, price, time, place and method of performance, liabilities for breach of contract, and method of dispute resolution. If any of these terms are omitted, the UCL specifies default rules that govern, which are similar to those provided by the UCC. For example, market price is substituted for an omitted price term.

Lawfulness As under the UCC, contracts that are the result of fraud, mistake, coercion, or duress are not valid. However, the UCL also invalidates contracts with illegitimate purposes. Article 7 of the UCL provides that "In concluding or performing a contract, the parties shall abide by the relevant laws and administrative regulations, as well as observe social ethics, and may not disrupt social and economic order or harm the public interests." "Social ethics" and "social and economic order" can be interpreted broadly by the Chinese courts and lead to state interference in contracts.

Statute of Frauds The UCL follows the civil law practice of not requiring contracts to be in writing, as required by the UCC's Statute of Frauds provision for many contracts. Under UCL Art. 10, contracts may be formed by "a writing, in an oral conversation, as well as in any other form." A writing is required only if required by some other law or if the parties have agreed that writings are needed. The UCL broadly defines "writing" as a "memorandum of contract, letter or electronic message, which is capable of expressing its contents in a tangible form." It also allows contracting by exchange of electronic data.

Risk of Loss Under the UCC, merchant sellers have a greater burden compared to nonmerchant sellers; under Chinese law there is no difference. The UCL provides that "the risk of damage to or loss of the subject matter is borne by the seller prior to delivery, and by the buyer after delivery. ..." Under the UCC, the risk of loss shifts from the seller to the buyer based on the shipping terms agreed to; under the UCL, the risk shifts with delivery to an independent carrier, unless the parties have agreed otherwise. This has a major impact on who must purchase insurance for the goods.

Warranties The UCL provides for express warranties only when there is an express description of the good, sample, or model in the contract. There may be some implied warranties in the UCL similar to the UCC's warranty of merchantability, but the language of the statute is ambiguous. Similar to other parts of the UCL, experience under the law has not been significant, so caution is in order.

company, the contract is automatically governed by the CISG—unless the parties specify that they want to exclude application of the CISG, or some parts of it, and choose another law to govern their contract. The parties could specify German law, Florida law, or even some other relevant law. If they do not specify the law, then the CISG automatically governs the contract.

Sales Covered by the CISG The CISG applies to contracts for commercial sale of goods made by parties who have places of business in different countries that have ratified the CISG. It does not matter what the citizenship of the parties is; it is the location of the businesses that matters. Unlike the UCC, which applies to goods sold to the consuming public, the CISG governs only commercial sales or sales between merchants. However, even among merchants, certain sales are excluded from the CISG:

- Auction sales
- Consumer goods bought for personal or household use
- Contracts that are primarily for the supply of labor or of other services
- Electricity
- Ships and aircraft
- Securities such as stocks, negotiable instruments, and money

Again, parties to contracts that would normally be covered by the CISG can pick another law to govern their contract for the sale of goods if they so desire. Because of their lack of experience under the CISG, few parties wish to fall under its rules; courts are not familiar with it, and there is little case law precedent.

Similarities to UCC The CISG is not greatly different from the UCC or the commercial civil codes used in most nations. It is based on the business reality that many deals are not detailed in contracts that account for all possibilities. It instructs judges to look at the plain meaning of words and to look for consistency.

Formality Contracts need not be formal; the CISG states that "A contract of sale need not be concluded in or evidenced by writing and is not subject to any other requirements as to form. It may be proved by any means, including witnesses." Judges are told to look at the circumstances of past dealings, such as the negotiations, the practices of the parties in dealing with each other, and "any practices which they have established between themselves." However, if parties to a contract made under the CISG desire, they can insert a statement that judges are not to consider parol evidence and should not look beyond the words in the contract.

Offers Advertisements under the CISG are not offers that can be accepted to form a contract; they are only offers to enter into negotiations. However, offers made to "one or more specific persons" are valid offers to make a contract. Offers become effective when they reach the offeree, but they can be revoked any time before acceptance is communicated.

Much like the UCC, the CISG holds that an offer "is sufficiently definite if it indicates the goods and expressly or implicitly fixes or makes provision for determining the quantity and price." When a contract does not expressly include the price, the parties are held "to have impliedly made reference to the price generally charged at the time of the conclusion of the contract for such goods sold under comparable circumstances in the trade concerned." Similarly, if there is uncertainty over a term, the courts will look to the practices "in the particular trade concerned." For example, in one case, the parties argued about what was meant by "chicken." One party claimed it meant young fryers, but the court found that industry practice meant a cooking chicken of any size.

Acceptance Acceptance of an offer must be made within the time stated in the offer, or, if not stated, within a reasonable time. Acceptance can be sent by any reasonable means. Any statement or conduct by the offeree to indicate acceptance is sufficient to form the contract. The acceptance is effective when it is received by the offeror, so an offer may be withdrawn up to the point the offeror receives acceptance. As with the UCC and common law, silence is normally not acceptance, but many contracts are formed by performance without stating that there will be performance. For example, if an offeror sends an order asking for 500 boxes of fried grasshoppers, shipping the grasshoppers serves as acceptance.

ISSUE SPOTTER
What Law Applies, and Where, to Your Contract?

Your store buys interesting products from around the world, and you try to track down unusual items that are not found in major retail chains. So you are in international commerce. You have a line of credit at a bank. It makes payments to the sellers once the goods have been accepted in the United States. But what if something goes wrong? You accept a shipment of bamboo furniture from Malaysia. It looks great, the bill is paid, but three months later, the furniture falls apart. You complain and get the runaround. The contract said nothing about jurisdiction or law. Can you sue? Where? What are you likely to do? What can you do to minimize such problems?

Battle of the Forms It is common in business for orders (offers) to be sent that are accepted by the seller (offeree) returning a different standard form. When a dispute arises, the contract is based upon two forms with different terms. The CISG holds that if the differences are material, then the second form is a counteroffer, not an acceptance, so there was no contract. Terms that are not material are a part of the contract unless specifically rejected by the offeror. In this sense, the CISG is less flexible than the UCC and more like the common law of contracts. Under the UCC, courts are more likely to fill in material terms than they are under the CISG.

Duties of the Parties The obligations that parties to a contract have under the CISG are similar to those under the UCC. The seller must fulfill the obligation to deliver the goods with good title according to the terms specified, given reasonable commercial practices. If there is a problem, the buyer must notify the seller of defects "within as short a period as is practicable" after delivery. The seller may cure any defects in the delivered goods, so long as it is not costly to the buyer. If the goods are delivered properly, the buyer must take delivery and pay the price specified.

Remedies In the event of a breach of contract, parties are expected to behave in a reasonable manner and give the breaching party notice of the alleged breach and an opportunity to cure the defect. In this sense, the CISG is like German commercial law, which requires that a Nachfrist (i.e., period of grace) notice—a notice of the problem and a chance to perform properly—be given to the nonconforming party before suit for breach is filed. As under the common law and the UCC, if there is a failure to perform, there is an obligation to try to minimize the damages and make the best out of a bad situation so that the waste is minimized. If damages must be paid, they are usually the difference between the contract price and the value or cost incurred at the time of the breach. In the *Dingxi Longhai Dairy* case, we see an example of U.S. courts dealing with remedy issues under the CISG. Note how the court refers to the UCC and common law for comparison.

International Sales Disputes: The Dominance of Arbitration

There are not many cases in the courtson disputes under the CISG in part because most commercial sales contracts specify arbitration as the required method of dispute resolution. The United Nations encourages the use of arbitration in commercial dealings through the Convention on the Recognition and Enforcement of Foreign Arbitrable Awards.

DINGXI LONHAI DAIRY, LTD. V. BECWOOD TECHNOLOGY GROUP L.L.C.

United States Court of Appeals, Eighth Circuit, 635 F.3d 1106 (2011)

Case Background *Dingxi Longhai Dairy agreed to ship 612 metric tons of Inulin, a dietary fiber extract, to Becwood Technology, a Minnesota company. There would be four shipments from the port of Tianjin, China, to Londonderry, New Hampshire. Becwood received the first two shipments. It paid for one but refused to pay for the second because of mold on the packaging. Dingxi recalled shipments three and four before they reached their destination and sued Becwood for breach of contract.*

The district court held for Dingxi on the second shipment but dismissed its claims for damages relating to shipments three and four. Dingxi appealed.

Case Decision Per Curiam

* * *

It is undisputed that the contract was governed by the United Nations Convention on Contracts for the International Sale of Goods ("CISG"), the "international analogue" to Article 2 of the Uniform Commercial Code (UCC). In applying the Convention, we look to the language of its provisions and the "general principles on which it is based." CISG Art. 7(2). Caselaw interpreting analogous provisions of Article 2 ... may also inform a court where the language of the relevant CISG provisions tracks that of the UCC. With regard to pleading requirements, "the Convention's structure confirms what common sense (and the common law) dictate as the universal elements of [a breach-of-contract] action: formation, performance, breach and damages."

For its breach-of-contract claim, Dingxi's complaint alleged that it timely delivered all four shipments "F.O.B. to Tianjin–Xingang Port, China," as specified in the signed purchase order; that Becwood failed to pay for the last three shipments; and that Dingxi was therefore entitled to recover $1,415,086 "together with interest, disbursement,

costs, expenses and reasonable attorneys' fees." Under the UCC, this would plainly be a § 2–709 "Action for the Price" of the goods by the seller. Under the CISG, it was a claim by the seller for breach of contract subject to the remedy provisions in Articles 61–65 and 74–77.

Becwood moved to dismiss the claim regarding shipments three and four on the ground that a seller who recalls goods before they reach the buyer may not recover as damages, even if you assume that there's a breach from the buyer, the very contract price of those goods that the seller retained. The district court agreed. It dismissed the claim on the ground that damages following contract avoidance are governed by CISG Art. 76, and therefore "Dingxi has failed to assert cognizable damages on shipments 3 and 4."

We can agree that it is highly unlikely—though not inconceivable—that an aggrieved seller in this situation would recover the full contract price for shipments three and four. ...

Dingxi's complaint stated a breach-of-contract claim—performance of its contractual duty to deliver and the buyer's refusal to pay.... Dingxi recalled shipments three and four before they reached the buyer. That fact will likely preclude recovery of the full contract price. But if Dingxi proves that Becwood breached the contract as to shipments three and four, it is almost certain to be entitled to *some* monetary relief. ...

The order dismissing Dingxi's breach-of-contract claims relating to shipments three and four is reversed.

Questions for Analysis

1. Why would this case be tried under the CISG rather than the UCC or the UCL of China?
2. What damages would you think Dingxi might be due for the third and fourth shipments?

If a country has adopted the Convention, as the United States has, then courts are bound to recognize and enforce arbitration decisions that have followed proper procedure, unless the decision is in conflict with the law of the nation of one of the parties or goes beyond the scope of the matter covered by arbitration. So, as with domestic contracts in the United States, the parties to a contract written under the CISG who mandate arbitration have little reason ever to be in court, as it is the duty of the arbitrators to resolve the dispute under the rules of the CISG.

Full Circle

Centuries ago, when merchants could not rely on public courts for resolution of disputes and commercial law was not well developed, the law merchant developed. It was a voluntary set of common rules by which merchants across national boundaries could resolve disputes. It was based on the way most business was done. Disputes were resolved by a process similar to arbitration: private dispute resolution.

Over many decades, nations adopted commercial law based on business practices. Public courts were used to resolve some disputes. As international trade has grown, the

 TEST YOURSELF

1. In the case *Lee* v. *R & K Marine*, where Lee bought a new boat from *R & K* that literally fell apart in a few years, but *R & K* had a warranty disclaimer in the sales contract, the appeals court held that *R & K*:
   a. acted in "bad faith" in violation of its duty as a merchant under the UCC.
   b. could not disclaim all warranty in sales to consumers.
   c. had not made clear to Lee that the warranties were disclaimed, so they were held to still exist.
   d. had properly disclaimed all warranties.
2. Warranty of title to goods being purchased must be expressed in a contract, as the UCC does not presume that kind of warranty exists otherwise: T—F
3. A seller's promise or guarantee as to the quality, safety, performance, or durability of goods being sold is called _____.
4. In the case, *Dingxi Longhai Dairy, Ltd.* v. *Becwood Technology Group*, where the parties were in dispute over the shipment of goods from China to the United States, the court held that the CISG would determine responsibilities under the contract: T—F
5. The Convention on the Recognition and Enforcement of Foreign Arbitrable Awards has not been signed by the United States and a number of other major nations, making it not very useful so far: T—F
6. In *QVC* v. *MJC America*, where MJC provided defective heaters to QVC. The court held that because the UCC governed the relationship, QVC could:
   a. collect for lost profits, consequential damages, and all other costs involved.
   b. collect for consequential damages, but not for lost profits.
   c. collect for the costs to repair heaters only.
   d. not collect any damages due to the clear warranty disclaimer in the contract.
7. When a seller fails to deliver goods on time and the buyer must buy substitute goods as a result of the breach, the difference in the contract price and the price of the substitute goods is called _____.

Answers: d; F; express warranty; T; F; a; cover.

basic rules of law under which most contracts are formed is much the same, whether it is the law of a particular nation, such as the UCC is, or the civil code of a nation such as France, or the CISG. The rules do not vary radically from country to country.

Increasingly in recent years, merchants have turned again to private dispute resolution. As with contracts made in the United States, parties know that arbitration is quicker and cheaper than court litigation. In international dealings, parties worry that they may suffer discrimination—intentional or not—if they litigate disputes in the home courts of the other parties, so neutral arbitrators are again preferred. Courts around the world have come increasingly to enforce arbitration decisions, so parties have greater confidence in the integrity of the international legal system.

SUMMARY

- To make contract law more consistent with business practices and reduce the cost of operating businesses across state lines, the Uniform Commercial Code was developed. Article 2 of the UCC governs contracts for the sale of goods. Goods are tangible things that are movable at the time of the identification of the contract. Real estate, services, stocks, bank accounts, patents, and copyrights are not "goods" under the UCC. Transactions involving those things are governed by the common law of contracts.

- Under the UCC, merchants are held to a higher standard of conduct than are non-merchants. A person is a merchant if she deals, holds herself out as having special knowledge, or employs an agent, broker, or other intermediary who holds himself out as having special knowledge of the goods involved in the transaction. Merchants are required to conduct their activities in good faith and must follow business practices common in the trade.

- The common law governs a transaction unless the UCC modifies or specifically changes the effect of the common law. Generally, when the UCC modifies the common law, the effect is usually to be less demanding than the common law. An acceptance under the UCC, for example, does not have to be unequivocal to form a contract. An indefinite offer can form the basis of a contract (even with open price, quantity, delivery, or payment terms) under the UCC but not under the common law.

- The basic obligation of the seller is to transfer and deliver the goods. The buyer is obligated to accept and pay for them. In performing their obligations, in contract performance and enforcement, the parties are required by the UCC to act in good faith.

- In delivering conforming goods to the buyer, the seller is concerned with the appropriate manner and timeliness of delivery, place of tender, and the quality of tender. The UCC instructs the courts to provide such terms according to the apparent intent of the parties or the trade custom.

- The common law's perfect tender rule requires that the seller's tender of delivery conform in detail to the terms of the contract. The UCC modifies the buyer's common-law right to reject the goods by providing the seller with the right to cure defects within the time frame of the contract.

- The UCC obligates the seller to warrant title to goods being sold. The seller warrants good title, the absence of any interests or liens on the goods, and that the goods are free of any patent, copyright, or trademark infringements.

- A seller may create an express warranty under the UCC by making a statement to the buyer about the goods or by providing the buyer with a description of the goods or a sample or model of the goods.

- The UCC provides an implied warranty of merchantability and an implied warranty of fitness for a particular purpose. The good must conform to the contract description; be fit for the purposes for which it is intended; be of even kind, quality, and quantity; be adequately labeled; and conform to label descriptions. If a seller knows a buyer has a particular purpose for a good, and the buyer relies on the seller's skill or judgment in selecting a good, an implied warranty of fitness for a particular purpose may be created.

- The UCC extends to designated third parties any express warranty made by the seller to a buyer. To be consistent with other third-party beneficiary rules within a state, the UCC provides several alternative rules that states may adopt if they wish.

- When a buyer or seller breaches a contract for the sale of goods, the UCC provides the nonbreaching party with remedies designed to place them in the same position as if the contract had been performed. The seller may recover for losses suffered due to the buyer's failure to accept goods or to pay for goods. The buyer may recover the difference between what had to be paid to obtain substitute goods and the contract price. The seller and the buyer may seek incidental damages for recovery of costs resulting from the breach. The buyer is also allowed to recover consequential damages suffered, usually lost profits.

- The UN Convention on Contracts for the International Sale of Goods applies to contracts for commercial sale of goods by parties who have places of business in different countries that have ratified the CISG. Most major nations, including the United States, have ratified it. Such sales are covered by the CISG unless the parties specify that they want some other law to govern the contract.

- The CISG applies only to goods in commercial sales, that is, between merchants. Like the UCC, it does not require contracts to be formal writings, but gives priority to written terms in case of dispute. When terms are unclear, the courts are to look to the intent of the parties and to trade usage.

- In the event of a battle of the forms, under the CISG, when there are differences in material terms, no contract is formed; when changes are to minor terms, they may become incorporated into the contract unless a party to the contract object to them.

- As with commercial contracts in the United States, most international commercial sale contracts include an arbitration clause. Many nations have adopted the Convention on the Recognition and Enforcement of Foreign Arbitrable Awards, so courts will uphold arbitration clauses and enforce arbitration results unless they conflict with national policy or there was a serious problem with the arbitration process.

TERMS TO KNOW

Uniform Commercial Code, 276
goods, 278
good faith, 280
merchant, 280
sale, 280
title, 280
sales contract, 282
firm offer, 283
statute of frauds, 285

trade usage, 286
requirements contract, 287
output contract, 287
tender, 289
perfect tender rule, 289
cure, 289
warranty, 291
warranty of title, 291
express warranty, 291

implied warranty, 292
merchantable, 292
fitness for a particular
   purpose, 293
warranty disclaimer, 293
cover, 296
incidental damages, 296
consequential damages, 296

DISCUSSION QUESTION

What is the advantage of the UCC compared to the common law of contracts? Are there disadvantages to the adoption of a statute such as the UCC?

CASE QUESTIONS

1. Cal-Cut had dealt with Idaho Pipe for years. Idaho Pipe requested 30,000 feet of steel pipe from Cal-Cut. Cal-Cut sent written confirmation. Idaho Pipe accepted the offer by return mail, changed the delivery date from October 15 to December 15, and sent $20,000 in partial payment. Cal-Cut confirmed the order and did not change the October 15 delivery date, but wrote, "We will work it out," on the contract. Cal-Cut delivered 12,937 feet of pipe before October 5, which Idaho Pipe accepted. Then Cal-Cut refused to deliver any more pipe. The sale had become unprofitable, as the price of pipe had risen quickly. Was this deal enforced? Could Idaho Pipe recover damages? [*Southern Idaho Pipe and Steel* v. *Cal-Cut Pipe and Supply*, 567 P.2d 1246, Sup. Ct. Id. (1977)]

2. Polygram, a French company, made records, tapes, and CDs. 32-03, a New York distributor, ordered goods from Polygram that were

delivered in four shipments with written invoices. The invoices noted that payment was due in 60 days and that claims about problems must be made within three months of delivery. The companies had done business this way for years. 32-03 objected to the terms of sale for the first time in this incident, and refused to pay. It claimed there was no written contract in violation of the statute of frauds, and it was trade custom in the industry for distributors to be allowed to return any defective goods for credit. Polygram claims that the terms of the agreement were violated and sued for payment. Who was right? [*Polygram* v. *32-03 Enterprises*, 697 F. Supp. 132, E.D. NY (1988)]

3. Marquette agreed to provide all cement that Norcem would need for two years. The quantity and sales price for the first two shipments were specified in the contract. The third shipment, according to the contract, was to be negotiated for a price "not to exceed $38 per short ton." At the time of the third shipment, Marquette told Norcem the price would be $38; Norcem responded that Marquette's insistence on the maximum price was not in good faith and refused to buy the cement. Marquette sued for breach of contract. Was Marquette right? [*Marquette* v. *Norcem*, 494 N.Y.S.2d 511, Sup. Ct., App. Div., NY (1985)]
   ✓ Check your answer

4. Eureka Water in Oklahoma sold "Ozarka" branded water that it bottled and distributed for Nestle Waters. The companies got into a dispute. Would this case fall under the UCC or the common law? Much of the value of the contract arose from the use of the Ozarka trademark, but most of the work involved bottling and distributing water. [*Eureka Water Co.* v. *Nestle Waters North America*, 690 F.3d 1139, 10th Cir. (2012)]

5. Community Television Services (CTS) hired Dresser to build a 2,000-foot antenna tower in South Dakota for $385,000. The contract contained technical specifications warranting that the tower would withstand winds of 120 mph. During negotiations, Dresser had given CTS a sales brochure that stated:

   "Wind force creates the most critical loads to which a tower is normally subjected. When ice forms on the tower members, thereby increasing the surface area resisting the passage of wind, the load is increased. Properly designed towers will safely withstand the maximum wind velocities and ice loads to which they are likely to be subjected. Dresser … can make wind and ice load recommendations to you for your area based on U.S. Weather Bureau data. In the winter, loaded with ice and hammered repeatedly with gale force winds, these towers absorb some of the roughest punishment that towers take anywhere in the country … yet continue to give dependable, uninterrupted service."

   The tower was built according to the contract's technical specifications. Six years later, the tower collapsed during an 80-mph blizzard. Is Dresser liable for breach of an express warranty? [*Community Television Services* v. *Dresser*, 586 F.2d 637, 8th Cir. (1978)]
   ✓ Check your answer

6. Leavitt bought a new motor home. He told the dealer he would be driving in the mountains and wanted to be sure to have sufficient engine and brake power, which he was assured he would. He contended that there was not enough power to go uphill and the brakes overheated going downhill. Despite many warranty repairs, Leavitt concluded that the engine and brakes were not suitable, and he sued for breach of implied warranty of fitness for a particular purpose under the UCC. The jury awarded Leavitt $33,730 (the vehicle was worth about $80,000). The judge also awarded Leavitt attorney's fees under the Magnuson-Moss Warranty Act. Defendant appealed. Was the award justified under the UCC? [*Leavitt* v. *Monaco Coach*, 616 NW.2d 175, Ct. App., Mich. (2000)]
   ✓ Check your answer

7. The Bosarges purchased from J&J Mobile Homes Sales in Pascagoula a furnished mobile home manufactured by North River Homes. The home was described by a J&J salesman as the "Cadillac of mobile homes." But, upon moving into their home, the Bosarges discovered many defects. After arguing with North River for a year, during which time only a few repairs were made, the Bosarges refused to make further payments and sued North River for selling a mobile home of unmerchantable quality. North River countered that the Bosarges could not claim to reject the mobile home when they continued to live in it. Who was right? [*North River Homes* v. *Bosarge*, 594 So.2d 1153, Sup.Ct., Miss. (1992)]

8. Anhui, a Chinese company, contracted to sell dyed yarn to Hart, an American company. The contract contained a clause requiring arbitration of disputes before the China Council for the Promotion of International Trade in Beijing. When a dispute arose and Hart refused to pay Anhui, it began arbitration proceedings. Hart did not respond but sued Anhui in federal court in the United States. Hart claimed the arbitration clause was not enforceable because arbitration in Beijing would be a hardship and, even if it were not, the dispute was over the validity of the contract itself, an issue of contract law, not a payment dispute. Because that was a legal matter, it could be litigated. What resulted in federal court? [*Hart Enterprises Intl.* v. *Anhui Provincial Import and Export*, 888 F.Supp. 587, S.D. NY (1995)]

9. A textile mill in Bangladesh bought cotton from a broker in Tennessee. The contract stated that any problems with quality had to be resolved by arbitration at the Liverpool Cotton Association in England. Complaints had to be filed within two months, or the matter would not be heard. The buyer did not realize that the cotton was lower quality than paid for until six months had passed. Could it then sue under the CISG in federal court in Tennessee? [*Quasem Group, Ltd.* v. *W.D. Mask Cotton*, 967 F. Supp. 288, W.D. Tenn. (1997)]

ETHICS QUESTION

Many U.S. retailers include in their contracts with suppliers domestic and foreign, a requirement that the supplier agree not to violate any local labor laws or the contract can be terminated. Yet the illegal use of child labor is common in many countries, especially in carpet making in Pakistan and in sewing operations in many countries. The retailers have been criticized as using the codes of conduct for publicity purposes because enforcement is difficult and rare. Should such codes be used, and if so, how can they be enforced?

CHAPTER 12
Business Organizations

Three school acquaintances worked for different companies for five years when they decided to join together to start their own firm, a partnership developing real estate. They consulted a lawyer to help draw up the agreement for their new partnership, knowing that legal structure is important for any venture. They also knew that good intentions at the beginning of an operation often disappear when problems arise, which happened to them. The business did not do well, and the friends began to turn on each other. One partner did not do as much work as the other two thought he should. Another partner charged what the other two thought were personal expenses to the partnership. They could not agree on how to split the income or deal with certain expenses.

Could they have headed these problems off by forming a different kind of organization at the outset? Only in part. While form is important, managing an organization requires a complex set of abilities. Many people report that they would like to be their own boss some day. It is a great goal, but there is no magic key. You are often on your own because you cannot afford a team of lawyers, accountants, and other experts to guide you. This chapter examines the relative merits of different forms of organizations.

There are over 30 million businesses in the United States. Sole proprietorships—mostly businesses, such as consultants, dry cleaners, and restaurants—account for the majority, as Exhibit 12.1 shows. The data are not perfect as some proprietorships do not file tax returns, but the numbers give a sense of the dynamic nature of businesses in the United States.

We begin with a discussion of different types of business organizations, including sole proprietorships, partnerships, corporations, and limited liability companies. Every state has laws concerning aspects of corporation and partnership formation, operation, and dissolution, but organizations are primarily created by actions and contracts. The statutory requirements regarding business formation are not burdensome, but each form has legal advantages and disadvantages. This chapter considers factors that may influence a choice of business organization. Finally, we look at franchises, a popular business form that continues to grow.

EXHIBIT 12.1 BUSINESS ESTABLISHMENTS IN THE UNITED STATES

	NUMBER (BASED ON TAX RETURNS)	GROSS RECEIPTS ($ BILLION)	NET RECEIPTS ($ BILLION)	NET RECEIPTS AS PERCENTAGE OF GROSS RECEIPTS
Nonfarm Proprietorships	23 million	1,320	265	20.1
Partnerships	3.2 million	4,963	458	9.2
Corporations	5.9 million	27,266	984	3.6

Source: U.S. Internal Revenue Service.

Sole Proprietorships

A person doing business for himself or herself is a sole proprietor; the business organization is a **sole proprietorship**. It is the oldest and simplest form of business organization. As a proprietor, a person may simply begin to do business without formality in enterprises that do not require a government license or permit, although most states require business names to be registered if a fictitious business name is used. A fictitious name is a name other than the name of the individual. The proprietor generally owns all or most of the business property and is responsible for the control, liabilities, and management of the business.

In a sole proprietorship, legally and practically, the owner is the business; capital comes from the owner's own resources or is borrowed with the owner as debtor. Perhaps the two greatest disadvantages of the sole proprietorship are the fact that limited alternatives exist for raising capital and the owner is personally liable for all business debts. Because the profits of the business are taxed to the owner personally, a tax return in the business's name is not required so long as records of income and expenses are kept. The operational and record-keeping formalities of the business are at the owner's discretion as long as various taxing and licensing authorities are satisfied.

Partnerships

A **partnership** is defined as an association of two or more persons to carry on a business as co-owners for a profit. The partners or, more accurately, **general partners**, share control over the business's operations and profits. Many attorneys, doctors, accountants, and retail stores are organized as partnerships. A "person" who is a partner in a partnership may be another partnership, a corporation, or some other entity.

At common law, a partnership was not treated as an independent legal entity. As a consequence, a case could not be brought by or against the business. The partners had to sue or be sued individually. State law now provides that, for many purposes, a partnership may be treated as an independent, legal entity. Thus, a partnership may sue or be sued and collect judgments in its own name. There are many forms of partnerships, including joint ventures. As the Iowa Supreme Court has explained, joint ventures are a particular kind of partnership:

> A joint venture is defined as an association of two or more persons to carry out a single business enterprise for profit; also as a common undertaking in which two or more combine their property, money, efforts, skill or knowledge (43 NW2d at 136).

Partnership law originated in the common law but is now codified in the Uniform Partnership Act (UPA) and the Revised Uniform Partnership Act (RUPA). This act is offered to the states by the Uniform Law Commission (see www.uniformlaws.org). The

RUPA, which is often just called the UPA, has been adopted by most states and governs partnerships and partnership relations. It provides "default rules" that determine the operation of partnerships when a partnership agreement is silent on a particular issue or when no formal agreement exists among the partners.

Forming a Partnership

A partnership can begin with an oral agreement between two or more persons to do business as partners or with an implied agreement that may be inferred from the conduct of the partners as they do business together. If you and a friend start selling t-shirts together on the Internet, you have formed a partnership, although you may not think about it right away. However, if the business grows or a problem arises, it could become an issue. Typically, parties in a partnership formalize their relationship by a written agreement that likely covers the following points:

- *Basics*—name of the partnership, name of the business, place and date of formation; state law that applies to the partnership
- *Finances*—contributions of the partners (which may be money, facilities, or work); when payments are due; how additional capital contributions will be handled; the allocation of ownership shares; accounting rules; the distribution of profits; and priority rights in payments
- *Management*—voting rights of partners; appointment of managing partners with decision-making authority; and, in some cases, a compensation committee
- *Dissolution*—procedures to be followed if the partnership is terminated; rights of partners to leave the partnership; procedures to be followed if a partner dies; how partnership shares will be valued; limits on transfers of partnership shares; requirement to go to arbitration in case of dispute among partners

In the absence of a specific agreement, the UPA specifies and governs the relationship of the parties. Because the law does not require that a partnership have a name or that it be registered, outsiders might not know of its existence or who is involved.

Partnerships may be informal, and some come about by oral agreement; but courts prefer to follow documentary evidence of a partnership to make sure the parties have followed the requirements of state law, as the *Zhou* case discusses.

ZHOU V. BICKLEY

Court of Appeals of Kansas 286 P.3d 240 (2012)

Case Background *Bickley worked at Lawrence Yamaha. He frequently ate lunch at a Chinese restaurant where Zhou and Zhang, immigrants from China, worked. Bickley told Zhou and Zhang that the Yamaha shop was going out of business and suggested that they help him open a new motorcycle repair shop. The three of them signed a two-year lease on a building for the shop. Zhou and Zhang paid the security deposit and first month's rent. They helped pay for inventory and helped get the shop ready for business. They gave Bickley more money when he asked for it.*

Soon after, Zhou and Zhang asked for keys to the building; Bickley refused. They asked to see receipts and invoices; he refused. They asked to work at the shop; he refused. They demanded a written agreement; he refused. An attorney sent a demand letter on behalf of Zhou and Zhang that was ignored. Suit was filed demanding return of the funds expended. Bickley counterclaimed for breach of contract by his partners. The trial court held there was no partnership; there was only "a vague agreement to open a motorcycle repair shop." Bickley operated as a sole proprietor who borrowed money that he owed to Zhou and Zhang. Bickley appealed.

Case Decision Per Curiam

* * *

Generally, a partnership is the association of two or more persons to carry on as co-owners of a business for profit. The mere fact that the parties called themselves partners and referred to their business relation as a partnership will not necessarily make them partners, nor their business a partnership. Furthermore, an attempt to form a partnership can fail for numerous reasons.

Although Zhou, Zhang, and Bickley contributed money to the start-up expenses of the motorcycle repair shop and they signed a lease together, a reasonable person could conclude based on the evidence presented that no binding contract was ever formed—much less a binding contract to form a partnership.... Similarly, a reasonable person could conclude from the evidence—in particular their repeated requests for a written contract—that Zhou and Zhang simply intended to enter into a partnership agreement at some date in the future.

It was also reasonable for the district court to conclude that the parties had failed to form a partnership based on Bickley's actions in operating the business. As the evidence in the record reflects, Bickley denied Zhou and Zhang access to the building,

denied them access to financial records, and refused to let them participate in the operations of the business in any way. Certainly, such actions are not consistent with the fiduciary duties that partners owe to one another under the Kansas Uniform Partnership Act. Moreover, Bickley's own testimony was inconsistent on the type of partnership—general or limited—which he believed was formed.

"The existence of a partnership is not a question of the ... terminology the parties use to describe their relationship.... It is the intent to do the things which constitute a partnership that determines whether individuals are partners, regardless if it is their purpose to create or avoid the relationship." In the present case, there was sufficient evidence presented at trial upon which the district court could reasonably conclude that the parties did not intend to do those things which constitute a partnership.... Therefore, we will not substitute our judgment for that of the district court.

Affirmed.

Questions for Analysis

1. The appeals court affirmed that no partnership was ever created; what would have been necessary for that to happen? Did they need a signed document?
2. Suppose they had signed an agreement and the facts were the same. Would Bickley owe anything then?

Duty of Partners A partnership is a relationship based on extraordinary trust and loyalty. Partners owe a **fiduciary duty** to one another. A fiduciary relationship requires that each partner act in good faith for the benefit of the partnership. The partners must place their personal interests beneath those of the partnership. The Supreme Court stated the duty of partners as follows in *Latta* v. *Kilbourn*, 150 U.S. 524 (1893):

> *It is well settled that one partner cannot, directly or indirectly, use partnership assets for his own benefit; that he cannot, in conducting the business of a partnership, take any profit clandestinely for himself; that he cannot carry on the business of the partnership for his private advantage; that he cannot carry on another business in competition or rivalry with that of the firm, thereby depriving it of the benefit of his time, skill, and fidelity without being accountable to his copartners for any profit that may accrue to him....*

Control by Partners Unless otherwise specified in the partnership agreement, which can allocate control any way that the partners agree to, the presumption is that each partner has an equal voice in partnership management. Regardless of the size of the interest in the partnership, each partner has one vote in managerial decisions.

INTERNATIONAL PERSPECTIVE

Small Is Not So Beautiful in Japan

Each year, about 800,000 new businesses are started in the United States. If the population of Japan is adjusted for comparison to the United States, the number of new businesses would be less than one-third of the rate in the United States. Attitudes seem very different in the two countries. In the United States, small businesses are looked on with favor and are exempted from compliance with some laws; in Japan, they are discriminated against by government policy and are considered less desirable places to work.

Tetsu Anzai owned a few stores that pulled in $12 million a year. He reported that qualified people would not respond to his job ads even though unemployment is high. Worker wariness of small firms reflects government policy.

Government banking regulations favor big businesses. Small firms without large sums of cash to bankroll their operations, which include paying large deposits to rent office space, are usually out of luck. After paying taxes, it is hard for entrepreneurs to reinvest their earnings. The stock market is of limited help, as regulations make it difficult for new firms to be able to offer stock.

Because the Japanese economy has hit hard times, consideration is being given to rules that would help small businesses stimulate the growth that was for so many years generated by the big firms and smiled upon by public policy.

Except in the case of major decisions that require consent of all partners—such as decisions to change the nature of the partnership's business, to admit new partners, or to sell the business—a majority vote is presumed to be controlling under the UPA. In most large partnerships, the partners often delegate most management responsibilities to one person or group, often referred to as the managing partner or partners.

Regardless of who runs a partnership, the partners have a duty to one another to disclose all financial aspects of the business and to be completely honest, regardless of personal differences.

Termination of the Partnership

A change in the relationship of the partners that shows an unwillingness or an inability to continue with business may bring about termination or end of the partnership. By agreement, partners can allow partnership interests to be sold or assigned, usually with approval of existing partners. A complete termination comes about only after the partnership has been dissolved and its affairs have been wound up. The **dissolution** of the partnership occurs when an event takes place that precludes the partners from engaging in any new business. The **winding up** of partnership affairs involves completing any unfinished business and then collecting and distributing the partnership's assets.

Dissolution can come about in several ways. Change in the composition of the partners results in a new partnership and dissolution of the old one. Thus, the withdrawal or death of a partner causes the partnership to be dissolved. Similarly, the partnership is dissolved if a partner is bankrupt. Because it would be expensive and disruptive for partnerships to be terminated and re-formed because of the withdrawal, death, or bankruptcy of one partner, many agreements have provisions to allow the partnership to continue despite such events. One common way is for the partnership to purchase life insurance on the partners, with the proceeds to be used to buy back the interests of a deceased partner from her estate.

Limited Partnership

A limited partnership is a special form of a general partnership. Like a general partnership, a **limited partnership** is a business organization made up of two or more persons (partners) who have entered into an agreement to carry on a business venture for a profit. Unlike in a general partnership, however, not all partners in a limited partnership have the right to participate in the management of the enterprise and not all are liable for partnership debts.

Forming a Limited Partnership

Most states use some form of the Uniform Limited Partnership Act or the Revised Uniform Limited Partnership Act (both are generally referred to as the ULPA). Partners must execute a written agreement, called a certificate of limited partnership, and file it with the appropriate state official, usually the Secretary of State. The Uniform Act requires that certificates contain the following information:

- Name of the business
- Type or character of the business
- Address of an agent who is designated to receive legal process
- Names and addresses of each general and limited partner
- Contributions (cash, work, and property) of each partner
- Duration of the limited partnership
- The rights for personnel changes in the partnership and the continuance of the partnership upon those changes
- The proportion of the profits or other compensation that each partner is entitled to receive

The certificate puts third parties on notice that the limited partners' assets are not available to satisfy claims and that the limited partners lack the ability to commit the partnership to obligations. The name of the partnership must usually include the initials "L.P." or "LP" for the same reasons. Limited partnerships are attractive means of investing in a business where the limited partners do not wish to be actively involved in the business. For example, real estate investments are often set up as LPs, as we see in the *Eagles Landing* case. In addition to the terms listed above, the parties to the LP agreement may agree to bind themselves in ways not required by the certificate.

Relationship of the Parties

A limited partnership has at least one general partner and one or more **limited partners**. The general partners in a limited partnership are treated in the same manner as are partners in a general partnership. They have responsibility for managing the business and are personally liable to the partnership's creditors.

Limited partners are investors who may not participate in managing the business. Although they have the right to see the partnership books and to participate in the dissolution of the business, limited partners are not liable for the debts or torts of the LP beyond their capital contributions. Limited partners lose their limited liability and become general partners if they take an active role in managing the business. To avoid an inference of managerial control, limited partners may not take control of the firm, contribute services to the business, or allow their names to appear in the name of the business. So long as limited partners maintain their investor position, they are not liable for debts owed by the limited partnership (sometimes called limited liability partnerships), as noted in the *Eagles Landing* case.

EAGLES LANDING DEVELOPMENT, L.L.C. V. EAGLES LANDING APARTMENTS, L.P.

Court of Appeals of Tennessee 386 S.W.3d 246 (2012)

Case Background *Eagles Landing Development LLC (Eagles) contracted to build apartments for Eagles Landing Apartments, LP (ELA) for $1.4 million. ELA's general partner was Bluff City. There were two limited partners, PNC, a limited partnership, and Columbia, a corporation. Eagles completed the work but was still owed $931,000.*

The agreement stated that Bluff City's contribution would not exceed the net cash flow from the rental of the apartments. The cash flow was not good, so there was no money there. All cash invested in ELA by the partners was gone. Eagles sued for contribution by PNC and Columbia. The trial court held that the LP owed the $931,000. It appealed.

Case Decision Stafford, Judge

* * *

Columbia and PNC ... argue that even if the full developer's fee is due under the Development Agreement, that they were not parties to that agreement, and were only limited partners in the partnership. Consequently, they contend that they cannot be charged for any liability of the partnership under the Development Agreement. We agree.

The general rule, under the Tennessee Uniform Partnership Act (TUPA), is that "all partners are liable jointly and severally for all obligations of the partnership unless otherwise agreed by the claimant or provided by law." This general rule is modified by the Limited Liability Partnership (LLP) amendments to the TUPA for the protection of partners in registered limited liability partnerships. The LLP amendments to the TUPA provide that:

A partner in a registered limited liability partnership is not liable, directly or indirectly (including by way of indemnification, subrogation, contribution, assessment or otherwise), for debts, obligations and liabilities of or chargeable to the partnership or another partner, whether in tort, contract, or otherwise, arising from omissions, negligence, wrongful acts, misconduct or malpractice committed while the partnership is a registered limited liability partnership and in the course of the partnership business by another partner or an employee, agent, or representative of the partnership. ...

Consequently ... as partners in a limited liability partnership, neither Columbia nor PNC can be held liable for the debts of the partnership. In its order, the trial court ... appears to disregard PNC and Columbia's status as limited liability partners. ...

Therefore, while we affirm the trial court's judgment and the amount thereof, we reverse its assessment of that judgment to PNC and Columbia, and remand to the trial court for the sole purpose of entry of judgment against only the partnership, ELA. ...

Questions for Analysis

1. Does this decision mean Eagles will collect none of the $931,000 it is owed?
2. How could Eagles have protected itself better regarding PNC and Columbia?

Terminating a Limited Partnership

A limited partnership is terminated in much the same way as a general partnership. Events that affect a general partner and would bring about the dissolution of a general partnership also dissolve a limited partnership. While the bankruptcy of a general partner dissolves a limited partnership, the bankruptcy of a limited partner usually does not.

The business of the LP continues to operate while it is winding up, but it may not enter into any new commitments. In the final dispersal of the assets of the limited partnership, creditors' rights precede partners' rights. The limited partners receive their share

ISSUE SPOTTER
Sisterly Love?

You and your sister start a business. You rent a space and start teaching yoga classes. You have customers who pay fees, which you deposit into a joint checking account, from which you pay business bills. After six months, things are going pretty well; but you notice that a chunk of money seems to be missing, and your sister is driving a new car. It turns out that she made the down payment out of the joint account. You get into a fight about it. Whose money was it? Did she have the legal right to take it? It also occurs to you that one of your yoga clients could get twisted in knots and sue for an injury. Who could be liable for that? What else have you not thought about that you should?

of the profits and their capital contributions before general partners receive anything, unless the LP agreement holds otherwise.

Corporations

When most people think of a business, they think of a **corporation**. A corporation is an artificial person, or legal entity, created under state law. Most large, well-known businesses—such as Coca-Cola, General Motors, and Microsoft—are corporations. The corporation developed in the United States during the late 1700s. State governments issued **corporate charters** to selected businesses. Because the charter often granted special privilege, there was intense competition to receive charters. A charter might, for example, give a business the privilege of having the only bank in a town.

In the late 1800s, liberal general incorporation statutes began to be enacted in the United States. Those statutes established a simple procedure for incorporating a business and conferred no special privilege. Incorporation is now easily available to businesses regardless of their field of operation, size, or political influence.

Creating a Corporation

Every state has a general incorporation statute that sets the procedure for incorporation. Although it varies across the states, the basic requirements are similar. In general, a corporation's *articles of incorporation*, along with an application, must be filed with the appropriate state office (usually the Secretary of State), along with payment of a fee.

As Exhibit 12.2 shows, the articles of incorporation usually provide the following:

- Name and address of the corporation
- Name and address of the corporation's registered agent
- Purpose of the business
- The class(es) of stock to be issued and their par value
- Names and addresses of the incorporators

After reviewing the corporation's application for completeness, the state issues a **certificate of incorporation**. The incorporators then hold their first formal organizational meeting. At that meeting, the incorporators elect a board of directors, enact the corporation's bylaws, and issue the corporation's stock. The **bylaws** are the rules that regulate and govern the internal operations of the corporation. The shareholders, directors, and officers of the corporation must follow the bylaws in conducting corporate activities.

© Cengage Learning

EXHIBIT 12.2   EXAMPLE OF CERTIFICATE OF INCORPORATION

Certificate of Incorporation of _____ Corporation

1. **Name.** The name of the Corporation is _____ Corporation.

2. **Registered Office and Registered Agent.** The address of the Corporation's registered office in Delaware is _____ Street in the City of _____ and Country of _____, and the name of its registered agent at such address is _____.

3. **Purpose.** The purpose of the Corporation is to engage in any lawful act or activity for which Corporations may be now or hereafter organized under the General Corporation Law of Delaware.

4. **Capital Stock (providing for Two Classes of Stock, One Voting and One Nonvoting).** The total number of shares for all classes of stock the Corporation shall have authority to issue is _____, all of which are to be without par value. _____ of such shares shall be Class A voting shares and _____ of such shares shall be Class B nonvoting shares. The Class A shares and the Class B shares shall have identical rights except that the Class B shares shall not entitle the holder thereof to vote on any matter unless specifically required by law.

5. **Incorporators.** The names and mailing addresses of the incorporators are

Name	Mailing Address
_____	_____
_____	_____
_____	_____

6. **Regulatory Provisions.** [The Corporations may insert additional provisions for the management of the business and for the conduct of the affairs of the Corporation, and creating, defining, limiting, and regulating the powers of the Corporation, the Directors and the Stockholders, or any class of Stockholders.]

7. **Personal Liability.** The Stockholders shall be liable for the debts of the Corporation in the proportion that their stock bears to the total outstanding stock of the Corporation.

8. **Amendment.** The Corporation reserves the right to amend, alter, change or repeal any provision contained in the Certificate of INCORPORATION, in the manner now or hereafter prescribed by statute, and all rights conferred upon Stockholders herein are granted subject to this reservation.

We, the undersigned, being all of the incorporators above named, for the purpose of forming a Corporation pursuant to the General Corporation Law of Delaware, sign and acknowledge this Certificate of Incorporation this _____ day of _____, 20_____ .

Legal Entity Status Unlike a proprietorship, the corporation is a **legal entity** with rights and responsibilities separate from the owners. It is recognized under both federal and state law as a "person." Corporations are entitled to many constitutional protections, including free speech, equal protection under the law, and protections against unreasonable searches and seizures. As a "person," a corporation has the right of access to the courts as an entity that may sue and be sued. However, although the officers and employees of a corporation enjoy the privilege against self-incrimination under the Fifth Amendment, the corporation itself does not.

Relationship of the Parties

A corporation consists of three major groups: the shareholders, the board of directors, and the managers. Each owes specific duties and responsibilities to the other groups, to the corporation, and to third parties. An important feature of the corporation is the legal separation of ownership (the shareholders) and control (management and the board of directors). Members of other groups, such as employees, may be referred to as stakeholders, but they are generally not part of the basic legal structure of the entity.

Shareholders The **shareholders** own the corporation. Evidence of ownership is in the number of shares issued to various parties, which is now an electronic record rather than physical stock certificates. Shareholders have a limited right to inspect the corporation's books and records. As a rule, inspection is provided to shareholders if it is for a proper purpose and a request is made in advance. Finally, unless stated to the contrary on the stock certificate or the bylaws, shareholders are not restricted from selling or giving the stock to someone else.

The shareholders are not responsible for managing the corporation and, indeed, are not allowed to exercise day-to-day control. Instead, shareholders elect the board of directors and vote only on matters that change the corporation's structure or existence (such as a merger with another firm or an amendment to the corporation's articles of incorporation).

Elections take place at shareholder meetings, which are usually held annually. Notice of shareholder meetings must be provided in advance, and a **quorum**—usually more than half of the total shares—must be represented at the meeting. Most shareholders give third parties their **proxy**, a written authorization to cast their vote so that they do not have to attend the meeting in person. The proxy is often solicited by the corporation's management.

At the meeting, important corporate business is presented to the shareholders in the form of resolutions, which shareholders vote to approve or disapprove. The articles of incorporation establish voting rules. They usually require more than a simple majority for resolutions for actions such as amendments to the articles of incorporation and the bylaws or the dissolution or merger of the corporation.

The shareholder has no legal relationship with creditors of the corporation. A shareholder's obligation to creditors is limited to the shareholder's capital contributions, usually the amount paid to buy stock. A shareholder, however, may become a creditor of the corporation—for example, by supplying needed material or by working for the business—and enjoys the same rights of recovery against the corporation as any other creditor.

Lighter Side **of the Law**

Your Honor, I'll Turn Rocks into Gold

Marinov formed Amrox Corporation. He gave himself one-half of the stock for his secret knowledge and equipment. Four investors bought the rest of the stock for $330,000.

Marinov claimed to have a Ph.D. in physics from Russia and medical degrees from Bulgaria, Sweden, and Germany. He told investors that this education taught him how to turn corundum, which is cheap, into rubies and sapphires.

Nothing was ever produced, and the investors sued Marinov. The district court ruled for the investors; Marinov appealed. The appeals court upheld the verdict. Marinov told the court "he is developing a linear accelerator which he wishes to sell to the United Nations." The court found that claim and others "absolutely incredible" and that Marinov breached his fiduciary duty to the investors.

Source: Gizzi v. Marinov, 79 F.3d 1148.

Board of Directors The initial **board of directors**, the governing committee of a corporation, is specified in the articles of incorporation or chosen by the incorporators at the first corporate meeting. Thereafter, the selection of directors is a shareholder responsibility. Once elected, directors serve terms for a time specified in the articles, although the shareholders can remove a director from office for cause (generally for a breach of **duty** or misconduct). By law, the directors must meet at least once a year and keep records of meetings or the corporate status may be lost.

Legally, the board is the **principal** of a corporation; that is, on behalf of the corporation, it sets corporate policy and decides corporate business, such as the sale of assets, entrance into new product lines, major financing decisions, and appointment of corporate officers. The directors act, usually by majority vote, to exert top-level managerial authority. Directors are under a duty of care to make decisions on behalf of the corporation as a reasonably prudent person in the conduct of personal business affairs. Honest mistakes in judgment not resulting from negligence or disagreements about the appropriate strategy do not result in personal liability for the directors.

Business Judgment Rule   The **business judgment rule** makes directors and managers immune from liability when problems result from honest mistakes in judgment, so long as there is a reasonable basis for the decisions. It is in the shareholders' interest to offer sufficient protection to directors so that, as a practical matter, there is little risk that they will face liability if a business loss results if they acted in good faith. The practical reason for the rule was explained by the Second Circuit Court of Appeals:

> *First, shareholders to a very real degree voluntarily undertake the risk of bad business judgment. Investors need not buy stock, for investment markets offer an array of opportunities less vulnerable to mistakes in judgment by corporate officers ... the business judgment rule merely recognizes a certain voluntariness in undertaking the risk of bad business decisions.*
>
> *Second, courts recognize that after-the-fact litigation is a most imperfect device to evaluate corporate business decisions. The circumstances surrounding a corporate decision are not easily reconstructed in a courtroom years later, since business imperatives often call for quick decisions, inevitably based on less than perfect information. The entrepreneur's function is to encounter risks and to confront uncertainty, and a reasoned decision at the time made may seem a wild hunch viewed years later against a background of perfect knowledge.*
>
> *Third, because potential profit often corresponds to the potential risk, it is very much in the interest of shareholders that the law not create incentives for overly cautious corporate decisions (692 F.2d at 885).*

Fiduciary Duty   Directors are subject to a **fiduciary duty of loyalty**. This requires that directors place the interests of the corporation before their own interests. Directors have great leeway in making decisions. The courts understand that hindsight is better than foresight, so the business judgment rule protects directors against suits by shareholders claiming that the directors missed profit opportunities that they should have taken. However, if directors fail to let shareholders profit from opportunities, especially by taking advantage of opportunities for themselves that should have gone to the company, then liability may be imposed.

As the Delaware high court explained, a director's decision should be "based entirely on the corporate merits of the transaction and ... not be influenced by personal or extraneous considerations" (634 A.2d at 362). In many corporations, it is common for shareholders to be both directors and managers, giving them multiple roles to play. The kind of conflict that can arise is discussed in the *Storetrax* case.

STORETRAX.COM V. GURLAND

Court of Appeals of Maryland 915 A.2d 991 (2007)

Case Background *Gurland founded Storetrax.com, an Internet-based commercial real estate listing service, in Maryland. He incorporated it as a Delaware corporation. He then agreed for a group of investors to buy a majority share, and he became president and a member of the board. An employment contract spelled out some terms of employment, including a year's pay if he was ever fired. Two years later, he was removed as president, but stayed on the board for another year. He requested severance pay, but it was denied. He sued.*

The board claimed he was not due severance pay because his job duties, titles, and salary changed while he worked at Storetrax. Further, as a board member, it was a breach of fiduciary duty to sue the company. The lower court held for Gurland; Storetrax appealed.

Case Decision Harrell, Justice

* * *

It is well settled that directors of a corporation occupy a fiduciary relation to the corporation and its stockholders. This fiduciary relationship requires that a director perform his duties ... (1) in good faith; (2) in a manner he reasonably believes to be in the best interests of the corporation; and (3) with the care that an ordinarily prudent person in a like position would use under similar circumstances.

As such, directors of a corporation are entrusted with powers which are to be exercised for the common and general interest of the corporation, and not for their own private individual benefit. ...

This fiduciary duty, furthermore, is not intermittent or occasional, but instead the constant compass by which all director actions for the corporation and interactions with its shareholders must be guided. ...

Situations may arise where a corporate director, despite the requirement that a director adhere strictly to his or her fiduciary obligations, may proceed with an individual plan of action even though the director's interests conflict directly with those of the corporation on whose board he or she sits. ...

When a member of a corporation's board of directors conducts business with his or her own corporation, as was the case here, there is an appreciable possibility that, at some point, the director's interests will diverge from the interests of the corporation. Where such a conflict of interest arises, courts scrutinize closely those dealings in order to ensure that the transaction is carried out consistent with notions of good faith and fair dealing on the part of the director. With this in mind ... the director may find "safe harbor" by disclosing to the corporation the conflict of interest and pertinent facts surrounding the conflict so that a majority of the remaining disinterested shareholders or directors may ratify the transaction or, as the case may be, otherwise take action to protect the corporation's financial interests. ...

In the present case, there existed a conflict between Respondent's interests as an aggrieved former employee and his duty as a director of the corporation. His personal interests were adverse to those of the corporation, because threatened or actual litigation is adversarial in nature. While Gurland endeavored to obtain severance payment under the employment agreement, he held at the same time a position of trust with Storetrax and was impressed with an obligation to act in the best interests of the corporation. Gurland's seeking severance pay from Storetrax in the amount of $150,000 clearly was not in the corporation's best interests. Under the circumstances, however, we believe that Gurland notified Storetrax sufficiently of the imminence of a lawsuit such that he may claim the protections of the "safe harbor." ...

Affirmed.

Questions for Analysis

1. The Maryland high court held that a director did not breach his fiduciary duty by suing his own company board to fulfill a contractual obligation. Would it be good to have a rule that directors cannot do business with companies when they are board members?

2. Is there some way Gurland could cheat the company in this situation that he could not had he not been on the board?

Managers The corporation's board of directors hires **managers** to run the business. The extent of managerial control and the compensation enjoyed by managers are matters of contract and agency law between the board and the managers. Once hired, managers have the same broad duties of care and loyalty as the directors. There are potential conflicts of interest between managers and owners. The managers prefer to be paid more, receive more benefits, have beautiful offices, hold meetings at resorts, and so on. The owners would like the managers to be more frugal. In many instances, special provisions of the bylaws may address such conflicts. For example, there may be a special compensation committee made up of non-executive directors to review top management salaries and a similar audit committee to check the books for evidence of fraud.

Terminating the Corporation

The termination of a corporation, like the termination of a partnership, is conducted in two parts: the dissolution phase and the winding-up phase. Dissolution may be voluntary or involuntary, such as through bankruptcy, and marks the end of the corporation. Upon dissolution, the corporation may not take on any new business. A voluntary dissolution involves approval of the shareholders and the board of directors.

When a corporation is dissolved voluntarily, the board of directors is responsible for winding up the affairs of the corporation. After the corporation's affairs have been completed, the assets are liquidated. The proceeds of the liquidation are first used to satisfy creditors and any remainder goes to the shareholders.

Close Corporation

The law in 20 states allows the formation of a **close corporation**. This is often referred to a statutory close corporation to distinguish it from a closely held corporation, which is a corporation under a provision of securities law, which is discussed in Chapter 18.

Close corporations have a limited number of shareholders, usually 30 to 50, depending on state law. Shares may not be sold openly so there is a very limited market for shares. The shareholders must have an agreement that governs the affairs of the corporation, but these entities are not subject to formal rules regarding shareholder and director meetings as are required of regular corporations.

S Corporation

Regular corporations, which are referred to as C corporations, can elect, with the Internal Revenue Service, to be classified as an **S corporation**. Such corporations may have only one class of stock and may not have more than 100 shareholders. Only natural persons who are U.S. citizens or legal residents may be shareholders, not other corporations or partnerships.

This election is taken primarily for tax considerations. Profits and losses must be allocated to the shareholders who pay income taxes. The S corporation does not pay taxes, so it is like a partnership for tax purposes. This election is for active businesses only; if more than a quarter of gross receipts to the corporation are from passive (investment) income, the IRS can revert the company to regular C corporation status. This is a very popular form for smaller businesses.

Professional Corporations

Many professional businesses, such as groups of doctors in practice together, used to be partnerships. But all states have enacted statutes to allow **professional corporations** (PCs) to be formed. One reason is so the liability of the members of the group, such as the doctors, can be limited to what is invested in the PC. Therefore, each physician is not personally liable for the debts of all the others, which could arise from a costly malpractice judgment against one doctor in the group. A doctor who loses a malpractice case does not have limited liability because she is still personally liable for her negligence; but other members of the practice are protected because the joint entity cannot be used to attribute the negligent doctor's liability to others.

In most states, the owners of a PC can comprise only the professionals involved in the firm itself, that is, the doctors whose practices are tied together to some extent. Stock cannot be sold to outside investors. The tax treatment of PCs is complicated, but tax considerations are another reason many professionals choose this form of organization.

Benefit Corporation

A new class of corporation that voluntarily meets high standards of purpose, accountability, and transparency is called the **benefit corporation**. First made effective in Maryland in 2010, it is now an option in more than a dozen states, including California and New York.

Benefit corporations:

1. have a corporate purpose to create a material positive impact on society and the environment;
2. are required to consider the impact of their decisions not only on shareholders but also on workers, community, and the environment; and
3. are required to make available to the public an annual benefit report that assesses their overall social and environmental performance against a third-party standard.

This status allows company leadership greater leeway in making decisions that may not comport with the traditional standard of maximizing the financial interests of the firm.

? TEST YOURSELF

1. Legally, the principal of a corporation is _____.
2. In a general partnership, the partners usually have _____ liability.
3. Partners in a partnership are said to have a duty based on ordinary care to each other: T—F
4. In the case *Storetrax.com* v. *Gurland*, the appeals court held that when the board of directors refused to pay a large sum to a board member who was a former manager, the directors:
   a. were acting properly within their judgment.
   b. violated their fiduciary obligation not to interfere with the bylaws.
   c. illegally changed the status of the company from public to private.
   d. had an obligation to make the payment promised by contract.
5. The limited partners in a limited partnership may not manage the partnership: T—F
6. If the shares of stock in a company are held by a small group of shareholders and not actively traded, the company is said to be a(n) _____.
7. Sole proprietorships need not file Federal Sole Proprietorship tax returns: T—F

Answers: the board; unlimited; F; d; T; close corporation; T.

Limited Liability Companies

Compared with partnerships and proprietorships, the corporate form of organization presents entrepreneurs with a disadvantage—**double taxation** of profits—and an advantage—**limited liability**. The profits of corporations are taxed at the corporate level unless there is an S corporation election. Corporations must pay federal taxes and, in some states, state taxes. Then, if remaining profits are paid to the shareholders, the shareholders must pay income taxes on what they received. In contrast, a partnership pays no income taxes on its income, but instead passes the income through to the partners who pay tax on their share of the partnership income.

To deal with this problem and to encourage small business development, states enacted statutes authorizing limited liability companies. A **limited liability company** (LLC) is a business organization that is treated like a corporation for liability purposes but like a partnership for federal tax purposes. The profits are taxed only once as the earnings of the owners of the LLC. This form of organization has become very popular.

Lighter Side of the Law

Mad at Each Other? Sue the Insurance Company

Soon after Truck Insurance sold a policy to Marmac, an engineering company, Marmac's board members fell to fighting among themselves. Amey, a board member, 40 percent stockholder, and executive vice president, was demoted by the other board members. He sued Marmac and its officers for breach of fiduciary duty, intentional infliction of emotional distress, and other complaints.

Marmac insisted that Truck Insurance pay for the company and its officers' defense against Amey. Truck refused. The insurance policy covered torts inflicted by Marmac on outsiders; it did not provide coverage for torts board members committed against each other. The jury did not agree and awarded Marmac and its board members $61 million in damages from Truck.

The Supreme Court of California tossed out that decision, holding that "the Amey lawsuit sets forth nothing more than a business dispute." The board members would have to carry on their fight without their insurer.

Source: 44 Cal.Rptr.2d 370.

Method of Creation

As in the case of corporations, state laws provide the procedure to be followed in the creation of an LLC. The organizers file a document referred to as **articles of organization**, which is similar to a corporation's articles of incorporation and contains basic information:

1. Company name (must include "Limited Liability Company" or "LLC")
2. Address of the company or its registered agent
3. Whether the LLC is to be managed by its members or by a manager
4. Names and addresses of company members
5. Date (or event) upon which the company will be dissolved, if any
6. Whether any members are to be liable for company debts

Personal Liability

The state issues a certificate allowing the business to operate. The company must say LLC in its name so the public is on notice of its status. Under the statutes, no member or manager is personally liable for the debts of an LLC. However, members may agree by contract to be personally liable for the company's debts.

Relationship of the Parties

An LLC usually is formed by two or more **members**. (In Texas and Florida, it is possible to form an LLC with just one member.) The members have a **membership interest** in the company, somewhat like owning stock in a corporation or being a limited partner in a limited partnership. There are generally no restrictions on the number of members, but in practice the number is usually under 30. Individuals, corporations, partnerships, and other LLCs may be members. For example, BMW of North America, LLC, is largely owned by BMW of Germany. Unless the agreement says otherwise, members may not transfer membership interests without the consent of the other members.

INTERNATIONAL PERSPECTIVE

Offshore Businesses

Offshore businesses are often portrayed as shady organizations set up on tropical islands to hide ill-gotten gains. Actually, many offshore businesses are legitimate businesses created in jurisdictions that may check on them more rigorously than "onshore" countries such as the United States. It is more difficult to create a company in the "offshore" Cayman Islands than it is to create one in Delaware, where anonymous corporations can be created in hours.

The term "offshore" means that there is a difference in laws between two jurisdictions that can be used to someone's advantage by creating a legal entity or locating a transaction in one jurisdiction rather than another. For example, Latin Americans deposit tens of millions of dollars in tax-free accounts in U.S. bank each year. From the point of view of Venezuelan tax authorities, the United States is as much an "offshore" jurisdiction as Switzerland is with respect to the United States.

Much of the use of offshore business structures is tax-related. For example, the Irish band U2 moved the legal home of its music copyrights from Ireland to U2 Ltd., a holding company in the Netherlands. Because the Netherlands does not tax copyright royalty income, U2 Ltd. pays no tax on the royalties it collects for sales of U2's music. Artists are not alone in taking advantage of the Netherlands' tax system; companies that own patent rights find Dutch holding companies attractive as well.

There are important nontax reasons to use offshore jurisdictions as well. Many of those jurisdictions are successful because they offer convenient sources of high-quality professional services and solid legal systems. Appeals from Cayman courts go to Britain's Privy Council, one of the most respected business courts in the world.

Finally, offshore jurisdictions win business by offering choices of business entities. These range from simple "international business companies" offered by the British Virgin Islands, favored by Asian investors for their low cost and relative anonymity, to the sophisticated mutual funds and insurance laws in jurisdictions such as Bermuda and Cayman that enable companies to create entities with features not readily available in their home countries.

While major economies such as the United States and France complain about lost tax revenue caused by such competition, small countries such as Barbados contend that they have the same sovereign right to set their own tax rates and business organization laws. Efforts to prevent them from competing are modern forms of colonialism.

The members sign an **operating agreement**. Similar to the bylaws of a corporation, the agreement provides rules about the operation of the company and the relationships of the members. It establishes the company's method of management, allocation of profits and losses among members, restrictions on the transfer of membership interests, and the process to be followed in dissolving the company. State statutes provide default provisions to cover issues not stated in the agreement.

The LLC agreement may give each member an equal voice in management regardless of ownership percentage. More typically, the agreement provides that members may hire a manager to run the LLC. The manager need not be a member. The right to set management policy can be delegated to a group of members.

The Continuity-of-Life Factor

Unlike a corporation, an LLC is technically not allowed "perpetual" life. Although death, bankruptcy, retirement, resignation, or expulsion of any member terminates the membership of a member, similar to a partnership, the LLC itself can continue if all remaining members give their consent. In this way, although the company continues to exist, the relationship of the members has changed, which satisfies the IRS regulations regarding continuity of life and the application of partnership taxation. The ability of the members to consent to the continuation of the LLC must be set out in the articles of organization.

Termination

A limited liability company is dissolved and its affairs are wound up usually because of the occurrence of an event specified in the articles of the organization to bring about the dissolution of the company or by the consent of all the members. *In re 1545 Ocean Avenue, LLC* is a case in which the members of an LLC did not contemplate how things could go wrong, how disputes could be resolved, and when a termination could be triggered.

IN RE 1545 OCEAN AVENUE, LLC

Supreme Court, Appellate Division, Second Department, New York
893 N.Y.S.2d 590 (2010)

Case Background *1545 Ocean Avenue LLC was formed for a real estate development. It was owned 50-50 by two other companies, Ocean Suffolk and Crown Royal, which each had a membership certificate in 1545. The operating agreement contained no provisions relating to dissolution of the LLC.*

Two managers were appointed; Crown Royal appointed King, and Ocean Suffolk appointed Van Houten to operate 1545. As work progressed, King and Van Houten argued over the project. King announced that Crown Royal wanted to pull out of 1545 and sued for work to stop and the LLC to be dissolved. The trial court granted those requests. Van Houten and Ocean Suffolk appealed.

Case Decision Austin, Judge

* * *

LLCL [Limited Liability Company Law] § 702 provides for judicial dissolution as follows:

On application by or for a member, the Supreme Court in the judicial district in which the office of the limited liability company is located may decree dissolution of a limited liability company *whenever it is not reasonably practicable to carry on the business in conformity with the articles of organization or operating agreement....*

LLCL 702 is clear that unlike the judicial dissolution standards in the Business Corporation Law and the Partnership Law, the court must first examine the limited liability company's operating agreement to determine, in light of the circumstances presented, whether it is or is not "reasonably practicable" for the limited liability company to continue to carry on its business in conformity with the operating agreement Thus, the dissolution of a limited liability company under LLCL 702 is initially a contract-based analysis. . . .

Here, a single manager's unilateral action in furtherance of the business of 1545 LLC is specifically contemplated and permitted. Article 4.1 of the 1545 LLC Operating Agreement states:

> At any time when there is more than one Manager, *any one manager may take any action permitted under the Agreement*, unless the approval of more than one of the Managers is expressly required pursuant to the Agreement or the Act.

This provision does not require that the managers conduct the business of 1545 LLC by majority vote. It empowers each manager to act autonomously and to unilaterally bind the entity in furtherance of the business of the entity. The 1545 LLC operating agreement, however, is silent as to the issue of manager conflicts. Thus, the only basis for dissolution can be if 1545 LLC cannot effectively operate under the operating agreement to meet and achieve the purpose for which it was created. In this case, that is the development of the property which purpose, despite the disagreements between the managing members, was being met. . . .

Upon a review of the evidence submitted, we conclude that the Supreme Court did not providently exercise its discretion in granting the petition for dissolution. Thus, the order of the Supreme Court should be reversed, the petition denied, and the proceeding dismissed.

Questions for Analysis

1. The unhappy member, King (Crown Royal), cannot get out of the LLC this way. What options exist?
2. What should the members have done differently when they set up 1545 LLC?

Key Organizational Features

Several factors influence the choice of business organization, including the potential liabilities imposed on the owners, the transferability of ownership interests, the ability of the business organization to continue in the event of the death or withdrawal of one or more of the owners, the capital requirements of the business, and the tax rate applicable to the business organization selected. Exhibit 12.3 summarizes the differences between the major forms of business discussed so far. The following subsections review some of these factors in more detail.

Limited Liability

Limited liability allows persons to invest in a business without placing their personal wealth at risk. Limited liability can also allow investors to be passive toward the internal management of the business.

Businesses incur debts by contract—for example, by borrowing money and buying supplies on credit—and they may incur liability arising from tort suits, such as for having sold asbestos in the past. Limited liability means that if the sums owed are so large that the organization must go into bankruptcy, the owners—the shareholders or members—could lose their investments but cannot be held personally liable. No creditor of the business can assert that the owners must draw on their personal assets to pay the

EXHIBIT 12.3 COMPARING CHARACTERISTICS OF MAJOR FORMS OF BUSINESS ORGANIZATION

	PROPRIETORSHIP	PARTNERSHIP	CORPORATION	LIMITED LIABILITY COMPANY
Method of Creation	Owner begins business operations	Created by agreement of parties; statutes may apply	Chartered under state statute	Created under statute by agreement of members
Entity Status	Not separate from owner	Separate from owners for some purposes	Legal entity distinct from owners	Separate from owners for some purposes
Liability of Owners	Owner personally liable for debts	Unlimited liability except for limited partner in a limited partnership	Shareholders liable only to the extent of paid-in capital	Members liable to the extent of paid-in capital
Duration	Same as owner	Ended by agreement or by death or withdrawal of a partner	May have perpetual existence	Company dissolves after fixed time or a specific event
Transferability of Ownership Interests	May be sold at any time; new proprietorship formed	Generally, sale of partnership interest terminates partnership	Shares of stock can be transferred unless restricted by contract	Other members must consent to transfers
Control	Determined by owner	Partners have equal control unless otherwise agreed; limited partners have no management rights	Shareholders elect board of directors who set policy and appoint officers to manage	Operating agreement specifies management control
Capital	Limited to what owner can raise or borrow	Limited to what partners contribute or can borrow	Sale of more shares increases capital; may also borrow	Limited to what members contribute; may also borrow
Taxation	Profits taxed to owner as individual	Profits taxed to each owner's share	Double taxation; profits of corporation and shareholders' shares of profits are both taxed	If IRS conditions are met, same as a partnership

debts of the limited liability organization. In the case of a general partnership or proprietorship, the owners can face unlimited personal liability.

Courts can however, "pierce the corporate veil" of limited liability organizations and hold the owners personally liable under some circumstances. That is, the court disregards the corporate entity by finding that the entity is a sham and that the owner(s) actually operate the business as a proprietorship or partnership. The court can then impose liability on shareholders in instances of fraud, undercapitalization, or failure to follow corporate formalities. As the *K.C. Roofing* case illustrates, the court pierces the veil so the corporate form of business organization may not be used simply to avoid obligations.

Transferability of Ownership Interests

The transferability of ownership interests refers to the ability of an owner in a business venture to sell or pass that interest to others. The ability of owners to transfer ownership interests differs among the various forms of business organizations.

K.C. ROOFING CENTER V. ON TOP ROOFING, INC.

Missouri Court of Appeals, Western District 807 S.W.2d 545 (1991)

Case Background *The Nugents owned a series of roofing companies. Russell Nugent Roofing, Inc., was incorporated in 1977. Russell and his wife Carol were the only shareholders, directors, and officers. The corporation's name was changed to On Top Roofing in 1985. In 1987, it ceased doing business, and the Nugents did business through a new corporation, RNR Inc., which ceased to exist in 1988 and was replaced by RLN Construction, Inc., which was replaced by Russell Nugent, Inc. in 1989.*

During that time, Nugent worked continuously. The businesses were run out of the Nugent's home. In 1986, they paid themselves salaries of more than $100,000 each and charged the corporation $99,290 in rent for space in their home.

K.C. Roofing was owed $45,000 for roofing supplies sold to On Top Roofing. As On Top Roofing no longer existed, K.C. asked the court to pierce the corporate veil and hold the Nugents personally liable. The district court held for K.C. The Nugents appealed.

Case Decision Kennedy, Judge

* * *

Courts will pierce the corporate veil or disregard the corporate entity once a plaintiff shows:

(1) Control, not mere majority or complete stock control, but complete domination, not only of finances, but of policy and business practice in respect to the transaction attacked so that the corporate entity as to this transaction had at the time no separate mind, will or existence of its own; and

(2) Such control must have been used by the defendant to commit fraud or wrong, to perpetrate the violation of a statutory or other positive legal duty, or dishonest and unjust act in contravention of plaintiff's legal rights; and

(3) The aforesaid control and breach of duty must proximately cause the injury or unjust loss complained of.

Where a corporation is used for an improper purpose and to perpetrate injustice by which it avoids its legal obligations, "equity will step in, pierce the corporate veil and grant appropriate relief."

There was substantial evidence to support the trial court's finding that the three-part test for piercing the corporate veil was satisfied in this case. Russell Nugent was clearly in control of On Top Roofing, Inc. He and his wife were the sole shareholders of the corporation and he was the president and chief operating officer and clearly made all the decisions.

There also was substantial evidence to support the second and third prongs of the test. A court may pierce the corporate veil or disregard the separate legal entity of the corporation and the individual where the separateness is used as a subterfuge to defraud a creditor. But actual fraud is not necessarily a predicate for piercing the corporate veil; it may also be pierced to prevent injustice or inequitable consequences. From the evidence it appears that Russell Nugent was operating an intricate corporate shell game in which he would cease doing business as one corporate entity when he was unable to pay the corporation's creditors and he then would form another corporation in place of the prior one in order to get a "fresh start." ...

Through his domination and control over On Top, Russell Nugent was using it for the unfair or inequitable purpose of avoiding their debts to plaintiffs. Nugent continued to hold On Top out to the public as though it was still operating after it supposedly went out of business, yet he refused to honor On Top's obligations to its creditors. The actions of Nugent worked at least an injustice if not to defraud the plaintiffs. It would be unfair, unjust or inequitable to allow Nugent to hide behind the corporate shield and avoid his legal obligations to plaintiffs. We hold that the trial court did not err in piercing the corporate veil and holding Russell Nugent personally liable for the debts owed plaintiffs. ...

Judgment Affirmed.

Questions for Analysis

1. When a court pierces the corporate veil, doesn't that defeat the purpose of limited liability?

2. Could K.C. Roofing have protected itself by filing a lien against On Top Roofing?

Nontraded Entities The proprietor of a sole proprietorship is, in essence, the business. A decision to sell the business ends the existing proprietorship and initiates the creation of a new one. Selling proprietorships, partnerships, and other small businesses can be expensive (relative to the value of the business) because such businesses can be hard to price. Often, specialists are required to help determine the market value of the business.

If a partner sells or assigns his interest in a partnership, the partnership can continue, but the new person does not automatically become a partner. The person is entitled to receive the share of profits the partner would have received, but she does not gain the right to participate in the management of partnership affairs without permission of other partners. This protects the existing partners. Because partners have such broad powers with respect to the operation of the business, the law does not want to make someone a partner with someone else unless there is mutual agreement.

ISSUE SPOTTER
Keeping Things in Order

You have a small company. Whether it is a corporation or a limited liability company, you know there is always a chance that, should something go wrong, you can be sued by a supplier, customer, employee, or someone else for some problem. What steps should you take to ensure that your company keeps limited liability status?

Duration

A business's duration refers to its ability to continue to operate in the event of the death, retirement, or other incapacity of an owner of the business. The ability of a business to continue under such circumstances can depend on the form of business organization.

A sole proprietorship terminates with the death or incapacity of the proprietor. Similarly, at common law, a partnership is dissolved by the death, retirement, or other incapacity of a partner, but it is not necessarily terminated. To avoid liquidation, partners usually agree in advance to a continuation agreement. The same is true of LLCs. Most problems arise from disputes among partners or members. What is their right to exit if they are unhappy and how are they compensated for their portion of the entity? If that is not spelled out in the agreement, the court looks to the default rules in state law.

Unless its articles of incorporation provide for a specified period of duration, a corporation has the potential of **perpetual existence**. The death or retirement of a shareholder does not bring about the termination of the corporation. In most corporations, the death of a shareholder has no impact on the operations of the business.

Lighter Side of the Law

I Own the World!

Gopalan filed suit in federal court against Microsoft, Google, Apple, McDonald's, Starbucks, Coca-Cola, and 50 other U.S. corporations, claiming he was the actual owner of all of them. What had not been understood previously, he claimed, was that he used the I Ching system to invent the companies when he was "15 or 16" years old. "These companies were I Chinged in through a metaphysical layer created and owned by me," he claimed. Despite the lack of formal documentation of company creation, Gopalan asked the court to confirm his rightful ownership.

Source: Justica.com.

Franchises

About a third of retail sales in the United States take place in franchise operations, so they are a major form of business enterprise. Nationwide, there are about one million franchised businesses. Before the 1950s, only automobile manufacturers, soft-drink companies, and oil companies used franchising to market and distribute their goods. Later, many of today's most recognized companies began franchising, including 7-Eleven, Hampton Inns, The Gap, Subway, and McDonald's.

Generally a **franchise** exists whenever a franchisee, in return for payment of a franchise fee, is granted the right to sell goods or services by a franchisor according to a marketing plan. The plan must be substantially associated with the franchisor's trademark or trade dress. As a rule, a franchisee operates as an independent business, usually as a corporation or LLC, subject to the standards specified by the franchisor.

Successful franchises have two characteristics in common: a trademark that conveys authenticity and exclusivity, and a uniform product or service. For example, as consumers travel throughout the country, they recognize the Burger King name and expect the product to taste the same in California as it does in South Carolina. The franchisee benefits from the expertise and marketing of the franchisor. The franchisor benefits because the franchisee usually provides capital to fund the individual franchise location and works harder as the owner of the franchise than he would if he were only an employee of the parent company.

Types of Franchises

Franchises may be separated into three basic categories: (1) product distributorships, such as a car dealership, in which the franchisee has the right to sell the product of the parent company; (2) trademark or trade-name licensing, in which the franchisee has a license to market the company's brands, such as Coca-Cola; and (3) business format franchising, in which the franchisee follows the business model set out by the parent company, such as McDonald's, which also lends its trademark.

In business format franchising, the franchisor provides the franchisee with everything needed to begin the business, including how the franchisee operates the business according to set procedures.

The Law of Franchising

Federal and state laws are intended to protect investors from crooked or unethical operators. Franchise scams have defrauded investors of hundreds of millions of dollars. In response, federal and some state regulations require franchisors to register the franchise and to disclose relevant information necessary for franchisees to make informed investment decisions.

The FTC Franchise Rule Federal statutory protection is based on the Federal Trade Commission's Franchise Rule, which requires the franchisor to give prospective franchisees an offering circular—a detailed disclosure document—at least ten days before any money changes hands, or before a franchisee commits to a purchase. The Franchise Rule's disclosure document must provide the following information:

- Names, addresses, and telephone numbers of other franchisees
- An audited financial statement of the franchisor and its financial history
- The background and experience of the business's key executives
- The responsibilities that the franchisor and the franchisee will have to each other once the contract is signed
- The number of franchisees and how many have gone out of business

This document enables prospective investors to learn about the business. If the information provided is not true, it affords a legal basis for the FTC to bring an action against the franchisor. The investor would likely bring a cause of action for fraud or breach of contract against the franchise promoters. Most FTC actions against franchise operations are similar to this case summary from the FTC:

FTC v. Wealth Systems, Inc., CV 05-0394 PHX-JAT (D. Ariz. 2005) The Commission's complaint alleges that Wealth Systems ... violated Section 5 of the FTC Act in selling a home-based Internet business opportunity by misrepresenting that purchasers will earn substantial income. In addition, the complaint alleges that the defendants violated the Franchise Rule by: (1) failing to provide potential purchasers with a complete basic disclosure document; (2) failing to provide potential purchasers with an earnings claims document substantiating their earnings claims; and (3) making earnings claims in the general media without complying with the Franchise Rule's general media claims requirements, including disclosing the number and percentage of prior purchasers known by the defendants to have achieved the same or better results.

Such actions usually result in the promoted activity being closed down. There is rarely compensation for those who bought into franchises, as the operators usually burn through the cash they receive.

State Regulation California was the first state to regulate franchises. It requires franchisors to register with the state and to provide prospective franchisees with a prospectus disclosure document before selling any franchises. A dozen states have enacted similar laws. Many other states have business opportunity disclosure filing requirements. The information requirements imposed by the states differ from the FTC Franchise Rule. Most states use the Uniform Franchise Offering Circular (UFOC) written by the North American Securities Administrators Association as the basis for reporting. Those selling franchises must also pay a fee to franchise promotion in some states.

Most states have agencies, usually in the state attorney general's office, that have the authority to investigate franchise fraud among other bad business practices. If regulators suspect fraud, they can institute a civil lawsuit seeking damages, injunctions, and fines. Some franchisees are given extra protection by special state laws. Auto dealers and gas stations, for example, often have extra rights beyond those of most franchise owners.

The Franchise Agreement

The **franchise agreement** sets forth the rights and obligations of the franchisor and franchisee. Key elements that might be included in a business format franchise are shown

---

ISSUE SPOTTER
The Road to Riches?

You are offered a chance to have your own business: a franchise that would be the only one formed in your city for a new business that would deliver auto parts to auto repair shops in the city. The franchise promoter tells you great stories about the operation in other cities. For only $25,000 you can be your own boss and live well. This is not an uncommon situation. Facing this wonderful opportunity, what sorts of questions do you ask? Is the information provided via the FTC offering requirements a guarantee of security?

© Cengage Learning

in Exhibit 12.4. They include, among other things, the rights and limits associated with the use of the franchise trademarks or trade names, the use of the franchise operating manual, the location and designated territory of operation, fee and royalty payments, the advertising commitment, and termination procedures.

Some franchises, such as McDonald's, exercise tight control over their franchisees through the franchise agreement. Others, such as Dairy Queen, have fewer controls. This is why Dairy Queen restaurants in different locations vary more in menu, style, and layout than do McDonald's.

EXHIBIT 12.4   THE FRANCHISE AGREEMENT BETWEEN FRANCHISOR AND FRANCHISEE

Franchisee's Duties and Responsibilities

Grants franchisee the right to:

- Operate a franchiseed unit
- Use all of the franchisor's know-how related to the product
- Use trademarks or trade dress of the franchise
- Use franchise for a fixed period of time, perhaps with options for renewal

Furnishes franchisee with:

- Manual setting forth the franchise's operating procedures, including employee training
- Specifications regarding the building, accounting, advertising, and other procedures
- Training for how franchisee is to operate the business
- Company image

May provide franchisee with:

- Territorial exclusivity
- Source of product supply
- A regional or national advertising program
- Quality control inspections
- Group purchasing power

Promises to the franchisor to:

- Pay an initial franchise fee
- Pay a continuing royalty fee
- Pay an advertising fund contribution (1-4 percent of sales)
- Conduct the business according to the franchisor's standards
- Take the franchisor's training program
- Keep franchise information confidential
- Prepare franchise's books and records as franchisor requires
- Purchase certain products from franchisor
- Comply with employee hiring and training requirements

May promise the franchisor to:

- Build a facility to franchisor specifications
- Sell only the products of the franchisor
- Pay for national advertising
- Purchase supplies only from approved suppliers
- Exercise personal supervision of franchise operations
- Maintain facilities according to franchisor's requirements
- Maintain specified hours of operation
- Consent to periodic inspections

Trade Name and Procedure The agreement grants the franchisee the right to use the franchisor's name and identifying trademarks and trade dress. The franchisee normally must undergo training and is given the use of the franchisor's confidential operating manual. The franchisor may specify requirements regarding record keeping, advertising, hours of operation, hiring and training practices, and other details.

Territorial Rights The agreement may impose limits on the territorial rights of the franchisee and the franchisor. For example, the franchisor may not be allowed to operate additional outlets in the territory, unless the franchisee does not live up to certain performance standards. The franchisee may be limited to operating only one unit within the territory.

The agreement also states which party has the responsibility to select the site and to construct the facility. Major issues in many franchise contracts is whether the franchisor can open new stores in the area, whether the franchisee gets the first chance to buy any new units in the area, and how close new stores can be to existing ones.

Franchise Fees and Royalties Naturally, the initial franchise fee or up-front payment is specified. Once the business is operating, the franchisor may require a continuing royalty—generally a percentage of annual sales. The franchisor may also require payments for advertising. The advertising fees depend on whether the franchisor does local or national advertising on behalf of its franchises. To protect the trade name, most franchise agreements prohibit franchisees from engaging in any advertising or promotional programs not approved by the franchisor.

Although there are many federal and state regulations, most cases of conflict between franchisors and franchisees involve litigation over violations of the terms of the agreement. We see an example in the *Dunkin' Donuts* case, which also notes many common terms in franchise agreements.

DUNKIN' DONUTS FRANCHISED RESTAURANTS LLC V. SANDIP, INC.

United States District Court, Northern District of Georgia
712 F.Supp.2d 1325 (2010)

Case Background *Three individuals owned Sandip, Inc. which was a Dunkin' Donuts franchisee operating two donut shops in Norcorss, Georgia. "Dunkin' Donuts alleges that the defendants breached their franchise agreements by failing to remodel their shops, participate in mandatory system-wide programs, attend required training, and prepare immigration forms for new employees. Dunkin' Donuts also alleges that the defendants transferred a significant portion of the franchise without Dunkin' Donut's knowledge in violation of the franchise agreement." Sandip did not dispute these claims but protested that Dunkin' Donuts was not allowing the owners a reasonable chance to sell the franchise.*

Dunkin' Donuts entered into a settlement agreement to allow Sandip to try to find buyers for their shops. Sandip submitted a proposed sale agreement, but Dunkin' Donuts refused to accept the proposed buyer. Dunkin' Donuts moved for a court order for Sandip to turn over physical possession of the shops to Dunkin' Donuts. Sandip counterclaimed that Dunkin' Donuts rejected a reasonable proposal from a buyer to take over the shops.

Case Decision Thrash, District Judge

* * *

The 2008 settlement agreement provides that Dunkin' Donuts may not "unreasonably" reject a proposed sale agreement. The Defendants identify…ways in which they say Dunkin' Donuts acted unreasonably. First, they say Dunkin' Donuts did not consider the buyer's financial condition before rejecting the proposed sale agreement. However, Dunkin' Donuts offers a reasonable explanation for its actions. To determine whether to approve a sale, Dunkin' Donuts utilizes a two-step analysis. The first step is to evaluate whether the store is likely to "break even" the following year. During this step, Dunkin' Donuts considers the projected profits and liabilities of the store. If it appears the store will lose money, Dunkin' Donuts rejects the proposed sale agreement. If it appears the store will break even, Dunkin' Donuts moves to the second step. There, Dunkin' Donuts investigates the financial condition of the buyer to determine whether it is financially able to purchase and operate the store.

Here, Dunkin' Donut's analysis showed that the stores at issue would not break even. Therefore, Dunkin' Donuts did not complete the second step of the analysis. The Defendants may disagree with the sequence of Dunkin' Donut's analysis, but its decisions were made pursuant to a firmly established policy that is grounded in reasonable business considerations. Therefore, Dunkin' Donuts did not act unreasonably by failing to investigate the buyer's financial condition.

* * *

Dunkin' Donuts is entitled to terminate the franchise agreements pursuant to the termination clauses.

The lease agreements provide that Dunkin' Donuts may terminate the lease if the franchise agreement for the corresponding shop is terminated for any reason. ... Therefore, Dunkin' Donuts is also entitled to terminate the lease agreements.

The franchise agreements require the Defendants to stop using Dunkin' Donuts' proprietary marks and any methods associated with the Dunkin' Donuts system upon termination. Dunkin' Donuts says the Defendants have not done so and asks the Court for a permanent injunction ordering the Defendants to stop using its marks. Because the Court finds that Dunkin' Donuts is entitled to terminate the franchise agreements, Dunkin' Donuts is also entitled to summary judgment on its trademark claims. ...

The Plaintiff's Motion for Summary Judgment is granted.

Questions for Analysis

1. If Sandip had a willing buyer with sufficient cash to finance the operation, why would Dunkin' Donuts reject the buyer?
2. Aren't the terms of the franchise agreement favorable to Dunkin' Donuts?

Termination Franchise agreements are usually explicit about events that bring about the franchise's termination. Some have a fixed expiration time, such as 20 years. Typical provisions give the franchisor the right to terminate upon the occurrence of events, ranging from the bankruptcy of a franchisee to the failure of a franchisee to submit to inspection by the franchisor. Notice of termination must be given to the franchisee. In some states, franchisors must give the franchisees reasonable time to correct problems. In addition, several states have laws that restrict a franchisor's ability to terminate a franchise unless there is good cause. Upon termination, the franchisee loses the right to the franchisor's trade name.

CYBER LAW

Franchise Information on the Internet

Gathering information about many franchise opportunities is difficult. As in many other areas, the Internet provides some useful sources. Blue MauMau collects many stories about franchise operations and has contributions from experts.

Similarly, Franchise Chat gives updates about franchise businesses in the Unites States, Canada, Australia, and other nations. As in any area, horror stories can abound. In the area of franchises, Unhappy Franchisee provides many sad tales. The web can be a great source, but as with many franchise operations, be cautious.

? TEST YOURSELF

1. In the case *In re 1545 Ocean Avenue*, where the members in an LLC argued about how to run the business, the appeals court held that:
   a. the party who was unhappy with the business arrangement should be paid the fair market value of membership.
   b. the buy-sell agreement would be executed and either member could offer a price that the other party could accept or force the other to take.
   c. one member breached his fiduciary obligation to the others by engaging in fraud.
   d. there was no reason to terminate the LLC; it would continue to function.
2. The Federal Trade Commission regulation that guides disclosure when franchise offerings are made is called the _____.
3. In *Dunkin' Donuts* v. *Sandip, Inc.*, the court held that the parent company abused the rights of the franchisee by demanding unrealistic sales levels: T—F
4. Investors in a Limited Liability Company (LLC) are called _____.
5. If the owner of a corporation abuses the purpose of the corporation so as to avoid payments due to creditors, it is possible that the court will _____ of the corporation.
6. LLCs ordinarily, by law, have limited life: T—F

Answers: d; franchise rule; F; members; pierce the veil; T.

SUMMARY

- The most prominent forms of business organization are the sole proprietorship, partnership, limited partnership, corporation, and limited liability company.
- Sole proprietorships automatically come into existence whenever people begin to do business for themselves. Legally, the sole proprietor is the business, responsible for business's debts and torts, liable for its taxes, and in control of its operation and its transfer.
- General partnerships are composed of two or more people, general partners, who agree to carry on a business for profit. Partnerships may be structured in almost any way desired by the partners. When an agreement does not specify what happens in some instance, such as death of a partner, the law of partnership, codified in the Uniform Partnership Act, determines the result. In general, partners share in the managerial control, debts, tort liability, and profits of the business. They are taxed personally on partnership profits.
- Limited partnerships are governed by state law. They must have at least one general partner. The limited partners are investors who may not share

in managerial control of the business. Their liability is limited to the amount they invest, unless they try to exercise managerial control and become general partners, who are fully liable.
- Corporations are created under state law and are recognized as legal entities. They have their own legal life, which is potentially perpetual. They are responsible for their own debts and tort liabilities. Shareholders, as investors in corporations, are liable only to the amount they invest in the corporation.
- Shareholders vote to elect the board of directors and must vote on major issues such as selling the corporation. The board of directors is the principal of a corporation. It has responsibility for determining how the company is to be operated and for hiring and instructing the management. Managers are agents of the board and respond to the board's instructions.
- A limited liability company (LLC) provides limited liability for its members (investors) and is taxed as a partnership. Members are thus taxed on the income, rather than being subject to the double taxation of a corporation and its shareholders.

An LLC must restrict the transfer of member interests and is intended to operate for a fixed or definite time period, rather than have perpetual life.

- In addition to tax considerations, the other key factor in the choice of business form is limited liability, which investors in corporations, limited partnerships, and limited liability companies have, but proprietors and general partners do not have. Transfer of ownership interests is easiest in corporations with publicly traded stock. In other organizations, the value of interests is often not known, and often restrictions are placed on transfers. A corporation may have perpetual existence

as a legal entity. In practice, other organizations can exist for a long time under contracts that control what happens in case of death or retirement of an investor or partner.

- A franchise exists when a franchisee pays a fee and is granted the right to sell a franchisor's goods or services. Marketing is associated with the franchisor's trade name or trademark. The relationship is defined by a franchise agreement that sets forth the rights and duties associated with the use of the franchise marks or names, the use of the franchise operating manual, designated territory of operation, royalty payments, advertising commitment, and termination.

TERMS TO KNOW

sole proprietorship, 309
partnership, 309
general partner, 309
fiduciary duty, 311
dissolution, 312
winding up, 312
limited partnership, 313
limited partner, 313
corporation, 315
corporate charter, 315
certificate of incorporation, 315
bylaws, 315

legal entity, 316
shareholder, 317
quorum, 317
proxy, 317
board of directors, 317
duty, 318
principal, 318
business judgment rule, 318
fiduciary duty of loyalty, 318
managers, 320
close corporation, 320
S corporation, 320

professional corporation, 320
benefit corporation, 321
double taxation, 322
limited liability, 322
limited liability company, 322
articles of organization, 322
members, 323
membership interest, 323
operating agreement, 324
perpetual existence, 328
franchise, 329
franchise agreement, 330

DISCUSSION QUESTION

Four people jointly own a summer cottage and use it solely for their personal enjoyment. Is this a partnership? What if they rent the cottage to other people for part of the year? Suppose a renter dies in the cottage as a result of a gas leak. Could all owners be liable?

CASE QUESTIONS

1. Dr. Citrin had an agreement with Dr. Mehta for Mehta to work in Citrin's medical offices to see his patients when he was on vacation. While Citrin was on vacation, Mehta saw a patient and misdiagnosed the problem; the patient died. The heirs of the patient sued Citrin, claiming that Citrin and Mehta were partners. Were they? [*Impastato* v. *DeGirolamo*, 459 N.Y.S. 2d 512, N.Y. Sup. Ct. (1983)]

2. Covalt owned 25 percent and High owned 75 percent of CSI, a corporation that they operated together. They also entered into a

partnership to build an office building that they leased to CSI. Covalt resigned from CSI and went to work for a competitor. When the lease on the office building expired, Covalt demanded that High raise CSI's rent in a new lease, from $1,850 to $2,850 per month. High signed CSI to a new lease in the building at the old rent. Covalt sued High for breach of fiduciary duty to the partnership. Who was right? [*Covalt* v. *High*, 675 P.2d 999, Ct. App., NM (1983)]

✓ Check your answer

3. Former employees of the Castaways Hotel in Las Vegas sued to recover unpaid wages they lost when the hotel went bankrupt. They sued several high-level mangers who were also the owners of Castaways, which was incorporated as an LLC. The former employees contend that the managers were liable for their wages. Would the managers have legal liability for unpaid wages of employees? [*Bouchers* v. *Shaw*, 196 P.3d 959, Sup. Ct., Nev. (2008)]

4. When Dr. Witlin died, his wife inherited his 2.65 percent share of a partnership that owned a hospital. As the partnership agreement required, Witlin's share was paid. The amount paid was based on the finances at the time of payment. The partners did not reveal that they were in the process of selling the hospital, which soon happened, and more than tripled the value of the partners' shares. Was Mrs. Witlin due the sale price of the hospital or its value based on finances at the time of her husband's death? [*Estate of Witlin*, 83 Cal.App.3d 167, Ct. App., Calif. (1978)]
   ✓ Check your answer

5. A general partnership law firm signed a ten-year lease for office property with Sheehan, a partner in the law firm. Sheehan withdrew from the law firm and assigned his partnership interest to the remaining partners. Five years later, the law firm defaulted on the lease and filed for bankruptcy. Sheehan sued all past and present law firm partners for past due rent. The trial court held that the personal assets of the original partners who signed the lease were not at stake, nor were assets of current partners, only the assets of the bankrupt partnership were available. Is that correct? [*8182 Maryland Assoc. L.P.* v. *Sheehan*, 14 S.W.3d 576, Sup. Ct., Mo. (2000)]

6. The Haffs were sole shareholders of a business that often bought supplies from Cosgrove. When Haff ceased operations, it owed Cosgrove $9,000. Cosgrove sued the Haffs personally for the amount owed, contending that the corporate veil should be pierced. The two companies had done business for ten years. Cosgrove testified that it did not know what legal form Haff had. The phone was answered "J. Haff." The invoices sent from Cosgrove were made out to "J. A. Haff and Sons, Inc." Checks came from "J. A. Haff and Sons." Haff followed proper corporate procedures for annual meetings and separate accounts. Was the veil to be pierced? [*Cosgrove Distributors* v. *Haff*, 798 N.E.2d 139, App. Ct., Ill. (2003)]
   ✓ Check your answer

7. Four surgeons conducted their medical practices through an LLC they owned. The LLC obtained a $1.5 million loan from Emprise Bank. It was secured by personal guarantees of the four doctors, each for $200,000, plus an additional joint $375,000. Two doctors then moved away. When the LLC failed to pay, Emprise moved to enforce the personal guarantees by the two remaining doctors and won a judgment. Those two doctors contended that they had the right to sue the doctors who left as they injured the LLC. Are all four doctors liable? [*Emprise Bank* v. *Rumisek*, 215 P.3d 621, Ct. App., Kan. (2009)]

8. Domino's Pizza sold two franchises to experienced Domino's managers. The agreement stated that the franchisees agreed to "operate the Store in full compliance with all applicable laws, ordinances, and regulations." If not, Domino's had the right to terminate if problems were not corrected within 30 days. Later, the franchisees' books were a mess, reports were not filed on time, and they failed to pay city, state, or federal taxes. After six months of failure to correct the problems, Domino's gave 30 days' termination notice. The franchisees put the stores up for sale. When prospective buyers asked Domino's about the history of the stores, Domino's told the truth, which led to the sale price falling below what would have been offered if Domino's had not said anything and let the franchisees sell on their own. The franchisees sued Domino's; a jury awarded the franchisees over $2 million damages. Did this decision stand? [*Bennett Enterprises* v. *Domino's Pizza*, 45 F.3d 493, D.C. Cir. (1995)]

9. Several investors, organized through corporations, owned several Burger King restaurants in Wisconsin. The franchise agreement stated that franchise owners could not own competitor franchises. The investors formed other corporations and obtained Hardee's franchises. Burger King terminated its franchise agreements with the owners for violating the franchise agreements. The owners argued that because the Burger King and Hardee's franchises were owned by different corporations, the agreement had not been breached. Is that correct? [*Deutchland Enterprises* v. *Burger King*, 957 F.2d 449, 7th Cir. (1992)]

ETHICS QUESTION

Cook and Smith formed a limited partnership, called Trinty Development, to develop a shopping center. Adjacent to the shopping center was a ten-acre tract of undeveloped land that came up for sale after the limited partnership had begun its operations. Cook, the general partner, purchased the property from McCade, but only after McCade had refused to sell the property to Trinty. McCade stated that he did not want to do business with Smith. Cook then sold the property to another developer for a $60,000 profit. If Cook had sold the property to Trinty, Trinty could have profited. Smith objected to the purchase and sale by Cook. What alternatives did Cook have? With regard to his employment with Trinty, what was the ethical choice? How was Trinty damaged? With regard to Cook's relationship with McCade, what were Cook's alternatives?

CHAPTER **13**

Negotiable Instruments, Credit, and Bankruptcy

Most students know about student loans. Credit has never been as extensive as it is now. What's a little more debt? Some students have used student loans to finance spring break trips and other fun things. After all, when you graduate, the income will roll in to cover all that. And, if worse comes to worst, you can just file for bankruptcy! Unfortunately, bankruptcy does not get rid of your federal student loans—they are generally non-dischargeable debts, meaning they must be repaid.

Credit and its opposite—debt—are contractual relationships. Many credit contracts are common-law contracts, but some fall under the UCC and may be affected by federal or state regulations. Debt is usually incurred to purchase real property, such as an office building. Most companies rely on debt to get operations going or to expand. When in business, most firms extend credit to their customers. Sometimes the promises to pay are negotiable instruments that can be traded, as is true of most mortgages on property.

The downside of credit expansion is that each year more than one million individuals and many businesses file for bankruptcy. These are debtors whose financial problems overwhelm them. Their creditors, i.e., other individuals and businesses, share the pain by being forced to absorb more than $20 billion a year in unpaid debt.

Just as managing personal finance is important, controlling the cost of carrying debt and minimizing losses from bad credit are critical. Most businesses operate on thin profit margins, so decisions about borrowing and issuing credit can determine survival. This chapter considers the legal aspects of debt obligations and the financial instruments often used as proof of credit that has been granted; it ends with a look at the major parts of the bankruptcy code.

Negotiable Instruments

Like much law in the United States, the law of negotiable instruments has its origins in England. Five hundred years ago, the right to payment was a contract right that could not be sold to another. This inhibited trade because of the difficulty it created for merchants who worked on credit. Traders had to wait until the buyer paid them before they had the cash to acquire more goods to sell.

To resolve this problem, laws developed that allowed traders to assign a promise to pay to a third party. Typically, a merchant would sell to a third party, at a discount, his right to payment from his buyer. The trader could then buy more goods without waiting for the debtor to pay. The third party made her profit by collecting the amount owed from the debtor.

The law came to recognize assignments of promises to pay, and contractual promises to pay became tradable. Negotiable instruments became something that could be bought and sold. The law of negotiable instruments became responsive to the needs of business, and is now a part of the commercial law through Article 3 of the UCC.

The Functions of Negotiable Instruments

A **negotiable instrument** is a written promise or order to pay a certain sum of money. It functions as a substitute for cash. Few businesses today require cash in payment for all purchases. Because the law recognizes their validity, negotiable instruments such as checks are accepted as a substitute for cash for payment of goods and services. Negotiable instruments also provide a way for credit to be extended to debtors.

The Concept of Negotiability

Negotiable instruments are flexible in how they are used in business. Once issued, a negotiable instrument can be transferred to another party. If the instrument is assigned, the assignee has the same contract rights and responsibilities as the assignor. If the instrument is transferred by **negotiation**, the transferee takes the instrument free of any of the transferor's contract obligations. This way, the transferee may have more rights than the transferor.

If an instrument is made "to **bearer**," the party in possession is required only to deliver the instrument to transfer it. **Bearer instruments** can be created in different ways. For example, the maker (drawer) may create a bearer instrument by stating, "to bearer," "to the order of bearer," "payable to bearer," "to cash," or "pay to the order of cash."

Bearer instruments are risky because mere delivery creates a negotiation or transfer. Suppose a buyer of a car pays the seller with a check made out "to the order of cash." The seller loses the check. The check is found by Fallon, who uses it to buy goods from Leno Appliances. The check has been negotiated because delivery is sufficient for the transfer of a bearer instrument. Governments disfavor bearer instruments because it is difficult to trace money that has been transferred in bearer form.

Requirements for Negotiable Instruments

To be negotiable, a commercial instrument must meet the requirements of a negotiable instrument as provided by the UCC. Although commercial paper may be either negotiable or nonnegotiable, only negotiable instruments fall under the UCC. If the instrument is nonnegotiable, the common law of contracts applies. If a commercial instrument is negotiable, the UCC governs the resolution of the dispute.

The UCC Requirements According to UCC § 3-104, to be negotiable, an instrument must meet certain requirements. It must

1. be written;
2. be an unconditional order or promise to pay;
3. be signed by the maker or drawer;
4. be payable on demand or at a specified time;
5. be made out "to order" or "to bearer;" and
6. state a certain sum of money.

The UCC requires commercial instruments to be in writing for practical reasons. Oral promises would be nearly impossible to transfer to third parties and be very hard to prove. Under UCC § 3-105, the writing must be signed and unconditional, so the terms of payment are easily determined and not subject to the occurrence of another event or agreement. It must contain a clear statement of an order or promise to pay.

UCC § 3-106 requires that it state a specific sum of money. If the instrument stated that payment was to be made in goods, for example, it would be too difficult for third parties to determine its market value. The UCC also requires that it be payable on demand or at a definite time. It must be clear when payment is to be made and received.

Finally, the instrument must be "payable to order" (called **order paper** under UCC § 3-110), or "to bearer" (called **bearer paper** under UCC § 3-111), to ensure that it is freely transferable. With this language, or its equivalent, the parties acknowledge that a third party, who currently may be unknown, could become the owner of the instrument.

A negotiable instrument may be transferred in either of two ways according to UCC § 3-202(1). If the instrument is made "to the order" of the payee, the payee must (1) endorse and (2) deliver the instrument to a third party. Endorsement without delivery cannot bring about a transfer. Therefore, if a check is made "to the order of Johnny Depp," and Depp endorses the check but keeps it, there has not been a transfer.

INTERNATIONAL PERSPECTIVE

Mixing Religion and Finance

Laws limiting high interest rates (usury) in the United States can be traced to Christian views that the practice is sinful. Even more stringent are Islamic limits on interest.

Islamic countries have hundreds of billions of dollars in wealth, but some Islamic countries prohibit banking as we know it, which include charging interest on loans and paying interest to depositors. Many Muslims hold those activities to be banned (*haram*) by the Koran. Malaysian banks have been leaders in developing financial instruments that bring modern finance in line with Islamic rules.

In Malaysia and other Islamic countries, banks consult with advisers on Islamic law (*Shariah*) about what form of loans and repayments are acceptable. The result is that modern financial instruments are much more widely available than before, but the presentation is different from that of traditional financial institutions.

In conventional finance, a company may borrow $100 million from a bank for expansion and pay six percent interest ($6 million) per year on a 10-year note and then repay the principal. Under rules permitted (*halal*) by some Muslims, the borrowing company transfers assets, such as buildings, to a legal entity something like a trust (*ijara sukuk*). The company leases the assets back for payments of $6 million per year. The borrower also pledges to buy back the assets at the end of 10 years for $100 million. Not all Muslims agree that this procedure is acceptable, but banks using such instruments have exploded in growth.

Requirements for Holders in Due Course If an instrument is negotiable under the UCC, it may be freely traded in the market without concern for whether the parties earlier in the transaction have performed their other contract responsibilities—if the instrument is in the possession of a **holder in due course**. The person in possession of a negotiable instrument may be a holder in due course or an ordinary holder. An ordinary holder has the same contract responsibilities as an assignee under a nonnegotiable instrument. UCC § 3-302 states that to be a holder in due course, the transferee must:

1. give value for the negotiable instrument;
2. take the instrument without knowledge that it is overdue or defective; and
3. take the instrument in good faith.

Thus, a transferee may be an ordinary holder who transforms her position to that of a holder in due course by meeting these three requirements of the UCC. The drawer or maker is obligated to pay the instrument once it is in the possession of a holder in due course.

Suppose Pam agrees to buy the rights to a J-Right Car Wash franchise from Tammy. Pam signs the contract and gives Tammy $50,000 by cashier's check. Later, Pam learns that Tammy's business is going bankrupt. Pam tries to stop payment on the check. However, Tammy already transferred the check to a third party, Andy, who meets the UCC's requirements for a holder in due course. Tammy declares bankruptcy and J-Right is worthless. The bank pays Andy upon presentation of the check. The third party, Andy, is a holder in due course and, despite the fact that Tammy defrauded Pam, Andy has no legal obligation to repay Pam. This is why the business community has confidence in negotiable instruments as a substitute for cash.

Major Types of Negotiable Instruments

UCC § 3-104 identifies four negotiable instruments: drafts, checks, notes, and certificates of deposit. As Exhibit 13.1 shows, these instruments can be separated into two categories: orders to pay and promises to pay. Orders to pay, which include drafts and checks, are three-party instruments used instead of cash and as credit devices. Promises to pay, which include notes and certificates of deposit, are two-party instruments used as credit devices.

There is some common terminology for these instruments. The **drawer** issues or creates the document that requests payment, probably from a bank, but it could be from another party. The **drawee** agrees to make the payment, such as the bank making a payment based on a document presented to it. The drawee owes money to the drawer, such as the bank owing you the money you deposited in your account, and it will follow the wishes of the drawer of pay a third party. The party to receive payment is the **payee** or beneficiary who will be paid by the drawee.

For example, you import a load of furniture from Thailand, so you must pay for it. You are the drawer because you need to draw on money you have available, perhaps at a bank. You instruct the bank—the drawee—to make payment to the Thai company that

EXHIBIT 13.1 MAJOR FORMS OF NEGOTIABLE INSTRUMENTS

ORDERS TO PAY		PROMISES TO PAY	
Drafts 3 parties: drawer, drawee, and payee	**Checks** 3 parties: drawer, drawee, and payee	**Notes** 2 parties: maker and payee	**Certificates of Deposit** 2 parties: maker and payee

© Cengage learning

sent you the furniture, which is the payee or beneficiary. Not all transactions are that simple, so various instruments are used in business to make payments. We start with the most familiar one.

Orders to Pay: Checks According to UCC § 3-104(2), a **check** is a "draft drawn on a bank and payable on demand." The check is the most commonly used form of draft. However, unlike a draft—which may be payable at a later date and may have a bank, an individual, or a corporation as a drawee—a check must be paid on demand and must have a bank as its drawee.

Checks were once the major way for consumers to make purchases, but they pose risks for businesses because the consumer may not have sufficient funds in his account to enable the bank to pay the merchant when the merchant presents the check to the bank. Credit and debit cards have largely replaced checks in consumer transactions because they greatly reduce that problem.

Cashier's Check A **cashier's check** is one form of check in which the bank is both the drawer and the drawee. The customer gives money to the bank and designates a payee. The bank then writes a check on itself as drawee, with the check payable on demand to that payee. Cashier's checks are frequently used in transactions where the seller demands guaranteed payment.

An example is the purchase of real estate, where the owner/seller of the property requires that a guarantee of payment occur at the time title to the property is to pass to the buyer. To meet this requirement, a buyer gives the seller a cashier's check. Because the check is drawn by the bank ordering itself to pay money it has already collected from the buyer, the seller can be certain that the bank will honor the check when it is presented.

What happens if someone forges the signature on company checks? The court considers this in the *Associated Home and RV Sales* case, which discusses how the UCC allocates responsibility to try to reduce fraud.

ASSOCIATED HOME AND RV SALES, INC. V. BANK OF BELEN

Court of Appeals of New Mexico 294 P.3d 1276 (2012)

Case Background *Plaintiff sells recreational vehicles under the trade name Enchantment. It hired Ramos to assist with bookkeeping. In the next 20 months, Ramos forged 211 checks payable to herself or to cash, thereby stealing $283,547 from Enchantment before managers discovered the forgeries and notified the bank.*

The bank refused to cover the losses, noting that it sent monthly statements, including photocopies of canceled checks. Enchantment sued the Bank of Belen for common law fraud and negligence and for negligence under the UCC.

The trial court granted summary judgment to the bank. Enchantment appealed.

Case Decision Castillo, Chief Judge

* * *

The UCC states that "unless displaced by the particular provisions of the UCC, the principles of law and equity, including the law merchant and the law relative to capacity to contract, principal and agent, estoppel, fraud, misrepresentation, duress, coercion, mistake, bankruptcy and other validating or invalidating cause, supplement its provisions." [UCC 1-103] ... Common law principles are not preserved "in an area which is thoroughly covered by the UCC simply because they are not expressly excluded."

Article 4 of the UCC sets up a liability scheme and set of defenses to guide the relationship between a payor bank and its customers. A forged or altered check is not properly payable, and a bank is strictly liable for the resulting loss to a customer.

[UCC 4-406], however, sets up a scale of liabilities that shift depending on the actions of the parties, and a bank may seek "safe harbor" from the above strict liability scheme if it makes statements of account available to the customer on a regular basis. If a bank regularly provides a statement of account with information sufficient for the customer to identify the forgery, the customer must be reasonably prompt in notifying the bank of any forgeries; if the customer does so within thirty days of receiving the statement, the bank remains strictly liable for the loss. After that thirty-day period, however, the bank is liable only if the customer proves that the bank failed to exercise ordinary care in passing the forged item and that the bank's failure substantially contributed to the loss; in such a case, the loss is apportioned between the customer and the bank based on comparative negligence. Regardless of any lack of ordinary care on the part of the bank, if a year or more has passed from the customer's receipt of the statement identifying the forgery, the customer is precluded from bringing any claim under the UCC and must bear the entire loss....

In the case before us, we conclude that [UCC 4-406] adequately provides a scheme of liability and defenses and thus precludes common law claims brought by Enchantment....

We conclude that Enchantment was entitled to try to prove a lack of ordinary care by Bank for the forgeries that occurred within one year of Enchantment alerting Bank of the forgeries....

Enchantment contends that rather than mail monthly statements to Enchantment at its place of business, Bank provided the statements directly to [Ramos] who was committing the forgeries. Enchantment seems to be arguing that delivery to

an employee is not sufficient under the statute. We disagree. Delivery of statements to the customer does not require the mailing of statements but merely that the bank make them available "in a reasonable manner," such as allowing them to be picked up by an employee of the customer.... Bank made a *prima facie* case that it adequately provided monthly statements to Enchantment....

Enchantment's other evidence of negligence stems from an affidavit by its CEO alleging that (1) Bank promised not to accept checks made out to cash unless an officer presented the check; (2) signatures on the checks differed from those on signature cards kept on file by Bank; and (3) check amounts exceeded teller limits but were cashed without supervisor approval that had been promised by Bank....

The customer bears the burden of showing that a bank failed to exercise ordinary care and that issue is generally one for the factfinder to decide....

Enchantment, the party opposing summary judgment, brought forth some evidence of a lack of ordinary care on the part of Bank.... The CEO's allegations sufficiently raise a genuine issue of material fact such that, if proved, the jury might find that Bank breached a duty of ordinary care.... In sum, Enchantment did the bare minimum necessary to oppose the motion for summary judgment and raised genuine issues of material fact sufficient to survive Bank's motion, and it was error for the district court to grant the motion for summary judgment....

We reverse the motion for summary judgment in favor of Bank.

Questions for Analysis

1. What steps could the bank have taken to reduce the possibility of such a problem?
2. What steps should Enchantment have taken to reduce the possibility of such a problem?

Promises to Pay: Notes Another type of commercial paper is a **note**. A note is a promise—not an order—by one party, called the **maker**, to pay a certain sum of money to another party, the payee. Usually called **promissory notes**, these instruments involve two parties—the maker and the payee—rather than three parties (a drawer, a drawee, and a payee) required for a draft or check. An example of a simple promissory note is in Exhibit 13.2. Notes are important to finance the purchase of supplies. Often a business

EXHIBIT 13.2   A SAMPLE NOTE

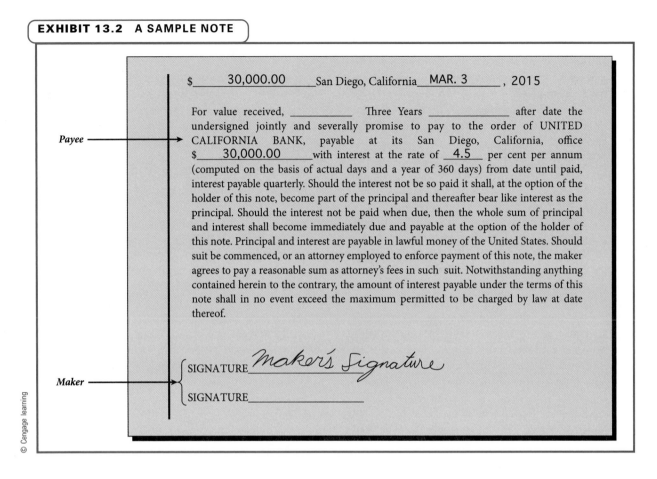

Payee

Maker

© Cengage learning

$_____30,000.00_____ San Diego, California __MAR. 3__ , 2015

For value received, _____ Three Years _____ after date the undersigned jointly and severally promise to pay to the order of UNITED CALIFORNIA BANK, payable at its San Diego, California, office $_____30,000.00_____ with interest at the rate of __4.5__ per cent per annum (computed on the basis of actual days and a year of 360 days) from date until paid, interest payable quarterly. Should the interest not be so paid it shall, at the option of the holder of this note, become part of the principal and thereafter bear like interest as the principal. Should the interest not be paid when due, then the whole sum of principal and interest shall become immediately due and payable at the option of the holder of this note. Principal and interest are payable in lawful money of the United States. Should suit be commenced, or an attorney employed to enforce payment of this note, the maker agrees to pay a reasonable sum as attorney's fees in such suit. Notwithstanding anything contained herein to the contrary, the amount of interest payable under the terms of this note shall in no event exceed the maximum permitted to be charged by law at date thereof.

SIGNATURE *Maker's Signature*

SIGNATURE_____

does not pay a supplier until after it has sold the goods made from the supplies, so notes help provide security about payment to be made in the near future.

Notes have different forms depending upon the transaction involved. Some notes are promissory notes—a promise by one party to pay money to another. Hundreds of billions of dollars worth of promissory notes have been issued to raise capital. These notes may be registered securities (see Chapter 18) and may be traded in the open market.

But promissory notes are used in many other ways. When personal property is used as collateral to back up a loan, the note created is a collateral note. The party seeking the loan (the maker) promises to pay the party giving the loan (the payee) according to the loan agreement. If repayment is not made, the payee has certain rights to the personal property of the maker to help repay the loan.

When real estate is used as collateral to secure the loan, the note is a real estate mortgage note. When the maker promises to repay the note in specified installments, the note is an installment note. A balloon note provides for installment payments, but often only of interest owed. It is possible that none of the debt is repaid until the final payment which may be for the entire principal of loan.

Orders to Pay: Drafts A **draft** is a binding order to pay a fixed sum of money that involves three parties. It is created by the drawer, who orders the drawee—usually a bank—to pay a certain sum to the payee. If you transfer your own funds from one bank account to another, then the drawer and payee are the same. When a draft guarantees payment for goods in international trade, the draft is called a **bill of exchange**.

A draft that requires immediate payment by the drawee to the payee is a **sight draft**. Banks have the right to check the legitimacy of a draft presented for payment, but usually they are paid "on sight."

Other drafts hold the payment until later, so there is time to make sure the goods ordered have been delivered. These are called time drafts or term drafts. They specify payment to be made in the future, such as 60 days from the date of the writing of the draft. The drafts are said to mature on the payment date set in the future.

When a payee is concerned about whether a draft is good, she may submit the draft to the drawee for **confirmation** that it is legitimate and that the drawee has funds to cover payment. This confirmation is called an acceptance. Because it usually happens at a bank, this confirmation is called a banker's acceptance. The draft is stamped as accepted by the bank, obligating the bank to make payment on the date the draft comes due.

The payee may sell a draft to another party to get cash immediately; the buyer then cashes the draft when it becomes due. To get cash for the draft immediately instead of at some point in the future, interest must be paid. This is called discounting the draft because it means paying less than the face value of the draft. For example, a business might sell a $10,000 draft for $9,800, which is a two percent discount. The payee is willing to sell at a discount because it needs the cash today.

Promises to Pay: Certificates of Deposit Another major form of commercial paper is a **certificate of deposit**. The UCC states that a certificate of deposit is an "acknowledgment by a bank" that it has received money from a customer with a promise by the bank that it will repay the money received at a date specified or, in some instances, on demand (§ 3-104(j)). The bank, as maker, creates the certificate and acknowledges receipt of the customer's money, promising to repay the customer as payee plus a certain rate of interest. Most large certificates of deposit (CDs) are negotiable, which allows them to be sold, used to pay debts, or used as collateral for a loan. Most are insured by the Federal Deposit Insurance Corporation (FDIC) for up to $250,000.

Lighter Side of the Law

How to Enforce a Judgment

The Nyerges paid cash directly to Bank of America to eliminate their mortgage and own their home outright. The bank then tried to foreclose, claiming the homeowners had not paid. The misunderstanding went on for a year and a half. Finally, the Nyerges sued and won a judgment for $2,534 for their expenses in dealing with the bank. Bank of America ignored the judgment.

The Nyerges obtained a seizure order. Two sheriff's deputies went to a Bank of America branch with a truck to remove furniture and computer equipment to cover the judgment. The bank manager soon issued a check for the judgment.

Source: Naples Daily News.

Credit

Not all promises to pay are negotiable instruments. There are many other payment arrangements. Whether a person or a business, a **creditor** is one who lends money to, or allows goods or services to be purchased on credit by, another party, the **debtor**.

? *TEST YOURSELF*

1. If a negotiable instrument may be freely traded in the market without concern for other contractual responsibilities, the party with the instrument is said to be _____.
2. A certificate of deposit is a draft drawn on a bank and payable on demand: T—F
3. In the *Associated Home and RV Sales* v. *Bank of Belen* case, where a bank honored bogus checks written by an employee on the company's account, the courts held that the bank:
   a. was strictly liable under the UCC for allowing the checks to be cashed.
   b. was liable under the common law and the UCC only because the signatures on the checks looked nothing like the real signatures.
   c. could be liable for negligence under the UCC for failing to follow proper procedure.
   d. could be liable under the UCC because Associated Home notified the bank within six months of the problem.
4. A legally binding written order to pay a fixed sum of money that involves three parties—a drawer, drawee, and a payee—is a draft: T—F
5. A promise by one party (the maker) to pay a certain sum of money to another party (the payee) is called a(n) _____.

Answers: a holder in due course; F; c; T; note.

Credit terms must specify the interest rate, if any, that applies to the sum owed, the **principal** of the debt, and payment dates, such as "in 30 days" for materials or more than 30 years for land. As discussed below, creditors want evidence of the debt's existence to use if they must sue to collect, such as a signed loan agreement, and may attach terms to debt that increase the probability of repayment.

While large corporations raise much of their funding by equity financing—that is, the sale of stock in the company or the sale of negotiable instruments that are subject to securities regulation (Chapter 18), smaller businesses tend to rely on debt financing, which usually means borrowing money evidenced by a contract.

The debt incurred by business includes long-term debt (such as financing of a building) and short-term debt (for inventory). Often, creditors want to see debt backed by something more solid than a promise to repay the money plus interest, and debtors would like to be able to get lower interest rates as well, so we discuss some of the devices used to strengthen the creditworthiness of the debtor.

Credit Policy

Some businesses, such as banks, are in the credit business. Other businesses extend credit as a part of their operations, whether the purpose of the business is to provide accounting services or to sell bricks. Because many businesses do not demand cash at the time of the sale of services or products, they have policies for credit standards and terms, as well as a collection policy. Credit policy focuses on such characteristics as the following:

1. Capacity (the debtor's ability to pay)
2. Capital (the debtor's financial condition)

3. Character (the debtor's reputation)
4. Collateral (the debtor's assets to secure debt)
5. Conditions (the economic situation affecting debtor's business)

Few lenders know much about a party seeking to borrow, but sources are available that provide such information (see Exhibit 13.3). Creditors can use credit-reporting agencies that sell **consumer reports** for business purposes about individuals and **credit ratings** for companies. Some consumers' rights about credit reports are specified by the Fair Credit Reporting Act (Chapter 19). **Credit reports** are not always accurate. Mistakes are made, so individuals and businesses should make sure their credit histories are accurate.

EXHIBIT 13.3   SOURCES OF CREDIT INFORMATION

Customer Financial Statements

It is normal practice to require a credit applicant to supply financial information. Individuals normally are asked to provide financial information such as tax returns, bank statements, and proof of income. Business applicants may be asked to provide financial statements such as audited balance sheets and income statements.

Banks

Banks may provide credit information about a customer. Credit departments of banks often share information about loan payment histories and related credit information about their customers.

Credit Reporting Agencies

Credit reporting agencies, such as Dun & Bradstreet Credibility Corp., specialize in providing credit reports and credit ratings on companies. Credit histories of individuals and businesses in many countries can be purchased from reporting agencies such as Experian, TransUnion, and Equifax.

Trade Associations

A number of trade associations provide information about the credit experiences of its members. They typically provide information about deals made on credit with suppliers and list the amount of credit and the repayment history.

© Cengage Learning

Credit Accounts   When a company extends credit to its customers, it usually offers credit terms according to the size of the account and the importance of the customer. Many accounts do not charge interest if the debt is paid within a certain time. Exhibit 13.4 lists some basic credit accounts offered by many companies.

EXHIBIT 13.4   COMMON TYPES OF CREDIT ACCOUNTS

Open Account

This is the most common form of credit. Goods are sold on an invoice that provides evidence of the transaction. Full payment is expected within a fixed time.

Installment Account

Generally used by consumers for the purchase of durable goods such as automobiles. Debtors repay by regular (generally monthly) payments.

Revolving Account

This is similar to the installment account, except that the debtor makes a minimum monthly payment, which is generally a fraction of the outstanding balance. More debt can be added to the account over time.

© Cengage Learning

In most cases, credit terms are determined by competitive conditions or industry standards. For credit under an **open account**, for example, the terms define the credit period available to the customer and any discounts offered for early payment. A typical industry standard is net 60 days from the date of invoice with a discount of two percent if paid within ten days of invoice. Consumer credit accounts—installment and revolving accounts—state the interest rate to be paid and the timing of the payments.

Collections Policy Most bills are paid on time. However, a collections policy is needed for debtors who fail to make timely payments. Usually, notification begins with a letter or e-mail stating that the account is past due. A telephone call or a second letter may follow. Depending on the business relationship, letters may be followed by a personal visit.

At times, additional action is necessary to protect the creditor's rights. The alternatives depend on whether the business is an unsecured or a secured creditor. In most transactions, the lender is an **unsecured** (general) **creditor**, who has little more than the customer's promise to pay securing the loan. If the customer proves to be insolvent, or unable to pay, the business receives nothing. If the customer simply will not pay, legal action must be considered. Next, we look at ways to establish more formal credit agreements.

Credit with Security

In contrast to unsecured creditor, a business is a **secured creditor** when it has the ability to take some of the nonpaying customers' property to satisfy the debt. The law provides two avenues through which the creditor can obtain the customers' property (referred to as security or **collateral**): (1) by agreement with the debtor; or (2) by operation of law.

By Agreement

The nature of the credit agreement depends upon whether the debtor's property is real property (real estate or other immovable property) or personal property (movable goods). The distinction between real and personal property is important for several reasons. Personal property is considered goods under the UCC, so such sales are usually governed by the Uniform Commercial Code (Chapter 11). As a result, sales of personal property can take place with relatively little or no formal documentation. On the other hand, because real property is governed by contract and property law, it requires documentation before a sale can be finalized. The agreement providing security in real property is a mortgage, which is examined later.

CYBER LAW

Innovations in Credit Scoring

The most common way to measure a borrower's creditworthiness is the FICO credit-rating score, which runs from 30 to 850. It is used by the consumer reporting agencies that follow the Fair Isaac Corp. system. The focus is on debt history, income, repayment records, and so on.

Scouring the Internet may be an alternative. Neo Finance of California prices car loans based on income and social data. It focuses on young adults, who have little credit history, but are likely to have good income in the future. The lender uses LinkedIn profiles as a measure of trustworthiness. The company Affirm searches Facebook and a hundred other databases in helping determine credit risk. An algorithm predicts likelihood of repayment.

ISSUE SPOTTER
Helping a Dream?

Your sister has opened her own store, fulfilling her dream. The store looks great and customer traffic seems good, but the up-front costs are high. She is deeply in debt and needs more credit to keep the store well stocked. The cash flow looks good and she believes, based on the trend and revenues, that within a year she will be turning a profit. To get more credit at a decent interest rate, she needs help. She asks you and your parents to cosign for an extension on her line of credit from a bank. She will sign a contract holding herself primarily liable on the debt and liable to you in case anything goes wrong. Is there much of a risk here? What is the downside?

Suretyship   Businesses often need to raise working capital to operate and expand. Owners of small businesses frequently must provide a personal **guaranty** or **suretyship** for debts to give the lender more confidence it will be repaid. If a business has a poor credit history, it may be required to provide a guaranty or suretyship for virtually any borrowing it does.

A guaranty may be a pledge of personal assets by business owners. In addition, a third party may provide the guaranty or suretyship. In either case, a promise is made to pay a debt of a business in the event the business does not pay. In this way, a suretyship or guaranty is created, and the credit of the party providing it becomes the security for the debt owed.

Surety Defined   A contract for a suretyship is a promise by a third party (the **surety**) to be responsible for the borrower's payment obligations, or performance, to a creditor. The borrower or debtor is referred to as the principal.

A surety could provide a suretyship for a fee or out of kindness, but could also be an owner or shareholder in the business. A suretyship can be created only by a contract between the surety and the creditor. The surety is obligated to pay the creditor if the principal fails to pay the debt or provide performance to the creditor. A common form of suretyship is a co-signature on a bank loan.

Guarantor Defined   A **guarantor** provides a guarantee of payment to a creditor should the principal debtor fail to pay and, therefore, can be the same as a surety. That is, to guarantee is to assume the obligation of a surety. In some states, the distinction between a guaranty and a surety is that a surety is primarily liable after the debtor, whereas the guarantor is secondarily liable.

In most states, one contract binds both the surety and the borrower, and the creditor is not obligated to exhaust legal remedies before demanding payment by the surety. In other states, the guarantor can be obligated to pay only after the creditor has exhausted legal remedies against the borrower and any surety.

Lighter Side **of the Law**

Do You Know Elvis Too?

Paul Allen is the billionaire co-founder of Microsoft. While he is not related to Brandon Price, an AWOL Army private, Price convinced Citibank that he was authorized by Allen to issue him, Price, a debit card and to change Allen's address from Seattle to Pittsburgh.

Fortunately, Price was not a wild spender. Before he was stopped, he had run up less than $1,000 in charges at GameStop and Family Dollar store.

Source: Pittsburgh Post-Gazette.

Defenses of Sureties Any contract defenses available to the principal also are available to the surety, including impossibility, illegality, duress, and fraud—but not the creditor's bankruptcy because the surety is providing financial protection to the creditor against such an event. A surety also is released when the creditor releases the borrower without the surety's consent. Similarly, the surety is released if material changes are made to the original contract between the creditor and the debtor without the surety's consent.

It must be emphasized that when one guarantees a loan, liability is imposed according to the terms of the documents signed, as the *General Electric Business Financial Services* case discusses.

GENERAL ELECTRIC BUSINESS FINANCIAL SERVICES V. SILVERMAN

United States District Court, Northern District of Illinois
693 F.Supp.2d 796 (2010)

Case Background *Warren Park Partners, Ltd., borrowed $34.8 million from GE Financial to buy land in Frisco, Texas. At the time the loan agreement was made, Silverman and his partners signed a guaranty by which each "absolutely, unconditionally and irrevocably guaranteed" the full payment of the principal and interest of all sums due under the loan agreement.*

Warren Park defaulted on the loan agreement and went into bankruptcy, so GE demanded payment from the partners. When they failed to pay, GE sued.

Silverman and his partners claimed affirmative defenses of fraud, extortion, theft, and economic duress. Affirmative defenses raise new facts that, if true, defeat the plaintiff's claim even if all statements in the plaintiff's claim are true. The basis for the defense was that hours before signing the documents, GE notified defendants of changes to the terms of the loan agreement that they did not have time to contest as the loan was needed immediately. They signed the agreement because they were trapped and claimed that a GE employee told them that the new terms would not be enforced. GE moved for summary judgment.

Case Decision Gettleman, District Judge

* * *

To establish a *prima facie* case for enforcement of a guaranty under Illinois law, plaintiff must "enter proof of the original indebtedness, the debtor's default, and the guarantee."

Plaintiff has offered evidence demonstrating all of the elements for [its] claims, which defendants do not contest. Instead, defendants assert four affirmative defenses that they claim preclude enforcement of the Guaranty. . . .

Plaintiff argues that [defendants'] allegations, which provide the foundation for each of defendants' affirmative defenses, even if taken as true, are barred by the Illinois Credit Agreement Act (ICAA) which bars all actions or defenses by a debtor based on or related to an oral credit agreement.

The ICAA has been described by the Seventh Circuit as a "strong form" of the Statute of Frauds because . . . it requires that the agreement be signed by both parties. . . .

The ICAA defines a credit agreement as "an agreement or commitment by a creditor to lend money or extend credit or delay or forebear repayment of money not primarily for personal, family or household purposes, and not in connection with the issuance of credit cards." The Illinois courts regard a guaranty agreement . . . as part of the "comprehensive credit agreement" between the parties and therefore governed by the ICAA. Applying this principle to the instant case, it is clear from the language of the Guaranty [was part of] the Loan. . . . Defendants do not dispute that the agreements are "credit agreements" under this definition. Therefore, the court finds that pursuant to the ICAA the Guaranty [is] part of the "credit agreement" between the parties.

Defendants argue that the ICAA does not apply to bar their affirmative defenses of fraudulent inducement and economic duress because defendants seek to invalidate, rather than modify, the underlying contract. Further, defendants argue that their defense of unclean hands simply seeks to prevent plaintiff from benefitting from its own wrongdoing. These arguments are specious at best....

Because the alleged oral promises that plaintiff made to defendants contradict the terms of the Guaranty..., the ICAA bars... defendants' affirmative defenses that rely on these allegations....

Plaintiff's motion for summary judgment... is granted.

Questions for Analysis

1. Suppose there were multiple witnesses to back up what Silverman said—that a GE representative told him the new terms of the loan really did not matter. Should that fact not be taken into consideration?
2. Does the Illinois Credit Agreement Act help or harm parties to loans?

Surety's Rights against the Principal If the principal (borrower) does not pay the creditor, and the surety has to satisfy the debt, the principal is obligated to repay the surety. If the borrower could pay the creditor but refuses to, the surety is entitled to **exoneration**, a court order requiring the principal to pay.

The surety is also entitled to be **subrogated** to the rights of the creditor against the debtor. This generally occurs when the surety pays part of the debt. In seeking repayment from the principal, the surety may assert any rights the creditor could have asserted against the debtor, including taking any security interests the creditor obtained from the borrower.

Secured Transactions The law governing the financing of commercial sales of goods is Article 9 of the UCC. When goods are sold to a customer, either a person or a business, the UCC provides that the goods may secure the debtor's obligation to pay. Called a **secured transaction**, it occurs when a buyer wants goods and does not pay cash, and the seller is leery of an unsecured debt.

By meeting the requirements of the UCC, the seller obtains the **perfection of security interest** in the goods sold to the customer as collateral to help secure payment in the event of default. That is, the seller can reclaim the goods. To make a security interest more easily enforceable, the seller must create the interest, or legal right, and make sure that the interest is attached and perfected.

Attachment According to the UCC, for there to be **attachment** of a security interest, the agreement must be signed by the customer; the seller must have provided value; and the customer must have legal, transferrable rights in the collateral. If the customer is unable to pay, the seller has rights against the customer that are superior to unsecured creditors but not necessarily superior to other secured creditors.

Perfection To establish superior rights—that is, to perfect the security interest—the creditor must give notice of the existence of the security interest so other potential creditors are aware that they will stand behind the creditor with the perfected interest in getting paid. The **perfection** of the interest establishes the date priority took effect. This way, when multiple creditors have claims, the priority order is clear.

The primary way to perfect is to file the financing statement with the secretary of state or other relevant official as required by state law, so it is available for public

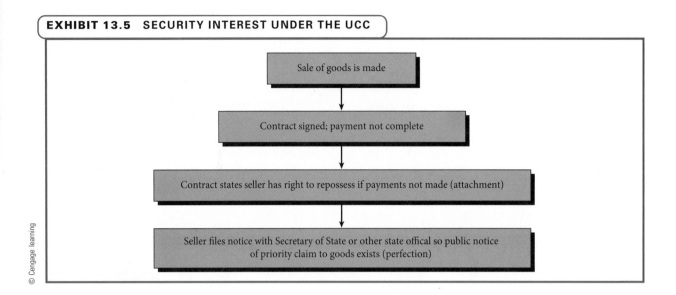

EXHIBIT 13.5   SECURITY INTEREST UNDER THE UCC

Sale of goods is made

Contract signed; payment not complete

Contract states seller has right to repossess if payments not made (attachment)

Seller files notice with Secretary of State or other state offical so public notice
of priority claim to goods exists (perfection)

inspection (see Exhibit 13.5). This process must be followed unless the goods being sold
are consumer goods. Under the UCC, a security interest for consumer goods is perfected
without filing. Normally, the financing statement contains little more than the names
and addresses of the firm and the customer, a description of the product, and the signature of the customer. The details of the credit transaction—such as the amount financed,
the payment schedule, and interest rate—are left to the security agreement.

Interests in Inventory   As collateral, supplies such as equipment, inventory, and raw
materials can be classified as **tangible property**—goods that are movable at the time a
security interest attaches or begins. To protect its interests, the lender extending credit
to a business obtains a security interest, sometimes called a **purchase money security
interest**. The procedure is nearly the same as the procedure followed by the business
when it extends credit to customers buying its product. As in that case, the security
interest gives the lender rights against the borrower—rights that are superior to other
creditors in the event the borrower fails to meet debt obligations.

A "Floating Lien" for Inventory   Under the UCC, inventory includes goods held for
sale as well as raw materials. Inventory is constantly changing. This could create a problem for a creditor that provides financing to a business with inventory as collateral. To
avoid the need to renew the financing contract every time something is sold or used, the
UCC allows a perfected security interest in property acquired after the security agreement is formed. This permits a **floating lien**. The security interest in any specific item
of inventory ends when the item is sold, but the interest attaches to new inventory.

Default by the Debtor A security interest helps to protect the interests of the seller in
the event the customer **defaults**, that is, cannot or will not meet payment obligations.
Because the seller has a security interest in the product, it has *priority* to the collateral
over all unsecured creditors and, depending on the priorities of other secured creditors,
perhaps over them as well.

The UCC provides that when repossessing goods, "a secured party may proceed without judicial process if this can be done without breach of peace." That is, if you do not
make payments on your car, it can be repossessed directly by the seller. In taking possession, the seller is not obligated to notify other parties who also may have a security

interest in the product. The creditor may keep the goods or resell them. If the product is resold, it must be sold in a "commercially reasonable manner." Any proceeds above what is owed must be returned to the customer. If it is sold for less than the debt plus the costs of sale, the debtor still owes the balance.

Default by a debtor often affects more than one party. Repossession may or may not be possible, and in searching for funds to repay the debt, creditors commonly argue over who is eligible for whatever funds are available. The UCC and state laws governing liens determine who gets what when a debtor cannot satisfy all creditors. Like anything else, a perfected security interest may not work as hoped, as the *Fordyce Bank* case illustrates.

FORDYCE BANK AND TRUST V. BEAN TIMBERLAND

Supreme Court of Arkansas 251 S.W.3d 267 (2007)

Case Background *Fordyce Bank made a series of loans to Bean Timberland so it could buy timber from landowners. Bean would cut timber from owners' lands and sell the logs to Potlatch and Idaho Timber, which milled the logs into lumber. Bean gave the bank security interests in the timber. The proceeds from timber sales were to repay the loans. The bank perfected its interests by filing UCC financing statements with the Secretary of State's office.*

Bean sold the timber but failed to repay the loans and went bankrupt. The bank sued Potlatch and Idaho because the bank had priority interest in the timber sale proceeds. The bank alleged that Potlatch and Idaho were negligent in their dealings for failing to do a lien search and "failed to exercise good faith" as required by the UCC.

The trial court held for Potlatch and Idaho, ruling that they were not negligent. They were not required to perform a security interest search in the ordinary course of business. The bank appealed.

Case Decision Glaze, Justice

* * *

Under [UCC 9-320], a buyer in the ordinary course of business "takes free of a security interest created by the buyer's seller, even if the security interest is perfected and the buyer knows of its existence." Thus, if Potlatch and Idaho were buyers in the ordinary course of business, they would be under no duty to perform a lien search because, even if they knew of a lien and had performed a lien search, they

could nonetheless take free of the Bank's security interest....

Evidence presented at trial clearly showed that Potlatch and Idaho's practices were "usual or customary" in the timber business.

Bean sold timber to various mills as "gatewood." Gatewood is severed timber that is brought to a lumber mill's front gate by a logger; the wood is weighed and inventoried, and if the timber meets the mill's specifications, the mill purchases it. If the wood does not meet specifications, the mill does not buy it. Numerous witnesses testified that purchases of gatewood are common in the Arkansas logging industry....

The procurement manager for Potlatch's Prescott mill, Jim Cornelius, testified that nothing in Potlatch's gatewood purchases from Bean did "anything to cause alarm." Cornelius also stated that he had no actual knowledge that the Bank had a security interest in Bean's inventory. He also declared that, in his 30 years in timber procurement, he had "never undertaken a search for security interests in gatewood," and that Potlatch "does not perform lien searches in any other state, either."...

In sum, the trial court had before it abundant evidence that purchasing gatewood without performing a lien search was the standard practice in the timber industry. Clearly, Bean's sales to Potlatch and Idaho, and Potlatch's and Idaho's practice of not conducting lien searches, "comported with the usual or customary practices in the kind of business in which the seller is engaged or with the seller's own usual or customary practices" [UCC § 9-320(a)]. As such, the trial court correctly determined that Potlatch and Idaho were buyers in the ordinary course of business. Further, because the mills were buyers in the ordinary course of business, they owed the Bank no duty to conduct a lien search. With no duty, there could be no breach of any duty....

   Affirmed.

Questions for Analysis

1. The high court affirmed that the buyers of the timber had no duty to do a search for a security interest on the timber and were not liable to the bank, which lost its potential collateral. What is the logic of not having buyers in the ordinary course of business not do a search?
2. What could the bank have done to protect itself against this sort of outcome?

Exempt Property   As discussed, it is not uncommon for business owners to pledge personal assets as security for the debts of the business (as a surety). If the business is not able to pay, the creditor may have assets pledged as collateral that may be seized and sold to repay the debt. If the debt is not fully paid after the sale, the creditor may sue the owners for the rest of the debt. To protect its interests, the creditor may ask the court for an attachment. After the judgment has been rendered and the owner is unable or unwilling to pay, the creditor may ask the court for a writ of execution.

The creditor moves against the owner's **nonexempt property**. That is, certain real and personal property is exempt from attachment proceedings. In the interest of ensuring that a debtor has housing, for example, states have a **homestead law** that provides an exemption that allows the debtor to retain the family home up to a specified amount free from creditors' claims. With regard to personal property, state statutes provide limited exemptions for, among other things, furniture, clothing, automobiles, and tools used in the debtor's trade or business.

Real Estate Financing

Buying real estate often involves a large outlay of money. Normally, much of the purchase price is borrowed. The real estate itself is used to secure the debt obligation and is evidenced by a mortgage. The **mortgage** is a lien that gives the lien holder the right to sell the property and repay the debt from sale proceeds in the event the borrower defaults. The debtor is the **mortgagor**, and the creditor is the **mortgagee**. State common law and real estate statutes govern such transactions because the UCC does not apply to real estate.

The Mortgage   According to the Statute of Frauds, a mortgage must be in writing. The mortgage contains a description of the property, sets forth any warranties relative to the property, states the debt, and the mortgagor's duties concerning taxes, insurance, and repairs. To protect the mortgagee's rights against other creditors, the mortgage should be recorded. State statutes typically require that the mortgage be placed in a county office, often called the recorder's office, clerk of the court, county clerk, or the register of deeds.

Default by the Mortgagor   If the borrower is unable to pay the mortgage, the mortgagee has the right to foreclose on the property. Foreclosure may be by judicial sale. In such situations, if the proceeds of the sale are sufficient to cover the costs of the foreclosure and the debt, any surplus must be returned to the mortgage holder. If the proceeds are not sufficient, the mortgagee may be able to seek to recover the remainder from the debtor by obtaining a **deficiency judgment** in a separate legal action after the foreclosure. However, most mortgages, while they are secured debt, are **non-recourse debt**. The lender can seize the collateral (the property), but not seek a deficiency judgment for any money owed not covered by the sale of the property.

Liens

Security obtained by a creditor through the operation of law is called a **lien**. Because the seller may obtain it without a specific agreement with the customer, the security may be a nonconsensual lien. The term lien is derived from the French language and means "tie" or "string." The legal meaning for lien is the legal right the seller has to the product now held by a customer. The lien helps to secure payment for goods or services, such as electrical work done in the construction of a new building or residence.

The procedures for using liens are mostly determined by state statutes. The most common liens are the mechanic's lien (applicable to real property), the possessory lien (applicable to personal property), and court-decreed liens. In each case, a creditor may obtain the lien without the debtor's consent by following statutory procedures. An additional remedy, **garnishment**, is a statutory procedure under which a creditor gains the right to attach up to 25 percent of a customer's net wages to be applied to an outstanding debt.

ISSUE SPOTTER
Lean on a Lien?

Your concrete company is offered a chance to get in on a huge construction project at a new shopping center. If it goes as planned, you will be able to double the size of your operation, allowing you to compete for more large-scale jobs. The builder will hire you as a subcontractor, and the price offered is fair. But the builder will not pay you or the other subcontractors until he is paid. So you have to carry debt as the project goes along. The contractor points out that the risk to you is minimal because the scale of the project is huge, and you are involved in only a small part of the total cost. Besides, he says, if there is a problem in your getting paid, you can slap a lien on the whole project. Would this action give you adequate protection? Is the gamble worth it?

Mechanic's Lien A **mechanic's lien** is the most common lien for work performed on real property. The party that furnishes material, labor, or services for the construction or repair of a building or other real property can place a lien on the property for unpaid bills (and becomes the lienor or lienholder). The lienholder must follow the steps that the law requires within a certain time. The requirements vary from state to state, but most require the lien to be filed within 90 days from the date that the work or services were completed. Should the lien not be paid, suit must be brought within six months after filing the lien. The *Summers Group* case illustrates some common issues in lien cases. Notice how the procedure is intended to settle all liens in one action.

SUMMERS GROUP, INC. V. TEMPE MECHANICAL, LLC

Court of Appeals of Arizona, 299 P.3d 743 (2013)

Case Background *Summers Group, dba Rexel, sold electrical materials for construction on property owned by Metro Lofts. Rexel was not paid for materials provided so on June 26, 2008, recorded a mechanic's lien on Metro Lofts' property. Other contractors on the work, including Tempe Mechanical,* *also filed liens against Metro Loft for non-payment. After not receiving payment, Rexel brought suit on December 24, 2008, against Metro Lofts and all other lienholders.*

Some lienholders (other contractors) did not respond and had default judgments entered against them. Tempe, which had filed a lien, answered Rexel's complaint. Metro Lofts was in bankruptcy and under the control of bankruptcy trustee, ML Manager. All parties agreed that the bankruptcy court would determine the priority of payment of all valid liens. Before the bankruptcy court could sort out priority of payments, the trial court had to determine the validity of the various liens. ML Manager argued that it stood first to receive payment, and because it should not be challenged, Rexel should pay all attorney fees related to the litigation. The trial court agreed. Rexel appealed.

Case Decision   Orozco, Judge

* * *

Mechanics' lien statutes and Arizona case law establish procedures to be followed when a mechanics' lien claimant initiates a foreclosure action on a lien. First, a mechanic lienor must sue each party against whom it seeks to assert its lien within six months after recording its lien. After an action is commenced by one mechanic lienor, "persons claiming liens who fail or refuse to become parties plaintiff shall be made parties defendant, and those not made a party, may, at any time before final hearing, intervene" [A.R.S. § 33–996]. After all the lien claimants are served, in order to assert their lien priority, each must file an answer or cross-claim. Finally, pursuant to A.R.S. § 33–998.A, if a lien claimant is made a party defendant to an action brought by another lien claimant, the timely filing of an answer or cross-claim asserting the lien, within six months of recording the lien, shall be deemed the commencement of an action.

In order to enforce its lien priority, Rexel named all of the other mechanics' lien claimants as parties in the complaint.

In this case, by filing answers to the allegations set forth in Rexel's complaint, the Remaining Lien Claimants each commenced an action asserting their lien priority. Because the Remaining Lien Claimants were involved in the litigation, the bankruptcy court's decision on the lien priority issue also affected their claims. Therefore, we hold that the Remaining Lien Claimants caused ML Manager to defend its lien priority....

The intent of the mechanics' lien statutes is for all lienholders to be treated on equal ground with one another regardless of the date the work was performed. Accordingly, [the statute] requires that when a sale is ordered in a mechanics' lien foreclosure action and the property is sold, the proceeds are prorated over the respective liens that have equal footing with the foreclosing lien. Moreover, in multi-issue litigation, it is common for attorney fees to be apportioned between successful and unsuccessful efforts.

The trial court erred in holding Rexel solely responsible for the payment of ML Manager's attorney fees. Similar to prorating sales proceeds, attorney fees for resolving priority should be prorated between lien claimants. The intent of the Legislature in adopting the mechanics' lien statutes was to create an even playing field for all laborers and materialmen who provide services and materials to enhance the value of another's property, regardless of the date the work was performed. All lien claimant parties are treated on equal footing in the sharing of the income collected after a mechanics' lien foreclosure sale and should also share in the potential expenditures.

Therefore, as unsuccessful parties in a lien priority contest, all the Remaining Lien Claimants should be liable for ML Manager's attorney fees award in proportion to their claims against the encumbered property....

Reversed and remanded.

Questions for Analysis

1. A number of contractors that had liens against Metro Lofts did not respond to the filing of this action to settle lien claims. Why would you think they failed to respond, as they lost all rights to collect by not doing so?

2. We look at bankruptcy law next, but why would you think the bankruptcy trustee imposed payment of all attorney fees on claimants?

Upon filing the lien, the creditor obtains security for the debt. Before a property can be sold, a lien must be removed, giving the creditor leverage over a real estate owner looking to sell. If the owner of the real property does not pay the lien, the creditor can move to force the sale of the property to satisfy the debt.

Possessory Lien The **possessory lien** is a lien that may apply to personal property. It provides a security interest for creditors that add value to or care for personal property. This lien offers the right to continue to hold goods on which work has been done, or for which materials have been supplied, until the customer pays. If the customer does not pay for the work or supplies, the creditor can force the sale of the property to fulfill payment of the debt.

Court-Decreed Liens When a debt is past due, a creditor may sue a debtor. Creditors prefer alternatives to litigation for collections because of the time and expense involved. If it is necessary to use the court system, creditors may use attachment and judgment liens as judicial means to try to protect their interests.

An **attachment lien** is a court-ordered seizure of goods from a customer to prevent the customer from disposing of the goods. Under state statute, the requirements are specific and limited. To obtain an attachment lien, the creditor must show that the debtor is likely to dispose of the product. If the court concurs, it issues a **writ** that allows attachment. The court may direct the sheriff to seize the good. Creditors must follow attachment procedures closely, or they could be liable for damages for wrongful attachment.

If the creditor is successful in an action against the debtor, the court awards a judgment. But the debtor may not pay, causing the creditor to then file a **judgment lien**. A lien is not put into effect simply by the existence of a court judgment. The creditor must record a lien against the debtor's real property based on the judgment. It provides notice to potential purchasers of the property of the existence of the judgment and lien, which is usually good for ten years.

If the debtor does not pay the judgment in a given time, the creditor may ask the court to issue a writ of execution. The writ is issued by the clerk of the court and directs the sheriff to seize and sell any of the debtor's nonexempt real or personal property, such as a car, to help settle the debt.

Bankruptcy

Financial ruin comes to many in the marketplace. Some consumers and businesses engage in fraud, causing financial messes that others pay for, but most **bankruptcy** is the result of bad luck, unexpected changes in financial conditions, or unintentional mismanagement. A person or a business is usually not able to pay debts that are due because liabilities exceed assets. At least some creditors refuse to extend the time for payment, so something must be done to resolve the financial mess.

Bankruptcy is not a new issue; the framers of the Constitution thought it such an important issue that they specifically made bankruptcy a matter of federal law. The purpose of bankruptcy law is to provide an orderly resolution where a debtor owes more than can be paid.

The bankruptcy code has been amended many times over the centuries. The most recent major revision was the Bankruptcy Abuse Prevention and Consumer Protection Act of 2005. The code states how matters are resolved when debts are greater than assets available. Because approximately 1.5 million people and 50,000 businesses file for bankruptcy each year, it is a major business issue. We review the major types of bankruptcy and then discuss non-bankruptcy choices for distressed debtors next.

? TEST YOURSELF

1. Under the UCC, open accounts for commercial transactions are permissible, but "revolving accounts" are not as the security is too uncertain: T—F
2. A promise by a third party to be responsible for a borrower's payment obligations to a creditor is called a(n) _____.
3. In *Fordyce Bank and Trust* v. *Bean Timberland*, where a security interest in timber held by the bank to secure a loan to a timber cutter was ignored by buyers of timber, the courts held that there was:
   a. no obligation for buyers to perform a lien search, so the buyers were not liable to the bank.
   b. an obligation for buyers to perform a lien search, so the buyers were liable to the bank.
   c. an obligation for buyers to perform a lien search only if the liens were perfected.
   d. an obligation for buyers to perform a lien search, but only for liens on file with the state.
4. A lien placed on personal property is called a(n) _____.
5. If a debt is past due, a court may order seizure of goods to prevent the goods from being disposed of by the debtor: T—F

Answers: F; suretyship; a; possessory lien; T.

Personal Bankruptcy

Before a person may file for bankruptcy, he must complete a credit counseling course. The Department of Justice's U.S. Trustee Program approves organizations to provide the mandatory credit counseling and debtor education. There are many in every state. Credit counseling and debtor education may not be provided together. A person must take credit counseling before filing bankruptcy. Debtor education is taken after filing.

Credit counseling before filing includes an evaluation of a person's financial situation, a discussion of alternatives to bankruptcy, and a personal budget plan. This usually takes about an hour. A certificate of credit counseling completion is provided, and one must have it to be able to file bankruptcy. The purpose is to try to head people off from filing bankruptcy if possible. But if one does file, then he or she must go through debtor education about budgeting, use of credit, and related issues.

Income and Means Testing If a person wishes to file for bankruptcy, there is an income test that helps determine if one files under Chapter 7 of the Bankruptcy Code (liquidation) or Chapter 13 of the Bankruptcy Code (reorganization of debts). If a person's monthly income is more than the state median, then Chapter 13 is more likely. That is, people with higher income are less likely to have debts extinguished. Furthermore, there is a test of income against reasonable expenditures for a person of a certain income level; that is, living above average for a given income level is held to be evidence that expenses can be cut and debts repaid under Chapter 13. The purpose of the test is to point people in the right direction. It is intended to reduce the number of higher-income people who file Chapter 7.

Chapter 7

Before the 2005 bankruptcy law, Chapter 7 of the bankruptcy code was the most commonly used alternative. But the reforms require more people to choose Chapter 13 instead. Chapter 7 means "liquidation" by discharge of most debts after sale and distribution of the sale proceeds of the debtor's non-exempt assets (such as stock in a company or a boat used for recreation) to the creditors. Assets that are exempt from proceedings include a car, clothing, appliances, some equity in a home, and a pension. While bankruptcy law is federal, states are allowed to set exemption levels. After the discharge, the debtor is not liable for the debts covered in the bankruptcy proceeding.

Most Chapter 7 bankruptcies, which total about one million a year, are **voluntary bankruptcies** filed by either individual or business debtors. A petition is filed with the bankruptcy court. The filing is a statement of the financial structure of the debtor, including the most recent tax returns. The petition provides the following:

- A list of all creditors and the amount and nature of their claims;
- The source, amount, and frequency of the debtor's income;
- A list of all of the debtor's property;
- A detailed list of the debtor's monthly living expenses, such as food, clothing, shelter, utilities, taxes, transportation, and medicine.

The filing of this petition means that a freeze, or automatic stay, is imposed on all actions against the debtor and the debtor's property by any creditors. A trustee is appointed to administer the debtor's estate. The trustee meets with creditors to review the accuracy of the information provided by the debtor. In practice, most Chapter 7 personal bankruptcies are quick and involve minimal participation by creditors as they know the likelihood of payment is near zero. In an **involuntary bankruptcy**, creditors file a petition with the court, forcing the declaration of bankruptcy and the beginning of proceedings.

Chapter 13

About 400,000 personal bankruptcies are handled under Chapter 13 each year. Sometimes this is referred to as the wage earner's plan. Only a voluntary option exists under Chapter 13, which is filed like a Chapter 7 bankruptcy, and it is available only for individuals. Because a sole proprietorship is owned by an individual, it may be handled under the Chapter 13 option.

In this proceeding, the debtor files a plan for the payment of creditors, usually over five years. Unlike Chapter 7, where the debtor is relieved of all non-property, in Chapter 13, the debtor retains her property and shares administration of the bankrupt estate with a court-appointed trustee. Payments are made to creditors as called for by the plan approved by the bankruptcy court. The trustee makes sure payments are made and that creditors do not try to go around the fixed payment schedule.

Chapter 13 is a court-protected debt repayment plan that usually must be accomplished within five years. It is possible that all debt will be repaid, but often only a portion is repaid under this installment plan. At the end of the payment period, certain unpaid debt is discharged. Long-term, secured debt, such as a house mortgage, is treated differently to increase the chance for the debtor to keep a home. If the plan fails to work, it is possible to shift to a Chapter 7 bankruptcy and have the financial issues cleared by hardship discharge.

While some people not familiar with bankruptcy have the impression that it can mean a return to living the high life, the *Darby* case indicates that is hardly so.

IN RE DARBY

United States Court of Appeals, Fifth Circuit, 470 F.3d 573 (2006)

Case Background *After Darby filed for Chapter 13 bankruptcy, Time Warner canceled his cable service. Darby filed a motion with the bankruptcy court to compel Time Warner to reinstate his service upon the offering of assurances of future payments. The bankruptcy court and district court held that cable service was not a utility that had to be provided as a necessity under the law. Darby appealed.*

Case Decision Stewart, Circuit Judge

* * *

The word "utility" as it is used in [the bankruptcy code] is not defined within the statute, but some guidance is provided by the legislative history of the provision. Both the House Judiciary Report and the Senate Report on the provision state in relevant part:

> This section gives debtors protection from a cutoff of service by a utility because of the filing of a bankruptcy case. This section is intended to cover utilities that have some special position with respect to the debtor, such as an electric company, gas supplier, or

telephone company that is a monopoly in the area so that the debtor cannot easily obtain comparable service from another utility. ...

The bankruptcy court did not err in determining that cable service is not a necessity. Therefore, cable service is not covered by [the bankruptcy code], and Time Warner is not required to reinstate Darby's service despite his offer of adequate assurances of future payment. ...

Even if Darby were correct in his assertion that he could not obtain an alternative to cable television, the fact that Time Warner is not a necessity is enough to exempt it from the requirements of [the bankruptcy code]. ...

Affirmed.

Questions for Analysis

1. The appeals court affirmed that a cable television company need not provide service to a person in bankruptcy. Would you think Internet service is a necessity?
2. How could Time Warner assure itself of payment from Darby?

The Bankruptcy Proceeding

Regardless of the kind of bankruptcy, a key feature is the emphasis on creditors receiving fair treatment. Once bankruptcy has been declared, a creditor cannot improve its position by getting to the debtor's property first. Nor can the debtor improve a favored creditor's position by transferring property to that creditor. It is the trustee's job to assure that no creditor has improved its relative position. Some creditors however, knowing bankruptcy may be coming, work with the debtor for favored treatment. But transfers of a debtor's property up to 90 days prior to the bankruptcy filing are void. Trustees can also go to court to undo earlier transactions by the bankrupt party to bring the assets back into the estate. The trustee's objective is to be sure the debtor provides accurate information and, if repayments are to be made, that the proper creditors receive payments.

ISSUE SPOTTER
Credit for the Bankrupt?

Some credit issuers have a policy of offering credit to people who have just gone through bankruptcy. Having had their debts cleared, they are not allowed to file for bankruptcy again for eight years. Are these folks in fact good credit risks because they cannot file for bankruptcy?

Priority Classes of Creditors Bankruptcy law states that certain creditors take priority over other creditors in receiving shares of the debtor's assets to pay for the debts owed them. Standing first in line are secured creditors. As discussed in Chapter 12, these creditors have a written security agreement that describes the specific property (collateral) that stands behind a particular debt. For a consumer, the most common collateral would be a home mortgage or an automobile loan. In bankruptcy, the secured creditor may request that the court grant permission for it to take possession of the property covered by the debt. The priority classes in bankruptcy are as follows:

1. Secured creditors
2. Costs of preserving and administering the debtor's estate
3. Unpaid wage claims
4. Certain claims of farmers and fishermen
5. Refund of security deposits
6. Alimony and child support
7. Taxes
8. General (unsecured) creditors who can file a proof of claim

All creditors of a particular class must be paid before the next-lower-priority creditors can be paid anything. Rarely is enough money received from the sale to pay general creditors what they are owed.

Discharge in Bankruptcy The final stage of the bankruptcy proceeding for individuals is discharge. **Discharge** means that the nonexempt assets have been liquidated and the proceeds distributed among certain creditors, who may not ask for more. The claimants are paid according to their priority, so unsecured creditors are rarely paid, and even secured creditors may get very little. The books have been cleared, and the debtor gets a fresh start. However, a declaration of bankruptcy remains on a person's credit history for ten years, and the debtor may not seek another discharge for eight years.

Some debts are not discharged by bankruptcy proceedings. The reason for these exceptions is to discourage the use of bankruptcy to evade certain responsibilities. The following are among the debts not extinguished by bankruptcy:

• Alimony and child support payments
• Back taxes
• Most student loans
• Some debts incurred immediately before filing bankruptcy
• Debts incurred by fraud against the creditors
• Fines owed to the government

Chapter 11

A portion of the bankruptcy code with a very different intent is Chapter 11, which applies to businesses that wish to remain in operation and not be liquidated. Many

INTERNATIONAL PERSPECTIVE

International Business Bankruptcy Complexities

Countries have different priorities for their bankruptcy laws. Some favor one type of creditor and some another, some favor employees of the bankrupt enterprise, and some give preference to keeping the business going. For example, Russia gives higher priority to intellectual property claims, and Scandinavian countries generally favor secured creditors to a greater degree than other countries. Most European countries force liquidation of businesses rather than allow reorganization of companies in trouble, although they are moving to rules more like Chapter 11.

These differences are important as businesses' assets are ever more scattered around the world. The complications are immense. Which country should have jurisdiction over a bank deposit of a bankrupt multinational firm when that deposit can move in seconds from the United States to the Netherlands? To deal with such issues, most countries have moved away from a "grab" theory of bankruptcy jurisdiction that gave control of assets to whichever bankruptcy court first got control to a "modified universalism" approach, based on the United Nations' Model Law on Cross-Border Insolvency bankruptcy law, which is largely incorporated into Chapter 15 of the U.S. Bankruptcy Code.

Under this approach, the courts take a worldwide perspective, looking for a solution that comes close to the theoretical ideal of having a single court determine all issues and avoid potentially conflicting rulings. To determine which court has jurisdiction, modified universalism asks which jurisdiction is the "principal place of business" or "center of the company's main interests" (COMI). Other countries' courts, following the same approach, defer to this court. Conversely, if a court in a jurisdiction where the debtor does not have COMI attempts to assert jurisdiction over assets elsewhere, it is likely to get a cold shoulder from foreign courts. Gradually, more and more countries have agreed to this approach.

© Cengage learning

businesses are worth more if they can be kept alive, generating revenue, than if they are liquidated in Chapter 7 when debts overwhelm assets. About 10,000 businesses each year use the Chapter 11 option.

The difference between the value of a business as a going concern compared with what is collected from selling its assets is known as a "going concern surplus." It is that surplus that the creditors hope to capture by allowing the business to remain in operation so that they have a greater chance of full repayment. There is a risk, of course, that keeping the business in operation will only worsen things, in which case the creditors lose even more. It is a judgment call, and creditors may disagree over whether to liquidate the business or not. In such cases, a court, with advice of a trustee, decides whether to allow the Chapter 11 proceeding or force liquidation.

Although Chapter 11 has been used to restructure some multibillion-dollar businesses, such as in the airline, asbestos, and automobile industries, most companies that file have assets worth less than $1 million. Well-planned Chapter 11 cases have good track records. There are often "prepackaged" bankruptcy filings, in which the debtor and creditors have already settled the issues before the filing and just need court approval to make it official. However, when businesses are in dire straits, it can be difficult to put together a reorganization plan to try to salvage operations as creditors press in.

Reorganization Process The filing under Chapter 11 automatically stays further financial actions by any parties involved. A hearing with the trustee determines whether the reorganization plan should be allowed to proceed or whether some creditors are due immediate payment or return of property. In most cases, managers of the debtor company are allowed by the court to continue operating the business. Thus, the debtor acts

Lighter Side of the Law

Home Sweet Home

Paul Bilzerian, a noted "corporate raider," was ordered to jail for contempt of court for allegedly hiding assets. He was being sued by the government, which was trying to collect a $62 million judgment against Bilzerian for securities fraud. Filing for bankruptcy protection against the judgment, Bilzerian claimed only $15,800 in assets, including a watch worth $5.

Fortunately for the destitute Bilzerian, Florida law allowed bankrupt persons to keep their homes. He lived in a 37,000 square-foot residence, which had an indoor basketball court, movie theater, nine-car garage, and an elevator. He offered to rent the home for $600,000 a week during a Super Bowl in Tampa.

Source: St. Petersburg Times.

as trustee of the operation, called a **debtor in possession**, attempting to generate income to cover debts owed. This means that the debtor's duty is to act in the best interests of the creditors as well as the owners.

Watching over the debtor is the creditors' committee composed of creditors with the largest claims. It supervises major management decisions of the reorganized business, cooperating with the debtor to try to make a success of the operation. The committee must review any unusual actions by the debtor; if the creditors object, the trustee and court review the matter.

As with Chapter 7, creditors in a class must be satisfied in order of priority of claims. However, unlike Chapter 7, where discharge of debts is the goal, under Chapter 11, the purpose is to have the business emerge as a profitable venture or to see it sold for its greatest value. But Chapter 11 proceedings mean many issues are fought in court, which is costly and adds significant delay to getting on with business. Judges and trustees can end up running companies. The *Kmart* case illustrates the kind of issues that arise, and this is just one of many rulings involving that one company.

IN THE MATTER OF KMART CORPORATION

United States Court of Appeals, Seventh Circuit, 359 F.3d 866 (2004)

Case Background *Kmart consists of the parent company and 37 affiliates and subsidiaries. When it filed for bankruptcy, it requested to pay, in full, the claims of selected "critical vendors." The request stated that some suppliers would be unwilling to do business in the future if past debts were not paid. To stay in operation, it needed to continue to receive such supplies. If it did not receive them, its ability to pay other creditors would be further impaired.*

The bankruptcy judge agreed and granted the order, without notifying the disfavored creditors.

The judge held that its decision was in the best interest of the debtors and creditors. Kmart was allowed to determine who were critical vendors. Kmart paid about $300 million to 2,330 suppliers. Another 2,000 vendors were not paid. They and 43,000 additional unsecured creditors got about 10 cents on the dollar, mostly in stock of the reorganized company.

Some of the creditors appealed to the district court. It reversed the order authorizing payments to critical vendors. Judge Grady concluded that neither the Bankruptcy Code nor the "doctrine of necessity" supported the order. That decision was then appealed to the 7th Circuit.

Case Decision Easterbrook, Circuit Judge

* * *

Appellants [Kmart and favored vendors] insist that, by the time Judge Grady acted, it was too late. Money had changed hands and we are told, cannot be refunded. But why not? Reversing preferential transfers is an ordinary feature of bankruptcy practice, often continuing under a confirmed plan of reorganization. ...

Section 105(a) [of the Bankruptcy Code] allows a bankruptcy court to "issue any order, process, or judgment that is necessary or appropriate to carry out the provisions of" the Code. This does not create discretion to set aside the Code's rules about priority and distribution. ... This statute does not allow a bankruptcy judge to authorize full payment of any unsecured debt, unless all unsecured creditors in the class are paid in full. ...

So does the Code contain any grant of authority for debtors to prefer some vendors over others? Many sections require equal treatment or specify the details of priority when assets are insufficient to satisfy all claims. ... Filing a petition for bankruptcy effectively creates two firms: the debts of the prefiling entity may be written down so that the postfiling entity may reorganize and continue in business if it has a positive cash flow. Treating prefiling debts as ... claims against the postfiling entity would impair the ability of bankruptcy law to prevent old debts from sinking a viable firm. ...

The foundation of a critical-vendors order is the belief that vendors not paid for prior deliveries will refuse to make new ones. ... For the premise to hold true, however, it is necessary to show not only that the disfavored creditors *will* be as well off with reorganization as with liquidation—a demonstration never attempted in this proceeding—but also that the supposedly critical vendors would have ceased deliveries if old debts were left unpaid while the litigation continued. ...

Some supposedly critical vendors will continue to do business with the debtor because they must. They may, for example, have long-term contracts, and the automatic stay prevents these vendors from walking away as long as the debtor pays for new deliveries. ...

Doubtless many suppliers fear the prospect of throwing good money after bad. It therefore may be vital to assure them that a debtor will pay for new deliveries on a current basis. Providing that assurance need not, however, entail payment for prepetition transactions. ...

Even if [the Code] allows critical-vendors orders in principle, preferential payments to a class of creditors are proper only if the record shows the prospect or benefit to the other creditors. This record does not, so the critical-vendors order cannot stand.

Affirmed.

Questions for Analysis

1. Assuming a vendor has no long-term obligation, would it continue to sell to Kmart if past debts were not paid?
2. Some critics of Chapter 11 contend that firms should be liquidated under Chapter 7, not operate under court supervision. Can you think of the reasons for that argument?

? *TEST YOURSELF*

1. Before a person may file for bankruptcy, they must complete a debtor education course: T—F
2. If a business files for bankruptcy and keeps operating in bankruptcy, it is said to be in _____.
3. Any person in financial difficulty has the right to file for Chapter 7 (liquidation) bankruptcy no more than every 10 years: T—F
4. In the case *In re Darby*, where Darby was in Chapter 13 bankruptcy and could not get cable television service, the court held that the cable company:
   a. must provide service to Darby, as it is considered to be a "utility."
   b. must provide service to Darby so long as he paid for the service in advance each month.
   c. need not provide service to Darby as it is not a necessity.
   d. need not provide service to Darby as his net income was too low.
5. Which of the following is a debt least likely to be extinguished by bankruptcy:
   a. back taxes.
   b. student loans.
   c. alimony.
   d. none of the other choices are likely to be extinguished by bankruptcy.

Answers: T; Chapter 11; F; c; d.

SUMMARY

- Negotiable instruments are flexible commercial instruments because of their ability to be transferred. Once issued, a negotiable instrument can be transferred by assignment or by negotiation. If the instrument is assigned, the assignee has the same contract rights and responsibilities as the assignor. If the instrument is transferred by negotiation, the transferee takes the instrument free of the transferor's contract responsibilities.

- To be negotiable, a commercial instrument must meet the general requirements of a negotiable instrument as provided by the UCC. It must be written, be an unconditional order or promise to pay, be signed by the maker or drawer, be payable on demand or at a specified time, be made out "to order" or "to bearer," and state a certain sum of money.

- If an instrument is negotiable under the requirements of the UCC, the instrument may be freely traded in the marketplace without concern for existing contract responsibilities as long as the instrument is in the possession of a holder in due course.

- As a creditor, a business monitors its credit extension and debt collection policies. As a debtor, a business borrows to pay for equipment, inventory, land, and buildings. Creditors are interested in being protected in the event a debtor is unable or unwilling to pay.

- A secured creditor has the right to take specific property of an insolvent debtor to satisfy the debt. The law provides two ways the creditor can obtain a debtor's property, referred to as security or collateral: (1) by agreement with the debtor, or (2) by operation of law and without an agreement between the lender and the borrower.

- A lender may require that a financially strong third party guarantee a loan. Such a guaranty may be a pledge of personal assets by business owners or from a third party. A promise is made to pay a particular debt of the business in the event it does not pay. A suretyship or guaranty is created, and the credit of the party providing it is the security for the debt owed.

- When a product is sold to a customer, Article 9 of the UCC provides that the product itself may secure the customer's obligation to pay. When credit is extended this way, the sale is called a secured transaction. By meeting the requirements of the UCC, the creditor obtains a security interest in the product to secure payment.

- To make a security interest enforceable, the lender must create the interest and make sure the interest is attached and perfected. When a creditor has a security interest in the product, it has priority to the product over some other creditors, including unsecured creditors. The lender can sue the debtor to recover the debt or repossess the product and resell it.

- In most credit transactions, except mortgages, creditors require that a security agreement and a financing statement be accepted and signed by the borrower. When money is borrowed for the purchase of real estate, the real estate itself secures the obligation and is evidenced by a mortgage. In most states, the mortgage is a lien, giving the holder the right to sell the property and repay the debt from proceeds in the event of default.

- Security obtained by a creditor through the operation of law is called a *lien*. The procedures for using liens are determined by state law. The most common liens are the mechanic's lien (applicable to real property), the possessory lien (applicable to personal property), and court-decreed liens. In each case, the lender may obtain the lien without the borrower's consent by following statutory procedures.

- The bankruptcy code governs bankruptcy procedure. There are several approaches to bankruptcy, including Chapter 7 (providing for liquidation and fair distribution of the debtor's assets for creditors), Chapter 11 (allowing businesses to reorganize rather than being liquidated), and Chapter 13 (personal bankruptcy for individuals that reorganizes debts, but does not discharge them).

- The trustee (or debtor in possession) is the person in charge of the bankruptcy. It is the trustee's objective, under bankruptcy court supervision, to maximize the amount of the debtor's assets available for distribution to the creditors.

- Bankruptcy law states that certain creditors take priority over other creditors in receiving shares of the debtor's assets. Secured creditors take priority over unsecured creditors.

TERMS TO KNOW

negotiable instrument, 339
negotiation, 339
bearer, 339
bearer instrument, 339
order paper, 340
bearer paper, 340
holder in due course, 341
drawer, 341
drawee, 341
payee, 341
check, 342
cashier's check, 342
note, 343
maker, 343
promissory note, 343
draft, 344
bill of exchange, 344
sight draft, 345
confirmation, 345
certificate of deposit, 345
creditor, 345
debtor, 345

principal, 346
consumer reports, 347
credit rating, 347
credit report, 347
open account, 348
unsecured creditor, 348
secured creditor, 348
collateral, 348
guaranty, 349
suretyship, 349
surety, 349
guarantor, 349
exoneration, 351
subrogated, 351
secured transaction, 351
perfection of security interest, 351
attachment, 351
perfection, 351
tangible property, 352
purchase money security
    interest, 352
floating lien, 352

default, 352
nonexempt property, 354
homestead law, 354
mortgage, 354
mortgagor, 354
mortgagee, 354
deficiency judgment, 354
non-recourse debt, 355
lien, 355
garnishment, 355
mechanic's lien, 355
possessory lien, 357
attachment lien, 357
writ, 357
judgment lien, 357
bankruptcy, 357
voluntary bankruptcy, 359
involuntary bankruptcy, 359
discharge, 361
debtor in possession, 363

DISCUSSION QUESTION

What are the basic differences between Chapters 7, 11, and 13 bankruptcy?

CASE QUESTIONS

1. Chung was at a racetrack operated by the New York State Racing Association. He bought a gambling voucher for use in SAMS, which are machines that take payments for gambling. The money credited to a voucher in a machine can be bet at once or can be used over time to make bets on SAMS. Chung forgot his voucher in a SAMS machine; it had several thousands of dollars credit on it. Someone found it and traded it in for cash. The betting system does not link a person to a voucher, so the thief was unknown. Chung sued, contending that the racetrack should be liable for failing to check the identity and ownership of vouchers prior to their use. Is the racetrack liable or is Chung out of luck? [*Chung* v. *New York State Racing Assn.*, 42 UCC Rep.Serv.2d 867, Dist. Ct., N.Y.C., NY (2000)]
   ✓ Check your answer

2. LaCombe practiced optometry as a sole proprietorship, LaCombe Eye Center. Slyfield worked for him at the front desk, but was not involved in bookkeeping. Over a four-year period, Slyfield embezzled checks made out to LaCombe by his patients, forged his signature, wrote her account number on it, and put the checks in her account at Bank One. LaCombe did not have an account at that bank. This worked for more than 500 checks totaling $70,000 until discovered. LaCombe sued Bank One for negligence for accepting the forged checks for deposit and negotiation. The district court held for LaCombe. The bank appealed. Was it liable? [*LaCombe* v. *Bank One Corp.*, 953 So.2d 161, Ct. App., La. (2007)]

3. McDowell owned and operated Big River Harley Davidson in Wapello, Iowa. As required by law, McDowell took out a motor vehicle dealer's surety bond for $35,000 with United Fire and Casualty Insurance. The bond protects retail customers who get stuck when a motor vehicle dealer, perhaps because of fraud, does not deliver a vehicle that has been paid for. The surety bond was in force when Big River went out of business and McDowell left the state. While in business,

Big River sold a Harley to Elworth Harley Davidson in Norfolk, Nebraska. Elworth paid $12,000 for the Harley that was never delivered. Elworth sued United Fire as surety for the $12,000. Can Elworth recover? [*United Fire and Casualty* v. *Acker*, 541 N.W.2d 517, Sup. Ct., Iowa (1995)]
   ✓ Check your answer

4. Bussewitz borrowed money from Citibank and signed a promissory note. Pitassi also signed the promissory note as co-maker of the note. When Bussewitz failed to make payments and defaulted on the note, Citibank, under the terms of the note, declared the entire unpaid balance due and sued both makers. Pitassi defended that he should not be liable because he signed the note only as a favor to Bussewitz and furthermore, the note did not state when the first installment payment was due; that term had been left blank. Is Pitassi liable? [*Citibank* v. *Pitassi*, 432 N.Y.S.2d 389, Sup. Ct., App. Div., NY (1980)]

5. Moody and three others bought a business and executed promissory notes for $8.17 million. Moody owned 20 percent of the business; the other three owned the other 80 percent of the business. Moody was unable to make several payments on schedule. The other owners covered the payments he was supposed to make so the notes would not go into default. Moody was sued by the others for his contribution. He asserted that he was the same as a surety. Because they made the payments that were due for the business, he was no longer obligated on those payments. Is that correct? [*Krumme* v. *Moody*, 910 P.2d 993, Sup. Ct., Ok. (1996)]
   ✓ Check your answer

6. Mollinedo's home was damaged by fire. Her insurance company, Sentry, recommended ServiceMaster as a repair company. An adjuster for Sentry visited the home with the home contractor from ServiceMaster and approved $30,000 worth of work, which ServiceMaster did with Mollinedo's approval. Sentry gave the $30,000 to Mollinedo's mortgage company. Mollinedo filed

for bankruptcy. ServiceMaster, which got nothing, sued Sentry for breach of contract and unjust enrichment. Did ServiceMaster, which never filed a lien, have a claim? [*Service-Master of St. Cloud v. GAB Business Services*, 544 N.W.2d 302, Sup. Ct., Minn. (1996)]

7. The Boggses were declared bankrupt under Chapter 13. Shortly after their discharge, Somerville Bank and Trust contended that the Boggses did not pay off the interest on a loan secured by a mortgage on their principal residence. The bank had not raised the issue until after the bankruptcy court had issued its discharge order covering the indebtedness. The bank attempted to collect the debt as though there had been no discharge. Is the bank entitled to collect the interest? [*Boggs v. Somerville Bank and Trust*, 51 F.3d 271, 6th Cir. (1995)]

8. Globe Building went into Chapter 7 bankruptcy, so a trustee was appointed to control the bankrupt estate. As a number of Globe employees had not been paid when the company went under, the state of Wisconsin, where Globe was located, filed a lien for wages against all property owned by Globe. Could the lien be enforced? [*In re: Globe Building Materials*, 463 F.3d 631, 7th Cir. (2006)]
   ✓ Check your answer

9. Susan Krieger had about $25,000 in student debts. It had been 11 years since she graduated from college. She never found work in the field for which she was trained and was destitute, living with her aged mother in a rural area. She applied to have the student debt forgiven under the "hardship" exception. Do you think that would apply in this case? [*Krieger v. Educational Credit Management Corp.*, 713 F.3d 882, 7th Cir. 2013)]

ETHICS QUESTION

Should a small business be allowed to seek discharge of debts through bankruptcy, when those debts were incurred as a consequence of an automobile accident caused by one of its drivers who was legally drunk at the time of the accident? [See *Matter of Wooten*, 30 *Bankr.* 357, N.D. Ala. (1983)]

PULLING IT TOGETHER

We have covered a number of key concepts in Chapters 6 through 13. Here we consider some cases that bring in legal issues from more than one area for you to identify.

Part 2 of the text reviewed the major areas of the common law that affect business. There is some statutory law in the chapters we covered, but most of the cases tended to reflect the way business practices were viewed, rather than being highly regulatory. Here, we consider cases that overlap more than one area that we covered and some that may raise issues going back to Part 1 of the text.

1. Two Men and a Truck (TMT) is a Michigan company that sells moving service franchises around the country. Mayes bought a TMT franchise in Indiana that operated under the TMT name. TMT sued Mayes for failure to pay royalties and advertising fees and for failure to file monthly sales reports for the franchise. TMT also terminated the franchise relationship, but Mayes continued to operate the franchise under the TMT name.

   Where would the suit be likely to be filed? What causes of action might TMT have against Mayes? Having read about franchises, take a guess what Mayes's likely defense may be with respect to the purchase of the franchise. List the possible actions TMT might file.

2. Miller was eating a Big Mac at a McDonald's franchise restaurant in Oregon when she bit into a sapphire stone and injured her teeth. She sued. Where could she file suit? Who would she sue? What would she sue them for? What defenses do you think may be relevant?

3. The Center for Behavioral Health rented a building for six years from Priskos. One day a water pipe burst, flooding much of the building. The Center hired Advanced Restoration to do repair work, and the bill was $9,300. Priskos was aware the work was being done but did not participate in the decision to hire Advanced or to authorize the work. The Center's insurer said it was not responsible for paying for such damage to the building. The Center gave the bill to Priskos, who contacted his insurance company. It paid the bill minus a $1,000 deductible. Priskos offered the $8,300 check to Advanced for the work as payment in full.

Advanced filed a mechanics' lien for the full amount. Priskos demanded a lien waiver from Advanced in exchange for the $8,300 as payment in full. Advanced sued Priskos and the Center for payment in full.

   Where would suit be filed? Did the tenant (the Center) have the right to have the work done and then expect the landlord to pay the bill, or is the tenant liable because it called Advanced to do the work? Was the tenant an agent authorized to call Advanced and thereby commit the principal, the landlord, to the contract? What kind of an agent would the Center be for Priskos, if there was an agency relationship?

4. Barry and Sandra Erlich hired Menezes to build their dream house on an ocean-view lot in California. They moved into the house in December 1990. Two months later, in the rainy season, "the house leaked from every conceivable location." Walls were so saturated that the plaster fell off, most windows leaked, and there were three inches of water in the living room. Despite various repair efforts by Menezes, water continued to leak in all parts of the house. Another contractor and an engineer found serious defects in the roof, walls, windows, and waterproofing, as well as structural problems with the walls, roof, and foundation.

   The Erlichs sued Menezes and testified that the problems with their house made them sick. Barry Erlich said that the distress worsened his heart condition, forcing him to resign from his job. Sandra was afraid the house might collapse on the family, especially in an earthquake. Their suit sought recovery on several theories, including breach of contract, fraud, negligent misrepresentation, negligent construction, emotional distress, and pain and suffering. Which of their tort and contract claims would seem most likely to stand?

5. Landham played the role of Billy, the Native American tracker, in the movie *Predator* starring Arnold Schwarzenegger. Fox licensed to Galoob Toys the right to produce and market a line of its "Micro Machine" toys based on *Predator*. One of three sets of toys contained a "Billy" action figure. It is

1.5 inches tall and bears no personal resemblance to Landham. Landham sued Galoob and Fox for false endorsement under the Landham Act and for violating his right of publicity (a part of the right to privacy). The district court dismissed the suit. Landham appealed. Does he have a suit in tort for the violation of his right of publicity and/or a suit for trademark infringement?

6. Barber erected a sign on his property facing Interstate 20 in west Texas. The sign said "Just Say NO to Searches" and gave a phone number. Callers received information about a citizen's constitutional rights regarding police searches of automobiles. The Texas Department of Transportation sent Barber a letter telling him that the sign violated the Highway Beautification Act and that he must remove the sign or obtain a permit from the Department to have a sign that complies with Department regulations. The trial court ordered Barber to remove the sign and to pay the Department's attorney's fees. He appealed.

7. Gateway sold computers and related products by mail, Internet, and telephone. With each PC, Gateway sent a "Standard Terms and Conditions Agreement" including a "Dispute Resolution" clause, stating that any dispute would be settled by arbitration under the rules of the International Chamber of Commerce (ICC) in Chicago. Several buyers of computers and software from Gateway sued for breach of contract and breach of warranty, contending the company falsely stated that technical support for products was available when in fact, the plaintiffs claimed, it was almost impossible to get technical support by phone.

The trial court dismissed the suit, holding that the parties had to go to arbitration. The plaintiffs appealed, contending that the arbitration clause violated UCC § 2-302 as an unconscionable contract because ICC rules require payment of a $4,000 advance fee when a claim is filed, of which $2,000 is nonrefundable regardless of outcome, and each plaintiff would have to bear the cost of travel to Chicago. These expenses are greater than the value of most of the products purchased. Is the arbitration clause valid under the UCC?

8. The Maretts owned Marett Properties, LLC. They hired Brice Building to work on two commercial real estate buildings that they intended to lease. The Maretts signed guaranties agreeing to be personally liable for Marett Properties' debt to Brice, but the construction contracts were never signed. After some time, Brice had been paid nothing for the $337,800 worth of work he had completed. The two properties were not leased and were unfinished. Because there was no completed contract, Brice sued the Maretts in quantum merit, an equity claim, and also to enforce their personal guaranty. The Maretts defended that there was a failure to complete a contract and that without a contract, the guaranty was not valid. Would Brice win the case?

9. Three accountants formed a partnership. Deodati was a client of McCreight, one of the partners. Deodati authorized McCreight to buy and sell certificates of deposit on his behalf. McCreight stole Deodati's money, generating fictitious income statements to conceal the fraud. The other partners knew nothing about the fraud. Deodati paid the partnership $3,500 for accounting services. When another partner uncovered the fraud, he notified Deodati, who sued the partnership for his losses. The trial court awarded Deodati $290,000 and imposed joint and several liability upon the partnership and the individual partners. The innocent partners then filed for bankruptcy. Deodati sought to prevent them from discharging the debt because it arose from fraud. The trial court held for the innocent partners. Deodati appealed. Are the innocent partners liable?

OVERVIEW

Some regulatory areas affect some businesses but other types of firms may be affected by the assorted rules only rarely. However, all businesses have agency and employment relationships. Labor markets in the United States are generally rated as the most free in the world, as employers and employees (or agents) come to whatever terms that are mutually advantageous.

The Supreme Court has noted many times that employment law is built on the common law of agency, so we begin this chapter with agency, which applies to more than just normal employment relationships. Then we examine the elements of employment law, including contractual agreements that can be attached to employment. Public policy limits on employment-at-will are considered, but, more importantly, the many federal (and some state) policies that impose requirements on employers, especially those designed to reduce discrimination in employment, are studied. Court interpretations of statutory requirements that apply to employment play a major role in determining how the rules work in practice.

CHAPTER **14**

Agency and the Employment Relationship

The Levine Cancer Institute, like most health care facilities, is concerned about cost control as patient payments from the government continue to be squeezed. One proposal for cost reduction is to reduce the number of professionals employed by the hospital. It recommends that nurses and doctors be encouraged to form companies to provide their services to the hospital. The hospital would then contract with the companies for nurses and doctors as independent contractors. While administrators believe that the plan could reduce costs, they are concerned about several legal matters. Would the new companies be agents of the hospital? By using the new companies, is it possible to designate the doctors and nurses as independent contractors, rather than as employees, and thus reduce potential liability for medical malpractice?

Another proposal recommends having an outside firm do all buying for the hospital, rather than have employees purchase supplies. One manager thinks that if the outside buying company makes a mistake in product choice or if a patient asserts that he was injured because a defective or inappropriate product was used, then the buying company would be liable for the mistake instead of the hospital. Is that correct?

These are among the subjects discussed in this chapter, which considers the range of possible employment relationships, how they are created, and the legal constraints on their formation and functions. We begin by considering agency relationships, which are the basis for an employment relationship, but can be more limited in purpose. Agency relationships are often critical in the formation of contracts and the employment relationship because businesses must assign various people to perform assorted services.

Agency Relationships

According to *Black's Law Dictionary,* an **agency relationship** is:

> *An employment [of an agent] for the purpose of representation in establishing relations between a principal and third parties.**

In other words, an agency is created when a person or company—the **agent**—agrees to act for, or in place of, another person or company—the **principal**—who provides the agent with authority to do so. The agent represents the principal. An agent may negotiate and legally bind a principal to contracts with third parties as long as he acts within the scope of authority granted by the principal. In dealing with third parties, normally customers or suppliers, the agent is granted certain authority to act for the principal. The typical agency relationship is compared with the typical two-party business transaction in Exhibit 14.1.

A principal's purpose for developing agency relationships is to expand business opportunities and use the expertise of agents. For example, the Don Reid Ford dealership in Orlando employs managers and sales representatives to make decisions about ordering cars, selling them to customers, buying and selling used cars, and running a repair shop.

EXHIBIT 14.1   A CONTRACT AND AN AGENCY RELATIONSHIP

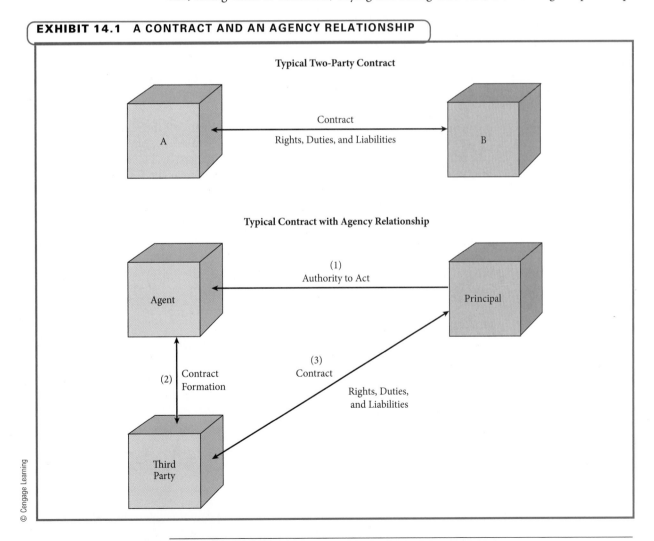

© Cengage Learning

---

*Reprinted from Black's Law Dictionary with permission of Thomson Reuters.

Don Reid and his customers enjoy business dealings that would not be possible without the ability to use agency relationships because Reid personally could not directly run everything needed in a large business. The managers, sales representatives, and mechanics all have certain responsibilities and limited scopes of authority. They can engage in certain transactions on behalf of the principal, Don Reid. Similarly, Don Reid may hire an attorney to perform certain legal duties, an accountant to deal with federal and state tax authorities, and other agents who have certain rights and responsibilities in business dealings.

Classification of Agents

An agent's authority is the power to change the principal's legal obligations. That is, when an agent uses authority, say, to enter into a contract with a third party, new rights and duties are created for the principal. A principal controls this by establishing the scope of an agent's authority to act for the principal.

Agents can have whatever duties they agree to accept, so classes of agents are nearly unlimited. Some commonly recognized ones are:

- **Universal agent**—someone designated to do all acts that can be legally granted to an agent. The agent is usually given a general power of attorney to do all business transactions on behalf of the principal.
- **General agent**—a person authorized to execute all transactions connected with a certain business, such as a manager who runs all aspects of a hotel. The principal may limit the extent of the general agent's authority to a portion of the business.
- **Special agent**—an agent with authority to represent the principal only for specific transactions, usually for a limited time.
- **Agency coupled with an interest**—when an agent pays for the right to have authority for a business. Suppose you lend someone money to buy a house to use as a rental. The borrower agrees that rent from the property will be sent to you to pay off the loan. The borrower has become the agent of the lender for the purpose of collecting rent.
- **Gratuitous agent**—when a person volunteers with no expectation of being paid for her services. The fact that there is no pay does not change the legal consequences of the agency relationship.
- **Subagents**—when a principal authorizes an agent to delegate authority to other agents, that is, to subagents who assist the agent. The subagents work for the agent but owe duties both to the agent and the principal.

Creating an Agency

No particular formal procedure is needed to establish an agency relationship. However, the principal must show a desire for the agent to act on her behalf, and the agent must consent to do so. Most agency relationships are created without formal statements such as "I will represent you," but can be based on a written agreement. An agency can be established by any of the following:

- Agreement of the parties
- Ratification of the agent's activities by the principal
- Application of the doctrine of estoppel
- Operation of law

Agency by Agreement of the Parties An agency is normally formed by an agreement of the parties. The principal and agent establish the agency by an oral or a written contract. As we have seen previously, the law requires a written contract in some instances. Generally, the agency is in writing when it is to last longer than one year or is for the sale of land. However, most agencies are established by agreements that do not qualify as contracts. The basis of the agency, its own area of law, is that the agent acts for the benefit of the principal and is subject to the principal's control.

One legal document that establishes an agency is the **power of attorney**, which authorizes a person or company to act as an agent for a principal. The power of attorney can be general or it can provide the agent with limited authority to act for the principal for one deal. The term, power of attorney, describes the document itself and does not mean that the agent, who may be called an attorney-in-fact, is actually an attorney.

Implied or Express Ratification by the Principal An agency relationship may be created by a principal's **ratification**—or acceptance of responsibility—of an agent's activities. This arises when a person who is not an agent, or an agent who is acting beyond her authority, enters into a contract on behalf of another—the alleged principal. In such circumstances, the alleged principal is ordinarily under no obligation to be bound by the person's actions. However, the alleged principal may become bound to the contract by ratifying the agreement.

By doing this, the alleged principal becomes the real principal and is bound by the contract as if an agent with the authority to enter into the contract had negotiated it. Suppose you advertised your car for sale for $9,000. A prospective buyer looked at it while you were away and offered $8,500, which your roommate accepted, thinking you would be happy to sell it for that. Because your roommate was not your agent, you would not be obligated to go through with the deal. However, you could also ratify the deal by selling for that price.

Ratification can be express or implied. An **express ratification** is a principal's clear signal to be bound to the otherwise unauthorized agreement. **Implied ratification** takes place when the principal behaves as if he has the intent of ratifying an unauthorized agreement. This usually occurs when the principal accepts the benefits of the agreement.

Express or implied ratification has limits as to what it covers. A principal can ratify agreements only when she knows the key facts. Furthermore, an agreement can be ratified only if the agent purported to act for the principal. The principal must ratify the agreement before the third party involved withdraws. Finally, if the agreement between the agent and the third party was required by law to be in writing, such as a sale of real estate, the ratification must be in writing.

Agency by Estoppel Similar to implied ratification, and legally identical in some states, is an **agency by estoppel**. In this case, an agency is created by the actions of a principal. Although no formal agency exists, the actions of the principal may lead one to reasonably believe that the presumed agent has authority to act for the principal. When the agent enters into a contract with a third party for the principal, the principal is bound to the contract and is stopped (prevented) from denying the existence of the agent's authority.

Agency by Operation of Law The courts may impose an agency relationship when an emergency exists. Suppose a hurricane is headed for Florida. Unable to talk to the boss who is traveling, an employee buys $500 worth of plywood to protect the windows and other business property. That purchase is beyond delegated authority, but the situation required an immediate decision. The agent, although acting beyond the authority granted by the principal, is given the authority to do so in emergencies through an **agency by operation of law** and must be compensated.

Lighter Side of the Law

Is Slavery an Employment Relationship?

Ruiz, a 60-year-old former schoolteacher from the Philippines, was a domestic servant for James Jackson and his wife. She claimed she was paid $300 a year for working 18 hours a day. She said she was hit and slept on a dog bed. She was told she would go to jail and never see her family again if she told anyone.

After she escaped and sued, a Los Angeles jury awarded her $825,000 damages for involuntary servitude and false imprisonment. She was helped by the Coalition to Abolish Slavery and Trafficking, which estimates that thousands of people are brought to the United States every year and kept in such conditions.

Jackson, who knows the law, filed for bankruptcy right before the trial began. When he lost the suit, his employer fired him from his position as vice president for legal affairs for Sony Pictures Entertainment.

Source: Associated Press.

Acts for the Principal

An agent's ability to transact business for a principal depends on the scope of authority given to the agent. Authority may be determined by statements by the principal, the principal's conduct, or the trade customs in business. An agent can have two general classes of authority: actual authority and apparent authority. If an agent claims to have authority but in fact has none, the principal is not responsible for the agent's dealings with third parties who have no reason to think the agent has authority. The problem is, do third parties know there is no authority?

Actual Authority **Actual authority**, sometimes called real authority, is given by the principal to the agent. Actual authority can come from express and implied authority. It confers the power and the right to change the principal's legal status on the agent.

Express authority is based on oral or written instructions given by the principal to an agent. Suppose the owner of an apartment complex hires a leasing agent and tells him or her to rent apartments at a certain price. The agent now has express authority to rent the apartments as instructed.

Often, when an agent receives express authority, he also receives **implied authority** to do whatever is reasonable to carry out the agency purpose. Suppose a landowner authorizes a real estate agent to find a buyer for some acreage. The landowner does not describe to the agent every step that could be taken. Even though the parties may not discuss the matter, the agent would have implied authority to post a "For Sale" sign on the property, advertise the offer for sale, and take possible buyers to see the property. The agent would have implied authority to use normal business practices unless instructed not to do so by the principal.

Apparent Authority A principal can be bound by unauthorized acts of an agent who appears to have authority to act. **Apparent authority** arises when the principal creates an appearance of authority in an agent that leads a third party to conclude reasonably that the agent has authority to act for the principal.

Apparent authority commonly arises when a principal hires a business manager as an agent. As a rule, the authority to manage a business gives the agent the implied authority—or the appearance of authority, as we see in the *Cove Management* case—to undertake usual business activities.

COVE MANAGEMENT V. AFLAC, INC.

Appellate Court of Illinois, 986 N.E.2d 1206 (2013)

Case Background *Galgano signed an "Associates Agreement" with AFLAC in 2004. It authorized him to solicit applications for insurance policies offered by AFLAC. The agreement stated that Galgano was an independent contractor without authority to bind AFLAC for his "debts, faults, or actions." It also stated that Galgano may not enter into contracts or incur debt on behalf of AFLAC. Another agreement, signed in 2005, stated that Galgano did not have authority to "rent any office space" or otherwise obligate AFLAC without "specific written authorization."*

In 2009, Galgano leased office space from Cove Management. The lease listed the tenant as AFLAC and listed Galgano as the guarantor for the office to be used for "insurance services." Galgano signed as lessee and as guarantor. When he later defaulted on lease payments, Cove sued AFLAC to recover losses. Cove noted that the office was clearly listed as an AFLAC office engaged in business for AFLAC. Cove asserted that it had the right to presume that Galgano had authority as an agent to bind AFLAC to the lease. The district court dismissed the suit; Cove appealed.

Case Decision Justice Gordon

* * *

In order to determine whether Galgano was an independent contractor or an agent of AFLAC, we must first determine Galgano's authority. An agent's authority may be either actual or apparent, and actual authority may be either express or implied. Express authority is actual authority granted explicitly by the principal to the agent, while implied authority is actual authority proven circumstantially by evidence of the agent's position. Apparent authority, by contrast, is authority imposed by equity.

Plaintiff's primary argument is that AFLAC clothed Galgano with apparent authority as its agent and thus AFLAC was liable as a lessee under the lease. Apparent authority is defined as follows:

Apparent authority in an agent is such authority as the principal knowingly permits the agent to assume or which he holds his agent out as posses-

sing—it is such authority as a reasonably prudent man, exercising diligence and discretion, in view of the principal's conduct, would naturally suppose the agent to possess." ...

Where a principal has created the appearance of authority in an agent, and another party has reasonably and detrimentally relied upon the agent's authority, the principal cannot deny it.

If there is no showing of reasonable and detrimental reliance upon the agent's authority, there can be no apparent authority.

The majority of evidence that plaintiff shows is evidence that came into existence after the signing of the lease, except for the statements and representations of Galgano, which cannot be considered. ... Likewise, we cannot consider the evidence (1) that when the office was set up, the parking sign had the AFLAC symbol and duck, (2) that AFLAC's stylized blue materials were in the office, inside and out, and (3) that AFLAC was listed on the directory of the building, because they all occurred after the lease was signed and thus there was not any reliance by plaintiff on that information when entering into the lease. ...

The record in the instant case does not show that plaintiff made any effort to determine whether Galgano was an independent contractor or an agent of AFLAC acting within the scope of his authority. Instead, plaintiff apparently relied exclusively on the statements and representations of Galgano that he had the authority to bind AFLAC to the lease on the premises. ...

We cannot find that Galgano was acting under apparent authority. In addition, plaintiff failed to make a reasonable inquiry as they were under a duty to make. ...

Affirmed.

Questions for Analysis

1. What should Cove Management have done to avoid this situation?
2. Did Galgano breach a duty he owed to AFLAC?

Duties of the Agency Parties

An agency relationship means that parties have duties that govern their conduct. For example, both parties are required to act in good faith toward each other and to share information having an important effect on the relationship. In addition, as Exhibit 14.2 summarizes, there are duties that each party owes the other.

Principal's Duties to an Agent

The law of agency emphasizes the duties an agent owes to his principal. This is understandable, as the acts central to the agency relationship are to be performed by the agent. Nevertheless, the principal owes the agent certain duties.

The principal has a **duty to cooperate** with her agent by performing responsibilities defined in the agreement forming the agency. If relevant, the principal must provide a safe working environment and warn the agent of any unreasonable risks associated with the agency. In addition, the principal must furnish goods of adequate quality to the agent, if the agreement calls for the sale of goods of a specific quality.

Unless the agent agrees to work for free, the principal is under a **duty to compensate** her agent. If the agency does not specify the compensation, the principal has a duty to pay the reasonable value of the services provided. In such circumstances, the agent is paid the "customary" rate for services provided.

A principal has a duty to pay the reasonable expenses incurred by an agent, for example, pay travel and lodging expenses. The principal has a **duty to reimburse** authorized payments the agent makes to third parties on behalf of the principal. However, the principal has no obligation to pay the agent for expenses incurred through misconduct, such as getting thrown in jail for driving drunk while on business for the principal.

The principal is under a **duty to indemnify**—to pay for damages or to insure the agent against losses suffered while undertaking authorized transactions. Suppose the principal has goods that belong to someone else and directs the agent to sell them. The agent sells the goods, believing they are the property of the principal. Later, if the legal owner sues the agent, the principal must indemnify the agent for costs incurred in the lawsuit.

EXHIBIT 14.2   DUTIES IN AN AGENCY RELATIONSHIP

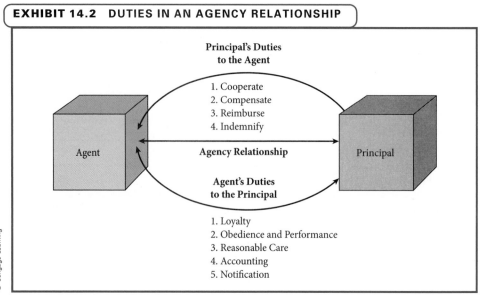

© Cengage Learning

Agent's Duties to the Principal An agent's duties to a principal arise because an agent is a **fiduciary** of the principal. That is, the agent occupies a position of trust, honesty, and confidence for the principal. In addition to taking on specific responsibilities for the principal in an agency relationship, the law presumes certain duties for agents.

The **duty of loyalty** requires an agent to place the principal's interests before the agent's personal interests or those of any third party. That is, the agent may not compete with the principal while working for the principal, unless the principal approves. It would be a violation of this duty if the agent also represented another party whose interests were in conflict with those of the principal.

Don Reid Ford in Orlando had a manager named Southern who handled inventory at Reid's "Get Ready Department." Southern received fake invoices from Stafford, who ran an operation that sold supplies to Reid. Southern would order the invoices paid, and then Stafford and Southern would split the cash—about $300,000 over a two-year period. The actions were criminal, but also violated Southern's duty to Reid. He was ordered to pay restitution.

The duty of loyalty applies to all employees, even CEOs of corporations. The Supreme Court of Massachusetts held that the CEO of a large company, Astra USA, would forfeit all compensation paid to him during his disloyalty to the company. He failed to disclose to the board the fact that he had been paying women with company money not to file sexual harassment charges (914 N.E.2d 36).

An agent must perform instructions provided by the principal. The agent violates the **duty of obedience and performance** by ignoring the principal's instructions and is liable to the principal for related losses. However, an agent has no obligation to engage in acts that could lead to personal liability.

An agent is required to exercise **reasonable care** in the performance of duties, i.e., to perform responsibilities with the degree of care that a reasonable person would exercise under the circumstances. An accountant hired to prepare an income tax return who fails to take advantage of a legal tax deduction would violate this duty of reasonable care.

An agent has a **duty to account** for the funds and property of his principal that have been entrusted to him or have come into his possession. The agent must be able to show where money or property comes from and goes to. An agent must also avoid mixing personal funds with funds belonging to the principal.

Finally, an agent is under a duty to keep her principal informed of all facts relevant to the agency. Suppose Linkin hires Eminem as her agent to sell some farmland at a given price. Eminem learns that in the next several months, the farmland will likely increase in value because of a new highway to be built nearby. Eminem is under a **duty to inform** Linkin of this information so that she can decide whether she still wants Eminem to sell according to her original instructions. We see an example of an agent violating duties to a principal in the *Bearden* case.

BEARDEN V. WARDLEY CORP.

Court of Appeals of Utah 72 P.3d 144 (2003)

Case Background *Bearden wanted to sell a rental house she owned. She listed the property with real estate agent Gritton, who worked for Wardley Corporation, a real estate brokerage firm. Gritton*

then told Bearden that he would buy the house. She agreed. The contract called for him to pay Bearden $400 a month followed by a balloon payment at the end of five years. Bearden would keep *title to the property until the balloon payment was made.*

Unknown to Bearden, when Gritton gave her multiple documents to sign, one was a warranty deed that transferred title to Gritton. He had the signature improperly notarized and recorded the deed. When he did not keep up on his payments to Bearden, she hired a lawyer. He discovered that Gritton had fraudulently obtained the warranty deed, that he had borrowed money against the property, and that the property was in foreclosure. Bearden paid $60,000 to keep the property from being lost.

She sued Gritton and Wardley for breach of contract, fraud, and breach of fiduciary duty. The jury awarded Bearden $75,000 in compensatory damages, $25,000 in punitive damages, $50,000 in attorney fees, plus costs and interest. Because the judgment was against both Gritton and Wardley, Wardley was stuck with paying the judgment. It appealed.

Case Decision Thorne, Judge

* * *

Wardley argues that the trial court erred ... because Bearden did not introduce evidence regarding Wardley's duty to Bearden or the resulting breach. Bearden introduced into evidence a listing contract drafted by Wardley and signed by Gritton, individually and as Wardley's agent. The listing Contract provided:

> Wardley Better Homes and Gardens and the Agent agree to act as agent for the seller and will work diligently to locate a Buyer for the Property. As the Seller's agent, they will act consistent with their *fiduciary duties to the*

Seller of loyalty, full disclosure, confidentiality, and reasonable care.

Bearden also introduced evidence that it was Wardley's policy to have management or a supervisor review the documents in its transition files and that Wardley had an internal policy that prohibited agents from purchasing properties that an agent listed. From this evidence, the jury could have found that Wardley owed Bearden the fiduciary duties of "loyalty, full disclosure, confidentiality, and reasonable care."

... Bearden introduced evidence that (1) Gritton was employed by Wardley, (2) Wardley was aware that Gritton had executed a listing agreement and a real estate purchase agreement with Bearden wherein Gritton acted as buyer and seller's agent and the purchaser of the property, (3) Wardley never questioned Gritton about violating its internal policy against an agent purchasing property listed by that agent, (4) Wardley never asked Gritton to stop representing Bearden, and (5) Wardley never informed Bearden of Gritton's violations of the internal policy. This evidence is sufficient for the jury to find that Wardley breached its duty of care to Bearden. ...

Affirmed.

Questions for Analysis

1. The appeals court affirmed that the principal was liable for damages incurred by fraud of one of its agents. Because there was no evidence that Wardley participated in Gritton's fraud, why should it be liable?
2. Suppose Gritton had told Wardley he wanted to buy the property he had listed. What should Wardley have done?

Liability for Contracts

The primary purpose of agency relationships is to help principals expand business activities. Agents enter into contracts on behalf of the principal. The rights and liabilities of the principal and agent may be determined by whether the principal is disclosed or undisclosed.

Disclosed Principals According to the *Restatement (Third) Agency*, a **disclosed principal** is one whose identity is known by the third party at the time a contract is entered into with an agent.

A disclosed principal is liable to a third party for a contract made by an agent who had actual authority to act on behalf of the principal. Suppose Antebellum instructs

CYBER LAW

Computer Abuse by Employees

Citrin worked for a real estate development company to help identify properties that the company could buy. He decided to go into business for himself in competition with his employer. To cover his tracks, he installed a program to scrub his company computer clean of all information. Some of the files would have shown how he was collecting information for himself; others were company files he developed. His computer had the only copy, so valuable information was destroyed.

The company sued him for violating the Computer Fraud and Abuse Act, which holds it illegal to intentionally damage a protected computer. The federal appeals court held that Citrin breached his duty of loyalty. Once he breached that duty by planning to use company resources for his own gain, he no longer had an agency relationship that gave him the right to access company files. He then was liable for destroying files by accessing a computer he had no right to use (440 F.3d 418). The Act gives employers additional legal weapons to go after those who damage company machines or files.

© Cengage Learning

Underwood, her agent, to buy her a car. Underwood contracts for a car with a seller who knows that Underwood is acting as an agent. Antebellum is bound by the contract and must honor it. The third-party seller may sue Antebellum if she fails to perform according to the agreement made for her by Underwood.

The principal is also liable if a third party enters into a contract with an agent with apparent authority. However, an agent who violates the duty of obedience to the principal is liable to the principal for any losses. To illustrate, suppose Antebellum did not give Underwood authority to buy a car, but Antebellum's conduct in the past led the seller to believe that Underwood had authority. If Underwood contracts for a car, Antebellum is bound by it. However, Underwood must indemnify Antebellum for losses incurred as a result.

Undisclosed Principals An **undisclosed principal** is one whose identity is unknown by the third party. The third party has no knowledge that the agent is acting for another when a contract is made. Thus, the third party is unaware of both the identity of the principal and of the agency relationship. In this situation, the agent is liable to the third party for the principal's nonperformance of the contract.

If the agent had authority to make a contract, the undisclosed principal is bound to the obligations formed with third parties by the agent just as if the identity had been disclosed.

If the agent is found liable to the third party, because the principal failed to perform and the third party sues the agent, the agent is entitled to be indemnified by the principal. However, the agent must have been operating within the scope of his authority. If the agent acted outside his authority, the undisclosed principal is under no obligation to accept responsibility for the agent's actions.

The issue of an undisclosed principal comes up in quite a few cases that are similar to the *Yim* case, where a buyer attempts to evade paying for goods purchased under the claim that the buyer was only an agent for a principal—a business. But the business is often controlled by the agent.

Terminating an Agency

The agency relationship is voluntary. Thus, when a party leaves or when the consent comes to an end, the agency is terminated; the agent's authority to act for the principal

YIM V. J'S FASHION ACCESSORIES, INC.
Court of Appeals of Georgia 680 S.E.2d 466 (2009)

Case Background *Benjamin Yim did business under the trade name Ho Tae. He ordered goods from J's Fashion. Invoices were sent to Ho Tae. When the account was not paid, Fashion sued Yim. He denied liability on the grounds that he was acting as an agent for a corporation, the principal, known as Hosung Enterprise, Inc. It did business under the name Ho Tae. J's Fashion replied that "at no time did Benjamin Yim disclose the existence of a corporation or other artificial entity with whom we were dealing. At all times, we dealt directly with Benjamin Yim using his trade name 'Ho Tae.'" The trial court entered summary judgment against Yim for the amount invoiced. He appealed, contending that he was only an agent for Hosung Enterprise.*

Case Decision Blackburn, Presiding Judge

* * *

"An agent who makes a contract without identifying his principal becomes personally liable on the contract." Thus, "in order to avoid personal liability, an agent is under a duty to disclose the fact of his agency and the identity of his principal, and one who deals with an agent who fails to disclose his principal may at his election recover from either the agent or the principal." Because the duty is on the agent to make this disclosure, it is "not on the party with whom he deals to discover it."

The agent must be specific in this disclosure. "The disclosure of an agency is not complete for the purpose of relieving the agent from personal liability unless it embraces the name of the principal." Nor is it sufficient if the agent merely uses the trade name of the principal. "The use of a trade name is not necessarily a sufficient disclosure of the identity of the principal and the fact of agency so as to protect the agent against personal liability." A "trade name is merely a name assumed or used by a person recognized as a legal entity. A judgment against one in an assumed or trade name is a judgment against him as an individual. An undertaking by an individual in a fictitious or trade name is the obligation of the individual." Accordingly, if the agent's only evidence of disclosing the fact of the agency and the identity of the principal is use of the principal's trade name, summary judgment against the agent individually is usually warranted.

Here, J's Fashion submitted the affidavit of its manager that at no point did Yim indicate he was acting other than as an individual doing business under the trade name "Ho Tae." …

The trial court did not err in granting summary judgment to J's Fashion. Judgment affirmed.

Question for Analysis

1. Suppose the court agreed that Yim was an agent for Hosung. If Hosung did not have the resources to pay the judgment, would J's Fashion have any other legal argument to make?

---

ends. It may be necessary to give notice of the termination to third parties to end the agent's apparent authority.

Parties may set a specific date for an agency to end. If no time is set, the agency ends when its purpose, such as the sale of real estate, is fulfilled. The parties may agree to end the agency or to extend it beyond its original time and scope of duties. An agency can be ended upon reasonable notice by either the agent or the principal.

Certain events automatically terminate an agency. Called termination by operation of law, an agency ends without any action by the principal or the agent if certain events occur. For example, if the principal or the agent dies, the agency ends. It also ends if the subject matter is destroyed, such as when a house for sale burns down.

❓ TEST YOURSELF

1. A person authorized to execute all transactions connected with a business is this class of agent: _____.
2. When a principal behaves as if she intended to allow an unauthorized agreement by an agent, there is said to be express ratification: T—F
3. In *Cove Management* v. *AFLAC*, where an AFLAC agent went beyond his authority and signed a lease for office space in AFLAC's name, the courts held that AFLAC:
   a. was excused from the lease because the agent was not a general agent.
   b. was excused from the lease because the agent lacked apparent authority.
   c. was bound to the lease because the agent had apparent authority.
   d. was bound to the lease by agency by estoppel.
4. One of the duties of a principal to an agent is paying travel expenses and other normal expenses incurred on behalf of the principal. This is called the _____.
5. In *Yim* v. *J's Fashions Accessories, Inc.*, where Yim was an agent for Ho Tae, which did not pay the bills sent by J's Fashion, and Yim was then sued, the courts held that Yim:
   a. had to pay J's because he failed to disclose the agency.
   b. had to pay J's because the court pierced the veil of Ho Tae.
   c. did not have to pay J's because it was industry practice for agents to buy without disclosing the principal.
   d. did not have to pay J's because the invoices were clearly marked Ho Tae.
6. If an agent acts on behalf of a principal in dealing with a third party, and the third party never knows of the principal, by law there cannot be an enforceable contract between the third party and the principal: T—F
7. If an agent receives oral or written instructions from the principal about the business that may be done on behalf of the principal, there is said to be _____ authority.

Answers: general; F; b; duty to reimburse; a; F; express.

The Essential Employment Relationship

Many agency relationships involve people hired to perform specific tasks. A professional baseball player hires an agent to negotiate salary. A homeowner hires an agent to market and help sell a house. You hire an accountant to prepare an annual audit statement for a business and do a tax return. All of these people may be employees, but they are not employees of the person who hired them to perform the particular job.

The employment relationship involves many aspects of agency. As we saw in the *Cove Management* case, an independent contractor—the AFLAC sales representative—went beyond his authority and claimed to have entered into a lease on behalf of his employer. Cove Management seemed unclear as to the authority of the agent to enter into a lease on behalf of the agent's principal.

When someone is an agent only for a specific task, the authority is usually clear. When we get into employment situations, the issues are more complex because there

EXHIBIT 14.3   DISTINGUISHING LEGAL RELATIONSHIPS

TYPES OF RELATIONSHIPS	CHARACTERISTICS
Principal–Agent	Agent acts on behalf of or for the principal, with a degree of personal discretion
Master–Servant (Employer–Employee)	The servant is an employee whose conduct is controlled by the employer; a servant can also be an agent
Employer–Independent Contractor	An independent contractor is not an employee, and the employer does not control the details of the independent contractor's performance; the contractor is usually not an agent

© Cengage Learning

are many possible relationships. Traditionally the employer–employee relationship was called, at law, a master–servant relationship. We next look at that and also at the employer–independent contractor relationship, which is more limited in scope. As Exhibit 14.3 shows, there are key differences in the major relationship categories. The categories are not always exclusive. As Exhibit 14.4 notes, there may be elements of more than one category in a position held by a person.

Employer–Independent Contractor

The employer–independent contractor relationship differs from the agency and employee–employer relationships in several ways. Consider how **independent contractor** is defined by the *Restatement (Second) Agency*:

> *An independent contractor is a person who contracts with another to do something for him but who is not controlled by the other nor subject to the other's right to control with respect to his physical conduct in the performance of the undertaking.*

As the definition explains, the independent contractor is distinguished by the extent of control the employer retains over work performance. The more control the employer retains, the less likely the worker can be characterized as an independent contractor. As a

EXHIBIT 14.4   EXAMPLES OF AGENCY AND EMPLOYMENT RELATIONSHIPS

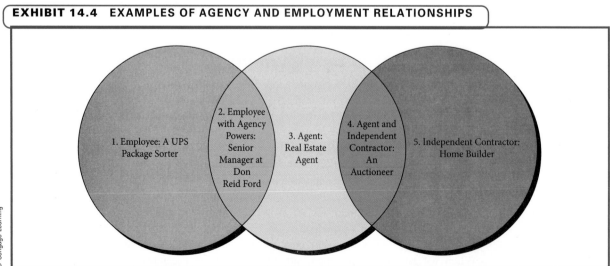

1. Employee: A UPS Package Sorter

2. Employee with Agency Powers: Senior Manager at Don Reid Ford

3. Agent: Real Estate Agent

4. Agent and Independent Contractor: An Auctioneer

5. Independent Contractor: Home Builder

© Cengage Learning

rule, the employer is not liable for the torts of an independent contractor. In the chapter on employment law, we see how a determination of employee or contractor status is likely to be determined by state or federal law.

Contractors as Agents   Some independent contractors are also agents. Contractors authorized to enter into contracts for the principal are agents. This often includes attorneys, auctioneers, and other such persons who conduct business on behalf of a principal. Some contractors do not have authority to enter into contracts for the principal and so, are not agents. This would usually include building contractors and others hired to perform certain tasks for an employer. As the *Southern Equipment* case indicates, hiring independent contractors may avoid what could otherwise be a costly liability.

FRANCE V. SOUTHERN EQUIPMENT CO.

Supreme Court of Appeals of West Virginia 689 S.E.2d 1 (2010)

Case Background *Hensley did business under the trade name Royalty Builders. He hired 16-year-old Robert France to do roofing work for him during a spring break from high school. Southern Equipment needed a new metal roof on a building and accepted a bid from Quality Metal Roof. Quality hired Royalty to do the work. Quality supplied the materials. France, working on the roof, fell off and suffered serious injuries. Among others, he sued Southern for exposing him to the inherently dangerous job of roofing. Southern was granted summary judgment in its favor by the trial (circuit) court. France appealed.*

Case Decision Ketchum, Justice

* * *

We have held that "the employer of an independent contractor is not liable for physical harm caused to another by an act or omission of the contractor or his servant."

…We stated [in an earlier case] that it is the power to control the subordinate's work that is determinative of whether an employer–employee relationship exists:

There are four general factors which bear upon whether a master–servant relationship exists … (1) Selection and engagement of the servant; (2) Payment of compensation; (3) Power of dismissal; and (4) Power of control. The first three factors are not essential to the existence of the relationship; the fourth, the power of control, is determinative.

In [another case] we specified that if a defendant establishes that it had no right to control a contrac-

tor's work, then the contractor is an "independent contractor":

One who would defend against tort liability by contending that the injuries were inflicted by an independent contractor has the burden of establishing that he neither controlled nor had the right to control the work, and if there is a conflict in the evidence and there is sufficient evidence to support a finding of the jury, the determination of whether an independent contractor relationship existed is a question for jury determination.

In [another case] we clarified that a defendant may exercise broad supervision of an independent contractor's work, and yet still not "control the work" to such a degree as to make the contractor an "employee." We stated that:

An owner who engages an independent contractor to perform a job for him or her may retain broad general power of supervision and control as to the results of the work so as to insure satisfactory performance of the contract—including the right to inspect, to stop the work, to make suggestions or recommendations as to the details of the work, or to prescribe alterations or deviations in the work—without changing the relationship from that of owner and independent contractor, or changing the duties arising from that relationship.

In the instant case, the circuit court concluded from an examination of the record that there was no question of material fact that Southern Equipment "neither engaged Royalty Builders to do the work nor had any power to control the work." The circuit court therefore concluded that Royalty Builders was an independent contractor, and concluded that Southern Equipment could not be held vicariously liable as Royalty Builders's—and, thereby, plaintiff Robert France's—employer....

Affirmed.

Questions for Analysis

1. Having France on the job violated federal and state employment law because of France's age on a dangerous worksite. Could that change Southern's liability?
2. France argued that Southern's managers should have noticed that a young person was working on the roof and inquired about it. Is that a credible argument?

Master–Servant or Employer–Employee

Master–servant is an old term still often used in law that means the same as employer–employee relationship. The **servant** (**employee**) is hired by a **master** (**employer**). Traditionally, servants or employees did manual labor; they were not in a position to act on behalf of the master or employer when dealing with third parties. The master–servant rules apply when an employee is under the direct control of an employer, such as a food service worker. When the employee does not have authority to represent the employer in business dealings, no agency exists; a master–servant relationship exists. Because employers are presumed to be in control of their employees, employers may be liable for the torts committed by employees in the course of employment.

Employees as Servants and Agents Many employees now are agents and servants; that is, many of us work under the control of employers, but in some capacities we act as agents, in which case the employers are also principals. Employees often make business decisions that affect their employer. Sales representatives at Don Reid Ford dealership who are authorized to sell cars within certain price ranges without permission of a supervisor are employees with certain agency powers to make contracts for their employer.

The distinction between agent-principal and master-servant is often blurred. Most employers do not specify to their employees that they are agents in certain matters and employees in others. What matters is what legal authority or responsibility exists when questions arise about the validity of a contract or the responsibility for a tort.

Employment-at-Will Under American common law, employees are presumed to work at will. That is, employers are free to discharge employees for any reason at any time, and employees are free to quit their jobs for any reason at any time. As explained by the Supreme Court of Tennessee in 1884, "All may dismiss their employees at will ... for good cause, for no cause, or even for cause morally wrong, without thereby being guilty of a legal wrong" (81 Tenn. 507).

The presumption that the employer may freely dismiss an employee, however, can be overcome if there is evidence to show a contract limiting dismissal exists or that there is a public policy against dismissal. In such cases, there may be a breach of contract that violates a statutory obligation. Many statutes that control certain aspects of the employment relationship affect the **employment-at-will** doctrine. In the next two chapters, we focus on statutory limits on the presumption of at-will, but we must stress that the employment-at-will doctrine remains strong in today's business.

Contracting to Limit At-Will Employment As we have discussed, if an employee is an at-will employee, she may be dismissed at any time without reason or cause. The employment contract exists only so long as the employee works and the employer pays. The arrangement can end at any time. However, the parties may have agreed to a contract that goes beyond at-will.

As we see in the new two chapters, there are statutory grounds for employees to sue for improper dismissal or treatment on the job. Here we consider suits claiming that an employment contract was violated by termination. Contract claims for wrongful discharge from employment can be summarized into three general categories, although other claims are possible:

1. An express contract exists when the employer and employee agree on employment for a guaranteed time. An employee may be hired for a fixed period, until a project is completed, or until some other event occurs according to the terms of the contract. Dismissing the employee without just cause (e.g., evidence of incompetence or proof of financial crisis) could be a breach of contract. This cause of action is not common.

2. An implied contract, based on written or oral statements, may restrict the grounds for termination or require specific procedures to be followed in a dismissal. Most states recognize this as a possible exception to the at-will presumption. Evidence includes the policies and past practices of the employer. Courts expect employers to behave consistently in such matters, not just follow procedure when it suits them to do so.

   For example, the Supreme Court of Connecticut found an implied contract was breached in *Coelho* v. *Post-Seal International* (544 A2d 170). An employee was fired without good cause, despite statements by the company president that he had job security and that the president supported him in conflicts with other employees. The court stated "there was sufficient evidence to permit the jury to find that the parties had an implied agreement that, so long as he performed his job properly, the plaintiff would not be terminated... ." Employers must be cautious about the statements they make to employees because what they say may be held to create an employment contract.

3. Similarly, covenants of good faith and fair dealing that can be extended to employment contracts are recognized in a minority of the states. Some successful suits have been brought against employers who misrepresented employment conditions to attract an employee, only to soon fire them with no good reason. This is not a common basis for successful suit, however.

The contract exceptions just noted do lead to litigation, but at-will employment is still the commonly presumed rule. The much-noted *Bechtel* case illustrates what usually happens when limits on the at-will rule are claimed.

GUZ V. BECHTEL NATIONAL
Supreme Court of California 8 P.3d 1089 (2000)

Case Background *Guz worked for Bechtel (BNI) for 22 years. He had a good employment record. Bechtel's personnel policy stated that its employees were at-will. It also stated that employees could be terminated for unsatisfactory performance or because of a reduction in workload or a reorganization. Management decided to cut the budget for Guz's division. Guz and others were fired. This occurred at a time of good profits for the company. The duties Guz performed were shifted to other employees. He applied for other positions at BNI, but he was rejected without reason.*

Guz sued, alleging breach of an implied contract to be terminated only for good cause and for breach of the implied covenant of good faith and fair dealing. The trial court dismissed the suit, holding that Guz was an at-will employee. The appeals court reversed, holding that "Guz's longevity, promotions, raises, and favorable performance reviews, together with Bechtel's written progressive discipline policy and Bechtel officials' statements of company practices, raised a triable issue: that Guz had an implied-in-fact contract to be dismissed only for good cause."

Bechtel appealed.

Case Decision Baxter, Judge

* * *

While the statutory presumption of at-will employment is strong, it is subject to several limitations. For instance, as we have observed, "the employment relationship is fundamentally contractual." ...

Among the many available options, the parties may agree that the employer's termination rights will vary with the particular circumstances. The parties may define for themselves what cause or causes will permit an employee's termination and may specify the procedures under which termination shall occur. The agreement may restrict the employer's termination rights to a greater degree in some situations, while leaving the employer freer to act as it sees fit in others.

The contractual understanding need not be express, but may be *implied in fact,* arising from the parties' *conduct* evidencing their actual mutual intent to create such enforceable limitations.... These factors might include "the personnel policies or practices of the employer, the employee's longevity of service, actions or communications by the employer reflecting assurances of continued employment, and the practices of the industry in which the employee is engaged." ...

We did not suggest, however, that every vague combination of ... factors, shaken together in a bag, necessarily allows a finding that the employee had a right to be discharged only for good cause, as determined in court.

On the contrary, "courts seek to enforce the *actual* understanding" of the parties to an employment agreement. Whether that understanding arises from express mutual words of agreement, or from the parties' conduct evidencing a similar meeting of minds, the exact terms to which the parties have assented deserve equally precise scrutiny. ...

We see *no* triable evidence of an implied agreement between Guz and Bechtel on *additional, differ-*

ent, or broader terms of employment security. As Bechtel suggests, the personnel documents themselves did not restrict Bechtel's freedom to reorganize, reduce, and consolidate its workforce for whatever reasons it wished.

* * *

Guz insists his own undisputed long and successful service at Bechtel constitutes strong evidence of an implied contract for permanent employment except upon good cause. Guz argues that by retaining him for over twenty years, and by providing him with steady raises, promotions, commendations, and good performance reviews during his tenure, Bechtel engaged in "actions ... reflecting assurances of continued employment." ...

An employee's *mere* passage of time in the employer's service, even where marked with tangible indicia that the employer approves the employee's work, cannot *alone* form an implied-in-fact contract that the employee is no longer at-will. Absent other evidence of the employer's intent, longevity, raises, and promotions are their own rewards for the employee's continuing valued service; they do not, *in and of themselves*, additionally constitute a contractual guarantee of future employment security. A rule granting such contract rights on the basis of successful longevity alone would discourage the retention and promotion of employees. ...

Guz points to the deposition testimony of Johnstone, BNI's president, who stated his understanding that Bechtel terminated workers only with "good reason" or for "lack of [available] work." But there is no evidence that Bechtel employees were aware of such an unwritten policy, and it flies in the face of Bechtel's general disclaimer. This brief and vague statement, by a single Bechtel official, that Bechtel sought to avoid arbitrary firings is insufficient as a matter of law to permit a finding that the company, by an unwritten practice or policy on which employees reasonably relied, had contracted away its right to discharge Guz at will. ...

Bechtel's written personnel documents—which, as we have seen, are the sole source of any contractual limits on Bechtel's rights to terminate Guz—imposed no restrictions upon the company's prerogatives to eliminate jobs or work units, for any or no reason, even if this would lead to the release of existing employees such as Guz.

The Judgment of the Court of Appeals is reversed.

Questions for Analysis

1. The high court held that employment-at-will is difficult to overcome by a claim of implied contract. Is there an incentive for employers to make it clear to employees that they are strictly at-will and there is no assurance of continued employment?

2. Is there an employment contract? Guz had to follow the requirements of his employer; what consideration did the employer give?

Employee Handbooks

Many employers issue **employee handbooks** or manuals to explain company policies, benefits, and procedures. The handbooks often discuss grounds for discipline and dismissal. Some explain policy about how such matters are handled. Some assert that employees will be dismissed only for good cause and that certain dismissal safeguards exist, such as review by a committee or managerial supervisor. Courts can hold that such handbooks create express or implied contracts that limit the presumption of employment at-will.

As the Supreme Court of California noted in *Foley* v. *Interactive Data* (765 P.2d 373), "breach of written 'termination guidelines' implying self-imposed limitations on employer's power to discharge at-will may be sufficient to state a cause of action for breach of employment contract." That is, in California and many other states, the courts look to employment practices, including statements in a handbook, as limits on the employer's ability to dismiss at-will.

Even if the handbook states that employment is at-will, if other provisions of the handbook or company practice indicate otherwise, the employer may have to show that dismissal was for good cause and that promised procedure was followed. Hence, managers should be sure that handbooks and policies are procedures actually followed by the company, or suits for damages for wrongful dismissal are likely to be filed (see Exhibit 14.5).

To reduce this possibility, many employers put a bold disclaimer at the front of the handbook that says it is not a contract and require employees to sign a disclaimer. Such

Lighter Side of the Law

The Ultimate Employment Gig

A Verizon risk team was searching for data breaches caused by presumed hackers in Shenyang, China. They discovered that a Verizon independent contractor had been doing nothing for months but turned in a lot of software work. He subcontracted his work to software writers in China for $50,000, a fraction of the fee he was paid for the work.

Verizon thought the Chinese were hacking their system for sensitive information, but they were just doing their job while the contractor was busy surfing the Web. His favorite videos, according to investigators, were of cats. Verizon reported that the Chinese did excellent work.

Source: L.A. Times.

EXHIBIT 14.5 COMMON PROBLEMS WITH EMPLOYEE HANDBOOKS

Using boilerplate forms that include material not relevant to the employer
Making promises about discipline procedures that are not followed consistently
Creating probationary periods that imply permanent status once probation has ended
Failing to change the handbook to comply with state and federal laws as they change
Listing specific offenses for which people may be fired can create the impression those are the only offenses that matter
Not giving a clear at-will employment statement and failing to specify that the employer has the right to change the terms at any time without notice

© Cengage Learning

disclaimers are generally upheld if they are prominent and known by the employees. However, poorly drafted handbooks and disclaimers may open the door to litigation.

For example, in a Utah case, the high court held that "a clear and conspicuous disclaimer in an employee handbook negates an employee's contention that the employment relationship is other than at will." However, in this instance, the disclaimer in the handbook could be interpreted to mean that it only applied to part-time employees, which would mean that the employer "intended to restrict its right to terminate full-time, core employees only for cause" (296 P.3d 760). Hence, the matter would go to a jury.

Despite cases that have been brought under theories of wrongful discharge that limit employment-at-will or that personnel policies in employee handbooks limit the right of employers to dismiss employees, unless specific steps to limit the right to fire employees have been promised to employees, the likelihood of a successful claim by an employee for wrongful termination is small.

Evaluations

Most employers have managers perform evaluations of personnel under their supervision. This can be an issue in litigation. Evaluations should be consistent with any statements in a handbook or, in case of dismissal, there can be a claim of wrongful discharge. This is most likely to happen if an employee consistently receives good evaluations and is suddenly terminated for non-performance. Even if the employee is at-will, courts frown on such inconsistency, so it creates more of an opportunity for litigation. This is an even bigger issue when it can be used as part of a claim of discrimination, a topic we cover in Chapter 16.

ISSUE SPOTTER
Can You Be Too Encouraging to Employees?

Your company is an at-will employer that has a handbook that makes clear the legal status of employees. But no one likes to think he or she is always on the verge of being fired, or there will be little reason for loyalty. To encourage employee retention, it is not uncommon for supervisors to approach employees whose personal problems have begun to affect their job performance to say that the company "wants you to stay" and "will provide help for you." Does this kind of supportive talk set the company up for a suit for violation of an implied contract if the employee is later fired? Would it be better to say nothing if it is clear there are problems? How are such matters best handled?

© Cengage Learning

Social Media

As technology and social norms change, companies adjust to take advantage of new innovations. Employers have the right to structure the workplace so as to reduce the likelihood of suit or bad image from improper actions. For example, most companies use Twitter, Facebook, and other social media. Such usage means that new legal issues arise and employers must adjust.

For example, after a director of Cisco System's intellectual property group identified himself as the author of the "Patent Troll Tracker" blog, both Cisco and the author were sued for defamation in two separate cases. The blog attacked "patent trolls"—companies that buy patents for the purpose of threatening others with lawsuits for patent infringement—and accused named attorneys of "criminal conduct, unethical conduct, and conduct unbefitting an officer of the Court." Cisco had not asked the author to create the blog, and company executives were unaware of it. However, because the author's supervisor knew about it, and it related to the author's duties at Cisco, the company could have been liable. Both cases were settled for undisclosed terms.

There is some protection under § 230 of the Communications Decency Act (CDA), which provides immunity for content posted or submitted by third parties, if the company is merely acting as a publisher. But this does not help if company employees post the content. Even if an employee is not tweeting in an official capacity, the company may be liable if the online activity is within the scope of employment or a reasonable reader would expect that the tweeter was authorized to speak on behalf of the company.

To minimize liability for online statements, companies may restrict unofficial company social media endeavors, limit who can post to official social media, limit what can be posted, and provide a means for addressing infringement and other claims. Companies may also want to restrict links to sites outside the official one, particularly regarding video clips on sites like YouTube. Control over practices such as "deep-linking" may also be important. In one case, Live Nation Motor Sports sued a website owner that included deep links to copyrighted webcasts, bypassing the home page and advertising of Live Nation.

A policy on editing potentially offensive content is important as well. Restricting comments may also be a good idea because such posts significantly increase the risk of infringement liability. At least one federal district court has held that the CDA does not protect an employer against sexual harassment claims based on objectionable e-mails and conduct on a corporate e-mail system. The CDA offers no protection to those hosting websites against claims based on third-party infringement of copyrighted material.

Finally, companies may wish to restrict their employees' non-work blogs to areas that do not involve the employees' work responsibilities or imply any company endorsement. Employees may resent such rules, but there are liability and reputation reasons for controls. As part of employment at-will, firms can impose restrictions on employees who wish to retain their jobs.

Tort Liability for Employers and Principals

Besides creating contractual liability, agents and employees can create tort liability. The principal or employer is liable for the tort of an agent or employee if the tort was authorized or, more commonly, liability may exist if the tort occurred within the scope of employment. If the agent or employee commits an unauthorized tort outside the scope of employment, the agent or employee is liable to the third party for damages incurred, and the principal or employer is usually not liable.

INTERNATIONAL PERSPECTIVE

Workplace Data Privacy in the EU

Based on Article 8 of the European Convention on Human Rights, the EU has privacy rules that are much more stringent than in the U.S. Companies with employees in Europe must conform or risk major penalties. Article 8 requires explicit consent by employee if the employer is dealing with data that reveals an employee's race, ethnicity, religion, political opinions, philosophical beliefs, union membership, health, or sex life. Consent requires "a genuine free choice" and the ability to later "withdraw the consent without detriment." This is very different from the United States, where an employer can make consent to waiving many such privacy rights a requirement of employment.

Interpreting EU cases, a "working group" (a body working on implementing EU legislation) set out three principles that should govern workplace privacy disputes:

1. Workers have a legitimate expectation of privacy at the workplace, which is not overridden by the fact that workers use communication devices or any other business facilities of the employer. However, the provision of proper information by the employer to the worker may reduce the workers' legitimate expectation of privacy.

2. The general principle of secrecy of correspondence covers communications at the workplace. This is likely to include electronic e-mail-related files and attachments thereto. Respect for private life also includes to a certain degree the right to establish and develop relationships with other human beings. The fact that such relationships, to a great extent, take place at the workplace puts limits on an employer's legitimate need for surveillance measures. When the European Court of Human Rights examined a case where there was surveillance of workplace e-mail, telephone use, and Internet usage, it found that there was a violation of Article 8. The employee had a reasonable expectation of privacy in her e-mail, Internet, and telephone use and she had not been given a warning that such usage was subject to monitoring (45 Eur. Ct. H.R. 253).

Principal's Liability

It is obvious that a principal or employer is liable for torts committed by an agent or an employee following orders. As the *Restatement (Third) Agency*, §7.03, explains, "A principal is subject to direct liability to a third party harmed by an agent's conduct when (a)...the agent acts with actual authority or the principal ratifies the agent's conduct and (i) the agent's conduct is tortious, or (ii) the agent's conduct, if that of the principal, would subject the principal to tort liability."

It is not often that an employer instructs an employee or a contractor, to commit a tort and the order is followed. Rather, liability tends to come from actions taken by agents or employees that the principal should have prevented so that injury would not have been inflicted. Liability may be imposed on the employer under the rule of vicarious liability or for a tort of negligent hiring.

ISSUE SPOTTER
Use of Company Cars

Your organization provides company cars for many sales reps so they can present the proper image for the organization. Occasionally, accidents happen. The company has insurance for the cars, but that rate goes up every time there is an accident. Should an accident be severe, there could be liability in the millions. Sometimes employees are in accidents when they are running personnel errands in the company cars. What is a sensible way to handle this liability that the employer faces?

Vicarious Liability Under the rule of **vicarious liability**, a principal or employer can be liable for the authorized or unauthorized intentional or negligent torts of agents and employees who were acting within the scope of employment. It is rare for an employer to be liable for a tort committed by an independent contractor. Courts consider many factors in determining whether an act was within the scope of employment. Some of the most important factors are whether:

- the act was of the same general nature as those authorized by the principal.
- the agent was authorized to be where he was at the time the act occurred.
- the agent was serving the principal's interests at the time of the act.

The rule of law imposing vicarious liability upon an innocent principal is known as ***respondeat superior*** (let the master answer). This doctrine has been justified on the grounds that the principal is in a better position to protect the public from such torts by controlling the actions of its agents and to compensate those injured. This rule also means that employers may be liable for torts of employees that can be attributed to negligent hiring or supervision.

This is one of the most difficult areas of agency and employment law. The line between when an employer may or may not be liable for torts or criminal acts committed by employees, agents, or independent contractors is hard to draw. The *Armstrong* case reviews some of the issues.

ARMSTRONG V. FOOD LION

Supreme Court of South Carolina 639 S.E.2d 50 (2006)

Case Background *Ronnie Armstrong went to a Food Lion store in Winnsboro with his mother, Tillie, to buy groceries. Three men in Food Lion uniforms approached Ronnie. One, Brown, had been in a fight with Ronnie two years before. He attacked Ronnie with a box cutter used to open cases of food. Another employee, Cameron, also attacked Ronnie. When Tillie tried to help Ronnie, Cameron punched her and knocked her down. Another shopper called for assistance.*

The Armstrongs sued Food Lion for numerous torts. The trial court held for Food Lion and the appeals court affirmed. The Armstrongs appealed.

Case Decision Moore, Justice

* * *

Petitioners contend Food Lion is legally responsible to them for the acts of its employees, Brown and Cameron. The doctrine of *respondeat superior* rests upon the relation of master and servant. A plaintiff seeking recovery from the master for injuries must establish that the relationship existed at the time of the injuries and also that the servant was then about his master's business and acting within the scope of his employment. An act is within the scope of a servant's employment where reasonably necessary to accomplish the purpose of his employment and in furtherance of the master's business. These general principles govern in determining whether an employer is liable for the acts of his servant.

The act of a servant done to effect some independent purpose of his own and not with reference to the service in which he is employed, or while he is acting as his own master for the time being, is not within the scope of his employment so as to render the master liable there for. Under these circumstances the servant alone is liable for the injuries inflicted. If a servant steps aside from the master's business for some purpose wholly disconnected with his employment, the relation of master and servant is temporarily suspended; this is so no matter how short the time, and the master is not liable for his acts during such time.

The trial court appropriately granted a directed verdict, because petitioners failed to produce any evidence that the Food Lion employees were acting within the scope of their employment or in furtherance of Food Lion's business when they attacked petitioners....

Two cases that have previously found an employer liable for its employee's assault of another person are distinguishable from the instant case. In *Crittenden* ... an employee assaulted another person in an attempt to collect a debt of the business. In *Jones*...a dairy farm's general manager assaulted the owner of a company contracted to provide a refrigerating system. The assault resulted from a dispute arising over problems with the system. The factor that distinguishes these cases from the instant case is that the assaults in *Jones* and *Crittenden* occurred, not merely in connection with the master's business, but with the purpose of in some way furthering the master's business. Here, there is no evidence that Brown and Cameron were furthering Food Lion's business in any manner. ... Therefore, the decision of the Court of Appeals is affirmed.

Questions for Analysis

1. What if the Food Lion employees had criminal records? Would that make a difference? Should employers place ex-felons in contact with the public?
2. Suppose a Food Lion employee carelessly dumps a heavy box on a customer and injures the customer. Would liability likely be imposed in that case?

Negligent Hiring An employer may be held liable for negligence in hiring and for putting in a position of trust or responsibility a person who could be expected to possibly cause problems. This is similar to *respondeat superior*. Most **negligent hiring** cases involve torts committed by an employee who is not acting in the scope of employment.

The *Restatement (Second) of Agency* §213 states: "A person conducting an activity through servants or other agents is subject to liability for harm resulting from his conduct if he is negligent or reckless...in the employment of improper persons...in work involving risks of harm to others." That is, we may have an obligation to check the background of an employee or independent contractor to see if there is a history that makes hiring doubtful.

Lighter Side of the Law

Who, Him? Must Be an Independent Contractor

Martinez worked for Singh at his doughnut shop in Sacramento. If Martinez was recognized as Singh's employee, Singh would be required to pay payroll taxes, such as workers' compensation and Social Security. Singh was not paying these taxes.

After Martinez was shot by gunmen who robbed Singh's store, Singh dragged him outside and told police Martinez was a customer. Singh then told an insurance agent that Martinez was a friend who had dropped by to watch him make doughnuts. Singh was fined $1,000 for falsifying information at a crime scene but was also sued by Martinez, who was, in fact, his employee.

Source: Sacramento Bee.

If a person has a history as a child molester, he should not be hired for a job in which he is routinely in contact with children. There would be an obligation to do a criminal background check when hiring for such positions. A bad-driving record would be irrelevant in that situation. However, if a company is hiring someone to drive a truck, the driving history would be relevant. Employers must use good judgment or face possible liability. Because background searches are not costly to perform, employers have an obligation to use such services.

❓ *TEST YOURSELF*

1. In modern language, a servant whose conduct is controlled by a master is generally called a(n) _____.
2. When someone is hired to do a job and is not an agent or servant and generally controls the details of the work done, the person is likely a(n) _____.
3. The doctrine of employment-at-will has been replaced in most states by laws that control proper methods of termination: T—F
4. In *Guz* v. *Bechtel National*, where Guz was terminated without cause after many years of good service, the California Supreme Court held the termination to:
   a. be a breach of an implied covenant of good faith.
   b. be a breach of an implied contract to terminate only for good cause.
   c. violate the California Fair Employment Act.
   d. create no cause of action.
5. In *Armstrong* v. *Food Lion*, where two grocery store workers assaulted two patrons in a store, the South Carolina Supreme Court held the employer not to be liable based on vicarious liability: T—F
6. Under the Communications Decency Act, employers may not control the use of social media, such as Facebook, by employees, unless obscene material is involved: T—F
7. If an employer issues an employee handbook, the employer may also issue a(n) _____ that it is not bound by the terms of the handbook and may change it any time.

Answers: employee; independent contractor; F; d; T; F; disclaimer.

SUMMARY

- An agency relationship is created when an agent agrees to act on behalf of, and to be subject to the control of, the principal. As the principal's representative, the agent may bind the principal to contracts with third parties. By using agents, a principal can expand business activities.
- No formal procedure exists for the creation of an agency relationship. There must, however, be an affirmative response on the part of the parties, with the principal manifesting a desire that the agent act on her behalf.

- Agents' authority can range from the extensive powers of a universal agent or the broad business authority of a general agent to the more limited powers of a special agent, a gratuitous agent, or a subagent.
- Agency relationships can be established by agreement of the parties, ratification of the agent's activities by the principal, application of the doctrine of estoppel, or operation of law.
- The agent's ability to act on behalf of the principal depends on the scope of authority granted by the

principal. An agent can have actual authority and apparent authority.

- The agent has actual authority if the principal has given the agent authority to act. For such actions, the principal is liable for contracts entered into by the agent on her behalf.

- Once an agency is created, the parties have the duty to share information and to act in good faith. The principal owes the agent the duties to cooperate, compensate, reimburse, and indemnify. The agent owes the principal the duties of loyalty, obedience and performance, reasonable care, accounting, and notification.

- The agent has apparent authority if the principal created the appearance of authority in the agent. While the principal is generally liable for the contracts of an agent with apparent authority, the agent may be obliged to indemnify the principal for losses incurred.

- Agency relationships may terminate through the activities of the parties or by operation of the law. Once an agency relationship is terminated, the agent's authority to act for the principal ceases. It may be necessary to notify third parties to end an agent's authority.

- Agency is distinguishable from master–servant (employer–employee) and employer–independent contractor relationships. Servants and independent contractors do not have authority to represent the employer in business dealings unless they are also authorized to be agents.

- Employment is presumed to be at-will, but the contract may extend beyond that based on oral or written promises that extend the relationship. An employment handbook may establish terms of an employment contract that prevent termination without cause.

- Employers have the right to impose controls on social media used by employees, especially when done on company time or property. Employers can impose controls on social media postings by employees that are not done at the workplace if they reflect negatively on the employer.

- An employer is rarely liable for the torts of an independent contractor but may be liable for the torts of an employee or agent if the act is committed in the course of business or if the employer fails to screen out employees who could pose a danger to others in certain situations.

TERMS TO KNOW

agency relationship, 375
agent, 375
principal, 375
universal agent, 376
general agent, 376
special agent, 376
agency coupled with an
     interest, 376
gratuitous agent, 376
subagent, 376
power of attorney, 377
ratification, 377
express ratification, 377
implied ratification, 377

agency by estoppel, 377
agency by operation of law, 377
actual authority, 378
express authority, 378
implied authority, 378
apparent authority, 378
duty to cooperate, 380
duty to compensate, 380
duty to reimburse, 380
duty to indemnify, 380
fiduciary, 381
duty of loyalty, 381
duty of obedience and
     performance, 381

reasonable care, 381
duty to account, 381
duty to inform, 381
disclosed principal, 382
undisclosed principal, 383
independent contractor, 386
servant, 388
master, 388
employment-at-will, 388
employee handbooks, 391
vicarious liability, 395
respondeat superior, 395
negligent hiring, 396

DISCUSSION QUESTION

An agent embezzles funds from his principal and uses the funds to buy a car. What duties has the agent violated? Who is entitled to ownership of the car?

CASE QUESTIONS

1. Zimmerman, a real estate salesman, asked Robertson if she was interested in selling her property. Robertson said she might be. Zimmerman came to Robertson with an offer by Velten to buy the property. Both parties signed a contract for sale. Zimmerman told Robertson he was being paid a commission by Velten. Before the deal on the property was to close, Robertson asked for a copy of the agreement between Zimmerman and Velten, but they refused. Robertson refused to go through with the deal. Velten sued, claiming there was a valid contract. Robertson said that Zimmerman violated his fiduciary duty to her to disclose his interests. Is the deal valid? [*Velten* v. *Robertson*, 671 P.2d 1011, Ct. App., Colo. (1983)]

2. Hunter Mining hired Hubco Data to customize computer equipment specific to Hunter's needs. Before the job was done, Hubco went out of business. Hunter sued MAI, the company that made the computer products that Hubco sold to Hunter, for breach of contract. Hubco was a licensed distributor of MAI when it sold Hunter the computer package. Was MAI liable as principal for Hubco's failure? [*Hunter Minings Laboratories, Inc.* v. *Management Assistance, Inc.*, 763 P.2d 350, Sup. Ct., Nev. (1988)]
   ✓ Check your answer

3. Dan Martin did business as Martin's Appliance. For years, he bought furniture from Independent Furniture. Martin's Appliance was sold to Struthers' Appliance, and Martin became the manager, but Independent did not know of the ownership change. Martin ordered furniture from Independent, which was never paid for the furniture. Independent sued Martin for the amount due. He claimed that he was only an agent for Struthers' so could not be personally liable. Is that argument correct? [*Independent Furniture Sales* v. *Martin*, 921 N.E.2d 718, Ct. App., Ohio (2010)]

4. Guardsmark, a private security company, hired Kadah as a security guard. His record was fine until one day he was accused of sexually assaulting Plancarte, a janitor at the office building where Kadah worked. No one witnessed the event, but one woman saw Plancarte running away. Plancarte sued Kadah in tort and sued Guardsmark based on *respondeat superior* because the attack occurred while Kadah was on duty. Guardsmark paid for Kadah's attorney. Did that payment imply Guardsmark's ratification of Kadah's wrongful actions? [*Plancarte* v. *Guardsmark*, 13 Cal. Rptr.3d 315, Ct. App., Calif. (2004)]
   ✓ Check your answer

5. Two stockbrokers, in clear violation of the rules of their employer, sold worthless stocks to unsuspecting customers. There was no question that the brokers did not have actual or implied authority to sell the stock. The customers who lost money sued the brokerage firm, contending it was liable for their losses because the brokers had apparent authority. Did they? [*Badger* v. *Paulson Investment Co.*, 803 P.2d 1178, Sup. Ct., Ore. (1991)]

6. Picard was a security guard for National Detective Agency. In violation of company rules, he had his own trained German shepherd dog with him while on duty. Meyers, a passerby, stopped to talk to Picard about the dog, which was in the back of a marked company car. Picard said he could show Meyers how well the dog was trained. When he took the dog from the car, it attacked and injured Meyers. Meyers sued National Detective, which argued that Picard's actions were outside the scope of his employment because he was violating company policy. Could the employer be liable? [*Meyers* v. *National Detective Agency*, 281 A.2d 435, Ct. App., D.C. (1971)]
   ✓ Check your answer

7. Neering was driving a truck for East Coast Furniture when he was in a minor accident with Valeo. Neering and Valeo pulled off the road and got into an argument. Neering hit Valeo with a padlock, inflicting injury on his eye. Valeo said Neering hit him for no good reason. Neering said he was afraid Valeo was going to steal the truck. Valeo sued East Coast for vicarious liability. Would it be liable for Neering's actions? [*Valeo* v. *East Coast Furniture*, 95 So.2d 921, Ct. App., Fla. (2012)]

8. Meyers, an at-will employee, complained to his employer that he was not being paid overtime when he should have been. He was fired, he claimed, for making that complaint. He sued for improper discharge because he claimed to have a right to overtime pay. What basis would he have for that

claim, and do you think it would stand? [*Meyers* v. *Meyers*, 861 N.E.2d 704, Sup. Ct., Ind. (2007)]

9. Vermeulen booked a trip to Machu Picchu in Peru through Worldwide Holidays travel agency in Florida. Worldwide received a commission from the Peruvian tour agency, Chasquitur. When in Peru, the driver of a Chasquitur van rear-ended another vehicle, and Vermeulen was injured. He sued Worldwide on the theory of vicarious liability for hiring unsafe drivers. Could he have a case? [*Vermeulen* v. *Worldwide Holiday*, 922 So.2d 271, Ct. App., Fla. (2006)]

ETHICS QUESTION

Clarence has been released from prison after a six-year term for armed robbery and assault. Having "paid his debt to society" for his crimes, he is now looking for work. You are advertising to hire workers for furniture-moving crews. Normally, two people work together all the time, so you know Clarence would be accompanied by another employee when on the job. However, you know of recent cases in which employers have been held liable for employees who have gone astray while on the job and have committed crimes. Because Clarence would be in people's homes, it is not impossible that this could happen. Should you not hire Clarence because of this worry?

CHAPTER 15

Employment and Labor Regulations

Years ago, anyone hired by IBM thought they had a job for life. The company had grown steadily and found ways even to care for employees who were not quality performers. But "Big Blue," as IBM was called, once the biggest firm in the computer world, was under siege by new competitors and their technology. Job security went out the window as the company cut back and changed to survive in the world of global competition that arose from firms that did not even exist a few years ago.

Like other firms in today's rapidly changing economy, IBM must deal with drug problems, family-leave issues, and a generation of workers that understand the lack of job security and are more likely to challenge decisions by superiors. The strict chain of command that existed in most firms has changed. Our labor market is more diverse in terms of race, sex, ethnicity, and employees expect that employers will accept more flexible working arrangements. Changes in the law reflect the changes in society. Managing people is more complex than in the days when most workers had assembly-line jobs that changed slowly.

In this chapter, we look at how statutes passed by legislatures and interpreted by courts have affected the nature of the employment relationship. We look at modern employment law and practice, such as substance abuse policy and other rules imposed on employers. The last part of the chapter looks at labor law, which primarily concerns relationships with labor unions, but which can also affect nonunion employees.

Public Policy Limits to At-Will Employment

As we saw in Chapter 14, the common law presumes that employers may hire and fire at will, and employees may quit at will. Those two parties to the employment relationship may contract around that presumption by an agreement that limits employers' ability to dismiss an employee without consequences.

Besides contractual agreements that place limits on the employment relationship, there are **public policy exceptions** that have arisen over the years. Most of these exceptions come from statutes, but some come from the application of common law rules.

Common Law and Statutory Exceptions

Employers violate public policy if they fire or punish an employee for certain actions. The courts craft some of the exceptions with the presumption of at-will employment; others are imposed by legislation. Under the most common of these exceptions, employers cannot fire an employee for:

- Refusing to commit an illegal act, such as falsifying reports required by a government agency or refusing to commit perjury (lie) at trial
- Performing a public duty, such as reporting for jury duty or military service
- Exercising a public right, such as filing a claim for workers' compensation or filing for bankruptcy

The first two of these issues arise rarely, but firing workers for filing workers' compensation claims is not uncommon. It rarely results in litigation because it mostly affects low-wage workers who are not sophisticated about their rights and, even if they do act, the damages are usually small because another job at about the same wage is usually available.

An exception to the rule that gets a lot of attention because it has involved some notable cases is the **whistle-blower** exception. This occurs when an employee reports an employer's illegal act. The general test of when this applies is that the whistle-blowing is primarily for the public good—to help law enforcement—rather than for private gain. This exception is more likely to apply to public-sector employees under state statute than to private-sector employees. For example, a government employee who reveals that bribes were taken by her supervisors could be rewarded for having taken that action if her charges are shown to be true.

When a firm dismisses an employee in violation of a public policy exception to the right of at-will discharge, the employee may sue for **wrongful discharge** or **retaliatory discharge**, which are torts. Most courts limit the public policy exceptions to cases in which there is a clear constitutional or statutory basis. That is, the wrongful discharge suits exist because the state wants to enforce and protect certain public goals, such as reporting for jury duty and reporting health violations, not because there is a desire to control the employment relationship. However, it must be emphasized that these cases are not easy to win. In the *Ballalatak* case, we see the Iowa Supreme Court discuss a particular limitation on this kind of action.

Contracts in Violation of Public Policy

As we discussed in Chapter 10, some contracts are not enforceable because they violate public policy; that same principle applies to employment contracts. The courts do not look with favor at **exculpatory agreements** that are part of an employment relationship. One party promises not to sue another in case of an injury caused by a tort or some other event. An employer may have employees sign an agreement not to sue the employer for any tort that occurs at the workplace. As the Connecticut Supreme Court

BALLALATAK V. ALL IOWA AGRICULTURE ASSOCIATION
Supreme Court of Iowa 781 N.W.2d 272 (2010)

Case Background *Ballalatak worked for Hawkeye Downs as a security supervisor. Two employees were injured in a work-related accident. They called Ballalatak and reported the injury. He drove to the scene, helped get the men to a hospital, and filled out an accident report. Later, the general manager, Nowers, told the three men to meet with him before returning to work. He told the men that their medical expenses would be taken care of without filing for workers' compensation. Later, the injured men told Ballalatak they were concerned they would not receive workers' compensation benefits. He relayed the concerns to Nowers and said the workers had a right to the benefits. Nowers fired him.*

Ballalatak sued, contending he was fired for inquiring into whether the company was fulfilling its workers' compensation obligation to the injured workers. Nowers claimed he was fired for insubordination. The district court dismissed the suit; Ballalatak appealed.

Case Decision Streit, Justice

* * *

Generally, an employer may fire an at-will employee at any time. However, under certain circumstances we recognize a common law claim for wrongful discharge from employment when such employment is terminated for reasons contrary to public policy. To support a claim of wrongful discharge, the employee must show:

> (1) existence of a clearly defined public policy that protects employee activity; (2) the public policy would be jeopardized by the discharge from employment; (3) the employee engaged in the protected activity, and this conduct was the reason for the employee's discharge; and (4) there was no overriding business justification for the termination.

The tort of wrongful discharge exists as a narrow exception to the general at-will rule, and this court is careful to ground recognition of such claims in "a well-recognized and defined public policy of the state." [In an earlier case, this court] explained that this court has recognized four categories of activities

protected by public policy in Iowa law: "(1) exercising a statutory right or privilege, (2) refusing to commit an unlawful act, (3) performing a statutory obligation, and (4) reporting a statutory violation."

Ballalatak claims he was fired for raising concerns to his employer, Hawkeye Downs, about potential mishandling of two employees' workers' compensation claims. ...

Ballalatak argues the public policy interest in allowing employees to pursue their statutory rights to workers' compensation benefits should be understood to extend to supervisors who advocate on behalf of or otherwise attempt to help those whom they supervise to receive such benefits. ...

This court has repeatedly recognized public policy protection for employees who exercise their own statutory rights. This court has also recognized that public policy protects employees who refuse to violate statutory or administrative regulations or to commit an unlawful act. Ballalatak was not fired for attempting to secure his own statutory rights nor was he fired for refusing to violate workers' compensation law. Instead ... he was fired for his attempt to ensure his employer did not violate the statutory rights of other employees. ...

Iowa law does not protect an employee who advocates internally for another employee's workers' compensation claim or internally raises concerns about the employer's compliance with workers' compensation statutes as it relates to another injured employee. Iowa law also does not protect an employee who asserts that other employees may contact an attorney regarding their workers' compensation rights. For these reasons, the district court did not err in granting summary judgment to Hawkeye Downs.

District court judgment affirmed.

Questions for Analysis

1. Could Ballalatak have sued the employer for breach of employment contract rather than for the tort of wrongful discharge?
2. Suppose employees could sue for "interfering" in the legal rights of other employees at work. What practical problems would that pose?

Lighter Side of the Law

Grounds for Termination?

Managers from Accountemps reported the following excuses from workers as reasons they could not come to work:

"I just got a new tattoo, and I need a few days to recover."

"I'm taking a few days off to start my own business."

"I need time to find myself."

"I'm going to be in a kick-boxing tournament."

"I need a leave of absence to try another job. But if it doesn't work out, I'd like to come back."

"I'm going to jail."

"My cat has hairballs."

Source: Inc. Magazine.

noted, such contracts are "almost universally rejected in the employment context [and] … are void as against public policy" (909 A.2d 43).

Noncompete Agreements It is not uncommon for employers to ask employees in certain positions to sign **noncompete agreements**. That is, the employee cannot leave and go into competition against the employer or go to work for a competitor for a certain time, usually one to three years. In states where such clauses are legal, some employers use them aggressively to discourage other companies from hiring their employees. They threaten suit against the employee and the new employer if there is such a move. The cost of fighting the litigation is often enough to discourage hiring people away from a competitor.

In many states, common law governs such covenants. As long as the restraints are reasonable in time and extent of coverage, the courts uphold them. Other states have statutory restrictions on agreements or covenants not to compete. The California Business and Professions Code, § 16600, states that, with few exceptions, every contract that restrains anyone from engaging in a lawful profession, trade, or business is void. So this is an area where employers must pay careful attention to state law. Where a restriction is struck as void, some states allow the court to imply reasonable terms into the covenant not to compete in order to save it in part. Other states do not and just eliminate any overly broad agreements entirely. In the *Zambelli Fireworks* case, we see a covenant not to compete upheld.

ZAMBELLI FIREWORKS MANUFACTURING CO. V. WOOD

United States Court of Appeals, Third Circuit, 592 F.3d 412 (2010)

Case Background *Zambelli is one of the oldest and largest fireworks companies in the United States, doing business in most states. Wood was hired by Zambelli in 2001 to work as a pyrotechnician and choreographer, executing fireworks displays in combination with music. While he had some background in* *fireworks, he had little experience in aerial fireworks displays. On the job, he learned many technical trade secrets, client lists, pricing, costs, and contract terms. Zambelli paid for Wood to become a certified trainer for the Pyrotechnic Guild International. A noncompete agreement, signed in 2005, specified that if Wood* *left Zambelli, he would not work for a competitor in the United States for two years; he would not solicit former clients; he would not disclose or use trade secrets; and if there was litigation, and Zambelli prevailed, Wood would pay all legal fees and costs.*

In 2007, Wood sought employment with Pyrotecnico, a major competitor. He was hired and signed an agreement that he would not take or use any Zambelli information or trade secrets. Pyrotecnico agreed to pay his salary for two years if needed as a result of the covenant, and it would cover legal expenses. In 2008, Wood resigned from Zambelli and went to Pyrotecnico. Zambelli sued to enforce the covenant not to compete. The district court held the agreement to be enforceable under Pennsylvania law and enjoined most technical work by Wood. He and Pyrotecnico appealed.

Case Decision Fisher, Circuit Judge

✳ ✳ ✳

Although restrictive covenants are a disfavored restraint on trade under Pennsylvania law, they are enforceable in equity where they are "incident to an employment relationship between the parties; the restrictions imposed by the covenant are reasonably necessary for the protection of the employer; and the restrictions imposed are reasonably limited in duration and geographic extent." To be "reasonably necessary for the protection of the employer," Pennsylvania law requires that the covenant be tailored to protect legitimate business interests.

Wood challenges on appeal the District Court's holding that Zambelli had two legitimate business interests in enforcing the restrictive covenant. First, the District Court concluded that "protection of Zambelli's customer goodwill is a legitimate business interest." Second, the District Court held that "the

specialized training, knowledge and skill Wood acquired during his seven years of employment with Zambelli is also a legitimate interest." Both interests, the Court reasoned, can be safeguarded through a reasonable restrictive covenant in Wood's employment agreement.

The District Court's holding is consistent with Pennsylvania law on legitimate business interests. We have held, applying Pennsylvania law, that legitimate business interests include trade secrets, confidential information, goodwill, unique or extraordinary skills, and specialized training that would benefit competitors. A business' goodwill entitled to protection is that which "represents a preexisting relationship arising from a continuous course of business."

Here, Wood's considerable amount of client contact, and attendant familiarity with Zambelli's confidential business information, are both legitimate and protectable parts of a business' goodwill relationship with its clients.... Wood had access to Zambelli's client list, pricing and business strategy, and had a long-standing relationship with Zambelli clients, who viewed him as a leader in the industry due, in part, to Zambelli's efforts to advertise Wood's specialized skills. Zambelli therefore had a legitimate business interest in ensuring that Wood did not transfer that goodwill to Pyrotecnico, its direct competitor....

Accordingly, we hold that the District Court did not err in holding that Zambelli had a legitimate business interest in its customer goodwill and Wood's specialized training and skills.

Questions for Analysis

1. Wood has valuable skills. Why should he not be able to sell those skills to the highest bidder?
2. How could Wood avoid this kind of situation?

Anti-Raiding Covenants A related area in which the law varies from state to state concerns the enforceability of **anti-raiding covenants**. In these cases, employees are required to sign, as a condition of employment, an agreement that they will not recruit fellow employees for another company when they leave their current place of employment.

Some courts have held such clauses to be in violation of public policy as an illegal restraint on competition; others have held them to be enforceable. For example, a New York court held that once an employee leaves a place of employment, continued restraints are not favored except to protect trade secrets. Other states, including California and Texas, have held that such covenants—if limited in time and coverage—are enforceable. In Missouri, the legislature specifically held such covenants to be legal. So, as in other policy areas, employers must be sure to consult state law.

Substance Abuse

Some abused substances, such as cocaine, are illegal; others, like OxyContin, are legal but can be obtained illegally. The most commonly abused substance, alcohol, is legal in most of the United States. The Department of Health and Human Services reports that about eight percent of workers are serious alcohol abusers. Add to this the estimated three to eight percent of the adult population who abuse or are addicted to illegal drugs or improperly dispensed drugs, such as pain killers, and it could mean that as many as one in eight working-age persons have a substance-abuse problem. This issue provides an example of how employers may change the employment relationship in response to a problem.

A Costly Issue for Business

Substance abuse directly affects employers because it can mean reduced productivity and higher medical insurance costs. The total economic cost of substance abuse is estimated to be more than $250 billion per year. The cost to employers is about $100 billion a year. The National Institute on Alcoholism and Alcohol Abuse estimates that health care (insurance) costs for families with an alcoholic are double the average. The huge cost of substance abuse does not include costs that arise from another widely used addictive legal drug, nicotine, which also reduces productivity and increases medical expenses.

The U.S. Chamber of Commerce reports that workers under the influence of alcohol or other drugs are 3.6 times more likely to suffer an injury or cause one than someone not under such influence. Those who abuse alcohol, even if not under the influence, are estimated to have a 70 percent greater chance of injury on the job, the RAND Institute reports. The Federal Railroad Administration found that alcohol- or other drug-impaired workers caused many railroad accidents. The National Transportation Safety Board found alcohol or other drugs to be a factor in one-third of all accidents involving truck drivers killed in highway accidents.

 ISSUE SPOTTER
What Attitude toward Drinking and the Office?

Many employers have office parties, either at the workplace or at a location picked by the employer. Such events can help build morale. Having alcoholic beverages makes it a more festive event for those who enjoy a few drinks. What legal issues can you see emerging from this? If a worker appears at any time, perhaps after lunch, to have consumed too much alcohol, or to otherwise be impaired, what should be done? Should the person be sent home?

© Cengage Learning

Legal Issues in Drug Testing

The discussion here largely concerns non-unionized places of employment. Companies that are unionized cannot impose a drug-testing program unless approved by the union in collective bargaining. Another issue we ignore at this point, but cover in the next chapter, are the rights of a substance abuser under disabilities laws.

Drug-Free Workplace Act The Drug-Free Workplace Act requires all companies with more than $25,000 worth of business with the federal government, which includes almost all large companies, to certify that they provide a "drug-free" workplace. The main requirements are that the employer:

- Publish and distribute a statement notifying employees that the use, distribution, or possession of drugs in the workplace is prohibited.

- State what action will be taken against employees who violate the policy, which may range from completion of a rehabilitation program to dismissal.
- Establish a drug-free awareness program and make an effort to make it work.
- Notify employees that, as a condition of employment, the employer must be notified of any drug-related convictions that occur, and the employer must notify the federal government of these.

Employers who fail to comply may lose their business with the federal government. In practice, this statute has been simple to deal with and is not regarded as having a significant effect in curtailing substance abuse.

The Omnibus Transportation Employee Testing Act requires employers who operate aircraft, public transportation, or commercial motor vehicles to test their employees for use of alcohol and illegal drugs. This includes pre-employment testing, random testing during employment, and testing after any accident. Confidentiality of test results is maintained, and the laboratory procedures used are highly accurate.

Employee Substance Abuse Policies

Court cases give guidance as to what private employers can do in a **substance-abuse policy**. Because the elements listed here may not be treated the same in all states, managers are advised to seek counsel or to employ an experienced drug-testing firm.

1. Pre-employment screening of job applicants for substance abuse is usually legal.
2. Testing of employees on an annual basis, or as a part of occasional physical examinations, is generally legal. However, physical examinations must be voluntary or directly related to the ability to perform the job. Drug tests are upheld when a job is safety-sensitive or when the policy is announced and applied consistently.
3. Random drug tests, when announced as a condition of employment, are upheld for jobs where safety is an issue, such as for truck drivers and pipeline welders. Drug tests for employees not in sensitive positions are more likely to be subject to challenge.
4. Drug tests after accidents have been upheld, again because public safety issues generally outweigh the employee's right to privacy.
5. Substance tests given because of "reasonable suspicion" of improper usage are likely to be allowed when there is an announced policy of such tests and when safety is an issue.
6. Use certified labs to give and process drug tests.
7. Give all employees a copy of the company policy and keep a signed receipt from the employee.

A substance-abuse policy should be clear and ensure that the testing is not discriminatory or done carelessly. The policy should state why the tests are done, what the test is

ISSUE SPOTTER

How Does an Employer Handle an Employee Who Flunks a Drug Test?

Company policy requires random drug testing of all employees. One employee, given a random test, tests positive for illegal drugs. Employees have been told that anyone flunking the test will be fired. Assuming you are in a state where that policy is allowed, as it is in most states, what steps should be in place to be sure the matter is handled properly?

looking for, what is done with the results, and the consequences of the test results. To eliminate the chance of a false test result, employees should be given an opportunity to have a second, high-quality test performed if they challenge positive test results.

❓ TEST YOURSELF

1. For an employer to be Certified Contractor under the Drug Free Workplace Act, all employees must be subject to an annual drug test: T—F
2. In the *Zambelli Fireworks Manufacturing Co.* v. *Wood* case, where Wood challenged the enforceability of a strict noncompetition clause in his employment contract, the appeals court held that under Pennsylvania law:
   a. such contracts were illegal.
   b. such contracts were legal but could be for no more than one year.
   c. such contracts were legal but could apply only to issues related to trade secrets.
   d. such contracts were legal if reasonable, which this one was.
3. If an employee signs an agreement that they will not recruit fellow employees for another company when they leave their current place of employment, it is called a(n) _____.
4. In the case, *Ballalatak* v. *All Iowa Agriculture*, the Iowa Supreme Court held that Ballalatak could not sue for wrongful dismissal for trying to enforce the workers' compensation rights of fellow employees: T—F
5. If an employee is fired for performing a public duty, such as reporting for military service, there is likely a right for a suit against the employer for _____.

Answers: F; d; anti-raiding covenant; T; wrongful discharge.

Worker Health and Safety

Concern about worker health and safety dates to the late 1800s. Federal regulations on coal mines were first enacted in the late 1800s, but most early job-safety legislation was at the state level. Early legislation concentrated on the major issues of job safety—accidents, injuries, and deaths. Between 1890 and 1920, most states enacted job safety laws, often together with workers' compensation laws (discussed later in this chapter). By the 1930s, concern had expanded from accidents to occupational health and concerns about long-term exposure to dusts and gases in the workplace. Most states began to address such exposure. Over the years, laws have imposed more requirements on employers to provide certain levels of safety and health protection to employees.

Occupational Safety and Health Act

Congress enacted the Occupational Safety and Health Act in 1970 (OSH Act). It created the Occupational Safety and Health Administration (OSHA), the Occupational Safety and Health Review Commission (OSHRC), and the National Institute for Occupational Safety and Health Council (NIOSH).

The OSH Act states that employers must provide employees a workplace "free from recognized hazards that are causing or are likely to cause death or serious physical harm" and that employers must "comply with occupational safety and health standards" issued by OSHA. OSHRC reviews administrative cases brought by OSHA, while NIOSH does studies to help set standards.

Inspections OSHA inspectors visit workplaces and respond to workers' reports of problems. In *Marshall* v. *Barlow's* (436 U.S. 307), the Supreme Court held that the Fourth Amendment prohibits warrantless searches. But because OSHA inspectors routinely obtain administrative warrants that do not require showing probable cause, unlike criminal search warrants, the warrant requirement has little impact in OSHA cases.

During a worksite visit, inspectors explain the purpose of the inspection and the procedures involved. The employer sends a representative to accompany the compliance officer on the walk around as the inspector looks for health or safety hazards. Some problems may be noted casually and not put in the formal report. At the end, the officer meets with the employer and, possibly, an employee representative to discuss findings. Employers may be given a chance to correct problems, or a citation may be issued as part of a formal report. The employer may contest the findings, as we see in the *Caterpillar Logistics* case.

CATERPILLAR LOGISTICS SERVICES, INC. V. SOLIS
United States Court of Appeals, Seventh Circuit, 674 F.3d 705 (2012)

Case Background *Caterpillar Logistics handles parts orders for Caterpillar products. Employees locate parts and put them on a conveyor belt. The packing department boxes parts for shipping. Each employee handles about 650 parts per day. The work requires repetitive hand, wrist, elbow, and shoulder movements, although most parts handled are light in weight.*

A month after MK began work in the packing department, she had pain in her elbow. The company doctor put her on leave for three months after a diagnosis showed that MK had swelling in ligaments and tendons around a joint. After she returned to work, the same problem arose, so she was transferred to a position that required less movement, which took care of the problem.

Caterpillar Logistics had a review panel of five specialists in musculoskeletal disorders determine if MK's injury was work related or not. The panel concluded the problem existed prior to MK's going to work, so was not work related. The Department of Labor disagreed and assessed a $900 fine for failing to report a work-related injury. An Administrative Law Judge (ALJ) held a four-day hearing on the matter and upheld the penalty. The OSHRC upheld that decision, which became the final decision of the Secretary of Labor. Caterpillar filed a petition for review of the order.

Case Decision Easterbrook, Chief Judge

* * *

Robert Harrison, the only physician to testify in support of the Department's position, provided the basis of the ALJ's decision. ... He testified that, nonetheless, the combination of moderate repetition plus pronation of the wrist, hand, and forearm must have caused MK's condition. He did not explain, however, why if this is so no other worker in the history of Caterpillar Logistics' operations has contracted epicondylitis. Nor did he discuss any epidemiological study, pro or con. Caterpillar Logistics' witnesses did discuss these matters. ...

The adjudicator ... must take account of competing evidence and inferences. That's essential to show why the agency credited one witness rather than another. This principle does not require elaborate discussion; the goal is not to produce tedious opinions that bury the analysis under an avalanche of detail. But it does require the agency to test its hypothesis against competing hypotheses. It may not simply ignore strong indications that its favored witness got things wrong. That's what happened here.

The big consideration missing from the ALJ's analysis is Caterpillar Logistics' 300-person-years of experience with its packing department.

Epicondylitis occurs at a rate of about 1% to 2% per year in the general population. This implies that Caterpillar Logistics should have encountered between three and six cases of epicondylitis among the staff of the packing department if work played no causal role at all. It actually had one case (MK's). If conditions in the packing department do cause or contribute to epicondylitis, the condition should occur at levels exceeding those of the populace at large. The record does not show an elevated incidence.

It might require a statistical analysis to determine whether the incidence of epicondylitis among the staff could have been the result of chance, and what frequency would imply a causal role for workplace conditions. Caterpillar Logistics did not perform tests for statistical significance—but the agency has the burden of proving causation by a preponderance of the evidence. Maybe a sample of 300 person-years is too small for the numbers to be significant when the background incidence of epicondylitis is so low—but the ALJ, having disregarded the experience at Caterpillar Logistics, did

not make a finding one way or the other about statistical significance. . . .

Dr. Harrison's failure to consider Caterpillar Logistics' actual experience matters. . . . It would be hard to know whether Caterpillar Logistics' own experience has any salience. What is certain is that the agency must choose among these possibilities; the judiciary cannot choose for it but must affirm, or not, based on the agency's rationale. The ALJ did not choose, indeed did not appreciate the need for choice, and the Commission as a whole has never discussed the subject. . . .

The petition for review is granted, the Secretary's decision is vacated, and the case is remanded for proceedings consistent with this opinion.

Questions for Analysis

1. Since the fine was only $900, why would the company spend vastly more than that on legal fees to contest the fine?
2. Poor use was made of statistical evidence. Should it be used when available?

Penalties Based on inspections by compliance officers, citations may be issued for violations of OSHA rules or for failure to meet the general standard of a workplace free of preventable hazards that could cause injury or death. Penalties may be imposed under Section 17 of OSH Act for the violations, running from small fines as in the Caterpillar Logistics case, to fines in the millions for serious multiple violations.

Because fines are often multiplied when violations continue over time, the total fine can be high. For example, Bridgestone/Firestone was fined $7.5 million for willful safety violations related to the death of a worker at an Oklahoma City plant.

 Lighter Side of the Law

How Dare You Work?

Smiley had worked at a Chicago real estate company as an administrative assistant for ten years. One day she decided to skip lunch and keep working. A manager told her she must leave her desk but she kept working. By Illinois law, hourly employees must be given at least a 30-minute lunch break away from their work station. The company was afraid it would get in trouble, so it fired Smiley.

She applied for unemployment compensation but was denied benefits because she was fired for misconduct. Her three appeals to the Illinois Department of Employment Security were denied. She finally won, three years later, at a court of appeals. The court found that her disinterest in lunch did not constitute a "wanton disregard of an employer's interests."

Source: Yahoo! News.

> **EXHIBIT 15.1 BIGGEST MISTAKES**
>
> **Ten Most Common Workplace Safety Violations**
>
> 1. No written hazard communication program
> 2. No information or training on hazardous chemicals
> 3. Electrical conductors not protected when entering boxes or fittings
> 4. Electrical covers missing
> 5. Guards missing on grinding wheels or spinning machinery
> 6. Hard hats not worn on construction sites
> 7. No fall protection for workers on elevated work surfaces
> 8. No portable fire extinguishers
> 9. Improper use of electrical cords
> 10. Not maintaining OSHA Injury and Illness Log
>
> *Source: National Federation of Independent Business.*

Workers and Toxic Substances

Most OSHA standards concern safety. However, health standards have been also issued, some of which have had major impacts. Protection from exposure to asbestos was one of the first health standards developed; compliance has cost billions of dollars. Other standards have been issued for exposure to vinyl chloride, coke-oven emissions, and other industrial carcinogens. The law calls for OSHA to issue standards that "most adequately assure, to the extent feasible … that no employee will suffer material impairment of health or functional capacity even if such employee has regular exposure to the hazard … for the period of his working life."

Besides listing exposure limits for some specific toxic substances, the **hazard communication standard** (HazCom) concerns exposure to hazardous chemicals. Failure to comply with HazCom properly is a common problem, as Exhibit 15.1 notes. Chemical producers and users must conduct a "hazard determination" of each chemical. Information about chemical hazards must be updated as new evidence becomes available. Where hazardous chemicals are used, employers must have the following:

1. A written plan that includes:
   - A list of hazardous chemicals in the workplace
   - The manner in which safety data sheets, chemical labels, and worker training about chemical safety will be handled
   - A description of how employees are trained to handle non-routine tasks, such as chemical spills or explosions
2. Labels for hazardous chemical containers that identify the chemical, hazard warnings, and the name and address of the producer or seller
3. Material safety data sheets (MSDSs) provided by chemical distributors with every container. MSDSs identify each chemical, its characteristics, its physical hazards (such as flammability) and health hazards, its primary route of entry (such as skin contact), exposure limits, cancer dangers, precautions for safe handling and use, control measures in the work place, emergency procedures, date of issue, and how to get more information
4. Programs to train employees at risk of exposure about the chemicals and proper procedures

Workers' Compensation

States adopted **workers' compensation law** in the early 1900s. They require employers to pay insurance premiums for injury and death benefits for employees. Workers'

Lighter Side of the Law

Rules Are Rules!

AutoZone employee McLean and his manager were alone on duty when a gun-wielding assailant herded them into the back room. Fearing they would be killed, McLean broke free, ran out to his truck, and retrieved his gun. He went back in to save the manager. The assailant saw him and took off.

McLean broke the company's "zero tolerance" rule against employees bringing firearms into a store, so he was fired.

Source: Fox News.

compensation was popular for workers because it provided a more certain recovery with benefits paid regardless of the cause of a work-related injury; that is, workers' comp is no-fault insurance. For employers, it reduced payments from tort damages to a schedule set by state law. In exchange for paying premiums, employers become immune from employee damage suits (torts) arising from on-the-job accidents. The objectives are to:

1. Provide sure, prompt, and reasonable income and medical benefits to work-accident victims or income benefits to their dependents, regardless of fault
2. Provide a certain remedy and reduce court costs and time delays associated with tort litigation
3. Prevent public and private charities from incurring the financial strains that would accompany uncompensated accidents
4. Reduce payment of fees to lawyers and expert witnesses
5. Encourage employer interest in safety and rehabilitation of workers through an insurance scheme that bases rates on the accident rating of the employer
6. Promote open discussion of the causes of accidents rather than encourage concealment of fault, thus helping to reduce accidents and health hazards

Compensation Claims

Workers' compensation laws cover most workers. To have a claim, a workers must show that he has: (1) an injury, (2) as a result of an accident or occupational disease, (3) that arose out of and in the course of employment. The negligence or fault of the employer in causing the injury is not an issue, and coverage is broad. Compensable injuries can include mental and nervous disorders and heart attacks that occur on the job.

ISSUE SPOTTER
Reducing Risks and Improving Looks

To reduce worker injuries and thereby reduce the likelihood of an OSHA safety violation as well as the number of workers' compensation claims, you would like to impose a dress code for employees that covers both safety and looks. You believe such a code would also improve professionalism in the workplace. Can you do what you want in this regard? Does a new dress code change the nature of the work contract you have with the workers? Must the workers agree to the new dress code?

Most courts are strict in interpreting state statutes that clearly state that the liability coverage of workers' compensation "shall be exclusive in place of any and all other liability to such employees...entitled to damages in any action at law or otherwise on account of any injury or death." The actions of the employer, employee, or third person become relevant only if there was an intentional tort.

Injured employees may want to sue in tort instead of accepting the workers' compensation payments because tort damages can be much larger. But, in general, suit outside of workers' compensation is rarely allowed. Exceptions may be for injury in case of intentional tort, injury caused by a defective product or toxic substance, or injury caused by the actions of a third party. Workers' compensation is generally considered the exclusive remedy.

Benefits and Incentives

Workers' compensation usually has major benefit categories: death, total disability, permanent partial disability, temporary partial disability, and medical expenses, including rehabilitation. While some injuries require only medical assistance, others take the worker out of the workplace for a recovery period, or possibly for life. Workers usually receive about two-thirds of their gross wages as disability income, up to a state-imposed weekly maximum—as low as $500 in some states to as much as $1,500 in others.

Premiums Tied to Safety Generally, workers' compensation provides employers with financial incentives to invest in safety at the worksite. Insurance premiums are based on injury claims records. Firms with the lowest number of injuries, and therefore the fewest claims, pay the lowest premiums. Different states have different systems, different rules, and different payout histories. Some states run the system directly, while others allow private insurers to compete for the business.

Premiums vary widely: North Dakota has the lowest rate in the nation at $1.01 per $100 of payroll; rates in Connecticut and California are about three times higher. Premiums also vary by occupation. For example, in Indiana, the rate is $0.30 per $100 in payroll for university workers and $19.61 per $100 in payroll for workers in logging operations. Rates also vary depending on how many claims an employer has had, which is called the business' experience rating. Because of the cost, some employers would like to not pay for workers' compensation or other obligations for employees, as we see in the *Long* case.

LONG V. SUPERIOR SENIOR CARE, INC.

Court of Appeals of Arkansas ---S.W.--- (2013)

Case Background *Long was an in-home certified nursing assistant (CNA). She had worked for one company for seven years before she began work for Superior Senior Care. The company had five employees in its office and about 100 independent contractors. Clients who needed in-home assistance would contact Superior. It would post the requirements to match CNAs with clients' needs. Superior operated as a referral service and received fees for that. Most clients deposited funds in escrow accounts with*

Superior, out of which CNAs were paid, so CNAs did not have to collect personally from each client.

Long was told her pay would be $10 an hour. Duties would be based on client needs. She did not have to take any given assignment; she could choose which one was most suited to her skills. Duties generally included cooking, house cleaning, laundry, and helping clients shower and move around.

The first day she was working at a client's home, she was helping the client move from a wheelchair to her bed when the client "went limp" and became dead weight. Long felt her back pop as she struggled to help the client. Although in pain, she stayed with the client for two more days. Afterwards she went to the hospital for tests and was given a back brace to wear. She was in pain and could not work, so she filed for workers' compensation.

Superior protested that Long was an independent contractor, not an employee. The Workers' Compensation Commission Administrative Law Judge held that Long was an employee. The Commission reversed that finding, ruling that she was an independent contractor not eligible for workers' compensation. She appealed.

Case Decision David M. Glover, Judge

* * *

[In an earlier case, the state Supreme Court] set forth the following factors that are to be considered in determining whether one is an employee or an independent contractor:

(1) the extent of control which, by the agreement, the master may exercise over the details of the work;

(2) whether or not the one employed is engaged in a distinct occupation or business;

(3) the kind of occupation, with reference to whether in the locality, the work is usually done under the direction of the employer or by a specialist without supervision;

(4) the skill required in the particular occupation;

(5) whether the employer or the workman supplies the instrumentalities, tools, and the place of work for the person doing the work;

(6) the length of time for which the person is employed;

(7) the method of payment, whether by the time or by the job;

(8) whether or not the work is a part of the regular business of the employer;

(9) whether or not the parties believe they are creating the relation of master and servant; and

(10) whether the principal is or is not in business. ...

The issue of whether an individual was functioning, at the time of an injury, as an employee or an independent contractor must depend on the particular facts of each case. ...

The terms of a contract, by themselves, cannot convert an employee into an independent contractor if the other surrounding facts do not support that conclusion. Here, however, the Commission determined that the facts supported Superior's position that Long was acting as an independent contractor, not as an employee. In accordance with our standard of review, we cannot say that fairminded persons using the same facts could not reach the same conclusion as the Commission. ...

Affirmed.

Questions for Analysis

1. Because Superior collected from clients and paid CNAs, does that not look like an employer-employee relationship?

2. How does Long receive income to help her while not able to work?

Besides workers' compensation, there are other tax and insurance obligations that an employer has for an employee that do not exist for an independent contractor. An employer must pay FICA (Social Security and Medicare) taxes and must withhold federal income taxes. Similar to workers' compensation is unemployment compensation. The premium rate for that generally runs one to five percent of payroll. Employers can avoid those costs and reporting obligations by using independent contractors. Both the Internal Revenue Service (IRS) and state agencies look closely at employer practices of declaring employees to be independent contractors rather than employees.

Family and Medical Leave

The Family and Medical Leave Act (FMLA) applies to private employers with 50 or more employees and applies to all governmental units. Employers must grant workers up to 12 weeks of unpaid leave per year after childbirth or adoption; to care for a seriously ill child,

CYBER LAW

Social Media Rules in the Workplace

As technology evolves, so do workplace rules and habits. The law also evolves as we determine legal standards that apply in the employment situation.

Many employers have policies making it clear that the organization has the right to access all e-mails that come to company computers or accounts. Software scans e-mails for red flag words—*sex, guarantee, social security number*, and so on. These controls help companies reduce lost work time, litigation from employees who claim harassment from e-mails with sexual content, and loss of information that should be secure.

In 2012, Maryland became the first state to ban employers from requesting access to social media accounts of employees and job applicants. Employers may not ask for user names or passwords to personal

sites such as Facebook. Giving your Facebook login information is a violation of the site's terms of service, and the Department of Justice considers it a federal crime to enter social media sites in violation of such terms However, in practice, there is no prosecution.

Some employers say they ask for voluntary access to social media sites but do not insist on it. The companies are not interested in personal items but indications of employment history or behavior that are not consistent with the information provided by the prospective employee.

Regardless of permission, employees and applicants should realize that there are firms that specialize in scouring the Internet for information that employers pay for as part of a background check. While it does not happen often, remember that anything once posted, despite removal, is in an archive that can be retrieved later.

spouse, or parent; or for an employee's own serious illness. Many states have similar laws, often applying to employers not covered by the federal statute.

A "serious health condition" that qualifies for FMLA leave includes illness, injury, a physical or mental condition that involves in-patient care (an overnight stay in a medical facility), or continuing treatment by a health care provider, which includes at least one of these:

1. More than three consecutive days of incapacity and treatment for a condition that involves two or more treatments, including exams, by a health care provider; or one treatment with continuing prescription medicine or special equipment
2. Incapacity due to pregnancy
3. Incapacity or treatment for a chronic, serious health condition
4. Any absence for multiple treatments and recovery for surgery or a condition that would likely result in more than a three-day period of incapacity if left untreated

While on leave, health care benefits, if provided, must remain in place. When employees return from leave, they must be returned to the same job or a comparable position.

Integration with Employment Rules

While the law does not seem that complicated, it has resulted in a lot of litigation, so employers should have clear policies that have been reviewed by a knowledgeable attorney. In general, an employer should designate a manager who is knowledgeable about the law to ensure compliance. Individual managers should not make determinations of eligibility because liability for FMLA violations may be imposed on individual managers as well as on the employing organization. As the *Callison* case indicates, employers can have policies to ensure such leave is not abused.

CALLISON V. CITY OF PHILADELPHIA

United Sates Court of Appeals, Third Circuit, 430 F.3d 117 (2005)

Case Background *Callison had worked for the city for two years when he was diagnosed with anxiety caused by stress at home and on the job. He used a lot of sick leave and was put on a Sick Abuse List. Employees on the list were required to get medical certification for all sick days and were subject to penalties for violations of the policy. Employees on sick leave were to call a hotline to report if they left home. A sick leave investigator would call homes to see if employees were there or not. Callison took three months FMLA leave; the city checked on him, and he was often not home. He was suspended for failure to follow policy.*

Callison sued, contending that he should not be subject to discipline while on FMLA leave and that to discipline him was retaliation in violation of the statute. The trial court held for the city. Callison appealed.

Case Decision Cowen, Circuit Judge

* * *

The FMLA is meant to prohibit employers from retaliating against employees who exercise their rights, refusing to authorize leave, manipulating positions to avoid application of the Act, or discriminatory applying policies to discourage employees from taking leave. In the instant case, the City did not engage in any of these prohibited acts. The City provided Callison with the entitlements set forth in the FMLA (e.g., a 12-week leave and reinstatement after taking medical leave).

Callison's contention that the FMLA's anti-abuse provisions ... preempt the City's procedures is meritless. The anti-abuse provisions in the FMLA permitting employers to request second opinions and certifications does not conflict with the City's provision requiring employees on medical leave to call in when leaving their home during business hours. These "certification" provisions merely outline some of the employer's rights and employee's corresponding obligations. ...

Contrary to Callison's assertion, there is no right in the FMLA to be "left alone." Nothing in the FMLA prevents employers from ensuring that employees who are on leave from work do not abuse their leave, particularly those who enter leave while on the employer's Sick Abuse List. ...

Because the City's internal call-in policy neither conflicts with nor diminishes the protections guaranteed by the FMLA, it is not invalidated by the Act. Accordingly, Callison was required to comply with the policy, and the City did not abrogate his FMLA rights by placing him on suspension for the violations.

For the foregoing reasons, the judgment of the District Court ... will be affirmed.

Questions for Analysis

1. The appeals court affirmed that the employer had the right to be sure an employee was in fact at home while taking FMLA leave. Why would the employer care where the employee was?
2. Is it not an invasion of privacy to call employees on sick leave to check on them?

FMLA coverage may be denied, on a case-by-case basis, to "key" employees. This may include only employees among the 10 percent highest paid, whose leave would cause "substantial and grievous economic injury to the operations of the employer." Also not covered are employees who have not worked for at least one year and who have not worked at least 1,250 hours in the past year.

Employees are required to notify employers at least 30 days in advance for foreseeable leave, such as for birth, adoption, or planned medical treatment. Workers with chronic conditions may be required to certify that they visit a doctor at least twice a year for that condition, but supervisors may not contact an employee's health-care provider directly to obtain medical certification of a condition. Workers who have been out on leave may be required to obtain a "fitness for duty" evaluation to ensure that they are qualified to return to their specific jobs.

General Regulation of Labor Markets

Besides the major laws already discussed, a variety of other laws restrict the labor market. Immigration laws limit who is allowed to work legally in the country. The minimum wage law sets a lower limit on what employees may be paid. States restrict entry into occupations by licensing requirements. Employers must warn employees of certain plant closings. Employee pensions are also subject to federal regulation. As there are many other regulations, and some are very detailed, we only cover some key points about certain employment regulations here.

Hiring Legally

To be hired legally in the United States, a person must present certain documents to show identity and authorization to work. Such documentary proof is required even if a person is a U.S. citizen. Because violations of the law can mean criminal penalties, employers must be sure to meet the basic requirements. Employers must collect evidence of citizenship or of legal work status for all new employees. For every person hired, the employer must have an I-9 form on file. The following documents are used as proof of identity and of employment eligibility:

- U.S. passport
- Permanent Resident Card
- Foreign passport with employment authorization

Combinations of other documents, such as a driver's license, school ID card, original Social Security card, or birth certificate, may provide satisfactory proof to the government immigration authorities of identity and employment eligibility requirements. See the U.S. Citizenship and Immigration Services (USCIS) web site for details.

General New Employment Procedure Employers must balance the need to obtain sufficient verification of a prospective employee's legal right to work in the United States with avoiding discrimination. The Department of Justice recommends three rules for striking that balance:

- Fill out an I-9 form for all new hires (which must be kept on file for three years or at least one year after the employee leaves the job, whichever is later).
- Allow the new employees to choose which documents from the I-9 list to use as proof; never insist on a specific document and accept any documents which appear genuine.
- Never ask for more documents than the I-9 requires.

The key to the I-9 system is the presentation by the prospective employee of documents specified on the I-9 form. The employer must accept documents offered that appear to be valid. Doing so creates a "safe harbor" that protects the employer from civil or criminal penalties unless the employer has been put on notice of its noncompliance or engages in a pattern or practice of violations.

In addition to the I-9 system, which relies exclusively on paper documents, USCIS operates an electronic verification system for employment eligibility. The E-Verify program allows employers to submit employee information electronically to the federal government. It then checks the information against a database containing citizenship and work authorization records. If the submitted information matches the Social Security database, and the employee is a U.S. citizen, the employer is notified that the employee is eligible to work.

Information on noncitizens is checked against the records of the USCIS. If the information is inconsistent with federal records, the employer is given a "tentative nonconfirmation," and the employee has eight working days to contest the result. During those days, the employer may not take any adverse action against the employee. This program has had accuracy issues since its inception, and employers have complained that the system is slow, which makes it particularly bad for hiring seasonal workers, such as for the Christmas shopping rush. Federal contracts may include a clause requiring E-Verify, so employers with such contracts must use the system. Some states, including Arizona and Mississippi, require employers to use E-Verify.

Costly Penalties Hiring unauthorized aliens can be expensive. Civil penalties range from $375 to $3,200 per worker for the first offense to $4,300 to $16,000 per worker for the third and subsequent offenses. Discriminating against authorized aliens can produce the same range of penalties. Failing to properly complete I-9 forms can lead to penalties between $110 and $1,100 per violation, so if an employer's record keeping is sloppy, the fines can be large.

When someone buys a business, the new owner becomes responsible for the previous owners' immigration compliance and so can be liable for any errors or omissions in employment verification for existing employees. The USCIS advises: "To avoid this liability, you may choose to complete a new I-9 Form for each acquired employee. If you do so, you must do so uniformly for all of your acquired employees without regard to actual or perceived citizenship status or national origin."

Federal Minimum Wage and Tax Requirements

Federal minimum wage requirements were initiated in 1938 as part of the Fair Labor Standards Act. Over the years, the minimum wage has averaged about 50 percent of the average manufacturing wage. The minimum wage was raised to $7.25 in 2009. Some states, such as California, have higher minimum wages. Some state laws also cover employers exempt from the federal law.

Supporters of the minimum wage contend that the law requires employers to pay a fair wage to employees and does not allow workers to be paid so little that they have trouble buying the necessities of life. Critics argue that the law results in lower demand for workers in the minimum wage category—usually young people, often minorities, with little education or job experience. The result is high unemployment among persons in those groups, who never get the chance to work to develop skills that command higher wages.

ISSUE SPOTTER
How Do You Count Hours for Telecommuters?

Working at home has become more common. There are over 10 million full-time telecommuters and 45 million more employees who do some work at home. This has raised problems in compliance with the Fair Labor Standards Act and other employment laws. How do you know for sure if an employee put in an 8-hour day? What if they claim a 10-hour day and expect overtime? What if they work through mandated break and meal times?

© Cengage Learning

INTERNATIONAL PERSPECTIVE

Flexibility in Labor Markets

The ability of labor markets to respond to changing conditions in a rapidly changing global economy means that flexibility is more important than ever. A group of researchers from Harvard, Yale, and the World Bank looked at labor laws in many nations to see how they compare.

The authors constructed a number of measures as shown in the table in the next column. In all indexes, the lower the score, the greater the flexibility in the labor market. The higher the score, the greater the regulatory barriers faced by an employer. The first measure, the Difficulty of Hiring Index, includes the ability to hire part-time labor and use other nontraditional labor terms. The second measure, the Difficulty of Firing Index, includes the expenses of terminating

a worker no longer needed. The third measure is the Rigidity of Hours—the ability to change schedules as needed. The fourth measure, the Rigidity of Employment Index, is a general measure that includes the first three measures. The fifth column, Firing Costs, is the average number of weeks of wages required by law to be incurred by an employer in severance pay and other costs.

Notice that many poor countries have the most restrictions on labor markets. How beneficial are these regulations for ordinary workers? Most such labor market controls are generally not helpful and present opportunities for corruption as government bureaucrats accuse employers of violating the law.

Country	Difficulty of Hiring Index	Rigidity of Hours Index	Difficulty of Firing Index	Rigidity of Employment Index	Firing Costs
U.S.	0	0	0	0	0
Singapore	0	0	0	0	4
Denmark	0	20	0	7	0
Canada	11	0	0	4	28
Mexico	33	20	70	41	52
Pakistan	78	20	30	43	90
Spain	78	40	30	49	56
Venezuela	67	40	100	69	Not Allowed

Source: www.doingbusiness.org.

Occupational Licensure and Regulation

Entry into many occupations is controlled by regulations and licensing requirements. Under **occupational licensure**, a person cannot simply set up and begin to operate a business. Permission from the regulating agency is required. Such permission usually requires some demonstration of competency or payment of a high entry fee. The purpose of these labor restrictions is to protect the consumer, and the restrictions are supposed to help guarantee that businesses are qualified to provide service of a certain quality. Today almost 30 percent of all full-time jobs require a state license compared to about 10 percent of jobs in 1970.

Regulations Set by State Law Although entry controls for a few occupations are set at the federal level, most restrictions are set at the state level. Generally, a person must have a license or certificate from the state to practice as a lawyer, doctor, dentist, nurse, veterinarian, optometrist, optician, or architect. In various states, an individual must be licensed to be a dog groomer, beekeeper, industrial psychologist, building contractor, electrician, plumber, or massage parlor operator. Usually, a state commission determines the criteria for a person to be licensed to practice. Employees in contact with children or other vulnerable individuals must often undergo criminal background checks. In most cases, there is a formal education requirement; in some cases, an apprenticeship period is required or a test of knowledge about the profession must be passed.

Many state laws regulate employment, ranging from laws affecting how businesses provide references to when employees must be paid their final paycheck. Many states require employees be given time off to vote if their work schedule would otherwise preclude getting to the polls and to attend parent-teacher conferences. These laws are important for three reasons. First, many small- to medium-size firms are unaware of the details of these laws and can find themselves inadvertently violating them. A company expanding into a new market in a different state needs to check the local laws carefully and not assume the same rules apply as in its home state.

Warning Employees of Plant Closings

The Worker Adjustment and Retraining Notification Act (WARN) requires employers with 100 or more full-time employees to give advance notice of a plant closing or mass layoff if 50 or more employees will be affected. The notice must be given to employees and local governments 60 days in advance of the closing or layoff. Such notices must be given for permanent terminations and reductions in work time of 50 percent or more for six months or longer.

Employees who do not receive proper notice of a plant closing or mass layoff may sue for up to 60 days' back pay and fringe benefits, interest, and attorney's fees. If the local government has not been properly notified, it may sue the company for up to $500 per day for each day there was no notice. If a firm fails to comply with WARN, it may be ordered not to cut its labor force. In several states, plant closing requirements go beyond the federal requirements.

Employee Retirement Plans

The key legislation regulating private employee retirement plans is the Employee Retirement Income Security Act (ERISA). Its main objective is to guarantee the expectations of retirement plan participants and to promote the growth of private pension plans. It has evolved into a very complex statute. One should not deal with such matters without expert guidance.

ERISA is directed at most employee benefit plans, including medical, surgical, or hospital benefits; sickness, accident, or disability benefits; death benefits; unemployment benefits; vacation benefits; apprenticeship or training benefits; day-care centers; scholarship funds; prepaid legal services; retirement income programs; and deferred income programs.

Vesting Requirements The law establishes vesting requirements. It guarantees that plan participants receive some retirement benefits after a certain length of employment. All plans must be adequately funded to meet their expected liabilities. A termination insurance program is to be provided in case of the failure of a plan.

The major problem addressed by ERISA was that of the loss of all benefits by employees who had many years of service with a company and then either quit or were fired. The law makes all full-time employees over the age of 25 with one year of service eligible for participation in employee benefit plans.

Mandatory **vesting**—when the employee becomes the owner of the funds in a retirement program—was established by ERISA. It provides the employer with three options: (1) to have 100 percent vesting after 10 years of employment; (2) to have 25 percent vesting after five years, then five percent vesting a year for five years, then 10 percent vesting a year for five years, to achieve 100 percent vesting in 15 years; and (3) vesting under the rule of 45, which states that if the age and years of service of an employee total 45, or if an employee has 10 years' service, that person must be at least 50 percent vested in the plan. Each added year of employment provides 10 percent more vesting so that an employee is fully vested in 15 years. Again, these rules are complex, so employers need reliable guidance on structuring benefit plans.

ISSUE SPOTTER
Hiring Documentation and Discrimination

Three men apply to manage the front desk of your hotel. One has more experience than the other two, but you refuse to hire him because all he has for the I-9 form is a French passport with an unexpired work authorization stamp. You ask him for "a driver's license, anything," but he has nothing else. The next person has only a temporary resident card that expires in nine days. That is too close for comfort. So, you hire the third applicant, who has a valid Canadian driver's license. Are you discriminating based on documentation?

© Cengage Learning 2015

? TEST YOURSELF

1. At the workplace, employees who work around dangerous chemicals must be trained about the chemicals and what to do in case of a problem under the _____.

2. In the case *Caterpillar Logistics Services, Inc. v. Solis*, where an employee suffered an arm injury, the appeals court affirmed that the worksite manager would be sentenced to six months in prison for failure to follow proper OSHA safety procedure: T—F

3. In the case *Long* v. *Superior Senior Care, Inc.*, where Long was injured on the job, the court held that because Long was an independent contractor, not an employee, she would not get workers' compensation benefits: T—F

(Continued)

4. In *Callison* v. *City of Philadelphia*, where Callison was fired for taking too much sick leave and sued for violation of the Family and Medical Leave Act, the appeals court held that the employer:
   a. did not violate Callison's FMLA rights.
   b. violated Callison's FMLA rights by its improper method of checking up on sick employees.
   c. violated Callison's FMLA rights by calling his doctor to obtain private medical information.
   d. did not violate Callison's FMLA rights because he did not have any; the employer had less than 50 full-time employees.
5. Federal minimum wage law only applies to workers over the age of 18: T—F
6. The federal law that regulates pensions and other worker benefits is commonly referred to as _____.
7. States may not regulate occupations by licensing unless Congress has approved such regulation due to the impact on Interstate Commerce: T—F

Answers: hazardous communication standard; F; T; a; F; ERISA; F.

Major Labor Relations Acts

Labor law generally refers to laws dealing with **unions**, while employment law refers to laws governing all employees. The federal labor code, the National Labor Relations Act (NLRA), was enacted by Congress in three major phases: the Wagner Act in 1935, the Taft-Hartley Act in 1947, and the Landrum-Griffin Act in 1959. The only major labor law passed before the NLRA was the Norris-La Guardia Act of 1932. While about 37 percent of public-sector employees belong to unions, less than 7 percent of private-sector workers do. Together, this means only about 12 percent of the workforce belongs to unions, but a greater proportionate represented by unions, and they play an important role in some industries.

Norris-La Guardia Act

Before passage of the Norris-La Guardia Act in 1932, there was little federal legislation that specifically addressed labor issues. Some courts held union activities to be criminal conspiracies, while others upheld the activities as legal. The most common tactic of employers was to plead for an injunction to stop strikes and other union activities as a violation of antitrust law. The Norris-La Guardia Act ended such court intervention. The Act declared that every worker should "have full freedom of association, self-organization, and designation of representatives of his own choosing, to negotiate terms and conditions of his employment."

Injunctions Prohibited Norris-La Guardia prohibits federal courts from issuing injunctions in nonviolent **labor disputes**. Management must deal with the union or begin administrative proceedings involving the National Labor Relations Board.

Specific acts not subject to court intervention include **strikes**, belonging to a union, paying strike or unemployment benefits to labor dispute participants, publicizing a labor dispute, picketing, peacefully assembling, and advising others to do any of these acts without violence or fraud. The Act also prohibits employers from requiring employees to sign **yellow-dog contracts**. Under such contracts, employees agree not to join a union or risk being fired if they do.

Wagner Act of 1935

The basic goal of the Wagner Act of 1935—the first phase of the NLRA—was to ensure workers the right to "self-organization, to form, join, or assist labor organizations, to bargain collectively through representatives of their own choosing, and to engage in other concerted activities for the purpose of collective bargaining or other mutual aid or protection...."

The National Labor Relations Board (NLRB) was created to monitor unfair labor practices and assure that union representation elections are fair. The NLRB does not regulate the substance of bargaining; the terms and conditions of employment are between employers and employees. It deals mostly with procedure and review of claims that the NLRA has been violated. Unlike most federal administrative agencies, the NLRB issues few rules, preferring instead to develop the law through decisions by the NLRB in a common law-like process. Because the Board's decisions vary with the political makeup of the NLRB, the outcomes of Board proceedings vary more over time than is the case with most agencies.

Lighter Side of the Law

Do What We Say, Not What We Do

Workers launched a protest, accusing their employer of improper layoffs, unlawful bans on union activities, and reclassifying workers in order to disempower the union. The workers were employed at the national Service Employees International Union (SEIU), headquartered in Washington, D.C.

A federal arbitrator held that, for years, an employer had "willfully" violated the Fair Labor Standards Act by not paying overtime properly to its workers. The employer was the U.S. Equal Employment Opportunity Commission.

Source: Washington Post.

The Taft-Hartley Act of 1947

The Taft-Hartley Act of 1947—the Labor-Management Relations Act—which amended the NLRA—marked a change in federal policy from actively encouraging labor union formation to a more balanced approach. The Act prohibits unions from the following activities:

- Coercing employees to support the union
- Refusing to bargain in good faith with employers about wages and working conditions
- Carrying out certain kinds of strikes, such as secondary boycotts; charging "excessive" union initiation fees or dues; or engaging in featherbedding (making employers pay for work not performed)
- Going on strike during a 30-day "cooling-off" period or during a 60-day period ordered by the president

The Landrum-Griffin Act of 1959

The Landrum-Griffin Act of 1959—Labor-Management Reporting and Disclosure Act—which amended the NLRA, increased regulation of internal union affairs. Senate investigations revealed the improper use of union funds by union leaders and election fraud. The Act was intended to assure that union members are protected from improper actions by union leaders.

Monitoring Leadership Union finances are subject to federal review, and a report is available to union members so they know how their dues are used. Union officials who betray the trust of their office are subject to prosecution. There are penalties if employers bribe union officials or attempt to prevent union activities by other illegal means.

Union Member Bill of Rights A "bill of rights" for union members is included in the Landrum-Griffin Act. The Act ensures members the right to nominate candidates for union offices, maintains fair election procedures—such as the use of secret ballots in union elections—and allows members to participate in union business, subject to "reasonable" union rules. Union dues and fees are to be set by majority vote of the members. If a union member is to be disciplined by the union, procedural safeguards protect the member's rights, and punishment may not be inflicted on those who challenge union leadership.

The National Labor Relations Board

The NLRB is an administrative agency charged with overseeing the National Labor Relations Act. It has five board members, a general counsel, regional directors, and administrative law judges. The board reviews unfair labor practice case decisions by regional directors and administrative law judges. The general counsel oversees the investigation and prosecution of unfair labor practice charges and represents the NLRB in court.

The NLRB has jurisdiction over all employers and all employees in labor disputes that affect interstate commerce. Certain classes of employees are not covered by the NLRA—federal, state, and municipal employees (the public sector), supervisors, managers, independent contractors, domestic servants, and agricultural laborers. The Railway Labor Act covers airline and railroad employees. It is similar to the NLRA.

Unfair Labor Practice Complaints

In general, **unfair labor practices** are actions by employers or unions that impair the goals of the NLRA. About 30,000 cases are filed each year with the NLRB. Most are charges of unfair labor practices. Charges filed against employers outnumber charges filed against unions by about two to one. A worker, a union, or an employer files each case. Examples of employer conduct that violates the NLRA:

- Threatening employees with loss of jobs or benefits if they join or support a union
- Threatening to close a plant if employees vote for unionization
- Questioning employees about union activities
- Promising benefits to employees if they do not support a union
- Giving employees worse assignments for participating in protected activities

Examples of union conduct that violates the NLRA:

- Threatening employees with loss of a job if they do not support the union
- Refusing to help employees with grievances who have criticized union leaders
- Engaging in picket line misconduct, such as threatening non-strikers
- Striking over issues unrelated to employment terms and conditions

In most cases, charges of unfair labor practices are filed at field offices that do investigations. If the investigation shows the case has merit, the regional director files a complaint. Many charges filed do not lead to a complaint being filed; they are dismissed by the regional director or withdrawn by the complaining party when they are informed of their likely lack of success. Of the charges that do lead to a complaint, most are settled before a hearing takes place.

Hearing Complaints An administrative law judge (ALJ), an employee of the NLRB, presides over complaints that are resolved at an administrative hearing. After taking evidence and receiving briefs, the ALJ issues a decision and order. The order either sets out the appropriate remedy or recommends the complaint be dismissed. Unless one of the parties involved files an exception, the decision is final.

If an exception to the decision is filed, the appeal is heard in Washington DC by a panel of three NLRB members if the case is routine; if the case is considered important, it is heard by the entire board. Board members hear no evidence and see no witnesses; in that sense, they are similar to an appellate court.

If one of the parties refuses to accept the board's decision, the case is referred to the U.S. Court of Appeals for enforcement or review of the order. In rare instances, the Supreme Court takes the case for final review.

Pivotal Role of NLRB

The NLRA gives the NLRB great leeway to make policy and remedies regarding unfair labor practices. Its determinations are not to be reversed unless they are arbitrary, capricious, or manifestly contrary to the NLRA.

Because of the board's powers to determine much of the substance of labor law in practice, appointment to the NLRB is politically sensitive. Presidents sympathetic to labor unions because of political support appoint pro-labor members; presidents who are more sympathetic to the interests of employers appoint pro-management members. As the composition of the NLRB changes, its rulings tend to swing in one direction or another.

Remedies

If the NLRB finds that an employer has engaged in an unfair labor practice, the remedies it may impose include

- Posting a notice in the workplace
- Issuing a cease-and-desist order
- Providing back pay for lost wages
- Reinstating dismissed workers
- Issuing an order to bargain with the union

Unionization

A major responsibility of the NLRB is to determine whether employees want to be represented by a union. The NLRA focuses on the rights of employees to "self-organization; to form, join, or assist labor organizations." To ensure that the employees' rights of self-organization can be exercised, the NLRB has rules governing employer and union conduct.

Unionization Process

If a union does not represent employees, a move to unionize may arise because some interested employees contact a union for assistance or by a union organizer who contacts employees to see if interest exists. The union then starts an organization drive. An employee committee is formed and, with the help of the organizer, calls informational meetings and distributes information.

Representation Elections If a union organizer collects **authorization cards** signed by 30 percent or more of the employees, asking for an election to be held to determine whether the union should represent them (the cards are kept secret from the employer), the organizer turns the cards over to the NLRB and requests a **representation election**.

The election determines whether a majority of employees in a bargaining unit wants the union as their agent. A bargaining unit may be all workers at a company, the workers at one plant, or workers in certain skills at one or more work sites, such as nurses at a hospital or at several hospitals. Managers may not be in a bargaining unit.

Before the election, a campaign is held. The union tells the workers of the benefits of unionization, and management tells the workers the benefits the company provides without a union. The company is prohibited from threatening those who favor unionization, nor may it promise, say, a large pay raise if the workers defeat the union. The company can argue about problems it sees from unionization. For example, if the union tells workers it will get them a 25 percent raise, the company can explain the likely consequences of such a demand.

The NLRB and the courts protect the interests of the employees, so they have access to union information, and it protects the employers' interest in controlling business without interference. As a rule, union organizers are not permitted access to company property. Like any other private property, the owner can control who is invited to come on the property.

Union Certification NLRB agents supervise the election, which is often held at the workplace. There are about 1,500 such elections around the country each year. After the election, the NLRB certifies the results. If more than 50 percent of the employees vote for the union, then the NLRB grants **union certification**. Unions win about 60 percent of the elections. The union is declared the exclusive **bargaining agent** for all employees in the bargaining unit and must be recognized by the company. All employees in the bargaining unit, even those who do not want the union, are bound by the recognition of the union as the exclusive bargaining agent for all employees. Exhibit 15.2 illustrates the process.

On the other side of the coin, 60 to 90 days before the expiration of a collective bargaining agreement, 30 percent of the workers can call for an election to attempt to **decertify** a union; that is, to get a majority of employees to vote to remove the union as bargaining agent.

Agency Shops

When a union is selected to be the collective bargaining agent, the workers who join the union must pay union dues. What about the workers who do not want to be union members? **Agency shops**—places of employment where a majority of employees have voted to be represented by a union in a collective bargaining agreement—are legal. In an agency shop, employees who belong to the union pay union dues, while employees who do not want to join the union pay **agency fees**. That is, nonunion employees are represented by the union and have fees deducted from their paychecks that go to cover the costs of union services, including collective bargaining and enforcing the bargain. Agency fees are a little lower than union dues.

EXHIBIT 15.2 UNIONIZATION PROCESS

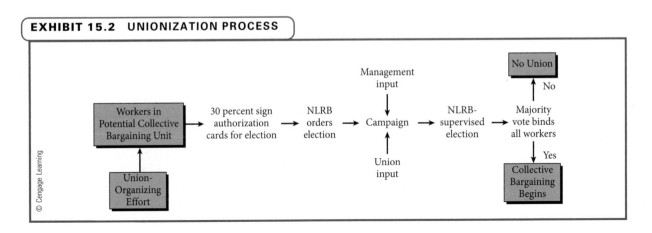

© Cengage Learning

INTERNATIONAL PERSPECTIVE

Labor Law in China

The People's Republic of China established three important new labor laws in 2007: the Employment Contracts Law (ECL), the Employment Promotion Law (EPL), and the Labor Dispute Mediation and Arbitration Law (LDMAL).

The ECL favors long-term employment relationships over short-term ones, providing job security and severance pay. It was aimed at the widespread practice of paying employees late to keep them employed at a firm. It attempts to change the practice of using short-term contracts to one of long-term or open-ended employment contracts with "just cause" termination provisions. For example, the ECL requires any employee with 10 years or more of service to be given an open-ended contract when a contract is renewed. Employees terminated without cause are entitled to reinstatement or double severance pay.

Under the ECL, unions' roles are focused on assisting employees in the negotiation of their individual contracts, not collective bargaining. Article 6 of the ECL provides:

A labor union shall assist and guide workers in the conclusion of employment contracts with their Employer and the performance thereof in accordance with the law, and establish a collective bargaining mechanism with the Employer in order to safeguard the lawful rights and interests of workers.

The EPL addresses employment discrimination issues, including a ban on discrimination based on race, ethnicity, gender, religion, and positive infectious disease status, such as employees with Hepatitis B.

The LDMAL covers employment disputes, making many decisions of arbitration commissions binding immediately, including decisions in cases where less than a year's salary is in dispute. The law also increased the time employees had to bring claims to a year.

With these changes, China has created a legal system for employment matters equivalent to that in most western countries. Implementing these laws effectively requires a similarly developed legal system, which is still a work in progress.

© Cengage Learning

Political Action The use of agency fees to support union political activities not directly related to the union's duties as a bargaining representative raises concerns about the constitutional rights of employees who are forced to provide financial support for political action. That is, unions devote significant sums to support favored political candidates. That money comes from union dues and from agency fees. Several Supreme Court cases have been heard on this issue. In *Chicago Teachers Union* (106 S.Ct. 1066), the Court listed four requirements regarding agency fees paid by nonunion workers to unions at unionized workplaces. There must be:

- An adequate explanation of the basis for the fee
- A reasonably prompt explanation of the basis for the fee
- An opportunity to challenge the fee before an impartial decision maker
- An escrow account for the amounts in dispute while challenges are pending

In the *Beck* decision (108 S.Ct. 2641), the Supreme Court found that 79 percent of the agency fees paid by Beck and other non-union AT&T employees represented by a union went to political action. The Court ordered the union to cut its agency fees, refund the excess fees collected from nonunion workers, and keep clear records about union expenditures by category. Justice Brennan noted that unions are not "free to exact dues equivalents from nonmembers in any amount they please, no matter how unrelated those fees may be to collective bargaining activities."

In practice, the Supreme Court decisions have not been enforced. Unions represent about two million workers who do not belong to the unions but must pay agency fees. Most agency fees, like union dues, go to support political action and other union

ISSUE SPOTTER
Moves to Help Keep Unions Out

Because most employers have little desire to see any of their workers unionize, employers generally are sensitive to indications that employees may be trying to generate interest in a union or that a union is actively seeking to get workers to sign authorization cards to force an election on unionization. What moves can a company make if it detects interest in unionizing among its employees? Prohibit distribution of all union material by e-mail or in employee boxes? Fire employees who are ringleaders? Make clear the company's total opposition to unionization? What is fair game?

activities not related to the expenses of collective bargaining at a workplace. Unions generally ignore the *Beck* ruling, forcing employees to go to the expense of litigation to enforce their rights as the NLRB rarely helps to enforce the Supreme Court's holdings.

Right-to-Work Laws The Taft-Hartley Act allows states to pass **right-to-work laws** to prohibit agency shops. In right-to-work states, if a majority of the employees vote for union representation and pay union dues, the union is the collective-bargaining agent for all employees. However, no employees can be required to pay agency fees, even though their wages and working conditions are determined by the collective-bargaining agreement. Because some employees receive the benefits of the union without paying union dues or agency fees, unions claim they are free riders. Right-to-work laws, in effect in half the states, clearly retard the effectiveness of unions in such states.

Collective Bargaining

Once employees choose a union, it becomes the legal representative of the employees. The employer must bargain with the union. **Collective bargaining** is the process by which the employer and the union, on behalf of all employees in a collective bargaining unit, negotiate a contract, setting forth the terms and conditions of employment for a given time period. Collective bargaining includes contract negotiation and contract administration as part of a continuous relationship between an employer and the employee representative.

Good-Faith Bargaining

The NLRA imposes a duty for employers and unions to bargain in good faith. Essentially, good faith means an obligation to meet and be willing to present proposals, to listen to and consider the proposals of the other party, and to search for common ground that can serve as the basis for an agreement—but there is no legal requirement that agreement be reached.

The Supreme Court has noted that under the NLRA that the NLRB and the courts should not become involved in the details of the bargaining process because Congress did not intend for direct intervention in the substance of labor bargains. Rather, the parties are free to reach an agreement of their own making.

Mandatory Subjects of Bargaining

The NLRA states that bargaining in good faith must occur with respect to **mandatory subjects of bargaining** about which employers and unions must bargain in good faith. However, either party may insist on its position and back that up with a strike or a lockout.

Employers and unions are free to bargain over any topics they agree to discuss. Among the topics that may be placed on the bargaining table because they have been determined by the NLRB or the courts to be subject to mandatory bargaining are the following:

- Pay rate
- Insurance plans
- Holidays
- Overtime pay
- Vacations
- Retirement plans
- Work hours
- Individual merit raises
- Breaks and lunch periods
- Safety practices
- Seniority rights
- Discipline procedures
- Termination procedures
- Layoff procedures
- Recall rights
- Union dues collection
- Grievance procedures
- Arbitration procedures
- No-strike clauses
- Drug testing

There is no requirement that every issue be covered in a collective bargaining contract, only that the employer must consider demands raised by the union. If the employer and the union cannot reach agreement, an arbitrator may be called in to help get the talks going, or either party may request help from the Federal Mediation and Conciliation Service. These mediators have no authority to impose a settlement, but often help the parties reach an agreement.

Arbitration Clauses Under grievance arbitration clauses in collective bargaining agreements, disputes between employers and unions or represented employees are resolved by an internal grievance procedure. If the results are not satisfactory, an outside labor arbitrator chosen under the contract hears disputes. Usually each side gets to veto nominees, helping to ensure both sides see the arbitrator as fair. If an arbitration decision is violated, the aggrieved party may then sue for enforcement. The right to grieve an issue belongs to the union, however, not the worker, as the union controls labor-management relations. If the union refuses to take an employee's concern to arbitration, the employee must sue the union for a violation of the "duty of fair representation." We see an example of this in the *Teamsters Local Union No. 523* case.

TEAMSTERS LOCAL UNION NO. 523 V. NATIONAL LABOR RELATIONS BOARD

United States Court of Appeals, Tenth Circuit, 590 F.3d 849 (2009)

Case Background *Interstate Brands made and distributed bakery products such as Hostess, Dolly Madison, and Wonder Bread. Different distribution systems handled different products. The employer consolidated its distribution so sales representatives, and distributors would handle all product lines. This meant that the union would now represent all distribution workers, rather than only some workers.*

Rammage had been a Dolly Madison sales representative for 15 years before consolidation and *was not represented by the union. Now that the union represented him, he was put at the bottom of its seniority list, which gave preference to workers that the union had represented previously. As a result, Rammage was "endtailed" to the bottom of the distribution system, lost his regular route, and was demoted.*

He complained to the NLRB that the union and employer were engaged in an unfair labor practice. The Board held in his favor. The union appealed.

Case Decision Tacha, Circuit Judge

* * *

In this case, the NLRB concluded that "in the context of a unit merger, a union and an employer are not lawfully permitted to dovetail the seniority of represented employees while endtailing previously unrepresented employees." This conclusion reflects a reasonable application of the NLRA and the legal principles articulated above. Indeed, the Union's insistence on Mr. Rammage's endtailing coupled with the Employer's acquiescence and its statements that Mr. Rammage was demoted because he was not in the Union reasonably suggest that the Union caused the Employer to discriminate against Mr. Rammage in a way that encourages Union participation.

… Accordingly, we find that the NLRB reasonably concluded that the Union's insistence on Mr. Rammage's endtailing and loss of seniority for route bidding purposes caused the Employer to discriminate against Mr. Rammage. …

Affirmed.

Questions for Analysis

1. Why would the union discriminate against Rammage?
2. Why would the employer go along with the union on this issue?

Almost all collective bargaining agreements contain dispute-resolution clauses. The federal courts encourage the use of the grievance arbitration process. This helps prevent the federal court system from being clogged with thousands of disputes.

Concerted Activities

To back up their positions, a union can call a strike, an employer can lock out the workers, or other steps can be taken to put pressure on the other party to settle. To promote productive collective bargaining, Congress provided that certain activities would be protected so the parties could back up bargaining demands.

Protected Activities The NLRA protects the rights of employees, individually or in groups, to engage in **concerted activities** for mutual aid or protection. Protected concerted activity includes most union-organizing efforts. It also involves actions by employees, unionized or not, such as a refusal to work because of unreasonable hazards or working conditions that endanger health or safety.

Unprotected Activities If workers engage in threats or acts of violence, they are not protected by the law. The Supreme Court has held that employers may fire employees for insubordination, disobedience, or disloyalty, unless the reason for such activity involves protected concerted activity. That is, a worker may not be fired for engaging in a union-organizing activity that the employer thinks is disloyal.

Strikes and Boycotts A **primary boycott**—a strike by a union against an employer whose collective bargaining agreement is in question—is legal. The law restricts **secondary boycotts**, which occur when a union uses economic pressure to try to force others to stop doing business with an employer not directly involved in a primary labor dispute. Examples include:

- A strike against an employer other than the one involved in the primary labor dispute, such as a strike against the steel companies that sell steel to the automakers if there is a strike against the automakers.
- Refusal to handle goods for a secondary employer, such as refusing to carry steel from steel companies to automakers during a strike against the automakers.

- Threats, coercion, or restraints against any person engaging in commerce—usually an employee—in an effort to spread the dispute beyond the primary employer. For example, in a strike against the food manufacturer Hormel, the union picketed local banks. The NLRB ruled that the union could not picket any banks as they were not directly involved with Hormel products. The picketing was an unfair labor practice.

Employer Economic Responses

Although employers may not retaliate against employees for engaging in protected activities, they have the right to use economic pressure. As previously noted, an employer may lock out the employees—refuse to let them work until the dispute with the union is settled.

A **lockout** is usually defensive—in response to a strike, to prevent a sit-down strike in the plant, or to prevent some other activity that would be destructive to the plant or its materials. So long as the lockout is seen as promoting the settlement of a collective bargaining agreement, it is most likely legal.

Replacement Workers A tactic successfully used by companies in recent years to weaken a union is the hiring of nonunion workers to replace striking workers. Once a collective-bargaining agreement expires, if the union and the employer have not agreed to a new contract, and the union calls for a strike, the employer may hire new workers and keep using existing workers who cross the picket line (crossovers). In some cases, there were enough replacement workers and crossovers that the union had lost substantial strength by the time a new agreement was signed.

? TEST YOURSELF

1. Under the Norris-LaGuardia Act, federal courts are prohibited against issuing _____ in case of nonviolent labor disputes.
2. If there is a dispute between a union and an employer that cannot be resolved by arbitration, a resolution will be imposed by the National Labor Relations Board after 90 days have passed: T—F
3. For a union representation election to be held, at least 50 percent of the employees must have signed authorization cards calling for an election: T—F
4. In *Teamsters Local Union No. 523* v. *National Labor Relations Board*, where an employee sued the union for removing his seniority when a merger of work-forces occurred, the appeals court held that:
   a. the union was correct because the employer agreed with the move.
   b. the union was correct because under the NLRA, unions may control seniority rankings of represented employees.
   c. the union was incorrect in removing seniority benefits as part of punishment for the employee's failure to be in the union.
   d. the union was incorrect in removing seniority benefits because the employer did not agree to the change.
5. In right-to-work states, _____ may be prohibited.
6. The NLRA, as amended, specifies that unions may not bargain over the terms of an employer's drug test policy: T—F
7. If a union uses economic pressure to try to force others to stop doing business with an employer not directly involved in a primary labor dispute, it is a(n) _____, and likely illegal.

Answers: injunctions; F; F; c; agency shops; F; secondary boycott.

SUMMARY

- There are public policy restrictions on employment-at-will, either by statute or by court determination. These include a right not to be fired or disciplined for refusing to commit an illegal act, for performing a public duty, or for exercising a public right. In limited circumstances, there is an exception for whistle-blowers.

- State law varies on employment contracts that may be in violation of public policy. Exculpatory agreements waiving tort rights or other causes of action are not looked on with favor. Anti-raiding covenants and noncompete agreements are allowed in many states, if reasonable, but are prohibited in some states.

- Most companies have policies regarding testing for substance abuse and steps that must be taken by an employee if abuse is detected. Generally, companies are free to require drug tests of job applicants and of employees in positions that affect health, safety, or large sums of money. Companies may wish to control substance abuse to reduce medical expenses, improve worker productivity, and reduce accidents.

- OSHA may impose work safety and health regulations. If a company fails to meet minimal safety standards, workers may walk off the job to protect their health. OSHA regulations must be justified by documented health or safety needs, but there is no requirement that they be cost-effective. Haz-Mat rules detail the handling of hazardous chemicals in the workplace.

- Most employers must pay for workers' compensation insurance to ensure that injured employees, regardless of fault, have medical expenses covered and receive partial compensation for lost wages. Workers' compensation prohibits tort suits against employers except in cases of intentional infliction of injury.

- Labor regulations require employers to collect evidence that all new employees are U.S. citizens or are noncitizens with legal work status. Employers must also comply with federal minimum wage requirements.

- Under the WARN Act, employers of more than 100 employees must notify employees at least 60 days in advance of any plant closings or layoffs that affect 50 or more employees. Employers with 50 or more employees must allow full-time employees to take up to 12 weeks unpaid leave for family or medical reasons under the FMLA.

- The Employee Retirement Income Security Act (ERISA) gives employees the right to their pension benefits after a certain time of service and provides federal inspection and guarantee of the solvency of pension funds.

- Under the Norris-La Guardia Act, federal courts may not issue injunctions against unions in labor disputes. Employers must bargain with unions according to the terms of the collective bargaining agreement, rather than seek relief in federal court.

- The National Labor Relations Act (NLRA) originated with the Wagner Act in 1935. Employees may organize unions and bargain collectively through the union of choice. Employers may not interfere in the exercise of those rights and employee actions may not interfere with the employer's interest in plant safety and efficiency. The Act created the National Labor Relations Board (NLRB), which is responsible for resolving unfair labor practice complaints and supervising matters of union representation.

- The Landrum-Griffin Act, a part of the NLRA, regulates internal union affairs. It covers the election of union leadership, protects the right of union members to speak out about union matters, and assures union members the right to see the books of the union, which are audited by the Department of Labor.

- If more than 30 percent of the workers at a workplace petition for a union representation election, the NLRB holds an election to determine whether a majority of the workers want union representation. Workers can also vote to end union representation. The employer and the union debate the pros and cons of union representation before workers vote.

- When a majority of the workers at a workplace vote for union representation, all workers are covered by the collective bargaining agreement settled by management and the union, and all workers must follow the procedures established for handling complaints. Workers who are not union members must follow the rules set by the collective bargaining contract.

- Workers who work at a unionized workplace must either join the union and pay dues or, if they do not want to join the union, pay agency fees to the union. In the 25 right-to-work states—a state statute allowed under the Taft-Hartley Act—workers at unionized work places cannot be forced to pay agency fees, making unions less effective in such states.

TERMS TO KNOW

public policy exception, 402	occupational licensure, 419	decertify, 426
whistle-blower, 402	vesting, 421	agency shop, 426
wrongful discharge, 402	union, 422	agency fee, 426
retaliatory discharge, 402	labor dispute, 422	right-to-work law, 428
exculpatory agreement, 402	strike, 422	collective bargaining, 428
noncompete agreement, 404	yellow-dog contract, 422	mandatory subjects of
anti-raiding covenant, 405	unfair labor practice, 424	bargaining, 428
substance-abuse policy, 407	authorization card, 425	concerted activity, 430
hazard communication	representation election, 425	primary boycott, 430
standard, 411	union certification, 426	secondary boycott, 430
workers' compensation law, 411	bargaining agent, 426	lockout, 431

DISCUSSION QUESTION

Do firms have the right to test all job applicants and refuse to hire applicants who test positive for drug use, even if the job in question has no safety or sensitivity concerns?

CASE QUESTIONS

1. Barbara Reynolds and Jason Stephens were at-will truck drivers for Ozark Motor Lines. They were fired when they refused to begin a trip from Memphis to Chicago without having adequate time to inspect the truck as required by safety provisions of the Tennessee Motor Carriers Act. The jury found this to be wrongful dismissal because Ozark violated statutory public policy. Do you think this was upheld on appeal? [*Reynolds* v. *Ozark Motor Lines*, 887 S.W.2d 822, Sup. Ct., Tenn. (1994)]

2. Rowan worked for TSC. She believed that her manager, Snider, and other employees were embezzling money from TSC. When Rowan expressed her concern to Snider, he twisted her arm and pushed her. Rowan reported the matter to Snider's supervisor, Carter, who told her to "keep her mouth shut." Rowan sued Snider for assault and was awarded damages. She also reported the assault to the police, and charges were filed against Snider. A TSC manager told Rowan to drop the criminal charges. She refused and was fired. Snider was convicted of criminal assault and battery. Rowan sued TSC for wrongful termination in violation of public policy. The federal district court certified a question to the Virginia Supreme Court, asking if the public policy exception to the employment-at-will doctrine applied in this case. Do you think it does? [*Rowan* v. *Tractor Supply*, 559 S.E.2d 709, Sup. Ct., Va. (2002)]

    ✓ Check your answer

3. Tanks was a bus driver for the Greater Cleveland Rapid Transit Authority (GCRTA). It had a substance abuse policy that required drivers to be tested after accidents. Tanks ran into a pole. As required, she submitted blood, saliva, and urine samples, which tested positive for cocaine. Under the terms of the policy, Tanks was fired. She sued, claiming that the drug test was an unreasonable search in violation of the Fourth Amendment to the Constitution. Did she have a case? [*Tanks* v. *GCRTA*, 930 F.2d 475, 6th Cir. (1991)]

4. A group of Boeing workers sued for injuries and disabilities from their four-year exposure to toxic chemicals. There was evidence that Boeing had

known of the problem but did nothing about it. Boeing asserted that the employees could only collect under workers' compensation; the employees sued for intentional tort. Could they bring such an action? [*Birklid* v. *Boeing*, 904 P.2d 278 Wash. Sup. Ct. (1995)]

✓ Check your answer

5. Vandenberg was at a party on company property. The company did not provide alcohol at the party, but Boyd was drinking. Boyd's boss, thinking he had drunk too much, told him not to drive home, but to call his wife to pick him up. Boyd ignored that, got in the truck the company provided him, and crashed into another company truck. Distraught over the accident, he grabbed a handgun he kept in the truck and killed himself. His wife filed an application for workers' compensation benefits due the survivor of a worker who died on the job. Do you think workers' compensation benefits would apply? [*Vandenberg* v. *Snedegar Construction*, 911 N.E.2d 681, Ct. App., Ind. (2009)]

6. Nastasi drove a propane gas truck for Synergy Gas. He had been active in getting a union certified as the bargaining agent for fellow employees. The unionization fight was bitter, and the NLRB cited the company for unfair labor practices. Soon after, Nastasi was in an accident in his truck. Synergy fired him, claiming that it fired all drivers in serious accidents because of the danger involved in driving such trucks. The union protested that the firing was because of Nastasi's union leadership. The NLRB ordered Nastasi reinstated to his job; Synergy appealed. What would you think was the result? [*Synergy Gas* v. *NLRB*, 19 F.3d 649, D.C. Cir. (1994)]

7. During a unionization campaign, a company told workers that no materials related to the union effort could be posted on employee bulletin boards. A supervisor told a union supporter "if we got a union in there, we'd be in the unemployment line." The union claimed these were unfair labor practices. The NLRB agreed; did the court? [*Guardian Industries* v. *NLRB*, 49 F.3d 317, 7th Cir. (1995)]

✓ Check your answer

8. Club Orleans was a "gentlemen's club" in Kansas. The owner classified the pole dancers as independent contractors. They worked only for tips from customers. A former dancer filed a claim for unemployment compensation. The state investigated and ruled that the club should be paying wages and, therefore, the former dancer could qualify for unemployment compensation. The state held that the dancers had to follow rules set by management. The club owner claimed the dancers were given creative freedom, so were not employees. What result do you think likely and why? [*Milano's* v. *Kansas Dept. of Labor*, 293 P.3d 707, Sup. Ct., Kan. (2013)]

9. When a collective bargaining agreement with IMT expired, the workers went on strike. The company announced it would take crossovers and then hire replacement workers, which it did. After the strike was settled, the union claimed the company had to take back all strikers in place of the replacement workers. Is that position correct? [*Iowa Mold Tooling Co.* v. *Teamsters Local Union No. 828*, 16 F.3d 311, 8th Cir. (1994)]

ETHICS QUESTION

Contemplating the opening of a factory, you discover that it appears to be a toss-up between building a plant that uses cheaper machinery and hiring 200 workers who will earn an average of $9 an hour and building a plant that uses more expensive, sophisticated machinery and hiring 80 workers likely to earn about $20 an hour. Is it more responsible to build one kind of factory than another? What if you know that the first kind of factory will probably never be unionized, but the second kind of factory is more likely to be unionized?

CHAPTER 16

Employment Discrimination

The owner of an Iowa electronics company made sexual advances to an employee after she had posed nude in a nationally distributed magazine. Could he have violated the law that restricts sex harassment in employment?

"John Doe" worked as an engineer at Boeing aircraft. After six years at Boeing—under the supervision of his physician—he decided to become "Jane Doe." Prior to sex-transformation surgery he began to live the social role of a woman. Boeing fired Doe for using the women's restroom and dressing as a woman despite company orders not to do so prior to sex-change surgery. Was Boeing guilty of disability or sex discrimination?

These cases illustrate the wide range of employment issues that can arise today. Years ago, neither of these cases would likely have existed, but now the law restricts employment practices with respect to discrimination based on many personal characteristics.

In this chapter, we focus on the Civil Rights Act of 1964, which is the basis of modern employment discrimination law. That landmark statute has been amended over the years. Case law has helped to clarify the rights and duties of employees and employers in dealing with race, sex, color, religion, national origin, age, and disability.

The answer to the first question, was the owner guilty of sex discrimination, is "yes." What the employee did on her own time was her business and violated no company policy. She did not invite his advances. The answer to the second question, was Boeing guilty of disability or sex discrimination, is "neither." There is no federal protection for transgender sex, and the company handled the matter properly—John/Jane Doe became a woman when that was declared to be a medical fact, as far as his employer was concerned, not when he made that a personal choice.

Origins of Discrimination Law

Discrimination in employment is a fact that occurs in varying degrees everywhere. Fifty years after passage of the most important antidiscrimination legislation in history, discrimination in employment still exists, but it is not as overt as it used to be. Disparities continue and are likely because of stereotyped assumptions about productivity based on personal characteristics.

The Civil Rights Movements

Historically, employers could hire and fire at will, subject to the limits we covered in the last chapter. Employers could discriminate because of race, sex, or any other personal characteristics. Similarly, labor unions could impose discriminatory membership rules. The situation was worsened by federal and state laws—Jim Crow laws—that supported or required segregation.

The drive for civil rights in employment and other aspects of life became a national movement in the early 1960s. Rising public concern provided support for the first federal employment discrimination statute in 1963, the Equal Pay Act, followed by the Civil Rights Act of 1964, which is the cornerstone of federal employment discrimination law.

The Equal Pay Act of 1963

The Equal Pay Act of 1963 was the first federal law to address employment discrimination. It is illegal to pay men and women employees different wages when their jobs require equal skill, effort, responsibility, and the same working conditions. Job titles are not relevant; job content is reviewed. The Equal Pay Act allows differences in wages if they are the result of "(i) a seniority system; (ii) a merit system; (iii) a system which measures earnings by quantity or quality of production; or (iv) a differential based on any factor other than sex." Some sex discrimination suits are brought based on the 1963 statute, but the vast majority of discrimination suits are brought under Title VII of the Civil Rights Act, which is larger in scope and has more remedies.

Title VII of the 1964 Civil Rights Act

The most important antidiscrimination employment law is **Title VII** of the Civil Rights Act of 1964. Major amendments to Title VII include the Equal Employment Opportunity Act of 1972 to give the Equal Employment Opportunity Commission (EEOC) the power to enforce the Act, by the Pregnancy Discrimination Act in 1978, and by the Civil Rights Act of 1991. Title VII makes it illegal for an employer of 15 or more workers:

1. to fail or refuse to hire or to discharge any individual, or otherwise to discriminate against any individual with respect to his compensation, terms, conditions, or privileges of employment; or
2. to limit, segregate, or classify his employees or applicants for employment in any way which would deprive or tend to deprive any individual of employment opportunities or otherwise adversely affect his status as an employee because of such individual's race, color, religion, sex, or national origin.

Many states have their own civil rights acts modeled on Title VII. They may protect additional classes of employees. For example, some states prohibit discrimination based on sexual orientation. Some cities also have civil rights laws that extend discrimination coverage. San Francisco prohibits employment discrimination based on height or weight.

Protected Classes

Title VII applies to employers, employment agencies, and labor unions in the private and public sectors. In general, it forbids **discrimination** in all aspects of employment on the basis of race, color, religion, sex, or national origin. The Supreme Court has held that law firms and other partnership organizations are covered by the law. Those are the characteristics that determine **protected classes** for purposes of Title VII coverage in the original statute. They do not apply to business relationships or to the selection of independent contractors.

Race The courts have little difficulty in determining **race** or racial status. Federal law recognizes five major racial groupings: black or African American, white, American Indian or Alaska Native; Native Hawaiian or other Pacific Islander, and Asian. The ethnic category Hispanic or Latino is protected as well and may overlap racial groups.

Contrary to some claims, whites are protected under Title VII. That was made clear by the Supreme Court in *McDonald* v. *Santa Fe Trail Transportation* (96 S.Ct. 2574). In *McDonald*, an African-American employee and a white employee stole property from their employer. The African-American employee was reprimanded but allowed to keep his job but the white employee was fired. The Court stated:

> *Title VII prohibits racial discrimination against the white petitioners.... While Santa Fe may decide that participation in a theft of cargo may render an employee unqualified for employment, this criteria must be applied alike to members of all races.*

Reverse discrimination—preferential treatment to members of protected classes—is illegal, but if minorities or women are underrepresented in a job category, it is legal for an employer to see that more minorities or women are hired to increase participation in a job category. Affirmative action programs, which are discussed later, that are implemented to remedy discrimination against minorities or women may be adopted if they are designed not to violate the rule against reverse discrimination. Race is the most common basis for a discrimination complaint. It is the claim in about 34 percent of the charges filed, or in about 34,000 per year. Note that when a discrimination claim is made, a person may claim more than one basis, such as race and sex.

Color Under Title VII, the term **color** refers generally to discrimination claims based on shade of skin. An example would be a department store's refusal to hire a Hispanic woman to work at a cosmetics counter because they would prefer to have a blue-eyed blonde with light skin in that position. Race and color discrimination charges are often brought together. Color discrimination claims are fewer than 3 percent of the total.

National Origin According to the Supreme Court in *Espinoza* v. *Farah Manufacturing* (94 S.Ct. 334), the term **national origin** is to be given its ordinary meaning:

> *[The term national origin] refers to the country where a person is born or ... the country from which his or her ancestors came.*

This has been held to exist where a person has a physical, cultural, or speech characteristic of a national origin group. Hispanics bring the most suits under this category, which represent about 11 percent of all charges. It may be discriminatory, for example, to require that English be spoken at all times in the workplace. If business necessity requires that

English be spoken, such as for reasons of safety or productivity, it may be a legitimate job requirement. Employment discrimination can also take place when an employer allows ethnic slurs to occur and does not take steps to stop such actions.

Religion Title VII does not define the term **religion** but states that "religion includes all aspects of religious observances and practice." This includes strong believers and atheists. The courts have defined the term broadly.

The employer is required to provide **reasonable accommodation** for an employee's religious practices. The employer may discriminate, however, if the accommodation imposes **undue hardship** on the conduct of business. Undue hardship is created by accommodations that would cost an employer more than a minimal amount. For example, if an employer has a strict dress code synonymous with a certain "look" to the public, the code need not be modified to allow certain employees to wear religious garb, such as a headdress. But if an employer does not have a strict dress code, then it could not tell an employee not to wear religious garb or to shave if the employee's religion requires members to be unshaven.

Among the most common complaints in religious discrimination is that the employer does not accommodate an employee's need to have certain times off from work to attend religious services. When an accommodation would disrupt a schedule designed to spread the burden of unpopular shifts, that can be an undue burden.

Discrimination because of religion is the charge in about 4 percent of the complaints filed annually. As with other protected classes, an employer must take steps to stop other employees from harassing an employee because of religion.

Sex The courts hold that the term **sex** should be given its ordinary meaning. Thus, Title VII prohibits sex discrimination simply on the basis of whether a person is male or female. This is the basis for complaints in about 30 percent of the charges files annually. Title VII does not protect discrimination on the basis of sexual preference or sexual identity, although the law in some states prohibits discrimination on such bases. Title VII does not prohibit

INTERNATIONAL PERSPECTIVE

EEOC Impact on Global Operations

American firms have operations in other countries, and foreign firms have operations in the United States. Americans work for American firms in other countries; foreign citizens work for American firms in the United States and in other countries. When does Equal Employment Opportunity (EEO) law apply? This is not a trivial matter because EEO law in the United States is much tougher than in many other nations.

Sayaka Kobayashi was a personal assistant in New York to Hideaki Otaka, president of Toyota's North American operations. She complained that Otaka groped her and made numerous sexual advances. When she complained, she was told she should meet with Otaka privately to discuss the matter, or she could quit. She sued in federal court because U.S. law applied to foreign operations in the United

States that employed foreign citizens. The president resigned and returned to Japan.

In general, U.S. law applies to anyone working for a company located in the United States and to U.S. citizens working for U.S. companies in other countries. But EEO does not apply to non-U.S. citizens working for U.S. companies in other countries. So, for example, when the Michigan company, Lear, ran an ad for a secretary for its operation in Mexico, it stated it wanted a woman, aged 20 to 28, unmarried, with "excellent presentation," and that she should submit a photo. Similarly, a large U.S. law firm, Baker and McKenzie, ran an ad for an attorney in Mexico. It wanted a man, the firm said, because Mexican clients expect to see a man. Those ads were legal in Mexico but probably were not good for public relations in the United States.

Lighter Side of the Law

A New Protected Class?

Curt Storey sued Burns International Security Services for wrongful discharge. He claimed he was fired for refusing to remove Confederate flags from his lunch box and pickup truck.

A lifelong resident of Pennsylvania, Storey claims protection to display such items because he is a "Confederate Southern American." However, Title VII does not recognize loyalty to the Confederacy as a protected class.

Source: Observer-Reporter (Washington, Pa.).

discrimination on the basis of marital status, as long as an employer applies employment rules evenly to employees of both sexes. However, many states prohibit discrimination on the basis of marital status.

Obvious examples of sex discrimination, or discrimination based on race or some other protected class, would include an employer allowing one protected class to work overtime but not another. It would be discrimination to hire men to be sales representatives but to hire women only for office-based positions. It would be discriminatory to require women to wear skirts, while allowing men generally to wear what they want.

Pregnancy Discrimination   Title VII was amended by the Pregnancy Discrimination Act. An employer may not discriminate against women because of pregnancy, childbirth, or related medical conditions. Women affected by these conditions "shall be treated the same for all employment-related purposes, including receipt of benefits under fringe benefit programs." Examples of pregnancy discrimination include:

- Denying a woman a job, assignment, or promotion because she is pregnant or has children
- Requiring a pregnant woman to go on leave when she is able to do her job
- Treating maternity leave differently from other leaves for temporary disabilities
- Discriminating in fringe benefits, such as health insurance, to discourage women of childbearing age from working

CYBER LAW

Your E-mail Is Your Boss's E-mail

In general, e-mail that is sent at work on company computers is available for company inspection. Whether the employee is told or not, employers have the right to monitor employee e-mail.

A sports writer for a Chicago newspaper was told by his employer to quit sending unwanted e-mail to a female coworker. When he did not quit sending her e-mail, the employer transferred the writer to another department. A federal court held that the paper was within its rights to do so; the employee could not complain about the interference with his e-mail, nor could he claim sex discrimination. The employer "was obviously trying to make the best of a difficult situation" (112 F.3d 853).

Why do employers care so much about e-mail transmissions at work? Chevron paid $2.2 million to settle sexual harassment claims of women employees for dirty jokes that were transmitted around the office via e-mail.

Sexual Harassment   A sexually hostile work environment is a form of sex discrimination. **Sexual harassment** is defined by the EEOC in the *Code of Federal Regulations* as unwelcome sexual advances, requests for sexual favors, and other verbal or physical conduct of a sexual nature when

1. submission to such conduct is made either explicitly or implicitly a term or condition of an individual's employment,
2. submission to or rejection of such conduct by an individual is used as a basis for employment decisions affecting such individual, or
3. such conduct has the purpose or effect of unreasonably interfering with an individual's work performance or creating an intimidating, hostile, or offensive working environment.

Sexual harassment falls into two major categories. The first is **quid pro quo**, or "this for that," where there is a promise of reward—such as promotion or pay raise—for providing sexual favors, or there is a threat of punishment for not going along with sexual requests. The second form is a **hostile environment** created at work by others (obviously, a hostile environment can exist because of race or some other characteristic). An abusive work environment is created by words or acts related to a person's sex. Examples are:

- Discussing sexual activities
- Commenting on physical attributes
- Unnecessary touching or gestures
- Using crude, demeaning, or offensive language
- Displaying sexually suggestive pictures

Trivial and isolated incidents usually are not sufficient grounds for a sexual harassment suit. The courts look to factors such as how often such conduct occurred; whether the harassment was by a supervisor who could control progress, pay, and working conditions or by a coworker; whether there was talk or actual touching; and whether more than one person was involved. The Supreme Court offered guidance in the *Harris* case about what constitutes a hostile work environment in general. This analysis would also apply if the situation were based on race or other protected class.

HARRIS V. FORKLIFT SYSTEMS

United States Supreme Court 510 U.S. 17, 114 S.Ct. 367 (1993)

Case Background *Harris worked as a rental manager for two years for Forklift Systems. Her boss, Hardy, often insulted her in front of others and made her the target of sexual slurs and suggestions. He said, "we need a man as the rental manager," and "you're a woman, what do you know?" He told her she was "a dumb-ass woman," and that they should "go to the Holiday Inn to negotiate her raise." Hardy asked Harris and other women employees to get coins from his front pants pocket. He threw things on the ground and asked women to pick them up. He made sexual comments about their clothing.*

Harris complained to Hardy about his comments. Hardy said that he was only kidding. When Harris arranged a deal with a customer, Hardy asked her, "What did you do, promise the guy sex Saturday night?" Harris quit and sued, claiming that Hardy's conduct created a hostile work environment. The district and appeals courts ruled against her. She appealed.

Case Decision O'Connor, Justice

* * *

When the workplace is permeated with "discriminatory intimidation, ridicule, and insult" that is "sufficiently severe or pervasive to alter the conditions of the victim's employment and create an abusive working environment," Title VII is violated.

This standard ... takes a middle path between making actionable any conduct that is merely offensive and requiring the conduct to cause a tangible psychological injury. ... Conduct that is not severe or pervasive enough to create an objectively hostile or abusive work environment—an environment that a reasonable person would find hostile or abusive—is beyond Title VII's purview. Likewise, if the victim does not subjectively perceive the environment to be abusive, the conduct has not actually altered the conditions of the victim's employment, and there is no Title VII violation.

... A discriminatorily abusive work environment, even one that does not seriously affect employees' psychological well-being, can and often will detract from employees' job performance, discourage employees from remaining on the job, or keep them from advancing in their careers. Moreover, even without regard to these tangible effects, the very fact that the discriminatory conduct was so severe or pervasive that it created a work environment abusive to employees because of their race, gender, religion, or national origin offends Title VII's broad rule of workplace equality. ...

This is not, and by its nature cannot be, a mathematically precise test. ... Whether an environment is "hostile" or "abusive" can be determined only by looking at all the circumstances. These may include the frequency of the discriminatory conduct; its severity; whether it is physically threatening or humiliating, or a mere offensive utterance; and whether it unreasonably interferes with an employee's work performance. The effect on the employee's psychological well-being is, of course, relevant to determining whether the plaintiff actually found the environment abusive. But while psychological harm, like any other relevant factor, may be taken into account, no single factor is required.

* * *

We therefore reverse the judgment of the Court of Appeals, and remand the case for further proceedings consistent with this opinion.

Questions for Analysis

1. The court held that the actions must be severe enough to create a hostile work environment to a reasonable person. If this issue were left to a jury, might not some people on the jury, especially men, be likely to think that Harris overreacted?
2. Two concurring opinions indicated that another standard is whether the abusive actions are sufficient to affect work performance. Would that provide better guidance?

The Supreme Court further clarified the law in *Oncale* v. *Sundowner Offshore Services* (118 S.Ct. 998). In that case, a male worker sued his employer because he suffered verbal and physical abuse of a sexual nature by other male workers. The Court held that Title VII prohibits same-sex harassment when it is motivated by the sex of the victim:

The law does not reach genuine but innocuous differences in the ways men and women routinely interact with members of the same sex and of the opposite sex. The prohibition of harassment ... forbids only behavior so objectively offensive as to alter the "conditions" of the victim's employment ... the objective severity of harassment should be judged from the perspective of a reasonable person in the plaintiffs position, considering "all the circumstances." ... Common sense, and an appropriate sensitivity to social context, will enable courts and juries to distinguish between simple teasing or roughhousing among members of the same sex, and conduct which a reasonable person in the plaintiffs position would find severely hostile or abusive.

Age Discrimination

Enacted in 1967 and amended since, the Age Discrimination in Employment Act (ADEA) prohibits discrimination in employment against persons on the basis of **age** for persons over age 40. All employers who have 20 or more employees must comply. The ADEA generally parallels Title VII in its prohibitions, exceptions, remedies, and enforcement. So, while the ADEA is a separate statute, we presume it acts the same way as Title VII unless specifically noted. The law prohibits failing or refusing to hire or promote because of age, terminating employees because of age, or other discrimination in the terms of employment. About 23 percent of the discrimination claims are in this category.

Often the courts must, as in other discrimination cases, look to see whether age discrimination can be inferred by studying practices at the place of employment. The following are examples of age discrimination:

- Forcing retirement because of age
- Requiring older workers to pass physical examinations as a condition of continued employment
- Indicating an age preference in advertisements for employees, such as "young, dynamic person wanted"
- Choosing to promote a younger worker rather than an older worker because the older worker may be retiring in several years
- Cutting health benefits for workers over age 65 because they are eligible for Medicare

Discrimination Based on Military Service

Since enactment of the Uniformed Services Employment and Reemployment Rights Act (USERRA) in 1994, it is illegal for an employer to deny "employment, reemployment, retention in employment, promotion, or any benefit of employment" based on a person's membership in or "obligation to perform service in a uniform service." As the Supreme Court noted in *Staub* v. *Proctor Hospital* (131 S.Ct. 1186), in a case involving hostility to a member of the military, an improper job action based on this law is a tort under federal law, so it is a form of discrimination that does not follow EEOC process.

Genetic Information Discrimination

The Genetic Information Nondiscrimination Act (GINA), which took effect in 2009, makes it illegal to discriminate in employment based on **genetic information**. Information about a person's genetic tests or those of a person's family members, which includes medical history, may not be obtained by an employer or used in any way to determine suitability for employment. As with other protected classes, it is illegal for a person to suffer harassment or retaliation on the basis of genetic information. The EEOC was assigned to enforce this statute, using the same procedure as it does for Title VII.

❓ *TEST YOURSELF*

1. Title VII was amended in 2010 to include sexual orientation to the list of protected classes in employment: T—F
2. Preferential treatment in favor of members of a protected class is known as _____.

(Continued)

3. The Pregnancy Discrimination Act requires employers to provide "reasonable accommodation" for pregnant women employees: T—F
4. In *Harris* v. *Forklift Systems*, where Harris quit work and sued for hostile work environment, the Supreme Court held that she:
    a. had no suit if she failed to take advantage of her company's human resource department's discrimination process.
    b. provided sufficient evidence of hostile work environment to allow a jury to find a *per se* violation of Title VII.
    c. could sue her supervisor who discriminated against her, but not the company, as it did not know of the situation.
    d. None of the above.
5. If an employee is promised a reward in the workplace in exchange for sexual favors, there is said to be _____ sexual harassment.

Answers: F; reverse discrimination; F; d; quid pro quo.

Bringing a Discrimination Charge

If someone believes they have suffered a discriminatory act in employment under Title VII or the Americans with Disabilities Act (which we look at later), a charge may be filed by mail or in person at an EEOC office or a similar state agency. For example, in Illinois, a complaint could be filed at the Illinois Department of Human Rights. The EEOC and state agencies, referred to as Fair Employment Practices Agencies (FEPAs), share the workload because most actions can be under either state or federal law. Under federal law, as amended by the Lily Ledbetter Fair Pay Act of 2009, a charge must be filed within 180 days of an alleged discriminatory event, but state law often extends this to 300 days.

Steps in the Process

At state and federal offices, there about 100,000 discrimination charges filed annually. If a charge appears to be particularly strong, then the case may get priority for staff investigation. When a claim seems more dubious, it is likely to sit on the back burner awaiting consideration or, of course, it may be dismissed.

As Exhibit 16.1 indicates, the EEOC investigates claims. This may involve interviews, requests for documents, and visits to places of employment. At any point, the EEOC can seek to settle a charge by mediation if the parties agree: otherwise, the process continues to completion.

The significant portion of charges are dismissed by the EEOC because, in the agency's judgment, no violation is likely to have occurred; that is, no reasonable cause exists. However, while not common, the party who brought the charge may still file suit. If the agency determines that a violation may have occurred, it can offer to mediate a settlement. In a small percent of cases, the agency brings suit itself. In most cases that proceed, the agency issues a **right to sue letter** that can be used in proceeding to court. The plaintiff, employing a private attorney, proceeds to state or federal court.

The agency sues on behalf of the complaining party or on behalf of that party and others who are similarly affected, creating a class of plaintiffs in a small number of cases. EEOC resources for such cases tend to be reserved for those in which a pattern of discriminatory behavior is believed present, not just for discrimination against one party.

EXHIBIT 16.1   USUAL STEPS IN A DISCRIMINATION COMPLAINT TO EEOC

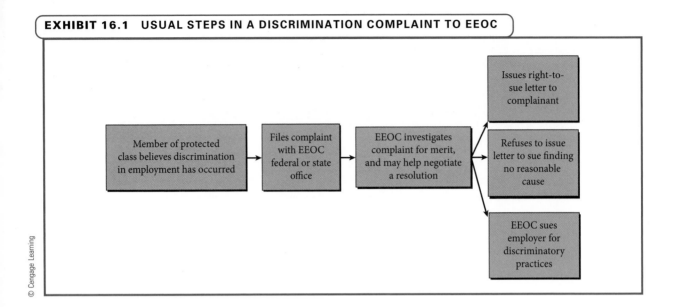

Forms of Discrimination

The laws against discrimination in employment cover most of the conditions of the employment process: hiring, promotion, transfers, discipline, pay raises, benefits, opportunities, and termination. When employers impose **differential standards** on the basis of a protected class status, a violation may have occurred.

As we saw in the *Harris* case, discrimination can also involve making life miserable for an employee, which is **harassment**. Even if there was no discrimination on the basis of pay, employees need not tolerate abusive behavior that is related to protected class status. If an employee quits because of harassment, as in the *Harris* case, then there was a **constructive discharge**. There is no obligation to stay and take abuse. However, as we see, internal company policy makes a big difference in this regard.

Traditionally, cases have been broken into two major groups: disparate treatment and disparate impact. Disparate treatment cases are the vast majority, so we address them first and more in depth, and then return to disparate impact.

Disparate Treatment   To recover for illegal discrimination—whether for race, color, religion, sex, national origin, or age—in a claim of **disparate treatment**, the plaintiff must prove that the employer intentionally discriminated. That is, a member of a protected class claims an employer treated the plaintiff differently from other employees because of the plaintiff's personal characteristics. Next, we go through the key steps of such a case.

Plaintiff Must Establish a Prima Facie Case   The Supreme Court established a four-part test in the *McDonnell-Douglas* decision (93 S.Ct. 1817). The plaintiff in a disparate treatment case must provide a ***prima facie*** **case** of discrimination. Exhibit 16.2 lists the four steps that must be met for a case to go forward. This test holds for all aspects of employment—hiring, promotion, compensation, conditions, discipline, and termination. In *Swierkiewicz* v. *Sorema* (122 S.Ct. 992), the Supreme Court made clear that only a "short and plain statement of the claim" is needed. Once the plaintiff meets the McDonnell-Douglas test, the case goes forward, and the burden shifts to the defendant to overcome the presumption of discrimination.

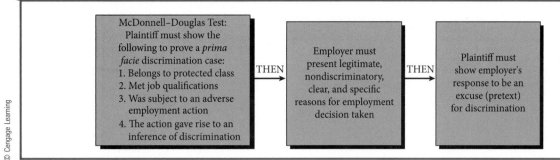

EXHIBIT 16.2   INITIAL STEPS IN DISPARATE TREATMENT CASES

© Cengage Learning

McDonnell–Douglas Test: Plaintiff must show the following to prove a *prima facie* discrimination case:
1. Belongs to protected class
2. Met job qualifications
3. Was subject to an adverse employment action
4. The action gave rise to an inference of discrimination

THEN

Employer must present legitimate, nondiscriminatory, clear, and specific reasons for employment decision taken

THEN

Plaintiff must show employer's response to be an excuse (pretext) for discrimination

Burden Shifts to Defendant   After a plaintiff shows a *prima facie* case of employment discrimination, the plaintiff wins unless the employer provides a successful defense. That is, the burden shifts to the defendant. The employer must show a legitimate, nondiscriminatory and reasonably specific reason for its decision to overcome the presumption of discrimination created by the *prima facie* case. The courts prefer clear standards for employment decisions, rather than vague claims that amount to "I felt like it." Legitimate reasons include such factors as seniority, education, performance, and experience.

Burden Shifts to Plaintiff to Attack Defense   After the employer offers a nondiscriminatory reason for the employment decision, the burden shifts back to the plaintiff to show that the defendant had an illegal motive. The plaintiff must show that the rationale offered by the employer was just a **pretext** or unacceptable excuse for disparate treatment. Such evidence can take many forms, such as showing inconsistency in decisions made by the employer, giving different reasons at different times for the decision, and presenting statistical evidence of discrimination based on sex or race. While discrimination is clear in some cases, it often requires a review of the employment situation and testimony from witnesses, usually other employees.

Lighter Side of the Law

Modify Your Body in Private

Cloutier worked for Costco for four years. While she was there, she kept adding to her collection of body piercings, tattoos, cuttings, and scars. She is a card-carrying member of the Church of Body Modification (see http://uscobm.com). Costco's dress code requires such personal decorations to be covered or removed. Cloutier refused to hide or remove some new facial piercings, so she was fired.

The EEOC tried to negotiate a compromise, but Cloutier refused to cover her piercings. She sued Costco for $2 million, claiming religious discrimination. The federal court held that while it would presume her religious beliefs were sincere, Costco had the right to a dress code so that customers see the workers as "reasonably professional in appearance."

Source: Cloutier v. Costco, 311 F.Supp.2d 190.

Possibility of Retaliation for Expression of Rights   Employees have the right to make complaints about discrimination, so if they are punished for doing so, then there is a basis for suit for **retaliation**. If workers are punished for participating in an official proceeding, such as filing a complaint or giving testimony in a discrimination investigation, then they have grounds for suit based on retaliation for a violation of a protected right. This occurs in more than a third of all discrimination complaints. We see an example in the *Heartland Inns of America* case, where a claim of sex discrimination and retaliation is made.

LEWIS V. HEARTLAND INNS OF AMERICA, L.L.C.

United States Court of Appeals, Eighth Circuit, 591 F.3d 1033 (2010)

Case Background *Brenda Lewis began working for Heartland Inns in 2005. She was promoted and received two merit pay increases. Her managers praised her work and said she "made a good impression" on customers.*

After she was promoted in December 2006, the Director of Operations, Cullinan, saw Lewis for the first time. She told Lewis's supervisor that she did not think Lewis was a "good fit" for the front desk because she lacked the "Midwestern girl look." She said that front desk girls should be pretty, and Lewis was not. In January 2007, Lewis' supervisor refused to remove Lewis from the front desk and was fired. Cullinan then met with Lewis to interview her for the position she already held and told her there would have to be a second interview, which had never happened before. Lewis was fired.

Lewis sued for violation of Title VII, contending that she was terminated for not conforming to sex stereotypes and in retaliation for opposing discriminatory practices. The district court granted summary judgment in favor of Heartland Inns. Lewis appealed.

Case Decision Murphy, Circuit Judge

* * *

The parties agree that Lewis' ICRA [Iowa Civil Rights Act] and federal claims are analytically indistinguishable....

The Supreme Court has stated that "the critical issue" in a sex discrimination case is "whether members of one sex are exposed to disadvantageous terms or conditions of employment to which members of the other sex are not exposed."... Cases [do not] compel a woman alleging sex discrimination to prove that men were not subjected to the same challenged discriminatory conduct or to show that the discrimination affected anyone other than herself. As the

Sixth Circuit succinctly stated, "an employer who discriminates against women because, for instance, they do not wear dresses or makeup, is engaging in sex discrimination *because the discrimination would not occur but for the victim's sex.*"...

Shortly after Cullinan's conversation ... about Lewis' appearance, Heartland procured video equipment so that Cullinan ... could inspect a front desk applicant's look before any hiring. Heartland's termination letter to Lewis only relied on the January 23 meeting she had with Cullinan. Only later did Heartland allege poor job performance would justify her termination. Lewis asserts further that Heartland did not follow its own written termination procedure, which includes assessing the employee's previous disciplinary record (Lewis had none) and conducting an investigation before making the termination decision. Kristi Nosbisch, Heartland's equal employment officer responsible for directing investigations of employment discrimination, knew that Lewis had complained that Cullinan's requirements were illegal, but she nonetheless relied on Cullinan's account of their meeting without asking Lewis for her own....

We turn next to Lewis' retaliation claim. Title VII prohibits employers from retaliating against employees who oppose discriminatory practices. The burden shifting *McDonnell Douglas* analytical framework applies to this inquiry as well, beginning with the three elements of a prima facie case of retaliation, whether: (1) the plaintiff engaged in protected conduct, including opposition to an action prohibited by Title VII; (2) she was subjected to an adverse employment action, and (3) there is a "causal nexus between the protected conduct and the adverse action."

In making out a prima facie retaliation claim, Lewis need not prove the merits of the underlying claim of sex discrimination. She can establish protected conduct "as long as [she] had a reasonable, good faith belief that there were grounds for a claim of discrimination." Lewis went into the January 23 meeting with Cullinan after learning about the "Midwestern girl look" comment. Lewis had already held her job for nearly a month and understood that other transferred employees in her situation had not been required to submit to a second interview. She observed Cullinan grow defensive after she asked her about the "Midwestern girl look" comment....

No one questions that Lewis was subjected to an adverse employment action, and there is ample record evidence to support a causal nexus between that and Lewis' protests at the January 23 meeting. Lewis received the termination notice a mere three days after the disputed conversation, and Heartland cited her objection to the second interview in her termination notice. The evidence of pretext already discussed applies with equal force in evaluating whether Lewis has made out a prima facie retaliation claim.

In sum, we conclude that Lewis has presented sufficient evidence to make out a prima facie case on her claims for sex discrimination and retaliation and a sufficient showing at this stage that Heartland's proffered reason for her termination was pretextual. Accordingly, we reverse the judgment of the district court and remand for further proceedings.

Questions for Analysis

1. What does the court mean when it says Heartland's reason for termination was pretextual?
2. Suppose Heartland had a policy of having a "Midwestern girl look" at their front desk as part of company strategy. Is that a legitimate business reason?

Key Defense for Employers In the *Ellerth* case, the Supreme Court makes clear how important it is for an employer to have clear, effective policy and procedures to reduce the likelihood of discrimination cases. Going to the roots of the employment relationship, agency law, the Court notes that without policies that can be shown to be meaningful, an employer is likely to have a more difficult defense and be more likely to incur vicarious liability for the actions of managers or employees who engage in discriminatory behavior against employees in a protected class. If an employer does not have an effective procedure in place to allow employees to take complaints about perceived discrimination, it also means there is a greater likelihood of punitive damages being imposed if the employer loses because of a lack of good-faith efforts to prevent discrimination.

BURLINGTON INDUSTRIES V. ELLERTH

Supreme Court of the United States 524 U.S. 742, 118 S.Ct. 2257 (1998)

Case Background *Ellerth worked for 15 months in sales at Burlington. One of her supervisors was Slowik, a mid-level manager with authority to hire, promote, and fire employees, subject to higher approval. Ellerth quit, claiming she was subject to sexually offensive remarks by Slowik and that his comments could be taken as threats to deny her job benefits. She refused his advances, did not suffer retaliation, and was promoted once. She did not tell anyone at Burlington about the problem until after she quit and filed suit. The district court granted Burlington*

summary judgment. The appeals court reversed, ordering a trial. Burlington appealed.

Case Decision Justice Kennedy delivered the opinion of the court.

* * *

We must decide ... whether an employer has vicarious liability when a supervisor creates a hostile work environment by making explicit threats to alter a subordinate's terms or conditions of employment, based on sex, but does not fulfill the threat. We turn to principles of agency law, for the term "employer" is defined under Title VII to include "agents." ...

Section 219(1) of the Restatement (Second) of Agency sets out a central principle of agency law:

> A master is subject to liability for the torts of his servants committed while acting in the scope of their employment.

An employer may be liable for both negligent and intentional torts committed by an employee within the scope of his or her employment. Sexual harassment under Title VII presupposes intentional conduct. ... The law now imposes liability where the employee's "purpose, however misguided, is wholly or in part to further the master's business." In applying scope of employment principles to intentional torts, however, it is accepted that "it is less likely that a willful tort will properly be held to be in the course of employment and that the liability of the master for such torts will naturally be more limited." ...

In order to accommodate the agency principles of vicarious liability for harm caused by misuse of supervisory authority, as well as Title VII's equally basic policies of encouraging forethought by employers and saving action by objecting employees, we adopt the following holding. ... An employer is subject to vicarious liability to a victimized employee for an actionable hostile environment created by a supervisor with immediate (or successively higher) authority over the employee. When no tangible employment action is taken, a defending employer may raise an affirmative defense to liability or damages, subject to proof by a preponderance of the evidence. The defense comprises two necessary elements: (a) that the employer exercised reasonable care to prevent and correct promptly any sexually harassing behavior, and (b) that the plaintiff employee unreasonably failed to take advantage of any preventive or corrective opportunities provided by the employer or to avoid harm otherwise. While proof that an employer had promulgated an antiharassment policy with complaint procedure is not necessary in every instance as a matter of law, the need for a stated policy suitable to the employment circumstances may appropriately be addressed in any case when litigating the first element of the defense. And while proof that an employee failed to fulfill the corresponding obligation of reasonable care to avoid harm is not limited to showing any unreasonable failure to use any complaint procedure provided by the employer, a demonstration of such failure will normally suffice to satisfy the employer's burden under the second element of the defense. No affirmative defense is available, however, when the supervisor's harassment culminates in a tangible employment action, such as discharge, demotion, or undesirable reassignment. ...

Given our explanation that the labels *quid pro quo* and hostile work environment are not controlling for purposes of establishing employer liability, Ellerth should have an adequate opportunity to prove she has a claim for which Burlington is liable.

Although Ellerth has not alleged she suffered a tangible employment action at the hands of Slowik, which would deprive Burlington of the availability of the affirmative defense, this is not dispositive. In light of our decision, Burlington is still subject to vicarious liability for Slowik's activity, but Burlington should have an opportunity to assert and prove the affirmative defense to liability. ...

The judgment of the Court of Appeals is affirmed.

Questions for Analysis

1. If a company has an effective in-house program to deal with discrimination complaints, it presents a strong defense for the employer if not used by the employee. The dissent in this case argued that this opens the door to cases that employers cannot defend themselves against—such as this case, where the company had a policy against discrimination that was apparently violated, but the injured employee did not take advantage of company policy. Is that likely to happen?
2. What steps should a company antidiscrimination policy include?

Justice Ginsburg repeated the key point of the *Ellerth* case in *Pennsylvania State Police* v. *Suders* (124 S.Ct. 2342). Suders claimed she was subject to sexual harassment by her supervisors, which caused her to resign. She sued, claiming constructive discharge based on hostile environment. The employer responded that it had an affirmative defense. It should not be held vicariously liable for the supervisors' conduct because Suders did not take advantage of the internal anti-harassment procedures before she quit.

ISSUE SPOTTER
Effective Sexual Harassment Policy

As the Supreme Court made clear in the *Ellerth* case, a critical part of a defense for an employer to avoid liability in a suit for sexual harassment is an effective in-house procedure to try to prevent such behavior and then deal with it should it arise. What steps would be reasonable to take to implement such a policy in an organization?

© Cengage Learning

The Court held that when harassment is "so intolerable as to cause a resignation" the employee need not "remain on the job while seeking redress." In such cases, constructive discharge is the same as being fired for an illegal reason. It is possible for an employer to establish the affirmative defense that it had a proper anti-harassment procedure in such a case, but it would be difficult. But, in general, an effective, secure, internal procedure to handle complaints about discrimination—that employees believe is trustworthy—helps provide a strong defense for the employer.

Effective Company Policy For a firm to claim, as in the *Ellerth* case, that the employee failed to take advantage of in-house protection against discrimination and harassment, it must have a credible program in place. It means there must be a credible, knowledgeable person or staff able to hear complaints. The process must be secure and separate from normal internal communication channels, and employees must believe it is trustworthy. That is, a firewall is needed to provide assurance of protection for an employee who is generally complaining about company policy or superiors. Some cases have involved the CEO of the company, so there must be ways around the standard chain of command.

While unwanted attempts at personal contact are clearly off limits, to attempt to reduce sexual harassment claims, some companies have policies against romances between employees. What starts out as a consensual relationship may end badly with a harassment claim. Having ground rules about co-worker dating may reduce corporate liability in such instances.

Disparate Impact Liability for employment discrimination may be based on a claim of **disparate impact**, which means that the employer used a decision rule that caused discrimination in some aspect of employment based on protected class status. The discrimination may have been unintentional, but the effect of the employer's action was to limit employment opportunities for a person or group of persons. There are fewer disparate impact cases than disparate treatment cases because they are more complex. But when they occur, they can be very costly to an employer because they involve a class of employees.

These cases involve employment practices that appear to be neutral on their face but have a disproportionately adverse impact on employees who are members of a protected class. Proof of intent to discriminate is not required, but the plaintiff must prove that the employment practice adversely affects employment opportunities for members of a protected class. The key issues are:

1. Does an employer have rules or practices that affect members of a protected group differently from other workers?
2. Are the rules or practices justified by business necessity, or because they relate to valid job requirements?

If it is asserted that the employer's hiring or promotion practices have a discriminatory impact on an applicant, the employer must show that the applicant was rejected not because of personal characteristics, but because the qualification requirements of the job were not met. The impact of employment rules must be neutral; that is, the rules must not have a disparate impact on a protected class. We see an example of an employment rule that fails to meet the test in the *Dial* case.

EQUAL EMPLOYMENT OPPORTUNITY COMM. V. DIAL CORPORATION

United States Court of Appeals, Eighth Circuit, 469 F.3d 735 (2006)

Case Background *Workers at the Dial plant in Iowa needed to be able to lift about 35 pounds of sausage at a time to a height between 30 and 60 inches. Doing this over and over meant injuries to workers, so the company began a Work Tolerance Screen (WTS) test for potential employees. Candidates had to demonstrate certain strength ability. For years, the workforce at Dial was about half men and half women. After the WTS was introduced, the number of women hired dropped to 15 percent. One applicant took the test and passed it, but was not hired. She complained to the EEOC.*

The EEOC brought suit on behalf of 54 women who had applied for work at Dial but were rejected despite passing the WTS. The trial court held that Dial had not demonstrated that the WTS was a business necessity, nor had it shown that it was valid. It awarded back pay to the women, ranging from $920 to $120,000. Dial appealed, contending that disparate impact had not been shown at trial.

Case Decision Murphy, Circuit Judge

* * *

Dial objects to the district court's findings of disparate impact and its conclusion that the company failed to prove the WTS was necessary to establish effective and safe job performance. ... In a disparate impact case, once the plaintiff establishes a prima facie case, the employer must show the practice at issue is "related to safe and efficient job performance and is consistent with business necessity." An employer using the business necessity defense must prove that the practice was related to the specific job and the required skills and physical requirements of the position. Although a validity study of an employment test can be sufficient to prove business necessity, it is not necessary if the employer demonstrates the procedure is sufficiently related to safe and efficient job performance. If the employer demonstrates business necessity, the plaintiff can still prevail by showing there is a less discriminatory alternative. ...

The district court was persuaded by EEOC's expert in industrial organization and his testimony "that a crucial aspect of the WTS is more difficult than the sausage making jobs themselves" and that the average applicant had to perform four times as many lifts as current employees and had no rest breaks. ...

Although Dial claims that the decrease in injuries shows that the WTS enabled it to predict which applicants could safely handle the strenuous nature of the work, the sausage plant injuries started decreasing before the WTS was implemented. Moreover, the injury rate for women employees was lower than that for men in two of the three years before Dial implemented the WTS. ...

Affirmed.

Questions for Analysis

1. The appeals court affirmed that the strength test discriminated against women job candidates. Because the job required strength, what could Dial have done to evaluate job candidates better?
2. Was the discrimination here intentional or unintentional?

Statutory Defenses under Title VII

As we saw in cases of disparate treatment, the employer must present a legitimate, nondiscriminatory, clear, and specific reason for the employment action taken. Title VII specifically protects certain business practices. Some specific defenses are provided by Title VII.

Business Necessity If employment practices can be shown to discriminate against some employees, the burden is on the employer to prove that the challenged practices are justified as a **business necessity** and are job related, as was claimed in the *Dial* case. Business necessity is evaluated with reference to the ability of the employee to perform a certain job.

Experience and skill requirements, frequently measured by seniority, are often accepted as necessary. For example, to be a skilled bricklayer requires experience usually gained only by long practice. To require such experience for certain positions is not a violation of Title VII. Similarly, if a job requires certain abilities of strength and agility, tests for such ability are legitimate.

Selection criteria for professional, managerial, and other white-collar positions must also meet the business necessity test. When objective standards (such as two years of brick-laying experience) cannot be used, subjective evaluations—such as impressions made by job interviews, references, and job performance evaluation—are recognized as necessary in hiring and promoting professional personnel. Similarly, positions may have an education requirement as long as it is, in fact, job-performance related. For example, to work as a CPA, one must have a degree in accounting.

Professionally Developed Ability Tests Employers often use tests to determine if job applicants possess the necessary skills and attributes. According to Title VII:

> *It shall not be an unlawful employment practice for an employer to give and to act upon the results of any professionally developed ability test provided that such test, its administration, or action upon the results is not designed, intended, or used to discriminate because of race, color, religion, sex, or national origin.*

Such tests must be shown to predict the work ability required for the job. Employers are usually required to supply statistical validation of the tests. Expert testimony from educational and industrial psychologists is often used to interpret the results.

Bona Fide *Seniority or Merit Systems* Employers often use differential treatment based on seniority or merit. Title VII requires the courts to uphold *bona fide* **seniority programs** and **merit systems**. Seniority is usually the length of time an employee has been with an employer and can be used to determine such things as eligibility for pension plans, length of vacations, security from layoffs, preference for rehire and promotion, and amount of sick leave.

ISSUE SPOTTER
Inadvertent Discrimination?

Some employers allow employee teams to decide whom to take on as new members. Management does not impose new members on teams. A major stock brokerage firm uses this method. The firm would hire new brokers, but then let teams invite their choice of individual to join a team. New African-American employees were not chosen as frequently to become team members as were new white employees. As a result, African-American employees often worked more on their own, which made it tougher to generate clients compared to working with an existing team with an existing client list.

The employer contends that management is not involved in any racial team-choice acceptance pattern. Does this practice raise unacceptable discriminatory practices, even if entirely unintentional?

The effects of seniority systems come under attack most often in cases involving layoffs on the basis of seniority. Many employers hold that in the event of a cutback in the workforce, workers with the most seniority have the most job protection—last hired, first fired. This means that minorities may suffer a greater share of the layoffs in a workforce cutback because they are likely to have less seniority, on average, than white workers. The Supreme Court recognizes this fact, but seniority rights are protected by statute.

Merit systems exist when employees are rewarded on the basis of job performance, such as meeting sales goals or other criteria that justifies differential rewards. Such a program, when properly designed, is an affirmative defense against a claim of discrimination by a person unhappy about their pay.

The Bona Fide *Occupational Qualification (BFOQ)* Another defense is a ***bona fide occupational qualification*** (BFOQ). Title VII states that discrimination is permitted in instances in which sex, religion, or national origin—but not race—is a BFOQ "reasonably necessary to the normal operation of that particular business." The employer has the burden of persuasion to establish the necessity of the BFOQ.

The EEOC gives this defense a narrow interpretation. Just because men have traditionally filled certain jobs does not mean that a legitimate defense exists for not hiring women for such positions. Simply because people were used to seeing, and may have preferred, female flight attendants did not mean that airlines could refuse to hire male flight attendants. No BFOQ on the basis of race is allowed. For example, an employer cannot assert that the business must have a white person for a particular job.

A BFOQ exists where hiring on the basis of a personal characteristic is needed to keep the "authenticity" of a position. For example, a topless bar can argue that the cocktail servers should be female because customers expect that as a part of the service. We expect to see male clothing modeled by a male model even though a woman could wear the clothes. In some, but not many, medical care situations, hospitals may restrict the sex of attendants for the comfort of patients or to protect sexual privacy.

Early Retirement Plans The ADEA was amended by the Older Workers Benefit Protection Act. Under the Act, employers may not force "involuntary retirement" on older workers, but if early retirement incentive plan (ERIP) benefits are so generous that an employee chooses to retire, the employee cannot claim to have been forced to retire. Employers may ask employees to sign "knowing and voluntary waivers" of age discrimination claims when they agree to retire early in response to an ERIP. The ADEA also exempts senior executives in high-level policy positions who are at least age 65 and are entitled to a company pension.

Remedies in Discrimination Cases

Title VII gives the courts leeway in the kinds of damages and equitable remedies that may be imposed when discrimination is found. The focus, as in most damage measures, is to try to put the plaintiffs in the position they would have held but for the discrimination. Specific remedies include:

- *Back pay*—to the date discrimination began, either the entire pay that would have been earned or the difference between pay received and what should have been received. Generally, employees must mitigate their damages by seeking other work. Failing to do so can reduce **back pay** or other damage awards.
- *Front pay*—if an employee was unlawfully fired, he may be ordered reinstated or the plaintiff may be ordered to be hired if she was improperly not hired. But often this is not realistic, so the plaintiff is given a sum, **front pay**, to compensate for

longer-term damage to a career for not having gained the experience or seniority of the position.

- *Compensatory damages*—for emotional distress, medical expenses, job-hunting costs, and loss of reputation. This is not available in ADEA cases.
- *Punitive damages*—may be granted to punish the employer for wrongdoing because the employer acted with malice or in reckless disregard for protected rights. This is not available in ADEA cases. These damages are capped by federal law to between $50,000 to $300,000, depending on the size of the employers.
- *Attorney's fees*—may be recovered, as well as costs such as filing fees, expert witness fees, and transcripts. Title VII plaintiffs who win usually get this; defendants who win rarely do. This does not apply in ADEA cases.

❓ TEST YOURSELF

1. A person bringing a discrimination suit in court must establish a(n) _____ for the matter to proceed.
2. If an employer is accused of intentional discrimination in violation of Title VII, that is referred to as a claim of *per se* discrimination: T—F
3. If an employee suffers intense harassment and quits because of it, there is said to be _____.
4. If an employment rule which, on its face is neutral, has the effect of causing illegal discrimination, there is said to be a disparate impact: T—F
5. Ellerth sued Burlington Industries for sex discrimination. The Supreme Court held in *Burlington Industries* v. *Ellerth* that Ellerth:
   a. must prove a "tangible employment action" that imposed a loss.
   b. was an independent contractor, so had no cause of action as she might if she were an employee.
   c. lost because she failed to take advantage of her employer's internal discrimination review process.
   d. None of the above.
6. In the case *EEOC* v. *Dial Corporation*, the court held that Dial's strength test for employees was justified as it was closely related to ability to perform the tasks assigned employees on the assembly line: T—F
7. There may be a defense of _____ in a situation where an employer rewards on the basis of productivity and it happens to produce the appearance of discrimination in pay.

Answers: prima facie case; F; constructive discharge; T; d; F; merit system.

Affirmative Action

An **affirmative action** program is a deliberate effort by an employer to remedy discriminatory practices in the hiring, training, and promotion of protected class members when a particular class is underrepresented in the employer's workforce. Such programs have been adopted based on race or sex only. Employers must walk a fine line between creating a legal affirmative action program and falling into a pattern of discrimination against members of another group.

After finding that members of a protected class are underrepresented in the company's workforce, an employer may voluntarily start an affirmative action program to ensure that the company provides more opportunities for women or minorities in certain job categories. The courts may impose an involuntary program as a remedy to correct past discriminatory employment practices by the company, but this is now quite rare.

Executive Order 11246

As the chief executive officer of the United States, the president has authority to determine certain conditions for government business that are set out in **executive orders**. Government contractors must abide by such orders. In 1965, President Johnson issued Executive Order 11246, a requirement that government contractors adopt affirmative action. Each president since then has continued the policy.

Enforced by the Office of Federal Contract Compliance Programs (OFCCP), the order requires companies with federal contracts of $10,000 per year to take affirmative action. Those with $50,000 in contracts and 50 or more employees must have a written affirmative action plan. That requires a contractor to conduct a **workforce analysis** for each job category within the organization. Jobs are studied by rank, salary, and the percent of those employed on the basis of race and sex.

Contractors must do an **underutilization analysis** comparing the percent of minorities and women in the community in each job category with the percent employed by a contractor. If underutilization is found—say, because 19 percent of the lab technicians are women compared with 41 percent of the lab technicians available in the relevant community—the contractor must establish a plan to increase the number of women in these positions.

Contractors who are not in compliance may be required to pay damages to affected employees. For example, in 2012 the OFCCP held that a meat packing plant owned by Hormel Food discriminated against women in hiring over a two-year period. The company was ordered to pay $439,530 in back wages to 1,988 qualified women applicants rejected for entry-level positions. The company would also make 700 job offers to affected women when positions became open.

Affirmative Action as a Remedy

Title VII provides that in the event an employer is found to have engaged in illegal discrimination, "the court may … order such affirmative action as may be appropriate." The court, EEOC or OFCCP, as we just saw, may require the employer to hire qualified employees in a protected class to make up for past discriminatory activities. The action may be oriented toward new employee recruitment, or it could be directed at using more resources to train current minority or women employees to become qualified candidates for promotion into positions in which they are underrepresented.

In recent years, as the worst vestiges of overt discrimination have been reduced, court-ordered affirmative action programs have become less common than voluntary affirmative action programs. Most employers adopt a program before one is forced upon them. The Supreme Court has approved mandated programs where a pattern of intentional discrimination makes it clear that a strong remedy is required under the flexible powers granted courts by the Civil Rights Act.

In *United States* v. *Paradise* (107 S.Ct. 1053), the Court upheld a court-ordered hiring and promotion goal program for the Alabama Department of Public Safety, which had failed to hire African-American troopers for years after passage of Title VII. Consistent with the state population, the Court upheld an ordered goal that 25 percent of all employees at all ranks should be qualified African Americans.

Disability Discrimination

The Rehabilitation Act of 1973 provides protection for disabled persons seeking employment with, or who are currently employed by, employers that receive federal funds. The Act is enforced similarly to Title VII employment discrimination suits. Section 503 of the Act is most important. It holds that all companies with federal contracts of $2,500 or more have a duty to ensure the disabled an opportunity in the workplace by providing reasonable accommodations.

The Americans with Disabilities Act (ADA) of 1990 expands the rights of persons with disabilities in employment and supplements access rights to public accommodations, such as hotels, restaurants, theaters, public transportation, telecommunications, and retail stores. The ADA incorporates most remedies and procedures set out in Title VII and applies to employers with 15 or more employees. States also have laws forbidding disability discrimination that can matter because they may apply to employees not covered by the federal law or have different procedural rules.

Compliance Process

Suits under the ADA arise the same way that discrimination suits brought under Title VII come about—by filing complaints with the EEOC. About 26,000 disability charges are filed annually with EEOC; the majority are dismissed as having "no reasonable cause." Complaints proceed much the same way as do Title VII charges. As explained by the Second Circuit Court of Appeals, "A plaintiff alleging a violation of the ADA has the burden of making out a *prima facie* case, which includes the following elements: "1) he was an 'individual who has a disability' within the meaning of the statute; 2) the employer had notice of his disability; 3) he could perform the essential functions of the job with reasonable accommodation; and 4) the employer refused to make such accommodation" (595 F.3d 102).

INTERNATIONAL PERSPECTIVE

Employment Discrimination in Europe and Japan

In many respects, European firms are years behind the United States in their treatment of minorities and women in the labor force. Most European countries and Japan have antidiscrimination statutes on the books, but the laws are not nearly as strict as the U.S. laws.

Employees in Europe can be forced to retire between ages 55 and 65, depending on the country. Europeans over age 45 who lose their jobs have a harder time finding employment again than do their counterparts in the United States.

The first sexual harassment case in Japan was not decided until 1992. A woman who was harassed by her boss for two years was fired for complaining. She was awarded $12,500 in damages. The case was a landmark in Japan.

Minority immigrants are treated as second-class citizens in most countries. In general, it is much harder for a noncitizen, especially a member of a racial minority, to obtain work and citizenship in Japan and in Europe than it is in the United States. Immigrants in France face blatant discrimination in the job market, reducing opportunities and economic integration.

Where affirmative action exists, it tends to be weak or even overtly discriminatory in favor of male-citizen workers who already dominate the labor force. Women are kept out of many higher-level jobs and are not paid as much as men for equal work.

European countries and Japan appear to treat women better in certain respects, such as by mandating generous maternity benefits, but one effect of those laws is to encourage employers not to hire women because of the high cost of the benefits to which women are entitled if they have children.

Lighter Side of the Law

Wicked Witch of the East?

Carole Smith is a Wiccan. After she had been working for the TSA at the Albany airport for seven months, a supervisor told her that he was investigating a claim of workplace violence. Another TSA employee accused Smith of casting spells on her. For example, one day the heater in her car did not work. What else could have caused it except a spell by Smith?

Smith, who was rated in the top 10 percent in detecting contraband carried by passengers, complained about harassment by numerous employees because of her beliefs. After carefully packing her record with negative comments, the TSA fired her.

Source: msnbc.com.

Definition of Disability

The Rehabilitation Act and the ADA define a person with a **disability** as

> *any person who (i) has a physical or mental impairment which substantially limits one or more of such person's major life activities [such as walking or hearing], (ii) has a record of such an impairment [such as cancer in remission], or (iii) is regarded as having such an impairment [even if there is none].*

Most states use the same definition. An amendment to the ADA that took effect in 2009 states that "disability" is to be construed "in favor of broad coverage of individuals ... to the maximum extent permitted."

The Supreme Court has recognized regulations by the Department of Health and Human Services as a guide to determining what constitutes a disability. The regulations define "major life activities" as "functions such as caring for one's self, performing manual tasks, walking, seeing, hearing, speaking, breathing, learning, and working." Examples of disabilities covered by the statutes may include people:

- Who have had cancer
- With a severe disfigurement
- Who have had a heart attack
- Who must use a wheelchair
- Who are hearing- or vision-impaired

Level of Disability ADA cases often involve individual evaluation of circumstances of what constitutes disability in relationship to particular employment. The courts have been clear that disabilities are major life conditions. If a person is partly impaired, it need not mean that person is considered disabled. It is a tough standard to meet, and, for those who are disabled, employers need only to make reasonable accommodations.

Employers need not retain employees who can no longer perform their jobs. For example, one dockworker whose weight rose to over 400 pounds was dismissed. He sued, claiming disability protection. The appeals court held that because his weight prevented him from going up and down ladders as needed, he could be terminated and had no grounds for suit because he could no longer perform the job (463 F.3d 436).

Considered Disabled Even if a person is not actually impaired, if other people think the person is impaired, the person is perceived as disabled. For example, former cancer patients have found that some employers are afraid to hire them because they think cancer is contagious or that the former patient will develop cancer again. As a result, even though no impairment exists, and even though doctors say there is no disease present, bias against the person who had the disease makes the person disabled for purposes of this law.

Reasonable Accommodation

Employers are obliged to make **reasonable accommodations** for persons with disabilities and are expected to incur expenses in making a position or workstation available to qualified disabled applicants and employees. Ford Motor Co. does not have to redesign its assembly line at high cost so that a worker in a wheelchair could work there because that would impose an undue hardship on business operations. However, when a workstation can be redesigned for just a few thousand dollars to accommodate a person with a disability, that must be done. The EEOC *Enforcement Guidance* provides this list of accommodations:

- Making existing facilities accessible
- Job restructuring
- Part-time or modified work schedules
- Acquiring or modifying equipment
- Changing tests, training materials, or policies
- Providing qualified readers or interpreters
- Reassignment to a vacant position

Besides explaining the law on point, the *Keith* case presents a good example of an effort at accommodation that was not followed.

KEITH V. COUNTY OF OAKLAND

United States Court of Appeals, Sixth Circuit, 703 F.3d 918 (2013)

Case Background *Nicholas Keith has been deaf since birth. He cannot speak verbally but can communicate using American Sign Language (ASL). He took and passed all portions of Oakland County's lifeguard training and applied for employment as a lifeguard. The head of lifeguard hiring, Stavale, approved his employment subject to the accommodation that Keith requested—presence of an ASL interpreter at staff and instructional meetings.*

Keith next passed a physical examination but the physician said Keith would require constant accommodation and expressed no opinion as to his suitability for employment. That delayed matters while a consultant was called. The consultant was dubious about Keith's ability to perform, but had no experience regarding the ability of deaf people to work as lifeguards. Stavale was sure Keith could do the job, as the court explained:

Stavale prepared a six-page outline setting forth the accommodations that she believed could success-

fully integrate Keith, and she sent it to Crokus for feedback. Stavale explained:

1. *Keith will carry laminated note cards in the pocket of his swim trunks to communicate with guests in non-emergency situations.*
2. *Keith does not need to hear to recognize and rescue a distressed swimmer; experience reveals that distressed swimmers do not cry out for help.*
3. *Keith will use his whistle and shake his head "no" to enforce pool rules.*
4. *Keith will briefly look at other lifeguards on duty when scanning his zone to see if they enter the pool for a save.*
5. *Because Keith cannot use the megaphone or radio, another lifeguard will have this responsibility when Keith is working.*
6. *Keith will not work the slide rotation, which should not be a problem because this is one of the favorite rotations and many lifeguards like to work more than one slide rotation.*

7. *The Emergency Action Plan ("EAP") will be modified, regardless of whether Keith is scheduled. To initiate the EAP, lifeguards will be required to signal with a fist in the air, opening and closing it like a siren. This will accommodate Keith and improve the effectiveness of the EAP for the entire team.*

The consultant was concerned the plan might not work, so the offer of employment was withdrawn. Keith sued for disability discrimination. The trial court granted summary judgment to the County. Keith appealed.

Case Decision Griffin, Circuit Judge

* * *

The ADA makes it unlawful for an employer to "discriminate against a qualified individual on the basis of disability." The ADA defines "discriminate" to include the failure to provide reasonable accommodation to an otherwise qualified individual with a disability, unless doing so would impose an undue hardship on the employer's business. To establish a prima facie case, a plaintiff must show that he is disabled and otherwise qualified for the position, either with or without reasonable accommodation. Once the plaintiff establishes a prima facie case, the burden shifts to the defendant to show that accommodating the plaintiff would impose an undue hardship on the operation of its business.

The parties do not dispute that Keith is disabled within the meaning of the ADA or that Oakland County rescinded the offer of employment because of his disability. The issues in dispute are whether Oakland County made an individualized inquiry, whether Keith is otherwise qualified for the position in question with or without reasonable accommodation, and whether Oakland County engaged in the interactive process.

As a threshold matter, the ADA mandates an individualized inquiry in determining whether an applicant's disability or other condition disqualifies him from a particular position. A proper evaluation involves consideration of the applicant's personal characteristics, his actual medical condition, and the effect, if any, the condition may have on his ability to perform the job in question. This follows from the ADA's underlying objective: "people with disabilities ought to be judged on the basis of their abilities; they should not be judged nor discriminated against based on unfounded fear, prejudice, ignorance, or mythologies; people ought to be judged on the relevant medical evidence and the abilities they have." The ADA requires employers to act, not based on stereotypes and generalizations about a disability, but based on the actual disability and the effect that disability has on the particular individual's ability to perform the job. ...

Keith has presented evidence from which a jury could reasonably find that he can communicate effectively despite his deafness. Like other lifeguards, Keith can adhere to the "10/20 standard of zone protection," a scanning technique taught to lifeguards in which they must scan their entire zone every ten seconds and be able to reach any part of their zone within twenty seconds. This method is purely visual. Further, by passing Oakland County's lifeguard training program and earning his lifeguard certification, Keith demonstrated his ability to detect distressed swimmers, which several experts testified is almost completely visually based. ...

Perhaps the most compelling evidence that Keith is "otherwise qualified" comes from his experts who have knowledge, education, and experience regarding the ability of deaf individuals to serve as lifeguards. They all opine that the ability to hear is unnecessary to enable a person to perform the essential functions of a lifeguard. The world record for most lives saved is held by a deaf man, Leroy Colombo, who saved over 900 lives in his lifeguarding career. One also cannot ignore that the American Red Cross certifies deaf lifeguards, and Gallaudet University, the only liberal arts university in the world dedicated to serving the needs of deaf individuals, has a lifeguard certification program.

In light of this evidence, we hold that reasonable minds could differ regarding whether Keith is "otherwise qualified" because he can perform the essential communication functions of a lifeguard. The district court erred when it decided that Keith's deafness disqualified him from the position as a matter of law. ...

Reversed and remanded.

Questions for Analysis

1. Is it an unreasonable expense for an employer to hire a qualified consultant to help evaluate the ability of a disabled person to perform a job?

2. Would the accommodations provided by Stavale not mean that other lifeguards would have to take on extra burdens?

Preemployment Guidance

The EEOC has issued *ADA Enforcement Guidance: Preemployment Disability-Related Questions and Medical Examinations.* The guidelines note that the ADA prohibits employers from asking disability-related questions or requiring medical exams before a job is offered. Hence, employers cannot ask questions about the nature or severity of a disability. The following are examples of questions that are illegal to ask during a job interview:

- Have you ever been treated for mental health problems?
- Have you ever filed for workers' compensation benefits?
- Do you have a disability that would interfere with your ability to perform the job?
- How many sick days were you out last year?
- Have you ever been unable to handle work-related stress?
- Have you ever been treated for drug addiction or drug abuse?

In the case of illegal drugs, past addiction is treated as a disability, but current use is not, so applicants may be asked about current use and may be given a drug test. However, alcoholism is a protected disability and applicants may not be asked questions about drinking habits, although it is permissible to ask whether an applicant has been arrested for driving under the influence of alcohol, if relevant.

If a disability is obvious, or if an applicant volunteers a disability, some questions may be asked about the need for reasonable accommodation. For example, if an applicant discloses that she needs breaks to take diabetes medication, the employer may ask how often such breaks are needed and how long they would be. Employers may make clear the requirements needed to perform a job, and if it is dubious that someone could perform a job function, an applicant may be asked to demonstrate how he or she could accomplish the task.

Once a job offer has been made, an employer may ask for documentation of a disability and may ask more questions about the reasonable accommodation needed for the employee. If a physical exam is given to new employees, similar exams must be given to all employees in the same job category, and the results must be kept confidential. Such exams can be given so long as they are related to the ability to do the job, not because an employer is trying to screen out employees with potential health problems. As we saw in the *Keith* case, when an applicant is qualified for employment, there may need to be a professional assessment of the person's limitations and how best to accommodate.

Violations by Employers As in the case of discrimination based on race, sex, or age, the law is broken if a qualified person is denied an opportunity primarily because

ISSUE SPOTTER
Accommodating Disabilities

The Americans with Disabilities Act does not give "bright lines" for exactly what accommodations are reasonable for employees with disabilities. Proper accommodations must be determined case-by-case. The key terms are "reasonable" and "undue hardship." What guidelines would you set for an organization in developing an accommodation policy?

Lighter Side of the Law

I Have the Right to Harass Women

Winston was fired after 19 years as an English teacher in the Maine Technical College System. While complaints had been made of sexual misconduct, he was dismissed because of a sexual harassment complaint, which was filed for kissing a female student "after a sexually suggestive conversation."

Winston sued, "claiming that he was terminated because of his 'mental handicap of sexual addiction'." His expert witness testified that this disorder, which had led to his seeking the services of prostitutes, was a permanent condition but that Winston could perform his job as a teacher. The supreme court of Maine tossed out the complaint, noting that the ADA specifically excludes "sexual behavior disorders" from the term *disability*.

Source: Winston v. Maine Technical College System, 631 A.2d 70.

of disability. However, in the case of disabilities, besides not discriminating, an employer must also make reasonable accommodations. In this sense, there is an affirmative action requirement, but it is not one tied to specific goals. This requirement works on a case-by-case basis. Employment situations that have been in violation of the law include:

- Using standardized employment tests that tend to screen out people with disabilities
- Refusing to hire applicants because they have a history of alcohol abuse, rather than because they are currently alcohol abusers
- Rejecting a job applicant because he or she is HIV-positive
- Asking job applicants if they have disabilities, rather than asking if they have the ability to perform the job
- Limiting advancement opportunities for employees because of their disabilities
- Not hiring a person with a disability because the workplace does not have a bathroom that can accommodate wheelchairs

Of all areas of employment discrimination law, disability assessment and accommodation is probably the most unsettled, so employers need to stay on top of developments in the area.

? TEST YOURSELF

1. Executive Order 11246, concerning proper utilization of workers on the basis of sex and minority status, applies to all companies with 50 or more employees: T—F
2. If a firm subject to Executive Order 11246 is not in compliance, it may be ordered to institute a(n) _____ program.

(Continued)

3. In *Keith* v. *County of Oakland,* where Keith sued for disability discrimination after he was rejected from being hired as a lifeguard, the appeals court held that:
   a. he was not disabled under the ADA.
   b. he was disabled under the ADA but the employer could not be expected to make reasonable accommodations.
   c. he was disabled under the ADA but was not qualified for employment even with attempts at accommodation.
   d. None of the above.
4. If an employee is disabled under the ADA, an employer is not expected to make a reasonable accommodation if it would impose a(n) _____ on business operations.
5. A person may be covered by the ADA even if one is not disabled if other people believe the person is disabled: T—F
6. Employers should, in the hiring process, collect "competent information" about applicants' disabilities so the employer can properly consider reasonable accommodations: T—F

Answers: F; affirmative action; d; undue hardship; T; F.

SUMMARY

- Title VII of the Civil Rights Act and the Age Discrimination in Employment Act requires employers not to discriminate on the basis of sex, race, color, religion, national origin, or age. This applies to all aspects of the employment process—hiring, promotion, discipline, benefits, and firing. The laws are enforced by the EEOC and private party suits.

- Legally, race means black or African American, White, American Indian or Alaska Native, Native Hawaiian or Other Pacific Islander, Asian, and the ethnic category Hispanic or Latino. Under federal law, sex means male or female. There is no consideration for sexual orientation, although some state laws cover it.

- Sex discrimination specifically includes discrimination with respect to childbearing plans, pregnancy, and related medical conditions.

- Sexual harassment poses a legal challenge for managers, who must take steps to inform employees of the seriousness and the consequences of harassment and establish internal procedures to allow claims to be investigated with an assurance of confidentiality.

- Key tests that the courts use to look for discrimination are disparate treatment, where, everything else being equal, employment decisions are illegally motivated by discrimination based on race, sex, national origin, religion, or age; and disparate impact, where the effect of hiring or promotion standards is to discriminate, even if unintentionally, on the basis of protected class status.

- A charge of discrimination must be filed at a federal or state EEO office within 180 days (300 under state law) of a discriminatory event. The EEOC may dismiss a charge, offer to mediate a dispute, file suit on behalf of an employee or group of employees, or give the employee a right-to-sue letter to go forward with litigation with their own attorney.

- An employee bringing suit must meet the *McDonnell-Douglas* test, which applies to all aspects of the employment process, to show that they (1) belong to a protected class; (2) met the qualifications of the job in question; (3) were rejected for the job, or suffered some other adverse job action; and (4) the employer sought other persons with similar qualifications or otherwise treated the employee differently.

- When employers are sued under the discrimination laws, they must present a preponderance of evidence that the practices they engage in are not discriminatory. The practices must be related to legitimate business necessity. Practices that, when properly designed, are allowed to stand include professionally developed ability tests, *bona fide* seniority and merit systems, and bona fide occupational qualifications that provide a rationale for personnel decisions.

- Employers may have affirmative action plans imposed on them by court order as a remedy for discrimination. Federal contractors must have affirmative action plans in place. These plans are designed to increase minority or female representation in certain job categories. This may be done by setting goals to be met within certain time frames.

- The Rehabilitation Act of 1973 and the Americans with Disabilities Act of 1990 require employers to take positive steps to make accommodations for disabled workers.

- A disability under the ADA means a limitation of a major life activity, such as walking, breathing, seeing, and hearing. It does not mean an impairment that a person can adjust to and not suffer a serious limitation on a major activity. The standard for disability is strict; the test is whether the disabled person can do the job in question with reasonable accommodation.

TERMS TO KNOW

Title VII, 436
discrimination, 437
protected classes, 437
race, 437
reverse discrimination, 437
color, 437
national origin, 437
religion, 438
reasonable accommodation, 438
undue hardship, 438
sex, 438
sexual harassment, 440
quid pro quo, 440

hostile environment, 440
age, 442
genetic information, 442
right to sue letter, 443
differential standard, 444
harassment, 444
constructive discharge, 444
disparate treatment, 444
prima facie case, 444
pretext, 445
retaliation, 445
disparate impact, 449
business necessity, 451

bona fide seniority program, 451
merit system, 451
bona fide occupational
    qualification, 452
back pay, 452
front pay, 452
affirmative action, 453
executive order, 454
workforce analysis, 454
underutilization analysis, 454
disability, 456
reasonable accommodation, 457

DISCUSSION QUESTION

Would a dress code that required men to wear three-piece suits, but stated only that women had to "look professional" be discriminatory against the male employees? What differences would be considered discriminatory?

CASE QUESTIONS

1. Parr applied for a position as an insurance representative for which he was well qualified. The manager who interviewed Parr told him he would probably be hired and also told him the company did not sell insurance to African Americans. Parr told the employment service that set up the interview of the manager's remarks and that he was married to an African-American woman. The employment service told the insurance company of Parr's marriage, at which point they declined to hire him. Was that a violation of Title VII? [*Parr v. Woodmen of the World Life Insurance*, 791 F.2d 888, 11th Cir. (1986)]
    ✓ Check your answer

2. Nelson worked for Dr. Knight as a dental assistant for 10 years. There was some sexual banter, but Nelson did not regard it as serious. Knight's wife demanded Nelson be fired because she could be a threat to their marriage, so Knight fired Nelson who then sued for sex discrimination. Do you think she had a case? [*Nelson v. Knight*, 2012 WL 6652747, Sup. Ct., Iowa (2012)]

3. Friedman applied for employment at a pharmaceutical warehouse. He was offered a position and told that, as a condition of employment, he would have to be vaccinated against the mumps. He refused to be vaccinated because the vaccine is grown in chicken embryos. He said that it would violate his system of beliefs as a vegan, which prohibits the use of any animal-related product. The employment offer was withdrawn: he sued for discrimination based on religion. The district court dismissed the case, holding that veganism is not a religion. Friedman appealed. Does he have a case? [*Friedman* v. *So. Cal. Permanente Medical Group*, 102 Cal.App.4th 39, Ct. App., Calif. (2002)]
✓ Check your answer

4. Lack sued his former employer, Walmart, and his former supervisor, Bragg, for sexual harassment. He contended that Bragg made "inappropriate and demeaning statements … of a sexual nature" and told vulgar jokes in front of Lack and others. When Lack complained, he suffered retaliation as Bragg made "his work schedule more burdensome and inconvenient." Wal-Mart ignored the problem. Other employees testified as to Bragg's behavior. The jury found for Lack and awarded him $80,000 in damages. Walmart appealed. Did Lack have a case? [*Lack* v. *Wal-Mart Stores*, 240 F.3d 255, 4th Cir. (2001)]

5. Breeden worked for a school district in Nevada. She attended a meeting with two male workers. One of the men made a sexist joke to the other male that was not directed at Breeden. She filed a sexual harassment complaint with the EEOC. Soon after, she was transferred to another position, a move that she had known for some time might occur. She added a charge of retaliation to her complaint. The district court dismissed the case. The court of appeals reversed for Breeden. The school district appealed to the Supreme Court. Does Breeden have a good case? [*Clark Co. School District* v. *Breeden*, 121 S.Ct. 1508, Sup. Ct. (2001)]
✓ Check your answer

6. Grosjean worked for First Energy since 1970. In 1997 he was promoted to a supervisory position. Two years later, when he was 54, his boss, Dressner, who was 41, removed Grosjean from his position, stating that he was not performing adequately. Grosjean kept the same pay, but had less status. The position was given to Riley, who

was 51. Grosjean sued for age discrimination for being denied the supervisory position. The trial court dismissed the suit. Grosjean appealed. Does he have a case? [*Grosjean* v. *First Energy*, 349 F.3d 332, 6th Cir. (2003)]

7. The Jackson, Michigan, Board of Education had a rule that in the event of a cutback in teachers, the layoffs would be proportional on the basis of race. That way, students would be guaranteed more minority teachers as role models. This was done because more of the older teachers were white; if the layoff was based on seniority only, more minority teachers would be laid off in proportion to the white teachers. The district court and court of appeals agreed with the school board, saying the rule helped to remedy past discrimination. What do you think the Supreme Court held? [*Wygant* v. *Jackson Board of Education*, 106 S.Ct. 1842 (1986)]
✓ Check your answer

8. Rene, who is openly gay, worked for the MGM Grand Hotel in Las Vegas for two years. He contended that his male supervisor and co-workers subjected him to a hostile work environment on a daily basis. He was subject to crude jokes, name-calling, and unwelcome physical touching. He sued the hotel for sexual harassment, noting that the reason for the harassment was his sexual orientation. The district court dismissed the suit, holding that his claim of sexual orientation discrimination is not recognized under Title VII. Rene appealed. Does he have a case? [*Rene* v. *MGM Grand Hotel*, 305 F.3d 1061, 9th Cir. (2002)]

9. J. B. Hunt Transport would not hire truck drivers who used prescription medications with side effects that might impair their driving ability. The EEOC sued Hunt, contending that this practice violated the ADA because Hunt discriminated against those with perceived disabilities. The district court held for Hunt; the EEOC appealed. Do you think Hunt's policy was permissible? [*EEOC* v. *J.B. Hunt Transport*, 321 F.3d 69, 2nd Cir. (2003)]

10. Dr. Fleming, an anesthesiologist, suffers from sickle cell anemia. He applied for a position as an anesthesiologist at the Yuma Regional Medical Center, but it refused to allow him to practice because of his disease. Fleming sued Yuma for employment discrimination in violation of the

Rehabilitation Act. The district court held for Yuma, noting that Fleming was an independent contractor. Fleming appealed. Do you think he should have a cause of action? [*Fleming* v. *Yuma Regional Medical Center*, 587 F.3d 938, 9th Cir. (2009)]

ETHICS QUESTION

You are a supervisor at a company that does not have an affirmative action program. In looking to hire a new person for a certain position, the person who best fits the job criteria is a white male, age 30. Two other candidates are also well qualified for the position but just slightly less so than the top candidate. One of the other candidates is African American; the third is a white woman, age 63. You believe that, in general, there is societal discrimination against minorities and older people. Should you give a little extra credit to the candidates who are in protected classes, given that you can justify whatever choice you make? How would you decide between the African-American man and the older white woman? Should you take into account that the man supports a wife and three children, whereas the woman has an employed husband and no children?

OVERVIEW

Decades ago, business was almost entirely governed by private relationships based upon common-law principles. Now the legal environment is much more complex. Federal regulation has expanded, often in bursts, over the past century. Regulation is now so common that businesses actively participate in the political process that determines the extent of regulations and how they are enforced.

A century ago, there was concern about the monopoly power of large corporations. After much political agitation, antitrust laws were passed. The 1960s saw social problems, such as race discrimination, that were not being resolved. The civil rights movement helped to promote the legislation that limits discrimination. Pollution became a major issue in the early 1970s, when most of the environmental statutes emerged. Today, as international trade expands, businesses must manage complexities that arise in legal relationships that were not imagined in times past.

PART 4

The Regulatory Environment of Business

Chapter 17:

The Regulatory Process Regulatory agencies are an increasingly important source of substantive law. Legislatures grant agencies the power to make and enforce laws through regulations, policy guidance documents, and other means. The processes that agencies and parties responding to them must follow are considered.

Chapter 18:

Securities Regulation Federal supervision of the securities markets began in the 1930s. Trillions of dollars of wealth are held in securities, and billions of dollars in securities are traded daily on securities markets. The markets and the professionals who work in the securities industry are subject to federal oversight. This affects how businesses raise money to fund operations.

Chapter 19:

Consumer Protection Food and drug regulations were the first major area of federal consumer safety protection to develop. Over the years, the Federal Trade Commission and other agencies have been given expanded control over other areas of consumer concern, including consumer credit.

Chapter 20:

Antitrust Law First established to bust the big trusts that dominated some areas of industry, antitrust law has evolved under Supreme Court direction to limit price fixing, market sharing, boycotts, and other business practices believed harmful to competition and consumers.

Chapter 21:

Environmental Law Before the 1970s, there were common-law restraints on abuse of air, water, and land. Passage of major environmental statutes introduced pervasive federal regulation related to most parts of the environment. More recently, global environmental issues have become of concern to many business operations.

Chapter 22:

The International Legal Environment of Business The globalization of business means that managers face an ever greater range of cross-boundary legal issues. This chapter focuses on domestic controls on international trade and on some of the major international legal rules that often affect international business.

CHAPTER 17
The Regulatory Process

The Kopczynski family has run a construction company in the state of Washington for many years. Chris, now the head of the company, deals with a more complex set of regulations than his father faced decades ago. Permits may be required from various federal agencies, such as the Army Corps of Engineers and the Soil Conservation Service, as well as many state and local agencies. Local zoning rules and construction codes must be followed. Safety, building, and environmental inspectors from assorted federal and state agencies are likely to show up on the job at any time. The state requires the company to pay workers' compensation and unemployment insurance taxes and to file numerous regular and special reports. The IRS requires tax filings on all employees and documentation of work eligibility for every employee. Special labor regulations must be followed on all projects involving government money. Such rules add greatly to the cost and complexity of operations.

Administrative agencies have a major impact on the legal environment of all businesses. Regulations concerning worker safety, discrimination, pollution, and many other activities have expanded significantly in recent decades. Some regulations, such as those on transportation, have been reduced in number, but others arise to deal with new enterprises, such as online businesses. Managers must stay up to date on regulatory developments in their areas of business.

Before we look at major areas of business regulation, this chapter reviews the development of administrative agencies. It then considers the powers delegated to agencies by Congress, including their legislative, investigative, adjudicatory, and enforcement authority. The last part of the chapter turns to the concept of judicial review, which is the power of the judicial branch of government to review agencies' actions or decisions.

Administrative Agencies

Administrative agencies are a major part of both state and federal government. They are the primary tools through which local, state, and federal governments perform regulatory functions. In the words of the Supreme Court in *FTC v. Ruberoid Company* (73 S.Ct. 245):

> *The rise of administration bodies probably has been the most significant legal trend of the last century and perhaps more values today are affected by their decisions than by those of all the courts. ... They have become a veritable fourth branch of the Government...*

The first federal regulatory agency was the Interstate Commerce Commission (ICC) created in 1887 to regulate railroads. Next, the Federal Trade Commission (FTC) and the Food and Drug Administration (FDA) were created in the early 1900s. During the Great Depression in the 1930s, many more agencies were created, such as the Securities and Exchange Commission (SEC) and the Federal Communications Commission (FCC), prompting talk of the "alphabet soup" of agencies. In the late 1960s and early 1970s, agencies were created to address new issues, including the Environmental Protection Agency (EPA) and the Equal Employment Opportunity Commission (EEOC). Today, more than 50 independent agencies and 14 cabinet departments issue tens of thousands of pages of regulations each year. Exhibit 17.1 is a list of a few agencies.

Creating an Administrative Agency

An **administrative agency** is an authority of the government, other than a legislature or a court, created to administer a particular law. Congress gives an agency power and authority through a **delegation of powers**. Congress grants to an agency the power to perform its regulatory purpose, which is to formulate, implement, and enforce policy relevant to its area of authority. A statute delegating those powers to the agency is an **enabling statute**, sometimes called an organic statute.

Why Create an Agency? Administrative agencies are created when a problem requires expertise and supervision. By 1970, for example, Congress decided the federal government should address the issue of air quality. But Congress has neither the time nor the expertise to determine how the law might be applied to thousands of different

---

EXHIBIT 17.1   SELECTED FEDERAL ADMINISTRATIVE AGENCIES AND WEBSITES

Commodity Futures Trading Commission (CFTC); *www.cftc.gov*
Consumer Product Safety Commission (CPSC); *www.cpsc.gov*
Department of Commerce (DoC); *www.doc.gov*
Department of Labor (DoL); *www.dol.gov*
Equal Employment Opportunity Commission (EEOC); *www.eeoc.gov*
Food and Drug Administration (FDA); *www.fda.gov*
Federal Trade Commission (FTC); *www.ftc.gov*
Health and Human Services (HHS); *www.hhs.gov*
Occupational Safety and Health Administration (OSHA); *www.osha.gov*
Securities and Exchange Commission (SEC); *www.sec.gov*

sources emitting many different air pollutants. Congress also lacks the ability to handle law enforcement and compliance directly.

Hence, when Congress passed the Clean Air Act, it delegated primary responsibility to the Environmental Protection Agency (EPA) to create and enforce the regulations implementing the broad guidelines Congress set down. The EPA has the legislative, investigative, adjudicatory, and enforcement powers to accomplish the task. It can consider technical details more effectively than can Congress and can monitor compliance. Congress monitors the EPA. If Congress is not satisfied with the results of EPA activities, it can force change. If voters are unhappy with regulations for being too lax or too stringent, they can pressure their representatives in Congress to change agency actions.

Lighter Side **of the Law**

Keep Pumping Out the Red Tape

The Texas State Library and Commission studied the filing of reports to the state. In a 668-page report, it concluded that of the 1,600 reports filed annually, about 400 duplicated another report, were filed even though the receiving agency no longer exists, or were so trivial that no one ever read the reports.

Source: Houston Chronicle.

Administrative Law

Administrative law consists of statutes that define the authority and structure of administrative agencies that then issue regulations. The primary sources of **administrative law** include:

- The enabling statutes of administrative agencies
- The Administrative Procedures Act (APA)
- Rules issued by administrative agencies
- Court decisions reviewing the validity of agency actions

The APA determines the primary structure of administrative law. Enacted in 1946, the APA defines the procedural rules and formalities for federal agencies. An agency must abide by APA requirements, unless Congress specifically imposes different requirements on the agency.

Congress has authority under the commerce clause and the necessary and proper clause in the Constitution to create agencies and give them powers to enact rules. Agencies are given authority to investigate violations of agency rules and to prosecute violators. Although specific powers differ from agency to agency, we can generalize a "typical" administrative agency. A summary of agency regulatory powers is provided in Exhibit 17.2.

Rulemaking

Agencies are usually authorized to engage in **rulemaking**. An agency develops materials that help those regulated understand what they are required to do to comply with the law. Agencies issue formal rules or **regulations**, provide policy guidance documents that explain how an agency views the law, and develop guidance for agency staff and the public arising from decisions in cases over time.

EXHIBIT 17.2	ADMINISTRATIVE AGENCIES: SUMMARY OF REGULATORY POWERS	
REGULATORY POWER	**DEFINITION**	**ADVANTAGES OF AGENCIES**
Legislative or Rulemaking Power	Develop rules to implement the agency's regulatory policies	Uses experts to consider technical details
Investigative Power	Obtain needed information to ensure that the statute and agency rules are observed	Can monitor regulated industries continuously, whether or not there has been a violation
Adjudicatory Power	Resolve disputes and violations through a judicial type of proceeding	Can bring actions quickly and enjoy flexibility and informality in their procedures
Enforcement Power	Impose sanctions to encourage compliance with statutes, an agency's rules, and an agency's adjudicatory outcomes	Flexibility to impose sanctions such as fines, prohibitions, restrictions on licenses, and threat of public exposure

© Cengage Learning

Types of Rules

The Administrative Procedures Act defines an **agency rule** as:

> *The whole or part of an agency statement of general or particular applicability and future effect designed to implement, interpret, or prescribe law or policy describing the organization, procedure, or practice requirements of an agency.*

In general, administrative rules are classified as substantive (legislative), interpretative, or procedural.

Substantive or Legislative Rules **Substantive or legislative rules** are administrative regulations with the same force of law as statutes enacted by Congress. When an agency issues a substantive rule (regulation), under its grant of authority by Congress, the rule is federal law. Regulations are not a lesser form of law than the laws written directly by Congress. Before issuing rules, an agency is generally required by the APA to provide public notice and the opportunity for interested parties to comment in writing for the public record. The agency then considers whether to change its proposal in response to the comments before issuing a final rule.

Businesses often belong to industry associations that monitor agencies' regulatory activity for new proposals that may affect their members. Large businesses have their own lobbyists in Washington DC to keep an eye on agencies' activities. Both associations and lobbyists can provide expert comments on proposed regulations.

Interpretative Rules **Interpretative rules** are statements issued by an agency to provide its staff and the public with guidance regarding the interpretation of a substantive rule or a statute. Interpretative rules range from informal policy statements to authoritative rulings that are binding on the agency.

In contrast to legislative rules, interpretative rules are exempt from the notice and comment requirements of the APA. An agency may issue interpretative rules without inviting input from interested parties. However, parties affected by rules may challenge an agency's interpretative rule by arguing that it is really a legislative rule. If the challenge is successful, the agency must go through the more complex process to adopt a formal rule.

Procedural Rules **Procedural rules** detail an agency's structure and describe its method of operation and its internal practices. The power to enact such rules is authorized by the agency's enabling statute. Once procedural rules are issued, they bind the agency. A challenge to an agency decision may be upheld if the challenging party can show that the agency did not comply with its own procedural rules in reaching a decision.

Rulemaking Procedure

Substantive rules are most important. An agency lays out the requirements of how a statute is to be applied in practice and the regulations that must be followed. Proposed rules are drafted by agency staff, reviewed internally, and approved by the head of the agency. After a new rule is approved and published in the *Federal Register* for public inspection, interested parties may submit written comments about the rule.

The public comment period is usually 60 to 90 days, after which the agency reviews the comments and finalizes the rule. Most substantive comments are contributed by trade associations and other professionals with expertise in the affected industry. These comments, which tend to be technical, are important because they form the basis of most legal challenges to rules. Submitting the comments is proof that the agency was put on notice of alleged defects in a rule.

Once an agency issues a final rule, it may be appealed to the agency itself, after which appeal is made to the U.S. Court of Appeals. The appeals court ensures that the agency has not exceeded its authority or violated proper procedure. The Supreme Court has made clear that the courts will defer to the expertise of agencies, so long as the rules issued are reasonable, given the language of the enabling statute. The leading case on this matter is the *Chevron* case. The result of this case is often referred to as the Chevron doctrine.

CHEVRON, U.S.A., INC. V. NATURAL RESOURCES DEFENSE COUNCIL, INC.

Supreme Court of the United States 467 U.S. 837 (1984)

Case Background *The Clean Air Act, as enacted by Congress, requires states with "nonattainment" (dirty air) areas to establish a permit program that regulates "new or modified major stationary sources of air pollution." Under EPA regulations, a state could allow a plant with multiple sources of pollution to be treated as one source of pollution. That is, an industrial facility would be treated as if it were under a "bubble." The pollution emitted by the facility under the bubble would be measured, rather than measuring emission from each emission point within the bubble.*

The National Resources Defense Council (NRDC) challenged the EPA "bubble rule" as inconsistent with the Clean Air Act. The Court of Appeals overturned the EPA regulation. That decision was appealed.

Case Decision Justice Stevens delivered the opinion of the Court.

✳ ✳ ✳

When a court reviews an agency's construction of the statute which it administers, it is confronted with two questions. First, always, is the question whether Congress has directly spoken to the precise question at issue. If the intent of Congress is clear, that is the end of the matter; for the court, as well as the agency, must give effect to the unambiguously expressed intent of Congress. If, however, the court determines Congress has not directly addressed the precise question at issue, the court does not simply impose its own construction on the statute, as would be necessary in the absence of an administrative interpretation. Rather, if the statute is silent or ambiguous with respect to the specific issue, the question for the court is whether the agency's answer is based on a permissible construction of the statute.

The power of an administrative agency to administer a congressionally created ... program necessarily requires the formulation of policy and the making of rules to fill any gap left, implicitly or explicitly, by Congress. If Congress has explicitly left a gap for the agency to fill, there is an express delegation of authority to the agency to elucidate a specific provision of the statute by regulation. Such legislative regulations are given controlling weight unless they are arbitrary, capricious, or manifestly contrary to the statute. Sometimes the legislative delegation to an agency on a particular question is implicit rather than explicit. In such a case, a court may not substitute its own construction of a statutory provision for a reasonable interpretation made by the administrator of an agency.

We have long recognized that considerable weight should be accorded to an executive department's construction of a statutory scheme it is entrusted to administer, and the principle of deference to administrative interpretations....

In light of these well-settled principles it is clear that the Court of Appeals misconceived the nature of its role in reviewing the regulations at issue. Once it determined, after its own examination of the legislation, that Congress did not actually have an intent regarding the applicability of the bubble concept to the permit program, the question before it was not whether in its view the concept is "inappropriate" in the general context of a program designed to improve air quality, but whether the Administrator's view that it is appropriate in the context of this particular program is a reasonable one. Based on the examination of the legislation and its history which follows, we ... conclude that the EPA's use of that concept here is a reasonable policy choice for the agency to make....

The judgment of the Court of Appeals is reversed.

Questions for Analysis

1. Congress did not specify that the EPA could use a "bubble" in measuring pollution emitted from an industrial facility, so why can EPA come up with such an idea?
2. If the courts did not grant such deference to agencies, what would be the practical result?

Enforcing Rules

The main job of agencies is to enforce laws written by Congress or by the agencies under the authority granted them by Congress. Enforcement means agencies must gather information and investigate. Agencies have various ways of doing this. While this chapter focuses on agency actions, most regulatory statutes give private parties the right to sue for violations of the law. In the following chapters, we review many examples of such litigation.

Investigative Powers

Information about compliance with federal laws is obtained in three basic ways:

- Regulated businesses are required to self-report.
- Direct observation determines if a business is following the law.
- Agency subpoena power is used to require a business to produce documents.

Monitoring and Self-Reporting Requirements Agencies may require businesses to monitor their own behavior. Those subject to a regulation can be required to report certain information to an agency at set times, such as monthly, or when certain events—often a violation—occur. The Clean Air Act, for example, requires businesses to monitor air pollution emissions and report the data to the Environmental Protection Agency:

The Administrator may require any person who owns or operates any emission source…to A) establish and maintain such records, B) make such reports, C) install, use, and maintain such monitoring equipment or methods, D) sample such emissions, and E) provide such other information as the Administrator may reasonably require. …

A party reporting its own violations can incur punishment. If, for example, a firm volunteers in its reports that it emitted too much of certain pollutants, the EPA can impose a fine. Businesses have contested fines resulting from mandatory **self-reporting** of violations, arguing that reporting self-incriminating evidence violates the Fifth Amendment. However, as pointed out in Chapter 4, the Supreme Court has ruled that the self-incrimination privilege does not provide strong protection for corporations. Failing to report violations or reporting false information almost always leads to heavier penalties than when a party volunteers violations.

Direct Observation by Agencies Agencies also acquire information by direct observation. Examples include worksite safety inspections by OSHA inspectors and testing by the EPA for excessive air pollution emissions. As discussed in Chapter 4, the Supreme Court has imposed limits on warrantless searches by administrative agencies, but administrative warrants are simple to obtain.

No warrant is required if evidence is obtained from an "open-field" observation, that is, if the evidence is gathered by an inspector through observations from areas where the public has access. In *Dow Chemical* v. *United States* (476 U.S. 227), the Supreme Court held it was legal for the EPA to fly over a Dow facility and take photographs for evidence of regulatory violations. Because the airspace over the facility was open to the public, there was no improper search in violation of the Fourth Amendment.

Agency Subpoena Power An agency may also obtain information by issuing a **subpoena**, a legal instrument that directs the person receiving it to appear at a specified time and place to testify or to produce documents. The Clean Air Act provides an example of a congressional authorization of the power to issue subpoenas and the procedure for enforcing them:

CYBER LAW

Do Old Regulations Apply to New Forms of Competition?

The growth of Internet-related technology raises tricky issues for regulators. If a new form of technology competes with existing regulated firms, and the new technology is not covered in the regulations that govern existing competitors, are the new competitors covered?

Bandwidth expansion over the air or through cable allows new forms of communication not covered by existing regulations. Existing firms want new competitors to be subject to rules so that they cannot expand so quickly. Even if the regulators agree with existing competitors, the way the laws were written and the regulations that implement the statutes did not include how to deal with new inventions.

In many cases, if regulation is to be maintained, Congress has to act. Such actions—as in the case of the Communications Decency Act of 1996, which was unanimously struck down by the Supreme Court as unconstitutional—indicate that Congress must not act too hastily lest it be defeated in its intent to control a new medium.

For purposes of obtaining information ... the Administrator may issue subpoenas for the attendance and testimony of witnesses and the production of relevant papers, books, and documents, and he may administer oaths. ... In case of ... refusal to obey a subpoena served upon any person ... the district court ... shall have jurisdiction to issue an order requiring such person to appear and give testimony before the Administrator ... and any failure to obey such an order may be punished by such court as a contempt thereof.

Unless the request for information by the agency is vague, or if the burden imposed on the business outweighs possible benefits to the agency, a business must comply with the subpoena. If a business asserts that the information requested by a subpoena deserves confidential treatment, such as a trade secret, an agency usually respects the request, or the business may seek a court order providing such protection.

Enforcement Power

Congress grants agencies many enforcement tools. The EPA, for example, can ensure compliance with air pollution control requirements by seeking civil and criminal penalties and injunctions.

In addition to having the authority to sue in federal court to seek civil and criminal penalties, agencies have authority to impose other sanctions. Consider the examples offered by the APA in its definition of sanction:

1. Prohibition, requirement, limitation, or other condition affecting the freedom of a person
2. Withholding of relief
3. Imposition of a penalty or fine
4. Destruction, taking, seizing, or withholding of property
5. Assessment of damages, reimbursement, restitution, compensation, costs, charges, or fees
6. Requirement, revocation, or suspension of a license
7. Taking other compulsory or restrictive action

Enforcement methods vary among agencies. Most rely on a mix of formal and informal ways to obtain compliance with regulatory requirements. Our discussion focuses on agency procedures, but when an agency brings criminal charges against a party, it works with the Department of Justice, which usually handles the prosecution of criminal cases that are heard in federal court. The *Black Beauty* case illustrates one enforcement process.

BLACK BEAUTY COAL COMPANY V. FEDERAL MINE SAFETY AND HEALTH REVIEW COMMISSION

United States Court of Appeals, District of Columbia Circuit, 703 F.3d 553 (2012)

Case Background *Mine Safety and Health Administration (MSHA) inspector Franklin entered a mine in Indiana operated by Black Beauty. The company assigned Hammond to escort Franklin. When he entered the mine he smelled burning coal. He asked some miners about it. One, Vogel,* *said he had smelled it about 30 minutes before. He investigated but did not find anything, so did not report a problem.*

Franklin proceeded and found a place where a conveyor belt dumped coal onto another belt. Because of a rip in a guard sheet, a pile of coal about

2'×2'×5' was packed around the transfer spot. Franklin thought it had begun to burn. Hammond said he would have someone come fix the problem. Franklin said to shut down the belts, but Hammond refused to do so as he did not see evidence of a fire. Franklin issued a citation for "high negligence."

MSHA sent Black Beauty a proposed penalty assessment, which it rejected, choosing to contest the matter to an Administrative Law Judge (ALJ). The ALJ agreed with the MSHA and imposed a $70,000 civil penalty as a result of the high negligence. Black Beauty petitioned for review.

Case Decision Karen LeCraft Henderson, Circuit Judge

* * *

30 C.F.R. §75.400 prohibits accumulations [of coal dust] but not mere spillages. No bright line differentiates the two terms. An accumulation exists if a reasonably prudent person, familiar with the mining industry and the protective purpose of the standard, would have recognized the hazardous condition that the regulation seeks to prevent. ...

After considering the facts ... the ALJ explained that none of the evidence explained the smell of burning coal that occurred at least thirty minutes before Franklin's arrival.

The lack of smoke ... does not mean that the ALJ's duration finding was unsupported by substantial evidence. ...

The ALJ's high negligence finding appears to be based on four facts: (1) Black Beauty had been cited for several past accumulations violations (including warnings for belt line accumulations); (2) the burning smell existed for a significant time period; (3) Villain [in charge of keeping the conveyor belts clean] "should have ... seen and noted" the coal turning in the tail roller; and (4) Vogel and the other miners did not alert management after noticing a burning smell. ...

For the foregoing reasons, Black Beauty's petition for review is denied.

Questions for Analysis

1. Don't the people working at the mine and running the mine have more expertise about safe operations than an inspector?
2. Why would the company fight the citation rather than pay? The cost of the fight is likely greater than the fine.

Informal Agency Procedures Agencies rely heavily on informal procedures that allow leeway in forcing compliance. Because informal procedures generally require less time and money than formal procedures, agencies prefer to use them when possible.

Informal procedures include tests and inspections, processing applications and permits, negotiations, settlements, and advice in the form of advisory opinions. Publicity, or the threat of it, can also be considered an informal procedure for an agency to get industry to comply with its rules.

In some instances, agencies may act on the spot. For example, an OSHA inspector, upon finding a situation that endangers workers, may order immediate changes. Many such incidents are handled this way, rather than involving time-consuming, more costly formal procedures. Perhaps the *Black Beauty* case would not have evolved into a formal matter if managers had responded to the inspector's conclusions about a problem on the spot. Similarly, manufacturers "voluntarily" withdraw products from the shelves and destroy them when a problem is discovered that would likely result in formal action by an agency.

Review of Informal Procedure Decisions A business unhappy with an agency sanction resulting from informal procedures may seek review. The agency head first reviews the decision. If dissatisfied with the agency's final decision, parties may seek review by the federal appeals court. In reviewing agency procedures, the courts are generally most concerned with whether the agency procedure was fair and whether the decision was consistent with the legislative intent of Congress.

Formal Agency Procedures Among the formal procedures used by most regulatory agencies are quasi-judicial powers, especially adjudicatory hearings. The APA dictates how hearings are conducted. In some instances, an agency's enabling statute may require procedures that differ somewhat from those provided by the APA.

Adjudicatory Hearings Formal agency process under APA rules provides for an **adjudicatory hearing** that follows rules similar to those followed in a trial, but is somewhat less formal in terms of procedure and evidence. As Exhibit 17.3 illustrates, an adjudicatory hearing is initiated by the agency filing a complaint. The business must respond to the complaint that alleges violation of the law enforced by the agency. If the matter is not settled by negotiation, a hearing may be necessary.

An **administrative law judge** (ALJ) from the agency presides over the hearing. The ALJ is a civil service employee of the agency, usually a staff attorney. Counsel for the agency presents the agency's evidence in support of the complaint; the business presents its evidence. Witnesses may be cross-examined, but the procedure is less formal than a court trial. The hearing must meet the due process guarantees of the Constitution, but there is no right to a jury trial, because these are not criminal or common-law causes.

After a hearing, the ALJ issues a written decision. If the business does not object to the decision, the agency normally adopts it. If the business is dissatisfied with the ALJ's decision and seeks review, the agency head (commissioners or administrator) reviews the decision. If the business is dissatisfied after this final agency review, it may then proceed to the federal appeals courts for further review, as in the *Black Beauty* case.

EXHIBIT 17.3 FORMAL AGENCY PROCEDURE: ADJUDICATORY HEARING

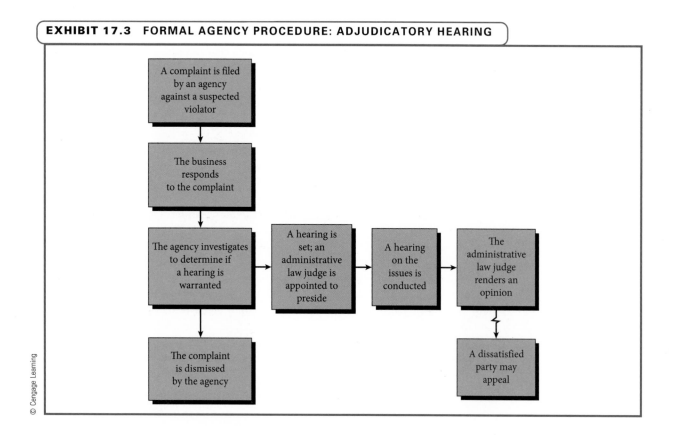

© Cengage Learning

ISSUE SPOTTER
Contest a Regulatory Order?

The Department of Labor contends that your firm has not been counting overtime work by employees properly. Labor demands the firm pay some back wages to employees to correct the calculation, pay a $1,000 fine, and promise not to violate the law concerning overtime work again. The matter can be settled quietly by accepting the Labor offer. One senior manager thinks Labor is wrong, and the matter should be contested. He suggests not only contesting the finding of Labor in this particular case, but contesting the validity of the regulation enforcing the overtime provisions of the Fair Labor Standards Act as written by the Department of Labor.

Would it make sense to contest Labor's administrative decision? What are the pros and cons of a challenge?

© Cengage Learning

The ALJ hearing a case is not an independent judge, as would be the case in a federal courtroom, but an employee of the same agency that brought the case against them. The courts have held that independence is not required by the Constitution. The rules that limit the ability of outsiders to discuss a case with a judge do not generally apply to ALJs, although there are some rules limiting such contacts.

❓ TEST YOURSELF

1. The primary structure of administrative law is determined by the _____ enacted by Congress in 1946.
2. Statements issued by an agency to provide its staff and the public with guidance regarding how an agency views the substance of a rule are interpretative rules: T—F
3. When an agency writes a new rule, before it is finalized, it is published in the Code of Federal Regulations: T—F
4. In the *Chevron* v. *Natural Resources Defense Council* case, the Supreme Court considered a challenge to an EPA rule that established "bubbles" over industrial plants as a part of measuring pollution. The Court held that the EPA's rule:
   a. violated the intent of Congress, so the bubble rule was invalid.
   b. violated the express words of Congress in the Clean Air Act, so the bubble rule was invalid.
   c. was within the "spirit" of the Clean Air Act, so was valid.
   d. was valid because courts generally defer to the expertise of an agency.
5. When a firm is subject to a regulation, an agency may not require a firm to report violations it commits, as that violates the Fifth Amendment: T—F
6. When an agency has an adjudicatory hearing about a matter, the hearing may be under the supervision of a(n) _____.
7. In the *Black Beauty Coal Company* v. *Federal Mine Safety and Health Review Commission* case, the appeals court held that the Mine Safety agency violated the APA by failing to provide "conclusive evidence" of a safety hazard: T—F

Answers: Administrative Procedures Act; T; F; d; F; administrative law judge; F.

Judicial Review

The APA sets the procedural requirements for a party seeking court of appeals review of an agency decision. Most appeals concern the legitimacy of regulations and whether a penalty issued by an agency for a violation was justified. That appeal is referred to as **judicial review**, an external check on agency power. This ensures that agencies follow required procedures, do not go beyond the authority granted them by Congress, can justify their actions, and respect constitutional rights.

When Judicial Review Can Occur

Before a court accepts an appeal to review an agency's action, the party making the request must satisfy some important procedural requirements. Without limits on judicial review, the courts could intrude into areas of agency responsibility, and they would be flooded with more cases. The most important of these procedural requirements are summarized in Exhibit 17.4.

Jurisdiction As in any lawsuit, the party challenging an agency action must select a court that has authority to hear the case. Most regulatory statutes declare which court has **jurisdiction** to review agency actions. Suppose, for example, that the EPA enacts a new regulation. The Clean Air Act states the following:

> *A petition for review of an action of the Administrator in promulgating any national ambient air quality standard…may be filed only in the United States Court of Appeals for the District of Columbia.*

A challenge filed anywhere else would be dismissed because the court lacked jurisdiction. Putting all challenges of a particular type in one court reduces the changes of inconsistent decisions across courts.

Reviewability An agency action that is challenged must be **reviewable** by the courts. Administrative agencies must follow required procedure rules or risk being found by the reviewing courts to have acted arbitrarily. Furthermore, agencies may not exceed

EXHIBIT 17.4 JUDICIAL REVIEW OF AGENCY ACTIONS: PROCEDURAL REQUIREMENTS

PROCEDURAL REQUIREMENT	DEFINITION
Jurisdiction	The complaining party may seek judicial review only in courts that have power to hear the case. Most statutes specify which courts have jurisdiction to hear appeals of agency actions.
Reviewability	An appellate court has the ability to reconsider an agency decision to determine whether correction or modification is needed.
Standing	A party seeking judicial review must demonstrate that it incurred an injury recognized by law as a result of the agency's action.
Ripeness	There can be no judicial review until the agency's decision is final so the court has the final issues in the case before it and not hypothetical questions or unresolved disputes.
Exhaustion	This is a "gatekeeping" device, requiring that a party seeking judicial review must have sought relief through all possible agency appeal processes before seeking review by the courts.

INTERNATIONAL PERSPECTIVE

Administrative Agencies in Japan

One of the most worrisome areas of Japanese legal culture for foreign companies is the body of administrative "law" known as "administrative guidance" (*gyosei shido*). This includes all procedural tools Japanese agencies can use to exert regulatory authority over businesses. An administrative agency, for example, may issue guidance by direction (*shiji*), request (*yobo*), warning (*keikoku*), encouragement (*kansho*), or suggestion (*kankoku*).

The power basis of administrative guidance is in the government's control of foreign trade. In theory, businesses are not forced to comply with guidance. But a business that ignores a suggestion might find that its quota of imported materials has been reduced, that it is being denied government financing for expansion, or that some other sanction is imposed.

The Foreign Exchange Control and Foreign Investment Acts of Japan, for example, require that the Foreign Investment Council must approve any agreement involving expenditures abroad. A business that has not complied with an agency's request that a pollution control device be installed might find that a contract requiring expenditures abroad has not been approved.

The Japanese judiciary has taken a hands-off policy toward administrative guidance. As long as the agency action is within its discretion, the action is not reviewed unfavorably, even if it is abusive. This gives Japanese administrative agencies more power than U.S. agencies.

© Cengage Learning

their regulatory objectives or risk being found to have violated the duties they were assigned by Congress. For these reasons, the APA authorizes the courts to review most agency actions. However, judicial review is not available if prohibited by statute or is a matter of agency discretion.

Review Prohibited by Statute   Just as Congress may specify in a statute which court has jurisdiction for judicial review, it can prohibit certain judicial review. Consider, for example, the following statutory provision regarding the authority of the Secretary of Veteran Affairs:

> *The decisions of the Secretary on any question of law or fact under any law administered by the Department of Veterans Affairs providing benefits for veterans and their dependents or survivors shall be final, and no other official or any court of the United States shall have the power or jurisdiction to review any decision.*

Lighter Side of the Law

Regulators Protecting Consumers?

Like most countries, Japan has regulations that claim to protect consumers that appear to do the opposite.

Japan's antitrust "watchdog," the Fair Trade Commission, does not allow retailers to give discounts below the listed price on CDs, books, or magazines. Discount coupons may not be issued because they might "confuse" consumers. One Japanese retailer tried to import small, plastic food containers from Thailand. The customs agency required every carton to be opened and the containers and their lids tested to make sure they worked. Now the company buys containers made in Japan. They do not have to be tested, and they cost consumers three to four times as much as the "untrustworthy" Thai imports.

Source: Wall Street Journal.

Thus, a party may not seek review of an administrative decision from the Department of Veteran Affairs in court. Congress can include such an exception in a statute as long as the exception does not violate constitutional rights.

Action Committed to Agency Discretion In addition to statutory exceptions to judicial review, there are exceptions for actions committed based on agency discretion for practical reasons. Some actions require speed, flexibility, and secrecy in decision making. For example, decisions affecting national defense and foreign policy may be committed to agency discretion and are not reviewable through the courts.

Standing A party seeking to challenge an agency action in court must have **standing** to seek judicial review. Section 2 of Article III of the Constitution limits judicial power to actual cases or controversies. Federal courts cannot hear complaints from parties who have no direct stake in a real dispute or who raise only hypothetical questions. Administrative law generally restricts the right of review to parties who can show an injury recognized by law as being entitled to protection.

The U.S. Supreme Court addressed this issue in *Lujan* v. *Defenders of Wildlife* (504 U.S. 555). In that case, environmental groups argued that U.S. aid to Egypt to build dams on the Nile River endangered the rare Nile crocodile. Plaintiffs asserted that the agencies providing the aid should comply with the Endangered Species Act. The Court refused the challenge because the plaintiffs lacked standing—they had suffered no "injury in fact." A concern about crocodiles in Egypt was too remote. Disagreement with an agency's policy is not the same as showing a concrete injury to the complaining party resulting from the policy. Policy disputes should be resolved through the political process. The Supreme Court reaffirmed the importance of standing when challenges were brought against agency decisions in the *Earth Island* case, which discusses some of the key issues involved.

SUMMERS V. EARTH ISLAND INSTITUTE

Supreme Court of the United States 129 S.Ct. 1142 (2009)

Case Background *The Forest Service Decision making and Appeals Reform Act of 1992 requires the Forest Service to establish a notice, comment, and appeals process for "proposed actions of the Forest Service concerning projects and activities implementing land and resource management plans." The regulations that implement the Act provide that certain procedures would not be applied to projects that the Forest Service considered excluded from the requirement to file an environmental impact statement (EIS), such as in the case of salvage-timber sales of 250 acres or less.*

After a forest fire in 2002, the Forest Service approved a salvage sale of burned timber on 238 acres. It did not prepare an EIS or provide for a formal notice of the sale. Earth Island challenged the sale and the district court ordered it stopped. The appeals court agreed with the injunction against

the sale. The government sought a review of the question whether Earth Island could challenge the Forest Service regulations at issue.

Case Decision Scalia, Justice

* * *

In limiting the judicial power to "Cases" and "Controversies," Article III of the Constitution restricts it to the traditional role of Anglo-American courts, which is to redress or prevent actual or imminently threatened injury to persons caused by private or official violation of law. Except when necessary in the execution of that function, courts have no charter to review and revise legislative and executive action. This limitation "is founded in concern about the proper-and properly limited-role of the courts in a democratic society."

The doctrine of standing is one of several doctrines that reflect this fundamental limitation. It requires federal courts to satisfy themselves that "the plaintiff has 'alleged such a personal stake in the outcome of the controversy' as to warrant *his* invocation of federal-court jurisdiction." He bears the burden of showing that he has standing for each type of relief sought. To seek injunctive relief, a plaintiff must show that he is under threat of suffering "injury in fact" that is concrete and particularized; the threat must be actual and imminent, not conjectural or hypothetical; it must be fairly traceable to the challenged action of the defendant; and it must be likely that a favorable judicial decision will prevent or redress the injury. This requirement assures that "there is a real need to exercise the power of judicial review in order to protect the interests of the complaining party," Where that need does not exist, allowing courts to oversee legislative or executive action "would significantly alter the allocation of power ... away from a democratic form of government," ...

The regulations under challenge here neither require nor forbid any action on the part of respondents. The standards and procedures that they prescribe for Forest Service appeals govern only the conduct of Forest Service officials engaged in project planning. "When the plaintiff is not himself the object of the government action or inaction he challenges, standing is not precluded, but it is ordinarily 'substantially more difficult' to establish." Here, respondents can demonstrate standing only if application of the regulations by the Government will affect *them* in the manner described above. ...

The judgment of the Court of Appeals is reversed. ...

Questions for Analysis

1. Given the words of the Court above, how could the plaintiff have demonstrated standing?
2. Does this indicate that standing is difficult to obtain?

Ripeness The **ripeness doctrine** concerns whether an agency action is final so as to allow judicial review. That is, agency decisions that are not completely finalized are not ripe for review because they could be changed. According to the Supreme Court in *Abbott Labs* v. *Gardner* (387 U.S. 136), the doctrine is designed "to protect agencies from judicial interference until an administrative decision has been formalized and its effects felt in a concrete way by the challenging parties."

Exhaustion The **exhaustion doctrine** requires a party to complete all agency appeals procedures before turning to a court for review. That is, parties may not go to the courts until they have exhausted all agency review procedures regarding a new rule or a disciplinary action. An action must be considered final by an agency before proceeding to court. This prevents unnecessary lawsuits by giving the agency the full chance to get the decision right.

Scope of Judicial Review

When all procedural requirements have been met, the court of appeals can review an agency action. The court's scope of review determines how far it can go in examining the action. The review depends on whether the issue before it involves a question of substantive law, statutory interpretation, or procedure. Each imposes different requirements on the reviewing court.

Review of Substantive Determination A court's review of an agency's substantive determination generally gets the lowest scope of judicial review. As the Supreme Court explained in the *Chevron* case earlier in the chapter, the courts yield to the agency's judgment in technical and scientific matters in working out the details of regulations. The courts generally do not find that an agency's actions or decisions are **arbitrary and capricious**, or an abuse of discretion, if the following are true:

- The agency has sufficiently explained the facts and its policy concerns.
- Those facts have some basis in the agency's record.
- On the basis of those facts and concerns, a reasonable person could reach the same judgments the agency has reached.

Review of Statutory Interpretation A court's review of an agency's statutory interpretation is given a greater scope of review. In contrast to the technical judgments required of the agency in implementing a statute, the courts have responsibility for the interpretation of the meaning of statutes enacted by Congress. The courts determine whether an agency has gone beyond the authority it was granted by Congress. Although the courts give great weight to the interpretation of a statute by the agency responsible for its implementation, they reject that interpretation if it does not comply with interpretations by established principles of statutory construction.

Review of Procedural Requirements The court's review of an agency's procedural requirements receives the most intense scope of review. The court is responsible for ensuring that the agency has not acted in disregard of statutorily prescribed procedures. The courts are the guardians of procedural fair play. Recall the *Black Beauty* case where the court upheld an administrative penalty imposed on a mining company by the Mine Safety and Health Administration (MSHA). The same court had a different view about another action against a mining company involving the same agency, as we see in the *Lone Mountain* case.

LONE MOUNTAIN PROCESSING, INC. V. SECRETARY OF LABOR

United States Court of Appeals, District of Columbia Circuit, 709 F.3d 1161 (2013)

Case Background *Lone Mountain, a mining firm, was cited for regulatory violations and was sent "notices of contest" that it did not respond to. Because it did not challenge the notices or respond within 30 days, the MSHA sent delinquency notices.*

Later, Lone Mountain filed motions to reopen the civil penalties that had become final. The agency denied Lone Mountain's motion because the company "failed to establish good cause" for reopening the matter. Lone Mountain appealed.

Case Decision Griffith, Circuit Judge

* * *

The Act [creating the MSHA] gives the Commission the power to set most of its own procedures, which it has done through a series of regulations. Of particular relevance to this dispute is a regulation that provides:

On any procedural question not regulated by the Act, these Procedural Rules, or the Administrative Procedure Act ..., the Commission and its Judges shall be *guided so far as practicable* by the Federal Rules of Civil Procedure. ...

Following the guidance of Federal Rule of Civil Procedure 60(b), the Commission has long held that it may reopen otherwise final orders, including those that have been rendered final Thus, by its own choice, the Commission must be "guided so far as practicable" by a rule that states that it "may" reopen final orders. This leaves the Commission with much discretion, but that discretion is not unfettered.

Lone Mountain argues that the Commission abused that discretion by departing from its own precedent without explanation, and we agree. ...

Over the years, mine operators have failed to respond to MSHA citations and proposed penalty assessments within the thirty-day windows prescribed by 30 U.S.C. §815(a) and subsequently have sought the Commission's lenience by filing motions to reopen. In turn, the Commission has developed a body of precedent regarding how to treat such motions based on the facts in each case.

If the Commission had been supplying a reasoned analysis regarding its prior policies and standards, it would have either held that ... [other] similar Commission orders involving timely citation contests cut in favor of Lone Mountain, or it would have explained why they do not apply in Lone Mountain's case. But despite their obvious relevance, the Commission failed even to mention or discuss, let alone distinguish, those orders. ... As we have long held, "an agency changing its course must supply a reasoned analysis indicating that prior policies and standards are being deliberately changed, not casually ignored." Failing to supply such analysis renders the agency's action arbitrary and capricious. ...

We grant the petition for review and remand the order to the Commission for reconsideration with this opinion.

Questions for Analysis

1. Does this decision mean Lone Mountain will likely prevail in its challenges to the citations?
2. What difference does this procedural rule make on agency operations?

Controls on Agencies

In addition to having checks imposed on them by judicial review, agencies are checked by Congress. Because it delegates powers to an agency, Congress may revoke those powers. This section discusses various measures that Congress uses, or has considered using, in providing those checks.

Direct Controls on Agencies

Public awareness and concern about the costs and effectiveness of regulation, as well as pressure from special interest groups, prompt responses from Congress. The most immediate control mechanism enjoyed by Congress is the ability to control agency activity through the budget process. The president, in appointing top agency officials, also helps control agency agendas. In addition, members of Congress have proposed bills calling for, among other things, mandatory cost-benefit analysis of agency regulations.

Agency Appropriations and Executive Orders Congress requires agencies to report on programs and activities on a regular basis. Congressional committees frequently hold oversight hearings. Administrative agencies submit annual budget requests for review by the president and by Congress. The president or Congress can recommend cuts in an agency's budget if either is opposed to some of the agency's activities. Through budget appropriations, Congress can mandate that an agency address specific issues. Congress can also prohibit an agency from working on specific issues. Budget control gives the president, and especially Congress, the ability to control details of agency regulatory policy.

Presidents have used Executive Orders to instruct administrative agencies to undertake certain tasks. Presidents issue several dozen Executive Orders each year. Many are trivial, but some have major policy implications, such as President Johnson's order that affirmative action programs in hiring were required of all companies that contract with the federal government. Congress can pass legislation to undo an Executive Order, or an Order may be challenged and stricken by the courts as an abuse of executive power, but it remains a strong tool for the president to use to allocate agency resources.

Cost-Benefit and Risk Analysis Mandatory **cost-benefit analysis** requires agencies to weigh the costs and benefits of new regulations. When the costs exceed the benefits derived from a regulation, the regulation is more easily challenged for reasonableness.

The same holds true for risk-assessment requirements that estimate the risk reduction achieved by regulations that affect health and safety.

The Data Quality Act, passed in 2000 and enforced by the Office of Management and Budget (OMB), requires agencies to ensure the quality of the analysis done to support regulations. If scientific, technical, and economic information standards are not met, affected parties may challenge a regulation as not supported by adequate analysis. OMB, reviewing proposed regulations, can also send a proposed regulation back to an agency for not having met sufficient scientific standards.

Lighter *Side* of the Law

We Will Teach You Not to Ask Questions

An open-government advocacy group's survey of agencies showed that eight had Freedom of Information Act requests unresolved after more than a decade. FOIA requires resolution within 20 days, but allows a 10-day extension under "unusual circumstances."

Sioux City, Iowa, requested documents from the Postal Service regarding its decision to move some jobs away from Sioux City. The Postal Service estimated that the fee for providing the documents would be $831,000.

Sources: National Security Archive; Sioux City Journal.

Indirect Controls on Agencies

Congress has passed several laws that can have the effect of indirectly controlling the power of administrative agencies. Through those acts, which include the Freedom of Information Act, the Privacy Act, and the Government in the Sunshine Act, Congress made it easier for parties outside an agency to obtain information in the possession of the agency. Most states have similar laws.

Freedom of Information Act The Freedom of Information Act (FOIA) makes most documents held by federal agencies available to the public. Unless the document falls within certain exempted categories, it must be released upon request from a citizen, although the process is often very slow. Exempted are trade secrets, documents related to national security, and documents that would, if disclosed, invade personal privacy.

Privacy Act The Privacy Act is gives citizens input about what information is collected about them and how that information is used. It requires that unless an exception applies, notice and prior consent are required before an agency can disclose information that concerns and identifies an individual. Individuals have the right to access agency records and to request amendments to correct inaccuracies. This may be enforced in federal district courts.

Government in the Sunshine Act The Government in the Sunshine Act limits secret meetings by agencies. The public is entitled to at least one week's notice of the time, place, and subject matter of agency meetings. An agency action taken at a meeting in violation of the Act is not invalid simply because of the violation; some other basis for overturning an agency action would have to be established. A court may grant an injunction against future violations of the Act. The Act lists situations in which meetings may be closed. An open meeting is not required, for example, when it concerns matters to be kept secret in the interest of national defense or when there may be disclosure of protected financial information.

? *TEST YOURSELF*

1. _____ means there can be no judicial review until the agency's decision is final so that the court will have the final issues in the case before it and not hypothetical disputes.
2. _____ means the complaining party may seek judicial review only in courts that have power to hear the case.
3. How far a court of appeals may go in examining an action undertaken by an agency is referred to as *statutory interpretation*: T—F
4. Congress may slash the budget of an administrative agency if it is not pleased with its performance: T—F
5. In *Summers* v. *Earth Island Institute*, where a decision by the Forest Service to log an area after a forest fire was challenged by an environmental group, the Supreme Court held that the Forest Service:
   a. could proceed as the challenging group did not have standing.
   b. could proceed as Congress stated in a statute that land burned by forest fires were no longer subject to environmental impact statements.
   c. could not proceed as the group showed it could suffer an "injury in fact."
   d. could not proceed as the group showed the agency violated the express intention of Congress.
6. In the *Lone Mountain Processing* case, the appeals court held that the mine safety agency violated its own procedure by refusing to hear an appeal from a company that had been issued citations: T—F
7. Congress requires cost-benefit analyses to be completed by any agency considering a regulation that would impose more than $100 million in cost: T—F
8. If a citizen wants access to government documents held by an agency, it may be necessary to file a(n) _____ request.

Answers: Ripeness; Jurisdiction; F; T; a; T; F; FOIA.

SUMMARY

- Administrative agencies are created by Congress and granted legislative, investigative, adjudicatory, and enforcement powers.
- The first federal agency was the Interstate Commerce Commission, established by Congress in 1887 to regulate railroads. The most significant growth periods of agencies took place during the Great Depression of the 1930s and the "social reform" era of the 1960s and 1970s.

- Administrative law consists of legal rules defining the authority and structure of administrative agencies, specifying procedural requirements, and defining the roles of government bodies, particularly the courts, in their relationship with agencies. The primary administrative law is the Administrative Procedures Act (APA).
- Administrative regulations are classified as legislative (substantive), which are major regulations

issued under grants of power from Congress; interpretative, which help to explain legislative regulations and statutes; and procedural, which detail the steps an agency uses in its rule-making procedures and enforcement.

- Agencies may require businesses that are subject to regulation to volunteer information related to the regulations on a regular basis, including reporting violations.

- Agencies may also watch for violations, including inspecting business property, and can gather information that is provided when requested or can force information from a business by use of subpoena.

- Agencies meet their regulatory responsibilities through informal and formal procedures. Informal procedures, which consist of tests and inspections, are not subject to the procedural requirements of the APA. Formal procedures, which include adjudicatory hearings, must meet the APA's procedural requirements.

- Agencies may issue fines, citations, or other penalties to rule violators. The violators can accept a penalty or contest it at an agency hearing before an administrative law judge, whose decision can be reviewed by the head of an agency and then by the federal courts of appeals. Criminal charges by an agency must be filed in federal court.

- Judicial review imposes a check on agency actions. To obtain review, the party challenging the action must meet the procedural requirements of jurisdiction, reviewability, standing, ripeness, and exhaustion.

- Congress provides direct and indirect checks on the administrative agencies. The direct checks provided by Congress include control over agency appropriations, reporting requirements, and cost-benefit analysis. Indirect checks include such acts as the Freedom of Information Act, the Privacy Act, and the Government in the Sunshine Act.

TERMS TO KNOW

administrative agency, 469
delegation of powers, 469
enabling statute, 469
administrative law, 470
rulemaking, 470
regulation, 470
agency rule, 471
substantive or legislative rules, 471

interpretative rules, 471
procedural rules, 471
self-reporting, 474
subpoena, 474
adjudicatory hearing, 477
administrative law
judge, 477
judicial review, 479

jurisdiction, 479
reviewable, 479
standing, 481
ripeness doctrine, 482
exhaustion doctrine, 482
arbitrary and
     capricious, 482
cost-benefit analysis, 484

DISCUSSION QUESTION

What advantages does an agency have over the judicial system in monitoring business behavior?

CASE QUESTIONS

1. TriMet provides mass transportation services in the Portland, Oregon area. Under the Americans with Disabilities Act (ADA), it developed a plan for providing paratransit service (LIFT) for disabled riders unable to use its fixed system of buses and light rail. The plan was approved by the Federal Transit Administration (FTA). Boose, who is disabled, is approved by TriMet to call on LIFT for her transportation needs. She requested that only sedans or taxis be sent, as riding buses caused her to suffer nausea and emotional stress.

TriMet refused. She sued, contending TriMet violated the ADA. The district court dismissed her suit. She appealed. Is it inconsistent for an agency to enact a plan that does not provide help needed by a disabled person who is supposed to benefit from the plan? [*Boose* v. *Tri-County Metropolitan Transportation District of Oregon*, 587 F.3d 997, 9th Circuit (2009)]

2. Prison inmates sentenced to death by lethal injection sued the Food and Drug Administration for refusing to take action against the makers and

users of the drugs used for lethal injection. The prisoners claimed that the drugs violated FDA standards and thus, should be subject to an enforcement action to prevent violations of FDA rules. The FDA claimed that it did not have to review drugs or undertake enforcement actions that it did not think necessary. The prisoners claimed that the FDA had to hold all drugs to the same standards and that enforcement action had to be taken. Were the prisoners correct? [*Heckler* v. *Chaney*, 105 S.Ct. 1649 (1985)]

✓ Check your answer

3. Ballanger bought a farm in Missouri. The seller told him that the farm had no wetlands on it. Ballanger cleared five acres of vegetation to extend the planting area on the farm. Later, the County Farm Service Agency asked the Conservation Service if Ballanger's farm complied with regulations concerning protection of wetlands. The Conservation Service determined that the five acres that had been cleared were wetlands and that Ballanger was not due the crop payments of $40,316 that he had received. He was ordered to repay the money. Ballanger contested the decision, but the Department of Agriculture ruled against him. Ballanger sued. The district court upheld the administrative ruling. Ballanger appealed that the process on the grounds that the agency was abusive. Is that a good argument? [*Ballanger* v. *Johanns*, 495 F.3d 866, 8th Cir. (2007)]

4. Congress passed a law that would force automakers to deal with the problem of underinflated tires. The law said "the Secretary of Transportation shall complete a rulemaking for a regulation to require a warning system in new motor vehicles to indicate to the operator when a tire is significantly underinflated." The rule the agency wrote said that automakers would be in compliance if they put a low-pressure sensor on any tire on a vehicle, not all four tires. This was contested as improper, stating that Congress meant for a sensor to be on every tire. How would you think the courts viewed the rule given the wording of the statute? [*Public Citizen* v. *Mineta*, 340 F.3d 39, 2nd Cir. (2003)]

✓ Check your answer

5. The Sierra Club sued the Secretary of the Interior for allowing the lease of federal land to be used for a ski resort. The secretary studied the issue and decided such use was appropriate. The Club claimed that the change in the use of the land would adversely change the area's aesthetics and ecology. The court of appeals held that the Club did not have standing to sue. Was that correct? [*Sierra Club* v. *Morton*, 405 U.S. 727 (1972)]

6. The Oregon Department of Fish and Wildlife (OFW) issued regulations that commercial crab catchers needed permits from OFW, as it would limit when crabbing could occur and how many crabs could be caught. The effect of the rule was to benefit commercial fishermen with small vessels over those with large vessels. Some vessel owners contested the authority of OFW to issue such rules. Could it issue regulations that discriminated against some producers compared to others? [*Fishermen Against Irresponsible Reallocation, Inc.* v. *Fish and Wildlife Comm.*, 22 Or.App. 353, Ct. App., Ore., (2008)]

7. A freedom of information request was filed with the Nuclear Regulatory Commission for information about nuclear plant operations that had been provided voluntarily by the plants to the commission on the agreement that the information be kept confidential, even though it did not involve trade secrets. The commission refused to release the information, claiming it would injure its working relationship with the plant operators. Was this a proper reason to refuse the information request? [*Critical Mass Energy Project* v. *Nuclear Regulatory Comm.*, 731 F.2d 554, D.C. Cir. (1990)]

ETHICS QUESTION

Most regulatory matters are settled informally: only a small number result in litigation. When a company is in a dispute with a federal agency, it knows that if it does not reach a settlement, there can be costly litigation. From the perspective of the government agency, the litigation is costless—the taxpayers foot the bill. Agencies know that the threat of costly litigation enhances their chance of extracting a settlement from the company. Should the government use this leverage to extract more in a settlement than it knows it would be likely to get in a court-resolved dispute?

Securities Regulation

When Enron and Worldcom collapsed in 2001 and 2002, each once valued in the tens of billions of dollars, the events were said to be the financial scandal of the ages. Thousands lost their jobs and their retirement funds evaporated. Congress responded by toughening federal securities laws.

That episode paled in comparison to when the stock market lost half its value between 2007 and 2009 and major Wall Street firms collapsed. Fearing a financial panic, the federal government rushed in with hundreds of billions of dollars in a program to save many financial institutions from similar fates.

The worst financial crisis since the 1930s raised questions about the role that government should play in the financial markets. Was a bailout a good thing or did it make non-investors pay for the mistakes of others? Would more regulatory oversight and restrictions on financial instruments help prevent market bubbles and bursts? In any event, Congress passed another major overhaul of financial regulations in 2010.

Securities markets handle tens of trillions of dollars in assets, so huge sums of money can be at risk. When that happens, confidence in securities is shaken. The Securities and Exchange Commission (SEC) is the primary regulator of U.S. securities markets. This chapter looks at the workings and legal control of some of the key elements of the securities industry.

The Elements of Securities

Securities are the financial backbone of the U.S. economy, so the efficient operation of the securities market is critical to economic growth. Business operations, especially larger companies, rely on securities for financing operations. Securities are also the main investment for pension funds, so the financial future of most people is tied to securities.

Corporate Finance

A **security** is almost always one of two things: First, it may be **debt** of certain forms, primarily money borrowed by a corporation usually as note or bond that can be traded. Second, it may be **equity**, the most well known being common stocks traded on stock exchanges. Securities provide capital for business operations, i.e., the money needed to get a business started or increased in size. Securities are usually records in computers that represent value in something real. This chapter opens with a look at the elements of debt and equity.

Debt When bonds are sold, there is usually an issue of a certain amount. For example, if General Motors issues 10,000 bonds that are each worth $10,000, the company raises $100 million, perhaps to help pay for a new factory. The bond issue means that GM has incurred debt that is to be repaid to the holders, or owners, of the bonds. The bonds are usually traded on the securities market, so they are **debt securities**. Debt financing may also be obtained by borrowing money from large lenders, such as banks and insurance companies. In that case, as we discussed in Chapter 12, a note may be issued to represent the debt. Because that note may be sold later to other parties, it can also be a security. A debt instrument issued by a corporation, such as a bond, specifies:

1. Amount of the debt
2. Length of the debt period
3. Debt repayment method
4. Rate of interest charged to the sum borrowed

Most purchases and sales are handled by professional bond traders who earn a commission for handling the trades of bonds.

Equity **Equity financing** is raising funds through the sale of company stock. It is called equity financing because a purchaser of shares of stock gains an ownership interest, or equitable interest, in the corporation. Shareholders have a claim on a portion of the future profits (if any) of the corporation. Unlike debt financing, a company has no specific obligation to repay shareholders the amount they have invested. For example, when Facebook sold stock for the first time, 421 million shares were bought by the public at $38 a share. Each share represents a right to a tiny fraction of the future value of the corporation.

Investors buy shares in the corporation if they think the profits will be sufficient to provide them a competitive rate of return on their investment. The officers of the corporation have a fiduciary obligation to make reasonable efforts to earn a profit. As in the case of bonds, unless prohibited by contract, stock can be traded, usually through a stock exchange.

Origins of Securities Regulation

Concern about fraud in the sale of securities to the public led to state laws regulating the sale of securities. The first securities statute was enacted in Kansas in 1911. State securities laws are called **blue sky laws**, which comes from a Supreme Court opinion describing the purpose of state securities laws as trying to prevent "speculative schemes which would have no more basis than so many feet of blue sky." Promoters had gone door-to-door selling worthless securities. After their money and the promoters were gone, the buyers found that the securities had nothing backing them other than the "blue sky."

Beginnings of Federal Regulation Federal regulation of securities began during a time of economic catastrophe. The stock market crashed in 1929. It was followed by the Great Depression. A quarter of all jobs disappeared and national income fell by a third. Many people blamed the depression on the stock market crash, but in fact, the market was correctly forecasting the coming depression. Nevertheless, there was a common belief that manipulators on Wall Street needed to be controlled and, indeed, there had been abusive practices.

Congress quickly enacted statutes to regulate securities markets. Most important were the Securities Act of 1933 and the Securities Exchange Act of 1934. The 1933 Act regulates the public offerings of securities when they are first sold. The Act requires that investors be given material information about new securities, and it prevents misrepresentation in the sale of securities. The 1934 Act regulates trading in existing securities and imposes disclosure requirements on corporations that have issued publicly held securities. It and later statutes also regulate securities markets and professionals.

The Securities and Exchange Commission The Securities and Exchange Commission (SEC) is the agency charged with enforcing and administering federal securities laws. The SEC is a bipartisan, independent agency that has five members appointed by the president for five-year terms. One is appointed as chairman. The SEC's staff is composed of attorneys, accountants, financial analysts and examiners, and other professionals. The staff is divided into divisions and offices, with regional offices around the country.

What Is a Security?

Although Congress often provides vague guidance to regulators, forcing the courts and regulatory agencies to define the terms and the scope of the legislation, this was not the case in defining the term "security" in the 1933 Act. Congress provided a detailed definition. According to the 1933 Act, a security includes:

> *... any note; stock; treasury stock; bond; debenture; evidence of indebtedness; certificate of interest or participation in any profit-sharing agreement; collateral-trust certificate; preorganization certificate or subscription; transferable share; investment contract; voting-trust certificate; certificate of deposit for a security; fractional, undivided interest in oil, gas, or other mineral rights; or, in general, any interest or instrument commonly known as a "security"; or any certificate of interest of participation in, temporary or interim certificate for, receipt for, guarantee of, or warrant or right to subscribe to or purchase any of the foregoing.*

Despite this detailed definition of a security, both the courts and the SEC look to the economic realities of an investment transaction to determine whether it is a security. That is, just because something is called a stock does not mean it is a security that falls within the jurisdiction of the federal security laws. Similarly, other things with names not included in the list written by Congress may be securities.

Supreme Court's *Howey* Test

If an investment instrument is a security, it must comply with the legal requirements imposed on securities issuers. Note that investors have incentives to sue to have the court declare that an investment instrument is a security. If an investment instrument is a security, investors have a higher degree of legal protection than that given to investments not qualifying as securities. In the 1946 case *SEC* v. *Howey*, the Supreme Court established a test to determine when an investment is a security for the purposes of federal regulation.

The ***Howey* test** developed by the Court is still the critical test. An investment is classified as a security for the purpose of federal regulation if it contains four basic elements:

1. The investment of money
2. In a common enterprise
3. With an expectation of profits
4. Generated by the efforts of persons other than the investors

The Four Elements The first element, "the investment of money," means an investor turns over money to someone else for an investment. The second element, "in a common enterprise," means that the investment is not the property of an investor, such as a car would be. Rather, an investor's capital is pooled with other investors' money so that each investor owns an undivided interest in the investment. An investor who owns Ford stock, for example, does not have the right to go to a Ford factory and demand a truck equal in value to the money he invested in the company. An investor has a claim only to a share of future earnings as established in the securities contract. Even though stock owners, or shareholders, own a portion of the company, they own an *undivided* interest in the company. That is, the shareholders cannot divide company property among themselves, unless they agree to liquidate (sell) the company.

The third and fourth elements, the expectation that profits will be generated by the efforts of persons other than the investor, mean that investors do not have direct control over the work that makes the investment a success or failure. That is, a board of directors controls the future of the organization. They hire managers to run the company. If an investment meets this definition, it is a security, and must be registered with the SEC before it is sold to the public.

CYBER LAW

Securities Offerings on the Web

There is no technological reason why new securities offerings cannot be posted on the Web, and some have been. The Capital Markets Efficiency Act, which preempts state registration of offers to "qualified purchasers," provides an opportunity for such offerings to develop. They are much cheaper than traditional offers presented on paper that go through full-blown SEC review.

Soon after the Jumpstart Our Business Startups (JOBS) Act was enacted in 2012, "crowdfunding" became popular. Hundreds of websites sprung up to take advantage of the ability to sell shares in small companies without the costly, traditional review. More funds from investors over the Internet became available through platforms such as AngelList, which selects legitimate, but risky, startups for listing. Scam artists also moved in quickly.

Securities Exempt from Regulation Some new securities sold to the public are exempt from regulation. The most important securities exempted by both the 1933 and the 1934 Acts are debts issued by or guaranteed by a federal, state, or local government. The 1933 Act also provides an exemption for securities issued by banks, religious and charitable organizations, insurance policies, and annuity contracts. Most of these securities are subject to control by other federal agencies, such as the Federal Reserve System.

In general, an exempted security is not subject to the registration requirements of the federal securities statutes. However, the securities may be subject to antifraud provisions. For example, the SEC brought fraud charges in 2013 against an alleged charitable organization that raised $75 million from investors in a so-called non-profit firm that claimed it would pay a nice return and donate to assorted charities.

Offering Securities to Investors

The 1933 Act, sometimes called the truth-in-securities law, requires that, before a security is sold, sellers disclose to prospective investors all material information about the security, its issuers, and the intended use of the funds to be raised. **Material information** is all relevant information that an investor would want to know about a company—its background, its executives, and its plan of operation. Filing a registration statement with the SEC fulfills **disclosure requirements**.

Among other purposes, securities regulation is aimed at reducing investment scams that offer impossibly high returns and tempt investors to "beat the market." Among other purposes, securities regulation is aimed at reducing investment scams that offer impossibly high returns and tempt investors to "beat the market." Seemingly respectable Wall Street firms have run such operations, notably the one run by Bernard Madoff that lost billions. But many scams run under the radar. Some are preposterous, offering quick 100 percent rates of return. Others are more sophisticated and thus, more believable. In most cases, the money people invested is long gone. The *Latta* case illustrates why securities laws exist, but by no means do the laws prevent such operations that may seem to be legitimate.

LATTA V. RAINEY

Court of Appeals of North Carolina 689 S.E.2d 898 (2010)

Case Background *From 2001 through 2004, Mobile Billboards of America (MBA) sold billboard "investments." Sales agents presented potential investors with an "offering circular" that allegedly complied with federal and state regulations regarding such opportunities.*

Investors could buy a "billboard unit" for $20,000. The "unit" would be leased for seven years to Outdoor Media Industries (OMI), a shell company owned and operated by MBA's principals. Investors were told that OMI would place billboards on trucks for display. The investors would receive an average return of 13.49 per-

cent annually. At the end of seven years, MBA would buy back the billboards and return the initial investment.

To further "protect" investors, MBA claimed that it had a Reserve Guaranty Trust (RGT) to insure that funds invested would be secure. $5,000 of each $20,000 invested would be placed in the RGT. It issued a "Trust Secured Certificate" that entitled investors to a share of money earned by funds invested in RGT, plus the right to their full $20,000 investment.

Rainey, a "Certified Senior Advisor," was a sales agent for MBA in North Carolina. He discussed *investments with the Lattas, who were retired and living on float income. They wanted a secure investment. Rainey recommended MBA billboards as a "safe company" with "absolutely no risk." The Lattas invested $100,000 in 2003. Rainey filled out the paperwork and told them what to sign. He never revealed that he received a commission of 16 to 20 percent on the sale. The first year, the Lattas received "lease payments" from OMI. In fact, it was a Ponzi scheme, where investments from new investors were used to send payments to earlier investors.*

The Secretary of State of North Carolina investigated. On April 7, 2004, MBA was ordered to stop making sales. On April 21, Rainey, knowing of the order, collected the Latta's final investment. Later, the state sent cease-and-desist letters to all MBA agents in the state. Rainey sent investors a letter telling them he had retained a lawyer to protect their "best interests," that he would sue MBA, and they stood "first in line" to collect a judgment.

The Lattas and other investors sued Rainey and others involved in the MBA sales. While the case was pending, Rainey filed for bankruptcy, and Mr. Latta died. The bankruptcy court allowed the suit to proceed. The trial court held that the MBA billboard sales were unregistered securities in violation of federal and state law, that Rainey sold securities as an unregistered salesperson or dealer, that he breached his fiduciary duty to the Lattas, and that he was engaged in fraudulent concealment, securities fraud, and conversion. The jury awarded Mrs. Latta $95,503.40 in compensatory damages, $750,000 in punitive damages, plus attorney's fees and costs. The court reduced the punitive damages to $286,510. Rainey appealed.

Case Decision Hunter, Judge

* * *

With respect to the actual fraud and securities fraud claims, defendant fails to differentiate between the two types of claims, lumping them together into one argument.

The essential elements of actual fraud are: (1) "False representation or concealment of a material fact, (2) reasonably calculated to deceive, (3) made with intent to deceive, (4) which does in fact deceive, (5) resulting in damage to the injured party."

In contrast to the elements of actual fraud [North Carolina securities law imposes] civil liability upon any person who: "Offers or sells a security by means of any untrue statement of a material fact or any omission to state a material fact necessary in order to make the statements made, in light of the circumstances under which they were made, not misleading (the purchaser not knowing of the untruth or omission), and who does not sustain the burden of proof that he did not know, and in the exercise of reasonable care could not have known of the untruth or omission...."

A. False Representation or Omission of Material Fact Defendant claims that the only "arguable misrepresentation" is that he told plaintiffs that there was "very little risk" involved in the MBA investments and that the only "material omission" attributable to defendant is his failure to disclose to plaintiffs the amount of his sales commission. Defendant thus concedes that he made at least one false representation and omission.

In addition, however, plaintiffs point to the fact that defendant was aware that the "lease payments" OMI made to investors like plaintiffs was not revenue from selling advertising but were actually funds transferred from MBA from more recent investments. At trial, defendant explained that he did not tell his clients, including plaintiffs, about the source of the purported lease payments because, as he was advised by MBA management, if he had told his clients, "people would not have invested in it...." From his testimony, the jury could reasonably conclude that defendant misrepresented or failed to disclose to plaintiffs the actual source of the purported lease payments....

B. Intent to Deceive Defendant also argues that there is no evidence that he acted with any intent to deceive plaintiffs. In the context of actual fraud, the required scienter is not present without both knowledge and an intent to deceive, manipulate, or defraud....Whether the defendant acts with the requisite scienter for fraud is generally a question of fact for the jury.

With respect to defendant's misrepresentations concerning the level of risk involved in the MBA investments, the evidence presented at trial tends to establish that defendant was aware of the high level of risk in investing in MBA and that plaintiffs would not invest in MBA if they knew that it was contrary to their personal financial goals of preserving principal....

C. Reasonable Reliance Defendant also claims that plaintiffs failed to establish the element of reasonable reliance. Defendant argues that plaintiffs should be estopped from bringing their fraud claims because plaintiffs admit that they received and reviewed the documentation disclosing the risk involved in the MBA investments. This argument is premised on defendant's assertion that the only misrepresentation he made was the "low risk"

assessment of the investment and that the only omission he made concerned the size of his commissions; it ignores the evidence that defendant was aware that OMI and MBA were paying earlier investors with investment funds from later investors....

No error [affirmed].

Questions for Analysis

1. Do you think this kind of investment scam is uncommon?
2. Could stronger securities regulations prevent this from happening?

Registration of securities is intended to provide investors with sufficient information about important facts regarding the security interest that a company is proposing to sell. With that financial information, investors can make an informed decision about the merits of new securities before buying them. The projections are designed to assist people in evaluating securities.

The Registration Statement

The **registration statement** for a new security offering has two parts: The first part is the prospectus, a document providing the legal offering of the sale of the security. The second part is detailed information required by the SEC.

The Prospectus A **prospectus** (called Schedule A) condenses the longer registration statement provided to the SEC and helps investors evaluate a security. The first version of the prospectus not yet approved by the SEC is called a **red herring** because of the red ink on the first page. The Facebook stock offering stated, in part, in red, "The information in this prospectus is not complete and may be changed. Neither we nor the selling stockholders may sell these securities until the registration statement filed with the SEC is effective." This is used by securities brokers to interest potential investors in a forthcoming offering. Every prospectus provides material information about:

- The security issuer's finances and business
- The purpose of the offering
- The plans for the funds collected
- The risks involved in the business venture
- The promoters' managerial experience and financial compensation
- Financial statements certified by independent public accountants

Regulation S-K The second part of the registration statement has more detailed information than the prospectus. The SEC spells out detailed requirements in Regulation S-K. More history on the financial background and past experience of the issuers is required. There is also more information about the proposed business and the issuers. Investment analysts who want to see more detail may use this information, and the disclosure document is available for public inspection.

ISSUE SPOTTER
What Are You Selling?

Your family cattle business, like many, has had a hard time making a profit. Your idea is to let city folks buy a piece of a cattle herd. You will sell young cows to investors for the going market price. Your family will keep possession of the cattle, raise them, and then market them. After costs are deducted, such as food and transport, you will split any profit (per cow) 50-50 with its buyer. As there are about 800 cattle in the herd at any time, that is the maximum number of cows you will sell. Investors may buy as many cows as they wish, up to the maximum, and they are welcome to come visit the herd. Assuming everything is done honestly, could there be a securities issue here?

Review by the SEC

The SEC does not rule on the merits of an offering; that is, it does not give an opinion about the likelihood of success of a proposed business. But it can require issuers to make high-risk factors clear in the prospectus so as to put buyers on notice. The registration becomes effective 20 days after it is filed. However, if the SEC issues a deficiency letter, the issuer needs extra time to amend the filing to provide more detail in the registration materials. The SEC can also issue a stop order to prohibit the sale of securities until the registration statement is amended to satisfy the examiners, but this is not common.

The Costs of Registration The registration process is expensive. The prospective issuer must hire professionals, including a securities attorney, a certified public accountant, and a printer for the prospectus. There is also the expense of hiring an **underwriter**—an investment banker, such as Morgan Stanley—to market the securities.

Stock underwriting fees may be less than 1 percent of the value of a large stock offering sold to the public, but the fee may be as high as 10 percent for a small offering by an unknown company. To avoid such costs, companies sometimes consider selling through a transaction that makes the security exempt from the registration process.

Exemptions from Registration

Some securities, such as government bonds, are exempt from the securities laws. All other securities are subject to the securities laws, but may qualify for an **exemption from registration**. Only the initial sale of the securities is exempt from registration; the securities are not exempt from other parts of the securities laws.

Private Placement The 1933 Act provides that registration is not necessary for new securities not offered to the public. In some years, more money is raised through **private placements** than through public offerings. The primary users of the exemption are those placing large blocks of securities with institutional investors, most often pension funds or insurance companies. For example, IBM might sell $250 million in new bonds directly to Prudential Insurance and MetLife, rather than offering the bonds to the general public.

Rule 144A Private placements are most common for large security issues, usually bonds, sold to **qualified institutional buyers** (QIBs). Rule 144A exempts U.S. and foreign security issuers from registration requirements for the sale of bonds and stocks to institutions with a portfolio of at least $100 million in securities. Further, securities issued to such large institutions may be traded among similar institutions without registration or disclosure requirements. A significant share of all new offerings have been sold under this registration exemption; close to $1 trillion is raised some years through what is referred to as 144A debt.

Regulation D   To explain what qualifies as a private placement exemption, the SEC adopted Regulation D. Such offerings may be made only to **accredited investors**. These investors are presumed to be sophisticated and wealthy enough to evaluate investment opportunities without an SEC-approved prospectus. Only accredited investors may participate in private placement offerings of securities. Institutions, such as banks and insurance companies, are accredited investors. Individual investors must have an annual income of at least $200,000 ($300,000 for a couple) or a net worth of at least $1 million. All other investors are unaccredited. In theory, accredited investors are better able to protect themselves in securities transactions than other investors and so, are not as likely to need the disclosures.

The most common form of Regulation D offerings are called Small Corporate Offering Registration. Companies may issue stock directly to accredited investors, and according to Rule 504, a company may raise up to $1 million within 12 month. This can be done on the Internet, as can larger offers that fall under Rule 505 ($1 to $5 million) or Rule 506 (over $5 million). Most states similarly allow such offerings without going through the registration process. However, the SEC must be notified of the fact that the sale is occurring by filing Form D.

The rules about private placements are complex. Even though the offerings may be exempt from registration, there is usually a reporting requirement to the SEC about the offers, and the law requires that investors be given relevant financial information—called a private-placement memorandum. Also, restrictions are placed on the resale of securities bought by investors in private placements, which can reduce their value.

WKSIs   Most securities are issued by **well-known seasoned issuers** (WKSIs). Formally, these are securities issuers that have offered at least $1 billion in debt securities previously or have a public-equity market capitalization of at least $700 million. This includes most well-known securities firms. They can file registration statements the day they announce a new offering, rather than submitting it beforehand to the SEC; there is no need to wait for SEC staff review. This does not make their securities exempt, but simplifies the registration process and makes it consistent with EU (European Union) securities rules for such issuers.

Further, WKSIs may use a free-writing prospectus that allows them to continuously update information, and it may be done on the Web. The standards are the same as for a traditional formal prospectus, but this allows communication with potential buyers at any time. Such securities are said to be under a **shelf registration**. That is, once registered, they may be sold at any time over the next three years. This helps firms market securities when conditions are favorable and when the firm needs the cash, rather than sell the entire issue immediately.

ISSUE SPOTTER
Can New Start-Up Firms Issue Securities?

We have heard of companies, such as Facebook, that came out of nowhere. Assume you are involved with a new, small company looking to expand. To do that, you need capital. A regular securities offering is complex and expensive. Without a reputation, it is highly unlikely to work. Would a private securities offering be likely to work? How about an online offering?

Regulation of Securities Trading

The 1933 Act imposes disclosure requirements on corporations issuing new securities. The 1934 Act imposes disclosure requirements on securities that are publicly traded. A security registered under the 1933 Act must be registered with the SEC under the 1934 Act. Even if exempt from registration under the 1933 Act, a security must be registered under the 1934 Act if it is listed on a **securities exchange**, such as the New York Stock Exchange, or if it is traded **over the counter** (OTC), and the company has $5 million or more in assets and 500 or more shareholders.

Any company that issued traded securities is a **publicly held company** subject to reporting requirements. A company that has fewer than 500 shareholders and does not allow its securities to be openly traded is called a **private company**. Its financial information is not available to the public. A company can go from being publicly held to privately held by buying up its stock so that it is held by fewer than 500 shareholders. Many multibillion-dollar corporations are in this category.

Disclosure requirements apply to thousands of publicly held companies, most of which have securities traded in the OTC market. They must file reports on their securities. The most important report is the 10-K annual report, an extensive audited financial statement similar in content to the information provided in the registration process under the 1933 Act.

Companies must also file quarterly 10-Q reports with unaudited financial information and 8-K reports whenever significant financial developments occur. The purpose of these reports is to ensure disclosure of financial information to investors. It must all be posted on company websites or social media sites such as Facebook and must include details about executive compensation.

Regulation FD

The SEC adopted Regulation Fair Disclosure (Reg FD) to create a more "level playing field." It requires public companies to release material information to the public, rather than reveal such information selectively. Reg FD restricts the traditional practice of firms giving private briefings to big investors and favored securities analysts. Such meetings may occur so that analysts can better understand company operations, but any material information provided at such meetings must also be released to the public at the same time.

The regulation requires open disclosure of material information that is revealed to anyone outside the company. Public disclosure of material information can be made by filing Form 8-K or by distributing the information in a way "reasonably designed to provide broad, non-exclusionary distribution of information to the public," such as by press release or on the web.

Proxies and Tender Offers

Most shares of stock, besides representing a share of future profits of a company, carry voting rights to elect boards of directors and to determine responses to major issues facing the company. Shares carry extra value because of voting rights, especially when major events, such as a takeover, occur. The SEC ensures that fair voting procedures are followed.

Proxies   A **proxy** is permission given by a shareholder to another party to vote his shares in the manner he instructs. Because it is not practical for many stock owners to attend corporate meetings at which shareholders vote to approve major decisions—such as whether to merge with another company, elect the board of directors, and the like—shareholders are sent proxies to be voted on their behalf.

Firms provide shareholders with proxy statements containing information about major proposed changes in the business.

Proxies are also solicited in fights for control of a company when a contest occurs, usually by an outside group that wishes to dispose of the existing board of directors and take the company in another direction. SEC regulations spell out the form and timing that proxy solicitations must take.

Tender Offers When one company attempts to take over another, it often uses a **tender offer**. Stockowners in the target company are offered stock in the acquiring company or cash in exchange for their stock. If successful, the acquiring company obtains enough stock to control the target company. Tender offers must be registered with the SEC, and certain procedures must be followed.

Lighter Side of the Law

The Magic Pill

Firepower International, out of Perth, Australia, advertised the Firepower Pill. Pop one in your gas tank and you would get better mileage, emissions would fall, and your engine would last longer. Its secret formula burned "the heavier elements of your fuel" to produce these wonderful results.

Hailed as socially responsible, Firepower received grants from the Australian government and raised more than $100 million from investors before the fraud came apart, and the Australian Securities and Investments Commission shut down the operation. The Aussies are still trying to track down money stashed overseas and hope to recover, at best, 40 cents on the dollar.

Source: Wikipedia.

? *TEST YOURSELF*

1. An instrument issued by a company that specifies the amount owed, when and how payments must be made, and the rate of interest to be charged is called _____.
2. The Supreme Court has provided a test for when an investment instrument is a security that must comply with federal securities laws. This is called the _____ test.
3. The SEC requires public companies to release material information to the public rather than reveal the information to selected parties, so that everyone has access to the information at the same time. This is called Regulation Equal Disclosure: T—F
4. In *Latta* v. *Rainey*, where Rainey was sued by Latta for securities fraud because an investment that Rainey sold that turned out to be worthless, the appeals court held that Rainey was:
   a. liable for fraud for knowingly selling an unregistered security.
   b. liable only for losses incurred by Latta once the North Carolina securities regulators ordered sales to stop.

(Continued)

c. not liable for losses as he was unaware of the scam nature of the investment being sold, so was an innocent seller.

d. not liable as the security was properly registered, but was high risk; investors take chances with such deals.

5. Well-known seasoned issuers that have issued a large amount of securities previously are not held to the same standard when issuing securities as are new securities issuers: T—F

6. When a new security is going to be offered to the public, as part of the registration process, the issuer must prepare a(n) _____, which is a condensed version of the full registration providing material information about the security offering.

7. All securities that are issued, including government bonds, must follow the same registration procedure with the SEC: T—F

8. Individual investors who have a certain level of wealth and income may be offered stock in private placements; these are called _____ investors.

Answers: dept; Howey; F; a; T; prospectus; F; accredited

Securities Fraud

Disclosure requirements do not prevent the sale or trading of securities in risky or poorly managed companies. Rather, the securities law helps ensure adequate and accurate disclosure of material facts concerning the securities of a publicly traded company. Failure to follow the disclosure requirements may result in suits for **securities fraud**. Some securities fraud cases arise from false and misleading information in the original registration materials, but most arise from information obtained during later disclosure, such as public statements made by corporate representatives.

Basis for Securities Fraud

Because legal obligations are created in the sale of a security, an investor can rely on common-law fraud for protection. However, common-law fraud can be more difficult to prove than securities fraud. Thus, injured investors generally rely on the antifraud provisions of the securities laws.

Section 11 of the 1933 Act imposes civil liability for **misstatements**. These include misleading statements and material omissions in securities registration material. Any person who buys a security covered by a registration statement that contains false or misleading information that would reasonably affect an investment decision, or that omits information that was important to a decision to purchase, may sue to recover losses incurred in that purchase.

Rule 10b-5 Section 10(b) of the 1934 Act makes it illegal for any person "to use or employ, in connection with the purchase or sale of any security registered on a national securities exchange or any security not so registered, any manipulative or deceptive device or contrivance in contravention of such rules and regulations as the Commission may prescribe…." It provides the broadest base for bringing a securities fraud action, and it is used in litigation more than any other part of the Act.

The SEC adopted Rule 10b-5 to enforce Section 10(b) of the 1934 Act. The rule is broad in scope:

It shall be unlawful for any person, directly or indirectly, by the use of any means or instrumentality of interstate commerce, or of the mails, or of any facility of any national securities exchange,

1. *To employ any device, scheme, or artifice to defraud;*
2. *To make any untrue statement of a material fact or to omit to state a material fact necessary in order to make the statements made, in the light of the circumstances under which they were made, not misleading; or*
3. *To engage in any act, practice, or course of business which operates or would operate as a fraud or deceit upon any person, in connection with the purchase or sale of any security.*

The rule applies to all securities, registered or not. Because the rule does not state specific offenses, it has been left to the SEC and the courts to decide how strict the standards are.

Liability for Securities Law Violations

Investors who lose money in the purchase or sale of securities because of omission of material information or misleading statements may sue parties connected with the preparation of disclosure documents or other important information about the securities. This includes directors of the company: the chief executive, financial, and accounting officers of the company; and accountants, lawyers, and other experts who helped prepare disclosure material. All parties are held to high standards of professional care, so significant expenses are incurred in the preparation of such materials.

SEC Action The SEC may sue those alleged to be violating securities laws. SEC actions may be remedial, such as an order to issue corrected financial statements. Because SEC action is public, the parties involved are exposed to publicity. Injury to reputation in financial dealings can be costly as people are likely to shy away from future dealings with people involved in SEC suits. Further, SEC action may lead to private suits to recover losses attributed to the error in information.

The SEC can also recommend that the Department of Justice bring criminal charges against those accused of committing securities fraud. Penalties may involve fines and imprisonment.

Liability for Misstatements

Securities law imposes liability for misstatements or omissions (failure to reveal information) about the financial status of a business that has issued securities. Misleading information that would reasonably affect investment decisions by securities buyers and sellers includes misinformation about the present financial status or the future prospects of the enterprise that would affect the price of the security.

For example, overly optimistic statements by executives can cause expectations of higher profits, leading investors to bid up the price of the stock. When the statements are found to be false, the stock price falls, thereby imposing losses on those who bought the stock on the basis of the positive statements. This is one of the most common grounds for private suits seeking damages based on a claim of securities fraud. Directors and senior managers of businesses know they may be responsible for the consequences of misstatements they make that cause the price of the securities issued by their company to rise or fall.

Safe Harbor The Securities Litigation Reform Act of 1995 amended the law to protect companies from liability for predictions about profits and the likely success of the company, so long as forecasts are accompanied by "meaningful cautionary statements identifying important factors that could cause actual results to differ materially from those in the forward-looking statement." This is called a **safe harbor** because it gives greater immunity from suit for corporate forecasts that turned out not to be accurate after the fact, but were made with disclaimers.

Federal Exclusivity The Securities Litigation Uniform Standards Act of 1998 requires securities suits involving nationally traded securities to be brought exclusively in federal court under federal law. The 1998 Act prohibits the pursuit of a class action suit under the law of any state if the suit alleges: (1) an untrue statement or omission of a material fact in connection with the purchase or sale of a covered security; or (2) that the defendant used or employed any deceptive device or contrivance in connection with the purchase or sale of a covered security.

The Act was passed in an effort to reduce the huge number of securities suits brought claiming losses due to misrepresentation. The *City of Livonia* case is a typical suit brought by unhappy investors suing on the theory that their losses can be tied to false information.

CITY OF LIVONIA EMPLOYEES RETIREMENT SYSTEM V. BOEING COMPANY

United States Court of Appeals, Seventh Circuit, 711 F.3d 754 (2013)

Case Background *A class action suit was filed on behalf of all persons who bought Boeing stock between May 4 and June 22, 2009. The key allegation was that Boeing was overly optimistic about its ability to get the new 787 Dreamliner into service as planned. When technical problems became known after test flights and the official first flight was delayed, the stock fell 10 percent on June 23.*

The suit claimed that company executives made false statements about when the plane would get into service and thereby committed securities fraud. The district court dismissed the suit; plaintiffs appealed.

Case Decision Posner, Circuit Judge

* * *

The Private Securities Litigation Reform Act of 1995 altered the landscape of federal securities fraud litigation in [ways] that bear on our case. First, it requires a plaintiff who is complaining about "forward-looking" statements—predictions or speculations about the future—to prove "actual knowledge" of falsity on the part of defendants, not merely reckless indifference to the danger that a statement is false.

Second, the complaint must "state with particularity facts giving rise to a *strong inference* that the defendant acted with the required state of mind," rather than a mere inference. But except with regard to "forward-looking" statements, the Act does not specify "the required state of mind," so it remains scienter.

The Supreme Court has glossed "strong inference" to mean that "a reasonable person would deem the inference of scienter cogent and at least as compelling as any opposing inference one could draw from the facts alleged." The plaintiff therefore "must plead facts rendering an inference of scienter *at least as likely as* any plausible opposing inference." ...

There is no securities fraud by hindsight. The law does not require public disclosure of mere *risks* of failure. No prediction—even a prediction that the sun will rise tomorrow—has a 100 percent probability of being correct. The future is shrouded in uncertainty. If a mistaken prediction is deemed a fraud, there will be few predictions, including ones that are well grounded, as no one wants to be held hostage to an unknown future.

Any sophisticated purchaser of a product that is still on the drawing boards knows, moreover, that its market debut may be delayed, or indeed that the project may be abandoned before it yields salable product. The purchasers of the Dreamliner protected themselves against the possibility of delay in delivery by reserving the right to cancel their orders; there are no allegations regarding cancellation penalties, or for that matter penalties imposed on Boeing for delivery delays....

There is no duty of total corporate transparency—no rule that every hitch or glitch, every pratfall, in a company's operations must be disclosed in "real time," forming a running commentary, a baring of the corporate innards, day and night.

Of course the fact that a prediction *may* prove untrue does not justify representing as true a prediction that one knows, to a reasonable certainty, is false. But unless the complaint created a strong

inference that [top executives], who made the allegedly false statements about the timing of the First
Flight, knew they were false, there would be no fraud
to impute either to them or to Boeing. No other employee of Boeing is accused of having made such
statements within the scope of his employment,
thereby triggering corporate liability in accordance
with the doctrine of respondeat superior. ...

The judgment dismissing the suit is affirmed....

Questions for Analysis

1. Would the result be different if plaintiffs could show
   that company leaders knew for sure the plane was
   not as far along as was claimed?
2. If a report is filled with cautionary statements
   about the future, does that provide strong
   protection to a company and its executives
   against such claims?

Sarbanes-Oxley Act

Congress added new requirements to securities law in 2002 with the Sarbanes-
Oxley Act. It requires that the chief executive officer (CEO) and chief financial
officer (CFO) of large companies that have publicly traded stock personally certify
that financial reports made to the SEC comply with SEC rules and that the
information in the reports is accurate. Knowingly making a misstatement is a
criminal offense with fines up to $5 million and up to 20 years in prison. The law
also provides protection for corporate whistle-blowers who report securities
violations.

Sarbanes-Oxley (SOX) established the Public Company Accounting Oversight
Board, which has authority to set accounting standards and discipline CPAs for
misconduct. Accountants now have a direct incentive to ensure comprehensive
reporting of risks and costs. This has caused tension between firms and their auditors. Some financial reports have been delayed as accountants have insisted on dig-
ging deeper than usual.

SOX has forced many firms to standardize procedures and accounting, which in
some cases has benefited firms because CEOs now better understand procedures in
some areas that had been unclear before. One impact of the law was change in the
practice of backdating executive stock options in which a favorable date of a low
purchase price for stock is chosen after the fact. SOX revealed such dealings and
forced many firms to reveal what had happened. Many firms discontinued the
practice as a result.

Lighter Side of the Law

Try, Try Again

Eric Stein was sentenced to eight years in prison in 2001 for an investment scam in
Nevada that pulled in $34 million. Deeply in remorse, soon after his release he began
a new operation called Return-a-Pet. People who subscribed would have their pets
returned to them!

But it was all a scam that investors plunked down between $5,000 to $50,000 to
support. When sentenced to another five years in prison, he was also ordered to pay
restitution to "investors."

Source: Wall Street Journal Law Blog.

INTERNATIONAL PERSPECTIVE

London, New York, and the Sarbanes-Oxley Act

London and New York compete for financial business. Both attempt to lure firms to list on their stock exchanges, establish offices, and spend money on lawyers, accountants, and bankers. After World War II, the growth of the American economy and the greater financial depth of U.S. capital markets lured firms to shift operations from London to New York. Some publicly held firms established "dual listings," putting their stock on both New York and London exchanges.

When the United States raised the costs of a New York listing with the requirements imposed by the Sarbanes-Oxley Act (SOX), the cost-benefit calculation shifted. Companies reported that SOX caused their audit costs to increase significantly. A survey of companies with more than $5 billion in annual revenues found that compliance costs just for section 404 (which requires the outside auditors and management to both certify that the firm's internal controls over financial disclosures meet the law's standards) averaged about $5 million per year. Smaller firms bear even higher proportionate costs. Such costs shifted corporate business away from the United States to competitors such as London.

SOX had many important impacts. First, it made private equity markets more attractive compared to public markets like the New York Stock Exchange. After SOX's passage, there was a significant number of NYSE delistings as firms went private to avoid the costs of compliance with SOX.

Second, SOX raised the cost of listing a stock in the United States relative to other stock exchanges. A number of companies with listings on both U.S. stock exchanges and foreign exchanges dropped their U.S. listings. Driving securities business to other countries does not increase the safety of investments for U.S. citizens.

Third, a study by former SEC Chief Economist Ken Lehn found that SOX had a chilling effect on managers' willingness to take risks. Lehn found that U.S. companies reduced spending on R&D and on capital expenditures, compared to companies in the United Kingdom, and increased their cash holdings.

The impact of SOX on New York's competitive position was negative. The London Stock Exchange and its junior market, the Alternative Investment Market, attributed more than £17 billion ($26 billion) in initial public offerings on their markets to firms that chose London over New York because of SOX.

Insider Trading

Rule 10b-5 is used to prohibit **insider trading**—the buying or selling of stock by persons who have access to information affecting the value of the stock that has not yet been revealed to the public. As the Supreme Court has noted, misappropriation of private information gives insiders an unfair advantage in the market over investors who do not have the information. It is illegal for an insider to trade on inside information until that information has been released to the public, and the stock price has had time to adjust to the new information.

Besides company insiders, Wall Street executives are most likely to be affected by Rule 10b-5. Regardless of how information is released, investment firms are more likely to have valuable information concerning the financial status of companies. The SEC brings about 50 such cases each year. Some are high profile, such as the case against SAC Capital Advisors that resulted in the company paying a $616 million penalty in 2013.

In Rule 10b-5-l, the SEC defines insider trading to include trading "on the basis of material, nonpublic information, which means "the person making the purchase or sale was aware of the material, nonpublic information when the person made the purchase or sale." To be aware of the information means "having knowledge: conscious; cognizant."

Executives in a firm, who almost always are aware of such information, may trade stock in their company and not be liable for insider trading if they contracted at an earlier date to have another person buy or sell the security at a specific time or on a "program" basis; that is, to make trades at specific time intervals.

SEC Prosecution

The SEC may prosecute insiders if they trade in the stock before the public has a chance to act on the information or they pass the information on to others so they can act. For example, suppose an attorney working for General Electric found out that GE was about to announce the sale of $1 billion worth of jet engines to Boeing in two days. Knowing that this good news would make GE stock rise, the attorney buys some GE stock before the announcement. This is insider trading for which the attorney could be sued for all profits earned from the stock transaction as well as incur other penalties.

Supreme Court Interpretation

The Supreme Court started to clarify the rules about insider trading in the 1980s. In *Chiarella* v. *U.S.* (445 U.S. 222), the Court said that the defendant was not a corporate insider who owed a fiduciary duty to the shareholders of his company. He was an outsider who was lucky enough to learn inside information. He could be responsible only if his position had a requirement that he could not use such information. He may have had an unfair advantage over other stock traders, but it did not constitute securities fraud.

In a 1983 case, *Dirks* v. *SEC* (463 U.S. 646), the Court held that not all breaches of fiduciary duty in a securities transaction indicate securities fraud. There must also be "manipulation or deception" and, in insider-trading cases, there must be "inherent unfairness involved, where one takes advantage of information intended to be available only for a corporate purpose and not for the personal benefit of anyone." An example of how the court applies the law to insider trading is seen in the *Ginsburg* case.

U.S. SECURITIES AND EXCHANGE COMMISSION V. GINSBURG

United States Court of Appeals, Eleventh Circuit, 362 F.3d 1292 (2004)

Case Background *Scott Ginsburg was CEO of Evergreen Media. He met with the CEO of EZ Communication to discuss "strategic alternatives." Ginsburg told his brother, Mark, who bought 3,800 shares of EZ stock. Ginsburg talked to his father, Jordan, who immediately bought 20,000 shares of EZ. The next day, Evergreen and EZ began discussing a merger under a confidentiality agreement. Scott again called Mark and Jordan. The calls were followed by more purchases of EZ stock. When EZ's stock rose 30 percent, Mark made a profit of $413,000 and Jordan made $664,000.*

The SEC sued Ginsburg for securities violations for communicating material, nonpublic information to his brother and father. The jury found that Ginsburg violated the rule against insider trading and ordered him to pay $1 million in penalties. The trial judge set aside the verdict, holding that the evidence was insufficient to find that Ginsburg had tipped off his brother and father. The SEC appealed.

Case Decision Carnes, Circuit Judge

* * *

The district court stated that "the phone records are insufficient to compel an inference that Scott Ginsburg conveyed material, nonpublic information to Mark," but that is not the issue. The SEC did not have the burden of putting in evidence that compelled the inference Ginsburg conveyed non-public information to Mark. All it was required to do was put in evidence that reasonably permitted that inference. It did that. The call/trade pattern occurrences coupled with the jury's right to disbelieve the innocent explanations of the calls and trades are enough to support the verdict....

Ginsburg contends that the SEC did not provide sufficient evidence to permit a reasonable jury to find that the information tipped was material and nonpublic, as required by Rule 10b-5. "An omitted fact is material if there is a substantial likelihood a reasonable shareholder would consider it important in deciding how to vote." Materiality is proved by showing a "substantial likelihood that the disclosure of the omitted fact would have been viewed by the reasonable investor as having significantly altered the 'total mix' of information made available."...

The jury could recognize as material ... nonpublic information about a private meeting between executives and the specific share price they discussed confidentially....

The district court's grant of judgment as a matter of law is reversed and the case is remanded with instructions that the court reinstate the civil penalty of $1,000,000, and enjoin Scott Ginsburg from future violations of the securities laws and regulations.

Questions for Analysis

1. The appeals court affirmed the conviction for insider trading. The Ginsburgs denied that the phone conversations were about a likely merger between Evergreen and EZ, and there is no recording of the conversations, so how could Ginsburg be found liable for insider trading for passing on private information?
2. Why was this a civil case and not a criminal case?

Insider Trading Acts

The Insider Trading Sanctions Act of 1984 gave the SEC authority to bring enforcement actions, as in the *Ginsburg* case, against violators who trade in securities while in possession of material, nonpublic information. The courts may order violators to pay triple damages based on a measure of the illegal profit gained or the loss avoided by the insider trading. Those convicted of violations may also have to pay back illegal profits to those who suffered the losses. In addition, criminal penalties may be assessed.

This law was strengthened by the Insider Trading and Securities Fraud Enforcement Act of 1988, which increased the maximum fine to $1 million for persons convicted of violating the law against insider trading and set the maximum prison term at 10 years per violation. As amended by SOX, the fine against corporations was raised to $5 million per "willful" violation, and lengthy prison terms may be imposed. A corporation may be fined up to $25 million for non-willful violations. The SEC may pay bounties—up to 10 percent of the penalty the government receives—to informants who give leads that produce insider-trading convictions.

ISSUE SPOTTER
Can You Exploit the Gossip?

Riding the elevator 42 floors in a New York City building, you overhear two people from the headquarters of a company located in the building discussing the fact that tomorrow they will announce that their company will be bought by another company. Price is not discussed, but you know that in such cases, the stock of the company being purchased often rises 20 to 30 percent when the announcement is made. You can immediately buy stock in that company and probably profit nicely from the information you overheard. Could you be accused of insider trading? Is there a breach of fiduciary duty if you trade?

INTERNATIONAL PERSPECTIVE

European Approaches to Insider Trading

The United Kingdom passed insider-trading legislation in 1980 and brings about the same number of suits as the SEC does, given the size of the two markets. In the U.K., these cases are often referred to as market abuse.

After a scandal involving high-ranking government officials, France adopted insider trading rules in 1989, giving the *Commission des Operations de Bourse* stronger powers than it had under older statutes. However, there have been only a few administrative sanctions and a few serious prosecutions.

Italy enacted its first insider trading law in 1991. While the terms of the statute appear to be stringent, in practice, enforcement is minimal, and the law has significant loopholes. There were only two convictions in ten years, and in 2001, false accounting was reduced to a misdemeanor.

Germany did not pass a law against insider trading until 1994. The law is enforced by the *Bundes aufsichtsamt fur den Wertpapierhandel*, which obtained its first conviction in 1995.

Compared to the United States, where the SEC is very active in insider trading actions, European nations still show minimal concern. The *Wall Street Journal* reports that the head of the German Association for Shareholder Protection says that the organization gives evidence of abuses to the authorities, but "more than 95 percent end up not being investigated. The cases are often too complicated for prosecutors to handle. They've not been trained in these matters."

The Investment Company Act

The Investment Company Act (ICA) of 1940 gives the SEC control over the structure of investment companies. It requires them to register as such with the SEC and be subject to regulations regarding operations and holds them liable to the SEC, and to private parties, for violations.

Investment Companies

An **investment company** invests and trades in securities. The ICA defines three types of investment companies: face-amount certificate companies, which issue debt securities paying a float return; unit investment trusts, which offer a float portfolio of securities; and management companies, the most important type of investment company.

Mutual Funds

The most common investment management company is the open-end company, or **mutual fund**. In 1980, $52 billion was invested in mutual funds. That has risen into the trillions. Most mutual funds are open-end companies that offer no specific number of shares and can expand as long as people invest with them. The money from these shares is invested in a portfolio of securities. The price of the shares is determined by the value of the portfolio divided by the number of shares sold to the public.

There are load and no-load mutual funds. The former are sold through a securities dealer and have a sales commission (load) of some percentage of the price. No-load funds are sold directly to the public with no sales commission. All funds charge an annual expense fee that covers costs of operation, including management fees. The fee usually runs about one percent per year.

Investment companies that do not offer securities to the public but are involved in internal investing, such as banks and insurance companies, are exempt from the regulations imposed on investment companies that deal with the public. They are subject to regulation by the Federal Reserve or other agencies.

Regulation of Investment Companies

Investment companies register with the SEC, stating their investment policy and providing financial information. Annual reports and other information must be provided on a continuing basis. Capital requirements, including how much debt such companies may have, are set by the SEC. Payment of dividends to investors must equal at least 90 percent of the taxable ordinary income of the company. A company must follow the investment rules laid out in its policy statements.

Registration and Disclosure Because investment companies sell securities, such as shares in mutual funds, to buy securities for investment purposes, their securities must be registered. Hence, companies under the ICA are subject to the disclosure requirements of the SEC for publicly traded securities. The sales literature used by mutual fund companies to promote investment strategies must be filed with the SEC. In general, no share of stock in an investment company may be sold for more than its current net asset value plus a maximum sales charge (load) of 8.5 percent.

Limiting Conflicts of Interest To reduce possible **conflicts of interest**, there are restrictions on who may be on the board of directors of an investment company. At least 74 percent of the members of the board must be outsiders; that is, persons with no direct business relationship with the company or its officers. The outsiders on the board are responsible for approving contracts with the investment advisers who are hired to manage the investment fund offered.

Further, investment companies may not use the funds invested for deals with any persons affiliated with the company. All deals are to be at "arm's length." Most major brokerage firms prohibit research analysts from trading in the securities of the firms they cover. So a Merrill Lynch analyst who covers Intel may not buy and sell that company's stock while making recommendations about that stock to clients of Merrill Lynch.

The Investment Advisers Act

The Investment Advisers Act (IAA) defines **investment adviser** as a "person who, for compensation, engages in the business of advising others ... as to the advisability of investing in, purchasing, or selling securities." Investment advisers direct the investment strategies of mutual funds.

Investment companies hire investment advisers registered with the SEC to manage operations. According to the ICA, investment advisers are "deemed to have a fiduciary duty with respect to the receipt of compensation for services" rendered to investment companies. The standard fee paid to advisers to manage an investment company fund is about 0.5 percent of the net assets of the fund each year.

Brokers and Dealers

The IAA regulates brokers, persons who make transactions in securities for the account of others; dealers, persons who buy and sell securities for their own account; and advisers, persons who charge fees for investment advice. They are all securities professionals and must be registered with the SEC. Violations of SEC rules can lead to suspension or loss of the right to do business in the industry; this happens hundreds of times a year.

Lighter Side **of the Law**

The Fall of a Blood Brother

R. Allen Stanford ran a Ponzi scheme out of the country of Antigua for a decade. Investors lost about $7 billion. Regulators in Antigua had consistently asserted that Stanford's operation was fine. When the scheme collapsed, Stanford's number-two executive said that Stanford and Antigua's chief bank regulator had taken an actual "blood oath" of loyalty to each other. While apparently there was no blood oath with U.S. regulators, the SEC was offered evidence several times over the years that a scam was going on but no action was taken.

After Stanford's operation was shut down, and his private jet and gold-plated helicopter were taken away, he was forced to fly commercial. He complained that before getting on a flight, "They make you take your shoes off … it's terrible."

Sources: New York Times; National Law Journal.

Professional Responsibility to Clients Primary concerns of the SEC in regulating securities professionals are obligations to clients and conflicts of interest. The Supreme Court has held that broker-dealers must make known to their customers any possible conflicts or other information that is material to investment decisions. Professionals violate their duty when they charge excessive markups on securities to unsuspecting customers. Markups over 5 percent are difficult to justify. Over 10 percent is not allowed.

Illegal practices include **churning**. That occurs when a broker who has control of a client's account buys and sells an excessive amount of stock to make money from the commissions earned on transactions. Also illegal is **scalping**: when a professional buys stock for personal benefit, then urges investors to buy the stock so that the price rises to the benefit of the professional.

Another concern of the SEC focuses on ensuring investors adequate information about available securities to make informed investment decisions. Generally, professionals violate the antifraud provisions of the regulations when they recommend securities without making adequate information available.

Stock Market Regulation

The volume and value of stock transactions have grown significantly over the years. Because trillions of dollars are changing hands on the New York Stock Exchange and the other securities markets, investors want to be assured that proper safeguards are in place.

Self-Regulation of Securities Markets

The 1934 Securities Exchange Act allows private associations of securities professionals to set rules for professionals dealing in securities markets. Congress gave the SEC the power to monitor these self-regulating organizations, which include the stock exchanges, such as the New York Stock Exchange (NYSE), NASDAQ, regional exchanges, and the over-the-counter (OTC) markets.

Rules for Exchange Members The stock exchanges have rules of conduct for their members. Rules govern the operation of an exchange; how securities are listed; obligations of issuers of securities, who may handle certain transactions; and how prices are set and reported. Other rules include how investors' accounts are to be managed and the qualifications of dealers and brokers.

Governing the exchanges is the Financial Industry Regulatory Authority (FINRA). It is an independent regulatory authority that sets rules of behavior for its traders and handles most disputes. FINRA helps oversee more than 17,000 brokerage firms with more than 1.3 million registered brokers. Its 3,000 employees are concentrated in Washington, D.C. and New York, but there are district offices around the country.

Liability and Penalties Punishment for violating rules can include suspension or expulsion from the exchange. If an exchange knows that a member is violating the rules—or the law—and ignores such a violation, causing investors to lose money, it can be held liable for the losses. The potential liability and SEC pressure have given the exchanges an incentive to watch securities professionals for bad behavior.

Regulations of Securities Transactions

FINRA, in conjunction with the SEC, regulates securities professionals who handle the actual trading of securities. To reduce problems, floor trading by professionals is limited to registered experts, as is off-floor trading. The difference between these two types of trading is that one is done on the floor of a securities exchange, while the other is done elsewhere, such as OTC. In either case, the professional securities dealers may not trade for their own advantage ahead of their customers.

Regulations also cover specialist firms. These firms generally do not deal directly with the public; rather, they handle transactions for brokers. Brokers may leave customers' orders with specialists to be filled. For example, if a stock is selling for $21 a share, and a stockowner is willing to sell at $22 dollars, the order may be left to be filled should the price rise to $22. SEC rules prohibit specialists from dealing for their own benefit in the orders they execute. Because they are the first to learn of price changes, they could buy and sell the stock left with them to take advantage of changes in stock prices.

Arbitration of Disputes

When investors establish accounts with investment firms or stockbrokers, they usually sign a standard form that states that disputes must be arbitrated, not litigated. SEC rules govern the arbitration process, which is the primary dispute resolution mechanism for brokers and investors. Although arbitration records are secret, the decisions are made public on the FINRA website.

As is generally the case, the Supreme Court has upheld the arbitration agreements. It would be unusual for an investor to be allowed to litigate a dispute with a broker. The Court has held that the arbitration agreements apply to security fraud claims against brokers and that there is a "strong endorsement of the federal statutes favoring this method of resolving disputes."

Dodd-Frank Wall Street Reform and Consumer Protection Act

The Dodd-Frank Act, passed in 2010, established new regulatory authority. Despite the name "Wall Street Reform," the law has more to do with consumer credit regulation. The impact on the operation of securities markets has been smaller.

Dodd-Frank increases regulatory oversight of financial markets, but not in the way securities are issued or generally handled. Regulators are to oversee general market conditions and be prepared to act in case of crisis. There is oversight of "systemic risk"—that is, the kind of market-wide problem that could lead to a general financial meltdown as occurred in 2007–2008—by the Financial Stability Oversight Council. Regulators have more authority to intervene in financial institutions in case of impending trouble.

The trading of derivatives—the buying and selling of a wide range of instruments, including futures and options—is subject to greater regulatory oversight, in part by increased transparency under Dodd-Frank. Such instruments must be traded on open exchanges, such as the New York Stock Exchange, where the existence of the contracts are known. Such financial instruments are treated more like equities that are already subject to SEC oversight.

As we noted at the start of the chapter, investment scams are common. The intent of the securities laws is to help provide investors with reliable information to make better-informed decisions. But the regulations can not prevent many problems from occurring, so investors need be wary.

❓ TEST YOURSELF

1. The SEC's definition of securities fraud is provided in Rule _____.
2. Securities law imposes liability for misstatements or _____ about the financial status of a firm that has issued securities.
3. In *City of Livonia* v. *Boeing*, where investors claimed securities fraud by Boeing for failing to reveal possible problems with getting the Dreamliner in the air on schedule, the appeals court held that Boeing:
   a. knowingly hid unfavorable flight tests, so was liable to investors.
   b. did not report unfavorable flight tests to the SEC, but did so "innocently."
   c. was not shown to make improper false statements about the status of the plane.
   d. could not be liable because the SEC had approved all information filings as in compliance with SEC procedures.
4. Sarbanes-Oxley requires the CEO and CFO of publicly-traded companies to personally certify financial reports made to the SEC: T—F
5. In *SEC* v. *Ginsburg*, where Ginsburg was accused of insider trading, the Supreme Court held he was not liable because he had no fiduciary obligation to protect the inside information: T—F
6. The stock exchange engaged in self-governance under a private regulator called FINRA: T—F
7. Most disputes with brokerage firms are resolved through _____.

Answers: 10b-5; omission; c; T; F; T; arbitration.

SUMMARY

- Securities include any (1) investment of money (2) in a common enterprise in which there is an expectation of profits (3) from the efforts of persons other than the investors. This definition includes any investment device that meets these general criteria.

- Registration of new securities requires public disclosure of financial and managerial information and of future business plans with the SEC. Beausse the disclosure is complicated, and mistakes can lead to serious legal consequences, skilled counsel is required.

- Securities that are sold under a private placement exemption do not have to be registered with the SEC prior to sale. Most securities sold this way are large bond issues sold directly to institutional investors, such as insurance companies. Some smaller stock offerings are sold in limited numbers to accredited (wealthy and sophisticated) investors to avoid the cost of registration. These securities are subject to SEC regulation after their sale.

- Companies that have publicly traded securities must file financial disclosure information with the SEC, including quarterly and annual reports.

Production of these reports is costly and exposes a company's finances to the public, including competitors.

- Takeover attempts and proxy battles for control of a company are subject to SEC regulations, as are certain voting rights of shareholders.
- All securities are subject to the law concerning securities fraud, which arises from the common law of fraud. They are also subject to the securities statutes that are expressed by the SEC in Rule 10b-5, which applies to a wide range of activities related to the handling of securities.
- Liability may be imposed on securities issuers or corporate officials for misstatements in corporate documents, including statements to the media. Material information that misleads investors about a company and causes profits in a security to be lost may be the basis of legal action. Executives and those who work with sensitive financial matters must address company matters with a high degree of care.
- Insider trading can lead to criminal and civil prosecution under securities law as well as private

liability. Liability is imposed when insiders violate a fiduciary duty. If one is in a position of trust that provides access to valuable information, then one may not exploit the information for personal gain because there exists a duty to protect the information and use it for the benefit of those to whom the duty is owed: the shareholders.

- Securities professionals—brokers, dealers, and financial advisers—are regulated by the SEC and must meet certain financial requirements. Those who give investment advice only through an investment newsletter are not subject to regulation.
- Firms that trade securities for investors (brokerage firms), firms that make investments for investors (investment companies, such as mutual funds), and the stock exchanges are regulated by the SEC. Self-regulatory organizations impose rules on industry members that are subject to SEC approval. Violations of regulatory requirements are subject to civil and criminal penalties. The Dodd-Frank Act is intended to provide additional protections against dubious practices in the securities industry.

TERMS TO KNOW

security, 490
debt, 490
equity, 490
debt securities, 490
equity financing, 490
blue sky laws, 491
Howey test, 492
material information, 493
disclosure requirements, 493
registration statement, 495
prospectus, 495
red herring, 495

underwriter, 496
exemption from registration, 496
private placement, 496
qualified institutional buyers, 496
accredited investor, 497
well-known seasoned issuers, 497
shelf registration, 497
securities exchange, 498
over the counter, 498
publicly-held company, 498
private company, 498
proxy, 498

tender offer, 499
securities fraud, 499
misstatements, 499
safe harbor, 501
insider trading, 504
investment company, 506
mutual fund, 507
conflicts of interest, 508
investment adviser, 508
churning, 509
scalping, 509

DISCUSSION QUESTION

What is the difference in the legal protection for purchasers of registered versus unregistered securities?

CASE QUESTIONS

1. A developer announced that a new apartment building was to be constructed. To have first chance at a unit in the building, you have to deposit $250 per room. Each room was called a

share of stock in the building. If you wanted a six-room apartment, you had to buy six shares of stock and later pay the sale price or rental rate. The stock price was to be refunded at the time

you sold your apartment or quit renting and left the building. You could not sell the stock directly to another person. Is this stock a security? [*United Housing Foundation* v. *Forman*, 95 S.Ct. 2051 (1975)]
✓ Check your answer

2. PTL (Praise the Lord, or People That Love) was a nonprofit ministry run by James Bakker. Bakker and his wife Tammy had a TV show on which they discussed, among other things, the availability of "Lifetime Partnerships" in PTL that cost from $500 to $10,000. About 153,000 people bought the partnerships, contributing $158 million to the construction of Heritage USA, a Christian retreat center for families. Based on the amount they contributed, purchasers were promised a short annual stay at a hotel at Heritage USA. Contributors were told that the number of partnerships sold was limited. However, the partnerships were oversold, and much of the money was spent on other facilities and lavish living by the Bakkers. Was the sale of the partnerships securities fraud? [*Teague* v. *Bakker*, 35 F.3d 978, 4th Cir. (1994)]

3. For ten years, a certified public accounting firm audited the books of an investment company to prepare disclosure documents required by the SEC. The head of the firm was stealing investors' funds and rigging the books, and the accountants never found out. One day, the head of the firm disappeared, leaving behind a mess and many unhappy investors. The investors sued the accounting firm to recover the money they lost, claiming that the firm was liable for securities fraud. Who do you think prevailed? [*Ernst and Ernst* v. *Hochfelder*, 96 S.Ct. 1375 (1976)]
✓ Check your answer

4. Novell merged with WordPerfect by issuing Novell stock in exchange for WordPerfect stock. After the merger, Novell's stock fell 7 percent. Grossman sued in a class-action suit alleging false and misleading statements and omissions from Novell, in the filing with the SEC related to the merger, that caused the stock price to be artificially inflated before the fall. Grossman cited statements from the company that the merger was "perhaps the smoothest of mergers in recent history" and that WordPerfect was "gaining market share … from less than 20 percent in 1992 to more than 40 percent today [1994]," and that the merger created a "compelling set of

opportunities." Did the case have merit? [*Grossman* v. *Novell*, 120 F.3d 1112, 10th Cir. (1997)]

5. Plains Resources' executives reported that the company found an unusually large natural gas field. As a result, the company's stock was bid up from $7.63 to $29 a share in a few months. Insiders were told that initial estimates were too high, however, and they sold more than 30,000 shares of stock. Information about the lower estimates was then released, driving the price down to about $15. Shareholders sued, claiming that the executives traded on insider information and misled investors by not revealing bad information about the gas find more quickly. Was that securities fraud? [*Rubinstein* v. *Collins*, 20 F.3d 160, 5th Cir. (1994)]
✓ Check your answer

6. SG ran "StockGeneration," a website offering the chance to buy shares in "virtual companies" listed on SGs "virtual stock exchange." SG arbitrarily set the buy-and-sell prices of each stock in the imaginary companies and allowed investors to buy and sell any quantity at posted prices. Millions of dollars were collected by SG, but participants had trouble redeeming their shares. SG suspended operations, and the SEC sued, contending that the sale of shares in a company that was claimed to be a "game without any risk" that had an average increase in value of 10 percent per month was, in fact, a sale of an unregistered security in violation of the Securities Exchange Act. The district court dismissed the complaint, holding that the shares were clearly marked and defined as a game lacking a business context. The SEC appealed. Were these unregistered securities? [*SEC* v. *SG Ltd.*, 265 F.3d 42, 1st Cir. (2001)]

7. Fleming, a publicly held company, and several officers of the company, were sued by various stockholders for securities fraud for filing documents that were materially misleading. The stockholders contended that information failed to discuss litigation lost by Fleming that resulted in a damage award of $200 million, which led to the company's stock falling by about 25 percent. The stock price recovered some after part of the trial verdict was set aside, and Fleming settled the case by paying $20 million. Stockholders contended that failure to fully reveal the risks of that litigation caused losses to investors in Fleming stock. The district court dismissed the suit

because the plaintiffs failed to show that Fleming made deliberate and materially misleading statements or omissions. Stockholders appealed; did they have a case? [*City of Philadelphia* v. *Fleming Co.*, 264 F.3d 1245, 10th Cir. (2001)]
   ✓ Check your answer

8.   Gebhart was an experienced securities sales person. For several years he sold a security that was recommended to him by a long-time friend in the industry. The friend told him the security was approved by the compliance office at Mutual of New York, where both had worked previously. Gebhart relied on that statement and did not investigate the security, which in fact had not been reviewed by Mutual's compliance office. It was a scam that collapsed. Securities regulators barred Gebhart from the industry for life for failure to investigate. He appealed, contending he did not commit securities fraud as he had no knowledge of the scam. Does he have an argument? [*Gebhart* v. *SEC*, 595 F.3d 1034, 9th Cir. (2010)]
   ✓ Check your answer

ETHICS QUESTION

You started the Triangular Frisbee Company as a small operation. When the product went over big, you decided to seek outside funding to build a larger company. Your lawyer explained to you the costs of SEC registration and securities disclosure in the case of a public stock offering. Your lawyer also explained that you could avoid this by organizing as a corporation on the Caribbean island nation of Torlaga and selling stock in the corporation from there. U.S. investors would simply buy your stock through a Torlaga stockbroker. This would be much cheaper and quicker than U.S. registration. What are the pros and cons of this arrangement? Is it ethical to avoid compliance with American laws in this manner?

CHAPTER 19

Consumer Protection

Look at a bottle of pills. The instructions say something like, "the maximum dose is two pills three times a day." But does it make sense for a person weighing 100 pounds to take the same dose as someone weighing 250 pounds? What if the drug is given to a 40-pound child? While there are some specific drugs for children, for many older drugs the proper dosage is not known. Why did the drug companies not test for proper dosage on children? Regulatory requirements in the U.S. largely prevented those tests.

More importantly, the long-term safety effects of almost all drugs given to children are entirely unknown. Children often take drugs for asthma, depression, ADHD, and high blood pressure for years, but no one has established the effects of years of exposure on the developing brain. The FDA and other regulatory agencies face huge political pressures as they attempt to fulfill their missions. Long-term studies are expensive, and if appropriate tests on children were required, there would be a firestorm of opposition, so ignorance continues. The regulatory process is far from perfect.

In any event, drug regulation, like other consumer protection laws covered in this chapter, including credit regulation, affect liability for producers and the decisions made by consumers and producers.

The FDA: Food and Drug Regulation

The Food and Drug Administration (FDA) is charged with monitoring food and drug safety. About one-third of its $4.5 billion annual budget is devoted to food safety, sanitation, and processing. One third of the budget is devoted to the study of the quality of marketed drugs and new-drug evaluations. The rest of the budget supports the study of biological products, veterinary products, medical devices, radiological products, cosmetics, and the National Center for Toxicological Research. Besides a large research staff, every year more than a thousand FDA inspectors inspect thousands of establishments that have annual sales of greater than $2 trillion.

Food Safety

The control of safety in commercial food, drink, drugs, and cosmetics affects a large sector of the economy. It began with the Pure Food and Drug Act of 1906. For years afterward, the primary concern was food safety as there were many horror stories of food poisoning.

The 1906 Act focused on sanitation and misbranding of food and drug products. The Bureau of Chemistry of the Department of Agriculture performed food analyses for identification of misbranded or impure foods and administered the Food and Drug Act until the FDA was created as a separate agency in 1927.

FDA and USDA Standards and Inspections After a drug disaster in which many people were poisoned by a nonprescription medicine, Congress passed the Federal Food, Drug, and Cosmetic Act in 1938. The Act greatly expanded the regulatory power of the FDA by providing the agency with the power not only to extend the standards for foods beyond certain goods but also to prohibit false advertising of drugs, classify unsafe food, add new enforcement powers, form inspection systems, and set safe levels of additives in foods.

The U.S. Department of Agriculture (USDA) has primary responsibility for sanitation of meat, poultry, and eggs. It works closely with the FDA, Centers for Disease Control and Prevention (CDC), and the EPA on food safety issues. The FDA and USDA have detailed regulations concerning inspection of foods, and both agencies inspect food processors. The agencies have the power to bring criminal charges against those who do not comply with their safety standards, as the *LaGrou* case shows.

UNITED STATES V. LAGROU DISTRIBUTION SYSTEMS

United States Court of Appeals, Seventh Circuit, 466 F.3d 585 (2006)

Case Background *LaGrou's cold storage warehouse in Chicago kept raw, fresh, and frozen meat, poultry, and other food products. LaGrou did not own the food, but stored products for commercial customers. Two million pounds of food went in and out daily.*

The manager became aware that rats were a problem. He talked to the company president, Stewart, about the problem. Rats were caught daily, and food the rats had gnawed on was thrown away. Customers were not told about the rats; they were told food

damaged in shipment was destroyed. An expert said structural changes were needed to eliminate holes in the building to stop rats from entering. Stewart thought it was too expensive to fix.

USDA inspectors saw rodent droppings and other problems. The next day, 14 USDA inspectors came, as well as inspectors from the FDA and the Illinois Department of Public Health. The night before the inspectors came, LaGrou threw away a lot of food and did a thorough cleaning, but employees told inspectors what had *gone on. A huge number of violations were found. The warehouse was ordered closed, and 22 million pounds of food destroyed. LaGrou was convicted of three felonies, put on probation for five years, and ordered to pay $8.2 million in restitution and $2 million in fines. The president and manager of the company were also convicted. LaGrou appealed.*

Case Decision Bauer, Circuit Judge

* * *

While LaGrou argues that the infested area was limited to the warehouse basement, the evidence illustrated that the situation at the warehouse was dire. The USDA and other government agencies found dangerous conditions *throughout* the ... facility. Dr. Rose testified that LaGrou's warehouse was the

"worst case" she had seen in her 28 years with the USDA. She further explained that given the ventilation system in the warehouse, the pathogens and viruses could have become airborne. In addition, the leaking roofs, condensation from overhead pipes and ceilings, and dripping pipes found throughout the warehouse could have also carried food-borne pathogens.

Affirmed.

Questions for Analysis

1. The appeals court affirmed the conviction of the company for violating food sanitation rules. People, not companies, make decisions; so what sense does it make to convict a company?
2. Who would restitution be paid to in such a case?

Food Quality Protection The Food Quality Protection Act of 1996 states that the FDA is to ensure a "reasonable certainty of no harm" (no more than a one-in-a-million lifetime chance of cancer) from any source that affects foods, raw or processed, whether added directly, such as food coloring, or indirectly, such as pesticide residues. The Food Quality Protection Act also expanded FDA jurisdiction to thousands of pesticides used in food production.

Nutrition Labeling

The FDA regulates **nutrition labeling**. The Nutrition Labeling and Education Act of 1990 requires the FDA to issue nutrition labels for hundreds of thousands of products. The Department of Agriculture, which regulates meat and poultry, works with the FDA to have regulations for those foods that are consistent with the FDA rules. The intent is to prevent misleading product claims and to help consumers make informed purchases.

Nutrients by Serving Size FDA regulations list over 100 categories of food, from soup to nuts, whose nutrients must be listed by standard serving size as defined in the regulations. The following must be listed per serving portion on labels:

- Total calories and calories from fat
- Total fat and saturated fat
- Carbohydrates (sugar and starch separately)
- Cholesterol
- Calcium
- Fiber
- Iron
- Sodium
- Protein
- Vitamins A and C

Producers may list other nutrients, such as potassium, other essential vitamins and minerals, and polyunsaturated fat. Vitamins that are so common that there is no shortage in American diets, such as thiamin, riboflavin, and niacin, do not have to be listed.

Standards for Health Claims Food labels must meet standards for words commonly used so that consumers can learn more about what they are buying. For example, "fresh" refers to raw food that has not been processed, frozen, or preserved; "low fat" means three or fewer grams of fat per serving and per 100 grams of the food; "low calorie" means fewer than 40 calories per serving and per 100 grams of food; and "light" or "lite" may be used on foods that have one-third fewer calories than comparable products. Similarly, for "organic" to be used in advertising a food, it must meet FDA and USDA specifications.

Further, health claims that are not well established, such as the claim that fiber reduces heart disease and cancer, may not be made unless sufficiently documented by the seller. The food health claims that may be noted on labels involve the health connection between calcium and the prevention of osteoporosis (weak bones), sodium (salt) and high blood pressure, fat and heart disease, and fat and cancer.

Lighter Side **of the Law**

Maybe Get a New Laptop

Dr. Armando Angulo was accused of being at the center of a large prescription drug fraud. He fled to Panama when indicted in Florida. Panama will not extradite him to the U.S.

The Drug Enforcement Administration decided later to drop the charges because the 400,000 paper documents and two terabytes of data took up 5 percent of the DEA's antiquated computer space. Plenty of evidence, but too costly to keep.

Source: Associated Press.

Drug Safety

Until 1938, drug controls existed to protect against quacks, false claims, mislabeling, and the sale of dangerous drugs such as heroin. The Food, Drug, and Cosmetic Act provided regulators with new powers. Those powers have been expanded over the years. The Act prohibits the sale of any drug until the FDA gives approval. An applicant must submit evidence that the drug is safe for its intended use. This prevents the sale of untested drugs in a market that generates $300 billion per year in sales.

A critical issue for a seller is whether its product is classified as a drug. This has become a major issue for the nutrition supplement industry. Its sales are largely unregulated. If a dietary supplement seller goes too far in its claims, then the FDA may classify the product as a drug, which makes it subject to significant regulations.

Designation of Prescription Drugs Before the 1938 Act, no drugs were designated as **prescription drugs**—that is, drugs that could used only with the permission of a physician. Drugs were either legal or illegal. Since 1938, the FDA has determined which drugs are prescription drugs; these are sold by pharmacies only with a physician's permission.

Drug Effectiveness Testing The **Kefauver Amendment** of 1962 requires the FDA to approve drugs based on their proven effectiveness—not just on their safety. The FDA has strict regulations concerning the testing process and adoption of new drugs. It costs

INTERNATIONAL PERSPECTIVE

Global Drug Controls

The United States sets the international standard for drug production. FDA standards are generally tougher than those in Europe or Japan, so anything that has made it through the FDA process is likely to be accepted worldwide. Foreign producers who wish to sell in the United States must meet FDA standards and allow inspection of facilities.

FDA-approved drugs are the gold standard. Development costs are so high that producers must charge high prices to cover investments. People in low-income countries cannot pay U.S. prices, so the firms sell drugs for less in such places. Governments in some nations, such as Canada, buy all the drugs for their markets and bargain with the drug companies, so drug prices in those countries are a little lower (but not much for most drugs).

Foreigners expect drugs that carry the name of a U.S. maker to be high quality, but forgery is common.

Some forgeries are good-quality illegal copies, but others are random ingredients mashed together and sold as the real thing. More than 50 people in Panama died from a cough syrup from China that contained a poison.

People waste money and injure their health taking worthless drugs they think are real. Some drug producers in China send the Chinese FDA real U.S. drugs, claiming they represent their products. The Chinese agency knows there are major problems in the Chinese drug industry, but cannot control tens of thousands of products on the market, especially when the agency has been known to take bribes to grant approval for products to enter the market. The head of the Chinese State Food and Drug Administration was executed a few years ago for taking bribes. When the regulatory process is corrupt, it can be worse than no regulation at all.

© Cengage Learning

more than $1 billion, and takes 10 to 15 years to develop many new drugs and to clear all FDA hurdles before a new product can be marketed.

A new compound averages three to six years in the making before the preclinical development stage. Only about 1 in 5,000 new compounds gets this far. The potential drug then goes to Phase I tests on 100 or fewer patients to determine the maximum tolerated dosage and likely side effects. If the drug still shows promise, in Phase II several hundred patients are tested to identify stages of the disease affected by the therapy. If approved, it goes to Phase III for testing on several thousand patients so comparisons can be made to existing drugs and placebos. Phase I, II, and III testing takes an average of seven years. Ninety percent of the drugs that get that far do not make it to final FDA approval, meaning that only 1 in 50,000 new compounds developed in the lab make it to market.

Medical Devices The FDA is also responsible for oversight of medical devices. A medical device is an instrument, machine, implant, or other article used in the diagnosis or treatment of a disease in humans or animals. Each one is assigned to a class based on the level of control needed to assure safety.

Class I devices present minimal potential for harm to the user and are usually of simple design, such as bandages and gloves. The makers are registered with the FDA, and the goods must be properly manufactured and labeled, but they are not subject to extensive controls. Class II devices are subject to special controls. In addition to assurances about manufacturing quality and proper labeling, there are performance standards and surveillance of the devices once in use. The devices are generally noninvasive, including X-ray machines, wheelchairs, and surgical materials. Class III devices are the most controlled. The FDA must give approval prior to marketing, and the agency tracks the devices once on the market to watch for problems that may require recalls. Examples include heart valves and bone implants.

Liability for Problems Does FDA approval of a drug reduce the liability of the producers if the drug creates problems? The courts give weight to the protection offered by the regulatory process. The number of liability suits from consumers injured by side effects of a drug is reduced because some effects are not preventable given the state of technology. But FDA approval is only evidence of safety, not a shield against liability. Can state tort law impose warning-label standards on FDA-approved drugs that vary from those required by the FDA? The Supreme Court reviewed this issue in the *Wyeth* v. *Levine* case.

WYETH V. LEVINE

United States Supreme Court 129 S.Ct. 1187 (2009)

Case Background *Phenergan is a drug approved by the FDA in 1955. The FDA also approved its use label. One form of Phenergan is used to treat nausea. It can be administered either by the "IV-push" method, where the drug is injected intravenously into a patient's vein, or by the "IV-drip" method, where it is administered intravenously using a drip feed in a saline solution.*

Diane Levine had Phenergan by IV-push into a vein to treat nausea. Because the needle penetrated an artery, she developed gangrene, a known problem from the IV-push injection. As a result, her forearm and hand were amputated.

Levine sued Wyeth in state court in tort for failure to warn. She requested damages for medical expenses and for the loss of her livelihood as a professional musician. She contended that the label on the drug was defective because, while it warned of the gangrene risk from IV-push, it did not instruct that the IV-drip method should be used. That is, Wyeth had a duty to instruct that the IV-drip method be used. Wyeth argued that federal law preempted the claims.

The trial court rejected that argument and found for Levine. The Vermont Supreme Court upheld the verdict. Wyeth appealed, contending that FDA approval of the drug use label under the Food, Drug, and Cosmetic Act (FDCA) should prevent the claim under state law.

Case Decision Stevens, Justice

* * *

The question presented by the petition is whether the FDA's drug labeling judgments "preempt state law product liability claims premised on the theory that different labeling judgments were necessary to make drugs reasonably safe for use."

* * *

Wyeth first argues that Levine's state-law claims are pre-empted because it is impossible for it to comply with both the state-law duties underlying those claims and its federal labeling duties. The FDA's premarket approval of a new drug application includes the approval of the exact text in the proposed label. Generally speaking, a manufacturer may only change a drug label after the FDA approves a supplemental application. There is, however, an FDA regulation that permits a manufacturer to make certain changes to its label before receiving the agency's approval. Among other things, this "changes being effected" (CBE) regulation provides that if a manufacturer is changing a label to "add or strengthen a contraindication, warning, precaution, or adverse reaction" or to "add or strengthen an instruction about dosage and administration that is intended to increase the safe use of the drug product," it may make the labeling change upon filing its supplemental application with the FDA; it need not wait for FDA approval....

... Wyeth could have revised Phenergan's label even in accordance with the amended regulation. As the FDA explained in its notice of the final rule, "'newly acquired information'" is not limited to new data, but also encompasses "new analyses of previously submitted data." The rule accounts for the fact that risk information accumulates over time and that the same data may take on a different meaning in light of subsequent developments.

... It has remained a central premise of federal drug regulation that the manufacturer bears responsibility for the content of its label at all times. It is charged both with crafting an adequate label and with ensuring that its warnings remain adequate as long as the drug is on the market....

Of course, the FDA retains authority to reject labeling changes made pursuant to the CBE regulation in its review of the manufacturer's supplemental application, just as it retains such authority in reviewing all supplemental applications. But absent clear evidence that the FDA would not have approved a change to Phenergan's label, we will not conclude that it was impossible for Wyeth to comply with both federal and state requirements....

In keeping with Congress' decision not to pre-empt common-law tort suits, it appears that the FDA traditionally regarded state law as a complementary form of drug regulation. The FDA has limited resources to monitor the 11,000 drugs on the market, and manufacturers have superior access to information about their drugs, especially in the post-marketing phase as new risks emerge. State tort suits uncover unknown drug hazards and provide incen-

tives for drug manufacturers to disclose safety risks promptly. They also serve a distinct compensatory function that may motivate injured persons to come forward with information. Failure-to-warn actions, in particular, lend force to the FDCA's premise that manufacturers, not the FDA, bear primary responsibility for their drug labeling at all times. Thus, the FDA long maintained that state law offers an additional, and important, layer of consumer protection that complements FDA regulation....

We conclude that it is not impossible for Wyeth to comply with its state and federal law obligations and that Levine's common-law claims do not stand as an obstacle to the accomplishment of Congress' purposes in the FDCA. Accordingly, the judgment of the Vermont Supreme Court is affirmed.

Question for Analysis

1. The dissent argued that the FDA was far more qualified than a state court jury to decide what drug warning was adequate. Expert analysis, under a regulatory scheme, which determined that the instructions were "safe" and "effective" should control the outcome, not the judgment of non-experts. Do you think that position has merit?

What if a drug is given to a patient improperly? The drug company is not likely to be liable, assuming it has given proper dosage instructions. If a physician ignores the instructions and changes the recommended dosage, or gives a drug in a situation that is not proper, and an injury results, the drug manufacturer is often shielded from liability by the **learned intermediary doctrine**. That is, the learned intermediary—the physician—would be liable for misuse of the product.

Enforcement Activities

Besides deciding when drugs are marketed, the FDA can force existing products, including food, cosmetics, and medical devices, to be removed from the market if claims are misleading or if new information becomes available that indicates the product was not as safe as previously thought. The FDA forces hundreds of products off the market each year and seizes thousands of import shipments.

ISSUE SPOTTER
How Much Can You Hype Health Supplements?

Your store sells "health foods" and many "health supplements," such as vitamins and herbs. It is common for new claims to be made about products. Several years ago, shark cartilage (ground up shark bones) was touted as preventing cancer. Many products grow popular at first, then fall by the wayside when the alleged benefits become less clear. For example, if the media reports that eating seaweed from the coast of Brazil can help prevent senility, can you repeat such a claim? Do you have the right to advertise a product for having such a benefit? Can you get in trouble for going too far to promote a product?

While enforcement has become tougher, the FDA has been allowing quicker approval for drugs that show some promise in life-threatening diseases such as AIDS. Rather than require the full, lengthy review process before the drugs may be sold to informed patients, the FDA allows the drugs to be carefully distributed.

? TEST YOURSELF

1. Nutrition labels, unlike drug labels, are primarily under the supervision of the USDA: T—F
2. In *United States* v. *LaGrou Distribution Systems*, the appeals court held that the USDA could shut down an unclean food facility and that the head of the company could be convicted of a felony: T—F
3. Since 1938, the FDA has had the authority to decide if a drug will be sold over the counter or if it will be sold only as a(n) _____ drug under the supervision of a physician.
4. In *Wyeth* v. *Levine*, where Levine lost an arm due to improper injection of a drug, and sued the maker of the drug, the Supreme Court held that drug makers are:
   a. immune from all liability claims if the FDA has approved the drug.
   b. immune from suit for claims that drug instructions are defective if the drug instructions were under FDA supervision.
   c. potentially liable if a defect in drug manufacturing can be shown, but not for improper administration of a drug.
   d. potentially liable for improper warnings about proper administration of a drug.
5. If a food product makes false claims about its contents, the FDA has the ability to have the product seized and removed from the market: T—F

Answers: F; T; prescription; d; T.

The FTC and Consumer Protection

The Federal Trade Commission (FTC) was established in 1915 to help enforce the antitrust laws (Chapter 20), but the FTC also devotes resources to its Bureau of Consumer Protection, which handles matters such as deceptive business advertising and marketing practices. Some responsibilities are specifically ordered by Congress, such as the consumer credit statutes. But most consumer protection efforts evolve as the FTC decides what Congress meant when it amended the FTC Act in the 1930s and said, in Section 5, that "unfair and deceptive acts or practices in or affecting commerce are hereby declared unlawful."

Based on experience and in response to pressure from Congress, the FTC investigates practices said to be unfair and deceptive. The FTC staff proposes complaints to the five commissioners, who decide by majority vote whether to issue a complaint. The complaint begins legal proceedings against a business engaged in practices the commission wants ended or modified.

Many complaints are settled by a **consent decree** agreed to by a party charged in an FTC complaint. The decree contains the terms of a settlement, which frequently include prohibition of certain practices, redress for consumers, and payment of civil penalties. Some cases result in administrative trials at the FTC. If the accused party or the FTC attorneys are not satisfied with the decision of the administrative law judge, they may appeal to the commissioners for review. An accused party who is not satisfied with the decision of the commissioners may appeal to a federal court of appeals.

Lighter Side of the Law

Protect Me from Myself!

Gary Null is described on *Quackwatch.com* as "one of the nation's leading promoters of dubious treatment for serious disease." He is the author of *The Joy of Juicing* and the marketer of many "health products" including "Gary Null's Ultimate Power Meal." It is loaded with Vitamin D.

Null sued Triarco Industries, manufacturer to *his* specifications of *his* "Ultimate Power Meal," for his "near-death experience" from consuming too much Vitamin D. His suit claims that Triarco should have tested the effects of high levels of Vitamin D because of the "excruciating fatigue" he experienced from his two servings a day.

Source: New York Daily News.

Unfair and Deceptive Acts or Practices

Congress ordered the FTC to fight "unfair and deceptive acts or practices." The lack of a clear definition for those terms means the FTC has leeway in deciding what cases to bring—what advertising is deceptive and what sales practices are unfair. The key term has always been "deceptive." Essentially, things held to be deceptive are also unfair, a term defined below.

Policy Statement on Deception To give the FTC staff guidance, the commissioners adopted a *deception policy statement* that summarizes a three-part test for deciding whether a particular act or practice is deceptive. There is **deception** if the following are true:

1. There is a misrepresentation or omission of information in a communication to consumers.
2. The deception is likely to mislead a reasonable consumer.
3. The deception is material; that is, it is likely to be misleading to the detriment of consumers.

Here are some points about what these points mean in practice:

- Omissions, or failure to reveal information, are not deceptive if there is no affirmative misrepresentation (false statement) or practice that takes advantage of consumer misunderstanding.
- To decide if an omission or representation (claim or statement) is deceptive, the FTC looks at what has been presented to consumers. Words in an advertisement are examined in the context of the entire ad, and consideration is given to evidence about what consumers think the ad means.
- A reasonable consumer is an "ordinary person" in the target audience of the advertisement. Hence, ads directed at children or ill people are held to a tougher standard.
- The false representation or omission is likely to affect a consumer's product choice.
- No proof of injury to consumers—usually financial loss—is needed if there is evidence that such injury is likely to occur, given the practice in question.

Defining Unfairness Section 5 of the FTC Act says "unfair or deceptive acts or practices in or affecting commerce, are declared unlawful." **Unfairness** is usually added to a charge of deception. The FTC has given operational meaning to unfair acts or practices in business by issuing a policy statement that gives a consumer injury standard:

1. It causes substantial harm to consumers.
2. Consumers cannot reasonably avoid injury.
3. The injury is harmful in its net effects.

That is, when the costs and benefits of the goods are compared, they are negative, so there is economic injury to the consumer.

The following are examples of FTC enforcement actions regarding different kinds of consumer-oriented scams:

Telemarketing Fraud The FTC obtained an injunction against five telemarketing firms for making misrepresentations in the sale of water purifiers and home security systems. The companies mailed postcards telling consumers they had won valuable awards, including $5,000 worth of merchandise. In fact, the "awards" were only certificates that required payment of large sums of money to get the goods. The telemarketers also made charges against consumers' credit cards without permission and billed customers for goods never sent.

Telemarketers are subject to the Telephone Consumer Protection Act and the Telemarketing and Consumer Fraud and Abuse Prevention Act that resulted in the FTC's Telemarketing Sales Rule. This allows consumers to sue telemarketers if they make telemarketing calls in violation of consumer instructions to be removed from call lists. If a consumer places a phone number on the National Do Not Call Registry, then it is improper if a company calls unless the consumer has had a business relationship with the company.

Oil and Gas Well "Investments" Several companies were involved in oil and gas well lease scams. More than 8,000 people invested $5,000 to $10,000 each in application fees to participate in a lottery for oil and gas rights on federal lands. The FTC obtained $47 million in refunds. Not only were the promoters sued, so were all the companies that worked with them in the scheme, such as banks and accounting firms. Because these "investments" were not securities, they did not fall under SEC jurisdiction.

Work-at-Home Opportunities A federal appeals court upheld a $16 million judgment against a company and its officers in *FTC* v. *Febre* (128 F.3d 530) for deceptive practices in four different work-at-home "opportunities." One involved mailing postcards, which supposedly could earn someone up to $15,000 per day. Almost 200,000 consumers paid the promoters more than $13 million, which was ordered rebated to the consumers, plus $3 million in damages.

Invention-Promotion Scams   The FTC sued 12 companies that raked in $90 million by claiming that they were consultants who help people make deals for valuable new inventions. "Project Mousetrap" discovered that people paid between $10,000 and $20,000 each to get "expert advice" in licensing and marketing such things as a toothbrush with bristles at both ends and a device that collects the shavings scratched off lottery tickets. While the operations were closed, only $250,000 remained for consumer redress.

As the *Federal Trade Commission* v. *John Beck Amazing Profits* case indicates, the courts tend to give the FTC substantial leeway in closing down operations that can fall under the general terms of unfair and deceptive operations. Restitution for consumers can be included, but scam operators rarely have enough money to pay much.

FEDERAL TRADE COMMISSION V. JOHN BECK AMAZING PROFITS, LLC

United States District Court, Central District, California
865 F.Supp.2d 1052 (2013)

Case Background *Beginning in 2004, several "wealth-creation" products were sold through infomercials and on the Internet. One was the "John Beck System" that promised to teach buyers how to get real estate cheap. Consumers paid $39.95 per month by credit card to receive an information kit and be a member of a "club" unless they took steps to cancel the membership.*

The FTC moved in 2009 to shut down the operations, alleging multiple violations of the Federal Trade Commission Act (FTCA). The FTC sought injunctive relief and monetary damages for customers of $300 million. It moved for summary judgment. Defendants objected.

Case Decision Jacqueline H. Nguyen, District Judge

* * *

Section 5 of the FTCA prohibits "unfair methods of competition in or affecting commerce ... and unfair or deceptive acts or practices in or affecting commerce...."

In demonstrating that a representation is likely to mislead, the FTC must establish that (1) such representation was false or (2) the advertiser lacked a reasonable basis for its claims. ...

The FTC alleges that in connection with the John Beck system, Defendant Beck, the "guru" of the system, and Defendants ... have expressly or implicitly represented that consumers who purchase and use the John Beck System are likely to be able to: (1) purchase homes, at government tax sales in their area, "free and clear" of all mortgages or liens, for just "pennies on the dollar;" (2) earn substantial amounts of money renting or selling homes they purchase at government tax sales; and (3) quickly and easily earn substantial amounts of money with little financial investment. The FTC claims that these representations were material and were either false or unsubstantiated at the time they were made. ...

The falsity of these representations is confirmed by the kit materials. Specifically, the materials teach consumers how to purchase tax liens and certificates, but the purchaser of a tax lien or certificate does not walk out of the tax sale with a deed or the right to turn around and sell the property. Instead, consumers have a right to collect delinquent taxes, and only in exceptional circumstances will the purchaser of a tax lien end up with title and the right to possess or sell the property. Additionally, tax sales are held only once a year and bidding typically starts at a very high percentage of the current fair market value of the property....

The falsity of the infomercials' representations is also confirmed by dozens of consumer witnesses, who testified that it is difficult or impossible to find government tax sales in their area, and it is difficult or impossible to earn substantial money by purchasing homes or land using the John Beck System. These consumers had to invest a significant amount of money if they were going to be able to use the system for a profit....

The Court finds that the misrepresentations in the John Beck infomercials are material, and no reasonable trier of fact could conclude that the misrepresentations were not likely to mislead consumers acting reasonably under the circumstances. Accordingly, summary adjudication ... is granted....

Questions for Analysis

1. Other schemes that were attacked almost never generated revenues for the buyers either. Why would people fall for such get-rich-quick schemes?
2. Do First Amendment free speech protections apply to such sales techniques?

Regulating Advertising Claims

Advertising has been defined as "the act ... of attracting public notice and attention. It includes all forms of public announcement that are intended to aid ... in the furtherance ... of directing attention to a business, commodity, service or entertainment." Legitimate advertisers and businesses have long advocated cracking down on false advertising. The FTC policy about advertising states that:

- Advertising must be truthful and nondeceptive.
- Advertisers must have evidence to back up their claims.
- Advertisements cannot be unfair.

To put this into effect, the FTC uses the **advertising substantiation program**. It requires advertisers and advertising agencies to have a reasonable basis before they make claims. When advertisers claim "studies show" or "tests prove," they must actually have evidence that provides a reasonable basis for the claims. The FTC considers the following factors to determine what a reasonable basis is:

- The kind of product
- The type of claim
- The consequences of a false claim and the benefits of a truthful claim
- The cost of developing substantiation for the claim
- The amount of substantiation that experts believe is reasonable

What Advertising Is Deceptive? Years ago, the FTC commissioners said: "Perhaps a few misguided souls believe ... that all 'Danish pastry' is made in Denmark. Is it therefore an actionable deception to advertise 'Danish pastry' when it is made in this country? Of course not." The point is that some people may misunderstand certain advertisements, but that does not mean that the FTC is always concerned. For example, hair dye is often advertised as "permanent." Someone may think it means that their hair will be the color of the dye forever, but no deception is involved. Most consumers know what is meant, and those who do not understand do not incur significant injury. The focus is on likely injury to the target of advertisements.

Examples of Deceptive Ad Cases Gateway Educational Products settled FTC charges that the claims about the ability of its "Hooked on Phonics" program to teach reading, including those with learning disabilities, were unsubstantiated. The FTC contended that consumer testimonials did not represent typical experiences. Experts on reading disability said that phonics instruction might not help people with dyslexia or other reading disabilities. The producer promised to stop the challenged claims and not make claims without substantiation.

The FTC helps enforce FDA definitions of food terms. The FTC sued Haagen-Dazs about the fat and calorie claims on its frozen yogurt products: "And each with just 1 gram of fat and 100 calories." In fact, the products contained up to 12 grams of fat per serving (compared to the FDA definition of low fat as 3 grams or less) and up to 230 calories per serving. The company agreed to meet FDA standards for labeling food products and not to misrepresent fat or calories.

Similarly, the FTC ordered Kellogg to stop claiming that Frosted Mini-Wheats cereal improved the attentiveness of children by 20 percent or that Rice Krispies improved immunity from diseases in children. The FDA also ordered General Mills to stop making health claims for Cheerios cereal or risk having the cereal classified as a drug.

Most deceptive advertising cases are settled in a similar manner—the advertiser agrees to stop making false claims. In some cases, a civil penalty is imposed, but large sums are not common. In rare instances, the FTC orders a company to engage in corrective advertising to make up for past false claims. The *Telebrands* case illustrates FTC action.

TELEBRANDS CORP. V. FEDERAL TRADE COMMISSION

United States Court of Appeals, Fourth Circuit, 457 F.3d 354 (2006)

Case Background *Telebrands direct markets assorted products. Its strategy was to compare its product to similar ones and note that its product cost less. Here the product was Ab Force, an electronic muscle stimulation (EMS) abdominal belt that sends a small electric current into the abdominal muscles. Telebrands was careful not to say directly that Ab Force did anything useful, but said it was part of "the latest fitness craze to sweep the country" and that other such belts "promise to get our abs into great shape fast— without exercise." Well-muscled models were used on TV to demonstrate the product.*

The FTC sued for false and misleading advertising claims. Telebrands had made unsubstantiated claims that Ab Force caused loss of weight, inches of fat to disappear, well-defined abs to form, and was an effective alternative to exercise. The Commission issued an order that included a "fencing-in" provision on Telebrands ads. It stated that Telebrands "shall not make any representation, in any manner... about weight, inch, or fat loss, muscle definition ... unless, at the time the representation is made, Telebrands possesses and relies upon competent and reliable evidence ... that substantiates the representation." Telebrands appealed.

Case Decision Duncan, Circuit Judge

* * *

The FTC considers three factors in determining whether order coverage bears a reasonable relationship to the violation it is intended to remedy: "(1) the seriousness and deliberateness of the violation; (2) the ease with which the violative claim may be transferred to other products; and (3) whether the respondent has a history of prior violations."...

Substantial evidence supports the FTC's finding that Telebrands' violations of [the FTC Act] were serious.... The violations involved claiming, with no substantiation, that the Ab Force could deliver certain results that Telebrands later admitted were beyond the device's capabilities. Telebrands [admitted] that "the Ab Force does not cause loss of weight, inches, or fat."...

Moreover, Telebrands mounted an expensive, nationwide advertising campaign for the Ab Force that was highly successful. Telebrands spent over four million dollars on the multimedia advertising campaign for the Ab Force, which included spots that aired more than 10,000 times on cable, satellite, and broadcast television outlets in major national markets. That campaign resulted in the sale of approximately

747,000 units with gross sales, including accessories, exceeding 19 million dollars. These facts militate in favor of a finding that the violations were serious....

The FTC found that the marketing strategy for the Ab Force has potential applicability to almost any kind of product or service, including many that Telebrands already markets. Indeed, the compare and save strategy is one of Telebrands's standard marketing tools. An unfair practice is transferable when other products can be marketed using similar techniques....

The order is enforced.

Questions for Analysis

1. The appeals court upheld the FTC order that restricted the advertising practices of Telebrands for a range of consumer products. Why would it apply to products other than Ab Force?
2. Suppose some doctor endorses such a product. Is that enough to substantiate claims about the benefits of the product?

False Advertising and the Lanham Act

Another way that false advertising claims may be struck down, and one that can be far more expensive to a false advertiser than most FTC, is when a private party brings a suit under the **Lanham Act**. Section 43 of the Act states:

Any person who, or in connection with any goods or services, or any container for goods, uses in commerce any word, term, name, symbol, or device ... or any false designation "of origin, false or misleading description of fact, or any false or misleading representation" of fact, which 1) is likely to cause confusion, or to cause mistake, or to deceive as to the affiliation, connection, or association of such person with another person, or as to the origin, sponsorship, or approval of his or her goods, services, or commercial activities by another person, or 2) in commercial advertising or promotion, misrepresents the nature, characteristics, qualities, or geographic origin of his or her or another person's goods, services, or commercial activities, shall be liable in a civil action by any person who believes that he or she is or is likely to be damaged by such act.

For example, Time Warner Cable won a suit against DirecTV (497 F.3d 144) for stating in ads that viewers could not get "the best picture out of some fancy big screen" without satellite television service. The court found that there was no basis for such a claim. The Act allows injured parties—the plaintiff who is a competitor—to collect double the value of the profits that the defendant earned from false advertising by luring business away.

 ISSUE SPOTTER
How Aggressive Can You Be in Advertising?

Different advertising tactics seem to work for various products and in different markets. Some small firms, to get noticed, directly take on the big firms in the industry by calling their products by name and saying that the small firm has a better product or service. If you really believe your product is better for the price, how explicit can you be in comparing it to your competitor without violating false advertising rules? How much risk is there in calling your competitor names?

© Cengage Learning

INTERNATIONAL PERSPECTIVE

Foreign Advertising Regulation

Advertising is subject to different controls around the world. Most countries impose fewer regulations on ads than is the case in the United States. In Europe, ad regulations tend to be tightest in northern Europe and loosest in the Mediterranean countries.

The U.K. has an Office of Fair Trading that operates somewhat like the FTC with respect to ad regulation. The general standard is that an ad is illegal if it misrepresents a product, whereas in the United States it may be illegal if it simply misleads. For an ad to misrepresent a product, there must be an estimation that consumers suffer damages because they have not been told the truth in the ad.

What is likely to be illegal varies across countries. A soup ad in the United States was held to be illegal by the FTC because the soup was photographed to look as though it had more chunky bits in it than a random bowl of the soup really would have. In most of Europe and Japan, that ad would not be illegal because, while it misleads, it does not injure consumers.

Beer ads in Japan promote the "extra strong" alcohol content, a practice that would be illegal in the United States under the alcohol advertising rules of the Bureau of Alcohol, Tobacco, and Firearms. As the chairman of a Japanese advertising firm explained, "When you come to Japan, you have to do as the Japanese do, especially in advertising."

© Cengage Learning

Trade Regulation Rules

Under Section 18 of the FTC Act, the Commission may issue **trade regulation rules** that set boundaries for practices when problems are common. Because many trade regulation rules from the FTC as well as other agencies are on the books, here we consider only a few.

As with most regulations, a proposed rule must be published in the *Federal Register* so interested parties may comment on it before it is finalized. When the rule is finalized, it becomes part of the **Code of Federal Regulations**. It gives the FTC grounds for charging that violators of the rule are committing an unfair and deceptive act because firms in an industry are required to know about rules that apply to them. Rules may limit certain contracts, as in the case of the rule that allows buyers to cancel contracts they agreed to in certain door-to-door sales. Next, we see some examples of trade rules.

The Insulation R-Value Rule The FTC's Trade Regulation Rule Concerning the Labeling and Advertising of Home Insulation (the R-value Rule) was written because it was difficult to understand insulation claims. By standardizing the insulation capacity of insulating materials—the R-value—the FTC helped consumers compare different products offered by different companies. If a company claims a product provides R-19-value insulation, there is a standard to measure the insulation value. The FTC sued Sears for violating the Rule. Sears advertised the thickness and price of insulation but did not disclose the R-value. In the settlement, Sears agreed to pay a civil penalty, to comply with the rule in the future, and to pay for advertisements to educate consumers about insulation and R-values.

The Mail-Order Rule One of the best-known trade regulation rules is the Mail-Order Rule. If a company sells merchandise by mail, it must ship goods in the time stated in its ads. Shipping dates must be stated on the offers (such as "allow five weeks for shipment") or shipment must be within 30 days of receipt of an order. If the goods cannot be shipped on time, customers must be sent a notice allowing them to cancel the order or to agree to a new shipping date. The rule gives the FTC a simple basis for issuing complaints against companies that fail to live up to the terms of their offers.

CYBER LAW

FTC Watches Tweets

© Cengage Learning 2015

The FTC issues rules regarding proper advertising on the Internet. Most recently it has noted possible problems with Tweets. Suppose a tweeter with many followers, such as a movie star or famous athlete, tweets that she used some product for something and it worked great. Because tweets are short, the FTC knows lengthy disclaimers do not work, so the FTC requires the word, "Ad" at the beginning of such tweets. Tweeters do not face prison time for violations, but fines and injunctions could beimposed if tweeters do not make it clear whether they are being compensated for peddling a product.

Kids' Online Privacy Rule The Children's Online Privacy Protection (COPPA) Rule focuses on websites, online services, and apps directed at children under age 13. It requires site and service operators to obtain parental consent before collecting personal information about a child, including photos and IP addresses. The rule is complex and, as in other areas, the FTC provides guidance on its website. Fines of up to $1 million have been imposed on firms that violate the rule.

Lighter Side of the Law

Wild Claims about Water in Europe

Bottled water makers asked the European Commission if ads could state that "regular consumption … of water can reduce the risk of development of dehydration." After a three-year investigation, a conference of 21 scientists convened in Italy and decreed no, and so the European Food Standards Authority has so ruled.

In the UK, the National Health Service (NHS) recommends drinking water to avoid dehydration and that people should drink at least 1.2 liters of water per day. An NHS spokesman said, "Of course water hydrates … we need to exercise common sense."

Source: The Telegraph (U.K.).

State Deceptive Practices Laws

We have focused on the FTC here, but the states play similar roles. All states give their attorneys general powers similar to the FTC to bring suit against those involved in scams or dubious business practices. Most states have some kind of business code or consumer protection act that restricts deceptive trade practices. These statutes can be applied to a wide range of activities.

Besides the state attorneys general having power to sue, consumers have private causes of action. For example, the Texas Business and Commerce Code states (§ 17.50):

A consumer may maintain an action where any of the following constitute a cause of economic damages or damages for mental anguish:

1. *the use or employment by any person of a false, misleading, or deceptive act or practice that is:*
   a. *specifically [listed later]; and*
   b. *relied on by a consumer to the consumer's detriment:*
2. *breach of an express or implied warranty:*
3. *any unconscionable action or course of action by any person; or*
4. *any [violation of the Insurance Code].*

As the *Schuchmann* case indicates, these state codes provide a statutory basis for a cause of action that goes beyond what may exist under contract law.

SCHUCHMANN V. AIR SERVICES HEATING AND AIR CONDITIONING

Missouri Court of Appeals, Southern District 199 S.W.3d 228 (2006)

Case Background *Schuchmann bought a heating and air conditioning unit for his house with a "lifetime warranty" from Air Services in 1998. Up to 2003, Air Services worked on the system when needed, but then refused to honor the warranty, saying it was too costly. Schuchmann sued and argued that Air's action violated the Missouri Merchandising Practices Act (MMPA). The court awarded Schuchmann $1,047 plus costs. Air Services appealed.*

Case Decision Shrum, Judge

* * *

Defendant is simply wrong, however, when it says we must reverse because Plaintiff did not prove Defendant intended from the beginning to default at some time on its promise of a lifetime warranty. Such an intent is not an element of an MMPA case. This follows from a reading of the last sentence of section 407.020.1: "Any act, use, or employment declared unlawful by this subsection violates this subsection *whether committed before, during, or after the sale*, advertisement, or solicitation. "Thus, the fact that Defendant's refusal to honor the warranty came after the sale is of no consequence.…

An unfair practice is defined as a practice that either: (1) offends any public policy as it has been established by the Constitution, statutes, or common law of this state, or by the Federal Trade Commis-

sion, or its interpretive decisions *or* (2) is unethical, oppressive, or unscrupulous; *and* (3) presents a risk of, or causes, substantial injury to consumers. Due to the unrestricted and all-encompassing nature of … the MMPA, the Supreme Court of Missouri, in speaking of the statute, has stated that "the literal words cover *every practice imaginable and every unfairness to whatever degree.*"

"The purpose of Missouri's Merchandising Practices Act is to preserve fundamental honesty, fair play, and right dealings in public transactions." As stated above, the MMPA supplements the definition of common law fraud, eliminating the need to prove an intent to defraud or reliance. The statute and the regulation paint in broad strokes to prevent evasion thereof due to overly meticulous definitions.…

Affirmed.

Questions for Analysis

1. The court affirmed that the seller violated the state deception law by refusing to honor the warranty on a product. The air conditioner was more than five years old. Is it reasonable to expect "lifetime" service?
2. What does the court mean that the state statute uses "broad strokes" to prevent evasion "due to overly meticulous definitions?"

? TEST YOURSELF

1. The FTC is empowered by Congress to fight _____ acts or practices.
2. In *Telebrands* v. *FTC*, the appeals court agreed that the company was engaged in an improper practice. As to remedies, the court held that the FTC:
   a. could issue an order to block deceptive advertisements.
   b. could get an injunction against further operations but not damages because consumers would not be repaid.
   c. could obtain damages from the company, but not an injunction because there was no "threat to human safety."
   d. could not obtain either damages because consumers would not be repaid, or obtain an injunction because there was no "threat to human safety."
3. The FTC attacks a practice as deceptive if it misleads any consumer: T—F
4. In the case *FTC* v. *John Beck Amazing Profits*, where a company was charged with deceptive sales practices, the court held that the FTC failed to show injury to consumers from false information: T—F
5. If a company makes false claims about another company's products in advertisements, suit for damages may be brought under the _____.
6. If there is a persistent problem in some area of consumer goods, and the FTC wishes to limit the problem, it may issue a(n) _____.

Answers: unfair or deceptive; a; F; F; Lanham Act; trade regulation rule.

Consumer Credit Protection

Congress first involved the federal government in the direct regulation of consumer credit with the Consumer Credit Protection Act (CCPA) of 1968. At that time, there was about $100 billion worth of consumer credit outstanding; now the figure is in the trillions. The CCPA is an umbrella law containing several credit-related laws. The laws provide rights for consumers and put requirements on creditors, including the following:

- Creditors must disclose all relevant terms in credit transactions (truth in lending).
- Procedures for correcting inaccurate and disputed bills and charges must be provided (fair credit billing).
- Credit-reporting agencies must provide accurate information in consumer reports (fair credit reporting).
- Creditors may not use certain personal characteristics, such as sex or race, in determining a person's creditworthiness (equal credit opportunity).
- Abusive debt collection techniques are prohibited (fair debt collection practices).

Truth-in-Lending Act

As Exhibit 19.1 shows, the first law to come under the CCPA was the Truth-in-Lending Act (TILA), which requires creditors in consumer transactions to disclose basic information about the cost and terms of credit to the consumer-borrower. By standardizing credit terms and methods of calculation, it helps people to shop for the most favorable credit terms.

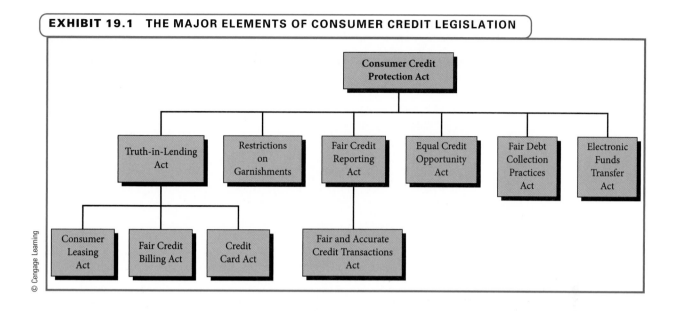

EXHIBIT 19.1   THE MAJOR ELEMENTS OF CONSUMER CREDIT LEGISLATION

Finance Charge Disclosures Until TILA was passed, creditors quoted interest in many ways. For example, an 8 percent "add-on interest rate" results in the same interest charges as a 15 percent "simple interest rate." This is because an add-on rate calculates interest on the initial amount of the loan regardless of the outstanding principal. The simple interest rate calculates interest only on the outstanding principal. Both methods are legitimate, but standardized terms let consumers make better comparisons.

TILA does not control interest rates; it requires standardized loan terms. TILA covers only consumer credit transactions because the debtor must be a "natural person," not a business organization. Because the creditor must be in the credit business, TILA does not apply to loans to friends. The law does not apply if the credit transaction does not include a finance charge unless the consumer repays the creditor in more than four installments. Finally, the Act does not apply to consumer credit transactions for more than $25,000, except real estate purchases.

Credit Cost Disclosure Transactions covered by TILA must disclose the credit costs in dollars (the finance charge) and the interest rate of that finance charge (the annual percentage rate, or APR). These items must be disclosed prominently in the agreement. **Regulation Z**, written by the Federal Reserve Board to implement the Truth-in-Lending Act, specifies items that must be listed if part of the finance charge:

1. Service, activity, carrying, and transaction charges
2. Loan fees and points (charges for making the loan)
3. Charges for credit life and credit accident and health insurance
4. In non-real-estate transactions, the fees for credit reports and appraisals

Certain other items, such as licenses and fees imposed by law, are not part of the finance charge if they are itemized and disclosed to the consumer in the transaction. Exhibit 19.2 shows the disclosure required in the sale of a car on credit.

Enforcement and Penalties TILA provides both civil and criminal penalties. A creditor can avoid liability for a violation, such as a failure to specify all finance charges, if the violation is corrected within 15 days from the time it is discovered by the creditor and before the consumer gives written notification of error.

EXHIBIT 19.2 SAMPLE CREDIT SALE DISCLOSURE FORM

Big Wheel Auto				Alice Green
ANNUAL PERCENTAGE RATE The cost of your credit as a yearly rate.	FINANCE CHARGE The dollar amount the credit will cost you.	Amount Financed The amount of credit provided to you or on your behalf.	Total of Payments The amount you will have paid after you have made all payments as scheduled.	Total Sale Price The total cost of your purchase on credit, including your down-payment of $ 1500 —
14.84 %	$ 1496.80	$ 6107.50	$ 7604.30	$ 9129.30

You have the right to receive at this time an itemization of the Amount Financed.

☐ I want an itemization. ☒ I do not want an itemization.

Your payment schedule will be:

Number of payments	Amount of Payments	When Payments Are Due
36	$211.23	Monthly, beginning 6-1-15

Insurance:
Credit life insurance and credit disability insurance are not required to obtain credit and will not be provided unless you sign and agree to pay the additional cost.

Type	Premium	Signature	
Credit Life	$120 —	I want credit life insurance.	_alice Green_ Signature
Credit Disability		I want credit disability insurance.	Signature
Credit Life and Disability		I want credit life and disability insurance.	Signature

Security: You are giving a security interest in:

☒ the goods being purchased.

☐ _____.

Filing Fees $_____   Non filing insurance $_____

Late Charge: If a payment is late, you will be charged $10.

Prepayment: If you pay off early, you

☐ may ☐ will not ☐ have to pay a penalty.

☒ may ☐ will not ☐ be entitled to a refund of part of the finance charge.

See your contract documents for any additional information about nonpayment, default, any required repayment in full before the scheduled date, and prepayment refunds and penalties.

I have received a copy of this statement.

alice Green   5-1-15

Signature   Date

_____

e means an estimate

Consumers may sue creditors who violate TILA disclosure rules for twice the amount of the finance charge (up to $1,000), court costs, and attorney's fees. A creditor who willfully or knowingly gives inaccurate information or fails to make proper disclosures is subject to criminal liability.

Consumer Leasing Act

The Consumer Leasing Act does for consumer leases, such as for automobiles, what the Truth-in-Lending Act does for consumer credit; that is, it provides standard terms for leases. The Act applies to leases of personal property for personal or household purposes, not for business use. The lease must have an obligation of no more than $50,000. Apartment leases are not covered by the Act because the property leased is real, not personal. Most car rentals are not covered because the term of the agreement is too short.

Disclosure Requirements The Consumer Leasing Act specifies information that must be given. The required disclosures include the following:

- Number, amount, and period of the payments and the payment total
- Express warranties offered by the leasing party or the manufacturer of the leased property
- Identification of the party responsible for maintaining the leased property
- Whether the consumer has an option to buy the leased property and, if so, the terms of that option
- What happens if the consumer terminates the lease before it expires

Fair Credit Billing Act

TILA includes the Fair Credit Billing Act (FCBA). Before the Act, some consumers complained they were unable to get creditors to correct inaccurate or unauthorized charges that appeared on their bills. Another problem was that credit cards were sent to people who did not request them. Some cards were lost or stolen, and consumers who never requested the cards were billed for unauthorized purchases. The FCBA addresses these problems:

1. In case of a billing error, a consumer must notify the creditor in writing within 60 days of the billing of a disputed charge. The creditor must answer the complaint within 30 days of receipt and has 90 days to resolve the problem and notify the consumer.
2. It prohibits the mailing of unsolicited credit cards.
3. It establishes procedures to report lost or stolen credit cards. Liability for unauthorized charges is $50.

Enforcement Most billing disputes are resolved through the procedures established by the FCBA. Dissatisfied consumers can also sue for civil penalties for FCBA violations. In successful actions, creditors are liable for twice the amount of the finance charge plus attorney's fees and court costs.

The FTC is a major FCBA enforcement agency, with jurisdiction over department stores, gasoline retailers, and non-bank-card issuers, such as American Express. Other federal agencies enforce the credit statutes for other credit-granting institutions. Most banks are regulated by the Federal Reserve Board.

Consumer Credit Card Act

The Credit Card Accountability Responsibility and Disclosure Act of 2009—better known as the Credit CARD Act—amended the Truth-in-Lending Act. It restricts certain practices by credit card companies:

- Issuers may not raise interest rates on an existing balance and promotional (low) rates must last at least six months.
- When companies raise rates, they must give cardholders 45 days' notice.
- Restrictions are placed on late fees and when they are imposed; no more than one fee may be charged in a billing cycle if a debtor goes over the card limit; and there may not be charges for Internet or telephone access when making payments.
- Cards may not be issued to consumers under age 21 unless they have independent means of income or get someone over 21 to cosign on the account.
- Finance charges may not be imposed on both the current and previous balance (double-cycle billing).
- Payments made on a credit card must be applied to the highest interest rate portion of the debt first.
- Statements must be sent at least 21 days before a payment is due.
- Gift cards may not expire for at least five years.

The Federal Reserve Board has primary responsibility for enacting regulations to make sure the law operates as Congress intended and has enforcement authority over card companies that violate provisions of the law.

Fair Credit Reporting Act

The Fair Credit Reporting Act (FCRA) regulates credit bureaus (consumer reporting agencies). It focuses on confidentiality and accuracy in consumer **credit reports**. No limit is placed on the information that consumer reporting agencies may include in their files, such as information on political beliefs or sexual practices, so long as the information is accurate.

Agencies may sell consumer reports only for business needs, such as to evaluate an applicant for credit, insurance, property rental, or employment. Nonbusiness use requires a court order or the consumer's permission.

Consumer Rights The FCRA gives consumers the right to see information reported about them that plays a role in credit being denied. As consumer reporting agencies collect some inaccurate information, it is wise to check your reports and take steps to correct the information. Credit bureaus must:

- Respond to consumer complaints about inaccurate information within 30 days.
- Tell consumers, on request, who has asked for copies of their credit history in the past year.
- Provide a toll-free consumer service number.
- Get the consumer's permission before giving a report to an employer or before releasing a report containing medical information.

When a consumer tells a reporting agency about incorrect information, the information must be deleted or changed or a statement from the consumer about the problem must be put in the file.

Shredding Documents The FTC's Disposal Rule applies to all businesses and persons that use consumer reports. It states that the information received in such reports must be properly destroyed after it has been used for its proper purpose. The information must

INTERNATIONAL PERSPECTIVE

Credit around the World

The United States has many laws governing credit, but how does it compare to other countries? Research by the World Bank, in the project Doing Business, looks at that.

In the table, we see four measures related to credit. The first, Legal Rights Index, measures the degree to which collateral and bankruptcy laws assist the lending process. The second, Credit Information Index, measures rules that affect the scope, access, and quality of credit information. Third is the percent of adults in a country covered by a public credit registry, which does not exist in the United States and some other countries; and the fourth measure is the percent of adults in a country covered by private credit bureaus.

Country	Legal Rights Index	Credit Information Index	Public Registry	Private Bureau
Brazil	3	5	46.8	62.2
Canada	7	6	0.0	100.0
China	6	4	27.7	0.0
Germany	7	6	1.3	100.0
Hong Kong	10	5	0.0	89.4
United Kingdom	10	6	0.0	100.0
United States	8	6	0.0	100.0

© Cengage Learning

be pulverized, shredded, or erased so the information cannot be read or reconstructed. This applies to paper and electronic documents. In general, businesses should do a document inventory and routinely destroy documents no longer needed to prevent them from getting into the wrong hands later.

Enforcement and Penalties The FTC has responsibility for enforcing the FCRA. The Act provides civil remedies to injured consumers, who may recover actual damages when noncompliance is negligent. When the credit agency is in willful noncompliance, the consumer may recover actual damages and a punitive penalty. In one suit, TRW was ordered to pay $290,000 in damages—of which $275,000 was punitive damages—for ignoring a consumer's attempt to correct errors in his credit report.

Fair and Accurate Credit Transactions Act

The Fair and Accurate Credit Transaction Act (FACT Act) amended the Fair Credit Reporting Act. It requires the major credit reporting services (Experian, TransUnion, and Equifax) to allow consumers to see their credit reports annually for free. That allows consumers to correct inaccurate information in the report as well as to think of ways to improve their credit score.

The primary concern of the FACT Act was to help deal with identity theft, which affects millions of people annually. The Act has numerous requirements, such as a rule that credit and debit card receipts may not include more than the last five digits of the card number, nor may the card's expiration date be printed on the cardholder's receipt. In addition, the Disposal Rule protects against unauthorized access to consumer information by prohibiting improper disposal of receipts, which would make it easier for "dumpster divers" to retrieve information from the trash to steal identities.

The FTC also coordinates with other financial regulators to have consistent rules about information disposal and protection. Lastly, there are rules that govern the disposal of information stored electronically. Because hard drives are difficult to securely and totally erase, their disposal must be given particular care.

Red Flag Rule The FACT Act required that the FTC come up with the regulation that is now called the Red Flag Rule. Because of intense opposition, its implementation was delayed until 2011. It requires all creditors—which means any business that collects payments, including physicians and other service providers—to have proactive protections in place. Specific to the kind of business, there must be procedures to catch "red flags" that tip one off about possible information thefts. The red flags fall into five categories:

- Alerts, notifications, or warnings from a consumer reporting agency
- Suspicious documents related to credit accounts
- Dubious identifying information, such as a peculiar address
- Unusual use of—or activity related to—a particular account
- Notices from customers, victims of identity theft, law enforcement authorities, or other businesses about possible identity thefts related to accounts.

As is true in most financial areas, there are firms that specialize in providing software and other services to credit providers to help with proper compliance by establishing a system that shows active steps taken to deal with problems and ensure compliance with the law.

 ISSUE SPOTTER
Dealing with Customer Records

Identity theft affects millions of people annually and costs billions of dollars. Businesses are becoming more sophisticated in the handling of information, so the volume of fraud has been dropping. If the information that a criminal has comes from your company records, you can be liable. What practical steps should be considered to help protect your customers and your business reputation?

© Cengage Learning

Equal Credit Opportunity Act

The Equal Credit Opportunity Act (ECOA) was added to the CCPA to prohibit credit discrimination on the basis of race, sex, color, religion, national origin, marital status, receipt of public benefits, the good-faith exercise of the applicant's rights under any part of the CCPA, or age (provided the applicant is old enough to sign a contract). Creditors are prohibited from using such criteria, known as *prohibited bases*, in determining creditworthiness.

Unlawful Credit Discrimination The guiding law for ECOA compliance is simple:

> A creditor shall not discriminate against an applicant on a prohibited basis regarding any aspect of a credit transaction.

Because this provision is broad, Regulation B, issued by the Federal Reserve Board, provides rules explaining what is unlawful discrimination:

- A creditor may not make statements related to a prohibited basis to discourage a person from applying for credit.
- A creditor may not use information concerning the likelihood that the applicant may have children or that the applicant is likely, for that reason, to have reduced or irregular income.
- Credit history must, at the applicant's request, consider not only the applicant's direct history but also the applicant's indirect credit history (for example, accounts that the applicant was liable for and accounts listed in the name of a spouse or former spouse that reflect his or her credit history).
- A creditor may not request information about a spouse or former spouse of the applicant unless: (1) the spouse will use the account or will be liable for the debt; (2) the applicant is relying on the spouse's income or on alimony or child support from the former spouse; or (3) the applicant lives in a community property state.

A violation of ECOA exists if a creditor used a factor prohibited by the Act. The consumer can sue the creditor for ECOA violations. If successful, the creditor is liable to the consumer for actual damages, limited punitive damages, attorney's fees, and court costs, whether the discrimination was intentional or not.

ECOA Notification Requirements When a consumer's credit application is denied or accepted at less favorable terms, the creditor must provide written notification containing the following:

1. The basic provisions of ECOA
2. Name and address of the federal agency regulating the creditor
3. Either a statement of the reasons for the action taken or a disclosure of the applicant's right to receive a statement of reasons

The first and second requirements tell rejected applicants that it is against the law to discriminate on a prohibited basis and point them to the federal agencies that enforce the Act. The third requirement is the most significant. By knowing why they were rejected, applicants can reapply when their situation changes or they can correct misinformation. By knowing the reasons for credit denial, applicants can better understand how credit decisions are made.

Lighter Side **of the Law**

Watch Who You Nickel and Dime

Wendy Ehringer bounced a check for $15.02. She got a notice from a debt collector (ACS) demanding the $15.02 plus $40 in fees, so she sent a money order for $55.02. Months later, she received notice of a lawsuit. Her payment was late, ACS claimed, so she was being sued for 18 cents—the interest on the original amount she owed because her payment arrived two days late—plus $311.26 in attorney fees.

Ehringer, a paralegal, knew her rights under the FDCPA and countersued. The court threw out ACS's claim and awarded Ehringer $500 damages plus $7,000 for attorney's fees.

Source: Seattle Times.

Fair Debt Collection Practices Act

Creditors have the right to collect debts they are owed. If not repaid, under state law they may go to court and ask for an order to **garnish** (set aside a portion of) the wages of the debtor to pay the debt, but that can be a costly process. If unsuccessful in collecting a debt, a creditor can sell the debt to a **debt collection agency** and pay the agency a commission for the funds it collects.

To collect accounts, debt collectors advise consumers by telephone or letter of the outstanding debt and urge them to pay. Sometimes, consumers are subjected to phone calls in the middle of the night, obscene language, and other harassment and abusive tactics. The Fair Debt Collection Practices Act (FDCPA) helps reduce unfair, deceptive, and abusive collection techniques used by some debt collectors.

Restrictions Imposed The FDCPA regulates the conduct of about 5,000 independent debt collection agencies that collect billions of dollars each year from consumers. In *Heintz* v. *Jenkins* (115 S.Ct. 1489), the Supreme Court held that the FDCPA "applies to attorneys who regularly engage in consumer-debt collection activity." The law does not apply to creditors attempting to collect their own debts, such as a department store trying to collect from a customer. The Act makes abusive debt collection practices illegal and contains a list of required actions.

Harassing, deceptive, and unfair debt collection practices—including threats of violence or arrest, obscene language, the publication of a list of delinquent consumers, and harassing phone calls—are prohibited. Debt collectors may not discuss the debts with other people, including the debtor's employer. The Act prohibits the use of false or misleading representations in collecting a debt.

What Must Be Communicated The FDCPA requires the debt collector to send certain information to the consumer within five days of the initial communication:

- Amount of debt
- Name of the creditor to whom the debt is owed
- A statement that unless the consumer disputes the validity of the debt within 30 days, the debt collector will assume the debt is valid
- A statement that the debt collector must show proof of the debt if the consumer advises the debt collector within 30 days of the notification that the consumer disputes the debt

Contact with the consumer must end when the collector learns that an attorney represents the consumer or when the consumer requests in writing that contact end. The debt collector then waits for payment or sues to collect the debt. Most cases that arise under the FDCPA concern improper language in debt collection letters. As the *Chuway* case shows, debt collectors must be careful in their choice of language to avoid violating the statute.

CHUWAY V. NATIONAL ACTION FINANCIAL SERVICE

United States Court of Appeals, Seventh Circuit, 362 F.3d 944 (2004)

Case Background *National Action, a debt collector, mailed Chuway, a debtor, a letter that identified a creditor (a credit card company) and stated that the "balance" on the debt was $367.52.*

The letter said that the creditor "has assigned your delinquent account to our agency for collec- tion. Please remit the balance listed above in the return envelope provided. To obtain your most current balance information, please call 1-800-916-9006. Our friendly and experienced representatives will be glad to assist you and answer any questions you have."*

Chuway sued National Action for violating the FDCPA because the communication was not proper under the Act. The district court granted summary judgment for National Action because the letter stated "the amount of the debt" and so did not violate the statute. Chuway appealed.

Case Decision Posner, Circuit Judge

* * *

Here ... the *entire* debt that the defendant was hired to collect was the $367.42 listed as the "balance."

So if the letter had stopped after the "Please remit" sentence, the defendant would be in the clear. But the letter didn't stop there. It went on to instruct the recipient on how to obtain "your most current balance information." If this means that the defendant was dunning her for something more than $367.42, it's in trouble because the "something more" is not quantified.... The credit card company, which is to say the creditor, not the debt collector, may charge the plaintiff interest on the $367.42 between when the debt accrued and when the plaintiff finally pays and may add the interest accruing in the interim to the plaintiff's current balance. But that would not be a part of "the amount of the debt" for which the *defendant* was dunning her....

It is not enough that the dunning letter state the amount of the debt that is due. It must state it clearly enough that the recipient is likely to understand it. Otherwise the collection agency could write the letter in Hittite and have a secure defense....

If the debt collector is trying to collect only the amount due on the date the letter is sent, then he complies with the Act by stating the "balance" due, stating that the creditor "has assigned your delinquent account to our agency for collection," and asking the recipient to remit the balance listed—and stopping there, without talk of the "current" balance. If, instead, the debt collector is trying to collect the listed balance plus the running interest on it or other charges, he should use the safe-harbor language [established in an earlier case]: "As of the date of this letter, you owe $ [the exact amount due]. Because of interest, alter charges, and other charges that may vary from day to day, the amount due on the day you pay may be greater. Hence, if you pay the amount shown above, an adjustment may be necessary after we receive your check, in which event we will inform you before depositing the check for collection. For further information, write the undersigned or call 1-800-[phone number]."

Reversed and remanded.

Questions for Analysis

1. The appeals court held the debt collection letter to violate the FDCPA. How could Chuway afford to sue National Action over such a small sum of money?
2. Why did National Action not use the language the court cited as providing a safe harbor because the words meet the specific requirements of the FDCPA?

Enforcement Consumers subjected to collection abuses enforce compliance by suing. A collector who violates the FDCPA is liable for actual damages caused. Consumers bringing action in good faith will have their attorney's fees and court costs paid by the collector. The FTC can sue collectors that violate the act, as can state attorneys general in states with similar laws.

When debt collection practices go overboard, the debtor may, of course, sue in tort, as well as for violations of the FDCPA. In a case in El Paso, a jury awarded debtors $11 million in damages against Household Credit Services, their creditor, and Allied

ISSUE SPOTTER
How Should You Handle Unpaid Accounts?

Your company sells furniture mostly to low-income people who buy on credit provided by your company. You know that the default rate, which is pretty high in your business, can determine whether the store is profitable or not. Should you sell or assign the debt to a debt collector or handle the collection internally? What difference is there legally? Are there advantages of going one way or another?

Adjustment Bureau, a collection agency used by Household Credit. Attempting to collect a $2,000 debt, death threats were made. Damages under the FDCPA were a tiny fraction of the jury tort verdict.

Electronic Fund Transfer Act

Many **electronic fund transfer** (EFT) services are available to consumers. Such transfers are larger in volume than are the funds transferred by check and cash. They include:

- ATM deposits or other transactions
- Direct deposits of paychecks
- Debit cards used to buy goods or services
- Automatic bill-paying services
- Telephone transfers to credit cards (presuming a written agreement exists)

As electronic innovations developed, Congress became concerned about the rights and liabilities of the consumers, financial institutions, and retailers who use electronic fund transfer systems. The Electronic Fund Transfer Act was passed and required the Federal Reserve Board to write Regulation E to implement the Act.

Liability for Stolen Cards One important protection provided by the Act is the liability limit when a consumer's ATM card is stolen and an unauthorized user drains the account. Unlike the Fair Credit Billing Act's $50 limit on liability for lost or stolen credit cards, the Electronic Fund Transfer Act's limit on liability is potentially greater.

Regulation E provides that the consumer's liability is no more than $50 if the financial institution is notified within two days after the consumer learns of the theft. The consumer's liability becomes $500 as long as the financial institution is notified within 60 days. If the consumer does not report the theft within 60 days after receiving the first statement containing unauthorized transfers, the consumer is liable for all amounts after that.

Liability for Mistakes The Act makes financial institutions liable to consumers for damages caused by failure to make electronic transfers. However, liability is limited to actual damages proved, such as costs incurred by a consumer if a car is repossessed for failure to make a required payment.

Consumers are to receive a monthly statement from financial institutions. Consumers have 60 days to report errors. When a consumer reports an error, the institution must resolve the dispute within 45 days. If an investigation takes more than 10 business days to complete, the institution must re-credit the disputed amount to the consumer's account; the consumer has use of the funds until the complaint is resolved. Failure to undertake a good-faith investigation of an alleged error makes the institution liable for triple the consumer's actual damages.

The Consumer Financial Protection Bureau

Congress enacted a major financial reform bill in 2010, popularly called the Dodd-Frank Act. The legislation is so complex that it is taking years for regulations authorized by it to be put into effect. The part of the legislation that has the largest impact on consumer credit markets established a new regulatory agency, the Consumer Financial Protection Bureau (CFPB), within the Federal Reserve.

The CFPB was granted wide rulemaking and enforcement authority over banks and other financial companies. The CFPB draws many employees from existing agencies, such as the FTC, the Comptroller of the Currency, and the Federal Deposit Insurance Corporation. Congress expressly stated that state attorneys general have authority to enforce rules issued by the CFPB.

Congress specifically instructed the CFPB to focus on several areas. First, the CFPB should crack down on financial scams and gimmicks that are aimed at ordinary consumers and debtors. By giving this agency authority that was fragmented across different agencies, the intent was to have more focus on practices deemed harmful to consumers. Second, the CFPB should ensure that the terms of financial documents, such as credit transactions, are transparent and can be understood by reasonable consumers. Third, the CFPB should focus on the practices of nonbank institutions, such as payday lenders, to limit practices deemed particularly unfair. Fourth, the CFPB should look at existing rules, such as those in place under the Equal Credit Opportunity Act, to ensure that various regulations are not in conflict with each other because credit regulation is highly complex. Lastly, the CFPB should work to ensure uniform application of credit rules.

❓ *TEST YOURSELF*

1. The focus of the Truth-in-Lending Act is that lenders provide correct information to borrowers; it does not control the way the information is presented: T—F
2. If you believe you are being charged for something improperly by a creditor, you should follow the procedure provided in the _____.
3. According to the Equal Credit Opportunity Act, a lender may not discriminate against a prospective borrower because the borrower receives welfare: T—F
4. In *Chuway* v. *National Action Financial Services*, where Chuway sued a debt collector for violating the Fair Debt Collection Practices Act, the appeals court held that the debt collector: T—F
   a. violated the FDCPA by continual harassing calls to Chuway.
   b. violated the FDCPA by using imprecise language in the debt collection letter.
   c. did not violate the FDCPA because all information in the collection process was true.
   d. did not violate the FDCPA for making a 17-cent error in listing the amount due; the mistake was *de minimis*.
5. If a credit card is stolen and the card holder immediately notifies the card issuer, the card holder liability for improper charges is _____.

Answers: F; Fair Credit Billing Act; T; b; $50.

SUMMARY

- The Food, Drug, and Cosmetic Act, enforced by the FDA, imposes liability on companies and persons involved in the production and distribution of food and drug products. The primary concern for food is safety. The FDA is helped by the U.S. Department of Agriculture in food sanitation inspection.

- The FDA must approve food additives before being sold to the public. Nutrition labels on processed foods must list by standard consumer portions fat, carbohydrates, cholesterol, and other nutrients, as well as certain vitamins and minerals and total calories.

- The FDA determines when drugs are safe and effective for sale and whether drugs are to be sold by prescription only or over the counter. Food, drugs, cosmetics, and medical devices that the FDA determines to be unsafe may be ordered off the market or seized.

- The FTC has broad authority to attack unfair or deceptive business practices. The consumer protection mission includes the advertising substantiation program, which requires advertisers to be able to demonstrate the truth of product claims.

- The FTC issues trade regulation rules to govern business practices that have raised problems. The rules set standards that businesses must meet. That makes prosecution for rule violations straightforward.

- The attorney general of a state has the authority to sue sellers involved in deceptive business practices. Most states have statutes that give consumers broad rights to sue for unfair and deceptive business practices. These statutes can provide legal rights beyond those provided by contract.

- The Truth-in-Lending Act, which applies to most consumer loans, requires that lenders meet requirements on how the details of loan amounts, interest charges, and other items are calculated and stated to the borrower. There is no defense for certain violations of this statute. The Consumer Leasing Act sets similar standards for consumer leases.

- The Fair Credit Billing Act details the rights of consumers to resolve billing errors. Creditors must follow requirements on how long they have to respond to the consumer and what they must do to resolve the dispute. As under other parts of the credit statutes, violations mean double damages, plus attorney's fees, for the plaintiff.

- Credit bureaus sell lenders the credit history about consumers seeking credit. The Fair Credit Reporting Act specifies consumers' rights to challenge the accuracy of reports issued by these bureaus. Credit bureaus must respond to inquiries from consumers about errors in credit reports.

- Under the Equal Credit Opportunity Act, creditors may not consider the following factors in determining who is granted credit: race, sex, age, color, religion, national origin, marital status, receipt of public benefits, or the exercise of legal rights. Specific regulations govern how lenders must comply with this statute.

- Debt collectors may not abuse the rights of debtors granted by the Fair Debt Collection Practices Act. They may not make abusive phone calls, threats, or claims of legal action not actually underway or use other forms of harassment. A debt collector informed by any debtor that no further contact is desired may not contact the debtor except for notice of legal action.

- Consumer rights and responsibilities for credit cards and ATM cards that have been stolen are spelled out in the law. To limit liability for unauthorized charges, the consumer must notify the card issuer of the theft of the card.

TERMS TO KNOW

nutrition labeling, 517
prescription drugs, 518
Kefauver Amendment, 518
learned intermediary doctrine, 521
consent decree, 523
deception, 523

unfairness, 524
advertising substantiation
    program, 526
Lanham Act, 528
trade regulation rules, 528
Code of Federal Regulations, 528

Regulation Z, 533
credit report, 536
garnish, 540
debt collection agency, 540
electronic fund transfer, 542

DISCUSSION QUESTION

If consumers think agencies such as the FTC prevent unfair and deceptive practices, will they become less careful in watching out for themselves, thereby encouraging more bad business practices?

CASE QUESTIONS

1. Laetrile was a drug not approved by the FDA for sale. Some people believed it helped fight cancer. Some cancer victims sued the FDA, saying they had a constitutional right to privacy that was being denied by the FDA's refusal to let them have access to Laetrile. A court of appeals held that it was not reasonable to apply the FDA's drug safety and effectiveness standards to dying cancer patients because they had nothing to lose and were willing to try the drug. The Supreme Court reviewed the case. What do you think the result was? [*U.S. v. Rutherford*, 99 S.Ct. 2470 (1979)]

2. Heath took Ortho-Novum oral contraceptives from 1967 to 1974, when, at age 28, she suffered kidney failure that required a kidney transplant. She sued, claiming the kidney failure was caused by the drug, which did not warn physicians to monitor blood pressure or watch for signs of kidney problems. Ortho defended that it was in compliance with FDA regulations in marketing the product, so it should not be subject to common-law strict liability or negligence. Did federal regulation of the drug remove common-law liability? [*Ortho Pharmaceutical v. Heath*, 722 P.2d 410, Colo. Sup. Ct. (1986)]
   ✓ Check your answer

3. Nutraceutical sold a dietary supplement containing ephedrine, a substance the FDA classified as a drug. The FDA said that because the dietary supplement contained the substance, the supplement would be treated as a drug and therefore, subject to the strict requirements of drugs. Nutraceutical countered that because the product was a dietary supplement, the FDA could not impose such strict rules. Which position do you think prevailed? [*Neutraceutical Corp. v. Von Eschenbach*, 459 F.3d 1033, 10th Circuit (2006)]

4. Cyberspace.com sent mailings to millions of people with a check for $3.50. On the back of the check, in fine print, it said if you signed and cashed the check, you subscribed to the company's Internet access service. A quarter million people signed the checks. Most never used the Internet service but were billed for it. Was it an unfair and deceptive trade practice as the FTC claimed? [*FTC v. Cyberspace.com LLC*, 453 F.3d 1196, 9th Cir. (2006)]
   ✓ Check your answer

5. Dr. Amrani performed two major back surgeries on Williamson to try to resolve a major back problem. After the surgeries, which were apparently not as successful as hoped, Williamson sued Amrani under the Kansas Consumer Protection Act. She claimed that Amrani made representations to her about the benefits of the surgery that were not true. He told her the surgery worked well, when in fact the record was not so good. She claimed this was deception to induce her to undergo the surgery. Could she use a consumer deception statute to bring an action for a medical procedure? [*Williamson v. Amrani*, 152 P.3d 60, Sup. Ct., Kan. (2007)]

6. Procter and Gamble sold a detergent, *Ace con Blanqueador*, in Puerto Rico. It advertised that *"Mas bianco no se puede"* (Whiter is not possible). Clorox sued Procter and Gamble, contending that the ad was false and misleading in violation of the Lanham Act. The district court dismissed the suit; Clorox appealed. Could it have a suit for false advertising against its competitor under the Lanham Act? [*Clorox Company Puerto Rico v. Procter and Gamble*, 228 F.3d 24, 1st Cir. (2000)]
   ✓ Check your answer

7. Fairbanks Capital acquired 12,800 mostly delinquent mortgages from a mortgage company, including a mortgage owned by the Schlossers. Identifying itself as a debt collector, Fairbanks sent the Schlossers a letter asserting that their mortgage was in default. In fact, the Schlossers were not in default and sued Fairbanks for failure to notify the debtors of their right to contest the debt as required by the Fair Debt Collections Practices Act (FDCPA). The district court held

that because the Schlossers were not in default, there was no debt to collect, so the FDCPA did not apply. The Schlossers appealed. Do they have a case? [*Schlossers* v. *Fairbanks Capital*, 323 F.3d 534, 7th Cir. (2003)]

8. Pfennig sued Household Credit Services for violations of the Truth-in-Lending Act. She contended that she was extended credit but was then charged a fee of $29 a month when she went over the $2,000 limit on her credit card. The fee was not listed in the finance charges disclosed on her monthly statements, but was listed as a new purchase on which additional finance charges were calculated. Does she have a case? [*Pfennig* v. *Household Credit Services*, 295 F.3d 522, 6th Cir. (2002)]

9. Sarah Grendahl planned to marry Lavon Phillips. Mary, Sarah's mother, believed Phillips was lying about his background, so she hired a private investigator to check him out. Using reports from a consumer-reporting agency, the investigator determined that Phillips had been convicted for writing bad checks, sued for paternity in one state, and was delinquent in child support in another state. When Phillips learned that the truth about his background being revealed, he sued Mary Grendahl, the detective agency, and the consumer-reporting agency for violating the Fair Credit Reporting Act. Would Phillips have a case? [*Phillips* v. *Grendahl*, 312 F.3d 357, 8th Cir. (2002)]

ETHICS QUESTION

The FTC is proposing a regulation that would hurt the sales of one of the products your company produces. The agency believes that there is a long-run consumer health issue that it should address. You estimate the regulation will cost your company $20 million a year in sales and $2 million a year in profits. The three other firms in the industry that make a similar product will also be hurt. Your Washington representative tells you that if all four firms are willing to spend $5 million in lobbying efforts, it can probably get Congress to kill the proposed regulation. All other firms agree to help foot the bill. This kind of lobbying is common. Should you pay to help get the regulation killed?

CHAPTER **20**
Antitrust Law

Business is tough. Trying to compete in the building supply business, you have cut prices to the bone, leaving no profit. Your competitors do the same. Some have gone out of business.

Stability would be better if you and the other suppliers agreed not to sell supplies at a loss. Construction is always boom-and-bust. If suppliers can hold on through bad times, everyone can survive and be ready to serve clients when things pick up again. Your clients will be better served at that time than if many suppliers go broke and only a few competitors remain to dominate the market when things return to normal.

What happens if you discuss this idea—not selling supplies at a loss—with your competitors to try to get an agreement? You are not looking to jack up prices, just not sustain losses. Would an agreement cause antitrust-law violations? Business people need to be aware of antitrust law in three main contexts:

- Avoiding violating antitrust statutes and rules by their own behavior
- Identifying illegal behavior by their suppliers and competitors
- Knowing when competitors wish to merge or combine operations

The antitrust statutes written by Congress do not state exactly what is illegal. Instead, the courts must interpret the language in the statutes to determine what activities are prohibited. Antitrust law, therefore, refers to the antitrust statutes, the interpretation of the statutes by the courts, and the enforcement policies of administrative agencies, especially the Department of Justice and the Federal Trade Commission. This chapter looks at how antitrust law is applied to both horizontal and vertical business arrangements.

Antitrust Statutes

The growth of large corporations in the late nineteenth century led to calls for constraints on business. The result was the passage of federal antitrust legislation: the Sherman Act, the Clayton Act, and the Federal Trade Commission (FTC) Act. The key parts of these broadly written statutes are excerpted in Appendix H. Except for a few actions that are clearly illegal under the statutes, it has been left largely to the federal agencies and courts to determine how the laws are applied in practice.

The Sherman Act

The Sherman Antitrust Act was passed by Congress in 1890 in response to the unpopularity of large business organizations. The most famous was the Standard Oil Trust, John D. Rockefeller's company, which at its peak controlled about 90 percent of the oil sales in the country. The word **antitrust** comes from Standard Oil, which was organized in the form of a trust. Sponsors of the Act saw it as a way to reduce concerns that a few large firms dominated some industries. The major sections of the Sherman Act are so broad that one could find almost any business activity to be illegal:

*Sec. 1: Every contract, combination in the form of trust or otherwise, or conspiracy, in **restraint of trade** or commerce among the several States, or with foreign nations, is hereby declared to be illegal.*

Sec. 2: Every person who shall monopolize, *or* attempt to monopolize, *or combine or conspire with any other person or persons, to monopolize any part of the trade or commerce among the several States, or with foreign nations, shall be deemed guilty of a felony.*

The Clayton Act

Enacted in 1914, the Clayton Act was added to the Sherman Act. The Clayton Act is intended to stop a business practice early in its use to prevent a firm from becoming a **monopoly** by making practices that "substantially lessen competition or tend to create a monopoly" illegal.

Under the antitrust laws, what is a monopoly? In general, a monopoly exists in a market when one firm or only a few dominate the sales of a product or service. As we see in this chapter, the fact that a company obtains such a position is not necessarily illegal. The laws focus more on actions that show an effort to eliminate competition. The Clayton Act holds some specific acts to be illegal. The most important sections of the Act include:

Sec. 2: It shall be unlawful for any person engaged in commerce ... to discriminate in price between different purchasers of commodities of like grade and quality ... where the effect of such discrimination may be substantially to lessen competition or tend to create a monopoly in any line of commerce.... [This section was added by the Robinson-Patman Act of 1936 and restricts price discrimination in the sale of goods. As we will see, this means when a producer sells the same good at different prices to different buyers.]

Sec. 3: It shall be unlawful for any person engaged in commerce ... to lease or make a sale ... on the condition ... that the lessee or purchaser thereof shall not use or deal in the goods ... or other commodities of a competitor ... where the effect ... may be to substantially lessen competition or tend to create a monopoly.... [This is a restriction on tying sales, where the sale of one good is tied to the sale of another good, and exclusive dealing, when a company is forbidden from dealing with other possible buyers or sellers.]

> *Sec. 7: No corporation...shall acquire the whole or any part of the assets of another corporation engaged also in commerce, where...the effect of such acquisition may be substantially to lessen competition, or to tend to create a monopoly.* [This restricts mergers of dominant competitors, such as McDonald's and Burger King.]
>
> *Sec. 8: No person at the same time shall be a director in any two or more corporations...if such corporations are or shall have been...competitors, so that the elimination of competition by agreement between them would constitute a violation of...the antitrust laws.* [This restricts interlocking directorates. For example, Eric Schmidt quit the Apple board because he was also on the Google board.]

The Federal Trade Commission Act

In 1914 Congress enacted the Federal Trade Commission Act. It established the Federal Trade Commission (FTC) as an agency to investigate and enforce violations of the antitrust laws. Although most of the Act provides for the structure, powers, and procedures of the FTC, it also provides a major addition to antitrust law:

> *Sec. 5: Unfair methods of competition in or affecting commerce, and unfair or deceptive acts or practices in commerce, are hereby declared unlawful.*

The **unfair methods of competition** referred to in the FTC Act have been interpreted by the courts as any business activity that may tend to create a monopoly by unfairly eliminating or excluding competitors from the marketplace.

Exemptions

Not all business activities are subject to the antitrust laws. In some cases, successful lobbying of Congress resulted in statutory exemptions from the antitrust laws. The following activities and businesses are provided exemptions:

- The Clayton Act exempts some activities of nonprofit organizations and of agricultural, fishing, and some other cooperatives.
- The Export Trading Company Act allows sellers of exports to receive limited antitrust immunity. For example, a group of domestic producers may be allowed to join together to improve their ability to sell their products in other countries.
- The **Parker doctrine**, or state action doctrine, allows state governments to restrict competition in industries such as public utilities (e.g., cable television), professional services (e.g., nursing), and public transportation (e.g., taxicabs). However, the Supreme Court held that for the doctrine to protect parties from antitrust actions, the state must play "a substantial role in determining the specifics of the economic policy." That is, the state must have intended to restrict competition and perhaps fix prices.
- The McCarran-Ferguson Act exempts the insurance industry from federal antitrust laws so long as the states regulate insurance.
- Under the Noerr-Pennington doctrine, lobbying to influence a legislature is not illegal. This is because the First Amendment gives persons the right to petition their government, even if the purpose is anticompetitive.
- Most labor unions' activities are exempt. The National Labor Relations Act protects collective bargaining to set conditions of employment.

Enforcement Individuals and businesses have the right to sue for the violations of the antitrust laws. Most antitrust suits are private civil suits. The Antitrust Division of the Justice Department brings dozens of criminal antitrust suits each year. For a civil lawsuit under the Sherman Act or Clayton Act, a choice must be made as to whether the Justice Department or the FTC brings the case. The agencies have agreed to divide the cases by industry, but may consult to decide which agency should handle a particular case. State attorneys general may also bring antitrust cases under federal or state law.

Sherman Act Violations of the Sherman Act carry the most severe penalties of the antitrust statutes. Most of the criminal cases involve price fixing or bid rigging by competitors.

- Violations of Sections 1 and 2 of the Sherman Act can be felonies. Individuals who violate the Act face up to 10 years in prison, a fine of $1 million, or both. Businesses can be fined up to $100 million. The Antitrust Division of the Department of Justice brings criminal cases. Some years, fines totaling over $1 billion have been collected.
- Private parties or the government can seek injunctive relief under the Act in a civil proceeding. An injunction would order a defendant (the party who violated the Act) to stop the illegal acts.
- Private parties harmed by a violation of the Sherman Act can sue for **treble damages**; if they win, they get three times their actual money damages, plus court costs and attorney's fees.

Clayton Act The Department of Justice or private parties may bring civil proceedings under the Clayton Act, but the normal procedure has been for the FTC, which shares jurisdiction with the Justice Department, to issue **cease and desist orders**, prohibiting further violation. The FTC has the authority to investigate suspect business dealings, hold hearings (rather than trials), and issue administrative orders approved in federal court that require parties to stop or change certain business acts. When these orders are ignored, there may be criminal penalties.

FTC Act Violations of the FTC Act carry a variety of penalties, ranging from an order preventing a planned merger to substantial civil penalties. It is much easier for the FTC to bring administrative actions against a company than for the Justice Department to bring a criminal suit under the Sherman Act, so the agencies decide which route is most appropriate to take in each case.

CYBER LAW

Software Replacing Lawyers

When Anheuser-Busch InBev, the largest beer company in the world, wanted to merge with Mexico's Grupo Modelo, the plan was reviewed by the Department of Justice (DOJ) for antitrust issues. The merger was allowed, but only after Modelo's U.S. operation was sold, as well as a brewery in Mexico.

Such cases can involve millions of documents reviewed by lawyers for relevance to the matter. In this case, as in a few others, software was trained to search for relevant documents. Manual searches were compared to software searches to fine-tune the software. kCura, the company that developed the software, has worked with the DOJ as it seeks better predictive coding tools to sift through the nearly endless data sources that exist. In the Modelo case, the savings was estimated to be more than 50 percent compared to traditional search methods.

Remedies Available

Whether an antitrust suit is brought by a private plaintiff or by the government, the courts can impose a variety of remedies besides monetary damages, including the following:

- Restrain a company or individuals from certain conduct
- Force a company to sell part of its assets (break up the company)
- Force a company to let others use its patents or facilities (licensing)
- Cancel or modify existing business contracts

For a firm to recover damages under the antitrust laws, the harm suffered by the plaintiff must be the kind of harm that the antitrust laws are meant to prevent. A firm that loses profits because a new competitor enters its market cannot sue for damages because antitrust law favors increased competition. Only plaintiffs suffering injuries caused by the anticompetitive behaviors of defendants can recover damages under antitrust law.

Per Se Rule and the Rule of Reason

One question the courts must address is whether, as a matter of policy, a certain business practice will be held to be illegal *per se* or whether a rule of reason is appropriate.

A ***per se* rule** means that certain business agreements or activities automatically are held to be illegal if found to exist. The classic example of a *per se* violation of antitrust law is a group of competitors agreeing on the prices to charge for their goods so they can eliminate price competition. In discussing *per se* illegality, the Supreme Court in *Northern Pacific Railway Co.* v. *United States* (356 U.S. 1) stated that there are certain activities that "because of their pernicious effect on competition and lack of any redeeming virtue are conclusively presumed to be unreasonable and therefore illegal without elaborate inquiry as to the precise harm they have caused or business excuse for their use."

A **rule of reason**, in contrast, means that the court looks at the facts surrounding business practices before deciding whether it helps or hurts competition. The court considers such factors as the business reasons for the restraint, the position in an industry of a firm accused of a restraint, and the structure of the industry.

If a court concludes that a business practice promotes competition, the court dismisses the case. But if the court finds that the practice on net reduces competition, then the court rules that it violates the antitrust laws.

Monopolization

The Sherman Act and Clayton Act are concerned with monopolization of markets but the statutes provide little guidance as to what behavior crosses the line to be illegal practices. Therefore, antitrust law has been built on many court cases over the years. The courts usually consider the structure of a market and the nature of the behavior that is attacked.

The focus of the law is on business practices that can lead to a monopoly. The law does not restrict the size of firms. The concern is to protect competition in a given market, not to protect individual competitors who complain about another competitor's behavior. The law favors competition because it lowers prices for consumers, it spurs companies to innovate, and it increases choice. Monopolies not only tend to charge higher prices but also offer inferior service and are slow to innovate. In the *Spanish Broadcasting* case we see a discussion of the factors that courts consider in a monopolization case brought under the Sherman Act.

SPANISH BROADCASTING SYSTEM OF FLORIDA V. CLEAR CHANNEL COMMUNICATIONS

United States Court of Appeals, Eleventh Circuit, 376 F.3d 1065 (2004)

Case Background *Spanish Broadcasting System (SBS) owns 14 Spanish-language stations, including five stations in the top-ten markets. Hispanic Broadcasting Corporation (HBC) owns 55 Spanish-language stations and is in all top-ten markets. Clear Channel (CC) owns the largest English-language radio network in the United States, with 1,200 stations, and it owns 26 percent of HBC.*

SBS sued CC and HBC, claiming they conspired to drive SBS out of the Spanish-language radio market in violation of the Sherman Act. SBS claimed that the two stations discouraged advertisers from placing ads with SBS and induced SBS employees to quit and then join HBC. SBS contended that the stations made it difficult for SBS to enter new markets by bidding up prices and taking away business opportunities, and interfered with SBS's ability to raise money in capital markets.

The district court dismissed the suit, holding that SBS did not meet the standards necessary to maintain an antitrust suit under the Sherman Act; SBS appealed.

Case Decision Barkett, Circuit Judge

* * *

Because the Sherman Act contains only general language, courts have played an extremely important role in shaping the reach of the Act and the requirements for stating a cause of action under each section. Critically, under both sections, an antitrust plaintiff must show harm to competition in general, rather than merely damage to an individual competitor.... This case turns in large part on whether SBS has met its obligation to allege facts that would support a showing of this harm to competition, rather than merely to itself....

SBS alleged that the practices [described above] constituted an agreement between CC and HBC to restrain trade in violation of Section One of the Sherman Act as well as attempted monopolization by both CC and HBC of the major Spanish-language radio markets in violation of Section Two of the Act....

Section One of the Sherman Act ... prohibits combinations and conspiracies that restrain interstate or foreign trade. This provision applies both to agreements between companies that directly compete with one another, called "horizontal" agreements, and to agreements between businesses operating at different levels of the same product's production chain or distribution chain, known as "vertical" agreements. In addition, although some restraints on trade remain illegal *per se*, such as certain agreements to fix prices, most asserted antitrust violations now require "the finder of fact to decide whether the questioned practice imposes an *unreasonable* restraint on competition, taking into account a variety of factors, including specific information about the relevant business, its condition before and after the restraint was imposed, and the restraint's history, nature, and effect." Section One claims that do not allege *per se* antitrust violations are analyzed under this "rule of reason," and the claims fail if the restraint on trade is reasonable. Both parties accept that the rule of reason applies to the Section One claims raised by SBS in this case....

Even if we were to assume that CC and HBC acted in concert for purposes of Section One, however, we would still affirm here, given that SBS failed to allege sufficient anticompetitive effect, a critical component of any antitrust claim....

Anticompetitive effects are measured by their impact on the market rather than by their impact on competitors.... In order to prove this anticompetitive effect on the market, the plaintiff "may either prove that the defendants' behavior had an actual detrimental effect on competition, or that the behavior had the potential for genuine adverse effects on competition."

In an attempt to meet this burden, SBS focuses upon the harm it allegedly suffered at the hands of HBC and CC, such as weakened stock prices, restricted access to capital markets, loss of employees, damaged reputation, and loss of advertising revenue. None of these allegations assert damage to competition itself rather than damage to SBS, one competitor in the Spanish-language advertising market....

Section Two makes it a crime to monopolize, to attempt to monopolize, or to conspire to monopolize any part of interstate or foreign trade. This provision covers behavior by a single business as well as coordinated action taken by several businesses.

The ... complaint alleged only attempted monopolization, which involves three distinct elements: "(1) the defendant has engaged in predatory or anticompetitive conduct with (2) a specific intent to monopolize and (3) a dangerous probability of achieving monopoly power."

Like claims under Section One, Section Two claims require harm to competition that must occur within a "relevant," that is, a distinct market, with a specific set of geographical boundaries and a narrow delineation of the products at issue.... SBS explained that it considered the relevant market to be advertising purchased in the top-ten Spanish-language markets and HBC earned 51 percent of the advertising revenue in that market....

There is no question that CC does not participate in the Spanish-language radio market. Thus, CC cannot attempt to monopolize that market. SBS attempted to overcome this hurdle by pointing out that CC owned 26 percent of HBC, implying that this either makes CC an effective participant in the relevant market or at least gives CC sufficient control over HBC to permit attempted monopolization.

We reject this contention. Absent allegations of significant control over the policies of a subsidiary, a minority ownership share does not convert a parent corporation into a competitor.... To be a competitor at the level of the subsidiary, the parent must have substantial control over the affairs and policies of the subsidiary.

As with Section One claims, conduct that injures individual firms rather than competition in the market as a whole does not violate Section Two. The Supreme Court has explained that "even an act of pure malice by one business competitor against another does not, without more, state a claim under the federal antitrust laws."...

Because SBS has not alleged any harm to competition in the market, nor explained how any of the actions taken by HBC could lead to monopolization of that market, SBS has not alleged anticompetitive conduct and thus has not stated a claim against HBC under Section Two....

Affirmed.

Questions for Analysis

1. The court focused on damage to competition in the market. What is the relevant product market that was under consideration?
2. If it is true that HBC lured away SBS employees, which weakened SBS's ability to compete, why was the court not concerned?

Mergers

Mergers are a source of monopolization concern. If companies that are competitors, will competition be significantly injured? A **merger** involves two or more firms coming together to form a new firm. A combination can be created by one firm's acquiring all or a large part of the stock or the assets of another firm. A merger is termed a **horizontal merger** when the two firms were competitors before they merged (e.g., Exxon and Mobil). One of the most famous merger decisions, *Standard Oil*, established the rule of reason as the approach the courts use in judging merger activities.

In the 1911 case, *Standard Oil* v. *United States* (221 U.S. 1), the Supreme Court ordered the breakup of the Standard Oil Trust, which was a combination of 72 companies that had joined to control as much as 90 percent of the production, shipping, refining, and selling of oil products. The court held that such a combination was a violation of Section 1 of the Sherman Act, which prohibits monopolization by a combination. Since that time, government authorities have challenged a number of mergers in part or in whole.

Premerger Notification Before firms merge, the Hart-Scott-Rodino (HSR) Antitrust Improvements Act requires the firms to notify the Antitrust Division of the Department of Justice or the Federal Trade Commission at least one month before the planned merger, if the value of the transaction is more than $70 million. The **premerger notification** requires payment of a filing fee.

Of the more than 1,000 HSR notices filed each year, a small number are subject to detailed examination by antitrust authorities, which may put the merger on hold while it is studied. The merging firms may be required to sell certain assets to allow the merger to go forward. For example, in a merger of gasoline producers, the resultant company was required to sell gas stations in some parts of the country where it would have had too much market power. Most mergers that are opposed, such as the proposed merger of Staples and Office Depot, are called off or changed in scope.

Determining Market Power To help businesses and regulators assess the antitrust implications of a merger, the Department of Justice has issued **merger guidelines** over the years. Revised by Justice and the FTC most recently in 2010, the guidelines discuss factors that arr considered in determining whether a merger will likely be challenged. Many factors considered by the Supreme Court in merger cases have been incorporated into the guidelines, which particularly focus on **market power**:

> *The unifying theme of the Guidelines is that mergers should not be permitted to create or enhance* market power *or to facilitate its exercise.... The ability of one or more firms profitably to maintain prices above competitive levels for a significant period of time is termed* market power.

Product and Geographic Markets To assess a firm's market power in antitrust cases, the courts determine the **market share** held by the firms involved in the merger. A firm's market share refers to the percentage of the relevant market controlled by the firm.

The Clayton Act states that the legality of a merger between two firms rests on whether "in any line of commerce in any section of the country, the effect of such acquisition may be substantially to lessen competition, or tend to create a monopoly." The phrase "in any line of commerce" refers to the particular **product market** in which the firms operate. For example, banks may be both in the credit market and the checking account market.

The phrase "in any section of the country" has reference to a **geographic market**. The relevant area may be one city or may be the nation. Therefore, in determining the relevant market, the courts and antitrust authorities take into account the appropriate product and geographic markets.

After determining the relevant market, a firm's market share can be determined by dividing the firm's sales by total sales within that market. In a merger case, the court often considers whether the combined market share of the merging firms exceeds some maximum market share and will, therefore, "substantially ... lessen competition" within the relevant market.

The determination of the product and geographic markets can be very complex. For example, is Apple in the market for computers that run the Apple operating system, in the personal computer market generally, or in the entertainment device market? Expert testimony about such issues usually plays a large role in deciding the outcome of cases.

Potential Competition Ordinarily, one thinks of competitors as offering similar products in the same market area. If the companies do not compete in this sense, should the courts be concerned about a merger? The Supreme Court has stated that the **potential competition** (the possibility that two companies can become competitors) may be enough to stop a merger.

The idea of potential competition was applied in *FTC* v. *Procter & Gamble* (386 U.S. 568), in which Procter & Gamble, a large household products maker, wanted to merge with Clorox, the leading maker of liquid bleach. After finding that bleach was the relevant product market, the Supreme Court held that even though Procter & Gamble did not make bleach, it could not merge with Clorox because Procter & Gamble could make bleach in the future. The Court wanted Clorox to face the threat of potential competition by a company such as Procter & Gamble.

When Mergers Are Allowed Merger guidelines take into consideration that a major reason to approve a merger is that it enhances efficiency in the market, benefiting consumers by a better allocation of resources.

The Supreme Court has also noted that if one of the firms involved in a merger is facing bankruptcy or other circumstances that threaten the firm, the Court will look more favorably upon the merger. This is called the **failing firm defense**. That defense is not in the statute but was created by the courts. To use the defense, the merging firms must establish that:

1. The firm being acquired is not likely to survive without the merger.
2. Neither the firm has any other prospective buyers or, if there are other buyers, the acquiring firm affects competition the least.
3. Other alternatives for saving the firm have been tried but have not succeeded.

Business Realities The courts weigh economic evidence and, like the FTC and Justice Department, often find mergers are not harmful to consumers. One defense used at times is the power buyer defense. Under this idea, a merger that increases concentration to high levels can be defended by showing that the firm's customers are sophisticated and powerful buyers. If the court finds that powerful buyers have sufficient bargaining power to ensure that the merged firm will be unable to charge monopoly prices, the merger might be allowed.

For example, in *United States* v. *Baker Hughes* (908 F.2d 981), the D.C. Circuit Court of Appeals denied the government's attempt to stop a merger of manufacturers of hard-rock hydraulic underground drilling rigs. Even though this industry had few sellers, the court found that the sophisticated and powerful buyers of such drilling rigs—oil companies—had sufficient bargaining power to ensure that the merged firm would be unable to charge monopoly prices for its rigs.

INTERNATIONAL PERSPECTIVE

The European Union and Antitrust Law

Antitrust law differs significantly across jurisdictions. Behavior that is legal in one country may be illegal in another. Because of the size of the European market, European Union (EU) antitrust law is an important consideration for businesses. Because EU and U.S. laws are different, companies operating in both jurisdictions must evaluate if their actions meet both sets of laws.

For example, U.S. antitrust regulators approved a merger by GE and Honeywell, two U.S.-based companies. However, EU antitrust regulators blocked the merger, prompting GE's CEO to complain that "The European regulators' demands exceeded anything I or our European advisers imagined and differed sharply from antitrust counterparts in the United States and Canada."

In another contrasting action, the EU demanded that Microsoft make available a version of Windows without a bundled Windows Media Player, disclose information to competitors about Windows that Microsoft considered confidential, and pay a fine of about $2 billion. A parallel U.S. investigation into the same issue led to minor penalties. Microsoft was later fined $732 million by the EU over browser choice tied to the Windows operating system.

The potentially aggressive nature of antitrust enforcement in the EU comes from its authority over any merger where the merging companies have a combined worldwide revenue of at least €5 billion, and receive annual revenue of €250 million within the EU, regardless of the companies' nationality. Thus, an American firm merging with a Mexican company that does a modest level of business in Europe, would be required to seek EU approval for a merger. An important difference between the U.S. and EU antitrust laws is that the EU Competition Commission can block mergers on its own, while U.S. regulators must go to court if they wish to do so.

Another criticism of EU antitrust law is that it is used strategically against foreign firms. In the past, there were few antitrust actions in Europe. The United States has had much tougher competition policies. Antitrust scholars contend that the emphasis of U.S. law is to promote competition, while the EU law focuses on protecting local competitors and extracting revenue from foreign firms.

Horizontal Restraints of Trade

When businesses at the same level of operation, such as retailers of a common product or producers of a raw material, come together in some manner—through contract, merger, or conspiracy—they risk being accused of restraining trade. A **horizontal restraint of trade** occurs when the businesses involved operate at the same level of the market and generally in the same market. It is easy to visualize a horizontal arrangement among competitors by examining the diagram in Exhibit 20.1. For example, think of three manufacturers of light bulbs who agree to charge the same price for bulbs or to split the market on a geographical basis.

The diagram could also show an arrangement among wholesalers or among retailers of a certain product. A collection of rival firms that come together by some form of agreement in an attempt to restrain trade by restricting output and raising prices is

---

EXHIBIT 20.1   HORIZONTAL BUSINESS RELATIONSHIPS

Product A Manufacturer X	⟷	Product A Manufacturer Y	⟷	Product A Manufacturer Z

© Cengage Learning

called a **cartel**. The most famous cartel of our day is the Organization of Petroleum Exporting Countries (OPEC), the group of oil-producing nations that banded together to control oil output. Becase that cartel consists of sovereign nations, American antitrust laws do not affect it. When private firms attempt to cartelize an industry, they are subject to antitrust law.

Price Fixing

Many antitrust cases have concerned **price fixing**. When firms sell the same product and agree to fix the price, there is a conspiracy that likely violates the Sherman Act. Price fixing has usually been held to be the worst violation of the antitrust laws. In *U.S.* v. *Trenton Potteries* (276 U.S. 392), the Supreme Court held that when competitors fix prices, there is a violation of the Sherman Act, whether the prices they set are reasonable or not. The Court decision held that agreements to set prices "may well be held to be in themselves unreasonable or unlawful restraints, without the necessity of minute inquiry whether a particular price is reasonable or unreasonable." That is, most price fixing is illegal *per se*. In the *Freeman* case, we see an application of this principle.

FREEMAN V. SAN DIEGO ASSOCIATION OF REALTORS
United States Court of Appeals, Ninth Circuit, 322 F.3d 1133 (2003)

Case Background *In most cities, a Multiple Listing Service (MLS) is used by real estate agents to share information about properties on the market through a computerized database. Agents subscribe to the MLS to list the properties they represent, as well as to see information about other properties on the market.*

Before 1992, there were 12 MLS associations in San Diego. The associations bought data services from four different database operators. Eleven associations decided to combine so all subscribing agents would have access to all San Diego properties; the combined database would also cost less to maintain than separate databases. The new entity, owned by the 11 associations, was called Sandicor. The 11 associations continued to sign up agents and collect subscription fees, but Sandicor set the rules. No price cutting was allowed. When the associations compared costs, they discovered that the largest MLS spent $10 per month per subscriber, while two small ones spent $50 per month per subscriber. The fee for all was set at $44 per subscribing agent, paid to Sandicor. That price was less than the $50 cost per subscriber that the small operators incurred, so the lower-cost associations agreed to cover the losses that the smaller MLS associations incurred.

Freeman and other San Diego real estate agents who subscribed to association services sued. They contended that Sandicor's central database was beneficial and efficient, but that the price of Sandicor's services was inflated. A service that had cost $10 a month at some associations was now $44. Plaintiffs contended that Sandicor was charging excessive service fees.

Freeman offered Sandicor the opportunity to market the MLS information to subscribers through a new service center at lower prices than the existing associations charged, but Sandicor refused. Freeman sued for Sherman Act violations for a conspiracy in restraint of trade by fixing prices, a violation of Section 1. The district court dismissed the suit; plaintiffs appealed.

Case Decision Kozinski, Circuit Judge

* * *

No antitrust violation is more abominated than the agreement to fix prices. With few exceptions, price-fixing agreements are unlawful *per se* under the Sherman Act and ... no showing of so-called competitive abuses or evils which those agreements were designed to eliminate or alleviate may be interposed as a defense." The dispositive question generally is not whether any price fixing was justified, but simply whether it occurred....

Sandicor charges subscribers for their use of the MLS; its MLS fee includes the support services provided by the associations. The support fee Sandicor pays the associations for support services was fixed at a level more than twice what it cost the most efficient association to provide them....

Were we to grant immunity from Section 1 merely because defendants nominally sell services through another entity rather than to consumers directly, we would risk opening a major loophole for ... retailer collusion.... Sandicor charges MLS subscribers $44 per month; an association collects this fee from each subscriber and hands it over to Sandicor, which then returns $22.50 to the associa-

tion as the support fee.... Defendants can't turn a horizontal agreement to fix prices into something innocuous just by changing the way they keep their books....

Reversed and remanded.

Questions for Analysis

1. The appeals court held that competitors improperly rigged prices. Sandicor claimed that the quality of its data was better because all associations contributed data, and the subscribers got superior service. Why did that argument not matter?

2. Sandicor claimed that it helped competition because the smallest, highest-cost associations were kept in business because the larger ones subsidized them. Why was that argument rejected?

While the courts take a hard line against collusion for the purpose of rigging prices, any one company has the right to charge whatever price it wishes for its products or services. The courts also recognize that certain organizations may help markets to work better. In some cases, a joint venture helps to set market prices. If a court finds that a good reason exists for this, it will allow the practice to stand.

Consider the problem faced by the thousands of owners of music copyrights, who have the right to earn royalties when thousands of radio stations and other commercial music users play their music. Because the owners could not possibly contract with every user of their music, they join organizations such as Broadcast Music, Inc. (BMI) or the American Society of Composers, Authors and Publishers (ASCAP). They issue "blanket licenses" that set the fees to be paid by any commercial users of the music. In *Broadcast Music* v. *CBS* (441 U.S. 1), the Supreme Court held that blanket licensing in such situations is not illegal price fixing because there is no other way for this market to work. Because the market works better than it would if BMI and ASCAP did not exist, the price fixing is not illegal.

Exchanges of Information

One problem in antitrust law is deciding whether the trading of information among businesses helps or restrains the competitive process. Some business information is collected and shared by the government, but many exchanges are done by private organizations, such as trade associations of firms in the same industry. If a business knows its competitors' sales, production, planned or actual capacities, cost accounting, quality standards, and research developments, is competition enhanced or is the information likely to be used to restrain trade?

Information Sharing The Supreme Court considered the issue of the sharing of information by competitors in *U.S.* v. *United States Gypsum* (438 U.S. 422). Six gypsum producers called each other to confirm prices being offered on gypsum products to various customers. That is, a buyer would tell Company B that Company A had offered to sell gypsum board at a certain price. Company B would call Company A to confirm the offer to make sure the buyer was telling the truth. The gypsum companies defended the practice as a good-faith effort to meet competition.

The Court said that a rule of reason may be applied, but the practice was not defensible. In an industry with only a few producers, sharing price information by competitors would most likely help to set prices and so could not be justified. The Court did not apply a *per se* rule against such price information exchanges. Instead, it held that exchanges would be examined closely and would be allowed in limited circumstances.

We see an example of illegal information sharing by competitors in the *Todd* case.

TODD V. EXXON CORPORATION

United States Court of Appeals, Second Circuit, 275 F.3d 191 (2001)

Case Background *Fourteen large oil companies organized surveys of salaries they paid to managerial, professional, and technical (MPT) employees. They used a "Job Match Survey" to be sure that the jobs at each company were compared properly. Representatives of the companies met to discuss job classifications and other data issues. A consultant analyzed, refined, and distributed the data to the 14 firms. The firms used the data in setting the salaries of MPT employees.*

Todd and other employees sued, contending that the information sharing was done to hold down MPT salaries. Plaintiffs contended this violated Section 1 of the Sherman Act. They did not claim that the companies conspired to fix wages, but that the sharing of information allowed the employers to control wages more than they could have without such information. The district court dismissed the suit. Plaintiffs appealed.

Case Decision Sotomayor, Circuit Judge

* * *

Information exchange is an example of a facilitating practice that can help support an inference of a price-fixing agreement....

The [Supreme Court has explained]: "The exchange of price data and other information among competitors does not invariably have anticompetitive effects; indeed such practices can in certain circumstances increase economic efficiency and render markets more, rather than less, competitive."...

Plaintiff argues that the relevant market in this case is the market for "the services of experienced, salaried, non-union, managerial, professional, and technical (MPT) employees in the oil and petrochemical industry, in the continental

United States and various sub-markets thereof." If the market is defined in this way, defendants would have a substantial market share of 80 to 90 percent....

The traditional horizontal conspiracy case involves an agreement among sellers with the purpose of raising prices to supracompetitve levels. The Sherman Act, however, also applies to abuse of market power on the buyer side—often taking the form of monopsony or oligopsony. Plaintiff is correct to point out that a horizontal conspiracy among buyers to stifle competition is as unlawful as one among sellers.... There is thus no reason to doubt that a ... data exchange claim—a close cousin of traditional price fixing—can be brought against a group of buyers....

If ... the plaintiff in this case could prove that (1) defendants engaged in information exchanges that would be deemed anticompetitive ... and (2) such activities did in fact have an anticompetitive effect on the market for MPT labor in the oil and petrochemical industry, we would not deny relief.... On remand, therefore, the court should consider whether plaintiff has demonstrated anticompetitive effects as part of the court's assessment of defendant's market power....

Another important factor to consider in evaluating an information exchange is whether the data are made publicly available. Public dissemination is a primary way for data exchange to realize its procompetitive potential.... Access to information may better equip buyers to compare products, rendering the market more efficient while diminishing the anticompetitive effects of the exchange. A court is therefore more likely to approve a data exchange where the information is made public.

In the instant case, dissemination of the information to the employees could have helped mitigate any anticompetitive effects of the exchange and possibly enhanced market efficiency by making employees more sensitive to salary increases. No such dissemination occurred, however. The information was not disclosed to the public nor to the employees whose salaries were the subject of the exchange....

Remanded.

Questions for Analysis

1. The appeals court held that the information sharing could violate the Sherman Act. Wage information is often gathered and published. Why is it normally legal?
2. The district court held that the oil companies did not control the MPT market, but that the appeals court rejected contention. Why might that court see it differently?

Conspiracy to Restrict Information Although the courts have indicated that it is generally legal to share price information in an open manner, and it is illegal to share information secretly among competitors or for the purpose of constructing a common price list for competitors, it may also be illegal to band together to restrict certain non-price information. Even the appearance of conspiring can cause problems, so, as Exhibit 20.2 indicates, companies and trade associations can take steps to avoid such problems.

In the Supreme Court decision *FTC* v. *Indiana Federation of Dentists* (476 U.S. 447) the Court held that the FTC justifiably attacked the policy of an Indiana dentists' organization requiring members to withhold X-rays from dental insurance companies. Insurance companies sometimes required dentists to submit patient X-rays to help evaluate patients' claims for insurance benefits. The X-rays helped the companies eliminate insurance fraud and make sure that dentists did not prescribe dental work not required. The FTC attack on this policy was upheld under a rule of reason analysis that showed the dentists' policy to be a conspiracy in restraint of trade. The Court noted that no pro-competitive reason for the anti-X-ray-sharing rule was found.

Lighter Side of the Law

We're Lawyers, and We're Here to Help You

Nineteen lawyers teamed together to bring a class-action antitrust suit on behalf of consumers against three gasoline retailers in Dothan, Alabama. In a trial that lasted six weeks in federal court, the jury found that there was a conspiracy to fix gasoline prices. Damages were found to be $1. However, under the law, the guilty party is also responsible for attorney's fees. The judge granted the attorneys $2 million in legal fees for their diligent efforts.

Source: Associated Press.

Territorial Restrictions

A horizontal market division occurs when firms competing at the same level of business reach an agreement to divide the market on geographic or other terms. The effect of the agreement is to eliminate competition among those firms. Firms competing in a national

EXHIBIT 20.2   AVOIDING ANTITRUST PROBLEMS AT TRADE MEETINGS

ANTITRUST REMINDER

Competitors often meet when attending industry conventions. This means firms could share information improperly and even plan to act together. Because of this possibility, it is common for meeting organizers to remind participants of antitrust problems that could emerge from their being together. Here is a list from one trade association meeting.

DON'T:

- Discuss with other members your own, or your competitors', prices or anything that might affect prices, such as costs, discounts, terms of sale, or profit margins.
- Make public announcements or statements about your own prices or those of competitors.
- Talk about what your company, or any other company, plans to do in particular geographic or product markets or with particular customers.
- Disclose to others at meetings any competitively sensitive information.
- Stay at a meeting where any such price, or competitively sensitive, talk occurs.

DO:

- Always look for and adhere to a written agenda, and limit discussion to agenda or non-business topics.
- Consult your corporate counsel in case of doubt about the propriety of a topic of discussion.
- State any reservations you have concerning remarks or discussion at a meeting; if the discussion is not terminated or resolved satisfactorily, leave the meeting.
- Avoid "rump sessions" involving the discussion of business matters.

© Cengage Learning

market, for example, may reach an agreement to divide the market into regional markets, with each firm being assigned one region. Each firm can then exercise monopoly power within its region.

Agreements intended to provide horizontal customer allocations or **territorial allocations** are often held to violate antitrust law. When the agreement does not involve price fixing by the firms participating in the agreement, the case may be considered under a rule of reason; that is, each challenged agreement is evaluated in light of its effect on consumer welfare. However, this has not been a common basis for antitrust cases in recent years.

ISSUE SPOTTER
Share and Share Alike

Your customers, retail housing construction supply firms, tell you that the price your pipe production company is asking for PVC pipe is too high and that they will be taking their business elsewhere. The profit margins are thin, and you are not interested in cutting prices unless it is absolutely necessary to retain business. When you go to the annual PVC pipe makers' convention, how might you legally find out what your competitors are charging? What type of action would be most likely to get you into trouble with the antitrust authorities?

© Cengage Learning

❓ TEST YOURSELF

1. Exchanges of market-relevant information among competitors is generally *per se* illegal: T—F

2. In *Freeman* v. *San Diego Assn. of Realtors*, where Multiple Listing Services (MLS) joined together to provide all information from all MLS services at one price, the appeals court held that the practice:
   a. was a *per se* violation of the Sherman Act as price fixing.
   b. violated the Sherman Act under a rule of reason analysis because it caused prices to increase.
   c. was not a violation of the Sherman Act under a rule of reason analysis because the price was reasonable.
   d. was not a violation of the Sherman Act under a rule of reason analysis because of the greater efficiency of one information provider compared to 12.

3. When two firms wish to join together to become one firm, it is called a(n) _____ and may be subject to antitrust review.

4. The Sherman Act was the first antitrust statute passed by Congress; the second was the Clayton Act. The third antitrust statute was the _____.

5. Congress has enacted a number of exemptions to the antitrust laws, such as exempting most labor union activity from antitrust inspection: T—F

6. In *Spanish Broadcasting System of Florida* v. *Clear Channel Communications*, where Clear Channel dominated that Spanish-language radio market, the appeals court held that Clear Channel must sell seven stations so as to increase competition in that market: T—F

7. In *Todd* v. *Exxon Corporation*, where large firms in the oil industry hired a consultant to provide information about wages for industry professionals, and Todd sued, contending a violation of the Sherman Act, the appeals court held that the:
   a. oil companies may have illegally kept the information private.
   b. oil companies conspired to fix wages artificially low and must pay damages to all affected employees.
   c. plaintiff had no cause of action because he could not show how he was harmed by the information sharing.
   d. plaintiff should have sued under the Robinson-Patman Act for price suppression.

8. If competitors in an industry get together to agree to chop up the market and not compete directly with each other, this is likely an illegal _____ or _____.

Answers: F; a; merger; FTC Act; T; F; a; customer allocation, territorial allocation.

Vertical Restraint of Trade

Until now, we have considered antitrust law as it applies to horizontal restraints of trade. We now turn to antitrust issues such as vertical restraint of trade, exclusionary practices, and price discrimination. **Vertical restraint of trade** concerns relationships between buyers and sellers, such as between the manufacturer and its wholesalers or the wholesalers and retailers. A key subject of this part of the chapter is how firms deal with each up and down of the business chain. We look at how producers', distributors' and retailers' dealings are controlled by antitrust law.

Vertical business arrangements govern relationships in the different stages of the production, distribution, and sale of the same product, as we see in Exhibit 20.3. For

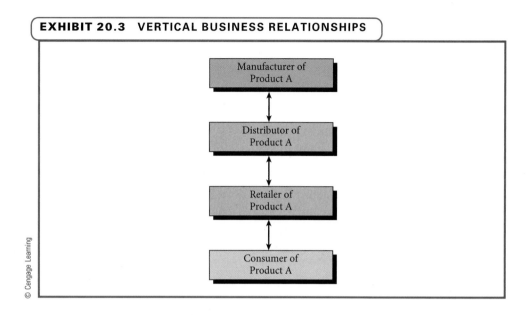

EXHIBIT 20.3 VERTICAL BUSINESS RELATIONSHIPS

Manufacturer of Product A

Distributor of Product A

Retailer of Product A

Consumer of Product A

© Cengage Learning

example, think of a manufacturer that imposes resale restrictions on the retailers. Many makers of luxury goods exercise considerable control over sellers of their products to protect their brand image. The producer tells the retailer the price it must set at retail (the resale price), the area in which there may be resale of products, or who the retailer's customers may be. Because these arrangements restrain actions, they may be challenged as contrary to the goals of antitrust law.

Vertical Price Fixing

Vertical price-fixing arrangements involve agreements between a manufacturer, its wholesalers, its distributors or other suppliers, and the retailers that sell the product to consumers. As a rule, these are intended to control the price at which the product is sold to consumers. In many cases, it has been the retailers that approach the manufacturer and request a price agreement. In other instances, the manufacturer requires the wholesaler (supplier) to control the price being charged by retailers. Agreements can call for the retailer to fix minimum prices or maximum prices.

Resale Price Maintenance An agreement between a manufacturer, a supplier, and retailers of a product under which the retailers agree to sell the product at not less than a minimum price is called **resale price maintenance** (RPM). One purpose of these arrangements is to prevent retailers from cutting the price of a brand-name product. Although manufacturers may contend that such arrangements make product distribution more efficient or competitive, such arrangements can be an illegal restraint of trade.

Dr. Miles Case In 1911, the Supreme Court pronounced a basic rule about RPM. It stated that once a producer or supplier sells a product to a retailer, it could not control the price the retailer charges consumers. In *Dr. Miles Medical* v. *John D. Park and Sons* (220 U.S. 373), the court held that a manufacturer can, of course, sell its product for whatever it wants, but it cannot "fix prices for future sales." That is, it cannot set prices further down the sales chain.

Pros and Cons of Resale Price Maintenance RPM has been the subject of political wrangling in Congress and debate among lawyers and economists since *Dr. Miles.* The groups favoring the ability to control resale prices have been the producers of quality, well-known products and small retailers. Opponents have been mass retailers and producers of lesser-known products.

Many small retailers favor RPM. They cannot match Wal-Mart prices, so they would like to see all retailers forced by manufacturers to sell goods at the same prices. If the retailers are strong enough, they may band together to demand that the producer impose RPM so that retailers do not compete with each other by price-cutting. RPM thus prevents cheating by members of the retail cartel.

Producers of well-known, established products may favor RPM because it allows retailers to earn higher profits from the sale of their products. These higher retail profits, in turn, encourage retailers to advertise the products more and to give good service.

Mass retailers oppose RPM because they have grown large by slashing retail prices. The mass retailers often offer little point-of-sale service; their concern is selling large volumes at lower markup. Similarly, the producers of lesser-known brands want to compete on the basis of price, so they like the chance to be on the mass retailers' shelves with the best-known products. They have not incurred the high costs of establishing a good reputation, so their prices are lower.

However, RPM may result in more full-service, higher-cost stores staying in business. Hence, RPM advocates claim that consumers and well-established brands may be better off by the information and service that may be provided under an RPM arrangement. Smaller-market retailers and producers may be able to compete more effectively with big box stores and lower-cost brands.

Vertical Maximum Price Fixing Some years ago, the Supreme Court held that some price fixing in vertical relationships is acceptable. In *State Oil Co.* v. *Khan* (118 S.Ct. 275), a gasoline distributor controlled the maximum gasoline sales markup that its gasoline station dealers could charge customers. One gas station owner wanted to charge more for retail gasoline than the distributor would allow and sued, claiming this was illegal price fixing. The Supreme Court upheld the maximum-price controls, noting that low prices benefit consumers regardless of how the prices are set. A rule of reason is applied in such cases.

Vertical Minimum Price Fixing After 96 years, the Supreme Court limited the rule from the *Dr. Miles* case by holding that vertical minimum price fixing, or RPM, was no long *per se* illegal. Since the *Leegin* case, it has been subject to a rule of reason analysis. That is, when a manufacturer imposes resale prices, such as retail prices to be set by stores on certain products, the courts look to see if the practice in a particular case is destructive to competition or not. As the Court explained, **intrabrand competition** must be considered as well as **interbrand competition**.

LEEGIN CREATIVE LEATHER PRODUCTS V. PSKS

United States Supreme Court 551 U.S. 877 (2007)

Case Background *Leegin designs, makes, and distributes leather goods. Most popular are belts with the brand name "Brighton." These are sold across the country in over 5,000 stores, mostly independent, small boutiques and specialty stores. Leegin refused to sell to retailers that*

discounted Brighton goods below its suggested retail prices. Leegin allowed products not selling well, that the retailer did not plan on reordering, to be discounted.

Leegin told the stores that bought from it: "In this age of mega stores like Macy's ... consumers are perplexed by promises of product quality and support of product which we believe is lacking in these large stores. Consumers are further confused by the ever popular sale, sale, sale, etc." In contrast, the Leegin policy was stable prices that would allow selected retailers to earn good profits. That would give them an incentive to support the Brighton brand.

Leegin discovere that Kay's Kloset, a retail store in Texas, was consistently discounting Brighton-brand products by 20 percent. It told Kay's to stop cutting prices below suggested retail prices, but it did not, so Leegin quit selling to it.

Kay's then sued Leegin for violating Section 1 of the Sherman Act. At trial, the court would not allow expert testimony about the economic benefits of the Leegin policy, holding that resale price maintenance was a per se violation. The jury awarded Kay's $1.2 million damages, which were then tripled. The appeals court affirmed. Leegin appealed.

Case Decision Kennedy, Justice

* * *

Though each side of the debate can find sources to support its position, it suffices to say here that economics literature is replete with procompetitive justifications for a manufacturer's use of resale price maintenance....

Minimum resale price maintenance can stimulate interbrand competition—the competition among manufacturers selling different brands of the same type of product—by reducing intrabrand competition—the competition among retailers selling the same brand. The promotion of interbrand competition is important because "the primary purpose of the antitrust laws is to protect [this type of] competition." A single manufacturer's use of vertical price restraints tends to eliminate intrabrand price competition; this in turn encourages retailers to invest in tangible or intangible services or promotional efforts that aid the manufacturer's position as against rival manufacturers. Resale price maintenance also has the potential to give consumers more options so that they can choose among low-price,

low-service brands; high-price, high-service brands; and brands that fall in between.

Absent vertical price restraints, the retail services that enhance interbrand competition might be under-provided. This is because discounting retailers can free ride on retailers who furnish services and then capture some of the increased demand those services generate. Consumers might learn, for example, about the benefits of a manufacturer's product from a retailer that invests in fine showrooms, offers product demonstrations, or hires and trains knowledgeable employees....

Resale price maintenance, in addition, can increase interbrand competition by facilitating market entry for new firms and brands....

While vertical agreements setting minimum resale prices can have procompetitive justifications, they may have anticompetitive effects in other cases; and unlawful price fixing, designed solely to obtain monopoly profits, is an ever present temptation. Resale price maintenance may, for example, facilitate a manufacturer cartel....

To the extent a vertical agreement setting minimum resale prices is entered upon to facilitate a ... cartel, it would need to be held unlawful under the rule of reason....

For these reasons the Court's decision in *Dr. Miles Medical Co.* v. *John D. Park & Sons Co.*, 220 U.S. 373, 31 S.Ct. 376 (1911), is now overruled. Vertical price restraints are to be judged according to the rule of reason....

The judgment of the Court of Appeals is reversed, and the case is remanded for proceedings consistent with this opinion.

Questions for Analysis

1. Assuming resale price maintenance to be generally legal, what kind of companies do you think would benefit the most from the practice?
2. This overturned a rule set in a case almost 100 years ago. Should courts overturn old rulings or should they leave it to the legislature to change the law?

Vertical Nonprice Restraints

Manufacturers frequently impose nonprice restraints on their distributors and retailers. Such vertical arrangements often take the form of territorial or customer restrictions on the sale of the manufacturer's products. Coca-Cola and PepsiCo, for example, set territorial restrictions on their bottlers. Each bottler is permitted to sell and deliver the product within its designated territory. Delivery outside that territory—that is, delivery in competition with another bottler—is grounds for loss or cancellation of the franchise agreement.

Customer restrictions may be imposed on distributors and retailers when the manufacturer sells directly to certain customers. A construction materials manufacturer, for example, may deal directly with large commercial accounts but allow distributors to deal with smaller accounts. The courts apply the rule of reason in such cases.

In most territorial restraint cases, the plaintiff is a retailer or distributor that has been terminated by a manufacturer changing its product distribution strategy. The manufacturer often eliminates some distributors so that the remaining distributors have the necessary territorial or customer base to be successful.

Exclusionary Practices

A principal concern of the antitrust laws is the extent to which firms with market power can control the markets in which they do business. Various business practices are designed to make it more difficult for competitors to challenge the market dominance of the firm using such tactics. Such practices, which include tying arrangements, exclusive-dealing agreements, and boycotts, can come under antitrust attack if the courts find them to be anticompetitive. Section 3 of the Clayton Act applies to tying arrangements and to exclusive-dealing agreements involving goods, while Section 1 of the Sherman Act, which covers goods and services, governs the antitrust aspects of group boycotts.

Tying Arrangements   In *Northern Pacific Railway Company* v. *United States* (356 U.S. 1), the Supreme Court defined a **tying arrangement** or **tie-in sale** as

> *an agreement by a party to sell one product [the tying product] but only on the condition that the buyer also purchases a different [complementary or tied] product, or at least agrees that he will not purchase that product from any other supplier.*

The Supreme Court held that where monopoly power exists, tying arrangements violate the antitrust laws; the arrangement extends a firm's market power over the tying product into the market for the tied product. The courts apply either Section 1 of the Sherman Act—viewing tying arrangements as an unreasonable restraint of trade—or Section 3 of the Clayton Act—viewing tying arrangements as a sales contract that may substantially lessen competition or tend to create a monopoly.

Rule of Reason Applied to Tie-in Cases   The Supreme Court has held that tie-ins meet a rule of reason test so long as competitive alternatives exist. That is, if a tie-in creates a monopoly, when there are no or few good alternatives, it is likely illegal; but if products or services are tied together when there are competitors, the tie-in likely passes the rule of reason test, as the Court held in *U.S. Steel* v. *Fortner Enterprises* (429 U.S. 610).

U.S. Steel produced mobile homes. Fortner needed $2 million to develop land on which to place mobile homes that he promised to buy from U.S. Steel if it would lend him the money. U.S. Steel made the loan. Later, Fortner's venture failed, and he claimed the contract with U.S. Steel violated antitrust law because there was a tie-in between the purchase of homes and the financing of the land. The mobile homes were the product tied to U.S. Steel's alleged power over the credit market. The Court rejected that argument, holding that U.S. Steel, while large, had no monopoly power over credit or over mobile homes, which are in highly competitive markets. Because the tie-in did not exploit any monopoly power, the actions of U.S. Steel did not violate the antitrust law under a rule of reason analysis.

Vertical Restraint Guidelines The Department of Justice's *Vertical Restraint Guidelines* claim that the Supreme Court is likely to impose a *per se* rule of illegality only when three conditions are met:

1. The seller has market power in the tying product.
2. Tied and tying products are separate.
3. There is evidence of substantial adverse effect in the tied product market.

In other situations, the rule of reason approach is to be employed. The Justice Department said that in such cases, the following test would hold:

> *The use of tying will not be challenged if the party imposing the tie has a market share of 30 percent or less in the market for the tying product. This presumption can be overcome only by a showing that the tying agreement unreasonably restrained competition in the market for the tied product.*

The Supreme Court found an illegal tie-in arrangement in *Eastman Kodak* v. *Image Technical Services* (504 U.S. 451). Kodak, a maker of complex photographic equipment, refused to sell replacement parts for its machines to independent companies that offered repair and maintenance service on the machines. Kodak required buyers of its machines to use its own repair personnel in order to obtain Kodak replacement parts. Independent repair companies lost business, and some went out of business. The Court held that Kodak used market power over the machines to extend the power to replacement parts. That would not be allowed unless Kodak could show that the practice promoted competition in the market for the machinery.

INTERNATIONAL PERSPECTIVE

China's Anti-Monopoly Law

The People's Republic of China enacted an Anti-Monopoly Law (AMD) that went into effect in 2008. It is under the supervision of the Anti-Monopoly Commission (AMC). Operationally, it is structured more like antitrust law in the EU than in the United States; decisions are made by a government agency, not private litigators.

Like most antitrust law, the AML may be applied to both horizontal and vertical agreements. Horizontal price fixing, output restrictions, market divisions, limits on technology, and boycotts are prohibited. Resale price fixing is a vertical arrangement that is prohibited, but there is less concern about vertical arrangements than about horizontal agreements among competitors. Violators face civil and administrative penalties, but not criminal penalties.

Just as EU antitrust enforcement can affect decisions of multinational firms, so can the AML. For example, when InBev of Belgium merged with Anheuser-Busch of the United States to create the world's largest beer company, the AMC placed restrictions of the ownership share the new company could have in Chinese breweries.

More surprising was the blockage of Coca-Cola's attempted purchase of Huiyuan Juice Group. The merger would have created the second largest juice maker in the country, with about 20 percent of the market. That would have allowed it to be a more effective competitor against the dominant firm in the market, but the AMC rejected the move, saying it would hurt small competitors in the market.

As is true of other countries, China intends to protect the position of domestic enterprises. When Chinese sellers of vitamin C were found guilty of price-fixing in the United States and ordered to pay $162 million in damages, the companies defended that prices were set by the Chinese government, which protested the application of U.S. law to Chinese companies selling in the U.S. market.

Boycotts A **boycott** occurs when a group conspires to prevent the carrying on of business or to harm a business. It can be promoted by any group—consumers, unions, retailers, wholesalers, or suppliers—who, when acting together, can inflict economic damage on a business. The boycott is used to force compliance with a price-fixing scheme or some other restraint of trade. Boycott cases usually fall under the *per se* rule against price fixing.

Unlike other vertical restrictions in which one manufacturer negotiates with individual dealers about terms of trade for its goods, boycotts may involve manufacturers getting together to tell dealers what they must do, or dealers getting together to tell manufacturers what they must do. The Supreme Court has made it clear that when horizontal competitors use a boycott to force a change in the nature of a vertical relationship, there is a *per se* violation of the law. Such cases are not common.

Lighter Side **of the Law**

Give Us What We Want, or We Will Throw a Tantrum

Where a website shows up in a search depends on many factors. The formulae are complex, but are partly a function of how many searchers have looked at a website. The algorithm is kept secret to try to reduce the gaming that website owners use to try to get a higher ranking for their sites than they can earn otherwise.

KinderStart.com is a specialty search engine designed for "children zero to seven." Google gave KinderStart.com a low Page Rank (PR) based on its formula. The low PR meant little traffic for KinderStart.

So KinderStart.com sued Google for Sherman Act violations in its PR system. It demanded money and that Google reveal its trade secrets about how it sets PRs. It got nowhere with the litigation.

Source: True Stella Awards.

The Robinson-Patman Act

The Robinson-Patman Act, enacted in 1936, amends the Clayton Act. Section 2 (a) states that "it shall be unlawful for any person engaged in commerce ... to discriminate in price between different purchasers of commodities of like grade and quality ... where the effect of such discrimination may be substantially to lessen competition or tend to create a monopoly in any line of commerce." Thus, a seller is said to engage in **price discrimination** when the same product is sold to different buyers at different prices.

Section 2(a) is a highly controversial part of antitrust law. The reason for its passage was to limit the ability of chain stores to offer merchandise at a price lower than their single-store competitors. The intent of the Act is to deny consumers the benefits from lower prices that result from mass merchandising. The Department of Justice and the FTC have been reluctant to enforce the Act. Most cases brought under the Robinson-Patman Act are private actions.

Price Discrimination

Most cases brought under the Robinson-Patman Act concern a firm charging different prices in different markets or offering bulk sale discounts to larger volume retailers. To illustrate, suppose that two sellers—Simpson's Wholesale and South Park Distributors—sell the same product in competition with each other in San Francisco. Simpson's also sells the product in Oakland, but South Park does not. If Simpson's reduces its price levels in San Francisco but not in Oakland, that price cut may violate the Robinson-Patman Act. Simpson's is engaging in price discrimination—charging different prices in different markets to the detriment of a competitor, South Park.

Predatory Pricing The business practice just described is sometimes called **predatory pricing.** That is, Simpson's attempts to undercut South Park in San Francisco and sells the product for a higher price in other markets in which it does not compete with South Park. Presumably, Simpson's intends to drive South Park from the San Francisco market and then raise prices there when South Park goes out of business.

Firms can file suits alleging predatory pricing under both the Robinson-Patman Act and Section 2 of the Sherman Act. However, because it is difficult to distinguish predatory prices from prices driven low by competition, the Supreme Court today is reluctant to rule in favor of plaintiffs alleging predation.

To win, a plaintiff must present strong evidence showing that:

1. The defendant priced below cost.
2. The defendant's below-cost prices created a genuine prospect that the defendant would monopolize the market.
3. The defendant would enjoy its monopoly at least long enough to recoup the losses it suffered during the price war.

The Court puts this heavy burden on predatory-pricing plaintiffs because it understands that firms might otherwise sue their price-cutting rivals for no reason other than to keep these rivals from lowering prices to competitive levels. As the Court said in *Brooke Group LTD.* v. *Brown & Williamson Tobacco Corporation* (113 S.Ct. 2578), "It would be ironic indeed if the standards for predatory pricing liability were so low that antitrust suits themselves became a tool for keeping prices high." In the *Weyerhaeuser* case, the Supreme Court extended the analysis to include what some have called **predatory bidding**—when a strong firm can outbid rivals.

WEYERHAEUSER V. ROSS-SIMMONS HARDWOOD LUMBER

Supreme Court of the United States 549 U.S. 312, 127 S.Ct. 1069 (2007)

Case Background *Ross-Simmons sued Weyerhaeuser for antitrust violation for driving it out of business. The claim was that Weyerhaeuser consistently outbid Ross for logs to process into lumber. Ross contended this was predatory behavior—Weyerhaeuser bid higher to get control of the logs, so Ross could not compete in the lumber market. Weyerhaeuser used state-of-the-art technology to increase efficiency and captured 65 percent of the red alder log market in the area around Longview, Washington.*

The jury held for Ross, awarding it $26 million, which was tripled. The appeals court affirmed. Weyerhaeuser appealed, claiming the holding violated the Supreme Court's previous decision in the Brooke Group case.

Case Decision Thomas, Justice

* * *

Predatory bidding, which Ross-Simmons alleges in this case, involves the exercise of market power on the buy side or input side of a market. In a predatory-bidding scheme, a purchaser of inputs "bids up the market price of a critical input to such high levels that rival buyers cannot survive (or compete as vigorously) and, as a result, the predating buyer acquires (or maintains or increases) its) monopsony power." Monopsony power is market power on the buy side of the market. As such, a monopsony is to the buy side of the market what a monopoly is to the sell side and is sometimes colloquially called a "buyer's monopoly."

A predatory bidder ultimately aims to exercise the monopsony power gained from bidding up input prices. To that end, once the predatory bidder has caused competing buyers to exit the market for purchasing inputs, it will seek to "restrict its input purchases below the competitive level," thus "reducing the unit price for the remaining inputs it purchases." The reduction in input prices will lead to "a significant cost saving that more than offsets the profits that would have been earned on the output." If all goes as planned, the predatory bidder will reap monopsonistic profits that will offset any losses suffered in bidding up input prices.

Predatory-pricing and predatory-bidding claims are analytically similar....

More importantly, predatory bidding mirrors predatory pricing in respects that we deemed significant to our analysis in *Brooke Group*.... Predatory pricing requires a firm to suffer certain losses in the short term on the chance of reaping supracompetitive profits

in the future. A rational business will rarely make this sacrifice. The same reasoning applies to predatory bidding. A predatory-bidding scheme requires a buyer of inputs to suffer losses today on the chance that it will reap supracompetitive profits in the future....

A predatory-bidding plaintiff also must prove that the defendant has a dangerous probability of recouping the losses incurred in bidding up input prices through the exercise of monopsony power. Absent proof of likely recoupment, a strategy of predatory bidding makes no economic sense because it would involve short-term losses with no likelihood of offsetting long-term gains....

For these reasons, we vacate the judgment of the Court of Appeals and remand the case for further proceedings consistent with this opinion.

Questions for Analysis

1. The Supreme Court held that there was no basis for an antitrust suit based on a claim of predatory bidding. Because Ross was driven from the market, why did its claim not hold?
2. If Weyerhaeuser was more profitable than Ross, why could Ross not show that Weyerhaeuser had an unfair advantage in the market?

Volume Discounts Legal? The Robinson-Patman Act is also concerned with sales discounts given to large-volume retailers. To illustrate, suppose Simpson's and South Park both buy the same product from Tweet Distributors for the purpose of selling it retail. Because Simpson's is a larger-volume retailer, Tweet gives Simpson's a bigger price discount on its larger purchases. The price discount gives Simpson's a competitive advantage over South Park in the sale of the product to customers in the area. The alleged injury to competition is the price discount given to Simpson's, the larger purchaser. This type of action generates numerous private actions against producers who discriminate in pricing to wholesalers or retailers.

 ISSUE SPOTTER

Who Do You Sell What to, and for How Much?

Your company sells appliances. You handle the selling of refrigerators to retailers. Your Big Box model has a wholesale price of $629, plus actual shipping cost. Home Depot calls and wants to buy 20,000 Big Box units over ten months. Bob's Home Store calls and wants to buy ten Big Box units over ten months. Home Depot wants a discount because of the size of its order. Can you give them a discount? What about Bob's? How might Robinson-Patman apply?

Defenses

A key defense for firms charged with violating the Robinson-Patman Act is to show a **cost justification** for different prices charged in different markets or to different buyers. An obvious cost-justification defense is a difference in transportation costs—it costs more to transport a refrigerator 300 miles than 30 miles. Similarly, on a per-unit basis, it is cheaper to deliver a thousand refrigerators than it is to deliver five refrigerators. The major problem with using the cost-justification defense is that it is virtually an accounting impossibility to assign specific costs of production to individual products. As a consequence, the cost-justification defense is rarely successful by itself.

The other defense that may be used is that of **meeting competition**. That is, a firm cuts its price in response to a competitor's cutting its price first. The problem with this defense can be that the original price cut is illegal under Robinson-Patman, which means that subsequent price cuts may also be illegal, at least at some point. Competitors must show that the meeting-competition price cut was done in good faith, not in an effort to injure competitors but to stay competitive.

? TEST YOURSELF

1. When a manufacturer tells a retailer the price to sell its product at the retail level, that practice is called _____.
2. The Supreme Court held that maximum price fixing in vertical relationships, as in *State Oil Co.* v. *Khan*, is generally legal if the effect is to lower prices to benefit consumers: T—F
3. In *Leegin Creative Leather Products* v. *PSKS*, where Leegin was controlling the minimum price at which many of its goods could be sold by retailers, the Supreme Court held that Leegin's actions were:
   a. *per se* illegal.
   b. *per se* legal.
   c. legal under a rule of reason analysis.
   d. illegal under a rule of reason analysis.
4. When the sale of one good is linked to the sale of another good, it is said to be a(n) _____ arrangement.
5. When a group conspires to prevent the carrying on of business or to harm a business, it is called a(n) _____ and is likely illegal.
6. If a company engages in price discrimination, where it sells a good to one buyer at a different price than it sells the same good to another buyer, there may be a violation of the Robinson-Patman Act: T—F
7. If a firm is charged with violating the Robinson-Patman Act, the most likely successful defense is called _____.

Answers: resale price maintenance; T; c; tying; boycott; T; meeting competition.

SUMMARY

- The three most important antitrust statutes—the Sherman Act of 1890, the Clayton Act of 1914, and the FTC Act of 1914—were enacted in response to concern about the economic power of the large industrial corporations and trusts that emerged during the late nineteenth century. Before the enactment of the statutes, common-law precedent was relied on to combat certain restraints on trade, but the government had little authority to intervene.

- Congress exempts labor unions and others from the antitrust laws. The state action doctrine allows states to regulate business in such a way as to fix prices or otherwise monopolize a market.

- Violations of the antitrust laws can expose defendants to criminal penalties, which can include prison sentences, as well as civil penalties. Defendants who lose antitrust suits in which damages are found must pay treble damages. The Antitrust Division of the Justice Department, the Federal Trade Commission, and private parties enforce the antitrust laws. Only the Justice Department can bring criminal charges for alleged antitrust violations.

- Most antitrust matters are determined by a rule of reason analysis, where the courts weigh the pros and cons of business practices alleged to be anti-competitive. Some practices, such as price fixing by competitors, are so clearly anticompetitive that they are declared to be illegal *per se*.

- Horizontal restraints of trade occur when business competitors at the same level of business, such as producers of similar products, agree to act together.

- Mergers of competitor companies are likely to be challenged only if the merger would significantly reduce competition in a market. The market is defined along both territory and product lines.

- Independent companies in the same industry are usually not allowed to agree to divide the market geographically, by type of customer, or in any other arrangement that reduces competition.

- Horizontal price fixing occurs when competitors agree to act together to set prices for their products or services. This can happen at any level of operation and is usually illegal *per se*.

- There is no defense for companies in the same industry that get together, by any means, to agree

on product prices in the markets in which they operate. Competitors may not fix prices at any level unless there are special circumstances that make the arrangement pro-competitive.

- Companies in an industry may share price and other market information through a trade association so long as the information is not used to control the market, and the information is available to the public.

- Vertical relationships are between sellers and buyers at different levels of business, such as between manufacturer and distributor. Vertical restraints of trade occur when a firm at one level of business controls the practices of a firm at another level, such as a distributor telling a retailer what price to charge its customers for its products.

- Vertical price fixing, or resale price maintenance, in which the producer tells the retailers of its products the minimum prices at which to sell the products, is illegal *per se*. Suggested retail prices are legal but may not be enforced by a threat to cut off a retailer who will not adhere to them.

- Vertical non-price restraints, such as granting exclusive territory to dealers, are viewed under a rule of reason. Manufacturers are given wide latitude in picking dealers and deciding the terms under which they retain them. The producer may not conspire with a dealer against another dealer.

- Tie-in sales, where the sale of one product is tied to the sale of another, are judged under a rule of reason. For such a sale to be illegal, it must be shown that monopoly power in one product existed and was extended to the other product.

- When any organized group at one level of business (such as hardware store owners) gets together to agree to a joint action (such as refusal to deal) against one or more businesses at another level of business (such as a particular hardware supplier), such action is a boycott, which is usually illegal *per se*.

- The Robinson-Patman Act holds that price discrimination—selling the same product to different buyers at different prices—must be justified by differences in the cost of selling to the different buyers or because the price difference was required to meet competition. This is one of the most troublesome areas of law for producers. The courts are not sympathetic to such cases.

TERMS TO KNOW

antitrust, 548
restraint of trade, 548
monopoly, 548
unfair methods of
    competition, 549
Parker doctrine, 549
treble damages, 550
cease and desist order, 550
per se rule, 551
rule of reason, 551
merger, 553
horizontal merger, 553

premerger notification, 554
merger guidelines, 554
market power, 554
market share, 554
product market, 554
geographic market, 554
potential competition, 554
failing firm defense, 555
horizontal restraint of trade, 556
cartel, 557
price fixing, 557
territorial allocation, 561

vertical restraint of trade, 562
resale price maintenance, 563
intrabrand competition, 564
interbrand competition, 564
tying arrangement, 566
tie-in sale, 566
boycott, 568
price discrimination, 568
predatory pricing, 569
predatory bidding, 569
cost justification, 571
meeting competition, 571

DISCUSSION QUESTION

Why was the Sherman Act written in such broad language? Is it possible that Congress wrote the legislation in an unclear manner to give the courts broad leeway in attacking monopolistic business practices? Would it have been better for Congress to have specified more of the terms of antitrust violations?

CASE QUESTIONS

1. Many professional engineers belong to the National Society of Professional Engineers, which governs technical aspects of the practice of engineering. The canon of ethics adopted by the Society held that engineers could not bid against one another for a particular job. The Society claimed that this rule was to prevent engineers from engaging in price-cutting to get engineering jobs, which could then give them incentives to cut corners on the quality of work. Such a practice could lead to inferior work that could endanger the public. The Justice Department sued, claiming that this was a violation of Section 1 of the Sherman Act. The government claimed that the ethical rule reduced price competition and gave an unfair advantage to engineers with well-established reputations. Who wins? [*National Society of Professional Engineers* v. *United States*, 98 S.Ct. 1355 (1978)]

2. Professional basketball players and their union sued the National Basketball Association (NBA) for various practices, such as the draft of college players and its salary-cap system. They claimed that this violated the antitrust law by restricting opportunities for professional basketball players. Could such practices survive a rule of reason

analysis? [*NBA* v. *Williams*, 45 F.3d 684, 2nd Cir. (1995)]
✓ Check your answer

3. A Wisconsin law, the Unfair Sales Act, long required that retail gasoline be marked up at least 9.18 percent over wholesale price. When gas went to more than $4 a gallon in 2008, the law required the price to be increased at retail by 38 cents more a gallon. Flying J, which runs travel plazas, sued to contest the law, as it did not wish to mark-up its gas or diesel that much. The state contended that it was immune from antitrust actions. Was that position correct? Can a state mandate a price markup? [*Flying J* v. *Van Hollen*, 578 F.3d 569, 7th Cir. (2009)]

4. Several companies operated downhill ski facilities in Aspen, Colorado. They all sold a joint ticket that allowed skiers to ski at all facilities: the receipts were later divided according to various use rates. Eventually, one firm owned all ski areas but one. The big firm stopped issuing the joint ticket and instead issued a ticket good only for its ski areas. The firm that owned only one ski facility saw its market share fall from 20 percent to 11 percent. It sued, claiming that the larger firm violated Section 2 of the Sherman Act by

attempting to monopolize skiing by ending the joint ticket arrangement. Is the sale of the joint ticket a violation of the antitrust law? [*Aspen Skiing Company* v. *Aspen Highlands Skiing Corporation*, 472 U.S. 585 (1985)]

✓ Check your answer

5. Coca-Cola required independent food distributors (IFDs) that sold its fountain syrup to sign a loyalty agreement that they would not sell any Pepsi products so long as they were selling Coke products. Pepsi sued, contending that the loyalty agreement was monopolization and attempted monopolization of the IFD market. Is this monopolization, or are there adequate alternatives in the relevant markets? [*Pepsico* v. *Coca-Cola*, 315 F.3d 102, 2nd Cir. (2002)]

6. Syufy bought all of Las Vegas's first-run movie theaters. The government sued Syufy for monopolization. While admitting that he had a substantial share of the market, he pointed out that: (1) movie prices in Las Vegas were no higher than movie prices in comparable cities; (2) no sooner did Syufy acquire all of Las Vegas's first-run theaters than other competitors successfully entered the market; and (3) movie studios (Paramount Pictures) are powerful and want to avoid theater monopolization so they will ensure that Syufy does not abuse market dominance. Evaluate Syufy's arguments. [*U.S.* v. *Syufy*, 903 F.2d 659, 9th Cir. (1990)]

✓ Check your answer

7. Dr. Johnson joined the obstetrics practice of Dr. Fadel. Johnson became unhappy with the arrangement, contending she was not being given enough patients. She wanted to set up her own practice, so she met with the physician recruiter at the hospital used by their patients. Johnson claimed the recruiter promised her an $800,000 line of credit and guaranteed annual income of at least $200,000 a year. The hospital board voted not to make her such an offer. Fadel fired her; she moved to another city and sued for conspiracy to restrain trade in violation of the Sherman Act. The district court dismissed the suit; Johnson appealed. Did she have grounds for suit? [*Johnson* v. *University Health Services*, 161 F.3d 1334, 11th Cir. (1998)]

✓ Check your answer

8. A maker of hamburger patty machines required its dealers to also purchase its hamburger patty paper. The manufacturer cut off a dealer that did not like this requirement. The dealer sued, claiming that his was an illegal tie-in sale. The dealer was awarded $300,000 damages for the value of its lost sales. Was this the correct decision? [*Roy B. Taylor Sales* v. *Hollymatic*, 28 F.3d 1379, 5th Cir. (1994)]

9. The Utah Pie Company made and sold frozen pies in the Salt Lake City area. It was very successful and soon had two-thirds of the frozen-pie market in that area. In response to the loss of their market shares, three large pie makers—Carnation, Pet, and Continental—cut their prices in the Salt Lake area but not elsewhere. As a result, their sales picked back up, and Utah Pie's fell to 45 percent of the market. The result was lower frozen-pie prices for consumers in that market. Utah Pie sued the other three companies for violating what part of the antitrust law? Did it win? [*Utah Pie Co.* v. *Continental Baking Co.*, 87 S.Ct. 1326 (1967)]

✓ Check your answer

ETHICS QUESTION

Your firm produces electric blenders. A certain popular model has a suggested retail price of $30. Your firm sells it wholesale for $18. Smaller stores tend to sell the blender at the suggested retail price. One large discount chain sells the blender for $26 and asks you to cut the price to them to $17.50. Because of that chain's large sales, your production and profits are up. You will earn even higher profits if you cut the price to them to $17.50—a possible violation of the Robinson-Patman Act. Should you cut the price for the chain? What if the chain says that it will cut its retail price to $25 if you cut the price to $17.50?

Environmental Law

The Environmental Protection Agency (EPA) and Amoco Corporation once cooperated on a four-year project to study pollution-control effectiveness. The EPA listened to company experts; the company revealed operation details to the EPA. The study showed that EPA regulations required Amoco to spend $41 million a year to trap air pollution from one refinery, when the same level of pollution reduction, using a better technology, could be achieved for $11 million. The regulations did not allow the cheaper control methods. The study also showed that no controls were required on one part of the refinery that emitted five times more pollution as the pollution being controlled at a cost of $41 million. EPA was as frustrated as Amoco by the results. Inflexible regulations and statutes that are slow to change trapped both.

Hundreds of billions of dollars are spent per year on pollution controls. Because controls are so costly, there are often fights between industry and regulators. Some expensive pollution controls achieve little, while some major sources of pollution are not effectively regulated, as was asserted after the BP oil well blowout in the Gulf of Mexico in 2010.

This chapter reviews the major federal laws providing environmental protection, but it begins with a discussion of common-law rules that regulate environmental quality, such as the application of nuisance law. The chapter then discusses the creation of the EPA and the most important environmental statutes, including the Clean Air Act, the Clean Water Act, the Resource Conservation and Recovery Act, the Superfund, and the Endangered Species Act.

Environmental Regulation

Federal control of the environment essentially began in 1970. Before then, some **pollution** laws were on the books, but they meant little in practice. Since 1970, an explosion of federal legislation has affected most aspects of the environment. Exhibit 21.1 lists only a fraction of the environmental statutes on the books now, but these have the greatest impact.

To implement and enforce federal environmental mandates, Congress created the EPA in 1970. Today, it is one of the largest federal agencies, with about 18,000 employees and a budget of about $9 billion. Add to that the state environmental agencies that are required to help enforce federal and state environmental laws. The EPA has primary responsibility for four major external environmental problems: air pollution, water pollution, land pollution, and pollution associated with certain products. This chapter reviews the key features of the major federal mandates, but before that, we review an important contribution of the common law that helps to protect environmental quality.

EXHIBIT 21.1 FEDERAL REGULATION OF ENVIRONMENTAL POLLUTION

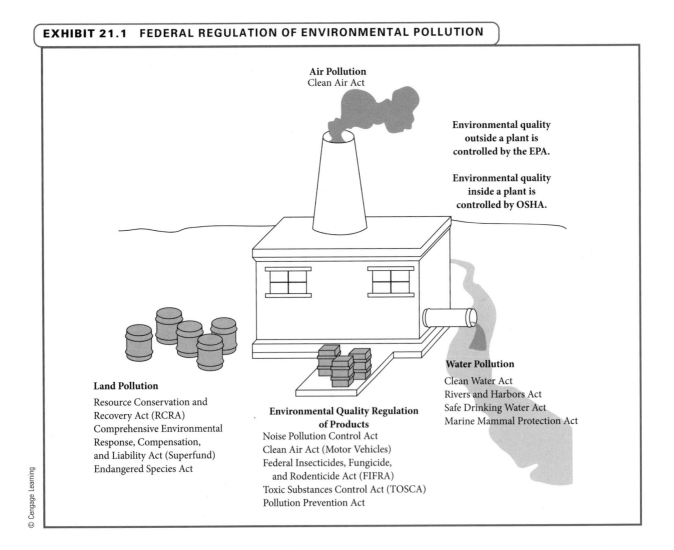

Air Pollution
Clean Air Act

Environmental quality outside a plant is controlled by the EPA.

Environmental quality inside a plant is controlled by OSHA.

Land Pollution

Resource Conservation and Recovery Act (RCRA)
Comprehensive Environmental Response, Compensation, and Liability Act (Superfund)
Endangered Species Act

Environmental Quality Regulation of Products
Noise Pollution Control Act
Clean Air Act (Motor Vehicles)
Federal Insecticides, Fungicide, and Rodenticide Act (FIFRA)
Toxic Substances Control Act (TOSCA)
Pollution Prevention Act

Water Pollution
Clean Water Act
Rivers and Harbors Act
Safe Drinking Water Act
Marine Mammal Protection Act

Pollution and the Common Law

Before 1970, pollution was a problem handled by the states. State statutes dealt with some of the worst problems, such as automobile emissions in California, but citizens primarily relied on the common law, especially nuisance and trespass.

Nuisance, Trespass, and Pollution

As discussed in the chapters on property and torts, nuisances may be public or private. A **public nuisance** is an unreasonable interference with a right held in common by the public. In a pollution case, the right held in common is a community's right to a reasonably clean and safe environment. As a rule, a public nuisance case may be brought against a polluter by a city or state attorney. A **private nuisance** is a substantial and unreasonable interference with the use and enjoyment of the land of another. It generally involves a polluter who is injuring one person or a group of people and may face private litigation.

For example, in the 1907 case *Georgia* v. *Tennessee Copper Company* (206 U.S. 230), the Supreme Court reviewed a complaint by the state of Georgia that a copper smelter in Tennessee was discharging gases that killed vegetation in Georgia and threatened human health. The Court held that an injunction to shut down the smelter could be issued if the smelter could not control the pollution enough to stop the damage.

A **trespass** is an unauthorized breach of the boundaries of another's land. The main difference between trespass and nuisance is that a trespass occurs whenever there is physical invasion of a plaintiff's property. A nuisance requires proof that interference with property is substantial and unreasonable. In practice, nuisance and trespass are difficult to distinguish in many pollution cases.

Negligence, Strict Liability, and Pollution

Both negligence and strict liability for **abnormally dangerous activities** may apply in pollution cases. Tort liability may be based on negligence, which is failure to use reasonable care to prevent pollution from causing a foreseeable injury. Strict liability for abnormally dangerous activities applies to businesses that produce or emit toxic pollutants. The courts emphasize the risks created by toxic pollutants and the location of the activity relative to where people live. Courts have found crop dusting, chemical leakage into groundwater, storing flammable substances in a populated area, and noxious gas emissions all to be abnormally dangerous.

Water Rights and Pollution

There is no common-law right to pollute water. Most states rely on **riparian water law**, although western states have a variety of other water laws. Riparian water law holds that people who live along rivers and bodies of water have the right to use the water in reasonable amounts but must allow the water to flow downstream in usable form. There is no right to pollute the water so it is not usable downstream. Hence, enforcement of water rights has long been a basis for suing polluters. The *Whalen* decision illustrates how the law works to protect water quality in the absence of any regulation. Note the New York high court's classic statement about how rights are to be protected.

This decision contrasts sharply with a famous decision 60 years later by the same court, *Boomers* v. *Atlantic Cement Company* (257 N.E.2d 870). The air pollution, noise, and vibration from a cement plant created a nuisance for nearby homes. The court refused to issue an injunction, only awarding damages to the homeowners. The court reasoned that the value of the cement plant was higher than the cost suffered by the homeowners, so no injunction should be issued.

WHALEN V. UNION BAG AND PAPER

Court of Appeals of New York, 208 N.Y.1, 101 N.E. 805 (1913)

Case Background *Whalen owned a farm on a creek in New York. He used water from the creek to water plants and livestock. Union Bag built a pulp mill upstream, employing about 500 people. The mill polluted the creek so that Whalen could not use the water.*

Whalen sued Union Bag for damages and requested that the court issue an injunction to stop the pollution. The trial court (special term) awarded damages of $312 per year and issued an injunction to take effect in one year. Either the pollution had to be stopped or the mill was to be shut down. The appellate court overturned the injunction and reduced damages to $100 per year. Whalen appealed to the highest court in New York.

Case Decision Werner, Justice

* * *

The setting aside of the injunction was apparently induced by a consideration of the great loss likely to be inflicted on the defendant by the granting of the injunction as compared with the small injury done to the plaintiff's land by that portion of the pollution which we regarded as attributable to the defendant. Such a balancing of injuries cannot be justified by the circumstances of this case.

...Although the damage to the plaintiff may be slight as compared with the defendant's expense of abating the condition, that is not a good reason for refusing an injunction. Neither courts of equity nor law can be guided by such a rule, for if followed to its logical conclusion, it would deprive the poor litigant of his little property by giving it to those already rich.

It is always to be remembered in such cases that "denying the injunction puts the hardship on the party in whose favor the legal right exists, instead of on the wrongdoer."...

The fact that the appellant has expended a large sum of money in the construction of its plant, and that it conducts its business in a careful manner and without malice, can make no difference in its rights to the stream. Before locating the plant, the owners were bound to know that every riparian proprietor is entitled to have the waters of the stream that washes his land come to it without obstruction, diversion, or corruption, subject only to the reasonable use of the water, by those similarly entitled, for such domestic purposes as are inseparable from and necessary for the free use of their land; they were bound also to know the character of their proposed business, and to take notice of the size, course, and capacity of the stream, and to determine for themselves at their own peril whether they should be able to conduct their business upon a stream of the size and character of Brandywine creek without injury to their neighbors; and the magnitude of their investment and their freedom from malice furnish no reason why they should escape the consequences of their own folly....

The judgment of the Appellate Division, insofar as it denied the injunction, should be reversed, and the judgment of the special term in that respect reinstated, with costs to the appellant.

Questions for Analysis

1. The New York high court held that the polluter must pay damages and stop harmful pollution or cease operation. With such tough rules, why would we need federal regulation of water pollution?

2. Should damages be the only resort in such cases? Assuming that the real loss to Whalen was $312 per year, why should he be able to get an injunction that would put hundreds of people out of work?

In the *Whalen* case, no price tag was put on rights, and costs and benefits were not compared. The *Boomer* court compared costs and benefits and made the economically "efficient" decision, rather than simply ordering the nuisance to be stopped. This kind of decision played a role in the push for federal regulation of pollution.

Clean Air Act

The Clean Air Act of 1970, with major amendments in 1977 and 1990, establishes federal authority to control air pollution. Although prior to 1970 many states had passed air pollution regulations, the Nixon Administration and Congress wanted to do more. In the words of the Supreme Court, Congress intended to "take a stick to the states" with this law. The Act requires the EPA to set pollution standards and, through forced cooperation of the states, to enforce standards across the country.

National Ambient Air Quality Standards

A key regulatory program for air quality is the **National Ambient Air Quality Standards** (NAAQS). The EPA determines NAAQS for air pollutants that "arise or contribute to air pollution which may reasonably be anticipated to endanger public health and welfare." The NAAQS set limits on how much of a pollutant is allowed in the air outside—ambient air—as air quality is measured at hundreds of sites around the country.

The primary factors for a pollutant's NAAQS are public health effects. Secondary factors are its public welfare effects (impact on plants, animals, soil, and constructed surfaces). The EPA has national standards for sulfur dioxide, particulates, ozone, carbon monoxide, nitrogen oxide, and lead. Exhibit 21.2 summarizes the principal characteristics, health effects, and sources of major air pollutants. Carbon dioxide (CO_2), considered to be the major greenhouse gas, was most recently added to the list. After EPA sets the NAAQS for a pollutant, it measures levels and declares states to be in or out of compliance with the standard. States not in compliance must take steps to improve or risk losing federal highway funding or other federal funds.

State Implementation Plans

When EPA sets limits for the NAAQS, each state develops a **State Implementation Plan** (SIP). The SIPs define the controls to be used in each state to achieve the standards. In theory, if each emission source in a state met its pollution control requirements, the

EXHIBIT 21.2   MAJOR AIR POLLUTANTS SUBJECT TO NAAQS

POLLUTANT	SOURCES	HEALTH EFFECTS
Sulfur Dioxide (SO_2)	Power and industrial plants that burn sulfur-containing fossil fuels; smelting of sulfur-bearing ores	Causes and aggravates respiratory ailments, inducing asthma, chronic bronchitis, emphysema
Particulates (PM)	Wind erosion; stationary sources that burn solid fuels; agricultural operations	Chest discomfort; throat and eye irritation; respiratory problems
Ozone (O_3)	Mostly from vehicle exhaust, refineries, and chemical plants	Aggravates respiratory ailments; causes eye irritation
Carbon Monoxide (CO)	Motor vehicle exhaust and other carbon-containing materials; natural sources	Reduces oxygen-carrying capacity of blood; impairs heart function, visual perception, and alertness
Nitrogen Oxide (NO_x)	Motor vehicle exhaust; power plants	Aggravates respiratory ailments
Lead (Pb)	Nonferrous metal smelters; motor vehicle exhaust	Can cause mental and physical disabilities (lead poisoning)
Carbon Dioxide (CO_2)	Primarily fossil fuels	At local level, can cause blood poisoning; globally, may cause climate change

© Cengage Learning

state's air quality would meet the national standards. The Act requires that regulated emission sources meet pollution control requirements as set by the SIP by a certain date. SIPs are usually tens of thousands of pages long, specifying what each factory and production process can emit, so they are of immense concern to many firms.

The Clean Air Act, like some other major environmental statutes, places the primary enforcement burden on the states. The EPA is an oversight agency that sets limits on what the states may do and sets the minimum regulations they must impose. When the EPA changes emission standards, states must revise their SIPs, which are then reviewed by the EPA. That review may occur at a regional office; there are ten EPA regional offices and branches of the regional offices in other cities. For example, the Region 8 headquarters is in Denver. It has, among other locales, a branch in Helena, Montana. If a state does not submit an adequate plan, the EPA writes one for it. All SIPs must include the following:

- Enforceable emission limits
- Schedules and timetables for compliance
- Measures for monitoring air quality and emissions from pollution sources
- Adequate funding, personnel, and authority for implementing and enforcing the SIP

The Permit System

The Clean Air Act sets rules for the construction of new industrial plants or for major renovations of existing facilities. The standards imposed on plant owners depend on the air quality of the area in which a plant is built. One set of rules applies if the plant is built in a "clean air area," and another set applies if a plant is built in a "dirty air area." In either case, the plant owner is required to obtain a preconstruction permit from the EPA or the state agency that enforces the Act.

Clean Air Areas Areas with clean air—air of better quality than required by the NAAQS—are called **attainment areas** or **prevention of significant deterioration (PSD) areas**. PSD areas are where air quality is better than the national standards. In such areas, only a slight increase in pollution is allowed from new construction. That slight increase is called the maximum allowable increase. Any activity, including the construction or expansion of a plant, that causes the maximum allowable increase to be exceeded is prohibited in a PSD area.

New construction is allowed in PSD areas if two basic requirements are met. First, the owner must agree to install the best available control technology (BACT)—as determined by the EPA—on the new operation to control its air pollution. Second, the owner must show that the pollution from its plant will not cause the maximum allowable increase in the area to be exceeded. The maximum allowable increase in the various forms of air pollution depends upon the classification of an area and the effect a particular pollutant would have on the air there. Some PSD classes, such as wilderness areas, are subject to much stricter controls than are less sensitive PSD areas.

Dirty Air Areas Dirty air areas are called **nonattainment areas**, meaning that they have not met the NAAQS. Businesses wanting to build in nonattainment areas are required to meet more restrictive standards than are imposed in PSD areas. The **emission offset** policy imposes three requirements on owners of new or expanded plants:

1. A new plant's pollution must be controlled to the maximum degree possible. The plant must use the lowest achievable emissions rate (LAER) technology. LAER can be a cleaner technology than the BACT requirement. Generally, the EPA designates the LAER as the cleanest emission technology in use by any similar plant.

2. New plant owners must certify that any other plants they have in the area meet SIP requirements.
3. A new plant can be built in a nonattainment area only if any increase in air pollution from the new plant is offset by reductions in the same pollutants from other plants in the area. That is, when the new plant is operating, the area must enjoy an overall air quality improvement.

Suppose Geely wants to build a new car assembly plant in Detroit, a nonattainment area for sulfur dioxide. Geely must obtain a preconstruction permit from the EPA. To obtain the permit, Geely will have to apply LAER technology and prove that other plants Geely owns in the area are in compliance with Michigan's SIP. For example, if Geely's new plant adds 10 units of pollution to the air, Geely must reduce pollution elsewhere in the area by more than 10 units. That may require Geely to buy existing pollution sources and shut them down. When the new plant begins operation, air quality in the area should improve.

Expanding Need for Air Quality Permits

While we hear most about air pollution permit issues from big projects, such as power plants, air pollution policies are built into state environmental policy at a much lower level. Many construction projects require environmental impact reports to be prepared that consider a wide range of effects of new projects. For example, suppose Walmart wishes to build a new store in California. The California Environmental Quality Act requires an environmental impact statement that considers the air pollution consequences of the change in traffic flows given the existence of a new store.

Mobile Sources of Pollution

Some major air pollutants, such as lead, have nearly disappeared from the atmosphere. Large reductions have occurred in particulates and carbon monoxide. But ozone at lower levels of the atmosphere has changed little; it is mostly produced by imperfect burning of petroleum products. Because vehicles are the primary source, the law has tightened controls on cars and trucks. While vehicles produce fewer hydrocarbons that help form ozone than they did when the Clean Air Act was passed, many more miles are driven by more vehicles today, keeping ozone emissions up.

The level of ozone allowed is determined by the NAAQS, but the law also imposes direct controls on **mobile sources** of pollution. Tailpipe exhaust standards for cars, trucks, and buses have become so stringent that newer vehicles cannot get much cleaner. Where ozone pollution is worst, in most major cities, SIPs impose tougher vehicle emission inspections, vapor recovery systems at gas stations, reformulated gasoline, and alternative fuel requirements.

The law often allows states to impose emissions standards that go beyond the federal requirements. California has set tougher auto emissions standards and requirements for cleaner-burning gasoline and has forced greater use of alternative fuel and electric-powered cars. Other states have adopted the California standards, which means that some California standards are likely to become the national standard. The *American Trucking Association* case discusses control of mobile sources of air pollution and the ability of EPA to grant states the ability to implement stronger control rules.

Toxic Pollutants

As amended in 1990, the Clean Air Act lists 189 substances declared to be hazardous air pollutants. The EPA sets maximum achievable control technology (MACT) standards for the pollutants. The goal is a 90 percent reduction in emissions for the pollutants and a 75 percent reduction in cancer caused by air pollution. If the EPA determines that a pollutant is a threat to public health or the environment, tighter control standards are to be imposed without regard

AMERICAN TRUCKING ASSOCIATION V. ENVIRONMENTAL PROTECTION AGENCY
United States Court of Appeals, District of Columbia Circuit, 600 F.3d 624 (2010)

Case Background *Congress gave California permission to regulate emissions from in-use mobile sources of pollution. This primarily applies to engines that run transportation refrigeration units (TRUs), such as the refrigeration units on trucks carrying perishable foods. Other states may follow a rule identical to the one in California or adopt no rule at all. EPA must approve a proposed California regulation unless EPA finds the standard unjustified, given air conditions in California or because the cost of compliance is too high.*

The California Air Resources Board devised a plan in 2004 to reduce particulate matter emissions from diesel TRU engines by 75 percent by 2010 and 85 percent by 2020. The rule began to take effect in 2009. It applies to trucks based in California and trucks operating in California—such as a truck from another state that picks up a load of fruit in California.

TRU owners must show that they are in compliance with the standard or replace an old engine with a new compliant engine. EPA approved the standard, finding that its cost was not unreasonable. The American Trucking Association (ATA) challenged EPA's decision as arbitrary and capricious.

Case Decision Kavanaugh, Circuit Judge

* * *

When it comes to regulating emissions from *stationary* pollution sources like waste incinerators and power plants, EPA sets national ambient air quality standards, and the individual states develop and implement plans to achieve those standards.

As to regulating emissions from *mobile* pollution sources like automobile engines, EPA and the States also share responsibility depending on the kind of engine at issue. From a regulatory perspective, and oversimplifying a bit for present purposes, mobile engines fall into one of four categories: (i) new on-road, (ii) new non-road, (iii) in-use on-road, and (iv) in-use non-road.

This case concerns the fourth category in-use non-road engines. ...

ATA argues that California's rule is a *de facto* national rule because many trucks pass through California and will be subject to the rule. As a result,

ATA contends that other states are effectively precluded from declining to follow California's lead, in contravention of those states' rights under the Act.

ATA's argument on this point is weak. The California rule does not require any other state to adopt California's approach, and it does "not apply anywhere but in California, and only to vehicles that have entered California. ..." If ATA's members operate trucks in California, they must comply while operating in California. If they do not operate in California, they need not comply. We find nothing about this approach to be inconsistent with the federal statutory scheme. ...

ATA also asserts that EPA, in applying the third criterion, failed to give "appropriate consideration to the cost of compliance" with California's TRU rule. Under that provision, EPA must assess the "economic costs" of California's proposed emissions standards, including the costs resulting from "the timing of a particular emission control regulation." In approving the California TRU rule, EPA adequately considered those costs. EPA explained that businesses can comply with the TRU rule for about $2,000 to $5,000 per unit. EPA also determined that the phased implementation of the rule would help minimize its cost. Although the costs of the TRU rule are not insignificant, EPA's duty under this portion of the statute is simply to consider those costs. It did so here. EPA's conclusion, namely that California's rule was consistent with [the Clean Air Act], was reasonable and reasonably explained.

In the realm of air quality regulation related to in-use non-road engines, "Congress consciously chose to permit California to blaze its own trail with a minimum of federal oversight." We have no legal basis in this case to disrupt that congressional scheme, overturn EPA's decision, or otherwise disturb the California rule.

We deny ATA's petition for review.

Questions for Analysis

1. Is it likely that most trucks with refrigeration units will, in fact, comply with the California standard, thereby making it nearly a national standard?
2. Is a cost of $2,000 to $5,000 per truck not significant?

to such economic factors as cost or technological feasibility. The EPA has issued tough standards for many pollutants, such as emissions from dry-cleaning establishments and commercial bakeries. These rules are highly technical.

Enforcement

The EPA and state environmental agencies have primary authority to enforce the Clean Air Act and other environmental statutes. Citizens, including environmental groups, have rights to bring **citizen suits** to enforce environmental statutes when government agencies fail to do so. Many such suits are brought every year. The environmental statutes list the penalties that may be imposed on violators.

Some environmental offenses are prosecuted as criminal matters. There are more than 200 criminal indictments per year. EPA and state environmental agencies collect hundreds of billions of dollars per year in fines in civil and criminal cases.

Carrot-and-Stick Approach Enforcement uses a carrot-and-stick approach. In the U.S. Sentencing Guidelines, punishment for environmental crimes imposes penalties on a company and its executives based on several factors. Punishment is reduced for companies that

- Cooperate with the government in investigations
- Voluntarily report illegal actions
- Educate their workforce about environmental standards
- Assist those who suffer from environmental wrongdoing
- Have a strong internal environmental compliance program

Clean Water Act

Federal authority over water pollution goes back to the Rivers and Harbors Act of 1886 and 1899 and the Federal Water Pollution Control Act of 1948. However, there was little effective federal control; primary responsibility was left to the states. By 1970, marine life in Lake Erie was almost gone, and many rivers were unfit as drinking water sources or for recreation.

INTERNATIONAL PERSPECTIVE

Industrialization Brings Environmental Problems to China

The pollution that afflicts the poorest people—breathing smoke-filled air from cooking fires in their living huts and drinking contaminated water—is reduced when industrialization occurs and economic conditions improve. But, at the same time, pollutants from rising industrial production create problems.

As the economy of China has grown rapidly in the past three decades, environmental damage has increased rapidly. The government of China understands the magnitude of the problem and has laws and agencies to deal with pollution. On the books, the structure looks much like the EPA. In practice, there is little enforcement.

At least 70 percent of the water in major rivers is rated as "severely polluted." The China National Environmental Monitoring Center reports that no major city has good air quality. Waters around coastal cities are badly polluted. The State Oceanographic Administration Marine Environment Protection Department warns that marine ecological systems near Shanghai and other major cities are "dangerously close to collapse."

Rules that have weak enforcement mean little. When a fertilizer plant dumped large quantities of ammonia and nitrate into a river, killing tons of fish and poisoning drinking water for downstream cities, nothing much happened. An official from the State Environmental Protection Administration said that there is no authority to shut down the worst offenders, most of which are government-owned companies: "We can only fine them, and such a small amount at that. They basically decide it's a cost that doesn't matter."

Sources: China Daily News; Wall Street Journal.

The Clean Water Act (CWA) was passed in 1972 and was substantially amended in 1977 and 1986. The objective of the Clean Water Act is to "restore and maintain the chemical, physical, and biological integrity of the Nation's waters." The Act has five main elements:

1. National **effluent** (pollution) standards set by the EPA for each industry
2. Water quality standards set by the states under EPA approval
3. A **discharge permit** program that sets water quality standards to reduce pollution
4. Special provisions for toxic chemicals and oil spills
5. Construction grants and loans from the federal government for **publicly owned treatment works** (POTWs), such as sewage treatment plants

The CWA makes it unlawful for any person, business, or government to dump pollutants into navigable waters without a permit. Although the Act does not define "navigable waters," the term is broadly interpreted for regulatory purposes. Except for isolated small bodies of water, all waters are considered to be under federal jurisdiction. **National Pollution Discharge Elimination System** (NPDES) permits are required not only for dumping waste water into water, but even for moving water from one place to another.

Cleaning the nation's waters has been much more expensive and has taken longer than was anticipated when the Clean Water Act was passed in 1972. At that time, Congress said that the discharge of pollutants into any waters would be completely eliminated by 1985. That was an impossible goal. Discharges have probably dropped to about half of what they were when the Act was passed. But because pollutants that are easiest to eliminate have been attacked first, the cost of removing more pollutants will be much higher in the future.

Point Source Pollution

The water pollution that is easiest to identify comes out of a pipe. We can see it, measure it, and, given technical knowledge, treat the discharge. Control of such **point source pollution** has been the primary focus of federal law since 1972. Sewage from homes and industrial sources (point sources) is often treated at publicly owned treatment works (POTWs). Billions are spent every year to improve existing POTWs (sewage treatment plants), and many cities require businesses to pretreat their emissions to reduce the need for treatment at the POTW. Because most effluents treated at POTWs are not toxic, the sludge—the glop that is removed during sewage treatment—is often used for fertilizer. The treated water is pumped back into rivers or lakes. Exhibit 21.3 illustrates primary water effluent sources.

Under the Clean Water Act, states must designate the intended use of all surface water. If the use is drinking water, treated water dumped into a bay, lake, or river must be quite pure; if the body of water is designated for recreation, the treated water must be clean enough so it does not contaminate swimmers or fish.

Industrial Permits Industrial discharges are subject to a permit process. As we have seen already, the EPA and state environmental agencies, under the National Pollutant Discharge Elimination System (NPDES), require industrial polluters to list the amount and type of their discharges. The polluters are issued permits to release various pollutants in specified quantities.

Control Technology Each firm in an industry must meet the effluent (pollutant) limits set by the EPA for each chemical dumped into wastewater. The list of controlled substances is expanding, and the degree to which the substances must be controlled grows gradually tighter. Conventional pollutants, like human waste, are controlled by the best

EXHIBIT 21.3   PRIMARY SOURCES OF WATER EFFLUENTS

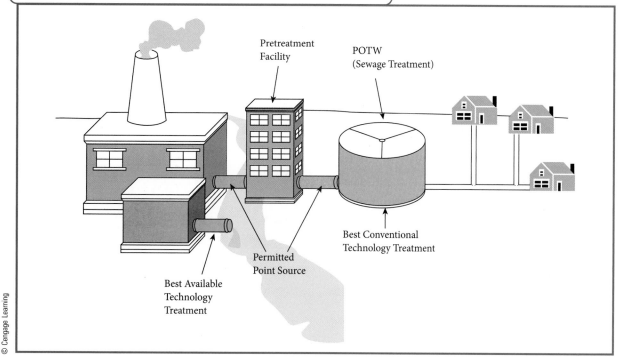

Pretreatment Facility

POTW (Sewage Treatment)

Best Conventional Technology Treatment

Permitted Point Source

Best Available Technology Treatment

© Cengage Learning

conventional technology (BCT). Congress ordered the EPA to consider cost-effectiveness when setting such standards.

Cost considerations are not as important for toxic or unconventional pollutants, which are subject to tighter control, called best available technology (BAT)—defined by the EPA as the "very best control and treatment measures that have been or are capable of being achieved." Hence, as better technology is invented to control pollutants, polluters must use it to reduce their pollution. Regardless of the kind of pollutants, if a polluter is located on a particularly sensitive waterway, even more stringent controls may be ordered.

When a new plant is built or a new source of pollution is created, it is subject to even tighter controls—called **New Source Performance Standards** (NSPS). The law says that the standard is "the greatest degree of effluent reduction ... achievable through application of the best available demonstrated control technology, processes, operating methods, and other alternatives, including, where practicable, standards permitting no discharge of pollutants." Using BAT controls for the pollution produced is not enough; the entire production process must use the best technology that exists to minimize pollution output. This is true both for air pollution and water pollution for new construction.

Enforcement

Because point-source water pollution control is based on a permit system, the permits are the key to enforcement. Under the NPDES, the states have primary responsibility for enforcing the permit system, subject to EPA monitoring and approval.

Operating without a permit or discharging more pollution than is allowed under a permit violates the law. Firms that have pollution permits must monitor their own performance and file **discharge monitoring reports** (DMRs), available for public inspection. Hence, firms must report violations of the amount they are allowed to pollute under their permits. Lying about violations is more serious than admitting to violations. Serious violations can lead to criminal prosecution. Every year, prison sentences are handed down for violators who dump toxic wastes.

Citizen suits against polluters are common under the Clean Water Act. The "citizen," which usually means an environmental organization, must notify the EPA and the alleged permit violator of the intent to sue. If the EPA takes charge of the situation, the citizen suit is blocked. If the EPA does not act diligently and violations continue, the private suit to force enforcement of the law may proceed. If the plaintiff wins, the loser pays attorneys' fees. The Supreme Court considered what may be a point source in the *Decker* case.

DECKER V. NORTHWEST ENVIRONMENTAL DEFENSE CENTER

United States Supreme Court 133 S.Ct. 1326 (2013)

Case Background *The Clean Water Act requires that NPDES permits be held by entities that discharge pollutants from any point source into navigable waters. One EPA regulation in this regard is the Silvicultural Rule concerning logging operations. It states that permits are required unless discharges are composed only of stormwater. Hence, permits are needed at sawmills and where logs are sorted, but are generally not required for runoff along logging roads.*

Georgia-Pacific (G-P) has a contract with the state of Oregon to harvest timber from state forests. When it rains, water runs off logging roads used by G-P. That water flows into various rivers. The Northwest Environmental Defense Center (NEDC) brought a citizen suit against G-P, the state of Oregon, and the EPA because G-P was not required to obtain NPDES permits. The district court dismissed the suit, finding that permits were not needed because logging roads were not industrial operations. The court of appeals reversed, holding that rain runoff from the logging roads was "associated with industrial activity," so permits were required. Defendants appealed.

Case Decision Kennedy, Justice

* * *

Under the Clean Water Act, petitioners were required to secure NPDES permits for the discharges of channeled stormwater runoff only if the discharges were "associated with industrial activity," as that statutory term is defined in ... the Industrial Stormwater Rule. Otherwise, the discharges fall within the Act's general exemption of "discharges composed entirely of stormwater" from the NPDES permitting scheme.

NEDC ... contends that the statutory term "associated with industrial activity" unambiguously covers discharges of channeled stormwater runoff from logging roads. That view, however, overlooks the multiple definitions of the terms "industrial" and "industry." These words can refer to business activity in general, yet so too can they be limited to "economic activity concerned with the processing of raw materials and manufacture of goods in factories." The latter definition does not necessarily encompass outdoor timber harvesting. ...

The EPA takes a different view. It concludes that the earlier regulation invoked Standard Industrial Classification 24 "to regulate traditional *industrial* sources such as sawmills." It points to the regulation's reference to "facilities" and the classification's reference to "establishments," which suggest industrial sites more fixed and permanent than outdoor timber-harvesting operations. ...

It is well established that an agency's interpretation need not be the only possible reading of a regulation—or even the best one—to prevail. When an agency interprets its own regulation, the Court, as a general rule, defers to it "unless that interpretation is plainly erroneous or inconsistent with the regulation." The EPA's interpretation is a permissible one. Taken together, the regulation's references to "facilities," "establishments," "manufacturing," "processing," and an "industrial plant" leave open the rational interpretation that the regulation extends only to traditional industrial buildings such as factories and associated sites, as well as other relatively fixed facilities. …

The EPA's decision exists against a background of state regulation with respect to stormwater runoff from logging roads. The State of Oregon has made an extensive effort to develop a comprehensive set of best practices to manage stormwater runoff from logging roads. These practices include rules mandating filtration of stormwater runoff before it enters rivers and streams, requiring logging companies to construct roads using surfacing that minimizes the sediment in runoff, and obligating firms to cease operations where such efforts fail to prevent visible increases in water turbidity. Oregon has invested substantial time and money in establishing these practices. In addition, the development, siting, maintenance, and regulation of roads—and in particular of state forest roads—are areas in which Oregon has considerable expertise. In exercising the broad discretion

the Clean Water Act gives the EPA in the realm of stormwater runoff, the agency could reasonably have concluded that further federal regulation in this area would be duplicative or counterproductive. Indeed, Congress has given express instructions to the EPA to work "in consultation with State and local officials" to alleviate stormwater pollution by developing the precise kind of best management practices Oregon has established here. …

For the reasons stated, the judgment of the Court of Appeals is reversed, and the cases are remanded for proceedings consistent with this opinion.

Questions for Analysis

1. Because Oregon regulates logging operations, why would the environmental group want EPA regulations also under discharge permits?
2. Does road runoff seem like point source emission or nonpoint source?

Nonpoint Source Pollution

About half of all water pollution is from nonpoint sources—it is runoff from construction sites, logging and mining operations, streets, and agriculture. Pollutants are washed by rain into streams and lakes and seep into groundwater. Much **nonpoint source pollution** has only recently come under control efforts. The complexity of the problem requires multiple solutions. Nonpoint source pollution is often very expensive to treat because there is no easy way to capture the contaminated water to treat it.

Many cities have old-fashioned combined stormwater-sewage systems, in which the same pipes carry rainwater runoff and sewage. Because runoff from streets usually occurs during rainstorms, when sewage treatment plants do not have the capacity to treat all runoff water, holding tanks may have to be built so the water can be treated later.

The consequences of groundwater pollution that comes from agricultural fertilizers and sprays are considered by various agencies under statutes in addition to the Clean Water Act. These include the Safe Drinking Water Act; the Federal Insecticide, Fungicide, and Rodenticide Act; the Toxic Substances Control Act; and other laws that deal, one way or another, with pollution that shows up in water from nonpoint sources. Although regulations to reduce runoff have been gradually tightened, runoff pollution remains a problem that is difficult to resolve technologically or politically.

ISSUE SPOTTER
Does Obeying EPA Regulations Eliminate Litigation?

Your company's production facility produces certain water pollutants that are treated according to EPA standards. You have all the EPA permits that are required. Does this mean the treated water you pump into the river near the plant has no legal consequence? Are there legal problems that you could face even if EPA has no complaints about your operations? How can you be sure?

Wetlands

In years past, **wetlands** were seen as nuisances that bred mosquitoes, so the common view was that they should be drained and filled with dirt. Wetlands destruction was subsidized by agencies such as the Army Corps of Engineers. Now that the environmental value of wetlands is better known, developers and others must protect wetlands. The EPA defines wetlands as:

> *Those areas that are inundated or saturated by surface or groundwater at a frequency and duration sufficient to support, and that under normal circumstances do support, a prevalence of vegetation typically adapted for life in saturated soil conditions. Wetlands generally include swamps, marshes, bogs, and similar areas.*

This definition includes mangrove swamps of coastal saltwater shrubs in the South; prairie potholes in the Dakotas and Minnesota, where shallow depressions that hold water during part of the year are visited by migrating birds; and playa lakes in the Southwest that are flooded basins only rarely. Wetlands can be small holes or large areas and may contain one plant or dozens of important species.

Permit System Under the CWA, anyone wanting to change a wetland must receive a Section 404 permit from the Army Corps of Engineers. The EPA may block an Army Corps permit to prevent environmental damage. About 10,000 permits are issued each year to allow dredging or filling of wetlands. Often, a permit to dredge wetlands includes a requirement that other land be restored to wetland status in exchange. Tens of thousands of more permits are issued each year for activities that "cause only minimal adverse environmental effects" to wetlands. Hence, businesses in construction or other activities that disturb earth must make sure wetlands requirements have been met. Permits have become standard practice, even for ordinary building projects.

Because many construction projects result in some damage to wetlands, it is common for trading to be done—a builder "buys" other wetlands, or restores wetlands, in exchange for the right to fill some wetlands. This is referred to as wetlands mitigation banking. As the EPA explains: "A mitigation bank is a wetland, stream, or other aquatic resource area that has been restored, established, enhanced, or … preserved for the purpose of providing compensation for unavoidable impacts to aquatic resources permitted under Section 404 or a similar state or local wetland regulation." Some firms specialize in arranging such wetlands trades. The *Hearts Bluff* case illustrates the kind of issues that can arise in the mitigation process.

HEARTS BLUFF GAME RANCH, INC. V. UNITED STATES

United States Court of Appeals, Federal Circuit, 669 F.3d 1326 (2012)

Case Background *Hearts Bluff bought 4,000 acres of land in Titus County, Texas, for use in a mitigation bank. It is used as an offset to preserve and restore wetlands to compensate for the environmental impact of more destructive use of land in other locations. Such work is done under the supervision of the Army Corps of Engineers. It issues section 404 permits for work that involves wetlands damage.*

Before buying Hearts Bluff, the company contacted the Corps seeking assurances that the land would be suitable for mitigation banking. The Corps held that it was suitable, but that the land was in an area on which the State of Texas planned to build a large reservoir. Two years later, when Texas announced it would build the reservoir, the Corps held that the Hearts Bluff property could not be used for mitigation.

Hearts Bluff sued the government for an uncompensated taking under the Fifth Amendment, as the value of the land was much lower when the mitigation bank status was denied. The Claims Court, which handles suits for compensation against the government, denied the claim. Plaintiff appealed.

Case Decision Lourie, Circuit Judge

* * *

The government is of course correct that section 404 permits are separate and distinct from the mitigation banking program. Section 404 permits allow landowners to conduct environmentally destructive activity on their land that they would normally be able to do but for the existence of government regulations. We have held that the denial of a section 404 permit could amount to a taking of a cognizable property right as it deprives the landowner of a right inherent in land ownership, as might certain zoning decisions.

Mitigation bank operators, on the other hand, do not necessarily possess section 404 permits; they sell credits from the mitigation banking program to section 404 permit holders or applicants so that the section 404 permit holders or applicants can satisfy the compensatory mitigation obligations of section 404. As discussed below, the mitigation banking program does not restrict land use at all prior to entering into a mitigation banking instrument. The mitigation banking program merely gives access to the credit-swapping program....

Hearts Bluff has not been disturbed in the use of its property. Hearts Bluff purchased land, not a mitigation bank instrument or mitigation bank credits. At no point did Hearts Bluff possess a right to sell or transfer mitigation bank credits or a mitigation bank instrument. It is possible at some point in the future that the Corps could grant a mitigation bank instrument applicable to the property. But without such an instrument, Hearts Bluff is still able to sell, assign, or transfer the land, or exclude others from its use, as it always was able to do. Hearts Bluff is even free to create and preserve environmentally friendly wetlands on the same property, as it desired to do under the mitigation banking program. In short, the Corps' denial did not diminish in any way the rights Hearts Bluff possessed the day it purchased the land, after it applied for the permit, or after the Corps denied the permit. Owning land in and of itself does not give rise to a right to run a mitigation bank, and obtaining a mitigation instrument is therefore not a cognizable property interest....

We affirm.

Questions for Analysis

1. Why would the value of the land be different if it was used for mitigation banking?
2. When the Corp initially told Hearts Bluff that the land was suitable for mitigation, did that not create a property interest?

Wetlands Takings The wetlands permit system can result in prohibitions on building or modifying land that was purchased with the expectation that certain uses were allowed. Some landowners have discovered their land to be worthless because they cannot get a permit for the land to be modified. Several cases, such as *Loveladies Harbor* v. *United States* (28 F.3d 1171), have resulted in decisions that the government must pay for land it forces out of circulation for wetlands protection.

In *Loveladies*, a New Jersey coastal development that had been under construction for 30 years was halted when the Army Corps prohibited any further construction because of wetlands destruction. Fifty acres of wetlands fell from $2.66 million in value to nearly nothing. The Federal Circuit Court of Appeals ordered the government to pay the developer for the land as a taking for public benefit.

Land Pollution

Millions of tons of hazardous waste are generated each year. Some waste can be recycled as inputs into other products, and EPA has a program to encourage companies to find

❓ TEST YOURSELF

1. State Implementation Plans under the Clean Air Act are rewritten by the EPA every five years: T—F
2. If a firm emits pollution that goes on to a neighbor's property, the neighbor may have a suit for _____ or for _____.
3. In *Whalen* v. *Union Bag and Paper*, where a paper mill imposed a few hundred dollars worth of damages on a downstream water user, the New York high court held that the value of the water to the mill was much greater than the benefits of the water to the downstream user, so the mill could continue operation: T—F
4. Areas that have "dirty air" because they have not met Clean Air Act standards are called _____.
5. In the *American Trucking Association* v. *EPA* case, where EPA did not block California from passing new, strict regulations that would apply to engines used on trucks to cool the cargo, the appeals court held that the EPA:
   a. violated the instructions of Congress that it, not a state, devise such standards.
   b. could allow California to adopt new standards, but failed to consider the reasonableness of the costs, so must revise the standards.
   c. properly considered the California standard and could allow it to take effect.
   d. was "arbitrary and capricious" in its review because it did not consider scientific evidence about the effect on air quality if the regulation took effect.
6. Under the Clean Water Act, a point-source emitter of effluent must obtain a(n) _____ that specifies how much may be dumped.
7. Pollution that runs off from agriculture is subject to much less regulation than pollution emitted by point sources, such as factories: T—F
8. In *Hearts Bluff Game Ranch, Inc.* v. *United States*, where a wetlands mitigation company sued the government for failing to provide approval for mitigation banking status on its property, the court held that the Army Corps of Engineers had not denied the property owner of any compensable right: T—F

Answers: F; trespass, nuisance; F; nonattainment areas; c; discharge permit; T; T.

uses for chemical wastes. Improperly stored hazardous waste can get into lakes, streams, and groundwater. Modern waste disposal sites are heavily regulated, high-tech operations with monitoring wells, layers of impermeable liners, and other safety measures. As a result, proper disposal is quite costly.

To reduce the amount of toxic substances that are dumped and to limit exposure to chemicals that are toxic to people or animals, controls are imposed on the production, distribution, use, and disposal of toxic chemicals. Older waste sites, where chemicals and other materials were carelessly disposed of have required the expenditure of billions to clean them up. As Exhibit 21.4 indicates, managers must be aware of the liability that can arise from using chemicals today and from the ownership of property that may contain toxic wastes.

EXHIBIT 21.4   REGULATION OF HAZARDOUS SUBSTANCE

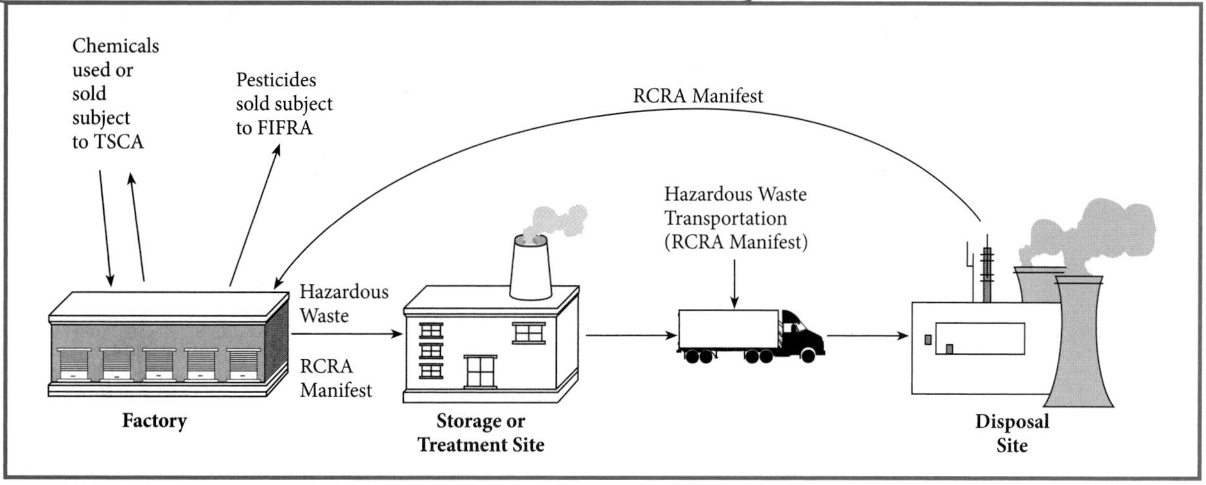

Toxic Substances Control Act

Tens of thousands of chemicals are registered with EPA. Under the Toxic Substances Control Act (TSCA) passed in 1976, the EPA keeps track of these chemicals. Because some chemicals can cause health hazards, accurate information about their possible impact is vital.

When a producer wants to sell a new chemical, it must notify the EPA. As the agency explains: "Anyone who plans to manufacture or import a new chemical substance for a non-exempt commercial purpose is required by section 5 of TSCA to provide EPA with notice before initiating the activity. This premanufacture notice, or PMN, must be submitted at least 90 days prior to the manufacture or import of the chemical." Under TSCA, there is a presumption of innocence; EPA must show that a chemical poses a health hazard before restricting or banning it. About 200 chemicals have been fully tested by EPA for safety, and five have been banned.

Biotechnology, the manipulation of biological processes to produce chemicals or living organisms for commercial use, is also subject to TSCA regulation. Because biotechnology research results may be eligible for patents, this is a field with potentially valuable products worth billions of dollars. Genetic engineering produces materials like enzymes that can purify water and consume the oil in oil spills. The EPA monitors such efforts to use natural organisms in new ways and to use genetically altered microorganisms.

Pesticides

Pesticides are used to repel, kill, or disable pests, including undesirable plants, insects, rodents, fungi, and molds. Most pesticides are toxic to people and the environment if improperly used. Congress originally passed the Federal Insecticide, Fungicide, and Rodenticide Act (FIFRA) in 1947 and has amended it several times since. States also regulate pesticides and are allowed to give additional registration for special or emergency needs. States also license related businesses, such as pesticide applicators, distributors, dealers, and the users of particularly dangerous pesticides.

The EPA has registered more than 20,000 products under FIFRA; the classes of products are shown in Exhibit 21.5. Registration means that before a pesticide is sold, the EPA has examined scientific data from multiple tests about a product's effects. The label

EXHIBIT 21.5 TYPES OF PESTICIDES REGULATED BY FIFRA

TYPE	TARGETS
Insecticides	Flying and crawling insects
Herbicides	Undesirable plants/weeds
Rodenticides	Mice, rats, and other rodents
Fungicides	Fungi that cause plant disease/wood rot, etc.
Nematicides	Invertebrates (worms)
Fumigants	Insects/fungi
Antimicrobials	Microorganisms such as bacteria, molds, fungi
Biopesticides	Natural materials such as animals, plants, bacteria, and certain minerals that target a variety of pests
Plant or insect growth regulators	Plant (accelerate or retard, the rate of growth of a plant); insect (affect the growth of insects)

© Cengage Learning

on the product must be accurate as to proper use and precautions. Registration is approved for five years at a time for pesticides that meet these conditions:

1. The product does what the producers claim it will do.
2. The registration materials and the label are accurate as to proper use.
3. The product, when used properly, will not have "unreasonable adverse effects on the environment."

FIFRA requires that the economic and environmental costs and benefits of each product be considered. The EPA determines what risk—such as groundwater contamination or skin irritation—might be posed by a pesticide in order to limit how the product is used and who may use it. Because some products pose a danger to certain species, the EPA may restrict use to locations that minimize exposure to those who could be harmed. Working with the FDA, the EPA sets usage requirements to take into account the residues that remain in food products to ensure that consumers are not exposed to unsafe levels of pesticides.

Lighter Side of the Law

Thanks for the Housing

Alison Murray enjoyed the first home she ever owned. Then bats moved into the roof. Authorities in Aberdeen, Scotland, told her in August that she would have to move out of the house because the bats are protected under Scottish and European Union law. Experts told her she would likely be able to move back in November when the bats would leave to hibernate elsewhere.

Source: The Scotsman.

Resource Conservation and Recovery Act

TSCA and FIFRA are primarily concerned with controlling toxic substances before they get to the market. How toxic substances are handled once they are in the market and when they are discarded is the concern of the Resource Conservation and Recovery Act (RCRA) passed in 1976 and amended in 1984.

"Out of sight, out of mind" was standard procedure for the disposal of many hazardous wastes before the environmental consequences of improper disposal were understood. RCRA requires that hundreds of thousands of generators, who create millions of tons of hazardous waste each year, comply with an EPA regulatory program dealing with the transportation, storage, treatment, and disposal of hazardous waste to reduce danger to health and the environment.

Hazardous Waste RCRA requires the EPA to identify and maintain a list of hazardous wastes. The Act defines **hazardous waste** as follows:

> *… a solid waste … which because of its quantity, concentration, or physical, chemical, or infectious characteristics may—*
>
> *(a) cause, or significantly contribute to, an increase in mortality or an increase in serious irreversible, or incapacitating reversible, illness; or, (b) pose a substantial present or potential hazard to human health or the environment when improperly treated, stored, transported, or disposed of, or otherwise managed.*

The characteristics of a hazardous waste are ignitability, such as in gasoline; corrosivity, such as in acids; reactivity, such as in unstable chemicals; and toxicity, such as is found in materials that threaten groundwater. Wastes that threaten groundwater, such as used batteries and unused pesticides, may be stored or disposed of only at sites whose owners or operators have EPA permits. To get permits, the owners of **treatment, storage, and disposal (TSD) sites** agree to meet all regulations regarding the handling of hazardous wastes.

Regulation of TSD Sites RCRA requires the EPA to regulate TSD sites. Certain hazardous wastes must be treated prior to disposal. A treatment facility is where a change is made in the physical, chemical, or biological character of hazardous waste to make it less hazardous or to recover energy or materials from it. A storage facility is where waste is held, such as in storage tanks, until it can be disposed of or treated. A disposal facility is where hazardous wastes are placed into controlled landfills.

The Manifest System RCRA forces compliance by hazardous waste generators, transporters, and TSD-site owners through a **manifest system**. The producer of a hazardous waste must complete a manifest—a form that states the nature of the hazardous waste and identifies its origin, shipping route, and final destination. The waste must be packaged in appropriate and properly labeled containers.

Generators must give transporters of hazardous waste a copy of the manifest. Transporters, such as trucking companies, must sign the manifest and, upon delivery, provide a copy to the owner of the TSD site, who must return a copy of the manifest to the generator, thereby closing the circle. If a generator is not informed of the proper disposal of the waste, it notifies the EPA. This reporting system provides regulators with the ability to track hazardous waste through its generation, transportation, and disposal phases. It also helps prevent disposal at unlicensed facilities.

Superfund

After publicity rose concerning hazardous waste at abandoned waste sites, Congress enacted the Comprehensive Environmental Response, Compensation, and Liability Act

(CERCLA) in 1980. Called the **Superfund**, the Act provides the authority to clean up abandoned hazardous sites. Congress amended the Superfund program in 1986 with the Superfund Amendments and Reauthorization Act (SARA). Private parties incur much of the cleanup costs.

Over the years, the EPA has evaluated tens of thousands of sites and, using a Hazard Ranking System, put those deemed most in need of action on the **National Priority List** (NPL). Those are the locations that receive the most attention. Some sites cost a few million dollars to clean up; others run as high as half a billion. The EPA has completed the cleanup at hundreds of sites; about 1,300 sites are in various stages of work.

Responsible Parties An abandoned dumpsite might contain hazardous wastes contributed by many waste generators. In addition, the dumpsite may have been operated by different parties over the years. Under the law, there are likely to be multiple **potentially responsible parties** (PRPs). The EPA publishes a "PRP Search Manual" to give guidance on finding parties who may be brought into a Superfund site cleanup. CERCLA defines PRPs, who can be held liable for both cleanup costs and damages to natural resources, to include:

1. Current owners of a hazardous waste site
2. Prior owners of a site at the time of hazardous waste disposal
3. Any hazardous waste generator who arranged for disposal at the site
4. Any transporter of hazardous waste who selected the site for disposal

The parties may be held strictly and jointly and severally liable for these costs; that is, each party can be liable for the entire cleanup cost regardless of the size of its contribution to the hazardous waste at the site. As a result, each party has a strong incentive to identify other PRPs, which often results in lengthy, expensive litigation.

Practical Problems Even before PRPs are identified or sued, the EPA may begin a cleanup if there is a threat to public health or the environment if cleanup is delayed. Later, the government can try to recover expenses by suing PRPs, if they can be located. More commonly, the EPA orders private parties to pay to clean up the site under EPA supervision. This has generated billions of dollars in litigation as parties wrangle over responsibility.

Hence, an important issue to consider when buying property is whether it contains toxic wastes that may have been buried years ago or, when buying a business, whether the business was involved in handling toxic materials. If so, the new owner may be held responsible for cleanup costs. Some new owners have been handed cleanup bills for more than the property is worth, even though the new owners did not generate the waste. If they cannot find other PRPs capable of paying the bill, the new owners are stuck. As a result, property buyers often have an environmental audit performed on land they intend to purchase.

Because of the nearly unlimited liability for unknown cleanup costs, no one wants to buy a site that might have to be cleaned up and so, useful property sits abandoned. For example, the Cleveland *Plain Dealer* built a new plant for newspaper production on farmland outside the city. The *Plain Dealer* had also considered an abandoned urban site, but it was found to have chemicals in the soil from years before. Such old sites are referred to as **brownfields**. The newspaper could not risk Superfund liability, so it moved out of town rather than run the operation in downtown Cleveland, where it would have helped restore the area.

The Brownfields Revitalization Act of 2002 was passed to help bring such brownfields back into use. It limits the liability to purchasers of contaminated sites for previous improper dumping of toxic wastes on the land.

Species Protection

Most environmental laws are written with a primary concern for the effect of pollutants on human health. But some laws address environmental protection for wildlife or, more broadly, for all species. The most important of these laws is the Endangered Species Act (ESA), enacted in 1973 and amended several times. In some respects, the ESA is the toughest environmental statute.

The ESA recognizes the value of species **habitat**. It authorizes designation of critical habitat—areas needed to preserve endangered species—and calls for recovery plans for listed species. The Fish and Wildlife Service (FWS) of the Department of the Interior, which has primary responsibility for the ESA, devises recovery programs for approximately 1,250 recognized threatened and endangered species in the United States. To give an idea of coverage, Exhibit 21.6 lists the threatened (T) and endangered (E) species identified by the FWS just for the state of Kansas.

Habitat Protection

The ESA authorizes the Secretary of the Interior to declare species of animal or plant life endangered and to establish the critical habitat of such species. An **endangered species** is

EXHIBIT 21.6	ANIMAL AND PLANT SPECIES LISTED IN KANSAS BY FISH AND WILDLIFE SERVICE

STATUS	SPECIES
E	Bat, gray *(Myotis grisescens)*
E	Beetle, American burying *(Nicrophorus americanus)*
E	Crane, whooping *(Grus americana)*
T	Madtom, Neosho *(Noturus placidus)*
T	Plover, piping *(Charadrius melodus)*
T	Shiner, Arkansas River Arkansas R. Basin *(Notropis girardi)*
E	Shiner, Topeka *(Notropis topeka [=tristis])*
E	Spectaclecase (mussel) *(Cumberlandia monodonta)*
E	Sturgeon, pallid *(Scaphirhynchus albus)*
E	Tern, least interior *(Sterna antillarum)*
E	Bat, Indiana *(Myotis sodalist)*
E	Mussel, snuffbox *(Epioblasma triquetra)*
E	Vireo, black-capped *(Vireo atricpalilla)*
E	Wolf, gray *(Canis lupus)*
E	Ferret, black-footed *(Mustela nigripes)*
T	Milkweed, Mead's *(Asclepias meadii)*
T	Orchid, western prairie fringed *(Platanthera praeclara)*
E	Clover, running buffalo *(Trifolium stoloniferum)*

Source: Fish and Wildlife Service.

defined as "any species which is in danger of extinction throughout all or a significant portion of its range." When a species is listed as endangered or threatened by the Interior Department, the Act imposes obligations on private and public parties. Under the ESA, no person may "take, import, or conduct commercial activity with respect to any endangered species." In most disputes involving an endangered species, parties generally agree that the species deserves protection; the conflict centers on how protection is provided.

Lighter Side of the Law

Protect Truly Rare Species

An office in the Parliament of Sweden was searching environmental records. It discovered a regional environmental court order from Jaemtland. The court had denied a resort-development permit because it could interfere with the "Storsjoe monster." The Storsjoe monster is something like the Loch Ness monster, with a serpent's body and cat-like head. It was first "seen" in 1635. The court held that "it is prohibited to kill, hurt, or catch animals of the Storsjoe monster species" or to "take away or hurt the monster's eggs, roe, or den."

Similarly, when Alcoa prepared to build an aluminum smelting plant in Iceland, the government required it to hire an expert to assure that none of the country's "hidden people" lived under the property. A six-month inspection determined that none of the elf-like goblins lived under the property, so construction could proceed.

Sources: Washington Post; Vanity Fair.

The ESA states that projects may not "result in the destruction or modification of habitat of [endangered] species." The full impact of that statement was not clear for years. However, in 1991, a federal court ordered logging stopped on federal lands in Oregon, Washington, and northern California. Environmental groups had sued to stop logging to protect the habitat and nesting areas of the spotted owl, a bird on the endangered species list. In 1995, the Supreme Court, in *Babbitt* v. *Sweet Home* (515 U.S. 2407), held that habitat protection is a key part of the ESA, so logging had to be stopped until a habitat protection plan was put in place. The reduction in logging on behalf of the spotted owl is estimated to have cost in the range of $25 to $50 billion.

Controversy and Uncertainty Endangered species protection joins wetlands in being one of the most controversial environmental issues. There is no clear legal definition of *endangered* or *species* or *habitat*. The legal requirements for adding a species to the list are minimal. Because listing a species can lead to very tight controls on private property use, landowners fear having their land removed from use as a result of uncompensated habitat protection.

Habitats have been clearly defined for only some listed species. Environmental agencies cannot address all problems. Citizen groups play a large role in pressing for enforcement of environmental statutes. The following case illustrates the potential reach of the ESA, as it is applied when climate change is taken into consideration.

Global Environmental Issues

Some major environmental issues—the ozone layer, global climate change, habitat destruction, and the marine environment—must be dealt with on an international scale. Even if the United States did not contribute to a particular global environmental

IN RE POLAR BEAR ENDANGERED SPECIES ACT LISTING

United States Court of Appeals, District of Columbia Circuit, 709 F.3d 1 (2013)

Case Background *In 2005, the Fish and Wildlife Service (FWS) was petitioned to list the polar bear under the Endangered Species Act (ESA) as threatened or endangered. The bear population is now healthy, and they are spread over 19 different areas in the Arctic. After a three-year review, the FWS found that as a result of the effects of global climate change, the polar bear is likely to become an endangered species over the next 45 years. It listed the species as threatened.*

Various groups challenged the listing as either overly restrictive or insufficiently protective. They attacked the listing as arbitrary and capricious in violation of the Administrative Procedure Act (APA). The District Court rejected the claims and upheld the FWS rule. Interested parties appealed.

Case Decision Edwards, Senior Circuit Judge

* * *

The appellate court's task in a case such as this is a "narrow" one. Our principal responsibility here is to determine, in light of the record considered by the agency, whether the Listing Rule is a product of reasoned decisionmaking. ...

The Listing Rule rests on a three-part thesis: the polar bear is dependent upon sea ice for its survival; sea ice is declining; and climatic changes have and will continue to dramatically reduce the extent and quality of Arctic sea ice to a degree sufficiently grave to jeopardize polar bear populations. No part of this thesis is disputed and we find that FWS's conclusion—that the polar bear is threatened within the meaning of the ESA—is reasonable and adequately supported by the record.

The Listing Rule is the product of FWS's careful and comprehensive study and analysis. Its scientific conclusions are amply supported by data and well within the mainstream on climate science and polar bear biology. Thirteen of the fourteen peer reviewers to whom FWS submitted the proposed rule found that it generally "represented a thorough, clear, and balanced review of the best scientific information available from both published and unpublished sources of the current status of polar bears" and that it "justified the conclusion that polar bears face threats throughout their range." ...

Appellants argue that FWS violated the APA and ESA by inadequately explaining how the predicted decrease in habitat would likely lead to such a dramatic population decline causing the species to be endangered within the next 45 years. ...

Appellants' claim fails because FWS clearly explained how the anticipated habitat loss renders this particular species likely to become endangered. The agency considered and explained how the loss of sea ice harms the polar bear. ...

Therefore, we reject this challenge and hold that FWS's conclusion that the species warranted listing throughout its range was not arbitrary and capricious. ...

Affirmed.

Questions for Analysis

1. Bear habitat does not appear to be in danger in many of the 19 areas in which they congregate, so why would it matter if there is a threat to only some areas?
2. If the problem may not occur for as much as 45 years, why should anything be done now?

---

problem, the consequences would still be borne here, so the United States must work with other countries to decide what to do about such issues. The ozone issue provides a good example of an international legal solution to an environmental problem.

The Ozone

Too much ozone (O_3) in the air we breathe is a problem caused largely by vehicle exhaust in a local area. Ozone depletion at high levels in the atmosphere is caused by

ISSUE SPOTTER
Picking a Sweet Spot

Your firm develops resort spots. Nice pieces of land are found for developing a hotel, golf course, and other facilities. Sometimes houses are also built for permanent residents. The plots of land purchased run between 100 and 600 acres. In considering land for development, what environmental issues should be considered before buying the property?

chlorofluorocarbons (CFCs), known commonly as Freon, among other names. CFCs were widely used as refrigerants in air-conditioning and in making computer chips. In the stratosphere, CFCs eat away at the ozone layer, which protects us from ultraviolet radiation. As ozone is depleted, possible effects on humans include increases in skin cancer and eye cataracts and injury to the immune system.

Evidence of a "hole" in the ozone layer over Antarctica in 1985 convinced industry and the government that CFCs were a serious problem. Ozone loss could cause tens of thousands of deaths per year. In the United States, the makers of CFCs, which produced one-third of the world supply, agreed with the EPA that CFC production had to be eliminated.

The producers supported the Montreal Protocol of 1987, which the United States signed. Under this international treaty, nations that produced CFCs agreed to cut production by 50 percent by 1998. The protocol was revised by the London treaty of 1990, requiring production of CFCs and Halon (the best firefighting chemical that existed) to be phased out completely by 2000.

A solution was achieved that resulted in producers giving up a multibillion-dollar-per-year market. Producers' cooperation was hastened by the promise from the government that existing producers would have a monopoly over the product during it final years. The total cost to the world's economy of the CFC phase-out was about $200 billion.

Lighter Side of the Law

Let the Sun Shine!

Carolynn Bissett and Richard Treanor see themselves as good environmentalists. They own a Toyota Prius and prided themselves on their California backyard, which contained beautiful redwood trees.

Invoking a 30-year-old law, California's Solar Shade Control Act, Santa Clara County officials brought criminal charges against them for allowing their trees to grow and block sunlight from their neighbor's solar panels. The trees were there first, but that did not matter. The tree owners were convicted and the judge ordered the death penalty for offending trees.

Source: Christian Science Monitor.

International Cooperation

CFC production occurred largely in the United States, Japan, and European nations—countries that could essentially force the decision on this issue. Other international environmental issues require more cooperation from less-developed nations because those nations will experience more of the effects of changes in policies to reduce environmental problems.

The Montreal Protocol provided a fund, set up by wealthier nations, to pay poorer nations to sign the agreement to ban CFCs. That is, the United States paid for environmental cooperation from other nations. If the United States and other nations are concerned about species preservation and other environmental issues, they must pay less-developed nations to protect species and to cover the costs of some pollution controls.

Climate Change

Greenhouse gases that many scientists link to climate change are at the heart of the recent environmental policy debate. A treaty drafted in Kyoto, Japan, in 1997 contains assertions by most nations that they would take steps to substantially reduce certain gas emissions—such as carbon dioxide—between 2008 and 2012. The treaty, however, did not achieve its goals. The Clinton administration approved the treaty in 1998, but did not submit it to Congress for ratification because it would not have passed. A Senate resolution passed 95 to 0 indicating strong opposition to the treaty.

The Kyoto Treaty has been more symbolic than a real commitment. Greenhouse gas emissions have increased faster in some signing nations in Europe than they have in the United States, where they have been falling for a decade. As the economies of the most populous nations, China and India, grow quickly, their emissions are rising quickly. If there is a consensus that the emissions must be addressed, it will require international action. Poor nations cannot afford advanced technology, so the United States, the European Union, and Japan may have to offer some solutions. The Supreme Court became involved in on the issue in 2007, which may be a signal of new trends in environmental law in the years to come, as the United States, like some other nations, may act unilaterally to reduce carbon emissions.

MASSACHUSETTS V. ENVIRONMENTAL PROTECTION AGENCY

Supreme Court of the United States 549 U.S. 497 (2007)

Case Background *Twelve states, some local governments, and private organizations sued the EPA, contending that it did not live up to its obligation under the Clean Air Act to regulate greenhouse gases that result from vehicle emissions. EPA responded that its regulations were sufficient and that it need not design more stringent regulations. The appeals court agreed; plaintiffs appealed.*

Case Decision Stevens, Justice

* * *

Congress has ordered EPA to protect Massachusetts (among others) by prescribing standards applicable to the "emission of any air pollutant from any class or classes of new motor vehicle engines, which in [the Administrator's] judgment cause, or contribute to, air pollution which may reasonably be anticipated to endanger public health or welfare."...

EPA's steadfast refusal to regulate greenhouse gas emissions presents a risk of harm to Massachusetts that is both "actual" and "imminent." There is, moreover, a "substantial likelihood that the judicial relief requested" will prompt EPA to take steps to reduce that risk.

The harms associated with climate change are serious and well recognized. Indeed, the National Research Council Report itself—which EPA regards as an "objective and independent assessment of the relevant science," identifies a number of environmental changes that have already inflicted significant harms, including "the global retreat of mountain glaciers, reduction in snow-cover extent, the earlier spring melting of rivers and lakes, [and] the accelerated rate of rise of sea levels during the twentieth century relative to the past few thousand years. ..."

EPA does not dispute the existence of a causal connection between man-made greenhouse gas emissions and global warming. At a minimum, therefore, EPA's refusal to regulate such emissions "contributes" to Massachusetts' injuries. ...

EPA does not believe that any realistic possibility exists that the relief petitioners seek would mitigate global climate change and remedy their injuries. That is especially so, because predicted increases in greenhouse gas emissions from developing nations, particularly China and India, are likely to offset any marginal domestic decrease. ...

And reducing domestic automobile emissions is hardly a tentative step. Even leaving aside the other greenhouse gases, the United States transportation sector emits an enormous quantity of carbon dioxide into the atmosphere ... more than 1.7 billion metric tons in 1999 alone. That accounts for more than 6 percent of worldwide carbon dioxide emissions. ...

In sum—at least according to petitioners' uncontested affidavits—the rise in sea levels associated with global warming has already harmed and will continue to harm Massachusetts. The risk of catastrophic harm, though remote, is nevertheless real. That risk would be reduced to some extent if petitioners received the relief they seek. We therefore hold that petitioners have standing to challenge the EPA's denial of their rule-making petition. ...

Because greenhouse gases fit well within the Clean Air Act's capacious definition of "air pollutant," we hold that EPA has the statutory authority to regulate the emission of such gases from new motor vehicles. ...

Questions for Analysis

1. The Supreme Court held that the EPA has authority to regulate greenhouse gases, such as carbon dioxide emissions from vehicles. If Massachusetts and other states feel strongly about it, why do those states not address the matter?
2. Does the Supreme Court have the authority to order EPA to control such emissions?

INTERNATIONAL PERSPECTIVE

CITES: Global Species Concerns May Conflict with Local Interests

The same year the Endangered Species Act (ESA) of 1973 was passed, a meeting was held in Washington, D.C., to establish a global initiative to help protect species. The Convention on International Trade in Endangered Species of Wild Fauna and Flora (CITES) was initiated. Since then, most nations have joined CITES. Unlike a treaty, the CITES is not binding law, and most nations agree to comply only with preservation measures. Little can be done to impose penalties for noncompliance if a nation does not take the matter seriously.

A key provision of CITES is its ban on transportation of products from endangered species through a signatory nation's territory. For example, because the United States belongs to CITES, no products from species it lists as endangered can be transported through cargo hubs at U.S. airports such as Miami, FL. This dramatically reduces the ability to ship such

products from Central and South America, effectively expanding CITES' reach.

CITES focuses on species preservation. Unlike the ESA, which allows habitat protection as part of species protection, CITES has no such provision. The focus is on discouraging trade in endangered species. The gorilla, red panda, rhinoceros, Asian elephant, and jaguar are among the hundreds of species covered by CITES. Nevertheless, like other contraband goods, trade in endangered species flourishes when there are willing buyers and sellers despite these formal legal protections.

Poor people can earn a huge amount of money, by their standards, by selling one illegally killed endangered animal. The rhinoceros horn is believed by some Asians to have amazing medical value, so people are willing to pay a high price for it. When revenue from such trade brings revenue to a country, it is not likely to suppress the market, which makes international controls ineffective. For example, wildlife authorities in Kenya have broad powers (including the authority to shoot to kill) to stop poaching. But some "poachers" shot were innocent bystanders who stumbled upon poaching operations run by game wardens.

A different route has been tried elsewhere. Elephants have been protected in Zimbabwe by a program that allows indigenous people who live near the herds the right to control the animals. They sell hunting rights to wealthy foreigners who want to hunt elephant. The local people profit from the hunt-

ing and have an incentive to protect the quality of the herd, so that large, healthy animals are available over time. They patrol to prevent poachers from killing elephants. Similarly, the endangered white rhino is protected in large areas in South Africa; the property owners sell limited hunting rights to big game hunters so they can afford to provide the habitat needed by the animals to survive.

Species protection under the CITES can be very costly. To obtain effective species protection in poor countries involves creative approaches to give incentives to people who may otherwise see little reason to care about such matters.

? TEST YOURSELF

1. Chemicals in commercial use are registered with the EPA under _____ .
2. Pesticides are registered with the EPA under the Resource Conservation and Recovery Act: T—F
3. Hazardous waste generators, transporters, and disposal site operators must keep track of the waste by use of a(n) _____ .
4. Much of the protection of endangered species focuses on the protection of their _____ .
5. In *In re Polar Bear Endangered Species Act Listing*, where groups challenged the Fish and Wildlife Service designation of the polar bear as threatened under the Endangered Species Act, the court held that:
   a. the rule was not arbitrary and capricious, so the court would defer to the expertise of the FWS.
   b. the groups protesting that the rule protecting the bear was not strong enough needed to be taken into account by FWS in a revision of the rule.
   c. the groups protesting that the rule protecting the bear was not justified because most of the bears do not live in U.S. jurisdiction were correct so the rule had to be modified.
   d. there was inadequate evidence of harm to the bears in the next 45 years, so a rule placing them on the ESA list was arbitrary and capricious.
6. Under CERCLA, or Superfund, if it is determined that an abandoned waste site needs remediation, it is placed on the _____ .
7. When urban land is abandoned as a result of the costs of compliance with environmental standards, the property is referred to as a(n) _____ .
8. To protect ozone in the upper atmosphere against destruction, an international treaty agreed to stop the production of chemicals that caused the change: T—F

Answers: TOSCA; F; manifest; habitat; a; National Priority List; brownfield; T.

SUMMARY

- Before passage of federal environmental laws, environmental protection relied on common-law remedies, including private and public nuisance actions, trespass, negligence, strict liability for hazardous activities, and riparian water rights. Actions could result in damages or an injunction ordering the offender to cease damaging activities. The EPA is the key regulator of the environment. It works with environmental agencies in all states to enforce federal requirements.

- The Clean Air Act sets air quality standards for several major pollutants: sulfur dioxide, particulates, ozone, carbon monoxide, nitrogen oxide, and lead. These standards are constantly tightened. New polluters must use the best pollution control technology available. In some areas, if a business is to produce any new air pollution, it must buy pollution rights from existing polluters, who are paid either to quit polluting or to install better pollution-control equipment.

- The Clean Water Act focuses on point-source pollution, which comes out of pipes from factories or sewer systems. Point sources must have permits that allow them to discharge certain amounts of pollution into water bodies. States must declare what standards all bodies of water in the state need to meet according to their use (e.g., drinking *versus* swimming quality). Nonpoint source pollution—runoff from farms, streets, construction sites, mining, and logging—is just beginning to be addressed.

- Wetlands are lands saturated with water at least part of the year. Prior to building on or disturbing a wetland, developers must obtain a permit from the Army Corps of Engineers. The EPA has final say on wetlands use.

- The Toxic Substances Control Act and the Federal Insecticide, Fungicide, and Rodenticide Act require EPA review and approval of toxic substances before they are sold. The EPA may restrict product usage and keep track of evidence of harm from such products.

- The Resource Conservation and Recovery Act requires comprehensive paperwork, called manifests, to follow the production, distribution, and disposal of hazardous substances. Hazardous waste treatment, storage, and disposal facilities are subject to strict licensing and regulatory control.

- The Superfund program provides federal support to clean up abandoned hazardous waste sites. Any parties that contributed to the disposal of the wastes, even if legal at the time, may be held liable for part or all of the cleanup costs. Land purchasers should consider an environmental audit to check for possibilities of hazardous wastes, wetlands, or endangered species.

- The Endangered Species Act can block any economic activity, without compromise, if the activity can harm the habitat of an endangered species. Compromises that demonstrate habitat protection may allow a project to go forward as approved by the Fish and Wildlife Service.

- Some environmental controls are imposed by international agreements. The Montreal Protocol required cessation of the production of chlorofluorocarbons (CFCs)—chemicals used in refrigeration systems, plastics production, and firefighting. Protection of biological diversity and reduction of greenhouse gases are international issues that require advanced nations to pay for environmental protection in poorer nations.

TERMS TO KNOW

DISCUSSION QUESTION

Were common-law actions—such as nuisance, trespass, and strict liability—against pollution too weak? That is, was federal statutory intervention needed to prevent serious environmental damage?

CASE QUESTIONS

1. A land developer started a retirement village in an area with large cattle feedlots. Later, after part of the village was built, the developer brought a nuisance action against the largest feedlot owner. The developer claimed that the feedlot was polluting the air with terrible odors, causing discomfort to the residents, and reducing the value of property. Assume the court found the feedlot to be a nuisance. What should be the remedy? Could the feedlot be a nuisance in one location and acceptable in another? [*Spur Industries* v. *Del Webb Development*, 494 P.2d 700, Sup.Ct., Ariz. (1972)]

2. For ten years, a company dumped millions of gallons of chemical wastes on its property in Tennessee. The state shut down the site. Residents around the property sued the company, claiming that their drinking water was contaminated. What basis for suit did they have, and could they win? [*Sterling* v. *Velsicol Chemical*, 647 F.Supp. 303, W.D. Tenn. (1986)]
    ✓ Check your answer

3. The EPA set emission standards for vinyl chloride, a toxic substance that is carcinogenic to humans. The Clean Air Act says such standards must be "at the level which ... provides an ample margin of safety to protect the public health." The exact threat from vinyl chloride was not known. The EPA said that the proper emissions requirement is the lowest level attainable by best available control technology. The Natural Resources Defense Council sued, contending that because there was uncertainty about the danger, the EPA had to prohibit all emissions. Which position do you think was held correct? [*NRDC* v. *EPA*, 824 F.2d 1146, D.C. Cir. (1987)]

4. As required by the Clean Water Act, the EPA issued standards for discharges from hundreds of sources. Despite the standards, the EPA issued variances to some polluters on a case-by-case basis, allowing them to exceed the discharge standards. The Natural Resource Defense Council sued to oppose such variances; the Chemical Manufacturers Association defended the variances. Who won? [*Chemical Manufacturers Assn.* v. *NRDC*, 470 U.S. 116 (1985)]
    ✓ Check your answer

5. Congress gave the EPA the power in RCRA to regulate "solid wastes." The EPA declared that this includes materials that are being recycled. This was challenged as incorrect, that Congress meant the regulation of materials being discarded or disposed of, not materials being reused. Which position would seem logical? [*American Mining Congress* v. *EPA*, 824 F.2d 1177, D.C.Cir. (1987)]

6. The City of Cochran, Georgia, operated a wastewater treatment facility under an NPDES permit. Treatment water is dumped into Jordan Creek in the Altamaha River basin. For five years, the city regularly exceeded the effluent limitations in its NPDES permit. A nonprofit organization, ARK, founded to protect the Altamaha River, sued Cochran under the citizen suit provision of the Clean Water Act. ARK sought injunctive relief against the pollution as well as civil penalties and attorney fees. ARK moved for partial summary judgment. Does the citizen group have the right to bring such a suit? [*Altamaha Riverkeepers* v. *City of Cochran*, 162 F.Supp.2d 1368, M.D. Ga. (2001)]
    ✓ Check your answer

7. A company ran a hazardous waste disposal and recycling operation. Several companies sent their hazardous wastes to the site. The facility was improperly managed: waste was dumped on the ground, chemicals were mixed, and records were

not kept about what was there. The EPA cleaned up the site under Superfund and sued the companies that sent their waste to the site because the owners of the site could not pay the bill. The companies responded that they were not liable under CERCLA because there was no evidence that the particular waste they sent had been improperly disposed of. Were they right? [*U.S. v. S.C. Recycling and Disposal*, 653 F.Supp. 984, Dist. S.C. (1984)]

8. Georgoulis owned White Farm Equipment (WFE) from 1980 to 1985. During those years, WFE dumped its hazardous waste in a dump in Iowa owned by another company. The EPA declared the dump to be a Superfund site. It claimed Georgoulis was a responsible party and so, had to contribute personally to the cleanup costs. The court found that Georgoulis did not "have any personal knowledge of the disposal practices at the dump site, or was in any way directly involved in waste disposal matters." Could Georgoulis be liable? [*U.S. v. TIC Investment*, 68 F.3d 1082, 8th Cir. (1995)]

9. Plaintiffs, residents, and owners of lands and property along the Mississippi Gulf sued major energy and chemical companies. Plaintiffs claim that defendants' operation of fossil fuel and chemical industries caused the emission of greenhouse gases that contributed to global warming, which changed weather patterns and caused Hurricane Katrina to be stronger than it would have been otherwise, thereby causing large losses. On claims of nuisance, trespass, and negligence, the plaintiffs contend that the firms injured them, so they demand compensatory and punitive damages. The district court dismissed the suit. Plaintiffs appealed; do you think they have a case? [*Comer* v. *Murphy Oil*, 585 F.3d 855, 5th Cir. (2009)]

ETHICS QUESTION

You are an executive with a leading manufacturing company, and one aspect of your business pollutes heavily. You know that you can build a plant in a third-world country to handle that aspect without pollution control. This would mean that for the same amount of production, you would add ten times more pollution to the environment than you do now, but it would be more profitable for the company. You can legally move the plant. Should you?

CHAPTER 22

The International Legal Environment of Business

The Foreign Corrupt Practices Act (FCPA) makes it illegal for businesses to bribe foreign officials to obtain business. The Department of Justice believed that an executive of the French engineering firm Alstom SA, who is a French citizen, bribed Indonesian officials for his company to get business. When the French citizen, Frederic Pierucci, came to the United States on business, did that make him subject to arrest and criminal prosecution for violation of the FCPA?

That is just one of issues that we focus on in this chapter on the international legal environment of business. We begin with a discussion of the nature of the international business environment. Then we consider the various ways that the U.S. government works to restrict imports and stimulate exports. The business organizations that may be considered before becoming involved in an international venture are then looked at. The constraints imposed by the FCPA are considered next. Finally, we discuss the nature of international contracting, insurance against loss, and procedures for the resolution of international disputes.

International Law and Business

Faster and cheaper transportation and communications have changed the nature of business. The percentage of U.S. gross domestic product involved in international trade has tripled over the years. For example, the Ford Motor Co. has hundreds of suppliers in other countries that make continuous deliveries. Most businesses are affected by events in other countries. Crop failures in Argentina, wars in the Middle East, currency devaluations in Mexico, and shipping strikes in Germany can all quickly and negatively affect U.S. business.

The International Business Environment

International business includes all business transactions that involve entities from two or more countries. In addition to the movement of goods between countries, international trade includes the movement of services, capital, and personnel by multinational enterprises.

The international business environment includes business activities that are affected by conditions and events in different countries. Even U.S. businesses that operate only in the domestic market can find themselves in direct competition with foreign firms. Initially, the main source of foreign competition came from imported products. However, foreign competitors now build factories in the United States to compete more effectively. For example, more parts for some Honda cars are made in the United States than parts for some Fords.

Major differences between domestic and international businesses include special financial, political, and regulatory risks in international enterprises. These arise from a variety of sources, including differences among countries in currencies, languages, customs, legal systems, social philosophies, and government policies.

Origins of International Law

Before the development of the international procedures that are discussed in this chapter, nations and merchants involved in international commerce had long developed rules for trade. Early trade customs centered on the law of the sea. They provided, among other things, for rights of shipping in foreign ports, salvage rights, fishing rights, and freedom of passage.

International commercial codes date back at least as far as 1400 BCE for Egyptians involved in trade. Merchants from various countries developed commercial codes among themselves to provide some legal certainty in international transactions. Greek and Roman civilizations had well-developed codes of practice for international trade.

During the Middle Ages, principles embodied in the *lex mercatoria* (law merchant) arose from trading customs that governed commercial transactions throughout Europe. The law merchant created a legal structure for the protection and encouragement of transactions across jurisdictions. Commerce codes in use today, such as those discussed in Chapter 11, are derived from trading codes dating back many centuries.

Sources of International Law

The main sources of international commercial law are the laws of individual nations, the laws defined by trade agreements between countries, and the rules enacted by worldwide or regional organizations, such as the United Nations or the European Union (EU). There is, however, no international system of courts generally accepted for resolving international conflicts between businesses. An overview of some international and U.S. organizations affecting the international legal environment is provided in Exhibit 22.1.

EXHIBIT 22.1   SELECTED ORGANIZATIONS AFFECTING THE INTERNATIONAL LEGAL ENVIRONMENT

WORLD ORGANIZATIONS	
World Bank	Promotes private foreign investment through loans and guarantees; provides technical and managerial assistance on large capital projects
International Monetary Fund (IMF)	Responsible for promoting international trade by working for stability of in government finances and currency exchange rates
World Trade Organization (WTO)	Promotes international trade by working to reduce trade barriers and to establish uniform tariff schedules and trade rules
Commission on International Trade Law	Promotes uniformity in laws; discourages legal obstacles to trade
World Intellectual Property Organization	Promotes protection of intellectual property worldwide and promotes uniformity in laws
International Court of Justice	Principal court of the United Nations, located in the Netherlands; only countries—not private parties—have standing to bring cases
UNITED STATES ORGANIZATIONS	
International Trade Administration (ITA)	Part of the Department of Commerce; promotes trade and U.S. products; provides companies with data, foreign license requirements, and other information
International Trade Commission (ITC)	Agency responsible for recommending trade restrictions to the president; examines the impact of a subsidized foreign import on domestic industry
Court of International Trade	Has jurisdiction to review findings of the ITC or ITA and over lawsuits against the United States regarding imports, tariffs, duties, or embargoes
Bureau of Export Administration (BEA)	Part of the Department of Commerce; responsible for maintaining the Commodity Control List and goods subject to export controls
United States Export-Import Bank (Ex-Im Bank)	Provides loans and loan guarantees to foreign purchasers of goods exported from the United States; mostly involved in heavy capital equipment projects
Overseas Private Investment Corporation (OPIC)	Provides insurance for U.S. projects that would be rejected by private insurers, largely projects in developing countries; coverage protects against currency exchange problems, expropriation or confiscation, and war
United States Trade Representative (USTR)	Appointed by the president to negotiate trade agreements that reduce trade barriers, including the WTO

International Trade Agreements

Most countries seek to improve their economic relations through trade agreements. The intent is to improve investment and trade climates among countries. For example, most industrialized countries have tax agreements to prevent double taxation of profits earned in international business. Two particularly important trade agreements for U.S. businesses are a regional treaty, the North American Free Trade Agreement (NAFTA), and an international treaty, the General Agreement on Tariffs and Trade, which created the World Trade Organization.

North American Free Trade Agreement   NAFTA was ratified by the governments of Canada, the United States, and Mexico and went into effect in 1994. It reduced or eliminated tariffs and trade barriers on most North American trade. The industries most affected by NAFTA are agriculture, automobiles, pharmaceuticals, and textiles. The agreement creates a huge trade area, with over 400 million consumers, and has fewer trade restrictions than most other countries.

NAFTA provides for greater Mexican protection of U.S. and Canadian intellectual property. It also ensures that the managers of U.S. companies do not use access to Mexico as a way to avoid U.S. environmental laws. NAFTA uses special panels to resolve disputes involving unfair trade practices, investment restrictions, and environmental issues.

World Trade Organization   After World War II, the General Agreement on Tariffs and Trade (GATT) worked to reduce trade barriers. GATT focused on trade restrictions, including import quotas and tariffs. It published tariff schedules to which countries agreed. Tariff schedules were developed in trade negotiations, or rounds. The Doha Round, which began in 2001, has made little progress on changes to global rules.

GATT was replaced by the World Trade Organization (WTO) in 1995. It has overseen trade agreements and has worked to set up a dispute-resolution system using three-person arbitration panels. The panels follow strict schedules for making decisions. WTO member nations agreed they should not veto WTO decisions. Trade agreements have lowered tariffs around the world. The United States, Japan, Canada, countries of the European Union, and other industrialized nations agreed to eliminate tariffs completely among themselves in ten industries, namely:

Beer	Medical equipment
Construction equipment	Paper
Distilled spirits	Pharmaceuticals
Farm machinery	Steel
Furniture	Toys

Intellectual Property   As we saw in Chapter 9, the WTO also helps provide worldwide protection for intellectual property. The WTO countries also agreed to reduce governmental subsidies on business research, civil aviation, and agriculture. Only in the entertainment arena was the United States not able to gain reductions in trade barriers by the Europeans. France especially wants to maintain the barrier because of its concerns about the domination of American films, music, and videos in Europe.

Subsidies and Countervailing Measures   To help enforce WTO rules, the organization has the authority to investigate and rule on a **subsidy** a government gives a producer in a country an unfair advantage in the market. But it is a long, slow process with measures that can be difficult to enforce, as the following example illustrates.

Example from Cotton   The United States is a major cotton producer; most output is exported. The Department of Agriculture pays cotton farmers as much as $5 billion a year in crop subsidies. Without the subsidies, it is unlikely that much cotton would be grown in the United States. The government of Brazil filed a complaint with the WTO in 2002, covering the years 1999 to 2002, showing that subsidies were a major part of the income received by U.S. cotton farmers in some years. The subsidies to U.S. farmers made it harder for Brazilian cotton farmers to compete in the world market.

The WTO report was released in 2004. The United States, which was found to have provided improper subsidies under WTO rules, appealed the finding to the WTO. The decision was upheld in 2005. Brazil and the United States argued about what should be done. A compliance panel was appointed and, in 2007, confirmed that the United States was wrong to provide the subsidies. The United States filed more appeals.

Finally, in 2009, the WTO issued a final judgment authorizing Brazil to impose trade sanctions against the United States. Those are **countervailing measures** that are legal under WTO rules. That is, Brazil was allowed to impose tariffs on imports that ordinarily would not be subject to the tariffs. In 2010 with WTO permission, Brazil announced tariffs on more than 100 goods sold from the United States to Brazil. Brazil said it might not impose the tariff if the United States changed its subsidy policy. To avoid the tariffs, the United States agreed to pay $150 million a year to a "cotton fund" for Brazilian cotton growers and to reform domestic cotton subsidies in the future. Brazil then agreed not to impose tariffs on U.S. goods.

U.S. Import Policy

Countries have long imposed restrictions on the import of certain products and services. Limits on imports usually protect domestic interests. For example, the United States restricts the import of sugar-based ethanol from Brazil because it is cheaper and more efficient than domestic corn-based ethanol. Some restrictions are also placed on exports, usually related to national security. The latest equipment and software used in weaponry is most likely to be restricted.

Taxes on Imports

Import restrictions are imposed to generate revenue for the government and to protect a country's domestic industries from foreign competition. Import licensing procedures, quotas, testing requirements, safety and manufacturing standards, government procurement policies, and complicated customs procedures are all ways to regulate imports.

Tariff Classes   A **tariff**, or duty, is a tax imposed by a government on imported goods. Tariffs are in two categories: specific tariffs—a fixed tax or duty on each unit of a product—and *ad valorem* tariffs—a tax as a percentage of the product price. Domestic producers argue that without a tariff foreign products will force them out of the market. Workers will lose their jobs, and the country will grow dependent on imports. Those arguing against tariffs assert that only through free trade will countries exploit their comparative advantage, have incentives to invent new goods and services, and help consumers by lowering prices on goods.

In the United States, the duty imposed is published in the tariff schedules, which are applied by the Customs and Border Protection to products entering U.S. ports. Customs officials classify products and determine the tariff rates when products enter the country. Any tariff must be paid before the goods enter the country.

Harmonized Tariff Schedules The United States uses the **harmonized tariff schedule** (the HTSUS, or Harmonized Tariff Schedule of the United States), developed to standardize how goods are classified by customs officials worldwide. Countries uses the same codes to classify goods traded. The process streamlines trade by reducing language and usage differences among countries, but different countries may impose different tariffs.

Importers file many requests with Customs each year for determination of the classification of goods. An appeal of a Customs' tariff determination goes first to the U.S. Court of International Trade and from there to the U.S. Court of Appeals for the Federal Circuit. The Supreme Court stated, in *United States* v. *Mead Corp.*, that tariff classifications are entitled to "respect" by the courts, but not the strong deference given to many agency regulations. As a result of this relatively weak support for tariff classifications, there are many challenges.

UNITED STATES V. MEAD CORPORATION
United States Supreme Court 533 U.S. 218 (2001)

Case Background *Mead imported "day planner" calendars. Under the tariff (HTSUS), there was a heading for "registers, account books, notebooks... and similar articles." Under subheading 4820.10, "diaries, notebooks and address books" were subject to a 4.0 percent tariff. Another subheading was for "other" items not subject to a tariff. The "other" heading was applied to the planners until 1993, when Customs changed the classification to the "diaries" subheading and applied the 4 percent tariff.*

Mead protested, but Customs stayed with the new classification. Mead sued in the Court of International Trade (CIT). It granted summary judgment for Customs. Mead appealed to the Court of Appeals for the Federal Circuit. It reversed, holding that tariff classifications by Customs do not get the high level of deference given to some agency regulations under the Chevron doctrine (see Chapter 17) because Customs can change classifications without a formal notice-and-rule process that occurs for most substantive regulations. The court held that the planners were not "diaries" as those are defined as bound volumes, whereas the planner was in a three-ring binder, so should be classified as "other" and not subject to a tariff. Customs appealed.

Case Decision Souter, Justice

* * *

There are...ample reasons to deny *Chevron* deference here. The authorization for classification

rulings, and Customs's practice in making them, present a case far removed not only from notice-and-comment process, but from any other circumstances reasonably suggesting that Congress ever thought of classification rulings as deserving the deference claimed for them here....

Indeed, to claim that classifications have legal force is to ignore the reality that 46 different Customs offices issue 10,000 to 15,000 of them each year. Any suggestion that rulings intended to have the force of law are being churned out at a rate of 10,000 a year at an agency's 46 scattered offices is simply self-refuting. Although the circumstances are less startling here, with a Headquarters letter in issue, none of the relevant statutes recognizes this category of rulings as separate or different from others; there is thus no indication that a more potent delegation might have been understood as going to Headquarters even when Headquarters provides developed reasoning, as it did in this instance.

Nor do the amendments to the statute made effective after this case arose disturb our conclusion. The new law requires Customs to provide notice-and-comment procedures only when modifying or revoking a prior classification ruling or modifying the treatment accorded to substantially identical transactions and under its regulations, Customs sees itself obliged to provide notice-and-comment procedures only when "changing a practice" so as to produce a tariff increase, or in the imposition of a restriction or prohibition, or when Customs

Headquarters determines that "the matter is of sufficient importance to involve the interests of domestic industry." The statutory changes reveal no new congressional objective of treating classification decisions generally as rulemaking with force of law, nor do they suggest any intent to create a *Chevron* patchwork of classification rulings, some with force of law, some without.

In sum, classification rulings are best treated like "interpretations contained in policy statements, agency manuals, and enforcement guidelines."...

Question for Analysis

1. What does the lower level of deference by the courts mean in practice?

Import Controls

Congress has given the Department of Commerce, through its International Trade Administration (ITA) and the International Trade Commission (ITC), the ability to restrict imports. Some imports are prohibited for safety or environmental reasons. Congress is also concerned with foreign companies that sell their products at prices lower in the U.S. market than in their home market—called dumping—or receive a subsidy from their government to lower costs of production, so they can produce more goods to sell in other countries.

Bans on Certain Products Importing certain products may be illegal. For example, some explosives and weapons cannot be imported. Banned products, such as narcotics, violate domestic laws and cannot legally be imported. Products made from endangered species are prohibited. Other items may not meet safety regulations or pollution requirements and cannot be imported. For example, foreign vehicles that do not meet U.S. safety or pollution standards are banned.

Antidumping Orders Under both the WTO and U.S. law, **dumping** is the practice of charging a lower price in the export market than in the home market, after taking into consideration important differences in the sale (such as credit terms and transportation) and the nature of the goods being sold.

If it is determined that goods from a country are being dumped, and domestic industries are losing sales as a result, an antidumping order may be issued. Under this order, the incoming goods may be subject to an **antidumping duty** or tax. The amount of the duty is determined by comparing the market price in the home market with the price charged in the United States. The difference between the two prices determines the tariff to be applied to the price of the product.

Similarly, the Commerce Department determines if a government is "providing, directly or indirectly, a subsidy with respect to the manufacture, production, or exportation of a class or kind of merchandise imported, or sold for importation into the United States." If so, and if the ITC determines that this injures U.S. producers, tariffs are imposed in an amount equal to the net subsidy.

ISSUE SPOTTER
Starting an Import Business

Having seen good quality wood furniture and handicrafts in Central America, you want to import them to the United States and try to develop a full-time business. Assuming you have some cash to get started, what key steps do you see as necessary to initiate such a venture in terms of international trade aspects?

© Cengage Learning

Lighter Side **of the Law**

Chop Shops

Autos and the parts that go into them are now produced around the world, but countries work to protect domestic markets. Ford passenger vans are produced at a Ford plant in Turkey. They are shipped to Baltimore. There, workers remove the non-driver seats and replace the side windows with steel walls. That converts the vans from passenger vans into cargo vans.

Why do this? The tariff on "delivery vans" is high; the tariff on "passenger vans" is low, so it is cheaper to bring in the passenger vans and refit them to become delivery vans. The tariff under which this is done was created in 1963 to protect U.S. van makers from cheap foreign imports.

Source: Wall Street Journal.

Duty orders generally remain in place until the importer can show three consecutive years of "fair market value" sales, and Commerce is convinced that there is little chance of "less than fair market value" sales in the United States in the future. Companies hoping to impose taxes on their competitors' imports file hundreds of antidumping requests each year. After a decision is made by Commerce, the decision may be appealed to the Court of International Trade and then to the Court of Appeals for the Federal Circuit. When a dumping tariff is imposed by the United States, or any other government, there may be an appeal to the WTO, which hears hundreds of complaints each year. It does not have the power to force nations to change restrictions on imports, but it can allow other nations to retaliate without violating international trade treaties.

Foreign Trade Zones and Duty-Free Ports **Foreign trade zones** are areas where businesses can import goods without paying tariffs. The zone is a secured area where goods may be processed, assembled, or warehoused. Tariffs are imposed only on the finished product, generally a much lower amount than what would be imposed on individual parts, and only when the product leaves the zone for sale in the domestic market. Products exported from the zone to other countries are generally not subject to tariffs.

Duty-free ports are ports of entry that do not assess duties or tariffs on products. They encourage the importation and sale of international goods within the country. Hong Kong is well known for such practices. Benefits to a country are the encouragement of trade with other countries and the attraction of businesses and tourists to the country to purchase products free of duties and other fees.

Export Promotion and Restrictions

Governments usually encourage the export of domestic products. They hope to stimulate employment and bring in foreign exchange from export sales. When the value of imports exceeds the value of exports, the country is said to be running a trade deficit. However, for reasons of national defense and foreign policy, governments may restrict exports of certain products.

Federal Government Efforts The Commerce Department is the major export-promotion agency in the United States. Primary responsibility for export promotion within Commerce falls upon the ITA. It manages the U.S. Foreign Commercial Service, which has offices in major cities around the world and export counselors in district offices around the United States. At its overseas offices, called Commercial Consulates, it supplies U.S. product information, arranges business meetings with local firms, accompanies U.S. company representatives to meetings, and gathers local market information. The Commercial Consulates, for example, might assist a U.S. company in finding a foreign agent to distribute its products. They also lead trade missions overseas each year and participate in hundreds of trade expositions.

ISSUE SPOTTER
Making the Deal Stick

You have worked for a long time to attract a client and have finally won an order for your company to supply financial services to Glorious, a large Chinese company headquartered in Shanghai. Glorious sends you an agreement drawn up by its attorney. Chinese law governs in all respects. Are you sure you want to sign? What changes in the agreement would be high on your list?

© Cengage Learning

Export Restrictions The U.S. government imposes restrictions on exports when the sale of a good may:

- Injure domestic industry (e.g., exporting a raw material in short supply)
- Jeopardize national security (e.g., selling military hardware to the wrong country)
- Conflict with national policy (e.g., selling goods to a country that supports terrorist activities)

The Arms Export Control Act, as implemented under the International Traffic in Arms Regulations (ITAR), imposes many restrictions on the export of weapons and technology that can be used to make weapons. Restrictions are implemented through licensing requirements in the Export Administration Act.

Congress delegated the power to enforce export licenses to the Secretary of Commerce. Licenses can be issued only according to strict standards. The standards reflect the tension between a desire to control exports of strategic goods for security reasons and the desire to encourage exports to reduce the trade deficit.

Export Controls Commerce maintains a list—the **Commodity Control List**—of the goods subject to restricted licenses. The restrictions imposed depend upon the country to which goods are to be sent and the reason for the export restriction. Goods not on the list are subject to a general license, which requires little more than filing a Shipper's Export Declaration with Commerce.

Application to Re-export U.S. Goods Commerce's export licensing requirements also apply to the re-export of U.S. goods. That is, an export license is needed to ship U.S.-origin controlled goods from, say, India to Iran. The intent is to prohibit the shipment of sensitive goods from the United States first to a "safe" country and then to a controlled country. In this way, the Export Administration Act reaches beyond U.S. boundaries.

Lighter Side **of the Law**

I Make Sure *Other* People Obey the Law

Lorraine Henderson was the Boston-area port director for the federal Customs and Border Protection who supervised 220 employees and was paid more than $132,000 a year. She was convicted of a felony in 2010 for hiring illegal immigrants to clean her house over a period of several years. According to court documents, she instructed one illegal cleaning lady who was wearing a bug, "You have to be careful, 'cause they [her agency] will deport you."

Source: Boston Globe.

Penalty Provisions   Penalties for violations of Commerce's licensing provisions include criminal and civil penalties. For example, ITT was fined $100 million for selling sophisticated night-vision goggle technology to a firm in Singapore that sold the technology to China. The company was also required to spend $50 million helping to develop new night-vision technology that will be owned by the U.S. government and was barred from selling certain exports for three years. An exporter that "willfully" violates the Act can receive up to 20 years in prison. As in the ITT case, penalties also can result in the suspension or revocation of an authority to export.

Business Structures in Foreign Markets

Businesses have two basic ways of selling products in foreign markets. They can either export products manufactured in this country to a foreign country or manufacture products in the foreign country for distribution there.

Foreign Manufacturing

Costs that may be reduced by foreign manufacturing include shipping, labor expenses, and raw materials. Operating in another country may also help secure long-term contracts to supply goods in that country. In addition, foreign manufacturing may be a way to avoid import restrictions or tariffs imposed by the host country.

Several leading Japanese companies decided to open manufacturing facilities in the United States. They feared that Congress might impose high tariffs on Japanese products. Because products made by a Japanese business located in the United States are made in America, they are not subject to duties. Businesses considering foreign manufacturing have several options, including:

- A wholly owned foreign subsidiary
- A joint venture
- A licensing agreement
- A franchise agreement
- Contract manufacturing

Wholly Owned Subsidiary By doing foreign manufacturing through a **wholly owned subsidiary**, a business owns the operation. A business may buy an existing facility or build a new one. Situations exist, however, in which complete ownership is not possible. Many countries impose limits on the percentage of ownership in a local enterprise by foreigners.

INTERNATIONAL PERSPECTIVE

Put the Shoe on the Other Foot

When we discuss international business it is, of course, from an American perspective looking at problems and issues peculiar to doing business in other countries. How do foreigners see doing business in the United States?

China Daily did a survey of Chinese executives doing business in the United States. The problems are much the same as Americans experience going overseas—unfamiliar rules, cultural barriers, and high operating costs. Nevertheless, the overall impression appears positive.

Thirty-three percent of respondents said they would describe their company's experience as very successful; 61 percent said somewhat successful. None thought it was a flop. How easy is it to conduct business in the United States? Twenty-eight percent said very easy, 33 percent said somewhat easy, and 35 percent said somewhat difficult.

The greatest problems are tough competition in the United States and the high cost of operating in the country. Few found a bias against Chinese enterprises and did not find regulations on investments much of a problem. Ease of entry is important as billions of dollars are beginning to make their way back to the United States from China, reversing what had been a one-way flow previously.

Joint Venture A **joint venture** means sharing ownership with foreign partners. For example, one party may supply the facilities, and the other party may supply the technological skills required for the operation. Although a joint venture requires less investment by the company than does a wholly owned subsidiary, it can mean loss of managerial control. A major advantage is a local partner who knows how to deal with regulations and is experienced in domestic markets.

Licensing Agreement A **licensing agreement** is a contract. One business—the licensor—grants another business—the licensee—access to its patents and other technologies. The licensor is usually granted a royalty on sales. Allowing the licensee to use the business's trademark could help establish a worldwide reputation. However, the licensing company needs to make sure that the agreement is enforceable in the licensee's country or the technology and trademark may be easily stolen.

Franchise Agreement Franchising is a popular vehicle for establishing a foreign market presence. Franchising is a form of licensing. The franchisor (the supplier) grants the franchisee (the foreign dealer) the right to sell products or services in exchange for a fee. The most visible franchises are fast-food restaurants. McDonald's, Pizza Hut, Coca-Cola, and KFC have made major inroads with franchises in China. The franchising company must work to make sure that the quality, and thus the reputation, of its products is maintained at overseas franchises.

Contract Manufacturing Companies may contract for the production of certain products in foreign facilities. U.S. retailers, for example, contract for the production of clothing and shoes in Malaysia, India, and China, where labor costs are low. Contract manufacturing has the advantage of requiring limited investment in production facilities.

Nike has made contract manufacturing an important part of its operations. The company does not own many of the manufacturing plants that produce its shoes. When demand for the products slows, it can end a manufacturing contract. The company does not have to worry about making payments on a plant that is not producing. However, when workers die in fires or collapsed buildings where the company's products were made, as occurred in Bangladesh, the American buyer that relied on the contractor who did not correct terrible working conditions suffers a lot of bad press.

? TEST YOURSELF

1. If a company is manufacturing goods in another country, and ownership of the manufacturing facility is owned with a local partner, that is generally referred to as contract manufacturing: T—F
2. The free trade agreement between Canada, Mexico, and the United States is common referred to as _____.
3. The major international body dedicated to opening exchange of goods and services globally is referred to as the _____.
4. A tariff that imposes a percentage tax on imported goods is called an *ad valorem* tariff: T—F
5. The policy of the U.S. government is not to subsidize the production of any goods that enter the export market: T—F
6. In *United States* v. *Mead Corp.*, where Mead contested the classification of a tariff imposed by Customs on the day planners it imported, the Supreme Court held that:
   a. it violated the First Amendment to impose a tax on printed matter.
   b. the courts would give the expertise of Customs a high level or *Chevron* deference when reviewing tariffs.
   c. the courts would look to the intent of Congress on the tariff rates imposed on any imported good.
   d. the courts could consider the expertise of Customs when reviewing tariff classifications.
7. Congress imposes restrictions on the imports of goods, especially military goods, and one can commit a felony by selling such goods without permission: T—F

Answers: F; NAFTA; WTO; T; F; d; T.

Foreign Corrupt Practices Act

Governments in most countries are involved in business activity. Government permission often is required before business transactions can be completed, which increases the likelihood of bribery. Corruption is a global problem, but is more common in less-developed nations.

In the United States, the Foreign Corrupt Practices Act (FCPA) prohibits U.S companies and their agents from bribing foreign officials. The law was enacted after exposure of cases in which U.S. corporations bribed foreign officials for favors. A study by the Securities and Exchange Commission found that the practice was widespread: more than 400 companies (117 of which were *Fortune* 500 companies) admitted to making substantial bribes to foreign officials.

Corruption

In many countries, corruption is so common that normal business is nearly impossible. It is a major barrier to economic development. There are measures of risk of investment

EXHIBIT 22.2   CORRUPTION PERCEPTION INDEX

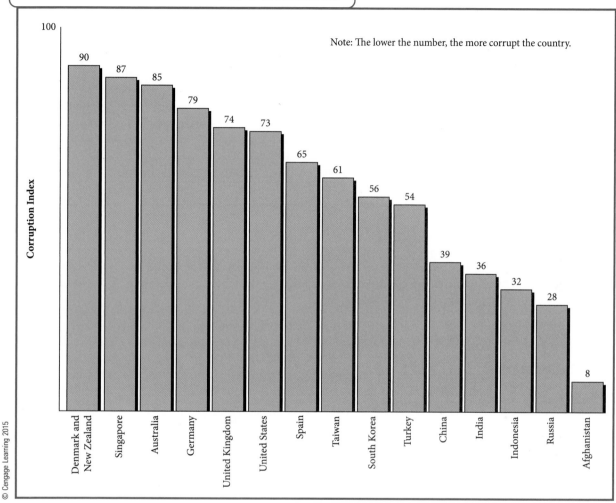

Note: The lower the number, the more corrupt the country.

around the world. One widely accepted measure comes from Transparency International (TI), an organization founded by a former World Bank director who was frustrated at the inability of countries to grow because of corruption. Exhibit 22.2 shows some of TI's Corruption Perception Index, from least to most corrupt, which is based on numerous surveys. A score of 100 would indicate a country that is completely corruption-free.

International Antibribery Movement Many nations signed a convention against corruption. All agreed to present legislation to their national legislatures that would make bribery a crime. In 1998, the U.S. Senate ratified the Convention on Combating Bribery of Foreign Officials in International Business Transactions. In 2006, Congress ratified the United Nations Convention against Corruption (UNCAC). It is supposed to bring international cooperation to corruption enforcement actions. Some nations have not been quick to act, and, even in countries that have laws on their books, enforcement is dubious. In a study of the large trading nations, Transparency International reported that firms from Belgium and Canada were least likely to pay bribes. The United States was tied with France and Singapore in the middle of the pack. Most likely to pay bribes, by a large margin, were Russian firms.

FCPA Antibribery Provisions

The FCPA prohibit U.S. companies from "corruptly" paying or offering to pay a foreign official to gain assistance in obtaining or retaining business. The Act also prohibits payments to a person, such as a foreign agent, when the U.S. company knows that payment will go toward bribing a foreign official.

The Act recognizes that some payments are necessary and routine. An exception exists for a "facilitating or expediting payment … the purpose of which is to expedite or secure the performance of a routine government action." Such "routine actions" normally include bribes for services such as processing visas and providing utilities or transportation services. If you guess wrong about what constitutes "necessary" or "routine" the consequences could be serious.

The basic test in determining whether a bribe is permissible focuses not on the person to whom payment is made, but on the purpose of the payment. This is complicated by the fact that such payments are often made by local agents without the knowledge of the U.S. manager.

Remember the question at the start of the chapter regarding the French manager of a French company accused of paying a bribe in Indonesia? He was indicted when he came to the United States as the government claimed that its jurisdiction applied to foreign firms and foreign nationals engaged in global operations. Because his firm had operations in the United States, jurisdiction applied.

Who Knows What? The most controversial part of the antibribery law is the "knowing" requirement. Congress stated that "simple negligence" or "mere foolishness" should not be the basis for liability. The FCPA provides that the knowing requirement covers "any instance where any reasonable person would have realized the existence of the circumstances or result and the [individual] has consciously chosen not to ask about what he had reason to believe he would discover." For example, managers should be concerned about foreign agents who work on a commission basis. The government is particularly suspicious that large commissions may be a cover for the agent to make bribes.

Lighter Side of the Law

All Corruption Is Not Created Equal

Under U.S. law, any foreigner *suspected of* corruption cannot get a visa to come into the country. There need not be a conviction for corruption, just good evidence of it. While the Department of Justice has a large file on the son of the very corrupt long-time president of Equatorial Guinea, the son is granted a visa by the Department of State so that he can come enjoy his $35 million estate in Malibu whenever he wishes.

Observers contend that the different policy toward the visitor may be due to the large oil reserves contained in the poverty-stricken country.

Source: New York Times.

Accounting Requirements

The FCPA requires companies to "make and keep books, records, and accounts which, in reasonable detail, accurately and fairly reflect the transactions and dispositions of [their] assets." The law also requires companies to "devise and maintain a system of internal accounting controls sufficient to provide reasonable assurances" that all

UNITED STATES V. KING

United States Court of Appeals, Eighth Circuit, 351 F.3d 859 (2003)

Case Background *The FBI investigated the dealings of Owl Securities and Investments (OSI), a Kansas City company that raised funds for a large real estate project in Costa Rica. The investigation focused on King, one of OSI's largest investors. The FBI obtained the cooperation of OSI executives, including Kingsley, OSI's president, who tape recorded conversations.*

King was convicted of planning to bribe senior Costa Rican officials to obtain the rights to the land to be developed. He was fined $60,000 and sentenced to 30 months in prison. He appealed.

Case Decision Beam, Circuit Judge

* * *

Viewing the evidence in the light most favorable to the verdict, there was ample evidence in the record to support the jury's conviction. The tape recordings, alone, support the jury's verdict. [Footnote, quoting King: "I think we could pay the top people enough, that the rest of the people won't bother us any. That's what I'm hoping this million and a half dollars does. I'm hoping it pays for enough top

people."] There was sufficient evidence to prove King's knowledge of the proposed payment long before Kingsley became an informant for the government. Moreover, the recordings show King's knowing participation in, approval of, and subsequent actions in furtherance of the conspiracy to offer the bribe. In addition, the testimony of six witnesses conducted over a five-day period, and the remaining exhibits, support the jury's conviction of King for conspiracy and substantive violations under the FCPA. ...

Affirmed.

Questions for Analysis

1. The appeals court affirmed the conviction for the FCPA violation. King contended that because Kingsley was a conspirator, his testimony should not be allowed because it could not be considered reliable. Is it?
2. Is it fair that King got prison time and Kingsley did not because Kingsley cooperated with the FBI?

transactions are authorized and that access to assets can be tracked. The accounting provisions were included in the Act in response to a study by the Securities and Exchange Commission that showed that many corporations maintained "slush funds" that were "off the books" to make bribes to foreign officials. The Act requires a "paper trail" to improve corporate accountability.

Penalties The Department of Justice is responsible for criminal enforcement of the FCPA. A violation leads to fines up to $100,000 and imprisonment for up to five years for individuals. Corporations convicted of violations can incur fines of up to $2 million per violation. Multiple violations run up the total; the German company Siemens agreed to pay an $800 million fine after an investigation showed it paid large bribes to government officials in Argentina in an effort to win contracts. Eight Siemans' executives and contractors were also charged. The *United States v. King* case is an example of a more normal FCPA action.

International Contracts

As in domestic business agreements, a contract is the basis for an international agreement. As we saw in Chapter 11, some sales of goods are under the CISC, but most international business contracts are not. Such contracts can differ from domestic contracts in complexity and use of unusual provisions. The distance between the parties often complicates contract negotiation, substance, and performance. The differing languages, currencies, legal systems, and business customs of parties can affect the nature of the contract and influence the way it is written.

Cultural Aspects

Sensitivity to cultural differences is important in international contracting. In Japan, for example, *meishi*, or business cards, are exchanged formally at a first meeting and treated with respect, while in the United States, business cards may be exchanged casually at any time and are only glanced at. In many countries, including China, hours may pass before the details of the business are mentioned, and it is considered rude to go directly to business matters. This is different from the U.S. approach, where the parties usually get right to the point.

The attitude toward relationships is another difference. Many countries have a cultural expectation that a relationship will be long-term. As a result, the negotiation process may be long because it is necessary for the parties to know one another before entering into a relationship. Contracts based on long-term expectations are often relatively short, with few contingencies expressly provided. The idea is that problems can be worked out as they arise, with the parties trying to maintain the relationship.

Language itself should not be a barrier to an international contract. However, it is important that the terms of the contract are clearly defined in a language that all parties understand. Interpreters can be an integral part of the negotiations and the final draft of the contract, where parties are not fluent in a common language. Significant issues can arise when contracts are executed in multiple languages when the versions differ in interpretation because the meaning of terms differs. A decision about which language is official is important.

Financial Aspects

To manage the financial risks that may arise in international contracts, care must be taken in specifying the method of payment. In addition, the parties may be concerned about removing profits from the countries in which they conduct business.

Exchange Markets In an international transaction, the seller often receives another country's currency. A business may want to exchange that currency into dollars, but the exchange is not always simple. Exchange risk is the potential loss or profit that occurs between the time currency is acquired and the time it is exchanged for another currency.

Suppose, for example, that U.S. Wine Company buys French wines. The contract calls for the payment of €3,000,000 in 180 days. When the contract is signed, the exchange rate is €1 per $1, or $3,000,000. Suppose that U.S. Wine waits several months to pay and the exchange rate falls to €0.85 to the dollar.

U.S. Wine now must pay $3,530,000. Change in the exchange rate costs the importer $530,000. To avoid such difficulties, businesses may require payment in dollars rather than in the currency of the other country. Alternatively, the parties may use financial instruments to hedge the risk. For example, U.S. Wine could sign a contract with a foreign exchange dealer to receive the difference in the value of $3 million in euros on the date payment is due. This would, for a price, put the currency risk on the foreign exchange dealer.

Financial Instruments Used in International Contracts International contracts often use special financial devices. These assure later payment or allow for the arrangement of credit when buyers are otherwise unable to come up with the cash necessary for the transaction. One device commonly used is the letter of credit.

A **letter of credit** is an agreement or assurance by the bank of the buyer to pay a specified amount to the seller upon receipt of certain documents that prove that the goods have been shipped and that contractual obligations of the seller have been fulfilled. The documentation usually required may include a certificate of origin, export license, certificate of inspection, bill of lading, commercial invoice, and insurance policy. Once the bank has received the required documentation, it releases payment to the seller. Exhibit 22.3 illustrates the route taken by a letter of credit and documentation in an international business transaction between an Italian seller and an American buyer, each using its own bank.

Letters of credit can be either revocable or irrevocable. As the label attached to each implies, a revocable letter of credit may be withdrawn before the specific date stated on it, while an irrevocable letter of credit may not be withdrawn. Exhibit 22.4 is an example of an irrevocable letter of credit.

EXHIBIT 22.3   LETTER OF CREDIT IN AN INTERNATIONAL TRANSACTION

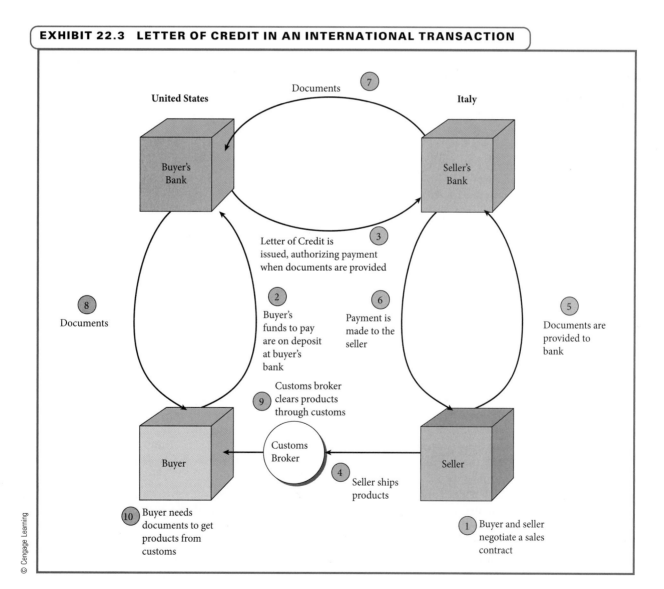

© Cengage Learning

EXHIBIT 22.4   EXAMPLE OF AN IRREVOCABLE LETTER OF CREDIT

LETTER OF CREDIT—CONFIRMED, IRREVOCABLE

Western Reserve Bank
Chicago, Illinois

Letter of Credit #59723
Issued on August 1, 2015

To: Exotica Company
Dallas, Texas

From: Tiramisu Import Company
Rome, Italy

Gentlemen:

We are instructed by Commercial Bank of Italy, Rome, Italy, to inform you that they have opened their irrevocable credit in favor of Tiramisu Import Company, Rome, Italy, for the sum in U.S. dollars not exceeding a total of about $55,000.00 (Fifty-five Thousand and 00/100 Dollars), available by your drafts on us, to be accompanied by:

1. Full Set on Board Negotiable Ocean Bills of Lading, stating: "Freight Prepaid" and made out to the order of Commercial Bank of Italy.
2. Insurance Policy or Certificate covering Marine and War Risk.
3. Packing List.
4. Commercial Invoice in triplicate:

   Covering 200 Pes. 1025 Electric Espresso Coffee Machines
   200 Pes. 750 Stove-Top Espresso Coffee Makers
   350 Pes. 420 Electric Pasta Makers

Total Value $54,702.75 C.I.F. Rome, Italy
Import Lic. No. 3792 Expires October 24, 2015
5. Shipper's Export Declaration.

   Partial Shipment Permitted. Transshipment Not Permitted.
   Merchandise must be shipped in SS Mercaso.
   All documents must indicate Letter of Credit No. 59723, Import License No. 3792, expires October 24, 2015.
   All drafts must be marked "Drawn under Letter of Credit No. 59723, issued by Western Reserve Bank. Drafts must be presented to this company not later than October 1, 2015."
   This credit is subject to the Uniform Customs and Practices for Documentary Credits (1984 Revision) International Chamber of Commerce Publication No. 400.
   We confirm the credit and thereby undertake that all drafts drawn and presented as above specified will be duly honored by us.

By
International Credit Department

Exchange Controls A factor to consider when making an investment in a foreign jurisdiction is whether you can get money out of that country later. The ability of a business to return money earned in a foreign country back to its home country is called **repatriation**. The ability to repatriate money can be limited by some form of currency control, such as **foreign exchange controls** that restrict the ability to change one country's currency into another. These laws remain popular with many Asian, African, and Latin American governments that wish to control the flow of money in and out of their economies.

For example, an investor in China who wants to put money in a business out of the country may need government permission to move funds because the Yuan is not a freely convertible currency. As a result, many Chinese firms raise money through Hong Kong in Hong Kong dollars, where there are no exchange controls. Exchange controls affect firms' decisions on where to locate assets. Firms do not want cash reserves in a bank in a country with exchange controls because that would make it hard to move the cash when and to where it is needed. As countries sometimes change currency rules quickly, one must pay close attention to economic and political conditions.

Transfer Pricing   When a multinational firm sells goods from a division located in one country to a division in the United States, it has to determine and record the price. Because the transaction takes place within the firm, there is no "market" price to use. The firm must create an artificial price to use in its accounts. This practice is referred to as **transfer pricing**.

Suppose a firm is exporting wine from its French vineyard to its U.S. wine distributor. If tax rates are higher in France than in the United States, the firm may transfer the wine at a low price, so that the profits accrue in the United States, not in France. Transfer pricing can be done without physically moving goods. Many pharmaceutical firms assign their patent rights to subsidiaries in low-tax countries, shifting profits to those jurisdictions. Similarly, the band U2 assigned its copyrights to a holding company in the Netherlands where taxes are lower than in its home country of Ireland.

To attempt to prevent such transactions from lowering tax bills, tax authorities such as the Internal Revenue Service have guidelines as to what they consider a reasonable price for such transactions. When firms use prices for internal transactions that the tax authorities think are too low or too high, the tax authority recalculates the taxpayer's income to reflect what the government believes was a reasonable price. To help the tax service do this, the government usually requires considerable documentation of such transactions.

Where goods traded within a company are generally available, it is relatively easy to observe the market price for a transaction. But many firms move partially completed or proprietary goods among subsidiaries in different countries. Determining a price becomes an arbitrary exercise in allocating costs. Businesses engaged in transactions involving transfer pricing must be careful not to fall afoul of the tax authorities in either country, both of which wish to maximize their tax revenues and so, the profits allocated to their country. This can be difficult and creates a demand for accountants and lawyers skilled in such matters.

Key Clauses in International Contracts

The contract is the foundation of any business venture. As with domestic contracts, care should be taken that the intent of the parties is fully represented by the contract. International contracts should be in writing, even if they only state the positions and goals of the parties. Certain key clauses are generally considered critical in international deals.

Payment Clauses   The **payment clause** states the manner in which payment is to be received and the currency in which it is made. Because some nations restrict currencies from leaving the country, payments have special effects on the receiver of the currency that must be addressed. Problems with inflation and currency exchange risks, especially in unstable economies or in long-term agreements, should also be covered.

Choice-of-Language Clause   Even when parties speak the same language, complex contractual terms may exceed the understanding of one of the parties when the contract is made in another country. A word or phrase in one language or country may not be readily translatable to another. Technical terms should be defined. A contract should have a **choice-of-language clause**, which sets out the official language by which the contract is to be interpreted, as seen in Exhibit 22.5.

Force Majeure Clause   ***Force majeure*** is a French term meaning a "superior or irresistible force." This clause protects contracting parties from problems beyond their

---

EXHIBIT 22.5   MAJOR CLAUSES USED IN MANY INTERNATIONAL CONTRACTS

Example of Choice-of-Language Clause with Arbitration Provision

This Agreement is signed in two (2) originals in the English language, which shall be regarded as the authoritative and official text. Any matters referred to arbitration will also be in the English language, which will be the official language used in arbitration.

Example of Choice-of-Language with Translation Provision

This Agreement is signed in two (2) originals in the French language, which shall be regarded as the authoritative and official text. Parties hereto agree to provide an official translation of this Agreement in the English language. Both parties ratify this translation, and it may be relied upon as being an accurate representation of the official form.

Example of *Force Majeure* Clause

The parties hereto shall not be liable for failure of performance hereunder if occasioned by war, declared or undeclared; fire; flood; interruption of transportation; inflation beyond the expected rate; embargo, accident; explosion; inability to procure or shortage of supply of materials, equipment, or production facilities; prohibition of import or export of goods covered hereby; governmental orders, regulations, restrictions, priorities or rationing by strike or lockout or other labor troubles interfering with production or transportation of such goods; or with the supplies of raw materials entering into their production; or any other cause beyond the control of the parties.

Forum Selection and Choice-of-Law Clauses

All claims and disputes arising out of or in relation to this contract shall be litigated before the courts of the city of Paris, France. This contract shall be governed by the laws of the state of California, the country of the United States of America.

© Cengage Learning

---

control. Traditionally, this clause was used to protect the parties from the consequences of a natural disaster that interfered with performance. The clause also protects the parties against political upheavals. An illustration of a typical *force majeure* clause is given in Exhibit 22.5.

Forum Selection and Choice-of-Law Clauses To reduce uncertainties in the event of a dispute, companies usually put a **forum selection clause** and a **choice-of-law clause** in their contracts. (Examples are given in Exhibit 22.5.) The forum may be in one place (Paris), and the law to be applied may be from another place (California).

By selecting the court or place of arbitration in which disputes must be resolved and which law is to be applied, the possibility that the parties will go "forum shopping"— looking for the most favorable forum for the resolution of a dispute—is reduced.

Loss of Investment

Political upheavals, unstable monetary systems, and changes in laws are some of the risks encountered in other countries. In addition, businesses must be concerned about the loss of investment by nationalization, expropriation, and confiscation.

Nationalization **Nationalization** is when a country takes over, or nationalizes, a foreign investment in a country. The compensation paid by the government is often less than the true value of the business. The government of Venezuela, for example, nationalized Exxon-Mobil holdings in that country in 2007. Five years later, an arbitration panel held that Exxon should receive $900 million for the property, which was for only one of the claims brought by Exxon. The government of Venezuela announced it would pay only $255 million and refused to work with Exxon any longer. Such disputes often drag on for decades.

Expropriation Like nationalization, **expropriation** is the action of a country in taking foreign property in accordance with international law. Most countries agree that for a valid expropriation, there must be adequate compensation provided. International law recognizes a country's right to expropriate the property of foreigners within its jurisdiction, so long as payment is made. If a takeover is unlawful, it is a **confiscation**.

Insuring against Risk of Loss An all-risk insurance policy can provide financial relief in the event of nationalization, or if other problems occur. Short-term private insurance usually lasts from three to five years and is available for most investments. Risks such as currency blockages, embargoes, and a government's arbitrary decision to recall letters of credit may be insured by insurers such as Lloyd's of London. In addition, sellers may obtain rejection insurance in the event that a buyer rejects a product for reasonable cause, such as spoilage at sea.

ISSUE SPOTTER
Where to Produce?

Your company makes electric scooters for sale in the North American market. You import the motors from China, the tires from Brazil, the frames from the United States, and other parts come from suppliers around the world. Where might you consider building the scooters? What are the trade-offs?

Some countries have government agencies to assist in insuring exporters from risk of loss. In the United States, for example, the Overseas Private Investment Corporation (OPIC) insures investors willing to invest in less-developed countries friendly to the United States. OPIC offers investors insurance against expropriation, currency inconvertibility, and damage from wars or revolutions.

International Dispute Resolution

World trade is in the trillions of dollars. With that much commerce, disputes arise. They may be the result of unanticipated events, difficulties in performance, or changes in the political climate of a country that may affect a contract. Whatever the problem, parties to international contracts need help to try to resolve disputes and enforce their rights.

Litigation

Disputes often end up either in the court system at home or within the opposing party's country, although companies often settle on a neutral third legal system to avoid giving either an advantage. Litigation is complicated because evidence, witnesses, and documents central to resolving the dispute are often located in two or more countries. In some instances, these difficulties may be reduced by treaties or conventions between the two countries. These may allow for proper notice of the suit to the foreign party, appropriate service of process, issues of standing, methods for documentation certification, and procedures for taking evidence.

If the action is commenced in a foreign court, the U.S. participant often encounters a judicial system very different from that in this country. Courts in some countries are influenced more by political pressures than are U.S. courts. In addition, some courts will not enforce contract provisions that may be enforceable in the United States.

Arbitration

Judicial forums are not very effective in resolving many international commercial disagreements. Cost considerations, jurisdictional barriers, the length of time to litigate, legal uncertainties, and the inability of judicial systems to fashion appropriate relief have encouraged the use of alternative dispute resolution techniques, especially arbitration.

Attempts to standardize arbitral rules and procedures have resulted in the creation of organizations such as the International Chamber of Commerce and other arbitration organizations around the world. These organizations have rules to address issues concerning arbitration proceedings and awards. In many countries, including the United States, the enforcement of arbitral awards is facilitated by the United Nations Convention on the Recognition and Enforcement of Foreign Arbitral Awards (discussed in Chapter 11). Federal district courts have jurisdiction to hear motions to confirm or challenge an international arbitration award involving a U.S. business.

The International Court of Justice

Contrary to common belief, there are no "international courts" to handle business disputes, but certain disputes may be taken to the International Court of Justice (ICJ), headquartered at The Hague, Netherlands, and part of the United Nations. The ICJ has 15 judges, representing all of the world's major legal systems, with no two judges from the same country. Only nations may take claims to this court; it is rarely used for commercial disputes.

Doctrine of Sovereign Immunity

In international law, **sovereign immunity** doctrine allows a court to give up rights to jurisdiction over foreign enterprises or countries. The doctrine is based on traditional notions that a sovereign should not be subject to litigation in a foreign court. As a result, investors may not be able to obtain relief in their country's court system.

Some countries restrict the doctrine's application in commercial circumstances. If a foreign nation does not do this when it enters into a contract with a private party, then there is no recourse to U.S. courts in case of breach. The Foreign Sovereign Immunities Act provides a uniform rule for the determination of sovereign immunity in legal actions in this country's courts. The Act provides the following:

> *Under international law, [countries] are not immune from the jurisdiction of foreign courts insofar as their commercial activities are concerned, and their commercial property may be levied upon for the satisfaction of judgments rendered against them in connection with their commercial activities.*

Doing business with foreign partners can result in special problems that are not as common in domestic business. Issues of jurisdiction, the effect of statutes and treaties, and the ability to obtain a judgment—and collect on one—are not unique to international business but are major concerns that should not be ignored in the rush to grab what may look like easy money.

INTERNATIONAL PERSPECTIVE

Migrating to Australia

Allowing foreigners to migrate to a country can be politically charged. Australia seeks immigrants who contribute to the economy and embrace "Australian values." Potential immigrants are assessed under a point system to see if they are desirable. The system is more transparent than immigration rules in the United States. Australia gives points for:

- Having a skilled occupation (40-60 points depending on need for occupation)

- Age (30 points for 18-29; 25 points for 30-34; 20 points for 35-39; and 15 points for 40-44)

- English language ability (competent = 20 points; "vocational" language ability = 15 points)

- Working 3 years out of the past 4 in a 60-point occupation (10 points)

- Working 3 years out of the past 4 in a skilled occupation and having a current 40-60 point occupation (5 points)

- Working in an occupation on a government list of occupations "in demand" and already having a job offer from an employer that has employed at least 10 full-time employees for two years (20 points)

- Working in an occupation on a government list of occupations "in demand," but not having a job offer (15 points)

- Having a degree from an Australian university after full-time study in Australia: doctorate (15 points), Masters or Honours degree (10 points), other (5 points)

- Having lived and studied in a less populated area of Australia for two years (5 points)

- Having a spouse who satisfies the basic immigration requirements for language, age, ability, work experience, etc. (5 points)

- Having legally worked in Australia for at least 6 months in an occupation in demand (5 points)

- Fluency in certain languages (5 points)

- Potential immigrants generally need 120 points to be accepted.

To ensure that immigrants agree with Australians about what kind of society Australia is, the government requires new immigrants 18 or older to read a booklet it provides on Australia and sign a statement agreeing to respect and uphold Australian law and values.

© Cengage Learning

❓ *TEST YOURSELF*

1. The federal law that makes paying bribes to obtain business in other countries is called the _____.
2. Under the general principles of international law, if the rate of exchange changes during the term of a contract, so as to impose a loss on the buyer, the contract is considered voidable: T—F
3. An assurance by the bank of the buyer to pay a specific amount to the seller upon receipt of certain documents that prove the goods have been shipped and a contract fulfilled is called a(n) _____.
4. In *United States* v. *King*, where King was accused by the U.S. government of bribing officials in Costa Rica, the appeals court held that:
   a. his conviction and prison sentence stood.
   b. he could not be convicted unless the government of Costa Rica provided testimony that the bribes violated Costa Rican law.
   c. he could not be convicted for an act that may be illegal in the United States but occurred outside of U.S. jurisdiction.
   d. he could not be convicted because of the doctrine of sovereign immunity.

5. If a country expropriates the property of a foreign company, it is a violation of international law: T—F
6. If a foreign government were to seize property of a U.S. company in that country and not pay for the property, that is called _____.
7. To make sure a dispute over a contract will be tried in a court that a party to the contract desires, the party should make sure there is a proper *force majeure* clause: T—F
8. The United Nations has encouraged the use of arbitration of disputes among parties to international business disputes: T—F

Answers: Foreign Corrupt Practices Act; F; letter of credit; a; F; confiscation; F; T.

SUMMARY

- The international market is characterized by additional financial, political, and regulatory risks in addition to those present in domestic markets. Those risks arise from differences among countries in currencies, language, business customs, legal and social philosophies, and national economic goals.

- The principal sources of international trade law are the laws of individual countries, the laws arising from trade agreements between countries, and the rules enacted by worldwide or regional trade organizations.

- To reduce trade barriers, most nations participated in General Agreement on Tariffs and Trade (GATT), which resulted in the World Trade Organization (WTO), which now oversees some trade disputes.

- Most countries have import and export regulations. Import restrictions include import licensing requirements, import quotas, safety standards, government procurement policies, and customs procedures. To standardize tariff schedules and their application, most countries have adopted the harmonized tariff schedule to classify goods.

- The United States imposes prohibitions on the export of certain technologies that could be used by hostile nations or terrorists. The government monitors the exportation of weapons and computers.

- The most common international business arrangements are wholly owned subsidiaries, joint ventures, licensing agreements, franchise agreements, and contract manufacturing. The choice of business organization is influenced by the laws of a country, the purposes of the commercial venture, the financial resources of the parties, and the degree of managerial control desired by the company.

- The Foreign Corrupt Practices Act (FCPA) prohibits U.S. companies and their agents from bribing foreign officials. The FCPA makes the bribery of foreign officials a criminal offense and requires U.S. companies to establish internal accounting mechanisms to prevent such bribery. It is a criminal offense to make payments to foreign officials for the purpose of gaining business favor in a foreign country.

- To create an effective international contract, a business should consider differences in business customs, attitudes toward the contractual relationship, and languages. Specific clauses in international contracts worthy of special consideration are the payment, choice-of-language, *force majeure*, and forum selection and choice-of-law clauses.

- Business in foreign countries may face special risks. Currency exchange controls may limit the ability to repatriate profits. Political upheavals, unstable monetary systems, dramatic changes in laws, and other problems associated with doing business with a developing country must be considered. Losses may occur through nationalization, expropriation, or confiscation of the foreign investment.

- Although most international trade occurs without incident, disputes sometimes arise concerning contract performance. Various national and international institutions may assist a business in effective dispute resolution. Those institutions include judicial litigation in court systems and arbitration. The doctrine of sovereign immunity may bar recovery of losses through the judicial system.

TERMS TO KNOW

subsidy, 608
countervailing measures, 609
tariff, 609
harmonized tariff schedule, 610
dumping, 612
antidumping duty, 612
foreign trade zone, 612
duty-free port, 612
Commodity Control List, 614

wholly owned subsidiary, 614
joint venture, 615
licensing agreement, 615
letter of credit, 621
repatriation, 622
foreign exchange controls, 622
transfer pricing, 623
payment clause, 623
choice-of-language clause, 623

force majeure, 623
forum selection clause, 624
choice-of-law clause, 624
nationalization, 624
expropriation, 624
confiscation, 625
sovereign immunity, 626

DISCUSSION QUESTION

Compare the merits of arbitration and judicial litigation as methods of dispute resolution in international trade.

CASE QUESTIONS

1. A Houston corporation contracted for a German corporation to tow a drilling rig from Louisiana to the coast of Italy, where the Houston company was to drill wells. The contract provided that: "Any dispute arising must be treated before the London Court of Justice." While on its way to Italy, the rig was damaged by a storm. The German tug towed the rig to Tampa, Florida, the nearest port. The Houston company sued in the U.S. District Court, seeking $3.5 million damages from the German company. Is the use of the American court proper in this situation? What effect would the contract clause have on the lawsuit? [*M/S Bremen* v. *Zapata Off-Shore*, 92 S.Ct. 1907 (1972)]

2. Seawinds, a shipping company, was incorporated in Hong Kong with its principal place of business in California. It contracted with Nedlloyd Lines, a shipping company in the Netherlands, to "establish a joint venture company to carry on a transportation operation." The agreement had the following choice-of-law provision:

   This agreement shall be governed by and construed in accordance with Hong Kong law, and each party hereby irrevocably submits to the non-exclusive jurisdiction and service of process of the Hong Kong courts.

   Later, Seawinds sued in California state court, asserting that Nedlloyd had breached its duties under the contract by engaging in

activities that led to the cancellation of charter hires essential to the joint venture's business and by making and then reneging on commitments to contribute additional capital. Nedlloyd responded that Seawinds failed to state causes of action because Hong Kong law was to be applied. If the case is brought in California court, which law should be applied? The law of Hong Kong or of California? Does California have a substantial relationship to the parties or their transaction? Is there a reasonable basis for the selection of Hong Kong law by the parties in their original agreement? [*Nedlloyd Lines B.V.* v. *Superior Court*, 834 P.2d 1148, Sup. Ct., Cal. (1992)]
   ✓ Check your answer

3. Nettie Effron, a Florida resident, bought a 16-day cruise off the Brazilian coast from Sun Line Cruises. The cruise was on the 55 *Stella Solaris*, owned by Sun Line Greece. The cruise ticket stated "any action against the carrier must be brought only before the courts of Athens, Greece, to the jurisdiction of which the Passenger submits himself formally excluding the jurisdiction of all and other court or courts of any other country." Effron was injured when she fell while on the ship. She sued for damages in federal court in New York. Sun Line moved to have the case dismissed because of the forum selection clause in the ticket. The district court refused to dismiss; Sun Line appealed. What do you think

resulted? [*Effron* v. *Sun Line Cruises*, 67 F.3d 7, 2nd Cir. (1995)]

4. Farr, a U.S. company, contracted to buy sugar from CAV, a Cuban company owned by U.S. citizens. Because the government of Cuba nationalized its sugar industry, including CAV, it demanded that payments for sugar already shipped must be made to the Banco Nacional de Cuba. At CAV's insistence that it was the rightful owner of the sugar, and that the nationalization violated international law, Farr paid CAV. Banco Nacional sued to collect payment from Farr for the sugar delivered. The case went to the Supreme Court, where Banco Nacional was held to be correct. On what theory would the Supreme Court base its opinion? [*Banco Nacional de Cuba* v. *Sabbatino*, 84 S.Ct. 923 (1964)]
   ✓ Check your answer

5. The *F/V Cape Cod*, a commercial fishing vessel and the only asset of R&M, sank. During the accident, DiMercurio, a fisherman, was injured. He sued the company for his injuries and was awarded $350,000. R&M, having no assets, assigned DiMercurio all rights it had against Sphere Drake, the London-based insurer of the boat. DiMercurio took his claim to Sphere Drake, but it denied the demand and invoked the arbitration process specified in the policy, which called for arbitration of all coverage disputes in London. DeMercurio then sued, contesting the validity of the arbitration provision. The district court held for Sphere Drake. DiMercurio appealed. Does he have a valid claim? [*DiMercurio* v. *Sphere Drake Insurance PLC*, 202 F.3d 71, 1st Cir. (2000)]

6. Chisholm and Company and the Bank of Jamaica agreed that Chisholm was to arrange lines of credit from a number of banks and was to obtain Ex-Im Bank credit insurance. The Bank of Jamaica then "went around" Chisholm and dealt with Ex-Im Bank directly. It excluded Chisholm from receiving any benefit from the credit insurance that Ex-Im Bank provided. Chisholm sued the Bank of Jamaica. In its defense, the bank asserted that its actions were protected by sovereign immunity and the act of state doctrine. Were the bank's assertions correct? [*Chisholm and Company* v. *Bank of Jamaica*, 643 F.Supp. 1393, S.D. Fla. (1986)]
   ✓ Check your answer

7. *Pride Central America* (PCA), an American company, owned the ship *Pride Mississippi (PM)*. PCA leased *PM* to Pemex, the national oil company of Mexico, which used *PM* in its operations off the coast of Mexico in Mexican waters. Sandria, a citizen of Mexico, worked for a Mexican company, GOMPS, which provided maintenance support for Pemex. Sandria was killed on the *PM* during a storm. The Mexican Ministry of Labor and Social Security assumed jurisdiction over the accident. Sandria's family members were compensated in accordance with Mexican law. Sandria's representative sued PCA in federal court in Texas, contending that the conditions on *PM* were unsafe and that PCA should be liable to Sandria's family. PCA moved to dismiss, arguing that Mexican law should control the matter. Is that correct? [*Saqui* v. *Pride Central America*, 595 F.3d 206, 5th Cir. (2010)]

8. Robinson worked for the Shields Agency as a security guard at a building in New York owned by the government of Malaysia. While the building was being renovated, Robinson slipped and fell on something "that had been spilled on the floor." Contending that he suffered permanent injuries in the fall, he sued the Malaysian government in tort for his injuries. The district court dismissed the suit, holding that the government was immune due to the Foreign Sovereign Immunities Act. Robinson appealed. Does the Act bar his suit? [*Robinson* v. *Government of Malaysia*, 269 F.3d 133, 2nd Cir. (2001)]
   ✓ Check your answer

ETHICS QUESTION

In some countries, it is expected that businesses will pay off officials. Suppose these payoffs make the difference between getting the contract and not getting the contract? If a payoff is not made because of the Foreign Corrupt Practices Act, a foreign competitor that makes the bribe gets the deal. The American company that loses the deal would have to close a factory, putting 500 people out of work. The law aside, can you justify a bribe in that instance?

PULLING IT TOGETHER

In the last section of the text, we focused on statutory law, the regulations that follow from them, and how the courts and agencies interpret the laws in practice. When a statute imposes a rule different from the traditional common law, the statute dominates. So in certain areas of law, administrative rules are of key importance. Here, we consider some cases that cover at least two areas of law that we have considered in the text.

1. Morrison and Gugle opened a store together. The business was incorporated; each owned half the stock. Gugle was president; Morrison was secretary-treasurer. Both were employees of the corporation. They got into a dispute over money. Gugle did not trust Morrison and sent her a letter offering to buy her out. Morrison did not respond. Gugle fired her and denied her access to company records. Morrison sued Gugle for wrongful termination and defamation. The trial court held for Gugle. Morrison appealed. Does employment law, corporation law, or tort law control this matter?

2. Illinois Tool Works (ITW) has a patent on a printhead and ink container that uses unpatented ink in printing. ITW required its customers to buy ink only from ITW to use with their printheads and containers. They could not buy refill ink from other suppliers, such as Independent Ink, which sued ITW for antitrust violation for improperly tying the sale of ink to the sale of printheads and containers. Did the fact that the printheads and containers were patented give ITW the right to require buyers to buy only their ink, or was that an abuse of the patents that created an antitrust violation?

3. A federal statute, the Magnuson-Moss Warranty Act, requires sellers of consumer products to meet certain standards in the warranties they place on goods. Many states have lemon laws that concern the rights of consumers if they buy a vehicle that turns out to have problems that cannot be fixed in a reasonable number of attempts. Sales of goods are also covered by the UCC or possibly by the common law. The Edwards bought a new Hyundai that had a six-year, 72,000-mile bumper-to-bumper warranty. It had multiple problems over the next two years plus and, despite many repair attempts, still had problems. The Edwards sued for breach of written warranty, breach of implied warranty of merchantability, violation of the federal Magnuson-Moss Warranty Act, and violation of the Missouri Lemon Law. Can all of these claims, based on different sources of law, be brought together?

4. Kossol was a partner in Continental Food Network, which sold food plans to consumers. Consumers signed contracts to pay thousands of dollars for a plan to provide them a certain quantity of food over several years and give them a "free" freezer. The plan cost much more than the food and freezer were worth, and the food was not the quality claimed. The Attorney General of Maryland sued under state consumer protection law. The court ordered the operation shut down and $6 million in restitution paid to consumers. Kossol was held jointly and severally liable for the payments. He appealed, contending that only the parent company could be held liable, and that he could not be held personally liable. Assuming there was consumer fraud, could liability go against both the owners of the business as well as the business itself?

5. Ravenscroft worked for Westvaco for years when he was fired for sexual harassment of a co-worker in violation of company policy. He challenged his discharge as improper because he was represented in employment by a union. The collective bargaining agreement stated that the union could challenge discharges by arbitration. The arbitrator then held that Ravenscroft had harassed the woman, but ordered him reinstated in his job. The company sued, contending that the arbitrator exceeded his authority by substituting his judgment for that of management and that reinstatement violated public policy because it prevented the company from dealing effectively with sexual harassment. Who prevails? Does labor law or discrimination law control?

APPENDIX A

Legal Research and the Internet

Resources for Legal Research

There are several good starting points for finding free legal information on the Internet. FindLaw (www.findlaw.com) serves as an excellent legal information portal, especially for those lacking access to fee-based services, such as Westlaw and LexisNexis (www.westlaw.com and www.lexisnexis.com). The Legal Information Institute (LII) (www.law.cornell.edu) hosted by Cornell University Law School also provides legal information to the world. WashLaw WEB (www.washlaw.edu), hosted by the Washburn University School of Law, provides many links through its no-nonsense menu. HG.org (www.hg.org) is a world-wide legal directory that features links to foreign and international legal research resources. For legal newspapers via the Internet, visit Law.com (www.law.com).

If these sites do not produce the results you need, try PublicLegal (www.ilrg.com) at the Internet Legal Research Group, or a general search engine, such as Google (www.google.com), for which it helps to know and use the advanced search techniques.

Students should become familiar with their institution's library Web site. Virtually every law school library and university has a Web site with links to relevant reference sources. In addition to providing access to the library's online catalog, the library or its consortium of regional libraries may allow affiliated students access to legal databases, full-text journal databases, indexes to legal journals, and general reference databases.

Primary sources of U.S. law consist of cases, legislation (statutes), and administrative regulations. The Internet is a potential source for each type of law, but not every statute or case can be found for free on the Internet. Courts (e.g., the U.S. Supreme Court, federal appellate courts, and some federal district courts) have been releasing their opinions via the Internet in vendor-neutral formats since 1994. Government agencies, such as the Library of Congress and the Government Printing Office (GPO), have provided free, online resources such as federal legislative materials (since the 104th Congress), the *Federal Register*, and the *Code of Federal Regulations*.

Secondary sources—such as encyclopedias, treatises, and the *American Law Reports*—are not likely to be found on the Web. Selected published law review articles can be found and accessed at no cost, including some recent international or technological law review articles. One may search FindLaw or ALSO! (American Law Sources On-Line, www.lawsource.com/also) to see if a desired law review article is available in full-text via the Internet. The savvy legal researcher realizes that consulting a relevant secondary source at the outset, even one not available on the Internet, may save time and effort in the long run.

Supreme Court opinions are available at FindLaw and LII. The U.S. Supreme Court also has a Web site (www.supremecourt.gov). Federal appellate courts began to place their opinions on the Internet in the early 1990s. For information and statistics pertaining to the federal courts, see the United States Courts Web site (www.uscourts.gov). Federal district court opinions may or may not be available; try searching FindLaw's index (http://www.find-law.com/10fedgov/judicial/district_courts.html). For coverage of state courts, a good starting point is the National Center for State Courts (www.ncsc.org) or state resources at FindLaw (www.findlaw.com/llstategov/index. html).

The U.S. Code is available at GPO Access (www.gpoaccess.gov). The Library of Congress provides the Thomas database (http://thomas.loc.gov), named for Thomas

Jefferson, allows users to access to federal legislative information, such as bill summaries and status, bill text, public laws by law number, roll call votes, committee reports, House and Senate committee information, and the *Congressional Record* and *Congressional Record Index.*

Administrative law resources are readily available on the Internet. The GPO provides access to the *Federal Register*, the *Code of Federal Regulations*, the *List of CFR Sections Affected* (LSA), the *United States Government Manual*, and other administrative law databases. Most, if not all, federal administrative agencies have Web pages that allow access to pertinent statutory and regulatory sources, as well as agency-specific information. USA.gov (www.usa.gov) is a good starting point for access to federal agency information on the Internet. A Spanish-language version of the portal is available at www.usa.gov/gobiernousa/index.shtml.

Researching a new topic? Visit the online journal *LLRX.com* (www.llrx.com) and see if any of the research guides are relevant. Or, if you are unfamiliar with both the jurisdiction and the legal issue or process you are researching, search for a research guide from a library in that jurisdiction. For example, the New York State Library has a very useful guide to research legislative history in New York (www.nysl.nysed.gov/leghist).

The Internet is home to many law-oriented blogs (called *blawgs*) that have expert and non-expert commentary on any topic under the sun. Wikipedia, a free, open-source encyclopedia is also an excellent research tool as are other collaborative wikis dedicated to legal topics. While these tools may help manage your research and access background research information, remember that such Internet resources are not always peer-reviewed and should not be considered the best tools for accurate, in-depth legal research.

Try to find statutes from the official Web site of the jurisdiction you are researching. Likewise, try to find court opinions (cases) from official court Web sites. Remember the fee-based services, such as Westlaw, LexisNexis, LoisLaw, and VersusLaw, and databases licensed by your institutional or public library may be an appropriate starting point. Westlaw and LexisNexis are especially valuable in providing trustworthy sources and tools called *citators*—such as KeyCite and Shepard's—that help you confirm that the statute or case you are citing is still "good law." Many academic libraries allow patrons working in the library to access Westlaw, LexisNexis, or some version thereof.

Resources for Business Information

Academic institutions offer the starting point for effective business research via the Internet. Most business school Web sites offer a mix of proprietary information accessible only to currently affiliated members of their communities, as well as an assortment of generally accessible Web sites. Academic institutions that offer extensive business research guides—with selected, related Web sites—include the Jackson Library of the Stanford University Graduate School of Business (www.gsb.stanford.edu/jacksonlibrary/research) the Lippincott Library of the Wharton School of the University of Pennsylvania (www.library.upenn.edu/Lippincott), and the OSU Virtual Finance Library (http://fisher.osu.edu/fin/overview.htm), hosted by Ohio State University's Department of Finance, which provides, among other information, a Finance Site List for researchers.

The Securities and Exchange Commission's EDGAR database (www.sec.gov/edgar.shtml) is a major governmental source for finding such information as registration statements and periodic reports on large public companies. Another nonprofit, human-edited source of business information links is the Internet Public Library (www.ipl.org).

Companies, big and small, have Web pages presenting their mission statements, product descriptions, and annual reports. Larger companies also post press releases and messages from company executives. Corporate Web sites, while primarily marketing tools, may shed light on corporate America's reaction to and opinions regarding specific government policy measures or rules of law. Many corporate sites provide an e-mail address for a company official. With a little creativity, one can often acquire information unavailable through traditional research methods.

There are also commercial Internet providers of business information. BRINT.com (www.brint.com) claims to be "the premier business and technology knowledge portal and global community network for the new world of business." CEOExpress (www.ceoexpress.com) is "designed by a busy executive for busy executives" and provides links to daily news and information, as well as business research.

General News Resources

Keeping up on recent news developments is easy with the many commercial news sites: ABC News, CBS News, CNN, MSNBC, Bloomberg, Fox News, as well as independent sources, such as the Drudge Report, and various blogs. Many newspapers have Web sites that offer some free content, such as the *Wall Street Journal* (www.wsj.com) and *New York Times* (www.nytimes.com). The extent of archival coverage on newspapers' Web sites varies, so students doing in-depth news research may wish to use an index of newspaper articles, which are readily available from most libraries for registered patrons. Newspapers.com (www.newspapers.com) is the place to see if one's local newspaper has an Internet presence.

APPENDIX B

Case Analysis and Legal Sources

The legal environment of business is often one's first encounter with the law and the legal process in detail. Legal citations, the organization of legal materials, and opinion analysis can be bewildering at first. This appendix provides a look at the structure of a court opinion, plus a bit more detail on legal sources.

Reading a Legal Opinion

In resolving disputes, courts often report their decisions in written opinions. Decisions of appellate courts are most frequently reported. Usually only important decisions at the trial court level are reported. Through a written opinion, a judge explains the legal basis for the decision reached. Published opinions provide legal precedents in the common law.

An opinion can exceed 100 pages and involve several complex issues or it can be short and involve only a simple issue. To help analyze an opinion, law students often prepare a summary of the opinion, called a case brief, essentially an abstract of the opinion setting forth its most essential parts.

To brief an opinion, there is no formal procedure. Here, we provide a basic approach to assist in briefing the opinions excerpted in this text. It is an effective way to study legal opinions.

Before you brief an opinion, read it carefully. Then separate the opinion into its five fundamental parts by asking yourself questions about those parts:

(1) A Statement of the Significant Facts:
   Who is the plaintiff? The defendant?
   Who did what to whom?
   What relief is being sought from the court?
(2) A Statement of the Relevant Procedural History:
   Who prevailed in the lower court?
   What kind of ruling was it (summary judgment, dismissal, etc.)?
   Which party is appealing?
(3) A Statement of the Legal Issue in the Dispute:
   What are the specific legal questions the court is being asked to address?
   What is the standard of review?
(4) A Statement of the Court's Decision:
   How did the court respond to the question(s) posed to it?
   Did the plaintiff or the defendant prevail on the appeal?
(5) An Explanation of the Court's Reasoning:
   What is the legal basis for the court's decision?

This basic procedure is illustrated in the following opinion. We have provided numbered section headings to the five major parts of the opinion and have inserted some notes to help clarify a few points. As in the chapters, this opinion is extracted from a longer document (a long deletion of material from a holding is indicated by asterisks [***]; a deletion of a smaller part of a decision is indicated by an ellipsis [...]) so that the essence is retained in the condensed version.

DALLAS PARKS V. GEORGE STEINBRENNER AND NEW YORK YANKEES, INC.

New York Supreme Court, Appellate Division, First Department, 520 N.Y. 2d 374 (1987)

Citation The citation for the case includes the names of the primary parties. In this case the plaintiff, Dallas Parks, is listed first, but in appeals cases, the plaintiff may become the respondent to an appeal by a defendant and be listed on the right-hand side of the citation. The defendants, Steinbrenner and the Yankees, are listed on the right-hand side here. In some cases there are multiple parties, but not all names are listed in the short case citation.

The name of the court follows as does the legal citation, 520 NY2d 374, That means the court decision appears in volume 520 of the New York Reporter, Second Series, beginning on page 374. All citations appear in similar form; some are reported in multiple reporters and may have multiple citations to where the decisions appear.

Brief and Explanation Begin by summarizing the essential facts in the opinion. In the text, the facts and procedural history are summarized for you in the Case Background section provided with each opinion.

1. Facts Dallas Parks, the plaintiff, alleges that he was defamed by the defendant, George Steinbrenner, owner of the New York Yankees. The alleged defamation occurred when the defendant issued a press release criticizing Park's abilities as a baseball umpire. The plaintiff seeks damages on the grounds that the press release falsely attacked his abilities as an umpire.

> Note: The procedural history summarizes how the lower court(s) ruled on the dispute. In the text, the procedural history is summarized in the Case Background section.

2. Procedural History The defendant argued that the press release represented a constitutionally protected expression of opinion. The Special Term (the lower court) disagreed, finding that although the press release expressed an opinion, it was not backed

up by an adequate statement of the facts to support that opinion. The defendant appealed to the New York Supreme Court.

> Note: The legal issue in the opinion is the question the parties are asking the court to resolve. Some opinions state exactly what the issue is that the court is being asked to resolve. In the text, the issue is generally found in our summary of the lower court's decision or from the stated contentions of the parties. In analyzing an opinion in the text, state the issue in your own words to aid your understanding of the opinion. Next we see the names of the four appeals judges who heard the appeal. Then we see the first part of their decision.

Before Carro, J. P., and Kassal, Ellerin, Wallach, JJ.

Memorandum Decision This action for defamation brings into play one of the most colorful of American traditions—the razzing of the umpire.

The Plaintiff, Dallas Parks, served as an American League baseball umpire from 1979 through 1982. He alleges that he was defamed by George Steinbrenner, principal owner of the New York Yankees, when Steinbrenner, on August 29, 1982, issued a press release, excerpts of which were published in newspapers throughout the United States, criticizing Park's abilities as an umpire. The press release, which was issued after the Yankees had played a two-game series with the Toronto Blue Jays in Toronto, Canada, on August 27th and 28th, at which Parks officiated, reads as follows:

> Judging on his last two days' performance, my people tell me that he is not a capable umpire. He is a member of one of the finest crews umpiring in the American League today, but obviously he doesn't measure up.
>
> We are making no excuse for the team's play this season, but this weekend our team has had several key injuries and for umpire

Dallas Parks to throw two of our players out of ball-games in two days on plays he misjudges is "ludicrous."

This man, in my opinion, has had it in for the Yankees ever since I labeled him and several of the umpires as "scabs" because they worked the American League games in 1979 during the umpires' strike.

Parks must learn that the word *scab* is a commonly used phrase. It is in no way meant as a personal insult. However, because he worked during the strike for baseball management does not mean he should be protected by them and annually given a job he is not capable of handling.

3. Issue Does the press release constitute a constitutionally protected statement of pure opinion?

Note: After stating the issue, state the court's decision, both procedural (e.g., judgment for the defendant) and substantive (a yes or no response to the issue presented).

4. The Court's Decision Yes, the press release is a constitutionally protected expression of pure opinion. Judgment for the defendant; the Special Term's trial court's decision is reversed.

Note: The court's rationale is the heart of the opinion. The court generally discusses the relevant law surrounding the question presented to it. Then the court applies that law to the facts of the dispute before it. In reaching its decision, the court explains its rationale—why and how it reached the conclusion that the facts in this dispute do or do not fall within the existing law. In the text, the court's rationale is presented in excerpts from the actual opinions in the Case Decision section.

5. Court's Reasoning Quoting the court: A statement of pure opinion is a statement that is accompanied by the facts upon which it is based, or it does not imply that it is based on undisclosed facts.

Statements that constitute pure opinion whether false or libelous may not serve as the basis for an action for defamation.

In determining whether a statement is fact or opinion, consideration is given to what an average person hearing or reading the statement will take it

to mean, the circumstances surrounding its use, and the way it is written.

The press release must be evaluated within the broader social context of baseball. It is an American tradition to verbally abuse umpires. In this context, the average reader would perceive the release as opinion and not fact. The release is the kind of statement that generally accompanies a voicing of displeasure at an umpire's calls.

The statement by the defendant represents the view of an owner of a baseball team that is doing poorly and who has chosen to vent his frustration by baiting the umpire.

There is no indication that defendant's opinions are based on some other undisclosed facts unknown to the reader.

This less than complimentary critical assessment appears to have been the "final straw" in the rhubarb that had long simmered between the umpire and the owner and resulted in commencement of the instant action, against Steinbrenner and the Yankees, wherein plaintiff seeks damages for defamation on the ground that the press release falsely impugned his ability, competence, conduct, and fairness as a baseball umpire.

In subsequently moving to dismiss the complaint for failure to state a cause of action, defendants argued that the press release represented a nonactionable, constitutionally protected expression of opinion. While Special Term [lower court] found that the statement was "clearly expressed as an opinion," it nevertheless held that the complaint sufficiently pleaded a cause of action in defamation because the press release did not set forth an adequate statement of fact contained in the statement—i.e., that Parks expelled two Yankee players from the game—did "not in any way support the opinions proffered" that plaintiff was incompetent and biased and, further, that no factual basis was set forth for the conclusory assertion that plaintiff misjudged plays.

We disagree with Special Term's assessment of the press release in question and find that it constituted a constitutionally protected expression of pure opinion.

In all defamation cases, the threshold issue which must be determined, as a matter of law, is whether the complained of statements constitute fact or opinion. If they fall within the ambit of "pure opinion," then even if false and libelous, and no matter how pejorative or pernicious they may be, such statements are safeguarded and may not serve as the basis for an action in defamation. A nonactionable "pure opinion" is defined as a statement of opinion which either is accompanied by a recitation of the facts upon which it is based, or, if not so accompanied, does not imply that it is based upon undisclosed facts. Alternatively, when a defamatory statement of opinion implies that it is based upon undisclosed detrimental facts which justify the opinion but are unknown to those reading or hearing it, it is a "mixed opinion" and actionable. Similarly actionable as a "mixed opinion" is a defamatory opinion which is ostensibly accompanied by a recitation of the underlying facts upon which the opinion is based, but those underlying facts are either falsely misrepresented or grossly distorted.

Determining whether particular statements, or particular words, express fact or opinion is oft-times an exercise beset by the uncertainties engendered by the imprecision and varying nuance inherent in language. While mechanistic rules and rigid sets of criteria have been eschewed as inappropriate vehicles for the sensitive process of separating fact from opinion, reference to various general criteria has been found helpful in resolving the issue. Predominant among these is that the determination is to be made on the basis of what the average person hearing or reading the communication would take it to mean, and what significance is to be accorded the purpose of the words, the circumstances surrounding their use and the manner, tone, and style with which they are used. An approach which was favorably commented upon in the *Steinbrenner* case is that set forth by Judge Starr in his plurality opinion in *Oilman* v. *Evans* which enunciates four factors which should generally be considered in differentiating between fact and opinion. They are summarized … as follows:

1) an assessment of whether the specific language in issue has a precise meaning which is readily understood or whether it is indefinite and ambiguous;
2) a determination of whether the statement is capable of being objectively characterized as true or false;
3) an examination of the full context of the communication in which the statement appears; and
4) a consideration of the broader social context or setting surrounding the communication including the existence of any applicable customs or conventions which might signal to readers or listeners that what is being read or heard is likely to be opinion, not fact.

These factors have particular relevance to the statement here in issue, which must be evaluated within the broader social context of a baseball club owner versus an umpire, and special attention should be accorded to whether there exist any customs and conventions regarding the status of an umpire in the great American pastime which would signal to readers that what is being read is likely to be opinion not fact.

* * *

From the late nineteenth century on, the baseball umpire has come to expect not only verbal abuse, but in many cases, physical attack as well, as part of the "robust debate" ingrained in the profession … .

Judges, too, have expressed their acceptance of this American tradition. In dismissing a minor league general manager's defamation action on other grounds, a federal court noted that harsh insults, especially those directed at an umpire, are accepted commonplace occurrences in baseball.

* * *

When Steinbrenner's remarks are viewed in this context, it is clear that they would be perceived by the average reader as a statement of opinion, and not fact. The negative characterizations of the plaintiff umpire as "not capable," that "he doesn't measure up," that he "misjudges" plays and that his decision to "throw two of our players out of ball games" was "ludicrous" are readily understood to be the kind of "rhetorical hyperbole" that generally accompany the communication of displeasure at an umpire's "calls." While the subjective and emotional character of such sentiments is commonly recognized and construed as "opinion" rather than fact, that view is expressly emphasized upon a reading of the entire press release with its qualifying phrases of "my people tell me" immediately evident that the statement represents the view of the owner of an embattled baseball team who is obviously chafing at "the team's (poor) play this season," which has been exacerbated by a weekend of injuries and ejections of players, and who is venting his frustrations in the venerated American tradition of "baiting the umpire." Indeed, even if the assertions in the statement implying that plaintiff was incompetent and biased in performing his duties were to be viewed as statements of fact, it is questionable whether they could be construed as defamatory, i.e., exposing the plaintiff to public contempt, ridicule, aversion, and disgrace and inducing an evil opinion of him in the minds of right thinking persons—in light of the generally "critical" attitudes which baseball umpires, in any event, ordinarily inspire in both the game's fans and its participants.

Although acknowledging that the statement in issue was "clearly expressed as opinion," Special Term held that it was actionable, because the accompanying underlying facts were found by Special Term not to adequately support the opinions proffered. That one may dispute the conclusions drawn from the specified facts is not, however, the test. So long as the opinion is accompanied by a recitation of the facts upon which it is based, it is deemed a "pure opinion" and is afforded complete immunity even though the facts do not support the opinion. The

rationale for this broad protection of an expression of opinion accompanied by a recitation of the facts upon which it is based is that the reader has the opportunity to assess the basis upon which the opinion was reached in order to draw his or her own conclusions concerning its validity.

* * *

The reverence which the First Amendment accords to ideas has properly resulted in the determination that, "however pernicious an opinion may seem, we depend for its correction not on the conscience of judges and juries but on the competition of other ideas." Those competing ideas about baseball's arbiters will undoubtedly continue to abound aplenty both on the playing fields and in the sports columns, albeit not in the courtroom.

Accordingly the Order, Supreme Court, Bronx County (Alfred J. Callahan, J.), entered May 9, 1986, which denied the defendants' motion to dismiss the complaint and supplemental complaint for failure to state a cause of action, should be reversed, on the law, and the complaint dismissed, without costs.

Major Sources of the Law

There are several important sources of law in the United States, including the U.S. Constitution; case law established by the written opinions of judges; statutes enacted by legislative bodies; regulatory agency orders, opinions, and regulations; treatises; law review articles; and Restatements of Law. At one time or another, we reference these sources in explaining the laws making up the legal environment of business. This section provides a guide to reading a citation to a source of law. If you decide to study an aspect of the legal environment in more detail, this section provides guidance in locating appropriate material.

Case Law

The published judicial opinions of all federal courts and the appellate state courts are available in court reporters. As a rule, opinions appear in hardback volumes of the reporters about a year after a court has delivered its decision. The opinions are available more quickly in paperback volumes published shortly after the case is decided, even more quickly through computer research services (such as Westlaw and LexisNexis), and in the form of *slip opinions*, which are copies of a decision as soon as it is made public by the court. Appendix A discusses availability of this information on the Internet.

Supreme Court decisions are published in *United States Reporter* (U.S.), *Supreme Court Reporter* (S.Ct), *Lawyers' Edition of Supreme Court Reports* (L.Ed.), and *U.S. Law Week*. A citation reads as follows: *Arnett* v. *Kennedy*, 416 U.S. 134, 94 S.Ct. 1633, 40 L.Ed.2d 15 (1974). This tells us that Arnett appealed a decision of a lower court to the U.S. Supreme Court. In 1974, the Supreme Court decided the case (which was argued in 1973), and its decision is reported in volume 416 of *United States Reporter* beginning on page 134 and in volume 94 of *Supreme Court Reporter* beginning on page 1633. A reference to a point cited on a particular page in that opinion might read 416 U.S. 134, 137, which means that the case begins on page 134 and the particular point referenced is on page 137.

Decisions of U.S. Circuit Courts of Appeals are reported in *Federal Reporter* (F.), now in its third series (F.3d). The following is an example of a citation: *Easton Publishing Co.* v. *Federal Communications Commission*, 175 F.2d 344 (D.C. Cir., 1949). The decision in this case can be found in volume 175 of *Federal Reporter* (second series), beginning on page 344. The decision was issued by the Court of Appeals of the District of Columbia circuit in 1949.

Opinions of U.S. district courts that the judges decide to publish are reported in *Federal Supplement* (F.Supp.) now in its second (2d) series. An example is *Amalgamated Meat Cutters* v. *Connally*, 337 F.Supp. 737 (S.D. NY 1971). The decision can be found in volume 337 of *Federal Supplement* beginning on page 737. The case was decided by the federal district court in the Southern District of New York in 1971.

State appellate court decisions are reported in regional reporters published by West Publishing Company. Decisions of the state supreme courts and courts of appeals for Arkansas, Kentucky, Missouri, Tennessee, and Texas, for example, are reported in *South Western Reporter* (S.W.). Other state court opinions are reported in *Atlantic Reporter* (A.), *North Eastern Reporter* (N.E.), *North Western Reporter* (N.W.), *Pacific Reporter* (P.), *South Eastern Reporter* (S.E.), and *Southern Reporter* (S.), all of which are in the second (2d) or third (3d) series. Because they handle so many cases, California and New York have individual reporters, *New York Supplement* and *California Reporter*. Some states publish their own reporters in addition to the West series.

Statutory Law

Statutes, laws passed by Congress, are published in the *United States Code* (U.S.C.) and printed by the U.S. Government Printing Office. The U.S.C. contains the text of all laws passed by Congress and signed by the president. A reference to this source might read 40 U.S.C. § 13.1 (volume 40, *United States Code*, section 13.1). As noted in Appendix A, these are available on the Internet.

A popular source of statutory law is the *United States Code Annotated* (U.S.C.A.). In the U.S.C.A., each section of a statute contains helpful annotations that provide references to the legislative history of the section and to court decisions using and interpreting it. A reference to this source might read 14 U.S.CA. § 45.3 (volume 14, *United States Code Annotated*, section 45.3). Both the U.S.C. and the U.S.CA., which report the same laws, are organized and integrated in a pattern that makes the laws relatively easy to find and to read.

The U.S. Government Printing Office also publishes *Statutes at Large*, a chronological list of all laws enacted by Congress. This list is not often used unless it is necessary to look up a law that has just been passed by Congress, but is not yet reported in the U.S.C. or U.S.CA. A full citation might read: Voting Rights Act of 1965, Pub.L. No. 89-110, 79 Stat. 437, 42 U.S.C. §§ 1971, 1973. The Voting Rights Act of 1965 was the 110th *Public Law* enacted by the 89th Congress and appears in volume 79 of *Statutes at Large*, page 437. In addition, it appears in volume 42 of the U.S.C., sections 1971 and 1973. Also, remember that there is often a difference between the number of the section in the statute as written by Congress and the number of the section in the Code. For example, the "National Environmental Policy Act of 1969, § 102, 42 U.S.C. § 4332" means that section 102 of the statute as passed by Congress is found in section 4332 of volume 42 of the U.S.C.

Regulatory Law

Regulations, rules passed by agencies subsequent to a congressional statute, are published in the *Code of Federal Regulations* (C.F.R.). These regulations are intended to implement a particular statute enacted by Congress. The C.F.R., revised annually, is organized by subject matter and contains the text of regulations in effect as of the date of publication. A citation reading 7 C.F.R § 912.65 refers to Title 7 of the *Code of Federal Regulations*, section 912.65. Different titles refer to different government agencies. These are all available on the Internet.

To keep up-to-date on new and proposed regulations, one needs to consult the *Federal Register* (Fed.Reg.). Printed five days a week by the U.S. Government Printing Office, the *Federal Register* lists all proposed regulations and all new and amended regulations. A citation might read 46 Fed.Reg. 26,501 (1981). This refers to volume 46 of the *Federal Register*, published in 1981, page 26,501 (which has to do with a new environmental standard).

Agency Orders and Opinions

Agency orders and opinions are official regulatory materials that go beyond the regulations. Orders may be issued by the top officials (e.g., the commissioners) of a regulatory agency, while opinions are generally issued by an agency's administrative law judge in adjudicatory hearings (discussed in Chapter 17). While agencies usually have official publications published on the Internet, the agency materials are also published by private companies such as Commerce Clearing House (CCH) and Bureau of National Affairs (BNA). Each reporter covers a single topic, such as environmental law or federal tax law. The reporters are up-to-date and contain new regulations, orders, opinions, court decisions, and other materials of interest to anyone following regulations in a certain area. These reporters, which are usually large loose-leaf binders, cover hundreds of topics, such as chemical regulations, hazardous materials, transportation, noise regulations, collective bargaining negotiations, securities regulations, patents, and antitrust laws.

Treatises, Law Reviews, and Restatements of the Law

Important secondary sources of law are legal treatises, law reviews, and Restatements of Law. Most of these are available on the Internet but many require payment. Treatises generally cover one area or topic of law, summarizing the principles and rules dealing with the topic. An example of a treatise is W. Jaeger, *Williston on Contracts* (3d ed. 1957).

Law reviews, published by law schools and usually edited by law students, contain articles written by legal scholars, judges, law students, and practitioners on virtually all aspects of the law. An example of a legal citation to a law review is Mark J. Roe, "Corporate Strategic Reaction to Mass Tort," 72 *Virginia Law Review* 1 (1986), which means that the article "Corporate Strategic Reaction to Mass Tort" written by Mark J. Roe can be found in volume 72 of *Virginia Law Review* beginning on page 1.

Like a treatise, a Restatement is limited in its coverage to a single area of law. Restatements are the consequence of intensive study on a specific topic by legal scholars, culminating in a written statement of the law. That statement includes rules stated in bold type—often referred to as *black-letter law*—along with explanatory comments. The rules presented are usually synthesized from opinions of the courts in all jurisdictions. An example is *Restatement (Second) of Torts.*

The Constitution of the United States of America

Preamble

We the People of the United States, in Order to form a more perfect Union, establish Justice, insure domestic Tranquility, provide for the common defence, promote the general Welfare, and secure the Blessings of Liberty to ourselves and our Posterity, do ordain and establish this Constitution for the United States of America.

Article I

Section 1. All legislative Powers herein granted shall be vested in a Congress of the United States, which shall consist of a Senate and House of Representatives.

Section 2. The House of Representatives shall be composed of Members chosen every second Year by the People of the several States, and the Electors in each State shall have the Qualifications requisite for Electors of the most numerous Branch of the State Legislature.

No Person shall be a Representative who shall not have attained to the Age of twenty five Years, and been seven Years a Citizen of the United States, and who shall not, when elected, be an Inhabitant of that State in which he shall be chosen.

Representatives and direct Taxes shall be apportioned among the several States which may be included within this Union, according to their respective Numbers, which shall be determined by adding to the whole Number of free Persons, including those bound to Service for a Term of Years, and excluding Indians not taxed, three fifths of all other Persons. The actual Enumeration shall be made within three Years after the first Meeting of the Congress of the United States, and within every subsequent Term of ten Years, in such Manner as they shall by Law direct. The number of Representatives shall not exceed one for every thirty Thousand, but each State shall have at Least one Representative: and until such enumeration shall be made, the State of New Hampshire shall be entitled to chuse three, Massachusetts eight, Rhode Island and Providence Plantations one, Connecticut five, New York six, New Jersey four, Pennsylvania eight, Delaware one, Maryland six, Virginia ten, North Carolina five, South Carolina five, and Georgia three.

When vacancies happen in the Representation from any State, the Executive Authority thereof shall issue Writs of Election to fill such vacancies.

The House of Representatives shall chuse their Speaker and other Officers: and shall have the sole Power of Impeachment.

Section 3. The Senate of the United States shall be composed of two Senators from each State, chosen by the Legislature thereof, for six Years; and each Senator shall have one Vote.

Immediately after they shall be assembled in Consequence of the first Election, they shall be divided as equally as may be into three Classes. The Seats of the Senators of the first Class shall be vacated at the Expiration of the second Year, of the second Class at the Expiration of the fourth Year, and of the third Class at the Expiration of the sixth Year, so that one third may be chosen every second Year; and if Vacancies happen by

Resignation, or otherwise, during the Recess of the Legislature of any State, the Executive thereof may make temporary Appointments until the next Meeting of the Legislature, which shall then fill such Vacancies.

No Person shall be a Senator who shall not have attained to the Age of thirty Years, and been nine Years a Citizen of the United States, and who shall not, when elected, be an Inhabitant of that State for which he shall be chosen.

The Vice President of the United States shall be President of the Senate, but shall have no Vote, unless they be equally divided.

The Senate shall chuse their other Officers, and also a President pro tempore, in the Absence of the Vice President, or when he shall exercise the Office of President of the United States.

The Senate shall have the sole power to try all Impeachments. When sitting for that Purpose, they shall be on Oath or Affirmation. When the President of the United States is tried, the Chief Justice shall preside: And no Person shall be convicted without the Concurrence of two thirds of the Members present.

Judgment in Cases of Impeachment shall not extend further than to removal from Office, and disqualification to hold and enjoy any Office of honor, Trust or Profit under the United States: but the Party convicted shall nevertheless be liable and subject to Indictment, Trial, Judgment and Punishment, according to Law.

Section 4. The Times, Places and Manner of holding Elections for Senators and Representatives, shall be prescribed in each State by the Legislature thereof: but the Congress may at any time by Law make or alter such Regulations, except as to the Places of chusing Senators.

The Congress shall assemble at least once in every Year, and such Meeting shall be on the first Monday in December, unless they shall by Law appoint a different Day.

Section 5. Each House shall be the Judge of the Elections, Returns and Qualifications of its own Members, and a Majority of each shall constitute a Quorum to do Business; but a smaller Number may adjourn from day to day, and may be authorized to compel the Attendance of absent Members, in such Manner, and under such Penalties as each House may provide.

Each House may determine the Rules of its Proceedings, punish its Members for disorderly Behaviour, and, with the Concurrence of two thirds, expel a Member.

Each House shall keep a Journal of its Proceedings, and from time to time publish the same, excepting such Parts as may in their Judgment require Secrecy; and the Yeas and Nays of the Members of either House on any question shall, at the Desire of one fifth of those Present, be entered on the Journal.

Neither House, during the Session of Congress, shall, without the Consent of the other, adjourn for more than three days, nor to any other Place than that in which the two Houses shall be sitting.

Section 6. The Senators and Representatives shall receive a Compensation for their Services, to be ascertained by Law, and paid out of the Treasury of the United States. They shall in all Cases, except Treason, Felony and Breach of the Peace, be privileged from Arrest during their Attendance at the Session of their respective Houses, and in going to and returning from the same; and for any Speech or Debate in either House, they shall not be questioned in any other Place.

No Senator or Representative shall, during the Time for which he was elected, be appointed to any civil Office under the Authority of the United States, which shall have been created, or the Emoluments whereof shall have been en creased during such time; and no Person holding any Office under the United States, shall be a Member of either House during his Continuance in Office.

Section 7. All Bills for raising Revenue shall originate in the House of Representatives; but the Senate may propose or concur with Amendments as on other Bills.

Every Bill which shall have passed the House of Representatives and the Senate, shall, before it become a Law, be presented to the President of the United States; If he approve he shall sign it, but if not he shall return it, with his Objections to that House in which it shall have originated, who shall enter the Objections at large on their Journal, and proceed to reconsider it. If after such Reconsideration two thirds of that House shall agree to pass the Bill, it shall be sent, together with the Objections, to the other House, by which it shall likewise be reconsidered, and if approved by two thirds of that House, it shall become a Law. But in all such Cases the Votes of both Houses shall be determined by Yeas and Nays, and the Names of the Persons voting for and against the Bill shall be entered on the Journal of each House respectively. If any Bill shall not be returned by the President within ten Days (Sundays excepted) after it shall have been presented to him, the Same shall be a Law, in like Manner as if he had signed it, unless the Congress by their Adjournment prevent its Return, in which Case it shall not be a Law.

Every Order, Resolution, or Vote to which the Concurrence of the Senate and House of Representatives may be necessary (except on a question of Adjournment) shall be presented to the President of the United States; and before the Same shall take Effect, shall be approved by him, or being disapproved by him, shall be repassed by two thirds of the Senate and House of Representatives, according to the Rules and Limitations prescribed in the Case of a Bill.

Section 8. The Congress shall have Power to lay and collect Taxes, Duties, Imposts and Excises, to pay the Debts and provide for the common Defence and general Welfare of the United States; but all Duties, Imposts and Excises shall be uniform throughout the United States;

To borrow Money on the credit of the United States;

To regulate Commerce with foreign Nations, and among the several States, and with the Indian Tribes;

To establish an uniform Rule of Naturalization, and uniform Laws on the subject of Bankruptcies throughout the United States;

To coin Money, regulate the Value thereof, and of foreign Coin, and fix the Standard of Weights and Measures;

To provide for the Punishment of counterfeiting the Securities and current Coin of the United States;

To establish Post Offices and post Roads;

To promote the Progress of Science and useful Arts, by securing for limited Times to Authors and Inventors the exclusive Right to their respective Writings and Discoveries;

To constitute Tribunals inferior to the supreme Court;

To define and punish Piracies and Felonies committed on the high Seas, and Offenses against the Law of Nations;

To declare War, grant Letters of Marque and Reprisal, and make Rules concerning Captures on Land and Water;

To raise and support Armies, but no Appropriation of Money to that Use shall be for a longer Term than two Years;

To provide and maintain a Navy;

To make Rules for the Government and Regulation of the land and naval Forces;

To provide for calling forth the Militia to execute the Laws of the Union, suppress Insurrections and repel Invasions;

To provide for organizing, arming, and disciplining, the Militia, and for governing such Part of them as may be employed in the Service of the United States, reserving to the States respectively, the Appointment of the Officers, and the Authority of training the Militia according to the discipline prescribed by Congress;

To exercise exclusive Legislation in all Cases whatsoever, over such District (not exceeding ten Miles square) as may, by Cession of particular States, and the Acceptance of Congress, become the Seat of the Government of the United States, and to exercise like Authority over all Places purchased by the Consent of the Legislature of the State in which the Same shall be, for the Erection of Forts, Magazines, Arsenals, dock-Yards, and other needful Buildings;—And

To make all Laws which shall be necessary and proper for carrying into Execution the foregoing Powers, and all other Powers vested by this Constitution in the Government of the United States, or in any Department or Officer thereof.

Section 9. The Migration or Importation of such Persons as any of the States now existing shall think proper to admit, shall not be prohibited by the Congress prior to the Year one thousand eight hundred and eight, but a Tax or Duty may be imposed on such Importation, not exceeding ten dollars for each Person.

The Privilege of the Writ of Habeas Corpus shall not be suspended, unless when in Cases of Rebellion or Invasion the public Safety may require it.

No Bill of Attainder or ex post facto Law shall be passed.

No Capitation, or other direct, Tax shall be laid, unless in Proportion to the Census or Enumeration herein before directed to be taken.

No Tax or Duty shall be laid on Articles exported from any State.

No Preference shall be given by any Regulation of Commerce or Revenue to the Ports of one State over those of another; nor shall Vessels bound to, or from, one State, be obliged to enter, clear, or pay Duties in another.

No Money shall be drawn from the Treasury, but in Consequence of Appropriations made by Laws; and a regular Statement and Account of the Receipts and Expenditures of all public Money shall be published from time to time.

No Title of Nobility shall be granted by the United States: And no Person holding any Office of Profit or Trust under them, shall, without the Consent of the Congress, accept of any present, Emolument, Office, or Title, of any kind whatever, from any King, Prince, or foreign State.

Section 10. No State shall enter into any Treaty, Alliance, or Confederation: grant Letters of Marque and Reprisal; coin Money; emit Bills of Credit; make any Thing but gold and silver Coin a Tender in Payment of Debts; pass any Bill of Attainder, ex post facto Law, or Law impairing the Obligation of Contracts, or grant any Title of Nobility.

No State shall, without the Consent of the Congress, lay any Imposts or Duties on Imports or Exports, except what may be absolutely necessary for executing its inspection Laws: and the net Produce of all Duties and Imposts, laid by any State on Imports or Exports, shall be for the Use of the Treasury of the United States; and all such Laws shall be subject to the Revision and Control of the Congress.

No State shall, without the Consent of Congress, lay any Duty of Tonnage, keep Troops, or Ships of War in time of Peace, enter into any Agreement or Compact with another State, or with a foreign Power, or engage in War, unless actually invaded, or in such imminent Danger as will not admit of delay.

Article II

Section 1. The executive Power shall be vested in a President of the United States of America. He shall hold his Office during the Term of four Years, and, together with the Vice President, chosen for the same Term, be elected, as follows:

Each State shall appoint, in such Manner as the Legislature thereof may direct, a Number of Electors, equal to the whole Number of Senators and Representatives to which the State may be entitled in the Congress: but no Senator or Representative, or Person holding an Office of Trust or Profit under the United States, shall be appointed an Elector.

The Electors shall meet in their respective States, and vote by Ballot for two Persons, of whom one at least shall not be an Inhabitant of the same State with themselves. And they shall make a List of all the Persons voted for, and of the Number of Votes for each; which List they shall sign and certify, and transmit sealed to the Seat of the Government of the United States, directed to the President of the Senate. The President of the Senate shall, in the Presence of the Senate and House of Representatives, open all the Certificates, and the Votes shall then be counted. The Person having the greatest Number of Votes shall be the President, if such Number be a Majority of the whole Number of Electors appointed; and if there be more than one who have such Majority, and have an equal Number of Votes, then the House of Representatives shall immediately chuse by Ballot one of them for President; and if no Person have a Majority, then from the five highest on the List the said House shall in like Manner chuse the President. But in chusing the President, the Votes shall be taken by States, the Representation from each State having one Vote; a quorum for this Purpose shall consist of a Member or Members from two thirds of the States, and a Majority of all the States shall be necessary to a Choice. In every Case, after the Choice of the President, the Person having the greatest Number of Votes of the Electors shall be the Vice President. But if there should remain two or more who have equal Votes, the Senate shall chuse from them by Ballot the Vice President.

The Congress may determine the Time of chusing the Electors, and the Day on which they shall give their Votes; which Day shall be the same throughout the United States.

No Person except a natural born Citizen, or a Citizen of the United States, at the time of the Adoption of this Constitution, shall be eligible to the Office of President; neither shall any Person be eligible to that Office who shall not have attained to the Age of thirty five Years, and been fourteen Years a Resident within the United States.

In Case of the Removal of the President from Office, or of his Death, Resignation, or Inability to discharge the Powers and Duties of the said Office, the Same shall devolve on the Vice President, and the Congress may by Law provide for the Case of Removal, Death, Resignation or Inability, both of the President and Vice President, declaring what Officer shall then act as President, and such Officer shall act accordingly, until the Disability be removed, or a President shall be elected.

The President shall, at stated Times, receive for his Services, a Compensation, which shall neither be encreased nor diminished during the Period for which he shall have been elected, and he shall not receive within that Period any other Emolument from the United States, or any of them.

Before he enter on the Execution of his Office, he shall take the following Oath or Affirmation:—"I do solemnly swear (or affirm) that I will faithfully execute the Office of President of the United States, and will to the best of my Ability, preserve, protect and defend the Constitution of the United States."

Section 2. The President shall be Commander in Chief of the Army and Navy of the United States, and of the Militia of the several States, when called into the actual Service of the United States; he may require the Opinion, in writing, of the principal Officer in each of the executive Departments, upon any Subject relating to the Duties of their respective Offices, and he shall have Power to grant Reprieves and Pardons for Offences against the United States, except in Cases of Impeachment.

He shall have Power, by and with the Advice and Consent of the Senate, to make Treaties, providing two thirds of the Senators present concur; and he shall nominate, and by and with the Advice and Consent of the Senate, shall appoint Ambassadors, other public Ministers and Consuls, Judges of the supreme Court, and all other Officers of the United States, whose Appointments are not herein otherwise provided for, and which shall be established by Law: but the Congress may by Law vest the Appointment of such inferior Officers, as they think proper, in the President alone, in the Courts of Law, or in the Heads of Departments.

The President shall have Power to fill up all Vacancies that may happen during the Recess of the Senate, by granting Commissions which shall expire at the End of their next Session.

Section 3. He shall from time to time give to the Congress Information of the State of the Union, and recommend to their Consideration such Measures as he shall judge necessary and expedient; he may, on extraordinary Occasions, convene both Houses, or either of them, and in Case of Disagreement between them, with Respect to the Time of Adjournment, he may adjourn them to such Time as he shall think proper; he shall receive Ambassadors and other public Ministers; he shall take Care that the Laws be faithfully executed, and shall Commission all the Officers of the United States.

Section 4. The President, Vice President and all civil Officers of the United States, shall be removed from Office on Impeachment for, and Conviction of Treason, Bribery, or other high Crimes and Misdemeanors.

Article III

Section 1. The judicial Power of the United States, shall be vested in one supreme Court, and in such inferior Courts as the Congress may from time to time ordain and establish. The Judges, both of the supreme and inferior Courts, shall hold their Offices during good Behaviour, and shall, at stated Times, receive for their Services, a Compensation, which shall not be diminished during their Continuance in Office.

Section 2. The judicial Power shall extend to all Cases, in Law and Equity, arising under this Constitution, the Laws of the United States, and Treaties made, or which shall be made, under their Authority;—to all Cases affecting Ambassadors, other public Ministers and Consuls;—to all Cases of admiralty and maritime Jurisdiction;—to Controversies to which the United States shall be a Party;—to Controversies between two or more States;—between a State and Citizens of another State;—between Citizens of different States;—between Citizens of the same State claiming Lands under Grants of different States, and between a State, or the Citizens thereof, and foreign States, Citizens or Subjects.

In all Cases affecting Ambassadors, other public Ministers and Consuls, and those in which a State shall be Party, the supreme Court shall have original Jurisdiction. In all the other Cases before mentioned, the supreme Court shall have appellate Jurisdiction, both as to Law and Fact, with such Exceptions, and under such Regulations as the Congress shall make.

The Trial of all Crimes, except in Cases of Impeachment, shall be by Jury; and such Trial shall be held in the State where the said Crimes shall have been committed; but when not committed within any State, the Trial shall be at such Place or Places as the Congress may by Law have directed.

Section 3. Treason against the United States, shall consist only in levying War against them, or in adhering to their Enemies, giving them Aid and Comfort. No Person shall be convicted of Treason unless on the Testimony of two Witnesses to the same overt Act, or on Confession in open Court.

The Congress shall have Power to declare the Punishment of Treason, but no Attainder of Treason shall work Corruption of Blood, or Forfeiture except during the Life of the Person attainted.

Article IV

Section 1. Full Faith and Credit shall be given in each State to the public Acts, Records, and judicial Proceedings of every other State. And the Congress may by general Laws prescribe the Manner in which such Acts, Records and Proceedings shall be proved, and the Effect thereof.

Section 2. The Citizens of each State shall be entitled to all Privileges and Immunities of Citizens in the several States.

A Person charged in any State with Treason, Felony, or other Crime, who shall flee from Justice, and be found in another State, shall on Demand of the executive Authority of the State from which he fled, be delivered up, to be removed to the State having Jurisdiction of the Crime.

No Person held to Service or Labour in one State, under the Laws thereof escaping into another, shall, in Consequence of any Law or Regulation therein, be discharged from such Service or Labour, but shall be delivered up on Claim of the Party to whom such Service or Labour may be due.

Section 3. New States may be admitted by the Congress into this Union; but no new State shall be formed or erected within the Jurisdiction of any other State; nor any State be formed by the Junction of two or more States, or Parts of States, without the Consent of the Legislatures of the States concerned as well as of the Congress.

The Congress shall have Power to dispose of and make all needful Rules and Regulations respecting the Territory or other Property belonging to the United States; and nothing in this Constitution shall be so construed as to Prejudice any Claims of the United States, or of any particular State.

Section 4. The United States shall guarantee to every State in this Union a Republican Form of the Government, and shall protect each of them against Invasion; and on Application of the Legislature, or of the Executive (when the Legislature cannot be convened) against domestic Violence.

Article V

The Congress, whenever two thirds of both Houses shall deem it necessary, shall propose Amendments to this Constitution, or, on the Application of the Legislatures of two thirds of the several States, shall call a Convention for proposing Amendments, which, in either Case, shall be valid to all Intents and Purposes, as Part of this Constitution, when ratified by the Legislatures of three fourths of the several States, or by Conventions in three fourths thereof, as the one or the other Mode of Ratification may be proposed by the Congress; Provided that no Amendment which may be made prior to the Year One thousand eight hundred and eight shall in any Manner affect the first and fourth Clauses in the Ninth Section of the first Article; and that no State, without its Consent, shall be deprived of its equal Suffrage in the Senate.

Article VI

All Debts contracted and Engagements entered into, before the Adoption of this Constitution, shall be as valid against the United States under this Constitution, as under the Confederation.

This Constitution, and the Laws of the United States which shall be made in Pursuance thereof; and all Treaties made, or which shall be made, under the Authority of the United States, shall be the supreme Law of the Land; and the Judges in every State shall be bound thereby, any Thing in the Constitution or Laws of any State to the Contrary notwithstanding.

The Senators and Representatives before mentioned, and the Members of the several State Legislatures, and all executive and judicial Officers, both of the United States and of the several States, shall be bound by Oath or Affirmation, to support this Constitution; but no religious Test shall ever be required as a Qualification to any Office or public Trust under the United States.

Article VII

The Ratification of the Conventions of nine States, shall be sufficient for the Establishment of this Constitution between the States so ratifying the Same.

AMENDMENT I [1791]

Congress shall make no law respecting an establishment of religion, or prohibiting the free exercise thereof; or abridging the freedom of speech, or the press; or the right of the people peaceably to assemble, and to petition the Government for a redress of grievances.

AMENDMENT II [1791]

A well regulated Militia, being necessary to the security of a free State, the right of the people to keep and bear Arms, shall not be infringed.

AMENDMENT III [1791]

No Soldier shall, in time of peace be quartered in any house, without the consent of the Owner, nor in time of war, but in a manner to be prescribed by law.

AMENDMENT IV [1791]

The right of the people to be secure in their persons, houses, papers, and effects, against unreasonable searches and seizures, shall not be violated, and no Warrants shall issue, but upon probable cause, supported by Oath or affirmation, and particularly describing the place to be searched, and the persons or things to be seized.

AMENDMENT V [1791]

No person shall be held to answer for a capital, or otherwise infamous crime, unless on a presentment or indictment of a Grand Jury, except in cases arising in the land or naval forces, or in the Militia, when in actual service in time of War or public danger; nor shall any person be subject for the same offence to be twice put in jeopardy of life or limb; nor shall be compelled in any criminal case to be a witness against himself, nor be deprived of life, liberty, or property, without due process of law; nor shall private property be taken for public use, without just compensation.

AMENDMENT VI [1791]

In all criminal prosecutions, the accused shall enjoy the right to a speedy and public trial, by an impartial jury of the State and district wherein the crime shall have been committed, which district shall have been previously ascertained by law, and to be informed of the nature and cause of the accusation; to be confronted with the Witnesses against him; to have compulsory process for obtaining witnesses in his favor, and to have the Assistance of counsel for his defence.

AMENDMENT VII [1791]

In Suits at common law, where the value in controversy shall exceed twenty dollars, the right of trial by jury shall be preserved, and no fact tried by a jury, shall be otherwise re-examined in any Court of the United States, than according to the rules of the common law.

AMENDMENT VIII [1791]

Excessive bail shall not be required, nor excessive fines imposed, nor cruel and unusual punishments inflicted.

AMENDMENT IX [1791]

The enumeration in the Constitution, of certain rights, shall not be construed to deny or disparage others retained by the people.

AMENDMENT X [1791]

The powers not delegated to the United States by the Constitution, nor prohibited by it to the States, are reserved to the States respectively, or to the people.

AMENDMENT XI [1798]

The Judicial power of the United States shall not be construed to extend to any suit in law or equity, commenced or prosecuted against one of the United States by Citizens of another State, or by Citizens or Subjects of any Foreign State.

AMENDMENT XII [1804]

The Electors shall meet in their respective states and vote by ballot for President and Vice President, one of whom, at least, shall not be an inhabitant of the same state with themselves; they shall name in their ballots the person voted for as President, and in distinct ballots the person voted for as Vice President, and they shall make distinct lists of all persons voted for as President, and of all persons voted for as Vice President, and of the number of votes for each, which lists they shall sign and certify, and transmit sealed to the seat of the government of the United States, directed to the President of the Senate;—The President of the Senate shall, in the presence of the Senate and House of Representatives, open all the certificates and the votes shall then be counted;—The person having the greatest number of votes for President, shall be the President, if such number be a majority of the whole number of Electors appointed; and if no person have such majority, then from the persons having the highest numbers not exceeding three on the list of those voted for as President, the House of Representatives shall choose immediately, by ballot, the President. But in choosing the President, the votes shall be taken by states, the representation from each state having one vote; a quorum for this purpose shall consist of a member or members from two-thirds of the states, and a majority of all the states shall be necessary to a choice. And if the House of Representatives shall not choose a President whenever the right of choice shall devolve upon them, before the fourth day of March next following, then the Vice President shall act as President, as in the case of the death or other constitutional disability of the President. The person having the greatest number of votes as Vice President, shall be the Vice President, if such number be a majority of the whole number of Electors appointed, and if no person have a majority, then from the two highest numbers on the list, the Senate shall choose the Vice President; a quorum for the purpose shall consist of two-thirds of the whole number of Senators, and a majority of the whole number shall be necessary to a choice. But no person constitutionally ineligible to the office of President shall be eligible to that of the Vice President of the United States.

AMENDMENT XIII [1865]

Section 1. Neither slavery nor involuntary servitude, except as a punishment for crime whereof the party shall have been duly convicted, shall exist within the United States, or any place subject to their jurisdiction.

Section 2. Congress shall have power to enforce this article by appropriate legislation.

AMENDMENT XIV [1868]

Section 1. All persons born or naturalized in the United States, and subject to the jurisdiction thereof, are citizens of the United States and of the State wherein they reside. No State shall make or enforce any law which shall abridge the privileges or immunities of citizens of the United States; nor shall any State deprive any person of life, liberty, or property, without due process of law; nor deny to any person within its jurisdiction the equal protection of the laws.

Section 2. Representatives shall be appointed among the several States according to their respective numbers, counting the whole number of persons in each State, excluding Indians not taxed. But when the right to vote at any election for the choice of electors for President and Vice President of the United States, Representatives in Congress, the Executive and Judicial officers of a State, or the members of the Legislature thereof, is denied to any of the male inhabitants of such State, being twenty-one years of age, and citizens of the United States, or in any way abridged, except for participation in rebellion, or other crime, the basis of representation therein shall be reduced in the proportion which the number of such male citizens shall bear to the whole number of male citizens twenty-one years of age in such State.

Section 3. No person shall be a Senator or Representative in Congress, or elector of President and Vice President, or hold any office, civil or military, under the United States, or under any State, who, having previously taken an oath, as a member of Congress, or as an officer of the United States, or as a member of any State legislature, or as an executive or judicial officer of any State, to support the Constitution of the United States, shall have engaged in insurrection or rebellion against the same, or given aid or comfort to the enemies thereof. But Congress may by a vote of two-thirds of each House, remove such disability.

Section 4. The validity of the public debt of the United States, authorized by law, including debts incurred for payment of pensions and bounties for services in suppressing insurrection or rebellion, shall not be questioned. But neither the United States nor any State shall assume or pay any debt or obligation incurred in aid of insurrection or rebellion against the United States, or any claim for the loss or emancipation of any slave; but all such debts, obligations and claims shall be held illegal and void.

Section 5. The Congress shall have power to enforce, by appropriate legislation, the provisions of this article.

AMENDMENT XV [1870]

Section 1. The right of citizens of the United States to vote shall not be denied or abridged by the United States or by any State on account of race, color, or previous condition of servitude.

Section 2. The Congress shall have power to enforce this article by appropriate legislation.

AMENDMENT XVI [1913]

The Congress shall have power to lay and collect taxes on incomes, from whatever source derived, without apportionment among the several States, and without regard to any census or enumeration.

AMENDMENT XVII [1913]

The Senate of the United States shall be composed of two Senators from each State, elected by the people thereof, for six years; and each Senator shall have one vote. The electors in each State shall have the qualifications requisite for electors of the most numerous branch of the State legislatures.

When vacancies happen in the representation of any State in the Senate, the executive authority of each State shall issue writs of election to fill such vacancies; Provided, That the legislature of any State may empower the executive thereof to make temporary appointments until the people fill the vacancies by election as the legislature may direct.

This amendment shall not be so construed as to affect the election or term of any Senator chosen before it becomes valid as part of the Constitution.

AMENDMENT XVIII [1919]

Section 1. After one year from the ratification of this article the manufacture, sale, or transportation of intoxicating liquors within, the importation thereof into, or the exportation thereof from the United States and all territory subject to the jurisdiction thereof for beverage purposes is hereby prohibited.

Section 2. The Congress and the several States shall have concurrent power to enforce this article by appropriate legislation.

Section 3. This article shall be inoperative unless it shall have been ratified as an amendment to the Constitution by the legislatures of the several States, as provided in the Constitution, within seven years from the date of the submission hereof to the States by the Congress.

AMENDMENT XIX [1920]

The right of citizens of the United States to vote shall not be denied or abridged by the United States or by any State on account of sex.

Congress shall have power to enforce this article by appropriate legislation.

AMENDMENT XX [1933]

Section 1. The terms of the President and Vice President shall end at noon on the 20th day of January, and the terms of Senators and Representatives at noon on the 3d day of January, of the years in which such terms would have ended if this article had not been ratified; and the terms of their successors shall then begin.

Section 2. The Congress shall assemble at least once every year, and such meeting shall begin at noon on the 3d day of January, unless they shall by law appoint a different day.

Section 3. If, at the time fixed for the beginning of the term of the President, the President elect shall have died, the Vice President elect shall become President. If a President shall not have been chosen before the time fixed for the beginning of his term, or if the President elect shall have failed to qualify, then the Vice President elect shall act as President until a President shall have qualified: and the Congress may by law provide for the case wherein neither a President elect nor a Vice President elect shall have qualified, declaring who shall then act as President, or the manner in which one who is to act shall be selected, and such person shall act accordingly until a President or Vice President shall have qualified.

Section 4. The Congress may by law provide for the case of the death of any of the persons from whom the House of Representatives may choose a President whenever the right of choice shall have devolved upon them, and for the case of the death of any of the persons from whom the Senate may choose a Vice President whenever the right of choice shall have devolved upon them.

Section 5. Sections 1 and 2 shall take effect on the 15th day of October following the ratification of this article.

Section 6. This article shall be inoperative unless it shall have been ratified as an amendment to the Constitution by the legislatures of three-fourths of the several States within seven years from the date of its submission.

AMENDMENT XXI [1933]

Section 1. The eighteenth article of amendment to the Constitution of the United States is hereby repealed.

Section 2. The transportation or importation into any State, Territory, or possession of the United States for delivery or use therein of intoxicating liquors, in violation of the laws thereof, is hereby prohibited.

Section 3. This article shall be inoperative unless it shall have been ratified as an amendment to the Constitution by conventions in the several States, as provided in the Constitution, within seven years from the date of the submission hereof to the States by the Congress.

AMENDMENT XXII [1951]

Section 1. No person shall be elected to the office of the President more than twice, and no person who has held the office of President, or acted as President, for more than two years of a term to which some other person was elected President shall be elected to the office of the President more than once. But this Article shall not apply to any person holding the office of President when this Article was proposed by the Congress, and shall not prevent any person who may be holding the office of President, or acting as President, during the term within which this Article becomes operative from holding the office of President or acting as President during the remainder of such term.

Section 2. This article shall be inoperative unless it shall have been ratified as an amendment to the Constitution by the legislatures of three-fourths of the several States within seven years from the date of its submission to the States by the Congress.

AMENDMENT XXIII [1961]

Section 1. The District constituting the seat of Government of the United States shall appoint in such manner as the Congress may direct:

A number of electors of President and Vice President equal to the whole number of Senators and Representatives in Congress to which the District would be entitled if it were a State, but in no event more than the least populous State; they shall be in addition to those appointed by the States, but they shall be considered, for the purposes of the election of President and Vice President, to be electors appointed by a State; and they shall meet in the District and perform such duties as provided by the twelfth article of amendment.

Section 2. The Congress shall have power to enforce this article by appropriate legislation.

AMENDMENT XXIV [1964]

Section 1. The right of citizens of the United States to vote in any primary or other election for President or Vice President, for electors for President or Vice President, or for Senator or Representative in Congress, shall not be denied or abridged by the United States or any State by reason of failure to pay any poll tax or other tax.

Section 2. The Congress shall have power to enforce this article by appropriate legislation.

AMENDMENT XXV [1967]

Section 1. In case of the removal of the President from office or of his death or resignation, the Vice President shall become President.

Section 2. Whenever there is a vacancy in the office of the Vice President, the President shall nominate a Vice President who shall take office upon confirmation by a majority vote of both Houses of Congress.

Section 3. Whenever the President transmits to the President pro tempore of the Senate and the Speaker of the House of Representatives his written declaration that he is unable to discharge the powers and duties of his office, and until he transmits to them a written declaration to the contrary, such powers and duties shall be discharged by the Vice President as Acting President.

Section 4. Whenever the Vice President and a majority of either the principal officers of the executive departments or of such other body as Congress may by law provide, transmit to the President pro tempore of the Senate and the Speaker of the House of Representatives their written declaration that the President is unable to discharge the powers and duties of his office, the Vice President shall immediately assume the powers and duties of the office as Acting President.

Thereafter, when the President transmits to the President pro tempore of the Senate and the Speaker of the House of Representatives his written declaration that no inability exists, he shall resume the powers and duties of his office unless the Vice President and a majority of either the principal officers of the executive department or of such other body as Congress may by law provide, transmit within four days to the President pro tempore of the Senate and the Speaker of the House of Representatives their written declaration that the President is unable to discharge the powers and duties of his office. Thereupon Congress shall decide the issue, assembling within forty-eight hours for that purpose if not in session. If the Congress, within twenty-one days after receipt of the latter written declaration, or, if Congress is not in session, within twenty-one days after Congress is required to assemble, determines by two-thirds vote of both Houses that the President is unable to discharge the powers and duties of his office, the Vice President shall continue to discharge the same as Acting President; otherwise, the President shall resume the powers and duties of his office.

AMENDMENT XXVI [1971]

Section 1. The right of citizens of the United States, who are eighteen years of age or older, to vote shall not be denied or abridged by the United States or by any State on account of age.

Section 2. The Congress shall have power to enforce this article by appropriate legislation.

AMENDMENT XXVII [1992]

No law varying the compensation for the services of the senators and representatives shall take effect, until an election of representatives shall have intervened.

APPENDIX D

The Uniform Commercial Code (Excerpts)

Article 1. General Provisions

Section 1-101. Short Title.

This Act shall be known and may be cited as Uniform Commercial Code.

Section 1-102. Purposes; Rules of Construction; Variation by Agreement.

(1) This Act shall be liberally construed and applied to promote its underlying purposes and policies.

(2) Underlying purposes and policies of this Act are

    (a) to simplify, clarify and modernize the law governing commercial transactions;

    (b) to permit the continued expansion of commercial practices through custom, usage, and agreement of the parties;

    (c) to make uniform the law among the various jurisdictions.

(3) The effect of provisions of this Act may be varied by agreement, except as otherwise provided in this Act and except that the obligations of good faith, diligence, reasonableness and care prescribed by this Act may not be disclaimed by agreement but the parties may by agreement determine the standards by which the performance of such obligations is to be measured if such standards are not manifestly unreasonable.

(4) The presence in certain provisions of this Act of the words **"unless otherwise agreed"** or words of similar import does not imply that the effect of other provisions may not be varied by agreement under subsection (3).

(5) In this Act unless the context otherwise requires

    (a) words in the singular number include the plural, and in the plural include the singular;

    (b) words of the masculine gender include the feminine and the neuter, and when the sense so indicates, words of the neuter gender may refer to any gender.

Section 1-106. Remedies to Be Liberally Administered.

(1) The remedies provided by this Act shall be liberally administered to the end that the aggrieved party may be put in as good a position as if the other party had fully performed but neither consequential or special nor penal damages may be had except as specifically provided in this Act or by other rule of law.

(2) Any right or obligation declared by this Act is enforceable by action unless the provision declaring it specifies a different and limited effect.

Section 1-201. **General Definitions.**

Subject to additional definitions contained in the subsequent Articles of this Act which are applicable to specific Articles or Parts thereof, and unless the context otherwise requires, in this Act:

(1) **"Action"** in the sense of a judicial proceeding includes recoupment, counterclaim, set-off, suit in equity, and any other proceedings in which rights are determined.

(2) **"Aggrieved Party"** means a party entitled to resort to a remedy.

(3) **"Agreement"** means the bargain of the parties in fact as found in their language or by implication from other circumstances including course of dealing or usage of trade or course of performance as provided in this Act (Sections 1-205 and 1-206). Whether an agreement has legal consequences is determined by the provisions of this Act, if applicable; otherwise by the law of contracts (Section 1-103). (Compare "Contract".)

(4) **"Bank"** means any person engaged in the business of Banking.

(5) **"Bearer"** means the person in possession of an instrument, document of title, or certificated security payable to bearer or endorsed in blank.

(6) **"Bill of lading"** means a document evidencing the receipt of goods for shipment issued by a person engaged in the business of transporting or forwarding goods, and includes an airbill. "Airbill" means a document serving for air transportation as a bill of lading does for marine or rail transportation, and includes an air consignment note or air waybill.

(7) **"Branch"** includes a separately incorporated foreign branch of a bank.

(8) **"Burden of establishing"** a fact means the burden of persuading the triers of fact that the existence of the fact is more probable than its nonexistence.

(9) **"Buyer in ordinary course of business"** means a person who in good faith and without knowledge that the sale to him is in violation of the ownership rights or security interest of a third party in the goods buys in ordinary course from a person in the business of selling goods of that kind but does not include a pawnbroker. All persons who sell minerals or the like (including oil and gas) at wellhead or mine head shall be deemed to be persons in the business of selling goods of that kind. "Buying" may be for cash or by exchange of other property or on secured or unsecured credit and includes receiving goods or documents of title under a preexisting contract for sale but does not include a transfer in bulk or as security for or in total or partial satisfaction of a money debt.

(10) **"Conspicuous":** A term of clause is conspicuous when it is so written that a reasonable person against whom it is to operate ought to have noticed it. A printed heading in capitals (as: Non-Negotiable Bill of Lading) is conspicuous. Language in the body of a form is "conspicuous" if it is in larger or other contrasting type or color. But in a telegram any stated term is "conspicuous". Whether a term or clause is "conspicuous" or not is for decision by the court.

(11) **"Contract"** means the total legal obligation which results from the parties' agreement as affected by this Act and any other applicable rules of law. (Compare "Agreement".)

(12) **"Creditor"** includes a general creditor, a secured creditor, a lien creditor and any representative of creditors, including an assignee for the benefit of creditors, a trustee in Bankruptcy, a receiver in equity, and an executor or administrator of an insolvent debtor's or assignor's estate.

(13) **"Defendant"** includes a person in the position of defendant in a cross-action or counterclaim.

(14) **"Delivery"** with respect to instruments, documents of title, chattel paper, or certificated securities means voluntary transfer of possession.

(15) **"Document of title"** includes bill of lading, dock warrant, dock receipt, warehouse receipt, or order for the delivery of goods, and also any other document which in the regular course of business or financing is treated as adequately evidencing that the person in possession of it is entitled to receive, hold, and dispose of the document and the goods it covers. To be a document of title, a document must purport to be issued by or addressed to a bailee and purport to cover goods in the bailee's possession which are either identified or are fungible portions of an identified mass.

(16) **"Fault"** means wrongful act, omission, or breach.

(17) **"Fungible"** with respect to goods or securities means goods or securities of which any unit is, by nature or usage of trade, the equivalent of any other like unit. Goods which are not fungible shall be deemed fungible for the purposes of this Act to the extent that under a particular agreement or document unlike units are treated as equivalents.

(18) **"Genuine"** means free of forgery or counterfeiting.

(19) **"Good faith"** means honesty in fact in the conduct or transaction concerned.

(20) **"Holder"** with respect to a negotiable instrument means the person in possession if the instrument is payable to bearer or, in the case of an instrument payable to an identified person, if the identified person is in possession. "Holder" with respect to a document of title means the person in possession if the goods are deliverable to bearer or to the order of the person in possession.

(21) To **"honor"** is to pay or to accept and pay, or where a credit so engages to purchase or discount a draft complying with the terms of the credit.

(22) **"Insolvency proceedings"** include any assignment for the benefit of creditors or other proceedings intended to liquidate or rehabilitate the estate of the person involved.

(23) A person is **"insolvent"** who either has ceased to pay his debts in the ordinary course of business or cannot pay his debts as they become due or is insolvent within the meaning of the federal bankruptcy law.

(24) **"Money"** means a medium of exchange authorized or adopted by a domestic or foreign government and includes a monetary unit of account established by an intergovernmental organization or by agreement between two or more nations.

(25) A person has **"notice"** of a fact when

    (a) he has actual knowledge of it; or

    (b) he has received a notice or notification of it; or

    (c) from all the facts and circumstances known to him at the time in question, he has reason to know that it exists.

A person "knows" or has "knowledge" of a fact when he has actual knowledge of it. "Discover" or "learn" or a word or phrase of similar import refers to knowledge rather than to reason to know. The time and circumstances under which a notice or notification may cease to be effective are not determined by this Act.

(26) A person **"notifies"** or "gives" a notice or notification to another by taking such steps as may be reasonably required to inform the other in ordinary course whether or not such other actually comes to know of it. A person "receives" a notice or notification when

    (a) it comes to his attention; or

    (b) it is duly delivered at the place of business through which the contract was made or at any other place held out by him as the place for receipt of such communications.

(27) Notice, knowledge, or a notice or notification received by an organization is effective for a particular transaction from the time when it is brought to the attention of the individual conducting that transaction, and in any event from the time when it would have been brought to his attention if the organization had exercised due diligence. An organization exercises due diligence if it maintains reasonable routines for communicating significant information to the person conducting the transaction, and there is reasonable compliance with the routines. Due diligence does not require an individual acting for the organization to communicate information unless such communication is part of his regular duties or unless he has reason to know of the transaction and that the transaction would be materially affected by the information.

(28) **"Organization"** includes a corporation, government or governmental subdivision or agency, business trust, estate, trust, partnership or association, two or more persons having a joint or common interest, or any other legal or commercial entity.

(29) **"Party,"** as distinct from **"Third Party,"** means a person who has engaged in a transaction or made an agreement within this Act.

(30) **"Person"** includes an individual or an organization (Section 1-102).

(31) **"Presumption"** or **"presumed"** means that the trier of fact must find the existence of the fact presumed unless and until evidence is introduced which would support a finding of its non existence.

(32) **"Purchase"** includes taking by sale, discount, negotiation, mortgage, pledge, lien, issue or reissue, gift, or any other voluntary transaction creating an interest in property.

(33) **"Purchaser"** means a person who takes by purchase.

(34) **"Remedy"** means any remedial right to which an aggrieved party is entitled with or without resort to a tribunal.

(35) **"Representative"** includes an agent, an officer of a corporation or association, and a trustee, executor, or administrator of an estate, or any other person empowered to act for another.

(36) **"Rights"** includes remedies.

(37) **"Security interest"** means an interest in personal property or fixtures which secures payment or performance of an obligation. The retention or reservation of title by a seller of goods notwithstanding shipment or delivery to the buyer (Section 2-401) is limited in effect to a reservation of a "security interest." The term also includes any interest of a buyer of accounts or chattel paper which is subject to Article 9. The special property interest of a buyer of goods on identification of those goods to a contract for sale under Section 2-401 is not a "security interest," but a buyer may also acquire a "security interest" by complying with Article 9. Unless a consignment is intended as security, reservation of title there under is not a "security interest," but a consignment in any event is subject to the provisions on consignment sales (Section 2-326).

Whether a transaction creates a lease or security interest is determined by the facts of each case; however, a transaction creates a security interest if the consideration the lessee is to pay the lessor for the right to possession and use of the goods is an obligation for the term of the lease not subject to termination by the lessee, and

(a) the original term of the lease is equal to or greater than the remaining economic life of the goods,

(b) the lessee is bound to renew the lease for the remaining economic life of the goods or is bound to become the owner of the goods,

(c) the lessee has an option to renew the lease for the remaining economic life of the goods for no additional consideration or nominal additional consideration upon compliance with the lease agreement, or

(d) the lessee has an option to become the owner of the goods for no additional consideration or nominal additional consideration upon compliance with the lease agreement.

A transaction does not create a security interest merely because it provides that

(a) the present value of the consideration the lessee is obligated to pay the lessor for the right to possession and use of the goods is substantially equal to or is greater than the fair market value of the goods at the time the lease is entered into,

(b) the lessee assumes risk of loss of the goods, or agrees to pay taxes, insurance, filing, recording, or registration fees, or service or maintenance costs with respect to the goods,

(c) the lessee has an option to renew the lease or to become the owner of the goods,

(d) the lessee has an option to renew the lease for a fixed rent that is equal to or greater than the reasonably predictable fair market rent for the use of the goods for the term of the renewal at the time the option is to be performed, or

(e) the lessee has an option to become the owner of the goods for a fixed price that is equal to or greater than the reasonably predictable fair market value of the goods at the time the option is to be performed.

For purposes of this subsection (37):

(x) Additional consideration is not nominal if (i) when the option to renew the lease is granted to the lessee the rent is stated to be the fair market rent for the use of the goods for the term of the renewal determined at the time the option is to be performed, or (ii) when the option to become the owner of the goods is granted to the lessee, the price is stated to be the fair market value of the goods determined at the time the option is to be performed. Additional consideration is nominal, if it is less than the lessee's reasonably predictable cost of performing under the lease agreement if the option is not exercised;

(y) **"Reasonably predictable"** and **"remaining economic life of the goods"** are to be determined with reference to the facts and circumstances at the time the transaction is entered into; and

(z) **"Present Value"** means the amount as of a date certain of one or more sums payable in the future, discounted to the date certain. The discount is determined by the interest rate specified by the parties, if the rate is not manifestly unreasonable at the time the transaction is entered into; otherwise, the discount is determined by a commercially reasonable rate that takes into account the facts and circumstances of each case at the time the transaction was entered into.

(38) **"Send"** in connection with any writing or notice means to deposit in the mail or deliver for transmission by any other usual means of communication with postage or cost of transmission provided for and properly addressed and in the case of an instrument to an address specified thereon or otherwise agreed, or if there be none to any address reasonable under the circumstances. The receipt of any writing or notice within the time at which it would have arrived if properly sent has the effect of a proper sending.

(39) **"Signed"** includes any symbol executed or adopted by a party with present intention to authenticate a writing.

(40) **"Surety"** includes guarantor.

(41) **"Telegram"** includes a message transmitted by radio, teletype, cable, any mechanical method of transmission or the like.

(42) **"Term"** means that portion of an agreement which relates to a particular matter.

(43) **"Unauthorized"** signature means one made without actual, implied, or apparent authority and includes a forgery.

(44) **"Value."** Except as otherwise provided with respect to negotiable instruments and bank collections (Sections 3-303, 4-208 and 4-209), a person gives "value" for rights if he acquires them

    (a) in return for a binding commitment to extend credit or for the extension of immediately available credit whether or not drawn upon and whether or not a charge back is provided for in the event of difficulties in collection; or

    (b) as security for or in total or partial satisfaction of a preexisting claim; or

    (c) by accepting delivery pursuant to a preexisting contract for purchase; or

    (d) generally, in return for any consideration sufficient to support a simple contract.

(45) **"Warehouse receipt"** means a receipt issued by a person engaged in the business of storing goods for hire.

(46) **"Written"** or **"writing"** includes printing, typewriting, or any other intentional reduction to tangible form.

Section 1-202. **Prima Facie Evidence by Third-Party Documents.**

A document in due form purporting to be a bill of lading, policy or certificate of insurance, official weigher's or inspector's certificate, consular invoice, or any other document authorized or required by the contract to be issued by a third party shall be prima facie evidence of its own authenticity and genuineness and of the facts stated in the document by the third party.

Section 1-203. **Obligation of good faith.**

Every contract or duty within this Act imposes an obligation of good faith in its performance or enforcement.

Section 1-204. **Time; Reasonable Time; "Seasonably."**

(1) Whenever this Act requires any action to be taken within a reasonable time, any time which is not manifestly unreasonable may be fixed by agreement.

(2) What is a reasonable time for taking any action depends on the nature, purpose, and circumstances of such action.

(3) An action is taken **"seasonably"** when it is taken at or within the time agreed or if no time is agreed at or within a reasonable time.

Section 1-205. **Course of Dealing and Usage of Trade.**

(1) A course of dealing is a sequence of previous conduct between the parties to a particular transaction which is fairly to be regarded as establishing a common basis of understanding for interpreting their expressions and other conduct.

(2) A usage of trade is any practice or method of dealing having such regularity of observance in a place, vocation, or trade as to justify an expectation that it will be observed with respect to the transaction in question. The existence and scope of such a usage are to be proved as facts. If it is established that such a usage is embodied in a written trade code or similar writing, the interpretation of the writing is for the court.

(3) A course of dealing between parties and any usage of trade in the vocation or trade in which they are engaged, or of which they are or should be aware, give particular meaning to and supplement or qualify terms of an agreement.

(4) The express terms of an agreement and an applicable course of dealing or usage of trade shall be construed wherever reasonable as consistent with each other; but when such construction is unreasonable, express terms control both course of dealing and usage of trade, and course of dealing controls usage of trade.

(5) An applicable usage of trade in the place where any part of performance is to occur shall be used in interpreting the agreement as to that part of the performance.

(6) Evidence of a relevant usage of trade offered by one party is not admissible unless and until he has given the other party such notice as the court finds sufficient to prevent unfair surprise to the latter.

Article 2. Sales

Part 1 **Short Title, General Construction and Subject Matter**

Section 2-101. **Short Title.**

This Article shall be known and may be cited as Uniform Commercial Code-Sales.

Section 2-102. **Scope; Certain Security and Other Transactions Excluded from This Article.**

Unless the context otherwise requires, this Article applies to transactions in goods; it does not apply to any transaction which, although in the form of an unconditional contract to sell or present sale, is intended to operate only as a security transaction, nor does this Article impair or repeal any statute regulating sales to consumers, farmers, or other specified classes of buyers.

Section 2-103. **Definitions and Index of Definitions.**

(1) In this Article, unless the context otherwise requires,

(a) "Buyer" means a person who buys or contracts to buy goods.

(b) "Good faith" in the case of a merchant means honesty in fact and the observance of reasonable commercial standards of fair dealing in the trade.

(c) "Receipt" of goods means taking physical possession of them.

(d) "Seller" means a person who sells or contracts to sell goods.

Section 2-104. **Definitions: "Merchant"; "Between Merchants"; "Financing Agency."**

(1) "Merchant" means a person who deals in goods of the kind or otherwise by his occupation holds himself out as having knowledge or skill peculiar to the practices or goods involved in the transaction or to whom such knowledge or skill may be attributed by his employment of an agent or broker or other intermediary who by his occupation holds himself out as having such knowledge or skill.

(2) "Financing agency" means a bank, finance company, or other person who in the ordinary course of business makes advances against goods or documents of title or who by arrangement with either the seller or the buyer intervenes in ordinary course to make or collect payment due or claimed under the contract for sale, as by purchasing or paying the seller's draft or making advances against it or by merely taking it for collection whether or not documents of title accompany the draft. "Financing agency" includes also a bank or other person who similarly intervenes between persons who are in the position of seller and buyer in respect to the goods (Section 2-707).

(3) "Between merchants" means in any transaction with respect to which both parties are chargable with the knowledge or skill of merchants.

Section 2-105. **Definitions: Transferability; "Goods"; "Future" Goods; "Lot"; "Commercial Unit."**

(1) "Goods" means all things (including specially manufactured goods) which are movable at the time of identification to the contract for sale other than the money in which the price is to be paid, investment securities (Article 8), and things in action. "Goods" also includes the unborn young of animals and growing crops and other identified things attached to realty as described in the section on goods to be severed from realty (Section 2-107).

(2) Goods must be both existing and identified before any interest in them can pass. Goods which are not both existing and identified are "future" goods. A purported present sale of future goods or of any interest therein operates as a contract to sell.

(3) There may be a sale of a part interest in existing identified goods.

(4) An undivided share in an identified bulk of fungible goods is sufficiently identified to be sold although the quantity of the bulk is not determined. Any agreed proportion of such a bulk or any quantity thereof agreed upon by number, weight, or other measure may to the extent of the seller's interest in the bulk be sold to the buyer who then becomes an owner in common.

(5) "Lot" means a parcel or a single article which is the subject matter of a separate sale or delivery, whether or not it is sufficient to perform the contract.

(6) "Commercial unit" means such a unit of goods as by commercial usage is a single whole for purposes of sale and division of which materially impairs its character or value on the market or in use. A commercial unit may be a single article (as a machine) or a set of articles (as a suite of furniture or an assortment of sizes) or a quantity (as a bale, gross, or carload) or any other unit treated in use or in the relevant market as a single whole.

Part 2 **Form, Formation, and Readjustment of Contract**

Section 2-201. **Formal Requirements; Statute of Frauds.**

(1) Except as otherwise provided in this section, a contract for the sale of goods for the price of $500 or more is not enforceable by way of action or defense unless there is some writing sufficient to indicate that a contract for sale has been made between the parties and signed by the party against whom enforcement is sought or by his authorized agent or broker. A writing is not insufficient because it omits or incorrectly states a term agreed upon, but the contract is not enforceable under this paragraph beyond the quantity of goods shown in such writing.

(2) Between merchants if within a reasonable time a writing in confirmation of the contract and sufficient against the sender is received and the party receiving it has reason to know its contents, it satisfies the requirements of subsection (1) against such party unless written notice of objection to its contents is given within ten days after it is received.

(3) A contract which does not satisfy the requirements of subsection (1) but which is valid in other respects is enforceable

   (a) if the goods are to be specially manufactured for the buyer and are not suitable for sale to others in the ordinary course of the seller's business and the seller, before notice of repudiation is received and under circumstances which reasonably indicate that the goods are for the buyer, has made either a substantial beginning of their manufacture or commitments for their procurement; or

   (b) if the party against whom enforcement is sought admits in his pleading, testimony, or otherwise in court that a contract for sale was made, but the contract is not enforceable under this provision beyond the quantity of goods admitted; or

   (c) with respect to goods for which payment has been made and accepted or which have been received and accepted (Section 2-606).

Section 2-202. **Final Written Expression: Parol or Extrinsic Evidence.**

Terms with respect to which the confirmatory memoranda of the parties agree or which are otherwise set forth in a writing intended by the parties as a final expression of their agreement with respect to such terms as are included therein may not be contradicted by evidence of any prior agreement or of a contemporaneous oral agreement but may be explained or supplemented

(a) by course of dealing or usage of trade (Section 1-205) or by course of performance (Section 2-208); and

(b) by evidence of consistent additional terms unless the court finds the writing to have been intended also as a complete and exclusive statement of the terms of the agreement.

Section 2-203. **Seals Inoperative.**

The affixing of a seal to a writing evidencing a contract for sale or an offer to buy or sell goods does not constitute the writing of a sealed instrument, and the law with respect to sealed instruments does not apply to such a contract or offer.

Section 2-204. **Formation in General.**

(1) A contract for sale of goods may be made in any manner sufficient to show agreement, including conduct by both parties which recognizes the existence of such a contract.

(2) An agreement sufficient to constitute a contract for sale may be found even though the moment of its making is undetermined.

(3) Even though one or more terms are left open, a contract for sale does not fail for indefiniteness if the parties have intended to make a contract and there is a reasonably certain basis for giving an appropriate remedy.

Section 2-205. **Firm Offers.**

An offer by a merchant to buy or sell goods in a signed writing which by its terms gives assurance that it will be held open is not revocable, for lack of consideration, during the time stated or if no time is stated for a reasonable time, but in no event may such period of irrevocability exceed three months; but any such term of assurance on a form supplied by the offeree must be separately signed by the offeror.

Section 2-206. **Offer and Acceptance in Formation of Contract.**

(1) Unless otherwise unambiguously indicated by the language or circumstances

  (a) an offer to make a contract shall be construed as inviting acceptance in any manner and by any medium reasonable in the circumstances;

  (b) an order or other offer to buy goods for prompt or current shipment shall be construed as inviting acceptance, either by a prompt promise to ship or by the prompt or current shipment of conforming or nonconforming goods, but such a shipment of non-conforming goods does not constitute an acceptance if the seller seasonably notifies the buyer that the shipment is offered only as an accommodation to the buyer.

(2) Where the beginning of a requested performance is a reasonable mode of acceptance, an offeror who is not notified of acceptance within a reason able time may treat the offer as having lapsed before acceptance.

Section 2-207. **Additional Terms in Acceptance or Confirmation.**

(1) A definite and seasonable expression of acceptance or a written confirmation which is sent within a reasonable time operates as an acceptance even though it states terms additional to or different from those offered or agreed upon, unless acceptance is expressly made conditional on assent to the additional or different terms.

(2) The additional terms are to be construed as proposals for addition to the contract. Between merchants such terms become part of the contract unless:

    (a) the offer expressly limits acceptance to the terms of the offer;

    (b) they materially alter it; or

    (c) notification of objection to them has already been given or is given within a reasonable time after notice of them is received.

(3) Conduct by both parties which recognizes the existence of a contract is sufficient to establish a contract for sale although the writings of the parties do not otherwise establish a contract. In such case the terms of the particular contract consist of those terms on which the writings of the parties agree, together with any supplementary terms incorporated under any other provisions of this Act.

Section 2-208. Course of Performance or Practical Construction.

(1) Where the contract for sale involves repeated occasions for performance by either party with knowledge of the nature of the performance and opportunity for objection to it by the other, any course of performance accepted or acquiesced in without objection shall be relevant to determine the meaning of the agreement.

(2) The express terms of the agreement and any such course of performance, as well as any course of dealing and usage of trade, shall be construed whenever reasonable as consistent with each other; but when such construction is unreasonable, express terms shall control course of performance, and course of performance shall control both course of dealing and usage of trade (Section 1-205).

(3) Subject to the provisions of the next section on modification and waiver, such course of performance shall be relevant to show a waiver or modification of any term inconsistent with such course of performance.

Section 2-209. Modification, Rescission, and Waiver.

(1) An agreement modifying a contract within this Article needs no consideration to be binding.

(2) A signed agreement which excludes modification or rescission except by a signed writing cannot be otherwise modified or rescinded, but except as between merchants such a requirement on a form supplied by the merchant must be separately signed by the other party.

(3) The requirements of the statute of frauds section of this Article (Section 2-201) must be satisfied if the contract as modified is within its provisions.

(4) Although an attempt at modification or rescission does not satisfy the requirements of subsection (2) or (3), it can operate as a waiver.

(5) A party who has made a waiver affecting an executory portion of the contract may retract the waiver by reasonable notification received by the other party that strict performance will be required of any term waived, unless the retraction would be unjust in view of a material change of position in reliance on the waiver.

Section 2-305. Open Price Term.

(1) The parties if they so intend can conclude a contract for sale even though the price is not settled. In such a case the price is a reasonable price at the time for delivery if

    (a) nothing is said as to price; or

    (b) the price is left to be agreed by the parties and they fail to agree; or

    (c) the price is to be fixed in terms of some agreed market or other standard as set or recorded by a third person or agency, and it is not so set or recorded.

(2) A price to be fixed by the seller or by the buyer means a price for him to fix in good faith.

(3) When a price left to be fixed otherwise than by agreement of the parties fails to be fixed through fault of one party, the other may at his option treat the contract as cancelled or himself fix a reasonable price.

(4) Where, however, the parties intend not to be bound unless the price be fixed or agreed, and it is not fixed or agreed, there is no contract. In such a case, the buyer must return any goods already received or, if unable so to do, must pay their reasonable value at the time of delivery, and the seller must return any portion of the price paid on account.

Section 2-309. **Absence of Specific Time Provisions; Notice of Termination.**

(1) The time for shipment or delivery, or any other action under a contract if not provided in this Article or agreed upon, shall be a reasonable time.

(2) Where the contract provides for successive performances but is indefinite in duration, it is valid for a reasonable time but unless otherwise agreed may be terminated at any time by either party.

(3) Termination of a contract by one party except on the happening of an agreed event requires that reasonable notification be received by the other party, and an agreement dispensing with notification is invalid if its operation would be unconscionable.

Section 2-311. **Options and Cooperation Respecting Performance.**

(1) An agreement for sale which is otherwise sufficiently definite (subsection 3 of Section 2-204) to be a contract is not made invalid by the fact that it leaves particulars of performance to be specified by one of the parties. Any such specification must be made in good faith and within limits set by commercial reasonableness.

(2) Unless otherwise agreed specifications relating to assortment of the goods are at the buyer's option, and except as otherwise provided in subsections (1)(c) and (3) of Section 2-319, specifications or arrangements relating to shipment are at the seller's option.

(3) Where such specification would materially affect the other party's performance but is not seasonably made or where one party's cooperation is necessary to the agreed performance of the other but is not seasonably forthcoming, the other party in addition to all other remedies

    (a) is excused for any resulting delay in his own performance; and

    (b) may also either proceed to perform in any reasonable manner or after die time for a material part of his own performance treat die failure to specify or to cooperate as a breach by failure to deliver or accept the goods.

Section 2-312. **Warranty of Tide and Against Infringement; Buyer's Obligation Against Infringement.**

(1) Subject to subsection

(2) there is in a contract for sale a warranty by the seller that

    (a) the title conveyed shall be good, and its transfer rightful; and

    (b) the goods shall be delivered free from any security interest or other lien or encumbrance of which the buyer at the time of contracting has no knowledge.

(3) A warranty under subsection (1) will be excluded or modified only by specific language or by circumstances which give the buyer reason to know that the person selling does not claim title in himself or that he is purporting to sell only such right or title as he or a third person may have.

(4) Unless otherwise agreed a seller who is a merchant regularly dealing in goods of the kind warrants that the goods shall be delivered free of the rightful claim of any third person by way of infringement or the like, but a buyer who furnishes

specifications to the seller must hold the seller harmless against any such claim which arises out of compliance with the specifications.

Section 2-313. **Express Warranties by Affirmation, Promise, Description, Sample.**

(1) Express warranties by the seller are created as follows:

    (a) Any affirmation of fact or promise made by the seller to the buyer which relates to the goods and becomes part of the basis of the bargain creates an express warranty that the goods shall conform to the affirmation or promise.

    (b) description of the goods which is made part of the basis of the bargain creates an express warranty that the goods shall conform to the description.

    (c) Any sample or model which is made part of the basis of the bargain creates an express warranty that the whole of the goods shall conform to the sample or model.

(2) It is not necessary to the creation of an express warranty that the seller use formal words such as "warrant" or "guarantee" or that he have a specific intention to make a warranty, but an affirmation merely of the value of the goods or a statement purporting to be merely the seller's opinion or commendation of the goods does not create a warranty.

Section 2-314. **Implied Warranty: Merchantability; Usage of Trade.**

(1) Unless excluded or modified (Section 2-316), a warranty tiiat the goods shall be merchantable is implied in a contract for their sale if the seller is a merchant with respect to goods of that kind. Under this section the serving for value of food or drink to be consumed either on the premises or elsewhere is a sale.

(2) Goods to be merchantable must be at least such as

    (a) pass witthout objection in the trade under the contract description; and

    (b) in the case of fungible goods, are of fair average quality within the description; and

    (c) are fit for the ordinary purposes for which such goods are used; and

    (d) run, within the variations permitted by the agreement, of even kind, quality, and quantity within each unit and among all units involved; and

    (e) are adequately contained, packaged, and labeled as the agreement may require; and

    (f) conform to the promises or affirmations of fact made on the container or label if any.

(3) Unless excluded or modified (Section 2-316) other implied warranties may arise from course of dealing or usage of trade.

Section 2-315. **Implied Warranty: Fitness for Particular Purpose.**

Where the seller at the time of contracting has reason to know any particular purpose for which the goods are required and that the buyer is relying on the seller's skill or judgment to select or furnish suitable goods, there is unless excluded or modified under the next section an implied warranty that the goods shall be fit for such purpose.

Section 2-316. **Exclusion or Modification of Warranties.**

(1) Words or conduct relevant to the creation of an express warranty and words or conduct tending to negate or limit warranty shall be construed wherever reasonable as consistent with each other; but subject to the provisions of this Article on parol

or extrinsic evidence (Section 2-202), negation or limitation is inoperative to the extent that such construction is unreasonable.

(2) Subject to subsection (3), to exclude or modify the implied warranty of merchantability or any part of it, the language must mention merchantability and in case of a writing must be conspicuous, and to exclude or modify any implied warranty of fitness the exclusion must be by a writing and conspicuous. Language to exclude all implied warranties of fitness is sufficient if it states, for example, that "There are no warranties which extend beyond the description on the face hereof."

(3) Notwithstanding subsection (2)

    (a) unless the circumstances indicate otherwise, all implied warranties are excluded by expressions like "as is," "with all faults," or other language which in common understanding calls the buyer's attention to the exclusion of warranties and makes plain that there is no implied warranty; and

    (b) when the buyer before entering into the contract has examined the goods or the sample or model as fully as he desired or has refused to examine the goods, there is no implied warranty with regard to defects which an examination ought in the circumstances to have revealed to him; and

    (c) an implied warranty can also be excluded or modified by course of dealing or course of performance or usage of trade.

(4) Remedies for breach of warranty can be limited in accordance with the provisions of this Article on liquidation or limitation of damages and on contractual modification of remedy (Sections 2-718 and 2-719).

Part 4 Tide, Creditors, and Good Faith Purchasers

Section 2-401. Passing of Tide; Reservation for Security; Limited Application of This Section.

Each provision of this Article with regard to the rights, obligations, and remedies of the seller, the buyer, purchasers, or other third parties applies irrespective of title to the goods except where the provision refers to such title. Insofar as situations are not covered by the other provisions of this Article and matters concerning title became material, the following rules apply:

(1) Title to goods cannot pass under a contract for sale prior to their identification to the contract (Section 2-501), and unless otherwise explicitly agreed, the buyer acquires by their identification a special property as limited by this Act. Any retention or reservation by the seller of the title (property) in goods shipped or delivered to the buyer is limited in effect to a reservation of a security interest. Subject to these provisions and to the provisions of the Article on Secured Transactions (Article 9), title to goods passes from the seller to the buyer in any manner and on any conditions explicitly agreed on by the parties.

(2) Unless otherwise explicitly agreed, title passes to the buyer at the time and place at which the seller completes his performance with reference to the physical delivery of the goods, despite any reservation of a security interest and even though a document of title is to be delivered at a different time or place; and in particular and despite any reservation of a security interest by the bill of lading

    (a) if the contract requires or authorizes the seller to send the goods to the buyer but does not require him to deliver them at destination, title passes to the buyer at the time and place of shipment; but

    (b) if the contract requires delivery at destination, tide passes on tender there.

(3) Unless otherwise explicitly agreed, where delivery is to be made without moving the goods,

    (a) if the seller is to deliver a document of title, title passes at the time when and the place where he delivers such documents; or

    (b) if the goods are at the time of contracting already identified and no documents are to be delivered, title passes at the time and place of contracting.

(4) A rejection or other refusal by the buyer to receive or retain the goods, whether or not justified, or a justified revocation of acceptance revests title to the goods in the seller. Such revesting occurs by operation of law and is not a "sale".

Part 5 Performance

Section 2-507. **Effect of Seller's Tender; Delivery on Condition.**

(1) Tender of delivery is a condition to the buyer's duty to accept the goods and, unless otherwise agreed, to his duty to pay for them. Tender entitles the seller to acceptance of the goods and to payment according to the contract.

(2) Where payment is due and demanded on the delivery to the buyer of goods or documents of title, his right as against the seller to retain or dispose of them is conditional upon his making the payment due.

Section 2-508. **Cure by Seller of Improper Tender or Delivery; Replacement.**

(1) Where any tender or delivery by the seller is rejected because non conforming and the time for performance has not yet expired, the seller may seasonably notify the buyer of his intention to cure and may then within the contract time make a conforming delivery.

(2) Where the buyer rejects a non conforming tender which the seller had reasonable grounds to believe would be acceptable with or without money allowance, the seller may if he seasonably notifies the buyer have a further reasonable time to substitute a conforming tender.

Section 2-513. **Buyer's Right to Inspection of Goods.**

(1) Unless otherwise agreed and subject to subsection (3), where goods are tendered or delivered or identified to the contract for sale, the buyer has a right before payment or acceptance to inspect them at any reasonable place and time and in any reasonable manner. When the seller is required or authorized to send the goods to the buyer, the inspection may be after their arrival.

(2) Expenses of inspection must be borne by the buyer but may be recovered from the seller if the goods do not conform and are rejected.

(3) Unless otherwise agreed and subject to the provisions of this Article on C.I.F. contracts (subsection 3 of Section 2-321), the buyer is not entitled to inspect the goods before payment of the price when the contract provides

    (a) for delivery "C.O.D." or on other like terms; or

    (b) for payment against documents of title, except where such payment is due only after the goods are to become available for inspection.

(4) A place or method of inspection fixed by the parties is presumed to be exclusive, but unless otherwise expressly agreed, it does not postpone identification or shift the place for delivery or for passing the risk of loss. If compliance becomes impossible, inspection shall be as provided in this section, unless the place or method fixed was clearly intended as an indispensable condition failure of which avoids the contract.

Part 6 **Breach, Repudiation, and Excuse**

Section 2-601. **Buyer's Rights on Improper Delivery.**
Subject to the provisions of this Article on breach in installment contracts (Section 2-612) and unless otherwise agreed under the sections on contractual limitations of remedy (Sections 2-718 and 2-719), if the goods or the tender of delivery fail in any respect to conform to the contract, the buyer may

(a) reject the whole; or

(b) accept the whole; or

(c) accept any commercial unit or units and reject the rest.

Section 2-606. **What Constitutes Acceptance of Goods.**

(1) Acceptance of goods occurs when the buyer

    (a) after a reasonable opportunity to inspect the goods signifies to the seller that the goods are conforming or that he will take or retain them in spite of their non conformity; or

    (b) fails to make an effective rejection (subsection 1 of Section 2-602), but such acceptance does not occur until the buyer has had a reasonable opportunity to inspect them; or

    (c) does any act inconsistent with the seller's ownership; but if such act is wrongful as against the seller, it is an acceptance only if ratified by him.

(2) Acceptance of a part of any commercial unit is acceptance of that entire unit.

Section 2-607. **Effect of Acceptance; Notice of Breach; Burden of Establishing Breach After Acceptance; Notice of Claim or Litigation to Person Answerable Over.**

(1) The buyer must pay at the contract rate for any goods accepted.

(2) Acceptance of goods by the buyer precludes rejection of the goods accepted and if made with knowledge of a non conformity cannot be revoked because of it, unless the acceptance was on the reasonable assumption that the non conformity would be seasonably cured but acceptance does not of itself impair any other remedy provided by this Article for non conformity.

(3) Where a tender has been accepted

    (a) the buyer must within a reasonable time after he discovers or should have discovered any breach notify the seller of breach or be barred from any remedy; and

    (b) if the claim is one for infringement or the like (subsection 3 of Section 2-312) and the buyer is sued as a result of such a breach, he must so notify the seller within a reasonable time after he receives notice of the litigation or be barred from any remedy for liability established by the litigation.

(4) The burden is on the buyer to establish any breach with respect to the goods accepted.

(5) Where the buyer is sued for breach of a warranty or other obligation for which his seller is answerable over

    (a) he may give his seller written notice of the litigation. If the notice states that the seller may come in and defend, and that if the seller does not do so he will be bound in any action against him by his buyer by any determination of fact common to the two litigations, then unless the seller after seasonable receipt of the notice does come in and defend he is so bound.

    (b) if the claim is one for infringement or the like (subsection 3 of Section 2-312) the original seller may demand in writing that his buyer turn over to him control of the litigation including settlement or else be barred from any remedy over, and if he also agrees to bear all expense and to satisfy any adverse judgment, then unless the buyer after seasonable receipt of the demand does turn over control, the buyer is so barred.

(6) The provisions of subsections (3), (4) and (5) apply to any obligation of a buyer to hold the seller harmless against infringement or the like (subsection 3 of Section 2-312).

Section 2-608. **Revocation of Acceptance in Whole or in Part.**

(1) The buyer may revoke his acceptance of a lot or commercial unit whose non conformity substantially impairs its value to him if he has accepted it

    (a) on the reasonable assumption that its non conformity would be cured and it has not been seasonably cured; or

    (b) without discovery of such non conformity if his acceptance was reasonably induced either by the difficulty of discovery before acceptance or by the seller's assurances.

(2) Revocation of acceptance must occur within a reasonable time after the buyer discovers or should have discovered the ground for it and before any substantial change in condition of the goods which is not caused by their own defects. It is not effective until the buyer notifies the seller of it.

(3) A buyer who so revokes has the same rights and duties with regard to the goods involved as if he had rejected them.

Part 7 **Remedies**

Section 2-703. **Seller's Remedies in General.**

Where the buyer wrongfully rejects or revokes acceptance of goods or fails to make a payment due on or before delivery or repudiates with respect to a part or the whole, then with respect to any goods directly affected and, if the breach is of the whole contract (Section 2-612), then also with respect to the whole undelivered balance, the aggrieved seller may

    (a) withhold delivery of such goods;

    (b) stop delivery by any bailee as hereafter provided (Section 2-705);

    (c) proceed under the next section respecting goods still unidentified to the contract;

    (d) resell and recover damages as hereafter provided (Section 2-706);

    (e) recover damages for non-acceptance (Section 2-708) or in a proper case the price (Section 2-709);

    (f) cancel.

Section 2-710. **Seller's Incidental Damages.**

Incidental damages to an aggrieved seller include any commercially reasonable charges, expenses, or commissions incurred in stopping delivery; in the transportation, care, and custody of goods after the buyer's breach, in connection with return or resale of the goods or otherwise resulting from the breach.

Section 2-711. **Buyer's Remedies in General; Buyer's Security Interest in Rejected Goods.**

(1) Where die seller fails to make delivery or repudiates, or die buyer rightfully rejects or justifiably revokes acceptance then with respect to any goods involved, and with respect to the whole if the breach goes to the whole contract (Section 2-612), the buyer may cancel and, whether or not he has done so, may in addition to recovering so much of the price as has been paid

    (a) "cover" and have damages under the next section as to all the goods affected whether or not they have been identified to the contract; or

    (b) recover damages for non delivery as provided in this Article (Section 2-713).

(2) Where the seller fails to deliver or repudiates, the buyer may also

    (a) if the goods have been identified recover them as provided in this Article (Section 2-502); or

    (b) in a proper case obtain specific performance or replevy the goods as provided in this Article (Section 2-716).

(3) On rightful rejection or justifiable revocation of acceptance, a buyer has a security interest in goods in his possession or control for any payments made on their price and any expenses reasonably incurred in their inspection, receipt, transportation, care, and custody and may hold such goods and resell them in like manner as an aggrieved seller (Section 2-706).

Section 2-712. "Cover"; Buyer's Procurement of Substitute Goods.

(1) After a breach within the preceding section, the buyer may "cover" by making in good faith and without unreasonable delay any reasonable purchase of or contract to purchase goods in substitution for those due from the seller.

(2) The buyer may recover from the seller as damages the difference between the cost of cover and the contract price together with any incidental or consequential damages as hereinafter defined (Section 2-715), but less expenses saved in consequence of the seller's breach.

(3) Failure of the buyer to effect cover within this section does not bar him from any other remedy.

Section 2-715. Buyer's Incidental and Consequential Damages.

(1) Incidental damages resulting from the seller's breach include expenses reasonably incurred in inspection, receipt, transportation, and care and custody of goods rightfully rejected, any commercially reasonable charges, expenses, or commissions in connection with effecting cover and any other reasonable expense incident to the delay or other breach.

(2) Consequential damages resulting from the seller's breach include

    (a) any loss resulting from general or particular requirements and needs of which the seller at the time of contracting had reason to know and which could not reasonably be prevented by cover or otherwise; and

    (b) injury to person or property proximately resulting from any breach of warranty.

Article 3. Negotiable Instruments

Part 1 General Provisions and Definitions

Section 3-104. Form of Negotiable Instruments; "Draft"; "Check"; "Certificate of Deposit"; "Note."

(1) Any writing to be a negotiable instrument within this Article must

    (a) be signed by the maker or drawer; and

    (b) contain an unconditional promise or order to pay a sum certain in money and no other promise, order, obligation, or power given by the maker or drawer except as authorized by this Article; and

    (c) be payable on demand or at a definite time; and

    (d) be payable to order or to bearer.

(2) A writing which complies with the requirements of this section is

   (a) a "draft" ("bill of exchange") if it is an order;
   (b) a "check" if it is a draft drawn on a bank and payable on demand;
   (c) a "certificate of deposit" if it is an acknowledgment by a bank receipt of money with an engagement to repay it;
   (d) a "note" if it is a promise other than a certificate of deposit.

(3) As used in other Articles of this Act, and as the context may require, the terms "draft," "check," "certificate of deposit," and "note" may refer to instruments which are not negotiable within this Article as well as to instruments which are so negotiable.

Section 3-105. **When Promise or Order Unconditional.**

(1) A promise or order otherwise unconditional is not made conditional by the fact that the instrument

   (a) is subject to implied or constructive conditions; or
   (b) states its consideration, whether performed or promised, or the transaction which gave rise to the instrument, or that the promise or order is made, or the instrument matures in accordance with or "as per" such transaction; or
   (c) refers to or states that it arises out of a separate agreement or refers to a separate agreement for rights as to prepayment or acceleration; or
   (d) states that it is drawn under a letter of credit; or
   (e) states that it is secured, whether by mortgage, reservation of title, or otherwise; or
   (f) indicates a particular account to be debited or any other fund or source from which reimbursement is expected; or
   (g) is limited to payment out of a particular fund or the proceeds of a particular source, if the instrument is issued by a government or governmental agency or unit; or
   (h) is limited to payment out of the entire assets of a partnership, unincorporated association, trust, or estate by or on behalf of which the instrument is issued.

(2) A promise or order is not unconditional if the instrument

   (a) states that it is subject to or governed by any other agreement; or
   (b) states that it is to be paid only out of a particular fund or source except as provided in this section.

Section 3-106. **Sum Certain.**

(1) The sum payable is a sum certain even though it is to be paid

   (a) with stated interest or by stated installments; or
   (b) with stated different rates of interest before and after default or a specified date; or
   (c) with a stated discount or addition if paid before or after the date fixed for payment; or
   (d) with exchange or less exchange, whether at a fixed rate or at the current rate; or
   (e) with costs of collection or an attorney's fee or both upon default.

(2) Nothing in this section shall validate any term which is otherwise illegal.

Section 3-110. **Payable to Order.**

(1) An instrument is payable to order when by its terms it is payable to the order or assigns of any person therein specified with reasonable certainty, or to him or his order, or when it is conspicuously designated on its face as "exchange" or the like and names a payee. It may be payable to the order of

(a) the maker or drawer; or

(b) the drawee; or

(c) a payee who is not maker, drawer, or drawee; or

(d) two or more payees together or in the alternative; or

(e) an estate, trust, or fund, in which case it is payable to the order of the representative of such estate, trust, or fund or his successors; or

(f) an office, or an officer by his title as such, in which case it is payable to the principal, but the incumbent of the office or his successors may act as if he or they were the holder; or

(g) a partnership or unincorporated association, in which case it is payable to the partnership or association and may be endorsed or transferred by any person thereto authorized.

(2) An instrument not payable to order is not made so payable by such words as "payable upon return of this instrument properly endorsed."

(3) An instrument made payable both to order and to bearer is payable to order unless the bearer words are handwritten or typewritten.

Section 3-111. **Payable to Bearer.**

An instrument is payable to bearer when by its terms it is payable to

(a) bearer or the order of bearer; or

(b) a specified person or bearer; or

(c) "cash" or the order of "cash", or any other indication which does not purport to designate a specific payee.

Part 2 **Negotiation, Transfer, and Endorsement**

Section 3-201. **Negotiation.**

(1) (a) "Negotiation" means a transfer of possession, whether voluntary or involuntary, of an instrument by a person other than the issuer to a person who thereby becomes its holder.

(2) (b) Except for negotiation by a remitter, if an instrument is payable to an identified person, negotiation requires transfer of possession of the instrument and its endorsement by the holder. If an instrument is payable to bearer, it may be negotiated by transfer of possession alone.

Section 3-202. **Negotiation Subject to Rescission.**

(1) (a) Negotiation is effective even if obtained (i) from an infant, a corporation exceeding its powers, or a person without capacity, (ii) by fraud, duress, or mistake, or (iii) in breach of duty or as part of an illegal transaction.

(2) (b) To the extent permitted by other law, negotiation may be rescinded or may be subject to other remedies, but those remedies may not be asserted against a subsequent holder in due course or a person paying the instrument in good faith and without knowledge of facts that are a basis for rescission or other remedy.

National Labor Relations Act (Excerpts)

* * *

Rights of Employees

Section 7. Employees shall have the right to self-organization, to form, join, or assist labor organizations, to bargain collectively through representatives of their own choosing, and to engage in other concerted activities for the purpose of collective bargaining or other mutual aid or protection, and shall also have the right to refrain from any or all of such activities requiring membership in a labor organization as a condition of employment as authorized in section 8(a)(3).

Unfair Labor Practices

Section 8.
(a) It shall be an unfair labor practice for an employer—

    (1) to interfere with, restrain, or coerce employees in the exercise of the rights guaranteed in section;

    (2) to dominate or interfere with the formation or administration of any labor organization or contribute financial or other support to it: *Provided*, That ... an employer shall not be prohibited from permitting employees to confer with him during working hours without loss of time or pay;

    (3) by discrimination in regard to hire or tenure of employment or any term or condition of employment to encourage or discourage membership in any labor organization....

    (4) to discharge or otherwise discriminate against an employee because he has filed charges or given testimony under this Act;

    (5) to refuse to bargain collectively with the representatives of his employees, subject to the provisions of section 9(a).

(b) It shall be an unfair labor practice for a labor organization or its agents—

    (1) to restrain or coerce (A) employees in the exercise of the rights guaranteed in section 7: *Provided*, That this paragraph shall not impair the right of a labor organization to prescribe its own rules with respect to the acquisition or retention of membership therein; or (B) an employer in the selection of his representatives for the purposes of collective bargaining or the adjustment of grievances;

    (2) to cause or attempt to cause an employer to discriminate against an employee ... or to discriminate against an employee with respect to whom membership in such organization has been denied or terminated on some ground other than his failure to tender the periodic dues and the initiation fees uniformly required as a condition of acquiring or retaining membership;

(3) to refuse to bargain collectively with an employer, provided it is the representative of his employees subject to the provisions of section 9(a);

(4) (i) to engage in, or to induce or encourage any individual employed by any person engaged in commerce or in an industry affecting commerce to engage in, a strike or a refusal in the course of his employment to use, manufacture, process, transport, or otherwise handle or work on any goods, articles, materials, or commodities or to perform any services; or (ii) to threaten, coerce, or restrain any person engaged in commerce or in an industry affecting commerce, where in either case an object thereof is—

(A) forcing or requiring any employer or self-employed person to join any labor or employer organization or to enter into any agreement which is prohibited by section 8(e);

(B) forcing or requiring any person to cease using, selling, handling, transporting, or otherwise dealing in the products of any other producer, processor, or manufacturer, or to cease doing business with any other person, or forcing or requiring any other employer to recognize or bargain with a labor organization as the representative of his employees unless such labor organization has been certified as the representative of such employees under the provisions of section 9: *Provided*, That nothing contained in this clause (B) shall be construed to make unlawful, where not otherwise unlawful, any primary strike or primary picketing;

(C) forcing or requiring any employer to recognize or bargain with a particular labor organization as the representative of his employees if another labor organization has been certified as the representative of such employees under the provisions of section 9;

(D) forcing or requiring any employer to assign particular work to employees in a particular labor organization or in a particular trade, craft, or class rather than to employees in another labor organization or in another trade, craft, or class, unless such employer is failing to conform to an order or certification of the Board determining the bargaining representative for employees performing such work:

Provided, That nothing contained in this subsection (b) shall be construed to make unlawful a refusal by any person to enter upon the premises of any employer (other than his own employer), if the employees of such employer are engaged in a strike ratified or approved by a representative of such employees whom such employer is required to recognize under this Act: *Provided further*, that for the purposes of this paragraph (4) only, nothing contained in such paragraph shall be construed to prohibit publicity, other than picketing, for the purpose of truthfully advising the public, including consumers and members of a labor organization, that a product or products are produced by an employer with whom the labor organization has a primary dispute and are distributed by another employer, as long as such publicity does not have an effect of inducing any individual employed by any person other than the primary employer in the course of his employment to refuse to pick up, deliver, or transport any goods, or not to perform any services, at the establishment of the employer engaged in such distribution;

(5) to require of employees covered by an agreement authorized under subsection (a)(3) the payment, as a condition precedent to becoming a member of such organization, of a fee in an amount which the Board finds excessive or discriminatory under all the circumstances. In making such a finding, the Board shall consider, among other relevant factors, the practices and customs of labor organizations in the particular industry, and the wages currently paid to the employees affected;

(6) to cause or attempt to cause an employer to pay or deliver or agree to pay or deliver any money or other thing of value, in the nature of an exaction, for services which are not performed or not to be performed; and

(7) to picket or cause to be picketed, or threaten to picket or cause to be picketed, any employer where an object thereof is forcing or requiring an employer to recognize or bargain with a labor organization as the representative of his employees, or forcing or requiring the employees of an employer to accept or select such labor organization as their collective bargaining representative, unless such labor organization is currently certified as the representative of such employees:

(A) where the employer has lawfully recognized in accordance with this Act any other labor organization and a question concerning representation may not appropriately be raised under section 9(c) of this Act,

(B) where within the preceding twelve months a valid election under section 9(c) of this Act has been conducted, or

(C) where such picketing has been conducted without a petition under section 9(c) being filed within a reasonable period of time not to exceed thirty days from the commencement of such picketing....

Nothing in this paragraph (7) shall be construed to permit any act which would otherwise be an unfair labor practice under this section 8(b).

(c) The expressing of any views, argument, or opinion, or the dissemination thereof, whether in written, printed, graphic, or visual form, shall not constitute or be evidence of an unfair labor practice under any of the provisions of this Act, if such expression contains no threat of reprisal or force or promise of benefit.

(d) (i) For the purposes of this section, to bargain collectively is the performance of the mutual obligation of the employer and the representative of the employees to meet at reasonable times and confer in good faith with respect to wages, hours, and other terms and conditions of employment, or the negotiation of an agreement, or any question arising there under, and the execution of a written contract incorporating any agreement reached if requested by either party, but such obligation does not compel either party to agree to a proposal or require the making of a concession....

(e) It shall be an unfair labor practice for any labor organization and any employer to enter into any contract or agreement, express or implied, whereby such employer ceases or refrains or agrees to cease or refrain from handling, using, selling, transporting, or otherwise dealing in any of the products of any other employer, or to cease doing business with any other person, and any contract or agreement entered into heretofore or hereafter containing such an agreement shall be to such extent unenforceable and void....

Representatives and Elections

Section 9.

(a) Representatives designated or selected for the purposes of collective bargaining by the majority of the employees in a unit appropriate for such purposes, shall be the exclusive representative of all the employees in such unit for the purposes of collective bargaining in respect to rates of pay, wages, hours of employment, or other conditions of employment: *Provided,* That any individual employee or a group of employees shall have the right at any time to present grievances to their employer and to have such grievances adjusted, without the intervention of the bargaining representative, as long as the adjustment is not inconsistent with the terms of a collective-bargaining contract or agreement then in effect: *Provided further,* That the bargaining representative has been given opportunity to be present at such adjustment.

(b) The Board shall decide in each case whether, in order to assure to employees the fullest freedom in exercising the rights guaranteed by this Act, the unit appropriate for the purposes of collective bargaining shall be the employer unit, craft unit, plant unit, or subdivision thereof...

(c) (1) Whenever a petition shall have been filed, in accordance with such regulations as may be prescribed by the Board—

(A) by an employee or group of employees or an individual or labor organization acting in their behalf, alleging that a substantial number of employees (i) wish to be represented for collective bargaining and that their employer declines to recognize their representative as the representative defined in section 9(a), or (ii) assert that the individual or labor organization, which has been certified or is being currently recognized by their employer as the bargaining representative, is no longer a representative as defined in section 9(a); or

(B) by an employer, alleging that one or more individual or labor organizations have presented to him a claim to be recognized as the representative defined in section 9(a); the Board shall investigate such petition and if it has reasonable cause to believe that a question of representation affecting commerce exists shall provide for an appropriate hearing upon due notice. Such hearing may be conducted by an officer or employee of the regional office, who shall not make any recommendations with respect thereto. If the Board finds upon the record of such hearing that such a question of representation exists, it shall direct an election by secret ballot and shall certify the results thereof.

(2) In determining whether or not a question of representation affecting commerce exists, the same regulations and rules of decision shall apply irrespective of the identity of the persons filing the petition or the kind of relief sought and in no case shall the Board deny a labor organization a place on the ballot by reason of an order with respect to such labor organization or its predecessor not issued in conformity with section 10(c).

(3) No election shall be directed in any bargaining unit or any subdivision within which, in the preceding twelve-month period, a valid election shall have been held. Employees engaged in an economic strike who are not entitled to reinstatement shall be eligible to vote under such regulations as the Board shall find are consistent with the purposes and provisions of this Act in any election conducted within twelve months after the commencement of the strike. In any election where none of the choices on the ballot receives a majority, a run-off shall be conducted, the ballot providing for a selection between the two choices receiving the largest and second largest number of valid votes cast in the election.

(4) Nothing in this section shall be construed to prohibit the waiving of hearings by stipulation for the purpose of a consent election in conformity with regulations and rules of decision of the Board.

(5) In determining whether a unit is appropriate for the purposes specified in subsection (b) the extent to which the employees have organized shall not be controlling.

(d) Whenever an order of the Board made pursuant to section 10(c) is based in whole or in part upon facts certified following an investigation pursuant to subsection (c) of this section and there is a petition for the enforcement or review of such order, such certification and the record of such investigation shall be included in the transcript of the entire record required to be filed under section 10(e) or 10(f), and thereupon the decree of the court enforcing, modifying, or setting aside in whole or in part the order of the Board shall be made and entered upon the pleadings, testimony, and proceedings set forth in such transcript.

(e) (1) Upon the filing with the Board, by 30 per centum or more of the employees in a bargaining unit covered by an agreement between their employer and a labor organization made pursuant to section 8(a)(3), of a petition alleging they desire that such authority be rescinded, the Board shall take a secret ballot of the employees in such unit, and shall certify the results thereof to such labor organization and to the employer.

(2) No election shall be conducted pursuant to this subsection in any bargaining unit or any subdivision within which, in the preceding twelve-month period, a valid election shall have been held.

* * *

Title VII of Civil Rights Act of 1964 (Excerpts)

Definitions

Section 701.

(j) The term "religion" includes all aspects of religious observance and practice, as well as belief, unless an employer demonstrates that he is unable to reasonably accommodate to an employee's or prospective employee's religious observance or practice without undue hardship on the conduct of the employer's business.

(k) The terms "because of sex" or "on the basis of sex" include, but are not limited to, because of or on the basis of pregnancy, childbirth or related medical conditions; and women affected by pregnancy, childbirth, or related medical conditions shall be treated the same for all employment-related purposes, including receipt of benefits under fringe benefit programs, as other persons not so affected but similar in their ability or inability to work, and nothing in Section 703(h) of this title shall be interpreted to permit otherwise. This subsection shall not require an employer to pay for health insurance benefits for abortion, except where the life of the mother would be endangered if the fetus were carried to term, or except where medical complications have arisen from an abortion: *Provided*, That nothing herein shall preclude an employer from providing abortion benefits or otherwise effect bargaining agreements in regard to abortion.

Unlawful Employment Practices

Section 703.

(a) It shall be unlawful employment practice for an employer—

    (1) to fail or refuse to hire or to discharge any individual, or otherwise to discriminate against any individual with respect to his compensation, terms, conditions, or privileges of employment, because of such individual's race, color, religion, sex, or national origin; or

    (2) to limit, segregate, or classify his employees or applicants for employment in any way which would deprive or tend to deprive any individual of employment opportunities or otherwise adversely affect his status as an employee, because of such individual's race, color, religion, sex, or national origin.

(b) It shall be unlawful employment practice for an employment agency to fail or refuse to refer for employment, or otherwise to discriminate against, an individual because of his race, color, religion, sex, or national origin, or to classify or refer for employment any individual on the basis of his race, color, religion, sex, or national origin.

(c) It shall be an unlawful employment practice for a labor organization—

    (1) to exclude or to expel from its membership, or otherwise to discriminate against, any individual because of his race, color, religion, sex, or national origin;

    (2) to limit, segregate, or classify its membership or applicants for membership or to classify or fail or refuse to refer for employment any individual, in any way

which would deprive or tend to deprive any individual of employment opportunities, or would limit such employment opportunities or otherwise adversely affect his status as an employee or as an applicant for employment, because of such individual's race, color, religion, sex, or national origin; or

(3) to cause or attempt to cause an employer to discriminate against an individual in violation of this section.

(d) It shall be an unlawful employment practice for any employer, labor organization, or joint labor-management committee controlling apprenticeship or other training or retraining, including on-the-job training programs to discriminate against any individual because of his race, color, religion, sex, or national origin in admission to, or employment in, any program established to provide apprenticeship or other training.

(e) Notwithstanding any other provision of this title, (1) it shall not be an unlawful employment practice for an employer to hire and employ employees, for an employment agency to classify, or refer for employment any individual, or for any employer, labor organization, or joint labor-management committee controlling apprenticeship or other training or retraining programs to admit or employ any individual in any such program, on the basis of his religion, sex, or national origin in those certain instances where religion, sex, or national origin is a bona fide occupational qualification reasonably necessary to the normal operation of that particular business or enterprise, and (2) it shall not be an unlawful employment practice for a school, college, university, or other educational institution or institution of learning to hire and employ employees of a particular religion if such school, college, university, or other educational institution or institution of learning is, in whole or in substantial part, owned, supported, controlled, or managed by a particular religion or by a particular religious corporation, association, or society, or if the curriculum of such school, college, university, or other educational institution or institution of learning is directed toward the propagation of a particular religion.

* * *

(h) Notwithstanding any other provision of this title, it shall not be an unlawful employment practice for an employer to apply different standards of compensation, or different terms, conditions, or privileges of employment pursuant to a bona fide seniority or merit system, or a system which measures earnings by quantity or quality of production or to employees who work in different locations, provided that such differences are not the results of an intention to discriminate because of race, color, religion, sex, or national origin; nor shall it be an unlawful employment practice for an employer to give and to act upon the results of any professionally developed ability test provided that such test, its administration or action upon the results is not designed, intended, or used to discriminate because of race, color, religion, sex, or national origin. It shall not be an unlawful employment practice under this title for any employer to differentiate upon the basis of sex in determining the amount of wages or compensation paid or to be paid to employees of such employer if such differentiation is authorized by the provision of section 6(d) of the Labor Standards Act of 1938, as amended (29 U.S.C. 206(d)).

(i) Nothing contained in this title shall apply to any business or enterprise on or near an Indian reservation with respect to any publicly announced employment practice of such business or enterprise under which a preferential treatment is given to any individual because he is an Indian living on or near a reservation.

(j) Nothing contained in this tide shall be interpreted to require any employer, employment agency, labor organization, or joint labor-management committee subject to this tide to grant preferential treatment to any individual or to any group because of the race, color, religion, sex, or national origin of such individual or group on account of an imbalance which may exist with respect to the total number or percentage of persons of any race, color, religion, sex, or national origin employed by any employer, referred or classified for employment by any employment agency or labor organization, admitted to membership or classified by any labor organization, or admitted to, or employed in, any apprenticeship or other training program, in comparison with the total number or percentage of persons of such race, color, religion, sex, or national origin in any community, State, section, or other area, or in the available work force in any community, State, section, or other area.

Other Unlawful Employment Practices

Section 704.

(a) It shall be an unlawful employment practice for an employer to discriminate against any of his employees or applicants for employment, for an employment agency, or joint labor-management committee controlling apprenticeship or other training or retraining, including on-the-job training programs, to discriminate against any individual, or for a labor organization to discriminate against any member thereof or applicant for membership, because he has opposed any practice, made an unlawful employment practice by this title, or because he has made a charge, testified, assisted, or participated in any manner in an investigation, proceeding, or hearing under this title.

(b) It shall be an unlawful employment practice for an employer, labor organization, employment agency, or joint labor-management committee controlling apprenticeship or other training or retraining, including on-the-job training programs, to print or cause to be printed or published any notice or advertisement relating to employment by such an employer or membership in or any classification or referral for employment by such a labor organization, or relating to any classification or referral for employment by such an employment agency, or relating to admission to, or employment in, any program established to provide apprenticeship or other training by such a joint labor-management committee indicating any preference, limitation, specification, or discrimination, based on race, color, religion, sex, or national origin, except that such a notice or advertisement may indicate a preference, limitation, specification, or discrimination based on religion, sex, or national origin when religion, sex, or national origin is a bona fide occupational qualification for employment.

Americans with Disabilities Act (Excerpts)

Title I—Employment

SECTION 101. DEFINITIONS

(8) Qualified individual with a disability. The term "qualified individual with a disability" means an individual with a disability who, with or without reasonable accommodation, can perform the essential functions of the employment position that such individual holds or desires. For the purposes of this title, consideration shall be given to the employer's judgment as to what functions of a job are essential, and if an employer has prepared a written description before advertising or interviewing applicants for the job, this description shall be considered evidence of the essential functions of the job.

(9) Reasonable Accommodation. The term "reasonable accommodation" may include—

(A) making existing facilities used by employees readily accessible to and usable by individuals with disabilities; and

(B) job restructuring, part-time or modified work schedules, reassignment to a vacant position, acquisition or modification of equipment or devices, appropriate adjustment or modifications of examinations, training materials or policies, the provision of qualified readers or interpreters, and other similar accommodations for individuals with disabilities.

(10) Undue Hardship.

(A) In general: The term "undue hardship" means an action requiring significant difficulty or expense, when considered in light of the factors set forth in subparagraph (B).

(B) Factors to be considered: In determining whether an accommodation would impose an undue hardship on a covered entity, factors to be considered include—

(i) the nature and cost of accommodation needed under this Act;

(ii) the overall financial resources of the facility or facilities involved in the provision of the reasonable accommodation; the number of persons employed at such facility; the effect on expenses and resources, or the impact otherwise of such accommodation upon the operation of the facility;

(iii) the overall financial resources of the covered entity; the overall size of the business of a covered entity with respect to the number of its employees; the number, type, and location of its facilities; and

(iv) the type of operation or operations of the covered entity, including the composition, structure, and functions of die workforce of such entity; the geographic separateness, administrative, or fiscal relationship of the facility or facilities in question to the covered entity.

SECTION 102. DISCRIMINATION

(a) General Rule. No covered entity shall discriminate against a qualified individual with a disability because of the disability of such individual in regard to job application procedures, the hiring, advancement, or discharge of employees, employee compensation, job training, and other terms, conditions, and privileges of employment.

(b) Construction. As used in subsection (a), the term "discriminate" includes—

   (1) limiting, segregating, or classifying a job applicant or employee in a way that adversely affects the opportunities or status of such applicant or employee because of the disability of such applicant or employee;

   (2) participating in a contractual or other arrangement or relationship that has the effect of subjecting a covered entity's qualified applicant or employee with a disability to the discrimination prohibited by this title (such relationship includes a relationship with an employment or referral agency, labor union, an organization providing fringe benefits to an employee of the covered entity, or an organization providing training and apprenticeship programs);

   (3) utilizing standards, criteria, or methods of administration—

      (A) that have the effect of discrimination on the basis of disability; or
      (B) that perpetuate the discrimination of others who are subject to common administrative control;

   (4) excluding or otherwise denying equal jobs or benefits to a qualified individual because of the known disability of an individual with whom the qualified individual is known to have a relationship or association;

   (5) (A) not making reasonable accommodations to the known physical or mental limitations of an otherwise qualified individual with a disability who is an applicant or employee, unless such covered entity can demonstrate that the accommodation would impose an undue hardship on the operation of the business of such covered entity; or

      (B) denying employment opportunities to a job applicant or employee who is an otherwise qualified individual with a disability, if such denial is based on the need of such covered entity to make reasonable accommodation to the physical or mental impairments of the employee or applicant;

   (6) using qualification standards, employment tests or other selection criteria that screen out or tend to screen out an individual with a disability or a class of individuals with disabilities unless the standard, test or other selection criteria, as used by the covered entity, is shown to be job-related for the position in question and is consistent with business necessity; and

   (7) failing to select and administer tests concerning employment in the most effective manner to ensure that, when such test is administered to a job applicant or employee who has a disability that impairs sensory, manual, or speaking skills, such test results accurately reflect the skills, aptitude, or whatever other factor of such applicant or employee that such test purports to measure, rather than reflecting the impaired sensory, manual, or speaking skills of such employee or applicant (except where such skills are the factors that the test purports to measure).

* * *

SECTION 104. ILLEGAL USE OF DRUGS AND ALCOHOL

(b) Rules of Construction. Nothing in subsection (a) shall be construed to exclude as a qualified individual with a disability an individual who—

(1) has successfully completed a supervised drug rehabilitation program and is no longer engaging in the illegal use of drugs, or has otherwise been rehabilitated successfully and is no longer engaging in such use;

(2) is participating in a supervised rehabilitation program and is no longer engaging in such use; or

(3) is erroneously regarded as engaging in such use, but is not engaging in such use; except that it shall not be a violation of this Act for a covered entity to adopt or administer reasonable policies or procedures, including but not limited to drug testing, designed to ensure that an individual described in paragraph (1) or (2) is no longer engaging in the illegal use of drugs.

APPENDIX H

The Antitrust Statutes (Excerpts)

Sherman Act

RESTRAINTS OF TRADE PROHIBITED

Section 1—Trusts, etc., in restraint of trade illegal; penalty. Every contract, combination in the form of trust or otherwise, or conspiracy, in restraint of trade or commerce among the several States, or with foreign nations, is declared to be illegal. Every person who shall make any contract or engage in any combination or conspiracy declared by sections 1 to 7 of this title to be illegal shall be deemed guilty of a felony, and, on conviction thereof, shall be punished by fine not exceeding $10,000,000 if a corporation, or if any other person, $350,000, or by imprisonment not exceeding three years, or both said punishments, in the discretion of the court.

Section 2—Monopolizing trade a felony; penalty. Every person who shall monopolize, or attempt to monopolize, or combine or conspire with any other person or persons, to monopolize any part of the trade or commerce among the several States, or with foreign nations, shall be deemed guilty of a felony, and, on conviction thereof, shall be punished by fine not exceeding $10,000,000 if a corporation, or, if any other person, $350,000, or by imprisonment not exceeding three years, or by both said punishments, in the discretion of the court.

Clayton Act

REFUSALS TO DEAL

Section 3—Sale, etc., on agreement not to use goods of competitor. It shall be unlawful for any person engaged in commerce, in the course of such commerce, to lease or make a sale or contract for sale of goods, wares, merchandise, machinery, supplies, or other commodities, whether patented or unpatented, for use, consumption, or resale within the United States or any Territory thereof or the District of Columbia or any insular possession or other place under the jurisdiction of the United States, or fix a price charged thereof, or discount from, or rebate upon, such price, on the condition, agreement, or understanding that the lessee or purchaser thereof shall not use or deal in the goods, wares, merchandise, machinery, supplies, or other commodities of a competitor or competitors of the lessor or seller, where the effect of such lease, sale, or contract for sale or such condition, agreement or understanding may be to substantially lessen competition or tend to create a monopoly in any line of commerce.

PRIVATE SUITS

Section 4—Suits by persons injured; amount of recovery. Any person who shall be injured in this business or property by reason of anything forbidden in the antitrust laws may sue there for in any district court of the United States in the district in which the defendant resides or is found or has an agent, without respect to the amount in controversy, and shall recover threefold the damages by him sustained, and the cost of suit, including a reasonable attorney's fee....

MERGERS

Section 7—Acquisition by one corporation of stock of another. No corporation engaged in commerce shall acquire, directly or indirectly, the whole or any part of the stock or other share capital and no corporation subject to the jurisdiction of the Federal Trade Commission shall acquire the whole or any part of the assets of another corporation engaged also in commerce, where in any line of commerce in any section of the country, the effect of such acquisition may be substantially to lessen competition, or to tend to create a monopoly.

No corporation shall acquire, directly or indirectly, the whole or any part of the stock or other share capital and no corporation subject to the jurisdiction of the Federal Trade Commission shall acquire the whole or any part of the assets of one or more corporations engaged in commerce, where in any line of commerce in any section of the country, the effect of such acquisition, of such stocks or assets, or of the use of such stock by the voting or granting of proxies or otherwise, may be substantially to lessen competition, or to tend to create a monopoly.

This section shall not apply to corporations purchasing such stock solely for investment and not using the same by voting or otherwise to bring about, or in attempting to bring about, the substantial lessening of competition. Nor shall anything contained in this section prevent a corporation engaged in commerce from causing the formation of subsidiary corporations for the actual carrying on of their immediate lawful business, or the natural and legitimate branches or extensions thereof, or from owning and holding all or part of the stock of such subsidiary corporations, when the effect of such formation is not to substantially lessen competition.

INTERLOCKING DIRECTORATES

Section 8—Interlocking directorates and officers. No person at the same time shall be a director in any two or more corporations, any one of which has capital, surplus, and undivided profits aggregating more than $1,000,000, engaged in whole or in part in commerce, other than banks, banking associations, trust companies, and common carriers subject to the Act to regulate commerce approved February fourth, eighteen hundred and eighty-seven, if such corporations are or shall have been theretofore, by virtue of their business and location or operation, competitors, so that the elimination of competition by agreement between them would constitute a violation of any of the provisions of any of the antitrust laws. The eligibility of a director under the foregoing provision shall be determined by the aggregate amount of the capital, surplus, and undivided profits, exclusive of dividends declared but not paid to stockholders, at the end of the fiscal year of said corporation next preceding the election of directors, and when a director has been elected in accordance with the provisions of this Act it shall be lawful for him to continue as such for one year thereafter.

Federal Trade Commission Act

UNFAIR METHODS OF COMPETITION PROHIBITED

Section 5—Unfair methods of competition unlawful; prevention by commission—declaration.

Declaration of unlawfulness; power to prohibit unfair practices.

(a) (1) Unfair methods of competition in or affecting commerce, and unfair or deceptive acts or practices in or affecting commerce, are declared unlawful....

(b) Any person, partnership, or corporation who violates an order of the Commission to cease and desist after it has become final, and while such order is in effect, shall forfeit and pay to the United States a civil penalty of not more than $5,000 for each violation, which shall accrue to the United States and may be recovered in a civil action brought by the Attorney General of the United States. Each separate violation of such an order shall be a separate offense, except that in the case of a violation through continuing failure or neglect to obey a final order of the Commission each day of continuance of such failure or neglect shall be deemed a separate offense.

Robinson-Patman Act (an Amendment to the Clayton Act)

PRICE DISCRIMINATION; COST JUSTIFICATION; CHANGING CONDITIONS

Section 2—Discrimination in price, services, or facilities.

(a) Price; selection of customers.

It shall be unlawful for any person engaged in commerce, in the course of such commerce, either directly or indirectly, to discriminate in price between different purchases of commodities of like grade and quality, where either or any of the purchasers involved in such discrimination are in commerce, where such commodities are sold for use, consumption, or resale within the United States or any Territory thereof or the District of Columbia or any insular possession or other place under the jurisdiction of the United States, and where the effect of such discrimination may be substantially to lessen competition or tend to create a monopoly in any line of commerce, or to injure, destroy, or prevent competition with any person who either grants or knowingly receives the benefit of such discrimination, or with customers of either of them: *Provided*, That nothing herein contained shall prevent differentials which make only due allowance for differences in the cost of manufacture, sale, or delivery resulting from the differing methods or quantities in which such commodities are to such purchasers sold or delivered: *Provided*, however, That the Federal Trade Commission may, after due investigation and hearing to all interested parties, fix and establish quantity limits, and revise the same as it finds necessary as to particular commodities or classes of commodities, where it finds that available purchasers in greater quantities are so few as to render differentials on account thereof unjustly discriminatory or promotive of monopoly in any line of commerce; and the foregoing shall then not be construed to permit differentials based on differences in quantities greater than those so fixed and established: And provided further, That nothing herein contained shall prevent persons engaged in selling goods, wares, or merchandise in commerce from selecting their own customers in bona fide transactions and not in restraint of trade: And provided fruitier, That nothing herein contained shall prevent price changes from time to time where in response to changing conditions affecting the market for or the marketability of the goods concerned, such as but not limited to actual or imminent deterioration of perishable goods, obsolescence of seasonal goods, distress sales under court process, or sales in good faith in discontinuance of business in the goods concerned.

MEETING COMPETITION

(b) Burden of rebutting prima-facie case of discrimination.

Upon proof being made, at any hearing on a complaint under this section, that there has been discrimination in price or services or facilities furnished, the burden of rebutting the prima-facie case thus made by showing justification shall be upon the person charged with a violation of this section, and unless justification shall be affirmatively shown, the Commission is authorized to issue an order terminating the discrimination: *Provided*, however, That nothing herein contained shall prevent a seller rebutting the prima-facie case thus made by showing that his lower price or the furnishing of services or facilities to any purchaser or purchasers was made in good faith to meet an equally low price of a competitor, or the services or facilities furnished by a competitor.

BROKERAGE PAYMENTS

(c) Payment or acceptance of commission, brokerage or other compensation.

It shall be unlawful for any person engaged in commerce, in the course of such commerce, to pay or grant, or to receive or accept, anything of value as a commission, brokerage, or other compensation, or any allowance of discount in lieu thereof, except for services rendered in connection with the sale or purchase of goods, wares, or merchandise, either to the other party to such transaction or to an agent, representative, or other intermediary therein where such intermediary is acting in fact for or in behalf, or is subject to the direct or indirect control, of any party to such transaction other than the person by whom such compensation is so granted or paid.

PROMOTIONAL ALLOWANCES

(d) Payment for services or facilities for processing or sale.

It shall be unlawful for any person engaged in commerce to pay or contract for the payment of anything of value to or for the benefit of a customer of such person in the course of such commerce as compensation or in consideration for any services or facilities furnished by or through such customer in connection with the processing, handling, sale, or offering for sale of any products or commodities manufactured, sold, or offered for sale by such person, unless such payment of consideration is available on proportionally equal terms to all other customers competing in the distribution of such products or commodities.

PROMOTIONAL SERVICES

(e) Furnishing services or facilities for processing, handling, etc.

It shall be unlawful for any person to discriminate in favor of one purchaser against another purchaser or purchasers of a commodity bought for resale, with or without processing, or by contracting to furnish or furnishing, or by contributing to the furnishing of, any services or facilities connected with the processing, handling, sale, or offering for sale of such commodity so purchased upon terms not accorded to all purchasers on proportionally equal terms.

BUYER DISCRIMINATION

(f) Knowingly inducing or receiving discriminatory price.

It shall be unlawful for any person engaged in commerce, in the course of such commerce, knowingly to induce or receive a discrimination in price which is prohibited by this section.

PREDATORY PRACTICES

Section 3—Discrimination in rebates, discounts, or advertising service charges; underselling in particular localities; penalties.

It shall be unlawful for any person engaged in commerce, in the course of such commerce, to be a party to, or assist in, any transaction of sale, or contract to sell, which discriminates to his knowledge against competitors of the purchaser, in that, any discount, rebate, allowance, or advertising service charge is granted to the purchaser over and above any discount, rebate, allowance, or advertising service charge available at the time of such transaction to said competitors in respect of a sale of goods of like grade, quality, and quantity; to sell, or contract to sell, goods in any part of the United States at prices lower than those exacted by said person elsewhere in the United States for the purpose of destroying competition, or eliminating a competitor in such part of the United States; or, to sell, or contract to sell, goods at unreasonably lower prices for the purpose of destroying competition or eliminating a competitor.

Securities Statutes (Excerpts)

Securities Act of 1933

DEFINITIONS

Section 2. When used in this title, unless the context requires—

(1) The term "security" means any note, stock, treasury stock, bond, debenture, evidence of indebtedness, certificate of interest or participation in any profit-sharing agreement, collateral-trust certificate, preorganization certificate or subscription, transferable share, investment contract, voting-trust certificate, certificate of deposit for a security, fractional undivided interest in oil, gas, or other mineral rights, any put, call, straddle, option, or privilege on any security, certificate of deposit, or group or index of securities (including any interest therein or based on the value thereof), or any put, call, straddle, option, or privilege entered into on a national securities ex change relating to foreign currency, or, in general, any interest or participation in, temporary or interim certificate for, receipt for, guarantee of, or warrant or right to subscribe to or purchase, any of the foregoing.

* * *

EXEMPTED SECURITIES

Section 3. (a) Except as hereinafter expressly provided the provisions of this title shall not apply to any of the following classes of securities:

* * *

(2) Any security issued or guaranteed by the United States or any territory thereof, or by the District of Columbia, or by any State of the United States, or by any political subdivision of a State or Territory, or by any public instrumentality of one or more States or Territories, or by any person controlled or supervised by and acting as an instrumentality of the Government of the United States pursuant to authority granted by the Congress of the United States; or any certificate of deposit for any of the foregoing; or any security issued or guaranteed by any bank; or any security issued by or representing an interest in or a direct obligation of a Federal Reserve Bank....

(3) Any note, draft, bill of exchange, or banker's acceptance which arises out of a current transaction or the proceeds of which have been or are to be used for current transactions, and which has a maturity at the time of issuance of not exceeding nine months, exclusive of days of grace, or any renewal thereof the maturity of which is likewise limited;

(4) Any security issued by a person organized and operated exclusively for religious, educational, benevolent, fraternal, charitable, or reformatory purposes and not for pecuniary profit, and no part of the net earnings of which inures to the benefit of any person, private stockholder, or individual;

* * *

PROHIBITIONS RELATING TO INTERSTATE COMMERCE AND THE MAILS

Section 5. (a) Unless a registration statement is in effect as to a security, it shall be unlawful for any person, directly or indirectly—

    (1) to make use of any means or instruments of transportation or communication in interstate commerce or of the mails to sell such security through the use or medium of any prospectus or otherwise; or

    (2) to carry or cause to be carried through the mails or in interstate commerce, by any means or instruments of transportation, any such security for the purpose of sale or for delivery after sale.

(b) It shall be unlawful for any person, directly or indirectly—

    (1) to make use of any means or instruments of transportation or communication in interstate commerce or of the mails to carry or transmit any prospectus relating to any security with respect to which a registration statement has been filed under this title, unless such prospectus meets the requirements of section 10, or

    (2) to carry or to cause to be carried through the mails or in interstate commerce any such security for the purpose of sale or for delivery after sale, unless accompanied or preceded by a prospectus that meets the requirements of subsection (a) of section 10.

(c) It shall be unlawful for any person, directly, or indirectly, to make use of any means or instruments of transportation or communication in interstate commerce or of the mails to offer to sell or offer to buy through the use or medium of any prospectus or otherwise any security, unless a registration statement has been filed as to such security, or while the registration statement is the subject of a refusal order or stop order or (prior to the effective date of the registration statement) any public proceeding of examination under ... this title.

Securities Exchange Act of 1934

DEFINITIONS AND APPLICATION OF TITLE

Section 3. (a) When used in this title, unless the context otherwise requires—

★ ★ ★

    (4) The term "broker" means any person engaged in the business of effecting transactions in securities for the account of others, but does not include a bank. ...

    (5) The term "dealer" means any person engaged in the business of buying and selling securities for his own account, through a broker or otherwise, but does not include a bank, or any person insofar as he buys or sells securities for his own account, either individually or in some fiduciary capacity, but not as part of a regular business.

★ ★ ★

    (7) The term "director" means any director of a corporation or any person performing similar functions with respect to any organization, whether incorporated or unincorporated. ...

    (8) The term "issuer" means any person who issues or proposes to issue any security; except that with respect to certificates of deposit for securities, voting-trust

certificates, or collateral-trust certificates, or with respect to certificates of interest or shares in an unincorporated investment trust not having a board of directors or the fixed, restricted management, or unit type, the term "issuer" means the person or persons performing the acts and assuming the duties of depositor or manager pursuant to the provisions of the trust or other agreement or instrument under which such securities are issued; and except that with respect to equipment-trust certificates or like securities, the term "issuer" means the person by whom the equipment or property is, or is to be, used. ...

(9) The term "person" means a natural person, company, government, or political subdivision, agency, or instrumentality of a government.

REGULATION OF THE USE OF MANIPULATIVE AND DECEPTIVE DEVICES

Section 10. It shall be unlawful for any person, directly or indirectly, by the use of any means or instrumentality of interstate commerce or of the mails, or of any facility of any national securities exchange—

(a) To effect a short sale, or to use or employ any stop-loss order in connection with the purchase or sale, of any security registered on a national securities exchange, in contravention of such rules and regulations as the Commission may prescribe as necessary or appropriate in the public interest or for the protection of investors.

(b) To use or employ, in connection with the purchase or sale of any security registered on a national securities exchange or any security not so registered, any manipulative or deceptive device or contrivance in contravention of such rules and regulations as the Commission may prescribe as necessary or appropriate in the public interest or for the protection of investors.

Sarbanes-Oxley Act of 2002

(PUBLIC COMPANY ACCOUNTING REFORM AND CORPORATE RESPONSIBILITY ACT) TITLE 15, CH. 98, UNITED STATES CODE

Sec. 7241.—Corporate responsibility for financial reports

(c) Regulations required

(d) The Commission shall, by rule, require, for each company filing periodic reports under section 78m (a) or 78o (d) of this title, that the principal executive officer or officers and the principal financial officer or officers, or persons performing similar functions, certify in each annual or quarterly report filed or submitted under either such section of this title that—

(1) the signing officer has reviewed the report;

(2) based on the officer's knowledge, the report does not contain any untrue statement of a material fact or omit to state a material fact necessary in order to make the statements made, in light of the circumstances under which such statements were made, not misleading;

(3) based on such officer's knowledge, the financial statements, and other financial information included in the report, fairly present in all material respects the financial condition and results of operations of the issuer as of and for, the periods presented in the report;

(4) the signing officers—

    (A) are responsible for establishing and maintaining internal controls;

    (B) have designed such internal controls to ensure that material information relating to the issuer and its consolidated subsidiaries is made known to such officers by others within those entities, particularly during the period in which the periodic reports are being prepared;

    (C) have evaluated the effectiveness of the issuer's internal controls as of a date within 90 days prior to the report; and

    (D) have presented in the report their conclusions about the effectiveness of their internal controls based on their evaluation as of that date;

(5) the signing officers have disclosed to the issuer's auditors and the audit committee of the board of directors (or persons fulfilling the equivalent function)—

    (A) all significant deficiencies in the design or operation of internal controls which could adversely affect the issuer's ability to record, process, summarize, and report financial data and have identified for the issuer's auditors any material weaknesses in internal controls; and

    (B) any fraud, whether or not material, that involves management or other employees who have a significant role in the issuer's internal controls; and

(6) the signing officers have indicated in the report whether or not there were significant changes in internal controls or in other factors that could significantly affect internal controls subsequent to the date of their evaluation, including any corrective actions with regard to significant deficiencies and material weaknesses.

Glossary

A

Abnormally dangerous activity *see* Ultrahazardous activity.

Absolute privilege a defense in a defamation suit affirming that the defendant had an unconditional right to make the statements in question and be free from litigation. This most often applies to statements made by members of a legislature as part of the deliberation process.

Acceptance the offeree's notification or expression to the offeror that he agrees to be bound by the terms of the offeror's proposal, thereby creating a contract. The trend is to allow acceptance by any means that reasonably notifies the offeror of the acceptance.

Accord in a debtor/creditor relationship, an agreement between the parties to settle a dispute for some partial payment. The creditor has a right of action against the debtor.

Accord and satisfaction in a debtor/creditor agreement, an agreement between the parties to right of action against subsequent payment. The isfaction are complete when payment the creditor has a tendered. and sat-

Accredited investor in securities law, investors permitted to buy certain securities, often offered in private placements without SEC registration. An individual must have a net worth of at least $1 million or have made at least $200,000 each year for the last two years ($300,000 with his or her spouse if married).

Actual authority power of an agent to bind a principal; the power is from an express or implied agreement between principal and agent.

Actual malice the intentional doing of a wrongful act, without a legal excuse, with the intent to inflict injury.

Actus reus Latin, for "guilty act;" the wrongful deed that constitutes the physical component of a crime; usually must be joined with *mens rea* to establish criminal liability.

Adjudicatory hearing in administrative law, a formal process involving a regulatory agency and the private parties involved in a complaint; procedures are more informal than a court trial but protect due process rights.

Administrative agency a governmental bureau established by Congress (or the president) to execute certain functions of Congress. Agencies transact government business and may write and enforce regulations under the authority of Congress or the president.

Administrative law rules and regulations established by administrative agencies to execute the functions given them by Congress or the president; also the law governs how agencies must operate.

Administrative law judge a person appointed to conduct an administrative hearing about a regulatory matter. Usually attorneys who work for the administrative agency, such as the Federal Trade Commission, serve in this capacity. They run a trial-like proceeding and issue a decision in the matter based on the facts determined at the hearing.

Adversary system of justice   a legal system in which the parties to a dispute present their own arguments and are responsible for asserting their legal rights.

Adverse possession   (easement by prescription) a method by which one obtains the right to property by following specific rules under which a nonowner may be declared to be the lawful owner. This normally requires open possession of the property and restraining others from use of the properly for a period of time required by state law and may require payment of properly taxes.

Advertising substantiation program   a policy of the Federal Trade Commission to review advertisements for content to ensure they are not deceitful.

Affirm   in a court of appeals, or supreme court, a decision to declare that a judgment entered by a lower court is valid and will stand as decided.

Affirmative action   taking constructive steps to remedy discriminatory employment practices affecting racial minorities and women.

Affirmative defense   defendant's response to plaintiffs claim that attacks the plaintiffs legal right to bring the action rather than attacking the truth of the claim. An example of an affirmative defense is the running of the statute of limitations.

Age   under federal employment discrimination law, all persons over age 40 are covered.

Agency by estoppel   an agency created by operation of law that arises when the principal, by failing to properly supervise the agent, allows the agent to exercise too many powers, thereby allowing others to be justified in thinking that the agent possesses the powers the agent claimed to have.

Agency by operation of law   when the law imposes on a principal the consequence of an agency that was not otherwise accepted, usually in an emergency or other unusual situation.

Agency coupled with an interest   when an agent has an interest in the subject matter that is relevant to the agency relationship; this is often an interest in a specific piece of properly.

Agency fees   in labor law, the right of a union to charge fees to employees who are not union members, instead of union dues, to cover the cost of representing such employees; such fees are illegal in right-to-work states.

Agency relationship   is where a principal employs an agent to carry out various duties on his or her behalf by delegating decision making powers.

Agency rule   in administrative law, a rule issued by a regulatory agency under its powers granted by Congress and subject to procedural requirements that detail the legal obligations of affected parties.

Agency shop   in labor law, a unionized workplace where employees who are not union members must pay agency fees to the union for being the sole bargaining agent for all employees; illegal in states that have right-to-work laws.

Agent   a person authorized to act for or to represent another, called the principal. Agreement a "meeting of the minds;" a mutual understanding between the parties as to the substance of a contract.

Alibi   claim or evidence provided that defendant was elsewhere when an act, typically a criminal one, is alleged to have taken place.

Alternative dispute resolution   a process by which the parties to a dispute resolve it through a mechanism other than litigation in court; includes arbitration, negotiation, and mediation.

Amount in controversy   the damages claimed or the relief demanded by the injured party in a dispute.

Answer   the response of a defendant to the plaintiff's complaint, denying in part or in whole the charges made by the plaintiff.

Anticipatory breach   the assertion by a party to a contract that she will not perform a future obligation as required by the contract.

Antidumping duty   a tariff to equalize the difference between the price at which the product is sold in the exporting country and the price at which the importer will sell the product in the importing country; designed to prevent foreign businesses from artificially lowering their prices and gaining unfair advantages outside their home market.

Anti-raiding covenant   in employment law, when employees are required to sign, as a condition of continued employment, an agreement that in the future, should they no longer work for the employer, they will not attempt to hire away other employees from the company; these are looked at closely by the courts as possible restraints of trade.

Antitrust federal and state statutes to protect commerce from certain restraints of trade, such as price fixing and monopolization.

Apparent authority the authority a reasonable person would assume an agent possesses in light of the principal's conduct.

Appellate jurisdiction the power of a court to revise or correct the proceedings in a case already acted upon by a lower court or administrative agency.

Arbiter in an arbitration proceeding, the person granted the authority to decide a controversy.

Arbitrary and capricious a judgment or decision, by an administrative agency or judge, which is without basis in fact or in law. Such a decision is often referred to as being without a rational basis.

Arbitrary and fanciful a trademark that is either inherently distinctive or a word that is not related to the product.

Arbitration a means of settling disputes between parties when they submit the matter to a neutral third party of their choosing, who resolves the dispute by issuing a binding award. A popular alternative to the court system for resolving disputes due at lower cost and greater speed.

Arraignment the initial step in a criminal prosecution; the defendant is brought before the court to hear the charges and enter a plea.

Articles of organization limited liability companies must produce this document, and submit a copy to the state, to be recognized as a legal entity; generally provides minimal information necessary, such as name of LLC, its purpose, life, and names and addresses of organizers.

Assault any word or action intended to cause another to be in fear of immediate physical harm.

Assault and battery intentionally causing another to anticipate immediate physical harm through some threat and then carrying out the threatened activity.

Assignment a transfer of one's interest in property or a contract to another person.

Assumption of risk common-law doctrine under which a plaintiff may not recover for the injuries or damages that result from an activity in which the plaintiff willingly participated. A defense used by the defendant in a negligence case, when the plaintiff had knowledge of the danger, voluntarily exposed himself to the danger, and was injured.

Attachment the legal process of seizing another's property in accordance with a writ or judicial order for the purpose of security satisfaction of a judgment to be rendered.

Attachment In UCC, when the requirements of a security interest (agreement, value, and conveyable rights in the collateral) exist, the security agreement becomes enforceable between parties and is said to attach.

Attachment lien a lien on property seized by attachment; usually made final upon entry of a judgment in favor of the attaching creditor.

Attainment areas under the Clean Air Act, areas that meet federal standards for major pollutants; they are designated "prevention of significant deterioration areas," because they are not allowed to become more polluted.

Authorization card a card signed by an employee at a worksite targeted for possible unionization; the card authorizes the union to request that an election be held to determine if all workers will be represented by the union.

Award the decision that settles an arbitration proceeding. It is normally the determination of a single arbiter, but it can be the decision of the panel of arbitrators that heard the dispute. The decision may be in writing but need not give a rationale.

B

Back pay compensation for past economic losses (lost wages and fringe benefits) caused by an employer's discriminatory employment practices, such as limiting promotion opportunities for older workers.

Bankruptcy a proceeding under the law that is initiated by an insolvent individual or business (a voluntary bankruptcy) or by creditors (an involuntary bankruptcy) seeking to have the insolvent's assets distributed among the creditors and to then discharge the insolvent from further obligation or to reorganize the insolvent's debt structure.

Bargaining agent the union recognized and certified by the National Labor Relations Board, upon election by a majority of the workers, to be the exclusive representative of employees in a bargaining unit (worksite) to determine working conditions and wages.

Battery   the intentional unallowed touching of another. The "touching" may involve a mere touch that is offensive or an act of violence that causes serious injury.

Bearer   In UCC the person in possession of an instrument, document of title, or certificated security payable to bearer or indorsed in blank.

Bearer instrument   an instrument payable to bearer (the person in possession); it must specify that it is payable to bearer, to cash, or to a specific bearer.

Bearer paper   a financial instrument payable to the person who holds it rather than to the order of a specific person; it is negotiated by delivery of the instrument to a transferee.

Beneficiary   a person for whose benefit property is held in trust; usually a person designated to benefit from an assignment, such as in a will or insurance policy, or to receive something by a legal arrangement or instrument.

Benefit corporation   a corporate form that voluntarily meets high standards of purpose, accountability, and transparency.

Beyond a reasonable doubt   in criminal law, the general rule that for a judge or jury to find a defendant guilty, there can be no significant doubt that the defendant violated a criminal statute.

Bilateral contract   a contract formed by the mutual exchange of promises of the parties.

Bill of exchange   an unconditional order in writing, addressed by one person to another, signed by the person giving it, requiring the person to whom it is addressed to pay on demand, or at a fixed or determinable future date, a certain sum of money. Same as a draft under the UCC.

Blue sky laws   name given to state laws that regulate the offer and sale of securities.

Board of directors   the principals of a corporation, elected by shareholders, responsible for governing the business, especially as to major decisions; directors appoint corporate officers and agents to act on their behalf in running the business day to day. Boards are usually composed of inside directors, such as the president of the company, and outside or independent directors, who have no employment relationship with the company.

***Bona fide* occupational qualification**   or BFOQ, employment in particular jobs may not be limited to persons of a particular sex or religion, unless the employer can show that sex or religion is an actual qualification for performing the job. Not permitted on the basis of race.

***Bona fide* seniority program**   in employment, a system that recognizes length of service in deciding promotions, layoffs, and other job actions; protection of workers based on length of service is protected by Title VII.

Boycott   an effort to organize a group to not deal with some party, such as a group of retailers refusing to buy products from manufacturers who do certain things not liked by the retailers, or a group of labor unions agreeing not to handle any products made by a certain company.

Breach of contract   failure, without a legal excuse, of a promisor to perform the terms agreed to in a contract.

Bribery   the offering, giving, receiving, or soliciting of something of value for the purpose of influencing the action of an official in the discharge of public or legal duties.

Brownfield   in environmental law, real properly, the expansion, redevelopment, or reuse of which may be complicated by the presence or potential presence of a hazardous substance, pollutant, or contaminant.

Bulk-supplier doctrine   one who sells to an intermediary in large quantities can fulfill the duty to warn ultimate users if adequate instructions are provided to the distributor or if the wholesaler or manufacturer is trained and knowledgeable of the properties of the product and safe ways to handle it, and can pass on the information to users.

Business judgment rule   a principle of corporate law under which a court will not challenge the business decisions of a corporate officer or director made with ordinary care and in good faith.

Business necessity   justification for an otherwise prohibited discriminatory employment practice based on employer's proof that (1) the otherwise prohibited employment practice is essential for the safety and efficiency of the business, and (2) no reasonable alternative with a lesser impact exists.

Business trust   a business organization, similar to a corporation, by which investors receive transferable certificates of beneficial interest instead of shares of stock.

in corporation law, the rules that regulate and govern the internal operations of a corporation with respect to directors, shareholders, and officers rights and duties.

C

Cartel   a combination of independent producers in an industry attempting to limit competition by acting together to fix prices, divide markets, or restrict entry into the industry.

Case   a dispute between two or more parties that is resolved through the legal process.

Case reporters   books containing the decisions issued by federal and state courts in which judges provide the legal reasoning for decisions issued.

Cashier's check   a bank's check, drawn on itself, signed by the cashier of the bank or other bank official obligating the bank to pay the payee a certain sum of money on demand.

Cause in fact   an act or omission without which an event would not have occurred. Courts express this in the form of a rule commonly referred to as the "but for" rule: the injury to a person would not have happened but for the conduct of the wrongdoer.

Causation   the causing or producing of an effect; in law, something that may be related to legal consequences.

Caveat emptor   Latin for "let the buyer beware."

Cease and desist order   an order by an administrative agency or a court prohibiting a firm from conducting activities that the agency or court deems illegal.

Certificate of deposit   a written bank document that provides evidence of a deposit made at a bank, for a certain time, that pays a certain rate of interest that is promised to be paid to the depositor or to another party as ordered.

Certificate of incorporation   *see* Corporate charter.

Certification mark   in trademark law, any symbol, name, or word used to identify the location or other aspect of the origin of a product.

Charges   the direction or guideline that a judge gives a jury concerning the law of the case being deliberated.

Charter   *see* Corporate charter.

Check   a draft or order drawn upon a bank, payable on demand, signed by the maker or drawer, that is an unconditional promise to pay a certain sum of money to the order of the payee named on the instrument. It normally must say "pay to the order" of on the face of the check.

Choice-of-language clause   in international contracts especially, a clause that specifies the language that will apply to the contract between parties in the event of a dispute, so that there will be an official version in one language only.

Choice-of-law clause   a common provision in a contract that specified what law must be used to resolve a dispute that arises between the parties to a contract.

Choice of laws   *see* Conflict of laws.

Churning   refers to the excessive buying and selling of securities in a securities investment account by a broker, for the purpose of generating commissions and without regard to investment objectives.

Citizen-suit provisions   in regulatory law, a right provided by Congress for private citizens to bring a suit before a federal court to force compliance with a law passed by Congress; in some instances, the cost of the suit is borne by the government or the defendant if the private party wins the case.

Civil law   (l) laws, written or unwritten, that specify the duties that exist between and among people, as opposed to criminal matters; or (2) codified or statutory law, used in many Western European countries and Japan, as distinguished from the common or judge-made law used in the United Kingdom and the United States.

Close corporation   a closely held corporation; a corporation that has stock that is not allowed to be widely held; the number of shareholders is limited and usually, unlike a publicly held corporation, the shareholders are active in oversight of the firm.

Closing argument   oral presentation to the jury by the attorneys after the plaintiff and defendant have stated their cases and before the judge charges the jury.

Code of Federal Regulations   or CFR, the codification of the general and permanent rules and regulations (administrative law) published in the *Federal Register* by the executive departments and agencies of the federal government.

Collateral   property pledged as a secondary security for the satisfaction of a debt in the event the debtor does not repay as expected.

Collective bargaining   the process by which a union and an employer arrive at and enforce agreements regarding employment of workers represented by a union.

Collective mark   a trademark or service mark used by the members of a cooperative association to identify the goods and services they produce.

Color   under federal employment discrimination law, the shade of one's skin.

Commerce clause   that part of the U.S. Constitution that gives Congress the power to regulate interstate commerce; the basis of much federal regulation.

Commercial speech   expressions made by businesses about commercial matters or about political matters; the First Amendment protects most truthful speech in this category.

Commodity Control List   or CCL, a list maintained by the Department of Commerce that classifies restrictions on the exportation of certain goods to certain nations.

Common law   law developed by American and English courts by decisions in cases. Unlike statutes, it is not passed by a legislative body and is not a specific set of rules; rather, it must be interpreted from the many decisions that have been written over time.

Comparative negligence   a defense to negligence whereby the plaintiffs damages are reduced by the proportion his fault bears to the total injury he has suffered.

Compensatory damages   a sum awarded to an injured party that is equivalent to her actual damages or injuries sustained. The rationale is to restore the injured party to the position she was in before the injury.

Complaint   the initial pleading by the plaintiff in a civil action that informs the defendant of the material facts on which the plaintiff bases the lawsuit.

Compliance program   under the federal Sentencing Guidelines, a company that maintains a compliance program with regulations that apply to the company will be subject to less punishment in case of violations of the law than if there is no good-faith effort to have internal procedures to help ensure that the law is followed within the organization.

Concerted activity   in labor law, actions by employees, such as a strike or other mutual activity that furthers their employment interests, protected by the National Labor Relations Act.

Concurrent jurisdiction   when two different courts are each empowered to deal with the subject matter at issue in a dispute.

Concurring opinion   at the appellate court level, an opinion filed by one or more of the justices in which the justices agree with the majority opinion but state separate views or reasons for the decision.

Conditional privilege   also called qualified privilege; a defense in defamation cases affirming that the defendant published in good faith or as part of a duty to publish; it protects the defendant in a case that may otherwise be actionable.

Confirmation   in commercial law, a bank's agreement to honor a letter of credit issued by another bank.

Confiscation   the act whereby a sovereign takes private properly without a proper public purpose or just compensation.

Conflicts of interest   a real or seeming incompatibility between one's private interests and one's public or fiduciary duties; for example, in securities, when a broker has a personal stake in an investment that is promoted to clients.

Conflict of laws   body of law establishing the circumstances in which a state or federal court shall apply the laws of another state, rather than the laws of the state in which it is sitting, to decide a case before it.

Consent   a voluntary agreement, implied or expressed, to submit to a proposition or act of another.

Consent decree   a judgment entered by consent of the parties and approval of a court, whereby the defendant agrees to stop alleged illegal activity without admitting guilt or wrongdoing. Often used to settle complaints by regulatory agencies.

Consequential damages   in UCC, losses that do not flow directly from a breach of contract but that result indirectly from the act and should have been foreseeable by the seller.

Consideration   in a contract, the thing of value bargained for in exchange for a promise; the inducement or motivation to a contract; the element that keeps the contract from being gratuitous and, therefore, makes it legally binding on the parties.

.tion the fundamental law of a nation; a written document establishing the powers of the government and its basic structure; the controlling authority over all other law.

Constitutional privilege speech that is protected by the First Amendment; generally applies to members of the media attempting to protect news sources; also applies to comments made about public officials or public figures, who have reduced rights to sue for defamation for comments made about them.

Constructive discharge under federal employment discrimination law, when an employee quits employment due to pervasive abuse or discriminatory treatment in violation of Title VII.

Consumer reports often called credit reports; files maintained by companies concerning consumers' credit history and evidence of income and debt; sold for legitimate business purposes.

Contempt of court any act that obstructs a court in the administration of justice or that is calculated to lessen the court's authority.

Contract a legal relationship consisting of the rights and duties of contracting parties; a promise or set of promises constituting an agreement between the parties that gives each a legal duty to the other and also the right to seek a remedy for the breach of those duties. The elements of a contract include agreement, consideration, legal capacity, lawful subject matter, and genuine consent.

Contractual capacity the mental capacity required by law for a party entering into a contract to be bound by that contract. Minors, intoxicated persons, and the insane generally lack capacity to contract.

Contributory negligence as a complete defense to negligence, an act or a failure to act that produces a lack of reasonable care on the part of the plaintiff that is the proximate cause of the injury incurred.

Conversion the unauthorized taking of properly, permanently or temporarily, that deprives its rightful owner of its lawful use.

Copyright a grant to an author or a publisher of an exclusive right to print, reprint, publish, copy, and sell literary work, musical compositions, works of art, and motion pictures for the life of the author plus an additional 50 years.

Corporate charter a certificate issued by a state government recognizing the existence of a corporation as a legal entity; it is issued automatically upon filing the information required by state law and payment of a fee.

Corporate social responsibility the belief that businesses have a duty to society that goes beyond obeying the law and maximizing profits.

Corporation a business organized under the laws of a state that allow an artificial legal being to exist for purposes of doing business in its name.

Cost-benefit analysis computing the costs of an activity compared to the estimated monetary value of the benefits from the activity.

Cost justification in antitrust law, a defense available in price discrimination (Robinson-Patman) cases to show that a buyer was offered a good at a lower price than another buyer because of differences in the costs of serving the two customers.

Counterclaim a claim a defendant asserts against the plaintiff.

Counterfeiting to imitate, forge, or copy without authority and to pass off as original with an intent to deceive. This may be done for money, securities, copyrights, patents, trademarks, and other protected property.

Counteroffer an offeree's response to an offeror rejecting the offeror's original offer and at the same time making a new offer.

Countervailing measures the WTO Agreement on Subsidies and Countervailing Measures restricts the use of subsidies and regulates the actions countries can take to counter the effects of subsidies. A country can use the WTO's process to seek the withdrawal of a subsidy, or a country can charge extra duties ("countervailing duty") on subsidized imports that hurt domestic producers.

Court of original jurisdiction *see* Original jurisdiction.

Covenant in property law, an agreement by two or more parties, in writing, that places certain restrictions on the use of property or obligates the owner of the property to take specific actions with respect to the land. These obligations normally go with the property as it passes from owner to owner over time.

Covenant not to compete   part of an agreement in the sale of a business for the seller not to compete with the buyer for a given time in a given market; in employment law, it is an agreement, not enforceable in all states, for an employee not to go to work for a competitor for a certain time after leaving current employment.

Cover   In UCC, the buyer can recover from the seller the difference between the cost of the substituted goods and the original contract price. It is the purchase on the open market, by the buyer in a breach-of-contract case, of goods to substitute for those promised but not delivered.

Credit rating   an opinion as to the reliability of a person in paying debts.

Credit report   a report made by a consumer reporting agency concerning the financial condition and credit character of a person or business.

Creditor   a person to whom a debt is owed by a debtor.

Crime   a violation of the law that is punishable by the state or nation; classified as felonies or misdemeanors.

Criminal law   governs or defines legal wrongs, or crimes, committed against society. Wrongdoers are punished for violating the rules of society. A person found guilty of a criminal offense is usually fined or imprisoned.

Criminal negligence   gross negligence so extreme that it is punishable as a crime. For example, involuntary manslaughter can be based on criminal negligence, such as when an extremely careless automobile driver kills someone.

Cross-complaint   during the pleadings, a claim the defendant asserts against the laintiff. *See also* Counterclaim.

Cross examination   examination by the attorney representing the adverse party after the other party has examined her witness.

Cure   in UCC, the right of a seller to make good on an improper delivery of goods if done within the time allowed by contract and with notification to the buyer in a timely manner.

Cybersquatting   when a trademark is improperly used in a domain name; this is in violation of federal law that extends trademark protection to include domain name usage.

D

Damages   money compensation sought or awarded as a remedy for a breach of contract or for tortious acts.

Danger-invites-rescue doctrine   the principle that a tortfeasor who is liable for endangering a person is also liable for injuries to someone who reasonably attempted to rescue the person in danger.

Debt   a sum of money due by an express agreement.

Debt collection agency   a business that is paid to or buys the right to collect the debts owed by consumers to a business.

Debt securities   an obligation of a corporation, usually in the form of a bond, issued for a certain value at a certain rate of interest to be repaid at a certain time.

Debtor   a person who owes a debt to a creditor.

Debtor in possession   in bankruptcy law, the debtor in Chapter 11 bankruptcy who remains in control of a business or assets or the trustee appointed to control a business or assets.

Deception   in consumer protection law, a claim, practice, or omission likely to mislead a reasonable consumer and cause the consumer to suffer a loss.

Decertification   a process by which employees vote to withdraw their consent to union representation; an election is conducted by the National Labor Relations Board.

Deed   a conveyance of really; a writing signed by a grantor, whereby title to really is transferred from one to another.

Defamation   an intentional false communication, either published or publicly spoken, that injures another's reputation or good name.

Defamation *per se*   a statement that is libel or slander in and of itself and is not capable of an innocent meaning.

Default   the omission or failure to perform a contractual duty to fulfill a promise or discharge an obligation to pay interest or principal on a debt when due. In UCC, when default occurs may be defined by the parties to the agreement.

Default judgment   judgment entered against a party who failed to appear in court to defend against a claim brought by another party.

Defendant   the party against whom an action or lawsuit is brought.

Deficiency judgment   a judgment against a debtor for the unpaid balance of the debt if a foreclosure sale or a sale of repossessed personal properly fails to yield the full amount due on the debt.

Delegation   the legal transfer of power and authority to another to perform duties.

Delegation of powers   the constitutional right of Congress to authorize government agencies to perform certain legal duties.

Demurrer   an older term for a motion to dismiss a claim for failure to state a cause of action. *See* Motion to dismiss.

Deposition   sworn testimony, written or oral, of a person taken outside the court.

Descriptive   a trademark that describes the good or service in question; a mark must have strong market recognition to receive legal protection.

Design defect   in product liability litigation, a claim that a consumer suffered an injury because a safer product design was not used.

Detrimental reliance   *see* Promissory estoppel.

Differential standard   in federal employment discrimination law, when an employer sets rules to make it more difficult for a person who is a member of a protected class to meet job requirements than for similarly situated employees.

Dilution   a violation of trademark rights that occurs by blurring or tarnishing a famous mark regardless of intent on the part of the violator; specific rights are provided by federal law for strong marks.

Direct examination   the initial examination of a witness by the party on whose behalf the witness has been called.

Directed verdict   verdict granted by the court on the grounds that the jury could reasonably reach only one conclusion on the basis of the evidence presented during the trial.

Directors   *see* Board of directors.

Disability   under the Americans with Disabilities Act, a physical or mental condition that affects a major life activity that limits the ability of a person to perform a particular job function.

Discharge   the termination of one's obligation. Under contract law, discharge occurs either when the parties have performed their obligations in the contract, or

when events, the conduct of the parties, or the operation of law releases parties from performing.

Discharge monitoring reports   or DMR, under the Clean Water Act, firms with pollution permits must file these reports with the EPA and have them available for public inspection to show the level of emissions actually dumped into bodies of water or treatment facilities.

Discharge permit   under the Clean Water Act, the EPA controls many effluent sources by limiting, through a permit program, dumping into any body of water.

Disclosed principal   a principal whose identity is revealed by the agent to a third party.

Disclosure requirements   in securities law, the revealing of financial and other information relevant to investors considering buying securities; the requirement that sufficient information be provided prospective investors so that they can make an informed evaluation of a security.

Discovery   the process by which the parties to a lawsuit gather information from each other to reduce the scope of what will be presented in court; process is determined by rules of procedure and may be limited by the court hearing the case.

Discrimination   illegal treatment of a person or group (intentional or unintentional) based on race, color, national origin, religion, sex, disability, or age. This includes the failure to remedy the effects of past discrimination.

Disparate impact   in employment discrimination law, when an apparently neutral rule regarding hiring or treatment of employees works to discriminate against a protected class of employees.

Disparate treatment   differential treatment of employees or applicants on the basis of their race, color, religion, sex, national origin, or age; for example, when applicants of a particular race are required to pass tests not required of other applicants.

Dissenting opinion   an opinion written by one or more appellate judges or justices explaining why they disagree with the decision of the majority of the court in a given case.

Dissolution   the process of terminating or winding up a corporation or partnership that changes the nature of the organization or ends it completely. This may come about involuntarily, such as through forced bankruptcy, or may be voluntary, as when a board of directors approves the end of the life of a company.

Diversity jurisdiction   when parties to a suit are from different jurisdictions (states or nations), it may create a basis for having a case heard in federal court.

Diversity-of-citizenship   an action in which the plaintiff and the defendant are citizens of different states.

Doctrine of judicial immunity   an official or a judge perform regulatory duties is absolutely immune from suit for damages for judicial acts.

Double jeopardy   when a defendant is prosecuted or sentenced twice for the same offense. Double jeopardy is prohibited by the Fifth Amendment.

Double taxation   the imposition of two taxes on the same property or income during the same period; especially the taxation of corporate profits that are then subject to taxation again when remainder of profits are paid as income (dividends) to the shareholders.

Draft   a written order signed by a party (the drawer), instructing another party (the drawee, usually a bank) to pay a certain sum of money, on demand, to a third party (the payee).

Drawee   the party that a draft is directed to and that is requested to pay the amount stated on it; normally a bank (the payor) that is directed to pay a sum of money on an instrument.

Drawer   the party who directs a person or entity, usually a bank, to pay a sum of money stated in an instrument; e.g., a person (the maker) who writes a check.

Due care   the degree of care that a reasonable person can be expected to exercise to avoid harm reasonably foreseeable if such care is not taken.

Due process clause   constitutional limitation requiring that a person not be deprived of life, liberty, or property without a fair and just hearing.

Dumping   when a seller provides a large quantity of goods at less than fair market value or less than the cost of production; selling goods in another country for less than the market price at home.

Duress   when coercion or threats are used to get another person to act in a way, such as sign a contract, that the person would not otherwise agree to.

Duty   a legal obligation that is owed to another and that must be satisfied; an obligation for which somebody else has a corresponding right.

Duty-free port   a special economic zone in a nation where goods may be imported or exported without being subject to usual tariffs; often done for transshipment of goods or to encourage processing in a country.

Duty of loyalty   in agency law, the obligation an agent has to put the interests of the principal before the interests of the agent in matters related to the agency relationship.

Duty of obedience and performance   the obligation of an agent to execute the obligations of an agency in the manner instructed by the principal.

Duty to account   in an agency relationship, the obligation of an agent to report with accuracy about all financial matters related to the relationship, including expenditures and revenues.

Duty to compensate   in an agency, the obligation of a principal to pay an agent a reasonable fee for services performed or to pay the amount agreed upon by the parties.

Duty to cooperate   the obligation of a principal in an agency relationship to act in a manner so as not to impede the ability of the agent to fulfill the purpose of the agency.

Duty to indemnify   in an agency, the obligation of a principal to pay for damages or losses suffered by an agent in the execution of transactions allowed under the relationship.

Duty to inform   in an agency relationship, the legal requirement an agent has to inform a principal of any matters related to the agency that can affect its success.

Duty to reimburse   in agency law, the obligation a principal has, unless otherwise agreed upon, to pay the agent for reasonable expenses incurred in carrying out agency obligations.

E

Easement   the right to use the property of another in a particular manner. Most commonly, this is a right of access to cross one piece of property to reach another piece of property or the right to have utilities go across, on, or under property. It is a right that is said to "run with the land."

Easement by prescription   *see* Adverse possession.

Economic espionage   when commercial trade secrets are stolen for use by a competitor; this is specifically in violation of federal law.

Economic loss rule   the principle that a plaintiff cannot sue in tort to recover for purely monetary loss (damages) that occur in breach of contract instances. An exception to this rule is when the defendant commits fraud or negligent misrepresentation, which brings in a tort cause of action to what would otherwise only be a contract matter.

Effluent   liquid waste (pollution under the Clean Water Act) that is discharged into a river, lake, or other body of water.

Electronic fund transfer   monetary transactions made electronically, usually by telephone or computer.

Embezzlement   statutory offense when a person fraudulently appropriates for her own use the property or money entrusted to her by another.

Eminent domain   the power of the government to take private property for public use for fair compensation.

Emission offset   under the Clean Air Act, a requirement that for a polluting facility to be built or expanded, the owner must reduce certain pollutants by as much or more than the new pollution to be generated; this may be done by paying other polluters to reduce emissions.

Emotional distress   also called *mental distress*; a tort action for damages to compensate a person for mental injury suffered due to another's actions.

Employee handbooks   manuals issued by employers to inform employees of their duties and rights as employees; often used as evidence of an employment contract that must be followed by both parties.

Employment-at-will   a doctrine under the common law providing that unless otherwise explicitly stated, an employment contract was for an indefinite term and could be terminated at any time by either party without notice.

Enabling statute   legislative enactment granting power to an administrative agency.

En banc   legal proceedings before or by the court as a whole rather than before or by a single judge or a panel of judges.

Endangered species   in environmental law, a list of animals and plants declared by the government to be in danger of becoming extinct; violators may be prosecuted for killing endangered animals or plants or injuring their habitat.

Entrapment   a law-enforcement officer's inducement of a person to commit a crime, by fraud or undue persuasion, in an attempt to bring a criminal prosecution against that person. It provides an affirmative defense that the crime would not have been committed but for the set up.

Equal protection clause   Section 1 of the Fourteenth Amendment to the Constitution, providing that states treat all persons subject to state laws in a similar manner. "No State shall … deny to any person within its jurisdiction the equal protection of the laws."

Equitable remedies   the means by which a court enforces a right adjudicated in equity or prevents or redresses the violation of such a right. Remedies include specific performance, injunction, recission, reformation, and declaratory judgment.

Equity   (1) in securities law, an ownership claim on a business interest, usually a security with no repayment terms; and (2) a legal system that operates alongside the "law," and is concerned with achieving justice in cases when courts of law are incompetent to act.

Equity financing   when a business obtains funds by issuing ownership shares to investors in the organization.

Error of law   a determination by an appeals court that a lower court, usually a trial court, made a mistake in applying the law to the facts that were established at trial.

Estate   the amount, nature, and quality of a person's interest in land or other properly.

Ethics   rules or standards governing the conduct of members of a profession and how such standards are put into action within an organization.

Excessive fines   an excessive penalty that is held to violate the Eighth Amendment. This occurs when a fine or penally, such as a prison term, is too large relative to the legal violation that occurred.

Exclusionary rule   under the Fourth Amendment, as interpreted by the courts, evidence that has been gathered in violation of the search-and-seizure rules cannot be used against a defendant at trial.

Exclusive jurisdiction   the power of a court over a particular subject matter as provided by statute to the exclusion of other courts.

Exculpatory clause or agreement   a part of a contract that releases one of the parties from liability for their wrongdoings; not favored at laws. *See also* Liability waiver.

Executive orders   under powers granted by the Constitution, or by Congress in legislation, an order by the president to establish or enforce a legal requirement.

Exemplary damages   *see* Punitive damages.

Exemptions from registration   in securities law, provisions that allow certain securities to be sold without meeting the usual registration requirements with the Securities and Exchange Commission; does not exempt the securities from other aspects of securities laws.

Exhaustion doctrine   a rule that when a statute provides an administrative remedy, relief must be sought through appropriate agency process before a court can act to consider other relief.

Exoneration   the right to be reimbursed by reason of having paid money that another person should have paid. Also, the right of a surely to compel the principal debtor to satisfy the obligation when possible.

Expectancy damages   compensation awarded in litigation, usually in contract cases, for the loss of what a party reasonably anticipated from a transaction that was not completed.

Express authority   in agency law, when an agent has clear authority, verbal or written, to act on behalf of a principal for certain matters.

Express contract   a contract that is oral or written, as opposed to being implied from the conduct of the parties. *See* Implied contract.

Express ratification   when a principal clearly accepts responsibility for an agency relationship.

Express warranty   a promise, in addition to an underlying sales agreement, that goes beyond the terms of the sales agreement and under which the promisor assures the description, performance, or quality of the goods.

Expropriation   the taking of a privately-owned properly by a government. Governments are required to, but at times do not, pay compensation for such takings.

F

Failing firm defense   in antitrust law, a rule that firms may be allowed to merge that would not be allowed to do so otherwise, because one of the firms is in danger of going out of business anyway.

Failure to warn   in product liability cases, when a producer is found liable in tort for not warning consumers of dangers the producer knew existed or should have known existed.

Fair use   the right of persons other than the owner of copyrighted material to use it in a reasonable manner without the consent of the owner; factors include the purpose of the use, the extent of the use, and the economic effect of the use.

False imprisonment   also called *false arrest*; the intentional detention or restraint of an individual by another.

Federal question   a question in a case in which one of the parties, usually the plaintiff, is asserting a right based on a federal law.

Fee simple   in property law, an absolute ownership interest in an estate (real properly) without restrictions; the strongest form of properly ownership.

Felony   a serious class of crime—such as rape, murder, or robbery—that may be punishable by imprisonment in excess of one year or death.

Fiduciary   a person having a duty, generally created by his own undertaking, to act in good faith for the benefit of another in matters related to that undertaking. A fiduciary duty is the highest standard of duty implied by law.

Fiduciary duty of loyalty   the duty of loyalty stands for the principle that directors and officers of a corporation in making all decisions in their capacities as corporate fiduciaries, must act without personal economic conflict. The duty of loyalty can be breached either by making a self-interested transaction or taking a corporate opportunity.

Firm offer   in UCC, a signed writing by a merchant promising to keep an offer open. In contrast to an option, a firm offer does not require consideration to make the offer irrevocable.

Fitness for a particular purpose   in UCC, a buyer may rely on a seller's skill or judgment in selecting goods for a special use, thereby creating a warranty that the goods are fit for the intended use.

Floating lien   a security interest retained in collateral even when the collateral changes in character, classification, or location. An inventory loan in which the lender receives a security interest or general claim on a company's inventory. Under the UCC, such security is not only in inventory or accounts of the debtor at the time of the original loan, but also in inventory or accounts acquired after the loan.

Force majeure   a common clause in contracts that essentially frees both parties from liability or obligation when an extraordinary event beyond the control of the parties, such as a war, strike, riot, crime, or "act of God" (flooding, earthquake, volcanic eruption), prevents one or both parties from fulfilling obligations under the contract.

Foreign exchange controls   restrictions imposed by a government on the purchase/sale of foreign currencies by residents or on the purchase/sale of local currency by nonresidents.

Foreign trade zones   or FTZ, designed areas that provide special customs procedures to plants engaged in international trade-related activities. Duty-free treatment is accorded items that are processed in FTZs and then reexported.

Forum   a public place where a trial or judicial proceeding is held.

Forum non conveniens   a rule that allows a court, in equity, to decline jurisdiction over a case when it believes that the matter would be better resolved in another forum. Usually this is invoked when most of the parties and witnesses to a case are in another location, making it more convenient for the trial to be held there, rather than where the case was filed.

Forum selection clause   a contractual provision in which the parties establish the place—such as the country, state, or type of court—for specified litigation or arbitration in the event of a dispute.

Franchise   a contract between a parent company (franchisor) and an operating company (franchisee) to allow the franchisee to run a business with the brand name of the parent company, so long as the terms of the contract concerning methods of operation are followed.

Franchise agreement   the contract between a franchisor and franchisee that sets forth the terms and conditions of the franchise relationship. Federal law, and some state laws, regulate some terms of such agreements.

Fraud   an intentional misrepresentation of a material fact designed to induce the person receiving the miscommunication to rely upon it to her detriment, so that a loss is suffered.

Front pay   compensation for future economic losses arising from employment discrimination that cannot be remedied by traditional relief, such as hiring, promotion, or reinstatement.

Frustration   a doctrine in contract law that allows a party to be relieved of a duty to perform because the purpose of the contract no longer exists. Circumstances occurred after the contract was formed that make performance irrelevant or impossible.

G

Garnishment   a legal process by which a creditor appropriates a debtor's wages or property in the hands of a third party.

General agent   a person serving as an agent who is authorized to act for the principal in all matters relating to a particular business or employment relationship.

General jurisdiction   a power of a court to hear all controversies that may be brought before it.

General partner   a partner in a limited partnership or any partner in a general partnership who accepts, or has imposed by law, personal liability for all debts of the partnership.

Generic   a trademark used to identify a good that has no legal protection; it may have been a valid trademark at one time, but was not protected against common use.

Genetic information   a basis for employment discrimination based on exploitation of genetic information about a current or potential employee that affects employment decisions.

Genuine consent   *see* Reality of consent.

Geographic market   in antitrust law, the area in the country in which a business has market power.

Good faith   in UCC, honesty in fact in the conduct or transaction in question.

Goods   UCC manufactured things (not services) that are movable and have physical existence (not intangible).

Goodwill   an intangible properly that is generally considered to be the expected continued business that will come due to the existing reputation of a firm.

Grand jury   a body of people, often 23, who are chosen to sit periodically for at least a month and as long as a year to decide whether to issue indictments. If evidence presented by the prosecutor is sufficient, an indictment will issue. The jury may screen possible charges and may participate in an investigation that may lead to an indictment.

Gratuitous agent   an agent who volunteers services without an agreement or expectation of compensation, but whose voluntary consent creates the rights and liabilities of the agency relationship.

Gross negligence   a conscious and voluntary disregard for the need to use reasonable care, likely to cause foreseeable injury or harm to person, property or both.

Guarantor   one who makes a guaranty. Person who becomes secondarily liable for another's debt; in contrast to a surety, who is primarily liable with the debtor. One who promises to answer for the debt in case of default.

Guaranty   a collateral agreement for performance of another's undertaking. An agreement in which the guarantor agrees to satisfy the debt of a debtor, only if the debtor fails to repay the debt (secondary liability).

H

Habitat   an ecological or environmental area inhabited by a particular species of animal, plant or other type of organism; taken into consideration in designing protection programs for endangered or threatened species.

Harmonized tariff schedule   a set of definitions to classify goods; adopted by many countries so that they share common terminology when setting tariffs.

Harassment   unwelcome conduct based on race, color, religion, sex (including pregnancy), national origin, age (40 or older), disability or genetic information in violation of employment discrimination law.

Hazard communication standard   also called HazCom in employment law; the requirement that an employer provide training and information about hazardous chemicals employees will be exposed to on the job.

Hazardous waste   a substance that may cause or contribute to an increase in mortality or pose a hazard to human health or the environment when improperly treated.

Holder in due course   in UCC, a holder of an instrument who took it for value in good faith and without any notice of any claim against the instrument; the holder is free of any claims against the instrument.

Homestead law   a statute exempting a homestead from judicial sale for debt, unless the owners have jointly mortgaged the property.

Horizontal merger   a merger between two companies that compete in the same product market.

Horizontal restraint of trade   anticompetitive action by businesses at the same level of operation. Rival firms that come together by agreement in an attempt to restrain trade by restricting output and raising prices is called a *cartel*.

Hostile environment   in federal employment discrimination law, creating or allowing to exist a climate at work that is abusive to a person based on their protected class status.

***Howey* test**   the rule established by the Supreme Court to determine what a security is under the federal securities law: an investment of money in a common enterprise with the expectation that profits will be generated by the efforts of others.

Hung jury   a jury so divided in opinion that it cannot agree upon a verdict.

I

Implied authority   in agency law, when the right of an agent to act on behalf of a principal is inferred from past actions or from the current position of the agent.

Implied contract   a contract formed on the basis of the conduct of the parties.

Implied ratification   when the acceptance of an agency relationship by a principal is reasonably presumed given the actions of the principal.

Implied warranty   an unwritten, unexpressed promise or guarantee that a court infers to exist and that accompanies a good.

Impossibility of performance   a doctrine used to discharge the obligations of parties to a contract when an event—such as a law being passed that makes the contract illegal or the subject matter of the contract is destroyed (called objective impossibility)—makes performance impossible for one or both parties.

Impracticability   an interpretation of the doctrine of impossibility in contracts that allows a party to a contract to be relieved of the duty to perform, when the basis of the contract no longer exists due to un-forseen events.

Incidental damages   in UCC losses that are reasonably related to actual damages, such as a seller's commercially reasonable expenses incurred in stopping delivery or in transporting and caring for goods after a buyer's breach.

Independent contractor   one who provides service in the course of an occupation, who follows the employer's direction as to the result of the work but does the work according to her own methods, unlike a servant or employee, who is subject to detailed control in the performance of work.

Indictment   a formal written charge issued by a grand jury asserting that the named person has committed a crime.

Infringement   in patent, copyright, and trademark law, the unauthorized use or imitation of another's recognized right to the properly involved.

Injunction   an order issued by a court that restrains a person or business from doing some act or orders the person to do something; may be permanent or temporary.

In personam jurisdiction   the power the court has over the person(s) involved in the action.

***In rem* jurisdiction**   an action taken by a court against the properly of the defendant.

Insider trading   the buying or selling of securities of a firm by persons who have information about the firm not yet available to the public and who expect to make a profit through those transactions.

Instructions   *see* Charges.

Intangible asset   property that is a "right," such as a patent, copyright or trademark, or an asset that is lacking physical evidence, such as goodwill in a firm.

Intangible property   property that has no value because of its physical being but is evidence of value, such as securities, promissory notes, copyrights, patents, and certain contracts.

Integrity   living according to a moral code and standards of ethics.

Intellectual property   property recognized at law that arises from mental processes, such as inventions and works of art.

Intentional misrepresentation   *see* Fraud.

Intentional tort   a wrong committed upon the person or properly of another, where the actor is expressly or impliedly judged to have intended to commit the act that led to the injury.

Interbrand competition   competition among various brands of a particular product. Interference with business relationship a tort in which a defendant commits an intentional and unjustified interference with a plaintiffs valid business dealings that inflicts monetary damage.

Interference with contract   a tort in which there is a valid contract, and the defendant knew of the contract but intentionally caused a breach of the contract, resulting in damages to the plaintiff.

Interference with prospective advantage   (or with a business relationship) a tort where there is an intentional and unjustified intervention with a relationship that a party had been developing with others in an effort to obtain new business or more business.

Interpretative rules   statements issued by administrative agencies that explain how the agency understands its statutory authority to operate; these may be advisory or binding.

Interrogatories   in the discovery process, a set of written questions for a witness or a party for which written answers are prepared with assistance of counsel and signed under oath.

Interstate commerce   the carrying on of commercial activity that affects business in more than one state.

Intervening conduct   in tort, an independent cause that comes between the original wrongful act and the injury that relieves liability that would otherwise exist for the original act; a legal break in the causal connection.

Intrabrand competition   competition among retailers in the sales of a particular brand of product.

Invasion of privacy   in tort, the encroachment on the right of a person to their solitude, the appropriation of a person's reputation for commercial purposes, or the public disclosure of facts that the person had a legal right to keep private.

Investment adviser   under securities law, a person who, for compensation, engages in the business of advising others as to the advisability of investing in, purchasing, or selling securities. This includes securities brokers and dealers.

Investment company   any corporation in business to own and hold the stock of other corporations.

Invitee   a person who has an invitation, express or implied, to enter on to another's premises, such as a business visitor.

Involuntary bankruptcy   a bankruptcy proceeding against an insolvent debtor that is initiated by creditors.

J

Joint and several liability   liability that a person or business either shares with other tortfeasors or bears individually.

Joint tenancy   a tenancy with two or more co-owners who take identical interests by the same instrument and with the same right of possession. It differs from a tenancy in common in that each joint tenant has a right of survivorship to the other's share.

Joint venture   a business agreement between two or more individuals or companies engaged in a solitary business enterprise for profit without actual partnership or incorporation

Judgment   the official decision of a court of law upon the rights and claims of the parties to an action litigated in and submitted to the court for its determination.

Judgment as a matter of law   *see* Directed verdict.

Judgment lien   a lien binding the real estate of a judgment debtor, in favor of the judgment holder, and giving the latter a right to levy on the properly for the satisfaction of his judgment to the exclusion of others.

Judgment notwithstanding the verdict   judgment entered by the court for a party following a jury verdict against the party.

Judicial review   authority of a court to reexamine a dispute considered and decided previously by a lower court or by an administrative agency.

Jurisdiction   the right of a court or other body to hear a case and render a judgment.

Jurisdiction over the person   power of a court to lawfully bind a party involved in a dispute before it.

Jurisdiction over the subject   power of a court to lawfully affect the thing or issue in dispute.

Jury   a body of people selected to hear the evidence in a case presented in court and who are given the power to apply the law to the facts established at trial in determining which party prevails in the matter in dispute, whether civil or criminal.

Just compensation   the portion of the Fifth Amendment that states "nor shall private properly be taken for public use, without just compensation." The requirement that when the government uses its power to force a private party to give up a properly interest, fair market value should be paid.

K

Kefauver Amendment   the portion of the Food, Drug, and Cosmetic Act that requires the Food and Drug Administration to approve drugs only after their safely and effectiveness have been established.

L

Labor dispute   under labor law, specific actions by employers, a union, or employees that are subject to coverage by standards set by the National Labor Relations Act.

Landlord   the owner of real properly (an estate) that has been leased to another party, the tenant.

Lanham Act   provides a private cause of action for a party injured by misappropriation of trademark and for one injured by false advertising that injures the sale of a competitor's product.

Law   enforceable rules of conduct set forth by a government to be followed by the citizens of the society.

Law merchant   in commercial law, the rules devised by merchants in Europe over several centuries to govern their trade; many of these rules were formally adopted into law.

Learned intermediary doctrine   the rule that a physician or other qualified medical professional will be held liable for misapplication of a prescription medication if ordered for a use not recommended by the producer, who is relieved of liability in such instances when a patient is injured by the medicine.

Lease   an agreement, usually a contract, that gives the right to a party to take exclusive possession of property for a specific time for a certain payment. This normally creates a landlord and tenant relationship.

Leasehold   refers to the real properly, an estate, that is under the lawful control of a tenant for the term of the lease agreed to with the landlord.

Legal detriment   when a promisee gives up the right to retain control of something he was entitled to keep, or to give up the right to do something, in exchange for a promise by the other party to the contract.

Legal entity   the existence of a thing, other than a natural person, that has legal existence so that it can function in a legal capacity, such as a corporation doing business.

Legislative rules   *see* Substantive rules.

Letter of credit   a written document in which the party issuing the document—usually a bank—promises to pay third parties in accordance with the terms of the document.

Liability waiver   similar to an exculpatory clause, in that a party contracts to waive certain tort rights that may otherwise exist against another party; these can be valid if limited in scope and the risks involved are clearly understood by the party who agrees to the waiver, which is found to be reasonable by the court.

Libel   a defamation that is in the form of a printing, writing, pictures, or broadcast on radio or television.

Licensing agreement   a contract whereby one firm, the licensor, grants another firm, the licensee, the right to exploit certain assets of the licensor, such as a patent or trademark.

Lien   a claim or encumbrance on properly for payment of some debt, obligation, or duty. Qualified right that a creditor has in or over specific properly of a debtor as security for the debt or for performance of some act. Right to retain properly for payment of a debt.

Life estate   in property law, when a life tenant (the beneficiary of the arrangement) has the right to occupy a piece of properly for life or earn income from a piece of properly for life, after which control of the properly passes to the designated owner.

Limited jurisdiction   also called *special jurisdiction;* the power of a court to hear cases only of particular types—such as small claims courts or family courts—where judgments may be issued that only cover certain kinds of disputes.

Limited liability   the fact that shareholders of a corporation are not liable for the debts of the corporation beyond the amount of money they have invested in the corporation.

Limited liability company   or LLC, is a form of organization authorized by statute at the state level that is characterized by limited liability, management by members or managers, and limitations on ownership transfer.

Limited partner   a partner in a limited partnership whose liability for partnership debts is limited to the amount of his contribution to the partnership.

Limited partnership   a business organization consisting of one or more general partners, who manage and contribute assets to the business and who are personally liable for the debts of the business, and one or more limited partners, who contribute assets only and are liable only up to the amount of that contribution.

Liquidated damages   amounts specified in a contract to be paid in the event of a breach. They represent a reasonable estimation by the parties of the damages that will occur in the event of breach.

Lockout   refusal by an employer to allow employees to work.

Long-arm statute   a state statute permitting courts to obtain personal jurisdiction over nonresidents as long as the requirements of the statute are met.

M

Magistrates   judicial officers appointed by the judges of federal district courts pursuant to the United States Magistrates Act.

Mail fraud   an act of fraud using the Postal Service, as in making false representations through the mail to exploit another party.

Majority opinion   when an appeals court issues an opinion in a case that affirms or reverses the decision of the lower court, a majority of the judges join in an opinion that expresses the legal rationale for the decision of the court. If all judges agree, it is a unanimous opinion.

Maker   a person who signs a note (promissory note) promising to pay money to another.

Managers in businesses, persons hired to perform certain functions in a firm who are given discretion to control certain business assets; ultimately responsible to the board of directors of a corporation or the owner of a proprietorship or partnership.

Mandatory subjects of bargaining under the National Labor Relations Act, all terms and conditions of employment that must be discussed by employers and unions or an unfair labor practice occurs.

Manifest system in environmental and occupational safety law, the requirement that certain chemicals have documentation concerning their production, distribution, and disposal to ensure proper handling and disposal of toxic substances.

Market power in antitrust law, the ability to raise prices significantly above the competitive level without losing much business.

Market share the percentage of a market, by sales volume of a product nationally or in a geographic area, that is controlled by a firm.

Master a principal who hires another to perform services and who has the right to control the conduct of that person in the performance of the service; more commonly, an employer. *See also* Servant.

Material breach *see* Breach of contract.

Material fact information that is substantially relevant to the consideration of a contract or to securities or to the decision made in a trial.

Material information *see* Material fact.

Mechanic's lien a claim under state law to secure priority of payments for the value of work performed and materials supplied in building on or improving land and buildings.

Mediation a form of alternative dispute resolution in which a third party is hired by parties to a dispute with the intent to persuade them to settle their dispute.

Mediator a neutral person, usually paid, who attempts to help other parties reach an agreement to resolve a dispute.

Meeting competition in antitrust law, a defense in price discrimination (Robinson-Patman) cases in which a firm shows that prices were cut to meet the prices of competitors.

Members in LLCs, owners of the enterprise have this title rather than shareholder as in the case of a corporation; members report income or losses from the LLC on their personal tax returns.

Membership interest shares of ownership in limited liability; much like shares in a corporation or shares in a partnership; the legal claim to a portion of an LLC's profits.

Mens rea Latin for "the state of mind" of the actor.

Mental distress *see* Emotional distress.

Merchant in UCC, one who regularly deals in goods covered by contract for sale, who holds himself out to buyers as having specialized knowledge about particular goods; held to a standard of good-faith dealing.

Merchantability in commercial law, the notion that goods are reasonably fit for the ordinary purposes for which such goods are used.

Merger a contract through which one firm acquires the assets and liabilities of another firm.

Merger guidelines internal rules issues by the Antitrust Division of the Department of Justice in conjunction with the Federal Trade Commission. The rules govern the extent to which these regulatory bodies will study and/or challenge a potential merger on grounds of market concentration or threat to competition.

Merit system in employment discrimination law, the right of an employer to have a system to reward employees based on performance; often used as an affirmative defense in a Title VII discrimination cases.

Mineral rights also called *subsurface rights;* in property law, an interest in minerals in land, usually underground, that is separate from ownership of the surface of the land. There is a right to take the minerals from the land or to receive a royalty from the sale of minerals.

Miranda rights from a 1966 Supreme Court case, the doctrine that a criminal suspect in police custody must be informed of certain constitutional rights before interrogation. The suspect must be advised of the right to remain silent, the right to have an attorney present during questioning, and the right to have an attorney appointed if he cannot afford one. If not advised of these rights, evidence obtained from the suspect during the interrogation cannot be used.

Mirror-image rule   the common-law principle that the acceptance of a contract offer must be positive, unconditional, and clear, and must not change the terms of the offer.

Misappropriation   an unauthorized taking of another's properly that denies the rightful owner the full use an benefit of the properly.

Misdemeanor   a lesser crime that is neither a felony nor treason, punishable by a fine and/or imprisonment in other than state or federal penitentiaries.

Misrepresentation   words or conduct by a person to another that, under the circumstances, amount to a false statement.

Misstatements   in securities law, liability may be imposed on those responsible for issuing information about securities that misleads a reasonable investor in investment decisions to her detriment; may be part of fraud.

Mistake   in contracts, when the parties to a contract did not mean the same thing, or one party had an incorrect belief about the facts or law. May be grounds for voiding a contract.

Mistrial   a trial that cannot stand in law because the court lacks jurisdiction, because of juror misconduct, or because of disregard for some other procedural requirement.

Mitigation of damages   doctrine that imposes a duty upon an injured party to exercise reasonable diligence in attempting to minimize damages after being injured.

Mobile source   under the Clean Air Act, a pollution source such as automobiles, trucks, and airplanes.

Modify   in an appeals court, to change some detail of a lower court holding, but to leave the primary finding in place. For example, the decision of the lower court is likely to be affirmed, but the legal reasoning for the decision is amended.

Monetary damages   *see* Damages.

Money laundering   the act of transferring illegally obtained money through legitimate people or accounts so that its original source cannot be traced; a federal crime that is often involved in illegal international transactions.

Monopoly   a market structure in which the output of an industry is controlled by a single seller or a group of sellers making joint decisions regarding production and price.

Morality   concerns conformity to rules of correct conduct within the context of a society, religion, or other institution.

Moral right   the right of an author or artist, by copyright, to guarantee the integrity of a creation. This may include rights of attribution or credit; integrity— the right to ensure that the work is not changed without the artist's consent.

Mortgage   an interest in real properly created by a written instrument providing security for the payment of a debt. In many states, a mortgage is a lien; it is a pledge or security of particular properly to help ensure payment of a debt or other obligation.

Mortgagee   party who holds or receives a mortgage; the creditor.

Mortgagor   one who, having all or part of a title to real properly, pledges the property in writing for a particular purpose, such as to secure a debt; the party who mortgages properly; the debtor.

Motion to dismiss   a request that a complaint be dismissed, because it does not state a claim for which the law provides a remedy or is in some other way legally deficient.

Mutual fund   an investment vehicle regulated by the Investment Company Act, where many investors pool their money to be managed by a professional staff.

N

National Ambient Air Quality Standards   or NAAQS, federal standards under the Clean Air Act that set the maximum concentration levels in the atmosphere for several air pollutants.

National origin   under federal employment discrimination law, the country a person or a person's ancestors are from.

National Priority List   or NPL, contaminated sites, as determined by the Environmental Protection Agency under the Superfund law, that must be cleaned up and returned to nearly original condition.

National Pollutant Discharge Elimination System or NPDES, federal standards under the Clean Water Act that set the water pollution effluent standards for every industry that discharges liquid wastes into the nation's waterways.

Nationalization   the act of bringing an industry under governmental control or ownership; often this is applied to foreign-owned firms.

Necessary and proper clause   the part of the U.S. Constitution that gives Congress the authority to use various powers to execute its functions under the Constitution.

Negligence   the failure to do something that a reasonable person, guided by the ordinary considerations that regulate human affairs, would do or the doing of something that a reasonable person would not do.

Negligent hiring   a basis for tort that may arise from an employer's lack of care in selecting an employee who the employer knew or should have known was unfit for the position, thereby creating an unreasonable risk of harm to others.

Negotiable instrument   a signed, written, unconditional promise to pay, to the bearer of the instrument or to order of a certain party, a specific sum of money on demand or on a certain date.

Negotiation   voluntary discussion of the terms and conditions of a proposed agreement or a form of alternative dispute resolution to resolve a dispute and avoid litigation; under the UCC, the transfer of an instrument to another party who becomes the holder, or the act of putting into circulation a check or promissory note.

New Source Performance Standards   or NSPS, under the Clean Water Act, the level of allowable wastewater discharges from new industrial facilities. The EPA determines the best available demonstrated control technology for each industrial category.

Nolo contendere   Latin for "I do not wish to contend;" that is, a party pleads no contest. It is often shortened to *nob.*

Nominal damages   a damage award whereby a court recognizes that the plaintiff has suffered a breach of duty but has not suffered any actual financial loss or injury as a result. Plaintiffs recovery for such breaches is often as little as one dollar.

Nonattainment area   under the Clean Air Act, an area in which the air quality for certain pollutants fails to meet the National Ambient Air Quality Standards.

Noncompete agreement   in employment law, when an employer requires an employee, as a condition of employment, to agree not to compete with the employer in the future for a certain time and in a certain location; such agreements are not favored in some states.

Nonexempt property   a debtor's possessions that a creditor can attach to satisfy a debt.

Nonpoint source pollution   under the Clean Water Act, sources of pollution that are diverse, such as urban and agricultural runoff from rainstorms.

Non-recourse debt   a debt that is secured by a pledge of collateral for which the borrower is not personally liable.

Note   a written promise by one party (the maker) to pay money to another party (the payee) or to bearer; a two-party negotiable instrument.

Novation   an agreement between the parties to a contract to discharge one of the parties and create a new contract with another party to be responsible for the discharged party's obligations.

Nutrition labeling   by statute, nutritional facts labels must list the percentage supplied required in one day of human nutrients based on the average 2,000 calorie a day diet.

O

Occupational licensure   requirement at the state level that for one to practice a certain profession, one must meet certain educational or experience guidelines, pass an entry examination, and show evidence of continuing educational accomplishments.

Offer   a proposal to do or refrain from doing some specified thing by a party, called the offeror, to another party, called the offeree. The proposal creates in the offeree a legal power to bind the offeror to the terms of the proposal by accepting the offer.

Offeree   the party to whom an offer is made.

Offeror   the party making an offer to another party to enter into a contract.

Omission   a failure to do something, especially a neglect of duty; leaving something out that may be critical to a decision.

Open account   credit extended by a seller to a buyer that permits buyer to make purchases without security.

Opening statement or argument   oral presentations made to the jury by the attorneys before the parties present their cases.

Operating agreement   a contract among members of a limited liability company setting forth the parties' agreements about funding, development, operations, and other key issues of the LLC.

Option contract   in contract law, an offer that is included in a formal or informal contract that creates an obligation to keep an offer open for a specified period, so that the offeror cannot revoke the offer during that period. To be valid, the option must be supported by consideration.

Oral argument   presentations made in an appeals court or supreme court, usually by attorneys, in support of or objecting to the decision of a lower court as part of the appeals process.

Order paper   an instrument payable to a specific payee or to any person that the payee designates.

Ordinary care   *see* Due care.

Original jurisdiction   power of a court to take a lawsuit at its beginning, try it, and pass judgment upon the law and facts.

Output contract   when a seller promises to supply, and a buyer promises to buy, all the goods or services that a seller produces during a certain time and at a set price.

Over the counter   a stock market for securities generally not sold in large daily volumes so that they are not listed on a stock exchange, such as the New York Stock Exchange; a securities market created by stockbrokers who relay information to a central location about offers to buy or sell certain amounts of a stock.

P

Parker doctrine   an exemption from liability for engaging in antitrust violations. It applies when the state exercises legislative authority in creating a regulation with anticompetitive effects, and to private actors when they act at the direction of the state.

Parol evidence rule   a rule that prohibits the introduction into a lawsuit of oral evidence that contradicts the terms of a written contract intended to be the final and complete expression of the agreement between the parties.

Partnership   a business owned by two or more persons that is not organized as a corporation.

Patent   a grant from the government conveying and securing for an inventor the exclusive right to make, use, and sell an invention for 20 years from the time of application.

Payee   one to whom money is paid or payable; usually a party named in commercial paper as recipient.

Payment clause   the portion of a contract that specifies how and when payment is to be made and, important in international business, what currency will be used.

Penalty   excessive damages specified in a contract that are to be impose on a breaching party. Courts often reject enforcement of such clauses, which are treated as punishment, not actual damages, regardless of the terminology given in the contract.

Perfect tender rule   at common law, seller's offer of delivery must conform to every detail of contract with buyer; under the UCC, parties may agree to limit the operation of this rule, or the seller may cure a defective tender if the time for performance has not ended; the seller notifies the buyer quickly of intent to cure defect, or the seller repairs or replaces defective goods within performance time limits.

Perfection   the validation of a security interest as against other creditors; normally accomplished by filing a statement with some public office or possibly by taking possession of the collateral.

Perfection of security interest   in a secured transaction, the process by which a security interest is protected against competing claims to the collateral. It usually requires the secured party to give notice of the interest by filing it in the appropriate government office, usually the secretary of state.

Performance   in contract law, the fulfilling of obligations or promises according to the terms agreed to or specified by parties to a contract. Complete performance of those obligations or promises by both parties discharges the contract.

Permanent injunction   *see* Injunction.

Perpetual existence   a general presumption in corporation law that a corporation will exist forever; i.e., most organizations do not have a specific date fixed for termination.

Per se rule   in antitrust, a violation held to be so pernicious as to have no defense if a violation is shown to have occurred.

Personal jurisdiction   *see* Jurisdiction over the person.

Personal service   in the pleadings stage, personal service of the complaint is accomplished by physically delivering it to the defendant.

Plaintiff   the party who initiates a lawsuit.

Plea bargain   also called *negotiated plea;* a negotiated agreement between a prosecutor and a criminal defendant for the defendant to plead guilty to a lesser offense or to only one of multiple charges in exchange for concessions such as a lighter sentence or a dismissal of the other charges.

Pleading   statement of the plaintiff and the defendant that details their facts, allegations, and defenses, which create the issues of the lawsuit.

Point source pollution   under the Clean Water Act, any definitive place of discharge of a water pollutant, such as pipes, ditches, or channels.

Police power   a general power of the states to enact laws to protect public safely, health, and order so long as due process and equal protection are not violated.

Political speech   in constitutional law, speech that concerns political, as opposed to commercial, matters; given a high level of protection by the First Amendment.

Pollution   the release of substances into the air, water, or land that cause physical change.

Possessory lien   also called *artisan's lien*; a lien in which the creditor has the right to the possession of specific properly until a debt is satisfied or an obligation is performed.

Potential competition   in antitrust law, consideration given to the degree of competitiveness that exists in a market because of the possibility that firms not now in the market will enter it and compete with existing producers.

Potentially responsible party   a possible polluter who may be held liable under CERCLA for contributing to the contamination or misuse of a particular properly or resource.

Power of attorney   a document authorizing another person to act as one's agent or attorney with respect to the matters stated in the document.

Precedent   a decision in a case that is used to guide decisions in later cases with similar fact situations.

Predatory bidding   in antitrust law, similar to predatory pricing; when a dominant firm bids up the price of an input to get sufficient control of it to be able to dominate a market that relies on the input, so as to drive out competitors and then be able to raise prices later.

Predatory pricing   in antitrust law, pricing below an accepted measure of cost (such as average variable cost) to drive competitors from the market in the short run to reduce competition in the long run.

Premerger notification   the Hart-Scott-Rodino (HSR) Act requires parties to certain mergers to submit a "Notification and Report Form for Certain Mergers and Acquisitions," with information about each company's business. Parties may not close their deal until the waiting period outlined in the HSR Act has passed, or the government grants and end to the waiting period.

Premises liability   an intentional tort, or a tort based on negligence, when the owner or party with responsibility for maintaining certain properly fails to provide adequate safely for visitors to the properly against criminal attacks or accidents.

Preponderance of the evidence   in civil trials, the burden of persuasion to win a verdict requires that the plaintiff prove its claim by having the majority or bulk of the evidence on its side.

Prescription drugs   a medicine licensed by the Food and Drug Administration that should be dispensed to consumers only with permission of a physician or other qualified medical personnel.

Pretext   under federal employment discrimination law, an attack made by a plaintiff against a defense offered by an employer to a charge of discrimination, holding that the rationale given is a false excuse to cover discriminatory treatment.

Prevention of significant deterioration (PSD) area   under the Clean Air Act, an area where the air quality is better than required by the national ambient air standards, such as national parks and wilderness areas. Air quality is not allowed to fall.

Price discrimination   in antitrust law, charging different prices to different customers for the same product without a cost justification for the price difference.

Price fixing   an agreement among participants in a market to buy or sell a product or service only at a fixed price, or to control market conditions such that the price is maintained at a given level; generally held to be *per se* illegal under antitrust statutes.

***Prima facie* case**   in federal employment discrimination law, the requirement that a plaintiff show they are a member of a protected class, met relevant job qualifications, suffered some adverse job action, and was treated differently with respect to the same issue by an employer.

Primary boycott   in labor law, a union action that tries to convince people not to deal with an employer with which the union has a grievance.

Principal   in an agency relationship, a person who, by explicit or implicit agreement, authorizes an agent to act on his behalf and perform acts that will be binding on the principal.

Principal (suretyship)   the person primarily liable, for whose performance of her obligation the surely has become bound.

Private company   also called close corporation; a firm owned by a relatively small number of shareholders that does not offer or trade its company stock on the stock exchanges; the company's stock is offered and traded privately, subject to restrictions imposed when the stock was issued.

Private law   a classification of law, generally denoting laws that affect relationships between people.

Private nuisance   in tort law, when an activity reduces the right of one person, or a small number of persons, to enjoy properly without unreasonable interference.

Private placement   when securities are sold to investors without registration with the Securities and Exchange Commission; primarily used by large institutional investors, not for sales to the public.

Privilege   in tort law, the ability to act contrary to another's legal right without that party having legal redress for the consequences of that act; usually raised as a defense.

Privity   a legal relationship between parties, such as between parties to a contract.

Privity of contract   the immediate relationship that exists between the parties to a contract.

Probable cause   reasonable ground to believe the existence of facts warranting the undertaking of certain actions, such as the arrest or search of a person.

Procedural law   the rules of the court system that deal with the manner in which lawsuits are initiated and go forward. Court systems generally have rules regarding pleadings, process, evidence, and practice.

Procedural rules   under the Administrative Procedure Act or other legislation, the process that an administrative agency must follow for its actions to be valid.

Product liability   a general category of cases in which the producer or seller of products may be held responsible to buyers, users, or innocent third parties, who suffer injuries due to defects in the goods.

Product market   in antitrust law, the product market includes all products that can be reasonably substituted by consumers for the product of the business under investigation.

Professional corporation   in most states, a category of corporations that may be used by those providing a personal service that require a license, such as physicians, dentists, architects, and accountants. The primary reason to adopt this status is for tax benefits.

Profit   a servitude that gives the right to pasture cattle, dig for minerals, or otherwise take away some part of the soil.

Promise   a statement or declaration that binds the party making it (the promisor) to do or refrain from doing a particular act or thing. The party to whom the declaration is made (the promisee) has a right to demand or expect the performance of the act or thing.

Promisee   party to whom a promise is made.

Promisor   party who makes a promise.

Promissory estoppel   a doctrine that allows promises to be enforced in the absence of consideration, if a promise is made which the promisor reasonably expects will induce action or forbearance on the part of the promisee and, which in fact, does cause such action or forbearance to the detriment of the promisee.

Promissory note   an unconditional promise, in writing, to pay a certain sum at a specific time, or on demand, to a person named on the instrument or to the bearer of the instrument; such notes are negotiable.

Property   at law, the right to possess, use, and enjoy a specific thing, such as a piece of land or chattel.

Prospectus   under securities law, a pamphlet that must be produced for distribution to prospective buyers of securities that contains information about the background of the security being offered.

Protected classes   under Title VII of the Civil Rights Act of 1964, those groups the law seeks to protect, including groups based on race, sex, national origin, religion, and color.

Protective order   a decree by a court to protect a person or a legal entity against harassment by another person or to protect certain documents, such as trade secrets, against discovery in the litigation process.

Proximate cause   in tort law, the action of the defendant that produces the plaintiffs injuries, without which the injury or damage in question would not have existed.

Proxy   giving another person the right to vote on one's behalf; in stock votes, when a person gives another the right to vote in a certain manner, such as for candidates for board of directors.

Public law   a classification of law, generally denoting laws that affect relationships between people and their governments.

Public nuisance   in tort law, when an activity reduces the right of the public in general to enjoy properly without unreasonable interference.

Public policy exception   in employment law, statutory or court-mandated exceptions to the presumption of employment-at-will that goes beyond contract issues in employment; for example, it is illegal for an employer to dismiss an employee for reporting for jury duty.

Publicly-held company   a company that has permission to offer its registered securities (stock, bonds) for sale to the public, usually through a stock exchange or traded over-the-counter via market makers who use non-exchange quotation services.

Publicly owned treatment works   under the Clean Water Act, a heavily funded federal program to bring local water treatment facilities up to federal standards, usually the best conventional technology level.

Punitive damages   also called *exemplary damages*; compensation awarded to a plaintiff beyond actual damages; awarded to punish the defendant for doing a particularly offensive act.

Purchase money security interest   a secured interest created when a buyer uses the money of a lender to make a purchase and gives the lender a security interest in the properly purchased.

Q

Qualified institutional buyers   purchaser of securities deemed financially sophisticated and recognized by the SEC to need less protection from issuers than most public investors.

Qualified Privilege   *see* conditional privilege.

Quantum meruit   a concept in equity that a party should not be unjustly enriched by not paying for goods or services received that do not clearly fall under a contract; it is the recovery a plaintiff is allowed to be granted under an implied contract to pay for the reasonable value of services provided.

Quasi contract   a contract imposed by law, in the absence of an actual contract, to prevent unjust enrichment. A contract implied in law.

Quid pro quo   Latin for "what this for that," or "something for something;" the giving of something valuable for something valuable, such as consideration in a contract. Also refers to sexual discrimination, when sexual favors are exchanged for employment favors.

Quitclaim deed   a deed that conveys the grantor's complete interest or claim in real properly but that does not warrant that the title is valid.

Quorum   the minimum number of members of a body, such as a board of directors or shareholders of a company, necessary to conduct the business of that group.

R

Race   also called *racial status*, under federal employment discrimination law: black, white, American Indian or Alaska Native, Native Hawaiian or Other Pacific Islander, Asian, and Hispanic or Latino.

Racketeer Influenced and Corrupt Organizations Act   or RICO, a law designed to attack organized criminal activity by prosecuting persons who participate or conspire to participate in racketeering. The federal RICO statute of 1970 applies to activity involving interstate or foreign commerce. Many states have adopted laws—"little RICO" acts—based on the federal statute. The federal and most state RICO acts provide for enforcement not only by criminal prosecution but also by civil lawsuit, in which plaintiffs can sue for treble damages.

Racketeering   a pattern of illegal activity, such as bribery, that is part of an operation owned or controlled by those engaged in the illegal activity. RICO extends it to include activities such as mail fraud and securities frauds.

Ratification   in contract law, the act of accepting responsibility for a previous act that would not constitute an enforceable contractual obligation but for the ratification. Ratification causes the obligation to be binding as if it were valid and enforceable in the first place.

Real property   land, the products of land (such as timber), and property that cannot be moved (such as houses).

Reality of consent   in contract law, a contract must have been entered into freely based upon correct information about the matter to be valid; if duress, misrepresentation, or fraud was present when the agreement was made, there is no contract.

Reasonable accommodation   in employment discrimination law, the requirement that employers take steps that are not very costly to make employment possible for persons with disabilities.

Reasonable care   the degree of care that a person of ordinary prudence would use in the same or similar circumstances or in the same line of business.

Reasonable person   the standard which one must observe to avoid liability for negligence; often includes the duty to foresee harm that could result from certain actions.

Red herring   in securities law, a prospectus that has not yet been approved by the Securities Exchange Commission. It has a red border on its front to signal to interested parties that it is not yet approved for final distribution; used as an advertising device.

Registration statements   in securities law, the financial information that must be filed with the Securities and Exchange Commission for review prior to the sale of securities to the public.

Regulation   a rule or order, having legal force, issued by an administrative agency; the act or process of controlling by rule.

Regulation Z   a rule issued by the Federal Reserve Board to implement the Truth-in-Lending Act requiring systematic disclosure of the costs associated with credit transactions.

Regulatory takings   when a government action results in a reduction in the value of private property; such instances are usually not subject to compensation under the Constitution, unless most of the value of property is destroyed.

Religion   under federal employment discrimination law, any sincere and meaningful belief a person possesses.

Remand   the act of an appellate court in sending a case back to a trial court ordering it to take action according to the appellate court's decision. The order usually requires a new trial or limited hearings on specified subject matter.

Remedy   the legal means by which a right is enforced or the violation of a right is prevented or compensated.

Repatriation   the process used to transfer assets or earnings from a host nation to another nation.

Representation election   in labor law, when at least 30 percent of workers in a current or proposed bargaining unit sign a request to have an election to determine if all workers in that workplace will be represented by a particular union.

Repudiation   a rejection, disclaimer, or renunciation of a contract before performance is due, but which does not operate as an anticipatory breach, unless the promisee elects to treat the rejection as a breach and brings a suit for damages.

Requirements contract   when a buyer promises to buy, and a seller promises to supply, all of the goods that a buyer needs during a certain time.

Resale price maintenance   when a manufacturer or wholesaler sets the price of a good at the next level, such as at the retail level; if the price set is not charged by the retailer, the manufacturer or wholesaler will no longer sell the good to the retailer.

Rescission   to cancel or nullify a contract; it is the unmaking of a contract, as if it never existed. It may occur because both parties agree to avoid the contract, or because one party gives the other party grounds for canceling the contract, such as by an act that would create grounds for not fulfilling the obligations.

Res ispa loquitur   Latin for "the thing speaks for itself;" given the facts presented, it is clear that the defendant's actions were negligent and were the proximate cause of the injury incurred.

Res judicata   a rule that prohibits the same dispute between two parties from being relitigated by a court after final judgment has been entered and all appeals exhausted.

Respondeat superior   doctrine of vicarious liability under which an employer is held liable for the wrongful acts of his employees committed within the scope of their employment.

Restitution   a remedy in equity to restore a person to his original position had there been no loss or injury or to the position he would have enjoyed had there been no breach of contract.

Restraint of trade   any contract, agreement, or combination that eliminates or restricts competition.

Retaliation   when a worker suffers a adverse employment decision because the worker exercised a right under an employment discrimination statute.

Retaliatory discharge   *see* Wrongful discharge.

Reverse   a decision by an appellate court that overturns or vacates the judgment of a lower court.

Reverse discrimination   when discrimination is employed against majority groups so as to favor certain minority groups, often in affirmative action programs.

Reviewability   the ability for the decision of a court or an agency to be appealed to a higher court or administrative level.

Revocation   the recall of some power, authority, or thing granted; in contract law, the withdrawal by the offeree of an offer that had been valid until withdrawn.

Right-to-sue letter   a document issued by a federal or state employment discrimination agency, after an investigation of a complaint, stating that the plaintiff has raised issues that merit review by a court.

Right-to-work law   state laws that prohibit unions from forcing employees who do not want to pay union dues or agency fees to pay such dues or fees even if the employees are represented by the union under a collective bargaining agreement.

Riparian water law   at common law, relating to the bank of a river or stream; the owner of land bounded by a river or body of water has the right to reasonably use the water next to the land or that passes over the land.

Ripeness doctrine   in administrative law, a doctrine that before a matter may be appealed to the court system, an agency must have finalized its decision, so the matter is ready for court review.

Risk-utility test   when evidence shows that a reasonable person would conclude that the benefits of a product's particular design compared to a reasonable alternative design did not outweigh the dangers inherent in the original design.

Rulemaking   in administrative law, the procedures that agencies must follow when issuing rules to interpret or enforce the statutory authority they were granted by Congress.

Rule of reason   in antitrust law, the court considers all facts and decides whether what was done was reasonable and did not harm competition in net; compare to the *per se* rule.

S

Safe harbor   a provision of a statute or a regulation that reduces or eliminates a parly's liability under the law, on the condition that the party performed its actions in good faith.

Sale   in UCC, when there is a passing of title of a good from the seller to the buyer for a price.

Sales contract   in UCC, "the passing of title from the seller to the buyer for a price."

Satisfaction   the performance of a substituted obligation in return for the discharge of the original obligation.

S corporation   a corporation may be granted S status if it does not own any subsidiaries, has only one class of stock, and has no more than seventy-five shareholders, all of whom must be U.S. citizens or U.S. residents.

Scalping   when a securities professional buys (or sells) a number of shares of an investor's security at the bid (or ask) price and then, when the price moves, quickly sells (or buys) the same security from the professional's own account for a higher (or lower) price for a profit generated by trading the client's account.

Scienter   Latin for "knowingly;" usually meaning that the defendant knew that the act in question was illegal.

Secondary boycott   a union's refusal to handle products of or work for a secondary company with whom the union has no dispute; to force that company to stop doing business with another company with which the union has a dispute.

Secondary meaning   when a trademark or trade dress is distinctive and receives public recognition by itself, not just as a means of identifying the origins of the good or service it represents.

Secured creditors   a person who has loaned money to another and has a legally recognized interest in the properly of the debtor until fulfillment of the terms of the debt agreement.

Secured transaction   any transaction, regardless of form, intended to create a security interest in personal properly, including goods, documents, and other intangible properly.

Securities   in securities law, a debt or equity instruments that are evidence of a contribution of money by a group of investors into a common enterprise that will be operated for profit by professional managers.

Securities exchange   a regulated market where securities, such as stocks, are traded.

Securities fraud   in securities law, the statutory basis for charging anyone involved in the issuance or trading of securities with fraud, which is usually due to misleading issuance of information or failure to disclose material information that causes investors to suffer losses.

Security   a negotiable financial instrument that represents some type of financial value; freely exchangeable for or replaceable in the satisfaction of an obligation.

Self-defense   generally, a legal excuse for the use of force to resist an attack on one's person or to defend another person who is under attack or properly that is under attack. This defense may apply in common-law cases and in criminal cases.

Self-incrimination   the rule that a witness is not bound to give testimony that would incriminate him with respect to a criminal act.

Self-reporting   the requirement under many laws that one subject to the law must volunteer certain matters, including violations, that have occurred to the relevant regulatory agency.

Sentencing Guidelines   a federal statute that provides detailed instructions for judges to determine appropriate sentences for federal crimes; it includes factors such as the nature of the crime and the history of the defendant.

Servant   a person who works in the service of another person (the employer) under an express or implied contract of hire, usually at-will, under which the employer has the right to control the details of work performance.

Service mark   under trademark law, any symbol, word, or name used in the sale of goods to distinguish the services available from a particular source; service marks apply to services; trademarks apply to goods.

Service of process   in the pleadings stage, the delivery of the complaint to the defendant either to her personally or, in most jurisdictions, by leaving it with a responsible person at her place of residence.

Servitude   a burden that rests on one estate for the benefit of another. Servitudes on land may impose obligations on the owner of land to permit something to be done on the properly by another, or it may be a restriction on the use of properly that would normally be permitted.

Sex   under federal employment discrimination law, male and female; under some state laws, sexual orientations may be recognized categories.

Sexual harassment   discrimination in employment in violation of Title VII of the 1964 Civil Rights Act that may be evidenced by sexual advances, requests for sexual favors, and other conduct of a sexual nature.

Shareholder   the owner of one or more shares of stock in a corporation.

Shelf registration   a Securities and Exchange Commission rule that allows certain companies to file a single registration statement for the future sale of securities. This registration allows the company to react quickly to favorable market conditions.

Sight draft   a draft payable upon proper presentment.

Sine qua non   Latin for "without which not;" an indispensable thing; something on which something else relies upon.

***Sine qua non* rule**   *see* Cause in fact.

Slander   an oral defamation of one's reputation or good name.

Sole proprietorship   a business owned by a person who is not organized as a corporation.

Sophisticated user   in tort law, a defense that when a manufacturer sells a product to a sophisticated buyer, such as another manufacturer, the purchaser is responsible for instructing its employees about the dangers in using the product.

Sovereign immunity   the doctrine under which a non-sovereign party is precluded from engaging in a legal action against a sovereign party, unless the sovereign gives its consent.

Special agent   one employed as an agent to conduct a specific transaction or business act for a principal; while there may be more than one action involved, it is not expected to be a continuous relationship.

Special warranty deed   a deed by which the grantor promises to defend the title against only those claims and demands of the grantor and those claiming through the grantor.

Specific performance   an equitable remedy, whereby the court orders a party to a contract to perform his duties under the contract. Usually granted when money damages are inadequate as a remedy, and the subject matter of the contract is unique.

Standing   the right to sue in a particular court.

Stare decisis   the use of precedent by courts; the use of prior decisions to guide decision making in cases before the courts.

State implementation plan   under the Clean Air Act, a requirement that each state prepare, under Environmental Protection Agency supervision, a plan to control certain air pollutants by certain dates to meet national air quality standards.

Statute of Frauds   a statutory requirement that certain types of contracts be in writing to be enforceable.

Statute of limitations   a statute setting maximum time periods from the occurrence of an event, during which certain actions can be brought or rights enforced. If an action is not filed before the expiration of that time period, the statute bars the use of the courts for recovery.

Strict liability   in tort a legal theory that imposes responsibility for damages regardless of the existence of negligence; in tort law, any good sold that has a defect that causes injury leads to the imposition of liability.

Strike   a work stoppage by employees for the purpose of coercing their employer to give in to their demands.

Subagent   one authorized by an agent to help perform agency duties for a principal. When an agent has authority to appoint a subagent, he is subject to control by both the agent and the principal.

Subject-matter jurisdiction   *see* Jurisdiction over the subject.

Subpoena   an order by a court or other legal authority empowered to require a person to appear to give testimony about a certain civil or criminal matter. A subpoena *duces tecum* orders the production of documents.

Subrogation   the substitution of one party in place of another with respect to a lawful claim, so that the party substituted succeeds to the rights of the other in relation to the debt or claim and its rights and remedies.

Subsidy   a government monetary grant to a favored industry.

Substance-abuse policy   in employment law, workplace rules adopted by an employer with respect to any required tests and the consequences of abuse of drugs, alcohol, or other substances; must comply with certain federal and state laws.

Substantial factor   a standard adopted in several states in place of proximate cause; a jury may hold a defendant liable in tort if it finds that defendant's conduct was a major cause of the injury in question.

Substantial performance   a doctrine that recognizes that a party that performs a contract, but with a slight deviation from the contract's terms, is entitled to the contract price less any damages caused by the deviation.

Substantive law   law that defines the rights and duties of persons to each other, as opposed to procedural law, which is law that defines the manner in which rights and duties may be enforced.

Substantive rules   administrative rulings based on statutory authority granted an agency by Congress; the rules have the same legal force as statutes passed by Congress.

Suggestive   a trademark which, by its name, suggests the use or purpose of the good it represents; legal protection is due such marks but can be more difficult to establish than for arbitrary and fanciful marks.

Summary judgment a judgment entered by a trial court as a matter of law, when no genuine issue of law is found to exist.

Summons process through which a court notifies and compels a defendant to a lawsuit to appear and answer a complaint.

Superfund in environmental law, the Comprehensive Environmental Response, Compensation, and Liability Act; it concerns requirements about when hazardous waste sites must be cleaned up and who is liable for the costs.

Superseding cause the act of a third party, or an outside force, that intervenes to prevent a defendant from being liable for harm to another due to negligence.

Supremacy clause Article VI, paragraph 2 of the U.S. Constitution, which states that the Constitution and federal laws are supreme over the laws of all states.

Surety one who undertakes to pay money or otherwise act in the event that her principal fails to pay or act as promised. A surely is usually bound with her principal by the same contract, executed at the same time and for the same consideration. Under the UCC, this includes a guarantor. However, liability of guarantor, depending on state law, is secondary and collateral, whereas liability of surely is primary and direct.

Suretyship the relationship among three parties in which one party, the surely, guarantees payment of a debtor's debt owed to a creditor or acts as a co-debtor.

T

Takings clause *see* Just compensation.

Tangible property property that has physical form and substance, such as real estate and goods.

Tariff a tax imposed on imported goods by the government to encourage domestic industry or to raise revenues. *See also* Excise tax.

Preliminary injunction *see* Injunction.

Temporary restraining order a court order in equity to restrain a particular action while the court considers a request to issue an injunction.

Tenancy in common an ownership interest in which each tenant (owner) has an undivided interest in properly. More than one party owns the properly in joint possession, but there are separate titles so that when an owner dies, her interest passes to her heirs.

Tenant one who possesses (rents) real properly for a period of time, usually under a lease. The properly or estate is normally owned by the landlord.

Tender a valid and sufficient offer of performance of a contract, especially for the delivery of goods under the UCC.

Tender offer an offer open to current stockholders to buy a stock at a certain price; offer may be contingent upon receiving a certain amount of stock before any purchase is completed or may be an open offer; a method used to obtain enough stock to control a corporation.

Termination in contract law, the ending of an offer or contract, usually without liability.

Territorial allocation in antitrust law, the boundaries specified by contract or other agreement in which a wholesaler or retailer may sell a product.

Third-party-beneficiary contract a contract that benefits a third party and that gives that party a right to sue in the event of breach.

Tie-in sale in antitrust law, the requirement that if one product or service is purchased then another product or service must also be purchased, even if it is not desired by the customer.

Title generally, the legal right of ownership; under the UCC, title is determined by rules regarding identification of goods, the risk of loss of goods, and insurable interest in the goods.

Title VII the major section of the Civil Rights Act of 1964 that provides the primary basis for suits for employment discrimination based on race, sex, religion, color, or national origin.

Toll refers to a time period, usually set by statute, required to meet an obligation or to be met for a right to exist, such as a statute of limitation that must be met to have the right to have a cause of action. If something has tolled, the right has been lost.

Tort an injury or wrong committed with or without force against another person or his properly; a civil wrong that is a breach of a legal duty owed by the person who commits the tort to the victim of the tort.

Tortfeasor an individual or business that commits a tort.

Trade dress intellectual properly protected by trademark law and the Lanham Act that concerns the total appearance and image of products and of service establishments, including shape, size, graphics, and color.

Trademark a distinctive design, logo, mark, or word that a business can register with a government agency for its exclusive use in identifying its product or itself in the marketplace.

Trade name a word or symbol that has become sufficiently associated with a product over a period of time that it has lost its primary meaning and has acquired a secondary meaning; once so established, the company has a right to bring a legal action against those who infringe on the protection provided the trade name.

Trade regulation rules administrative rulings by the Federal Trade Commission or other agencies that hold certain practices to be illegal or create standards that must be met by sellers of certain products or services.

Trade secrets in tort law, valuable, confidential data—usually in the form of formulas, processes, and other forms of information not patented or not patentable—that are developed and owned by a business.

Trade usage in UCC, standard practices or terminology in an area of business that the courts may presume to exist between parties when a contract is unclear about a particular aspect of a business relationship.

Transfer pricing the setting, documentation, and adjustment of charges made between related parties for good, services, or use of property. Transfer prices among parts of a business may be used to reflect allocation of resources across components, or for other purposes; the prices are often artificial, not real market prices.

Treatment, storage, and disposal (TSD) sites under the Resource Conservation and Recovery Act, a requirement that producers, transporters, and disposers of hazardous wastes keep records (manifests) and meet federal standards in all phases of such operations.

Treble damages a money damage award allowable under some statutes that is determined by multiplying the jury's actual damage award by three.

Trespass an unauthorized intrusion upon the property rights of another.

Trespass to personal property an unlawful interference with the rights of another person to possess their personal property, such as movable objects.

Trial a judicial examination of a dispute between two or more parties under the appropriate laws by a court or other appropriate tribunal that has jurisdiction.

Trial *de novo* Latin for "a new" trial, or retrial at an appellate court in which the entire case is examined as though no trial had occurred.

Trust the right, enforceable in equity, to the beneficial enjoyment of property to which another person holds legal title; a property interest held by one person (*trustee*) at the request of another (*settlor*) for the benefit of a third party (*beneficiary*).

Trustee a person who has legal title in some property, such as the property of a bankrupt business, held in trust for the benefit of another person (the beneficiary).

Tying arrangements an agreement between a buyer and a seller in which the buyer of a specific product is obligated to purchase another good. *See also* Tie-in sale.

U

Ultrahazardous activity in tort law, a rule that when an activity involves a risk of serious harm, such as the use of explosives or toxic chemicals, strict liability will be imposed when any harm is caused to other persons or property.

Unconscionable contract a contract, or a clause in a contract, that is grossly unfair to one of the parties because of stronger bargaining powers of the other party; usually held to be void as against public policy.

Underutilization analysis a statistical review of workforce categories to look for evidence of underrepresentation of women and/or minorities; usually performed as part of affirmative action requirements.

Underwriter a professional firm that handles the marketing of a security to the public; it either buys all of a new security offering and then sells it to the public, or it takes a commission on the securities it actually sells.

Undisclosed principal when the identity of a principal is unknown to a third party, so that the third party is unaware that the agent being dealt with is representing the agency.

Undue hardship an accommodation to employees, based on an effort to satisfy religious beliefs, that would either alter the nature of the enterprise or affect its viability due to the costs imposed on the employer or other employees.

Undue influence the misuse of one's position of confidence or relationship with another individual to overcome that person's free will thereby taking advantage of that person to affect decisions.

Unenforceable contract a contract that was once valid but, because of a subsequent illegality, will not be enforced by the courts.

Unfair labor practice in labor law, a wide range of actions that violates the rights of workers to organize and engage in collective activities or that violates the rights of employers to be free from practices defined as illegal under the National Labor Relations Act.

Unfair methods of competition under the Federal Trade Commission Act, a range of business practices found to violate the public interest; they may be based on fraud, deception, or a violation of public policy, because competition is injured.

Unfairness in a consumer protection law, a charge under Section 5 of the Federal Trade Commission Act that a business practice causes harm that consumers cannot reasonably avoid.

Uniform Commerical Code or UCC, a statute passed in similar form by the states that sets many rules of commercial sales agreements and negotiable debt instruments.

Unilateral contract an offer or promise of an offeror that is binding only after completed performance by the offeree. The offeree's completed performance serves as acceptance of the offer and performance of the contract.

Union an association of workers that is authorized to represent them in bargaining with their employers.

Union certification in labor law, when a majority of the workers at a workplace vote to have a union be their collective bargaining agent, the National Labor Relations Board certifies the legal standing of the union for that purpose.

Universal agent one serving as an agent who is authorized to conduct every transaction that can be lawfully delegated by a principal to an agent.

Unknown hazard in products liability, a claim that tort liability should be assigned to a producer for injuries suffered by a consumer due to a defect or hazard in a product that was not known by the producer at the time the product was made.

Unsecured creditor a party owed money but who has no collateral, lien, or other security to secure the debt or claim in the event of default by the debtor.

Usury the practice of lending money and requiring the borrower to pay a high amount of interest, considered to be illegal by law.

Utility patent a patent granted for the invention of a process, machine, manufacture, or composition of matter; the most common form of patent.

V

Venue the geographic area in which an action is tried and from which the jury is selected.

Vertical restraint of trade in antitrust law, contracts or combinations which reduce or eliminate competition among firms in the production, distribution, and sale of some good.

Vesting under the Employee Retirement Income Security Act, the requirement that pension benefits become the properly of workers after a specific number of years of service to an employer.

Vicarious liability liability that arises from the actions of another person who is in a legal relationship with the party upon whom liability is being imposed.

Void contract a contract that does not exist at law; a contract having no legal force or binding effect.

Voidable contract a contract that is valid but which may be legally voided at the option of one of the parties.

Voir dire to "speak the truth." In the trial stage, preliminary examination of a juror in which the attorneys and the court attempt to determine bias, incompetency, and interest.

Voluntary bankruptcy a bankruptcy proceeding that is initiated by the debtor.

W

Warrant   a judicial authorization for the performance of an act that would otherwise be illegal.

Warranty   an assurance or guaranty, either expressed in the form of a statement by a seller of goods or implied by law, having reference to and ensuring the character, quality, or fitness of purpose of the goods.

Warranty deed   a deed containing one or more covenants of title; a deed that expressly guarantees good, clear title and that contains covenants concerning the quality of title, including defense of title against all claims.

Warranty disclaimer   in UCC, the ability of goods to be sold as is, or with fewer warranty rights that would normally exist, based upon clear communication to the buyer that warranty rights are reduced or eliminated at the time of sale.

Warranty of title   in general, the duty of a seller to provide good title or legal right of ownership of goods to the buyer; under the UCC, specific warranty rights are provided when title to goods passes.

Waste   physical harm to real property committed by a tenant. May occur whether intentional or negligent and may include the failure to maintain or repair properly.

Well-known seasoned issuers   security issuers with a track-record of successful past issues who are allowed to use a quicker securities registration process for new issues.

Wetlands   in environmental law, land covered by water at least part of the year; exact coverage by various environmental statutes is still unresolved.

Whistle-blower   an employee who alerts the authorities to the fact that her employer is undertaking an activity that is contrary to the law.

White-collar crime   a wide range of nonviolent crimes, often involving cheating or dishonesty in commercial matters. Examples would be fraud, embezzlement, and insider trading.

Wholly owned subsidiary   a business, often in another country, that is organized as a legal entity but is completely owned by another company, the "parent" firm, or by a government.

Winding up   process of settling the accounts and liquidating the assets of a partnership or corporation for the purpose of dissolving the concern.

Wire fraud   fraud involving the use of electronic communications, such as by making false representations on the telephone or the Internet to obtain money. The federal Wire Fraud Act holds that any fraud by wire or other electronic communications, such as radio or television in foreign or interstate commerce is a crime.

Workers' compensation laws   state statutes that provide for awards to workers or their dependents if a worker incurs an injury or an illness in the course of employment. Under such laws, the worker is freed from bringing a legal action to prove negligence by the employer.

Workforce analysis   a statistical breakdown of the composition of employees in an organization, by job category, by EEOC protected class status.

Writ   a mandatory precept issued by a court of justice.

Writ of execution   a writ to put into force the judgment of a court.

Written brief   an appellate brief is a written document, prepared by an attorney, to be the basis for an appeal of a case to an appellate court. It contains the points of law the attorney wants to establish, with the arguments and authorities to support that view.

Wrongful discharge   a cause of action an employee may have if dismissed for an improper reason, such as exercising a public right or other interest protected in the employment relationship, such as protected class status under Title VII.

Y

Yellow-dog contract   an agreement between an employer and an employee under which the employee agrees not to join a union, and that if he joins a union, there is a breach of contract and the employee is dismissed.

Z

Zoning   when the land in an area, usually a city, is divided into categories according to the kinds of structures that may be built, the purposes of the use of the land, and other regulations that may apply to different parcels of property.

Index